West's Law School Advisory Board

JESSE H. CHOPER
Professor of Law,
University of California, Berkeley

DAVID P. CURRIE
Professor of Law, University of Chicago

YALE KAMISAR
Professor of Law, University of San Diego
Professor of Law, University of Michigan

MARY KAY KANE
Chancellor, Dean and Distinguished Professor of Law,
University of California,
Hastings College of the Law

LARRY D. KRAMER
Dean and Professor of Law, Stanford Law School

WAYNE R. LaFAVE
Professor of Law, University of Illinois

JONATHAN R. MACEY
Professor of Law, Yale Law School

ARTHUR R. MILLER
Professor of Law, Harvard University

GRANT S. NELSON
Professor of Law,
University of California, Los Angeles

JAMES J. WHITE
Professor of Law, University of Michigan

PRODUCTS LIABILITY

CASES AND MATERIALS

Fourth Edition

By

David A. Fischer
Associate Dean and James Lewis Parks Professor of Law
University of Missouri-Columbia

Michael D. Green
Bess & Walter Williams Distinguished Chair
Wake Forest University School of Law

William Powers, Jr.
President, Hines H. Baker and Thelma Kelley Baker Chair in Law
University Distinguished Teaching Professor
University of Texas at Austin

Joseph Sanders
A.A. White Professor
University of Houston Law Center

AMERICAN CASEBOOK SERIES®

Mat #40368451

Thomson/West have created this publication to provide you with accurate and authoritative information concerning the subject matter covered. However, this publication was not necessarily prepared by persons licensed to practice law in a particular jurisdiction. Thomson/West are not engaged in rendering legal or other professional advice, and this publication is not a substitute for the advice of an attorney. If you require legal or other expert advice, you should seek the services of a competent attorney or other professional.

American Casebook Series and West Group are trademarks registered in the U.S. Patent and Trademark Office.

COPYRIGHT © 1988, 1994 WEST PUBLISHING CO.
© West, a Thomson business, 2002
© 2006 Thomson/West
    610 Opperman Drive
    P.O. Box 64526
    St. Paul, MN 55164-0526
    1-800-328-9352

Printed in the United States of America

ISBN-13: 978-0-314-16123-9
ISBN-10: 0-314-16123-6

D.A.F. to
Elizabeth Fischer

and M.G. to
Robert Green and Marion Ewald

and W.P. to
Kim Heilbrun

and J.S. to
Beth, Tom, and Rob Sanders

*

Preface

As with the prior editions of this book, we seek to focus on the major products liability issues that exist today. While we hope to provide a flavor of the history and development of products liability, there has been enormous change in the decades since the American Law Institute adopted § 402A in 1964. This book emphasizes the issues of the modern day, including the law that developed and is reflected in the Restatement (Third) of Torts: Products Liability, the trend toward comparative responsibility for apportionment of liability among all parties, reflected in the Restatement (Third) of Torts: Apportionment of Liability, the growth of toxic substances litigation, with its attendant scientific evidence and expert witness issues, and the procedural issues reflected in modern mass products liability litigation. Beyond providing students familiarity with these doctrinal developments, we hope to facilitate students' honing their legal reasoning skills.

The book is designed to be sufficiently flexible to meet differing course needs. The book is readily adaptable for either a two or three hour course. Depending on the coverage of products liability in the basic Torts class and an instructor's particular interests, the course can focus on the basics of products liability, contained in Chapters 1–4, 8, and 12, cover the application of first-year Torts principles to the products liability context in Chapters 5, 7, 9, and 10, or deal with advanced aspects of products liability, including scientific evidence and mass torts in Chapters 6, 11, and 13.

To facilitate coverage and avoid duplication of the products liability standards and the different types of defects, we provide a straightforward, streamlined, logical organization. Chapter 1 provides an introduction and review of basic tort principles, including negligence and misrepresentation. Chapter 2 addresses warranty issues in more depth because of its relative lack of coverage in first year Torts classes. The book proceeds with the elements of a products liability claim, including defect, cause in fact, proximate cause, damages, affirmative defenses, and contribution and indemnity, after a Chapter that covers the emergence of products liability and its policy bases. We also include separate Chapters on proof, the role of legislation and regulation, statutes of limitations, the boundaries of products liability, and complex litigation.

Most footnotes are omitted from the main cases and other quoted material without indication. We have renumbered the footnotes that are used. Citations are sometimes omitted without indication, and at other times are indicated by brackets. Editor's footnotes are indicated by an asterisk. All other omissions of textual material are indicated by asterisks.

Throughout the book we use the phrase "products liability" to describe the rules of modern products liability imposing liability on the basis of defect. Use of the older term "strict liability" to describe these rules is both outdated and misleading. Moreover the older term is confusing when we contrast products liability with "true" strict liability.

In a number of places we have cited to the current version of the Restatement (Third) of Torts: Liability for Physical Harm (Proposed Final Draft No. 1, 2005). That Draft received final approval in May, 2005, but will not be published for several years and then under a different name to reflect its expansion to cover emotional distress.

We would like to thank several dedicated people who were enormously helpful in preparing this edition of the book: Sandra Jackson at the University of Houston; Scott Walls at the University of Missouri; Kathy Bartsch at the University of Texas; and Arlene McClannon, John Vermitsky, and Michael Schrader at Wake Forest University.

DAVID A. FISCHER
MICHAEL D. GREEN
WILLIAM POWERS, JR.
JOSEPH SANDERS

June 2006

Acknowledgments

The authors would like to thank the publishers and authors of the following works for allowing them to include excerpts:

American Law Institute, Restatement (Third) of Torts: Products Liability: §§ 2 and comments a, d, e, f, p, 4(a), 3, 5 and comments a and e, 6 and comments c and f, 7 and comment b, 8 and comments a, b, and k, 10 and comment b, 11 and comment c, 13, 14 and comment d, 16, and comment d, 18, 19 and comments c and e, 20 and comments c, d, and f. Copyright 1998 by The American Law Institute. Reprinted with permission.

American Law Institute, Restatement (Third) of Torts: Liability for Physical Harm (Proposed Final Draft No. 1, 2005) §§ 14, 15, 16, 26 and comments e and j, 27 and comments d, f, g, and l, 28 and 36. Copyright 2005 by The American Law Institute. Reprinted with permission.

American Law Institute, Restatement (Third) of Torts: Apportionment of Liability § 8, comment a. Copyright 2000 by The American Law Institute. Reprinted with permission.

American Law Institute, Restatement (Second) of Torts §§ 321, and 402A and comments f, g, n, p, q and caveat. Copyright 1965 by The American Law Institute. Reprinted with permission.

American Law Institute and National Conference of Commissioners on Uniform State Laws, Uniform Commercial Code §§ 2–313, 2–316, 2–318, 2–715, comment 5, and 2–725. Copyright 1978 and 2001 by The American Law Institute and National Conference of Commissioners on Uniform State Laws. Reprinted with permission.

Ausness, Unavoidably Unsafe Products and Strict Products Liability: What Liability Rule Should be Applied to the Sellers of Pharmaceutical Products? 78 Ky.L.J. 705, 720–23, 745, 747–48, 749–51 (1989/1990). Copyright 1990 by the Kentucky Law Journal. Reprinted with permission.

Epstein, Product Liability: The Search for the Middle Ground, 56 N.C.L.Rev. 643, 651. Copyright 1978 by North Carolina Law Review. Reprinted with permission.

Fischer, Proportional Liability: Statistical Evidence and the Probability Paradox, 46 Vand. L. Rev. 1201, 1202. Copyright 1993 by Vanderbilt University School of Law. Reprinted with permission.

Fischer, Products Liability—Proximate Cause, Intervening Cause, and Duty, 52 Mo.L.Rev. 547. Copyright 1987 by David A. Fischer. Reprinted with permission.

Green, The Inability of Offensive Collateral Estoppel to Fulfill its Promise: An Examination of Estoppel in Asbestos Litigation, 70 Iowa L. Rev. 141, 221–23. Copyright 1984 by the University of Iowa. Reprinted with permission.

Klemme, The Enterprise Liability Theory of Torts, 47 U.Colo.L.Rev. 153, 158–165 (1976). Copyright 1976 by the University of Colorado Law Review, Inc. Reprinted with permission.

Landes and Posner, A Positive Economic Analysis of Products Liability, 14 J.Legal Stud. 535, 553–56 (1985). Copyright 1985 by the University of Chicago. Reprinted with permission.

Noel, Products Defective Because of Inadequate Directions or Warnings, 23 S.W.L.J. 256, 289. Copyright 1969 by South West Law Journal. Reprinted with permission.

Owen, Problems in Assessing Punitive Damages Against Manufactures of Defective Products, 49 U.Chi.L.Rev. 1, 15–25. Copyright 1982 by University of Chicago Law Review. Reprinted with permission.

Posner, Economic Analysis of Law, 161 (3d Ed. 1986). Copyright 1986 by Richard A. Posner. Reprinted with permission of Richard A. Posner and Little, Brown and Company.

Posner, Strict Liability: A Comment, 2 J.Legal Studies 205–212 (1973). Copyright 1973 by the University of Chicago. Reprinted with permission.

Powers, A Modest Proposal to Abandon Strict Products Liability, 1991 U.Ill.L.Rev. 639, 644–651, 653–654. Copyright 1991 by the Board of Trustees of the University of Illinois. Reprinted with permission.

Powers, Texas Products Liability Law. Copyright 1985 by Butterworth Publishers. Reprinted with permission.

Sanders, Benedectin on Trial: A Study of Mass Tort Litigation (1998). Copyright 1998 by University of Michigan Press. Reprinted with permission.

Shavell, Strict Liability Versus Negligence, 9 J.Legal Studies 1, 2–9 (1980). Copyright 1980 by the University of Chicago. Reprinted with permission.

Summary of Contents

	Page
PREFACE	v
ACKNOWLEDGMENTS	vii
TABLE OF CASES	xix
TABLE OF STATUTES	xxxvii
TABLE OF RESTATEMENTS	xliii

Chapter 1. Introduction — 1
Sec.
- A. History — 1
- B. Negligence — 3
- C. Misrepresentation — 8

Chapter 2. Warranty — 13
Sec.
- A. Introduction — 13
- B. Express Warranty — 15
- C. Implied Warranty of Merchantability — 25
- D. Implied Warranty of Fitness for Particular Purpose — 30
- E. Persons Who Are Protected: Privity of Contract — 34
- F. Remedies — 37
- G. Disclaimers — 37
- H. Remedy Limitations — 47
- I. Notice and Statutes of Limitation — 51

Chapter 3. Emergence of Product Liability — 53
Sec.
- A. Adoption — 53
- B. Policies Underlying Products Liability — 59

Chapter 4. Defect — 86
Sec.
- A. Introduction — 86
- B. Manufacturing Defects — 87
- C. Design Defects — 98
- D. Proof of Non–Specific Defect (in Manufacture or Design) by Circumstantial Evidence — 223
- E. Warning Defects — 234

Chapter 5. Causation in Fact — 339
Sec.
- A. Tests for Determining Causation — 339

Sec.
B. Proof of Causation 341

Chapter 6. Proof of Defect and Causation 390
Sec.
A. Industry Standard and Custom 390
B. Post-Accident Remedial Measures 403
C. Expert Witnesses 409

Chapter 7. Proximate Cause 480
Sec.
A. Introduction 480
B. Product Alteration 487
C. Effect of Apportionment of Fault on Superseding Cause 497

Chapter 8. The Effect of Statutes and Regulations 507
Sec.
A. Relevance of Statutes 507
B. Regulation 515
C. Preemption 532

Chapter 9. Damages 548
Sec.
A. In General 548
B. Pecuniary Loss and Harm to Property 550
C. Mental Distress 561
D. Punitive Damages 575

Chapter 10. Apportionment of Liability Among Multiple Parties 599
Sec.
A. Consumer Conduct Defenses and Comparative Responsibility 599
B. Apportioning Liability Among Defendants and the Special Role of Employers: Contribution and Indemnity 638

Chapter 11. Statutes of Limitation and Repose 665
Chapter 12. Parties and Transactions Governed by Strict Liability 691
Sec.
A. Parties Who Can Be Sued 691
B. Transactions Covered by Product Liability and Warranty 714

Chapter 13. Complex Litigation 777
Sec.
A. Issue Preclusion/Collateral Estoppel 778
B. Multidistrict Litigation 791
C. Class Actions 796

INDEX 861

Table of Contents

	Page
PREFACE	v
ACKNOWLEDGMENTS	vii
TABLE OF CASES	xix
TABLE OF STATUTES	xxxvii
TABLE OF RESTATEMENTS	xliii

Chapter 1. Introduction — 1
Sec.

A. History — 1
B. Negligence — 3
    MacPherson v. Buick Motor Co. — 5
    Note — 8
C. Misrepresentation — 8

Chapter 2. Warranty — 13
Sec.

A. Introduction — 13
B. Express Warranty — 15
    Hauter v. Zogarts — 18
    Notes — 20
C. Implied Warranty of Merchantability — 25
    Notes — 29
D. Implied Warranty of Fitness for Particular Purpose — 30
    Problem — 33
E. Persons Who Are Protected: Privity of Contract — 34
F. Remedies — 37
G. Disclaimers — 37
    Henningsen v. Bloomfield Motors, Inc. — 37
    Note — 42
H. Remedy Limitations — 47
I. Notice and Statutes of Limitation — 51

Chapter 3. Emergence of Product Liability — 53
Sec.

A. Adoption — 53
    Greenman v. Yuba Power Products, Inc. — 53
    Notes — 57
B. Policies Underlying Products Liability — 59
    Klemme, The Enterprise Liability Theory of Torts — 61
    Posner, Strict Liability: A Comment — 66
    R. Posner, Economic Analysis of Law — 72
    Shavell, Strict Liability Versus Negligence — 73

TABLE OF CONTENTS

Sec.

Powers, A Modest Proposal to Abandon Strict Products Liability 79

Chapter 4. Defect 86

Sec.

A. Introduction 86
B. Manufacturing Defects 87
    Lee v. Electric Motor Division 87
    Notes 88
    Landes and Posner, A Positive Economic Analysis of Products Liability 91
    Hunt v. Ferguson–Paulus Enterprises 93
    Notes 95
C. Design Defects 98
    1. Consumer Expectations 98
        Gray v. Manitowoc Co., Inc. 98
        Notes 103
        Brawner v. Liberty Industries, Inc. 104
        Keller v. Welles Department Store of Racine 106
        Notes 108
    2. Risk–Utility 114
        Phillips v. Kimwood Machine Co. 114
        Notes 120
        Fallon v. Clifford B. Hannay & Son, Inc. 124
        Notes 129
        Landes and Posner, A Positive Economic Analysis of Products Liability 132
        Notes 133
        Barker v. Lull Engineering Co. 134
        Notes 138
        Note Regarding the Foresight/Hindsight Distinction 141
        (a) Ignorance of Risk Caused by Misuse 144
            Romito v. Red Plastic Co., Inc. 144
            Notes 150
        (b) Changes in Technology 152
            Boatland of Houston, Inc. v. Bailey 152
            Notes 158
            Smith v. Louisville Ladder Co. 158
            Notes 162
            Kallio v. Ford Motor Co. 163
            Notes 168
            O'Brien v. Muskin Corp. 170
            Notes 175
        (c) Delegability of the Design Process 181
            Bexiga v. Havir Manufacturing Corp. 181
            Notes 184
            Mott v. Callahan Ams Machine Co. 188
            Notes 192
        (d) Special Problems with Medical Devices and Pharmaceuticals 199
            Grundberg v. Upjohn Co. 199
            Notes 213
            Ausness, Unavoidably Unsafe Products and Strict Products Liability: What Liability Rule Should Be Applied to the Sellers of Pharmaceutical Products? 217
            Notes 222

Sec.		Page
D.	Proof of Non–Specific Defect (in Manufacture or Design) by Circumstantial Evidence	223
	Myrlak v. Port Authority of New York and New Jersey	223
	Notes	230
E.	Warning Defects	234
	1. Duty to Warn	234
	Hollister v. Dayton Hudson Corp.	234
	Notes	241
	Dosier v. Wilcox & Crittendon Co.	247
	Notes	249
	2. Adequacy of Warning	249
	Spruill v. Boyle–Midway, Inc.	250
	Notes	256
	Edwards v. California Chemical Co.	257
	Notes	261
	Rhodes v. Interstate Battery System of America, Inc.	262
	Notes	268
	Broussard v. Continental Oil Co.	270
	Notes	275
	3. Obvious or Known Dangers	279
	Burke v. Spartanics Ltd.	279
	Notes	286
	Campos v. Firestone Tire & Rubber Co.	289
	Notes	294
	4. Who to Warn	295
	(a) Users, Consumers, and Bystanders	295
	Humble Sand & Gravel, Inc. v. Gomez	295
	Notes	308
	(b) Learned Intermediaries	311
	Perez v. Wyeth Laboratories Inc.	311
	Notes	322
	(c) Allergies and Idiosyncratic Reactions	326
	Kaempfe v. Lehn & Fink Products Corp.	326
	Notes	330
	(d) The Continuing Duty to Warn	332
	Cover v. Cohen	332
	Notes	334

Chapter 5. Causation in Fact 339

Sec.		Page
A.	Tests for Determining Causation	339
B.	Proof of Causation	341
	1. Reliance on Warnings	341
	Anderson v. F.J. Little Machine Co.	341
	Notes	345
	Town of Bridport v. Sterling Clark Lurton Corp.	346
	Notes	350
	2. Enhanced Injuries	352
	Trull v. Volkswagen of America, Inc.	352
	Notes	356
	3. Linking the Defendant to the Product	357
	Mulcahy v. Eli Lilly & Co.	357
	Notes	366

	Page
Sec.	
Rutherford v. Owens–Illinois, Inc.	370
Notes	382

Chapter 6. Proof of Defect and Causation — 390
Sec.
A. Industry Standard and Custom — 390
Bruce v. Martin–Marietta Corp. — 390
Notes — 393
Union Supply Co. v. Pust — 395
Notes — 397
Alevromagiros v. Hechinger Co. — 398
Notes — 402
B. Post–Accident Remedial Measures — 403
First Premier Bank v. Kolcraft Enterprises, Inc. — 403
Notes — 407
C. Expert Witnesses — 409
Daubert v. Merrell Dow Pharm., Inc. — 409
Sanders, Bendectin on Trial: A Study of Mass Tort Litigation 45–60 (1998) — 417
Notes — 432
Kumho Tire Co., Ltd. v. Carmichael — 435
Notes — 444
Jaurequi v. Carter Manufacturing Co., Inc. — 445
Notes — 451
Westberry v. Gislaved Gummi Ab — 452
Notes — 459
Howerton V. Arai Helmet, Ltd. — 464
Notes — 477

Chapter 7. Proximate Cause — 480
Sec.
A. Introduction — 480
B. Product Alteration — 487
Robinson v. Reed–Prentice Div. of Package Mach. Co. — 487
Notes — 492
Southwire Co. v. Beloit Eastern Corp. — 494
Note — 497
C. Effect of Apportionment of Fault on Superseding Cause — 497
Barry v. Quality Steel Products, Inc. — 497
Notes — 504

Chapter 8. The Effect of Statutes and Regulations — 507
Sec.
A. Relevance of Statutes — 507
Lorenz v. Celotex Corp. — 507
Notes — 511
B. Regulation — 515
Southland Mower Co. v. Consumer Product Safety Commission — 516
Notes — 531
C. Preemption — 532
Bates v. Dow Agrosciences LLC — 532
Notes — 544

	Page
Chapter 9. Damages	**548**

Sec.
- A. In General 548
- B. Pecuniary Loss and Harm to Property 550
  - Alloway v. General Marine Industries 550
  - Notes 560
- C. Mental Distress 561
  - Gnirk v. Ford Motor Co. 561
  - Notes 565
  - Burns v. Jaquays Mining Corp. 567
  - Notes 573
- D. Punitive Damages 575
  - Acosta v. Honda Motor Co., Ltd. 575
  - Owen, Problems in Assessing Punitive Damages Against Manufacturers of Defective Products 580
  - Notes 581
  - Romo v. Ford Motor Co. 585
  - Notes 596

Chapter 10. Apportionment of Liability Among Multiple Parties **599**

Sec.
- A. Consumer Conduct Defenses and Comparative Responsibility 599
  - 1. Contributory Negligence 600
  - 2. Contributory Negligence Under 402a 603
    - McCown v. International Harvester Co. 603
    - Notes 606
  - 3. Assumption of Risk 606
    - Heil Co. v. Grant 609
    - Notes 612
  - 4. Comparative Responsibility 613
    - Daly v. General Motors Corp. 613
    - Notes 621
  - 5. Product Misuse 627
    - Jimenez v. Sears, Roebuck & Co. 628
    - Notes 635
- B. Apportioning Liability Among Defendants and the Special Role of Employers: Contribution and Indemnity 638
  - 1. Apportionment Within the Distributive Chain: Indemnity 641
    - Tromza v. Tecumseh Products Co. 641
    - Notes 644
  - 2. Apportionment Outside the Distributive Chain: Contribution 649
  - 3. Partial Settlements 653
    - Duncan v. Cessna Aircraft Co. 653
    - Notes 655
  - 4. The Special Case of Employers 657
    - Lambertson v. Cincinnati Welding Corp. 658
    - Notes 663

Chapter 11. Statutes of Limitation and Repose **665**
- Raymond v. Eli Lilly & Co. 665
- Notes 671
- Heath v. Sears, Roebuck & Co. 672
- Notes 676

Sec.

Pustejovsky v. Rapid–American Corp. 678
Notes 688

Chapter 12. Parties and Transactions Governed by Strict Liability ... 691

Sec.

A. Parties Who Can Be Sued 691
   1. Retailers, Wholesalers, and Distributors 691
      Vandermark v. Ford Motor Co. 691
      Notes 693
   2. Government Contractors 695
      Boyle v. United Technologies Corp. 695
      Notes 702
      Problem 704
   3. Successor Corporations 705
      Savage Arms, Inc. v. Western Auto Supply Co. 705
      Notes 711

B. Transactions Covered by Product Liability and Warranty 714
   1. Leases and Bailments 715
      Martin v. Ryder Truck Rental, Inc. 715
      Notes 719
      Armstrong Rubber Co. v. Urquidez 720
      Notes 723
   2. Franchises and Trademark Licenses 726
      Kosters v. Seven–Up Co. 726
      Notes 729
   3. Publications 731
      Winter v. G.P. Putnam's Sons 731
      Notes 735
   4. Used Products 736
      Tillman v. Vance Equipment Co. 736
      Notes 740
   5. Real Estate 745
      Kriegler v. Eichler Homes, Inc. 745
      Notes 747
      Peterson v. Superior Court 750
      Notes 761
   6. Services 761
      Hoffman v. Simplot Aviation, Inc. 763
      Notes 766
      Hoover v. Montgomery Ward & Co., Inc. 767
      Notes 769
      Barbee v. Rogers 772
      Notes 775

Chapter 13. Complex Litigation 777

Notes 777

Sec.

A. Issue Preclusion/Collateral Estoppel 778
   Hardy v. Johns–Manville Sales Corp. 778
   Notes 787
   Green, The Inability of Offensive Collateral Estoppel to Fulfill Its
      Promise: An Examination of Estoppel in Asbestos Litigation 789

TABLE OF CONTENTS

	Page
Chapter 9. Damages	**548**

Sec.
- A. In General 548
- B. Pecuniary Loss and Harm to Property 550
  - Alloway v. General Marine Industries 550
  - Notes 560
- C. Mental Distress 561
  - Gnirk v. Ford Motor Co. 561
  - Notes 565
  - Burns v. Jaquays Mining Corp. 567
  - Notes 573
- D. Punitive Damages 575
  - Acosta v. Honda Motor Co., Ltd. 575
  - Owen, Problems in Assessing Punitive Damages Against Manufacturers of Defective Products 580
  - Notes 581
  - Romo v. Ford Motor Co. 585
  - Notes 596

Chapter 10. Apportionment of Liability Among Multiple Parties **599**

Sec.
- A. Consumer Conduct Defenses and Comparative Responsibility 599
  1. Contributory Negligence 600
  2. Contributory Negligence Under 402a 603
     - McCown v. International Harvester Co. 603
     - Notes 606
  3. Assumption of Risk 606
     - Heil Co. v. Grant 609
     - Notes 612
  4. Comparative Responsibility 613
     - Daly v. General Motors Corp. 613
     - Notes 621
  5. Product Misuse 627
     - Jimenez v. Sears, Roebuck & Co. 628
     - Notes 635
- B. Apportioning Liability Among Defendants and the Special Role of Employers: Contribution and Indemnity 638
  1. Apportionment Within the Distributive Chain: Indemnity 641
     - Tromza v. Tecumseh Products Co. 641
     - Notes 644
  2. Apportionment Outside the Distributive Chain: Contribution 649
  3. Partial Settlements 653
     - Duncan v. Cessna Aircraft Co. 653
     - Notes 655
  4. The Special Case of Employers 657
     - Lambertson v. Cincinnati Welding Corp. 658
     - Notes 663

Chapter 11. Statutes of Limitation and Repose **665**
- Raymond v. Eli Lilly & Co. 665
- Notes 671
- Heath v. Sears, Roebuck & Co. 672
- Notes 676

	Page
Sec.	
Pustejovsky v. Rapid–American Corp.	678
Notes	688

Chapter 12. Parties and Transactions Governed by Strict Liability — 691

Sec.

A. Parties Who Can Be Sued — 691
   1. Retailers, Wholesalers, and Distributors — 691
      Vandermark v. Ford Motor Co. — 691
      Notes — 693
   2. Government Contractors — 695
      Boyle v. United Technologies Corp. — 695
      Notes — 702
      Problem — 704
   3. Successor Corporations — 705
      Savage Arms, Inc. v. Western Auto Supply Co. — 705
      Notes — 711

B. Transactions Covered by Product Liability and Warranty — 714
   1. Leases and Bailments — 715
      Martin v. Ryder Truck Rental, Inc. — 715
      Notes — 719
      Armstrong Rubber Co. v. Urquidez — 720
      Notes — 723
   2. Franchises and Trademark Licenses — 726
      Kosters v. Seven–Up Co. — 726
      Notes — 729
   3. Publications — 731
      Winter v. G.P. Putnam's Sons — 731
      Notes — 735
   4. Used Products — 736
      Tillman v. Vance Equipment Co. — 736
      Notes — 740
   5. Real Estate — 745
      Kriegler v. Eichler Homes, Inc. — 745
      Notes — 747
      Peterson v. Superior Court — 750
      Notes — 761
   6. Services — 761
      Hoffman v. Simplot Aviation, Inc. — 763
      Notes — 766
      Hoover v. Montgomery Ward & Co., Inc. — 767
      Notes — 769
      Barbee v. Rogers — 772
      Notes — 775

Chapter 13. Complex Litigation — 777

Notes — 777

Sec.

A. Issue Preclusion/Collateral Estoppel — 778
   Hardy v. Johns–Manville Sales Corp. — 778
   Notes — 787
   Green, The Inability of Offensive Collateral Estoppel to Fulfill Its Promise: An Examination of Estoppel in Asbestos Litigation — 789

Sec.		Page
B.	Multidistrict Litigation	791
	In Re Silicone Gel Breast Implants Products Liability Litigation	792
	Notes	795
C.	Class Actions	796
	Note	801
	Valentino v. Carter–Wallace, Inc.	802
	Notes	809
	Jenkins v. Raymark Industries, Inc.	810
	In Re Rhone–Poulenc Rorer Inc.	815
	Notes	822
	Amchem Products, Inc. v. Windsor	823
	Notes	841
	Note on the Class Action Fairness Act of 2005	845
	Note on Mandatory Class Actions	845
	Note on Bankruptcy Option for Mass Torts	849
	In Re Joint Eastern & Southern District Asbestos Litigation	851
	In Re Asbestos Litigation	853
	Notes	857
INDEX		861

Table of Cases

The principal cases are in bold type. Cases cited or discussed in the text are roman type. References are to pages. Cases cited in principal cases and within other quoted materials are not included.

Acme Pump Co., Inc. v. National Cash Register Co., 32 Conn.Supp. 69, 337 A.2d 672 (Conn.Com.Pl.1974), 31

Acosta v. Honda Motor Co., Ltd., 717 F.2d 828 (3rd Cir.1983), **575**

Adams v. American Cyanamid Co., 1 Neb. App. 337, 498 N.W.2d 577 (Neb.App. 1992), 49

Adams v. G.D. Searle & Co., Inc., 576 So.2d 728 (Fla.App. 2 Dist.1991), 213

Adams v. Johns–Manville Sales Corp., 727 F.2d 533 (5th Cir.1984), 689

Adams Van Service, Inc. v. International Harvester Corp., 1973 WL 21443 (Pa. Com.Pl.1973), 49

Advance Chemical Co. v. Harter, 478 So.2d 444 (Fla.App. 1 Dist.1985), 331

Akers v. Kelley Co., 173 Cal.App.3d 633, 219 Cal.Rptr. 513 (Cal.App. 6 Dist.1985), 111

Albertson v. Volkswagenwerk Aktiengesellschaft, 230 Kan. 368, 634 P.2d 1127 (Kan.1981), 689

Alevromagiros v. Hechinger Co., 993 F.2d 417 (4th Cir.1993), **398**

Alfred N. Koplin & Co., Inc. v. Chrysler Corp., 49 Ill.App.3d 194, 7 Ill.Dec. 113, 364 N.E.2d 100 (Ill.App. 2 Dist.1977), 11

Aller v. Rodgers Machinery Mfg. Co., Inc., 268 N.W.2d 830 (Iowa 1978), 120

Allison v. McGhan Medical Corp., 184 F.3d 1300 (11th Cir.1999), 434

Alloway v. General Marine Industries, L.P., 149 N.J. 620, 695 A.2d 264 (N.J. 1997), **550**, 560

Alm v. Aluminum Co. of America, 717 S.W.2d 588 (Tex.1986), 308

Ambrosini v. Labarraque, 101 F.3d 129, 322 U.S.App.D.C. 19 (D.C.Cir.1996), 460

Amchem Products, Inc. v. Windsor, 521 U.S. 591, 117 S.Ct. 2231, 138 L.Ed.2d 689 (1997), **823**, 841, 842, 844, 845, 846, 848, 850

American Elec. Power Co., Inc. v. Westinghouse Elec. Corp., 418 F.Supp. 435 (S.D.N.Y.1976), 49

American Laundry Machinery Industries v. Horan, 45 Md.App. 97, 412 A.2d 407 (Md.App.1980), 484

American Motorcycle Assn. v. Superior Court, 146 Cal.Rptr. 182, 578 P.2d 899 (Cal.1978), 645

American Safety Equipment Corp. v. Winkler, 640 P.2d 216 (Colo.1982), 9

American Tel. & Tel. Co. v. New York City Human Resources Admin., 833 F.Supp. 962 (S.D.N.Y.1993), 50

Anderson v. F.J. Little Mach. Co., 68 F.3d 1113 (8th Cir.1995), **341,** 346

Anderson v. Klix Chemical Co., 256 Or. 199, 472 P.2d 806 (Or.1970), 249

Anderson v. Minneapolis, St. P. & S. S. M. Ry. Co., 146 Minn. 430, 179 N.W. 45 (Minn.1920), 340

Anderson v. Olmsted Utility Equipment, Inc., 60 Ohio St.3d 124, 573 N.E.2d 626 (Ohio 1991), 742

Anderson v. Somberg, 67 N.J. 291, 338 A.2d 1 (N.J.1975), 230

Apex Supply Co., Inc. v. Benbow Industries, Inc., 189 Ga.App. 598, 376 S.E.2d 694 (Ga.App.1988), 49

Armstrong v. Cione, 69 Haw. 176, 738 P.2d 79 (Hawai'i 1987), 761

Armstrong Rubber Co. v. Urquidez, 570 S.W.2d 374 (Tex.1978), **720,** 723, 725

Asbestos and Asbestos Insulation Material Products Liability Litigation, In re, 431 F.Supp. 906 (Jud.Pan.Mult.Lit.1977), 857

Asbestos Litigation, In re, 90 F.3d 963 (5th Cir.1996), **853**

Askey v. Occidental Chemical Corp., 102 A.D.2d 130, 477 N.Y.S.2d 242 (N.Y.A.D. 4 Dept.1984), 574

Austin v. Will–Burt Co., 361 F.3d 862 (5th Cir.2004), 346, 393

xix

Ayers v. Jackson Township, 106 N.J. 557, 525 A.2d 287 (N.J.1987), 574

Azzarello v. Black Bros. Co., Inc., 480 Pa. 547, 391 A.2d 1020 (Pa.1978), 122

Bagel v. American Honda Motor Co., Inc., 132 Ill.App.3d 82, 87 Ill.Dec. 453, 477 N.E.2d 54 (Ill.App. 1 Dist.1985), 560

Bailey v. McDonnell Douglas Corp., 989 F.2d 794 (5th Cir.1993), 703

Bainter v. Lamoine LP Gas Co., 24 Ill. App.3d 913, 321 N.E.2d 744 (Ill.App. 3 Dist.1974), 725

Baker v. International Harvester Co., 660 S.W.2d 21 (Mo.App. E.D.1983), 482

Balido v. Improved Machinery, Inc., 29 Cal. App.3d 633, 105 Cal.Rptr. 890 (Cal.App. 2 Dist.1972), 334

Barb v. Wallace, 45 Md.App. 271, 412 A.2d 1314 (Md.App.1980), 34

Barbee v. Rogers, 425 S.W.2d 342 (Tex. 1968), 769, **772,** 775, 776

Barker v. Lull Engineering Co., 143 Cal. Rptr. 225, 573 P.2d 443 (Cal.1978), 113, **134,** 138, 140, 141, 214, 482

Barnard v. Saturn Corp., a Division of General Motors Corp., 790 N.E.2d 1023 (Ind. App.2003), 636

Barr v. Rivinius, Inc., 58 Ill.App.3d 121, 15 Ill.Dec. 591, 373 N.E.2d 1063 (Ill.App. 3 Dist.1978), 485, 486

Barry v. Ivarson Inc., 249 So.2d 44 (Fla. App. 2 Dist.1971), 36

Barry v. Quality Steel Products, Inc., 263 Conn. 424, 820 A.2d 258 (Conn. 2003), **497,** 504, 505, 506

Basko v. Sterling Drug, Inc., 416 F.2d 417 (2nd Cir.1969), 331, 339

Bates v. Dow Agrosciences LLC, 544 U.S. 431, 125 S.Ct. 1788, 161 L.Ed.2d 687 (2005), **532,** 544, 545, 546

Batts v. Tow–Motor Forklift Co., 978 F.2d 1386 (5th Cir.1992), 109

Beale v. Hardy, 769 F.2d 213 (4th Cir. 1985), 310

Becker v. National Health Products, Inc., 896 F.Supp. 100 (N.D.N.Y.1995), 460

Bednarski v. Hideout Homes & Realty Inc., a Division of United States Homes & Properties, Inc., 711 F.Supp. 823 (M.D.Pa.1989), 748

Bell Helicopter Co. v. Bradshaw, 594 S.W.2d 519 (Tex.Civ.App.-Corpus Christi 1979), 335

Berardi v. Johns–Manville Corp., 334 Pa.Super. 36, 482 A.2d 1067 (Pa.Super.1984), 671

Berry By and Through Berry v. Beech Aircraft Corp., 717 P.2d 670 (Utah 1985), 676

Beshada v. Johns–Manville Products Corp., 90 N.J. 191, 447 A.2d 539 (N.J.1982), 244

Best v. Taylor Mach. Works, 179 Ill.2d 367, 228 Ill.Dec. 636, 689 N.E.2d 1057 (Ill. 1997), 676

Beverly Hills Fire Litigation, In re, 695 F.2d 207 (6th Cir.1982), 797

Bexiga v. Havir Mfg. Corp., 60 N.J. 402, 290 A.2d 281 (N.J.1972), 150, **181,** 184, 601, 657

Bickett v. W.R. Grace & Co., 1972 WL 20845 (W.D.Ky.1972), 32

Bigbee v. Pacific Tel. & Tel. Co., 192 Cal. Rptr. 857, 665 P.2d 947 (Cal.1983), 482

Bigelow v. Agway, Inc., 506 F.2d 551 (2nd Cir.1974), 22

Bilotta v. Kelley Co., Inc., 346 N.W.2d 616 (Minn.1984), 90

Bishop v. Firestone Tire & Rubber Co., 814 F.2d 437 (7th Cir.1987), 294

Blackburn v. Dorta, 348 So.2d 287 (Fla. 1977), 613

Blevins v. New Holland North America, Inc., 128 F.Supp.2d 952 (W.D.Va.2001), 451

BMW of North America, Inc. v. Gore, 517 U.S. 559, 116 S.Ct. 1589, 134 L.Ed.2d 809 (1996), 596

Boatland of Houston, Inc. v. Bailey, 609 S.W.2d 743 (Tex.1980), **152,** 158

Bobka v. Cook County Hospital, 97 Ill. App.3d 351, 52 Ill.Dec. 790, 422 N.E.2d 999 (Ill.App. 1 Dist.1981), 485

Booker v. Revlon Realistic Professional Products, Inc., 433 So.2d 407 (La.App. 4 Cir.1983), 330

Booth v. Mary Carter Paint Co., 202 So.2d 8 (Fla.App. 2 Dist.1967), 657

Borel v. Fibreboard Paper Products Corp., 493 F.2d 1076 (5th Cir.1973), 215, 257, 269, 787, 788

Bourelle v. Crown Equipment Corp., 220 F.3d 532 (7th Cir.2000), 452

Bowling v. Heil Co., 31 Ohio St.3d 277, 511 N.E.2d 373 (Ohio 1987), 626

Boyle v. United Technologies Corp., 487 U.S. 500, 108 S.Ct. 2510, 101 L.Ed.2d 442 (1988), **695,** 702, 703, 705

Braun v. Soldier of Fortune Magazine, Inc., 968 F.2d 1110 (11th Cir.1992), 735

Brawner v. Liberty Industries, Inc., 573 S.W.2d 376 (Mo.App.1978), **104,** 111

Bray v. Marathon Corp., 356 S.C. 111, 588 S.E.2d 93 (S.C.2003), 566

Breast Implant Litigation, In re, 11 F.Supp.2d 1217 (D.Colo.1998), 460

Brech v. J.C. Penney Co., Inc., 698 F.2d 332 (8th Cir.1983), 511

Brescia v. Great Road Realty Trust, 117 N.H. 154, 373 A.2d 1310 (N.H.1977), 719

Bridport, Town of v. Sterling Clark Lurton Corp., 166 Vt. 304, 693 A.2d 701 (Vt.1997), **346,** 350

Brim v. State, 695 So.2d 268 (Fla.1997), 477

Brochu v. Ortho Pharmaceutical Corp., 642 F.2d 652 (1st Cir.1981), 324

TABLE OF CASES

Brooks v. Beech Aircraft Corp., 120 N.M. 372, 902 P.2d 54 (N.M.1995), 397
Brooks v. Howmedica, Inc., 273 F.3d 785 (8th Cir.2001), 546
Broussard v. Continental Oil Co., 433 So.2d 354 (La.App. 3 Cir.1983), **270,** 275, 279, 308
Brown v. Asgrow Seed Co. of Texas, 379 S.W.2d 412 (Tex.Civ.App.-San Antonio 1964), 31
Brown v. Quick Mix Co., Division of Koehring Co., 75 Wash.2d 833, 454 P.2d 205 (Wash.1969), 111
Brown v. Superior Court, 245 Cal.Rptr. 412, 751 P.2d 470 (Cal.1988), 213, 369
Brown v. United States Stove Co., 98 N.J. 155, 484 A.2d 1234 (N.J.1984), 482
Brownlee v. Louisville Varnish Co., 641 F.2d 397 (5th Cir.1981), 257
Broyles v. Brown Engineering Co., 275 Ala. 35, 151 So.2d 767 (Ala.1963), 767
Bruce v. Martin–Marietta Corp., 544 F.2d 442 (10th Cir.1976), **390,** 393, 740
Bruce Farms, Inc. v. Coupe, 219 Va. 287, 247 S.E.2d 400 (Va.1978), 749
Buckman Co. v. Plaintiffs' Legal Committee, 531 U.S. 341, 121 S.Ct. 1012, 148 L.Ed.2d 854 (2001), 545
Builders Supply Co. v. McCabe, 366 Pa. 322, 77 A.2d 368 (Pa.1951), 644
Burke v. Spartanics, Ltd., 252 F.3d 131 (2nd Cir.2001), **279,** 286, 287, 341, 346
Burleson v. Texas Dept. of Criminal Justice, 393 F.3d 577 (5th Cir.2004), 460
Burnett v. James, 564 S.W.2d 407 (Tex.Civ. App.-Dallas 1978), 17
Burns v. Jaquays Mining Corp., 156 Ariz. 375, 752 P.2d 28 (Ariz.App. Div. 2 1987), **567,** 689

Calloway v. City of Reno, 116 Nev. 250, 993 P.2d 1259 (Nev.2000), 560
Calloway v. Manion, 572 F.2d 1033 (5th Cir.1978), 28, 30
Camacho v. Honda Motor Co., Ltd., 741 P.2d 1240 (Colo.1987), 407
Campos v. Firestone Tire & Rubber Co., 98 N.J. 198, 485 A.2d 305 (N.J. 1984), **289,** 294, 295
Capital Holding Corp. v. Bailey, 873 S.W.2d 187 (Ky.1994), 574
Cardwell v. Hackett, 579 S.W.2d 186 (Tenn. Ct.App.1978), 28
Carley v. Wheeled Coach, 991 F.2d 1117 (3rd Cir.1993), 703
Carney v. Sears, Roebuck & Co., 309 F.2d 300 (4th Cir.1962), 17
Carter v. Johns–Manville Sales Corp., 557 F.Supp. 1317 (E.D.Tex.1983), 142, 176
Castano v. American Tobacco Co., 84 F.3d 734 (5th Cir.1996), 809
Castillo v. E.I. Du Pont De Nemours & Co., Inc., 854 So.2d 1264 (Fla.2003), 479
Castrignano v. E.R. Squibb & Sons, Inc., 546 A.2d 775 (R.I.1988), 213

Caterpillar, Inc. v. Shears, 911 S.W.2d 379 (Tex.1995), 187
Caterpillar Tractor Co. v. Beck, 593 P.2d 871 (Alaska 1979), 138, 214
Cavallo v. Star Enterprise, 100 F.3d 1150 (4th Cir.1996), 460
Cavallo v. Star Enterprise, 892 F.Supp. 756 (E.D.Va.1995), 459, 460
Centex Homes v. Buecher, 95 S.W.3d 266 (Tex.2002), 748, 749
Chisholm v. J.R. Simplot Co., 94 Idaho 628, 495 P.2d 1113 (Idaho 1972), 638
Christian v. Gray, 65 P.3d 591 (Okla.2003), 460
Chrysler Corp. v. Alumbaugh, 168 Ind.App. 363, 342 N.E.2d 908 (Ind.App. 3 Dist. 1976), 485
Chubb Group v. C.F. Murphy & Associates, Inc., 656 S.W.2d 766 (Mo.App. W.D. 1983), 771, 775
Cipollone v. Liggett Group, Inc., 505 U.S. 504, 112 S.Ct. 2608, 120 L.Ed.2d 407 (1992), 544, 545, 546
Cipollone v. Liggett Group, Inc., 644 F.Supp. 283 (D.N.J.1986), 130, 131
Clarke Industries, Inc. v. Home Indem. Co., 591 So.2d 458 (Ala.1991), 198, 199
Clarys v. Ford Motor Co., 592 N.W.2d 573 (N.D.1999), 560
Clausen v. M/V New Carissa, 339 F.3d 1049 (9th Cir.2003), 460
Cleveland v. Square–D Co., 613 S.W.2d 790 (Tex.Civ.App.-Hous (14 Dist.) 1981), 52
Coffer v. Standard Brands, Inc., 30 N.C.App. 134, 226 S.E.2d 534 (N.C.App. 1976), 17, 26
Colvin v. Red Steel Co., 682 S.W.2d 243 (Tex.1984), 637
Combustion Engineering, Inc., In re, 391 F.3d 190 (3rd Cir.2005), 859
Compaq Computer Corp. v. Lapray, 135 S.W.3d 657 (Tex.2004), 22
Connelly v. Uniroyal, Inc., 75 Ill.2d 393, 27 Ill.Dec. 343, 389 N.E.2d 155 (Ill.1979), 729
Cook v. Minneapolis, St. P. & S.S.M.R. Co., 98 Wis. 624, 74 N.W. 561 (Wis.1898), 340
Cooley v. Quick Supply Co., 221 N.W.2d 763 (Iowa 1974), 693
Copley Pharmaceutical, Inc., In re, 161 F.R.D. 456 (D.Wyo.1995), 822
Cotton v. Buckeye Gas Products Co., 840 F.2d 935, 268 U.S.App.D.C. 228 (D.C.Cir.1988), 243
Couch v. Astec Industries, Inc., 132 N.M. 631, 53 P.3d 398 (N.M.App.2002), 408
County Asphalt, Inc. v. Lewis Welding & Engineering Corp., 323 F.Supp. 1300 (S.D.N.Y.1970), 50
Court v. Grzelinski, 72 Ill.2d 141, 19 Ill.Dec. 617, 379 N.E.2d 281 (Ill.1978), 485, 486
Cover v. Cohen, 473 N.Y.S.2d 378, 461 N.E.2d 864 (N.Y.1984), **332,** 334

TABLE OF CASES

Cowgill v. Raymark Industries, Inc., 780 F.2d 324 (3rd Cir.1985), 672
Crandell v. Larkin and Jones Appliance Co., Inc., 334 N.W.2d 31 (S.D.1983), 740
Cratsley v. Commonwealth Edison Co., 38 Ill.App.3d 55, 347 N.E.2d 496 (Ill.App. 1 Dist.1976), 770
Crocker v. Winthrop Laboratories, Division of Sterling Drug, Inc., 514 S.W.2d 429 (Tex.1974), 331
Cropper v. Owens–Corning Fiberglas Corp., 1997 WL 1433782 (Pa.Com.Pl.1997), 383
Crossfield v. Quality Control Equipment Co., Inc., 1 F.3d 701 (8th Cir.1993), 198, 199
CSX Transportation, Inc. v. Easterwood, 507 U.S. 658, 113 S.Ct. 1732, 123 L.Ed.2d 387 (1993), 544
Culbert v. Sampson's Supermarkets Inc., 444 A.2d 433 (Me.1982), 566
Curcio v. Caterpillar, Inc., 344 S.C. 266, 543 S.E.2d 264 (S.C.App.2001), 257

Dague v. Piper Aircraft Corp., 275 Ind. 520, 418 N.E.2d 207 (Ind.1981), 676
Daly v. General Motors Corp., 144 Cal. Rptr. 380, 575 P.2d 1162 (Cal.1978), **613,** 621, 622, 627, 649, 650
Dambacher by Dambacher v. Mallis, 336 Pa.Super. 22, 485 A.2d 408 (Pa.Super.1984), 123, 242
Dannenfelser v. DaimlerChrysler Corp., 370 F.Supp.2d 1091 (D.Hawai'i 2005), 357
D'Antona v. Hampton Grinding Wheel Co., Inc., 225 Pa.Super. 120, 310 A.2d 307 (Pa.Super.1973), 493
Dare v. Sobule, 674 P.2d 960 (Colo.1984), 652
Dart v. Wiebe Mfg., Inc., 147 Ariz. 242, 709 P.2d 876 (Ariz.1985), 90, 138
Daubert v. Merrell Dow Pharmaceuticals, Inc., 509 U.S. 579, 113 S.Ct. 2786, 125 L.Ed.2d 469 (1993), 162, 346, **409,** 432, 433, 434, 444, 452, 460, 462, 464, 479
Davis v. Avondale Industries, Inc., 975 F.2d 169 (5th Cir.1992), 246
Davis v. Berwind Corp., 547 Pa. 260, 690 A.2d 186 (Pa.1997), 492
Davis v. Whiting Corp., 66 Or.App. 541, 674 P.2d 1194 (Or.App.1984), 676
Davis v. Wyeth Laboratories, Inc., 399 F.2d 121 (9th Cir.1968), 244, 323, 334
De Bardeleben Marine Corp. v. United States, 451 F.2d 140 (5th Cir.1971), 736
Decatur Co-op. Ass'n v. Urban, 219 Kan. 171, 547 P.2d 323 (Kan.1976), 30
Deffebach v. Lansburgh & Bro., 150 F.2d 591, 80 U.S.App.D.C. 185 (D.C.Cir. 1945), 31
DeKalb Agresearch, Inc. v. Abbott, 391 F.Supp. 152 (N.D.Ala.1974), 44
Delaney v. Towmotor Corp., 339 F.2d 4 (2nd Cir.1964), 724

DeLuryea v. Winthrop Laboratories, a Div. of Sterling Drug, Inc., 697 F.2d 222 (8th Cir.1983), 408
Dennis v. Ford Motor Co., 471 F.2d 733 (3rd Cir.1973), 492
Denny v. Ford Motor Co., 639 N.Y.S.2d 250, 662 N.E.2d 730 (N.Y.1995), 27, 121
Densberger v. United Technologies Corp., 297 F.3d 66 (2nd Cir.2002), 703
DeSantis v. Parker Feeders, Inc., 547 F.2d 357 (7th Cir.1976), 485
Devlin v. Smith, 89 N.Y. 470, 11 Abb. N. Cas. 322 (N.Y.1882), 2
Dewberry v. LaFollette, 598 P.2d 241 (Okla. 1979), 750
Dewick v. Maytag Corp., 296 F.Supp.2d 905 (N.D.Ill.2003), 408
Diamond v. E.R. Squibb and Sons, Inc., 397 So.2d 671 (Fla.1981), 676
Diehl v. Blaw–Knox, 360 F.3d 426 (3rd Cir. 2004), 408
DiIenno v. Libbey Glass Div., Owens–Illinois, Inc., 668 F.Supp. 373 (D.Del.1987), 31
Dillon v. Legg, 68 Cal.2d 728, 69 Cal.Rptr. 72, 441 P.2d 912 (Cal.1968), 566
Dix & Associates Pipeline Contractors, Inc. v. Key, 799 S.W.2d 24 (Ky.1990), 663
Dobias v. Western Farmers Ass'n, 6 Wash. App. 194, 491 P.2d 1346 (Wash.App. Div. 3 1971), 33
Dole v. Dow Chemical Co., 331 N.Y.S.2d 382, 282 N.E.2d 288 (N.Y.1972), 286
Donald v. City Nat. Bank of Dothan, 295 Ala. 320, 329 So.2d 92 (Ala.1976), 32
Dosier v. Wilcox–Crittendon Co., 45 Cal.App.3d 74, 119 Cal.Rptr. 135 (Cal. App. 1 Dist.1975), **247,** 249, 637
Drayton v. Jiffee Chemical Corp., 395 F.Supp. 1081 (N.D.Ohio 1975), 16
Ducko v. Chrysler Motors Corp., 433 Pa.Super. 47, 639 A.2d 1204 (Pa.Super.1994), 232
Dudley Sports Co. v. Schmitt, 151 Ind.App. 217, 279 N.E.2d 266 (Ind.App. 2 Dist. 1972), 730
Duncan v. Cessna Aircraft Co., 665 S.W.2d 414 (Tex.1984), 608, 622, 650, **653,** 655, 656
Durrett v. Baxter Chrysler–Plymouth, Inc., 198 Neb. 392, 253 N.W.2d 37 (Neb. 1977), 26
Dyer v. Best Pharmacal, 118 Ariz. 465, 577 P.2d 1084 (Ariz.App. Div. 1 1978), 484

Edwards v. California Chemical Co., 245 So.2d 259 (Fla.App. 4 Dist.1971), **257,** 261
Eimann v. Soldier of Fortune Magazine, Inc., 880 F.2d 830 (5th Cir.1989), 736
Eisen v. Carlisle and Jacquelin, 417 U.S. 156, 94 S.Ct. 2140, 40 L.Ed.2d 732 (1974), 801, 802, 822

Elgin Airport Inn, Inc. v. Commonwealth Edison Co., 89 Ill.2d 138, 59 Ill.Dec. 675, 432 N.E.2d 259 (Ill.1982), 771
Ellington v. Coca Cola Bottling Co. of Tulsa, Inc., 717 P.2d 109 (Okla.1986), 565
Elmore v. American Motors Corp., 70 Cal.2d 578, 75 Cal.Rptr. 652, 451 P.2d 84 (Cal.1969), 485
Elmore v. Owens–Illinois, Inc., 673 S.W.2d 434 (Mo.1984), 142
Embs v. Pepsi–Cola Bottling Co. of Lexington, Kentucky, Inc., 528 S.W.2d 703 (Ky. 1975), 485
Emsco Screen Pipe Co. of Texas v. Heights Muffler Co., 420 S.W.2d 179 (Tex.Civ. App-Hous (14 Dist.) 1967), 33
Energy Investors Fund, L.P. v. Metric Constructors, Inc., 351 N.C. 331, 525 S.E.2d 441 (N.C.2000), 36
Epstein v. Official Committee of Unsecured Creditors of Estate of Piper Aircraft Corp., 58 F.3d 1573 (11th Cir.1995), 850
Erdman v. Johnson Bros. Radio & Television Co., 260 Md. 190, 271 A.2d 744 (Md.1970), 601, 602
E.R. Squibb & Sons, Inc. v. Cox, 477 So.2d 963 (Ala.1985), 351
Escola v. Coca Cola Bottling Co. of Fresno, 24 Cal.2d 453, 150 P.2d 436 (Cal.1944), 57
Eshbach v. W.T. Grant's & Co., 481 F.2d 940 (3rd Cir.1973), 482, 483
Ethicon, Inc. v. Parten, 520 S.W.2d 527 (Tex.Civ.App-Hous (14 Dist.) 1975), 723, 775
Exxon Co., U.S.A. v. Sofec, Inc., 517 U.S. 830, 116 S.Ct. 1813, 135 L.Ed.2d 113 (1996), 505

Fairchild v. Glenhaven Funeral Services Ltd (t/a GH Dovener & Son) (HL 2002), 386, 388
Fallon v. Clifford B. Hannay & Son, Inc., 153 A.D.2d 95, 550 N.Y.S.2d 135 (N.Y.A.D. 3 Dept.1989), **124,** 185
Fargo Mach. & Tool Co. v. Kearney & Trecker Corp., 428 F.Supp. 364 (E.D.Mich.1977), 49
Farina v. Niagara Mohawk Power Corp., 81 A.D.2d 700, 438 N.Y.S.2d 645 (N.Y.A.D. 3 Dept.1981), 770
Fear Ranches, Inc. v. Berry, 470 F.2d 905 (10th Cir.1972), 32
Feldman v. Lederle Laboratories, 97 N.J. 429, 479 A.2d 374 (N.J.1984), 213, 243, 244, 481
Fetter v. Beal, 1 Ld. Raymond 339, 91 Eng. Rep. 1122 (King's Bench 1697), 688, 689
Fiorito Bros., Inc. v. Fruehauf Corp., 747 F.2d 1309 (9th Cir.1984), 50
First National Bank of Mobile v. Cessna Aircraft Co., 365 So.2d 966 (Ala.1978), 724

First Premier Bank v. Kolcraft Enterprises, Inc., 686 N.W.2d 430 (S.D. 2004), **403,** 407, 408
Fischer v. Johns–Manville Corp., 103 N.J. 643, 512 A.2d 466 (N.J.1986), 583
Fischer v. Moore, 183 Colo. 392, 517 P.2d 458 (Colo.1973), 652
Fisher v. Ford Motor Co., 224 F.3d 570 (6th Cir.2000), 547
Flowers v. Viking Yacht Co., 366 N.J.Super. 49, 840 A.2d 291 (N.J.Super.L.2003), 560
Fluor Corp. v. Jeppesen & Co., 170 Cal. App.3d 468, 216 Cal.Rptr. 68 (Cal.App. 2 Dist.1985), 736
Folz v. State, 110 N.M. 457, 797 P.2d 246 (N.M.1990), 565
Ford Motor Co. v. Pool, 688 S.W.2d 879 (Tex.App.-Texarkana 1985), 90
Ford Motor Co. v. Ridgway, 135 S.W.3d 598 (Tex.2004), 232, 452
Ford Motor Co. v. Taylor, 60 Tenn.App. 271, 446 S.W.2d 521 (Tenn.Ct.App. 1969), 31
Forma Scientific, Inc. v. BioSera, Inc., 960 P.2d 108 (Colo.1998), 407, 408
Fred's Excavating & Crane Service, Inc. v. Continental Ins. Co., 340 So.2d 1220 (Fla.App. 4 Dist.1976), 31
Freeman v. Hoffman–La Roche, Inc., 260 Neb. 552, 618 N.W.2d 827 (Neb.2000), 213
Freightliner Corp. v. Myrick, 514 U.S. 280, 115 S.Ct. 1483, 131 L.Ed.2d 385 (1995), 544
Frey v. Harley Davidson Motor Co., Inc., 734 A.2d 1 (Pa.Super.1999), 741
Frye v. Medicare–Glaser Corp., 153 Ill.2d 26, 178 Ill.Dec. 763, 605 N.E.2d 557 (Ill.1992), 324
Frye v. United States, 293 F. 1013 (D.C.Cir. 1923), 432, 479
Fulbright v. Klamath Gas Co., 271 Or. 449, 533 P.2d 316 (Or.1975), 725

Gagne v. Bertran, 43 Cal.2d 481, 275 P.2d 15 (Cal.1954), 766
Galindo v. Precision American Corp., 754 F.2d 1212 (5th Cir.1985), 695, 741
Garcia v. Halsett, 3 Cal.App.3d 319, 82 Cal. Rptr. 420 (Cal.App. 1 Dist.1970), 719
Gardner v. Q.H.S., Inc., 448 F.2d 238 (4th Cir.1971), 256, 268
Garfield v. Furniture Fair–Hanover, 113 N.J.Super. 509, 274 A.2d 325 (N.J.Super.L.1971), 725
Garrison v. Rohm & Haas Co., 492 F.2d 346 (6th Cir.1974), 188
Gatto v. Walgreen Drug Co., 61 Ill.2d 513, 337 N.E.2d 23 (Ill.1975), 657
Geier v. American Honda Motor Co., Inc., 529 U.S. 861, 120 S.Ct. 1913, 146 L.Ed.2d 914 (2000), 544, 545, 546, 547
Genaust v. Illinois Power Co., 62 Ill.2d 456, 343 N.E.2d 465 (Ill.1976), 770

TABLE OF CASES

General Electric Co. v. Joiner, 522 U.S. 136, 118 S.Ct. 512, 139 L.Ed.2d 508 (1997), 432, 432, 433
General Motors Corp. v. Hopkins, 548 S.W.2d 344 (Tex.1977), 637, 638
General Motors Corp. v. Sanchez, 997 S.W.2d 584 (Tex.1999), 626
General Supply & Equipment Co., Inc. v. Phillips, 490 S.W.2d 913 (Tex.Civ.App.-Tyler 1972), 17
George v. Parke-Davis, 107 Wash.2d 584, 733 P.2d 507 (Wash.1987), 367
Gibbs v. General Motors Corp., 450 S.W.2d 827 (Tex.1970), 742
Gilbert v. Stone City Const. Co., Inc., 171 Ind.App. 418, 357 N.E.2d 738 (Ind.App. 1 Dist.1976), 485, 486
Gilchrist Timber Co. v. ITT Rayonier, Inc., 696 So.2d 334 (Fla.1997), 602
Gilliam v. Indiana Nat. Bank, 337 So.2d 352 (Ala.Civ.App.1976), 44
Givens v. Lederle, 556 F.2d 1341 (5th Cir. 1977), 323
Glittenberg v. Doughboy Recreational Industries, 441 Mich. 379, 491 N.W.2d 208 (Mich.1992), 346
Global Truck & Equipment Co., Inc. v. Palmer Mach. Works, Inc., 628 F.Supp. 641 (N.D.Miss.1986), 22
Gnirk v. Ford Motor Co., 572 F.Supp. 1201 (D.S.D.1983), **561,** 565, 566, 567
Goeb v. Tharaldson, 615 N.W.2d 800 (Minn. 2000), 478
Goebel v. Denver and Rio Grande Western R.R. Co., 215 F.3d 1083 (10th Cir.2000), 444
Goodbar v. Whitehead Bros., 591 F.Supp. 552 (W.D.Va.1984), 308, 310
Goodlin v. Medtronic, Inc., 167 F.3d 1367 (11th Cir.1999), 546
Grahn v. Dillingham Const., Inc., 2004 WL 2075570 (Cal.App. 1 Dist.2004), 383
Gramling v. Baltz, 253 Ark. 352, 253 Ark. 361, 485 S.W.2d 183 (Ark.1972), 49
Grams v. Milk Products, Inc., 283 Wis.2d 511, 699 N.W.2d 167 (Wis.2005), 561
Gray v. Manitowoc Co., Inc., 771 F.2d 866 (5th Cir.1985), **98,** 110
Green v. Smith & Nephew AHP, Inc., 245 Wis.2d 772, 629 N.W.2d 727 (Wis.2001), 104
Greenberg v. Lorenz, 213 N.Y.S.2d 39, 173 N.E.2d 773 (N.Y.1961), 3, 34
Greenman v. Yuba Power Products, Inc., 59 Cal.2d 57, 27 Cal.Rptr. 697, 377 P.2d 897 (Cal.1963), 2, 3, 51, **53,** 57, 58, 81, 627, 717
Green Oil Co. v. Hornsby, 539 So.2d 218 (Ala.1989), 585
Greeves v. Rosenbaum, 965 P.2d 669 (Wyo. 1998), 748
Griggs v. Firestone Tire & Rubber Co., 513 F.2d 851 (8th Cir.1975), 483, 493
Grillo v. Burke's Paint Co., Inc., 275 Or. 421, 551 P.2d 449 (Or.1976), 657

Grimes v. Hoffmann-LaRoche, Inc., 907 F.Supp. 33 (D.N.H.1995), 460
Grimshaw v. Ford Motor Co., 119 Cal. App.3d 757, 174 Cal.Rptr. 348 (Cal.App. 4 Dist.1981), 583
Gross v. Nashville Gas Co., 608 S.W.2d 860 (Tenn.Ct.App.1980), 215
Grundberg v. Upjohn Co., 813 P.2d 89 (Utah 1991), **199,** 213
Guarino v. Mine Safety Appliance Co., 306 N.Y.S.2d 942, 255 N.E.2d 173 (N.Y. 1969), 485
Gupta v. Ritter Homes, Inc., 646 S.W.2d 168 (Tex.1983), 749
Guy v. Crown Equipment Corp., 394 F.3d 320 (5th Cir.2004), 452
G-W-L, Inc. v. Robichaux, 643 S.W.2d 392 (Tex.1982), 747, 769

Habecker v. Clark Equipment Co., 942 F.2d 210 (3rd Cir.1991), 143
Haberly v. Reardon Co., 319 S.W.2d 859 (Mo.1958), 484
Hagans v. Oliver Machinery Co., 576 F.2d 97 (5th Cir.1978), 187
Hagenbuch v. Snap-On Tools Corp., 339 F.Supp. 676 (D.N.H.1972), 22
Hall v. Baxter Healthcare Corp., 947 F.Supp. 1387 (D.Or.1996), 460
Halphen v. Johns-Manville Sales Corp., 484 So.2d 110 (La.1986), 176
Hamilton v. Asbestos Corp., Ltd., 95 Cal. Rptr.2d 701, 998 P.2d 403 (Cal.2000), 688
Hammond v. International Harvester Co., 691 F.2d 646 (3rd Cir.1982), 185
Hanberry v. Hearst Corp., 276 Cal.App.2d 680, 81 Cal.Rptr. 519 (Cal.App. 4 Dist. 1969), 736
Hansen v. Mountain Fuel Supply Co., 858 P.2d 970 (Utah 1993), 574
Happel v. Wal-Mart Stores, Inc., 199 Ill.2d 179, 262 Ill.Dec. 815, 766 N.E.2d 1118 (Ill.2002), 325
Hardman v. Helene Curtis Industries, Inc., 48 Ill.App.2d 42, 198 N.E.2d 681 (Ill. App. 1 Dist.1964), 28, 638
Hardy v. Johns-Manville Sales Corp., 681 F.2d 334 (5th Cir.1982), **778,** 787, 788
Harris v. Great Dane Trailers, Inc., 234 F.3d 398 (8th Cir.2000), 546
Harrison v. Bill Cairns Pontiac of Marlow Heights, Inc., 77 Md.App. 41, 549 A.2d 385 (Md.App.1988), 232
Hasler v. United States, 718 F.2d 202 (6th Cir.1983), 460
Haugen v. Minnesota Mining & Mfg. Co., 15 Wash.App. 379, 550 P.2d 71 (Wash. App. Div. 2 1976), 612
Hauter v. Zogarts, 120 Cal.Rptr. 681, 534 P.2d 377 (Cal.1975), **18,** 21, 22
Hawk Industries, Inc. v. Bausch & Lomb, Inc., 59 F.R.D. 619 (S.D.N.Y.1973), 848

TABLE OF CASES

Hawkins Const. Co. v. Matthews Co., Inc., 190 Neb. 546, 209 N.W.2d 643 (Neb. 1973), 720

Heath v. Sears, Roebuck & Co., 123 N.H. 512, 464 A.2d 288 (N.H.1983), **672,** 677

Heaton v. Ford Motor Co., 248 Or. 467, 435 P.2d 806 (Or.1967), 111

Heckman v. Federal Press Co., 587 F.2d 612 (3rd Cir.1978), 257

Hedges v. Public Service Co. of Indiana, Inc., 396 N.E.2d 933 (Ind.App. 1 Dist. 1979), 770

Hefferin v. Stempkowski, 247 Pa.Super. 366, 372 A.2d 869 (Pa.Super.1977), 663

Heil Co. v. Grant, 534 S.W.2d 916 (Tex. Civ.App.-Tyler 1976), **609**

Helene Curtis Industries, Inc. v. Pruitt, 385 F.2d 841 (5th Cir.1967), 485

Heller v. Shaw Industries, Inc., 167 F.3d 146 (3rd Cir.1999), 462

Hemet Dodge v. Gryder, 23 Ariz.App. 523, 534 P.2d 454 (Ariz.App. Div. 1 1975), 657

Hempstead v. General Fire Extinguisher Corp., 269 F.Supp. 109 (D.Del.1967), 736

Henderson v. Ford Motor Co., 519 S.W.2d 87 (Tex.1974), 611

Henningsen v. Bloomfield Motors, Inc., 32 N.J. 358, 161 A.2d 69 (N.J.1960), 3, 14, 34, **37,** 42, 43

Hensley v. Sherman Car Wash Equipment Co., 33 Colo.App. 279, 520 P.2d 146 (Colo.App.1974), 608

Heritage v. Pioneer Brokerage & Sales, Inc., 604 P.2d 1059 (Alaska 1979), 142

Hiigel v. General Motors Corp., 190 Colo. 57, 544 P.2d 983 (Colo.1975), 262

Hill v. General Motors Corp., 637 S.W.2d 382 (Mo.App. E.D.1982), 493, 494

Hiner v. Deere and Co., Inc., 340 F.3d 1190 (10th Cir.2003), 346

Hinton v. Monsanto Co., 813 So.2d 827 (Ala.2001), 575

Hoffman v. Simplot Aviation, Inc., 97 Idaho 32, 539 P.2d 584 (Idaho 1975), **763,** 766, 767, 769

Hollister v. Dayton Hudson Corp., 201 F.3d 731 (6th Cir.2000), **234**

Holloway v. General Motors Corp., Chevrolet Division, 399 Mich. 617, 250 N.W.2d 736 (Mich.1977), 26

Holowaty v. McDonald's Corp., 10 F.Supp.2d 1078 (D.Minn.1998), 346

Holt v. Stihl, Inc., 449 F.Supp. 693 (E.D.Tenn.1977), 602

Hoover v. Montgomery Ward & Co., Inc., 270 Or. 498, 528 P.2d 76 (Or. 1974), **767,** 769, 770, 775

Hopkins v. Dow Corning Corp., 33 F.3d 1116 (9th Cir.1994), 433

Horn v. Thoratec Corp., 376 F.3d 163 (3rd Cir.2004), 546

Hornbeck v. Western States Fire Apparatus, Inc., 280 Or. 647, 572 P.2d 620 (Or.1977), 613

Horner v. Spalitto, 1 S.W.3d 519 (Mo.App. W.D.1999), 325

Hovenden v. Tenbush, 529 S.W.2d 302 (Tex.Civ.App.-San Antonio 1975), 741

Howerton v. Arai Helmet, Ltd., 358 N.C. 440, 597 S.E.2d 674 (N.C.2004), **464,** 478, 479

Howes v. Hansen, 56 Wis.2d 247, 201 N.W.2d 825 (Wis.1972), 485

Huddell v. Levin, 537 F.2d 726 (3rd Cir. 1976), 356

Hudgens v. Bell Helicopters/Textron, 328 F.3d 1329 (11th Cir.2003), 703

Huffman v. Caterpillar Tractor Co., 908 F.2d 1470 (10th Cir.1990), 408

Humber v. Morton, 426 S.W.2d 554 (Tex. 1968), 747, 748

Humble Sand & Gravel, Inc. v. Gomez, 146 S.W.3d 170 (Tex.2004), **295,** 308

Hunt v. Blasius, 74 Ill.2d 203, 23 Ill.Dec. 574, 384 N.E.2d 368 (Ill.1978), 187

Hunt v. Ferguson–Paulus Enterprises, 243 Or. 546, 415 P.2d 13 (Or.1966), **93**

Hunt v. Guarantee Elec. Co. of St. Louis, 667 S.W.2d 9 (Mo.App. E.D.1984), 771

Huppe v. Twenty–First Century Restaurants of America, Inc., 130 Misc.2d 736, 497 N.Y.S.2d 306 (N.Y.Sup.1985), 398

Hymowitz v. Eli Lilly and Co., 541 N.Y.S.2d 941, 539 N.E.2d 1069 (N.Y.1989), 369

Hyundai Motor America, Inc. v. Goodin, 822 N.E.2d 947 (Ind.2005), 36

Hyundai Motor Co. v. Rodriguez ex rel. Rodriguez, 995 S.W.2d 661 (Tex.1999), 26

Incollingo v. Ewing, 444 Pa. 263, 444 Pa. 299, 282 A.2d 206 (Pa.1971), 269

In re (see name of party)

Insolia v. Philip Morris Inc., 216 F.3d 596 (7th Cir.2000), 109

Jackson v. Nestle–Beich, Inc., 147 Ill.2d 408, 168 Ill.Dec. 147, 589 N.E.2d 547 (Ill.1992), 96

Jackson v. New Jersey Mfrs. Ins. Co., 166 N.J.Super. 448, 400 A.2d 81 (N.J.Super.A.D.1979), 335

Janssen v. Hook, 1 Ill.App.3d 318, 272 N.E.2d 385 (Ill.App. 2 Dist.1971), 31

Jaroslawicz v. Prestige Caterers, Inc., 292 A.D.2d 232, 739 N.Y.S.2d 670 (N.Y.A.D. 1 Dept.2002), 29

Jaurequi v. Carter Mfg. Co., Inc., 173 F.3d 1076 (8th Cir.1999), 162, **445,** 451

Jeannelle v. Thompson Medical Co., Inc., 613 F.Supp. 346 (E.D.Mo.1985), 565

Jeld–Wen, Inc. v. Gamble by Gamble, 256 Va. 144, 501 S.E.2d 393 (Va.1998), 635

Jenkins v. Raymark Industries, Inc., 782 F.2d 468 (5th Cir.1986), **810**

TABLE OF CASES

Jimenez v. Sears, Roebuck and Co., 183 Ariz. 399, 904 P.2d 861 (Ariz.1995), **628,** 636, 638

Jiminez v. Dreis & Krump Mfg. Co., Inc., 736 F.2d 51 (2nd Cir.1984), 187

Johnson v. Ford Motor Co., 29 Cal.Rptr.3d 401, 113 P.3d 82 (Cal.2005), 596, 597

Johnson v. Johnson Chemical Co., Inc., 183 A.D.2d 64, 588 N.Y.S.2d 607 (N.Y.A.D. 2 Dept.1992), 351

Johnson v. Michelin Tire Corp., 812 F.2d 200 (5th Cir.1987), 231

Joint Eastern and Southern Dist. Asbestos Litigation, In re, 14 F.3d 726 (2nd Cir.1993), **851**

Joint Eastern and Southern Dist. Asbestos Litigation, In re, 982 F.2d 721 (2nd Cir. 1992), 853

Joint Eastern and Southern Districts Asbestos Litigation, In re, 878 F.Supp. 473 (E.D.N.Y.1995), 850

Joint Eastern and Southern Districts Asbestos Litigation, In re, 237 F.Supp.2d 297 (E.D.N.Y.2002), 778

Jones v. Hutchinson Mfg., Inc., 502 S.W.2d 66 (Ky.1973), 482

Jones, Inc. v. W. A. Wiedebusch Plumbing & Heating Co., 157 W.Va. 257, 201 S.E.2d 248 (W.Va.1973), 31

Jones & McKnight Corp. v. Birdsboro Corp., 320 F.Supp. 39 (N.D.Ill.1970), 49, 50

Jordan v. Sunnyslope Appliance Propane & Plumbing Supplies Co., 135 Ariz. 309, 660 P.2d 1236 (Ariz.App. Div. 1 1983), 741

Jordon by Jordon v. K–Mart Corp., 417 Pa.Super. 186, 611 A.2d 1328 (Pa.Super.1992), 123

Joyce v. A.C. and S., Inc., 785 F.2d 1200 (4th Cir.1986), 688

Jurado v. Western Gear Works, 131 N.J. 375, 619 A.2d 1312 (N.J.1993), 635, 637

Kaempfe v. Lehn & Fink Products Corp., 21 A.D.2d 197, 249 N.Y.S.2d 840 (N.Y.A.D. 1 Dept.1964), **326**

Kallas Millwork Corp. v. Square D Co., 66 Wis.2d 382, 225 N.W.2d 454 (Wis.1975), 676

Kallio v. Ford Motor Co., 407 N.W.2d 92 (Minn.1987), 163, **163,** 169

Kamarath v. Bennett, 568 S.W.2d 658 (Tex. 1978), 749, 761

Kannankeril v. Terminix International, Inc., 128 F.3d 802 (3rd Cir.1997), 460, 461

Kately v. Wilkinson, 148 Cal.App.3d 576, 195 Cal.Rptr. 902 (Cal.App. 5 Dist.1983), 565, 566

Kealoha v. E.I. du Pont de Nemours and Co., Inc., 82 F.3d 894 (9th Cir.1996), 197

Keen v. Dominick's Finer Foods, Inc., 49 Ill.App.3d 480, 7 Ill.Dec. 341, 364 N.E.2d 502 (Ill.App. 1 Dist.1977), 723

Keener v. Dayton Electric Mfg. Co., 445 S.W.2d 362 (Mo.1969), 693

Keller v. Welles Dept. Store of Racine, 88 Wis.2d 24, 276 N.W.2d 319 (Wis.App. 1979), **106,** 109, 111

Kelley v. American Heyer–Schulte Corp., 957 F.Supp. 873 (W.D.Tex.1997), 461

Kelley v. R.G. Industries, Inc., 304 Md. 124, 497 A.2d 1143 (Md.1985), 177, 178, 179

Kemp v. Medtronic, Inc., 231 F.3d 216 (6th Cir.2000), 546

Kemp v. Wisconsin Electric Power Co., 44 Wis.2d 571, 172 N.W.2d 161 (Wis.1969), 770

Kennedy v. Cumberland Engineering Co., Inc., 471 A.2d 195 (R.I.1984), 676

Kennedy v. Guess, Inc., 806 N.E.2d 776 (Ind.2004), 730

Kentucky Utilities Co. v. Auto Crane Co., 674 S.W.2d 15 (Ky.App.1983), 770

Kerstetter v. Pacific Scientific Co., 210 F.3d 431 (5th Cir.2000), 703

Killeen v. Harmon Grain Products, Inc., 11 Mass.App.Ct. 20, 413 N.E.2d 767 (Mass. App.Ct.1980), 151

Kimbell Foods, Inc., United States v., 440 U.S. 715, 99 S.Ct. 1448, 59 L.Ed.2d 711 (1979), 698

King v. Damiron Corp., 113 F.3d 93 (7th Cir.1997), 740

Kingston v. Chicago & N.W. Ry. Co., 191 Wis. 610, 211 N.W. 913 (Wis.1927), 341

Kirsch v. Picker Intern., Inc., 753 F.2d 670 (8th Cir.1985), 322

Klages v. General Ordnance Equipment Corp., 240 Pa.Super. 356, 367 A.2d 304 (Pa.Super.1976), 609

Klein v. Continental–Emsco, 445 F.2d 629 (5th Cir.1971), 232

Klem v. E.I. DuPont De Nemours & Co., 19 F.3d 997 (5th Cir.1994), 197

Klimas v. International Tel. & Tel. Corp., 297 F.Supp. 937 (D.R.I.1969), 485

Knab v. Alden's Irving Park, Inc., 49 Ill. App.2d 371, 199 N.E.2d 815 (Ill.App. 1 Dist.1964), 31

Knitz v. Minster Mach. Co., 69 Ohio St.2d 460, 432 N.E.2d 814 (Ohio 1982), 111, 138

Knowles v. Harnischfeger Corp., 36 Wash. App. 317, 674 P.2d 200 (Wash.App. Div. 3 1983), 257

Koehring Co. v. A.P.I., Inc., 369 F.Supp. 882 (E.D.Mich.1974), 49, 50

Kohlenberger, Inc. v. Tyson's Foods, Inc., 256 Ark. 584, 510 S.W.2d 555 (Ark. 1974), 50

Kolb v. Texas Employers' Ins. Ass'n, 585 S.W.2d 870 (Tex.Civ.App.-Texarkana 1979), 609

Kopper Glo Fuel, Inc. v. Island Lake Coal Co., 436 F.Supp. 91 (E.D.Tenn.1977), 32

Korean Air Lines Disaster of Sept. 1, 1983., In re, 597 F.Supp. 619 (D.D.C.1984), 736

Kosters v. Seven–Up Co., 595 F.2d 347 (6th Cir.1979), **726,** 729

Kotecki v. Cyclops Welding Corp., 146 Ill.2d 155, 166 Ill.Dec. 1, 585 N.E.2d 1023 (Ill.1991), 663

Kozlowski v. John E. Smith's Sons Co., 87 Wis.2d 882, 275 N.W.2d 915 (Wis.1979), 335

Kramer v. Lewisville Memorial Hosp., 858 S.W.2d 397 (Tex.1993), 340

Kriegler v. Eichler Homes, Inc., 269 Cal. App.2d 224, 74 Cal.Rptr. 749 (Cal.App. 1 Dist.1969), **745,** 748

Kuhn v. Sandoz Pharmaceuticals Corp., 270 Kan. 443, 14 P.3d 1170 (Kan.2000), 477

Kuisis v. Baldwin–Lima–Hamilton Corp., 457 Pa. 321, 319 A.2d 914 (Pa.1974), 483

Kumho Tire Co., Ltd. v. Carmichael, 526 U.S. 137, 119 S.Ct. 1167, 143 L.Ed.2d 238 (1999), 162, **435,** 479

Kuziw v. Lake Engineering Co., 586 F.2d 33 (7th Cir.1978), 493

Laaperi v. Sears, Roebuck & Co., Inc., 787 F.2d 726 (1st Cir.1986), 288, 351

LaGorga v. Kroger Co., 275 F.Supp. 373 (W.D.Pa.1967), 150

Lambertson v. Cincinnati Welding Corp., 312 Minn. 114, 257 N.W.2d 679 (Minn.1977), 658, **658,** 663, 664

Lamendola v. Mizell, 115 N.J.Super. 514, 280 A.2d 241 (N.J.Super.L.1971), 485, 486

Landers v. East Texas Salt Water Disposal Co., 151 Tex. 251, 248 S.W.2d 731 (Tex. 1952), 640

Lane v. C.A. Swanson & Sons, 130 Cal. App.2d 210, 278 P.2d 723 (Cal.App. 2 Dist.1955), 16

Lankford v. Sullivan, Long & Hagerty, 416 So.2d 996 (Ala.1982), 676

Larosa v. Superior Court, 122 Cal.App.3d 741, 176 Cal.Rptr. 224 (Cal.App. 1 Dist. 1981), 740

Larsen v. Pacesetter Systems, Inc., 74 Haw. 1, 837 P.2d 1273 (Hawai'i 1992), 613

Lasley v. Shrake's Country Club Pharmacy, Inc., 179 Ariz. 583, 880 P.2d 1129 (Ariz. App. Div. 1 1994), 325

Latimer v. General Motors Corp., 535 F.2d 1020 (7th Cir.1976), 493

Layne–Atlantic Co. v. Koppers Co., Inc., 214 Va. 467, 201 S.E.2d 609 (Va.1974), 32

Leahy, People v., 34 Cal.Rptr.2d 663, 882 P.2d 321 (Cal.1994), 477

Lee v. Electric Motor Division, 169 Cal. App.3d 375, 215 Cal.Rptr. 195 (Cal.App. 2 Dist.1985), **87,** 97

Lee v. State Farm Mut. Ins. Co., 272 Ga. 583, 533 S.E.2d 82 (Ga.2000), 565

Lee v. Volkswagen of America, Inc., 688 P.2d 1283 (Okla.1984), 356

Leichtamer v. American Motors Corp., 67 Ohio St.2d 456, 424 N.E.2d 568 (Ohio 1981), 584

Lenhardt v. Ford Motor Co., 102 Wash.2d 208, 683 P.2d 1097 (Wash.1984), 393, 397

Lenherr v. NRM Corp., 504 F.Supp. 165 (D.Kan.1980), 188

Lesnefsky v. Fischer & Porter Co., Inc., 527 F.Supp. 951 (E.D.Pa.1981), 188

Lester v. Magic Chef, Inc., 230 Kan. 643, 641 P.2d 353 (Kan.1982), 113

Lewis v. Babcock Industries, Inc., 985 F.2d 83 (2nd Cir.1993), 703

Lewis v. Big Powderhorn Mountain Ski Corp., 69 Mich.App. 437, 245 N.W.2d 81 (Mich.App.1976), 767

Lewis v. Coffing Hoist Division, Duff–Norton Co., Inc., 515 Pa. 334, 528 A.2d 590 (Pa.1987), 397

Lewis & Sims, Inc. v. Key Industries, Inc., 16 Wash.App. 619, 557 P.2d 1318 (Wash. App. Div. 1 1976), 32

Lexecon Inc. v. Milberg Weiss Bershad Hynes & Lerach, 523 U.S. 26, 118 S.Ct. 956, 140 L.Ed.2d 62 (1998), 796

Li v. Yellow Cab Co., 119 Cal.Rptr. 858, 532 P.2d 1226 (Cal.1975), 615

Libbey–Owens Ford Glass Co. v. L & M Paper Co., 189 Neb. 792, 205 N.W.2d 523 (Neb.1973), 484

Lincoln Pulp & Paper Co., Inc. v. Dravo Corp., 436 F.Supp. 262 (D.Me.1977), 50

Lindstrom v. A–C Product Liability Trust, 424 F.3d 488 (6th Cir.2005), 383

Linegar v. Armour of America, Inc., 909 F.2d 1150 (8th Cir.1990), 186

Liriano v. Hobart Corp., 170 F.3d 264 (2nd Cir.1999), 286, 287

Liriano v. Hobart Corp., 677 N.Y.S.2d 764, 700 N.E.2d 303 (N.Y.1998), 494

Liriano v. Hobart Corp., 132 F.3d 124 (2nd Cir.1998), 286, 287

Lish v. Compton, 547 P.2d 223 (Utah 1976), 30

Little Lake Misere Land Co., Inc., United States v., 412 U.S. 580, 93 S.Ct. 2389, 37 L.Ed.2d 187 (1973), 698

Lobianco v. Property Protection, Inc., 292 Pa.Super. 346, 437 A.2d 417 (Pa.Super.1981), 122

Loeb & Co., Inc. v. Schreiner, 294 Ala. 722, 321 So.2d 199 (Ala.1975), 30

Logerquist v. McVey, 196 Ariz. 470, 1 P.3d 113 (Ariz.2000), 479

Lonon v. Pep Boys, Manny, Moe & Jack, 371 Pa.Super. 291, 538 A.2d 22 (Pa.Super.1988), 613

Lopez v. Precision Papers, Inc., 107 A.D.2d 667, 484 N.Y.S.2d 585 (N.Y.A.D. 2 Dept. 1985), 494

Lorenz v. Celotex Corp., 896 F.2d 148 (5th Cir.1990), **507,** 511

Loughan v. Firestone Tire & Rubber Co., 749 F.2d 1519 (11th Cir.1985), 288

Lukaszewicz v. Ortho Pharmaceutical Corp., 510 F.Supp. 961 (E.D.Wis.1981), 324

Lum v. Stinnett, 87 Nev. 402, 488 P.2d 347 (Nev.1971), 657

MacDonald v. Mobley, 555 S.W.2d 916 (Tex. Civ.App.-Austin 1977), 44

MacDonald v. Ortho Pharmaceutical Corp., 394 Mass. 131, 475 N.E.2d 65 (Mass. 1985), 324, 515

Mackowick v. Westinghouse Elec. Corp., 373 Pa.Super. 434, 541 A.2d 749 (Pa.Super.1988), 613

MacPherson v. Buick Motor Co., 217 N.Y. 382, 111 N.E. 1050 (N.Y.1916), 2, 3, 5, **5**, 8

Magee v. Wyeth Laboratories, Inc., 214 Cal. App.2d 340, 29 Cal.Rptr. 322 (Cal.App. 2 Dist.1963), 485

Magrine v. Krasnica, 94 N.J.Super. 228, 227 A.2d 539 (N.J.Co.1967), 769, 770

Maize v. Atlantic Refining Co., 352 Pa. 51, 41 A.2d 850 (Pa.1945), 269

Malsch v. Vertex Aerospace, LLC, 361 F.Supp.2d 583 (S.D.Miss.2005), 703

Management Computer Services, Inc. v. Hawkins, Ash, Baptie & Co., 206 Wis.2d 158, 557 N.W.2d 67 (Wis.1996), 585

Mancuso v. Consolidated Edison Co. of New York, Inc., 56 F.Supp.2d 391 (S.D.N.Y. 1999), 460

Martens v. MCL Construction Corp., 347 Ill.App.3d 303, 282 Ill.Dec. 856, 807 N.E.2d 480 (Ill.App. 1 Dist.2004), 748

Martin v. Abbott Laboratories, 102 Wash.2d 581, 689 P.2d 368 (Wash.1984), 366

Martin v. Ryder Truck Rental, Inc., 353 A.2d 581 (Del.Supr.1976), **715**, 719

Martinez v. Dixie Carriers, Inc., 529 F.2d 457 (5th Cir.1976), 287

Matter of (see name of party)

Matthews v. Celotex Corp., 569 F.Supp. 1539 (D.N.D.1983), 688

Matthews v. Stewart Warner Corp., 20 Ill. App.3d 470, 314 N.E.2d 683 (Ill.App. 1 Dist.1974), 397

Mauch v. Manufacturers Sales & Service, Inc., 345 N.W.2d 338 (N.D.1984), 151, 622

Maxted v. Pacific Car & Foundry Co., 527 P.2d 832 (Wyo.1974), 158

McCarty v. E.J. Korvette, Inc., 28 Md.App. 421, 347 A.2d 253 (Md.App.1975), 48, 49

McClain v. Chem-Lube Corp., 759 N.E.2d 1096 (Ind.App.2001), 514

McClain v. Metabolife International, Inc., 401 F.3d 1233 (11th Cir.2005), 460

McCormack v. Abbott Laboratories, 617 F.Supp. 1521 (D.Mass.1985), 366

McCown v. International Harvester Co., 463 Pa. 13, 342 A.2d 381 (Pa.1975), **603**, 606, 653

McCroy ex rel. McCroy v. Coastal Mart, Inc., 207 F.Supp.2d 1265 (D.Kan.2002), 346

McDaniel v. Bieffe USA, Inc., 35 F.Supp.2d 735 (D.Minn.1999), 335

McDougald v. Garber, 538 N.Y.S.2d 937, 536 N.E.2d 372 (N.Y.1989), 549

McGonigal v. Gearhart Industries, Inc., 851 F.2d 774 (5th Cir.1988), 703

McGraw v. Furon Co., 812 So.2d 273 (Ala. 2001), 695

McKisson v. Sales Affiliates, Inc., 416 S.W.2d 787 (Tex.1967), 232, 724

McLaughlin v. Mine Safety Appliances Co., 226 N.Y.S.2d 407, 181 N.E.2d 430 (N.Y. 1962), 262

McNally v. Nicholson Mfg. Co., 313 A.2d 913 (Me.1973), 35

Medtronic, Inc. v. Lohr, 518 U.S. 470, 116 S.Ct. 2240, 135 L.Ed.2d 700 (1996), 545, 546

Meister v. Medical Engineering Corp., 267 F.3d 1123, 347 U.S.App.D.C. 361 (D.C.Cir.2001), 460

Mekdeci By and Through Mekdeci v. Merrell Nat. Laboratories, a Div. of Richardson–Merrell, Inc., 711 F.2d 1510 (11th Cir.1983), 788

Menard v. Newhall, 135 Vt. 53, 373 A.2d 505 (Vt.1977), 350

Mendez v. Honda Motor Co., 738 F.Supp. 481 (S.D.Fla.1990), 151

Meracle v. Children's Service Society of Wisconsin, 149 Wis.2d 19, 437 N.W.2d 532 (Wis.1989), 565

Metro–North Commuter R.R. Co. v. Buckley, 521 U.S. 424, 117 S.Ct. 2113, 138 L.Ed.2d 560 (1997), 574

Mettinger v. Globe Slicing Mach. Co., Inc., 153 N.J. 371, 709 A.2d 779 (N.J.1998), 693

Mexicali Rose v. Superior Court, 4 Cal. Rptr.2d 145, 822 P.2d 1292 (Cal.1992), 97

Micallef v. Miehle Co., 384 N.Y.S.2d 115, 348 N.E.2d 571 (N.Y.1976), 4

Michael v. Warner/Chilcott, 91 N.M. 651, 579 P.2d 183 (N.M.App.1978), 323

Michalko v. Cooke Color and Chemical Corp., 91 N.J. 386, 451 A.2d 179 (N.J. 1982), 188

Midgley v. S.S. Kresge Co., 55 Cal.App.3d 67, 127 Cal.Rptr. 217 (Cal.App. 3 Dist. 1976), 261

Miles v. Bell Helicopter Co., 385 F.Supp. 1029 (N.D.Ga.1974), 35

Miller v. Anetsberger Bros., Inc., 124 A.D.2d 1057, 508 N.Y.S.2d 954 (N.Y.A.D. 4 Dept.1986), 262

Miller v. Preitz, 422 Pa. 383, 221 A.2d 320 (Pa.1966), 35

Miller v. United States Steel Corp., 902 F.2d 573 (7th Cir.1990), 561

Mitchell v. Gencorp Inc., 165 F.3d 778 (10th Cir.1999), 460

Mitchell v. Lone Star Ammunition, Inc., 913 F.2d 242 (5th Cir.1990), 703

Mitchell v. Miller, 26 Conn.Supp. 142, 214 A.2d 694 (Conn.Super.1965), 485

Mix v. Ingersoll Candy Co., 6 Cal.2d 674, 59 P.2d 144 (Cal.1936), 97

Mohrdieck v. Village of Morton Grove, 94 Ill.App.3d 1021, 50 Ill.Dec. 409, 419 N.E.2d 517 (Ill.App. 1 Dist.1981), 484

Moody v. City of Galveston, 524 S.W.2d 583 (Tex.Civ.App.-Hous (1 Dist.) 1975), 771

Moore v. Remington Arms Co., Inc., 100 Ill.App.3d 1102, 56 Ill.Dec. 413, 427 N.E.2d 608 (Ill.App. 4 Dist.1981), 584

Moran v. Faberge, Inc., 273 Md. 538, 332 A.2d 11 (Md.1975), 484

Morgan v. Wal–Mart Stores, Inc., 30 S.W.3d 455 (Tex.App.-Austin 2000), 325

Morrissette v. Sears, Roebuck & Co., 114 N.H. 384, 322 A.2d 7 (N.H.1974), 672

Morrow v. New Moon Homes, Inc., 548 P.2d 279 (Alaska 1976), 36

Morton v. Owens–Corning Fiberglas Corp., 40 Cal.Rptr.2d 22 (Cal.App. 1 Dist.1995), 104

Moss v. Crosman Corp., 136 F.3d 1169 (7th Cir.1998), 278

Mott v. Callahan AMS Mach. Co., 174 N.J.Super. 202, 416 A.2d 57 (N.J.Super.A.D.1980), **188,** 192, 193, 196

Mugavero v. A–1 Auto Sales, Inc., 130 Idaho 554, 944 P.2d 151 (Idaho App.1997), 36

Mulcahy v. Eli Lilly & Co., 386 N.W.2d 67 (Iowa 1986), **357,** 389

Mull v. Ford Motor Co., 368 F.2d 713 (2nd Cir.1966), 484, 505

Murphy v. E.R. Squibb & Sons, Inc., 221 Cal.Rptr. 447, 710 P.2d 247 (Cal.1985), 369, 775

Murray v. Fairbanks Morse, 610 F.2d 149 (3rd Cir.1979), 622

Myrlak v. Port Authority of New York and New Jersey, 157 N.J. 84, 723 A.2d 45 (N.J.1999), **223,** 230, 231

Naporano Iron & Metal Co. v. American Crane Corp., 79 F.Supp.2d 494 (D.N.J. 1999), 560

National Bank of Commerce v. Associated Milk Producers, Inc., 22 F.Supp.2d 942 (E.D.Ark.1998), 460

Needleman v. Pfizer Inc., 2004 WL 1773697 (N.D.Tex.2004), 547

Nelson v. American Home Products Corp., 92 F.Supp.2d 954 (W.D.Mo.2000), 461

Nelson v. Krusen, 678 S.W.2d 918 (Tex. 1984), 676

Nelson v. Tennessee Gas Pipeline Co., 243 F.3d 244 (6th Cir.2001), 444

Nelson v. Union Equity Co-op. Exchange, 548 S.W.2d 352 (Tex.1977), 29, 30

Nelson v. Wilkins Dodge, Inc., 256 N.W.2d 472 (Minn.1977), 31

Nelson v. Nelson Hardware, Inc., 160 Wis.2d 689, 467 N.W.2d 518 (Wis.1991), 741

Nesselrode v. Executive Beechcraft, Inc., 707 S.W.2d 371 (Mo.1986), 123

Netland v. Hess & Clark, Inc., 284 F.3d 895 (8th Cir.2002), 546

Newman v. Utility Trailer & Equipment Co., Inc., 278 Or. 395, 564 P.2d 674 (Or.1977), 482

Newmark v. Gimbel's Inc., 54 N.J. 585, 258 A.2d 697 (N.J.1969), 769, 770

Newmark v. Gimbel's Inc., 102 N.J.Super. 279, 246 A.2d 11 (N.J.Super.A.D.1968), 769

Newton v. Roche Laboratories, Inc., 243 F.Supp.2d 672 (W.D.Tex.2002), 460

Nielsen v. George Diamond Vogel Paint Co., 892 F.2d 1450 (9th Cir.1990), 703

Nolan v. Johns–Manville Asbestos, 85 Ill.2d 161, 52 Ill.Dec. 1, 421 N.E.2d 864 (Ill. 1981), 671

Noonan v. Buick Co., 211 So.2d 54 (Fla. App. 3 Dist.1968), 483

Norplant Contraceptive Products Liability Litigation, In re, 215 F.Supp.2d 795 (E.D.Tex.2002), 325

Norris v. Baxter Healthcare Corp., 397 F.3d 878 (10th Cir.2005), 434, 460

Northern Power & Engineering Corp. v. Caterpillar Tractor Co., 623 P.2d 324 (Alaska 1981), 560

O'Brien v. Muskin Corp., 94 N.J. 169, 463 A.2d 298 (N.J.1983), **170,** 175, 176, 179, 216, 217

Oddi v. Ford Motor Co., 234 F.3d 136 (3rd Cir.2000), 444, 452

Odgers v. Ortho Pharmaceutical Corp., 609 F.Supp. 867 (E.D.Mich.1985), 324

Oehler v. Davis, 223 Pa.Super. 333, 298 A.2d 895 (Pa.Super.1972), 480, 481

Oglesby v. General Motors Corp., 190 F.3d 244 (4th Cir.1999), 452

O'Laughlin v. Minnesota Natural Gas Co., 253 N.W.2d 826 (Minn.1977), 771

Olsen v. Royal Metals Corp., 392 F.2d 116 (5th Cir.1968), 26

Olson v. A.W. Chesterton Co., 256 N.W.2d 530 (N.D.1977), 294

O'Malley v. American LaFrance, Inc., 2002 WL 32068354 (E.D.N.Y.2002), 724, 725

Oman v. Johns–Manville Corp., 764 F.2d 224 (4th Cir.1985), 309, 310

O'Mara v. Dykema, 328 Ark. 310, 942 S.W.2d 854 (Ark.1997), 748

Orrox Corp. v. Rexnord, Inc., 389 F.Supp. 441 (M.D.Ala.1975), 49

Ortiz v. Fibreboard Corp., 527 U.S. 815, 119 S.Ct. 2295, 144 L.Ed.2d 715 (1999), 822, 846, 847, 848, 849, 850, 851, 853, 854, 857

Outboard Marine Corp. v. Schupbach, 93 Nev. 158, 561 P.2d 450 (Nev.1977), 663

Owens v. Allis–Chalmers Corp., 414 Mich. 413, 326 N.W.2d 372 (Mich.1982), 402

Owens v. Patent Scaffolding Co., 77 Misc.2d 992, 354 N.Y.S.2d 778 (N.Y.Sup.1974), 720

Owens–Corning Fiberglas Corp. v. Malone, 972 S.W.2d 35 (Tex.1998), 597

Owens–Illinois, Inc. v. Zenobia, 325 Md. 420, 601 A.2d 633 (Md.1992), 583, 584

Padillas v. Stork–Gamco, Inc., 186 F.3d 412 (3rd Cir.1999), 444

Pako Corp. v. Thomas, 855 S.W.2d 215 (Tex.App.-Tyler 1993), 52

Palsgraf v. Long Island R.R. Co., 248 N.Y. 339, 162 N.E. 99 (N.Y.1928), 484, 485

Paoli R.R. Yard PCB Litigation, In re, 35 F.3d 717 (3rd Cir.1994), 433, 478

Parker v. Brush Wellman, Inc., 377 F.Supp.2d 1290 (N.D.Ga.2005), 574

Parker v. Mobil Oil Corp., 793 N.Y.S.2d 434 (N.Y.A.D. 2 Dept.2005), 460

Parklane Hosiery Co., Inc. v. Shore, 439 U.S. 322, 99 S.Ct. 645, 58 L.Ed.2d 552 (1979), 778, 788

Pasquale v. Speed Products Engineering, 166 Ill.2d 337, 211 Ill.Dec. 314, 654 N.E.2d 1365 (Ill.1995), 566

Passa v. Derderian, 308 F.Supp.2d 43 (D.R.I.2004), 796

Passwaters v. General Motors Corp., 454 F.2d 1270 (8th Cir.1972), 485

Payne v. Soft Sheen Products, Inc., 486 A.2d 712 (D.C.1985), 243

Payton v. Abbott Labs, 386 Mass. 540, 437 N.E.2d 171 (Mass.1982), 574

Peck v. Ford Motor Co., 603 F.2d 1240 (7th Cir.1979), 484

Pegg v. General Motors Corp., 258 Pa.Super. 59, 391 A.2d 1074 (Pa.Super.1978), 483

Pemberton v. American Distilled Spirits Co., 664 S.W.2d 690 (Tenn.1984), 286

People v. _____ (see opposing party)

Perez v. McConkey, 872 S.W.2d 897 (Tenn. 1994), 613

Perez v. Wyeth Laboratories Inc., 161 N.J. 1, 734 A.2d 1245 (N.J.1999), **311,** 324, 325

Perkins v. Northeastern Log Homes, 808 S.W.2d 809 (Ky.1991), 676

Petersen v. Hubschman Const. Co., Inc., 76 Ill.2d 31, 27 Ill.Dec. 746, 389 N.E.2d 1154 (Ill.1979), 749

Peterson v. Lou Bachrodt Chevrolet Co., 61 Ill.2d 17, 329 N.E.2d 785 (Ill.1975), 740

Peterson v. Superior Court, 43 Cal. Rptr.2d 836, 899 P.2d 905 (Cal.1995), **750**

Petroski v. Northern Indiana Public Service Co., 171 Ind.App. 14, 354 N.E.2d 736 (Ind.App. 3 Dist.1976), 770

Phillips v. Allen, 427 F.Supp. 876 (W.D.Pa. 1977), 608

Phillips v. Duro–Last Roofing, Inc., 806 P.2d 834 (Wyo.1991), 602

Phillips v. Kimwood Machine Co., 269 Or. 485, 525 P.2d 1033 (Or.1974), 112, **114,** 120, 121, 123, 141, 142, 151, 163, 243, 482

Pierce v. Pacific Gas & Electric Co., 166 Cal.App.3d 68, 212 Cal.Rptr. 283 (Cal. App. 3 Dist.1985), 770, 771

Pierringer v. Hoger, 21 Wis.2d 182, 124 N.W.2d 106 (Wis.1963), 656

Pike v. Frank G. Hough Co., 85 Cal.Rptr. 629, 467 P.2d 229 (Cal.1970), 111

Pilkington v. Hendricks County Rural Elec. Membership Corp., 460 N.E.2d 1000 (Ind.App. 1 Dist.1984), 770

Pines v. Perssion, 14 Wis.2d 590, 111 N.W.2d 409 (Wis.1961), 761

Pittsburg Coca–Cola Bottling Works of Pittsburg v. Ponder, 443 S.W.2d 546 (Tex.1969), 693

Plummer v. Lederle Laboratories, Division of American Cyanamid Co., 819 F.2d 349 (2nd Cir.1987), 324

Potomac Elec. Power Co. v. Westinghouse Elec. Corp., 385 F.Supp. 572 (D.D.C. 1974), 49, 50

Potter v. Chicago Pneumatic Tool Co., 241 Conn. 199, 694 A.2d 1319 (Conn.1997), 394

Potter v. Eli Lilly and Co., 926 S.W.2d 449 (Ky.1996), 788

Potter v. Firestone Tire & Rubber Co., 25 Cal.Rptr.2d 550, 863 P.2d 795 (Cal. 1993), 574

Praytor v. Ford Motor Co., 97 S.W.3d 237 (Tex.App.-Hous. (14 Dist.) 2002), 461

Presbrey v. Gillette Co., 105 Ill.App.3d 1082, 61 Ill.Dec. 816, 435 N.E.2d 513 (Ill.App. 2 Dist.1982), 330

Pride v. BIC Corp., 218 F.3d 566 (6th Cir. 2000), 452

Pridgett v. Jackson Iron & Metal Co., 253 So.2d 837 (Miss.1971), 740

Prince v. LeVan, 486 P.2d 959 (Alaska 1971), 30, 31

Pritchard v. Liggett & Myers Tobacco Co., 350 F.2d 479 (3rd Cir.1965), 608

Promaulayko v. Johns Manville Sales Corp., 116 N.J. 505, 562 A.2d 202 (N.J.1989), 694

Providence Hospital v. Truly, 611 S.W.2d 127 (Tex.Civ.App.-Waco 1980), 776

Pust v. Union Supply Co., 38 Colo.App. 435, 561 P.2d 355 (Colo.App.1976), 483

Pustejovsky v. Rapid–American Corp., 35 S.W.3d 643 (Tex.2000), **678,** 688, 689

Putensen v. Clay Adams, Inc., 12 Cal. App.3d 1062, 91 Cal.Rptr. 319 (Cal.App. 1 Dist.1970), 21

Quintana–Ruiz v. Hyundai Motor Corp., 303 F.3d 62 (1st Cir.2002), 141

Ramirez v. Amsted Industries, Inc., 86 N.J. 332, 431 A.2d 811 (N.J.1981), 552

Ransome v. Wisconsin Electric Power Co., 87 Wis.2d 605, 275 N.W.2d 641 (Wis. 1979), 770

Ray v. Alad Corp., 136 Cal.Rptr. 574, 560 P.2d 3 (Cal.1977), 714

TABLE OF CASES

Raymond v. Eli Lilly & Co., 117 N.H. 164, 371 A.2d 170 (N.H.1977), **665,** 671
Rexrode v. American Laundry Press Co., 674 F.2d 826 (10th Cir.1982), 398
Reyes v. Wyeth Laboratories, 498 F.2d 1264 (5th Cir.1974), 323, 324
Rhodes v. Interstate Battery System of America, Inc., 722 F.2d 1517 (11th Cir. 1984), **262,** 268, 279
Rhone–Poulenc Rorer Inc., Matter of, 51 F.3d 1293 (7th Cir.1995), **815,** 822, 842, 845
Rich Products Corp. v. Kemutec, Inc., 66 F.Supp.2d 937 (E.D.Wis.1999), 561
Rickey v. Chicago Transit Authority, 98 Ill.2d 546, 75 Ill.Dec. 211, 457 N.E.2d 1 (Ill.1983), 565
Rios v. Niagara Mach. and Tool Works, 12 Ill.App.3d 739, 299 N.E.2d 86 (Ill.App. 1 Dist.1973), 187
Ritter v. Narragansett Elec. Co., 109 R.I. 176, 283 A.2d 255 (R.I.1971), 484
Rix v. General Motors Corp., 222 Mont. 318, 723 P.2d 195 (Mont.1986), 129
Rix v. Reeves, 23 Ariz.App. 243, 532 P.2d 185 (Ariz.App. Div. 1 1975), 740
R.N. Thompson & Associates, Inc. v. Wickes Lumber Co., 687 N.E.2d 617 (Ind.App. 1997), 749
Robertson v. General Tire and Rubber Co., 123 Ill.App.3d 11, 78 Ill.Dec. 587, 462 N.E.2d 706 (Ill.App. 5 Dist.1984), 142
Robinson v. Reed–Prentice Division of Package Machinery Co., 426 N.Y.S.2d 717, 403 N.E.2d 440 (N.Y.1980), **487,** 492, 493, 494
Rodriguez v. Besser Co., 115 Ariz. 454, 565 P.2d 1315 (Ariz.App. Div. 1 1977), 335
Rogers v. Ford Motor Co., 952 F.Supp. 606 (N.D.Ind.1997), 451
Rogers v. Toro Mfg. Co., 522 S.W.2d 632 (Mo.App.1975), 151, 636
Roll v. Tracor, Inc., 102 F.Supp.2d 1200 (D.Nev.2000), 703
Romito v. Red Plastic Co., 44 Cal. Rptr.2d 834 (Cal.App. 2 Dist.1995), **144,** 636
Romo v. Ford Motor Co., 6 Cal.Rptr.3d 793 (Cal.App. 5 Dist.2003), **585,** 596, 598
Rose v. A.C. & S., Inc., 796 F.2d 294 (9th Cir.1986), 671
Roupp v. Acor, 253 Pa.Super. 46, 384 A.2d 968 (Pa.Super.1978), 745
Rowson v. Kawasaki Heavy Industries, Ltd., 866 F.Supp. 1221 (N.D.Iowa 1994), 351
Rudd v. General Motors Corp., 127 F.Supp.2d 1330 (M.D.Ala.2001), 462
Ruiz–Guzman v. Amvac Chemical Corp., 141 Wash.2d 493, 7 P.3d 795 (Wash. 2000), 162, 163
Rusin v. Glendale Optical Co., Inc., 805 F.2d 650 (6th Cir.1986), 308
Russell v. G.A.F. Corp., 422 A.2d 989 (D.C. 1980), 241

Russo v. Hilltop Lincoln–Mercury, Inc., 479 S.W.2d 211 (Mo.App.1972), 50
Rutherford v. Owens–Illinois, Inc., 67 Cal.Rptr.2d 16, 941 P.2d 1203 (Cal. 1997), 340, **370,** 383, 384, 386, 389

Salk v. Alpine Ski Shop, Inc., 115 R.I. 309, 342 A.2d 622 (R.I.1975), 16
Saloomey v. Jeppesen & Co., 707 F.2d 671 (2nd Cir.1983), 736
Sam Shainberg Co. of Jackson v. Barlow, 258 So.2d 242 (Miss.1972), 693
Samuels v. American Cyanamid Co., 130 Misc.2d 175, 495 N.Y.S.2d 1006 (N.Y.Sup.1985), 324
Sanderson v. Eckerd Corp., 780 So.2d 930 (Fla.App. 5 Dist.2001), 324
Sandford v. Chevrolet Division of General Motors, 292 Or. 590, 642 P.2d 624 (Or. 1982), 623, 626
Santiago v. E.W. Bliss Div., Gulf and Western Mfg. Co., 201 N.J.Super. 205, 492 A.2d 1089 (N.J.Super.A.D.1985), 695
Santor v. A & M Karagheusian, Inc., 44 N.J. 52, 207 A.2d 305 (N.J.1965), 560
Saratoga Fishing Co. v. J.M. Martinac & Co., 520 U.S. 875, 117 S.Ct. 1783, 138 L.Ed.2d 76 (1997), 560
Saunders System Birmingham Co. v. Adams, 217 Ala. 621, 117 So. 72 (Ala. 1928), 340
Saupitty v. Yazoo Mfg. Co., Inc., 726 F.2d 657 (10th Cir.1984), 492, 493
Savage Arms, Inc. v. Western Auto Supply Co., 18 P.3d 49 (Alaska 2001), **705,** 711, 713, 714
Schafersman v. Agland Coop, 262 Neb. 215, 631 N.W.2d 862 (Neb.2001), 461
Scheuler v. Aamco Transmissions, Inc., 1 Kan.App.2d 525, 571 P.2d 48 (Kan.App. 1977), 729
Schipper v. Levitt & Sons, Inc., 44 N.J. 70, 207 A.2d 314 (N.J.1965), 748
Schmaltz v. Norfolk & Western Ry. Co., 878 F.Supp. 1119 (N.D.Ill.1995), 461
Schreier v. Merrell Dow Pharmaceutical, Inc., 745 F.2d 58 (6th Cir.1984), 846
Seattle–First Nat. Bank v. Tabert, 86 Wash.2d 145, 542 P.2d 774 (Wash.1975), 90
Self v. General Motors Corp., 42 Cal.App.3d 1, 116 Cal.Rptr. 575 (Cal.App. 2 Dist. 1974), 150
Sell v. Bertsch and Co., Inc., 577 F.Supp. 1393 (D.Kan.1984), 740
Sessa v. Riegle, 427 F.Supp. 760 (E.D.Pa. 1977), 32
Sexton By and Through Sexton v. Bell Helmets, Inc., 926 F.2d 331 (4th Cir.1991), 402
Shackil v. Lederle Laboratories, a Div. of American Cyanamid Co., 116 N.J. 155, 561 A.2d 511 (N.J.1989), 369
Shaffer v. Debbas, 21 Cal.Rptr.2d 110 (Cal. App. 4 Dist.1993), 602

Shanks v. Upjohn Co., 835 P.2d 1189 (Alaska 1992), 214, 243
Shawver v. Roberts Corp., 90 Wis.2d 672, 280 N.W.2d 226 (Wis.1979), 193
Sheldon v. West Bend Equipment Corp., 718 F.2d 603 (3rd Cir.1983), 492
Shepard v. Superior Court, 76 Cal.App.3d 16, 142 Cal.Rptr. 612 (Cal.App. 1 Dist. 1977), 566
Shibuya v. Architects Hawaii Ltd., 65 Haw. 26, 647 P.2d 276 (Hawai'i 1982), 676
Shields v. Morton Chemical Co., 95 Idaho 674, 518 P.2d 857 (Idaho 1974), 602
Shoshone Coca–Cola Bottling Co. v. Dolinski, 82 Nev. 439, 420 P.2d 855 (Nev. 1966), 232
Siemen v. Alden, 34 Ill.App.3d 961, 341 N.E.2d 713 (Ill.App. 2 Dist.1975), 29, 32
Signal Oil and Gas Co. v. Universal Oil Products, 572 S.W.2d 320 (Tex.1978), 601
Siharath v. Sandoz Pharmaceuticals Corp., 131 F.Supp.2d 1347 (N.D.Ga.2001), 460
Silicone Gel Breast Implants Products Liability Litigation, In re, 793 F.Supp. 1098 (Jud.Pan.Mult.Lit.1992), **792**
Sills v. Massey–Ferguson, Inc., 296 F.Supp. 776 (N.D.Ind.1969), 308
Silverstein v. Northrop Grumman Corp., 367 N.J.Super. 361, 842 A.2d 881 (N.J.Super.A.D.2004), 703
Simeone ex rel. Estate Of Albert Francis Simeone, Jr. v. Bombardier-Rotax GmbH, 360 F.Supp.2d 665 (E.D.Pa. 2005), 693
Simmons v. Mark Lift Industries, Inc., 366 S.C. 308, 622 S.E.2d 213 (S.C.2005), 713
Simmons v. Pacor, Inc., 543 Pa. 664, 674 A.2d 232 (Pa.1996), 574
Sindell v. Abbott Laboratories, 163 Cal. Rptr. 132, 607 P.2d 924 (Cal.1980), 640
Singer v. Walker, 39 A.D.2d 90, 331 N.Y.S.2d 823 (N.Y.A.D. 1 Dept.1972), 638
Smith v. E.R. Squibb & Sons, Inc., 405 Mich. 79, 273 N.W.2d 476 (Mich.1979), 241
Smith v. Home Light and Power Co., 695 P.2d 788 (Colo.App.1984), 770
Smith v. Ingersoll–Rand Co., 14 P.3d 990 (Alaska 2000), 626, 627
Smith v. Ingersoll–Rand Co., 214 F.3d 1235 (10th Cir.2000), 451
Smith v. Louis Berkman Co., 894 F.Supp. 1084 (W.D.Ky.1995), 493
Smith v. Louisville Ladder Co., 237 F.3d 515 (5th Cir.2001), **158**, 162, 163, 164
Snell v. Bell Helicopter Textron, Inc., 107 F.3d 744 (9th Cir.1997), 703
Soaper v. Hope Industries, Inc., 309 S.C. 438, 424 S.E.2d 493 (S.C.1992), 31

Soler v. Castmaster, Div. of H.P.M. Corp., 98 N.J. 137, 484 A.2d 1225 (N.J.1984), 492
Sopha v. Owens–Corning Fiberglas Corp., 230 Wis.2d 212, 601 N.W.2d 627 (Wis. 1999), 688
Soule v. General Motors Corp., 34 Cal. Rptr.2d 607, 882 P.2d 298 (Cal.1994), 139, 140
Southland Mower Co. v. Consumer Product Safety Commission, 619 F.2d 499 (5th Cir.1980), **516**, 532
Southwire Co. v. Beloit Eastern Corp., 370 F.Supp. 842 (E.D.Pa.1974), **494**
Speed Fastners, Inc. v. Newsom, 382 F.2d 395 (10th Cir.1967), 22
Sperry–New Holland, a Div. of Sperry Corp. v. Prestage, 617 So.2d 248 (Miss.1993), 111
Spiegel v. Saks 34th St., 43 Misc.2d 1065, 252 N.Y.S.2d 852 (N.Y.Sup.App.Term 1964), 331
Sprietsma v. Mercury Marine, a Div. of Brunswick Corp., 537 U.S. 51, 123 S.Ct. 518, 154 L.Ed.2d 466 (2002), 547
Spruill v. Boyle–Midway, Inc., 308 F.2d 79 (4th Cir.1962), **250**, 256, 257, 278
Stackiewicz v. Nissan Motor Corp. in U.S.A., 100 Nev. 443, 686 P.2d 925 (Nev. 1984), 232
Stafford v. Nipp, 502 So.2d 702 (Ala.1987), 775
Stahl v. Novartis Pharmaceuticals Corp., 283 F.3d 254 (5th Cir.2002), 408
Stanback v. Parke, Davis and Co., 657 F.2d 642 (4th Cir.1981), 286, 346
Stanfield v. Medalist Industries, Inc., 34 Ill.App.3d 635, 340 N.E.2d 276 (Ill.App. 2 Dist.1975), 158
Stang v. Hertz Corp., 83 N.M. 217, 490 P.2d 475 (N.M.App.1971), 22, 24
Stanley v. Schiavi Mobile Homes, Inc., 462 A.2d 1144 (Me.1983), 750
Stanton v. Astra Pharmaceutical Products, Inc., 718 F.2d 553 (3rd Cir.1983), 514
Stanton v. Carlson Sales, Inc., 45 Conn. Supp. 531, 728 A.2d 534 (Conn.Super.1998), 741
State Farm Mut. Auto. Ins. Co. v. Campbell, 538 U.S. 408, 123 S.Ct. 1513, 155 L.Ed.2d 585 (2003), 596, 597
States Steamship Co. v. Stone Manganese Marine, Ltd., 371 F.Supp. 500 (D.N.J. 1973), 197
Statler v. George A. Ray Mfg. Co., 195 N.Y. 478, 88 N.E. 1063 (N.Y.1909), 2
Stephens v. G.D. Searle & Co., 602 F.Supp. 379 (E.D.Mich.1985), 324
Sternhagen v. Dow Co., 282 Mont. 168, 935 P.2d 1139 (Mont.1997), 243
Stillie v. AM Intern., Inc., 850 F.Supp. 960 (D.Kan.1994), 742
Stones v. Sears, Roebuck & Co., 251 Neb. 560, 558 N.W.2d 540 (Neb.1997), 31

TABLE OF CASES   xxxiii

Stovall & Co. v. Tate, 124 Ga.App. 605, 184 S.E.2d 834 (Ga.App.1971), 36
Straub v. Fisher and Paykel Health Care, 990 P.2d 384 (Utah 1999), 566
Summers v. Tice, 33 Cal.2d 80, 199 P.2d 1 (Cal.1948), 389
Swallow v. Emergency Medicine of Idaho, P.A., 138 Idaho 589, 67 P.3d 68 (Idaho 2003), 460, 461
Sylvestri v. Warner & Swasey Co., 398 F.2d 598 (2nd Cir.1968), 17

Tate v. Boeing Helicopters, 140 F.3d 654 (6th Cir.1998), 703
Tauber–Arons Auctioneers Co. v. Superior Court, 101 Cal.App.3d 268, 161 Cal.Rptr. 789 (Cal.App. 2 Dist.1980), 740
Taylor v. Hawkinson, 47 Cal.2d 893, 306 P.2d 797 (Cal.1957), 788
Technical Chemical Co. v. Jacobs, 480 S.W.2d 602 (Tex.1972), 350
Telectronics Pacing Systems, Inc., In re, 172 F.R.D. 271 (S.D.Ohio 1997), 823
Tennessee Carolina Transp., Inc. v. Strick Corp., 283 N.C. 423, 196 S.E.2d 711 (N.C.1973), 31, 44
Terhune v. A.H. Robins Co., 90 Wash.2d 9, 577 P.2d 975 (Wash.1978), 322
Terry v. Moore, 448 P.2d 601 (Wyo.1968), 22
Tetracycline Cases, In re, 107 F.R.D. 719 (W.D.Mo.1985), 809
Tetterton v. Long Mfg. Co., Inc., 314 N.C. 44, 332 S.E.2d 67 (N.C.1985), 676
Texsun Feed Yards, Inc. v. Ralston Purina Co., 447 F.2d 660 (5th Cir.1971), 31
Thate v. Texas & Pacific Railway Co., 595 S.W.2d 591 (Tex.Civ.App.-Dallas 1980), 723
Thibault v. Sears, Roebuck & Co., 118 N.H. 802, 395 A.2d 843 (N.H.1978), 397
Thiry v. Armstrong World Industries, 661 P.2d 515 (Okla.1983), 583
Thomas v. Bove, 687 P.2d 534 (Colo.App. 1984), 771
Thomas v. St. Joseph Hospital, 618 S.W.2d 791 (Tex.Civ.App.-Hous (1 Dist.) 1981), 723, 775
Thomas v. Winchester, 6 N.Y. 397 (N.Y. 1852), 2, 5
Thompson v. Package Machinery Co., 22 Cal.App.3d 188, 99 Cal.Rptr. 281 (Cal. App. 2 Dist.1971), 492
Thornton v. Mono Mfg. Co., 99 Ill.App.3d 722, 54 Ill.Dec. 657, 425 N.E.2d 522 (Ill.App. 2 Dist.1981), 676
Tillman v. Vance Equipment Co., 286 Or. 747, 596 P.2d 1299 (Or.1979), **736**
Times Mirror Co. v. Sisk, 122 Ariz. 174, 593 P.2d 924 (Ariz.App. Div. 2 1978), 736
Toner v. Lederle Laboratories, a Division of American Cyanamid Co., 112 Idaho 328, 732 P.2d 297 (Idaho 1987), 213
Toole v. Baxter Healthcare Corp., 235 F.3d 1307 (11th Cir.2000), 434

Torres v. Northwest Engineering Co., 949 P.2d 1004 (Hawai'i App.1997), 21, 602
Torsiello v. Whitehall Laboratories, Division of Home Products Corp., 165 N.J.Super. 311, 398 A.2d 132 (N.J.Super.A.D.1979), 323
Torstenson v. Melcher, 195 Neb. 764, 241 N.W.2d 103 (Neb.1976), 31
Town of (see name of town)
Trampe v. Wisconsin Tel. Co., 214 Wis. 210, 252 N.W. 675 (Wis.1934), 657
Trent v. Brasch Mfg. Co., Inc., 132 Ill. App.3d 586, 87 Ill.Dec. 784, 477 N.E.2d 1312 (Ill.App. 1 Dist.1985), 748
Trimble v. Asarco, Inc., 232 F.3d 946 (8th Cir.2000), 575
Tri–State Ins. Co. of Tulsa, Oklahoma v. Fidelity & Cas. Ins. Co. of New York, 364 So.2d 657 (La.App. 2 Cir.1978), 294
Troja v. Black & Decker Mfg. Co., 62 Md. App. 101, 488 A.2d 516 (Md.App.1985), 163
Tromza v. Tecumseh Products Co., 378 F.2d 601 (3rd Cir.1967), **641,** 649
Trull v. Volkswagen of America, Inc., 320 F.3d 1 (1st Cir.2002), 356
Trull v. Volkswagen of America, Inc., 145 N.H. 259, 761 A.2d 477 (N.H.2000), **352,** 356, 357
Tucci v. Bossert, 53 A.D.2d 291, 385 N.Y.S.2d 328 (N.Y.A.D. 2 Dept.1976), 484
Turner v. Central Hardware Co., 353 Mo. 1182, 186 S.W.2d 603 (Mo.1945), 17
Turner v. General Motors Corp., 584 S.W.2d 844 (Tex.1979), 112
Turner v. International Harvester Co., 133 N.J.Super. 277, 336 A.2d 62 (N.J.Super.L.1975), 741, 742
Tuttle v. Lorillard Tobacco Co., 377 F.3d 917 (8th Cir.2004), 351
Tyrrell v. Prudential Ins. Co. of America, 109 Vt. 6, 192 A. 184 (Vt.1937), 350

Union Carbide Corp. v. Holton, 136 Ga.App. 726, 222 S.E.2d 105 (Ga.App.1975), 493
Union Supply Co. v. Pust, 196 Colo. 162, 583 P.2d 276 (Colo.1978), 193, 194, 195, 196, **395**
United Pacific Co. v. Southern Cal. Edison Co., 163 Cal.App.3d 700, 209 Cal.Rptr. 819 (Cal.App. 2 Dist.1985), 770, 771
United States v. _____ (see opposing party)
United States Fibres, Inc. v. Proctor & Schwartz, Inc., 358 F.Supp. 449 (E.D.Mich.1972), 50
Unterburger v. Snow Co., Inc., 630 F.2d 599 (8th Cir.1980), 408
Urland v. Merrell–Dow Pharmaceuticals, Inc., 822 F.2d 1268 (3rd Cir.1987), 671

Valentino v. Carter–Wallace, Inc., 97 F.3d 1227 (9th Cir.1996), **802,** 809

Valiga v. National Food Co., 58 Wis.2d 232, 206 N.W.2d 377 (Wis.1973), 32

Valley Datsun v. Martinez, 578 S.W.2d 485 (Tex.Civ.App.-Corpus Christi 1979), 17, 745

Valley Iron & Steel Co. v. Thorin, 278 Or. 103, 562 P.2d 1212 (Or.1977), 31

Vallillo v. Muskin Corp., 212 N.J.Super. 155, 514 A.2d 528 (N.J.Super.A.D.1986), 295

Vandermark v. Ford Motor Co., 61 Cal.2d 256, 37 Cal.Rptr. 896, 391 P.2d 168 (Cal.1964), **691,** 693

Van Dike v. AMF, Inc., 146 Mich.App. 176, 379 N.W.2d 412 (Mich.App.1985), 351

Vanek v. Kirby, 253 Or. 494, 450 P.2d 778 (Or.1969), 26

Ventricelli v. Kinney System Rent A Car, Inc., 411 N.Y.S.2d 555, 383 N.E.2d 1149 (N.Y.1978), 483

Vintage Homes, Inc. v. Coldiron, 585 S.W.2d 886 (Tex.Civ.App.-El Paso 1979), 51

Vlases v. Montgomery Ward & Co., 377 F.2d 846 (3rd Cir.1967), 27

Wagner v. International Ry. Co., 232 N.Y. 176, 133 N.E. 437 (N.Y.1921), 485

Walker v. Clark Equipment Co., 320 N.W.2d 561 (Iowa 1982), 566

Walker v. Merck & Co., Inc., 648 F.Supp. 931 (M.D.Ga.1986), 322, 323

Walker v. Stauffer Chemical Corp., 19 Cal. App.3d 669, 96 Cal.Rptr. 803 (Cal.App. 2 Dist.1971), 196, 197, 215

Walton v. Harnischfeger, 796 S.W.2d 225 (Tex.App.-San Antonio 1990), 198, 199

Wangen v. Ford Motor Co., 97 Wis.2d 260, 294 N.W.2d 437 (Wis.1980), 583

Ward v. Ochoa, 284 So.2d 385 (Fla.1973), 657

Warner Fruehauf Trailer Co., Inc. v. Boston, 654 A.2d 1272 (D.C.1995), 613

Waters v. Barry, 711 F.Supp. 1125 (D.D.C. 1989), 848

Webb v. Navistar Intern. Transp. Corp., 166 Vt. 119, 692 A.2d 343 (Vt.1996), 622, 626

Weisgram v. Marley Co., 528 U.S. 440, 120 S.Ct. 1011, 145 L.Ed.2d 958 (2000), 445

Welch v. Hesston Corp., 540 S.W.2d 127 (Mo.App.1976), 485

Welge v. Planters Lifesavers Co., 17 F.3d 209 (7th Cir.1994), 231

Werwinski v. Ford Motor Co., 286 F.3d 661 (3rd Cir.2002), 561

Wesley, People v., 611 N.Y.S.2d 97, 633 N.E.2d 451 (N.Y.1994), 477

West v. G.D. Searle & Co., 317 Ark. 525, 879 S.W.2d 412 (Ark.1994), 324

Westberry v. Gislaved Gummi AB, 178 F.3d 257 (4th Cir.1999), **452,** 460

Westbrock v. Marshalltown Mfg. Co., 473 N.W.2d 352 (Minn.App.1991), 187

White v. First Federal Sav. & Loan Ass'n of Atlanta, 158 Ga.App. 373, 280 S.E.2d 398 (Ga.App.1981), 44

White v. Ford Motor Co., 312 F.3d 998 (9th Cir.2002), 452

White v. Johns–Manville Corp., 103 Wash.2d 344, 693 P.2d 687 (Wash.1985), 672

Whitehead v. St. Joe Lead Co., Inc., 729 F.2d 238 (3rd Cir.1984), 310

White Motor Credit Corp., In re, 75 B.R. 944 (Bkrtcy.N.D.Ohio 1987), 714

Whiting v. Boston Edison Co., 891 F.Supp. 12 (D.Mass.1995), 460

Whitmer v. Schneble, 29 Ill.App.3d 659, 331 N.E.2d 115 (Ill.App. 2 Dist.1975), 16

Wilber v. Owens–Corning Fiberglas Corp., 476 N.W.2d 74 (Iowa 1991), 688

Wilkinson v. Bay Shore Lumber Co., 182 Cal.App.3d 594, 227 Cal.Rptr. 327 (Cal. App. 2 Dist.1986), 215

Williams v. Beechnut Nutrition Corp., 185 Cal.App.3d 135, 229 Cal.Rptr. 605 (Cal. App. 2 Dist.1986), 109

Williams v. Detroit Edison Co., 63 Mich. App. 559, 234 N.W.2d 702 (Mich.App. 1975), 770

Williams Ford, Inc. v. Hartford Courant Co., 232 Conn. 559, 657 A.2d 212 (Conn. 1995), 602

Wills v. Amerada Hess Corp., 379 F.3d 32 (2nd Cir.2004), 460

Wilson v. Piper Aircraft Corp., 282 Or. 61, 577 P.2d 1322 (Or.1978), 176, 511

Winnett v. Winnett, 57 Ill.2d 7, 310 N.E.2d 1 (Ill.1974), 485

Winter v. G.P. Putnam's Sons, 938 F.2d 1033 (9th Cir.1991), **731,** 736

Winterbottom v. Wright, 1842 WL 5519 (Unknown Court 1842), 2, 4, 5

Wirth v. Mayrath Industries, Inc., 278 N.W.2d 789 (N.D.1979), 770

Wiseman v. Goodyear Tire and Rubber Co., 29 Wash.App. 883, 631 P.2d 976 (Wash. App. Div. 3 1981), 90

Witczak v. Pfizer, Inc., 377 F.Supp.2d 726 (D.Minn.2005), 547

Wolfe v. Ford Motor Co., 6 Mass.App.Ct. 346, 376 N.E.2d 143 (Mass.App.Ct. 1978), 35, 241

Wood v. Public Service Co. of New Hampshire, 114 N.H. 182, 317 A.2d 576 (N.H. 1974), 770

Wood v. Wyeth–Ayerst Laboratories, Div. of American Home Products, 82 S.W.3d 849 (Ky.2002), 575

Wooderson v. Ortho Pharmaceutical Corp., 235 Kan. 387, 681 P.2d 1038 (Kan.1984), 334

Woods v. Fruehauf Trailer Corp., 765 P.2d 770 (Okla.1988), 103, 113

Worrell v. Barnes, 87 Nev. 204, 484 P.2d 573 (Nev.1971), 771

Wright v. Carter Products, Inc., 244 F.2d 53 (2nd Cir.1957), 331

Wynacht v. Beckman Instruments, Inc., 113 F.Supp.2d 1205 (E.D.Tenn.2000), 459

Young v. Tide Craft, Inc., 270 S.C. 453, 242 S.E.2d 671 (S.C.1978), 483

Zaremba v. General Motors Corp., 360 F.3d 355 (2nd Cir.2004), 452

Zerand–Bernal Group, Inc. v. Cox, 23 F.3d 159 (7th Cir.1994), 714

Zerby v. Warren, 297 Minn. 134, 210 N.W.2d 58 (Minn.1973), 600

*

Table of Statutes

UNITED STATES

UNITED STATES CONSTITUTION

Amend.	This Work Page
7	822

UNITED STATES CODE ANNOTATED
11 U.S.C.A.—Bankruptcy

Sec.	This Work Page
Ch. 11	849
Ch. 11	850
Ch. 11	859
524(g)	850
524(h)	850

15 U.S.C.A.—Commerce and Trade

Sec.	This Work Page
1191—1204	547
1261 et seq.	547
1381 et seq.	545
2301 et seq.	1
7001 et seq.	24
7901—7903	179
7901	179
7903	179

21 U.S.C.A.—Food and Drugs

Sec.	This Work Page
151—159	547
1601	198

28 U.S.C.A.—Judiciary and Judicial Procedure

Sec.	This Work Page
1332	845
1332(d)	845

UNITED STATES CODE ANNOTATED
28 U.S.C.A.—Judiciary and Judicial Procedure

Sec.	This Work Page
1369	796
1404	796
1404(a)	796
1407	791
1407	796
1407(a)	433
1442	703
1453	845
1711—15	845

45 U.S.C.A.—Railroads

Sec.	This Work Page
421—447	544

46 U.S.C.A.—Shipping

Sec.	This Work Page
4301—4311	547

47 U.S.C.A.—Telegraphs, Telephones, and Radiotelegraphs

Sec.	This Work Page
151 et seq.	547

49 U.S.C.A.—Transportation

Sec.	This Work Page
20301—20306	547
20701—20903	547
40101	677

STATUTES AT LARGE

Year	This Work Page
2005, P.L. 109-2	845

TABLE OF STATUTES

UNIFORM COMMERCIAL CODE

Sec.	This Work Page
1–203(1)	24
1–205	29
Art. 2	14
Art. 2	15
Art. 2	24
Art. 2	34
Art. 2	35
Art. 2	48
Art. 2	49
Art. 2	601
Art. 2	695
Art. 2	714
Art. 2	715
Art. 2	720
Art. 2	745
Art. 2	747
Art. 2	762
Art. 2	767
Art. 2	769
2–102	14
2–102	15
2–102	714
2–102	747
2–102	767
2–103(a)(4)	15
2–104	29
2–104(1)	30
2–105	14
2–105	747
2–106(1)	15
2–106(1)	720
2–106(1)	725
2–201	22
2–201	30
2–201(a)	30
2–202	22
2–202	45
2–202(2)	45
2–209	45
2–302	48
2–302	49
2–313	15
2–313	15
2–313	17
2–313	21
2–313	22
2–313	28
2–313	29
2–313	30
2–313	36
2–313	48
2–313	49
2–313	714
2–313	720
2–313	725
2–313(1)(a)	17
2–313(1)(c)	16
2–313(2)	17
2–313(2)	24
2–313A	36

UNIFORM COMMERCIAL CODE

Sec.	This Work Page
2–313B	36
2–313, Comment 3	20
2–313, Comment 5	16
2–313, Comment 6	21
2–313, Comment 7	22
2–313, Comment 9	22
2–313, Comment 10	24
2–313A	23
2–313A	24
2–313A, Comment 1	24
2–313B	24
2–314	15
2–314	25
2–314	26
2–314	27
2–314	28
2–314	29
2–314	30
2–314	31
2–314	121
2–314	638
2–314	714
2–314	720
2–314	725
2–314(2)	25
2–314(2)	27
2–314(2)(a)	29
2–314(2)(b)	29
2–314(2)(c)	26
2–314(2)(c)	27
2–314(2)(f)	17
2–314(2)(f)	28
2–314(3)	28
2–314(3)	29
2–314, Comment 3	745
2–314, Comment 6	25
2–314, Comment 7	26
2–314, Comment 12	28
2–314, Comment 13	601
2–314, Comment 13	608
2–315	15
2–315	29
2–315	30
2–315	31
2–315	33
2–315	714
2–315	720
2–315	725
2–315, Comment 2	31
2–315, Comment 5	32
2–316	3
2–316	29
2–316	43
2–316	43
2–316	44
2–316	46
2–316	47
2–316	49
2–316	51
2–316	607

UNIFORM COMMERCIAL CODE

Sec.	This Work Page
2–316(1)	45
2–316(2)	44
2–316(2)	47
2–316(3)	47
2–316(3)(a)	44
2–316(3)(b)	32
2–316(3)(b)	44
2–316(3)(b)	601
2–316(3)(c)	44
2–316, Comment 1	45
2–316, Comment 2	45
2–316, Comment 2	47
2–316, Comment 8	601
2–316, Comment 8	608
2–316, Comment 9	32
2–318	34
2–318	35
2–318	36
2–318	43
2–318	749
2–607	3
2–607(3)(a)	51
2–715	37
2–715(2)(b)	601
2–715, Comment 5	601
2–719	43
2–719	47
2–719	48
2–719	49
2–719	51
2–719	607
2–719–2	49
2–719(3)	48
2–719(3)	49
2–725	51
2–725	52
2–725	677
2–725(b)	52

REVISED UNIFORM COMMERCIAL CODE

Sec.	This Work Page
1–203(1)(n)	22

MODEL UNIFORM PRODUCT LIABILITY ACT

Sec.	This Work Page
102(J)	583
114	664

UNIFORM SALES ACT

Sec.	This Work Page
12	21

STATE STATUTES

ALABAMA CODE

Tit.	This Work Page
7, § 2–316(5)	45

ARIZONA REVISED STATUTES

Sec.	This Work Page
12–683(3)	635

WEST'S ANNOTATED CALIFORNIA CIVIL CODE

Sec.	This Work Page
3294	589

WEST'S ANNOTATED CALIFORNIA CODE OF CIVIL PROCEDURE

Sec.	This Work Page
340.2	653
875	647
877	648

WEST'S COLORADO REVISED STATUTES ANNOTATED

Sec.	This Work Page
13–21–402(1)	694
13–21–402(2)	694
13–21–403	514

CONNECTICUT GENERAL STATUTES ANNOTATED

Sec.	This Work Page
14–100a(c)	652

DELAWARE CODE

Tit.	This Work Page
18, § 7001	694

DISTRICT OF COLUMBIA CODE

Sec.	This Work Page
7–2551.02	179

WEST'S FLORIDA STATUTES ANNOTATED

Sec.	This Work Page
768.76	550

OFFICIAL CODE OF GEORGIA ANNOTATED

Sec.	This Work Page
51–11.1	694

ILLINOIS REVISED STATUTES

Ch.	This Work Page
83, § 22.2	52

WEST'S ANNOTATED INDIANA CODE

Sec.	This Work Page
34–20–5–1	514

KANSAS STATUTES ANNOTATED

Sec.	This Work Page
60–3702	585

KENTUCKY REVISED STATUTES

Sec.	This Work Page
411.186	585
411.340	694

LOUISIANA STATUTES ANNOTATED—REVISED STATUTES

Tit.	This Work Page
9, § 2800.51 et seq.	176

MAINE REVISED STATUTES ANNOTATED

Tit.	This Work Page
11, § 2–316(5)	45

MARYLAND ANNOTATED CODE

Art.	This Work Page
27, § 36–I(h)	179

MARYLAND ACTS

Year	This Work Page
1988, c. 533	179

MASSACHUSETTS GENERAL LAWS ANNOTATED

Ch.	This Work Page
106, § 2–316A	45

MISSISSIPPI CODE ANNOTATED

Sec.	This Work Page
11–1–65	584

NEW HAMPSHIRE CONSTITUTION

Art.	This Work Page
14, Pt. 1	676
14, Pt. 1	677

NEW JERSEY STATUTES ANNOTATED

Sec.	This Work Page
2A:15–97	550
2A:58C–3	176
2A:58C–4	315

NEW YORK, MCKINNEY'S CIVIL PRACTICE LAW AND RULES

Sec.	This Work Page
1601—02	663

OHIO REVISED CODE

Sec.	This Work Page
2315.19	626

VERNON'S ANNOTATED TEXAS CIVIL STATUTES

Art.	This Work Page
5236f	761

V.T.C.A., CIVIL PRACTICE AND REMEDIES CODE

Sec.	This Work Page
33.004	664
33.012	656
41.008	585
41.009	585
41.011	585
82.002	694
82.003	694
90.001 et seq.	690

V.T.C.A., LABOR CODE

Sec.	This Work Page
417.001	664

TEXAS RULES OF CIVIL EVIDENCE

Rule	This Work Page
407	408

WEST'S REVISED CODE OF WASHINGTON ANNOTATED

Tit.	This Work Page
62A, § 2–316(4)	45

FEDERAL RULES OF CIVIL PROCEDURE

Rule	This Work Page
23	797
23	822
23	836
23	838
23(a)	809
23(a)	823
23(b)(1)	809
23(b)(1)	845
23(b)(1)	846
23(b)(1)	847
23(b)(1)(B)	845
23(b)(1)(B)	846
23(b)(1)(B)	847
23(b)(1)(B)	848
23(b)(1)(B)	849
23(b)(1)(B)	853
23(b)(1)(B)	857
23(b)(3)	797
23(b)(3)	809
23(b)(3)	810
23(b)(3)	823
23(b)(3)	845
23(b)(3)	846
23(c)(2)	801
23(c)(4)(A)	809
23(f)	822

FEDERAL RULES OF EVIDENCE

Rule	This Work Page
104(a)	444
403	408
407	407
407	408
702	403
702	462
702	464
703	462
706	434

CODE OF FEDERAL REGULATIONS

Tit.	This Work Page
21, § 130.35(e)	514
21, § 130.35(f)	514

Table of Restatements

RESTATEMENT 2ND JUDGEMENTS

Sec.	This Work Page
24, Comment h	688
27	778

RESTATEMENT 3RD LAW GOVERNING LAWYERS

Sec.	This Work Page
128, Comment (d)(i)	778

RESTATEMENT 2ND TORTS

Sec.	This Work Page
295A	397
310	10
311	10
321	337
321	338
328D	234
388	241
388	256
388, Comment n	301
395, Comment j	638
395, Comment k	638
402, Comment f	693
402A	3
402A	57
402A	58
402A	188
402A	193
402A	397
402A	407
402A	485
402A	563
402A	599
402A	603
402A	606
402A	694
402A(1)(b)	492
402A(1), Comment g	483
402A(2)(a)	89
402A, Caveat (2)	193
402A, Caveat (2)	492
402A, Caveat (3)	193
402A, Caveat (3)	492
402A, Comment (g)	110
402A, Comment h	627
402A, Comment (i)	110

RESTATEMENT 2ND TORTS

Sec.	This Work Page
402A, Comment i	241
402A, Comment j	241
402A, Comment j	243
402A, Comment j	350
402A, Comment k	213
402A, Comment k	214
402A, Comment k	215
402A, Comment k	216
402A, Comment k	222
402A, Comment n	606
402A, Comment n	609
402A, Comment p	193
402A, Comment p	492
402A, Comment q	193
402A, Comment q	492
402B	8
402B	9
402B	10
402B	11
402B	602
402B	627
402B	736
402B, Comment j	11
404, Comment a	188
431	340
432(2)	339
432, Comment d	340
500	583
520, Comment l	174
545A	602
549	10
552A	602
552B	10
552C	11
552C	12
908, Comment e	585
918	652

RESTATEMENT 3RD TORTS: APPORTIONMENT OF LIABILITY

Sec.	This Work Page
2, Comment i	613
8	656
8, Comment a	622
16	656
16, Comment g	656
17	640

RESTATEMENT 3RD TORTS: APPORTIONMENT OF LIABILITY

Sec.	This Work Page
22	645
23, Comment g	641
24, Comment i	657
26	357
26	651
B19, Comment l	664

RESTATEMENT 3RD TORTS: LIABILITY FOR PHYSICAL HARM

Sec.	This Work Page
13 (proposed)	397
14 (proposed)	515
15 (proposed)	515
16 (proposed)	511
26	384
26, Comment e	383
26, Comment j	383
26 (proposed)	383
27	384
27, Comment d (proposed)	340
28, Comment g	389
28 (proposed)	389
34, Comment c (proposed)	505
36	385
42 (proposed)	713

RESTATEMENT 3RD TORTS: PRODUCTS LIABILITY

Sec.	This Work Page
1	714
1, Comment a	1
1, Comment c	693
1, Comment c	694
1, Comment e	693
2	88
2	143
2	243
2	407
2	482
2	492
2(a)	95
2(b)	168
2, Comment d	397
2, Comment e	176
2, Comment f	129
2, Comment f	169
2, Comment i	351
2, Comment l	257

RESTATEMENT 3RD TORTS: PRODUCTS LIABILITY

Sec.	This Work Page
2, Comment j	286
2, Comment j	345
2, Comment k	330
2, Comment n	1
2, Comment p	151
2, Comment p	493
2, Illustration 2	694
3	229
3	231
3	232
3	233
3	234
3, Comment b	231
3, Illustration 3	231
4(a)	515
4(b)	511
5	195
5	196
5, Comment c	197
6	215
6(c)	217
6, Comment f	217
6(d)	322
7	95
7, Comment b	95
8	743
8(c)	744
9	8
9	9
9	10
9	11
9, Comment b	8
9, Comment b	11
9, Comment c	11
10	336
10	338
11	336
11	338
13	712
14	729
15, Comment b	493
17	626
18	607
19	217
19	747
19	771
19, Comment c	217
19, Comment e	747
20	723
20(b)	719
20, Comment c	719
20, Comment d	772
20, Comment f	720

PRODUCTS LIABILITY

CASES AND MATERIALS

Fourth Edition

Chapter 1

INTRODUCTION

SECTION A. HISTORY

"Products liability" refers to civil liability for injuries caused by defective products. It generally covers several different theories of liability—including negligence, breach of warranty so-called strict liability, and misrepresentation—which are not mutually exclusive but can be combined in the same lawsuit.[1] The Restatement (Third) of Torts: Products Liability, adopted by the American Law Institute in 1998, and whose provisions are an important topic in this casebook, suggests that courts may combine some of these traditional theories into a single theory of liability for selling a "defective product."[2] Nevertheless, most courts still speak the language of the traditional categories.

Negligence, warranty, and misrepresentation were developed primarily outside of the context of products liability litigation. Negligence applies to products liability litigation pretty much the same way it applies to other personal injury litigation. Warranty law was developed primarily in the context of commercial dealings, and its roots are in contract law. The law of misrepresentation was also developed primarily in the context of commercial dealings, but its roots are in tort law. Unlike the other three theories, so-called strict tort liability was developed as a special theory to deal with injuries caused by defective products. In this book we generally refer to this theory as products liability.

The main historic advantage of product liability has been that the plaintiff can recover without a showing of fault. The defendant is not an insurer, however. The plaintiff must still prove that the product was defective at the time it left the defendant's hands, that the product was used in a foreseeable manner, and that the defect was both the cause in fact and the proximate cause of the injury. The theory can only be used

---

1. Product cases are also governed by the federal Magnuson–Moss Act, 15 U.S.C. § 2301 *et seq.* and in several states by state consumer protection or deceptive trade practices laws.

2. Restatement (Third) of Torts: Products Liability § 1, cmt. *a*; § 2 cmt. *n* (1998).

1

against certain classes of potential defendants, e.g., those in the business of selling or leasing products. Recovery is generally limited to cases involving personal injury or property damage. Most courts do not allow recovery in cases involving pure economic loss, and some do not permit recovery for damage to the product itself. After the new Restatement, differences between product liability and negligence are not as important as they once were.

Breach of warranty is similar to products liability, both in terms of what a plaintiff has to prove and the type of conduct that is recognized as a defense. Warranty law, however, imposes three additional obstacles to recovery that arise from the contractual nature of the remedy. Privity of contract is sometimes required, a plaintiff must give a reasonably prompt notice of breach of warranty, and disclaimers are permitted. Another difference is that the four year warranty statute of limitations begins to run at the time of sale. Tort statutes of limitations generally begin to run at the time of the injury. Warranty theory is important primarily in cases where product liability does not apply, such as those involving pure economic loss.

Two landmark cases—*MacPherson v. Buick Motor Co.*[3] and *Greenman v. Yuba Power Products, Inc.*[4]—divide the history of modern products liability law into three eras. Before *MacPherson*, product manufacturers were given special protection: a plaintiff could recover for injuries caused by *negligently* manufactured products only if he or she was in privity of contract with the defendant. Privity of contract is an appropriate requirement for actions based on contractual obligations, but foreseeability of injury normally defines a defendant's scope of liability in negligence. Nevertheless, before *MacPherson*, American courts usually required a plaintiff to prove privity of contract with the defendant in order to recover damages from a negligent seller.[5]

Even before *MacPherson*, courts developed an exception to the privity requirement: negligent manufacturers of *inherently dangerous* products could be held liable to remote plaintiffs with whom they were not in privity of contract.[6] In the late nineteenth and early twentieth centuries, courts applied this exception to increasingly innocuous products[7]. In *MacPherson*, Justice Cardozo applied this exception to an automobile with a defective wheel, holding that the privity rule is not applicable to any product that is dangerous when defective. Since most products that cause injury are dangerous when defective, *MacPherson* effectively sounded the death knell of the privity rule.

After *MacPherson*, American products liability law entered its second phase. Privity was no longer a hurdle to recovery in products

---

3. 217 N.Y. 382, 111 N.E. 1050 (1916). *See infra* page 5.

4. 59 Cal.2d 57, 27 Cal.Rptr. 697, 377 P.2d 897 (1963). *See infra* Chapter 3, p. 53.

5. The source of the rule was the English case of Winterbottom v. Wright, 10 M. & W. 109, 152 Eng.Rep. 402 (Ex. 1842).

6. *See e.g.* Thomas v. Winchester, 6 N.Y. 397 (1852) (poisonous drug).

7. *See e.g.* Devlin v. Smith, 89 N.Y. 470 (1882) (scaffolding); Statler v. George A. Ray Mfg. Co., 195 N.Y. 478, 88 N.E. 1063 (1909) (coffee urn).

liability cases. During this second phase of American products liability law, product cases were treated like other negligence cases, and a plaintiff was still required to prove that the defendant had failed to use reasonable care. Plaintiffs often faced a difficult burden in proving negligence because the manufacturer's alleged negligent conduct usually occurred prior to the plaintiff's connection with the product or the manufacturer. Moreover, the manufacturer's alleged negligent conduct usually occurred at a location under the manufacturer's control.

During this era a plaintiff could also sue for breach of implied or express warranty. A plaintiff was not required to prove negligence in a suit for breach of warranty, but this theory of recovery posed its own obstacles: a plaintiff was required to prove privity of contract and to give notice of breach, sellers had the ability to disclaim warranties, and statutes of limitations often ran from the time of sale, not injury. *MacPherson* abolished the privity rule in cases based on negligence, not in cases based on breach of warranty. Nevertheless, courts began to whittle away at the privity requirement in warranty cases, first in cases involving implied warranties for food purchased by a member of the plaintiff's family,[8] and then more generally.[9] Courts also began to whittle away at some of the other obstacles, for example, by limiting a seller's ability to disclaim.[10]

Greenman v. Yuba Power Products, Inc.,[11] decided by the California Supreme Court in 1963, ushered in the third stage of modern products liability law by adopting product liability for sellers of defective products. Product liability requires neither privity of contract nor proof of negligence, and it is not subject to disclaimers or the requirement of notice that are applicable to warranties under the Uniform Commercial Code.[12] In 1964, the American Law Institute adopted section 402A of the Restatement (Second) of Torts, which followed *Greenman* and embodied its theory of product liability for sellers of defective products.

See generally Priest, The Invention of Enterprise Liability: A Critical History of the Intellectual Foundations of Modern Tort Law, 14 J.Legal Stud. 461 (1985); Schwartz, The Beginning and the Possible End of the Rise of Modern American Tort Law, 26 Ga.L.Rev. 601 (1992); Spacone, The Emergence of Strict Liability: A Historical Perspective and Other Considerations, Including Senate 100, 8 J.Prod.Liab. 1 (1985).

SECTION B. NEGLIGENCE

Actionable negligence requires unreasonable conduct that is both a cause in fact and a proximate (or legal cause) of damages. The reason-

8. Greenberg v. Lorenz, 9 N.Y.2d 195, 213 N.Y.S.2d 39, 173 N.E.2d 773 (1961).

9. *See* Henningsen v. Bloomfield Motors, Inc., 32 N.J. 358, 161 A.2d 69 (1960); Prosser, The Assault Upon the Citadel (Strict Liability to the Consumer), 69 Yale L.J. 1099 (1960).

10. See Henningsen v. Bloomfield Motors, Inc., 32 N.J. 358, 161 A.2d 69 (1960).

11. 59 Cal.2d 57, 27 Cal.Rptr. 697, 377 P.2d 897 (1963).

12. *See* Uniform Commercial Code (U.C.C.) §§ 2–316, 2–607.

ableness of the conduct is a question for the jury. The plaintiff must prove that a reasonable person in the position of the defendant, before the alleged negligent act, would have recognized that the act would create a risk of harm to others, and that this foreseeable risk is unreasonable, that is, is not justified by the benefit gained by taking it.

Not Reasonable Person but Reasonable Manufacturer of This product

Recall from your first-year torts class that courts evaluate the forseeability and reasonableness of the risks created by the defendant's conduct from the perspective of a "reasonable person," not from the idiosyncratic perspective of the individual defendant. One exception to this rule, however, is that a particular defendant's superior skill and knowledge are taken into account. This is important in cases involving product manufacturers. They are held to the standard of a reasonable manufacturer of the particular product, which means that they should keep reasonably abreast of scientific research and developments in the field.

Contributory negligence is the most important defense. The defendant must prove that the plaintiff engaged in conduct that created a foreseeable, unreasonable risk of harm, and that the unreasonable conduct was an actual and proximate cause of plaintiff's harm. Contributory negligence is no longer a complete defense in most jurisdictions but, under comparative negligence, merely reduces the plaintiff's recovery in accordance. There are two types of comparative negligence. Under modified comparative negligence, a plaintiff is completely barred if his or her negligence exceeds a certain threshold, e.g., more than fifty percent. Under pure comparative negligence, a plaintiff can always recover something, as long as some actionable negligence is attributable to defendant.

As described briefly in Section A, product manufacturers historically were given a number of immunities that narrowly restricted the scope of potential liability. One such rule was that product sellers were not liable for harm caused by products with known or obvious dangers. In other words, dangerous products could give rise to liability only if they possessed latent or unknown dangers. Most courts now have abandoned that rule, holding that the obviousness of a risk is just a factor the jury can take into account when evaluating how dangerous a product is. *See, e.g.*, Micallef v. Miehle Co., 39 N.Y.2d 376, 384 N.Y.S.2d 115, 348 N.E.2d 571 (1976).

The second and most important such rule was the requirement that the plaintiff and defendant be in privity of contract. The origin of this rule was Winterbottom v. Wright, 10 M. & W. 109, 152 Eng.Rep. 402 (1842). That case held that a person who negligently repaired a stagecoach could not be liable to a passenger injured in an accident because the passenger did not have a contract with the defendant. The court stated:

> There is no privity of contract between these parties; and if the plaintiff can sue, every passenger, or even any person passing along the road, who was injured by the upsetting of the coach, might bring a similar action. Unless we confine the operation of such contracts

as this to the parties who entered into them, the most absurd and outrageous consequences, to which I can see no limit, would ensue.

Even though *Winterbottom v. Wright* was not a products liability case, courts subsequently applied the rule to negligence claims against product sellers. Courts gradually began to recognize some exceptions to the privity requirement, the most important of which was for products that were "imminently" or "inherently" dangerous. This body of doctrine led to Justice Cardozo's landmark opinion in *MacPherson v. Buick Motor Co.*, which follows.

MacPHERSON v. BUICK MOTOR CO.
Court of Appeals of New York, 1916.
217 N.Y. 382, 111 N.E. 1050.

CARDOZO, J. The defendant is a manufacturer of automobiles. It sold an automobile to a retail dealer. The retail dealer resold to the plaintiff. While the plaintiff was in the car it suddenly collapsed. He was thrown out and injured. One of the wheels was made of defective wood, and its spokes crumbled into fragments. The wheel was not made by the defendant; it was bought from another manufacturer. There is evidence, however, that its defects could have been discovered by reasonable inspection, and that inspection was omitted. There is no claim that the defendant knew of the defect and willfully concealed it. * * * The charge is one, not of fraud, but of negligence. The question to be determined is whether the defendant owed a duty of care and vigilance to any one but the immediate purchaser.

The foundations of this branch of the law, at least in this state, were laid in Thomas v. Winchester, 6 N.Y. 397, 57 Am.Dec. 455. [This case created an exception to the rule that the seller of a product is liable in negligence only to his immediate purchaser.] A poison was falsely labeled. The sale was made to a druggist, who in turn sold to a customer. The customer recovered damages from the seller who affixed the label. "The defendant's negligence," it was said, "put human life in imminent danger." A poison, falsely labeled, is likely to injure any one who gets it. Because the danger is to be foreseen, there is a duty to avoid the injury. Cases were cited by way of illustration in which manufacturers were not subject to any duty irrespective of contract. The distinction was said to be that their conduct, though negligent, was not likely to result in injury to any one except the purchaser.

[The court discusses two of the first cases to apply the rule of Thomas v. Winchester.]

These early cases suggest a narrow construction of the rule. Later cases, however, evince a more liberal spirit. First in importance is Devlin v. Smith, 89 N.Y. 470, 42 Am.Rep. 311. The defendant, a contractor, built a scaffold for a painter. The painter's servants were injured. The contractor was held liable. He knew that the scaffold, if improperly constructed, was a most dangerous trap. He knew that it was to be used by the workmen. He was building it for that very purpose. Building it for their use, he owed them a duty, irrespective of his contract with their master, to build it with care.

From Devlin v. Smith we pass over intermediate cases and turn to the latest case in this court in which Thomas v. Winchester was followed. That case is Statler v. Ray Mfg. Co., 195 N.Y. 478, 480, 88 N.E. 1063. The defendant manufactured a large coffee urn. It was installed in a restaurant. When heated, the urn exploded and injured the plaintiff. We held that the manufacturer was liable. We said that the urn "was of such a character inherently that, when applied to the purposes for which it was designed, it was liable to become a source of great danger to many people if not carefully and properly constructed."

It may be that Devlin v. Smith and Statler v. Ray Mfg. Co. have extended the rule of Thomas v. Winchester. If so, this court is committed to the extension. The defendant argues that things imminently dangerous to life are poisons, explosives, deadly weapons—things whose normal function it is to injure or destroy. But whatever the rule in Thomas v. Winchester may once have been, it has no longer that restricted meaning. A scaffold (Devlin v. Smith, supra) is not inherently a destructive instrument. It becomes destructive only if imperfectly constructed. A large coffee urn (Statler v. Ray Mfg. Co., supra) may have within itself, if negligently made, the potency of danger, yet no one thinks of it as an implement whose normal function is destruction. What is true of the coffee urn is equally true of bottles of aerated water. Torgesen v. Schultz, 192 N.Y. 156, 84 N.E. 956, 18 L.R.A. (N.S.) 726, 127 Am.St.Rep. 894. * * *

We hold, then, that the principle of Thomas v. Winchester is not limited to poisons, explosives, and things of like nature, to things which in their normal operation are implements of destruction. If the nature of a thing is such that it is reasonably certain to place life and limb in peril when negligently made, it is then a thing of danger. Its nature gives warning of the consequences to be expected. If to the element of danger there is added knowledge that the thing will be used by persons other than the purchaser, and used without new tests, then, irrespective of contract, the manufacturer of this thing of danger is under a duty to make it carefully. That is as far as we are required to go for the decision of this case. There must be knowledge of a danger, not merely possible, but probable. It is possible to use almost anything in a way that will make it dangerous if defective. That is not enough to charge the manufacturer with a duty independent of his contract. Whether a given thing is dangerous may be sometimes a question for the court and sometimes a question for the jury. There must also be knowledge that in the usual course of events the danger will be shared by others than the buyer. Such knowledge may often be inferred from the nature of the transaction. But it is possible that even knowledge of the danger and of the use will not always be enough. The proximity or remoteness of the relation is a factor to be considered. We are dealing now with the liability of the manufacturer of the finished product, who puts it on the market to be used without inspection by his customers. If he is negligent, where danger is to be foreseen, a liability will follow.

* * *

There is here no break in the chain of cause and effect. In such circumstances, the presence of a known danger, attendant upon a known use, makes vigilance a duty. We have put aside the notion that the duty to safeguard life and limb, when the consequences of negligence may be foreseen, grows out of contract and nothing else. We have put the source of the obligation where it ought to be. We have put its source in the law.

From this survey of the decisions, there thus emerges a definition of the duty of a manufacturer which enables us to measure this defendant's liability. Beyond all question, the nature of an automobile gives warning of probable danger if its construction is defective. This automobile was designed to go 50 miles an hour. Unless its wheels were sound and strong, injury was almost certain. It was as much a thing of danger as a defective engine for a railroad. The defendant knew the danger. It knew also that the car would be used by persons other than the buyer. This was apparent from its size; there were seats for three persons. It was apparent also from the fact that the buyer was a dealer in cars, who bought to resell. The maker of this car supplied it for the use of purchasers from the dealer just as plainly as the contractor in Devlin v. Smith supplied the scaffold for use by the servants of the owner. The dealer was indeed the one person of whom it might be said with some approach to certainty that by him the car would not be used. Yet the defendant would have us say that he was the one person whom it was under a legal duty to protect. The law does not lead us to so inconsequent a conclusion. Precedents drawn from the days of travel by stagecoach do not fit the conditions of travel today. The principle that the danger must be imminent does not change, but the things subject to the principle do change. They are whatever the needs of life in a developing civilization require them to be.

* * *

In this view of the defendant's liability there is nothing inconsistent with the theory of liability on which the case was tried. It is true that the court told the jury that "an automobile is not an inherently dangerous vehicle." The meaning, however, is made plain by the context. The meaning is that danger is not to be expected when the vehicle is well constructed. The court left it to the jury to say whether the defendant ought to have foreseen that the car, if negligently constructed, would become "imminently dangerous." Subtle distinctions are drawn by the defendant between things inherently dangerous and things imminently dangerous, but the case does not turn upon these verbal niceties. If danger was to be expected as reasonably certain, there was a duty of vigilance, and this whether you call the danger inherent or imminent. In varying forms that thought was put before the jury. We do not say that the court would not have been justified in ruling as a matter of law that the car was a dangerous thing. If there was any error, it was none of which the defendant can complain.

We think the defendant was not absolved from a duty of inspection because it bought the wheels from a reputable manufacturer. It was not merely a dealer in automobiles. It was a manufacturer of automobiles. It was responsible for the finished product. It was not at liberty to put the finished product on the market without subjecting the component parts to ordinary and simple tests. Richmond & Danville R.R. Co. v. Elliott, 149 U.S. 266, 272, 13 Sup.Ct. 837, 37 L.Ed. 728. Under the charge of the trial judge nothing more was required of it. The obligation to inspect must vary with the nature of the thing to be inspected. The more probable the danger the greater the need of caution.

* * *

Other rulings complained of have been considered, but no error has been found in them.

The judgment should be affirmed, with costs.

Note

By interpreting the exception to the privity rule so broadly, the court, in effect, eliminated the rule. Any product that is likely to be dangerous if negligently made can now give rise to a cause of action for negligence without a showing of privity. Courts in virtually all states have followed *MacPherson*. Courts also impose products liability without requiring privity of contract. In warranty cases, privity can still play a role. Of course, many other issues can arise in a products case, just as they can arise in any negligence case. You studied those issues in your first-year torts course. We will not rehearse them all here, but you should keep them in mind when analyzing any negligence claim in a products case.

SECTION C. MISREPRESENTATION

Restatement (Third) of Torts: Products Liability § 9 provides:

One engaged in the business of selling or otherwise distributing products who, in connection with the sale of a product, makes a fraudulent, negligent, or innocent misrepresentation of material fact concerning the product is subject to liability for harm to persons or property caused by the misrepresentation.

Section 9 of the new Restatement is expressly based on Section 402B of the Restatement (Second) of Torts. See Restatement (Third) of Torts: Products Liability § 9, cmt *b*. Section 402B provided:

One engaged in the business of selling chattels who, by advertising, labels, or otherwise, makes to the public a misrepresentation of a material fact concerning the character or quality of a chattel sold by him is subject to liability for physical harm to a consumer of the chattel caused by justifiable reliance upon the misrepresentation, even though (a) it is not made fraudulently or negligently, and (b) the consumer has not bought the chattel from or entered into any contractual relation with the seller.

A succinct history of section 402B is to be found in American Safety Equipment Corp. v. Winkler, 640 P.2d 216, 219–20 (Colo. 1982).

The theory of innocent misrepresentation embodied in Section 9 was not cut from whole cloth. It is an outgrowth of the law of intentional misrepresentation (fraud) and negligent misrepresentation, both of which were developed primarily in non-product cases. The law of fraud and negligent misrepresentation is important in products cases for two reasons.

First, a plaintiff can rely directly on the law of fraud and negligent misrepresentation in a product case. A product seller who fraudulently or negligently misrepresents a product may be liable for any resulting damages, including purely economic damages. Consequently, a plaintiff who can prove fraud or negligent misrepresentation has this advantage over a plaintiff who can prove only products liability or ordinary negligence, though not over a plaintiff who can prove breach of warranty.

Second, other than the issues specifically addressed by section 9—such as the defendant's state of mind—many of the rules governing fraud and negligent misrepresentation are applicable to innocent misrepresentation under section 9.

To establish a common law action for fraud, a plaintiff must prove (a) that the defendant made a false representation of a material fact, (b) that the defendant knew the statement was false, knew that he had no knowledge of its truth or falsity, or knew that he did not have as strong a basis for his statement as he implied, (c) that the defendant intended the plaintiff to rely on the statement, (d) that the plaintiff justifiably relied on the statement, and (e) that the plaintiff suffered damage.

An action for fraud or negligent misrepresentation differs from an action for breach of contract because the absence of a contract (due to lack of consideration, for example) does not defeat recovery. Moreover, the defendant's mere failure to perform a promise will not support recovery in an action for misrepresentation. To recover for fraud, the plaintiff must prove that the defendant knowingly or recklessly deceived him. To recover for negligent misrepresentation, the plaintiff must prove that the defendant negligently deceived him.

In addition to the different requirements concerning the defendant's state of mind (scienter), most courts also distinguish between fraud and negligent misrepresentation in terms of the defendant's scope of liability. Most courts have held that a defendant's liability for fraud extends to any person who the defendant had "reason to know" would rely. However, a defendant's liability for negligent misrepresentation extends only to individuals within the class of persons that the defendant actually knew would rely. Most courts also use a different measure of damages depending on the defendant's state of mind. For fraud under section 549 of the Second Restatement of Torts, a plaintiff can choose between out-of-pocket loss or benefit-of-the-bargain damages. For negligent misrepresentation under section 552B, the plaintiff can recover both. However, in a fraud case a plaintiff can also recover consequential economic loss.

The other elements of a cause of action for misrepresentation—such as the requirement of a false statement of material fact—are the same, irrespective of whether the action is based on fraud, negligent misrepresentation, or innocent misrepresentation under section 9.

Sections 310 and 311 of the Restatement (Second) of Torts provide for liability for "physical harm" caused (respectively) by "conscious representation" and "negligent misrepresentation."

Section 402B applies only to defendants who are "engaged in the business of selling or otherwise distributing products." Other sellers, even if they sell to the public, are not covered.

Most misrepresentations are made with words, but a deed—such as masking a defect—can also constitute a misrepresentation. Normally, non-disclosures do not constitute misrepresentations, but this general rule has several exceptions. A duty to speak and disclose facts exists when a confidential or fiduciary relationship exists between the parties. A duty to disclose also exists when, during the course of negotiations, a party learns that his earlier representations were false, or when a party gives a false impression by revealing some facts while withholding others.

To be actionable, a misrepresentation must be a matter of fact. Opinions concerning quality or value (or other "sales talk") constitute "puffing" and are not actionable. Predictions of future events are opinions and therefore are not actionable, although some courts have held otherwise if the speaker purports to have special knowledge. A promise to perform a future act is not a statement of fact, and a failure to perform such a promise is actionable only in contract, unless the defendant made the promise with an intent not to carry it out. Statements of law are opinions rather than facts, except (a) when they are intended to be statements of fact and are understood as such, (b) when a special relationship of trust exists between the parties, or (c) when the defendant represents himself to have special knowledge of the law.

The misrepresentation of fact must also be material. The test of materiality in cases involving common law fraud is whether the statement would be important to a reasonable person. This is an objective test, and it applies unless the defendant actually knows that the plaintiff regards a matter as being important even though a reasonable person would not. The requirement of materiality is designed to prevent a party from using a trivial misrepresentation as an excuse to set aside a bad bargain.

In products liability cases, a statement might be material if it significantly affects the manner in which the plaintiff uses the product, thereby increasing its danger. Most cases addressing the requirement of materiality arise in the context of fraud or negligent misrepresentation. It is possible that slightly different rules will evolve in personal injury cases under section 9.

Section 402B of the Second Restatement required that a plaintiff show justifiable reliance on the misrepresentation. According to Comment j, liability does not exist "where the misrepresentation is not known, or there is indifference to it, and it does not influence the purchase or subsequent conduct." The representation need not, however, be the "sole inducement to purchase, or to use the chattel, and it is sufficient that it has been a substantial factor in that inducement." Comment c to section 9 of the new Restatement incorporates by reference Comment j of the Second Restatement.

Justifiable reliance is also an element of fraud and negligent misrepresentation, and Comment j to section 402B explicitly incorporates the rules concerning reliance developed under those theories. In cases involving fraud or negligent misrepresentation, a plaintiff who is aware of the truth cannot recover. Moreover, some courts have held that if a reasonably prudent person would have been aware of the facts or investigated further, the plaintiff will be deemed to have knowledge of the facts and cannot recover for the misrepresentation.

The injured consumer need not be the one to rely on the misrepresentation. It is enough that the purchaser relies on the misrepresentation and then passes the product along to the injured consumer.

Section 9 provides for liability only in cases involving harm to persons or property. Most courts have interpreted section 402B strictly and permitted recovery only for physical harm. *See, e.g.,* Alfred N. Koplin & Co. v. Chrysler Corp., 49 Ill.App.3d 194, 7 Ill.Dec. 113, 364 N.E.2d 100 (1977). In any event, lost wages or profits caused by physical harm are recoverable as normal personal injury damages.

Section 402B of the Second Restatement provided for liability to a "consumer," but a "consumer" need not have actually purchased the product. Comment i provides that an employee or family member of the purchaser who uses the product is also a consumer, as is anyone "who makes use of the chattel in the manner which a purchaser may be expected to use it." A caveat to section 402B stated that "[t]he Institute expresses no opinion as to whether the rule stated in this Section may apply * * * where physical harm is caused to one who is not a consumer of the chattel." Comment b to Section 9 of the new Restatement leaves this question open.

Section 552C of the Restatement (Second) of Torts provides:

Misrepresentation in Sale, Rental or Exchange Transaction

(1) One who, in a sale, rental, or exchange transaction with another, makes a misrepresentation of a material fact for the purpose of inducing the other to act or to refrain from acting in reliance upon it, is subject to liability to the other for pecuniary loss

caused to him by his justifiable reliance upon the misrepresentation, even though it is not made fraudulently or negligently.

(2) Damages recoverable under the rule stated in this section are limited to the difference between the value of what the other has parted with and the value of what he has received in the transaction.

Note that section 552C is limited to pecuniary damages, which are covered in subsection (2) by an out-of-pocket measure of damages. One commentator has suggested section 552C can support recovery of more extensive damages. *See* Hill, Damages for Innocent Misrepresentation, 73 Colum.L.Rev. 679 (1973).

Chapter 2

WARRANTY

SECTION A. INTRODUCTION

Warranties have a dual significance for products liability law. First, they have historical importance. They provided a basis for liability in product cases before the adoption of products liability, and while products liability has shed most of its warranty heritage, warranty law spawned product liability and influenced its early development.

Second, warranty law still provides an effective remedy for injured consumers. Plaintiffs usually can join claims of product liability and breach of warranty, and an action for breach of warranty can provide a victim with certain remedies that are not available under product liability, such as recovery of pure economic damages. Breach of warranty can also trigger a variety of remedies available under some states' consumer protection statutes.

Warranty law covers many issues that are not relevant to products liability litigation. Indeed, most of warranty law was developed to regulate commercial dealings. Consequently, the material in this chapter does not offer a systematic survey of warranty law. Instead, it addresses those aspects of warranty law that affect products liability litigation.

Breach of warranty arose in the fourteenth century as a tort. The cause of action was based on the notion that the seller had made a misrepresentation. It was a form of strict liability because the seller was liable for breach of warranty without regard to intent or negligence. By the late eighteenth century, courts recognized breach of warranty as a *contract* claim, not just as a tort, although the tort action was still available. Because of their tort heritage, warranty obligations can arise as a matter of law without regard to whether the parties intend to create them. Because of their contract heritage, privity of contract between the plaintiff and defendant is sometimes an issue, and a seller is sometimes permitted to disclaim a warranty or to limit any available remedy. Moreover, a plaintiff may be required to give reasonably prompt notice of breach.

The common law eventually recognized three types of warranties: the implied warranty of merchantability, the implied warranty of fitness for a particular purpose, and the express warranty. These warranties were codified in the Uniform Sales Act in 1906 and then in Article 2 of the Uniform Commercial Code in 1951. The legislatures of 49 states (all but Louisiana) have adopted some version of the UCC, which is a joint product of the American Law Institute and the National Conference of Commissioners on Uniform State Laws. In 2003, the ALI and NCCUSL proposed several changes to Article 2, including changes to several of the warranty provisions. Thus far, the changes have not been adopted in any state but as you do research in this area in the next few years, you should be alert to possible changes in your state's version of the UCC. We will note some of the potential changes in the following discussion.

Although a product seller was subject to strict liability for breach of warranty, the usefulness of warranty law was limited because of the requirements of privity and notice and because of the seller's right to disclaim. Reform began when courts started to relax these impediments to recovery. They first relaxed the privity requirement, historically in cases involving impure food. The first case was in 1913, and by 1960 seventeen jurisdictions imposed liability without privity. Courts used a variety of methods to accomplish this result, such as "fictitious agencies or third-party-beneficiary contracts * * * [or warranties] running with the goods from the manufacturer to the consumer, by analogy to a covenant running with the land." Prosser, The Assault Upon the Citadel (Strict Liability to the Consumer), 69 Yale L.J. 1099, 1106 (1960). In the 1950s a few courts began imposing liability without privity even in cases not involving food.

Henningsen v. Bloomfield Motors, Inc., 32 N.J. 358, 161 A.2d 69 (1960), is a landmark case. *Henningsen* gave a woman injured in an automobile accident a cause of action for breach of an implied warranty of merchantability against the automobile manufacturer even though she was not in privity of contract with the defendant. The court also refused to enforce a disclaimer and remedy limitation in the standard form contract. In addition to deciding these specific issues, *Henningsen* was important because it helped lead to modern products liability. Courts recognized that the strict liability they imposed under warranty law was really based on tort because privity of contract was not required and because normal contract defenses such as disclaimers and remedy limitations were not recognized. *See generally* Ames, The History of Assumpsit, 2 Harv.L.Rev. 1 (1888); Prosser, The Assault Upon the Citadel (Strict Liability to the Consumer), 69 Yale L.J. 1099 (1960); Prosser, The Implied Warranty of Merchantable Quality, 27 Minn.L.Rev. 117 (1943).

The warranty provisions of Article 2 apply only to the sale of goods. Section 2–102 provides that Article 2 itself applies to "transactions in goods." Section 2–105 defines "goods" as

> all things (including specifically manufactured goods) which are movable at the time of identification to the contract for sale other

than the money in which the price is to be paid, investment securities * * * and things in action. "Goods" also includes the unborn young of animals and growing crops and other identified things attached to realty as described in the section on goods to be severed from realty (Section 2–107).

Consequently, Article 2 is not applicable to services or to real estate transactions.

The specific warranty provisions of Article 2—section 2–313 governing express warranties, section 2–314 governing implied warranties of merchantability, and section 2–315 governing implied warranties of fitness—refer to "sales" or "sellers." A "sale" is defined in subsection 2–106(1) as "the passing of title from the seller to the buyer for a price (Section 2–401)." A "seller" is defined in subsection 2–103(a)(4) as "a person who sells or contracts to sell goods." Section 2–102 expressly excludes from Article 2 any transaction "intended to operate only as a security transaction." Consequently, transactions in "goods" other than sales, such as leases and bailments, are not expressly governed by the Article 2 warranties. They may, however, be governed by common law warranties or by product liability.

Issues concerning the types of transactions governed by the Article 2 warranties can be quite complicated, and various states differ in their interpretation of Article 2. These issues are addressed in more detail in Chapter 12, along with issues concerning the types of transactions governed by product liability. It is important at this point simply to recognize that the Article 2 warranties are applicable to transactions involving a sale of goods.

SECTION B. EXPRESS WARRANTY

Uniform Commercial Code

§ 2–313. Express Warranties by Affirmation, Promise, Description, Sample

(1) Express warranties by the seller are created as follows:

(a) Any affirmation of fact or promise made by the seller to the buyer which relates to the goods and becomes part of the basis of the bargain creates an express warranty that the goods shall conform to the affirmation or promise.

(b) Any description of the goods which is made part of the basis of the bargain creates an express warranty that the goods shall conform to the description.

(c) Any sample or model which is made part of the basis of the bargain creates an express warranty that the whole of the goods shall conform to the sample or model.

(2) It is not necessary to the creation of an express warranty that the seller use formal words such as "warrant" or "guarantee" or that he

have a specific intention to make a warranty, but an affirmation merely of the value of the goods or a statement purporting to be merely the seller's opinion or commendation of the goods does not create a warranty.

The *raison d'etre* of express warranties is to permit the parties to a transaction to structure their own deal. Consequently, a lawyer's first task in any case involving an express warranty is to interpret the warranty itself. This issue has been the principal source of litigation about express warranties. In interpreting an express warranty, the entire context of the transaction should be taken into account, including other dealings between the parties and trade practices. Comment 5 to section 2–313 provides that "all descriptions by merchants must be read against the applicable trade usages with the general rules as to merchantability resolving any doubts."

A sample of cases is instructive about the types of interpretation issues that can arise. In Salk v. Alpine Ski Shop, Inc., 115 R.I. 309, 342 A.2d 622 (1975), the plaintiff bought skis with bindings that release "whichever way you fall" and "at the exact tension you set." The court interpreted the warranty to mean only that the release was uniform in all directions, not that the bindings would always release, no matter what tension. On the other hand, in Lane v. C.A. Swanson & Sons, 130 Cal.App.2d 210, 278 P.2d 723 (1955), the plaintiff was injured when a hidden bone from a can of "boned chicken" lodged in his throat. The defendant argued that the term "boned chicken" was merely descriptive of the type of product, not an affirmation that the chicken was absolutely devoid of bone fragments. Relying on the word "boned" on the label and on advertisements referring to "No bones," the Court held for the plaintiff.

Some courts have held that a general assurance of safety constitutes an express warranty that the product will not injure the user. For example, in Drayton v. Jiffee Chem. Corp., 395 F.Supp. 1081 (N.D.Ohio 1975), the court held that an advertisement claiming that a drain cleaner is "safe for household use" constituted an express warranty. Other courts have interpreted express warranties more strictly. For example, in Whitmer v. Schneble, 29 Ill.App.3d 659, 331 N.E.2d 115 (1975), the seller of a Doberman puppy told the buyers that it was "docile." Two years later it bit a child, and the buyers sued for breach of express warranty. The court held that even a docile Doberman will bite children under some circumstances, so the express warranty, if any, was not breached. Moreover, the warranty, if any, described the Doberman when it was sold and did not warrant that the dog's personality would not change.

The point of these cases is not their particular results. It is that, like all other contract provisions, warranties are subject to disputes about interpretation, based on the language of the warranty and the circumstances of the transaction.

As section 2–313(1)(c) indicates, an express warranty can be made by sample or model. An "affirmation of fact or promise" or a "description of goods" can be made by pictures or other forms of communication, as well as by words. For example, in Sylvestri v. Warner & Swasey Co., 398 F.2d 598 (2d Cir.1968), the plaintiff was thrown from a backhoe when a support gave way. The court held that an advertisement with a picture of the backhoe lifting pipe constituted an express warranty that it was suitable for lifting heavy objects, including boulders. The court stated that "[i]t is the 'essential idea' conveyed by the advertising representations which is relevant." But in Coffer v. Standard Brands, Inc., 30 N.C.App. 134, 226 S.E.2d 534 (1976)—where the plaintiff was injured when he bit down on an unshelled nut sold in a glass jar of otherwise shelled mixed nuts—the court held that the clear glass jar revealing shelled nuts did not constitute an express warranty that the whole jar was devoid of shells.

Express warranties are created under section 2–313(1)(a) only for promises or affirmations of "fact." Section 2–313(2) makes clear that opinions, especially of value, do not constitute express warranties. As in the law of misrepresentation, which is addressed in the previous chapter, it is often difficult to distinguish between "facts" and "opinions." Courts have found that the following statements constitute affirmations of fact and therefore express warranties: that a product will not deteriorate, General Supply and Equip. Co. v. Phillips, 490 S.W.2d 913, 917 (Tex.Civ. App. 1972); that a product is in "excellent condition," Valley Datsun v. Martinez, 578 S.W.2d 485 (Tex.Civ.App. 1979); and that a product is "adequate" for the job, Burnett v. James, 564 S.W.2d 407, 409 (Tex.Civ. App. 1978). In Carney v. Sears, Roebuck & Co., 309 F.2d 300 (4th Cir.1962), the court held that a statement that a ladder was "good" quality was an "opinion," but in Turner v. Central Hardware Co., 353 Mo. 1182, 186 S.W.2d 603 (1945), the court held that a statement that a ladder was "strong and durable" was a "fact." Neither court was explicitly applying section 2–313.

To constitute an express warranty, a promise or affirmation of fact must "relate[ ] to the goods." Promises unrelated to the goods may still create contractual obligations, but they do not constitute warranties. The distinction can be important, because "warranties" are governed by special provisions concerning waiver, privity of contract, and limitations on damages.

Unlike an implied warranty of merchantability, which is applicable only to sellers who are merchants, an express warranty is applicable to merchants and non-merchants alike. Additionally, an express warranty is applicable only to a seller who actually makes a representation. Thus, a retailer is not automatically liable under section 2–313 for a manufacturer's express warranties, although a retailer might be liable for breach of an implied warranty of merchantability under section 2–314(2)(f) if the product fails to conform to a manufacturer's promise on the label. A retailer who makes a representation as part of a manufacturer's promotion may create liability for the manufacturer under agency principles, and a retailer who reiterates a manufacturer's promise may be liable for his own express warranty.

If a defendant breaches an express warranty, it is irrelevant that she was not at fault or that the goods were nevertheless reasonably safe.

HAUTER v. ZOGARTS
Supreme Court of California, En Banc, 1975.
14 Cal.3d 104, 120 Cal.Rptr. 681, 534 P.2d 377.

TOBRINER, JUSTICE.

* * *

Defendants[1] manufacture and sell the "Golfing Gizmo" (hereinafter Gizmo), a training device designed to aid unskilled golfers improve their games. Defendants' catalogue states that the Gizmo is a "completely equipped backyard driving range." In 1966, Louise Hauter purchased a Gizmo from the catalogue and gave it to Fred Hauter, her 13 1/2–year-old son, as a Christmas present.

The Gizmo is a simple device consisting of two metal pegs, two cords—one elastic, one cotton—and a regulation golf ball. After the pegs are driven into the ground approximately 25 inches apart, the elastic cord is looped over them. The cotton cord, measuring 21 feet in length, ties to the middle of the elastic cord. The ball is attached to the end of the cotton cord. When the cords are extended, the Gizmo resembles the shape of a large letter "T," with the ball resting at the base.

The user stands by the ball in order to hit his practice shots. The instructions state that when hit correctly, the ball will fly out and spring back near the point of impact; if the ball returns to the left, it indicates a right-hander's "slice"; a shot returning to the right indicates a right-hander's "hook." If the ball is "topped," it does not return and must be retrieved by the player. The label on the shipping carton and the cover of the instruction booklet urge players to "drive the ball with full power" and further state: "COMPLETELY SAFE BALL WILL NOT HIT PLAYER."

On July 14, 1967, Fred Hauter was seriously injured while using defendants' product. Thereafter, plaintiffs filed the instant suit on his behalf, claiming false representation, breach of express and implied warranties and strict liability in tort.

Fred Hauter testified at trial that prior to his injury, he had practiced golf 10 to 20 times at driving ranges and had played several rounds of golf. His father instructed him in the correct use of the Gizmo. Fred had read the printed instructions that accompany the product and had used the Gizmo about a dozen times. Before the accident, Fred set up the Gizmo in his front yard according to the printed instructions. The area was free of objects that might have caused the ball to ricochet, and no other persons were nearby. Fred then took his normal swing with a

---

1. Defendants are Rudy C. Zogarts, who does business as House of Zog [manufacturer] and Miles Kimball Company [seller].

seven-iron. The last thing he remembers was extreme pain and dizziness. After a period of unconsciousness, he staggered into the house and told his mother that he had been hit on the head by the ball. He suffered brain damage and, in one doctor's opinion, is currently an epileptic.

* * *

We first treat the claim for breach of express warranty, which is governed by California Commercial Code section 2313. The key under this section is that the seller's statements—whether fact or opinion—must become "part of the basis of the bargain."[2] (See Cal.U.Com.Code, § 2313, com. 8; Ezer, *supra,* at p. 287, fn. 39.) The basis of the bargain requirement represents a significant change in the law of warranties. Whereas plaintiffs in the past have had to prove their reliance upon specific promises made by the seller (Grinnell v. Charles Pfizer & Co. (1969) 274 Cal.App.2d 424, 440, 79 Cal.Rptr. 369), the Uniform Commercial Code requires no such proof. According to official comment 3 to the Uniform Commercial Code following section 2313, "no particular reliance * * * need be shown in order to weave [the seller's affirmations of fact] into the fabric of the agreement. Rather, any fact which is to take such affirmations, once made, out of the agreement requires clear affirmative proof."

The commentators have disagreed as to the impact of this new development. (See generally, Note, "Basis of the Bargain"—What Role Reliance? (1972) 34 U.Pitt.L.Rev. 145, 149–150.) Some have said that the basis of the bargain requirement merely shifts the burden of proving non-reliance to the seller. (See 1 Carroll, Cal.Commercial Law, *supra,* § 6.7, p. 210; Boyd, Representing Consumer—The Uniform Commercial Code and Beyond (1968) 9 Ariz.L.Rev. 372, 385.) Indeed, the comments to section 2313 seem to [bear] out this analysis; they declare that "all of the statements of the seller [become part of the basis of the bargain] *unless good reason is shown to the contrary."* (Cal.U.Com.Code, § 2313, com. 8 (emphasis added).)[3]

Other writers, however, find that the code eliminates the concept of reliance altogether. (See Note, *supra,* 34 U.Pitt.L.Rev. at p. 150; Nordstrom, Sales (1970) §§ 66–68.) Support can be found in the comments to the code for this view also; they declare that "[i]n view of the principle

---

2. As we explained above, defendants' statement is one of fact and is subject to construction as an express warranty. It is important to note, however, that even statements of opinion can become warranties under the code if they become part of the basis of the bargain. (Cal.U.Com.Code, § 2313, com. 8; Ezer, *supra,* at p. 287, fn. 39.) Thus the California Uniform Commercial Code expands sellers' liability beyond the former Uniform Sales Act (former Civ. Code §§ 1732–1736) and provides greater coverage than Restatement Second of Torts, section 402B, discussed earlier.

3. The code relegates "the metaphysical 'buyer's reliance' requirement to secondary status, where it properly belongs." (Ezer, The Impact of the Uniform Commercial Code on the California Law of Sales Warranties (1961) 8 U.C.L.A.L.Rev. 281, 285.) Ezer also notes: "The Code's implicit premise is that buyer's reliance is prima facie established from the fact that he made the purchase. If the seller can establish that the buyer in fact did not rely on the seller, that the affirmation or promise was not the 'basis of the bargain,' to use the Code language, then there is no express warranty." (*Id.,* at p. 285, fn. 30.)

that the whole purpose of the law of warranty is to determine what it is that the seller *has in essence agreed to sell,* the policy is adopted of those cases which refuse except in unusual circumstances to recognize a material deletion of the seller's obligation. Thus, a contract is normally a contract for a sale of something describable and described." (Cal.U.Com. Code, § 2313, com. 4 (emphasis added).) To these observers, the focus of the warranty shifts from the buyer, who formerly had to rely upon specific statements in order to recover, to the seller, who now must stand behind his words if he has failed adequately to disclaim them. "[T]he seller must show by clear affirmative proof either that the statement was retracted by him before the deal was closed or that the parties understood that the goods would not conform to the affirmation or description. Under such an interpretation, the affirmation, once made, is a part of the agreement, and lack of reliance by the buyer is not a fact which would take the affirmation out of the agreement." (Note, *supra,* 34 U.Pitt.L.Rev. at p. 151.)[4]

We are not called upon in this case to resolve the reliance issue.[5] The parties do not discuss the changes wrought by the Uniform Commercial Code, and plaintiffs are fully able to meet their burden regardless of which test we employ. Fred Hauter's testimony shows that he read and relied upon defendants' representation; he was impressed by "something on the cover dealing with the safety of the item." More importantly, defendants presented no evidence which could remove their assurance of safety from the basis of the bargain. The trial court properly concluded, therefore, that defendants expressly warranted the safety of their product and are liable for Fred Hauter's injuries which resulted from a breach of that warranty.

* * *

Notes

1. Did Fred have a bargain with anyone?
2. Comment 3 to section 2–313 states:

> The present section deals with affirmations of fact by the seller, descriptions of the goods or exhibitions of samples, exactly as any other part of a negotiation which ends in a contract is dealt with. No specific

---

4. Thus if a seller agrees to sell a certain quality of product, he cannot avoid liability for selling lower grade goods. No longer can he find solace in the fact that the injured consumer never saw his warranty. (See Lonzrick v. Republic Steel Corp. (1966) 6 Ohio St.2d 227, 237, 218 N.E.2d 185.)

5. Although the code has been the law in California since 1965, we know of no California case which analyzes the basis of the bargain requirement. The scattered cases from other jurisdictions generally have ignored the significance of the new standard and have held that consumer reliance still is a vital ingredient for recovery based on express warranty. (See, e.g., Stang v. Hertz Corp. (1971) 83 N.M. 217, 219, 490 P.2d 475, revd. on other grounds, 83 N.M. 730, 497 P.2d 732; Gillette Dairy, Inc. v. Hydrotex Indus., Inc. (8th Cir.1971) 440 F.2d 969, 974; Capital Equip. Enterprises, Inc. v. North Pier Term. Co. (1969) 117 Ill.App.2d 264, 254 N.E.2d 542, 545; Speed Fastners, Inc. v. Newsom (10th Cir.1967) 382 F.2d 395, 397.)

intention to make a warranty is necessary if any of these factors is made part of the basis of the bargain. In actual practice affirmations of fact made by the seller about the goods during a bargain are regarded as part of the description of those goods; hence no particular reliance on such statements need be shown in order to weave them into the fabric of the agreement. Rather, any fact which is to take such affirmations, once made, out of the agreement requires clear affirmative proof. The issue normally is one of fact.

Comment 6 states in part:

In general, the presumption is that any sample or model just as any affirmation of fact is intended to become a basis of the bargain. But there is no escape from the question of fact.

Section 12 of the Uniform Sales Act provided:

Any affirmation of fact or any promise by the seller relating to the goods is an express warranty if the natural tendency of such affirmation or promise is to induce the buyer to purchase the goods, and if the buyer purchases the goods relying thereon. No affirmation of the value of the goods, nor any statement purporting to be a statement of the seller's opinion only shall be construed as a warranty.

3. Does the difference in language between section 12 of the Uniform Sales Act and section 2–313 of the Uniform Commercial Code require a conclusion that reliance is no longer required? Does the difference affect the underlying standard, or does it merely affect the burden of proof? For a relatively recent case of first impression on whether reliance is required, *see* Torres v. Northwest Engineering Co., 86 Hawai'i 383, 949 P.2d 1004, 1014 (App.1997) ("The gist of a breach of express warranty action thus focuses on (1) what the seller agreed to sell; and (2) whether the product delivered by the seller complied with the statements or description of what the seller agreed to sell." No reliance is required.)

4. Footnote 4 in *Hauter* suggests that an express warranty may be created even though the consumer never saw it. Obviously, there could be no reliance. Are there reasons to enforce a warranty that the consumer has not seen? Do you suppose a court would refuse to enforce a provision of an automobile warranty that the consumer had not read? A product's price presumably reflects the value of a standardized warranty even if the consumer has not read or relied on it. Since a non-relying buyer pays the higher price, should he be given the benefit of the warranty even though he has not relied on it?

An affirmation or promise made to one person who then supplies the product to another person who is unaware of the affirmation or promise can create an express warranty. For example, in Putensen v. Clay Adams, Inc., 12 Cal.App.3d 1062, 91 Cal.Rptr. 319 (1970), the court held that a patient could sue for breach of an express warranty made to his doctor, even though the patient himself was unaware of the warranty. Such cases are appropriately addressed as raising issues concerning the scope of liability for breach of a warranty, not as raising issues concerning the creation of the warranty itself.

5. Does Comment 7, which states that post-sale statements can be express warranties, undermine the argument that a consumer must rely on a pre-sale affirmation or promise in order to claim that it is a warranty?

6. One of the authors has a Golfing Gizmo in its original box. Unfortunately, it must have been manufactured subsequent to the Hauter case because neither the box it came in nor the instructions claim the product is "completely safe" and that the ball "will not hit [the] player." After reading the remainder of this chapter, revisit this case and ask yourself if the product lends itself to any other warranty claims.

7. Some courts have continued to require the plaintiff to show some type of reliance to establish an express warranty. *See, e.g.,* Speed Fastners, Inc. v. Newsom, 382 F.2d 395, 397 (10th Cir.1967); Hagenbuch v. Snap–On Tools Corp., 339 F.Supp. 676, 680 (D.N.H.1972); Stang v. Hertz Corp., 83 N.M. 217, 219, 490 P.2d 475, 477 (App.1971), judgment reversed, 83 N.M. 730, 497 P.2d 732 (1972); Terry v. Moore, 448 P.2d 601, 602 (Wyo.1968); Global Truck & Equip. Co. v. Palmer Machine Works, Inc., 628 F.Supp. 641 (N.D.Miss.1986). *See* Compaq Computer Corp. v. Lapray, 135 S.W.3d 657 (Tex. 2004) for a discussion of the current position in a number of states.

8. Section 2–313 does not require express warranties to be in writing. Express warranties are, however, subject to the statute of frauds in section 2–201 and the parol evidence rule of section 2–202.

9. Comment 7 to section 2–313 provides that post-sale representations may be considered part of the bargain even if they are not supported by independent consideration. Should a court nevertheless require some form of reliance, such as the purchaser foregoing other safety precautions? *See* Bigelow v. Agway, Inc., 506 F.2d 551 (2d Cir.1974); Terry v. Moore, 448 P.2d 601 (Wyo.1968).

10. For general discussions of the role of reliance in the analysis of express warranties, see Adler, The Last Best Argument for Eliminating Reliance from Express Warranties: "Real World" Consumers Don't Read Warranties, 45 S.C.L.Rev. 429 (1994); Note, "Basis of the Bargain"—What Role Reliance, 34 U.Pitt.L.Rev. 145 (1972).

11. The proposed revisions to section 313 contains a new provision on remedial promises.

> (4) Any remedial promise made by the seller to the immediate buyer creates an obligation that the promise will be performed upon the happening of the specified event.

Revised UCC section 1–203(1)(n) defines a remedial promise as "a promise by the seller to repair or replace goods or to refund all or part of the price of goods upon the happening of a specified event." Comment 9 expands on the meaning of this term:

> A "remedial promise" is a promise by the seller to take a certain remedial action upon the happening of a specified event. The types of remedies contemplated by this term as used in this Article are specified in the definition-repair or replacement of the goods, or refund of all or part of the price. No other promise by a seller qualifies as a remedial promise. Furthermore, the seller is entitled to specify precisely the event that will precipitate the obligation. Typical examples include a commit-

ment to repair any parts of the goods that are defective, or a commitment to refund the purchase price if the goods fail to perform in a certain manner. A post-sale promise to correct a problem with the goods that the seller is not obligated to correct that is made to placate a dissatisfied customer is not within the definition of remedial promise. Whether the promised remedy is exclusive, and if so whether it has failed its essential purpose, is determined under Section 2–719.

12. What about the situation where a warranty is contained within shrink wrapped packaging that the consumer is very unlikely to see until after the sale is completed and the product is unwrapped at home? A new proposed section of the U.C.C. is designed to deal with these "pass-through" warranties.

§ 2–313A. Obligation to Remote Purchaser Created by Record Packaged with or Accompanying Goods.

(1) This section applies only to new goods and goods sold or leased as new goods in a transaction of purchase in the normal chain of distribution. In this section:

(a) "Immediate buyer" means a buyer that enters into a contract with the seller.

(b) "Remote purchaser" means a person that buys or leases goods from an immediate buyer or other person in the normal chain of distribution.

(2) If a seller in a record packaged with or accompanying the goods makes an affirmation of fact or promise that relates to the goods, provides a description that relates to the goods, or makes a remedial promise, and the seller reasonably expects the record to be, and the record is furnished to the remote purchaser, the seller has an obligation to the remote purchaser that:

(a) the goods will conform to the affirmation of fact, promise or description unless a reasonable person in the position of the remote purchaser would not believe that the affirmation of fact, promise or description created an obligation; and

(b) the seller will perform the remedial promise.

(3) It is not necessary to the creation of an obligation under this section that the seller use formal words such as "warrant" or "guarantee" or that the seller have a specific intention to undertake an obligation, but an affirmation merely of the value of the goods or a statement purporting to be merely the seller's opinion or commendation of the goods does not create an obligation.

(4) The following rules apply to the remedies for breach of an obligation created under this section:

(a) The seller may modify or limit the remedies available to the remote purchaser if the modification or limitation is furnished to the remote purchaser no later than the time of purchase or if the modification or limitation is contained in the record that contains the affirmation of fact, promise or description.

> (b) Subject to a modification or limitation of remedy, a seller in breach is liable for incidental or consequential damages under Section 2–715, but the seller is not liable for lost profits.
>
> (c) The remote purchaser may recover as damages for breach of a seller's obligation arising under subsection (2) the loss resulting in the ordinary course of events as determined in any manner that is reasonable.
>
> (5) An obligation that is not a remedial promise is breached if the goods did not conform to the affirmation of fact, promise or description creating the obligation when the goods left the seller's control.

Comment 1 to section 2–313A notes that it uses the term "obligation" rather than "warranty" to avoid any inference that the obligation arises as part of the basis of the bargain.

The proposed revisions to Article 2 also include a companion provision, section 2–313B, creating obligations through advertising. However, this proposed section requires that the buyer enters into the transaction with knowledge of and the expectation that the goods will conform to affirmations or fact or promises made in the advertisement.

13. As do many other sections of the proposed revisions to Article 2, section 2–313A contains the word "record." Record is defined in section 1–203(1) as "information that is inscribed on a tangible medium or that is stored in an electronic or other medium and is retrievable in perceivable form." The definition and the definition of "electronic record" are based on provisions in the Uniform Electronic Transactions Act and are consistent with the federal Electronic Signatures in Global and National Commerce Act (15 U.S.C. § 7001 *et seq.*).

14. Recall that section 2–313(2) notes that "an affirmation merely of the value of the goods or a statement purporting to be merely the seller's opinion or commendation of the goods does not create a warranty." In Stang v. Hertz, 83 N.M. 217, 219, 490 P.2d 475, 477 (App.1971), judgment reversed, 83 N.M. 730, 497 P.2d 732 (1972), after the customer had leased the defendant's car she walked outside to pick it up. An employee casually commented, "you've got good tires there." Did this comment create a warranty or was it mere "puffing?" Comment 10 of the proposed revisions to section 2–313 provides a list of considerations for determining when a comment is a mere puff.

> There are a number of factors relevant to determine whether an expression creates a warranty under this section or is merely puffing. For example, the relevant factors may include whether the seller's representations taken in context, (1) were general rather than specific, (2) related to the consequences of buying rather than the goods themselves, (3) were "hedged" in some way, (4) were related to experimental rather than standard goods, (5) were concerned with some aspects of the goods but not a hidden or unexpected nonconformity, (6) were informal statements made in a formal contracting process, (7) were phrased in terms of opinion rather than fact, or (8) were not capable of objective measurement.

SECTION C. IMPLIED WARRANTY OF MERCHANTABILITY

Uniform Commercial Code

§ 2–314. Implied Warranty: Merchantability; Usage of Trade

(1) Unless excluded or modified (Section 2–316), a warranty that the goods shall be merchantable is implied in a contract for their sale if the seller is a merchant with respect to goods of that kind. Under this section the serving for value of food or drink to be consumed either on the premises or elsewhere is a sale.

(2) Goods to be merchantable must be at least such as

    (a) pass without objection in the trade under the contract description; and

    (b) in the case of fungible goods, are of fair average quality within the description; and

    (c) are fit for the ordinary purposes for which such goods are used; and

    (d) run, within the variations permitted by the agreement, of even kind, quality and quantity within each unit and among all units involved; and

    (e) are adequately contained, packaged, and labeled as the agreement may require; and

    (f) conform to the promises or affirmations of fact made on the container or label if any.

(3) Unless excluded or modified (Section 2–316) other implied warranties may arise from course of dealing or usage of trade.

As we have seen, an important issue in a case involving an express warranty is interpreting the warranty to determine whether it has been breached. Similarly, an important issue in a case involving an implied warranty of merchantability is ascertaining the "content" of the warranty to determine whether it has been breached. How good must a product be in order to be merchantable? This question is similar to the question in negligence of determining how a reasonable person would have behaved.

Subsection 2–314(2) provides some guidelines, but they are not exhaustive. Comment 6 provides:

Subsection (2) does not purport to exhaust the meaning of "merchantable" nor to negate any of its attributes not specifically mentioned in the text of the statute, but arising by usage of trade or through case law. The language used is "must be at least such as * * *," and the intention is to leave open other attributes of merchantability.

Proposed Change to Section 2–314

The only proposed change to the black letter of Section 2–314 is in subsection 2–314(2)(c). It would read " ... are fit for the ordinary purposes for which goods *of that description* are and...." However, the comments have undergone considerable revision.

As in the case of negligence—and as we shall see, products liability—an implied warranty of merchantability does not require perfection, and a plaintiff must show more than that the product caused injury. Like the standard of defectiveness in product liability, merchantability requires only that a product be of reasonable quality. Coffer v. Standard Brands, Inc., 30 N.C.App. 134, 226 S.E.2d 534 (1976), is typical. The plaintiff was injured when he bit down on a piece of shell from a bottle of otherwise unshelled mixed nuts. The court held that the nuts were merchantable because normal industry practice permitted some variations from an absolute absence of shell fragments. Unlike the standard of defectiveness in product liability, however, courts have not carefully defined the standard of merchantability. Some courts have suggested that merchantability should be equated with defectiveness under product liability. *See, e.g.,* Hyundai Motor Co. v. Rodriguez, 995 S.W.2d 661 (Tex.1999); Durrett v. Baxter Chrysler–Plymouth, Inc., 198 Neb. 392, 253 N.W.2d 37 (1977); Holloway v. General Motors Corp., 399 Mich. 617, 250 N.W.2d 736 (1977); Vanek v. Kirby, 253 Or. 494, 450 P.2d 778 (1969); Olsen v. Royal Metals Corp., 392 F.2d 116 (5th Cir.1968). This position has been adopted in the comments of the revisions to UCC section 314. Comment 7 states:

> Suppose that an unmerchantable lawn mower causes personal injury to the buyer, who is operating the mower. Without more, the buyer can sue the seller for breach of the implied warranty of merchantability and recover for injury to person "proximately resulting" from the breach. Section 2–715(2)(b).

> This opportunity does not resolve the tension between warranty law and tort law where goods cause personal injury or property damage. The primary source of that tension arises from disagreement over whether the concept of defect in tort and the concept of merchantability in Article 2 are coextensive where personal injuries are involved, *i.e.,* if goods are merchantable under warranty law, can they still be defective under tort law, and if goods are not defective under tort law, can they be unmerchantable under warranty law? The answer to both questions should be no, and the tension between merchantability in warranty and defect in tort where personal injury or property damage is involved should be resolved as follows:

> When recovery is sought for injury to person or property, whether goods are merchantable is to be determined by applicable state products liability law. When, however, a claim for injury to person or property is based on an implied warranty of fitness under Section 2–315 or an express warranty under Section 2–313 or an obligation arising under Section 2–313A or 2–313B, this Article determines

whether an implied warranty of fitness or an express warranty was made and breached, as well as what damages are recoverable under Section 2–715.

To illustrate, suppose that the seller makes a representation about the safety of a lawn mower that becomes part of the basis of the buyer's bargain. The buyer is injured when the gas tank cracks and a fire breaks out. If the lawnmower without the representation is not defective under applicable tort law, it is not unmerchantable under this section. On the other hand, if the lawnmower did not conform to the representation about safety, the seller made and breached an express warranty and the buyer may sue under Article 2.

Not all courts agree that merchantability should be equated with defectiveness under products liability. In Denny v. Ford Motor Co., 87 N.Y.2d 248, 662 N.E.2d 730, 639 N.Y.S.2d 250 (1995) the court held that whether a product is merchantable because it is "fit for the ordinary purposes for which such goods are used" is determined by the consumer expectations test because implied warranty originates in contract law and is concerned with fulfilling expectations. Products liability in New York is different. It uses the risk-utility test because it is based on "social policy and risk allocation." Thus, it is possible in New York for a product to be unmerchantable because it violates consumer expectations even though it is not defective under the risk-utility test. Under these circumstances the manufacturer could be held liable for breach of implied warranty of merchantability even though it is not liable in tort.

It is normally not a defense to a claim for breach of an implied warranty of merchantability that the seller (even the retailer) could not have done anything to detect or prevent the defect. Thus, in Vlases v. Montgomery Ward & Co., 377 F.2d 846 (3d Cir.1967), the plaintiff purchased one-day-old chicks from the defendant's mail order catalogue. After a few weeks, he discovered that the chicks had avian leukosis disease, a form of cancer, and sued defendant. Defendant, the retailer, argued that it is impossible to detect avian leukosis in one-day-old chicks. The court held that the retailers' argument might defeat a claim of negligence, but not one of breach of an implied warranty of merchantability.

The most commonly cited subsection under section 2–314 is 2–314(2)(c), which requires that goods be "fit for the ordinary purposes for which such goods are used." As comment 8 states, "[f]itness for the ordinary purposes for which goods of the type are used is a fundamental concept of [subsection 2–314(2)]." Fitness for ordinary purposes is difficult to define, however, because it varies with the purposes for which a particular product is ordinarily used. Once determined, this issue in turn raises the issue of whether a product has been used for its ordinary purpose. If the product has not been used for its ordinary purposes, the product's use is not covered by an implied warranty of merchantability. It may, however, be covered by an implied warranty of fitness. A determination of a product's ordinary purposes depends on the circumstances of each case. For example, in Hardman v. Helene Curtis Industries, Inc., 48 Ill.App.2d 42, 198 N.E.2d 681 (1964), the plaintiff, a small child, was burned after she sprayed flammable hair spray on her clothing and hair because the hair spray smelled good. The court held it was a jury question whether the hair spray had been used for an "ordinary purpose."

Subsection 2–314(2)(f) is interesting. It requires that goods "conform to the promises or affirmations of fact made on the container or label if any." Although this requirement is similar to an express warranty under section 2–313, two situations exist in which subsection 2–314(2)(f) might be independently important.

First, a representation made on a package or label might not be a part of the basis of the bargain—because it was not read or relied upon by the buyer—and therefore would not constitute an express warranty. Such a representation might nevertheless be covered by subsection 2–314(2)(f). One goal of subsection 2–314(2)(f) is to police consumer markets by insuring that goods conform to representations on their labels. This goal might be advanced under a "private attorney general" theory by permitting buyers to sue even if they have not themselves read or relied on the representation. This rationale is plausible for express warranties as well, but a court might be more inclined to apply it under subsection 2–314(2)(f), where the seller is a merchant, rather than under section 2–313, where the seller is not necessarily a merchant. Courts have not actually relied on this rationale, however, and they may in fact require a buyer to show knowledge of or reliance on a representation to trigger subsection 2–314(2)(f).

The second situation in which subsection 2–314(2)(f) might have independent significance is when the defendant is a retailer. Unless a retailer adopts representations a manufacturer has put on a label, the retailer is not responsible for them as express warranties under section 2–313. Section 2–314, however, applies to all sellers in the chain of distribution if they are merchants in the goods in question. Consequently, a retailer might be liable under section 2–314(2)(f), even if it is not liable under subsection 2–313.

Even if goods are *not* reasonably fit for their ordinary purpose, they might still be merchantable. If a defect is obvious and the buyer inspects the goods, they are not unmerchantable. *See, e.g.,* Cardwell v. Hackett, 579 S.W.2d 186 (Tenn.App.1978). Similarly, there is no liability for breach of an implied warranty of merchantability if the buyer accepts the goods after having been given an opportunity to inspect, if the inspection would reasonably be expected to reveal the product's condition. *See, e.g.,* Calloway v. Manion, 572 F.2d 1033 (5th Cir.1978).

Subsection 2–314(3) provides that "other implied warranties may arise from course of dealing or usage of trade." Comment 12 states that the purpose of "[s]ubsection 3 is to make explicit that usage of trade and course of dealing can create warranties and that they are implied rather than express warranties and thus subject to exclusion or modification under section 2–316."

Subsection 2–314(3) overlaps with section 1–205, which provides generally that course of dealing and usage of trade affect the construction and interpretation of contract provisions. It also overlaps with subsection 2–314(2)(a), which provides that goods are not merchantable if they do not "pass without objection in the trade.* * * " Nevertheless, subsection 2–314(3) may have some independent significance. For example, unlike the obligations created by section 1–205, the obligations created by subsection 2–314(3) are "warranties" that are subject to the special waiver provisions of section 2–316. Even so, subsection 2–314(3) does not create an "implied warranty of merchantability," and thus its warranties may not be subject to the special provisions in section 2–316 directed specifically to implied warranties of merchantability, as opposed to the provisions of section 2–316 directed to warranties generally.

Courts seldom rely on subsection 2–314(3), and its precise relationship to section 1–205 and subsections 2–314(2)(a) and (b) is unclear.

Unlike section 2–313 (and as we shall see section 2–315), section 2–314 applies only to sellers who are merchants with respect to the goods in question. Obviously, Ford is a merchant with respect to automobiles, whereas an individual selling a used car through a classified ad is not. But there can be close cases. For example, in Siemen v. Alden, 34 Ill.App.3d 961, 965, 341 N.E.2d 713, 716 (1975), the defendant who operated a sawmill bought a new rip saw and sold the old one. The purchaser of the old saw argued that the sawmill was a merchant in saws because it had expertise. The sawmill argued that it was not a merchant in saws because it did not regularly sell saws; instead, this was an isolated transaction. The court agreed with the sawmill.

Notes

1. On the other hand, in Jaroslawicz v. Prestige Caterers, 292 A.D.2d 232, 739 N.Y.S.2d 670 (2002) the plaintiff, a guest on a hotel and meal package tour, suffered food poisoning that lead to the development of Guillian–Barre Syndrome. He sued the tour operator, Leisure Time for breach of the implied warranty of merchantability. Leisure Time moved for summary judgment, arguing it was not a merchant with respect to the food served on the tour. However, the court found evidence that Leisure Time assumed responsibility for preparing meals, provided the dishes, utensils and cooking equipment, oversaw the kitchen, and provided suggestions to the caterers in preparing the meals. Under these circumstances, the appellate court found that Leisure Time's actions were more than general supervision and affirmed the trial court's refusal to grant the tour operator a summary judgment on the merchantability claim.

2. In Nelson v. Union Equity Co–Op. Exchange, 548 S.W.2d 352 (Tex.1977), the court was required to decide whether a farmer who sells his crop is a merchant under section 2–104. The ultimate issue in the case was whether a grain futures contract was governed by the statute of frauds in

section 2–201. Subsection 2–201(a) exempts some contracts "between merchants." Although *Nelson* did not involve an implied warranty of merchantability under section 2–314, the court gave no indication that the definition of merchant under section 2–104 differs depending on whether the case involves the statute of frauds under section 2–201 or an implied warranty of merchantability under section 2–314.

The court held that the farmer was a merchant with respect to his crop:

> [A] person is a "merchant" if he (1) deals in goods of the kind, or (2) by his occupation holds himself out as having knowledge or skill peculiar to the *practices* involved in the transaction, or (3) by his occupation holds himself out as having knowledge or skill peculiar to the *goods* involved in the transaction, or (4) employs an intermediary who by his occupation holds himself out as having such knowledge or skill, and that knowledge or skill may be attributed to the person whose status is in question. If the facts show that a person satisfies any of the above criteria, then we are bound to hold that person to be a merchant.

548 S.W.2d at 355. The court concluded that Nelson, the farmer, satisfied the first three criteria, any one of which made him a "merchant."

Two aspects of the court's reasoning are significant. First, the court held that to be a merchant, a seller need not represent himself as having special skill or knowledge; the fact that he is engaged in an *occupation* that would normally require such skill or knowledge is sufficient. Second, the court observed that the "broad language of section [2–104(1)] and the accompanying text of the Official Comment suggest that the term 'merchant' was intended to apply to all but the most casual or inexperienced sellers." 548 S.W.2d at 357. The court did, however, recite the seller's actual expertise in some detail.

Several other courts have held that a farmer is not a merchant with respect to his crop. *See, e.g.*, Loeb and Company, Inc. v. Schreiner, 294 Ala. 722, 321 So.2d 199 (1975); Decatur Cooperative Association v. Urban, 219 Kan. 171, 547 P.2d 323 (1976); Lish v. Compton, 547 P.2d 223 (Utah 1976). *But see* Calloway v. Manion, 572 F.2d 1033 (5th Cir.1978); Prince v. LeVan, 486 P.2d 959, 964 (Alaska 1971).

SECTION D. IMPLIED WARRANTY OF FITNESS FOR PARTICULAR PURPOSE

Uniform Commercial Code

§ 2–315. Implied Warranty: Fitness for Particular Purpose

Where the seller at the time of contracting has reason to know any particular purpose for which the goods are required and that the buyer is relying on the seller's skill or judgment to select or furnish suitable goods, there is unless excluded or modified under the next section an implied warranty that the goods shall be fit for such purpose.

Like an express warranty under section 2–313, but unlike an implied warranty of merchantability under section 2–314, an implied warranty of fitness applies to merchants and non-merchants alike. Moreover, like an express warranty and unlike an implied warranty of merchantability, an implied warranty of fitness does not automatically apply to all sellers in the chain of distribution. It applies only to sellers whose conduct creates the warranty.

Some courts have held that section 2–315 applies only when the buyer actually has a special purpose for the goods, not an ordinary purpose, even if the other requirements of section 2–315 are met. *See* Fred's Excavating and Crane Serv., Inc. v. Continental Ins. Co., 340 So.2d 1220 (Fla.App.1976); Ford Motor Co. v. Taylor, 60 Tenn.App. 271, 446 S.W.2d 521 (1969); DiIenno v. Libbey Glass Div., Owens–Illinois, Inc., 668 F.Supp. 373 (D.Del. 1987); Stones v. Sears, Roebuck & Co., 251 Neb. 560, 558 N.W.2d 540, 547 (1997). Other courts have held that both an implied warranty of fitness and an implied warranty of merchantability can apply to goods that are used for their ordinary purpose, as long as the other requirements of sections 2–314 and 2–315 are met. *See* Deffebach v. Lansburgh & Bro., 150 F.2d 591 (D.C.Cir.1945) (seller should have known that lounging robe is likely to come into contact with flames as part of its ordinary purpose) (pre-code, relying upon D.C. code's implied warranty of fitness); Acme Pump Co. v. National Cash Register Co., 32 Conn.Sup. 69, 73, 337 A.2d 672, 675–76 (1974); Knab v. Alden's Irving Park, Inc., 49 Ill.App.2d 371, 199 N.E.2d 815 (1964) (brought under Illinois version of Uniform Sales Act); Nelson v. Wilkins Dodge, Inc., 256 N.W.2d 472, 476 n. 2 (Minn.1977); Torstenson v. Melcher, 195 Neb. 764, 771–72, 241 N.W.2d 103, 107 (1976); Tennessee Carolina Transp., Inc. v. Strick Corp., 283 N.C. 423, 196 S.E.2d 711 (1973); Jones, Inc. v. W.A. Wiedebusch Plumbing & Heating Co., 157 W.Va. 257, 201 S.E.2d 248, 253–54 (1973); Soaper v. Hope Industries, Inc., 309 S.C. 438, 440 424 S.E.2d 493 (1992). Comment 2 to section 2–315 provides that a "contract may of course include both a warranty of merchantability and one of fitness for a particular purpose," but that may mean only that different warranties might apply to different characteristics of the goods. Does this resolve the issue?

Parties to a transaction seldom explicitly agree that the buyer is relying on the seller's skill and judgment in selecting the goods. Consequently, courts must determine whether the buyer has in fact relied by looking at the circumstances of the transaction. One relevant factor is the parties' relative expertise. *See* Brown v. Asgrow Seed Co., 379 S.W.2d 412 (Tex.Civ.App. 1964); Texsun Feed Yards, Inc. v. Ralston Purina Co., 447 F.2d 660 (5th Cir.1971); ACME Pump Co., Inc. v. National Cash Register Co., 32 Conn.Sup. 69, 73, 337 A.2d 672, 676 (1974); *but see* Valley Iron & Steel Co. v. Thorin, 278 Or. 103, 109, 562 P.2d 1212, 1216 (1977) (although more familiar with goods than manufacturer, buyer relied upon manufacturer).

Some courts have required that the buyer prove that the seller actually has skill and expertise. *See* Prince v. LeVan, 486 P.2d 959, 963 (Alaska 1971); Janssen v. Hook, 1 Ill.App.3d 318, 272 N.E.2d 385 (1971). Nothing in section 2–315 or its comments supports this conclusion, however. Even so, a seller's actual skill and expertise might be a factor in determining both whether the buyer actually relied on the seller's judgment and whether the seller had reason to know of the buyer's reliance.

Another factor is whether the buyer participated in the selection of the goods. If the buyer or his agent examined the goods, she is less likely to have relied on the seller's judgment, and the seller is less likely to have known of any reliance. *See, e.g.,* Fear Ranches, Inc. v. Berry, 470 F.2d 905, 908 (10th Cir.1972); Sessa v. Riegle, 427 F.Supp. 760, 770 (E.D.Pa.1977) (buyer relying upon his own agent's examination of horse did not rely upon seller); Kopper Glo Fuel, Inc. v. Island Lake Coal Co., 436 F.Supp. 91, 95 (E.D.Tenn.1977); Donald v. City Nat'l Bank, 295 Ala. 320, 325, 329 So.2d 92, 96 (1976) (no reliance where buyer had boat inspected at his own expense); Valiga v. National Food Co., 58 Wis.2d 232, 257, 206 N.W.2d 377, 390–91 (1973). Subsection 2–316(3)(b), which addresses disclaimers, provides that

> when the buyer before entering into the contract has examined the goods or the sample or model as fully as he desired or has refused to examine the goods there is no implied warranty with regard to defects which an examination ought in the circumstances to have revealed. * * *

The specificity with which the buyer ordered the goods is also a factor in determining whether he relied on the seller's expertise. A buyer's claim that he relied on the seller's judgment and that the seller had reason to know of this reliance is weakened if the buyer had control over the good's specifications, *see* Layne–Atl. Co. v. Koppers Co., Inc., 214 Va. 467, 473–74, 201 S.E.2d 609, 614–15 (1974); Lewis & Sims, Inc. v. Key Indus., Inc., 16 Wash.App. 619, 557 P.2d 1318 (1976), or if he selected a product by brand name, *see* Siemen v. Alden, 34 Ill.App.3d 961, 965, 341 N.E.2d 713, 716 (1975); Bickett v. W.R. Grace & Co., 12 U.C.C.Rep.Serv. (Callaghan) 629, 1972 WL 20845 (W.D.Ky.1972).

Comment 5 to section 2–315 provides:

> Under the present section the existence of a patent or other trade name and the designation of the article by that name, or indeed in any other definite manner, is only one of the facts to be considered on the question of whether the buyer actually relied on the seller, but it is not of itself decisive of the issue. If the buyer himself is insisting on a particular brand he is not relying on the seller's skill and judgment and so no warranty results. But the mere fact that the article purchased has a particular patent or trade name is not sufficient to indicate nonreliance if the article has been recommended by the seller as adequate for the buyer's purposes.

Comment 9 to section 2–316, which addresses disclaimers, provides:

> The situation in which the buyer gives precise and complete specifications to the seller is not explicitly covered in this section, but this is a frequent circumstance by which the implied warranties may be

excluded. The warranty of fitness for a particular purpose would not normally arise since in such a situation there is usually no reliance on the seller by the buyer.

These factors are neither exhaustive nor conclusive. Whether a buyer relied on a seller's judgment and whether a seller had reason to know of this reliance are usually questions of fact that depend on the totality of a transaction's circumstances, including previous dealings between the parties and trade usage. *See* Dobias v. Western Farmers Ass'n, 6 Wash.App. 194, 199, 491 P.2d 1346, 1349 (1971); *cf.* Emsco Screen Pipe Co. v. Heights Muffler Co., 420 S.W.2d 179 (Tex.Civ.App. 1967) (holding that a seller who habitually accepted returned mufflers for credit impliedly warranted to do so).

NCCUSL has not proposed any changes to section 2–315.

Problem

Planning to build a go-cart, a sixteen year old boy bought a motor for five dollars from a neighbor who know of the child's intended use. The boy's deposition described the circumstances attendant to his purchase.

Q. At the time that you purchased the motor, did you have any conversation with the Defendant Mr. Wallace about it?

A. Yes.

Q. Do you recall what that conversation was?

A. Yes. I asked him if the engine ran good, and he said he had been using it for uses around the farm, and he said it ran real good.

Q. Did you indicate to him what use you were going to make of it?

A. Yes.

Q. And what was that?

A. A go-cart.

Q. What else can you recall now of any conversation you had with Mr. Wallace about that motor?

A. That was about all we talked about. He told me it ran good. And I told him I was, you know, wanted it for a go-cart. And he said it would work cause the shaft was out of the side of the engine.

Q. You did not try to start it at that time?

A. No. I told him I didn't want to start it. I took his word that it ran good. Because I didn't want to put it in the car hot and run it home.

* * *

Q. Did you in fact install this engine in a go-cart?

A. No, I didn't.

* * *

Q. When did you first attempt to start it?

A. About twenty minutes after I was home.

* * *

Q. And what happened when you did that?

A. I heard it start, and then that's all I remember.

Q. What happened to the engine?

A. I have no idea. I guess it blew up. Cause that's all I remember is hearing it start, and then it just that was it.

Is there a breach of any warranty? Why or why not? *See* Barb v. Wallace, 45 Md.App. 271, 412 A.2d 1314 (1980).

SECTION E. PERSONS WHO ARE PROTECTED: PRIVITY OF CONTRACT

Unlike product liability, recovery by remote plaintiffs for breach of an Article 2 warranty can still be affected by the concept of privity. The problem of recovery by plaintiffs other than the purchaser is called "horizontal privity." "Vertical privity" refers to the problem of a plaintiff recovering from a defendant further up than the retailer in the chain of distribution.

Historically, the contractual underpinnings of warranty law led courts to enforce warranties only for the benefit of persons who were in privity of contract with the defendant. Even before the adoption of the Uniform Commercial Code, several courts relaxed the privity requirement in cases in which one member of the family purchased a product for other members of the family. For example, in Greenberg v. Lorenz, 9 N.Y.2d 195, 213 N.Y.S.2d 39, 173 N.E.2d 773 (1961), the New York Court of Appeals held that a plaintiff who was injured by adulterated food could recover for breach of implied warranty even though her father had purchased the food. The court presumed that the father had purchased the food as an agent for the other family members. Similarly, in the landmark case of Henningsen v. Bloomfield Motors, Inc., 32 N.J. 358, 161 A.2d 69 (1960), the New Jersey Supreme Court held that a plaintiff who was injured while driving a defective automobile could recover for breach of implied warranty even though her husband had actually purchased the automobile.

Article 2 does not expressly address the problem of vertical privity. The problem of horizontal privity for warranties governed by Article 2 is addressed by section 2–318.

Uniform Commercial Code
§ 2–318. Third Party Beneficiaries of Warranties Express or Implied

Alternative A

A seller's warranty whether express or implied extends to any natural person who is in the family or household of his buyer or who is a guest in his home if it is reasonable to expect that such person may use, consume or be affected by the goods and who is injured in person by breach of the warranty. A seller may not exclude or limit the operation of this section.

Alternative B

A seller's warranty whether express or implied extends to any natural person who may reasonably be expected to use, consume or be affected by the goods and who is injured in person by breach of the warranty. A seller may not exclude or limit the operation of this section.

Alternative C

A seller's warranty whether express or implied extends to any person who may reasonably be expected to use, consume or be affected by the goods and who is injured by breach of the warranty. A seller may not exclude or limit the operation of this section with respect to injury to the person of an individual to whom the warranty extends.

Section 2–318 lumps the three Article 2 warranties together. Nevertheless, an express warranty is more "contractual" than an implied warranty of merchantability, and it might be argued that privity limitations make more sense in the context of express warranties—especially if the damages are purely economic and the parties are commercial entities—than in the context of implied warranties of merchantability—especially if the damages are due to personal injury and the plaintiff is a consumer.

Like express warranties, implied warranties of fitness are more "contractual" than implied warranties of merchantability because they depend on actual, albeit often amorphous, representations, and because they depend on reliance. Nevertheless, section 2–318 does not distinguish between implied warranties of fitness and implied warranties of merchantability on the issue of horizontal privity. You should recall that to recover under an implied warranty of fitness, the plaintiff must prove that the *buyer* relied on the seller's judgment in selecting the product for a particular purpose known to the seller. The plaintiff need not have been the buyer, however.

Courts in states that have adopted Alternative A to section 2–318 have been required to determine who qualifies as a family member, a household member, or a guest. *See, e.g.,* McNally v. Nicholson Mfg. Co., 313 A.2d 913, 920 (Me.1973) (employees of the purchaser are part of the "business family"); Miles v. Bell Helicopter Co., 385 F.Supp. 1029, 1031 (N.D.Ga.1974) (soldier injured by equipment purchased by the military not part of the "military family"); Miller v. Preitz, 422 Pa. 383, 221 A.2d 320 (1966) (nephew of purchaser held part of family for injury caused by product loaned by aunt who lived next door); Wolfe v. Ford Motor Co., 6

Mass.App.Ct. 346, 376 N.E.2d 143, 149 (1978) (niece who did not live in purchaser's household held to be part of family); Barry v. Ivarson Inc., 249 So.2d 44 (Fla.App.1971) (tenant of purchaser not within the scope of Alternative A); Stovall & Co. v. Tate, 124 Ga.App. 605, 184 S.E.2d 834 (1971) (student injured by product purchased by school not within the scope of Alternative A); Mugavero v. A–1 Auto Sales, Inc., 130 Idaho 554, 944 P.2d 151, 156 (1997) (driver and passenger of vehicle which rear-ended disabled truck on road were not third party beneficiaries of any express warranty given to buyer of truck).

Even in states that have adopted Alternative C or that have by judicial decision extended the scope of liability for breach of warranty to bystanders, liability does not extend to all persons for all injuries caused by the breach of warranty. Only injuries that are proximately caused by the breach are recoverable.

Proposed Changes to Section 2–318

NCCUSL's proposed changes to section 318 retains the three alternatives in the existing section but expands them to reflect obligations arising under sections 2–313A and 2–313B and section 313's provision concerning remedial promises.

Vertical Privity

Some courts require vertical as well as horizontal privity in cases involving only economic loss, and others permit recovery for *direct* economic loss without privity if plaintiff is a consumer, but do not permit recovery for *consequential* economic loss without privity. But in Morrow v. New Moon Homes, Inc., 548 P.2d 279 (Alaska 1976), the court held that lack of vertical privity did not bar recovery in an action for pure economic loss based on breach of an implied warranty of merchantability. The court noted that privity is not required in Alaska in an action for personal injury damages for breach of an implied warranty of merchantability and reasoned that "there is no satisfactory justification for a remedial scheme which extends the warranty action to a consumer suffering personal injury or property damage but denies similar relief to the consumer 'fortunate' enough to suffer only direct economic loss." More recently, in Hyundai Motor America, Inc. v. Goodin, 822 N.E.2d 947 (Ind.2005) the state Supreme Court extended previous decisions that Indiana's Alternative A version of section 318 did not create a vertical privity barrier in cases involving personal injury to cases involving only economic loss. In Goodin, the only injury was to the good itself, a new car with defective breaks. On the other hand, some states have retained vertical privity requirements in these cases. *See* Energy Investors Fund, L.P. v. Metric Constructors, Inc., 351 N.C. 331, 525 S.E.2d 441, 446 (2000).

SECTION F. REMEDIES

Uniform Commercial Code

§ 2–715. Buyer's Incidental and Consequential Damages

(1) Incidental damages resulting from the seller's breach include expenses reasonably incurred in inspection, receipt, transportation and care and custody of goods rightfully rejected, any commercially reasonable charges, expenses or commissions in connection with effecting cover and any other reasonable expense incident to the delay or other breach.

(2) Consequential damages resulting from the seller's breach include

(a) any loss resulting from general or particular requirements and needs of which the seller at the time of contracting had reason to know and which could not reasonably be prevented by cover or otherwise; and

(b) injury to person or property proximately resulting from any breach of warranty.

NCCUSL has not proposed any changes to section 2–715.

SECTION G. DISCLAIMERS

HENNINGSEN v. BLOOMFIELD MOTORS, INC.
Supreme Court of New Jersey, 1960.
32 N.J. 358, 161 A.2d 69.

[Mr. Henningsen purchased an automobile from defendant Bloomfield Motors and gave it to his wife as a gift. The automobile was manufactured by defendant Chrysler Corporation. Ten days after delivery of the car, Mrs. Henningsen was injured in an accident that resulted when the steering failed suddenly and without warning. Up to this time the car had functioned properly. Mrs. Henningsen sued both defendants for breach of express and implied warranties and for negligence. Her husband joined in the action seeking compensation for his consequential losses. The trial judge dismissed the negligence counts because of insufficient evidence. He gave the case to the jury on the implied warranty theory only. The jury rendered verdicts against both defendants in favor of the plaintiffs. Defendants appealed and plaintiffs cross-appealed, claiming that the negligence count should not have been dismissed.]

[The sales contract signed by Mr. Henningsen was a standard printed form. It contained the following language concerning the warranty. It was in fine print and located on the back of the form:]

"7. It is expressly agreed that there are no warranties, express or implied, *made* by either the dealer or the manufacturer on the motor vehicle, chassis, of parts furnished hereunder except as follows.

" 'The manufacturer warrants each new motor vehicle (including original equipment placed thereon by the manufacturer except tires), chassis or parts manufactured by it to be free from defects in material or workmanship under normal use and service. Its obligation under this warranty being limited to making good at its factory any part or parts thereof which shall, within ninety (90) days after delivery of such vehicle *to the original purchaser* or before such vehicle has been driven 4,000 miles, whichever event shall first occur, be returned to it with transportation charges prepaid and which its examination shall disclose to its satisfaction to have been thus defective; *this warranty being expressly in lieu of all other warranties expressed or implied, and all other obligations or liabilities on its part*, and it neither assumes nor authorizes any other person to assume for it any other liability in connection with the sale of its vehicles. * * * ' " (Emphasis ours.)

* * *

The terms of the [express] warranty are a sad commentary upon the automobile manufacturers' marketing practices. Warranties developed in the law in the interest of and to protect the ordinary consumer who cannot be expected to have the knowledge or capacity or even the opportunity to make adequate inspection of mechanical instrumentalities, like automobiles, and to decide for himself whether they are reasonably fit for the designed purpose. * * * But the ingenuity of the Automobile Manufacturers Association, by means of its standardized form, has metamorphosed the warranty into a device to limit the maker's liability.

[The court considered whether an implied warranty of merchantability should be applied to the sale–the case was decided before the adoption of the UCC. Surveying other jurisdictions, primarily in cases involving the sale of food and drink, the court concluded that a warranty of merchantability should be implied and that it extended to remote purchasers, such as the Henningsens, who were not in vertical privity with the manufacturer.]

The Effect of the Disclaimer and Limitation of Liability Clauseson the Implied Warranty of Merchantability.

* * *

In view of the cases in various jurisdictions suggesting the conclusion which we have now reached with respect to the implied warranty of merchantability, it becomes apparent that manufacturers who enter into promotional activities to stimulate consumer buying may incur warranty obligations of either or both the express or implied character. These developments in the law inevitably suggest the inference that the form of express warranty made part of the Henningsen purchase contract was devised for general use in the automobile industry as a possible means of avoiding the consequences of the growing judicial acceptance of the thesis that the described express or implied warranties run directly to the consumer.

In the light of these matters, what effect should be given to the express warranty in question which seeks to limit the manufacturer's liability to replacement of defective parts, and which disclaims all other warranties, express or implied? In assessing its significance we must keep in mind the general principle that, in the absence of fraud, one who does not choose to read a contract before signing it, cannot later relieve himself of its burdens. And in applying that principle, the basic tenet of freedom of competent parties to contract is a factor of importance. But in the framework of modern commercial life and business practices, such rules cannot be applied on a strict, doctrinal basis. The conflicting interests of the buyer and seller must be evaluated realistically and justly, giving due weight to the social policy evinced by the Uniform Sales Act, the progressive decisions of the courts engaged in administering it, the mass production methods of manufacture and distribution to the public, and the bargaining position occupied by the ordinary consumer in such an economy. This history of the law shows that legal doctrines, as first expounded, often prove to be inadequate under the impact of later experience. In such case, the need for justice has stimulated the necessary qualifications or adjustments.

* * * It is apparent that the public has an interest not only in the safe manufacture of automobiles, but also, as shown by the Sales Act, in protecting the rights and remedies of purchasers, so far as it can be accomplished consistently with our system of free enterprise. In a society such as ours, where the automobile is a common and necessary adjunct of daily life, and where its use is so fraught with danger to the driver, passengers and the public, the manufacturer is under a special obligation in connection with the construction, promotion and sale of his cars. Consequently, the courts must examine purchase agreements closely to see if consumer and public interests are treated fairly.

* * * As we have said, warranties originated in the law to safeguard the buyer and not to limit the liability of the seller or manufacturer. It seems obvious in this instance that the motive was to avoid the warranty obligations which are normally incidental to such sales. The language gave little and withdrew much. In return for the delusive remedy of replacement of defective parts at the factory, the buyer is said to have accepted the exclusion of the maker's liability for personal injuries arising from the breach of warranty, and to have agreed to the elimination of any other express or implied warranty. An instinctively felt sense of justice cries out against such a sharp bargain. But does the doctrine that a person is bound by his signed agreement, in the absence of fraud, stand in the way of any relief?

In the modern consideration of problems such as this, Corbin suggests that practically all judges are "chancellors" and cannot fail to be influenced by any equitable doctrines that are available. And he opines that "there is sufficient flexibility in the concepts of fraud, duress, misrepresentation and undue influence, not to mention differences in economic bargaining power" to enable the courts to avoid enforcement of unconscionable provisions in long printed standardized contracts. 1 Corbin on Contracts (1950) § 128, p. 188. Freedom of contract is not such an immutable doctrine as to admit of no qualification in the area in which we are concerned.

* * *

The traditional contract is the result of free bargaining of parties who are brought together by the play of the market, and who meet each other on a footing of approximate economic equality. In such a society there is no danger that freedom of contract will be a threat to the social order as a whole. But in present-day commercial life the standardized mass contract has appeared. It is used primarily by enterprises with strong bargaining power and position. "The weaker party, in need of the goods or services, is frequently not in a position to shop around for better terms, either because the author of the standard contract has a monopoly (natural or artificial) or because all competitors use the same clauses. His contractual intention is but a subjection more or less voluntary to terms dictated by the stronger party, terms whose consequences are often understood in a vague way, if at all."

* * *

The warranty before us is a standardized form designed for mass use. It is imposed upon the automobile consumer. He takes it or leave it, and he must take it to buy an automobile. No bargaining is engaged in with respect to it. In fact, the dealer through whom it comes to the buyer is without authority to alter it; his function is ministerial—simply to deliver it. The form warranty is not only standard with Chrysler but, as mentioned above, it is the uniform warranty of the Automobile Manufacturers Association. * * *

The gross inequality of bargaining position occupied by the consumer in the automobile industry is thus apparent. There is no competition among the car makers in the area of the express warranty. Where can the buyer go to negotiate for better protection? Such control and limitation of his remedies are inimical to the public welfare and, at the very least, call for great care by the courts to avoid injustice through application of strict common-law principles of freedom of contract. Because there is no competition among the motor vehicle manufacturers with respect to the scope of protection guaranteed to the buyer, there is no incentive on their part to stimulate good will in that field of public relations. Thus, there is lacking a factor existing in more competitive fields, one which tends to guarantee the safe construction of the article sold.

* * *

The task of the judiciary is to administer the spirit as well as the letter of the law. On issues such as the present one, part of that burden is to protect the ordinary man against the loss of important rights through what, in effect, is the unilateral act of the manufacturer. The status of the automobile industry is unique. Manufacturers are few in number and strong in bargaining position. In the matter of warranties on the sale of their products, the Automotive Manufacturers Association has enabled them to present a united front. From the standpoint of the purchaser, there can be no arms length negotiating on the subject. Because his capacity for bargaining is so grossly unequal, the inexorable conclusion which follows is that he is not permitted to bargain at all. He must take or leave the automobile on the warranty terms dictated by the maker. He cannot turn to a competitor for better security.

* * *

It is undisputed that the president of the dealer with whom Henningsen dealt did not specifically call attention to the warranty on the back of the purchase order. The form and the arrangement of its face, as described above, certainly would cause the minds of reasonable men to differ as to whether notice of a yielding of basic rights stemming from the relationship with the manufacturer was adequately given. The words "warranty" or "limited warranty" did not even appear in the fine print above the place for signature, and a jury might well find that the type of print itself was such as to promote lack of attention rather than sharp scrutiny. The inference from the facts is that Chrysler placed the method of communicating its warranty to the purchaser in the hands of the dealer. If either one or both of them wished to make certain that Henningsen became aware of that agreement and its purported implications, neither the form of the document nor the method of expressing the precise nature of the obligation intended to be assumed would have presented any difficulty.

But there is more than this. Assuming that a jury might find that the fine print referred to reasonably served the objective of directing a buyer's attention to the warranty on the reverse side, and, therefore, that he should be charged with awareness of its language, can it be said that an ordinary layman would realize what he was relinquishing in return for what he was being granted? Under the law, breach of warranty against defective parts or workmanship which caused personal injuries would entitle a buyer to damages even if due care were used in the manufacturing process. Because of the great potential for harm if the vehicle was defective, that right is the most important and fundamental one arising from the relationship. Difficulties so frequently encountered in establishing negligence in manufacture in the ordinary case make this manifest. * * * Any ordinary layman of reasonable intelligence, looking at the phraseology, might well conclude that Chrysler was agreeing to replace defective parts and perhaps replace anything that went wrong because of defective workmanship during the first 90 days or 4,000 miles of operation, but that he would not be entitled to a new car. It is not unreasonable to believe that the entire scheme being conveyed was a proposed remedy for physical deficiencies in the car. In the context of this warranty, only the abandonment of all sense of justice would permit us to hold that, as a matter of law, the phrase "its obligation under this warranty being limited to making good at its factory any part or parts thereof" signifies to an ordinary reasonable person that he is relinquishing any personal injury claim that might flow from the use of a defective automobile. Such claims are nowhere mentioned. The draftsmanship is reflective of the care and skill of the Automobile Manufacturers Association in undertaking to avoid warranty obligations without drawing too much attention to its effort in that regard. No one can doubt that if the will to do so were present, the ability to inform the buying public of the intention to disclaim liability for injury claims arising from breach of warranty would present no problem.

* * *

Public policy at a given time finds expression in the Constitution, the statutory law and in judicial decisions. In the area of sale of goods, the legislative will has imposed an implied warranty of merchantability as a general incident of sale of an automobile by description. The warranty does not depend upon the affirmative intention of the parties. It is a child of the law; it annexes itself to the contract because of the very nature of the transaction. Minneapolis Steel & Machinery Co. v. Casey Land Agency, 51 N.D. 832, 201 N.W. 172 (Sup.Ct.1924). The judicial process has recognized a right to recover damages for personal injuries arising from a breach of that warranty. The disclaimer of the implied warranty and exclusion of all obligations except those specifically assumed by the express warranty signify a studied effort to frustrate that protection. True, the Sales Act authorized agreements between buyer and seller qualifying the warranty obligations. But quite obviously the Legislature contemplated lawful stipulations (which are determined by the circumstances of a particular case) arrived at freely by parties of relatively equal bargaining strength. The lawmakers did not authorize the automobile manufacturer to use its grossly disproportionate bargaining power to relieve itself from liability and to impose on the ordinary buyer who in effect has no real freedom of choice, the grave danger of injury to himself and others that attends the sale of such a dangerous instrumentality as a defectively made automobile. In the framework of this case, illuminated as it is by the facts and the many decisions noted, we are of the opinion that Chrysler's attempted disclaimer of an implied warranty of merchantability and of the obligations arising therefrom is so inimical to the public good as to compel an adjudication of its invalidity. * * *

Note

According to the Court, exactly what is wrong with the warranty in *Henningsen*? Consider the following possibilities:

a) the disclaimer is not sufficiently conspicuous.

b) the buyer is likely to be surprised by the nature and scope of the disclaimer

c) the unequal bargaining strength of the parties

d) the harshness of the terms

e) the lack of alternative products with different warranties

f) the lack of alternative (extended) warranties

Which of these objections would have to be met for the Court to uphold the disclaimer? What does your answer reveal about the limitations of a warranty solution to product disappointment?

Henningsen was decided under the Uniform Sales Act. How would the disclaimers and remedy limitations fare under sections 2–316 and 2–719 of the UCC, which are addressed below? How would the Henningsens fare under section 2–318, which was addressed above?

Uniform Commercial Code

§ 2–316. Exclusion or Modification of Warranties

(1) Words or conduct relevant to the creation of an express warranty and words or conduct tending to negate or limit warranty shall be construed wherever reasonable as consistent with each other; but subject to the provisions of this Article on parol or extrinsic evidence (Section 2–202) negation or limitation is inoperative to the extent that such construction is unreasonable.

(2) Subject to subsection (3), to exclude or modify the implied warranty of merchantability or any part of it the language must mention merchantability and in case of a writing must be conspicuous, and to exclude or modify any implied warranty of fitness the exclusion must be by a writing and conspicuous. Language to exclude all implied warranties of fitness is sufficient if it states, for example, that "There are no warranties which extend beyond the description on the face hereof."

(3) Notwithstanding subsection (2)

(a) unless the circumstances indicate otherwise, all implied warranties are excluded by expressions like "as is", "with all faults" or other language which in common understanding calls the buyer's attention to the exclusion of warranties and makes plain that there is no implied warranty; and

(b) when the buyer before entering into the contract has examined the goods or the sample or model as fully as he desired or has refused to examine the goods there is no implied warranty with regard to defects which an examination ought in the circumstances to have revealed to him; and

(c) an implied warranty can also be excluded or modified by course of dealing or course of performance or usage of trade.

(4) Remedies for breach of warranty can be limited in accordance with the provisions of this Article on liquidation or limitation of damages and on contractual modification of remedy (Sections 2–718 and 2–719).

* * *

Some courts have held that the purpose of the conspicuousness requirement is met if the buyer actually sees the disclaimer. See Tennessee Carolina Transp., Inc. v. Strick Corp., 283 N.C. 423, 196 S.E.2d 711 (1973). Two leading commentators have the following observations concerning this issue.

> Comment 1 to 2–316 indicates that the purpose of the conspicuousness requirement is to "protect the buyer from surprise" and "unexpected and unbargained language of disclaimers." This purpose is accomplished when the buyer learns of the seller's disclaimer–conspicuous or inconspicuous. On the other hand, section 1–201(10) says, "A term or clause is conspicuous when so *written* * * *." (Emphasis added)
>
> * * *
>
> Giving legal effect to knowledge or lack of knowledge might reward the convincing liar who claims that the buyer was–or was not–made award of the disclaimer. * * * On the other hand, where the buyer–particularly a commercial buyer–admits to reading and understanding inconspicuous clauses or admits that the seller drew those clauses to his attention, the clauses should be valid and binding notwithstanding their inconspicuousness.

J. White & R. Summers, Uniform Commercial Code § 12–5 at 435 (5th ed. 2000).

A literal reading of section 2–316 suggests that "as is" disclaimers under subsection 2–316(3)(a) are not subject to the requirements in subsection 2–316(2) concerning specific language and conspicuousness. Subsection 2–316(2) explicitly states that its own requirements are "subject to subsection (3)," and subsection (3) explicitly states that its provisions are effective "notwithstanding subsection (2)." Consequently, some courts have read section 2–316 literally to conclude that "as is" disclaimers need not be conspicuous. See DeKalb Agresearch, Inc. v. Abbott, 391 F.Supp. 152, 154–55 (N.D.Ala.1974), aff'd, 511 F.2d 1162 (5th Cir.1975); Gilliam v. Indiana Nat'l Bank, 337 So.2d 352 (Ala.Civ. App.1976). Other courts have argued that the purposes of section 2–316 require that "as is" disclaimers be conspicuous or that conspicuousness at least be a factor in determining whether an "as is" disclaimer is valid. See MacDonald v. Mobley, 555 S.W.2d 916, 919 (Tex.Civ.App.1977); White v. First Federal Savings and Loan Assn. of Atlanta, 158 Ga.App. 373, 280 S.E.2d 398 (1981). The proposed changes to section 2–316, reproduced below, correct this ambiguity.

Note that section 2–316(3)(b) provides that a buyer's opportunity to inspect prior to purchase negates an implied warranty with regard to defects that an inspection would reasonably have revealed. Section 2–316(3)(c) provides that course of dealing or usage of trade can also exclude or modify an implied warranty. Obviously, neither subsection is subject to the "conspicuousness" requirement of subsection 2–316(2).

To be effective, a warranty disclaimer must be part of the parties' bargain. Post-sale disclaimers, like other post-sale modifications, are subject to the requirements of section 2–209. Although section 2–209 does not require post-sale modifications to be supported by consideration, it does require that the parties in fact agree to the modification, which may create a difficult obstacle for a seller attempting to enforce a post-sale disclaimer.

Some states have statutes that forbid disclaimers altogether in consumer transactions or in consumer transactions involving personal injury. *See, e.g.,* Ala.Code tit. 7, § 2–316(5); Mass.Gen.Laws Ann. ch. 106, § 2–316A; Wash.Rev.Code Ann. tit. 62A, § 2–316(4); Me.Rev.Stat. Ann. tit. 11, § 2–316(5).

Given the language of section 2–316(1), it is very difficult for a seller to disclaim an express warranty. Comment 1 to section 2–316 elaborates:

> This section is designed principally to deal with those frequent clauses in sales contracts which seek to exclude "all warranties, express or implied." It seeks to protect a buyer from unexpected and unbargained for language of disclaimer by denying effect to such language when inconsistent with language of express warranty and permitting the exclusion of implied warranties only by conspicuous language or other circumstances which protect the buyer from surprise.

Nevertheless, a disclaimer may affect both the interpretation of an express warranty and the decision of whether it is part of the "basis of the bargain." If an express warranty is part of the basis of the bargain and its meaning is unambiguous, however, a contradictory disclaimer is not effective.

Disclaimers of oral express warranties raise special problems. The parol evidence rule contained in section 2–202 provides:

> Terms with respect to which the confirmatory memoranda of the parties agree or which are otherwise set forth in a writing intended by the parties as a final expression of their agreement with respect to such terms as are included therein may not be contradicted by evidence of any prior agreement or of a contemporaneous oral agreement but may be explained or supplemented
>
>   (1) by course of dealing or usage of trade (Section 1–205) or by course of performance (Section 2–208); and
>
>   (2) by evidence of consistent additional terms unless the court finds the writing to have been intended also as a complete and exclusive statement of the terms of the agreement.

Section 2–202 is as applicable to express warranties as it is to other oral provisions. Comment 2 to section 2–316 provides that "[t]he seller is protected under this Article against false allegations of oral warranties by its provisions on parol and extrinsic evidence * * *," and subsection 2–316(1) refers explicitly to section 2–202. Section 2–202(2) requires, however, that "the court [find] the writing to have been intended also as a complete and exclusive statement of the terms of the agreement" in order for the parol evidence rule to exclude consideration of the oral warranty. A written disclaimer under section 2–316 might lead a court to determine that the parties intended the writing to represent their entire agreement concerning warranties, thereby excluding oral warranties under the parol evidence rule.

Proposed Changes to Section 2–316

§ 2–316. Exclusion of Modification of Warranties.

(1) Words or conduct relevant to the creation of an express warranty and words or conduct tending to negate or limit warranty shall be construed wherever reasonable as consistent with each other; but subject to ~~the provisions of this Article on parol or extrinsic evidence (Section 2–202)~~ Section 2–202, negation or limitation is inoperative to the extent that such construction is unreasonable.

(2) Subject to subsection (3), to exclude or modify the implied warranty of merchantability or any part of it <u>in a consumer contract the language must be in a record, be conspicuous, and state "The seller undertakes no responsibility for the quality of the goods except as otherwise provided in this contract," and in any other contract</u> the language must mention merchantability and in case of a ~~writing~~ <u>record</u> must be conspicuous ~~, and to~~. Subject to subsection (3), to <u>exclude or modify the</u> implied warranty of fitness, the exclusion must be ~~by a writing~~ <u>in a record</u> and <u>be</u> conspicuous. Language to exclude all implied warranties of fitness <u>in a consumer contract must state "The seller assumes no responsibility that the goods will be fit for any particular purpose for which you may be buying these goods, except as otherwise provided in the contract," and in any other contract the language</u> is sufficient if it states, for example, that "There are no warranties ~~which~~ <u>that</u> extend beyond the description on the face hereof." <u>Language that satisfies the requirements of this subsection for the exclusion or modification of a warranty in a consumer contract also satisfies the requirements for any other contract.</u>

(3) Notwithstanding subsection (2)<u>:</u>

(a) unless the circumstances indicate otherwise, all implied warranties are excluded by expressions like "as is", "with all faults" or other language ~~which~~ <u>that</u> in common understanding calls the buyer's attention to the exclusion of warranties ~~and~~<u>,</u> makes plain that there is no implied warranty<u>, and, in a consumer contract evidenced by a record, is set forth conspicuously in the record</u>; ~~and~~

(b) ~~when~~ <u>if</u> the buyer before entering into the contract has examined the goods or the sample or model as fully as ~~he~~ desired or has refused to examine the goods <u>after a demand by the seller</u> there is no implied warranty with regard to defects ~~which~~ <u>that</u> an examination ~~ought~~ in the circumstances ~~to~~ <u>should</u> have revealed to ~~him~~ <u>the buyer</u>; and

(c) an implied warranty ~~can~~ may also be excluded or modified by course of dealing or course of performance or usage of trade.

(4) Remedies for breach of warranty ~~can~~ may be limited in accordance with ~~the provisions of this article on liquidation or limitation of damages and on contractual modification of remedy (Sections 2–718 and 2–719)~~ Sections 2–718 and 2–719.

The proposed changes to section 2–316 clarify some ambiguities that emerged after the passage of this section. As noted above, they make it clear that disclaimers under paragraph (3) must be conspicuous if they are evidenced in a record. Likewise, Comment 2 of the proposed revisions clarifies the relationship between paragraphs (2) and (3).

The general test for disclaimers of implied warranties remains in subsection (3)(a), and the more specific tests are in subsection (2). A disclaimer that satisfies the requirements of subsection (3)(a) need not also satisfy any of the requirements of subsection (2).

Perhaps most importantly, in consumer contracts the proposed revisions replace the stilted and, for most consumers, the uninformative requirement that disclaimers of the merchantability warranty must use the word "merchantability" with the requirement that the disclaimer state that "The seller undertakes no responsibility for the quality of the goods except as otherwise provided in this contract." Similar common usage language is required to disclaim the fitness warranty.

SECTION H. REMEDY LIMITATIONS

Uniform Commercial Code

§ 2–719. Contractual Modification or Limitation of Remedy

(1) Subject to the provisions of subsections (2) and (3) of this section and of the preceding section on liquidation and limitation of damages,

(a) the agreement may provide for remedies in addition to or in substitution for those provided in this Article and may limit or alter the measure of damages recoverable under this Article, as by limiting the buyer's remedies to return of the goods and repayment of the price or to repair and replacement of non-conforming goods or parts; and

(b) resort to a remedy as provided is optional unless the remedy is expressly agreed to be exclusive, in which case it is the sole remedy.

(2) Where circumstances cause an exclusive or limited remedy to fail of its essential purpose, remedy may be had as provided in this Act.

(3) Consequential damages may be limited or excluded unless the limitation or exclusion is unconscionable. Limitation of consequential damages for injury to the person in the case of consumer goods is prima facie unconscionable but limitation of damages where the loss is commercial is not.

In McCarty v. E.J. Korvette, Inc., 28 Md.App. 421, 424,347 A.2d 253, 256 (1975), the seller offered the following "Korvette Tire Centers All-Road–Hazards Tire Guarantee."

> The tires identified hereon are guaranteed for the number of months (or miles) designated (36,000 miles) against all road hazards including stone bruises, impact bruises, blow out, tread separation, glass cuts and fabric breaks, only when used in normal, non-commercial passenger car service. If a tire fails to give satisfactory service under the terms of this guarantee, return it to the nearest Korvette Tire Center. We will replace the tire charging only the proportionate part of the sale price for each month elapsed (or mileage used) from date of purchase, plus the full federal tax.
>
> The above guarantee does not cover tires run flat, or simply worn out; tires injured by a fire, collision, vandalism, misalignment or mechanical defects of the vehicle. Radial or surface fissures, discoloration or ordinary repairable punctures, do not render tires unfit for service. Punctures will be repaired free.
>
> Neither the manufacturer nor Korvette Tire Centers shall be liable for any consequential damage and our liability is limited solely to replacement of the product.

On its face, this limitation purported to exclude remedies for personal injury. The court held that it was unconscionable under subsection 2-719(3), even though the plaintiff did not suffer any personal injury. Applying section 2-302—the general Article 2 provision governing unconscionability that gives courts considerable leeway to remedy unconscionable contract provisions—the court struck the limitation even as applied to economic consequential damages. The court's approach might not be common, but it demonstrates that lawyers drafting remedy limitations in commercial dealings must be careful not to use language that might be read to exclude personal injury damages.

Subsection 2-719(3) provides that limitations of consequential damages for personal injury are "prima facie" unconscionable, not "per se" unconscionable. It is not altogether clear whether a seller could even overcome the presumption of unconscionability.

Recall that an express warranty usually is not enforced beyond its own terms as interpreted by the court, which creates an interesting issue about the relationship between section 2-313 and 2-719. For example, if the seller in *McCarty* had simply promised that "the seller agrees to repair any blowouts," and then did repair any blowout, presumably there would be no breach. In the same vein, consider the entire category of service contracts. Presumably, an automobile dealer who sells a five-year service contract is not subject to personal injury liability on the basis of the service contract alone. In fact, such a promise is probably not a warranty at all. It is an enforceable contract provision, but it is not a representation about the quality of the product. Thus, section 2-719 is not even applicable.

Is it fair to say that what the seller in *McCarty* was attempting to create was a "repair and replacement" clause or what the proposed revisions to Article 2 refer to as a "remedial promise?" (see p. 22 *infra*). If so, the proposed revisions to section 2–313 make it clear that such promises are not a warranty, limitations of which might run afoul of section 2–719 or section 2–302.

Most courts have held that the language and conspicuousness requirements of section 2–316 do not apply to remedy limitations under section 2–719. *See* Orrox Corp. v. Rexnord, Inc., 389 F.Supp. 441, 445–46 (M.D.Ala.1975); Gramling v. Baltz, 253 Ark. 361, 362, 485 S.W.2d 183, 189 (1972), affirmed on rehearing, 253 Ark. 352, 485 S.W.2d 183 (1972); Fargo Mach. & Tool Co. v. Kearney & Trecker Corp., 428 F.Supp. 364, 381 (E.D.Mich.1977); Adams Van Serv., Inc. v. International Harvester Corp., 14 U.C.C.Rep.Serv. (Callaghan) 1142, 1147–49, 1973 WL 21443 (Pa.Com.Pl.1973) (limitation of remedy upheld although it appears in same clause and same size print as inconspicuous disclaimer); Apex Supply Co., Inc. v. Benbow Industries, Inc., 189 Ga.App. 598, 376 S.E.2d 694, 697 (1988). *But see* Adams v. American Cyanamid Co., 1 Neb.App. 337, 498 N.W.2d 577, 588 (1992). Nevertheless, a lack of conspicuousness might be a factor concerning unconscionability under section 2–302. *See generally,* Weintraub, Disclaimer of Warranties and Limitation of Damages for Breach of Warranty Under the U.C.C., 53 Tex.L.Rev. 60 (1974). Other factors, such as lack of bargaining power or gross unfairness, might render a limitation on damages unconscionable under section 2–302 even though the limitation does not violate section 2–316 or 2–719. It is unclear whether section 2–719(3) excludes these factors from consideration.

"Repair and replacement" clauses are common remedy limitations. Subsection 2–719(2) provides that any remedy limitation that "fail[s] of its essential purpose" is ineffective, and the buyer has the remedies provided for in the other provisions of Article 2. This is a common issue in cases involving "repair and replacement clauses" when the seller refuses to repair or replace the product.

Courts have split on the issue of whether a "repair or replacement" clause fails its essential purpose when a seller makes a good faith effort to repair or replace goods but is unable to do so. Some courts and commentators have suggested that a seller's motivation is irrelevant. *See* Fargo Mach. & Tool Co. v. Kearney & Trecker Corp., 428 F.Supp. 364 (E.D.Mich.1977); Special Project, Article Two Warranties in Commercial Transactions, 64 Cornell L.Rev. 30, 235–36 (1978). Other courts have held that a seller's good faith attempt is a factor that should be considered. *See* American Elec. Power Co. v. Westinghouse Elec. Corp., 418 F.Supp. 435, 453–54 (S.D.N.Y.1976); Potomac Elec. Power Co. v. Westinghouse Elec. Corp., 385 F.Supp. 572, 578–79 (D.D.C.1974), rev'd mem., 527 F.2d 853 (D.C.Cir.1975); Koehring Co. v. A.P.I., Inc., 369 F.Supp. 882 (D.Mich.1974); Jones & McKnight Corp. v. Birdsboro Corp., 320 F.Supp. 39 (N.D.Ill.1970).

In Russo v. Hilltop Lincoln–Mercury, Inc., 479 S.W.2d 211 (Mo.App. 1972), the plaintiff's car was destroyed by an electrical fire caused by a defective electrical part. The court permitted the plaintiff to recover the value of the car. In response to the defendant's argument that a "repair and replacement" provision limited the plaintiff's remedy to replacement of the electrical part, the court stated:

> That provision of the warranty implies the car was repairable. Here it could not be; it was worthless junk. At trial time the defendant had the car, still not repaired. It would be ludicrous to require plaintiff to ask defendant to do the impossible. "Laws governing warranties, express and implied, should be so administered as to be fair to all parties concerned. Such warranties should be meaningful." Jacobson v. Broadway Motors, Inc., Mo.App., 430 S.W.2d 602.

The contract also expressly excluded liability for car rental expenses. The court rejected the plaintiff's argument that the defendant's failure to repair constituted a "failure of purpose" that could be used to trigger the UCC remedy of incidental damages (here the cost of a rental car).

Courts have split on the effect of an independent limitation on consequential damages when a "repair or replacement" clause fails its essential purpose. Some courts have held that a separate and explicit consequential damage exclusion is effective even if the "repair and replacement" clause fails its essential purpose. *See* Lincoln Pulp & Paper Co., Inc. v. Dravo Corp., 436 F.Supp. 262, 278 (D.Me.1977) (under theory that location of exclusion contained in "independent contractual clause" precluded recovery of consequential damages); County Asphalt, Inc. v. Lewis Welding & Eng'g Corp., 323 F.Supp. 1300 (S.D.N.Y.1970), aff'd, 444 F.2d 372 (2d Cir.1971), cert. denied, 404 U.S. 939, 92 S.Ct. 272, 30 L.Ed.2d 252 (1971); Kohlenberger, Inc. v. Tyson's Foods, Inc., 256 Ark. 584, 510 S.W.2d 555 (1974); American Tel. & Tel. Co. v. New York City Human Resources Admin., 833 F.Supp. 962, 987 (S.D.N.Y. 1993). Other courts have held that a seller's bad faith failure to repair undermines even an explicit, independent limitation of consequential damages. *See* Koehring Co. v. A.P.I., Inc., 369 F.Supp. 882, 890 (E.D.Mich.1974); United States Fibres, Inc. v. Proctor & Schwartz, Inc., 358 F.Supp. 449, 465 (E.D.Mich.1972), affirmed on other grounds, 509 F.2d 1043 (6th Cir.1975); Jones & McKnight Corp. v. Birdsboro Corp., 320 F.Supp. 39, 43 (N.D.Ill.1970) (buyer entitled to expectation that seller "would not be unreasonably or willfully dilatory" in making repairs under warranty); Fiorito Bros., Inc. v. Fruehauf Corp., 747 F.2d 1309, 1315 (9th Cir. 1984) (manufacturer arbitrarily declined to make necessary repairs and thus arbitrarily and unreasonably declined to live up to its contractual promises). *See also* Potomac Elec. Power Co. v. Westinghouse Elec. Corp., 385 F.Supp. 572, 578–79 (D.D.C.1974) (seller's conscientious repair efforts preclude liability for consequential damages), reversed memorandum decision, 527 F.2d 853 (D.C.Cir.1975). One commentator has suggested that an independent limitation on consequential damages should fail when the seller's attempt to repair fails, even if the seller has made a good faith effort to repair. *See* Special Project, Article Two Warranties in Commercial Transactions, 64 Cornell L.Rev. 30, 239 (1978).

See generally, Anderson, Failure of Essential Purpose and Essential Failure on Purpose: A Look at Section 2–719 of the Uniform Commercial Code, 31 Sw.L.J. 758 (1977); Eddy, On the "Essential" Purposes of Limited Remedies: The Metaphysics of UCC Section 2–719(2), 65 Cal. L.Rev. 28, 39 (1977); Note, Failure of the Essential Purpose of a Limited Repair Remedy Under Section 2–719 of the Uniform Commercial Code, 32 Baylor L.Rev. 292, 296–98 (1980); Special Project, Article Two Warranties in Commercial Transactions, 64 Cornell L.Rev. 30, 239 (1978).

Note that a seller can effectively escape liability for personal injury damages by disclaiming a warranty under section 2–316, but cannot do so by limiting damages under section 2–719.

NCCUSL has not proposed any changes to section 2–719.

SECTION I. NOTICE AND STATUTES OF LIMITATION

Subsection 2–607(3)(a) provides that "the buyer must within a reasonable time after he discovers or should have discovered any breach notify the seller of breach or be barred from any remedy." This can be a pitfall for an unwary plaintiff. Recall that in Greenman v. Yuba Power Products, Inc., 59 Cal.2d 57, 27 Cal.Rptr. 697, 377 P.2d 897 (1963), Justice Traynor referred to this pitfall in his argument that the court should create an action for product liability, rather than force plaintiffs to rely on warranty law. Some courts have held that the notice requirement of section 2–607(3)(a) applies only between a buyer and an immediate seller. Consequently, these courts do not require a buyer to notify a remote seller. *See, e.g.,* Vintage Homes, Inc. v. Coldiron, 585 S.W.2d 886, 888 (Tex.Civ.App.1979).

One purpose underlying the notice requirement of section 2–607(3)(a) is to give the seller a chance to cure the defect. Arguably, there is no good reason to apply the requirement to a situation in which the plaintiff's first notice of the defect is an accident that causes personal injury. This issue might more appropriately be governed by a statute of limitations.

Section 2–725 provides:

(a) An action for breach of any contract for sale must be commenced within four years after the cause of action has accrued. By the original agreement the parties may reduce the period of limitation to not less than one year but may not extend it.

(b) A cause of action accrues when the breach occurs, regardless of the aggrieved party's lack of knowledge of the breach. A breach of warranty occurs when tender of delivery is made, except that where a warranty explicitly extends to future performance of the goods and discovery of the breach must await the time of such performance the cause of action accrues when the breach is or should have been discovered.

Notwithstanding the clear language of section 2–725(b), a few courts have calculated the statute of limitations from the time of injury in breach of warranty cases involving personal injury. *See* Cleveland v. Square–D Co., 613 S.W.2d 790 (Tex.Civ.App. 1981). *But see* Pako Corp. V. Thomas, 855 S.W.2d 215, 219 (Tex.App.1993).

If a court calculates the statute of limitation from the time of injury, it might also use the "discovery rule" (which is the normal rule in tort cases), counting only from the time the plaintiff discovered or should have discovered the injury.

Some states have adopted statutes of repose for product injuries, which provide that suit is barred, for example, ten years after the sale, even if the injury did not take place or was not discovered within the time period. *See, e.g.,* Ill.Rev.Stat. ch. 83, § 22.2. Such statutes are superfluous in light of the wording of section 2–725, because the four-year provision of section 2–725 runs from the time of sale, unless the warranty specifically refers to future performance.

Chapter 3

EMERGENCE OF PRODUCT LIABILITY

SECTION A. ADOPTION

GREENMAN v. YUBA POWER PRODUCTS, INC.
Supreme Court of California, 1963.
59 Cal.2d 57, 27 Cal.Rptr. 697, 377 P.2d 897.

TRAYNOR, JUSTICE.

Plaintiff brought this action for damages against the retailer and the manufacturer of a Shopsmith, a combination power tool that could be used as a saw, drill, and wood lathe. He saw a Shopsmith demonstrated by the retailer and studied a brochure prepared by the manufacturer. He decided he wanted a Shopsmith for his home workshop, and his wife bought and gave him one for Christmas in 1955. In 1957 he bought the necessary attachments to use the Shopsmith as a lathe for turning a large piece of wood he wished to make into a chalice. After he had worked on the piece of wood several times without difficulty, it suddenly flew out of the machine and struck him on the forehead, inflicting serious injuries. About ten and a half months later, he gave the retailer and the manufacturer written notice of claimed breaches of warranties and filed a complaint against them alleging such breaches and negligence.

After a trial before a jury, the court ruled that there was no evidence that the retailer was negligent or had breached any express warranty and that the manufacturer was not liable for the breach of any implied warranty. Accordingly, it submitted to the jury only the cause of action alleging breach of implied warranties against the retailer and the causes of action alleging negligence and breach of express warranties against the manufacturer. The jury returned a verdict for the retailer against plaintiff and for plaintiff against the manufacturer in the amount of $65,000. The trial court denied the manufacturer's motion for a new trial and entered judgment on the verdict. The manufacturer and plaintiff appeal. Plaintiff seeks a reversal of the part of the judgment in favor of the retailer, however, only in the event that the part of the judgment against the manufacturer is reversed.

Plaintiff introduced substantial evidence that his injuries were caused by defective design and construction of the Shopsmith. His expert witnesses testified that inadequate set screws were used to hold parts of the machine together so that normal vibration caused the tailstock of the lathe to move away from the piece of wood being turned permitting it to fly out of the lathe. They also testified that there were other more positive ways of fastening the parts of the machine together, the use of which would have prevented the accident. The jury could therefore reasonably have concluded that the manufacturer negligently constructed the Shopsmith. The jury could also reasonably have concluded that statements in the manufacturer's brochure were untrue, that they constituted express warranties,[1] and that plaintiff's injuries were caused by their breach.

The manufacturer contends, however, that plaintiff did not give it notice of breach of warranty within a reasonable time and that therefore his cause of action for breach of warranty is barred by section 1769 of the Civil Code. Since it cannot be determined whether the verdict against it was based on the negligence or warranty cause of action or both, the manufacturer concludes that the error in presenting the warranty cause of action to the jury was prejudicial.

Section 1769 of the Civil Code provides: "In the absence of express or implied agreement of the parties, acceptance of the goods by the buyer shall not discharge the seller from liability in damages or other legal remedy for breach of any promise or warranty in the contract to sell or the sale. But, if, after acceptance of the goods, the buyer fails to give notice to the seller of the breach of any promise or warranty within a reasonable time after the buyer knows, or ought to know of such breach, the seller shall not be liable therefor."

Like other provisions of the uniform sales act (Civ.Code, §§ 1721–1800), section 1769 deals with the rights of the parties to a contract of sale or a sale. It does not provide that notice must be given of the breach of a warranty that arises independently of a contract of sale between the parties. Such warranties are not imposed by the sales act, but are the product of common-law decisions that have recognized them in a variety of situations. * * * It is true that in many of these situations the court has invoked the sales act definitions of warranties (Civ.Code, §§ 1732, 1735) in defining the defendant's liability, but it has done so, not because the statutes so required, but because they provided appropriate standards for the court to adopt under the circumstances presented. * * *

---

1. In this respect the trial court limited the jury to a consideration of two statements in the manufacturer's brochure. (1) "WHEN SHOPSMITH IS IN HORIZONTAL POSITION—Rugged construction of frame provides rigid support from end to end. Heavy centerless-ground steel tubing insurers [sic] perfect alignment of components." (2) "SHOPSMITH maintains its accuracy because every component has positive locks that hold adjustments through rough or precision work."

The notice requirement of section 1769, however, is not an appropriate one for the court to adopt in actions by injured consumers against manufacturers with whom they have not dealt. (La Hue v. Coca–Cola Bottling, 50 Wash.2d 645, 314 P.2d 421, 422; Chapman v. Brown, D.C., 198 F.Supp. 78, 85, affd. Brown v. Chapman, 9 Cir., 304 F.2d 149.) "As between the immediate parties to the sale [the notice requirement] is a sound commercial rule, designed to protect the seller against unduly delayed claims for damages. As applied to personal injuries, and notice to a remote seller, it becomes a booby-trap for the unwary. The injured consumer is seldom 'steeped in the business practice which justifies the rule,' [James, Product Liability, 34 Texas L.Rev. 44, 192, 197] and at least until he has had legal advice it will not occur to him to give notice to one with whom he has had no dealings." (Prosser, Strict Liability to the Consumer, 69 Yale L.J. 1099, 1130, footnotes omitted.) It is true that in Jones v. Burgermeister Brewing Corp., 198 Cal.App.2d 198, 202–203, 18 Cal.Rptr. 311; Perry v. Thrifty Drug Co., 186 Cal.App.2d 410, 411, 9 Cal.Rptr. 50; Arata v. Tonegato, 152 Cal.App.2d 837, 841, 314 P.2d 130, and Maecherlein v. Sealy Mattress Co., 145 Cal.App.2d 275, 278, 302 P.2d 331, the court assumed that notice of breach of warranty must be given in an action by a consumer against a manufacturer. Since in those cases, however, the court did not consider the question whether a distinction exists between a warranty based on a contract between the parties and one imposed on a manufacturer not in privity with the consumer, the decisions are not authority for rejecting the rule of the La Hue and Chapman cases, supra. (Peterson v. Lamb Rubber Co., 54 Cal.2d 339, 343, 5 Cal.Rptr. 863, 353 P.2d 575; People v. Banks, 53 Cal.2d 370, 389, 1 Cal.Rptr. 669, 348 P.2d 102.) We conclude, therefore, that even if plaintiff did not give timely notice of breach of warranty to the manufacturer, his cause of action based on the representations contained in the brochure was not barred.

Moreover, to impose strict liability on the manufacturer under the circumstances of this case, it was not necessary for plaintiff to establish an express warranty as defined in section 1732 of the Civil Code.[2] A manufacturer is strictly liable in tort when an article he places on the market, knowing that it is to be used without inspection for defects, proves to have a defect that causes injury to a human being. Recognized first in the case of unwholesome food products, such liability has now been extended to a variety of other products that create as great or greater hazards if defective. * * *

Although in these cases strict liability has usually been based on the theory of an express or implied warranty running from the manufacturer to the plaintiff, the abandonment of the requirement of a contract between them, the recognition that the liability is not assumed by

---

2. "Any affirmation of fact or any promise by the seller relating to the goods is an express warranty if the natural tendency of such affirmation or promise is to induce the buyer to purchase the goods, and if the buyer purchases the goods relying thereon. No affirmation of the value of the goods, nor any statement purporting to be a statement of the seller's opinion only shall be construed as a warranty."

agreement but imposed by law * * * and the refusal to permit the manufacturer to define the scope of its own responsibility for defective products * * * make clear that the liability is not one governed by the law of contract warranties but by the law of strict liability in tort. Accordingly, rules defining and governing warranties that were developed to meet the needs of commercial transactions cannot properly be invoked to govern the manufacturer's liability to those injured by their defective products unless those rules also serve the purposes for which such liability is imposed.

We need not recanvass the reasons for imposing strict liability on the manufacturer. They have been fully articulated in the cases cited above. (See also 2 Harper and James, Torts, §§ 28.15–28.16, pp. 1569–1574; Prosser, Strict Liability to the Consumer, 69 Yale L.J. 1099; Escola v. Coca Cola Bottling Co., 24 Cal.2d 453, 461, 150 P.2d 436, concurring opinion.) The purpose of such liability is to insure that the costs of injuries resulting from defective products are borne by the manufacturers that put such products on the market rather than by the injured persons who are powerless to protect themselves. Sales warranties serve this purpose fitfully at best. (See Prosser, Strict Liability to the Consumer, 69 Yale L.J. 1099, 1124–1134.) In the present case, for example, plaintiff was able to plead and prove an express warranty only because he read and relied on the representations of the Shopsmith's ruggedness contained in the manufacturer's brochure. Implicit in the machine's presence on the market, however, was a representation that it would safely do the jobs for which it was built. Under these circumstances, it should not be controlling whether plaintiff selected the machine because of the statements in the brochure, or because of the machine's own appearance of excellence that belied the defect lurking beneath the surface, or because he merely assumed that it would safely do the jobs it was built to do. It should not be controlling whether the details of the sales from manufacturer to retailer and from retailer to plaintiff's wife were such that one or more of the implied warranties of the sales act arose. (Civ.Code, § 1735.) "The remedies of injured consumers ought not to be made to depend upon the intricacies of the law of sales." (Ketterer v. Armour & Co., D.C., 200 F. 322, 323; Klein v. Duchess Sandwich Co., 14 Cal.2d 272, 282, 93 P.2d 799.) To establish the manufacturer's liability it was sufficient that plaintiff proved that he was injured while using the Shopsmith in a way it was intended to be used as a result of a defect in design and manufacture of which plaintiff was not aware that made the Shopsmith unsafe for its intended use.

* * *

The judgment is affirmed.

GIBSON, C.J., and SCHAUER, MCCOMB, PETERS, TOBRINER and PEEK, JJ., concur.

Notes

1. **Historical note.** Before 1963 plaintiffs in products liability cases had to rely on negligence, breach of warranty, or misrepresentation. These theories were not developed as special causes of action for product cases, and they presented plaintiffs with certain obstacles. Negligence required a plaintiff to prove an act of negligence on the part of the defendant. Warranty law required a plaintiff to contend with privity, notice, and disclaimers.

In 1944, in a famous concurring opinion in *Escola v. Coca Cola Bottling Co. of Fresno*, 24 Cal.2d 453, 150 P.2d 436 (1944), Justice Roger Traynor of the California Supreme Court argued that these traditional theories were inadequate and that the court should adopt a special theory for product cases. Nineteen years later, in *Greenman*, Justice Traynor had the opportunity to write for a majority of the court and expressly adopted strict products liability for manufacturers of defective products.

Two years after that, in 1965, the American Law Institute embraced *Greenman* in section 402A of the Restatement (Second) of Torts. Work on this section was begun prior to the *Greenman* decision. Justice Traynor was a member of the Reporter's Advisory Committee and the Council of the American Law Institute when the section was developed. Wade, On Product "Design Defects" and Their Actionability, 33 Vand.L.Rev. 551, 554 (1980). Early drafts of the section applied only to food and drink. Because of the trend of the recent case law, it was eventually expanded to include all products. The history of the development of the section is traced in Wade, On the Nature of Strict Tort Liability for Products, 44 Miss.L.J. 825, 830–831 (1973). *See also,* Page, Generic Product Risks: The Case Against Comment k and for Strict Tort Liability, 58 N.Y.U.L.Rev. 853, 860–872 (1983).

With the imprimatur of a leading court and the American Law Institute, strict product liability swept the country. Nearly every American jurisdiction adopted it.

A major attraction of strict products liability was that it avoided the contractual strictures of warranty law, such as the rules about privity, notice, and disclaimers. A debate quickly arose about whether it was proper for courts to avoid these statutory limits by adopting a parallel tort theory that did not include them. *Compare* Wade, Tort Liability for Products Causing Physical Injury and Article 2 of the UCC, 48 Mo.L.Rev. 1 (1983), *with* Franklin, When Worlds Collide: Liability Theories and Disclaimers in Defective Product Cases, 18 Stan.L.Rev. 974 (1966). *See also* Dickerson, Products Liability: Dean Wade and the Constitutionality of Section 402A, 44 Tenn.L.Rev. 205 (1977); Donovan, Recent Developments in Products Liability Litigation in New England: The Emerging Confrontation Between the Expanding Law of Torts and the Uniform Commercial Code, 19 Me.L.Rev. 181 (1967); McNichols, Who Says That Strict Tort Disclaimers Can Never Be Effective? The Courts Cannot Agree, 28 Okla.L.Rev. 494 (1975); Miller, The Crossroads: The Case for the Code in Products Liability, 21 Okla.L.Rev. 411 (1968); Titus, Restatement (Second) of Torts Section 402A and the Uniform Commercial Code, 22 Stan.L.Rev. 713 (1970). The debate, however, was mainly academic. Few courts even mentioned this problem when adopting strict products liability, much less accepted the argument that strict liability is preempted by the UCC.

The history of product liability can be divided roughly into four periods. The first period, roughly the decade or so after *Greenman* was dominated by the question of whether states should even adopt product liability. The answer was almost always "yes." Cases in this era are important not only because they adopted strict products liability, but also because they give us insight into a particular court's views about the rationales underlying this theory of recovery. These rationales are useful in current litigation to help resolve specific issues of implementation. The second period, overlapping with the first and continuing roughly through the 1970s, saw courts spending much time and energy addressing the central question of strict products liability: what constitutes a "defective" product? The third period, which we are still in, is one in which courts are continuing to work out the details of strict products liability, by addressing issues such as defenses, causation, and the applicability of strict products liability to particular products and situations. The fourth period, which overlaps with the third, was ushered in by the American Law Institute's adoption in 1998 of the Restatement (Third) of Torts: Products Liability. The new Restatement is addressed throughout this book.

2. The Restatement of Torts (Second) § 402A (1965) provides:

§ 402A. Special Liability of Seller of Product for Physical Harm to User or Consumer

(1) One who sells any product in a defective condition unreasonably dangerous to the user or consumer or to his property is subject to liability for physical harm thereby caused to the ultimate user or consumer, or to his property, if

(a) the seller is engaged in the business of selling such a product, and

(b) it is expected to and does reach the user or consumer without substantial change in the condition in which it is sold.

(2) The rule stated in Subsection (1) applies although

(a) the seller has exercised all possible care in the preparation and sale of his product, and

(b) the user or consumer has not bought the product from or entered into any contractual relation with the seller.

3. The *Greenman* decision and the Restatement § 402A provided the intellectual basis for the transition from warranty to strict liability in tort, and represent the beginning of modern products liability law. A great many developments, however, have taken place since 1965. As a result, many courts today depart substantially from the Restatement rule.

4. The basic elements of a strict product liability cause of action under section 402A are as follows:

1. The defendant was in the business of producing or selling the product.

2. The product was expected to and did reach the purchaser without substantial change in the condition in which it was sold.

3. The product was defective at the time it left the defendant's control.

4. The harm resulted when the product was being used in a reasonably foreseeable manner.

5. The person harmed was foreseeable.

6. The defect was the cause in fact and proximate cause of physical harm to plaintiff's person or property.

The requirement of defect, the third element, represents the most important restriction on liability. This issue is treated in Chapter 4. Causation in fact (element 6) is addressed in Chapter 5. Proximate cause and foreseeability of the plaintiff (elements 5 and 6) are addressed in Chapter 7. The first element, that the defendant be in the business of selling the product, is covered in Chapter 12.

The fourth element, misuse, will not be treated in a separate section of the book. It is really not a concept that stands on its own. Rather, it is relevant to a variety of issues including defect, proximate cause, and contributory negligence. This book will deal with each of these aspects of misuse in the section of the book dealing with the subjects to which it relates.

The second element, substantial change, is also treated in two places in the book. This is because courts deal with this issue differently, depending on such variables as the type of defect, the type of product (i.e., whether it is a finished product or, on the other hand, raw material or a component part), and the time when the change is made.

All of this represents a very general statement of the elements of a product liability action. As we shall see, courts vary dramatically in the way they interpret and apply these elements.

SECTION B. POLICIES UNDERLYING PRODUCTS LIABILITY

Courts and scholars have advanced a variety of policy justifications for product liability. Six of them are briefly summarized below.

1. **Compensation (or loss spreading).** Losses inevitably result from the use of complex modern products. These losses can have a disastrous effect on the individual who experiences them. It is humane and fair to shift these losses to all consumers of the product. This can be accomplished by imposing liability on manufacturers, thus, forcing them to raise prices enough to pay for the losses or insure against them. *See* Holford, The Limits of Strict Liability for Product Design and Manufacture, 52 Tex.L.Rev. 81, 82–84, 87–88 (1973); Wade, On The Nature of Strict Liability for Products, 44 Miss.L.J. 825, 826 (1973).

2. **Deterrence.** Tort liability increases costs, but competition induces manufacturers to minimize them. Imposing liability on manufacturers, therefore, provides them with an incentive to market safer

products. In theory, strict liability may create more deterrence than negligence-based liability since negligence imposes liability only if the defendant fails to take measures that a reasonable person would take. Strict liability induces manufacturers to go beyond this if the cost of the added safety measures is less than the potential cost of liability for failing to take them. *See* Holford, The Limits of Strict Liability for Product Design and Manufacture, 52 Tex.L.Rev. 81, 82–84, 87–88 (1973); Wade, On The Nature of Strict Liability for Products, 44 Miss.L.J. 825, 826 (1973).

3. **Encouraging useful conduct.** The first two policies listed, compensation and deterrence, are most commonly cited as the bases for product liability. They are clearly not the only considerations, however, because they almost always point in the direction of imposing liability. Yet, no court has imposed the liability of an insurer on manufacturers by requiring them to pay for all harm caused by their products. This is because of the fear that such absolute liability would place unreasonable burdens on manufacturers and discourage them from producing useful products. The policy of avoiding over-deterrence by balancing the needs of defendants against the needs of plaintiffs is clearly at work, although it is seldom articulated. *See* Epstein, Products Liability: The Search for the Middle Ground, 56 N.C.L.Rev. 643 (1978); Fischer, Products Liability—An Analysis of Market Share Liability, 34 Vand.L.Rev. 1623, 1628–1629 (1981); Klemme, The Enterprise Liability Theory of Torts, 47 U.Colo.L.Rev. 153 (1976).

4. **Proof problems.** Quite often the manufacturer of a defective product is negligent. The modern complexities of manufacturing, however, frequently make it very difficult for plaintiff to establish this. This is particularly so because he is usually at a relative disadvantage because the manufacturer has greater access to expertise, information, and resources. Imposing strict liability relieves plaintiff of the burden of proving fault. *See* Keeton, Product Liability and the Meaning of Defect, 5 St. Mary's L.J. 30, 34–35 (1973); Schwartz, Foreword: Understanding Products Liability, 67 Calif.L.Rev. 435, 459–61 (1979).

The policy of helping plaintiffs avoid proof problems has been quite influential. Throughout these materials you will see instances where courts either eliminate the need to prove a particular element of plaintiff's case, or they shift the burden of proof on the issue to defendant. Examples include proof of causation in warning cases, proof of identity of defendant as the person who manufactured the product, proof that a risk inherent in the product was scientifically unknowable, and proof that the utility of a product design outweighs its benefits. Indeed, the most significant difference between negligence and product liability may turn out to be where the burden of proof lies with respect to such issues.

5. **Protection of consumer expectations.** Consumers should be protected from unknown dangers in products. This is particularly true since modern advertising and marketing techniques induce consumers to rely on manufacturers to provide them with safe, high-quality products.

Shapo, A Representational Theory of Consumer Protection: Doctrine, Function and Legal Liability for Product Disappointment, 60 Va.L.Rev. 1109 (1974).

6. **Cost internalization.** Forcing manufacturers to raise prices in order to pay for harm caused by their products will lead to a more efficient allocation of resources. The prices of products will then more nearly include all of their true costs, including accident costs. Being aware of the true costs of products, consumers will make more intelligent decisions about which products to purchase. *See* Franklin, Tort Liability for Hepatitis: An Analysis and a Proposal, 24 Stan.L.Rev. 439, 462–463, 465–472 (1972); Katz, The Function of Tort Liability in Technology Assessment, 38 U.Cin.L.Rev. 587, 636, 662 (1969).

Each of these policies has its strengths and weaknesses. None of them, singly or in combination, provides a completely satisfactory basis for product liability. This may help explain why the doctrine continues to evolve. For a general evaluation of these policies see, Owen, Rethinking the Policies of Strict Products Liability, 33 Vand.L.Rev. 681 (1980); Powers, A Modest Proposal to Abandon Strict Products Liability, 1991 U.Ill.L.Rev. 639; Powers, Distinguishing Between Products and Services in Strict Liability, 62 N.C.L.Rev. 415, 423–428 (1984).

The following readings discuss the major policies in greater detail. As you study product liability consider whether these policies are valid and whether the courts are effectively implementing them.

KLEMME, THE ENTERPRISE LIABILITY THEORY OF TORTS
47 U.Colo.L.Rev. 153, 158–165 (1976).

II. THE THEORY OF ENTERPRISE LIABILITY STATED GENERALLY

In its broadest terms the theory of enterprise liability in torts is that losses to society created or caused by an enterprise or, more simply, by an activity, ought to be borne by that enterprise or activity. Stated somewhat more precisely, the theory contemplates that losses historically recognized as compensable when caused by an enterprise, or activity, such as producing, distributing and using automobiles, ought to be borne by those persons who have some logical relationship with that enterprise or activity. The underlying justification for this theory, most ably articulated and illustrated by Guido Calabresi some years ago,[1] is a well known ethical premise of classical economics. This postulate is that, recognizing at any one point in time that the total resources available to a society are limited, the "best" way for the members of a community to decide collectively how they want those limited resources to be used and distributed in order to satisfy most efficiently the greatest possible number of the members' individual wants and desires is through an

---

1. Calabresi, [*Some Thoughts on Risk Distribution and the Law of Torts,* 70 Yale L.J. 499, 500–06 (1961)]. *See also* James, [*An Evolution of the Fault Concept,* 32 Tenn.L.Rev. 394, 400–01 (1965)].

open, competitive market system. The various competing uses to which the community's limited resources might be allocated in order to satisfy the maximum possible individual wants and desires will accordingly be determined through operation of the laws of supply and demand.

To illustrate: at any point in time, the steel available to a society will be limited. Whether more steel should be used to produce refrigerators rather than be used to produce cars will depend on whether or not those desiring more refrigerators are willing to pay a higher price for those refrigerators than others will be willing to pay for cars.

For the pricing mechanism of the market place to achieve this goal of the "best" allocation of the community's total limited resources, a supplier of goods or services must accurately reflect in the prices he seeks for his goods or services the "true" costs of making them available. If, for example, a druggist consistently sells his aspirin below his costs because of inaccurate cost accounting, but he nonetheless is able to stay in business because he more than offsets his aspirin-sales losses from the total profit he makes on his sales of other articles, the "best" allocation of the community's limited resources has not occurred. Ideally, the druggist should raise his price for aspirin. The labor and other resources allocated to the production of aspirin will be reduced because of a decrease in demand for the higher-priced aspirin. These resources will in turn become available for use in the production of other goods for which, at a lower price, there would be a greater demand. With the increased production of these other goods, the price at which they are sold should decline. As a consequence of all this, the community ends up with a better allocation of its limited resources (available labor, materials, etc.) than it had before, that is, one which does more to maximize the total individual desires of the society's members at less expense to them.

The distortions which can occur in this ideal pricing, resource allocation process are numerous and varied. Government tax policies and subsidies (whether to suppliers or purchasers) as well as its borrowing and expenditure practices and other monetary policies have the potential for distorting the process. Unrealistic cost accounting by suppliers and irrational considerations influencing purchasers, whether induced by fair or unfair advertising or other similar causes, will result in a distortion. Monopolistic business practices, control over large amounts of investment capital, and the existence of corporate conglomerates (where the losses of an unprofitable division are in part written off against the more profitable operations of another division), likewise have the potential for distorting the process.

The relevance of these considerations to tort law is that virtually every kind of loss which tort law has historically considered compensable is a loss of part of the community's total, though limited, available resources. Whether the law shifts the loss to the defendant or leaves it on the plaintiff, the loss will (1) not be eliminated and (2) will not remain entirely on whichever party the law chooses to place the loss on, or leave it on, initially. Today, especially through one or more of the diverse public and private insurance systems available, the initial loss-bearer, whether it be the plaintiff or the defendant, will be able in most cases to pass on all or a significant part of the loss to other persons in society.

In short, the theories of liability which the tort law uses for the purpose of deciding whether the loss should be left on the plaintiff or reallocated to the defendant will also determine how such losses, or costs, are to be distributed among various segments of the society. In almost all instances these losses will be reflected as costs in the pricing mechanism of the market place and ultimately in the allocation of the community's resources and in the distribution of its wealth among its members.

III. THE THEORY OF ENTERPRISE LIABILITY STATED GENERALLY AND THE RULE OF ACTUAL CAUSE

The rules of liability and nonliability of the tort law therefore function in most instances as cost accounting, i.e., cost distribution rules. In large measure they determine who will ultimately, through the pricing mechanism of the market place, bear the costs of the tort losses generated by the numerous activities people carry on in society.

Looking at the tort liability rules as cost accounting rules and then trying to fit this idea into the theory of enterprise liability as one which says the costs of an activity ought to be borne by the activity which creates or causes them immediately presents a problem. The problem is: no compensable tort loss is ever the "but for" result of only one enterprise or activity. It is always the result of an infinite number of "but for" causes or activities. But for the plaintiff's grandparents immigrating to this country; but for his parents meeting, marrying and conceiving him; but for the plaintiff's decision to get out of bed in the morning; but for his decision to walk to the post box to mail a letter, etc., the plaintiff would not have been struck and injured by the defendant's car, regardless of whether the defendant's driving is characterized as good or bad. To which, if any, of the plaintiff's "but for" activities, or to which one of the comparable universe of "but for" activities of the defendant, should the plaintiff's losses (as well as those of the defendant) be assigned? All these infinite "but for" activities "created" the loss in the sense that "but for" any one of them the losses would probably not have occurred. How should the tort law through its rules of liability and nonliability "cost account" for these losses? On what rational basis should the law decide which particular enterprise the loss should be treated as a cost of having engaged in?

One thing is clear. The theory of enterprise liability as it is usually put does not provide a rational answer to this basic question. An infinite number of enterprises created the loss, and the general statement of the enterprise liability theory alone provides no rational criteria for making an intelligent selection among them.

The general statement of the theory that the costs of an activity or enterprise ought to be borne by the activity or enterprise which created them should not, however, be rejected as devoid of analytic value. It has at least two uses. First, the underlying economic assumptions and values of the general statement of the theory also underlie the specific criteria of the theory, which will be considered later. Second, these assumptions and values also provide an explanation for why, as long as the tort law has been around and regardless of the changing theories of liability upon which the courts have shifted losses from plaintiffs to defendants, it has been "elementary policy that a defendant should not be held liable for the harm the plaintiff complains of unless the plaintiff can at least show that the defendant in fact caused the harm."[2]

Why should this "elementary policy" of the tort law—the "but for" rule of actual cause—have been so constant? Throughout the development of tort law, theories and rules for labeling conduct tortious have changed. So, too, the law governing the kinds of losses the courts have been willing to consider compensable, that is, worthy of being shifted, has changed. With but a few recently developed and very limited exceptions,[3] however, the rule has been: no matter how tortious the defendant's conduct may have been and no matter how long or how strongly a given loss has been considered compensable, unless the plaintiff is able to persuade the fact finder by a preponderance of the evidence that the defendant's activity was at least *one* of the infinite "but for" causes of his losses, the plaintiff cannot recover.

This requirement of "but for" cause cannot be explained on the ground that it is essential to having a tort judgment provide a deterrent effect on the defendant's future conduct. On the contrary, exactly the opposite seems true. A more valid explanation of the rule lies in the theory of enterprise liability and its rationale of using the market place as a tool for "best" allocating the community's limited resources. A case illustrating this point is *New York Central Railroad v. Grimstad*.[4] In that case the court held, notwithstanding the probable negligence of the railroad in not providing adequate life saving equipment on one of its barges, the trial court should have granted what today would be a motion for [judgment as a matter of law] against the plaintiff, because the plaintiff, as the widow of a deceased employee who had drowned, had not offered sufficient evidence from which a jury could reasonably have

---

2. C. Gregory & H. Kalven, Cases and Materials on Torts 5 (2d ed. 1969).

3. *See, e.g.,* the rule of Summers v. Tice, 33 Cal.2d 80, 199 P.2d 1 (1948), stated and more fully explained in Haft v. Lone Palm Hotel, 3 Cal.3d 756, 478 P.2d 465, 91 Cal. Rptr. 745 (1970). Where the plaintiff has established a prima facie case of (1) tortious conduct on the defendant's part toward the plaintiff and (2) that the conduct might *possibly* have caused plaintiff's loss, but (3) the plaintiff has not been able to establish a prima facie case of probable cause because the very nature of defendant's tortious conduct has made it extremely difficult, if not impossible, for the plaintiff to do so, and (4) the plaintiff has otherwise done all that could reasonably be expected to establish such a case, then the burden of proof shifts to the defendant to prove that his conduct was not in fact an actual cause of the plaintiff's loss. * * *

4. 264 F. 334 (2d Cir.1920).

found that "but for" the defendant's negligent omission the deceased would not have died.

Now if deterrence is the rationale behind the "but for" rule, the *Grimstad* result is wrong because, whether or not the defendant's conduct caused the loss, had liability been imposed the defendant would have understood it was being imposed because of his doing a tortious act, that is, because of his having engaged in a socially undesirable, risk creating act. That would have provided the deterrence, except for the possible dysfunctional effect which might have arisen because the defendant might have felt it "unjust" to hold him liable without adequate proof of actual cause. Aside from this consideration, however, the objective of deterrence would seem to have little to do with "but for" cause.

Consider though what might have happened in *Grimstad* if the law had not required proof of actual cause, but only proof of tortious conduct by the defendant (towards anyone) and proof of compensable loss by the plaintiff (loss of her husband's financial support). Mrs. Grimstad could then have sued, say a negligent cab driver (and his employer), and recovered simply upon proof of his negligence and her loss. Having been negligent, the cab driver is fairly in need of deterrence; having him understand he was being required to pay Mrs. Grimstad because of that negligence would provide the deterrence. I have little doubt that if the tort law were to abandon the "but for" rule, the risks of tort liability would become so much greater that the tort law would have a far greater, rather than lesser, deterrent effect on human behavior.

The theory of enterprise liability suggests a more plausible explanation for the "but for" rule. Suppose, not being burdened by a "but for" rule, Mrs. Grimstad was allowed to shift her loss to the negligent cab driver who in no way was a "but for" cause of her otherwise compensable loss. Who, ultimately, would pay for the loss? The likely answer is the cab owners (through smaller profits), the cab drivers (through lower wages), or the cab users (through higher fares). In any event, a significant distortion would occur in the pricing mechanism of the market place as it relates to cab services, with a consequent distortion in the "best" allocation of the community's total, limited resources.

While the general statement of the theory of enterprise liability does not tell us from among all the infinite "but for" causes which may have brought about the plaintiff's loss *which particular* "but for" activity or enterprise the loss should be assigned to, it does tell us we ought not assign it to an activity which had no "but for" causal relationship with that particular loss at all.[5]

---

5. For one court's recognition of the proposition that rules of "but for" cause do have an impact on the allocation of resources and the distribution of wealth, and that therefore such matters should be taken into account, particularly the "fairness" question of who ultimately should bear the costs of tort-like losses, see Haft v. Lone Palm Hotel, 3 Cal.3d 756, 478 P.2d 465, 91 Cal.Rptr. 745 (1970). In justification of the exception to the normal rules of "but for" cause which the court was articulating (see note 38 *supra* for the rule), the court observed:

This result is also consistent with the emerging tort policy of assigning liability to

POSNER, STRICT LIABILITY: A COMMENT
2 J.Legal Studies 205–212 (1973).

Within the last year there have appeared several major articles[1] that, while otherwise extremely diverse, share a strong preference (in one case implicit) for using the principle of "strict liability" to resolve legal conflicts over resource use.[2] I shall argue in this comment that the authors of these articles fail to make a convincing case for strict liability, primarily because they do not analyze the economic consequences of the principle correctly.

I

To explicate these consequences I shall use the now familiar example of the railroad engine that emits sparks which damage crops along the railroad's right of way. I shall assume that the costs of transactions between the railroad and the farmers are so high that the liability imposed by the law will not be shifted by negotiations between the parties.

The economic goal of liability rules in such a case is to maximize the joint value of the interfering activities, railroading and farming.[3] To identify the value-maximizing solution requires a comparison of the costs to the railroad of taking steps to reduce spark emissions to various levels, including zero, and the costs to farmers of either tolerating or themselves taking steps to reduce the damage to their property from the sparks. The value-maximizing solution may turn out to involve changes by both parties in their present behavior; for example, the railroad may have to install a good but not perfect spark arrester and the farmer may

---

a party who is in the best position to distribute losses over a group which should reasonably bear them. See generally Calabresi, *Some Thoughts on Risk Distribution and the Law of Torts* (1961) 70 Yale L.J. 499. In the instant case the defendant motel owner, and more generally the entire class of those who frequent defendants' motel, were, in an economic view, the beneficiaries of the "cost savings" accompanying the non-employment of a lifeguard. It is better that this entire group bear the burden of the loss resulting from the "economy," rather than to require one particular guest to absorb the entire loss. By assigning liability to the motel in those cases in which no direct evidence establishes causation, we make sure that all motel guests bear their fair share of these damages, since the motel owner is likely to treat either the costs of liability insurance, or the actual costs of litigation, as a direct expense of its business and establish its fees accordingly.

Id. at 775 n. 20, 478 P.2d at 477 n. 20, 91 Cal.Rptr. at 757 n. 20.

1. William F. Baxter & Lillian R. Altree, Legal Aspects of Airport Noise, 15 J.Law & Econ. 1 (1972); Guido Calabresi & Jon T. Hirschoff, Toward a Test for Strict Liability in Torts, 81 Yale L.J. 1055 (1972); George P. Fletcher, Fairness and Utility in Tort Theory, 85 Harv.L.Rev. 537 (1972); Richard A. Epstein, A Theory of Strict Liability, 2 J.Leg. Studies 151 (1973). My analysis is also an implicit criticism of Marc A. Franklin, Tort Liability for Hepatitis: An Analysis and Appraisal, 24 Stan.L.Rev. 439 (1972), especially *id.* at 462–64, and of much judicial writing on the subject; *see, e.g.,* Escola v. Coca–Cola Bottling Co., 24 Cal.2d 453, 462, 150 P.2d 436, 440–41 (1944) (Traynor, J., concurring).

2. The concept of strict liability is a various one, but at its core is the notion that one who injures another should be held liable whether or not the injurer was negligent or otherwise at fault.

3. Or, stated otherwise, to maximize the joint value of the railroad's right of way and the farmer's land.

have to leave an unplanted buffer space between the railroad right of way and his tilled fields. Or, the value-maximizing solution may involve changes by the railroad only, by the farmer only, or by neither party.

Let us consider what, if any, different effects negligence and strict liability—competing approaches to the design of liability rules—might have in nudging railroad and farmer toward the value-maximizing (efficient) solution, under various assumptions as to what that solution is.

The railroad will be adjudged negligent if the crop damage exceeds the cost to the railroad of avoiding that damage.[4] But the farmer will still not prevail if the cost of the measures *he* might have taken to avoid the damage to his crops is less than the crop damage; this is the rule of contributory negligence.

If the efficient solution requires only that the railroad take some measure to reduce the farmer's crop damage, then the negligence approach leads us toward the efficient solution. Since the railroad is liable for the damage and the damage is greater than the cost to the railroad of preventing it,[5] the railroad will adopt the preventive measure in order to avoid a larger damage judgment. If the efficient solution is either that the railroad do nothing or that both parties do nothing, the negligence standard will again lead to the efficient solution. Not being liable, the railroad will have no incentive to adopt preventive measures; the farmer will have no incentive to take precautions either, since by hypothesis the cost of doing so would exceed the crop damage that he suffers. If the efficient solution requires only the farmer to take precautions, the negligence approach again points in the right direction. The railroad is not liable and does not take precautions. The farmer takes precautions, as we want him to do, because they cost less than the crop damage they prevent.

That leaves only the case where the efficient solution involves avoidance by both parties. Again the negligence standard should lead toward an efficient solution. The farmer will adopt his cost-justified avoidance measure so as not to be barred by the contributory negligence rule and once he has done so the railroad will adopt its cost-justified avoidance measure to avoid liability for the accidents that the farmer's measure does not prevent.

The foregoing discussion must be qualified in one important respect. If the efficient solution requires only the railroad to take precautions but the farmer could take a precaution that, although more costly than the railroad's (otherwise *it* would be the optimum solution), would be less costly than the crop damage, the farmer's failure to adopt the measure

---

4. The meaning of negligence is explored in Richard A. Posner, A Theory of Negligence, 1 J.Leg. Studies 29 (1972). The example in text assumes that the probability of the damage occurring is one; the assumption is not essential to the analysis. It also assumes that the only possibilities are no crops or no sparks; this assumption, which is again not essential to the analysis, will be relaxed.

5. If the cost of prevention exceeded the damage cost, prevention would not be the efficient solution. The efficient solution would be to permit the damage to take place.

will, nonetheless, be deemed contributory negligence. He will therefore adopt it and the railroad will have no incentive to adopt what is in fact the cheaper method of damage prevention.

A principle of strict liability, with no defense of contributory negligence, would produce an efficient solution where that solution was either for the railroad alone to take precautions or for neither party to do so,[6] but not in the other two cases. In the case where the efficient solution is for the farmer alone to take avoidance measures, strict liability would not encourage efficiency, for with the railroad liable for all crop damage the farmer would have no incentive to avoid such damage even if it was cheaper for him to do so; he would be indifferent between the crops and compensation for their destruction. Similarly, in the case where the efficient solution consists of precautions by both railroad and farmer, strict liability would give the farmer no incentive to shoulder his share of the responsibility. But we need only add a defense of contributory negligence in strict liability cases in order to give the farmer an incentive to take precautions where appropriate. There would still be the problem of inefficient solutions where the farmer's precaution, although less costly than his crop damage, was more costly than the railroad's precaution; but this could be remedied by redefining the contributory negligence defense—a step that should be taken in any event.

At least as a first approximation, then, a strict liability standard with a defense of contributory negligence is as efficient as the conventional negligence standard, but not more efficient. This conclusion would appear to hold with even greater force where, as in a products liability case, there is (or can readily be created) a seller-buyer relationship between injurer and victim. Indeed, it can be shown that in that situation an efficient solution is likely to be reached not only under either strict liability (plus contributory negligence) or negligence, but equally with no tort liability at all.

The cost of a possibly dangerous product to the consumer has two elements: the price of the product and an expected accident cost (for a risk-neutral purchaser, the cost of an accident if it occurs multiplied by the probability of occurrence). Regardless of liability, the seller will have an incentive to adopt any cost-justified precaution, because, by lowering the total cost of the product to the buyer, it will enable the seller to increase his profit.[7] Where, however, the buyer can prevent the accident at lower cost than the seller, the buyer can be counted on to take the

---

6. In the first case, the railroad would be liable and would have an incentive to adopt the precaution. In the second case, the railroad would still be liable but it would have no incentive to adopt precautions; it would prefer to pay a judgment cost that by hypothesis would be lower than the cost of the precautions.

7. Suppose the price of a product is $10 and the expected accident cost 10¢; then the total cost to the (risk-neutral) consumer is $10.10. If the producer can reduce the expected accident cost to 5¢—say at a cost of 3¢ to himself—then he can increase the price of the product to $10.05, since the cost to the (risk-neutral) consumer remains the same. Thus his profit per unit is increased by 2¢. (In fact, he will be able to increase his total profits even more by raising price less.) The extra profit will eventually be bid away by competition from producers but that is in the nature of competitive advantages.

precaution rather than the seller, for by doing so the buyer will minimize the sum of the price of the product (which will include the cost of any precautions taken by the seller) and the expected accident cost.[8]

Although both strict liability and negligence appear to provide efficient solutions to problems of conflicting resource uses, they do not have identical economic effects. The difference comes in cases where the efficient solution is for neither party to the interference to do anything. This is the category of interferences known in negligence law as "unavoidable accidents." They are rarely unavoidable in the literal sense. But frequently the cost either to injurer or to victim of taking measures to prevent an accident exceeds the expected accident cost and in such a case efficiency requires that the accident be permitted to occur. Under a negligence standard, the injurer is not liable; under strict liability, he is. What if any economic difference does this make?

It can be argued that unless an industry is liable for its unavoidable accidents, consumers may be led to substitute the product of the industry for the safer product of another industry. Suppose the only difference between railroads and canals as methods of transportation were that railroads had more unavoidable accidents. If the railroad industry were not liable for those accidents, the price of railroad transportation would be the same as the price of transportation by canal, yet we would want people to use canals rather than railroads because the former were superior in the one respect—safety—in which the two methods differed. In principle, a negligence standard would require the railroad to bear the cost of those accidents. They are not unavoidable. In fact, they could be avoided at zero cost by the substitution of canal for railroad transportation. But perhaps courts are incapable of making inter-industry comparisons in applying the negligence standard. Nonetheless the argument affords no basis for preferring strict liability to negligence, since an identical but opposite distortion is created by strict liability. Compare two different tracts of land that are identical in every respect except that one is immediately adjacent to a railroad line and one is well back from any railroad line. If the railroad is strictly liable for crop damage inflicted by engine sparks there will be no incentive to use the tract near the railroad line for fire-insensitive uses and to shift the growing of flammable crops to the tract that is remote from a railroad line, even though such a rearrangement may eliminate all crop damage at zero cost.

A related misconception involves the question of the comparative safety level in the long run under strict liability versus negligence liability. The level of safety is unaffected in the short run by which liability rule is chosen. Even if the injurer is strictly liable, he will not try to prevent an accident where the cost of prevention exceeds the accident cost; he will prefer to pay the victim's smaller damages. Howev-

---

8. This is actually a more efficient solution than either negligence or strict liability, since it avoids the problem we noted earlier of the law's economically incorrect definition of contributory negligence. * * *

er, he will have an incentive to invest in research and development efforts designed to develop a cost-justified method of accident prevention, for such a method would lower the cost of complying with a rule of strict liability. It is tempting to conclude that strict liability encourages higher, and in the long run more efficient, levels of safety, but this is incorrect. Rather than creating an incentive to engage in research on safety, a rule of strict liability merely shifts that incentive. Under the negligence standard the cost of unavoidable accidents is borne by the victims of accidents. They can reduce this cost in the long run by financing research into and development of cost-justified measures by which to protect themselves. The victims will not themselves organize for research, but they will provide the market for firms specializing in the development of new safety appliances.[9]

Let us consider some other possible differences, in economic effect, between strict liability and negligence. It might appear that strict liability would reduce the costs of tort litigation, both by simplifying the issues in a trial and thereby reducing its costs and by removing an element of uncertainty and thereby facilitating settlements, which are cheaper than trials. But the matter is more complex than this. By increasing the scope of liability, strict liability enlarges the universe of claims, so even if the fraction of cases that go to trial is smaller the absolute number may be larger. And, by increasing the certainty that the plaintiff will prevail, strict liability encourages him to spend more money on the litigation; conceivably, therefore, the costs of trials might actually increase.[10]

Under strict liability, in effect the railroad (in our example) insures the farmer against the loss of his crops; under negligence liability, the farmer must obtain and pay for insurance himself (or self-insure). Thus, although strict liability, under the name "enterprise liability," has long been defended on the ground[11] that it permits accident losses to be spread more widely, there is little to this argument: the farmer can avoid a concentrated loss by insuring. However, if we were confident that the cost of insuring was lower for the railroad than for the farmer, we might on this ground prefer strict liability.[12]

9. In principle, the costs of research should be included in the basic negligence calculus; in practice, we may assume they are not.

10. On the determinants of the choice to litigate rather than to settle and of expenditures on litigation see Richard A. Posner, The Behavior of Administrative Agencies, 1 J.Leg. Studies 305–23 (1972); see also William M. Landes, An Economic Analysis of the Courts, 14 J. Law & Econ. 61 (1971).

11. Not an economic ground. See Richard A. Posner, Book Review, 37 U.Chi. L.Rev. 643 (1970).

12. The farmer may not want to insure; he may be a risk preferrer. A risk preferrer is someone who likes to take chances. He will pay $1 for a lottery ticket although the prize is $1000 and his chances of winning only one in 2000. And he may prefer to accept a one one-thousandth chance of a $1000 loss rather than pay $1 to insure against the loss. He will be especially hostile to the idea of paying $1.10 for that insurance, a more realistic example since insurance involves administrative expenses that consume a part of the premium. Hence, if many farmers are risk preferring and do not want insurance, the benefits of strict liability, as perceived by them, may be slight.

Strict liability increases the costs of railroading, in our example, and negligence the costs of farming. But the implications for the overall distribution of income and wealth are uncertain, at least in the example, so intertwined were the economic interests of railroads and farmers during the period when the modern system of negligence liability was taking shape. Any increase in the cost of railroading would be borne in significant part by farmers since they were the railroads' principal customers. The intertwining of economic interests is characteristic of many modern tort contexts as well, such as automobile and product accidents. Most victims of automobile accidents are owners of automobiles; victims of defective products are also consumers.

Additional considerations come into play where there is a buyer-seller relationship between victim and injurer; but they relate primarily to the question whether sellers' liability (either strict liability or negligence) has different consequences from no liability (*i.e.,* buyers' liability). There are two reasons for believing that there might be different safety consequences. First, if the buyers of a product are risk preferring, they may be unwilling to pay for a safety improvement even if the cost is less than the expected accident cost that the improvement would eliminate. Under a rule of no liability, the improvement will not be made; under a rule either of strict liability or of negligence liability, the improvement will be made.[13] But the higher level of safety is not optimum in the economic sense, since it is higher than consumers want.

Second, consumers may lack knowledge of product safety. Criticisms of market processes based on the consumer's lack of information are often superficial, because they ignore the fact that competition among sellers generates information about the products sold. There is however a special consideration in the case of safety information: the firm that advertises that its product is safer than a competitor's may plant fears in the minds of potential consumers where none existed before. If a product hazard is small, or perhaps great but for some reason not widely known (*e.g.,* cigarettes, for a long time), consumers may not be aware of it. In these circumstances a seller may be reluctant to advertise a safety improvement, because the advertisement will contain an implicit representation that the product is hazardous (otherwise, the improvement would be without value). He must balance the additional sales that he may gain from his rivals by convincing consumers that his product is safer than theirs against the sales that he may lose by disclosing to consumers that the product contains hazards of which they may not have been aware, or may have been only dimly aware. If advertising and marketing a safety improvement are thus discouraged, the incentive to adopt such improvements is reduced. But make the producer liable for the consequences of a hazardous product, and no question of advertising safety improvements to consumers will arise. He will adopt cost-justified

---

13. This assumes that the producer cannot disclaim liability; the effect of a disclaimer is to shift liability to the consumer.

precautions not to divert sales from competitors but to minimize liability to injured consumers.

In principle, we need not assume that the only possible sources of information about product safety are the manufacturers of the product. Producers in other industries would stand to gain from exposing an unsafe product, but if their products are not close substitutes for the unsafe product, as is implicit in our designation of them as members of other industries, the gain will be small and the incentive to invest money in investigating the safety of the product and disseminating the results of the investigation slight. Firms could of course try to sell product information directly to consumers; the problem is that because property rights in information are relatively undeveloped, the supplier of information is frequently unable to recover his investment in obtaining and communicating it.

The information problem just discussed provides an arguable basis for rejecting *caveat emptor* in hazardous-products cases, but not for replacing negligence with strict liability in such cases, which is the trend of the law. The traditional pockets of strict liability, such as respondeat superior and the liability of blasters and of keepers of vicious animals, can be viewed as special applications of negligence theory.[14] The question whether a general substitution of strict for negligence liability would improve efficiency seems at this stage hopelessly conjectural; the question is at bottom empirical and the empirical work has not been done.

R. POSNER, ECONOMIC ANALYSIS OF LAW
178 (6th Ed. 2003).

And yet there are significant economic differences between negligence and strict liability. Think back to our distinction between more care and less activity as methods of reducing the probability of an accident. One way to avoid an auto accident is to drive more slowly; another is to drive less. But rarely do courts in a negligence case try to determine the optimal level of the activity that gives rise to an accident; they do not ask, when a driver is in an accident, whether the benefit of the particular trip (maybe he was driving to the grocery store to get some gourmet food for his pet iguana) was equal to or greater than the costs, including the expected accident cost to other users of the road; or whether driving was really cheaper than walking or taking the train when all social costs are reckoned in. Such a judgment is too difficult for a court to make in an ordinary tort case. Only if the benefits of the activity are obviously very slight, as where a man runs into a burning building to retrieve an old hat and does so as carefully as he can in the circumstances but is seriously burned nonetheless, will the court find that engaging in the activity was itself negligence, even though once the decision to engage in the activity was made, the actor (plaintiff or defendant) conducted himself with all possible skill and circumspection.

14. See * * * Richard A. Posner, *supra* note 4, at 42–44, 76.

SHAVELL, STRICT LIABILITY VERSUS NEGLIGENCE
9 J.Legal Studies 1, 2–9 (1980).

UNILATERAL CASE

This case (as well as the bilateral case) will be considered in each of several situations distinguished by the nature of the relationship between injurers and victims.

*Accidents between strangers * * *:* In this subcase it is supposed that injurers and victims are strangers, that neither are sellers of a product, and that injurers may choose to engage in an activity which puts victims at risk.

By definition, under the negligence rule all that an injurer needs to do to avoid the possibility of liability is to make sure to exercise due care if he engages in his activity.[1] Consequently *he will not be motivated to consider the effect on accident losses of his choice of whether to engage in his activity or, more generally, of the level at which to engage in his activity;* he will choose his level of activity in accordance only with the personal benefits so derived. But surely any increase in his level of activity will typically raise expected accident losses (holding constant the level of care). Thus he will be led to choose too high a level of activity;[2] the negligence rule is not "efficient."

Consider by way of illustration the problem of pedestrian-automobile accidents (and, as we are now discussing the unilateral case, let us imagine the behavior of pedestrians to be fixed). Suppose that drivers of automobiles find it in their interest to adhere to the standard of due care but that the possibility of accidents is not thereby eliminated. Then, in deciding how much to drive, they will contemplate only the enjoyment they get from doing so. Because (as they exercise due care) they will not be liable for harm suffered by pedestrians, drivers will not take into account that going more miles will mean a higher expected number of accidents. Hence, there will be too much driving; an individual will, for example, decide to go for a drive on a mere whim despite the imposition of a positive expected cost to pedestrians.

However, under a rule of strict liability, the situation is different. Because an injurer must pay for losses whenever he is involved in an accident,[3] he will be induced to consider the effect on accident losses of both his level of care *and* his level of activity. His decisions will therefore be efficient. Because drivers will be liable for losses sustained by pedes-

---

1. It is assumed for ease of exposition that courts have no difficulty in determining if a party did in fact exercise due care; the reader will have no trouble in appropriately modifying the arguments to be made so as to take into account relaxation of such simplifications as this.

2. Specifically, while he will choose to engage in the activity just up to the level at which the personal benefit from a marginal increase would equal zero, it would be best from society's viewpoint for him to engage in the activity only up to the level at which his benefit from a marginal increase would equal the (positive) social marginal cost in terms of accident losses.

3. Causal or other reasons for limiting the scope of liability are ignored.

trians, they will decide not only to exercise due care in driving but also to drive only when the utility gained from it outweighs expected liability payments to pedestrians.

*Accidents between sellers and strangers * * ***: In this subcase it is assumed that injurers are sellers of a product or service and that they conduct their business in a competitive market. (The assumption of competition allows us to ignore monopoly power, which is for the purposes of this article a logically tangential issue). Moreover, it is assumed that victims are strangers; they have no market relationship with sellers either as their customers or as their employees.

Under the negligence rule the outcome is inefficient, but the reasoning is slightly different from that of the last subcase. While it is still true that all a seller must do to avoid liability is to take due care, why this results in too high a level of activity has to do with market forces. Because the seller will choose to avoid liability, the price of his product will not reflect the accident losses associated with production. This means that buyers of the product will face too low a price and will purchase too much, which is to say that the seller's level of activity will be too high. Imagine that the drivers are engaged in some business activity—let us say that they are taxi drivers. Then, given that they take due care, the taxi drivers will not have liability expenses, will set rates equal to "production" cost (competition among taxi drivers is assumed), will experience a greater demand than if rates were appropriately higher, and will therefore carry too many fares and cause too many accidents.

Under strict liability, the outcome is efficient, and again the reasoning is a little different from that in the last subcase. Since sellers have to pay for accident losses, they will be led to take the right level of care. And since the product price will reflect accident losses, customers will face the "socially correct" price for the product; purchases will therefore be appropriately lower than what they would be if the product price did not reflect accident losses. Taxi drivers will now increase rates by an amount equal to expected accident losses suffered by pedestrians, and the demand for rides in taxis will fall.

*Accidents between sellers and customers—or employees * * ***: It is presumed here that victims have a market relationship with sellers as either their customers or their employees; and since both situations are essentially the same, it will suffice to discuss only that when victims are customers. In order to understand the role (which is important) of customers' knowledge of risk, three alternative assumptions will be considered: customers know the risk presented by each seller; they do not know the risk presented by each seller but they do know the average seller's risk;[4] they misperceive even this average risk.

---

4. If sellers are assumed to be identical (as they are in the formal model) and therefore to act identically, the average risk will in fact be the risk presented by each seller. But it will be seen from the discussion of the situation when sellers are not liable that the first and second assumptions are nevertheless different.

Under the negligence rule, the outcome is efficient only if customers correctly perceive risks. As before, when the victims were strangers, sellers will take due care in order to avoid liability, so that the product price will not reflect accident losses. However, now the accident losses are borne by the customers. Thus, the "full" price in the eyes of customers is the market price plus imputed perceived accident losses. Therefore, if risks are correctly perceived, the full price equals the socially correct price, and the quantity purchased will be appropriate. But if risks are not correctly perceived, the quantity purchased will be inappropriate; if customers underestimate risks, what they regard as the full price is less than the true full price and they will buy too much of the product, and conversely if they overestimate risks.[5]

Think, for example, of the risk of food poisoning from eating at restaurants. Under the negligence rule, restaurants will decide to avoid liability by taking appropriate precautions to prepare meals under sanitary conditions. Therefore, the price of meals will not reflect the expected losses due to the (remaining) risk of food poisoning. If customers know this risk, they will correctly consider it in their decisions over the purchase of meals. But if they underestimate the risk, they will purchase too many meals; and if they overestimate it, too few.

Under strict liability, the outcome is efficient regardless of whether customers misperceive risks. As in the last subcase, because sellers have to pay for accident losses, they will decide to take appropriate care and will sell the product at a price reflecting accident losses. Thus customers will face the socially correct price and will purchase the correct amount. Their perception of the risk is irrelevant since it will not influence their purchases; as they will be compensated under strict liability for any losses, the likelihood of losses will not matter to them. Restaurant-goers will face a price that reflects expected losses due to food poisoning when meals are prepared under sanitary conditions; they will buy the same—and appropriate—number of meals whether they think the probability of food poisoning is low or high, for they will be compensated for any losses suffered.[6]

When sellers are simply not liable for accident losses, then the outcome is efficient only if customers know the risk presented by each seller. For, given this assumption, because customers will seek to buy

---

5. It may be instructive to mention the parallel situation in regard to employee victims. If employees correctly perceive risks at the workplace, then they will (appropriately) choose to work for a firm only if the "net" wage—the market wage less the expected accident losses they bear—is at least equal to their opportunity elsewhere. But if, say, they underestimate risks, they might choose to work for a firm when the net wage is in fact below their opportunity elsewhere.

6. However, it is worthwhile noticing that if they could not possibly be compensated for a kind of loss from food poisoning, then misperception of risk certainly would matter. For instance, if there were a risk of death from food poisoning and if restaurant-goers underestimated it, then they would expose themselves to a higher risk of death by eating restaurant meals than they would truly want to bear. Thus, the conclusion of this paragraph that misperception of risk does not matter under strict liability holds only in respect to risks compensable by payment of money damages.

products with the lowest full price (market price plus expected accident losses), sellers will be induced to take appropriate care (since this will lower the accident-loss component of the full price). While it is true that if a restaurant took inadequate precautions to prevent food poisoning, it could offer lower-priced meals, it is also true that customers would respond not just to the market price of meals but also to the likelihood of food poisoning—which they are presumed to know. Therefore customers would decide against giving the restaurant their business. Consequently, restaurants will be led to take adequate precautions and to charge accordingly. Moreover, because customers will base purchases on the correctly perceived full price, they will buy the correct amount.

If, however, customers do not know the risk presented by individual sellers, there are two sources of inefficiency when sellers are not liable. The first is that, given the risk of loss, the quantity purchased by customers may not be correct; of course, this will be true if customers misperceive the risk. The second source of inefficiency is that sellers will not be motivated by market forces to appropriately reduce risks. To understand why, consider the situation when customers do correctly perceive the average risk (when they do not correctly perceive this risk, an explanation similar to the one given here could be supplied). That is, assume that customers know the risk presented by sellers as a group but do not have the ability to "observe" the risk presented by sellers on an individual basis. Then sellers would have no inducement to exercise adequate care. Suppose that restaurant-goers know the risk of food poisoning at restaurants in general and it is, say, inappropriately high. Then if a *particular* restaurant were to take sufficient precautions to lower the risk, customers would not recognize this (except insofar as it eventually affected the average risk—but under the assumption that there are many competing restaurants, this effect would be negligible). Thus the restaurant could not charge a higher price for its meals—customers would have no reason not to go to the cheaper restaurants. In consequence, a situation in which sellers take inadequate care to reduce risks would persist; and similar reasoning shows that a situation in which they take adequate care would not persist. (Notice, however, that since customers are assumed to correctly perceive the average risk, at least they will purchase the correct number of meals—correct, given the high risk.)

Finally, it should be observed that the discussion of liability in the present subcase bears on the role of tort law in a contractual setting. When customers make purchases, they are willingly entering into a kind of contract—in which they agree to a price and pay it, receive goods, and expose themselves to a risk (in the absence of liability).[7] Therefore, our

---

7. It should be remarked that the possibility of contractual arrangements that go beyond mere agreement on price is not considered here; for example, the possibility that sellers might give customers some form of guarantee is not allowed for in the discussion or in the analysis. However, our conclusions do have some relevance to what contractual arrangements might be made. This is because what is "efficient" is, by definition, what maximizes benefits minus costs, which is in turn what is in the mutu-

conclusions may be generally expressed by the statement that, when customers' knowledge of risks is perfect, the rule of liability does not matter; the "contractual" arrangement arrived at in the market is appropriate. But when the knowledge is not perfect, there is generally scope for the use of liability, and the relative performance of liability rules depends on the precise nature of the imperfection in knowledge. The force of this point, and the fact that it is not always an obvious one, is perhaps well illustrated by the situation described in the previous paragraph. In that situation, customers did correctly perceive average risk, so that there was "assumption of risk," but this did not lead to a desirable result. The situation was one therefore in which, under our assumptions, courts ought not to allow the defense of assumption of risk to be successfully asserted.

BILATERAL CASE

In this case, account is taken of the possibility that potential victims as well as injurers may influence the probability or magnitude of accident losses by their choice of both level of care and of level of activity.

Accidents between strangers * * *:[8] Under the negligence rule,[9] the outcome is not efficient. As was true in the unilateral case, since all that an injurer needs to do to avoid liability is to exercise due care, he will choose too high a level of activity. In regard to victims, however, the situation is different. Since a victim bears his accident losses, he will choose an appropriate level of care *and* an appropriate level of his activity, given the (inefficient) behavior of injurers. The drivers will exercise due care but will go too many miles. And the pedestrians, knowing that they must bear accident losses, will exercise due care (in crossing streets and so forth) and they will also reduce the number of miles they walk in accordance with expected accident losses per mile.

Under strict liability with a defense of contributory negligence, the outcome is symmetrical to the last—and again inefficient.[10] Because all

al interest of the sellers and customers to do. (To illustrate, if customers *realize* that they do not know the risk of loss, then they might wish for, and insist on, a blanket guarantee, in effect making the seller strictly liable, and thereby giving him an incentive to reduce the risk of loss.) Of course, the reason this is not considered here is that a satisfactory treatment would require us to study at the least the value of explicit arrangements over the arrangements that inhere in the applicable tort and contract law, the costs of making explicit arrangements as opposed to the expected costs of reliance on the applicable law, and the willingness of courts to enforce what is at variance with the applicable law.

8. The explanation given in this and in the next subcase for why neither strict liability with a defense of contributory negligence nor the negligence rule results in an efficient outcome is in its essence that given by Richard Posner, Economic Analysis of Law 139–40 (2d ed. 1977). See also Duncan Kennedy, A History of Law and Economics or the Fetishism of Commodities (1979) (unpublished mimeographed paper at Harvard University) which makes related points at 54–63.

9. In the present discussion, it will make no difference whether or not the reader thinks of this rule as incorporating the defense of contributory negligence.

10. It is of course clear that under strict liability without the defense the outcome is inefficient, for victims would have no motive to take care.

that a victim needs to do to avoid bearing accident losses is to take due care, he will have no motive to appropriately reduce *his* level of activity; this is the inefficiency. However, because injurers now bear accident losses, they will take the appropriate amount of care and choose the right level of activity, given the inefficient behavior of victims. Drivers will exercise due care and go the correct number of miles. Pedestrians will also exercise due care but will walk too many miles.

From this discussion it is apparent that the choice between strict liability with a defense of contributory negligence and the negligence rule is a choice between the lesser of two evils. Strict liability with the defense will be superior to the negligence rule when it is more important that injurers be given an incentive through a liability rule to reduce their activity level than that victims be given a similar incentive; that is to say, when it is more important that drivers go fewer miles than that pedestrians walk fewer miles.

Because neither of the familiar liability rules induces efficient behavior, the question arises, "*Is there any conceivable liability rule depending on parties' levels of care and harm done that induces efficient behavior?* " * * * The answer is "*No.*" The problem in essence is that for injurers to be induced to choose the correct level of activity, they must bear all accident losses; and for victims to choose the correct level of their activity, they also must bear all accident losses. Yet it is in the nature of a liability rule that both conditions cannot hold simultaneously; clearly, injurers and victims cannot each bear all accident losses.[11]

Accidents between sellers and strangers * * *: Because the reader will be able to appeal to arguments analogous to those already made and in order to avoid tedious repetition, explanation of the results stated in this and the next subcase will be abbreviated or will be omitted.

Under both the negligence rule and strict liability with a defense of contributory negligence, the outcome is inefficient, as was true in the last subcase. Under the negligence rule, sellers will take appropriate care, but since the product price will not reflect accident losses, too much will be purchased by customers. Also, since victims bear accident losses, they will take appropriate care and choose the right level of activity. Under strict liability with the defense, sellers will take appropriate care and the product price will reflect accident losses, so the right amount will be purchased. Victims will exercise due care but will choose too high a level of activity. In addition, as in the last subcase, there does not exist any liability rule that induces efficient behavior.

Accidents between sellers and customers—or employees * * *: As before it will be enough to discuss here only the situation when victims are customers. If customers have perfect knowledge of the risk presented by each seller, then the outcome is efficient under strict liability with a

---

11. However, when other means of social control are also employed, it is possible to achieve an efficient outcome. For example, if use of the negligence rule were supplemented by imposition of a tax on the level of injurer activity, an efficient outcome could be achieved.

defense of contributory negligence or the negligence rule or if sellers are not subject to liability at all. For instance, in the latter situation, since customers wish to buy at the lowest full price, sellers will be led to take appropriate care; and since customers will make their purchases with the full price in mind, the quantity they buy will be correct; and since they bear their losses, they will take appropriate care.

There is, however, a qualification that needs to be made concerning the way in which it is imagined that customers influence accident losses. If one assumes that customers influence losses only by their choice of level of care and of the amount purchased, then what was stated in the previous paragraph is correct; and in regard to services and nondurables (such as meals at restaurants) this assumption seems entirely natural. But in regard to durable goods, it might well be thought that customers influence accident losses not only by their choice of level of care and of purchases, but also by their decision as to frequency of use per unit purchased. The expected number of accidents that a man will have when using a power lawn mower would seem to be influenced not only by whether he in fact purchases one (rather than, say, a hand mower) and by how carefully he mows his lawn with it, but also by how frequently he chooses to mow his lawn. In order for customers to be led to efficiently decide the frequency of use, they must bear their own accident losses. Thus, in regard to durables, the outcome is efficient under the negligence rule or if sellers are not liable, but the outcome is inefficient under strict liability with a defense of contributory negligence; for then if the man buys a power lawn mower, he will have no motive to appropriately reduce the number of times he mows his lawn.

Now suppose that customers correctly perceive only average risks. Then, subject again to a qualification concerning durables, the results are as follows. The outcome is efficient under strict liability with a defense of contributory negligence or under the negligence rule, but the outcome is not efficient if sellers are not liable, for then they will not take sufficient care. The qualification is that if the sellers produce durables, strict liability with the defense is inefficient, leaving the negligence rule as the only efficient rule.

Last, suppose that customers misperceive risks. Then the outcome is efficient only under strict liability with a defense of contributory negligence; and the qualification to this is that, if sellers produce durables, even strict liability with the defense is inefficient, so that there does not exist a liability rule which is efficient.

POWERS, A MODEST PROPOSAL TO ABANDON STRICT PRODUCTS LIABILITY
1991 U.Ill.L.Rev. 639, 644–651.

Courts have relied on various rationales to support strict products liability. One rationale for strict products liability is that it promotes product safety by requiring manufacturers to bear accident costs, thus giving manufacturers an incentive to produce safer products. This argument is controversial even on its own terms. It is debatable, both analytically and empirically, whether strict liability increases product safety, much less whether it tends to *optimize* product safety. More important for the present inquiry, however, is that this argument fails to distinguish between product injuries and other personal injuries. Strict liability also could be used to transform the cost of automobile accidents into a cost of driving, thereby providing an incentive for safety.[1] Incentives for safety might support strict liability generally (depending on the empirical evidence), but they do not explain the *selective* application of strict liability to product injuries.

A second common rationale for strict products liability is that it helps internalize accident costs into the price of products, thereby spreading a victim's loss among an entire group of consumers. Even if this is a desirable goal, which is itself controversial, it is not a goal that is specific to product injuries. Strict liability could also spread losses from nonproduct accidents. For example, losses from automobile accidents that are not currently covered by negligence could be spread through strict liability and nearly universal liability insurance.[2] Indeed, losses from disease and natural disaster seem to be as worthy of spreading as losses from product injuries, solely from the perspective of spreading risks.

Equally telling in the present context is that, although the argument for spreading risks is as powerful for injuries caused by nondefective products, courts uniformly deny recovery in these cases. Although the rhetoric of risk spreading is often used to support strict products liability for victims of defective products, it does not actually justify the selective

---

1. We might distinguish product cases from nonproduct cases on the basis that a liability rule has *less* impact on product manufacturers than on nonproduct tort-feasors. In transactions that are subject to market forces, we might be less concerned with an allocative inefficiency created by a liability rule because the parties can bargain their way back to an efficient result. For example, entitlements given to real property owners permit them to use their land frivolously, but they "pay" the price of foregoing a sale or rental at a value reflecting the more efficient use.

To the extent that strict liability is theoretically inefficient, it might be more tolerable in product cases in which a market can mitigate the inefficiency. The absence of a market among strangers prevents a similar mitigation of inefficiency in automobile accidents. Consequently, we might insist on a theoretically more efficient liability rule, such as negligence. *See generally* R. H. Coase, *The Problem of Social Cost*, 3 J.L. & Econ. 1 (1960); William C. Powers, Jr., *A Methodological Perspective on the Duty to Act*, 57 Tex. L. Rev. 523, 529 & n.21 (1979) (reviewing Marshall S. Shapo, The Duty to Act: Tort Law, Power, & Public Policy (1977)). No court has relied on this distinction, possibly because the *actual* impact of liability rules and markets on behavior is too uncertain, regardless of the theoretical models.

2. Strict liability for product injuries spreads losses by raising a product's price. Strict liability for automobile accidents would spread losses by raising liability insurance rates. The current system of automobile insurance spreads losses only if they are caused by negligent drivers, except for the meager level of first-party coverage.

Another argument for giving product injuries special treatment is that, unlike victims of automobile injuries, victims of product injuries do not have insurance. Consequently, they need another mechanism for spreading losses. One response to this argument is that people could insure against product injuries. Moreover, people typically do not insure against most types of loss through first-party automobile insurance.

use of strict liability for victims of defective products in the context of a system that declines to use strict liability for other injuries, including injuries from nondefective products.

A third rationale for strict products liability reflects strict products liability's warranty heritage: defective products frustrate consumer expectations. Especially in early cases, courts relied on consumer expectations created by general assurances of safety and quality that were found in advertising or that were inherent in the mere fact that a product was placed on the market. The emphasis on consumer expectations has waned, however, both as a test of defectiveness and as a reason for liability. One problem with this rationale is that it is difficult to ascertain consumer expectations in all but the simplest cases. Moreover, consumer expectations fail to explain why courts should treat products differently than services. Consequently, courts have been willing to free products liability from its warranty moorings.

I will have more to say about consumer expectations when I address defectiveness in Part III. The point there will be that in most product cases—especially cases not involving manufacturing defects—consumer expectations do not provide a meaningful test of defect and therefore do not provide an adequate ground for strict products liability. In *some* cases, however, consumer expectations may be sufficiently concrete to support liability, and to the extent that the manufacturer created these expectations, they provide a reason for distinguishing product cases. Though defendants in other personal injury cases may also create expectations—such as drivers creating an expectation of following the rules of the road—expectations created in a sales situation may warrant special treatment.

Nevertheless, consumer expectations have limitations as a ground for strict products liability. In most cases, consumer expectations are too vague; in those in which they are not, strict products liability is not a necessary response. Consumer expectations are likely to be well formed only in cases involving manufacturing defects or in cases involving explicit or implicit representations by manufacturers. I already have stated that negligence law can accommodate cases involving manufacturing defects. Similarly, the law of warranty or misrepresentation adequately can address cases involving real representations, either explicit or implicit. These solutions do not have as a by-product the problems inherent in maintaining strict products liability as a separate cause of action—that is, problems created by treating *all* product cases separately, simply because they involve products.

A fourth rationale for strict products liability is that it places the burden of injuries on manufacturers who are in a better position to prevent injury, "rather than [on] the injured persons who are powerless to protect themselves."[3] This rationale is itself controversial, but even

---

3. [Greenman v. Yuba Power Prods., Inc., 59 Cal.2d 57, 27 Cal.Rptr. 697, 701, 377 P.2d 897, 901 (1963)].

more important, it does not distinguish product injuries from other types of personal injuries. Victims of automobile accidents are often "powerless" to protect themselves, and the tort-feasor is in a better position to prevent the loss. Indeed, in consumer transactions the victim often has had at least the opportunity to select the manufacturer, a choice not usually given to the victim of an automobile accident.

A fifth rationale of strict products liability is that fairness requires a manufacturer to compensate victims because the manufacturer deliberately has imposed risks on consumers for its own benefit. Similar arguments have been used to explain tort liability generally, and therein lies its weakness as a justification for special treatment of product injuries. Motorists deliberately impose risks on pedestrians for the motorists' own benefit, yet we do not impose liability on motorists absent proof of negligence.

A final rationale for strict products liability is that plaintiffs face an unduly difficult burden of proving specific acts of negligence in product cases. The "proof" rationale for strict products liability does not necessarily deny that fault is the underlying motivation for liability. Instead, it posits that negligence is a common cause of defective products and that a plaintiff's inability to *prove* negligence is more likely to be a consequence of the difficulty of proof than of the manufacturer's actual freedom from negligence.[4] Proving negligence is difficult in any personal injury case. Witnesses might give conflicting accounts of the events, and the mechanism of the injury might have been destroyed in the accident. The problem of proof is more acute in product cases, however, because the alleged negligence normally occurred at a place controlled by the defendant and at a time before the plaintiff had any connection with the defendant or the product. These conditions *sometimes* exist in non-product cases, such as when a motorist fails to maintain his brakes adequately, but product injuries present this problem more acutely than other types of injuries. Consequently, courts can make a principled argument for relieving plaintiffs of the burden of proving negligence in

---

4. Other arguments might be constructed to support strict tort liability. For example, strict products liability might rest on an argument similar to unit pricing in supermarkets. If accident costs are reflected in a product's price, they are more visible to consumers, although the actual cost of the product (including risk) is unchanged. The increased visibility of actual product costs might help consumers shop comparatively and make better allocative decisions. The problem with this argument is that, like the risk-spreading argument, it is incompatible with the requirement of defectiveness. Of course, this could be remedied by dropping the requirement of defectiveness, but that solution is very unlikely. Moreover, no court has actually relied on this argument.

Another possible rationale is that strict tort liability avoids technical obstacles (such as timely notice) that plaintiffs face under the Uniform Commercial Code. *See* Greenman v. Yuba Power Prods., Inc., 377 P.2d 897, 899 (Cal.1963). It is difficult to take this argument seriously, however, because the obvious solution is to amend the UCC. Furthermore, this rationale does not itself explain the existence of implied warranties in the Code.

Sometimes we will find "smoke without fire," but experience and intuition might suggest that defectiveness implies negligence more often than not, even when the plaintiff cannot prove it. The plaintiff's failure might simply be due to the acute problems of proof presented by a product injury.

product cases while requiring proof of negligence in other types of personal injury cases.

The "proof" rationale is especially attractive because it harmonizes specific internal features of strict products liability in a way that the other rationales do not. For example, the "unavoidable danger" and "state-of-the-art" "defenses" are grounded implicitly on a judgment that we could not have expected the manufacturer to have made the product safer. (Risk spreading does not explain these defenses, because these risks are as worthy of spreading as any other risks.) Notwithstanding the normal inference of negligence from defectiveness, we are not convinced that a manufacturer was negligent in cases involving "unavoidable dangers" or "state-of-the-art" technology. The plaintiff's failure to prove negligence in these cases is not due to mere problems of proof.

Unlike some other rationales, the proof rationale is also consistent with courts' refusal to compensate victims of nondefective products. A defect raises a much stronger inference of negligence than does a mere injury. Moreover, while defectiveness is not always easy to prove, a plaintiff at least has contemporaneous access to the product itself, mitigating the special problems of proving specific acts of negligence in the manufacturing process.[5]

The proof rationale is important not because it necessarily represents good policy, but because it is the one rationale that offers at least a plausible reason to distinguish product injuries from other personal injuries. For this reason, I will give it close attention throughout the article. Nevertheless, it has problems of its own as a foundation for strict products liability. First, it may have been a stronger rationale when courts first adopted strict products liability than it is today. Discovery techniques have improved, the plaintiffs' bar has become more sophisti-

---

5. * * * The "proof" rationale can be generalized into an argument that includes other concerns about the litigation process. Requiring plaintiffs to prove negligence has the risk of creating too many false negatives, that is, cases in which a plaintiff is unable to prove negligence even though the defendant actually was negligent. But it also consumes resources, including the time and effort of parties and the court. The uncertainty of the outcome also diffuses the regulatory effect this body of law has on persons whose conduct we want to influence. It may be that these "administrative" considerations are more important in product cases than other personal injury cases.

Landes and Posner rely on concerns of this sort to explain strict liability for products based on long-term economic efficiency. [William M. Landes & Richard A. Posner, The Economic Structure of Tort Law 273–311 (1987)]; *see also* [William Powers, Jr., *On Positive Theories of Tort Law*, 66 Tex. L. Rev. 191, 205–11 (1987)]. Ultimately, the force of this argument depends on empirical data, but three initial observations are in order. First, courts have not, in fact, relied on an expanded "administrative" argument of this sort. Second, it is not at all clear why these "administrative" concerns (other than the fear of false negatives) should be more acute in a product case. Third, and most important, they depend mainly on differences between negligence and true strict liability, which, as a true entitlement system, would be more predictable and easier to apply. *See* Powers, [*A Methodological Perspective on the Duty to Act*, 57 Tex. L. Rev. 523, 534–36 (1979)]. But as we shall see in the next part, strict products liability is not a system of true strict liability. By depending on a jury finding of defectiveness, it lacks the formal clarity necessary to reap the administrative advantages this argument envisions.

cated, and trial courts may be more willing to permit juries to draw inferences of negligence from circumstantial evidence.

Second, the proof rationale applies only to manufacturing defects (flaws). It does not apply to design defects or warnings. In a case involving a manufacturing defect, the offending product is different from other products in the line. We may never know why. But a design defect or warning is common to all products in the line. They were the result of design decisions that are as susceptible to documentation and discovery as any other business decision. While the proof rationale distinguishes cases involving manufacturing defects from other personal injury cases, it also distinguishes them from other product cases. Third, to the extent the proof rationale does support special treatment of cases involving flaws, permitting the jury to draw an inference of negligence from the existence of a flaw, creating a presumption of negligence, or holding that flaws constitute negligence *per se* can all remedy proof problems. Doing so would keep product cases within the framework of negligence law and avoid certain problems that I will address below. The proof rationale does offer some support for distinguishing some product cases—cases involving manufacturing defects—from other personal injury cases. But that problem is so easily remedied within negligence law that it does not, on balance, provide an adequate basis for giving special treatment to *all* product cases under an independent cause of action.

In short, the rationales courts have offered to justify strict products liability do not adequately support a distinction between product cases and other personal injury cases. The proof rationale and consumer expectations offer some support for distinguishing *some* product cases from other personal injury cases, but they do not apply to most product cases as an integral group, and they can be satisfied by other means.[6]

---

6. A different type of argument, however, might be advanced in favor of strict products liability. Why should we make such a fuss about consistency? We would prefer, the proponent might argue, to apply strict liability (or some other version of expanded liability) to all personal injury cases. But as a political matter, we have been able to prevail only in product cases. At a deep level, law can never be perfectly rational, so we should accept this distinction as one of many inevitable, arbitrary compromises among social interests. After all, half a loaf is better than none; perfection is often an enemy of goodness. In fact, if we do not like the distinction between strict products liability and negligence, we should argue for applying strict liability to other cases, not for abandoning it in product cases.

There are several responses to this line of argument. First, it is true that my argument has attacked only the *distinction* between using strict liability in product cases and using negligence in other cases. I believe strict liability in other cases would be unworkable and pernicious; if a uniform theory is applied to all cases, it should be negligence. Moreover, applying strict liability to other cases is not politically feasible. But all of this is another matter. It is true that my real objection is the distinction between product cases and other cases.

Second, the distinction between product cases and other personal injury cases is not *merely* a failure in coherence. As I will demonstrate below, it affirmatively generates pernicious consequences. The effort to maintain the distinction has itself created serious problems, as we shall see. Sometimes half a loaf is not better than none.

Third, I agree that law cannot be perfectly rationalized. Sometimes courts (or society) must pick certain areas for reform because reform cannot take place everywhere at once. For example, advocates of universal social accident insurance may not be able to implement such a scheme everywhere, so they might try to begin with one area, such as automobile accidents, workplace accidents, or medical accidents. It is not clear, however, why pragmatic considerations such as this are applicable to strict products liability as a common law doctrine. Moreover, lack of coherence, in the sense that plausible reasons do not support important doctrinal distinctions, should at least count against a doctrinal scheme, even if it does not *ipso facto* condemn the scheme. For an interesting discussion of this issue, see [Ronald Dworkin, Law's Empire 177–90 (1986)].

At the very least, careful analysis of the reasons usually given to support strict products liability reveals that they are not as powerful as they seem. In fact, some courts have held that it is an unconstitutional violation of equal protection to distinguish between product cases and other personal injury cases when giving defendants relief through tort reform legislation. [Citation] While I do not endorse this conclusion as a matter of constitutional mandate, it does reflect the theme of this part: It is difficult to justify a distinction between product cases and other personal injury cases. * * *

Chapter 4

DEFECT

SECTION A.   INTRODUCTION

The key to understanding modern products liability law is to recognize the nature of the restriction on the scope of liability that results from the requirement that the product be defective in order to give rise to liability. Logically, courts could have adopted a regime holding product manufacturers strictly liable for all harm caused by their products. Yet, strict products liability in the United States evolved in a much more restrictive way, imposing "strict" liability only for "defective" products. Defect has become the core concept upon which liability turns. The same policy questions that are handled in negligence cases as a matter of "breach of duty" are handled in strict liability cases as a matter of "defect." It follows that how courts define defect, and how they apply that definition, has vitally important policy implications. Perhaps equally important is which party is assigned the burden of proving the various issues created by the definition of defect. Courts have developed several tests for determining when products are defective. This Chapter examines those tests, the policies underlying them, and the burden of proving them.

A product defect can be one of three types, and courts often employ different tests of defect depending on the type. First, a product can have a manufacturing defect. This is an unintended flaw in the product. Usually, only a small percentage of a manufacturer's products contain manufacturing defects. Such defects are easy to identify because the product differs from other similar products in the line.

Second, a product can be defective because it was improperly designed. The theory is that the manufacturer should have adopted a different design—perhaps an additional safety feature—that would have reduced the risk of accidental injury.

Third, a product can be defective because it is not accompanied by an adequate warning. Many products present risks even when properly designed. The dangers can often be minimized, however, if such products are accompanied by adequate warnings and instructions for use. Without such warnings and instructions, these products are defective.

86

Design and warning defects present more difficult problems than manufacturing defects. For one thing, it is harder to identify when such products are defective. Some external standard is needed because these products cannot be identified as being defective by simply comparing them to the manufacturer's other products. In addition, the repercussions of declaring that a product is defective because of its design or a failure to warn are more serious for the manufacturer. The determination condemns all products in the line rather than an isolated few.

The following three sections of this Chapter cover manufacturing defects, design defects, and warning defects respectively. Chapter 6 covers the kinds of evidence that may be used to prove that products are defective. As you read these cases you will see that the lines between the types of defect are sometimes blurred, and the determination of defectiveness is often complex. There is no single rule that applies in all cases. Jurisdictions vary widely as to the approach used. Furthermore, even within a given jurisdiction, the approach used often varies over time and according to type of defect.

SECTION B. MANUFACTURING DEFECTS

LEE v. ELECTRIC MOTOR DIVISION

Court of Appeals of California, Second District, 1985.
169 Cal.App.3d 375, 215 Cal.Rptr. 195.

THOMPSON, ASSOCIATE JUSTICE.

Plaintiffs Yong Lee and In Hak Lee appeal the adverse summary judgment granted on their consolidated actions seeking to impose liability for personal injury and loss of consortium against defendant component part manufacturer, Electric Motor Division, an unincorporated division of Gould, Inc., who manufactured and supplied the motor installed in the machine that injured Yong Lee.

* * *

Plaintiff Yong Lee was injured on January 15, 1979, while using the machine to grind meat. Her right hand was caught and crushed in the grinding mechanism, resulting in the amputation of her right hand and part of her forearm.

Plaintiffs filed their respective consolidated complaints for personal injury and loss of consortium based on theories of negligent design, manufacture and failure to warn, strict liability, and breach of warranty, against several parties, including defendant and Lasar.

Defendant's motion for summary judgment was granted on August 30, 1983. Summary judgment was filed on September 16, 1983, and notice was duly served and filed. Plaintiffs appeal from the summary judgment.

We will conclude that no triable issue of fact exists, and affirm the summary judgment.

* * *

Discussion

Plaintiffs contend that the defective design and manufacture of the motor and the lack of a warning proximately caused Yong Lee's injury because had the motor stopped immediately when turned off, her injuries would have been less severe.

* * *

Although plaintiffs have phrased their complaints in terms of both defective manufacture and design, they have not properly alleged a cause of action based on a manufacturing defect. A manufacturing defect is readily identifiable in general, because the defective product is one that "comes off the assembly line in a substandard condition" in comparison with the other identical units. (*Barker, supra,* 20 Cal.3d at p. 429, 143 Cal.Rptr. 225, 573 P.2d 443.) Plaintiffs do not contend that the motor, as compared to the other identically manufactured motors, came off the assembly line in a substandard condition. Hence, we find that defendant is entitled to summary judgment as a matter of law on the causes of action based on the allegation of defective manufacture.

* * *

The summary judgment is affirmed.

LILLIE, P.J., and JOHNSON, J., concur.

Notes

1. California has approved the following jury instruction for manufacturing defect cases:

The essential elements of a claim based upon an alleged manufacturing defect are:

    1. The defendant was the (manufacturer, supplier, etc.) of a product, namely _____ (identify the product);

    2. The product possessed a defect in its manufacture;

    3. The defect in manufacture existed when the product left the defendant's possession;

    4. The defect in manufacture was a cause of injury to the plaintiff; and

    5. Plaintiff's injury resulted from a use of the product that was reasonably foreseeable to the defendant[s].

A defect in the manufacture of a product exists if the product differs from the manufacturer's intended result or if the product differs from apparently identical products from the same manufacturer.

BAJI 9.00.3 (1994 Revision).

2. Section 2 of the Restatement (Third) of Torts: Products Liability provides:

§ 2. Categories of Product Defect

A product is defective when, at the time of sale or distribution, it contains a manufacturing defect, is defective in design, or is defective because of inadequate instructions or warnings. A product:

(a) contains a manufacturing defect when the product departs from its intended design even though all possible care was exercised in the preparation and marketing of the product; * * *

* * *

Comment:

   a. Rationale. * * * The rule for manufacturing defects stated in Subsection (a) imposes liability whether or not the manufacturer's quality control efforts satisfy standards of reasonableness. Strict liability without fault in this context is generally believed to foster several objectives. On the premise that tort law serves the instrumental function of creating safety incentives, imposing strict liability on manufacturers for harm caused by manufacturing defects encourages greater investment in product safety than does a regime of fault-based liability under which, as a practical matter, sellers may escape their appropriate share of responsibility. Some courts and commentators also have said that strict liability discourages the consumption of defective products by causing the purchase price of products to reflect, more than would a rule of negligence, the costs of defects. And by eliminating the issue of manufacturer fault from plaintiff's case, strict liability reduces the transaction costs involved in litigating that issue.

   Several important fairness concerns are also believed to support manufacturers' liability for manufacturing defects even if the plaintiff is unable to show that the manufacturer's quality control fails to meet risk-utility norms. In many cases manufacturing defects are in fact caused by manufacturer negligence but plaintiffs have difficulty proving it. Strict liability therefore performs a function similar to the concept of res ipsa loquitur, allowing deserving plaintiffs to succeed notwithstanding what would otherwise be difficult or insuperable problems of proof. Products that malfunction due to manufacturing defects disappoint reasonable expectations of product performance. Because manufacturers invest in quality control at consciously chosen levels, their knowledge that a predictable number of flawed products will enter the marketplace entails an element of deliberation about the amount of injury that will result from their activity. Finally, many believe that consumers who benefit from products without suffering harm should share, through increases in the prices charged for those products, the burden of unavoidable injury costs that result from manufacturing defects.

* * *

3. The Restatement of Torts (Second) § 402A(2)(a) (1965) provides that the seller of a product "in a defective condition unreasonably dangerous" is liable for physical harm even if it has "exercised all possible care in the preparation" of its product. With respect to their treatment of manufacturing flaws, therefore, both Restatements regard negligence by the seller as unnecessary for liability.

4. Some jurisdictions apply the consumer expectations test of defect in manufacturing defect cases and the risk-utility test in design defect cases. See Ford Motor Co. v. Pool, 688 S.W.2d 879 (Tex.App. 1985), affirmed in part and reversed in part on other grounds, 715 S.W.2d 629 (1986). The court stated:

> There are two different definitions of defectiveness for use in products liability cases in Texas. In cases involving manufacturing defects, defectiveness is defined according to a consumer expectancy test * * *. In design defect cases, defective design must be defined according to the risk-utility test * * *.
>
> * * *
>
> The two definitions reflect the differences between the theories of recovery underlying manufacturing and design defect cases. The application of Section 402A of the Restatement (Second) of Torts (1965) to cases involving not only flawed products, but also to perfectly made but ill-designed products, has necessarily divided what was ostensibly a single theory of liability into two distinct theories. The distinction arises partly because of the inherent difference between the analysis centered on a flawed product and a product defectively designed.
>
> Manufacturing defect cases involve products which are flawed, i.e., which do not conform to the manufacturer's own specifications, and are not identical to their mass-produced siblings. The flaw theory is based upon a fundamental consumer expectancy: that a mass-produced product will not differ from its siblings in a manner that makes it more dangerous than the others. Defective design cases, however, are not based on consumer expectancy, but on the manufacturer's design of a product which makes it unreasonably dangerous, even though not flawed in its manufacture. See Powers, The Persistence of Fault in Products Liability, 61 Texas L.Rev. 777 (1983); Keeton, Product Liability and the Meaning of Defect, 5 St. Mary's L.J. 30 (1973). * * *

688 S.W.2d at 881. See also Dart v. Wiebe Manufacturing, Inc., 147 Ariz. 242, 709 P.2d 876 (1985); Bilotta v. Kelley Co., Inc., 346 N.W.2d 616 (Minn.1984).

5. In Wiseman v. Goodyear Tire & Rubber Co., 29 Wash.App. 883, 631 P.2d 976 (1981) plaintiff was injured in a motor vehicle accident involving a blowout. He sued the tire manufacturer claiming that a flaw in the tire caused the blowout. The jury found for defendant after being instructed that they must find that the tire was both 1) defective and 2) unreasonably dangerous. Plaintiff appealed, claiming that the judge erred by requiring the jury to find both elements. He should, instead, have required the jury to find only that the tire was defective. Plaintiff relied on Seattle–First National Bank v. Tabert, 86 Wash.2d 145, 542 P.2d 774 (1975) (en banc), holding that in a design defect case plaintiff need not prove both defect and unreasonable danger because a product that is "unreasonably dangerous" is "necessarily defective." The court ruled against plaintiff, stating:

> In effect, [Plaintiff] urges us to state the converse of Tabert as the law, namely, that if a product has a manufacturing defect, it must necessarily be unreasonably dangerous. We decline to do so. Although

there is some validity in equating the two concepts in a design defect case, *see Seattle–First National Bank v. Tabert, supra* at 151, the connection between defect in a product and unreasonable danger from the product assumes a different meaning in a manufacturing defect case. * * * Some products defectively manufactured are still reasonably safe for the consumer. A car with an inadequate heater is defective but not unreasonably dangerous; a defective toaster which always chars bread is not unreasonably dangerous; a defective television set which receives only half the channels because of frequency limitations is not unreasonably unsafe. Thus, in order for a product to be defective in a manufacturing sense, it must be "'in a condition not contemplated by the ultimate consumer, [and] which [is] unreasonably dangerous to him.'" Bombardi v. Pochel's Appliance & TV Co., 10 Wash.App. 243, 246, 518 P.2d 202 (1973), citing Restatement (Second) of Torts § 402A, comment g at 351 (1965); *see* Curtiss v. YMCA, 82 Wash.2d 455, 511 P.2d 991 (1973). * * *

29 Wash.App. at 887–88, 631 P.2d at 979–80.

6. We have seen that in manufacturing flaw cases, liability is truly strict. The inability to discover the flaw by using reasonable care is no excuse. The economic justification for strict liability in such cases is set out in the following article.

LANDES AND POSNER, A POSITIVE ECONOMIC ANALYSIS OF PRODUCTS LIABILITY

14 J. Legal Stud. 535, 555–56 (1985).

* * *

2. *Process Failure.* Here the concept of strict liability has bite, as it does not in the defective design setting. Take the case where the cost-justified level of hygiene in a soft-drink plant allows mouse parts to get into one in every million bottles. By assumption there is no negligence; yet the bottle that contains the mouse parts is "defective" as a matter of products liability law, and if the consumer is made ill, the manufacturer will be liable. This result makes economic sense, however, because of the asymmetrical position of the manufacturer and the consumer with regard to avoiding this type of accident. The consumer can do nothing at reasonable cost, in the short or long run, to prevent the accident. It is out of the question that he should minutely inspect each soda bottle on the one in a million chance that it contains mouse parts. (Of course, if he does notice the mouse parts and drinks the soda anyway, he would be barred by assumption of risk from obtaining damages.) But while by assumption there is nothing cost justified the manufacturer can do *at present* to reduce the probability of the accident (otherwise he would be negligent), advances in technology may someday enable him to reduce it at a lower cost than the benefit in reducing expected accident costs. Under a negligence standard the manufacturer will simply wait till the technology is developed; strict liability will give him an incentive to foster its development. True, it will simultaneously reduce the incentive of the consumer (or of businesses that might sell to the consumer) to

develop better inspection methods, but it is a reasonable guess that preserving such an incentive would lead nowhere. In addition, strict liability will result in a small price increase (to cover the cost of the occasional tort judgment), which will in turn result in a small reduction in output and in a substitution by consumers of other, safer products.

It is true that, to a perfectly informed consumer, the price increase resulting from strict liability would not be a net cost. It would just offset the benefit he would be receiving from shifting to the manufacturer the cost of injuries caused by the product; the full cost of the product to the consumer (the price adjusted for any expected accident cost he bears) would be unchanged. But now the point recurs that it does not pay consumers to obtain information about small product risks. Suppose that in making his purchasing decisions the consumer will treat minute risks as zero risks; that is, they will not affect his decisions. This is not because of any psychological peculiarity but simply because it does not pay to figure out and possibly take measures against extremely remote contingencies. Then in a world of no liability output will exceed the optimal output (see equation (5)), and the manufacturer will not have an incentive to take due care. Shifting to strict liability will result in a price increase to cover the manufacturer's expected products liability costs, and the higher price will be perceived by the consumer as an increase in the full cost of the product (because he does not realize that the price increase is compensating him for an expected accident cost), and there will be some substitution away from the product. Thus, as noted earlier, the information about risk is impounded in the higher price and "communicated" to the consumer in a form that he can understand without investing in costly information. Finally, because the manufacturer aggregates the expected accident costs of all his present and future customers, an imperceptible cost to the individual consumer becomes a noticeable cost to the manufacturer, inducing him to look for ways of making long-run improvements in safety.

The process just described illustrates our earlier point that strict liability is a sensible rule when one wants to influence the level of the potential injurer's activity. Assuming that the costs of information are much higher to the buyer than to the seller, a negligence rule would not give the buyer the correct incentive to substitute away from the product. A rule of strict liability, by inducing the seller to sell less, automatically reduces the buyer's purchases. The only way to induce a change in the mutual activity of seller and buyer is to give the seller an incentive to change the activity level, and strict liability does that.

3. *Component Defect or Failure.* The analysis here is similar to that of process failure. The consumer can do little to detect a failure in a component of the product he buys. The manufacturer of the final product, though by definition not negligent in failing to detect the defect in the component (if he were, again there would be no need to invoke a distinctive body of products liability law), is less helpless than the consumer. The manufacturer can identify the component that failed more easily than the consumer can, and can take appropriate action,

legal or business, against the supplier of the component. He can also raise his price to cover potential liability costs and so induce substitution by the consumer away from products that have this hazard. And he has an incentive to explore long-run improvements in inspecting for component defects.

HUNT v. FERGUSON–PAULUS ENTERPRISES
Supreme Court of Oregon, Department 2, 1966.
243 Or. 546, 415 P.2d 13.

LUSK, J.

The plaintiff bought a cherry pie from the defendant through a vending machine owned and maintained by the defendant. On biting into the pie one of plaintiff's teeth was broken when it encountered a cherry pit. He brought this action to recover damages for the injury, alleging breach of warranty of fitness of the pie for human consumption. In a trial to the court without a jury the court found for the defendant and plaintiff has appealed.

Plaintiff assigns error to the court's failure to sustain his objection to a general finding entered in favor of the defendant and to the court's refusal to enter special findings requested by the plaintiff [that plaintiff did not and a reasonable consumer would not] expect to find a pit in the cherry pie.

* * *

Under ORS 72.3150 if the cherry pie purchased by the plaintiff from the defendant was not reasonably fit for human consumption because of the presence of the cherry pit there was a breach of warranty and plaintiff was entitled to recover his damages thereby caused.

In the consideration of similar cases some of the courts have drawn a distinction between injury caused by spoiled, impure, or contaminated food or food containing a foreign substance, and injury caused by a substance natural to the product sold. In the latter class of cases, these courts hold there is no liability on the part of the dispenser of the food. Thus in the leading case of Mix v. Ingersoll Candy Co., 6 Cal.2d 674, 59 P.2d 144, the court held that a patron of a restaurant who ordered and paid for chicken pie, which contained a sharp sliver or fragment of chicken bone, and was injured as a result of swallowing the bone, had no cause of action against the restaurateur either for breach of warranty or negligence. Referring to cases in which recovery had been allowed the court said:

> "All of the cases are instances in which the food was found not to be reasonably fit for human consumption, either by reason of the presence of a foreign substance, or an impure and noxious condition of the food itself, such as for example, glass, stones, wires or nails in the food served, or tainted, decayed, diseased, or infected meats or vegetables."

The court went on to say that:

> "* * * despite the fact that a chicken bone may occasionally be encountered in a chicken pie, such chicken pie, in the absence of some further defect, is reasonably fit for human consumption. Bones which are natural to the type of meat served cannot legitimately be called a foreign substance, and a consumer who eats meat dishes ought to anticipate and be on his guard against the presence of such bones."

* * *

The so-called "foreign-natural" test of the *Mix* case has been applied in the following cases: Silva v. F.W. Woolworth Co., 28 Cal.App.2d 649, 83 P.2d 76 (turkey bone in "special plate" of roast turkey); Musso v. Picadilly Cafeterias, Inc. (La.App.), 178 So.2d 421 (cherry pit in a cherry pie); Courter v. Dilbert Bros., Inc., 19 Misc.2d 935, 186 N.Y.S.2d 334 (prune pit in prune butter); Adams v. Great Atlantic & Pacific Tea Co., 251 N.C. 565, 112 S.E.2d 92 (crystalized [sic] grain of corn in cornflakes); Webster v. Blue Ship Tea Room, Inc., 347 Mass. 421, 198 N.E.2d 309 (fish bone in a fish chowder).

Other courts have rejected the so-called foreign-natural test in favor of what is known as the "reasonable expectation" test, among them the Supreme Court of Wisconsin, which, in Betehia v. Cape Cod Corp., 10 Wis.2d 323, 103 N.W.2d 64, held that a person who was injured by a chicken bone in a chicken sandwich served to him in a restaurant, could recover for his injury either for breach of an implied warranty or for negligence. "There is a distinction," the court said, "between what a consumer expects to find in a fish stick and in a baked or fried fish, or in a chicken sandwich made from sliced white meat and in roast chicken. The test should be what is reasonably expected by the consumer in the food as served, not what might be natural to the ingredients of that food prior to preparation. What is to be reasonably expected by the consumer is a jury question in most cases; at least, we cannot say as a matter of law that a patron of a restaurant must expect a bone in a chicken sandwich either because chicken bones are occasionally found there or are natural to chicken." 10 Wis.2d at 331–332.

Among other decisions adopting the reasonable expectation test are: Bonenberger v. Pittsburgh Mercantile Co., 345 Pa. 559, 28 A.2d 913, 143 A.L.R. 1417, Annotation at page 1421 (oyster shell in canned oysters used in making oyster stew); Bryer v. Rath Packing Co., 221 Md. 105, 156 A.2d 442, 77 A.L.R.2d 1 (chicken bone in chow mein); Varone v. Calarco, 22 Misc.2d 1085, 199 N.Y.S.2d 755 (struvite in canned tuna).

* * *

The foreign-natural test is criticized in Dickerson, Products Liability and the Food Consumer 184–189, and in an article by Mitchel J. Ezer, "The Impact of the Uniform Commercial Code on the California Law of Sales Warranties," 8 UCLA California Law Review 281.

In view of the judgment for the defendant, we are not required in this case to make a choice between the two rules. Under the foreign-natural test the plaintiff would be barred from recovery as a matter of law. The reasonable expectation test calls for determination of a question of fact * * *. The court has found the fact in favor of the defendant and this court has no power to disturb the finding.

Plaintiff argues that the court based its decision on the foreign-natural rule. The court did so indicate in a letter to counsel announcing its decision, but in the same letter the court also spoke of what can be "reasonably anticipated and guarded against by the consumer" and said that the question was a "mixed question of law and facts." Further, the court, as above stated, refused to make a finding of fact requested by the plaintiff that the plaintiff "did not reasonably expect to find a pit in the cherry pie." The general finding entered by the court covered all the issues of fact in the case.

* * *

There are no other assignments of error and the judgment is affirmed.

Notes

1. The courts remain split over whether to apply the consumer expectations test or the foreign-natural test in impure food cases. The cases are collected in, Annotation, 2 A.L.R.5th 189 (1992). Most courts that decline to impose liability for natural substances found in food apply the rule regardless of whether the action is based on breach of warranty, negligence, or products liability.

2. Section 7 of the Restatement (Third) of Torts: Products Liability adopts the consumer expectations test, although consumer expectations were rejected as the test for defectiveness for all other types of product defect. The Restatement provides that a food product containing a "harm-causing ingredient" is defective in manufacture under § 2(a) [the section that defines manufacturing defects] if "a reasonable consumer would not expect the food product to contain that ingredient." Comment b. to section 7 explains the rationale for the use of the consumer expectations test in this context.

b. The special problem under § 2(a). When a plaintiff suffers harm due to the presence in food of foreign matter clearly not intended by the product seller, such as a pebble in a can of peas or the pre-sale spoilage of a jar of mayonnaise, the claim is readily treated under § 2(a), which deals with harm caused by manufacturing defects. Food product cases, however, sometimes present unique difficulties when it is unclear whether the ingredient that caused the plaintiff's harm is an unanticipated adulteration or is an inherent aspect of the product. For example, is a one-inch chicken bone in a chicken enchilada, or a fish bone in fish chowder, a manufacturing defect or, instead, an inherent aspect of the product? The analytical problem stems from the circumstance that food products in many instances do not have specific product designs that may be used as a basis for determining whether the offending product ingredient constitutes a departure from design, and is thus a manufacturing defect. Food recipes vary over time, within the same restaurant or other commercial food-preparation facility, from facility to facility, and from locale to locale.

Faced with this indeterminacy, some courts have attempted to rely on a distinction between "foreign" and "natural" characteristics of food products to determine liability. Under that distinction, liability attaches only if the alleged adulteration is foreign rather than natural to the product. Most courts have found this approach inadequate, however. Although a one-inch chicken bone may in some sense be "natural" to a chicken enchilada, depending on the context in which consumption takes place, the bone may still be unexpected by the reasonable consumer, who will not be able to avoid injury, thus rendering the product not reasonably safe. The majority view is that, in this circumstance of uncertainty, the issue of whether a food product containing a dangerous but arguably natural component is defective under § 2(a) is to be determined by reference to reasonable consumer expectations within the relevant context of consumption. A consumer expectations test in this context relies upon culturally defined, widely shared standards that food products ought to meet. Although consumer expectations are not adequate to supply a standard for defect in other contexts, assessments of what consumers have a right to expect in various commercial food preparations are sufficiently well-formed that judges and triers of fact can sensibly resolve whether liability should be imposed using this standard.

3. Jackson v. Nestle–Beich, Inc., 147 Ill.2d 408, 168 Ill.Dec. 147, 589 N.E.2d 547 (1992), affirming, 212 Ill.App.3d 296, 155 Ill.Dec. 508, 569 N.E.2d 1119 (1991) rejected the foreign-natural test in favor of the consumer expectations test. Justice Heiple dissented. He offered the following defense of the foreign-natural test:

> The majority opinion in the instant case discards the foreign-natural doctrine and substitutes the reasonable expectation test. * * *
>
> In truth, the reasonable expectation test is what gave rise to the foreign-natural doctrine. That is to say, since it would be reasonable to expect to find a nut shell in a product containing nuts, there would be no liability. Rather than approach each broken tooth or other injury on a case-by-case basis, it was deemed more expeditious and efficient to crystallize the matter into the foreign-natural doctrine. That doctrine both did justice and promoted judicial economy.
>
> A reversion to the reasonable expectation test simply means that each food-related injury in this State will be subject to a lawsuit to determine whether the consumer's reasonable expectation was violated. The costs will be significant, first to the manufacturers and second to the consuming public. It is axiomatic that all production costs eventually end up in the price of the product. Additionally, if the costs exceed profitability, the product leaves the market place altogether and the consumers lose choice, selection and availability of products.
>
> The effects of this decision will go far beyond the defendant Nestle–Beich Company, whose candy caused a broken tooth. It extends to all

manufacturers and purveyors of food products including the neighborhood baker, the hot dog vendor and the popcorn man. Watch out Orville Redenbacher!

The continued march towards strict and absolute liability for others (others meaning anyone not injured who has assets) and the absence of any responsibility by the injured for their own welfare takes yet another step with this majority ruling.

147 Ill.2d at 417, 168 Ill.Dec. at 152–53, 589 N.E.2d at 552–53.

4. California originated the foreign-natural test in Mix v. Ingersoll Candy Co., 6 Cal.2d 674, 59 P.2d 144 (1936). It modified the test in Mexicali Rose v. Superior Court (Clark), 1 Cal.4th 617, 4 Cal.Rptr.2d 145, 822 P.2d 1292 (1992), and adopted the following test:

> The strict foreign-natural test of *Mix, supra*, 6 Cal.2d 674, 59 P.2d 144, should be rejected as the exclusive test for determining liability when a substance natural to food injures a restaurant patron. We conclude instead that in deciding the liability of a restaurateur for injuries caused by harmful substances in food, the proper tests to be used by the trier of fact are as follows:
>
> If the injury-producing substance is natural to the preparation of the food served, it can be said that it was reasonably expected by its very nature and the food cannot be determined unfit or defective. A plaintiff in such a case has no cause of action in strict liability or implied warranty. If, however, the presence of the natural substance is due to a restaurateur's failure to exercise due care in food preparation, the injured patron may sue under a negligence theory.
>
> If the injury-causing substance is foreign to the food served, then the injured patron may also state a cause of action in implied warranty and strict liability, and the trier of fact will determine whether the substance (i) could be reasonably expected by the average consumer and (ii) rendered the food unfit or defective. * * *
>
> Thus, we conclude that to the extent *Mix* precludes a cause of action in negligence when injuries are caused by substances natural to the preparation of the food served, it is overruled.

4 Cal.Rptr.2d at 157–58, 822 P.2d at 1303–04.

5. California normally uses the "deviation from the norm" test of defect in manufacturing flaw cases. *See Lee v. Electric Motor Division, supra,* page 87. This test could be applied in food cases. Instead, the California court applies a specialized combination of the "foreign-natural" test and "consumer expectations" test in food cases. Why?

SECTION C. DESIGN DEFECTS

1. CONSUMER EXPECTATIONS

GRAY v. MANITOWOC CO., INC.
United States Court of Appeals, Fifth Circuit, 1985.
771 F.2d 866.

W. EUGENE DAVIS, CIRCUIT JUDGE:

Earnest M. Gray brought this action for injuries which he sustained when he was struck by the boom of a construction crane manufactured by defendant, The Manitowoc Company, Inc. (Manitowoc). Gray's wife, Hughlene Gray, joined in this action seeking damages for loss of consortium and companionship. The Grays sought recovery under Mississippi law on theories of strict liability, implied warranty and negligence asserting that Gray's injuries were caused by a defect in the design of the crane and that Manitowoc had provided inadequate warnings of this defect. After the jury returned a verdict for the Grays, Manitowoc moved for judgment notwithstanding the verdict and for a new trial, asserting that the Grays failed to establish either the existence of a defect or a breach of a duty to warn. The district court denied Manitowoc's motion and entered judgment for the Grays. We conclude that the evidence was insufficient to establish that the crane possessed a latent hazard, as required by Mississippi law, for recovery on any of the theories of liability presented by the Grays and, therefore, reverse.

I.

Gray was struck in two separate incidents by the butt end of the boom of a Manitowoc 4100W crane while working as an ironworker foreman on a construction project near Port Gibson, Mississippi. These incidents occurred while Gray's crew was changing sections of the crane's boom and had placed the boom in a plane roughly parallel to the ground (the "boom down" position). Gray was standing on the left side of the crane, supervising this operation, as the crane operator swung the lowered boom in Gray's direction, striking Gray in the back.

Testimony at trial established that the operator's vision to the left side of the Manitowoc crane is obscured by the boom when the crane is operated in the "boom down" position. To compensate for the operator's incomplete field of vision, users of cranes such as the 4100W place a signal-man at various locations on the ground to guide the operator. This procedure was followed by Gray's employer during both incidents in which Gray alleged that he was struck. Gray contends, however, that Manitowoc should have provided mirrors, closed circuit television cameras or other devices to enable the operator to see to the left side of the crane when the crane is operated in the "boom down" position. Gray asserts that had these safety devices been placed on the crane, the crane operator would have seen Gray standing on the left side of the boom and would have avoided hitting him with the boom.

Manitowoc responds that even if mirrors or other devices would have permitted the operator to observe the area on the left side of the crane, the omission of these devices did not render the crane defective. Manitowoc argues that the hazards of operating the crane in the boom down position were open and obvious to ordinary users of the crane and that Mississippi law does not permit recovery under any theory of products liability for a manufacturer's failure to correct such patent dangers.

* * *

III.

Under Mississippi's version of strict liability for hazardous products, manufacturers are not insurers of the products they produce; the existence of a product defect must be established before recovery may be obtained for a resulting injury. * * * Mississippi has adopted the following formulation of the doctrine of strict liability for product defects (as it applies to manufacturers) from *The Restatement (Second) of the Law of Torts*, § 402A(1) (1965): "One who sells any product in a defective condition unreasonably dangerous to the consumer or to his property is subject to liability for physical harm thereby caused to the ultimate user or consumer, or to his property. * * *" *Jackson v. Johns–Manville Sales Corp.*, 727 F.2d 506, 511 (5th Cir.1984), *reinstated en banc in relevant respects*, 750 F.2d 1314, 1317 (1985); *State Stove Manufacturing Co. v. Hodges*, 189 So.2d 113, 118 (Miss.1966), *cert. denied, sub nom. Yates v. Hodges*, 386 U.S. 912, 87 S.Ct. 860, 17 L.Ed.2d 784 (1967); *Ford Motor Co. v. Matthews*, 291 So.2d 169, 171 (Miss.1974).

Comment (g) to the Restatement § 402A defines the term "defective condition": "The rule stated in this Section applies only where the product is, at the time it leaves the seller's hands, in a condition not contemplated by the ultimate consumer, which will be unreasonably dangerous to him." Comment (i), in turn, gives substance to the phrase "unreasonably dangerous":

> The rule stated in this Section applies only where the defective condition of the product makes it unreasonably dangerous to the user or consumer. * * * The article sold must be dangerous to an extent beyond that which would be contemplated by the ordinary consumer who purchases it, with the ordinary knowledge common to the community as to its characteristics.

As these comments illustrate, the consumer expectation test of section 402A is rooted in the warranty remedies of contract law, and requires that harm and liability flow from a product characteristic that frustrates consumer expectations. *See* Keeton, *Product Liability and the Meaning of Defect*, 5 St. Mary's L.J. 30, 37 (1973).

In the seminal Mississippi case for strict liability for defective products, *State Stove,* 189 So.2d at 118, the Mississippi Supreme Court indicated that the patent danger bar adopted by the Restatement was incorporated into Mississippi's doctrine of strict liability. The court quoted the consumer expectation definition of defectiveness set forth in comment (g) to section 402A of the Restatement. In *Ford Motor Co.,* 291 So.2d 169, the Mississippi Supreme Court expounded on the concept of a product defect. The court quoted the relevant portions of comments (g) and (i) to the Restatement § 402A and also quoted the following passage from W. Prosser, *Handbook of the Law of Torts* § 99, at 659–60 (4th Ed.1971): "The prevailing interpretation of 'defective' is that the product does not meet the reasonable expectations of the ordinary consumer as to its safety."[1] Id. The *State Stove* and *Ford* courts' commitment to the consumer contemplation test for product defects has not been undermined by any subsequent decision of the Mississippi Supreme Court, nor have we discovered any reported decisions in which Mississippi courts or we have permitted recovery in strict liability for a patently dangerous product design. See *Page v. Barko Hydraulics,* 673 F.2d 134, 137–39 (5th Cir.1982).

We recognize that excluding patent hazards from the definition of a product design defect has been subject to much scholarly criticism, and has been rejected in a number of jurisdictions. Nonetheless, the patent danger bar was, until recent years, generally thought to be the prevailing rule in the various states and, in the face of scholarly criticism, has been reaffirmed in a number of jurisdictions.[2] In the absence of any sign that this rule has been, or would be, rejected by the Mississippi Supreme Court, we are bound to apply it in this case. See *Wansor v. George Hantscho Co., Inc.,* 595 F.2d 218, 220–21 and n. 7 (5th Cir.1979). Hence, we conclude that the Gray's right to recover under the theory of strict liability depends upon whether the evidence was sufficient to permit the jury to find that the 4100W crane was "dangerous to an extent not contemplated by the ordinary consumer who purchased it, with the ordinary knowledge common to the community as to its characteristics." See *Ford Motor Co.,* 291 So.2d at 169.

IV.

We are persuaded that the record does not support a finding that the blind spot in the 4100W was a latent hazard. The evidence was overwhelming that the existence of this blind spot was common knowl-

---

1. Dean Prosser expanded on the language quoted above. He explained that the existence of a requirement that a hazard disappoint the expectations of the ordinary consumer "is borne out by the cases of conditions 'natural' to food, such as a fish bone in a plate of chowder, or a cherry pit in cherry pie, which the ordinary consumer would expect to encounter, and against which he would normally take his own precautions." Prosser, Section 99 at 660. Dean Prosser continued in a footnote: "It is not the fact that the defect is a natural one which is important, but the fact that the ordinary consumer would expect that he might encounter it." Id. at 660 n. 76.

2. See, e.g., *Delvaux v. Ford Motor Co.,* 764 F.2d 469 (7th Cir.1985) (Wisconsin law); *Young v. Tide Craft, Inc.,* 270 S.C. 453, 242 S.E.2d 671 (1978).

edge in the construction industry. Gray's supervisor, testifying as Gray's witness, stated that the existence of a blind spot in the crane operator's field of vision had been widely discussed at the Grand Gulf job site. The business manager of Gray's union local, again testifying as Gray's witness, indicated that the left side of the 4100W crane was referred to as the "blind side". Indeed, the photographs and physical evidence introduced at trial plainly reveal that if a workman standing in the blind spot on the left side of the 4100W had attempted to look at the crane operator, he would have been unable to see him; the record suggests no reason why, in this circumstance, the workman should expect that the crane operator would be able to see him. Finally, uncontested evidence concerning the universal industry practice of using a signalman on the ground to guide operators of cranes clearly demonstrated a common awareness in the construction industry of both the limitation on the operator's field of vision inherent in the design of such cranes and the dangers posed by this limitation. Plaintiff adduced no evidence that manufacturers of other cranes of the vintage of the 4100W equipped them with mirrors, television cameras or other similar devices. Rather, the evidence showed that there was no such industry custom of providing such devices. Industry custom therefore could not serve as a basis for a consumer to expect a crane manufacturer to furnish such devices.

Balanced against this evidence favorable to Manitowoc was Gray's testimony that he did not learn of the blind spot until after his second accident and the testimony of one inexperienced co-worker of Gray's that he also was unaware of the blindspot. Under the *Boeing* standard, we must, of course, credit this testimony. Nonetheless, both the Restatement's theory of strict liability and Mississippi's theories of negligence and implied warranty require an objective appraisal of the obviousness of a product hazard.[3] See *Restatement*, § 402A, comment (i) (the product "must be dangerous to an extent beyond that which would be contemplated by the ordinary consumer who purchases it, with the ordinary knowledge common to the community as to its characteristics"); *Harrist*, 140 So.2d at 561 (defects were "apparent and obvious to a casual observer"). Gray and his inexperienced co-worker's testimony concerning their subjective ignorance has little significance to this objective inquiry. In light of the overwhelming evidence indicating that the existence of a blind spot in the 4100W was common knowledge in the construction trade, we must conclude that the testimony of Gray and his inexperienced co-worker did not create a jury question as to the knowledge or expectations of the *ordinary* observer or consumer. We conclude that no reasonable jury could have found that the blind spot of the Manitowoc 4100W was not open and obvious, nor could any reasonable jury have concluded that the 4100W was dangerous to a degree not anticipated by the ordinary consumer of that product.

3. Gray's actual ignorance or awareness of the crane's blind spot hazard would be dispositive only if an assumption of risk issue were before us. See *Alexander v. Conveyors & Dumpers, Inc.*, 731 F.2d 1221, 1223–24 (5th Cir.1984).

Since the Grays failed to establish that the Manitowoc 4100W crane was defectively designed under any proper theory of Mississippi law,[4] the district court erred in refusing to grant defendant's motion for judgment notwithstanding the verdict. We therefore

REVERSE and RENDER the judgment.

Manitowoc 4100W cranes in "boom up" position

4. With respect to the verdict on theories of negligence and implied warranty, no serious contention is made that Manitowoc might be liable on the ground that the 4100W crane did not function properly for its intended purpose. Like the meatgrinder which adequately ground meat in *Ward*, it is not disputed that this crane adequately performed the construction tasks for which it was designed. See *Ward*, 450 F.2d at 1180.

Manitowoc 4100W crane in "boom down" position

Notes

1. This is a traditional statement of the consumer expectations test in its most conservative form. Under the test there is no liability for obvious or generally known dangers. The test is objective. The court looks to the expectations of the ordinary person who uses the product, rather than the individual plaintiff, or the public generally. Thus, if workers who use a particular tool are generally aware of its dangers, it is not defective notwithstanding that the average member of the public would not know of them. *See* Woods v. Fruehauf Trailer Corp., 765 P.2d 770 (Okl.1988) (gasoline tanker manufacturer was not subject to strict liability for failing to equip tanker with an automatic shutoff on the nozzle because the ordinary persons who used it, experienced truck drivers, were fully aware of the risk of gasoline catching on fire).

2. Are the following products defective under the consumer expectations test?

    A. In an automobile rollover accident the driver is injured because the roof collapses.

    B. A special rotary lawn mower had a removable front blade guard so that the mower could be used to cut tall weeds along fence rows. The mower did not have a blade brake that would automatically stop the blade when the operator let go of the steering bars. While using the mower without the guard, the operator stopped cutting and walked in front of the running mower to move a barrel without first releasing the clutch controlling the blade. He slipped on freshly cut weeds and came into contact with the blade.

C. An extruding machine did not have a guard over the intake hopper. The operator's arm was amputated when material being fed into the extruder became wrapped around his arm and drew it into the moving parts of the machine.

D. A punch press did not have a safety guard. While the worker put his hand below the ram to clean out scraps of metal, without warning or activation by him, the ram suddenly descended and crushed his fingers.

E. A gas stove was equipped with one-motion burner controls rather than two-step or self-latching controls. The one-motion controls can easily be turned on by accidentally brushing against them. A very young child climbed on the stove. Her clothes caught fire when she accidentally turned on the burner.

F. A new drug which is very beneficial to a large number of people causes a serious side-effect in a small number of people. Plaintiff takes the drug and suffers the side-effect. Prior to plaintiff's illness, the risk was not known.

3. **Ignorance of Risk.** The consumer expectations test is concerned with the consumer's perception of risk, not the manufacturer's perception. Courts impose liability if the consumer is ignorant of the pertinent danger, but the manufacturer's justifiable ignorance of risk is no excuse. *See*, Green v. Smith & Nephew AHP, Inc., 245 Wis.2d 772, 629 N.W.2d 727, 2001 WI 109 (2001) (liability for allergy to latex gloves; justifiable ignorance by the health care community that persons could develop latex allergy is no excuse). In Morton v. Owens–Corning Fiberglas Corp., 33 Cal.App.4th 1529, 1535, 40 Cal.Rptr.2d 22, 24 (1995), a case involving cancer caused by asbestos, the court stated:

> [E]vidence as to what the scientific community knew about the dangers of asbestos and when they knew it is not relevant to show what the ordinary consumer of OCF's product reasonably expected in terms of safety at the time of * * * exposure. It is the knowledge and reasonable expectations of the consumer, not the scientific community, that is relevant under the consumer expectations test.

BRAWNER v. LIBERTY INDUSTRIES, INC.

Missouri Court of Appeals, St. Louis District, 1978.
573 S.W.2d 376.

SMITH, JUDGE.

Plaintiff appeals the order of the trial court dismissing with prejudice his suit against defendants brought under a theory of strict liability in tort. We affirm.

Plaintiff is seven years old and was burned when he and Ray Middleton, Jr., also seven years old, removed the lid from a gasoline storage container and the gasoline ignited. The gasoline container was manufactured by defendant Liberty Industries, Inc., and purchased by Ray Middleton (presumably the younger Middleton boy's father) from defendant National Food Stores, Inc. and its store manager defendant Ippellito. The allegation upon which plaintiff sought to invoke the strict liability doctrine was:

> "That the failure of said gasoline storage container to be equipped with an opening device which would render same to unable to be opened by a child of seven years constitutes a defect in design and an unreasonably dangerous condition of said gasoline storage container."

In *Keener v. Dayton Electric Mfg. Co.*, 445 S.W.2d 362 (Mo.1969), Missouri adopted the theory of strict liability in tort set forth in Restatement of Torts 2d, Sec. 402A as follows:

> "One who sells any product in a defective condition unreasonably dangerous to the user or consumer or to his property is subject to liability for physical harm thereby caused to the ultimate user or consumer or to his property, * * *."

In Missouri a defect in design can meet the requirement of "defective condition". See *Keener, supra; Higgins v. Paul Hardeman, Inc.*, 457 S.W.2d 943 (Mo.App.1970).

Under Comments to Sec. 402A para. (g), we find that a defective condition is a "condition not contemplated by the ultimate consumer which will be unreasonably dangerous to him." Paragraph (i) of the Comments states that "Unreasonably dangerous" means "The article sold must be dangerous to an extent beyond that which would be contemplated by the ordinary consumer who purchases it, with the ordinary knowledge common to the community as to its characteristics." A gasoline container which does not have a child-proof spout does not meet the definition of either defective or unreasonably dangerous. A manufacturer is not an insurer nor must he create a product which is accident proof. See *Royal v. Black and Decker Manufacturing Co.*, 205 So.2d 307 (Fla.App.1968); *Vincer v. Esther Williams All–Aluminum Swimming Pool*, 69 Wis.2d 326, 230 N.W.2d 794 (1975); *Bellotte v. Zayre Corp.*, 116 N.H. 52, 352 A.2d 723 (1976). We have found no case, nor have we been cited to one, where a product made for adult use is deemed defective and unreasonably dangerous solely because it has not been made child-proof. The trial court correctly dismissed plaintiff's petition.

Plaintiff objects to the trial court's failure to allow plaintiff an opportunity to amend. Initially, the record does not indicate plaintiff ever requested such an opportunity. Secondly, plaintiff has not indicated what amendment he would or could make to state a cause of action.

Judgment affirmed.

CLEMENS, P.J., and McMILLIAN, J., concur.

KELLER v. WELLES DEPARTMENT STORE OF RACINE

Court of Appeals of Wisconsin, District II, 1979.
88 Wis.2d 24, 276 N.W.2d 319.

BODE, JUDGE.

This is a products liability case. On October 21, 1971, two and one-half year old Stephen Keller was playing with two year old William Sperry in the basement of the Sperry home. The boys were playing with a gasoline can which had been filled with gasoline by Wayne Sperry, William's father. The can was manufactured by Huffman Manufacturing Company, Inc. (Huffman) and was purchased by Wayne Sperry at Welles Department Store (Welles). The children were near a gas furnace and a hot water heater when gasoline, which they had poured from the can, was ignited. Stephen Keller was severely burned. Although Mrs. Sperry was home at the time of the accident, the two boys were unsupervised.

* * *

The cause of action against Huffman and Welles is pleaded both in negligence and strict liability. The defendants, Huffman and Welles, moved to dismiss the complaint for failure to state a claim upon which relief could be granted. The motion was denied and an order to that effect was entered on April 14, 1978. The defendants appeal.

The sole issue before this court is whether the complaint states a cause of action against the manufacturer and retailer of a gasoline can, * * * for injuries sustained by Stephen Keller resulting from the ignition of gasoline poured from a gasoline can without a child-proof cap.

STRICT LIABILITY

In *Dippel v. Sciano*, 37 Wis.2d 443, 155 N.W.2d 55 (1967), the Wisconsin Supreme Court adopted sec. 402A of Restatement, 2 *Torts* 2d, thereby accepting the concept of strict liability. * * *

* * *

To state a cause of action under strict liability then, the plaintiff must essentially allege that the product was defective and unreasonably dangerous. In the present case, the complaint clearly alleges that the defendants respectively manufactured or sold a gasoline can which was defective and unreasonably dangerous to children such as the plaintiff. The defect complained of was the failure to design the can with a cap sufficient to prevent children from removing it.

* * *

The defendants contend that the motion to dismiss should have been granted because, as a matter of law, no jury could have reasonably concluded that the gasoline can was either defective or unreasonably dangerous. In support of their argument, the defendants rely on *Vincer v. Esther Williams All–Aluminum Swimming Pool Co.,* 69 Wis.2d 326, 230 N.W.2d 794 (1975).

In *Vincer,* a young boy was visiting his grandparents' home. While unsupervised, he fell into a swimming pool, remained there for a prolonged period of time, and sustained severe brain damage. The allegation was that a retractable ladder to the aboveground pool had been left in the down position, thereby providing easy access to the pool. The parents brought suit against the manufacturer of the swimming pool claiming that the pool was defectively designed in that it failed to provide a self-latching and closing gate to prevent entry to the pool. The Esther Williams Company demurred to the complaint for failure to state a cause of action. The trial court sustained the demurrer and the supreme court affirmed.

In its opinion, the court determined as a matter of law that the pool did not contain an unreasonably dangerous defect. The defendants believe the principles enunciated in *Vincer* mandate a similar outcome in the instant case. We disagree.

Comment *g* to sec. 402A of Restatement, 2 *Torts* 2d, states that a product is in a defective condition when "at the time it leaves the seller's hands, [it is] in a condition not contemplated by the ultimate consumer, which will be unreasonably dangerous to him." While this comment serves as a guideline, there is no general definition for "defect," and a decision on whether a defect exists must be made on a case-by-case basis. *Jagmin v. Simonds Abrasive Co.,* 61 Wis.2d 60, 66, 211 N.W.2d 810, 813 (1973).

The *Vincer* court concluded that the swimming pool could not have been defective for failure to have the suggested gate because it had a retractable ladder which rendered the pool "as safe as it reasonably could be." *Vincer,* 69 Wis.2d at 331, 230 N.W.2d at 798. The product at issue here, a gasoline can, was not as safe as was reasonably possible since the cap was not designed in such a way as to prevent young children from removing it. Equipping the gasoline can with a child-proof cap would have rendered the can substantially safer and entailed only a nominal additional cost. The practical value of such a cap may readily be seen since gasoline cans, while not intended to be used by children unable to appreciate the attendant dangers of gasoline, are customarily stored in places accessible to children.

The second element to be considered is whether the defective product, the gasoline can, was unreasonably dangerous. Comment *i* to sec. 402A of the Restatement, in part, describes an article as unreasonably dangerous when it is "dangerous to an extent beyond that which would be contemplated by the ordinary consumer who purchases it, with the ordinary knowledge common to the community as to its characteristics." In *Arbet v. Gussarson,* 66 Wis.2d 551, 225 N.W.2d 431 (1975), the distinction between dangers which are latent or hidden and those which are obvious was explored in the context of this Restatement comment. The court observed that since an ordinary consumer would expect a

Volkswagon to be less safe in an accident than a larger car, the small size would not make the Volkswagon unreasonably dangerous. *Arbet* itself dealt with a design defect in a Rambler Station Wagon which resulted in gasoline being retained in the passenger compartment. Since the danger arising from this defect was hidden rather than obvious, the supreme court reversed the trial court and upheld the complaint as against the demurrer of the car manufacturer.

Vincer noted the patent-danger rule discussed in *Arbet* and stated that the Wisconsin test of whether a product contains an unreasonably dangerous defect was as follows: "If the average consumer would reasonably anticipate the dangerous condition of the product and fully appreciate the attendant risk of injury, it would not be unreasonably dangerous and defective." *Vincer*, 69 Wis.2d at 332, 230 N.W.2d at 798. The court then concluded that the swimming pool did not contain an unreasonably dangerous defect for two reasons: first, because the absence of a self-latching gate was an obvious condition and second, because the average consumer would recognize the inherent danger of a retractable ladder in the down position when unsupervised children are about.

We think a different result is warranted in the present case. While the defect in the gasoline can was not concealed, this court is unable to conclude, as a matter of law, that the absence of a child-proof cap was an obvious as opposed to a latent condition. Nor do we believe the dangers to unsupervised children from a gasoline can without a child-proof cap are so apparent that the average consumer would be completely aware of them.

In this regard the factual circumstances in this case are clearly distinguishable from those in *Vincer*. It is common knowledge that children are attracted to swimming pools and that precautions must therefore be taken. See *McWilliams v. Guzinski,* 71 Wis.2d 57, 62, 237 N.W.2d 437, 439 (1976) (holding that an insufficiently guarded swimming pool in a residential area is an attractive nuisance to a four year old child). The danger to a young child from a swimming pool is obvious. The hazards to a child arising from a gasoline can without a child-proof cap are not so readily apparent. A child is not so clearly attracted to this product that an adult would immediately be put on guard to take precautions for the child's safety.

Based on the foregoing discussion, we conclude the complaint stated a cause of action in strict liability.

* * *

Order affirmed.

Notes

1. Some courts have broadened the scope of liability under the consumer expectations test by being very reluctant to find that a risk is generally known or obvious. Phillips, Products Liability: Obviousness of Danger Revis-

ited, 15 Ind.L.Rev. 797 (1982). *See also,* Pardieck & Hulbert, Is the Danger Really Open and Obvious?, 19 Ind.L.Rev. 383 (1986); Note, An Analysis of *Koske v. Townsend Engineering*: The Relationship Between the Open and Obvious Danger Rule and the Consumer Expectation Test, 25 Ind.L.Rev. 235 (1991).

2. Courts accomplish this by a process of characterization. The way a court characterizes the risk that must be contemplated by the ordinary consumer will have a dramatic effect on the scope of liability. Jurisdictions requiring only that a generalized risk of injury be known or obvious will find the fewest products defective. On the other hand, jurisdictions requiring full appreciation of the details of the accident will find many more products defective. In cases where the accident is at all unusual, they can find the product defective because the average consumer would not have contemplated the exact occurrence.

A similar issue of characterization is whether the user must fail to appreciate the condition of the product (no child-proof cap) or whether he must fail to appreciate the danger of the product (the risk that a child will ignite the gasoline).

3. The characterization of whose expectations are protected has the same effect. *Keller* looked to "adult" expectations. Another approach would be to look at the expectations of the child who was injured. In Williams v. Beechnut Nutrition Corp., 185 Cal.App.3d 135, 229 Cal.Rptr. 605 (1986) Daniel, a three and one-half-year-old child, fell while holding a baby bottle. It broke, and he was cut by the glass. The court held that "the inherent danger posed by a glass container, while obvious to an adult, is not cognizable by a child Daniel's age." *See* Note, Unreasonably Dangerous Products From a Child's Perspective: A Proposal for a Reasonable Child Consumer Expectation Test, 20 Rutgers L.J. 433 (1989).

An analogous problem arises when a bystander is injured. Should the product be evaluated by looking the expectations of the product-user or the bystander? *See* Batts v. Tow–Motor Forklift Co., 978 F.2d 1386 (5th Cir. 1992) (Mississippi law; forklift, without any mirror or back-up warning device, backed into a bystander. The bystander could not recover because the absence of such devices, and the danger of the operator not facing in the direction of travel, was open and obvious to the forklift operator).

Applying Wisconsin law, Insolia v. Philip Morris Inc., 216 F.3d 596, 559–600 (7th Cir.2000) discusses these issues in the context of tobacco litigation involving smokers who began smoking long before the first health warnings appeared on cigarette packages:

> The plaintiffs propose that in this context the "average consumer" should be a beginning smoker, maybe even a beginning teenage smoker. The Restatement incorporates the common-sense notion that if a consumer knows ahead of time that a product might be dangerous but goes ahead and uses it anyway, the consumer takes the risk upon himself and the manufacturer will not be held strictly liable. Nicotine's addictive grip makes it difficult to quit smoking. Consequently, the state of knowledge of the average consumer must be measured before the average person is hooked and is no longer capable of making a rational choice. We agree with the plaintiffs that, when it comes to an addictive

product like cigarettes, the "average consumer" is the beginning smoker.

The plaintiffs also believe the average consumer should be a teenager because that is when many people begin smoking and become addicted. The defendants argue that *Todd v. Societe Bic, S.A.*, 21 F.3d 1402, 1408 (7th Cir.1994) (*en banc*), holds that children may never be the standard to measure consumer expectations. *Todd* interpreted Illinois law, which, like Wisconsin, adopted the Second Restatement of Torts, Section 402A. *Id.* at 1405. In *Todd*, a 22–month-old child was killed by a fire started by a 4–year-old child using a cigarette lighter that belonged to one of the adults in the household. *Id.* at 1404. The estate of the deceased child sued the manufacturer of the cigarette lighter, arguing that though the ordinary adult consumer would have appreciated the lighter's danger, children—who were foreseeable users—would not have understood the product's hazards. *Id.* at 1407–08. The court refused to expand the Restatement's consumer contemplation test from ordinary consumers to foreseeable users. *Id.* at 1408.

Contrary to the defendants' interpretation, *Todd* does not mean there is a universally fixed definition of the ordinary consumer that bears no relationship to the product in question. Because the primary consumers, users, and purchasers of cigarette lighters are adults, gauging the perceived risks of cigarette lighters from the average adult's viewpoint makes sense. The same logic holds true even for a product— like diapers—that is used primarily by children but that is purchased and the use of which is supervised by adults. But suppose there was a product—say, bubble gum—of which children were not only the primary users, but also the primary purchasers, independent of any parental control. It would defy reason to excuse bubble gum manufacturers for bubble-gum-related injuries to children on the grounds that adults who rarely use the product would have appreciated bubble gum's hazards. Likewise, if the facts demonstrate that the ordinary beginning smoker is a teenager, then the consumer contemplation test should be measured from the average pre-smoking teenager's perspective.

A related issue of characterization is whether the relevant expectations are those of the consumer who buys the product or the consumer who uses the product. *Gray v. Manitowoc Co., Inc., supra* page 98 quotes from both Comments (g) and (i) of the Restatement (Second) § 402A. Note that Comment (g) refers to "a condition not contemplated by the ultimate consumer, which will be unreasonably dangerous to him." Comment (i), refers to a danger not "contemplated by the ordinary consumer who purchases it." This difference in language could be making a distinction between the product user and the product buyer. If so, the distinction is important. In an accident involving an industrial machine that injures the machine operator, the consumer who buys the machine is the owner of the business. The consumer who uses the machine is the operator. Did the drafters of the Restatement (Second) intend to make this distinction?

4. In a vehicle accident case, should we look to the expectations of the owner, driver, passenger, bystander, or all of them? Should infant passengers be treated differently than adult passengers?

5. What characterizations did the courts in *Brawner* and *Keller* rely on to achieve their differing results?

6. Many courts have now rejected consumer expectations as a sole test of defect. *See, e.g.,* Sperry–New Holland, a Division of Sperry Corp. v. Prestage, 617 So.2d 248 (Miss.1993). Courts have criticized the rule on the following grounds:

A. The test may not always further the policies underlying strict liability. Rather than discouraging unreasonably dangerous designs, the rule might have the effect of encouraging them in an obvious form. Knitz v. Minster Machine Co., 69 Ohio St.2d 460, 432 N.E.2d 814 (1982).

B. The test may be unfair to third parties in some situations. For example, in some cases the user is aware of a danger that presents a risk to a third party who is ignorant of it and powerless to protect himself. The user may not be as strongly motivated to protect the third party as he would be to protect himself from a similar danger. In addition, the hazard may impair the user's ability to protect the bystander. *E.g.,* Pike v. Frank G. Hough Co., 2 Cal.3d 465, 85 Cal.Rptr. 629, 467 P.2d 229 (1970) (earthmoving machine backed over worker because of blind spot to rear of machine). Another example of unfairness are cases where a person purchases an obviously dangerous machine for use by an employee. The employee may have no real choice but to use the machine, and his knowledge of the risk may not fully protect him. *E.g.,* Brown v. Quick Mix Co., Division of Koehring Co., 75 Wash.2d 833, 454 P.2d 205 (1969).

C. With respect to many complex modern products the consumer has no expectations as to how safe it is. Knitz v. Minster Machine Co., 69 Ohio St.2d 460, 432 N.E.2d 814 (1982). Is the consumer expectations test incapable of resolving such cases? Why not deny recovery on the basis that expectations were not frustrated? *Cf.,* Heaton v. Ford Motor Co., 248 Or. 467, 435 P.2d 806 (1967). Or should courts grant recovery on the basis that the result was unexpected? Consider the following statement from Akers v. Kelley Co., Inc., 173 Cal.App.3d 633, 651, 219 Cal.Rptr. 513, 524 (1985):

> There are certain kinds of accidents—even where fairly complex machinery is involved—which are so bizarre that the average juror, upon hearing the particulars, might reasonably think: 'Whatever the user may have expected from that contraption, it certainly wasn't that.'

7. Professor Powers has criticized the consumer expectations test as follows:

> The consumer expectation test reflects the warranty heritage of strict products liability and is embodied in comment i of Restatement (Second) of Torts section 402A. It provides that a product is defective if the product is more dangerous than an ordinary consumer would contemplate. At first glance, the consumer expectation test seems clearly different from both true strict liability and negligence, and it consequently promises a stable middle ground to serve as a foundation for strict products liability. In fact, this promise is largely illusory.

True, consumer expectations can sometimes provide an independent ground of analysis. Sometimes consumer expectations about product safety are sufficiently concrete that they can serve as a standard for evaluating a product. A manufacturer's advertising or other communications might create concrete expectations that a product can perform safely a specific task.[1] Even when a manufacturer does not affirmatively create concrete consumer expectations, the offending condition might be sufficiently simple that ordinary consumers have concrete expectations to the contrary—such as when a soft drink contains foreign material. At a more abstract level, consumers might expect at least that a product meets the manufacturer's own specifications, although even here consumers are unlikely to be aware of those specifications or even the range of details they cover.

In most cases, however, consumer expectations do not provide an independent standard against which to judge a product. In most design cases the offending product feature is too complex to generate concrete consumer expectations. Even in simpler cases, consumers are unlikely to have thought much about the specific offending product. Actual consumer expectations about safety are likely to be vague and, more importantly, to oscillate between "it will never happen to me" and "of course, some products are poorly made." The former expectation proves too much, for it treats every offending product as defective. The latter expectation proves too little, for it treats no product as defective.

Without actual, specific consumer expectations, courts might use the consumer expectation test as a rubric for determining what consumers have a right to expect—for example, that consumers have a right to expect that a product will have cost-effective safety features, will not be negligently manufactured, or at least will meet the manufacturer's own specifications. But this approach still would require courts to determine what consumers have a right to expect. The consumer expectation test itself would not provide the standard.

The consumer expectation test's inability to provide an independent standard of defectiveness for complicated products may explain why its early popularity waned as cases began to involve increasingly complex design features. Some courts have expressly abandoned the consumer expectation test;[2] others have expressly held that it is synonymous with the risk-utility test.[3]

The consumer expectation test does not provide a powerful reason for eschewing negligence as the underlying standard of liability in product cases. When a manufacturer creates concrete consumer expectations, the law of express warranties or misrepresentation can evaluate

---

1. The law of express warranties could handle cases in which the manufacturer has affirmatively created a consumer's expectations. *See* [Powers, The Persistence of Fault in Products Liability, 61 Tex.L.Rev. 777, 795–797 (1983)].

2. *See generally* Turner v. General Motors Corp., 584 S.W.2d 844 (Tex.1979). This is certainly not the only explanation. Another motivation has been substantive, that is, that the consumer expectation test deprived plaintiffs of recovery when a "bad" product had a dangerous feature that was nevertheless obvious to ordinary consumers.

3. *See, e.g.*, Phillips v. Kimwood Mach. Co., 269 Or. 485, 525 P.2d 1033, 1036–37 (1974).

those expectations. Some people may be dissatisfied with the substantive law of express warranties and misrepresentation, but that is a different issue; such dissatisfaction provides shaky support for an independent theory of strict products liability that circumvents direct confrontation of the issues.

Powers, A Modest Proposal to Abandon Strict Products Liability, 1991 U.Ill.L.Rev. 639, 653–654. For other articles criticizing the consumer expectations test, *See* Fischer, Products Liability—The Meaning of Defect, 39 Mo.L.Rev. 339 (1974); Keeton, Products Liability—Liability Without Fault and the Requirement of Defect, 41 Tex.L.Rev. 855, 861 (1963); Marschall, An Obvious Wrong Does Not Make a Right: Manufacturers' Liability for Patently Dangerous Products, 48 N.Y.U.L.Rev. 1065 (1973); Phillips, Products Liability: Obviousness of Danger Revisited, 15 Ind.L.Rev. 797 (1982); Wade, On the Nature of Strict Tort Liability for Products, 44 Miss.L.J. 825, 829 (1973); Comment, The Consumer Expectations Test: A Critical Review of its Application in California, 17 Sw.U.L.Rev. 823 (1988).

8. In a classic article, Professor James Henderson offered the best defense of the consumer expectations test. Henderson, Judicial Review of Manufacturers' Conscious Design Choices: The Limits of Adjudication, 73 Colum.L.Rev. 1531 (1973). The test delegates to the marketplace responsibility for deciding how much safety should be designed into a product. *Id.* at 1558–1562. That is, under the test, courts do not attempt to evaluate the design itself. They merely require full disclosure of risks so that buyers can make intelligent decisions about how much safety to pay for. Presumably, products with excessive safety features will be driven off the market because they do not sell. On the other hand, if the public desires that the safety of a product be improved, manufacturers will respond to that demand by marketing safer products. This approach is preferable to an attempt by courts to evaluate design through the process of adjudication. *Id.* at 1557–1558. Courts are not equipped to deal with all of the considerations that must be taken into account in making design choices about products. *Id.* at 1539–1542. Because courts would be unable to develop meaningful design standards, cases would ultimately be decided on the basis of the whim of individual juries. *Id.* at 1558. This will ultimately cause a serious loss of confidence in the courts. *Id.*

9. The consumer expectations test remains viable. A small number of common law courts continue to use the test as the primary test of defect. *E.g.*, Lester v. Magic Chef, Inc., 230 Kan. 643, 641 P.2d 353 (1982); Woods v. Fruehauf Trailer Corp., 765 P.2d 770 (Okl.1988). Several legislatures have enacted statutes mandating that the consumer expectations test be used. The following notes discuss two such statutes. Note, The Consumer Expectations Test in New Jersey: What Can Consumers Expect Now?, 54 Brook. L.Rev. 1381 (1989); Note, An Analysis of *Koske v. Townsend Engineering*: The Relationship Between the Open and Obvious Danger Rule and the Consumer Expectation Test, 25 Ind.L.Rev. 235 (1991). Some jurisdictions reject consumer expectations as the exclusive test of defect, but continue to use it as an alternative test. *See Barker v. Lull Engineering Co., infra* page 134. Other courts restrict the use of the consumer expectations test to manufacturing flaw cases. *See* Section B of this chapter. Cases using the

2. RISK–UTILITY

PHILLIPS v. KIMWOOD MACHINE CO.
Supreme Court of Oregon, 1974.
269 Or. 485, 525 P.2d 1033.

HOLMAN, JUSTICE.

Plaintiff was injured while feeding fiberboard into a sanding machine during his employment with Pope and Talbot, a wood products manufacturer. The sanding machine had been purchased by Pope and Talbot from defendant. Plaintiff brought this action on a products liability theory, contending the sanding machine was unreasonably dangerous by virtue of defective design. At the completion of the testimony, defendant's motion for a directed verdict was granted and plaintiff appealed.

As is required in such a situation, the evidence is recounted in a manner most favorable to the plaintiff. The machine in question was a six-headed sander. Each sanding head was a rapidly moving belt which revolved in the direction opposite to that which the pieces of fiberboard moved through the machine. Three of the heads sanded the top of the fiberboard sheet and three sanded the bottom. The top half of the machine could be raised or lowered depending upon the thickness of the fiberboard to be sanded. The bottom half of the machine had powered rollers which moved the fiberboard through the machine as the fiberboard was being sanded. The top half of the machine had pinch rolls, not powered, which, when pressed down on the fiberboard by use of springs, kept the sanding heads from forcefully rejecting it from the machine.

On the day of the accident plaintiff was engaged in feeding the sheets of fiberboard into the sander. * * * During the sanding of * * * thick sheets, a thin sheet of fiberboard, which had become mixed with the lot, was inserted into the machine. The pressure exerted by the pinch rolls in the top half of the machine was insufficient to counteract the pressure which the sanding belts were exerting upon the thin sheet of fiberboard and, as a result, the machine regurgitated the piece of fiberboard back at plaintiff, hitting him in the abdomen and causing him the injuries for which he now seeks compensation.

Plaintiff asserts in his complaint that the * * * machine was defective and was unreasonably dangerous because there were no safety devices to protect the person feeding the machine from the regurgitation of sheets of fiberboard.

[T]here was evidence from which the jury could find that at a relatively small expense there could have been built into, or subsequently installed on, the machine a line of metal teeth which would point in the direction that the fiberboard progresses through the machine and which would press lightly against the sheet but which, in case of attempted regurgitation, would be jammed into it, thus stopping its backward motion. The evidence also showed that after the accident such teeth were installed upon the machine for that purpose by Pope and Talbot, whereupon subsequent regurgitations of thin fiberboard sheets were prevented while the efficiency of the machine was maintained. There was also evidence that defendant makes smaller sanders which usually are manually fed and on which there is such a safety device.

It was shown that the machine in question was built for use with an automatic feeder * * *. [A]t the time of the purchase by Pope and Talbot, defendant had automatic feeders for sale but that Pope and Talbot did not purchase or show any interest in such a feeder. Pope and Talbot furnished a feeding device of their own manufacture for the machine which was partially automatic and partially manual but which, the jury could find, at times placed an employee in the way of regurgitated sheets.

* * *

In defense of its judgment based upon a directed verdict, defendant contends there was no proof of a defect in the product, and therefore strict liability should not apply. This court and other courts continue to flounder while attempting to determine how one decides whether a product is "in a defective condition unreasonably dangerous to the user."[1] It has been recognized that unreasonably dangerous defects in products come from two principal sources: (1) mismanufacture and (2) faulty design.[2] Mismanufacture is relatively simple to identify because the item in question is capable of being compared with similar articles made by the same manufacturer. However, whether the mismanufactured article is dangerously defective because of the flaw is sometimes difficult to ascertain because not every such flaw which causes injury makes the article dangerously defective.[3]

The problem with strict liability of products has been one of limitation. No one wants absolute liability where all the article has to do is to cause injury. To impose liability there has to be something about the article which makes it dangerously defective without regard to whether

---

1. 2 Restatement (Second) of Torts § 402A, at 347 (1965).

2. Wade, On the Nature of Strict Tort Liability for Products, 44 Miss.L.J. 825, 830 (1973) (including failure to warn as a design defect).

3. The California Supreme Court recognized this problem and attempted to eliminate it by requiring only a defect that causes injury, and not an unreasonably dangerous defect. In Cronin v. J.B.E. Olson Corp., 8 Cal.3d 121, 104 Cal.Rptr. 433, 501 P.2d 1153 (1972), the court felt that requiring proof of an *unreasonably dangerous* defect would put an additional burden on plaintiff which the court deemed improper.

We, however, feel that regardless of whether the term used is "defective," as in *Cronin,* or "defective condition unreasonably dangerous," as in the Restatement, or "dangerously defective," as used here, or "not duly safe," as used by Professor Wade, the same considerations will necessarily be utilized in fixing liability on sellers; and, therefore, the supposedly different standards will come ultimately to the same conclusion. *See* Wade, Strict Tort Liability of Manufacturers, 19 Sw.L.J. 5, 14–15 (1965); Wade, *supra* note 2.

the manufacturer was or was not at fault for such condition. A test for unreasonable danger is therefore vital. A dangerously defective article would be one which a reasonable person would not put into the stream of commerce *if he had knowledge of its harmful character.*[4] The test, therefore, is whether the seller would be negligent if he sold the article *knowing of the risk involved.*[5] Strict liability imposes what amounts to constructive knowledge of the condition of the product.

On the surface such a test would seem to be different than the test of 2 Restatement (Second) of Torts § 402A, Comment *i.*, of "dangerous to an extent beyond that which would be contemplated by the ordinary consumer who purchases it." This court has used this test in the past. These are not necessarily different standards, however. As stated in Welch v. Outboard Marine Corp.,[6] where the court affirmed an instruction containing both standards:

> "We see no necessary inconsistency between a seller-oriented standard and a user-oriented standard when, as here, each turns on foreseeable risks. They are two sides of the same standard. A product is defective and unreasonably dangerous when a reasonable seller would not sell the product if he knew of the risks involved or if the risks are greater than a reasonable buyer would expect."

To elucidate this point further, we feel that the two standards are the same because a seller acting reasonably would be selling the same product which a reasonable consumer believes he is purchasing. That is to say, a manufacturer who would be negligent in marketing a given product, considering its risks, would necessarily be marketing a product which fell below the reasonable expectations of consumers who purchase it. The foreseeable uses to which a product could be put would be the same in the minds of both the seller and the buyer unless one of the parties was not acting reasonably. The advantage of describing a dangerous defect in the manner of Wade and Keeton is that it preserves the use of familiar terms and thought processes with which courts, lawyers, and jurors customarily deal.

4. *See* Borel v. Fibreboard Paper Products Corp., 493 F.2d 1076, 1088 (5th Cir. 1973); Welch v. Outboard Marine Corp., 481 F.2d 252, 254 (5th Cir.1973); Helene Curtis Industries, Inc. v. Pruitt, 385 F.2d 841, 850 (5th Cir.1967), cert. denied, 391 U.S. 913, 88 S.Ct. 1806, 20 L.Ed.2d 652 (1968); Olsen v. Royal Metals Corporation, 392 F.2d 116, 119 (5th Cir.1968); Dorsey v. Yoder, 331 F.Supp. 753, 759–760 (E.D.Pa. 1971), aff'd, 474 F.2d 1339 (3 Cir.1973).

See generally, P. Keeton, Manufacturer's Liability: The Meaning of "Defect" in the Manufacture and Design of Products, 20 Syracuse L.Rev. 559, 568 (1969); P. Keeton, Products Liability—Inadequacy of Information, 48 Tex.L.Rev. 398, 403–404 (1970); Wade, Strict Tort Liability of Manufacturers, 19 Sw.L.J. 5, 15–16 (1965).

5. *Cf.* Welch v. Outboard Marine Corp., 481 F.2d 252, 254 (5th Cir.1973). *See generally,* Wade, *supra* note 2, at 834–835; P. Keeton, Products Liability—Some Observations About Allocation of Risks, 64 Mich. L.Rev. 1329, 1335 (1966).

The Wade and Keeton formulations of the standard appear to be identical except that Keeton would impute the knowledge of dangers at time of trial to the manufacturer, while Wade would impute only the knowledge existing at the time the product was sold. *Compare* P. Keeton, Product Liability and the Meaning of Defect, 5 St. Mary's L.J. 30, 38 (1973), with Wade, *supra* note 3, at 15, and Wade, *supra* note 2, at 834.

6. 481 F.2d 252, 254 (5th Cir.1973).

Sec. C DESIGN DEFECTS 117

While apparently judging the seller's conduct, the test set out above would actually be a characterization of the product by a jury. If the manufacturer was not acting reasonably in selling the product, knowing of the risks involved, then the product would be dangerously defective when sold and the manufacturer would be subject to liability.

In the case of a product which is claimed to be dangerously defective because of misdesign, the process is not so easy as in the case of mismanufacture. All the products made to that design are the same. The question of whether the design is unreasonably dangerous can be determined only by taking into consideration the surrounding circumstances and knowledge at the time the article was sold, and determining therefrom whether a reasonably prudent manufacturer would have so designed and sold the article in question had he known of the risk involved which injured plaintiff. The issue has been raised in some courts concerning whether, in this context, there is any distinction between strict liability and negligence. The evidence which proves the one will almost always, if not always, prove the other. We discussed this matter recently in the case of Roach v. Kononen, 99 Or.Adv.Sh. 1092, 525 P.2d 125 (1974), and pointed out that there is a difference between strict liability for misdesign and negligence. We said:

"However, be all this as it may, it is generally recognized that the basic difference between negligence on the one hand and strict liability for a design defect on the other is that in strict liability we are talking about the condition (dangerousness) of an article which is designed in a particular way, while in negligence we are talking about the reasonableness of the manufacturer's actions in designing and selling the article as he did. The article can have a degree of dangerousness which the law of strict liability will not tolerate even though the actions of the designer were entirely reasonable in view of what he knew at the time he planned and sold the manufactured article. As Professor Wade points out, a way of determining whether the condition of the article is of the requisite degree of dangerousness to be defective (unreasonably dangerous; greater degree of danger than a consumer has a right to expect; not duly safe) is to assume that the manufacturer knew of the product's propensity to injure as it did, and then to ask whether, with such knowledge, something should have been done about the danger before it was sold. In other words, a greater burden is placed on the manufacturer than is the case in negligence because the law assumes he has knowledge of the article's dangerous propensity which he may not reasonably be expected to have, had he been charged with negligence." 99 Or.Adv.Sh. at 1099, 525 P.2d at 129.

To some it may seem that absolute liability has been imposed upon the manufacturer since it might be argued that no manufacturer could reasonably put into the stream of commerce an article which he realized might result in injury to a user. This is not the case, however. The manner of injury may be so fortuitous and the chances of injury occurring so remote that it is reasonable to sell the product despite the danger. In design cases the utility of the article may be so great, and the change of design necessary to alleviate the danger in question may so impair such utility, that it is reasonable to market the product as it is, even though the possibility of injury exists and was realized at the time of the sale. Again, the cost of the change necessary to alleviate the danger in design may be so great that the article would be priced out of the market and no one would buy it even though it was of high utility. Such an article is not dangerously defective despite its having inflicted injury.

In this case defendant contends it was Pope and Talbot's choice to purchase and use the sander without an automatic feeder, even though it was manufactured to be used with one, and, therefore, it was Pope and Talbot's business choice which resulted in plaintiff's injury and not any misdesign by defendant. However, it is recognized that a failure to warn may make a product unreasonably dangerous.[7] Comment j, Section 402A, 2 Restatement (Second) of Torts, has the following to say:

> "In order to prevent the product from being unreasonably dangerous, the seller may be required to give directions or warning, on the container, as to its use. The seller may reasonably assume that those with common allergies, as for example to eggs or strawberries, will be aware of them, and he is not required to warn against them. Where, however, the product contains an ingredient to which a substantial number of the population are allergic, and the ingredient is one whose danger is not generally known, or if known is one which the consumer would reasonably not expect to find in the product, the seller is required to give warning against it, if he had knowledge, or by the application of reasonable, developed human skill and foresight should have knowledge, of the presence of the ingredient and the danger. Likewise in the case of poisonous drugs, or those unduly dangerous for other reasons, warning as to use may be required."

Although the examples cited in the comment do not encompass machinery or such products, it has been recognized that a piece of machinery may or may not be dangerously defective, depending on the directions or warnings that may be given with it.[8]

---

7. See Borel v. Fibreboard Paper Products Corp., 493 F.2d 1076, 1088–1090, (5th Cir.1973). See generally, P. Keeton, Products Liability—Inadequacy of Information, 48 Tex.L.Rev. 398, 403–404 (1970); P. Keeton, Product Liability and the Meaning of Defect, 5 St. Mary's L.J. 30, 33–34 (1973).

8. Hursh & Bailey, 1 American Law of Products Liability 2d, § 4.13 and cases cited therein (1974); see Berkebile v. Brantly Helicopter Corp., 225 Pa.Super. 349, 311 A.2d 140, 143 (1973).

In fact, in the leading case in the area of strict liability, Greenman v. Yuba Power Products, 59 Cal.2d 57, 27 Cal.Rptr. 697, 377 P.2d 897, 13 A.L.R.3d 1049 (1963), the California Supreme Court stated:

" * * * To establish the manufacturer's liability it was sufficient that plaintiff proved that he was injured while using the Shopsmith in a way it was intended to be used as a result of a defect in design and manufacture *of which plaintiff was not aware* that made the Shopsmith unsafe for its intended use." (Emphasis added.) 27 Cal.Rptr. at 701, 377 P.2d at 901.

Thus it appears that the piece of machinery might not have been "defective" had the purchaser been made aware of its propensities through proper warnings.

It is our opinion that the evidence was sufficient for the jury to find that a reasonably prudent manufacturer, knowing that the machine would be fed manually and having the constructive knowledge of its propensity to regurgitate thin sheets when it was set for thick ones, which the courts via strict liability have imposed upon it, would have warned plaintiff's employer either to feed it automatically or to use some safety device, and that, in the absence of such a warning, the machine was dangerously defective. It is therefore unnecessary for us to decide the questions that would arise had adequate warnings been given.

In Anderson v. Klix Chemical, 256 Or. 199, 472 P.2d 806 (1970), we came to the conclusion that there was no difference between negligence and strict liability for a product that was unreasonably dangerous because of failure to warn of certain characteristics. We have now come to the conclusion that we were in error. The reason we believe we were in error parallels the rationale that was expressed in the previously quoted material from Roach v. Kononen, *supra,* where we discussed the difference between strict liability for misdesign and negligence. In a strict liability case we are talking about the condition (dangerousness) of an article which is sold without any warning, while in negligence we are talking about the reasonableness of the manufacturer's actions in selling the article without a warning. The article can have a degree of dangerousness because of a lack of warning which the law of strict liability will not tolerate even though the actions of the seller were entirely reasonable in selling the article without a warning considering what he knew or should have known at the time he sold it. A way to determine the dangerousness of the article, as distinguished from the seller's culpability, is to assume the seller knew of the product's propensity to injure as it did, and then to ask whether, with such knowledge, he would have been negligent in selling it without a warning.

It is apparent that the language being used in the discussion of the above problems is largely that which is also used in *negligence* cases, *i.e.*, "unreasonably dangerous," "have reasonably anticipated," "reasonably prudent manufacturer," etc. It is necessary to remember that whether the doctrine of negligence, ultrahazardousness, or strict liability is being used to impose liability, the same process is going on in each instance, *i.e.*, weighing the utility of the article against the risk of its use. Therefore, the same language and concepts of reasonableness are used by courts for the determination of unreasonable danger in products liability cases. For example, see the criteria set out in Roach v. Kononen, *supra.*[9] The difference between the three theories of recovery is in the

---

9. (1) The usefulness and desirability of the product—its utility to the user and to the public as a whole.

(2) The safety aspects of the product—the likelihood that it will cause injury, and the probable seriousness of the injury.

(3) The availability of a substitute product which would meet the same need and not be as unsafe.

(4) The manufacturer's ability to eliminate the unsafe character of the product without impairing its usefulness or making it too expensive to maintain its utility.

(5) The user's ability to avoid danger by the exercise of care in the use of the product.

(6) The user's anticipated awareness of the dangers inherent in the product and their

manner in which the decisional functions are distributed between the court and the jury. * * *

It is important to point out * * * that while the decision is made by the court whether an activity is abnormally dangerous and strict liability of the Rylands v. Fletcher[10] type is to be applied, the determination of whether a product is dangerously defective and strict liability is to be applied has been treated as one primarily for the jury, similar to the manner in which negligence is determined. Therefore, the factors set forth by Wade and used in Roach v. Kononen, *supra*, are not the bases for instructions to the jury but are for the use of the court in determining whether a case has been made out which is submissible to the jury. If such a case has been made out, then it is submitted to the jury for its determination under instructions as to what constitutes a "dangerously defective" product, much in the same manner as negligence is submitted to the jury under the "reasonable man" rule.[11]

* * *

The case is reversed and remanded for a new trial.

Notes

1. Many jurisdictions have adopted a risk-utility test of defect in recent years. There has been some quibbling over terminology, such as whether to use such terms as "reasonable" or "unreasonably dangerous" in describing the way the product is evaluated. Some courts avoid using such terms because they "ring of negligence." Regardless of the terminology, the basic approach is the same.

2. Note the language in *Phillips* to the effect that there is no difference between the consumer expectations test and the risk-utility test. Other courts have agreed. *E.g.*, Aller v. Rodgers Machinery Manufacturing Co., 268 N.W.2d 830 (Iowa 1978). In essence, they have converted the consumer expectations test into a risk-utility test by stating that consumers expect products to be reasonably safe. How would such courts deal with cases where a product contains an obvious danger (such as a punch press without a point of operation guard) that could easily be corrected?

avoidability, because of general public knowledge of the obvious condition of the product, or of the existence of suitable warnings or instructions.

(7) The feasibility, on the part of the manufacturer, of spreading the loss by setting the price of the product or carrying liability insurance.

10. Fletcher v. Rylands, 3 H & C 774, 159 Eng.Rep. 737 (Ex.1865), *reversed in* Fletcher v. Rylands, LR 1 Ex. 265 (1866), *affirmed in* Rylands v. Fletcher, LR 3 HL 330 (1868).

11. Wade, *supra* note 2, at 834–835. Professor Wade also suggests an appropriate jury instruction which embodies the new standard. We have taken the liberty of modifying his suggestion to a form which seems to us more appropriate for use by a jury. It is as follows:

"The law imputes to a manufacturer [supplier] knowledge of the harmful character of his product whether he actually knows of it or not. He is presumed to know of the harmful characteristics of that which he makes [supplies]. Therefore, a product is dangerously defective if it is so harmful to persons [or property] that a reasonable prudent manufacturer [supplier] with this knowledge would not have placed it on the market."

3. Courts are not always free to employ the risk-utility test. Some legislatures have explicitly adopted the consumer expectations test in tort cases. *See* note 9, *supra* page 113. Claims for breach of implied warranty of merchantability are also governed by a statute, the Uniform Commercial Code. In Denny v. Ford Motor Co., 87 N.Y.2d 248, 662 N.E.2d 730, 639 N.Y.S.2d 250 (1995) the court held that whether a product is merchantable because it is "fit for the ordinary purposes for which such goods are used" is determined by the consumer expectations test because implied warranty originates in contract law and is concerned with fulfilling expectations. Strict tort liability in New York is different. It uses the risk-utility test because it is based on "social policy and risk allocation." Thus, it is possible in New York for a product to be unmerchantable because it violates consumer expectations even though it is not defective under the risk-utility test. Under these circumstances the manufacturer could be held liable for breach of implied warranty of merchantability even though it is not liable in tort.

Almost all implied warranty claims for physical harm to person or property are brought on the basis that the goods are not "fit for the ordinary purposes for which such goods are used." Recall from Chapter 2, however, that § 2–314 specifies five additional ways that a good can be non-merchantable: The statute provides in part:

(2) Goods to be merchantable must be at least such as

(a) pass without objection in the trade under the contract description; and

(b) in the case of fungible goods, are of fair average quality within the description; and

(c) are fit for the ordinary purposes for which such goods are used; and

(d) run, within the variations permitted by the agreement, of even kind, quality and quantity within each unit and among all units involved; and

(e) are adequately contained, packaged, and labeled as the agreement may require; and

(f) conform to the promises or affirmations of fact made on the container or label if any.

In theory, a plaintiff who could establish any of these six bases, and could meet the other requirements for an implied warranty claim, could recover for personal injury for breach of warranty even though she were unable to establish a claim under strict liability in tort.

4. *Phillips* creates a distinction between negligence and strict liability by using hindsight rather than foresight to impute knowledge of risk to the manufacturer. It does this on both the design defect claim and the failure to warn claim. We treat the use of hindsight versus foresight in more detail in the Note Regarding the Foresight/Hindsight Distinction, *infra* page 141.

5. Judge Holman's opinion in *Phillips* points out that whether an activity gives rise to strict liability because it is abnormally dangerous is a question of law for the judge, but that strict products liability under the risk-utility test is a question of fact for the jury. Virtually all courts agree that

liability under the risk-utility test is a jury question. The Pennsylvania Supreme Court is a notable exception. In Azzarello v. Black Bros. Co., 480 Pa. 547, 391 A.2d 1020 (1978) the court ruled that the fundamental question as to whether to impose strict liability in a given case is to be made by the judge rather than the jury. The court stated:

> While a lay finder of fact is obviously competent in resolving a dispute as to the condition of a product, an entirely different question is presented where a decision as to whether that condition justifies placing liability upon the supplier must be made. * * * Thus the mere fact that we have approved Section 402A, and even if we agree that the phrase "unreasonably dangerous" serves a useful purpose in predicting liability in this area, it does not follow that this language should be used in framing the issues for the jury's consideration. Should an ill-conceived design which exposes the user to the risk of harm entitle one injured by the product to recover? Should adequate warnings of the dangerous propensities of an article insulate one who suffers injuries from those propensities? When does the utility of a product outweigh the unavoidable danger it may pose? These are questions of law and their resolution depends upon social policy. It is a judicial function to decide whether, under plaintiff's averment of the facts, recovery would be justified; and only after this judicial determination is made is the cause submitted to the jury to determine whether the facts of the case support the averments of the complaint. They do not fall within the orbit of a factual dispute which is properly assigned to the jury for resolution. A standard suggesting the existence of a "defect" if the article is unreasonably dangerous or not duly safe is inadequate to guide a lay jury in resolving these questions.

Id. at 1025–27. The court approved the following jury instruction:

> "The [supplier] of a product is the guarantor of its safety. The product must, therefore, be provided with every element necessary to make it safe for [its intended] use, and without any condition that makes it unsafe for [its intended] use. If you find that the product, at the time it left the defendant's control, lacked any element necessary to make it safe for [its intended] use or contained any condition that made it unsafe for [its intended] use, then the product was defective, and the defendant is liable for all harm caused by such defect."

Id. at 1027 n. 12.

6. *Azzarello v. Black Bros. Co.* created considerable confusion as to exactly what the judge was to decide and what the jury was to decide. *See* Henderson, Renewed Judicial Controversy Over Defective Product Design: Toward the Preservation of an Emerging Consensus, 63 Minn.L.Rev. 773, 797–801 (1979); Wade, On Product "Design Defects" and Their Actionability, 33 Vand.L.Rev. 551, 560–561 (1980). Not all of the subsequent cases clearly articulate the reasons for deciding the products liability issue as they did. An exception is Lobianco v. Property Protection, Inc., 292 Pa.Super. 346, 437 A.2d 417 (1981) which decided the issue by directly considering the policies underlying strict liability. In that case a homeowner sued a burglar alarm manufacturer for a theft loss that occurred because the burglar alarm malfunctioned. The court decided for the manufacturer on the basis that the

homeowner was best able to spread the loss by buying insurance. *See also* Dambacher by Dambacher v. Mallis, 336 Pa.Super. 22, 485 A.2d 408 (1984), appeal dismissed, 508 Pa. 643, 500 A.2d 428 (1985). Other courts have more narrowly restricted themselves to applying the accepted tests for determining defect. *See, e.g.*, Jordon by Jordon v. K–Mart Corp., 417 Pa.Super. 186, 611 A.2d 1328 (1992) where a ten-year-old boy lost control of his plastic sled and hit a tree. He claimed that the sled was defective in design because it lacked any independent steering or braking mechanisms. The court upheld the trial court's determination that the sled was not defective. The court said:

> The trial court, citing social policy, meticulously weighed the relative risks and utility of the sled in question and the type of sled, a toboggan, to determine whether liability should be imposed. The Court found that like most recreational activities, sledding involves a degree of risk and even changing the design to require brakes or steering would not remove the inherent risk in the activity. We agree with the trial court's analysis of social policy and hold that the trial court correctly applied the Azzarello threshold in determining the strict liability claim based on product design.

7. Should defect be a question for the judge or the jury? If it is a question for the jury, how much guidance should the court give to the jury? Compare the suggested jury instruction in *Phillips* with the approach taken by Nesselrode v. Executive Beechcraft, Inc., 707 S.W.2d 371, 377–78 (Mo. 1986), in which the court stated:

> Under Missouri's rule of strict tort liability, a product's design is deemed defective, for purposes of imposing liability, when it is shown by a preponderance of evidence that the design renders the product unreasonably dangerous. * * *

> Though Missouri has adopted the rule of strict tort liability as set forth in the *Restatement,* we have not yet formally incorporated, in any meaningful way, the *Restatement's* consumer expectation test into the lexicon of our products liability law. * * * Nor have we yet decided to travel or require plaintiffs to travel the path of risks and utilities. * * *

> Under our model of strict tort liability the concept of unreasonable danger, which is determinative of whether a product is defective in a design case, is presented to the jury as an ultimate issue without further definition. See Aronson's Men's Stores v. Potter Electric Signal Company, Inc., 632 S.W.2d at 472. Accordingly, our approved jury instruction which governs in a design defect case, MAI 25.04 (3rd) does not contain as one of its component elements a definitional paragraph which gives independent content to the concept of unreasonable danger.

> Notwithstanding the minority character of this approach, Professor Leon Green, in his 1976 Texas Law Review article, *Strict Liability Under Sections 402A and 402B: A Decade of Litigation,* explains why an approach that avoids the use of an external standard by which to determine unreasonable danger—*i.e.,* defectiveness—is preferable to one which does use an external standard. He points out first that juries do not have "a fictitious standard by which to determine assault, battery, false imprisonment, nuisance, entry upon land, or the taking of a

chattel" and then he suggests that "[n]or do juries need an external standard by which to determine the danger of a product in an unreasonably dangerous defective condition." Green, Strict Liability Under Sections 402A and 402B: A Decade of Litigation, 54 Tex.L.Rev. 1185, 1206 (1976). He concludes his discussion with the judgment that "the ritual indulged in by the giving of abstract, abstruse standards, impossible to comply with, only perpetuates the mystical trial by ordeal and *may conceal a hook in a transcendental lure that will snag an appellate court." Id.* at 1206. (emphasis added)

As we noted previously, at the trial of a design defect case, the concept of unreasonable danger is treated as an ultimate issue. The jury gives this concept content by applying their collective intelligence and experience to the broad evidentiary spectrum of facts and circumstances presented by the parties.

FALLON v. CLIFFORD B. HANNAY & SON, INC.

Supreme Court of New York, Appellate Division, Third Department, 1989.
153 A.D.2d 95, 550 N.Y.S.2d 135.

Before MAHONEY, P.J., and CASEY, YESAWICH, LEVINE and HARVEY, JJ.

LEVINE, JUSTICE.

Plaintiff brought this action for products liability * * * against defendant, the manufacturer of the "Hannay Reel", a power reel installed in propane gas delivery trucks upon which the hose used to convey the propane gas from the truck to the tank of the customer is wound, stored and unwound. The facts upon which plaintiff based his causes of action can be garnered from the allegations of the complaint, bill of particulars and the transcript of plaintiff's examination before trial. Briefly summarized, plaintiff claims that, at the time when he sustained the injuries for which he sues, he was employed as a propane gas delivery person for Agway Petroleum Corporation and had been so employed for several years. When the injury-producing incident happened, he was delivering gas to a residence in the Town of Otsego, Otsego County, and in the process of bringing the hose line from the truck to the customer's tank. He was " 'running' with [the] hose", i.e., accelerating his forward movement to overcome the inert weight of the hose as it unrolled from the vehicle, when an entanglement of the hose on the reel caused it to lock abruptly, which in turn caused plaintiff to fall and sustain serious injuries to his back.

According to plaintiff, the Hannay Reel was defective in not being equipped with a "guide master", a piece of optional equipment manufactured and offered for sale by defendant with the power reel. The function of a guide master is to mechanically direct the laying of the hose back and forth on the reel when the hose is being automatically rewound and thereby prevent the snarling of the hose on the reel, which plaintiff claims ultimately caused his injuries. In his bill of particulars, plaintiff further explained the entanglement problem of the reel without a guide master as being one wherein, upon rewinding, "the hose occasionally, depending on the angle of the hose to the revolving reel, overlaps at various angles, which occasionally results in an overlapping entanglement". * * *

After joinder of issue and pretrial discovery, defendant moved for summary judgment. The moving papers consisted of affidavits of defendant's vice-president of manufacturing and a manager of plaintiff's employer, the pleadings, a bill of particulars and the transcript of plaintiff's examination before trial. The evidentiary facts in admissible form in those papers show that defendant had manufactured and sold the power reel and guide master, with the guide master as optional equipment, since the early 1950s and had sold reels both with and without guide masters to plaintiff's employer for several years prior to plaintiff's accident. As a matter of deliberate choice of plaintiff's employer, several of its trucks were equipped with guide masters while others were not. The purpose of the guide master device, to avoid entanglement of the hose on the reel and resultant lock of the hose upon unwinding, was well known by plaintiff's employer and by plaintiff and his coemployees. * * *

Plaintiff opposed defendant's motion by submitting the affidavits of plaintiff and of a university professor of mechanical and aerospace engineering. In his affidavit, plaintiff admitted knowing the potential of the Hannay Reel not equipped with a guide master to entangle and suddenly lock when running with the hose to service a customer, but denied being "aware that it would knock me down". The affidavit of plaintiff's expert opined that the guide master was an "essential safety item that should, in fact, be a part of the standard equipment of the Hannay Reel and that it's [sic] purpose is to prevent the exact occurrence * * * which caused this accident". Supreme Court denied defendant's motion in its entirety on the ground that issues of fact were presented as to whether the guide master was actually a safety device and whether the absence of the device as a standard feature of defendant's reel created an unreasonable risk of harm to the user. This appeal by defendant ensued.

In our view, defendant was entitled to summary judgment * * *. * * * [P]laintiff's * * * claim in strict products liability [is] for a design defect and a failure to warn. The design defect claim refers to defendant's duty not to market the Hannay Reel without the guide master. Thus, it was plaintiff's burden to make out a prima facie case that, *inter alia*, absent the guide master, defendant's power reel was "not reasonably safe" (*Voss v. Black & Decker Mfg. Co.*, 59 N.Y.2d 102, 108, 463 N.Y.S.2d 398, 450 N.E.2d 204). A defectively designed product "is one which, at the time it leaves the seller's hands, is in a condition not reasonably contemplated by the ultimate consumer and is unreasonably dangerous for its intended use; that is one whose utility does not outweigh the danger inherent in its introduction into the stream of commerce" (*Robinson v. Reed–Prentice Div. of Package Mach. Co.*, 49 N.Y.2d 471, 479, 426 N.Y.S.2d 717, 403 N.E.2d 440). In applying the risk-utility facet of the definition of an unreasonably unsafe product, the

Court of Appeals has identified seven factors to be considered (*Voss v. Black & Decker Mfg. Co.*, *supra*, 59 N.Y.2d at 109, 463 N.Y.S.2d 398, 450 N.E.2d 204). Basically, and as relevant here, these factors refer to the magnitude and seriousness of the danger in using the product, the product's utility to the public and the individual user, the technological and economic feasibility of a safer design and the plaintiff's awareness of the danger and ability to have avoided injury by careful use of the product. These risk-utility factors are to be considered in the first instance by the court to determine whether a plaintiff has made out a prima facie case and, if so, then submitted in some reasonably simple fashion to the jury [citations].

Here, the facts and reasonable inferences to be drawn from the evidence submitted in support of defendant's motion negated plaintiff's claim that the Hannay Reel without a guide master was not reasonably safe. The reel, sans guide master, was exactly in the condition contemplated by the consumer at the time of purchase, i.e., a useful device whose mechanical efficiency was less than if it had been equipped with a guide master, a quality common to reels of all varieties. Plaintiff himself recognized that entanglement would only occur "occasionally". Even more remote was the likelihood that the sudden locking upon unwinding of a twisted hose would result in a gas deliverer losing balance and then falling with sufficient force to sustain any significant injury. Thus, defendant also successfully demonstrated in its moving papers that the magnitude of danger factor in the risk-utility test was insubstantial. While the existence of the guide master itself established the technical feasibility of a safer reel, the economic feasibility of marketing defendant's product only with the guide master was cast in doubt by the invoices submitted by defendant on the motion, tending to show that inclusion of the guide master substantially increases the cost of the product sold by defendant. Finally, as to the factors to be considered in the risk-utility test, plaintiff's awareness of the possibility of the hose locking and the simple precautions which could have been taken to avoid the disastrous fall also militated against a finding that the reel without a guide master was unreasonably dangerous [citation].

Moreover, it is readily inferrable that the risks both of an entangled hose locking and then causing any significant injury to a delivery person will vary from one job site to another, depending upon such factors as the distance from the delivery truck to the customer's tank and the conditions of the terrain traversed. Purchasers of the reels, knowing their clientele and the conditions under which deliveries to them would be made, were in a better position than defendant, as the manufacturer, to assess the necessity of the protection against snarling and locking afforded by a guide master, even if it were to be considered a safety device. For these reasons also, defendant's proof supported the conclusion that the reel alone was reasonably safe and that defendant satisfied its duty not to market a defective product by giving purchasers the option to buy its reel with or without the guide master [citations].

What has previously been discussed also largely disposes of the failure to warn claim in plaintiff's first cause of action. On defendant's proof, the danger of injury was insubstantial and, to whatever degree there was such a risk, it was an obvious one, likely to be appreciated by the user to the same extent as any warning of it would have provided [citations].

* * *

Thus, defendant submitted evidence in admissible form establishing a prima facie defense to each of the causes of action alleged in the complaint. Therefore, the burden shifted to plaintiff to submit contradictory proof to withstand defendant's motion by creating one or more issues of fact. * * * As to plaintiff's cause of action for products liability in tort, the opposing affidavits were insufficient to create a question of fact as to whether the Hannay Reel was not reasonably safe. Since plaintiff's personal affidavit conceded prior awareness of the property of the reel without a guide master of which he complains, it failed to controvert defendant's proof on this issue. The affidavit of plaintiff's expert contained only a bare, conclusory statement that the reel was unsafe without a guide master. No foundational facts, such as a deviation from industry standards, or statistics showing some frequent incidence of injuries in using this type of reel, are averred in support of this conclusion. No inference that the conclusion of plaintiff's expert was based upon his own personal knowledge can be drawn from the summary of his qualifications attached to his affidavit, which disclosed at most a general expertise in mechanical design for heating and other energy systems not vaguely related to the manufacturer of the product which is the subject of plaintiff's action. Without even the semblance of a foundation based upon facts in the record or personal knowledge, the opinion of plaintiff's expert was purely speculative and, thus, lacked sufficient probative force to constitute prima facie evidence that the Hannay Reel was not reasonably safe for its intended use [citations]. In the absence of such a prima facie showing that defendant's reel was not reasonably safe, plaintiff failed to create an issue of fact precluding summary judgment.

Order reversed, on the law, with costs, motion granted, summary judgment awarded to defendant and complaint dismissed.

MAHONEY, P.J., and CASEY, YESAWICH, and HARVEY, JJ., concur.

Hannay Reel without guide master

Hannay Reel with guide master

Notes

1. **Product Cost and Product Performance.** Courts consider the cost of making the product safer as part of the risk-utility balance. In Rix v. General Motors Corp., 222 Mont. 318, 723 P.2d 195 (1986), the braking system on a truck failed because of a hydraulic brake fluid leak. Plaintiff argued that the truck was defective because it was not equipped with a dual braking system so that the truck would have a back-up braking system in the event of such a failure. The technology for such a system was available and known to General Motors at the time of manufacture. The court stated that the jury should be instructed to consider, in addition to other factors, "[t]he relative costs both to the manufacturer and the consumer of producing, distributing and selling the original product as compared to the product with the alternative design."

Courts also consider the way performance is affected by suggested design changes. Cars, for example, would be much safer if they had a top speed of five miles per hour. Yet, they are not defective because they are capable of going faster.

2. The Restatement (Third) of Torts: Products Liability § 2 and Comment f. summarize how the various risk-utility factors interrelate:

§ 2. Categories of Product Defect

A product is defective when, at the time of sale or distribution, it contains a manufacturing defect, is defective in design, or is defective because of inadequate instructions or warnings. A product:

* * *

(b) is defective in design when the foreseeable risks of harm posed by the product could have been reduced or avoided by the adoption of a reasonable alternative design by the seller or other distributor, or a predecessor in the commercial chain of distribution, and the omission of the alternative design renders the product not reasonably safe; * * *

* * *

Comment:

f. Design defects: factors relevant in determining whether the omission of a reasonable alternative design renders a product not reasonably safe. Subsection (b) states that a product is defective in design if the omission of a reasonable alternative design renders the product not reasonably safe. A broad range of factors may be considered in determining whether an alternative design is reasonable and whether its omission renders a product not reasonably safe. The factors include, among others, the magnitude and probability of the foreseeable risks of harm, the instructions and warnings accompanying the product, and the nature and strength of consumer expectations regarding the product, including expectations arising from product portrayal and marketing. See Comment g. The relative advantages and disadvantages of the product as designed and as it alternatively could have been designed may also be considered. Thus, the likely effects of the alternative design on production costs; the effects of the alternative design on product longevity, maintenance, repair, and esthetics; and the range of consumer choice among products are factors that may be taken into account. A plaintiff is not necessarily required to introduce proof on all of these factors; their relevance, and the relevance of other factors, will vary from case to case. Moreover, the factors interact with one another. For example, evidence of the magnitude and probability of foreseeable harm may be offset by evidence that the proposed alternative design would reduce the efficiency and the utility of the product. On the other hand, evidence that a proposed alternative design would increase production costs may be offset by evidence that product portrayal and marketing created substantial expectations of performance or safety, thus increasing the probability of foreseeable harm. Depending on the mix of these factors, a number of variations in the design of a given product may meet the test in Subsection (b). On the other hand, it is not a factor under Subsection (b) that the imposition of liability would have a negative effect on corporate earnings or would reduce employment in a given industry.

* * *

3. **Benefits to the Economy.** Cipollone v. Liggett Group, Inc., 644 F.Supp. 283 (D.N.J.1986) supports the Third Restatement position that in evaluating the utility of the product the jury may not consider the economic benefits to society created in the course of producing the product. Plaintiffs claimed that defendant's cigarettes were defective, under the New Jersey risk-utility test, because the risks of smoking outweighed the utility of cigarettes. On the question of the utility of cigarettes, defendants planned to introduce evidence of the economic benefits of the cigarette industry including "consideration of profits made, employees hired, benefits to suppliers of goods and services, taxes generated and even charitable activities or contributions made by the defendant manufacturer." Plaintiffs made a motion in limine to bar such evidence. The trial court granted the motion, saying:

> Defendants' proposed evidence, when distilled to its essence, aims to establish that their product is profitable, that some of those profits are disseminated to others in society, and that such benefits would be reduced or eliminated if liability were imposed. But strict liability law is, if anything, intended to temper the profit motive by making a manufacturer or marketer aware that it may be less costly in the long run to market a product more safely, or not to market it at all. See Holford, The Limits of Strict Liability for Product Design and Manufacture, 52 Tex.L.Rev. 81, 86 (1973). As noted by Dean Wade, "Manufacturers are frankly in the business of making and selling products for the profit involved." Wade, On Product Design Defects and their Actionability, 33 Vand.L.Rev. 551, 569 (1980). To permit defendants to introduce the evidence that they here propose would undercut the very goals of strict liability law insofar as it suggests that defendants' interest in making a profit could transform an otherwise insufficient evaluation of their product's safety into a reasonable one.

Secondly, a fundamental purpose behind the imposition of strict liability is to require that a product "pay its way" by compensating for the harms it causes. * * * For this purpose to be furthered it is of course necessary to accept that a product's profitability will be reduced as it bears the costs attendant to its use, and indeed that its true costs to society may so outweigh its usefulness that those costs, when reflected in the product's price, will ultimately lead to that product's withdrawal from the market. That some economic dislocation may thereby result in the short run is, in turn, an accepted fact of life in the operation of a free market system in which those entities who profit from the marketing of a product—rather than its individual victims, or the government, or society—are the ones who are expected to bear the risks that such products are not economically viable. Indeed, any avoidance of product liability for reasons unrelated to the inherent value of the product itself would permit the continued marketing of products that do not truly pay their way, thus discouraging the profiting entities from devoting their energies to making their product safer, or to producing products that are more socially beneficial in the long term. To permit a manufacturer or marketer to introduce evidence of a product's profitability, and to suggest that such profitability will be endangered if legal liability is found, would thus undermine these goals of greater overall economic efficiency and product safety. * * *

The analysis was never meant to balance the risk to the consumer against the general benefit to society. Rather, the sole question presented is whether the risk to the consumers exceeds the utility to those consumers. * * *

644 F.Supp. at 288–90. This issue is discussed in Note, The Smoldering Issue in *Cipollone v. Liggett Group, Inc.*: Process Concerns in Determining Whether Cigarettes are a Defectively Designed Product, 73 Cornell L.Rev. 606, 615–619 (1988).

4. **Time of Ascertaining Costs and Benefits.** The costs and benefits of products can vary over time. The utility of a vaccine against a disease is much higher during an epidemic than when the disease is under control. The relevant time for evaluating a product's utility is the time of marketing. Likewise the costs of producing a safe product can either increase or decrease. These costs should be considered as they existed at the time the product was marketed. That is, courts consider how costly it would have been initially to build the product safely. They do not consider either the cost of building it safely today or the present cost of going back and making the product safe.

Be careful to distinguish the issue raised in this note—that the utility of taking a known risk can vary over time—from the issue discussed in the Note Regarding the Foresight/Hindsight Distinction, *infra* page 141. That note deals with the question of whether a manufacturer can be held liable for failing to protect against a risk that was not known at the time the product was marketed.

5. Are the following products defective under the risk-utility test of defect?

A. A gasoline can that does not have a child-proof top. A four-year-old child opened the can and was burned when the gasoline vapors accidentally caught fire.

B. A press without a point of operation safety guard. The worker was required to put a piece of metal stock between two halves of a die with her hand, and then activate the machine with a foot pedal. This would cause the two halves of the die to close with great force and shape the metal stock. The worker lost two fingers when she accidentally activated the foot pedal control while her hand was below the ram.

C. A riding lawn mower that does not have a dead man switch. The operator was thrown from the mower. His thumb and two fingers of his left hand were severed when he attempted to stop his fall.

D. A gas stove equipped with one-motion burner controls rather than two-step or self-latching controls. The one-motion controls can easily be turned on by accidentally brushing against them. A young child climbed on a chair in front of the stove and leaned over to get a spoon out of a fudge pan. The front burner ignited, and her clothes caught fire.

E. A beer bottle that is not strong enough to withstand the force of being thrown against a telephone pole.

F. A new drug which is very beneficial to a large number of people causes a serious side-effect in a small number of people. Plaintiff takes the drug and suffers the side-effect. Prior to plaintiff's illness, the risk was not known. The manufacturer did not warn about the risk of the side-effect.

G. A baseball base that is firmly secured at its location by a spike in the ground, such that the base remains in place whenever a runner slides into it, even if the runner begins the slide too late.

6. Characterization can play an important role in the way the test is applied. The adoption of a global versus a narrow characterization of the factor to be evaluated can influence the result. In note 5.A., *supra*, for example, the question of defect could be analyzed in terms of the usefulness of gasoline containers, or in terms of the availability and cost of child-proof tops.

7. For an economic appraisal of the risk-utility test of defect, consider the excerpt from the following article.

LANDES AND POSNER, A POSITIVE ECONOMIC ANALYSIS OF PRODUCTS LIABILITY
14 J. Legal Stud. 535, 553–54 (1985).

1. *Defective Design.* Here rather little need be said because the courts follow an explicit Hand formula approach.[1] This may surprise the reader, since the Hand formula is designed for negligence, and defective design cases are decided under the standard of strict liability. But it

---

1. See, for example, * * * Phillips v. Kimwood Mach. Co., 269 Ore. 485, 495–96, 525 P.2d 1033, 1038 (1974) * * *.

must be understood, first, that liability is strict in products cases only if a "defect" is shown (or, as we shall see, if the product, though not defective in the sense of improvable at a cost lower than the reduction in accident costs that the improvement would bring about, if "unreasonably [though unavoidably] dangerous"), and, second, that "defect" is determined in cost-benefit terms: a product is defective if it could have been made safer at a lower cost than the benefit in reducing expected accident costs.

Recall from Section II that negligence tends to be the preferred liability rule in joint care situations (that is, when it is efficient for both the consumer and manufacturer to take some care). It might seem paradoxical, therefore, that negligence rather than strict liability would be (in effect) the applicable rule for design defects, for the consumer would appear to be quite helpless to prevent accidents arising from such defects. The explanation lies in the fact that design defects typically involve durable goods, where the likelihood of an accident depends both on the product's design and on the method and intensity of consumer use. For example, a person who drives too fast and is injured when his car runs off the road could argue that his injury would have been avoided if the car had been designed differently (say, more like a tank). No doubt he is right. It is always possible to alter a product's design to make it safer. Yet in this example it is more efficient for the driver to avoid speeding than for the manufacturer to turn the car into a tank. If the manufacturer were liable for any and every injury that could have been avoided by a different design, consumers would have less incentive either to take care or to alter their activity level, for they would know they would be compensated for their injury. That is, if we are right that many product accidents that could be avoided by a different design are joint care situations, then negligence is the more efficient rule than strict liability for design defects.

Notes

1. We saw in Section B of this Chapter that courts impose true strict liability for manufacturing defects without regard to the reasonableness of the manufacturer's behavior. As Landes and Posner point out, by using the risk-utility test, courts accord very different treatment to design cases. The manufacturer that invests the optimal amount of money in design safety will not be liable for accidents resulting from reasonably safe designs. Yet, the manufacturer that invests the optimal amount of money in the quality control system used in the manufacturing process will be strictly liable for accidents resulting from flawed products that escape detection by the quality control system. In both cases the manufacturer's conduct is reasonable. Is the difference in treatment between manufacturing defects and design defects justifiable? Recall the earlier excerpt from Landes and Posner, *supra* page 91, offering a rationale for strict liability for harm caused by manufacturing flaws. Do you agree with their rationale? Is there a better explanation for the distinction?

2. Consider the following problem: A manufacturer can make a product component either out of copper (which will result in microscopic cracks developing in a small number of components) or out of platinum (which will never produce components with cracks). The manufacturer uses copper because platinum would make the product prohibitively expensive. A crack in a component causes a product failure that injures plaintiff. Plaintiff sues the manufacturer for her injuries, claiming that the product was defective. The evidence shows that the cracks could not have either been prevented or detected by the use of the best technology available. Should the court treat the case as one involving an allegation of design defect or of manufacturing defect? Does your answer depend on whether the cracks developed before or after the product was sold? Should this make any difference?

BARKER v. LULL ENGINEERING CO.
Supreme Court of California, 1978.
20 Cal.3d 413, 143 Cal.Rptr. 225, 573 P.2d 443.

TOBRINER, ACTING CHIEF JUSTICE.

[Plaintiff was injured at a construction site while operating a high-lift loader manufactured by defendant. The loader tipped partially over, and plaintiff jumped off the loader and attempted to scramble away. He was injured when some lumber on the lift fell and hit him. Plaintiff claimed that the loader was defectively designed in several respects, including that it should have been equipped with "outriggers," a roll bar, and seat belts. Plaintiff] instituted the present tort action seeking to recover damages for his injuries. The jury returned a verdict in favor of defendants, and plaintiff appeals from the judgment entered upon that verdict, contending primarily that in view of this court's decision in *Cronin v. J.B.E. Olson Corp.* (1972) 8 Cal.3d 121, 104 Cal.Rptr. 433, 501 P.2d 1153, the trial court erred in instructing the jury "that strict liability for a defect in design of a product is based on a finding that the product was unreasonably dangerous for its intended use * * *."

* * *

As we noted in *Cronin*, the Restatement draftsmen adopted the "unreasonably dangerous" language primarily as a means of confining the application of strict tort liability to an article which is "dangerous to an extent beyond that which would be contemplated by the ordinary consumer who purchases it, with the ordinary knowledge common to the community as to its characteristics." (Rest.2d Torts, § 402A, com. i.) In *Cronin*, however, we flatly rejected the suggestion that recovery in a products liability action should be permitted *only* if a product is more dangerous than contemplated by the average consumer, refusing to permit the low esteem in which the public might hold a dangerous product to diminish the manufacturer's responsibility for injuries caused by that product. As we pointedly noted in *Cronin*, even if the "ordinary consumer" may have contemplated that Shopsmith lathes posed a risk of loosening their grip and letting a piece of wood strike the operator, "another Greenman" should not be denied recovery. (8 Cal.3d at p. 133,

104 Cal.Rptr. 433, 501 P.2d 1153.) Indeed, our decision in *Luque v. McLean* (1972) 8 Cal.3d 136, 104 Cal.Rptr. 443, 501 P.2d 1163—decided the same day as *Cronin*—aptly reflects our disagreement with the restrictive implications of the Restatement formulation, for in *Luque* we held that a power rotary lawn mower with an unguarded hole could properly be found defective, in spite of the fact that the defect in the product was patent and hence in all probability within the reasonable contemplation of the ordinary consumer.

Thus, our rejection of the use of the "unreasonably dangerous" terminology in *Cronin* rested in part on a concern that a jury might interpret such an instruction, as the Restatement draftsman had indeed intended, as shielding a defendant from liability so long as the product did not fall below the ordinary consumer's expectations as to the product's safety.[1] As *Luque* demonstrates, the dangers posed by such a misconception by the jury extend to cases involving design defects as well as to actions involving manufacturing defects: indeed, the danger of confusion is perhaps more pronounced in design cases in which the manufacturer could frequently argue that its product satisfied ordinary consumer expectations since it was identical to other items of the same product line with which the consumer may well have been familiar.

Accordingly, contrary to defendants' contention, the reasoning of *Cronin* does not dictate that that decision be confined to the manufacturing defect context. Indeed, in *Cronin* itself we expressly stated that our holding applied to design defects as well as to manufacturing defects (8 Cal.3d at pp. 134–135, 104 Cal.Rptr. 433, 501 P.2d 1153), and in *Henderson v. Harnischfeger Corp.* (1974) 12 Cal.3d 663, 670, 117 Cal. Rptr. 1, 527 P.2d 353, we subsequently confirmed the impropriety of instructing a jury in the language of the "unreasonably dangerous" standard in a design defect case. (See also *Foglio v. Western Auto Supply* (1976) 56 Cal.App.3d 470, 475, 128 Cal.Rptr. 545.) Consequently, we conclude that the design defect instruction given in the instant case was erroneous.

* * *

Defendants contend, however, that if *Cronin* is interpreted as precluding the use of the "unreasonably dangerous" language in defining a design defect, the jury in all such cases will inevitably be left without any guidance whatsoever in determining whether a product is defective in design or not. * * * Amicus California Trial Lawyer Association (CTLA) on behalf of the plaintiff responds by suggesting that the precise intent of our *Cronin* decision was to preclude a trial court from formulating any

---

1. This is not to say that the expectations of the ordinary consumer are irrelevant to the determination of whether a product is defective, for as we point out below we believe that ordinary consumer expectations are frequently of direct significance to the defectiveness issue. The flaw in the Restatement's analysis, in our view, is that it treats such consumer expectations as a "ceiling" on a manufacturer's responsibility under strict liability principles, rather than as a "floor." As we shall explain, past California decisions establish that *at a minimum* a product must meet ordinary consumer expectations as to safety to avoid being found defective.

definition of "defect" in a product liability case, thus always leaving the definition of defect, as well as the application of such definition, to the jury. As we explain, neither of these contentions represents an accurate portrayal of the intent or effect of our *Cronin* decision.

* * *

Our decision in *Cronin* did not mandate such confusion. Instead, by observing that the problem in defining defect might be alleviated by reference to the "cluster of useful precedents," we intended to suggest that in drafting and evaluating instructions on this issue in a particular case, trial and appellate courts would be well advised to consider prior authorities involving similar defective product claims.

* * *

In general, a manufacturing or production defect is readily identifiable because a defective product is one that differs from the manufacturer's intended result or from other ostensibly identical units of the same product line. For example, when a product comes off the assembly line in a substandard condition it has incurred a manufacturing defect. * * * A design defect, by contrast, cannot be identified simply by comparing the injury-producing product with the manufacturer's plans or with other units of the same product line, since by definition the plans and all such units will reflect the same design. Rather than applying any sort of deviation-from-the-norm test in determining whether a product is defective in design for strict liability purposes, our cases have employed two alternative criteria in ascertaining, in Justice Traynor's words, whether there is something "wrong, if not in the manufacturer's manner of production, at least in his product." (Traynor, *The Ways and Meanings of Defective Products and Strict Liability, supra,* 32 Tenn.L.Rev. 363, 366.)

First, our cases establish that a product may be found defective in design if the plaintiff demonstrates that the product failed to perform as safely as an ordinary consumer would expect when used in an intended or reasonably foreseeable manner. This initial standard, somewhat analogous to the Uniform Commercial Code's warranty of fitness and merchantability (Cal.U.Com.Code, § 2314), reflects the warranty heritage upon which California product liability doctrine in part rests. As we noted in *Greenman,* "implicit in [a product's] presence on the market * * * [is] a representation that it [will] safely do the jobs for which it was built." (59 Cal.2d at p. 64, 27 Cal.Rptr. at p. 701, 377 P.2d at p. 901.) When a product fails to satisfy such ordinary consumer expectations as to safety in its intended or reasonably foreseeable operation, a manufacturer is strictly liable for resulting injuries. * * * Under this standard, an injured plaintiff will frequently be able to demonstrate the defectiveness of a product by resort to circumstantial evidence, even when the accident itself precludes identification of the specific defect at fault. * * *

As Professor Wade has pointed out, however, the expectations of the ordinary consumer cannot be viewed as the exclusive yardstick for evaluating design defectiveness because "[i]n many situations * * * the consumer would not know what to expect, because he would have no idea how safe the product could be made." (Wade, *On the Nature of Strict Tort Liability for Products, supra,* 44 Miss.L.J. 825, 829.) Numerous California decisions have implicitly recognized this fact and have made clear, through varying linguistic formulations, that a product may be found defective in design, even if it satisfies ordinary consumer expectations, if through hindsight the jury determines that the product's design embodies "excessive preventable danger," or, in other words, if the jury finds that the risk of danger inherent in the challenged design outweighs the benefits of such design. * * *

A review of past cases indicates that in evaluating the adequacy of a product's design pursuant to this latter standard, a jury may consider, among other relevant factors, the gravity of the danger posed by the challenged design, the likelihood that such danger would occur, the mechanical feasibility of a safer alternative design, the financial cost of an improved design, and the adverse consequences to the product and to the consumer that would result from an alternative design. * * *

Although our cases have thus recognized a variety of considerations that may be relevant to the determination of the adequacy of a product's design, past authorities have generally not devoted much attention to the appropriate allocation of the burden of proof with respect to these matters. * * * The allocation of such burden is particularly significant in this context inasmuch as this court's product liability decisions, from *Greenman* to *Cronin,* have repeatedly emphasized that one of the principal purposes behind the strict product liability doctrine is to relieve an injured plaintiff of many of the onerous evidentiary burdens inherent in a negligence cause of action. Because most of the evidentiary matters which may be relevant to the determination of the adequacy of a product's design under the "risk-benefit" standard—e.g., the feasibility and cost of alternative designs—are similar to issues typically presented in a negligent design case and involve technical matters peculiarly within the knowledge of the manufacturer, we conclude that once the plaintiff makes a prima facie showing that the injury was proximately caused by the product's design, the burden should appropriately shift to the defendant to prove, in light of the relevant factors, that the product is not defective. Moreover, inasmuch as this conclusion flows from our determination that the fundamental public policies embraced in *Greenman* dictate that a manufacturer who seeks to escape liability for an injury proximately caused by its product's design on a risk-benefit theory should bear the burden of persuading the trier of fact that its product should not be judged defective, the defendant's burden is one affecting the burden of proof, rather than simply the burden of producing evidence. * * *

Thus, to reiterate, a product may be found defective in design, so as to subject a manufacturer to strict liability for resulting injuries, under either of two alternative tests. First, a product may be found defective in design if the plaintiff establishes that the product failed to perform as safely as an ordinary consumer would expect when used in an intended or reasonably foreseeable manner. Second, a product may alternatively be found defective in design if the plaintiff demonstrates that the product's design proximately caused his injury and the defendant fails to establish, in light of the relevant factors, that, on balance, the benefits of the challenged design outweigh the risk of danger inherent in such design.

* * *

Finally, contrary to the suggestion of amicus CTLA, an instruction which advises the jury that it may evaluate the adequacy of a product's design by weighing the benefits of the challenged design against the risk of danger inherent in such design is not simply the equivalent of an instruction which requires the jury to determine whether the manufacturer was negligent in designing the product. (See, e.g., Wade, *On the Nature of Strict Tort Liability for Products, supra,* 44 Miss.L.J. 825, 835.) It is true, of course, that in many cases proof that a product is defective in design may also demonstrate that the manufacturer was negligent in choosing such a design. As we have indicated, however, in a strict liability case, as contrasted with a negligent design action, the jury's focus is properly directed to the condition of the product itself, and not to the reasonableness of the manufacturer's conduct. * * *

Thus, the fact that the manufacturer took reasonable precautions in an attempt to design a safe product or otherwise acted as a reasonably prudent manufacturer would have under the circumstances, while perhaps absolving the manufacturer of liability under a negligence theory, will not preclude the imposition of liability under strict liability principles if, upon hindsight, the trier of fact concludes that the product's design is unsafe to consumers, users, or bystanders. * * *

* * *

The judgment in favor of defendants is reversed.

Mosk, Clark, Richardson, Wright (Retired Chief Justice of California assigned by the Acting Chairperson of the Judicial Council), and Sullivan (Retired Associate Justice of the Supreme Court sitting under assignment by the Chairperson of the Judicial Council), JJ., concur.

Notes

1. A number of other jurisdictions have adopted the *Barker v. Lull* test of defect. Caterpillar Tractor Co. v. Beck, 593 P.2d 871 (Alaska 1979); Dart v. Wiebe Manufacturing, Inc., 147 Ariz. 242, 709 P.2d 876 (1985); Knitz v. Minster Machine Co., 69 Ohio St.2d 460, 432 N.E.2d 814 (1982).

2. California has approved the following jury instruction for design defect cases:

The _____ of a product is liable for injuries caused by a defect in its design which existed when it left the possession of the _____ provided that they resulted from a use of the product that was reasonably foreseeable by the _____.

A product is defective in design:

[if it fails to perform as safely as an ordinary consumer would expect when used in an intended or reasonably foreseeable manner]. [or]

[if there is a risk of danger inherent in the design which outweighs the benefits of that design].

[In determining whether the benefits of the design outweigh such risks you may consider, among other things, the gravity of the danger posed by the design, the likelihood that such danger would cause damage, the mechanical feasibility of a safer alternate design at the time of manufacture, the financial cost of an improved design, and the adverse consequences to the product and the consumer that would result from an alternate design.]

BAJI 9.00.5 (1992 Revision)

3. California does not apply the consumer expectations branch of the Barker test where the common experience of consumers cannot answer the question of how safely the product should have performed. In Soule v. General Motors Corp., 8 Cal.4th 548, 882 P.2d 298, 34 Cal.Rptr.2d 607 (1994) the court stated:

In some cases, therefore, "ordinary knowledge ... as to ... [the product's] characteristics" (Rest.2d Torts, *supra*, § 402A, com. i., p. 352) may permit an inference that the product did not perform as safely as it should. *If* the facts permit such a conclusion, and *if* the failure resulted from the product's design, a finding of defect is warranted without any further proof. The manufacturer may not defend a claim that a product's design failed to perform as safely as its ordinary consumers would expect by presenting expert evidence of the design's relative risks and benefits.[1]

However, as we noted in *Barker*, a complex product, even when it is being used as intended, may often cause injury in a way that does not engage its ordinary consumers' reasonable minimum assumptions about safe performance. For example, the ordinary consumer of an automobile simply has "no idea" how it should perform in all foreseeable situations, or how safe it should be made against all foreseeable hazards. (*Barker, supra*, 20 Cal.3d at p. 430, 143 Cal.Rptr. 225, 573 P.2d 443.)

* * *

As we have seen, the consumer expectations test is reserved for cases in which the *everyday experience* of the product's users permits a

---

1. For example, the ordinary consumers of modern automobiles may and do expect that such vehicles will be designed so as not to explode while idling at stoplights, experience sudden steering or brake failure as they leave the dealership, or roll over and catch fire in two-mile-per-hour collisions. If the plaintiff in a product liability action proved that a vehicle's design produced such a result, the jury could find forthwith that the car failed to perform as safely as its ordinary consumers would expect, and was therefore defective.

conclusion that the product's design violated *minimum* safety assumptions, and is thus defective *regardless of expert opinion about the merits of the design*. It follows that where the minimum safety of a product is within the common knowledge of lay jurors, expert witnesses may not be used to demonstrate what an ordinary consumer would or should expect. Use of expert testimony for that purpose would invade the jury's function (*see* Evid.Code, § 801, subd. (a)), and would invite circumvention of the rule that the risks and benefits of a challenged design must be carefully balanced whenever the issue of design defect goes beyond the common experience of the product's users.

Soule v. General Motors Corp., 8 Cal.4th 548, 567, 882 P.2d 298, 309, 34 Cal.Rptr.2d 607, 617 (1994).

4. How would a court using the *Barker v. Lull* test of defect decide the following cases?

    A. A punch press without a point of operation safety guard. The worker lost two fingers when she accidentally activated the foot pedal control while her hand was below the ram.

    B. A new drug that is very beneficial to a large number of people causes a serious side-effect in a small number of people. Plaintiff takes the drug and suffers the side-effect. Prior to plaintiff's illness, the risk was not known.

    C. A beer bottle, that is not strong enough to withstand the force of being thrown against a telephone pole, shatters and injures a bystander when it hits a pole.

5. The *Barker v. Lull* test significantly expands the scope of liability in two ways. First, by using the two tests of defect in the disjunctive, it insures that plaintiff will recover if the product fails either test. Some products are defective under risk-utility but not under consumer expectations, and some products are defective under consumer expectations but not risk-utility. By declaring that a product is defective if it violates either test, *Barker* carries liability further than courts that use either test singly.

6. The second way that *Barker* expands the scope of liability is by shifting the burden of proof on the question of whether the utility outweighs the risk. In analyzing this aspect of the *Barker v. Lull* test, Professor Epstein states:

> The careful division of burdens in the second portion of the test says that plaintiff need only show design *features* that might be implicated in the accident, leaving it to the defendant, at great expense, *routinely* to justify each feature as best he can. With this distribution of burden, the plaintiff can always show some way in which the product might have been changed in order to avert the accident, as it is always possible to generate some improvement at some price. All product related accidents have become presumptively actionable.

Epstein, Products Liability: The Search for the Middle Ground, 56 N.C.L.Rev. 643, 651 (1978). *See also,* Henderson, Renewed Judicial Controversy Over Defective Product Design: Toward the Preservation of an Emerging Consensus, 63 Minn.L.Rev. 773 (1979); Schwartz, Foreword: Understanding Products Liability, 67 Calif.L.Rev. 439 (1979).

7. Are there any cases that will not go to the jury under the *Barker v. Lull* test? Suppose plaintiff drops a typewriter on his toe, and he sues the manufacturer of the typewriter for the resulting injury. Would the case go to the jury? If not, why not?

8. In Quintana–Ruiz v. Hyundai Motor Corp., 303 F.3d 62 (1st Cir. 2002) plaintiff's arm and wrist were broken in four places by an automobile airbag when it deployed as intended in an automobile accident. Plaintiff sued the automobile manufacturer in a jurisdiction using the *Barker v. Lull* test, claiming the car was defective under the risk/utility branch of the test. Plaintiff presented no expert testimony. Defendant presented uncontradicted expert testimony that the benefits of the airbag's design outweighed the risks. The court of appeals reversed a jury verdict for plaintiff, finding the jury had insufficient evidence to reject the expert testimony. The court stated:

> [T]he plaintiff argues that when a plaintiff does not present her own expert testimony and convinces the jury to disregard the defense experts' testimony, a plaintiff can prevail on her design defect claim simply by showing that the product caused her injury. * * *
>
> * * *
>
> Generally, a jury may not reject testimony that is uncontradicted and unimpeached (directly, circumstantially, or inferentially) unless credibility is at issue[.] * * *
>
> * * *
>
> In this case, there is no such evidence as would support a jury's rejection of the experts' testimony. The experts, although paid by the defendants on an hourly basis, had no financial or personal interest in the outcome of the case. Nor is there a claim of fraud on the part of the expert witnesses. The only "bias" is in their retention by the defense. * * * There was no evidence, circumstantial or direct, tending to show that they were not credible witnesses. The testimony was not improbable, inconsistent, or otherwise facially unbelievable. In short, there is nothing in the record to support the jury's rejection of the experts' testimony.

Quintana–Ruiz v. Hyundai Motor Corp., 303 F.3d 62, 74–76 (1st Cir. 2002).

Note Regarding the Foresight/Hindsight Distinction

Phillips v. Kimwood Machine Co., supra page 114 states the traditional view about the distinction between negligence and strict liability in design and warning cases. Negligence requires that risks be foreseeable, but strict liability imputes knowledge of risk to the manufacturer. Numerous other cases agree. The issue, however, is not as simple as *Phillips* makes it sound.

The question is whether products will be judged in light of the knowledge and technology available at the time of distribution or at the time of trial. Consider all the types of information that would exonerate a manufacturer from liability for negligence if the information were truly unknowable at the time of distribution. The manufacturer might not know:

1) of a risk posed by a single product because of an undiscoverable manufacturing flaw; or

2) of a generic risk, a risk shared by all products in the line even when the product is used as intended, *e.g.*, exposure to a chemical in a product causes cancer; or

3) of a risk created by the misuse of the product, *e.g.*, the user of a bathtub drowns because she uses the tub as a boat, and the tub sinks because it is not seaworthy; or

4) of a risk created by unusual circumstances, *e.g.*, a defective dog chain breaks, but instead of a vicious dog attacking the plaintiff, a playful dog jumps on plaintiff and knocks him down, or

5) of technology that will reduce a known risk, *e.g.*, sale of a car equipped with mechanical brakes before hydraulic brakes were invented.

Strict products liability cases deal with some of the above-issues by using hindsight, but instances of courts actually using hindsight—in cases where it would make a difference—are actually quite rare. Issue 1, above, the undiscoverable manufacturing flaw, is the case where there is universal agreement. Courts impose true strict liability in that case. The manufacturer's inability to discover the flaw is no excuse. We saw that in Section B of this Chapter.

Issue 2, the generic risk, is more problematic. Courts are split on the question of whether inability to discover a generic risk associated with a product at the time of sale or distribution will excuse the manufacturer from liability. In design defect cases courts in most jurisdictions hold that justifiable ignorance of generic risk does not excuse the manufacturer. *E.g.*, Elmore v. Owens–Illinois, Inc., 673 S.W.2d 434 (Mo.1984) (asbestos). A minority of courts disagree. *E.g.*, Heritage v. Pioneer Brokerage & Sales, Inc., 604 P.2d 1059, 1063–64 (Alaska 1979) (design defect theory; formaldehyde fumes in mobile home).

Yet, even in majority-rule jurisdictions, there are very powerful restrictions on the use of hindsight in cases involving scientifically unknowable generic risk. First, the great majority of courts use foresight rather than hindsight in warning defect cases. *E.g.*, Robertson v. General Tire & Rubber Co., 123 Ill.App.3d 11, 78 Ill.Dec. 587, 462 N.E.2d 706 (1984) (design defect; wheel rim separation; noting that Illinois law requires that the risk be knowable in warning cases but not in design cases); Carter v. Johns–Manville Sales Corp., 557 F.Supp. 1317 (E.D.Tex.1983) (asbestos; knowledge requirement in warning cases but not in design cases); *See* note 7, *infra* page 243. That is, manufacturers are only liable for failing to warn about risks that they knew about or that they could have discovered by using the knowledge of an expert. Second, most courts exempt manufacturers of drugs and medical devices from strict liability. These cases are discussed in subsection (d) below. This exemption is very important because the issue of unknowable generic risks arises most frequently with new drugs and medical devices. Other kinds of products, such as machinery, almost never create new risks that could not have been discovered with due diligence. Thus, most cases that purport to apply hindsight to the generic risk issue are like

Phillips. There, the product's dangers were actually known at the time of manufacture; the result of the case would have been the same under a foresight test as under a hindsight test.

Issue 3, the failure to anticipate an accident caused by unforeseeable misuse of the product, is covered in subsection (a) below. Courts apply foresight here, holding manufacturers liable only for harm arising out of intended use or foreseeable use. The same is generally true with respect to issue 4, unexpected risk created by unusual circumstances. This issue is treated in Chapter 7, which deals with proximate cause. In products liability cases, courts often apply the foreseeability test of proximate cause as developed in negligence cases.

The remaining issue, knowledge of technology, is covered in subsection (b) below. All courts use foresight there, requiring manufacturers to use the best technology that was either available at the time of manufacture or that could have been developed at that time by an expert in the field. They do not hold manufacturers liable for failing to use technology available at the time of trial if it was impossible to have developed that technology at the time of manufacture.

All of this raises a number of important issues. Should justifiable ignorance excuse the manufacturer with respect to any or all of the five ways the question arises? Is there a defensible basis for applying foresight to some issues and hindsight to others? Should the resolution of these issues apply across the board to all products, or should certain products—such as drugs or asbestos—be dealt with differently? *See generally* Wade, On the Effect in Product Liability of Knowledge Unavailable Prior to Marketing, 58 N.Y.U.L.Rev. 734 (1983); Birnbaum and Wrubel, "State of the Art" and Strict Products Liability, 21 Tort & Ins.L.J. 30 (1985); Robb, A Practical Approach to Use of State of the Art Evidence in Strict Products Liability Cases, 77 Nw.U.L.Rev. 1 (1982); Spradley, Defensive Use of State of the Art Evidence in Strict Products Liability, 67 Minn.L.Rev. 343 (1982); Wertheimer, Unknowable Dangers and the Death of Strict Products Liability: The Empire Strikes Back, U.Cin.L.Rev. 1183 (1992).

In this regard, consider the facts of Habecker v. Clark Equipment Co., 942 F.2d 210 (3d Cir.1991). There, a forklift operator was thrown from a forklift and crushed beneath it. In the resulting lawsuit against the manufacturer, plaintiff claimed that the forklift was defective because it was not equipped with a seatbelt or harness. The evidence showed that, at the time of manufacture, it was impossible for the industry to determine whether operator restraint systems reduced the risk of injury to the operator or increased the risk. At the time of trial, however, modern computer modeling systems showed that operator restraint systems indeed reduced the risk. How should the case be decided? Does *Habecker* involve ignorance of generic risk (the manufacturer did not know the extent of the danger posed by a forklift without a seatbelt) or ignorance of technology (the manufacturer did not know that there was a safer alternative design)? Should the answer make any difference?

The Restatement (Third) of Torts: Products Liability § 2 takes the position that foresight should be used with respect to all issues in design and warning cases. The comments explain:

a. Rationale. * * * To hold a manufacturer liable for a risk that was not foreseeable when the product was marketed might foster increased manufacturer investment in safety. But such investment by definition would be a matter of guesswork. Furthermore, manufacturers may persuasively ask to be judged by a normative behavior standard to which it is reasonably possible for manufacturers to conform. For these reasons, Subsections (b) and (c) speak of products being defective only when risks are reasonably foreseeable.

* * *

m. Reasonably foreseeable uses and risks in design and warning claims. * * * In cases involving a claim of design defect in a mechanical product, foreseeability of risk is rarely an issue as a practical matter. Once the plaintiff establishes that the product was put to a reasonably foreseeable use, physical risks of injury are generally known or reasonably knowable by experts in the field. It is not unfair to charge a manufacturer with knowledge of such generally known or knowable risks.

The issue of foreseeability of risk of harm is more complex in the case of products such as prescription drugs, medical devices, and toxic chemicals. Risks attendant to use and consumption of these products may, indeed, be unforeseeable at the time of sale. Unforeseeable risks arising from foreseeable product use or consumption by definition cannot specifically be warned against. Thus, in connection with a claim of inadequate design, instruction, or warning, plaintiff should bear the burden of establishing that the risk in question was known or should have been known to the relevant manufacturing community. The harms that result from unforeseeable risks—for example, in the human body's reaction to a new drug, medical device, or chemical—are not a basis of liability. Of course, a seller bears responsibility to perform reasonable testing prior to marketing a product and to discover risks and risk-avoidance measures that such testing would reveal. A seller is charged with knowledge of what reasonable testing would reveal. If testing is not undertaken, or is performed in an inadequate manner, and this failure results in a defect that causes harm, the seller is subject to liability for harm caused by such defect.

Keep the issues raised in this note in mind as you study the materials in the rest of this chapter. As you examine those materials, ask yourself whether you agree with the conventional approach, the Restatement (Third) approach, or some other approach.

(a) Ignorance of Risk Caused by Misuse

ROMITO v. RED PLASTIC CO., INC.
Court of Appeals of California, Second District, 1995.
38 Cal.App.4th 59, 44 Cal.Rptr.2d 834.

ORTEGA, ACTING PRESIDING JUSTICE.

If the technological means exist, must a manufacturer improve its product to guard against injuries resulting from unforeseeable and accidental product misuse in order to stave off potential tort liability? We conclude as a matter of policy that despite the means to build a safer product, a manufacturer owes no duty to prevent injuries resulting from unforeseeable and accidental product misuse. We affirm summary judgment for the defendant manufacturer of a plastic skylight which lacked sufficient impact strength to bear the weight of a falling person.

BACKGROUND

This appeal involves a wrongful death action. On April 11, 1989, decedent Edward Romito, age 63, was employed as a journeyman electrician at the Santa Anita Race Track. Romito, who had 36 years of experience as an electrician, was removing television cables and wires that had been draped over the flat roof of the four-story Club Court building. The roof was not open to the public and was separated from an abutting terrace by a low wall. The roof contained a row of plastic skylights manufactured by defendant Red Plastic Company, Inc., d.b.a. Dur–Red Products.

The 6–foot tall and 228–pound Romito was wearing two fully-loaded tool belts and heavy work boots, but no safety line. As he was pulling the cable onto the roof through a small opening in a window below, the cable became tangled. He continued pulling until the cable suddenly broke free, causing him to lose his balance and stumble backwards onto a nearby plastic skylight. Romito fell through the skylight, landing 16 to 20 feet below on a concrete floor, fatally injured.

Romito's wife and two adult daughters * * * filed a wrongful death action against * * * defendant Dur–Red. The complaint alleged that Dur–Red * * * is liable in negligence and strict products liability for having failed to use an acrylic strong enough to bear the weight of a falling person.

The architect who designed the Club Court had specified, by make and model, 12 Dur–Red skylights. Defendant filled and delivered the order to the race track in July 1986, three years before the accident. The skylights, 3/16 of an inch thick, were 5–feet square with a 10–inch dome at the center, surrounded by metal frames. They met the applicable building code requirements, which neither specified an impact resistance rating for plastic skylights nor required that protective screens or railings be placed around them. Defendant, who was unfamiliar with the Club Court's design, had played no part in choosing the location of the skylights, installing them, or supervising the workers who would come near them.

Based on the above undisputed facts, defendant moved for summary adjudication of five issues: (1) falling through the skylight was an unforeseeable misuse of the product, (2) defendant owed no duty of care to the decedent, (3) defendant breached no duty of care, (4) the skylight was not defective, and (5) the skylight was not the legal cause of the accident.

In opposition to the motion, plaintiffs submitted the deposition of Russell Smith, avowedly Dur–Red's most knowledgeable employee regarding plastics technology. According to Smith, Dur–Red never considered whether its skylights can support a person's weight. Dur–Red's failure to use a stronger material in the accident skylight was not a calculated decision. Dur–Red subscribed to no trade publications regarding plastics technology and never consulted a chemical engineer or plastics specialist regarding the design, manufacture, or testing of its skylights before Romito's accident. Smith acknowledged, however, that skylights are often installed on flat roofs where people walk near them, and that he has heard of people falling through skylights and of skylights breaking.

Plaintiffs also submitted the declaration of a chemist and plastics industry consultant, James Mason. The skylight "had a Notched Izod impact strength of .34 foot pounds per inch of notch," which Mason believed was inadequate for its foreseeable use. Stronger acrylics were available for about the same price since the late 1970s. When the accident skylight was made, other manufacturers were using stronger but comparably priced materials with a 1.1 or greater impact strength, such as "Plexiglass D.R. by Rohm & Haas Corporation," (one of Dur–Red's suppliers), which would have held Romito's weight during the fall. In addition, "BASF's Luran, which had an impact strength of 5.6, over 15 times the strength" of defendant's skylight, was only "somewhat more expensive."

The trial court granted defendant's motion for summary adjudication on all issues. After concluding that no triable issues remained, the trial court entered summary judgment for defendant and this appeal followed.

DISCUSSION

* * *

A. *Negligence*

* * *

For the purpose of deciding this appeal, we accept plaintiffs' unrefuted evidence that in 1986 other manufacturers were using, and Dur–Red could have used, a comparably priced material strong enough to bear Romito's weight. We must decide whether Dur–Red may be absolved of negligence liability, as a matter of law, for failing to build a stronger skylight.

In *Rowland v. Christian* (1968) 69 Cal.2d 108, 113, 70 Cal.Rptr. 97, 443 P.2d 561, the California Supreme Court identified certain factors that should be considered in determining a landowner's duty of care: "[T]he major ones are the foreseeability of harm to the plaintiff, the degree of certainty that the plaintiff suffered injury, the closeness of the connection between the defendant's conduct and the injury suffered, the moral blame attached to the defendant's conduct, the policy of preventing future harm, the extent of the burden to the defendant and consequences to the community of imposing a duty to exercise care with resulting liability for breach, and the availability, cost, and prevalence of insurance for the risk involved. [Citations.]"

Applying these factors here, plaintiffs contend a triable issue of fact exists concerning the foreseeability of harm to the decedent. People have been known to fall through skylights, as Dur–Red's own employee admitted in his deposition testimony. The existence of protective devices (screens, rails, safety lines), also confirms there is some risk.

A triable issue of fact does not exist, however, merely because a jury could find the risk of a worker falling through the skylight was reasonably foreseeable. " 'The question of "duty" is decided by the court, not the jury. [Citations.]' *(Ballard v. Uribe* (1986) 41 Cal.3d 564, 572, fn. 6 [715 P.2d 624]....) In the typical negligence action, a determination that there is no duty giving rise to liability is essentially a conclusion that the weight of public policy warrants a departure from Civil Code section 1714." *(Thai v. Stang* (1989) 214 Cal.App.3d 1264, 1271, 263 Cal.Rptr. 202.)

"[I]t is often misleadingly stated that although duty is a question of law, foreseeability is a question of fact which must be decided by the trier of fact in any case about which reasonable minds can differ [citations]. To the contrary, where it is one factor to which a court looks in defining the boundaries of 'duty,' foreseeability of the particular kind of harm is strictly a question of law when evaluated within the general context of 'whether the category of negligent conduct at issue is sufficiently likely to result in the kind of harm experienced that liability may appropriately be imposed on the negligent party.' [Citations.]" *(Lopez v. McDonald's Corp.* (1987) 193 Cal.App.3d 495, 507, fn. 6, 238 Cal.Rptr. 436.)

" 'Defendant owes a duty, in the sense of a potential liability for damages, only with respect to those risks or hazards whose likelihood made the conduct unreasonably dangerous, and hence negligent, in the first instance. [Citations.]' " *(Lopez v. McDonald's Corp., supra,* 193 Cal.App.3d at pp. 507–508, 238 Cal.Rptr. 436.) "[T]he 'court's task—in determining "duty"—is not to decide whether a *particular* plaintiff's injury was reasonably foreseeable in light of a *particular* defendant's conduct, but rather to evaluate more generally whether the category of negligent conduct at issue is sufficiently likely to result in the kind of harm experienced that liability may appropriately be imposed on the negligent party.' *(Ballard v. Uribe* [1986] 41 Cal.3d [564,] 57[3], fn. 6 [224 Cal.Rptr. 664, 715 P.2d 624].) Viewed in this light, the question of foreseeability in a 'duty' context is a limited one for the court, and readily contrasted with the fact-specific foreseeability questions bearing on negligence (breach of duty) and proximate causation posed to the jury or trier of fact. *(Ibid.)*" *(Lopez v. McDonald's Corp., supra,* 193 Cal. App.3d at p. 507, 238 Cal.Rptr. 436, fns. omitted.)

We employ no rigid test for measuring the degree of foreseeability necessary to impose a duty of care. "The degree of foreseeability necessary to warrant the finding of a duty will ... vary from case to case. For example, in cases where the burden of preventing future harm is great, a high degree of foreseeability may be required. [Citation.] On the other hand, in cases where there are strong policy reasons for preventing the harm, or the harm can be prevented by simple means, a lesser degree of foreseeability may be required. [Citation.]" *(Gomez v. Ticor* (1983) 145 Cal.App.3d 622, 629–630, 193 Cal.Rptr. 600.)

Dur–Red's ability to prevent future harm is limited by its total lack of control over various external factors affecting the risk of harm. Those factors include, for example, the roof's design, the layout and installation of the skylights, the roof's accessibility to the public, the presence of screens or rails around the skylight, the training, skill, and safety equipment used by workers coming near the skylight, and the maintenance of the skylight and surrounding area. In this case, Dur–Red simply filled and delivered an order for 12 skylights, exercising no control over the circumstances of Romito's accidental fall through a skylight three years later. Romito's failure to tie himself to a safety line cannot be attributed to Dur–Red.

Even if Dur–Red had built the Club Court skylights with a 1.1 impact strength rated material and thus saved Romito from the consequences of his failure to wear a safety line and his accidental fall, the next worker coming near the same skylight might still be at risk depending on the circumstances of that accident. Perhaps even a 1.1 impact strength rated material would not save a 300–pound worker with a wheelbarrow of bricks who falls when a 40–foot scaffold collapses on top of a skylight. These and other myriad unpredictable circumstances make it necessary to impose a higher degree of foreseeability in this case as a matter of policy, lest we by judicial fiat transform skylight manufacturers into insurers of public safety.

We acknowledge the appeal of the logic that Dur–Red, in the interest of public safety, readily could have used a stronger material at no extra cost that would have saved Romito's life. This logic, however attractive in this case, fails to satisfy our broader policy concerns. Any product is potentially dangerous if accidentally misused or abused, and predicting the different ways in which accidents can occur is a task limited only by the scope of one's imagination. To require skylight manufacturers to adopt technological safety advances and recall, replace, or retrofit their older products or risk exposure to tort liability would be unreasonable in the absence of defined risks of harm.

Delineating the risks of harm to be eliminated by skylight manufacturers is a function better suited to the Legislature than the judiciary. Here, the skylight met all applicable building code requirements. It happened to be made of a weaker variety of plastic, but what if it had been made of glass? Should the manufacturer be subject to possible tort liability for having used glass rather than impact resistant plastic?

Should it matter that the architect had specified glass skylights without calling for any of the available safety devices, or that the building owner had failed to maintain the glass skylight which "was so covered with dust and paper that it appeared no different from the surrounding roof[?]" (*Hatheway v. Industrial Acc. Com.* (1939) 13 Cal.2d 377, 379, 90 P.2d 68.)

Here, the injury resulted from an accidental fall. If we were to impose a duty of care in this situation, should the manufacturer also owe a duty of care to a victim of crime? As the level of violence in modern society increases, even state of the art products may soon be rendered unsafe. For example, automobile windshields and home and office windows could be made of bulletproof glass but most are not. Must glass companies refuse to sell anything but bulletproof glass to auto manufacturers and construction companies simply because the stronger material exists and the risk of shootings is ever increasing in many urban neighborhoods? * * *

We conclude Dur–Red owed no duty of care to protect against the innumerable unforeseeable risks surrounding the accidental misuse of its product. * * *.

* * *

As a matter of law, we conclude the risk of harm to Romito was not reasonably foreseeable for reasons of policy, thus negating any duty of care. * * *.

Having found as a matter of law that Dur–Red had no legal duty to protect Romito against his unforeseeable and accidental misuse of the skylight, we conclude plaintiffs' negligence cause of action is barred.

B. Strict Products Liability

"[A] product may be found defective in design, so as to subject a manufacturer to strict liability for resulting injuries, under either of two alternative tests. First, a product may be found defective in design if the plaintiff establishes that the product failed to perform as safely as an ordinary consumer would expect when used in an intended or reasonably foreseeable manner. Second, a product may alternatively be found defective in design if the plaintiff demonstrates that the product's design proximately caused his injury and the defendant fails to establish, in light of the relevant factors, that, on balance, the benefits of the challenged design outweigh the risk of danger inherent in such design." (*Barker v. Lull Engineering Co.* (1978) 20 Cal.3d 413, 432, 143 Cal.Rptr. 225, 573 P.2d 443.)

Under the first prong of *Barker's* defective design test, the skylight was not defective. A skylight is not being used in an intended or reasonably foreseeable manner when a worker accidentally steps on and falls through it, as discussed in part A above. Accordingly, there is no triable issue of fact regarding the first prong of Barker's defective design test. * * *

The second prong of the design defect test is causation, which involves the same policy considerations that we relied upon to negate a duty of care. [Citation] Although in *Mitchell v. Gonzales* (1991) 54 Cal.3d 1041, 1 Cal.Rptr.2d 913, 819 P.2d 872, our Supreme Court disapproved the standard proximate cause instruction (former BAJI No. 3.75) in favor of the substantial factor test of causation, it did not eliminate the "normative or evaluative element" of proximate cause which asks the policy question of whether the defendant should be held liable for negligently causing the plaintiff's injury. [Citations]

Whether Dur–Red's failure to use a stronger material was a substantial factor in bringing about Romito's injury is irrelevant if Dur–Red owed no duty toward Romito due to the unforeseeability of the risk of harm. Having concluded no duty was owed, we need not discuss whether Dur–Red's conduct was a substantial factor in bringing about the injury.

* * *

For the policy reasons discussed in part A, defendant owed no legal duty to protect against Romito's unforeseeable and accidental misuse of the skylight. Accordingly, plaintiffs' product liability cause of action is also barred.

DISPOSITION

We affirm the summary judgment. Defendant is awarded costs.

MIRIAM A. VOGEL and MASTERSON, JJ., concur.

Notes

1. In many design defect cases decided under the risk-utility test of defect, the defectiveness of the product often turns on the question of whether the misuse is foreseeable. This is because manufacturers must design products to be reasonably safe in light of anticipated misuse. *See, e.g.,* Self v. General Motors Corp., 42 Cal.App.3d 1, 116 Cal.Rptr. 575 (1974) (automobiles must be designed to be reasonably safe when involved in collisions); Bexiga v. Havir Manufacturing Corp., 60 N.J. 402, 290 A.2d 281 (1972) (dangerous machinery must have adequate safety guards); LaGorga v. Kroger Co., 275 F.Supp. 373 (W.D.Pa.1967), affirmed, 407 F.2d 671 (3d Cir.1969) (child's jacket must be treated with flame retardant).

2. This same issue is sometimes dealt with as a question of proximate cause. Courts can characterize the act of misuse as an intervening cause, and hold that defendant is liable only if the act is foreseeable. Only then does the defendant have a duty to protect against the intervening cause. The result, of course, is the same whether the question is dealt with as an issue of defect or of proximate cause. There is no obligation to protect against risks created by unforeseeable misuse.

3. There is also a proximate cause issue that is unrelated to defect. This is where a clearly defective product produces an unexpected type of harm because it is misused in an unforeseeable way. Proximate cause issues arising out of misuse are dealt with in Chapter 7.

4. Is misuse an affirmative defense? Most courts say no, and place the burden of proving proper use on the plaintiff. *E.g.,* Rogers v. Toro Manufacturing Co., 522 S.W.2d 632 (Mo.App.1975). This is sensible in cases where the use is relevant to questions of defectiveness and proximate cause, both of which are elements of plaintiff's case. Should the answer be different in cases where misuse is solely relevant to the question of contributory fault because defect and proximate cause are present? *See Mauch v. Manufacturers Sales & Service, Inc., infra,* page 622.

5. Foreseeability is not always controlling. Manufacturers are not required to make products that are incapable of causing harm. Recall the language in *Phillips v. Kimwood Machine Co., supra* page 114, that the design only has to be reasonably safe, not completely safe. Certain products may not be defective in design, or because of a failure to warn, even though it is foreseeable that they can be used in such a way as to cause harm. *Cf.,* Mendez v. Honda Motor Co., 738 F.Supp. 481 (S.D.Fla.1990) (no duty to make it impossible for an inexperienced person, who failed to read owner's manual, to mount motorcycle shock absorbers upside down); Killeen v. Harmon Grain Products, Inc., 11 Mass.App.Ct. 20, 413 N.E.2d 767 (1980) (toothpick not defective because it has a sharp point).

6. The Restatement (Third) of Torts: Products Liability § 2 Comment p summarizes the many roles that misuse plays:

> *p. Misuse, modification, and alteration.* * * * Under the rule in Subsection (b), liability for defective design attaches only if the risks of harm related to foreseeable product use could have been reduced by the adoption of a reasonable alternative design. Similarly, under the rule in Subsection (c), liability for failure to instruct or warn attaches only if the risks presented by the product could have been reduced by the adoption of reasonable instructions or warnings. Foreseeable product misuse, alteration, and modification must also be considered in deciding whether an alternative design should have been adopted. The post-sale conduct of the user may be so unreasonable, unusual, and costly to avoid that a seller has no duty to design or warn against them. When a court so concludes, the product is not defective within the meaning of Subsection (b) or (c).
>
> A product may, however, be defective as defined in Subsection (b) or (c) due to the omission of a reasonable alternative design or the omission of an adequate warning, yet the risk that eventuates due to misuse, modification, or alteration raises questions whether the extent or scope of liability under the prevailing rules governing legal causation allow for the imposition of liability. See § 15.
>
> Moreover, a product may be found to be defective and causally responsible for plaintiff's harm but the plaintiff may have misused, altered, or modified the product in a manner that calls for the reduction of plaintiff's recovery under the rules of comparative responsibility. Thus, an automobile may be defectively designed so as to provide inadequate protection against harm in the event of a collision, and the plaintiff's negligent modification of the automobile may have caused the collision eventuating in plaintiff's harm. See § 17.

It follows that misuse, modification, and alteration are not discrete legal issues. Rather, when relevant, they are aspects of the concepts of defect, causation, and plaintiff's fault. Jurisdictions differ on the question of who bears the burden of raising and introducing proof regarding conduct that constitutes misuse, modification, and alteration. The allocation of burdens in this regard is not addressed in this Restatement and is left to local law.

7. Cases often involve ignorance of risk because of a failure to anticipate the use to which the product is put. In cases of this kind virtually all courts use foresight rather than hindsight to determine whether there is a duty to guard against misuse. The Note Regarding the Foresight/Hindsight Distinction, *supra* page 141 points out that justifiable ignorance of the harmful quality of a properly used product (generic risk) sometimes does not excuse the manufacturer from liability. Is there a logical justification for a court to use hindsight for generic risks and foresight for misuse?

(b) Changes in Technology

BOATLAND OF HOUSTON, INC. v. BAILEY

Supreme Court of Texas, 1980.
609 S.W.2d 743.

McGee, Justice.

This is a product defect case involving an alleged defect in the design of a 16-foot bass boat. The plaintiffs were the widow and adult children of Samuel Bailey, who was killed in a boating accident in May of 1973. They sued under the wrongful death statute, alleging that Samuel Bailey's death occurred because the boat he was operating was defectively designed. The boat had struck a partially submerged tree stump, and Bailey was thrown into the water. With its motor still running, the boat turned sharply and circled back toward the stump. Bailey was killed by the propeller, but it is unclear whether he was struck when first thrown out or after the boat circled back toward him.

Bailey's wife and children sought damages under a strict liability theory from the boat's seller, Boatland of Houston, Inc. At trial, they urged several reasons why the boat was defectively designed, including * * * the failure of the motor to automatically turn off when Bailey was thrown from the boat.

The trial court rendered a take-nothing judgment based on the jury's failure to find that the boat was defective and findings favorable to Boatland on several defensive issues. The court of civil appeals, with one justice dissenting, reversed and remanded the cause for a new trial because of errors in the admission of evidence and the submission of the defensive issues. 585 S.W.2d 805. We reverse the judgment of the court of civil appeals and affirm that of the trial court.

Evidence of Design Defect
* * *

In *Turner v. General Motors Corp.*, [584 S.W.2d 844 (Tex.1979),] this court discussed the strict liability standard of "defectiveness" as applied in design defect cases. Whether a product was defectively designed requires a balancing by the jury of its utility against the likelihood of and gravity of injury from its use. The jury may consider many factors before deciding whether a product's usefulness or desirability are outweighed by its risks. Their finding on defectiveness may be influenced by evidence of a safer design that would have prevented the injury.[1] *Turner v. General Motors Corp.*, supra at 849. See Keeton, *Product Liability and the Meaning of Defect*, 5 St. Mary's L.J. 30, 38 (1973); Wade, *Strict Tort Liability of Manufacturers*, 19 Sw.L.J. 5, 17 (1965). Because defectiveness of the product in question is determined in relation to safer alternatives, the fact that its risks could be diminished easily or cheaply may greatly influence the outcome of the case.

Whether a product was defectively designed must be judged against the technological context existing at the time of its manufacture. Thus, when the plaintiff alleges that a product was defectively designed because it lacked a specific feature, attention may become focused on the feasibility of that feature—the capacity to provide the feature without greatly increasing the product's cost or impairing usefulness. This feasibility is a relative, not an absolute, concept; the more scientifically and economically feasible the alternative was, the more likely that a jury may find that the product was defectively designed. A plaintiff may advance the argument that a safer alternative was feasible with evidence that it was in actual use or was available at the time of manufacture. Feasibility may also be shown with evidence of the scientific and economic capacity to develop the safer alternative. Thus, evidence of the actual use of, or capacity to use, safer alternatives is relevant insofar as it depicts the available scientific knowledge and the practicalities of applying that knowledge to a product's design. * * *

As part of their case-in-chief, the Baileys produced evidence of the scientific and economic feasibility of a design that would have caused the boat's motor to automatically shut off when Bailey fell out. According to the Baileys, the boat's design should have incorporated an automatic cut-off system or the boat should have been equipped with a safety device known as a "kill switch."

* * *

The deposition testimony of George Horton, the inventor of a kill switch designed for open-top carriers, was also introduced. Horton began developing his "Quick Kill" in November of 1972 and applied for a patent in January of 1973. According to Horton, his invention required no breakthroughs in the state of the art of manufacturing or production.

---

1. In *Turner*, this court stated that a number of evidentiary factors may be considered in determining whether a product's design is defective. The product's usefulness and desirability, the likelihood and gravity of injury from its use, the ability to eliminate the risk without seriously increasing the product's usefulness or cost, and the expectations of the ordinary consumer are some of these factors. *Turner v. General Motors Corp.*, 584 S.W.2d 844, 849 (Tex. 1979).

He stated that his invention was simple: a lanyard connects the operator's body to a device that fits over the ignition key. If the operator moves, the lanyard is pulled, the device rotates, and the ignition switch turns off. When he began to market his "Quick Kill," the response by boat dealers was very positive, which Horton perceived to be due to the filling of a recognized need. He considered the kill switch to be a necessary safety device for a bass boat with stick steering. If the kill switch were hooked up and the operator thrown out, the killing of the motor would prevent the boat from circling back where it came from. Horton also testified that for 30 years racing boats had been using various types of kill switches. Thus, the concept of kill switches was not new.

* * *

Boatland elicited evidence to rebut the Baileys' evidence of the feasibility of equipping boats with kill switches or similar devices in March of 1973, when the boat was assembled and sold. * * *

In response to the Baileys' evidence that the "Quick Kill" was readily available at the time of trial, Horton stated on cross-examination that until he obtained the patent for his "Quick Kill" in 1974 he kept the idea to himself. Before he began to manufacture them, he investigated the market for competitive devices and found none. The only applications of the automatic engine shut-off concept in use at the time were homemade, such as on racing boats. He first became aware of competitive devices in August of 1974.

Boatland introduced other evidence to show that kill switches were not available when Bailey's boat was sold. * * * Willis Hudson, who manufactured the boat operated by Bailey, testified that he first became aware of kill switches in 1974 or 1975 and to his knowledge no such thing was available before then. Ralph Cornelius, the vice-president of a marine appliance dealership, testified that kill switches were not available in 1973. The first kill switch he saw to be sold was in 1974, although homemade "crash throttles" or foot buttons had long been in use.

* * * After considering the feasibility and effectiveness of an alternative design and other factors such as the utility and risk, the jury found that the boat was not defective. The trial court rendered judgment for Boatland. The Baileys complained on appeal that the trial court erred in admitting Boatland's evidence that kill switches were unavailable when Bailey's boat was assembled and sold. The court of civil appeals agreed, holding that the evidence was material only to the care exercised by Boatland and thus irrelevant in a strict liability case.

In its appeal to this court, Boatland contends that the court of civil appeals misconstrued the nature and purpose of its evidence. According to Boatland, when the Baileys introduced evidence that kill switches were a feasible safety alternative, Boatland was entitled to introduce evidence that kill switches were not yet available when Bailey's boat was sold and thus were not a feasible design alternative at that time.

The primary dispute concerning the feasibility of an alternative design for Bailey's boat was the "state of the art" when the boat was sold. The admissibility and effect of "state of the art" evidence has been a subject of controversy in both negligence and strict product liability cases. In negligence cases, the reasonableness of the defendant's conduct in placing the product on the market is in issue. Evidence of industry customs at the time of manufacture may be offered by either party for the purpose of comparing the defendant's conduct with industry customs. An offer of evidence of the defendant's compliance with custom to rebut evidence of its negligence has been described as the "state of the art defense." *See generally* 2 L. Frumer & M. Friedman, Products Liability § 16A[4][i] (1980). In this connection, it is argued that the state of the art is equivalent to industry custom and is relevant only to the issue of the defendant's negligence and irrelevant to a strict liability theory of recovery.

In our view, "custom" is distinguishable from "state of the art." The state of the art with respect to a particular product refers to the technological environment at the time of its manufacture. This technological environment includes the scientific knowledge, economic feasibility, and the practicalities of implementation when the product was manufactured. Evidence of this nature is important in determining whether a safer design was feasible. The limitations imposed by the state of the art at the time of manufacture may affect the feasibility of a safer design. Evidence of the state of the art in design defect cases has been discussed and held admissible in other jurisdictions. *See, e.g., Raney v. Honeywell, Inc.,* 540 F.2d 932 (8th Cir.1976); *Caterpillar Tractor Co. v. Beck,* 593 P.2d 871 (Alaska 1979); *Barker v. Lull Engineering Co.,* 20 Cal.3d 413, 573 P.2d 443, 143 Cal.Rptr. 225 (1978); *Kerns v. Engelke,* 76 Ill.2d 154, 28 Ill.Dec. 500, 390 N.E.2d 859 (1979); *Cepeda v. Cumberland Engineering Co., Inc.,* 76 N.J. 152, 386 A.2d 816 (1978). *See generally* J. Sales & J. Perdue, The Law of Strict Tort Liability in Texas 41 (1977). Note, *The State of the Art Defense in Strict Products Liability,* 57 Marq.L.Rev. 491 (1974). Note, *Product Liability Reform Proposals: The State of the Art Defense,* 43 Albany L.Rev. 944, 944–45 (1979). In this case, the evidence advanced by both parties was relevant to the feasibility of designing bass boats to shut off automatically if the operator fell out, or more specifically, the feasibility of equipping bass boats with safety switches.

The Baileys offered state of the art evidence to establish the feasibility of a more safely designed boat: They established that when Bailey's boat was sold in 1973, the general concept of a boat designed so that its motor would automatically cut off had been applied for years on racing boats. One kill switch, the "Quick Kill," was invented at that time and required no mechanical breakthrough. The Baileys were also allowed to show that other kill switches were presently in use and that the defendant itself presently installed them.

Logically, the plaintiff's strongest evidence of feasibility of an alternative design is its actual use by the defendant or others at the time of manufacture. Even if a safer alternative was not being used, evidence that it was available, known about, or capable of being developed is relevant in determining its feasibility. In contrast, the defendant's strongest rebuttal evidence is that a particular design alternative was impossible due to the state of the art. Yet the defendant's ability to rebut the plaintiff's evidence is not limited to showing that a particular alternative was impossible; it is entitled to rebut the plaintiff's evidence of feasibility with evidence of limitations on feasibility. A suggested alternative may be invented or discovered but not be feasible for use because of the time necessary for its application and implementation. Also, a suggested alternative may be available, but impractical for reasons such as greatly increased cost or impairment of the product's usefulness. When the plaintiff has introduced evidence that a safer alternative was feasible because it was used, the defendant may then introduce contradictory evidence that it was not used.

Thus in response to the Baileys' evidence of kill switch use in 1978, the time of trial, Boatland was properly allowed to show that they were not used when the boat was sold in 1973. To rebut proof that safety switches were possible and feasible when Bailey's boat was sold because the underlying concept was known and the "Quick Kill," a simple, inexpensive device had been invented, Boatland was properly allowed to show that neither the "Quick Kill" nor any other kill switch was available at that time.

It could reasonably be inferred from this evidence that although the underlying concept of automatic motor cut-off devices was not new, kill switches were not as feasible an alternative as the Baileys' evidence implied. Boatland did not offer evidence of technological impossibility or absolute nonfeasibility; its evidence was offered to show limited availability when the boat was sold. Once the jury was informed of the state of the art, it was able to consider the extent to which it was feasible to incorporate an automatic cut-off device or similar design characteristic into Bailey's boat. The feasibility and effectiveness of a safer design and other factors such as utility and risk, were properly considered by the jury before it ultimately concluded that the boat sold to Bailey was not defectively designed.

In cases involving strict liability for defective design, liability is determined by the product's defective condition; there is no need to prove that the defendant's conduct was negligent. Considerations such as the utility and risk of the product in question and the feasibility of safer alternatives are presented according to the facts as they are proved to be, not according to the defendant's perceptions. Thus, even though the defendant has exercised due care his product may be found defective. When the Baileys introduced evidence of the use of kill switches, Boatland was entitled to introduce rebuttal evidence of non-use at the time of manufacture due to limitations imposed by the state of the art. Evidence offered under these circumstances is offered to rebut plaintiff's evidence that a safer alternative was feasible and is relevant to defectiveness. It was not offered to show that a custom existed or to infer the defendant's compliance therewith. We would be presented with a different question if the state of the art in 1973 with respect to kill switches had not been disputed and Boatland had attempted to avoid liability by offering proof that Bailey's boat complied with industry custom.

* * *

CONCLUSION

For the reasons stated above the judgment of the court of civil appeals is reversed. The judgment rendered by the trial court, that the Baileys take nothing against Boatland, is affirmed.

POPE, J., concurring, in which BARROW, J., joins.

[The concurring opinion of POPE, J. is omitted.]

ON REHEARING

CAMPBELL, JUSTICE, dissenting.

I dissent.

"State of the art" does not mean "the state of industry practice." "State of the art" means "state of industry knowledge." At the time of the manufacture of the boat in question, the device and concept of a circuit breaker, as is at issue in this case, was simple, mechanical, cheap, practical, possible, economically feasible and a concept seventy years old, which required no engineering or technical breakthrough. The concept was known by the industry. This fact removes it from "state of the art."

* * *

The manufacturer of the boat, Mr. Hudson, testified as follows as concerns the concept of a "kill switch." It is practically without dispute that this is one of the simplest mechanical devices and concepts known to man. Its function is, can be, and was performed by many and varied simple constructions. It is more a concept than an invention. The concept has been around most of this century. It is admittedly an easily incorporated concept. Was an invention required in order to incorporate a circuit breaker on a bass boat? Absolutely not! Did the manufacturer have to wait until George Horton invented his specific "Quick Kill" switch before it could incorporate a kill switch of some sort on its bass boats? Absolutely not! Mr. Hudson uses an even simpler electrical circuit breaker on his boats.

Mr. Hudson testified he could have made a kill switch himself, of his own, and of many possible designs, but simply did not do it. Why didn't he do it? He didn't think about it. He never had any safety engineer examine his boats. He hadn't heard of such, he puts them on now, but still thinks people won't use them.

* * *

What is this Court faced with in this case? Nothing more than a defendant seller attempting to avoid liability by offering proof that Bailey's boat complied with industry practice (which it did at that time) but not because of any limitations on manufacturing feasibility at that time. This is an industry practice case. The evidence does not involve "technological feasibility." * * *

* * * The important point is that there is no dispute that at the time of the manufacture of Mr. Bailey's boat, a circuit breaker, whether electrical or mechanical could have easily and cheaply been incorporated into the boat.

* * *

I would hold that the trial court erred in permitting such evidence by Boatland to go to the jury, and would affirm the judgment of the Court of Civil Appeals.

* * *

RAY, J., joins in this dissent.

Notes

1. Justice McGee asserts that the law is concerned with the condition of the product and not "defendant's perceptions." Therefore, there is no need to show that the defendant was negligent in order to prove that the product is defective. Is this true? Recall from Section B of Chapter 1 that, in negligence cases, courts hold manufacturers to the standard of an expert, and require them to keep abreast of all scientific advances.

2. Most courts agree with *Boatland,* and hold that the product must be evaluated in light of the technology available at the time of distribution. *E.g., Maxted v. Pacific Car & Foundry Co.,* 527 P.2d 832 (Wyo.1974). A few courts disagree. *E.g., Stanfield v. Medalist Industries, Inc.,* 34 Ill.App.3d 635, 340 N.E.2d 276 (1975) (unavailability of safety devices is no defense to a strict liability action). As we saw in the Note Regarding the Foresight/Hindsight Distinction, *supra* page 141, however, justifiable ignorance of the harmful quality of the product (generic risk) frequently does not excuse the manufacturer from liability in design defect cases. Is there a logical justification for a court to use hindsight for generic risks and foresight for technology in design cases?

SMITH v. LOUISVILLE LADDER CO.
United States Court of Appeals, Fifth Circuit, 2001.
237 F.3d 515.

Before DAVIS, SMITH and DENNIS, CIRCUIT JUDGES.

W. EUGENE DAVIS, CIRCUIT JUDGE:

This is an appeal from a judgment entered on a jury verdict for the plaintiff, Rodger Nelson Smith ("Smith"), in a products liability action against Louisville Ladder Corp. ("Louisville"). [Smith sought recovery against Louisville on three theories: defective design, failure to warn, and breach of implied warranty of merchantability.] Following a four day trial, the jury found in favor of Smith, and, after taking Smith's 15% contributory negligence into account, awarded Smith $1,487,500. We conclude that the record evidence does not support any of Smith's theories of recovery. We therefore reverse and render judgment for Louisville.

I.

Rodger Smith worked as a technician for Longview Cable Company ("Longview"), which provided cable television service in the Longview, Texas area. * * * Longview purchased the extension ladder and hook assembly in use at the time of Smith's accident from Louisville.

On the day of Smith's injury, he was assigned a routine repair job that required him to rest the ladder against a cable strand located some twenty feet off the ground. Smith placed the cable line inside the U-shaped hooks that extended from the top of the ladder and rested the ladder against the cable. The base of the ladder was on the ground approximately five feet from a utility pole to which the overhead cable was attached. Because of its weight, the cable sloped down slightly as it moved from the pole.

Smith climbed the ladder without securing the ladder to the pole or any other stationary object. Smith's plan was to secure himself to the ladder with his safety belt when he reached the top of the ladder and then use a hand line to attach the ladder to the utility pole. After Smith climbed to the top of the ladder, he reached for his safety belt and his weight shifted, causing the ladder to slide to his left down the natural slope of the cable. The ladder slid sideways for some distance with Smith hanging onto the ladder. When the ladder reached a position at or near the low point of the line between the two utility poles to which it was attached, one of the hooks came off the line, and the ladder twisted and came to an abrupt halt. Unable to maintain his grip on the ladder, Smith fell to the ground and was seriously injured.

Lateral slides of ladders along cables were well recognized risks in the telecommunications industry, and Smith, himself, had experienced several of these slides during his employment with Longview. However, in the earlier slides Smith had attached his safety belt to the ladder before the slide began and because he did not fall from the ladder he suffered no injury.

* * *

II

A. Design Defect

Smith focused most of his time and attention at trial on his theory that the Louisville extension ladder with hook assembly was defective because of the hook's ability to come off the cable during a slide. Smith's expert, Dr. Packman, testified that when the hook disengaged from the cable near the end of Smith's slide, the ladder to which Smith was clinging twisted more violently than it would had the hook remained attached to the cable and he concluded that this additional twist contributed to Smith's fall. Packman introduced the concept of a simple latching device that, when engaged, would close the opening in the hook, encircle the cable and prevent the hook from disengaging from the strand. Under Dr. Packman's concept, the latch remains disengaged until the hook is placed over the cable and the ladder is resting on the cable. The operator, from his position on the ground, would then remotely activate a spring loaded latch by pulling a line running from the latch to the bottom of the ladder. Once the latch was engaged, the hook would no longer be open and in the event of a slide, the hook could not disengage from the cable.

Louisville Ladder argues that Smith did not establish that the hook with Dr. Packman's latch was a "safer alternative design" within the meaning of the Texas statute. To establish a design defect, Section 82.005 of the Texas Civil Practice and Remedies Code requires a claimant "to prove by a preponderance of the evidence that: (1) there was a safer alternative design; and (2) the defect was a producing cause of the personal injury property damage or death for which the claimant seeks recovery." Subsection (b) states:

> (b) In this section, "safer alternative design" means a product design other than the one actually used that in reasonable probability:
>
> > (1) would have prevented or significantly reduced the risk of the claimant's personal injury, property damage, or death without substantially impairing the product's utility; and
> >
> > (2) was economically and technologically feasible at the time the product left the control of the manufacturer or seller by the application of existing or reasonably achievable scientific knowledge.

We found only one Texas case discussing the proof necessary to establish a safer alternative design under this statute. In *General Motors Corp. v. Sanchez,* 997 S.W.2d 584 (Tex.1999), the plaintiff's expert testified that his alternative design of the General Motors transmission would prevent internal forces in the transmission from moving the gear selector toward "reverse" rather than "park" when the driver inadvertently leaves the lever in a position between "reverse" and "park." According to plaintiff's expert, his proposed design change would eliminate this spontaneous movement 99% of the time. The court held that this testimony was sufficient to allow the jury to conclude that plaintiff had established a safer alternative design. *Id.* at 592.

In our case, Smith completely relies on Dr. Packman's evidence and testimony to establish a safer alternate design. Packman testified that his spring loaded latch, by preventing the hook from disengaging from the cable, would make the jolt at the end of the slide less violent, and, therefore, the worker would have a better chance of hanging onto the ladder. He conducted videotaped experiments for the purpose of establishing this fact. In the first experiment, he placed a 200-pound weight on a ladder with hooks like those found on the Louisville Ladder and then precipitated a slide to demonstrate the jerk that would occur when one of the hooks disengaged from the strand. For the second experiment, Dr. Packman videotaped a slide involving hooks that encircled the cable.[1] This experiment demonstrated a less violent jerk at the end of the slide.

The only conclusion Dr. Packman was able to reach was that his alternative design would result in a less violent jerk on the ladder at the end of the slide. Unlike the expert who testified in *General Motors*, Dr. Packman was unable to quantify this reduction in force and was unable to say that Smith or another worker could stay on the ladder in a slide where the hook was prevented from disengaging from the cable. The most Dr. Packman could say was that his design alteration would diminish the possibility of the worker's falling off because there was some reduction in the jerk.

Furthermore, Dr. Packman's concept of the latching device to close the open end of the hook around the cable was a preliminary concept. At the time of trial he admitted that he had considered several possible ways a man on the ground (or some distance up the ladder) could operate the latch mechanism but had not settled on any particular method. He agreed that his design was preliminary and that he was not ready to recommend it to a manufacturer. In addition, Packman conceded that a person climbing the ladder would find his proposed mechanism somewhat awkward and that using the mechanism could cause the ladder to get out of balance and slide. He was also questioned about a concern that the line to operate the latch mechanism running the length of the ladder has the potential of being a hazard to the person climbing the ladder. Packman agreed that he never evaluated the risks associated with his proposed alternate design due in part to the fact that it was never completed. Packman also conceded that he did not purport to conduct a risk-benefit analysis of his proposed redesign.

* * *

After careful review of the record, we conclude that no reasonable jury could have found from the evidence that the latching device Dr. Packman proposed adding to the hook assembly was a safer alternative design as defined by the Texas statute. Dr. Packman conceded that his proposed alternate design would not assist in preventing the hook from sliding on the cable. He also agreed that the only benefit a worker would derive from the alternate design was a reduced jerk at the end of the slide. He was therefore unable to say that his alternate design would have prevented Mr. Smith's fall. Therefore, we conclude that the evi-

---

1. As stated below, Dr. Packman never produced his proposed improvement—the spring loaded latching device. For this experiment he simply drilled holes in the hook, ran a bolt through the holes and closed the open end of the hook so that it would not disengage from the cable.

dence fails to establish that the alternative design would have "significantly" reduced the risk of Mr. Smith's injury.

Furthermore, Dr. Packman conceded that he made no risk-benefit analysis including what additional hazards would be created in implementing his proposed alternative design. Thus, Dr. Packman's testimony does not establish that his proposed design would not have substantially impaired the ladder's utility. The jury's finding of design defect, therefore, cannot stand.[2]

* * *

IV

For the above stated reasons, we conclude that Smith failed to present sufficient evidence at trial to support any of his theories of recovery. The district court's judgment is, therefore, reversed and judgment is rendered in favor of Louisville.

REVERSED and RENDERED.

[The dissenting opinion of DENNIS, CIRCUIT JUDGE, is omitted.]

Notes

1. **Reliability of expert testimony.** The *Smith* case indicated in footnote 2 that it did not have to rule on the reliability of the plaintiff's expert testimony. Yet, in light of *Daubert v. Merrell Dow Pharmaceuticals, Inc., infra* page 409, and *Kumho Tire Co., Ltd. v. Carmichael, infra* page 435, many courts have begun excluding expert evidence of a safer alternative design as unreliable even though the testimony, if admissible, would have been sufficient to establish a safer alternative design. *Jaurequi v. Carter Manufacturing Co., Inc., infra* page 445 is typical. Plaintiffs, therefore, have an additional concern in jurisdictions that apply the rigorous *Daubert/Kumho* standard of admissibility of expert testimony. In cases where expert testimony is needed to establish a safer alternative design, exclusion of expert evidence will prevent plaintiff from getting to the jury.

2. Can plaintiff show a safer alternative design by showing a safer alternative "product," rather than showing that the design of the product in question could be altered to make it safer? Ruiz–Guzman v. Amvac Chemical Corp., 141 Wash.2d 493, 7 P.3d 795 (En Banc 2000) answered this question in the affirmative. There, plaintiff was injured by Phosdrin, a pesticide for aphids. The evidence showed that Phosphamidon, a different aphid pesticide, was safer. The court held that this evidence was sufficient to show that Phosdrin was defective on the basis that Phosphamidon was a safer alternative design. This was the case even though Phosphamidon was a patented product; therefore, its chemical formulation was unavailable to the manufacturer of Phosdrin.

---

2. This disposition makes it unnecessary for us to reach appellant's argument that the district court erred in admitting Dr. Packman's testimony as reliable under *Daubert v. Merrell Dow Pharmaceuticals, Inc.*, 509 U.S. 579, 113 S.Ct. 2786, 125 L.Ed.2d 469 (1993).

Many nurseries sell aphid-eating ladybugs to gardeners to control aphids. Under the rationale of *Ruiz–Guzman*, are aphid-eating ladybugs a safer alternative design for both Phosdrin and Phosphamidon? Is a goat a safer alternative design for a lawnmower? Is a car a safer alternative design for a motorcycle? For a helicopter?

3. Even though *Smith* is based on a statute, the case is typical of an important line of common law cases that apply the risk-utility test rigorously, carefully weighing costs and benefits in deciding whether plaintiff's evidence of a safer alternative design is sufficient to create a jury question. *See, e.g.*, Troja v. Black & Decker, 62 Md.App. 101, 488 A.2d 516 (1985). This approach reflects the influence of economic analysis on legal thought. Other courts take a much softer approach in applying the risk-utility test, regarding the existence of a safer alternative design as simply one of several factors (not elements) that are relevant in determining defectiveness, which is to be determined by the jury under a generalized reasonable person standard. Dean John Wade's list of such factors has been the most influential with courts. His factors are set out in *Phillips v. Kimwood Machine Co.*, in footnote 9, *supra* page 119. The differences between the two approaches to risk-utility are analyzed in Green, The Schizophrenia of Risk-Benefit Analysis in Design Defect Litigation, 48 Vand.L.Rev. 609 (1995).

4. With *Smith*, compare *Kallio v. Ford Motor Co.*, the case that follows. *Kallio* takes the "soft" approach to dealing the existence of a safer alternative design.

KALLIO v. FORD MOTOR CO.
Supreme Court of Minnesota, 1987.
407 N.W.2d 92.

KELLEY, Justice.

While driving his 1977 Ford F–150 pickup truck home from work, Robert Kallio pulled over to the side of the road, shifted the automatic transmission lever into the "park" position, and left the cab to cover some tools in the open truck bed that had become exposed to the rain. He neither shut off the engine nor set the parking brake. As he jumped on the bumper to cover the tools, he suddenly realized the truck was moving in reverse. He leaped to the ground and ran to the truck's cab, but before he was able to re-enter the truck, he slipped on the pavement, fell, and the truck ran over both of his legs and one of his hands before a passenger sitting in the cab succeeded in stopping it. His subsequent action against Ford was bottomed on allegations of defective design of the truck's shifting mechanism and on Ford's failure to warn of the propensity of the truck not to go completely into the "park" position. The jury concluded both that the truck was defective and that Kallio was negligent.

1. Because it claims that Kallio failed to demonstrate the existence of a feasible, practicable, and safer alternative automatic transmission shift design, Ford asserts the trial court erred in denying Ford's motion for a directed verdict. Alternatively, Ford argues the trial court errone-

ously refused to give Ford's requested Instruction No. 11 relating to the issue.[1]

Whether the trial court erred in either case depends upon whether in a products liability alleged design defect case a plaintiff must establish as an element of his case that at the time of manufacture a safer, practicable, and technologically feasible alternative design existed—an issue of first impression for this court. Other courts of last resort, however, have addressed the issue. Ford buttresses its contention by reliance upon decisions from New York, Oregon, and Nebraska—all of which hold that in an alleged defective product design case, an element of plaintiff's case includes proof of the existence of a feasible, safer alternative design. These jurisdictions hold that initially the plaintiff has the onus of presenting evidence of the existence of substantial likelihood of harm and that when the product was manufactured, it was feasible to employ an alternative safer design. *Voss v. Black & Decker Mfg. Co.*, 59 N.Y.2d 102, 463 N.Y.S.2d 398, 450 N.E.2d 204 (1983); *Wilson v. Piper Aircraft Corp.*, 282 Or. 61, 577 P.2d 1322 (1978) *rehearing denied*, 282 Or. 411, 579 P.2d 1287 (1978); *Nerud v. Haybuster Mfg., Inc.*, 215 Neb. 604, 340 N.W.2d 369 (1983). This showing must be more than a "technical possibility [of the existence] of a safer design." *Piper Aircraft*, 282 Or. at 67–68, 577 P.2d at 1326.

The rule of strict liability in tort found in *Restatement (Second) of Torts* § 402(A) (1965) had its genesis more than 20 years ago. Almost since the rule's inception, courts have tended to borrow common law concepts of negligence in determining whether a manufactured product, as designed, is unreasonably dangerous. *See, e.g.*, Wade, *Strict Tort Liability of Manufacturers*, 19 Sw.L.J. 5, 17 (1965); *see also* Keeton, *Product Liability and the Meaning of Defect*, 5 St. Mary's L.J. 30 (1973); Steenson, *The Anatomy of Products Liability in Minnesota*, 6 Wm. Mitchell L.Rev. 1, 23–25 (1980); Wade, *On the Nature of Strict Tort Liability for Products*, 44 Miss.L.J. 825 (1973).

The design defect products liability cases arising in the three jurisdictions relied upon by Ford employ the negligence reasonable care test which requires the trier of fact to balance the product's risks against its utility and cost in determining whether it has been defectively designed. *See, e.g., Micallef v. Miehle Co.*, 39 N.Y.2d 376, 386, 384 N.Y.S.2d 115,

---

1. Defendant's requested Instruction No. 11 reads:

PLAINTIFF REQUIRED TO ESTABLISH THE AVAILABILITY OF A FEASIBLE, PRACTICABLE ALTERNATIVE

For you to conclude that the design of the park system in the subject Ford vehicle was defective and unreasonably dangerous at the time of sale by Ford Motor Company, the plaintiff must establish by a preponderance of the evidence that, at the time the vehicle was designed, there was available to the defendant a feasible practicable alternative design and that that design, if it had been chosen by Ford, would have avoided or materially reduced the plaintiff's injury. If the plaintiffs fail to prove the existence of such a feasible, practicable alternative design, they will be unable to prove that Ford's choice of design was unreasonable. The plaintiff cannot carry his burden in this regard merely by showing that an alternative design was possible. To succeed in this case the plaintiffs must establish that such a design would have been feasible and practicable, and that it would have avoided or materially reduced the plaintiff's injury.

121, 348 N.E.2d 571, 577–78 (1976); *Wilson v. Piper Aircraft Corp.*, 282 Or. 61, 66, 577 P.2d 1322, 1325–26 (1978); *Nerud v. Haybuster Mfg., Inc.*, 215 Neb. at 614, 340 N.W.2d at 375. We have likewise adopted a similar approach citing with approval *Micallef v. Miehle Co.* in *Holm v. Sponco Manufacturing, Inc.*, 324 N.W.2d 207, 212 (Minn.1982). Later, in *Bilotta v. Kelley Co.*, 346 N.W.2d 616 (Minn.1984), we reaffirmed our *Holm* holding that we had adopted the reasonable care balancing test. *Id.* at 622. Because this court in *Holm v. Sponco Manufacturing, Inc.* and in *Bilotta v. Kelley Co.* specifically adopted the reasonable care balancing test in design cases in reliance upon the analysis of the New York Court of Appeals in *Micallef v. Miehle Co.,* Ford here argues that we should likewise extend the reasonable care balancing test reasoning, as New York has done, to require preliminarily that a plaintiff must present evidence of the existence of a safer, feasible alternative design. On the other hand, Kallio urges that we should follow *Barker v. Lull Engineering Co.*, 20 Cal.3d 413, 143 Cal.Rptr. 225, 573 P.2d 443 (1978), which held that the burden of proving the nonexistence of a safer design should rest with the manufacturer.

We decline respondent's invitation to follow *Barker.* Instead, we concur in the observation made by the Oregon Supreme Court when, in the course of denying a petition for rehearing in *Wilson v. Piper Aircraft Corp.*, urging it to adopt the *Barker* rationale, it stated:

> Under that decision [*Barker*] it appears that a design defect case will always go to the jury if only the plaintiff can show that the product caused the injury. In this jurisdiction, however, it is part of plaintiff's case to show that a product which caused an injury was dangerously defective.

282 Or. at 413, 579 P.2d at 1287–88.

Unlike California, which in *Barker* specifically removed "unreasonable" as a limitation of the compensable dangerousness of a product, *see* 20 Cal.3d at 417, 573 P.2d at 446, 143 Cal.Rptr. at 228, Minnesota, like Oregon, maintains the requirement in a strict liability products case that a plaintiff must establish not only that the product was in a defective condition, but also that it was *unreasonably dangerous*. *O'Laughlin v. Minnesota Natural Gas Co.*, 253 N.W.2d 826, 832 (1977), *Bilotta v. Kelley Co.*, 346 N.W.2d at 622. Obviously, a factor bearing upon the latter requirement will be the existence or nonexistence of a feasible alternative design. To satisfy that requirement, the plaintiff ordinarily has the burden of showing the existence of an alternative design that was safer. If the manufacturer presents evidence disputing the contention, the trier of fact will resolve the "unreasonably dangerous" issue. As in other tort cases, plaintiffs asserting a strict liability tort claim based upon alleged defective design of a product ultimately have the burden to prove the elements of the asserted claim. Generally in a case based upon alleged improper design, one of those elements requires production of evidence that the design employed was unreasonably dangerous. To establish a prima facie case that it was unreasonably dangerous normally requires production of evidence of the existence of a feasible, alternative safer design.

In this case the trial court instructed the jury using JIG 117, 4 Minn.Dist. Judges Ass'n, *Minnesota Practice,* JIG III CIVIL (3d ed. 1986).[2] Additionally the court's instructions elaborated on other factors the jury could consider in deciding whether Ford's automatic transmission as designed was unreasonably dangerous. Included among those additional factors, the jury was informed it could consider the "state of the art" and the "practices of the automotive industry" at the time of the truck's sale. The tenor, if not the literal wording, of the instructions permitted the jury to consider availability of, and failure to use, an alternative, safer design as a factor. However, Ford complains the instructions didn't go far enough; that they should have informed the jury that plaintiff had the burden to prove the existence of a safer, feasible alternative design as an element of an alleged defective product design case. We disagree. The court's instruction correctly stated the law. *See, e.g., Bilotta v. Kelley Co.,* 346 N.W.2d at 621–22. Although normally evidence of a safer alternative design will be presented initially by the plaintiff, it is not necessarily required in all cases.[3] Such evidence is relevant to, and certainly may be an important factor in, the determination of whether the product was unreasonably defective. However, existence of a safer, practical alternative design is not an element of an alleged defective product design prima facie case.

Defendant's requested Instruction No. 11 is overly broad, not only because, in essence, it tends to elevate proof of the existence of a feasible alternative safer design from a factor properly for jury consideration to an element of the plaintiff's claim, but also because it tended to overemphasize that factor. As we have stated, such emphasis "is properly the function of counsel in closing argument, not by the court in its instructions." *Alholm v. Wilt,* 394 N.W.2d 488, 491 (Minn.1986). We note that counsel, indeed, made a vigorous final summation arguing Ford's position.

---

2. JIG 117 reads:
STRICT LIABILITY—DESIGN DEFECT
A manufacturer has a duty to use reasonable care when designing a product, so as to avoid any unreasonable risk of harm to (anyone who) (property that) is likely to be exposed to harm when the product is put to its intended use or to any use that is unintended but is reasonably foreseeable.

What constitutes reasonable care will vary with the surrounding circumstances. Reasonable care is the care that a reasonably prudent person would exercise under the same or similar circumstances.

The reasonable care to be exercised by a manufacturer when designing a product will depend on all the facts and circumstances, including, among others, the likelihood and seriousness of harm against the feasibility and burden of any precautions which would be effective to avoid the harm. You are instructed that the manufacturer is obligated to keep informed of scientific knowledge and discoveries in its field.

If the manufacturer did not use reasonable care when designing the product in question, then the product is in a defective condition unreasonably dangerous to the (user or consumer) (user's or consumer's property).

3. Conceivably, rare cases may exist where the product may be judged unreasonably dangerous because it should be removed from the market rather than be redesigned. *See, e.g., Wilson v. Piper Aircraft Corp.,* 282 Or. 61, 71 n. 5, 577 P.2d 1322, 1328 n. 5 (1978); *O'Brien v. Muskin Corp.,* 94 N.J. 169, 185, 463 A.2d 298, 306 (1983).

Finally, respondent did present some evidence, albeit weak, that a practical safer design was feasible through the testimony of William Barr and Michael Inden. Ford offered considerable evidence that, if believed, would permit the jury to conclude that, indeed, Ford had employed the state of the art in designing the transmission and that no safer practical design existed in 1977. Had we been jurors, we might have accepted Ford's position. However, the resolution of this disputed fact issue was for the trier of fact—here the jury. Sufficient evidence existed to support the conclusion it reached.

* * *

Accordingly, we affirm the court of appeals.

SIMONETT, J., specially concurs.

SIMONETT, JUSTICE (concurring specially).

* * *

My only reason for writing is to comment on further evidence offered by plaintiff on alternative design. In 1979, in a different trial, plaintiff's expert, William Barr, had testified that Ford's system was not unreasonably dangerous. In this case, however, Barr testified that he had now invented a device, as yet untested, never yet installed in any vehicle, containing some "bugs," but which he thought with "a good deal of work" might fix the problem. The majority opinion says this testimony of alternative design was "weak." In my view, Barr did not show his device was practical, and his testimony would not have withstood a motion to strike if one had been made. (Ford's expert, it might be added, thought Barr's device could not be made to work satisfactorily; that even if it could, it would not significantly reduce the problem; and that the device might make shifting more difficult.)

Conscious design defects present difficult problems of proof for both plaintiffs and manufacturers. There is much room for second guessing, and courts are being asked to establish standards of reasonableness for manufacturers (whether it be Ford or a fledgling family operation). Establishing standards entails a weighing of engineering, marketing, and financing factors, which, at times, may be a difficult task for courts to perform. *See* Henderson, *Judicial Review of Manufacturers' Conscious Design Choices: The Limits of Adjudication,* 73 Colum.L.Rev. 1531 (1973). On the other hand, the establishment of standards cannot always be avoided by passing the problem off to the jury under a general reasonable care instruction.

In any event, the limited issue before us is whether the trial court erred in refusing to give defendant's requested instruction that plaintiff was required to prove the existence of a feasible, practical alternative design. I agree with the majority opinion that the trial court's instructions on burden of proof were adequate and that it was unnecessary to give the requested instruction which would have unduly singled out one aspect of the proof. I also agree with the court's disposition of the other issues.

Sometimes where proof is lacking for a conscious design defect, plaintiff may still be able to show breach of a duty to warn. Henderson, *supra*, at 1562–63. Here, plaintiff knew his pickup might move if the shift lever was not completely in the park position, and there was no need to warn on this elementary, obvious fact. But what plaintiff did not know was that the shift lever would feel like it was in park when it was not. The jury could have found there should have been a warning placed in the owner's manual about this illusory effect.

Notes

1. Which approach to risk-utility is best, the economic approach or the soft approach? Suppose the alternative design was technologically impossible at the time of manufacture. Should this be an absolute bar to liability, or merely a factor to be considered in the risk-utility analysis?

2. If the existence of a feasible alternative design at the time of manufacture is an element rather than a factor, should plaintiff have the burden of proving the existence of the alternative, or should the absence of such an alternative be a defensive issue? As the main case indicates, the courts are split on the question of who has the burden of proof. The cases are collected in Annotation, 78 A.L.R.4th 154 (1990).

3. The Restatement (Third) of Torts: Products Liability § 2 (b) takes the position that plaintiff normally must prove the existence of a safer alternative design as an element of her prima facie case. Comment f explains how it would implement that requirement:

> While a plaintiff must prove that a reasonable alternative design would have reduced the foreseeable risks of harm, Subsection (b) does not require the plaintiff to produce expert testimony in every case. Cases arise in which the feasibility of a reasonable alternative design is obvious and understandable to laypersons and therefore expert testimony is unnecessary to support a finding that the product should have been designed differently and more safely. For example, when a manufacturer sells a soft stuffed toy with hard plastic buttons that are easily removable and likely to choke and suffocate a small child who foreseeably attempts to swallow them, the plaintiff should be able to reach the trier of fact with a claim that buttons on such a toy should be an integral part of the toy's fabric itself (or otherwise be unremovable by an infant) without hiring an expert to demonstrate the feasibility of an alternative safer design. Furthermore, other products already available on the market may serve the same or very similar function at lower risk and at comparable cost. Such products may serve as reasonable alternatives to the product in question.
>
> In many cases, the plaintiff must rely on expert testimony. Subsection (b) does not, however, require the plaintiff to produce a prototype in order to make out a prima facie case. Thus, qualified expert testimony on the issue suffices, even though the expert has produced no prototype,

if it reasonably supports the conclusion that a reasonable alternative design could have been practically adopted at the time of sale.

* * *

A test that considers such a broad range of factors in deciding whether the omission of an alternative design renders a product not reasonably safe requires a fair allocation of proof between the parties. To establish a prima facie case of defect, the plaintiff must prove the availability of a technologically feasible and practical alternative design that would have reduced or prevented the plaintiff's harm. Given inherent limitations on access to relevant data, the plaintiff is not required to establish with particularity the costs and benefits associated with adoption of the suggested alternative design.

* * *

Does Comment f reflect the economic approach to risk-utility, the "soft" approach to risk-utility, or is it somewhere between the two? *See*, Green, The Schizophrenia of Risk-benefit Analysis in Design Defect Litigation, 48 Vand.L.Rev. 609, 623–24 (1995). How would a court applying the philosophy of the Restatement (Third) have decided *Smith*? How would it have decided *Kallio*?

4. In light of the three preceding cases, and of the materials you have studied concerning the definition of defect, consider the following problem:

Philip, an eleven-year-old child, was severely injured when his left foot got caught in the agitator mechanism of a bulk chemical fertilizer spreader manufactured by the DDD Manufacturing Co. The spreader was designed for one-person operation, and was towed by a tractor. It was 7 feet long, 8 feet wide and more than 6 feet high. The agitator, at the bottom of the spreader, broke up fertilizer lumps into granules. It ran the length of the spreader, had sharp teeth, and rotated when the spreader was pulled forward. The sides of the spreader were V-shaped, so that gravity forced the fertilizer toward the agitator in the bottom. An auger below the agitator fed the granules into a spinner which distributed the fertilizer. A baffle formed a V-shaped roof several inches above the agitator to protect it from the weight of the fertilizer when the spreader was full. It was made of two pieces of metal, 4 inches wide and 85 inches long. They were joined lengthwise at a 90–degree angle. A metal bar designed to hold a canvas top ran above the hopper.

Philip's father was using the spreader to apply fertilizer to one of his fields. Philip was riding in the spreader, using his feet to break up lumps of fertilizer that were too large to go into the agitator. At the time of the accident, Philip was standing on the baffle and holding on to the metal bar above the hopper. His left foot slipped off of the baffle and was caught in the agitator.

The agitator was clearly visible below the baffle when the spreader was empty. Philip had not seen it and did not know of its existence. Philip's father knew about it, but did not warn him. A sign on the spreader stated that people should keep off the implement while it was in use. It also warned against getting near the moving parts without first disengaging the power.

Philip is represented by an attorney who plans to bring a strict products liability suit against DDD on the theory that the spreader was defectively designed. She has an expert witness who is a retired professor of agricultural engineering safety at a state university. The witness is willing to testify that, based on his inspection, the fertilizer spreader was unreasonably dangerous. His opinion is based upon (1) the known propensity of fertilizer to clog, interfering with the flow of fertilizer to the spinner (insofar as the lumps were too large to pass under the baffle to the agitator), and (2) insufficient guarding of the agitator to prevent one inside the spreader from getting hands or feet caught in the agitator. In his opinion, unless farmers carried a club-like instrument to break up fertilizer clumps, they would have to climb inside the spreader and crush them with their feet. If another person were assisting, he naturally would remain inside the spreader as they were fertilizing to avoid having to stop the tractor each time lumps interfered with the flow of fertilizer.

This witness believes that the spreader would have been reasonably safe if grids, grillwork, bars or the equivalent had been installed at some point at the top of or inside the spreader. Further testing, however, would be necessary to determine the ultimate form and feasibility of such devices. He nevertheless believes that, based on prior experience with similar problems, some such device was workable.

Philip's attorney also has, as witnesses, three farmers who will testify that farm personnel, household members and children frequently ride in fertilizer spreaders to break up lumps of fertilizer.

DDD has an expert engineer who will testify that the spreader was safe because it was designed for operation by one person. The operator would have to stop the tractor when it was necessary to break up lumps, and this would automatically terminate the agitator's rotation. The positioning of the agitator at the bottom of the spreader, and the warning sign on the machine are adequate safeguards. No bars or grillwork could be placed inside the machine without interfering with the flow of fertilizer. If asked on cross-examination, this expert will admit that he has never tested any of the devices suggested by plaintiff's expert.

Does Philip have sufficient evidence to get to a jury on his theory of liability in a jurisdiction that uses the consumer expectations test of defect? The risk-utility test?

O'BRIEN v. MUSKIN CORP.
Supreme Court of New Jersey, 1983.
94 N.J. 169, 463 A.2d 298.

The opinion of the Court was delivered by

POLLOCK, J.

[Plaintiff dove into an above-ground swimming pool with a vinyl liner. His outstretched hands hit the pool bottom, slid apart, and he struck his head on the bottom of the pool, sustaining injuries. He claimed that the pool was defective in design because the pool liner was slippery. Evidence indicated that there was no alternative lining material available for above-ground pools. The trial judge ruled that plaintiff had failed to prove a design defect in the pool, and refused to charge the jury on design defect. Instead, the court submitted the case to the jury solely on the adequacy of the warning. The jury found that the warning was inadequate, but that plaintiff was more at fault than defendant. Thus, because of the New Jersey modified comparative negligence rule, a judgement was entered for defendant.]

On appeal, the Appellate Division found that the trial court erred in removing from the jury the issue of design defect. Consequently, that court reversed the judgment against Muskin and remanded the matter for a new trial. * * *

* * *

The assessment of the utility of a design involves the consideration of available alternatives. If no alternatives are available, recourse to a unique design is more defensible. The existence of a safer and equally efficacious design, however, diminishes the justification for using a challenged design.

The evaluation of the utility of a product also involves the relative need for that product; some products are essentials, while others are luxuries. A product that fills a critical need and can be designed in only one way should be viewed differently from a luxury item. Still other products, including some for which no alternative exists, are so dangerous and of such little use that under the risk-utility analysis, a manufacturer would bear the cost of liability of harm to others. That cost might dissuade a manufacturer from placing the product on the market, even if the product has been made as safely as possible. Indeed, plaintiff contends that above-ground pools with vinyl liners are such products and that manufacturers who market those pools should bear the cost of injuries they cause to foreseeable users.

A critical issue at trial was whether the design of the pool, calling for a vinyl bottom in a pool four feet deep, was defective. The trial court should have permitted the jury to consider whether, because of the dimensions of the pool and slipperiness of the bottom, the risks of injury so outweighed the utility of the product as to constitute a defect. In removing that issue from consideration by the jury, the trial court erred. To establish sufficient proof to compel submission of the issue to the jury for appropriate fact-finding under risk-utility analysis, it was not necessary for plaintiff to prove the existence of alternative, safer designs. Viewing the evidence in the light most favorable to plaintiff, even if there are no alternative methods of making bottoms for above-ground pools, the jury might have found that the risk posed by the pool outweighed its utility.

In a design-defect case, the plaintiff bears the burden of both going forward with the evidence and of persuasion that the product contained a defect. To establish a prima facie case, the plaintiff should adduce sufficient evidence on the risk-utility factors to establish a defect. With respect to above-ground swimming pools, for example, the plaintiff might seek to establish that pools are marketed primarily for recreational, not therapeutic purposes; that because of their design, including their configuration, inadequate warnings, and the use of vinyl liners, injury is likely; that, without impairing the usefulness of the pool or pricing it out of the market, warnings against diving could be made more prominent and a liner less dangerous. It may not be necessary for the plaintiff to introduce evidence on all those alternatives. Conversely, the plaintiff may wish to offer proof on other matters relevant to the risk-utility analysis. It is not a foregone conclusion that plaintiff ultimately will prevail on a risk-utility analysis, but he should have an opportunity to prove his case.

* * *

In concluding, we find that, although the jury allocated fault between the parties, the allocation was based upon the consideration of the fault of Muskin without reference to the design defect. Perhaps the jury would have made a different allocation if, in addition to the inadequacy of the warning, it had considered also the alleged defect in the design of the pool.

* * *

We modify and affirm the judgment of the Appellate Division reversing and remanding the matter for a new trial.

[The opinion of CLIFFORD, J., concurring in result, is omitted.]

SCHREIBER, J., concurring and dissenting.

Until today, the existence of a defect was an essential element in strict product liability. This no longer is so. Indeed, the majority has transformed strict product liability into absolute liability and delegated the function of making that determination to a jury. I must dissent from that conclusion because the jury will not be cognizant of all the elements that should be considered in formulating a policy supporting absolute liability, because it is not satisfactory to have a jury make a value judgment with respect to a type or class of product, and because its judgment will not have precedential effect.

* * *

My research has disclosed no case where liability was imposed, utilizing the risk-utility analysis, as a matter of law for an accident ascribable to a product in the absence of a defect (manufacturing flaw, available alternative, or inadequate warning) other than in the absolute liability context. * * *

* * *

There are occasions where the court has determined as a matter of law because of policy reasons that liability should be imposed even though there is no defect in the product. This is the absolute liability model. The typical example is fixing absolute liability when an ultrahazardous activity causes injury or damage. Liability is imposed irrespective of any wrongdoing by the defendant. [Citation] In this situation the ultimate determination is that the industry should bear such costs, provided the jury has made the requisite findings on causation and damages.

Factors similar to those used in the risk-utility analysis for products liability are applied in the ultrahazardous activity case. The Restatement (Second) of Torts lists these elements:

§ 520. *Abnormally Dangerous Activities*

In determining whether an activity is abnormally dangerous, the following factors are to be considered:

(a) existence of a high degree of risk of some harm to the person, land or chattels of others;

(b) likelihood that the harm that results from it will be great;

(c) inability to eliminate the risk by the exercise of reasonable care;

(d) extent to which the activity is not a matter of common usage;

(e) inappropriateness of the activity to the place where it is carried on; and

(f) extent to which its value to the community is outweighed by its dangerous attributes.

It is conceivable that a court could decide that a manufacturer should have absolute liability for a defect-free product where as a matter of policy liability should be imposed. Suppose a manufacturer produced toy guns for children that emitted hard rubber pellets—an obviously dangerous situation. A court could reasonably conclude that the risks (despite warnings) outweighed the recreational value of the toy, that the manufacturer should bear the costs and that there should be absolute liability to a child injured by the toy.

The *Restatement* also cautions that whether an activity is an abnormally dangerous one so that it should be placed in the ultrahazardous category is to be settled by the court, not the jury. In its comment it states:

> The imposition of [absolute] liability, on the other hand, involves a characterization of the defendant's activity or enterprise itself, and a decision as to whether he is free to conduct it at all without becoming subject to liability for the harm that ensues even though he has used all reasonable care. This calls for a decision of the court;

and it is no part of the province of the jury to decide whether an industrial enterprise upon which the community's prosperity might depend is located in the wrong place or whether such an activity as blasting is to be permitted without liability in the center of a large city. [3 *Restatement (Second) of Torts* § 520 Comment l, at 43 (1965)]

* * *

[Today] * * * the Court * * * decides that a jury may speculate that, though there is no manufacturing flaw, the duty to warn has been satisfied and the manufacturer could not possibly have designed the item in a safer manner, the manufacturer can be absolutely liable because the jury finds that the risk outweighs the product's usefulness. It is not appropriate to forsake uniformity of treatment of a class or type of product by permitting juries to decide these questions. Nor is it appropriate for a jury to make this value judgment in addition to resolving factual issues. Unless the jury is to consider the feasibility of spreading the loss and the intricacies of cost avoidance, *see* Calabresi & Hirschoff, "Toward a Test for Strict Liability in Torts," 81 *Yale L.J.* 1055 (1972), the jury will conduct its inquiry in the absence of evidence of all the elements that should properly be considered in adopting a policy of having the manufacturer spread the loss by setting the price to cover the costs of claims or insurance premiums.

The majority holds that the jury should have been permitted to decide whether the risks of above-ground swimming pools with vinyl bottoms exceed their usefulness despite adequate warnings and despite unavailability of any other design. The plaintiff had the burden of proving this proposition. Yet he adduced no evidence on many of the factors bearing on the risk-utility analysis. There was no evidence on the extent that these pools are used and enjoyed throughout the country; how many families obtain the recreational benefits of swimming and play during a summer; how many accidents occur in the same period of time; the nature of the injuries and how many result from diving. There was no evidence of the feasibility of risk spreading or of the availability of liability insurance or its cost. There was no evidence introduced to enable one to gauge the effect on the price of the product, with or without insurance. The liability exposures, particularly if today's decision is given retroactive effect, could be financially devastating.

These factors should be given some consideration when deciding the policy question of whether pool manufacturers and, in the final analysis, consumers should bear the costs of accidents arising out of the use of pools when no fault can be attributed to the manufacturer because of a flaw in the pool, unavailability of a better design, or inadequate warning. If this Court wishes to make absolute liability available in product cases and not leave such decisions to the Legislature, it should require that trial courts determine in the first instance as a matter of law what products should be subject to absolute liability. In that event the court would consider all relevant factors including those utilized in the risk-utility analysis.

* * *

I join in the result, however. There was proof that the pool liner was slippery and that the vinyl bottom could have been thicker and the embossing deeper. As the majority states, a "fair inference could be drawn that deeper embossing would have rendered the pool bottom less slippery." * * * The plaintiff's theory was that the dangerous condition was the extreme slipperiness of the bottom. Viewing the facts favorably from the plaintiff's frame of reference, I would agree that he had some proof that the pool was incorrectly designed and therefore was defective. This issue, together with causation, should have been submitted to the jury.

Other than as stated herein, I join in the majority's opinion and concur in the judgment reversing and remanding the matter for a new trial.

CLIFFORD, J., concurring in the result.

For affirmance as modified—CHIEF JUSTICE WILENTZ, and JUSTICES CLIFFORD, HANDLER, POLLOCK and O'HERN—5.

Concurring and dissenting—JUSTICE SCHREIBER—1.

Notes

1. **Categorical Risk–Utility Balancing.** *O'Brien* differs from the other cases in this section in that it recognizes that a product can be defective because its risks outweigh its utility even though there is no safer alternative design. This theory has proven to be controversial. In 1987 the New Jersey Legislature passed a statute that severely restricts the *O'Brien v. Muskin* theory of recovery. The statute reads in pertinent part as follows:

> a. In any product liability action against a manufacturer or seller for harm allegedly caused by a product that was designed in a defective manner, the manufacturer or seller shall not be liable if:
>
> (1) At the time the product left the control of the manufacturer, there was not a practical and technically feasible alternative design that would have prevented the harm without substantially impairing the reasonably anticipated or intended function of the product * * *

* * *

> b. The provisions of paragraph (1) of subsection a. of this section shall not apply if the court, on the basis of clear and convincing evidence, makes all of the following determinations:
>
> (1) The product is egregiously unsafe or ultra-hazardous;
>
> (2) The ordinary user or consumer of the product cannot reasonably be expected to have knowledge of the product's risks, or the product poses a risk of serious injury to persons other than the user or consumer; and
>
> (3) The product has little or no usefulness.

N.J. Stat. Ann. 2A:58C–3

2. *Halphen v. Johns–Manville Sales Corp.*, 484 So.2d 110 (La.1986) ruled that a product could be defective in design even though there was not a safer alternative available. In 1988 the Louisiana legislature abolished this basis of liability. *See* Louisiana Revised Statutes Annotated Title 9, § 2800.51, et seq. In addition to *O'Brien* and *Halphen*, several other courts have indicated, at least in dictum, that a properly designed product can be defective because its risk outweighs its utility. *See* Carter v. Johns–Manville Sales Corp., 557 F.Supp. 1317, 1320 (E.D.Tex.1983); Wilson v. Piper Aircraft Corp., 282 Or. 61, 71 n. 5, 577 P.2d 1322, 1328, n. 5 (1978).

3. The Restatement (Third) of Torts: Products Liability § 2 Comment e provides for the possibility that a product could be defective under the risk-utility test even if there is no safer alternative design. The comment states:

> *e. Design defects: possibility of manifestly unreasonable design.* Several courts have suggested that the designs of some products are so manifestly unreasonable, in that they have low social utility and high degree of danger, that liability should attach even absent proof of a reasonable alternative design. In large part the problem is one of how the range of relevant alternative designs is described. For example, a toy gun that shoots hard rubber pellets with sufficient velocity to cause injury to children could be found to be defectively designed within the rule of Subsection (b). Toy guns unlikely to cause injury would constitute reasonable alternatives to the dangerous toy. Thus, toy guns that project ping-pong balls, soft gelatin pellets, or water might be found to be reasonable alternative designs to a toy gun that shoots hard pellets. However, if the realism of the hard-pellet gun, and thus its capacity to cause injury, is sufficiently important to those who purchase and use such products to justify the court's limiting consideration to toy guns that achieve realism by shooting hard pellets, then no reasonable alternative will, by hypothesis, be available. In that instance, the design feature that defines which alternatives are relevant—the realism of the hard-pellet gun and thus its capacity to injure—is precisely the feature on which the user places value and of which the plaintiff complains. If a court were to adopt this characterization of the product, and deem the capacity to cause injury an egregiously unacceptable quality in a toy for use by children, it could conclude that liability should attach without proof of a reasonable alternative design. The court would declare the product design to be defective and not reasonably safe because the extremely high degree of danger posed by its use or consumption so substantially outweighs its negligible social utility that no rational, reasonable person, fully aware of the relevant facts, would choose to use, or to allow children to use, the product.

4. With one very important exception, most courts have, for the most part, rejected the *O'Brien v. Muskin* theory. The question of whether to adopt the theory frequently arises in cases involving properly designed handguns. The issue is whether such weapons are defective because they create a risk of harm through foreseeable criminal misuse. No court has found such guns to be defective. *See* Lapp, The Application of Strict Liability

to Manufacturers and Sellers of Handguns: A Call for More Focused Debate, 10 J.Prod.Liab. 179 (1987); Note, Handgun Manufacturers' Tort Liability to Victims of Criminal Shootings: A Summary of Recent Developments in the Push for a Judicial Ban of the "Saturday Night Special", 31 Vill.L.Rev. 1577 (1986); Comment, Handguns and Products Liability, 97 Harv.L.Rev. 1912 (1984); Note, Manufacturers' Liability to Victims of Handgun Crime: A Common–Law Approach, 51 Fordham L.Rev. 771 (1983). Attempts to impose liability on an abnormally dangerous activity theory have also been unsuccessful. *See* Note, The Manufacture and Distribution of Handguns as an Abnormally Dangerous Activity, 54 U.Chi.L.Rev. 369 (1987).

The important exception is with respect to drugs and vaccines. Often, there is no safer alternative design for such products, and courts evaluate them according to the overall benefit and harm that they produce. These products are analyzed in subsection (d), *infra.*

5. In Kelley v. R.G. Indus., Inc., 304 Md. 124, 497 A.2d 1143 (1985) plaintiff was shot by a robber armed with a "Saturday Night Special" manufactured by defendant. According to the court:

> Saturday Night Specials are generally characterized by short barrels, light weight, easy concealability, low cost, use of cheap quality materials, poor manufacture, inaccuracy and unreliability. These characteristics render the Saturday Night Special particularly attractive for criminal use and virtually useless for the legitimate purposes of law enforcement, sport, and protection of persons, property and businesses.

304 Md. at 145–46, 497 A.2d at 1153–54. The court dismissed plaintiff's product liability design defect count, ruling that the handgun is not defective:

> [It is not defective under the consumer expectations test of defect because a] consumer would expect a handgun to be dangerous, by its very nature, and to have the capacity to fire a bullet with deadly force. Kelley confuses a product's *normal function,* which may very well be dangerous, with a defect in a product's design or construction. * * * For the handgun to be defective, there would have to be a problem in its manufacture or design, such as a weak or improperly placed part, that would cause it to fire unexpectedly or otherwise malfunction. * * * [Likewise, it is not defective under the risk/utility test because this] standard is only applied when something goes wrong with a product. * * * [I]n the case of a handgun which injured a person in whose direction it was fired, the product worked precisely as intended. Therefore, the risk/utility test cannot be extended to impose liability on the maker or marketer of a handgun which has not malfunctioned.

304 Md. at 136–37, 497 A.2d at 1148–49. The court's reasoning for finding no product defect is typical of the product liability cases exonerating manufacturers of properly designed handguns. Another feature of the *Kelley* opinion, however, is atypical. The court created a special cause of action, imposing strict liability on "manufacturers, as well as all in the marketing chain, of Saturday Night Specials." The court said:

> There is no clear-cut, established definition of a Saturday Night Special, although there are various characteristics which are considered

in placing a handgun into that category. Relevant factors include the gun's barrel length, concealability, cost, quality of materials, quality of manufacture, accuracy, reliability, whether it has been banned from import by the Bureau of Alcohol, Tobacco and Firearms, and other related characteristics. Additionally, the industry standards, and the understanding among law enforcement personnel, legislators and the public, at the time the weapon was manufactured and/or marketed by a particular defendant, must be considered. Because many of these factors are relative, in a tort suit a handgun should rarely, if ever, be deemed a Saturday Night Special as a matter of law. Instead, it is a finding to be made by the trier of facts.

On the other hand, before the question of liability may go to the trier of facts, a threshold question must be decided as a matter of law. Since both state and federal statutes reflect a policy that there are legitimate uses for handguns, the trial court must first find that the plaintiff has made a showing that the handgun in question possesses sufficient characteristics of a Saturday Night Special. Moreover, merely because a handgun is small and short barrelled is not itself sufficient for the issue to be submitted to the trier of facts. As stated earlier, the General Assembly of Maryland has recognized the need for certain persons to carry guns, for example, law enforcement personnel and persons with special permits. Non-uniformed law enforcement personnel and certain permit holders will of necessity be required to carry small, short barrelled handguns. A high-quality, small, short barrelled handgun, designed for such legitimate use, is not a Saturday Night Special, and the trier of facts should not be permitted to speculate otherwise. While the determination by the trial court that the plaintiff has passed the initial hurdle cannot be based on size and barrel length alone, these factors, coupled with evidence of low cost, poor quality of materials or workmanship, unreliability, or other identifying characteristics, may be sufficient for the trial court to allow the issue to go to the trier of facts.

Finally, once the trier of facts determines that a handgun is a Saturday Night Special, then liability may be imposed against a manufacturer or anyone else in the marketing chain, including the retailer. Liability may only be imposed, however, when the plaintiff or plaintiff's decedent suffers injury or death because he is shot with the Saturday Night Special. In addition, the shooting must be a criminal act. The shooting itself may be the sole criminal act, or it may occur in the course of another crime where the person firing the Saturday Night Special is one of the perpetrators of the crime. Although neither contributory negligence nor assumption of the risk will be recognized as defenses, nevertheless the plaintiff must not be a participant in the criminal activity. If the foregoing elements are satisfied, then the defendant shall be liable for all resulting damages suffered by the gunshot victim, consistent with the established law concerning tort damages.

304 Md. at 157–59, 497 A.2d at 1159–60. *Kelley* is noted in 16 Cumb.L.Rev. 593 (1985/86); 1986 Det.C.L.Rev. 565; 13 N.Ky.L.Rev. 519 (1987); 61 Notre Dame L.Rev. 478 (1986); 46 Md.L.Rev. 486 (1987); 60 St. John's L.Rev. 555 (1986); 21 Tort & Ins.L.J. 493 (1986); 43 Wash. & Lee L.Rev. 1315 (1986).

6. Does the result reached in *Kelley* represent good policy?

7. Could a court that adopts the analysis of *O'Brien* reach the same result as *Kelley*? Both cases impose strict liability for marketing products whose designs cannot be improved, but they use different approaches in reaching the decision to impose strict liability. Which approach is preferable?

8. Under the *O'Brien v. Muskin Corp.* theory, are the following products defective, even if they are carefully made, because their risk outweighs their utility: tobacco; whiskey; roller skates; hair dryers?

9. The cause of action created by *Kelley* was abolished by the Maryland General Assembly and the citizens of Maryland by the passage of Chapter 533 of the Acts of 1988 and its ratification in a public referendum. *See* Md.Code of 1957, Art. 27, § 36–I(h).

10. In a 1991 referendum the citizens of the District of Columbia passed the following statute:

> Any manufacturer, importer, or dealer of an assault weapon shall be held strictly liable in tort, without regard to fault or proof of defect, for all direct and consequential damages that arise from bodily injury or death if the bodily injury or death proximately results from the discharge of the assault weapon in the District of Columbia.

D.C. Code Ann. § 7–2551.02. For a discussion of the moral basis of liability of gun manufacturers, *see* Note, Corrective Justice and the D.C. Assault Weapon Liability Act, 19 J. Legis. 287 (1993).

11. In 2005 Congress passed the Protection of Lawful Commerce in Arms Act, 15 U.S.C §§ 7901–7903. With certain exceptions, this statute prohibits state or federal lawsuits and requires the immediate dismissal of pending suits:

> brought by any person against a manufacturer or seller of a qualified product, or a trade association, for damages, punitive damages, injunctive or declaratory relief, abatement, restitution, fines, or penalties, or other relief, resulting from the criminal or unlawful misuse of a qualified product by the person or a third party * * *.

15 U.S.C.A. § 7903 (2005).

In § 7901 of the act Congress made the following findings:

> (1) The Second Amendment to the United States Constitution provides that the right of the people to keep and bear arms shall not be infringed.

> (2) The Second Amendment to the United States Constitution protects the rights of individuals, including those who are not members of a militia or engaged in military service or training, to keep and bear arms.

> (3) Lawsuits have been commenced against manufacturers, distributors, dealers, and importers of firearms that operate as designed and intended, which seek money damages and other relief for the harm caused by the misuse of firearms by third parties, including criminals.

> (4) The manufacture, importation, possession, sale, and use of firearms and ammunition in the United States are heavily regulated by Federal,

State, and local laws. Such Federal laws include the Gun Control Act of 1968, the National Firearms Act, and the Arms Export Control Act.

(5) Businesses in the United States that are engaged in interstate and foreign commerce through the lawful design, manufacture, marketing, distribution, importation, or sale to the public of firearms or ammunition products that have been shipped or transported in interstate or foreign commerce are not, and should not, be liable for the harm caused by those who criminally or unlawfully misuse firearm products or ammunition products that function as designed and intended.

(6) The possibility of imposing liability on an entire industry for harm that is solely caused by others is an abuse of the legal system, erodes public confidence in our Nation's laws, threatens the diminution of a basic constitutional right and civil liberty, invites the disassembly and destabilization of other industries and economic sectors lawfully competing in the free enterprise system of the United States, and constitutes an unreasonable burden on interstate and foreign commerce of the United States.

(7) The liability actions commenced or contemplated by the Federal Government, States, municipalities, and private interest groups and others are based on theories without foundation in hundreds of years of the common law and jurisprudence of the United States and do not represent a bona fide expansion of the common law. The possible sustaining of these actions by a maverick judicial officer or petit jury would expand civil liability in a manner never contemplated by the framers of the Constitution, by Congress, or by the legislatures of the several States. Such an expansion of liability would constitute a deprivation of the rights, privileges, and immunities guaranteed to a citizen of the United States under the Fourteenth Amendment to the United States Constitution.

(8) The liability actions commenced or contemplated by the Federal Government, States, municipalities, private interest groups and others attempt to use the judicial branch to circumvent the Legislative branch of government to regulate interstate and foreign commerce through judgments and judicial decrees thereby threatening the Separation of Powers doctrine and weakening and undermining important principles of federalism, State sovereignty and comity between the sister States.

12. Why have attempts to impose liability for marketing products whose design cannot be improved met with so little success both in courts and legislatures? Are these attempts misguided efforts to regulate activity level rather than the level of care? *See* Posner, *supra* page 72; Note, The Smoldering Issue in *Cipollone v. Liggett Group, Inc.*: Process Concerns in Determining Whether Cigarettes are a Defectively Designed Product, 73 Cornell L.Rev. 606, 619–622 (1988). Is the use of political power by potential defendants the explanation? *See* Folio, The Politics of Strict Liability: Holding Manufacturers of Nondefective Saturday Night Special Handguns Strictly Liable After *Kelley v. R.G. Industries, Inc.*, 16 Hamline L.Rev. 147 (1992). Is there some other explanation?

(c) Delegability of the Design Process

BEXIGA v. HAVIR MANUFACTURING CORP.
Supreme Court of New Jersey, 1972.
60 N.J. 402, 290 A.2d 281.

The opinion of the Court was delivered by

PROCTOR, J.

This is a products liability case. Plaintiff John Bexiga, Jr., a minor, was operating a power punch press for his employer, Regina Corporation (Regina), when his right hand was crushed by the ram of the machine, resulting in the loss of fingers and deformity of his hand. [Plaintiff's father brought suit seeking damages on behalf of plaintiff] against Havir Manufacturing Corporation (Havir), the manufacturer of the machine * * *. The action was grounded in negligence, strict liability in tort and breach of warranty of fitness of purpose. The trial court dismissed the action at the close of the plaintiffs' case. The Appellate Division affirmed, and this Court granted plaintiffs' petition for certification.

The machine which caused the injuries was a 10-ton punch press[.] * * * [Plaintiff "testified that the punch press was approximately six or seven feet high with a ram, die and foot pedal."] With the exception of a guard over the flywheel there were no safety devices of any kind on the machine when it was shipped [to Regina, and Regina did not equip the press with any additional safety devices]. * * *[Plaintiff contends] that the punch press was so dangerous in design that the manufacturer was under a duty to equip it with some form of safety device to protect the user while the machine was being operated.

* * *

The particular operation John, Jr. was directed to do required him to place round metal discs, about three inches in diameter, one at a time by hand on top of the die. Once the disc was placed on the die it was held there by the machine itself. He would then depress the foot pedal activating the machine and causing the ram to descend about five inches and punch two holes in the disc. After this operation the ram would ascend and the equipment on the press would remove the metal disc and blow the trimmings away so that the die would be clean for the next cycle. It was estimated by John, Jr. that one cycle as described above would take approximately 10 seconds and that he had completed about 270 cycles during the 40 minutes he operated the machine. He described the accident as follows:

> Well, I put the round piece of metal on the die and the metal didn't go right to the place. I was taking my hand off the machine and I noticed that a piece of metal wasn't in place so I went right back to correct it, but at the same time, my foot had gone to the pedal, so I tried to take my hand off and jerk my foot off too and it was too late. My hand had gotten cut on the punch, the ram.

Plaintiffs' expert, Andrew Gass, a mechanical engineer, * * * described two 'basic types' of protective safety devices both of which were known in the industry at the time of the manufacture and sale. One was a push-button device with the buttons so spaced as to require the operator to place both hands on them away from the die area to set the machine in motion. The other device was a guardrail or gate to prevent the operator's hands from entering the area between the ram and die when the machine was activated. These and other safety devices were available from companies specializing in safety equipment.

On cross-examination Gass conceded that, in accordance with the custom of the trade, presses like the one in question were not equipped with safety devices by the manufacturer. Rather, he said safety devices were to be installed by the ultimate purchaser. However, in his opinion the custom of the trade was improper in that the machine was defectively designed for safety and that purchasers 'almost never' provided safety devices. * * * He concluded that the press here involved should have been equipped with a two-hand push-button device as are the larger presses. * * *

While pointing out that guardrails or gates might have to be 'modified' to suit the particular die or part used with the press, Gass stated that the push-button device would not have to be 'modified' no matter what die was used. In other words, the push-button device would be appropriate for any of the machine's normal uses. On Cross-examination he admitted that if the press were employed to punch holes in a 4–foot pipe a guardrail or gate would impede entry of the pipe into the die area and would have to be removed. He said that in such a case the guardrail or gate would not be needed because in holding the pipe the operator would be standing away from the machine. * * *

The Appellate Division in affirming the trial court's dismissal held that plaintiffs failed to make out a Prima facie case under strict liability, breach of warranty or negligence principles. On the issue of strict liability or breach of warranty the Court applied the rule set forth in the Restatement, which reads in pertinent part:

(1) One who sells any product in a defective condition unreasonably dangerous to the user or consumer or to his property is subject to liability for physical harm thereby caused to the ultimate user or consumer, or to his property if

(a) the seller is engaged in the business of selling such a product, and

(b) it is expected to and does reach the user or consumer without substantial change in the condition in which it is sold. Restatement, Torts 2d s 402A (1965).

The Court reasoned that since it was the custom of the trade that purchasers, rather than manufacturers, provide safety devices on punch presses like the one in question, Havir had no reason to believe that the press would be put to use without some additions[.] * * * It held liability could not be imposed under the Restatement rule because the manufacturer did not expect the product to reach the user without substantial change.

On the issue of negligence the Appellate Division * * * reasoned, 'Since the machine could be used to perform various tasks it conceivably could require a different group of safety devices in connection with each task.' Id. at 406, 276 A.2d at 594. Thus, it held, '(T)he imposition of such a duty upon Havir would have been impractical and that it did not act unreasonably in not equipping the press with safety devices 'on its own'.' Id.

[W]e cannot agree with the Appellate Division[.] * * * We have concluded that on either theory the proofs were sufficient to withstand a motion for dismissal.

There is no question but that the punch press here without any safety devices was dangerous to the user. From the evidence as to the guardrails or gates mentioned above we agree with the Appellate Division that it would be impracticable for the manufacturer to equip his presses with all of these protective devices, and therefore improper to place the responsibility for their installation upon the defendant. However, the expert testified that the alternative basic safety device, the push-button guard, would not have to be 'modified' to suit the die used with the press and there was no evidence that that device would have to be changed for any of the varied uses of the machine. * * *

On the basis of Gass' testimony the jury could infer that the two-hand device was appropriate for every normal operation of the machine and, thus, that it was not impracticable for Havir to equip its machine with such a device. Moreover, as noted above, the expert pointed out that larger punch presses are equipped by the manufacturer with push-button devices; that smaller presses, such as the one in question, were just as dangerous as the larger ones; and that they should be prepared for safety in the same manner. The jury could infer that the two-hand device was appropriate for all of the operations performed on the larger presses and,* * * it could also infer that the push-button device was equally appropriate for the normal uses of the smaller presses.

As we previously said on the issue of strict liability, the Appellate Division applied the rule set forth in the Restatement. To the extent that that rule absolves the manufacturer of liability where he may expect the purchaser to provide safety devices (Restatement, Supra, s 402A(1)(b)), it should not be applied. Where a manufacturer places into the channels of trade a finished product which can be put to use and which should be provided with safety devices because without such it creates an unreasonable risk of harm, and where such safety devices can feasibly be installed by the manufacturer, the fact that he expects that someone else will install such devices should not immunize him. The public interest in assuring that safety devices are installed demands more from the manufacturer than to permit him to leave such a critical phase of his manufacturing process to the haphazard conduct of the ultimate purchaser. The only way to be certain that such devices will be installed on all machines—which clearly the public interest requires—is to place the duty on the manufacturer where it is feasible for him to do so.

We hold that where there is an unreasonable risk of harm to the user of a machine which has no protective safety device, as here, the jury may infer that the machine was defective in design unless it finds that the incorporation by the manufacturer of a safety device would render the machine unusable for its intended purposes. As we have said, the jury could infer from plaintiffs' evidence that it was feasible for Havir to install the push-button device. Therefore, it was error for the trial court to dismiss the strict liability claim at the close of plaintiffs' case.

Of course the question of whether one is negligent depends on whether he acted reasonably under the circumstances of a particular case. Thus, aside from the question of the practicability of Havir's installation of a safety device on the press here involved as to negligence, we must consider whether Havir could reasonably foresee that Regina would not install a safety device. On this issue the custom of the trade—that the manufacturer did not install safety devices but relied on the purchaser to do so—while ordinarily evidential, is not conclusive. Nor would it be conclusive that N.J.S.A. 34:6—62 imposed the duty [to install the safety device] on the purchaser. While Havir may have thought that Regina would have taken adequate precautions to protect its employees or that it would be required to do so by statute, we do not think in view of the circumstances here that Havir had a right as a matter of law to assume such devices would be provided. As to negligence, we hold that a jury question was presented, and that it was error for the trial court to dismiss the action at the close of plaintiffs' case.

If the jury should find for the defendant on the issue of the defective or negligent design of the machine, the next question for it should be whether the defendant was negligent in failing to attach to the machine a suitable warning to the operator of the danger of using it without a protective device.

* * *

The judgment of the Appellate Division is reversed and the cause is remanded for a new trial.

* * *

Notes

1. *Bexiga* is the leading case holding that a manufacturer has a non-delegable duty to install necessary safety devices. This means that the manufacturer is liable if it sells the product without a necessary device even if it reasonably believes that some subsequent owner will install the device. A majority of courts are in accord with *Bexiga*.

2. Why have a non-delegable duty rule? One possible explanation is that in most jurisdictions Worker Compensation statutes immunize employ-

ers from tort liability to workers. Every state has enacted workers' compensation legislation that addresses injuries that arise in the workplace. First enacted early in the twentieth century, these statutes reflected two realities: 1) the industrial revolution produced an increased toll of occupational injury; and 2) most injured workers were unable to obtain any recovery through the tort system.

Although there is some variation among the states, workers' compensation statutes require employers to provide coverage for employees. Workers' compensation is a no-fault compensation scheme: An employee who suffers accidental injury arising out of his or her employment may recover for certain losses. The covered losses and amounts paid, however, are considerably more limited than the losses and damages provided by the tort system. Employees may recover for medical expenses, a percentage of lost wages (up to a statutory cap that is pegged to the average wage) and scheduled payments for permanent and temporary disabilities.

The quid pro quo for this guaranteed, albeit more modest, payment to injured employees is that it provides the exclusive remedy for an injured employee. Employees may not sue their employers in tort for workplace injuries, although this limitation does not prevent an injured employee from pursuing a "third-party" action against another, including a manufacturer of a product used in the workplace. Thus, for any given industrial injury we may have two systems of compensation involved: 1) the statutory workers' compensation scheme that governs between employee and employer; and 2) the tort system that addresses employee claims against anyone other than the employer. The meshing of these two systems, especially with regard to apportionment of liability in a tort action is addressed in Chapter 10.

Industrial accidents involving employees account for a significant percentage of serious injuries caused by products. Where immunity applies, an employer who negligently failed to equip a machine with a safety device could never be held liable to a worker who was injured by the machine. The non-delegable duty doctrine provides injured workers with a defendant (the manufacturer) who can be sued. If this explanation for the non-delegable duty rule is accurate, is it justifiable as a matter of policy? Is there a better explanation for the rule?

3. Of course the manufacturer is still free to argue that the product without the safety feature is not unreasonably dangerous. *See Fallon v. Clifford B. Hannay & Son, Inc., supra* page 124. Stated differently, the manufacturer can delegate design responsibility to the consumer by offering optional designs, some of which are safer than others, but only if all the models are reasonably safe. In this connection, consider the following cases. Can they be reconciled?

A. In Hammond v. International Harvester Co., 691 F.2d 646 (3d Cir.1982) defendant manufactured a tractor with a rollover protective structure (ROPS) as a standard feature. The buyer insisted that the ROPS be removed so that the tractor could move through a low barn door. The manufacturer complied with the request, and an employee of the purchaser was fatally injured in a subsequent accident. A ROPS would have averted the fatal injury. The court held the manufacturer liable for selling the tractor without the ROPS. The court stated:

> [T]he ROPS is standard equipment on the International Harvester Series 3300 loader tractor. This reflects the manufacturer's judgment that a [tractor] with a ROPS will not be unduly expensive or inconvenient to use, and that for safety's sake a loader tractor should come equipped with a ROPS. Without a ROPS, a loader tractor falls short of the optimal design; its design is legally defective and the defect is not cured because the removal of the safety device is specifically requested by the purchaser.

691 F.2d at 651.

B. In Linegar v. Armour of America, Inc., 909 F.2d 1150 (8th Cir.1990) defendant manufactured several styles of bullet-resistant vests. The contour style had a front and back panel held together with Velcro closures under the arms. It did not meet at the sides of the wearer's body, leaving an area along the sides of the body under the arms exposed when the vest was worn. The wrap-around style vest style provides greater coverage for the sides, but still must have an armhole that will be open four-inches below the armpit to allow freedom of movement. A State Highway Patrol trooper, who was wearing a contour style vest, was killed by a bullet that hit him in the side, an area that was unprotected by the vest. Plaintiff brought an action against the manufacturer, claiming that the contour style vest was defective because it did not cover the wearer's sides. The court held that the vest was not defective as a matter of law. The court stated:

> Trooper Linegar's protective vest performed precisely as expected and stopped all of the bullets that hit it. No part of the vest nor any malfunction of the vest caused Linegar's injuries. * * * The vest was designed to prevent the penetration of bullets where there was coverage, and it did so; the amount of coverage was the buyer's choice. The Missouri Highway Patrol could have chosen to buy, and Armour could have sold the Patrol, a vest with more coverage; no one contests that. But it is not the place of courts or juries to set specifications as to the parts of the body a bullet-resistant garment must cover. A manufacturer is not obliged to market only one version of a product, that being the very safest design possible. If that were so, automobile manufacturers could not offer consumers sports cars, convertibles, jeeps, or compact cars. All boaters would have to buy full life vests instead of choosing a ski belt or even a flotation cushion. Personal safety devices, in particular, require personal choices, and it is beyond the province of courts and juries to act as legislators and preordain those choices.
>
> In this case, there obviously were trade-offs to be made. A contour vest like the one here in question permits the wearer more flexibility and mobility and allows better heat dissipation and sweat evaporation, and thus is more likely to be worn than a more confining vest. It is less expensive than styles of vests providing more complete coverage. If manufacturers like Armour are threatened with economically devastating litigation if they market any vest style except that offering maximum coverage, they may decide, since one can always argue that more coverage is possible, to get out

of the business altogether. Or they may continue to market the vest style that, according to the latest lawsuit, affords the "best" coverage. Officers who find the "safest" style confining or uncomfortable will either wear it at risk to their mobility or opt not to wear it at all. * * * Law enforcement agencies trying to work within the confines of a budget may be forced to purchase fewer vests or none at all. * * * We are firmly convinced that to allow this verdict to stand would run counter to the law's purpose of promoting the development of safe and useful products, and would have an especially pernicious effect on the development and marketing of equipment designed to make the always-dangerous work of law enforcement officers a little safer.

909 F.2d at 1154–55.

4. A similar issue arises when a manufacturer sells a product with a removable guard. In Hagans v. Oliver Machinery Co., 576 F.2d 97 (5th Cir.1978) plaintiff was cut by the blade of a table saw because the blade guard had been removed. Plaintiff claimed that the saw was defective because the guard should have been permanently attached to the saw. The jury found for plaintiff, and defendant appealed. The appellate court reversed, holding that the saw was not defective as a matter of law. The evidence showed that the saw could not perform certain important operations with the guard in place. The court found that the removable guard represented a reasonable compromise between safety and utility. *See also* Caterpillar v. Shears, 911 S.W.2d 379 (Tex. 1995).

5. **Multi–Functional Machines**. Some multi-functional machinery cannot be equipped with a single guard or safety system that will work effectively with all functions. Therefore, different types of safeguards must be installed, depending on how the machine is to be used. May the manufacturer sell the machine without a guard, leaving it to the purchaser to install a guard that is appropriate for his use? Courts have dealt with this problem in a variety of ways. *See, e.g.,* Rios v. Niagara Machine & Tool Works, 12 Ill.App.3d 739, 299 N.E.2d 86 (1973), affirmed, 59 Ill.2d 79, 319 N.E.2d 232 (1974) (no duty as a matter of law to put a guard on a multi-functional machine if one guard cannot serve all uses); Westbrock v. Marshalltown Manufacturing Co., 473 N.W.2d 352, 358 (Minn.App. 1991) ("no duty to provide guards for a multi-purpose press where any single point-of-operation guard would impair the machine's multi-purpose utility"); Jiminez v. Dreis & Krump Manufacturing Co., Inc., 736 F.2d 51 (2d Cir.1984) (even where a safety guard limits the utility of a machine with multi-functional capabilities, the jury must decide whether the machine without a guard is reasonably safe. That the guard impairs the utility of the machine is relevant but not controlling because utility is only one factor to used in determining defectiveness).

6. **Custom Made Products**. Defendant manufactures a product according to plans and specifications supplied by its customer. The product as designed lacks a necessary safety feature. Is the manufacturer liable to a user who is injured by the product? There is general agreement that it is not liable on a negligence theory unless the plans create an obvious danger. *E.g.,* Hunt v. Blasius, 74 Ill.2d 203, 23 Ill.Dec. 574, 384 N.E.2d 368 (1978);

Restatement of Torts (Second) § 404, Comment a. (1965). This is because the contractor is justified in relying on the adequacy of the plans and specifications.

7. Is a contractor who follows its customer's plans and specifications exempt from strict liability by analogy to the above rule? The courts have disagreed. *See, e.g.,* Garrison v. Rohm & Haas Co., 492 F.2d 346 (6th Cir.1974) (no liability); Lesnefsky v. Fischer & Porter Co., Inc., 527 F.Supp. 951 (E.D.Pa.1981) (manufacturer of component part not liable under section 402A unless it knows or should know that the part is unsafe for the intended use); Lenherr v. NRM Corp., 504 F.Supp. 165 (D.Kan.1980) (liability under section 402A because the product is defective at the time it leaves the hands of the manufacturer); Michalko v. Cooke Color and Chemical Corp., 91 N.J. 386, 451 A.2d 179 (1982) (contractor who rebuilt part of a machine according to owner's specifications strictly liable).

MOTT v. CALLAHAN AMS MACHINE CO.
Superior Court of New Jersey, Appellate Division, 1980.
174 N.J.Super. 202, 416 A.2d 57.

The opinion of the court was delivered by LORA, P.J.A.D.

On March 22, 1974, plaintiff Shirley Mott was injured in the course of her employment for Clevepak Corporation as a "packer" on or near a punch press machine. At the time of her accident steel coil was being fed from a stock reel to the punch press at which she was working. Plaintiff turned and stepped between the reel and the roll feed at a point where the steel coil was running approximately ½ inch above the ground from the stock reel to the punch press to which the roll feed was affixed, and the tendon and nerves in her ankle and foot were severed by the sharp stock material.

Plaintiff brought suit against Callahan AMS Machinery Company (Callahan), Cooper Weymouth Company, Cooper Weymouth Maine, Inc., Cooper Weymouth Peterson Inc., Carl G. Peterson Co., Sterling Radiator Company Inc. and Reed National Corporation—all of which, except for Callahan, are related corporations through merger and consolidation. The machinery consisted of a punch press, a double roll feed and a double-motorized stock reel which were ordered by plaintiff's employer Clevepak from defendant Callahan and delivered on November 4, 1970. The punch press was manufactured by defendant Callahan, the roll feed by Cooper Weymouth Company and the stock reel by Cooper Weymouth Maine, Inc. When the roll feed was delivered to Callahan it was attached by bolts to the punch press by Callahan.

Callahan denies that it advised Clevepak how to install this equipment and, more particularly, the distance to be maintained between the stock reel and the punch press. The roll feed and the stock reel could be utilized with machines other than a punch press.

Plaintiff's products liability action is bottomed on alleged defective design in that it failed to provide safety guards between the stock reel and punch press, thereby exposing the steel coil notwithstanding it not

Sec. C   DESIGN DEFECTS   189

only permitted but contemplated that they be far enough apart so as to permit someone to walk between them. The instruction sheet for the motorized stock reel, issued by its manufacturer, Cooper Weymouth Maine, Inc., specified that when its stock reel is used there should be a distance of six to ten feet between the reel and the other machine to which material is being fed.

Callahan, by way of cross-claim, contends Cooper Weymouth was negligent in specifying the distance between the stock reel and punch press without providing a guard or barrier since it knew and should have foreseen that there would be a zone of danger created by the unguarded space. Callahan further asserts that it "simply supplied" both parts to Clevepak and did not inform Clevepak as to how far apart the machines should be when in operation.

Sterling Radiator, Reed National and Carl G. Peterson argued that it was Callahan's responsibility to place safety devices between the reel and the press machine since the reel is designed to feed different kinds of machines and a uniform guard rail would be inappropriate because some materials such as cloth that are fed with the Cooper Weymouth reel are not dangerous.

Summary judgments in favor of the Cooper Weymouth companies were granted below on the grounds that they had furnished only a component part rather than a separate machine and that Callahan sold the punch press, motorized reel and roll feed as a package and therefore was the only defendant responsible for installing safety devices. The remaining controversy between plaintiffs and Callahan was settled. Both plaintiffs and Callahan contend that the dismissal of the complaint as against all other defendants was error since there was a genuine issue of material fact as to the liability of the Cooper–Weymouth defendants precluding summary judgment. Defendants counter that as manufacturers of a component part, they may not be held liable for injuries proximately resulting from a design defect in a final assembled product.

Aside from the question of whether the stock reel and roll-feed furnished by the Cooper Weymouth defendants are component parts of the drill press rather than a separate machine used in tandem as a unit to perform the function of manufacturing the bottoms of chocolate cans, under the circumstances of this case there is a proper jury question as to the strict liability of the manufacturers of the stock reel and roll feed for their alleged defective design in failing to provide for a safety device between the motorized reel and the roll feed which was bolted to the punch press. *See, Prosser, Law of Torts* (4 ed. 1971), § 101 at 664; 2 *Frumer & Friedman, Products Liability*, § 16A[4][b][i] at 3B–38.2 (1979).

In *Roy v. Star Chopper Co., Inc.,* 584 F.2d 1124, 1134 (1 Cir.1978), *cert.* den. 440 U.S. 916, 99 S.Ct. 1234, 59 L.Ed.2d 466 (1979), the court, in ruling on Star Chopper's objection to the District Court's failure to instruct the jury that, as a manufacturer of a component part, it could not be held liable, held that the law was clear that a manufacturer of a component part could be held liable under strict liability. In that case plaintiff was injured by a motorized "take up" unit (two motor-driven pinch rolls and a spool) manufactured by Star Chopper and which had no safety guards. The *Roy* court noted that there was "considerable uncertainty" as to whether the "take up" unit was self-contained or a component. 584 *F*.2d at 1134, n. 12. The same uncertainty is present in the case at bar.

In *Verge v. Ford Motor Co.*, 581 *F*.2d 384 (3 Cir.1978), plaintiff had been pinned under a garbage truck that had been put into reverse gear. Ford had supplied the cab and chassis to a corporation (Leach) which then manufactured the garbage truck. Plaintiff had settled with that manufacturer. Ford appealed the trial court's denial of entry of a judgment *n.o.v.* in its favor. Plaintiff's central allegation was that Ford's cab and chassis was defective when it left Ford's hands because it did not contain a warning buzzer that would sound when the truck was put into reverse gear. Plaintiff's expert witness testified that a garbage truck without such a device is unreasonably dangerous.

The court stated the issue on appeal to be whether the responsibility for installing such a safety device should be placed solely upon the company that manufactured the cab and chassis, or solely upon the company that modified the chassis by adding the compactor unit or both. It went on to state

> * * * Where, as here, the finished product is the result of substantial work by more than one party, we must determine responsibility for the absence of a safety device by looking primarily to at least three factors:
>
> 1. Trade Custom—at what stage is that device generally installed. See *State Stove Mfg. Co. v. Hodges*, 189 *So.*2d 113 (Miss.1966), *cert. denied, sub nom. Yates v. Hodges*, 386 *U.S.* 912, 87 *S.Ct.* 860, 17 *L.Ed.*2d 784 (1967); *Schipper v. Levitt and Sons, Inc.*, 44 *N.J.* 70, 207 *A*.2d 314 (1965).
>
> 2. Relative expertise—which party is best acquainted with the design problems and safety techniques in question. *Cf. Schell v. AMF, Inc.*, 567 *F*.2d 1259, 1263 (3d Cir.1977) ("The expected expertise of the manufacturer in a highly specialized field" is a factor in determining whether the manufacturer is liable for failure to install a safety device.)
>
> 3. Practicality—at what stage is installation of device most feasible. See *Taylor, supra; Bexiga v. Havir Mfg. Corp.*, 60 *N.J.* 402, 290 *A*.2d 281 (1972); *State Stove Mfg. Co., supra.*

As we analyze these factors, we will remain mindful of the words of New Jersey Supreme Court Justice Nathan L. Jacobs, in *Schipper v. Levitt, supra*, 44 *N.J.* at 99, 207 *A*.2d at 330: "In developing steps toward higher consumer and user protection through higher trade morality and responsibility, the law should view trade relations realistically rather than mythically." [at 386–87]

In reviewing the evidence and entering judgment *n.o.v.* in favor of Ford, the court found that there was not an adequate basis for determining the trade custom; that the garbage truck manufacturer had more expertise than Ford in the design of refuse collection vehicles and installation of warning devices, and that it was much more practical for warning devices to be installed by the garbage truck manufacturer than by Ford.

The *Verge* court, in discussing the "practicality" prong of the three-part test, relied on the reasoning of *Bexiga v. Havir Mfg. Corp.*, 60 *N.J.* 402, 290 *A.*2d 281 (1972), but distinguished *Bexiga* on the facts. In *Bexiga* the trial court and the Appellate Division had held that the manufacturer of a punch press machine could not be strictly liable for failure to install a safety device because the machine could be used to perform various tasks and it would be impractical for the punch press manufacturer to install different safety devices for each separate use, 60 *N.J.* at 408–409, 290 *A.*2d 281. The Supreme Court, however, concluded that there was evidence from which a jury could have found that one safety device (a two-hand push button) could be installed for all uses of the machine. The court stated:

> Where a manufacturer places into the channels of trade a finished product which can be put to use and which should be provided with safety devices because without such it creates an unreasonable risk of harm, and where such safety devices can feasibly be installed by the manufacturer, the fact that he expects that someone else will install such devices should not immunize him. [at 410, 290 *A.*2d at 285].

Thus, the court stated, the trial judge had erred in granting defendant's motion for an involuntary dismissal at the close of plaintiff's case.

The *Verge* court noted, however, that the evidence in the case before it was that it would not be feasible to install the safety devices in question on all F-700 trucks and that there was no evidence that it would be feasible for Ford to determine which trucks were to be converted for refuse collection use; hence it was more practical for Leach to install the warning devices.

It should be noted that Cooper Weymouth Maine has taken the position that the "finished product" language in *Bexiga* limits the liability to Callahan. But we are of the view, as was the *Verge* court, that *Bexiga* should not be read so narrowly.

Our review of the record discloses that there are factual issues to be determined in applying the three-part test of *Verge*. As to trade custom, the report by plaintiff's expert stated:

> As a general rule of good safety practice, wherever there is a situation that is a continuous source of danger, one does not depend on the employee to exercise undue continuous caution. It behooved the manufacturers to safeguard the danger zone in order to eliminate, or at least, to minimize the hazard. This procedure is standard

practice, and many of the components of the press and take-off reel are so guarded.

Both manufacturers are obviously aware of the necessary physical separation and the creation of the expanse of slack stock. Both are also aware of the burrs and sharp edges that are prevalent on thin steel stock since Cooper Weymouth manufactures equipment that eliminates these sharp edges, and it is highly probable that Callahan has sold such equipment as part of a package. These sharp edges are common knowledge in the metal working industry.

The vice-president of Cooper Weymouth stated in his deposition, however, that he had never seen or heard of a safety device or guard of the material or stock that would go between the motorized reel and punch press. Then too, it is noted that the *Bexiga* court stated that the fact that it was a custom of the trade that the purchaser and not the manufacturer installed safety devices was only evidential and not conclusive. *Id.* at 411. As to expertise and practicality, the record is devoid of anything to support a finding therein.

In this respect, the report of plaintiff's expert stated:

In regard to Cooper Weymouth, it is, of course, very evident that their equipment must be operated utilizing a separation. In regard to Callahan AMS, they sold a "package", and thus were certainly aware of the conditions. Furthermore, the press, as factory fitted, was designed to be used in an automatic feed mode which made them as aware as Cooper Weymouth of the operative conditions.

It is our considered opinion that a plenary trial must be held to determine whether the facts to be developed at that trial will support the imposition of a duty on the Cooper Weymouth companies to install a safety device or to exercise a standard of conduct commensurate with a reasonably foreseeable hazard. * * *

Although the parts in question were manufactured by Cooper Weymouth Maine and Cooper Weymouth Company, the other named defendants are all related by merger or consolidation. As successor corporations they are responsible for the product liability claims against their predecessor. * * *

Reversed and remanded to the Law Division for trial and further proceedings consistent with this opinion. Jurisdiction is not retained.

Notes

1. As *Mott* reveals, a completed product is frequently the product of multiple entities' contributions, including raw materials, manufactured component parts, design, and assembly. Who is the "manufacturer" that is held strictly liable? When might more than one of the entities involved in the production of a finished product be held strictly liable? Quite obviously, this question cannot be answered without consideration of the factual context to

which it will be applied, and the type of defect and where it originated will be critical. The question that *Mott* addresses is but one aspect of the component part manufacturer issue: Who has the final design obligation to make sure the finished product includes sufficient safety devices to make it nondefective?

2. In some cases, the plaintiff's employer may be the designer and even final assembler of production machinery used in an occupational setting. To what extent was that true in *Mott*? As we discussed previously in note 2, *supra* page 184, suits by injured employees against their employers are barred by the "exclusive remedy" provision of workers compensation. Should enhanced design obligations be placed on those supplying parts, even substantial components, to an industrial purchaser who has designed the final product? *Compare* Union Supply Co. v. Pust, 196 Colo. 162, 583 P.2d 276 (Colo. 1978) *with* Shawver v. Roberts Corp., 90 Wis.2d 672, 280 N.W.2d 226 (Wis.1979).

3. Plaintiff was injured when a ram on a punch press descended, causing the die (which was attached thereto) to crush his hand. He brought a suit claiming that the manufacturer of the press was liable because it sold the press to plaintiff's employer without a point of operation guard. The manufacturer claimed that it was not responsible for equipping the press with a guard because it was a general purpose, multifunctional unit, having no point of operation because it was unequipped with dies. The manufacturer's evidence showed that the press was capable of performing thousands of functions. Until it was equipped with a die, and put to a specific use, its work area could not be adequately safeguarded. Each safety device had to be tailored to the manner in which the machine was used. How should the case be resolved?

4. **Substantial Change.** *Mott v. Callahan* offers one approach to the question of whether a manufacturer of a component part is required to provide the needed safety device. Another line of cases analyze the liability of a component part manufacturer in terms of whether its product has undergone a substantial change by virtue of having been incorporated into a final product. Under this approach, the component part manufacturer escapes liability if its product has undergone a substantial change.

Section 402A of the Restatement (Second) of Torts states that a seller of a defective product is liable if the product "is expected to and does reach the consumer without substantial change in the condition in which it is sold." Caveats (2) and (3) to section 402A state:

> The Institute expresses no opinion as to whether the rules stated in this Section may not apply
>
> * * *
>
> (2) to the seller of a product expected to be processed or otherwise substantially changed before it reaches the user or consumer; or
>
> (3) to the seller of a component part of a product to be assembled.

Comments p and q to section 402A elaborate:

> *p. Further processing or substantial change.* Thus far the decisions applying the rule stated have not gone beyond products which are sold

in the condition, or in substantially the same condition, in which they are expected to reach the hands of the ultimate user or consumer. In the absence of decisions providing a clue to the rules which are likely to develop, the Institute has refrained from taking any position as to the possible liability of the seller where the product is expected to, and does, undergo further processing or other substantial change after it leaves his hands and before it reaches those of the ultimate user or consumer.

It seems reasonably clear that the mere fact that the product is to undergo processing, or other substantial change, will not in all cases relieve the seller of liability under the rule stated in this Section. If, for example, raw coffee beans are sold to a buyer who roasts and packs them for sale to the ultimate consumer, it cannot be supposed that the seller will be relieved of all liability when the raw beans are contaminated with arsenic, or some other poison. Likewise the seller of an automobile with a defective steering gear which breaks and injures the driver, can scarcely expect to be relieved of the responsibility by reason of the fact that the car is sold to a dealer who is expected to "service" it, adjust the brakes, mount and inflate the tires, and the like, before it is ready for use. On the other hand, the manufacturer of pigiron, which is capable of a wide variety of uses, is not so likely to be held to strict liability when it turns out to be unsuitable for the child's tricycle into which it is finally made by a remote buyer. The question is essentially one of whether the responsibility for discovery and prevention of the dangerous defect is shifted to the intermediate party who is to make the changes. No doubt there will be some situations, and some defects, as to which the responsibility will be shifted, and others in which it will not. The existing decisions as yet throw no light upon the questions, and the Institute therefore expresses neither approval nor disapproval of the seller's strict liability in such a case.

q. Component parts. The same problem arises in cases of the sale of a component part of a product to be assembled by another, as for example a tire to be placed on a new automobile, a brake cylinder for the same purpose, or an instrument for the panel of an airplane. Again the question arises, whether the responsibility is not shifted to the assembler. It is no doubt to be expected that where there is no change in the component part itself, but it is merely incorporated into something larger, the strict liability will be found to carry through to the ultimate user or consumer. But in the absence of a sufficient number of decisions on the matter to justify a conclusion, the Institute expresses no opinion on the matter.

Union Supply Co. v. Pust, 196 Colo. 162, 583 P.2d 276 (1978) is a leading case using the substantial change analysis. In that case plaintiff was cleaning pulp off of a conveyor, and he was injured when his arm was caught in an unguarded "nip point" of the conveyor. Defendant sold many of the components of the conveyor system. The purchaser assembled them at its plant. The purchaser also added the parts necessary to complete the conveyor system, including the motor, conveyor belt, support legs, walkways and stairs, a counterweight, and the electrical controls. The conveyor was allegedly defective because it lacked an automatic cleaning device, a safety guard, and a warning at the "nip point." The court ruled that the defendant's liability was a question for the jury. Among the fact issues for the jury to resolve in deciding the case was whether defendant's product had undergone substantial change before it reached the plaintiff.

5. How do you think a jury would resolve the "substantial change" question in *Union Supply Co. v. Pust*? On what basis would they decide whether a substantial change had taken place in the components supplied by defendant?

6. **Substantial Participation.** The Restatement (Third) of Torts: Products Liability offers another approach to the question of whether a manufacturer of a component part is required to provide the needed safety device:

§ 5. Liability of Commercial Seller or Distributor of Product Components for Harm Caused by Products into Which Components Are Integrated

One engaged in the business of selling or otherwise distributing product components who sells or distributes a component is subject to liability for harm to persons or property caused by a product into which the component is integrated if:

(a) the component is defective in itself, as defined in this Chapter, and the defect causes the harm; or

(b)(1) the seller or distributor of the component substantially participates in the integration of the component into the design of the product; and

(2) the integration of the component causes the product to be defective, as defined in this Chapter; and

(3) the defect in the product causes the harm.

Comment:

a. Rationale. Product components include raw materials, bulk products, and other constituent products sold for integration into other products. Some components, such as raw materials, valves, or switches, have no functional capabilities unless integrated into other products. Other components, such as a truck chassis or a multi-functional machine, function on their own but still may be utilized in a variety of ways by assemblers of other products.

As a general rule, component sellers should not be liable when the component itself is not defective as defined in this Chapter. If the component is not itself defective, it would be unjust and inefficient to impose liability solely on the ground that the manufacturer of the integrated product utilizes the component in a manner that renders the integrated product defective. Imposing liability would require the component seller to scrutinize another's product which the component seller has no role in developing. This would require the component seller to develop sufficient sophistication to review the decisions of the business entity that is already charged with responsibility for the integrated product.

* * *

e. Substantial participation in the integration of the component into the design of another product. When the component seller is substantially involved in the integration of the component into the design of the integrated product, the component seller is subject to liability when the integration results in a defective product and the defect causes harm to the plaintiff. Substantial participation can take various forms. The manufacturer or assembler of the integrated product may invite the component seller to design a component that will perform specifically as part of the integrated product or to assist in modifying the design of the integrated product to accept the seller's component. Or the component seller may play a substantial role in deciding which component best serves the requirements of the integrated product. When the component seller substantially participates in the design of the integrated product, it is fair and reasonable to hold the component seller responsible for harm caused by the defective, integrated product. A component seller who simply designs a component to its buyer's specifications, and does not substantially participate in the integration of the component into the design of the product, is not liable within the meaning of Subsection (b). Moreover, providing mechanical or technical services or advice concerning a component part does not, by itself, constitute substantial participation that would subject the component supplier to liability. One who provides a design service alone, as distinct from combining the design function with the sale of a component, generally is liable only for negligence and is not treated as a product seller. See § 19(b).

7. How would *Mott v. Callahan* have decided the *Union Supply Co. v. Pust* case? How would the case be decided under Section 5 of the Restatement (Third)? Which approach is superior?

8. **Raw Materials.** Comment, Substantial Change: Alteration of a Product as a Bar to a Manufacturer's Strict Liability, 80 Dick.L.Rev. 245, 257–258 (1976) discusses the liability of a supplier of raw materials which are incorporated into a finished product:

> Determining responsibility for a defect is especially difficult when raw materials require processing to become usable products. Because of the great change from raw material to final product, the defect that actually caused an injury is often impossible to pinpoint. In these cases the liability of the seller of the raw material turns on "whether the responsibility for discovery and prevention of the dangerous defect is shifted to the intermediate party who is to make the change."[1]
>
> The two cases that have faced the question of change in raw material are excellent examples of how the burden of defect discovery and prevention can shift. In *Walker v. Stauffer Chemical Corp.*[2] the court held that a manufacturer of bulk sulfuric acid was not strictly liable for injury caused by an explosion of drain cleaner produced from the acid.
>
> We do not believe it realistically feasible or necessary to the protection of the public to require the manufacturer and supplier of a

---

1. Restatement § 402A, comment *p* at 357.

2. 19 Cal.App.3d 669, 96 Cal.Rptr. 803 (1971).

standard chemical ingredient such as bulk sulfuric acid, not having control over the subsequent compounding, packaging or marketing of an item eventually causing injury to the ultimate consumer, to bear the responsibility for that injury.[3]

Responsibility for prevention of the defect clearly lay with the processor, thus relieving the acid manufacturer of liability. *States Steamship Co. v. Stone Manganese Marine Ltd.*[4] provides a contrast to *Walker*. Defendant was a manufacturer of an alloy used in the production of ship propellers. Certain propellers were found defective and a ship owner brought suit for property damage. Noting that "a change in the shape of the product, however noticeable, is not dispositive of the change issue," the court denied defendant's motion for summary judgment and left the substantial change issue to the jury.[5]

In *States Steamship* the alloy was specifically produced for propellers. The manufacturer was aware of the minimum qualities necessary for adequate propeller strength. On the other hand, the acid in *Walker* was not solely for drain cleaners. The acid manufacturer was unable to determine the eventual characteristics of his product after its combination with other elements. Thus, in *States Steamship* the manufacturer had the best opportunity to prevent propeller defects, but in *Walker* that responsibility shifted to an intermediate party, the drain cleaner producer.

9. In part influenced by the litigation over jaw implants, known as the Proplast TMJ Implant, the Third Restatement § 5, Comment c protects the supplier of a raw material that is, by itself, not contaminated or otherwise defective. DuPont sold relatively small quantities of teflon to Vitek, Inc., which manufactured the TMJ Implant. Teflon is an inert and safe material that was used to fabricate the material out of which the TMJ Implant was made. The implants failed, caused serious problems in those in whom they were implanted, and ultimately had to be surgically removed. After Vitek went bankrupt, a number of TMJ Implant victims sued DuPont, claiming it had failed to warn them or their physicians of the dangers of using teflon for human implants. Dupont was aware of mixed success with teflon in human implants, informed Vitek of this, and required Vitek to sign an acknowledgment that it was assuming responsibility for assuring that teflon was an appropriate ingredient for the TMJ Implants it was going to manufacture. DuPont was successful in virtually every case brought against it. *See, e.g.,* Kealoha v. E.I. du Pont de Nemours and Co., 82 F.3d 894 (9th Cir.1996) (bulk supplier of safe component cannot be liable when that part is incorporated into a finished product that is defective, regardless of the foreseeability of the product's dangers); Klem v. E.I. DuPont De Nemours & Co.,19 F.3d 997 (5th Cir.1994).

In the wake of this litigation, DuPont and other raw material manufacturers threatened to cease selling their materials to medical device manufacturers. Sales to the biomedical industry were a small fraction of their market, and the liability concerns overshadowed the modest amount of sales. Senators Lieberman and McCain introduced a bill in Congress designed to

3. *Id.* at 674, 96 Cal.Rptr. at 806.
4. 371 F.Supp. 500 (D.N.J.1973).
5. *Id.* at 505.

protect biomedical raw materials suppliers from liability, arguing that although DuPont had successfully exonerated itself, it had to spend millions of dollars doing so. DuPont had sold less than $2,000 of teflon to Vitek for its jaw implants. *Lifesavers and Lawsuits*, Wash. Post (Apr. 3, 1996), at A19. The bill was enacted in a modified form in the Biomaterials Access Assurance Act of 1998, 21 USC § 1601 (1998).

10. **Duty to warn about another manufacturer's product**. Does a manufacturer have a duty to warn about another manufacturer's product? The courts have generally said no. Consider the following cases:

A. In Walton v. Harnischfeger, 796 S.W.2d 225 (Tex.App. 1990) plaintiff was injured when a nylon strap rigged to a load of tin and attached to a crane broke, and the load of tin dropped on him. Plaintiff alleged that the manufacturer of the crane was liable for failure to warn or to provide instructions regarding rigging of the crane. The court held that the crane manufacturer had no duty as a matter of law to warn or instruct concerning the nylon strap, a product manufactured by someone else.

B. In Crossfield v. Quality Control Equipment Co., Inc., 1 F.3d 701 (8th Cir.1993) plaintiff was injured by the chain/sprocket mechanism of a chitterling cleaning machine. The machine lacked a guard and an interlock that would have prevented the accident. The manufacturer of the machine was no longer in business. Plaintiff sued the supplier of the replacement chain that was on the machine at the time of the accident. The chain was specifically manufactured to fit the machine. Plaintiff alleged that the chain was defective because it lacked a warning stating that it could be hazardous when used on the machine. The court held that there was no duty to warn as a matter of law. The court stated:

> To impose responsibility on the supplier of the chain in the context of the larger defectively designed machine system would simply extend liability too far. This would mean that suppliers would be required to hire machine design experts to scrutinize machine systems that the supplier had no role in developing. Suppliers would be forced to provide modifications and attach warnings on machines which they never designed nor manufactured. Mere suppliers cannot be expected to guarantee the safety of other manufacturers' machinery.

1 F.3d at 704.

C. In Clarke Industries, Inc. v. Home Indemnity Co., 591 So.2d 458 (Ala.1991) plaintiff rented a floor sanding machine manufactured by defendant and did not empty the dust collection bag after use. A fire started by the spontaneous combustion of sawdust in the dust collection bag, and plaintiff's property was damaged. The dust collection bags manufactured by defendant for use with the sander contained a fire hazard warning. The bag that was on the machine was another brand that contained no warnings. There was testimony that the defendant was aware that the bags that came with the sander would routinely wear out and that replacement bags would be required. Further, there was testimony that defendant was aware that rental companies did not use its bags as replacements because they were too expensive. Plaintiff alleged that the sander was defective because a warning about the risk of spontaneous combustion should have been on the machine itself, rather than on the bag. The court upheld a jury verdict for plaintiff on this theory.

Can the holding in *Clarke Industries, Inc. v. Home Indemnity Co.* be reconciled with the holdings in *Walton v. Harnischfeger* and *Crossfield v. Quality Control Equipment Company*?

(d) Special Problems with Medical Devices and Pharmaceuticals

GRUNDBERG v. UPJOHN CO.
Supreme Court of Utah, 1991.
813 P.2d 89.

DURHAM, JUSTICE:

This case comes to us pursuant to rule 41 of the Utah Rules of Appellate Procedure as a question certified from the United States District Court for the District of Utah. The issue before us is whether Utah adopts the "unavoidably unsafe products" exception to strict products liability as set forth in comment k to section 402A of the Restatement (Second) of Torts (1965) ("comment k"). This question presents an unanswered issue of law for original disposition by this court.

We hold that a drug approved by the United States Food and Drug Administration ("FDA"), properly prepared, compounded, packaged, and distributed, cannot as a matter of law be "defective" in the absence of proof of inaccurate, incomplete, misleading, or fraudulent information furnished by the manufacturer in connection with FDA approval. We acknowledge that by characterizing all FDA-approved prescription medications as "unavoidably unsafe," we are expanding the literal interpretation of comment k.

The following facts are taken from the federal district court's certification order. Mildred Lucille Coats died at age 83 from gunshot wounds inflicted by her daughter, Ilo Grundberg, on June 19, 1988. Grundberg and Janice Gray, the personal representative of Coat's estate, brought this action, alleging that Grundberg shot her mother as a result of ingesting the drug Halcion, a prescription drug manufactured by defendant Upjohn to treat insomnia.

Plaintiffs allege that Grundberg took a .5 milligram dose of Halcion the day she shot her mother. They allege that this dose was recommended by her physician and was consistent with Upjohn's recommended dosage. Plaintiffs assert that Grundberg shot her mother while in a state of Halcion-induced intoxication, which allegedly included side effects such as depression, psychosis, depersonalization, aggressive assaultive behavior, and homicidal compulsion.

Plaintiffs' complaint states several causes of action, including common law negligence and strict liability. Plaintiffs claim that Upjohn failed to adequately warn about certain adverse side effects of Halcion and that Halcion was defectively designed. The failure-to-warn claim is scheduled for trial. The strict liability claim based on design defect is the subject of Upjohn's pending summary judgment motion, the outcome of which depends on this court's resolution of the certified question.

The parties agree that the Restatement (Second) of Torts section 402A, comment k (1965) and the principles it embodies provide an exemption from strict liability for a claimed design defect in the case of products that are "unavoidably unsafe." In moving for partial summary judgment, Upjohn argued that public policy supporting the research and development of new drugs requires a holding that *all* FDA-approved prescription medications are "unavoidably unsafe products" under comment k and, as such, manufacturers of those drugs would not be liable for a claim based on defective design. Plaintiffs argue that whether a drug is "unavoidably unsafe" must be determined on a case-by-case basis, with a determination in each case of whether the specific drug's benefit exceeded its risk at the time it was distributed. The district court found this to be a controlling question of law and certified it to this court.

* * *

I. Utah Law on Strict Liability

Section 402A of the Restatement (Second) of Torts (1965) addresses the strict liability of sellers of products. This court adopted section 402A, of which comment k is one provision, in *Ernest W. Hahn, Inc. v. Armco Steel Co.*, 601 P.2d 152, 158 (Utah 1979). Since then, we have adhered to section 402A and to at least one of its accompanying comments. [Citations] We have not addressed the application of comment k in the context of prescription drugs or otherwise. * * *

In its entirety, comment k reads:

k. *Unavoidably unsafe products.* There are some products which, in the present state of human knowledge, are quite incapable of being made safe for their intended and ordinary use. These are especially common in the field of drugs. An outstanding example is the vaccine for the Pasteur treatment of rabies, which not uncommonly leads to very serious and damaging consequences when it is injected. Since the disease itself invariably leads to a dreadful death, both the marketing and the use of the vaccine are fully justified, notwithstanding the unavoidable high degree of risk which they involve. Such a product, properly prepared, and accompanied by proper directions and warning, is not defective, nor is it *unreasonably dangerous*. The same is true of many other drugs, vaccines, and the like, many of which for this very reason cannot legally be sold except to physicians, or under the prescription of a physician. It is also true in particular of many new or experimental drugs as to which, because of lack of time and opportunity for sufficient medical experience, there can be no assurance of safety, or perhaps even of purity of ingredients, but such experience as there is justifies the marketing and use of the drug notwithstanding a medically recognizable risk. The seller of such products, again with the qualification that they are properly prepared and marketed, and proper warning is given, where the situation calls for it, is not to be held to strict liability for unfortunate consequences attending their use, merely because he has undertaken to supply the public with an apparently useful and desirable product, attended with a known but apparently reasonable risk.

Comment k establishes an exception to the strict products liability section 402A imposes on "[o]ne who sells any product in a defective condition unreasonably dangerous to the user or consumer or to his [or her] property. * * *" § 402A(1). This liability applies whether or not "the seller has exercised all possible care in the preparation and sale of his product. * * *" § 402A(2)(a). Comment g defines a "defective condition" as a condition "not contemplated by the ultimate consumer which will be unreasonably dangerous to [that consumer]." Comment k, however, defines a category of "unavoidably unsafe" products that "when properly prepared, and accompanied by proper directions and warning, [are] not defective, nor * * * *unreasonably* dangerous." (Emphasis in original.)

We agree with comment k's basic proposition—that there are some products that have dangers associated with their use even though they are used as intended. We also agree that the seller of such products, when the products are properly prepared and marketed and distributed with appropriate warnings, should not be held strictly liable for the "unfortunate consequences" attending their use. Thus, we adopt comment k's basic policy as the law to be applied in this state and must now turn to the issue of how to apply that policy.

II. APPLICATION OF COMMENT K

As a condition to its application, comment k requires that the product be "properly prepared, and accompanied by proper directions and warning. * * *" There are three types of product defects: manufacturing flaws, design defects, and inadequate warnings regarding use. [Citations] By its terms, comment k excepts unavoidably unsafe products from strict liability only to the extent that the plaintiff alleges a design defect; comment k's immunity from strict liability does not extend to strict liability claims based on a manufacturing flaw or an inadequate warning. The purpose of comment k is to protect from strict liability products that cannot be designed more safely. If, however, such products are mismanufactured or unaccompanied by adequate warnings, the seller may be liable even if the plaintiff cannot establish the seller's negligence. [Citation] Both parties agree in this case that the prerequisite to a comment k exemption—that the drug "was properly prepared and accompanied by warnings of its dangerous propensities"—must be established on a case-by-case basis. This limitation on the scope of comment k immunity is universally recognized.

Even in the case of a clearly alleged design defect, however, comment k is unclear on the scope of its protection. Until recently, most courts refrained from applying a design defect theory to products liability cases involving prescription drugs. Beginning with *Brochu v. Ortho Pharmaceutical Corp.*, 642 F.2d 652 (1st Cir.1981), however, and more recently in *Savina v. Sterling Drug, Inc.*, 247 Kan. 105, 795 P.2d 915 (1990), some states have permitted recovery for a strict liability claim based on the theory that the drug was defectively designed.

Some courts have applied comment k on a case-by-case basis, conditioning application of the exemption on a finding that the drug is in fact "unavoidably unsafe." *See Savina*, 795 P.2d 915; *Toner [v. Lederle Laboratories*, 112 Idaho 328, 732 P.2d 297 (1987)]; *see also Feldman v. Lederle Laboratories*, 97 N.J. 429, 479 A.2d 374, 382–83 (1984) (involving allegations of failure to warn, but stating, "Whether a drug is unavoidably unsafe should be decided on a case-by-case basis. * * * "); *Collins v. Eli Lilly Co.*, 116 Wis.2d 166, 342 N.W.2d 37, 52 (1984) (comment k applicable only if drug in question was placed on market without adequate testing because of exigent circumstances); *Patten v. Lederle Laboratories*, 676 F.Supp. 233 (D.Utah 1987) (federal district court predicting that Utah would adopt comment k).

California was the first state to fashion a risk/benefit test to determine which drugs are entitled to comment k protection. In *Kearl v. Lederle Laboratories*, 172 Cal.App.3d 812, 218 Cal.Rptr. 453 (1985),[1] the California Court of Appeal specifically discussed the problems society would face by subjecting drugs to the same accountability as other products, allowing unlimited redress for plaintiffs injured by pharmaceutical products. Such problems, the court noted, include delayed availability of needed drugs and imposition of the costs of research, development, and marketing of new products beyond that which manufacturers, especially small manufacturers, might be willing to risk. 218 Cal.Rptr. at 459 (quoting *Feldman*, 460 A.2d at 209).

The *Kearl* court expressed discomfort, however, with the "mechanical" method by which many appellate courts had concluded that drugs are entitled to special treatment. 218 Cal.Rptr. at 463. Thus, *Kearl* set forth a risk/benefit analysis to be carried out by the trial court on a case-by-case basis. *Id.* at 463–64. Under this approach, a product may be deemed unavoidably unsafe and thus exempt from a strict liability design defect cause of action only if the court concludes that (1) the product was intended to provide an exceptionally important benefit, and (2) the risk posed was substantial and unavoidable when distributed. *Id.* at 464.[2]

---

1. *Kearl* was overturned by the California Supreme Court in *Brown*, 751 P.2d at 470. Since *Brown*, the rule in California is that all prescription drugs are entitled as a matter of law to an exemption from strict liability claims based upon design defects.

2. The trial court would decide whether to exempt a product only after first taking

Idaho adopted and to some extent refined the *Kearl* approach in *Toner v. Lederle Laboratories*, 112 Idaho 328, 732 P.2d 297 (1987), a case addressing a suit against the manufacturer of a vaccine to immunize against diphtheria, pertussis, and tetanus ("DPT"). *Toner* required the drug manufacturer to prove at trial, on a case-by-case basis, that the benefits of the drug outweighed the risks at the time of marketing. 732 P.2d at 305–09. To qualify as an "unavoidably unsafe product" under this approach, "there must be, at the time of the subject products' distribution, no feasible alternative design which on balance accomplishes the subject product's purpose with a lesser risk." *Id.* at 306 (citing *Belle Bonfils Memorial Blood Bank v. Hansen*, 665 P.2d 118, 123 (Colo.1983)); *Kearl*, 218 Cal.Rptr. at 464. If there were alternative drug product designs that could have effectively achieved the same purpose, the court reasoned, the risk would not be "unavoidable" or "apparently reasonable" and the marketing and use of the product would not be justified. *Toner*, 732 P.2d at 306.

In direct contrast to those courts applying comment k's immunity on a case-by-case basis are courts holding that all prescription drugs are entitled as a matter of law to the exemption from strict liability claims based on design defect. In *Brown v. Superior Court*, 44 Cal.3d 1049, 245 Cal.Rptr. 412, 751 P.2d 470 (1988), the court addressed claims brought by plaintiffs who sued drug companies for injuries allegedly arising from their mothers' in utero exposure to diethystilbestrol, a synthetic hormone marketed for use during pregnancy. The court weighed the problem of whether imposing strict liability on drug manufacturers comports with the traditional goals of tort law, namely, deterrence and cost distribution. 751 P.2d at 478. The court acknowledged that a drug might be safer if pharmaceutical companies withheld it from the market until scientific skill and knowledge advanced to the point where all dangerous side effects could be discovered. *Id.* at 479. There was concern, however, that this delay, when added to the delay normally required for the FDA to approve a new drug, would not serve the public welfare. The court cited examples of several potentially useful drugs being withdrawn from the market or their availability seriously curtailed because of the liability crisis. *Id.* at 479–80.

The *Brown* court acknowledged the appeal of the *Kearl* cost/benefit approach, yet found the "mini-trial" procedure unworkable because of its negative impact on the development and marketing of new drugs. *Brown*, 751 P.2d at 481. Another of the *Brown* court's objections to *Kearl* was that it left the trial court to hear and resolve mixed questions of law and fact, placing the trial court in the role of fact finder. *Brown*, 751 P.2d at 481–82. The court found the cost/benefit test too open-ended

evidence out of the jury's presence, considering: (1) whether, when distributed, the product was intended to confer an exceptionally important benefit that made its availability highly desirable; (2) whether the then-existing risk posed by the product both was "substantial" and "unavoidable;" and (3) whether the interest in availability (again measured as of the time of distribution) outweighs the interest in promoting enhanced accountability through strict liability design defect review. *Kearl*, 218 Cal. Rptr. at 464.

and predicted that it would lead to disparate treatment of the same drug by different judges. *Id.* at 482.

The *Brown* court stressed three public policies mitigating against imposing strict liability for prescription drugs. First, drug manufacturers might stop producing valuable drugs because of lost profits resulting from lawsuits or the inability to secure adequate insurance. *Id.* at 479–80. Second, consumers have a vested interest in prompt availability of new pharmaceutical products. Imposing strict liability for design defects might cause manufacturers to delay placing new products on the market, even after those products receive FDA approval. *Id.* at 479. Finally, the added expense of insuring against strict liability and additional research programs might cause the cost of medication to increase to the extent that it would no longer be affordable to consumers. *Id.*

The plaintiffs and amici curiae in *Brown* asserted that the language of comment k cannot be interpreted to grant blanket immunity from strict liability to all prescription drugs. Rather, they asserted that only those drugs that are "unavoidably dangerous" are eligible for such protection. *Id.* at 482 n. 11. The court, although conceding that the comment is not entirely clear on this point, noted that "the comment was *intended* to and should apply to all prescription drugs." *Id.* (emphasis added). *Brown* concluded that "because of the public interest in the development, availability, and reasonable price of drugs, the appropriate test for determining responsibility is the test stated in comment k. * * *" *Id.* at 477.

In *Castrignano v. E.R. Squibb & Sons, Inc.*, 546 A.2d 775 (R.I.1988), the Rhode Island Supreme Court had the opportunity to review *Toner's* case-by-case risk/benefit analysis and *Brown's* broad exemption approach when formulating its own approach to drug products liability. The Rhode Island court opted for the more restrictive case-by-case approach, *id.* at 781, and developed a directed verdict standard to balance the roles of the judge and the jury in applying comment k. *Id.* at 781–82. Under the *Castrignano* test, if at the time of marketing the apparent benefit outweighed the apparent risk, comment k applies and recovery for design defect is precluded. *Id.* If a trial judge concludes that reasonable minds could not differ in deciding that a drug's benefit exceeds its risk, then as a matter of law, the trial judge can extend comment k protection. *Id.* at 782. If the judge feels that reasonable minds could differ on the question, the judge must submit the issue to the jury. *Id.*

In reviewing the approaches of other jurisdictions toward strict products liability for design defects in drug products, we are troubled by the lack of uniformity and certainty inherent in the case-by-case approach and fear the resulting disincentive for pharmaceutical manufacturers to develop new products. *Toner's* attempt to clarify the "unreasonably dangerous" standard seriously curtails the defendants' chances of success in establishing comment k immunity as a matter of law. One commentator notes that a defendant would have an easier time rebutting a plaintiff's prima facie case of design defect under the traditional standard than meeting the tough burden of "earning" the comment k exemption. *See* Reilly, *The Erosion of Comment k*, 14 U. Dayton L.Rev. 255, 266 (1989).

Toner applied a very literal and restrictive interpretation of comment k. For example, the comment cites examples of *certain* drugs and vaccines as products that "supply the public with an apparently useful and desirable product, attended with a known but apparently reasonable risk." Based on this language, *Toner* opined that (1) comment k "[c]learly * * * contemplates a weighing of the benefit of the product against its risk" and (2) was never intended to exempt *all* drugs from strict liability. *Toner*, 732 P.2d 297, 306. Even if we agree with the court in *Toner* that the comment contemplates a "weighing" of the drug's risks and benefits, we find it unnecessary to conclude that a *court* is the proper body to engage in that weighing process. Furthermore, we need not be bound by the specific language of comment k and may adopt and apply its fundamental policy without restricting ourselves to what we perceive to be its literal interpretation.

Castrignano's somewhat nebulous standard, designed to control when the question of comment k's application reaches the jury, leaves a great deal of room for plaintiffs to maneuver cases to the jury. Additionally, like the traditional case-by-case approach, this standard ignores the effectiveness of the FDA's regulatory process.

We agree with *Brown* that the case-by-case method first articulated in *Kearl* is unworkable, even in light of *Toner's* refinement of the test. We find the *Brown* result more in line with the public policy considerations in the important area of pharmaceutical product design. We do not agree, however, with the *Brown* court's apparent attempt to use the plain language of comment k as the vehicle for exempting all prescription drugs from strict liability rather than relying on the policies underlying that comment.

The American Law Institute's restatements are drafted by legal scholars who attempt to summarize the state of the law in a given area, predict how the law is changing, and suggest the direction the law should take. The restatement serves an appropriate advisory role to courts in approaching unsettled areas of law. We emphasize, however, that section 402A of the Restatement (Second) of Torts, as drafted in 1965, is not binding on our decision in this case except insofar as we explicitly adopt its various doctrinal principles. We agree with the principle comment k embodies, that manufacturers of unavoidably dangerous products should not be liable for a claim of design defect. We are persuaded that all prescription drugs should be classified as unavoidably dangerous in design because of their unique nature and value, the elaborate regulatory system overseen by the FDA, the difficulties of relying on individual lawsuits as a forum in which to review a prescription drug's design, and the significant public policy considerations noted in *Brown*. We therefore reach the same conclusion as did the California

Supreme Court in *Brown*, albeit pursuant to a slightly different rationale.

III. UNIQUE CHARACTERISTICS OF DRUGS

Because prescription drugs are chemical compounds designed to interact with the chemical and physiological processes of the human body, they will almost always pose some risk of side effects in certain individuals. Despite these risks, new drugs are continually approved by the FDA because of their social benefit in saving lives and alleviating human suffering. The health care system and general standard of living in this country, for example, would be seriously impaired without such essential drug products as antibiotics that allow quick recovery from ailments that were once debilitating or even fatal. *See* 37 Food, Drug & Cosmetic L.J. 15 (1982).

In addition, because the expansion of tort liability is justified primarily on the basis of deterring or transferring the cost of injuries, it is appropriate to consider the increased costs that could result from the curtailment of the production of prescription drugs. One commentator notes:

> [D]rugs are our most cost-effective input in supplying the demand for health. *A ten-dollar prescription is frequently a substitute for $2,000 worth of hospital services*—a substitute that produces a positive outcome with much higher frequency than hospital care. * * * *If we are serious about minimizing costs, our best bet is to increase the number of drug innovations.*

Brozen, *Statements, Drugs & Health: Economic Issues and Policy Objectives*, 305 (Helms ed. 1981) (emphasis added).

Despite inherent risks, *and in contrast to any other product*, society has determined that prescription medications provide a unique benefit and so should be available to physicians with appropriate warnings and guidance as to use. The federal government has established an elaborate regulatory system, overseen by the FDA, to control the approval and distribution of these drugs. *See* 21 U.S.C. §§ 301–393. No other class of products is subject to such special restrictions or protections in our society.

IV. FDA REGULATION

Congress created the FDA to "protect consumers from dangerous products." *United States v. Sullivan*, 332 U.S. 689, 696, 68 S.Ct. 331, 335, 92 L.Ed. 297 (1948). In its role as "both a health promoter * * * and * * * a public protector," the FDA employs a comprehensive scheme of premarket screening and post-market surveillance to ensure the safety and efficacy of all licensed medications. 50 Fed.Reg. 7452 (1985).

Before licensing a new medication, the FDA employs an extensive screening mechanism to ensure that the potential benefits of the product outweigh any associated risks. The manufacturer initiates the review by submitting an Investigational New Drug Application ("IND"), contain-

ing information about the drug's chemistry, manufacturing, pharmacology, and toxicology. *See* 21 U.S.C. § 355(b)(1) (Supp.1991); 21 C.F.R. § 312.21 (1990). If the FDA approves the IND, the drug's sponsor may gather data on clinical safety and efficacy needed for a New Drug Application ("NDA"), the formal license application. The NDA must include very detailed reports of all animal studies and clinical testing performed with the drug, reports of any adverse reactions, and any other pertinent information from world-wide scientific literature. 21 U.S.C. § 355(b) (Supp.1991); 21 C.F.R. § 314.50 (1990).

The new drug approval process can require years of testing and review. * * *

Elaborate premarket screening, however, does not ensure review of approved prescription medications where adverse reactions may appear after extensive preapproval testing. For this reason, the FDA also conducts extensive post-market surveillance. * * * In response to its surveillance findings, the FDA may require labeling changes or if necessary withdraw NDA approval and thereby revoke the license to market the medication. *Id.* at § 355(e).

We find this extensive regulatory scheme capable of and appropriate for making the preliminary determination regarding whether a prescription drug's benefits outweigh its risks. The structured follow-up program imposed by law ensures that drugs are not placed on the market without continued monitoring for adverse consequences that would render the FDA's initial risk/benefit analysis invalid. Allowing individual courts and/or juries to continually reevaluate a drug's risks and benefits ignores the processes of this expert regulatory body and the other avenues of recovery available to plaintiffs.

We note that the Utah Legislature has recognized the value of the FDA approval process and the public interest in the availability and affordability of prescription drugs by restricting the extent of liability for injuries resulting from the use of those drugs. Utah Code Ann. § 78–18–2(1) (Supp.1990) states that "punitive damages may not be awarded if a drug causing the claimant's harm: (a) received premarket approval or licensure by the Federal Food, Drug, and Cosmetic Act, 21 U.S.C. Section 301 et seq. * * *" This policy, designed to avoid discouraging manufacturers from marketing FDA-approved drugs, applies even to drugs marketed with inadequate warnings.

The legislature has also acknowledged the important role of governmental standards in Utah Code Ann. section 78–15–6(3). In that section, the legislature declared that there is a rebuttable presumption that a product which fully complies with the applicable government standards at the time of marketing is not defective.[3]

---

3. Plaintiffs argue that immunizing drug manufacturers from strict liability for design defects is contrary to this statute, because that conclusion would establish an "irrebuttable presumption" that the drug was not defective or unreasonably dangerous. We disagree. Plaintiffs may still recover under a strict liability claim by demonstrating that the product was unreasonably dangerous due to an inadequate warning, a

Our prior case law supports this approach as well. In *Barson v. E.R. Squibb & Sons, Inc.*, 682 P.2d 832 (Utah 1984), we addressed the sufficiency of evidence for a claim that a drug manufacturer negligently failed to warn of risks associated with its product. We held that even after meeting governmental requirements, if there are dangers about which the drug manufacturer knew or should have known, the manufacturer may be subject to liability. *Id.* at 836. Thus, consistent with our holding in this case, if a manufacturer knows or should know of a risk associated with its product, it is directly liable to the patient if it fails to adequately warn the medical profession of that danger. *Id.* at 835.

Moreover, the standard in Utah to which drug manufacturers must adhere to establish an adequate warning is very strict. In *Barson*, we stated:

> In determining whether a manufacturer has breached that duty [to adequately warn] and the extent to which a manufacturer is required to know of dangers inherent in its drug, it is important to point out that *the drug manufacturer is held to be an expert in its particular field and is under a "continuous duty * * * to keep abreast of scientific developments touching upon the manufacturer's product* and notify the medical profession of any additional side effects discovered from its use." *The drug manufacturer is responsible* therefore for not only "actual knowledge gained from research and adverse reaction reports," but also *for constructive knowledge as measured by scientific literature and other available means of communication.*

Barson, 682 P.2d at 835–36 (emphasis added).

V. PROPER FORUM FOR RISK/BENEFIT ANALYSIS

Finally, we do not believe that a trial court in the context of a products liability action is the proper forum to determine whether, as a whole, a particular prescription drug's benefits outweighed its risks at the time of distribution. In a case-by-case analysis, one court or jury's determination that a particular drug is or is not "defectively designed" has no bearing on any future case. As a result, differences of opinion among courts in differing jurisdictions leaves unsettled a drug manufacturer's liability for any given drug. Although the FDA may have internal differences of opinion regarding whether a particular new drug application should be approved, the individuals making the ultimate judgment will have the benefit of years of experience in reviewing such products, scientific expertise in the area, and access to the volumes of data they can compel manufacturers to produce. Nor is the FDA subject to the inherent limitations of the trial process, such as the rules of evidence, restrictions on expert testimony, and scheduling demands.[4]

manufacturing flaw, mismarketing, or misrepresenting information to the FDA. We cite these statutes only to demonstrate the legislature's similar deference to the expertise of certain governmental agencies, particularly that of the FDA.

4. There is also a certain moral question to be addressed when determining whether

One commentator has argued that courts as a whole are unsuited to render responsible judgments in the design defect area generally. *See* Henderson, *Judicial Review of Manufacturers' Conscious Design Choices: The Limits of Adjudication*, 73 Colum.L.Rev. 1531 (1973). He argues that decisions in this area are arbitrary due to their "polycentric" nature in which "each point for decision is related to all the others as are the strands of a spider web." *Id.* at 1536. These issues are difficult to litigate because

> [i]f one strand is pulled, a complex pattern of readjustments will occur throughout the entire web. If another strand is pulled, the relationships among all the strands will again be readjusted. A lawyer seeking to base [an] argument upon established principle and required to address himself in discourse to each of a dozen strands, or issues, would find [the] task frustratingly impossible.

Id.

Although we do not accept the notion that courts are unsuited to address design defect claims in any products liability action, we do agree that prescription drug design presents precisely this type of "polycentric" problem. A drug is designed to be effectively administered to specific individuals for one or a number of indications. To determine whether a drug's benefit outweighs its risk is inherently complex because of the manufacturer's conscious design choices regarding the numerous chemical properties of the product and their relationship to the vast physiologic idiosyncrasies of each consumer for whom the drug is designed. Society has recognized this complexity and in response has reposed regulatory authority in the FDA. Relying on the FDA's screening and surveillance standards enables courts to find liability under circumstances of inadequate warning, mismanufacture, improper marketing, or misinforming the FDA—avenues for which courts are better suited. Although this approach denies plaintiffs one potential theory on which to rely in a drug products liability action, the benefits to society in promoting the development, availability, and reasonable price of drugs justifies this conclusion.

In light of the strong public interest in the availability and affordability of prescription medications, the extensive regulatory system of the FDA, and the avenues of recovery still available to plaintiffs by claiming inadequate warning, mismanufacture, improper marketing, or misrepresenting information to the FDA, we conclude that a broad grant of a product's benefit outweighs its risk when faced with the reality of an injured plaintiff. For example, in the case of a vaccine, certain benefits of the drug's availability will accrue to group A, the individuals who are prevented from contracting the disease. A smaller number of individuals, however, may contract the disease and react violently to a component of the drug or, as some other result of the drug's properties, suffer terribly. Under a case-by-case approach, courts or juries must ask which is a more significant interest: efficacy with respect to group A versus harm to group B? The FDA must ask the same question: Does the benefit of this product outweigh its risk? The distinction is that the FDA is in a more objective and informed posture to make that determination. *See Toner*, 732 P.2d at 325–26 * * *.

immunity from strict liability claims based on design defects should be extended to FDA-approved prescription drugs in Utah.

HALL, C.J., and ZIMMERMAN, J., concur.

[JUSTICE HOWE's dissent is omitted.]

STEWART, JUSTICE (dissenting):

I dissent. The majority holds that a drug that is *avoidably* unsafe to human life or health is exempt from strict liability for design defects if approved by the FDA, even though alternative drugs can provide the same, or even better, therapy, with less risk to life or health. Thus, such FDA-approved drugs as various decongestants, expectorants, deodorants, hair growth stimulants, skin moisturizers, and cough and cold remedies, for example, have the same immunity as rabies or polio vaccines or medications essential in the treatment of cancer, heart disease, or AIDS. I see no basis for according drugs used to treat comparatively minor ailments a blanket immunity from strict liability for design defects if they are unreasonably dangerous to those who use them.

The limited immunity conferred by comment k on a few drugs was given only after thorough consideration by the American Law Institute. However, this Court gives blanket immunity for design defects to all FDA-approved drugs on the basis of blind reliance upon the efficacy and integrity of FDA procedures, about which the majority knows almost nothing. I agree with Justice Huntley of the Idaho Supreme Court, who stated:

> [N]o state supreme court has yet become convinced that the FDA has either adequate staffing, expertise, or data base to warrant its being substituted for the judicial system. * * * I fear the day when any supreme court can be convinced that an agency such as the FDA, no matter how well-intentioned, can supplant the American judicial system.

Toner v. Lederle Laboratories, 112 Idaho 328, 732 P.2d 297, 313 (1987) (Huntley, J., concurring specially). Indeed, in relying on FDA approval, the majority wholly ignores our statement in *Barson v. E.R. Squibb & Sons, Inc.*, 682 P.2d 832, 836 (Utah 1984), that FDA regulations for prescription drugs "are merely minimum standards."

In truth, FDA safety procedures do not justify abdication of judicial responsibility. For example, the FDA does not require existing drugs to undergo newly developed tests which would increase the likelihood that a product is in fact safe. * * *

Numerous congressional investigations have demonstrated that the FDA has often approved drugs in complete ignorance of critical information relating to the hazards of such drugs which was contained either in its own files or in the published medical literature, or both. For example, the FDA approved Oraflex on April 19, 1982, for the treatment of arthritis. The manufacturer withdrew the drug from the market on August 4, 1982, because eleven deaths were reported to be associated with the drug's use in the United States and sixty-one deaths were reported in the United Kingdom. Of principal concern were reports of serious and sometimes fatal Oraflex-associated liver and kidney disease. In *Deficiencies in FDA's Regulation of the New Drug "Oraflex"*, H.R.Rep. No. 511, 98th Cong., 1st Sess. (1983), the House Committee on Government Operations (hereinafter "H.C.G.O."), a congressional committee overseeing the FDA, found that the FDA was unaware that during the Oraflex clinical trials it had received four reports of serious concomitant liver and kidney disease and two reports of kidney disease unaccompanied by liver injury. At the time the FDA approved Oraflex for marketing, and for several months thereafter, it was unaware of the number of reports of Oraflex-associated adverse reactions it had received prior to its approval of the drug. *Id.* at 11–12. Prior to approving Oraflex, the FDA made no effort to obtain information on its safety from foreign countries in which the drug had already been marketed and was, therefore, unaware of a large number of reports of serious and sometimes fatal reactions to the drug submitted to the British and Danish regulatory authorities. *Id.* at 13. The FDA failed to enforce the legal requirement that drug manufacturers report all adverse reactions to a drug under clinical investigation, information essential to weigh the drug's risks against its potential benefits. *Id.* at 22.

[The discussion of similar experiences with three other FDA approved drugs, Merital, Versed, and Zomax, is omitted.]

Although the FDA has a mechanism for the withdrawal of pharmaceutical agents which are found to be dangerous, 21 U.S.C. § 355(e) (1988), the mechanism is slow and sometimes unreliable. For example, several studies were published in the early 1950s which should have put diethylstilbestrol (DES) manufacturers on notice that DES injured the reproductive systems of female fetuses whose mothers were exposed to the drug. However, it was not until 1971, nearly twenty years later, that the FDA finally banned the use of DES to prevent miscarriages, the most common use of the drug. *See Castrignano v. E.R. Squibb & Sons, Inc.*, 546 A.2d 775, 777 (R.I.1988). The lengthy wait by the FDA resulted in endangering a generation of women because their mothers had used DES during pregnancy.

In relying on the efficacy of FDA approval procedures as the basis for dispensing with the judicial remedy of product liability, the majority simply ignores FDA failures to protect the public against unnecessary and unacceptable risks. * * *

Proposals before Congress and rules promulgated by the FDA to make it easier for pharmaceutical companies to obtain FDA approval for new drugs would dilute even further the safety and efficacy standards for FDA approval of drugs. *See* Note, *Regulation of Investigational New Drugs: "Giant Step for the Sick and Dying?"*, 77 Georgetown L.J. 463 (1988). Perhaps truly unavoidably unsafe drugs intended to treat life-threatening ailments should be more easily available to the public, but a lessening of safety standards is an argument for strict liability, not against. Profit motivation is likely to lead to many more unnecessarily dangerous drugs.

Furthermore, not a shred of evidence has been presented to this Court that indicates that liability under the tort system has deterred pharmaceutical companies from introducing new drugs. Even if that were the case, the question that must be answered, given the majority's holding, is why comment k does not provide a proper accommodation of all the competing policy interests involved in the issue before the Court. Why should those who are seriously injured or suffer because of the death of another have to stand the expense of such losses to support the high profit margins in the drug industry?

In my view, the Rhode Island Supreme Court adopted a better approach in *Castrignano v. E.R. Squibb & Sons, Inc.*, 546 A.2d 775 (R.I.1988). The Rhode Island court held that only products that are truly unavoidably unsafe qualify for comment k protection. The court stated:

> This comment provides a risk-benefit test for products that, given the present state of human knowledge, are incapable of being made safe for their intended use. Products that satisfy the risk-benefit test are deemed unavoidably unsafe. These products, especially drugs, will not be considered defective and unreasonably dangerous under § 402A because their known or perceived benefits exceed their known or perceived risks. Therefore, the availability and marketing of these products is justified, not withstanding the risk. * * *

546 A.2d at 781.

Certain drugs clearly qualify for comment k exemption, even though the drugs' risk may be comparatively great. A drug's social utility may be so great, for example, a chemotherapeutic agent used for treatment of cancer, that it would obviously qualify for comment k exemption. Other drugs, such as sleeping compounds or dandruff cures, whose social utility may not be of such a high order, would not automatically qualify. The Rhode Island court stated that for a prescription drug to qualify for comment k exemption,

> the apparent benefits of the drug must exceed the apparent risks, given the scientific knowledge available when the drug was marketed. If the benefits outweigh the risks, then recovery for design-defect liability is precluded. If, however, the apparent risks exceed the apparent benefits, then the product is not exempt from design-defect liability and will be subject to the traditional design-defect analysis set forth in § 402A.

546 A.2d at 782.

Furthermore, Congress has never given broad immunity, as this Court does, to all prescription drugs, notwithstanding FDA approval. *See* Note, *A Prescription for Applying Strict Liability: Not all Drugs Deserve Comment k Immunization*, Brown v. Superior Court, 44 Cal.3d 1049, 751 P.2d 470, 245 Cal.Rptr. 412 (1988), 21 Ariz.St.L.J. 809, 830 (1989). Congress has, however, provided some immunity from tort law for some vaccines when the public interest required their widespread use. For example, Congress enacted the National Childhood Vaccine Injury Act, 42 U.S.C. §§ 300aa–1 to –34 (1988), which establishes a compensation scheme for children injured by vaccines as an alternative to pursuing tort claims against the manufacturers. However, even that Act does not completely foreclose strict liability for plaintiffs injured by vaccines; instead, it only establishes presumptions to aid the trier of fact. 42 U.S.C. §§ 300aa–22(b)(2), –23(d)(2).

The majority opinion states that a case-by-case analysis would leave drug companies uncertain regarding questions of immunity and would result in patchwork verdicts when a drug may be found to be subject to comment k exemption in one case but not subject to the exemption in another case. That consideration has little merit, in my view. We tolerate nonuniformity of result in negligence cases all the time. Nothing this Court does can bring about uniformity of result with respect to drugs. The states are already divided on the issue of whether FDA approval of a drug should confer immunity from design defects, although it appears that no state has gone as far as Utah now does. Suffice to say, a number of courts apply comment k on a case-by-case basis—a task that cannot be avoided even under the majority's position if a strict liability claim is coupled with a negligence claim, as is usually the case.

* * *

If Halcion was a causative agent, it is significant that *The Physicians' Desk Reference* (1990 ed.) lists nine other hypnotic agents available for use. At least two of the other hypnotics and one other medication listed as a sleeping aid are benzodiazepines and are, therefore, of the same general type as Halcion. In addition, the same reference lists thirteen sedatives that are on the market. The majority ignores the fact that the FDA found Halcion to be neither unique nor particularly essential and presented no advancement over existing therapeutic alternatives. Perhaps not all would have been appropriate medications, but with so many possible alternatives, it is doubtful that Halcion should be immune from strict liability.

Notes

1. Comment k to the Restatement (Second) of Torts § 402A creates an exception to strict liability for "unavoidably unsafe" products. Most courts evaluate each product on its own merits to determine whether it is unavoidably unsafe. *E.g.,* Adams v. G.D. Searle & Co., Inc., 576 So.2d 728 (Fla.App. 1991); Toner v. Lederle Laboratories, 112 Idaho 328, 336, 732 P.2d 297 (1987); Freeman v. Hoffman–La Roche, Inc., 260 Neb. 552, 618 N.W.2d 827 (2000); Feldman v. Lederle Laboratories, 97 N.J. 429, 479 A.2d 374 (1984); Castrignano v. E.R. Squibb & Sons, Inc., 546 A.2d 775 (R.I.1988). Other courts, like *Grundberg*, declare that all products within broad categories are unavoidably unsafe. *E.g.,* Brown v. Superior Court, 44 Cal.3d 1049, 245 Cal.Rptr. 412, 751 P.2d 470 (1988) (all prescription drugs if they are properly prepared and accompanied by adequate warnings).

2. In a jurisdiction that uses the risk-utility test of defect, is there any advantage to adopting Comment k and applying it on a case by case basis? In Shanks v. Upjohn Co., 835 P.2d 1189 (Alaska 1992) a person committed suicide shortly after taking a prescription drug. Plaintiff sued the prescription drug manufacturer for defective design and failure to warn. In design cases, the Alaska court normally uses the test of defect announced in *Barker v. Lull Engineering Co.*, supra page 134, *i.e.*, consumer expectations and risk-utility in the disjunctive. In *Shanks* the Alaska court declined to adopt Comment k, stating:

> In deciding whether a defendant has met the burden of proving that the benefits of the design outweigh the risk, we stated in [*Caterpillar Tractor Co. v. Beck*, 593 P.2d 871 (Alaska 1979)] that the fact finder must consider competing factors, including but not limited to
>
>> the gravity of the danger posed by the challenged design, the likelihood that such danger would occur, the mechanical feasibility of a safer alternative design, the financial cost of an improved design, and the adverse consequences to the product and to the consumer that would result from an alternative design.
>
> 593 P.2d at 886 (quoting *Barker*, 573 P.2d at 455). We believe these factors, with some modification and additions, should be considered in making the same determination in cases involving prescription drugs. Rephrasing these factors in language more appropriate to prescription drug products, the fact finder should consider the seriousness of the side effects or reactions posed by the drug, the likelihood that such side effects or reactions would occur, the feasibility of an alternative design which would eliminate or reduce the side effects or reactions without affecting the efficacy of the drug, and the harm to the consumer in terms of reduced efficacy and any new side effects or reactions that would result from an alternative design. In evaluating the benefits, the fact finder should be permitted to consider the seriousness of the condition for which the drug is indicated. In summary, what the trier of fact should determine in balancing these factors is whether the drug confers an important benefit and whether the interest in its availability outweighs the interest in promoting the enhanced accountability which strict products liability design defect review provides. See *Kearl v. Lederle Laboratories*, 172 Cal.App.3d 812, 218 Cal.Rptr. 453, 464 (1985).

* * *

While we accept the soundness of the policy underlying comment k that manufacturers of certain highly beneficial products which have inherent unavoidable risks of which the user is adequately warned should not be held strictly liable for injuries resulting from their products, we decline to formally adopt comment k * * *.

* * *

[W]e believe that the risk/benefit prong of the *Barker* test offers the manufacturers of those products intended to be protected by comment k an opportunity to avoid liability for strict liability claims based on a design defect theory. For these reasons, we find it undesirable and unnecessary to impose the additional layer of comment k on an area of law which is already strained under its own doctrinal weight. We recognize that by holding that the liability of drug manufacturers should be measured by the second prong of the *Barker* test, we are taking a position similar to those jurisdictions which apply comment k to prescription drugs on a case-by-case basis. However, we arrive at this result without specifically relying on comment k.

835 P.2d at 1196–98. On the possible difference between risk-utility analysis and Comment k analysis, *see* Ausness, Unavoidably Unsafe Products and Strict Products Liability: What Liability Rule Should be Applied to the Sellers of Pharmaceutical Products?, 78 Ky.L.J. 705, 738–740 (1990); Reilly, The Erosion of Comment K, 14 U.Dayton L.Rev. 255 (1989).

3. The vast majority of cases that apply Comment k have involved drugs, vaccines, blood, and medical devices. *See* Wilkinson v. Bay Shore Lumber Co., 182 Cal.App.3d 594, 227 Cal.Rptr. 327 (1986) (citing numerous cases). Many people believe that the comment only applies to such products. *E.g.*, Schwartz, Unavoidably Unsafe Products: Clarifying the Meaning and Policy Behind Comment k, 42 Wash. & Lee L.Rev. 1139, 1141 (1985).

4. Not everyone agrees. The language of Comment k is broad enough to apply to all types of products, not just drugs. A knife with a sharp blade, for example, could be regarded as unavoidably unsafe because it presents a risk that cannot be eliminated in the present state of human knowledge, and yet the risk is reasonable because knives are useful and desirable products. Courts have occasionally applied the doctrine to other products. Borel v. Fibreboard Paper Products Corp., 493 F.2d 1076, 1088–89 (5th Cir.1973), cert. denied, 419 U.S. 869, 95 S.Ct. 127, 42 L.Ed.2d 107 (1974) (asbestos); Walker v. Stauffer Chemical Corp., 19 Cal.App.3d 669, 674, 96 Cal.Rptr. 803, 806 (1971) (bulk sulfuric acid); Gross v. Nashville Gas Co., 608 S.W.2d 860 (Tenn.App.1980) (natural gas). For a comprehensive listing of products that have been held to be unavoidably unsafe, *see* Annotation, 70 A.L.R.4th 16 (1989).

5. In a jurisdiction that applies Comment k only to drugs, how would the court deal with a products liability claim against a knife manufacturer seeking damages for harm caused when a user accidentally cut himself on the sharp blade?

6. Because the Restatement (Third) of Torts: Products Liability uses foresight in all design and warning cases, it does not require a section exempting drug and medical device manufacturers from strict liability. It does, however, have a special provision applying to such manufacturers:

§ 6. Liability of Commercial Seller or Distributor for Harm Caused by Defective Prescription Drugs and Medical Devices

(a) A manufacturer of a prescription drug or medical device who sells or otherwise distributes a defective drug or medical device is subject to liability for harm to persons caused by the defect. A prescription drug or medical device is one that may be legally sold or otherwise distributed only pursuant to a health-care provider's prescription.

(b) For purposes of liability under Subsection (a), a prescription drug or medical device is defective if at the time of sale or other distribution the drug or medical device:

(1) contains a manufacturing defect as defined in § 2(a); or

(2) is not reasonably safe due to defective design as defined in Subsection (c); or

(3) is not reasonably safe due to inadequate instructions or warnings as defined in Subsection (d).

(c) A prescription drug or medical device is not reasonably safe due to defective design if the foreseeable risks of harm posed by the drug or medical device are sufficiently great in relation to its foreseeable therapeutic benefits that reasonable health-care providers, knowing of such foreseeable risks and therapeutic benefits, would not prescribe the drug or medical device for any class of patients.

* * *

Comment:

c. Manufacturers' liability for manufacturing defects. Limitations on the liability for prescription drug and medical-device designs do not support treating drug and medical-device manufacturers differently from commercial sellers of other products with respect to manufacturing defects. Courts have traditionally subjected manufacturers of prescription products to liability for harm caused by manufacturing defects.

* * *

f. Manufacturers' liability for defectively designed prescription drugs and medical devices. Subsection (c) reflects the judgment that, as long as a given drug or device provides net benefits for a class of patients, it should be available to them, accompanied by appropriate warnings and instructions. Learned intermediaries must generally be relied upon to see that the right drugs and devices reach the right patients. However, when a drug or device provides net benefits to no class of patients—when reasonable, informed health-care providers would not prescribe it to any class of patients—then the design of the product is defective and the manufacturer should be subject to liability for the harm caused.

* * * The issue is whether, objectively viewed, reasonable providers, knowing of the foreseeable risks and benefits of the drug or medical device, would prescribe it for any class of patients. Given this very demanding objective standard, liability is likely to be imposed only under unusual circumstances. * * *

7. **Categorical Risk–Utility Balancing**. Note that courts that do case by case balancing to determine whether a drug is exempt from design defect liability under Comment k of the Restatement (Second) § 402A are engaging in the kind of categorical risk-utility balancing that *O'Brien v. Muskin Corp.*, *supra* page 170, employed for above-ground swimming pools. That is, they are prepared to declare an unduly dangerous drug defective even though there is no safer alternative design for that drug. The Restate-

ment (Third) also endorses categorical risk-utility balancing for prescription drugs in § 6 (c) and Comment f, set out in the preceding note.

In the notes following *O'Brien*, we saw that courts and legislatures are reluctant to allow categorical risk-utility balancing for products other than drugs. Why are courts so willing to declare a drug like Benedictine defective because it causes birth defects when they are so reluctant to declare products like guns, alcohol, and tobacco defective because they harm people?

8. Blood Products. Virtually all jurisdictions exempt blood products from any form of strict liability. The Restatement (Third) of Torts: Products Liability § 19 reflects this rule. Comment c to § 19 explains:

> c. *Tangible personal property: human blood and human tissue.* Although human blood and human tissue meet the formal requisites of Subsection (a), they are specifically excluded from the coverage of this Restatement. Almost all the litigation regarding such products has dealt with contamination of human blood and blood-related products by the hepatitis virus or the HIV virus. Absent a special rule dealing with human blood and tissue, such contamination presumably would be subject to the rules of §§ 1 and 2(a). Those Sections impose strict liability when a product departs from its intended design even though all possible care was exercised in the preparation and marketing of the product. However, legislation in almost all jurisdictions limits the liability of sellers of human blood and human tissue to the failure to exercise reasonable care, often by providing that human blood and human tissue are not "products" or that their provision is a "service." Where legislation has not addressed the problem, courts have concluded that strict liability is inappropriate for harm caused by such product contamination.

What constitutes reasonable care for those engaged in providing professional services is defined in § 299A of the Restatement, Second, of Torts.

9. Since sellers of blood products are exempt from strict liability for manufacturing flaws (an unintended virus in the blood), should drug and medical-device manufacturers also be exempt from strict liability for such flaws? The excerpt from the following law review article discusses this issue.

AUSNESS, UNAVOIDABLY UNSAFE PRODUCTS AND STRICT PRODUCTS LIABILITY: WHAT LIABILITY RULE SHOULD BE APPLIED TO THE SELLERS OF PHARMACEUTICAL PRODUCTS?

78 Ky.L.J. 705, 720–23, 745, 747–48, 749–51 (1989/1990).

Ordinarily, product sellers are strictly liable for harm caused by mishaps in the production process even though they could not have discovered the condition or eliminated defective products by the exercise of due care. Strict liability is imposed on product sellers, particularly manufacturers, because they are in a good position to control production flaws. Additionally, because claims arising from manufacturing defects are relatively small in relation to the number of units produced, product sellers can usually obtain insurance at a reasonable cost.

Production flaws also occur in the pharmaceutical industry. One class of production flaw involves drugs that deviate from their accepted chemical formula. Since comment k requires that products be "properly prepared," it usually does not immunize against liability in such cases.[1] Product contamination is another type of production flaw. Although quality control standards are high in the pharmaceutical industry, impure or contaminated drugs sometimes enter the market. Although comment k shields sellers of "new and experimental drugs" from liability even when "purity of ingredients" cannot be assured,[2] it does not protect the purveyors of ordinary pharmaceutical products against liability when their products are contaminated.[3]

A more common risk arises from the failure to remove harmful byproducts from the finished product. This problem sometimes occurs in the manufacture of vaccines and other biologics.[4] For example, injuries can occur when substances used to culture vaccines are not completely removed from the finished product. This condition is associated with the Pasteur vaccine, which is cultured in the brains of small laboratory animals such as rats, mice, and rabbits.[5] Serious harm to the recipient can occur if small particles of animal brain material are left in the vaccine.[6] In such cases, however, the courts have found the Pasteur vaccine to be unavoidably unsafe.[7]

Virulent organisms in vaccines also can cause serious injuries. Vaccines typically use killed or weakened disease-producing organisms to create a natural immunity in the recipient's body.[8] A vaccine, however, can cause the very disease it is supposed to prevent if these harmful organisms are not neutralized. This problem has arisen in connection with the production of both Sabin and Salk polio vaccines.[9]

---

1. *See* Morris v. Parke, Davis & Co., 667 F.Supp. 1332, 1336 (C.D.Cal.1987); Toner v. Lederle Laboratories, 732 P.2d 297, 305 (Idaho 1987).

2. *See* Restatement (Second) of Torts § 402A comment k * * *.

3. *See* Abbott Laboratories v. Lapp, 78 F.2d 170, 174 (7th Cir.1935) (manufacturer held liable in negligence for allowing virulent bacteria to contaminate sterilized milk formula); David v. McKesson & Robbins, 253 A.D. 728, 300 N.Y.S. 635, 636 (1937) (manufacturer held liable in negligence for sodium fluoride in bicarbonate of soda), *aff'd*, 278 N.Y. 622, 16 N.E.2d 127 (1938); *see also* Note, [*Comment K Immunity to Strict Liability: Should All Prescription Drugs Be Protected?*, 26 Hous.L.Rev. 707, 736 (1989)](plaintiff can recover in strict liability if drug is adulterated).

4. Biologics are products that are cultured from living organisms. *See* Note, [Note, *Mass Immunization Cases: Drug Manufacturers' Liability for Failure to Warn*, 29 Vand.L.Rev. 235, n.2.245 (1976)].

5. *See* Comment, [*Torts—Strict Liability—A Hospital is Strictly Liable for Transfusions of Hepatitis*, 69 Mich.L.Rev. 1172, 1182 (1971)].

6. *Id.*

7. *See* Calabrese v. Trenton State College, 162 N.J.Super. 145, 392 A.2d 600, 604 (1978), *aff'd*, 82 N.J. 321, 413 A.2d 315 (1980).

8. *See* Note, *Vaccine Related Injuries: Alternatives to the Tort Compensation System*, 30 St.Louis U.L.J. 919, 920–21 (1986); *see also* Parke–Davis & Co. v. Stromsodt, 411 F.2d 1390, 1392–93 (8th Cir.1969).

9. *See* Franklin & Mais, *Tort Law and Mass Immunization Programs: Lessons from the Polio and Flu Episodes*, 65 Calif.L.Rev. 754, 765–66 (1977).

The Salk vaccine uses dead polio virus organisms to induce the formation of antibodies in the recipient's body. Killed polio virus is incapable of causing disease, but can act as an antigen to stimulate the production of antibodies that will attack any live polio viruses entering the body.[10] However, in *Gottsdanker v. Cutter Laboratories*,[11] Cutter Laboratories, a manufacturer of Salk vaccine, failed to exclude live polio virus from some of its vaccine even though it relied on government approved safety tests to prevent this from happening. As a result, a number of vaccine recipients contracted polio from the vaccine.[12] The defendant contended that liability should not be imposed because the vaccine was a "new" drug, and thus not subject to a strict liability rule. The court, however, rejected this argument and held in favor of the plaintiffs.

The Sabin vaccine uses a weakened live virus that causes the recipient's immune system to produce antibodies that are effective against ordinary polio virus.[13] As the weakened strain reproduces itself in the intestinal tract of the recipient, however, it occasionally produces a form of virulent strain instead.[14] This can cause the recipient, or those who come into close contact with the recipient, to contract polio.[15] Perhaps because the dangerous condition arises after the vaccine leaves the manufacturer's control, the courts generally have refused to impose strict liability in such cases.[16]

Another type of production flaw involves failure to detect and remove serum hepatitis from blood.[17] Only one case, *Cunningham v. MacNeal Memorial*,[18] has refused to apply comment k to serum hepatitis contamination. The Illinois Supreme Court declared in *Cunningham* that blood contaminated with serum hepatitis could not be treated as an

---

10. *See* Note, *supra* note [4], at 237.

11. 6 Cal.Rptr. 320 (Ct.App.1960).

12. *See* Note, *supra* note [4], at 238.

13. *See* Schwartz & Mahshigian, *National Childhood Vaccine Injury Act of 1986: An Ad Hoc Remedy or a Window for the Future?*, 48 Ohio St. L.J. 387, 388 (1987).

14. *Id.*

15. Plummer v. Lederle Laboratories, 819 F.2d 349, 351 (2d Cir.1987).

16. *See* Plummer, 819 F.2d at 356; Givens v. Lederle Laboratories, 556 F.2d 1341, 1345 (5th Cir.1977); Reyes v. Wyeth Laboratories, 498 F.2d 1264, 1274 (5th Cir. 1974), cert. denied, 419 U.S. 1096 (1974); Davis v. Wyeth Laboratories, 399 F.2d 121, 128–29 (9th Cir.1968); Williams v. Lederle Laboratories, 591 F.Supp. 381, 384 (S.D.Ohio 1984); Sheehan v. Pima County, 660 P.2d 486, 487 (Ariz.Ct.App.1982); Johnson v. American Cyanamid Co., 718 P.2d 1318, 1323 (Kan.1986); Dunn v. Lederle Laboratories, 328 N.W.2d 576, 579 (Mich. 1982); Cunningham v. Charles Pfizer & Co., 532 P.2d 1377, 1380 (Okla.1975).

Grinnell v. Charles Pfizer & Co., 79 Cal. Rptr. 369 (1969), represents an exception to this approach. The plaintiff contracted polio from the defendant's vaccine. The court held that the vaccine was defective because it contained virulent polio virus instead of the harmless variety, apparently assuming that the virulent strain was introduced into the vaccine during the production process rather than afterwards. *Id.* at 374.

17. Blood may be contaminated by serum hepatitis, a virus that cannot be detected in the blood under present medical technology. *See* Comment, *Blood Transfusions and the Transmission of Serum Hepatitis: The Need for Statutory Reform*, 24 Am. U. L. Rev. 367, 368 (1976). This condition differs from the vaccine cases because the contaminant exists in the donor's blood before the blood comes within the producer's control.

18. 266 N.E.2d 897 (Ill.1970).

unavoidably unsafe product because it was impure.[19] However, the *Cunningham* court's interpretation of comment k was widely criticized because comment k expressly mentioned impure drugs as one class of potentially unavoidably unsafe product.[20] For this reason, most courts apply comment k to cases involving blood impurities.[21]

* * *

3. THE ALLOCATIVE EFFICIENCY RATIONALE

The goal of allocative efficiency is to distribute society's economic resources in a way that maximizes social welfare.[22] Strict liability promotes allocative efficiency by encouraging product sellers to invest in product safety and thereby reduce the number of product-related injuries.[23] Additionally, strict liability causes product prices to reflect the true costs of production, including the cost of unavoidable product injuries, and thus ensures that members of the public will not "overconsume" dangerous products.[24]

* * *

The allocative efficiency rationale seems particularly applicable to production flaws in pharmaceutical products. Presently, suppliers of blood and vaccines often escape liability for production-related injuries because such injuries are considered unavoidable. However, if strict liability were imposed on product sellers, they would attempt to improve current production and detection technology in order to reduce or eliminate the risk of injury from harmful byproducts.

The contamination of transfused blood by serum hepatitis virus is an example of a risk that comment k treats as unavoidable. At the present time, serum hepatitis virus cannot be physically removed from the blood. Although tests can detect the presence of serum hepatitis in the blood, these tests are not completely accurate. Arguably, strict liability would encourage blood banks and hospitals to support the development of better detection methods. Strict liability also would provide an incentive for blood suppliers to implement better donor screening procedures. It is universally acknowledged that volunteer

---

19. *Id.* at 904; *see also* McDaniel v. Baptist Memorial Hospital, 352 F.Supp. 690 (W.D.Tenn.1971), *aff'd*, 469 F.2d 230 (6th Cir.1972). The McDaniel court questioned the application of comment k to contaminated blood. Apparently, the court felt that comment k should cover only characteristics that are common or indigenous to the product. *Id.* at 695.

20. *See* Hines v. St. Joseph's Hosp., 527 P.2d 1075, 1077 (N.M.1974); Comment, *supra* note [17], at 403.

21. *See* Belle Bonfils Memorial Blood Bank v. Hansen, 665 P.2d 118, 125–26 (Colo.1983); McMichael v. American Red Cross, 532 S.W.2d 7, 9 (Ky.1975); Moore v. Underwood Memorial Hosp., 371 A.2d 105, 107 (N.J.Super. Ct. 1977).

22. *See* R. Posner, Economic Analysis of Law 4 (1972).

23. *See* Owen, [*Rethinking the Policies of Strict Products Liability*, 33 Vand.L.Rev. 681, 711–13 (1980)]; Note, *Prescription Drugs and Strict Liability: The Flaw in the Ointment*, 19 Pac.L.J. 193, 198 (1987).

24. *See* Ausness, *Cigarette Company Liability: Preemption, Public Policy and Alternative Compensation Systems*, 39 Syracuse L.Rev. 897, 946–47 (1988); Henderson, [*Coping with the Time Dimension in Products Liability*, 69 Calif.L.Rev. 919, 933 (1981)].

donors are much less likely to transmit hepatitis virus than paid donors. Strict liability would encourage blood suppliers to search for new sources of volunteer donors and thereby reduce the risk of injury from impure blood.

* * *

4. THE LOSS-SPREADING RATIONALE

Loss-spreading provides yet another rationale for strict products liability. A large number of courts endorse strict liability because it shifts the costs of injuries from accident victims to product sellers, who can spread these costs among product buyers. Loss-spreading is based partly on the notion that those who benefit from an injury-producing activity should compensate those who suffer harm.[25] Loss-spreading also may be justified on secondary accident cost-avoidance grounds. According to this theory, the "secondary" or dislocation costs of injuries are reduced when they are spread among a large group of people instead of borne entirely by individual victims.[26]

Loss-spreading generally is most effective if liability for injuries is placed on the party who can best absorb and spread the cost of compensation. In the case of product-related injuries, product sellers are usually the best loss-spreaders because they can insure against such losses and treat them as a cost of production. Moreover, since product sellers typically sell to a mass market, the incremental cost to each consumer from such price increases is likely to be small.

Sellers of pharmaceutical products appear to be good loss-spreaders. The pharmaceutical industry is profitable, and the demand for its products is relatively inelastic. In theory, sellers of pharmaceutical products, like other product sellers, can obtain liability insurance and spread the cost of premiums through the pricing mechanism.

This reasoning seems especially applicable to risks associated with the production process. Production flaws in the manufacturing process are relatively rare and can be accurately predicted by statistical methods.[27] Arguably, production flaws in pharmaceutical products are similar to manufacturing defects. Consequently, the loss-spreading arguments that are made with respect to manufacturing defects in ordinary products also can be applied to production flaws in pharmaceutical products.[28]

25. * * * James, *General Products—Should Manufacturers Be Liable Without Negligence?*, 24 Tenn.L.Rev. 923, 924 (1956–57). * * *

26. *See* Calabresi, *Some Thoughts on Risk Distribution and the Law of Torts*, 70 Yale L.J. 499, 517–18 (1960–61); Kidwell, [*The Duty to Warn: A Description of the Model of Decision*, 53 Tex.L.Rev. 1375, 1386 (1974–75)].

27. *See* McClellan, *Strict Liability for Drug Induced Injuries: An Excursion Through the Maze of Products Liability, Negligence and Absolute Liability*, 25 Wayne L. Rev. 1, 30 (1978–79).

28. Contamination of blood by serum hepatitis virus may constitute an exception to this generalization because the incidence of hepatitis injuries is relatively high. *Cf.* Note, [*Liability for Serum Hepatitis in Blood Transfusions*, 32 Ohio St. L.J. 585 (1971).] (2% of blood transfusion recipients contract hepatitis); R. Titmuss, The Gift Relationship: From Human Blood to Social Policy 146 (1971) (3.5% of blood transfusion recipients contract hepatitis). According to

Notes

1. The following articles analyze comment k. Ausness, Unavoidably Unsafe Products and Strict Products Liability: What Liability Rule Should be Applied to the Sellers of Pharmaceutical Products?, 78 Ky.L.J. 705 (1990); Landes and Posner, A Positive Economic Analysis of Products Liability, 14 J.Legal Stud. 535, 556–560 (1985); Page, Generic Product Risks: The Case Against Comment K and For Strict Tort Liability, 58 N.Y.U.L.Rev. 853 (1983); Schwartz, Unavoidably Unsafe Products: Clarifying the Meaning and Policy Behind Comment k, 42 Wash. & Lee L.Rev. 1139 (1985); Comment, Comment K Immunity to Strict Liability: Should All Prescription Drugs be Protected? 26 Hous.L.Rev. 707 (1989).

2. In light of the materials you have studied concerning the definition of defect, and the materials in this section, consider the following problem:

Mrs. Paterson, an elderly woman, became extremely ill as a result of contracting Influenza Type Z induced by a vaccine designed to immunize her from the disease. This occurred because the dose of vaccine she was given contained some live virus. The vaccine was supposed to be comprised of killed virus. She desires to pursue a products liability claim against the manufacturer of the vaccine.

The vaccine is prepared by cultivating Influenza Type Z virus on a protein-free semisynthetic medium. Formaldehyde is then used to kill the virus. The formaldehyde and unwanted debris are removed, and the only thing left is the vaccine medium and the killed virus. For some unknown reason, in an extremely small number of cases, the formaldehyde fails to kill all the influenza virus. When this occurs, live virus will remain in the vaccine, and will occasionally infect recipients of the vaccine.

Prior to marketing the vaccine, the manufacturer knew about this risk. It nevertheless marketed the vaccine because there is no other known killing agent that will work to produce a vaccine against this particular strain of influenza. Furthermore, there is no way of telling which doses of the vaccine contain live virus. The vaccine is otherwise effective in preventing influenza. It is particularly important for elderly people because many of them become gravely ill when infected with this strain of influenza virus.

At the manufacturer's insistence, each person who received the vaccine was informed that a small percentage of doses contain live virus that can infect the recipient, but that it is not known which doses are contaminated.

Is the manufacturer liable for Mrs. Paterson's injuries?

one estimate, the cost of blood would double if blood suppliers were held strictly liable for injuries caused by contaminated blood. Note, [*Liability for Serum Hepatitis in Blood Transfusions*, 32 Ohio St. L.J. 585, 597 (1971)].

SECTION D. PROOF OF NON–SPECIFIC DEFECT (IN MANUFACTURE OR DESIGN) BY CIRCUMSTANTIAL EVIDENCE.

MYRLAK v. PORT AUTHORITY OF NEW YORK AND NEW JERSEY
Supreme Court of New Jersey, 1999.
157 N.J. 84, 723 A.2d 45.

COLEMAN, J.

In this strict products liability case involving one defendant, the primary issue is whether the doctrine of *res ipsa loquitur* should be applied when liability is based upon an alleged manufacturing defect. The trial court declined to instruct the jury regarding *res ipsa loquitur*. The Appellate Division held that the trial court should have given such an instruction. We disagree and reverse. We hold that the traditional negligence doctrine of *res ipsa loquitur* generally is not applicable in a strict products liability case. We adopt, however, the "indeterminate product defect test" established in Section 3 of the *Restatement (Third) of Torts: Products Liability* as the more appropriate jury instruction in cases that do not involve a shifting of the burden of persuasion.

I

On July 6, 1991, plaintiff, John Myrlak, was injured when his chair collapsed while he was at work. At that time, plaintiff was forty-three years old, six feet six inches tall, and weighed approximately 325 pounds. Plaintiff was employed as an assistant trainmaster for the Port Authority Trans–Hudson Corporation (PATH).

* * *

At the time of the accident, plaintiff had been seated in the chair performing his duties for approximately one hour and forty-five minutes. He suddenly heard a loud noise, and the back of his chair cracked and gave way. Plaintiff and the chair fell backwards, causing both to land parallel to the floor. Plaintiff grabbed the arms of the chair and pulled himself forward as he was falling. He injured his lower back and was hospitalized.

Although no one other than the plaintiff actually saw the accident, several PATH employees testified that they heard either a clicking or ratcheting sound, or a loud noise like a grinding of gears. After the accident, those employees observed that the back of the chair had collapsed and was parallel to the floor. A co-worker stated that he touched the back of the chair after the accident and it appeared to be flopping back and forth. Another co-worker testified that he sat in the chair the day following the accident and found it lacked back support.

The chair involved in the accident was manufactured by defendant Girsberger Industries, Inc. * * * [T]he chair that caused plaintiff's accident had been in use for five weeks.

The chair had a high backed seat with a triple joint construction that allowed the seat to follow the user's movement by adjusting two levers. One of the levers positioned the chair in either a locked or a "free flow" mode; the other lever adjusted the height of the chair. The chair was also equipped with a tension control mechanism underneath the seat to adjust the tension of the chair's back according to the user's need or desire. Plaintiff was familiar with the chair and its operation.

There was no evidence that the chair had been misused by plaintiff or any other PATH employee. The chair, however, was not used exclusively by plaintiff. On the contrary, it was customarily used by several different PATH employees twenty-four hours each day. Although some of the PATH employees who used the chair were similar in size to plaintiff, none of them ever reported any similar incidents or complaints with regard to the chair.

Plaintiff instituted the present litigation against PATH under the Federal Employer's Liability Act (FELA), claiming that PATH failed to provide a safe workplace and was negligent in providing him with a chair that was too small for a man his size. He also filed products liability claims against the manufacturer of the chair alleging both a manufacturing and a warning defect theory of liability. Pretrial discovery left some uncertainty concerning whether the chair examined by plaintiff's expert and displayed in the court room during the trial was the same chair that was involved in the accident. However, PATH maintains that they are one and the same. To support its position, PATH presented evidence regarding the chain of custody of the chair.

* * *

Plaintiff's expert was unable to duplicate the accident with the chair that was presented as evidence. Plaintiff's expert was not permitted to disassemble the chair, perform a failure analysis on it, or test any of its internal parts. He was allowed to operate the chair only by using the control levers. No application was addressed to the trial court to perform a more detailed analysis of the chair. The expert was unable to identify a specific defect in the chair; nor could he state that a defect caused the accident. On the issue of PATH's negligence, plaintiff's expert testified that the chair was too small for a person plaintiff's size and weight.

At the close of all of the evidence, plaintiff requested the court to charge the jury on *res ipsa loquitur* regarding the manufacturing defect claim. In denying the requested charge, the trial court stated that it wanted to avoid that phrase even though plaintiff relied on circumstantial evidence to infer that there was a manufacturing defect. The jury found PATH was negligent in failing to provide plaintiff with a safe workplace and awarded plaintiff 1.5 million dollars. The jury also found that plaintiff failed to establish a manufacturing defect in the chair.

PATH appealed and plaintiff cross-appealed. In a reported opinion, the Appellate Division reversed both verdicts and remanded for a new trial. 302 *N.J.Super.* 1, 694 *A.*2d 575 (1997). * * * The panel * * * reversed the verdict in favor of the manufacturer, concluding that the trial court should have instructed the jury on res ipsa loquitur. * * * We granted defendant Girsberger's petition for certification, limited to the issue whether *res ipsa loquitur* should apply to this strict products liability case.

II

* * *

-A-

The *res ipsa loquitur* doctrine derives its roots from the common law of England. The first reported decision to apply the doctrine in a case not involving railway collisions between two trains on the same line was *Byrne v. Boadle*, 159 *Eng. Rep.* 299, 300 (Exch. of Pleas 1863). That case involved a barrel of flour that fell and struck a passerby on a street as the barrel was being lowered from a window by a flour merchant. The court held that there "are certain cases [other than the train collision cases] of which it may be said *res ipsa loquitur,* and this seems one of them." *Ibid.* The court permitted a presumption of negligence, reasoning that it was "apparent that the barrel was in the custody of the defendant who occupied the premises, ... and ... the fact of its falling is *prima facie* evidence of negligence, ..., but if there are any facts inconsistent with negligence it is for the defendant to prove them." *Id.* at 301. * * *

Res ipsa loquitur, which in Latin means "the thing speaks for itself," is * * * not a theory of liability; rather, it is an evidentiary rule that governs the adequacy of evidence in some negligence cases. * * * The doctrine of *res ipsa loquitur,* where applicable, is a method of circumstantially proving the existence of negligence. Specifically, the doctrine permits an inference of defendant's want of due care when the following three conditions have been met: "(a) the occurrence itself ordinarily bespeaks negligence; (b) the instrumentality was within the defendant's exclusive control; and (c) there is no indication in the circumstances that the injury was the result of the plaintiff's own voluntary act or neglect." *Bornstein v. Metropolitan Bottling Co.*, 26 *N.J.* 263, 269, 139 *A.*2d 404 (1958). If the instrumentality has left the control of the defendant before the accident, the doctrine may nevertheless be invoked where applicable if plaintiff can present evidence that the instrumentality causing the harm neither was improperly handled, nor its condition changed after the defendant relinquished control. *Jakubowski v. Minnesota Mining and Mfg.*, 42 *N.J.* 177, 183, 199 *A.*2d 826 (1964).

Whether an occurrence ordinarily bespeaks negligence is based on the probabilities in favor of negligence. Hence, *res ipsa* is available if it is more probable than not that the defendant has been negligent. The doctrine does not shift the burden of persuasion to the defendant. Rather, what "is required of defendant is an explanation, not exculpation." *Buckelew, supra,* 87 *N.J.* at 526, 435 *A.*2d 1150. It shifts to the defendant the obligation to explain the causative circumstances because of defendant's superior knowledge. *Ibid.* The doctrine confers upon the plaintiff an inference of negligence sufficient to establish a *prima facie* case at the close of plaintiff's evidence. *Ibid.*

-B-

In a products liability case in which the plaintiff alleges a manufacturing defect under the Act, the plaintiff has the burden to prove "the product causing the harm was not reasonably fit, suitable or safe for its intended purpose." *N.J.S.A.* 2A:58C–2. In the typical manufacturing defect case, a plaintiff is not required to establish negligence. In other words, a plaintiff must impugn the product but not the conduct of the manufacturer of the product. *Prosser & Keeton on Torts,* § 99, at 695 (5th ed.1984); R. Keeton, *Products Liability—Inadequacy of Information,* 48 *Tex. L.Rev.* 398, 407–08 (1970).

* * *

Simply because a plaintiff is not required to prove fault in a strict liability case does not mean that absolute liability will be imposed upon a manufacturer. Although a plaintiff is relieved of proving fault, that plaintiff must nonetheless prove that the product was defective under our common law jurisprudence that was incorporated into the Act. Based on our well-established case law in this area, a plaintiff must prove that the product was defective, that the defect existed when the product left the manufacturer's control, and that the defect proximately caused injuries to the plaintiff, a reasonably foreseeable or intended user.

* * *

* * * [A] manufacturing defect under the Act occurs when the product comes off the production line in a substandard condition based on the manufacturer's own standards or identical units that were made in accordance with the manufacturing specifications. *N.J.S.A.* 2A:58C–2a. * * *

To prove both the existence of a defect and that the defect existed while the product was in the control of the manufacturer, a plaintiff may resort to direct evidence, such as the testimony of an expert who has examined the product, or, in the absence of such evidence, to circumstantial proof. *Scanlon v. General Motors Corp.,* 65 *N.J.* 582, 591, 326 *A.*2d 673 (1974). The law is "settled in this State that in a products liability case the injured plaintiff is not required to prove a specific manufacturer's defect." *Moraca v. Ford Motor Co.,* 66 *N.J.* 454, 458, 332 *A.*2d 599 (1975). Proof that a product is not fit for its intended purposes "requires only proof . . . that 'something was wrong' with the product." *Scanlon, supra,* 65 *N.J.* at 591, 326 *A.*2d 673. The mere occurrence of an accident and the mere fact that someone was injured are not sufficient to demonstrate the existence of a defect.

Under the *Scanlon* circumstantial evidence method of proving a product defect, the fact that a product is relatively new does not suffice by itself to establish a defective condition. The age and prior usage of the product in relation to its expected life span are factors to consider in conjunction with other evidence presented. Generally, the older a product is, the more difficult it is to prove that a defect existed while in the manufacturer's control. However, age of the product alone may not preclude a finding that the product was defective when the product is "of a type permitting the jury, after weighing all the evidence ..., to infer that in the normal course of human experience an injury would not have occurred at this point in the product's life span had there not been a defect attributable to the manufacturer." *Scanlon, supra*, 65 *N.J.* at 593, 326 *A.*2d 673. *Scanlon* held that this critical inference could not be drawn when the product in question, a complicated automobile, was nine months old and had only 4,000 miles of use.

In addition to the direct and circumstantial evidence methods of proving a product defect, a plaintiff has a third option. A plaintiff may establish a defect by "negat[ing] other causes of the failure of the product for which the defendant would not be responsible, in order to make it reasonable to infer that a dangerous condition existed at the time the defendant had control [of the product]." *Id.* at 593–94, 326 *A.*2d 673 (citing *Jakubowski, supra*, 42 *N.J.* at 184, 199 *A.*2d 826). Under that approach, a plaintiff does not have to negate all possible causes of failure, only those likely causes of failure. Both *Moraca* and *Scanlon* involved alleged defects in automobiles that were relatively new with low mileage. *Moraca* is similar to the present case in that the plaintiff there heard a "gink" while driving the car and the steering mechanism suddenly locked, causing the vehicle to skid off the road into a tree. Although *res ipsa* was not charged to the jury in *Moraca*, the jury was nonetheless allowed to infer a defect from the circumstances.

-C-

Based on the foregoing legal principles synthesized from our products liability and *res ipsa loquitur* jurisprudence, it is evident that there are some technical differences between using *res ipsa loquitur* as a method of proving negligence and using that doctrine to prove a product defect in strict products liability cases. Res ipsa loquitur is a doctrine created under the fault theory of negligence as a means of circumstantially proving a defendant's lack of due care. Strict products liability, on the other hand, is a theory of liability based upon allocating responsibility regardless of a defendant's unreasonableness, negligence, or fault. Nonetheless, except in those rare cases in which the application of *res ipsa loquitur* also involves a shifting of the burden of persuasion, there may be sound reasons to adopt a *res ipsa*-like method of circumstantially proving a product defect.

* * *

The doctrine of res ipsa loquitur * * * has been applied in cases involving multiple defendants and multiple theories of liability such as negligence and products liability. *See, e.g., Anderson v. Somberg*, 67 *N.J.* 291, 338 *A.*2d 1, *cert. denied*, 423 *U.S.* 929, 96 *S.Ct.* 279, 46 *L. Ed.*2d 258 (1975). The *Anderson*-type cases utilize collective *res ipsa loquitur* in that both the burden of coming forward with evidence and the burden of persuasion are shifted to the defendants.

Anderson and its progeny are cases involving unique circumstances in which a clearly helpless or anesthetized plaintiff suffered physical injury as a result of acts involving multiple defendants. In those cases, "it was apparent that at least one of the defendants was liable for plaintiff's injury because no alternative theory of liability was within reasonable contemplation." *Anderson, supra,* 67 N.J. at 298, 338 A.2d 1. The plaintiffs in those cases were clearly blameless. All of our reported decisions in which a *res ipsa* instruction was utilized in a products liability context involve the same set of highly fact-sensitive circumstances: a plaintiff sued multiple defendants on multiple theories of liability; all possible defendants were before the court; it was clear that at least one of those defendants was responsible for the plaintiff's injuries; and the plaintiff was either helpless, anesthetized, or in a situation in which he or she clearly had less information than the defendants concerning the cause of the injuries. Those special facts are simply not present in the vast majority of strict products liability cases, including the present one.

There is no precedent in this State permitting a *res ipsa loquitur* charge in a commonplace products liability case that involves only a single defendant. * * *

The majority of jurisdictions that have addressed the issue do not allow *res ipsa loquitur* to be used in a strict products liability cause of action. Jonathan M. Hoffman, *Res Ipsa Loquitur and Indeterminate Product Defects: If They Speak for Themselves, What Are They Saying?,* 36 S. Tex. L.Rev. 353, 373 (1995). * * *

We agree with the majority of jurisdictions that, ordinarily, the traditional *res ipsa loquitur* jury charge should not be used in strict products liability actions. As noted previously, *res ipsa loquitur* is a negligence doctrine; it is a circumstantial means of proving a defendant's lack of due care. Strict liability, on the other hand, is a theory of liability based on allocating responsibility regardless of a defendant's unreasonableness, negligence or fault. Thus, while *res ipsa* might demonstrate a manufacturer's negligence in failing to inspect or appropriately assemble a particular product, strict liability merely questions whether there is a defect in that product that existed before it left the manufacturer's control. Furthermore, a strict products liability case by its nature implies that the product will have left the control of the manufacturer. We reaffirm the Court's holding in the *Anderson*-type cases in which collective *res ipsa loquitur* is applied and the burden of persuasion is shifted to the defendants.

Even if we were to hold that the doctrine should be applied to a commonplace products liability case involving a single defendant, the trial court properly refused to give the jury a *res ipsa loquitur* charge in the present case. The chair had been in use for about five weeks. It was used twenty-four hours a day by at least three different persons of various weights and sizes. Although there was no evidence of misuse, multiple intended users had many opportunities to adjust the tension on the back of the chair to meet their personal needs. It cannot be said that simply because the back of the chair collapsed when plaintiff placed his weight against it, the chair was defective. The accident could not be replicated and no defect was found by any expert. The proofs—direct, circumstantial, and that negating of other causes—simply failed to show that collapse of the chair while the 325-pound plaintiff sat in it meant the chair was defective based on a balancing of the probabilities.

-D-

We recognize that as an alternative to a traditional *res ipsa loquitur* instruction, various states and commentators have advocated an intermediate-type approach for circumstantially proving the existence of a product defect. That approach appears to best serve the interest of all parties and is not inconsistent with the Act.

The *Scanlon* rule regarding circumstantial proof of a defect in a strict products liability case was adopted recently in the *Restatement (Third) of Torts: Products Liability*. It provides:

> It may be inferred that the harm sustained by the plaintiff was caused by a product defect existing at the time of sale or distribution, without proof of a specific defect, when the incident that harmed the plaintiff:
>
> (a) was of a kind that ordinarily occurs as a result of a product defect; and
>
> (b) was not, in the particular case, solely the result of causes other than product defect existing at the time of sale or distribution.

[*Restatement (Third) of Torts* § 3 (1997).]

The Restatement test for circumstantial evidence of a product defect is similar to *res ipsa loquitur* in that it is an inferential test. * * * [I]t permits the jury to draw two inferences: that the harmful incident was caused by a product defect, and that the defect was present when the product left the manufacturer's control. * * * [E]ven those jurisdictions that find that *res ipsa* is not specifically applicable to a strict products liability action have recognized that the inferences and principles that form the core of *res ipsa* "merely instantiates the broader principle, which is as applicable to a products case as to any other tort case, that an accident can itself be evidence of liability [,] ... if it is reasonably plain that the defect was not introduced after the product was sold." *Welge v. Planters Lifesavers Co.*, 17 F.3d 209, 211 (7th Cir.1994). We agree with that analysis.

Section 3 of the Restatement has been referred to as the "indeterminate product test" because its use is limited to those product liability cases in which the plaintiff cannot prove a specific defect. Hoffman, *supra*, 36 S. Tex. L.Rev. at 356. A plaintiff can satisfy the requirements of Section 3 of the Restatement the same way as in the case of *res ipsa loquitur,* by direct and circumstantial evidence as well as evidence that negates causes other than product defect.

* * *

We * * * adopt the indeterminate product defect test announced in Section 3 of the Restatement. * * * Section 3 of the Restatement in a products liability case does precisely what *res ipsa loquitur* does in a negligence context. We are persuaded, therefore, that our adoption of Section 3 of the Restatement is consistent with the policy that drives *res ipsa.* Like our traditional *res ipsa loquitur* charge, there is no shifting of the burden of proof under a jury charge based on Section 3 of the Restatement.

Our independent review of the record, including a consideration of the jury charge as a whole, convinces us that the trial court adequately informed the jury that it could rely on circumstantial evidence to "infer that there was a defect by reasoning from circumstances and the facts shown." Hence, plaintiff was not prejudiced by the absence of a *res ipsa loquitur* jury charge even if one had been required. Moreover, the circumstantial evidence charge that was given was equivalent to the indeterminate product test charge under Section 3 of the Restatement.

III

* * *

[The court remanded for a new trial because of an erroneous trial court decision to exclude evidence.]

Because we have adopted Section 3 of the Restatement, upon retrial, plaintiff need not prove a specific defect in the chair if he can establish that the incident that harmed him is of the kind that ordinarily occurs as a result of a product defect, and that the incident was not solely the result of causes other than product defect existing at the time the chair left Girsberger's control. *Restatement (Third) of Torts* § 3(a) and (b). If plaintiff cannot satisfy those requirements, he is not entitled to have the jury charged regarding an inference of a product defect, and plaintiff would be obligated to establish one or more manufacturing defects required by the Act, *N.J.S.A.* 2A:58C–2a.

* * *

For affirmance in part; reversal in part—Chief Justice PORITZ and Justices HANDLER, POLLOCK, O'HERN, GARIBALDI, STEIN, and COLEMAN.

Opposed—None.

Notes

1. In *Anderson*, discussed in *Myrlak*, a piece of a forceps-like instrument broke off and became embedded in the plaintiff's spine during surgery. The plaintiff sued the surgeon, the hospital, the medical supply distributor and the instrument manufacturer on various theories. The *Anderson* burden

shifting approach has some support in other jurisdictions, but the general rule remains that the plaintiff must establish the product was defective when in the possession of each defendant. This burden is easily met in most cases involving design and warning defect claims. In cases involving alleged manufacturing defects, however, defendants commonly claim that the product became flawed after it left the defendant's control.

2. As noted in *Myrlak*, the Restatement (Third) of Torts: Products Liability § 3 permits circumstantial evidence to support a finding of product defect. Comment *b* notes:

> The most frequent application of this section is to cases involving manufacturing defects. When a product unit contains such a defect, and the defect affects product performance so as to cause a harmful incident, in most instances it will cause the product to malfunction in such a way that the inference of product defect is clear. From this perspective, manufacturing defects cause products to fail to perform their manifestly intended functions. Frequently, the plaintiff is able to establish specifically the nature and identity of the defect and may proceed directly under [section] 2(a). But when the product unit involved in the harm-causing incident is lost or destroyed in that accident, direct evidence of specific defect may not be available. Under that circumstance, this section may offer the plaintiff the only fair opportunity to recover.

3. Plaintiff in *Myrlak* alleged the chair was defective in manufacture, meaning that it came off "the production line in a substandard condition". Could the chair have been defective in design instead? For example, its design might be deficient if the chair was not intended to be sufficiently sturdy to support a 325 pound person. Without additional evidence, is it possible to determine whether the problem was one of design or manufacture? Does it matter? Section 3 of the Products Liability Restatement permits an inference of defect even when it is not clear whether the defect is one in design or manufacture. *See*, Restatement (Third) of Torts: Products Liability § 3, Illustration 3 (automobile driver's seat suddenly collapsed backward while car was stopped at a stop light).

4. The problems that confront plaintiffs in manufacturing defect cases almost always involve proving the existence of a defect at the time the product left the possession of the defendant. The difficulty arises in several forms. In some cases the product is literally destroyed in the accident, leaving little evidence of what went wrong. In the *Welge* case, a glass jar of peanuts broke as the plaintiff tried to re-fasten the lid. The fragments were preserved and the parties agreed that it must have contained a defect but they could not find the fracture that caused the jar to shatter. More importantly, they did not agree when the defect had come into existence. Not surprisingly, the defendant argued that the defect was introduced due to rough handling and the plaintiff's evidence suggested nothing unusual had happened to the jar. Summary judgment against the plaintiff was held to be inappropriate.

In another group of cases there is a controversy as to whether the defect caused the accident or the accident caused the "defect." For example, in *Johnson v. Michelin Tire Corp.*, 812 F.2d 200 (5th Cir.1987) plaintiff was injured when his car, equipped with four-year-old tires crossed two lanes and ran into a guard rail. The question in the case was whether a defect in the tire caused a blow-out which led to the wreck, or, on the other hand, whether the tire damage was caused by the accident.

Some states explicitly have adopted a "malfunction doctrine" permitting the plaintiff to reach a jury when the circumstances surrounding the malfunctioning of a product establish prima facie the existence of a manufacturing defect. *See* Ducko v. Chrysler Motors Corp., 433 Pa.Super. 47, 639 A.2d 1204 (1994) (sudden steering failure in a two months old car); Stackiewicz v. Nissan Motor Corp., 100 Nev. 443, 686 P.2d 925 (1984) (automobile with 2,400 total miles; steering suddenly locked).

5. Harrison v. Bill Cairns Pontiac, Inc., 77 Md.App. 41, 549 A.2d 385 (1988) noted five factors to be considered in determining whether a product defect may be inferred from circumstantial evidence: (1) expert testimony on possible causes; (2) the length of time between the sale and the accident; (3) the occurrence of similar accidents in similar products; (4) the elimination of other causes of the accident; (5) whether the accident is a type that does not happen without a defect.

6. A common situation is a product sold in a sealed container. As the court said in McKisson v. Sales Affiliates, Inc., 416 S.W.2d 787 (Tex.1967), "[w]hen it is shown that the product involved comes in a sealed container, it is inferrable that the product reached the consumer without substantial changes in the conditions in which it was sold." If other evidence proves that the sealed container was invaded or that the product became flawed after it left the defendant's control, however, the inference breaks down. *See, e.g.* Klein v. Continental–Emsco, 445 F.2d 629 (5th Cir.1971).

7. What about "foreign" objects in sealed containers of food or drink? Typically, there are three major issues in deleterious food and drink cases: 1) is the food/drink defective?; 2) did the product's condition cause the plaintiff's damages?; and 3) is the product's condition attributable to the defendant? *See* Shoshone Coca–Cola Bottling Co. v. Dolinski, 82 Nev. 439, 420 P.2d 855 (1966) (dead mouse in Coke bottle).

8. Deterioration: A product's failure caused by normal wear and tear is not sufficient to establish that it was defective when sold. However, the plaintiff need not prove the product failed immediately upon delivery. If the product is designed or manufactured to have a propensity to deteriorate more quickly than normal, it might be defective when it is delivered, even though the danger is not manifested until later. In such cases, the defect is the propensity to deteriorate too quickly, which defect was present when the product was delivered.

9. Along these lines, the Texas Supreme Court refused to apply § 3 in Ford Motor Co. v. Ridgway, 135 S.W.3d 598 (Tex.2004). The case involved a fire in a two-year old pick-up that caught fire while being driven. At the time of the fire, the vehicle been driven approximately 55,000 miles by three owners and had undergone three repairs involving the truck's fuel system. Refusing to apply § 3, the court noted,

> Even if § 3 were the law in Texas, it would generally apply only to new or almost new products. Such products typically have not been modified or repaired, therefore making a product defect the likely cause of an

accident. The drafters of the Restatement realized this limitation and noted: "The inference of defect may not be drawn ... from the mere fact of a product-related accident.... Evidence that the product may have been used improperly or was altered by repair people weakens the inference [that there was a product defect]." Id. at reporters' notes to cmt. d (citations omitted). * * * Therefore, we reiterate that because section 3 is not applicable to the facts of this case, we need not decide if it is an accurate statement of Texas law.

In a concurring opinion, Justice Hecht offers a more fundamental critique of § 3.

> I join in the Court's opinion and write only to explain that while Texas law would allow proof of products liability by circumstantial evidence in certain cases, the black-letter rule of section 3 of the Restatement (Third) of Torts: Products Liability does not accurately restate Texas law.
>
> Section 3 states:
>
>> Circumstantial Evidence Supporting Inference of Product Defect
>>
>> It may be inferred that the harm sustained by the plaintiff was caused by a product defect existing at the time of sale or distribution, without proof of a specific defect, when the incident that harmed the plaintiff:
>>
>> (a) was of a kind that ordinarily occurs as a result of product defect; and
>>
>> (b) was not, in the particular case, solely the result of causes other than product defect existing at the time of sale or distribution.
>
> "It may be inferred" cannot mean "it is always proper to infer", as the present case demonstrates. * * *
>
> "It may be inferred" really means "it is sometimes proper to infer", but while this reading makes the rule stated in section 3 accurate, it also makes the rule not very helpful. Few would question the use of circumstantial evidence to prove products liability in appropriate cases. The hard issue is not whether it can be done, but when and how. The comments to section 3 and the cases cited in support of it illustrate the kinds of considerations courts have taken into account in deciding whether to allow an inference of pre-sale defect in a product, but these considerations are not reflected * * * in the black-letter rule itself. One looks to comments to explain the rule; one does not look to comments to find the rule.
>
> Section 3 is modeled on section 328D of the Restatement (Second) of Torts, which states:
>
>> Res Ipsa Loquitur
>>
>> (1) It may be inferred that harm suffered by the plaintiff is caused by negligence of the defendant when
>>
>> (a) the event is of a kind which ordinarily does not occur in the absence of negligence;

(b) other responsible causes, including the conduct of the plaintiff and third persons, are sufficiently eliminated by evidence; and

(c) the indicated negligence is within the scope of the defendant's duty to the plaintiff.

But the differences in the two provisions are such that section 3 is not an analogue of section 328D but rather a kind of res ipsa B lite! Sections 3(a) and (b) are less strict than the parallel provisions in sections 328D(1)(a) and (b), at least in a case like the present one. It cannot be said that fires in pickups do not ordinarily occur absent a product defect; they ordinarily occur for all sorts of reasons. Nor has Ridgway "eliminated by evidence" the existence of other responsible causes of the fire. The most he can say is that Ford has offered no evidence of another cause. He has not shown that, given the circumstances, another cause was impossible or even improbable. If section 3 were as strictly worded as section 328D, Ridgway's claim would clearly fail.

Texas law of res ipsa loquitur is at least as strict as section 328D. We require the first condition stated in section 328D(1)(a), and instead of the second condition stated in section 328D(1)(b), we require that the instrumentality causing harm have been under the defendant's management and control.

* * *

The rule of res ipsa loquitur allows an inference of negligence, absent direct proof, only when injury would ordinarily not have occurred but for negligence, and defendant's negligence is probable.

There is no reason to allow an inference of products liability any more freely than an inference of negligence. An inference of products liability is really two inferences: that the product was defective, and that the defect existed at the time of sale. Applying the principle underlying res ipsa loquitur, neither inference can be drawn without evidence that the injury would not ordinarily have occurred absent a product defect and that that defect probably existed when the product was sold. This is not what section 3 says.

Do you agree that § 3 creates a more liberal circumstantial evidence rule than § 328D?

SECTION E. WARNING DEFECTS

1. DUTY TO WARN

HOLLISTER v. DAYTON HUDSON CORP.
United States Court of Appeals, Sixth Circuit, 2000.
201 F.3d 731.

AMENDED OPINION

GILMAN, CIRCUIT JUDGE.

Laura Hollister, a citizen of Michigan, was severely burned when the shirt that she was wearing ignited upon contact with a hot electric burner on her apartment stove. She brought a lawsuit against Dayton Hudson Corporation, the Minnesota-based owner of the department store where the shirt was purchased, alleging negligence and breach of the store's implied warranty of merchantability. Her claims were based on allegations that (1) the shirt's design rendered it unreasonably dangerous, and (2) the shirt failed to carry a warning as to its extreme flammability. The district court granted Dayton Hudson's motion for summary judgment, concluding that Hollister had not established a prima facie case of design defect under Michigan law, and that any duty to warn was obviated by the open and obvious nature of the alleged defect.

Contrary to the decision of the district court, we believe that Hollister has adduced sufficient evidence to allow a reasonable juror to conclude that the shirt sold by Dayton Hudson was defective because of its failure to carry a warning regarding its extreme flammability. Although Hollister has failed to show any negligence on Dayton Hudson's part regarding this alleged defect, she need only establish a prima facie case that the shirt was defective and that it caused her injuries in order to pursue her claim for breach of implied warranty. We therefore AFFIRM the district court's entry of summary judgment on Hollister's negligence claim, REVERSE its entry of summary judgment on Hollister's breach of implied warranty claim to the extent that the claim is based upon a failure to warn, and REMAND for further proceedings consistent with this opinion.

* * *

B. Procedural background

* * *

On September 1, 1997, Hollister submitted reports pursuant to Rule 26 from the following four experts: David Hall (textile expert), Edmund Knight (expert on cause and origin of the fire), Anna Dutka (economic damages expert), and Alan Hedge (stove design expert). Dr. Hall's report stated that he was still looking for "exemplar" fabric identical to the rayon used in the shirt in question, and that in his opinion the fabric was dangerously flammable. The report identifies the fabric as 100% rayon, loosely woven with 1.5 denier threads.

Dr. Hall offered no opinion as to the feasibility of using a different fabric to construct a similar shirt, and acknowledged that he had no expertise in the use of fabrics in clothing. He initially testified that the flammability test promulgated by the Consumer Products Safety Commission (CPSC), set forth in 16 C.F.R. § 1610, determines whether a fabric is "unreasonably dangerous." The regulation's purpose is "to reduce danger of injury and loss of life by providing, on a national basis, standard methods of testing and rating the flammability of textiles and textile products for clothing use, thereby discouraging the use of any dangerously flammable clothing textiles." 16 C.F.R. § 1610.1. * * * Although Dr. Hall never tested the shirt remnants pursuant to 16 C.F.R.

§ 1610, Dayton Hudson's expert did. The fabric passed the test. Despite this fact, Dayton Hudson remained as a defendant. * * *.

In his deposition on October 31, 1997, Dayton Hudson's causation expert, John Campbell, acknowledged that he had located an "exemplar" shirt composed of fabric identical to that used in the shirt involved in the accident. Hollister's counsel subsequently purchased identical shirts to the one that Campbell had identified, and gave them to Dr. Hall for examination and testing.

Dr. Hall determined that the characteristics of the exemplar fabric were substantially identical to the shirt that Hollister had been wearing at the time of the accident. He then conducted a test comparing the exemplar fabric with fourteen other fabrics. The test utilized a stove-top electric burner set at 1100–1160 degrees, and involved sweeping 3.5 by 10–inch strips of the various fabrics across the burner. Hall then timed the rate of ignition and burning. The exemplar fabric ignited immediately, and burned completely within six seconds. Eleven of the fourteen non-exemplar samples failed to ignite at all. The three samples that did ignite were another 100% rayon sample, a rayon-polyester blend (both of which took about twelve seconds to burn completely), and a piece of newspaper (which burned in four seconds).

At the close of discovery, Dayton Hudson moved for summary judgment. One ground focused upon the requirement that a plaintiff such as Hollister must prove the effectiveness of a proposed alternative design. In response, Hollister acknowledged that she would not be calling an expert witness on the effectiveness of an alternative design. She claimed that this was a question of fact for the jury that did not require expert testimony. * * *

* * *

After briefing by both parties, the district court granted Dayton Hudson's motion for summary judgment on May 12, 1998. Hollister timely filed her notice of appeal to this court.

II. ANALYSIS

* * *

C. Breach of implied warranty

A plaintiff seeking to recover on a claim against a retailer for breach of implied warranty must establish two elements: (1) that the product was sold in a defective condition, and (2) that the defect caused her injury. *See Piercefield*, 133 N.W.2d at 134. Hollister contends that the shirt in question was defective because it was made of a fabric that was dangerously flammable (design defect) and because it should have carried a warning advising wearers of its extreme flammability (failure to warn).

1. *Hollister failed to establish a prima facie case of design defect*

a. The district court applied the proper analysis to Hollister's allegations of design defect

* * *

* * * The test applied by Michigan courts to design defect claims is set out in *Reeves v. Cincinnati, Inc.*, 176 Mich.App. 181, 439 N.W.2d 326, 329 (1989). * * * Reeves * * * calls for "a showing of alternative safety devices and whether those devices would have been effective as a reasonable means of minimizing the foreseeable risk of danger." *Id.*

* * *

b. Hollister failed to establish a prima facie case of design defect

Hollister's claim of design defect is primarily based upon the tests conducted by Dr. Hall, in which the exemplar fabric and fourteen other fabric samples were dragged across a hot burner at a prescribed rate. Those tests indicate that the exemplar fabric was significantly more flammable than other fabrics. Hollister presented no evidence, however, as to the availability of alternative fabrics when the shirt was manufactured, the cost of manufacturing the shirt with such fabrics, or the effect of a fabric change upon the wearability, durability, or appearance of the fabric. * * *

In sum, Dr. Hall never presented a "proposed alternative design" with any specificity. His only recommendation was that the weight of the fabric should have been heavier. Ignoring for the moment his silence on the practicality of such a suggestion, Dr. Hall also admitted "that he could not articulate the exact effect on flammability of the changes" he proposed. The district court thus properly dismissed Hollister's claims to the extent that they were premised on the shirt's allegedly defective design. *See Zettle v. Handy Mfg. Co.*, 998 F.2d 358, 362 (6th Cir.1993) (affirming a grant of summary judgment and holding that the plaintiff had failed to present sufficient evidence concerning the effectiveness of a proposed alternative design for a power washer under Michigan law).

* * *

2. *Hollister successfully established a prima facie case that the shirt was defective because it lacked a warning regarding its extreme flammability*

Hollister's second basis for asserting that the shirt was defective, and therefore sold in breach of Dayton Hudson's implied warranty of merchantability, is her claim that the shirt required a warning regarding its extreme flammability. Dayton Hudson counters that for Hollister to make out a failure to warn claim, she must first show that the shirt was defectively designed. It therefore maintains that Hollister's inability to establish a prima facie case of design defect is necessarily fatal to her claim. We find that Michigan law is contrary to Dayton Hudson's argument.

Conceptually, the two claims identify different types of defect. A design defect is the mark of a poorly designed product, which could reasonably have been designed in a safer manner. The category of failure to warn, on the other hand, applies to a product that may be designed in an optimally safe way, but nevertheless bears a latent danger that would not be apparent to an ordinary consumer. For example, without a warning as to its weight restrictions, a highway bridge might be legally "defective" even if it was designed safely and was in perfect working order. *See Wilson v. Bradlees of New England, Inc.*, 96 F.3d 552, 559 (1st Cir.1996). Similarly, a prescription drug might be well designed and effective for its intended use, but it would nevertheless be legally "defective" if it lacked appropriate warnings as to its proper dosage and possible side effects. *See* Restatement (Second) Torts § 402A, comment h (1972); *see also Barry v. Don Hall Labs.*, 56 Or.App. 518, 642 P.2d 685, 688 (1982) (holding that properly manufactured vitamins might still be found defective due to the absence of a warning as to their high sugar content).

Under Michigan law, design defect claims and failure to warn claims are governed by distinct analyses. *See Gregory v. Cincinnati Inc.*, 450 Mich. 1, 538 N.W.2d 325, 329 (1995) (holding that a manufacturer's failure to warn can support a product liability claim "even if it the design chosen does not render the product defective."); *Glittenberg v. Doughboy Recreational Indus.*, 441 Mich. 379, 491 N.W.2d 208, 216 (1992) (cautioning that "design defect analysis must not be used to evaluate failure to warn claims"). In the present case, the most relevant difference between the two claims is that a prima facie case of design defect requires that the plaintiff propose a reasonable alternative design, but a failure to warn claim does not. Thus Hollister's failure to propose a safer, alternative design for the rayon blouse, which was fatal to her design defect claim, does not support a grant of summary judgment against her claim for failure to warn.

In order to establish, under Michigan law, that a product is defective due to a failure to warn, a plaintiff must demonstrate that a manufacturer (1) had actual or constructive knowledge of the alleged danger, (2) had no reason to believe that consumers would know of this danger, and (3) failed to exercise reasonable care to inform consumers of the danger. *See Glittenberg*, 491 N.W.2d at 212–13 (holding that the dangers of diving headfirst into a manufacturer's aboveground swimming pool were open and obvious). If a product's danger is open and obvious to a reasonable consumer, the manufacturer has no duty to warn. *See id.* at 213. In such a case, a retailer who sells the product cannot be found liable for breach of implied warranty because the product is not defective.

The district court disposed of Hollister's failure to warn argument in a cursory manner, concluding that the danger inherent in having clothing come into contact with a hot stove is "open and obvious." We find this analysis to be oversimplified. It is true that a reasonable person would know that clothing is flammable; the question, however, is one of degree. *See Michigan Mut. Ins. Co. v. Heatilator Fireplace*, 422 Mich.

148, 366 N.W.2d 202, 205 (1985) (holding that even if a reasonable consumer would know that covering the vents on a fireplace presented a "vague danger," a jury might still reasonably find that a warning was required to give the consumer "a full appreciation of the seriousness of the life-threatening risks involved"). A consumer might reasonably be expected to know that a rayon shirt will catch fire more easily and burn more quickly than a shirt made of heavy flannel. An ordinary consumer would have no way of knowing, however, that a particular rayon shirt was substantially more combustible and flammable than another rayon shirt. *Cf. LaGorga v. Kroger*, 275 F.Supp. 373 (W.D.Pa.1967) (denying a retailer's motion for judgment as a matter of law where the plaintiff charged the retailer with breach of implied warranty for selling him a jacket that was unusually flammable and lacked a warning, noting that "[t]he public cannot be expected to possess the facilities or technical knowledge to apprehend inherent or latent dangers"), *aff'd,* 407 F.2d 671 (3d Cir.1969).

Hollister presented credible evidence that the exemplar fabric burned explosively, like newspaper, and that other comparable fabrics did not. In tests conducted by Hollister's expert, the exemplar fabric ignited instantly and burned completely within six seconds. Of the fourteen comparison samples, eleven failed to ignite at all when passed over a burner at the same rate. The three samples that did ignite were another 100% rayon sample and a rayon-polyester blend, both of which burned in about twelve seconds, and a piece of newspaper, which burned in four seconds. Thus the exemplar fabric burned twice as quickly as other rayon fabrics, and only two seconds slower than a piece of newspaper. A reasonable juror could conclude from this evidence that the shirt's manufacturer had a duty to know that the shirt possessed a latent danger, and a corresponding duty to warn consumers of that danger.

Once a plaintiff establishes that a product is defective—whether because of its design or because of a failure to warn—she must then demonstrate that this defect was a proximate cause of her injuries in order to make out a claim for breach of implied warranty. *See Piercefield,* 133 N.W.2d at 134. Hollister's mother stated in an affidavit that she would not have bought the shirt for her daughter if she had known that the shirt was extremely flammable, and Hollister herself maintained in an affidavit that she would not have worn the shirt in question if she had possessed such knowledge. A reasonable jury could find, based on this evidence, that the shirt's failure to carry a warning was a proximate cause of Hollister's injuries.

* * *

The Fourth Circuit's decision in *Howard v. McCrory Corp.,* 601 F.2d 133 (4th Cir.1979), is also instructive. In that case, a products liability action was brought by a mother whose infant son was fatally burned when his pajamas and bathrobe inexplicably caught fire. The mother sued the manufacturer and the retailer of the infant's pajamas, as well as the manufacturer and the retailer of his bathrobe, alleging strict liability, negligence, and breach of implied warranty. Judgment as a matter of law was entered in favor of the two retailers. The Fourth Circuit reversed for two distinct reasons, both of which are relevant to the instant case.

The district court had entered judgment in favor of Kresge, the retailer of the pajamas, because the plaintiff presented no expert testimony regarding the pajamas' flammability, only offering eyewitness testimony that the pajamas had ignited quickly and burned very rapidly. In reversing, the Fourth Circuit wrote:

> It has been held that, even where all the standard tests demonstrated that a product was not dangerously inflammable for use by infants, it is perfectly permissible for the jury to find that the product was dangerously inflammable from ... proof that the product "ignited easily, (and) burned rapidly and intensely with a high degree of heat."

Howard, 601 F.2d at 137 (citing *LaGorga*, 275 F.Supp. at 378).

McCrory, the retailer of the bathrobe, was granted judgment notwithstanding the verdict on the grounds that remnants of the robe had been tested and found to meet the standards of Class I fabrics under the CPSC flammability test. The Fourth Circuit reversed this holding as well, reasoning that "[c]ompliance with federal standards, while plainly relevant, is not conclusive on the issue of McCrory's liability and the jury is entitled to consider any other relevant evidence on the issue." *Howard*, 601 F.2d at 138.

This last holding is particularly significant because Dayton Hudson cites the fact that the exemplar fabric met federal flammability standards as a factor supporting the grant of summary judgment. Although such evidence would undoubtedly be relevant evidence for Dayton Hudson to introduce at trial, it is not dispositive of Hollister's claim at this stage. *See id.*; *Wilson v. Bradlees of New England, Inc.*, 96 F.3d 552 (1st Cir.1996) (holding that evidence of a garment meeting the federal flammability standards was relevant to, but not dispositive of, plaintiff's claims).

We therefore conclude that Hollister has established a prima facie case against Dayton Hudson for breach of implied warranty based upon a failure to warn, and that the district court erred in entering the grant of summary judgment on this claim. This is not to say, however, that Hollister will necessarily prevail at trial. She will still have to convince a jury that the shirt was considerably more flammable than a reasonable consumer would expect. *See Glittenberg*, 491 N.W.2d at 212–13. She will also have to convince a jury that the lack of a warning on the shirt was a proximate cause of her injuries. *See Moll v. Abbott Labs.*, 444 Mich. 1, 506 N.W.2d 816, 824 (1993). Finally, if Hollister does establish liability, the damages that Hollister sustained will be diminished in proportion to any amount of negligence attributed to her by the jury. *See* M.C.L. § 600.2949; *Karl v. Bryant Air Conditioning Co.*, 416 Mich. 558, 331

N.W.2d 456, 462 (1982) (holding that the Michigan comparative negligence statute applies to breach of implied warranty actions). These hurdles are likely to be significant ones. We are convinced, however, that Hollister has the right to proceed to the next stage of the litigation.

III. CONCLUSION

For all of the reasons set forth above, we AFFIRM the district court's entry of summary judgment on Hollister's negligence claim, REVERSE its entry of summary judgment on Hollister's breach of implied warranty claim to the extent that the claim is based upon a failure to warn, and REMAND for further proceedings consistent with this opinion.

Notes

1. **Negligence.** Under the law of negligence the supplier of a product must use reasonable care to warn product users of risks that they are unlikely to fully appreciate. Restatement of Torts (Second) § 388 (1965). Suppliers need only warn against significant risks, and not every conceivable accident that might occur. Madden, The Duty to Warn in Products Liability: Contours and Criticism, 89 W.Va.L.Rev. 221, 235 (1987); Noel, Products Defective Because of Inadequate Directions or Warnings, 23 Sw.L.J. 256, 264–265 (1969). In determining what warnings are necessary, courts balance the gravity and probability of the harm against the burden and feasibility of giving an effective warning. *Id.*

2. **Products Liability.** The duty to warn arises under the law of products liability because of the recognition that many useful products cannot be made completely safe. Yet it is often reasonable to market such products. Restatement of Torts (Second) § 402A, Comment i (1965). In order to prevent such products from being unreasonably dangerous, however, the seller must give appropriate directions and warnings with respect to risks that are not generally known and recognized. Restatement of Torts (Second) § 402A, Comment j (1965).

3. **Breach of Warranty.** Failure to warn can also give rise to a breach of implied warranty. This is because products unaccompanied by adequate instructions and warnings are not reasonably fit for the ordinary purposes for which such products are used. *See, e.g.,* Wolfe v. Ford Motor Co., 6 Mass.App.Ct. 346, 376 N.E.2d 143 (1978) (inadequate warnings concerning the effect of overloading a camper).

4. When the only alleged defect in the product is a failure to warn adequately, is there a difference among the three theories? Many courts hold that there is no difference because liability under all three theories turns on the question of whether the warning is reasonable. *E.g.,* Smith v. E.R. Squibb & Sons, Inc., 405 Mich. 79, 273 N.W.2d 476 (1979) (warning about the side-effects of a drug). In Russell v. G.A.F. Corp., 422 A.2d 989, 991 (D.C.App.1980) the court stated:

> A plaintiff may limit the claim to negligence in failing to warn about foreseeable harm from a product, *see* Burch v. Amsterdam Corporation, D.C.App., 366 A.2d 1079, 1086 (1976), or claim strict liability for injury

derived from the same failure. *See* Restatement (Second) of Torts § 402A, Comment j (1965). In either case, however, the duty is the same: ordinary care. *See* Basko v. Sterling Drug, Inc., 416 F.2d 417, 426 (2d Cir.1969) (Restatement, *supra* § 402A, Comment k, adopting the ordinary negligence standard of duty to warn). More specifically, whether a manufacturer can be held strictly liable for failure to warn, or held liable only for negligence, the threshold question whether there has been a "failure to warn" (triggering potential liability) is judged by the following standard of care:

> The seller or manufacturer of a product whose use could result in foreseeable harm has a duty to give a warning which adequately advises the user of attendant risks and which provides *specific* directions for safe use. [*Burch v. Amsterdam Corp., supra* at 1086 (emphasis in original).]

The trial court did not follow this standard but mistakenly added an element of "defectiveness" to the *Burch* test. One of the grounds for granting the directed verdict was the absence of evidence that the sheet was *defective* when it left G.A.F.'s hands. Of course, there must be a *danger* to warn about. *See* Beier v. International Harvester Co., 287 Minn. 400, 402, 178 N.W.2d 618, 620 (1970) (insufficient evidence to show danger of which defendant had a duty to warn in that it was impossible for bolts to become loose while outer nuts were tight). Evidence of a defect is unnecessary, however. A product can be perfectly made and still require directions or warnings on proper use in order to be safe. *See* Biller v. Allis Chalmers Manufacturing Co., 34 Ill.App.2d 47, 180 N.E.2d 46 (1962) (manufacturer owed duty to warn of latent limitations of even a perfectly made tractor).

5. **Risk–Utility Balancing.** Several courts have indicated that risk-utility balancing should not play an important role in products liability warning cases. Consider Dambacher by Dambacher v. Mallis, 336 Pa.Super. 22, 485 A.2d 408 (1984), appeal dismissed, 508 Pa. 643, 500 A.2d 428 (1985):

> As has been said, "In the case of an inadequate warning, * * * imposing the requirements of a proper warning will seldom detract from the utility of the product." Freund v. Cellofilm Properties, Inc., 87 N.J. 229, 238 n. 1, 432 A.2d 925, 930 n. 1 (1981). At the same time, the cost of adding a warning, or of making an inadequate warning adequate, will at least in most cases be outweighed by the risk of harm if there is no adequate warning.

In states that follow this view, must manufacturers warn against all conceivable product hazards, no matter how remote? If so this would represent a significant difference between negligence and products liability.

6. Is this difference desirable? Consider Twerski, Weinstein, Donaher, Piehler, The Use and Abuse of Warnings in Products Liability—Design Defect Litigation Comes of Age, 61 Cornell L.Rev. 495, 513–517 (1976). The authors argue that warnings cannot be effective unless they selectively focus on the most significant hazards. Therefore, courts should not induce manufacturers routinely to "overwarn" about trivial risks. If this should happen warnings would lose their credibility, and users will no longer pay attention to them. Keep this question in mind as you read the cases in the next

section. For a case agreeing with this view, *see* Cotton v. Buckeye Gas Products Co., 840 F.2d 935, 938 (D.C.Cir.1988) ("The primary cost [of a warning] is, in fact, the increase in time and effort required for the user to grasp the message. The inclusion of each extra item dilutes the punch of every other item. Given short attention spans, items crowd each other out; they get lost in fine print.")

7. **Foresight/Hindsight.** Under the law of negligence, manufacturers must only warn about foreseeable risks. One potential difference between negligence and products liability turns on whether, under the law of products liability, manufacturers must warn about unknowable risks. Courts are split on the question of whether to use foresight or hindsight in failure to warn cases. A majority of courts hold that ignorance of generic risk is an excuse. They hold that there is no liability for failing to warn about undiscoverable risks. *E.g.*, Payne v. Soft Sheen Products, Inc., 486 A.2d 712 (D.C.App.1985). This is the position of both the second and third Restatements. Restatement of Torts (Second) § 402A, Comment j (1965); Restatement (Third) of Torts: Products Liability § 2 (1997). The minority rule requires warnings about risks known at the time of trial even if they were not known or knowable at the time of manufacture. *E.g.*, Sternhagen v. Dow Co., 282 Mont. 168, 935 P.2d 1139 (1997); *Phillips v. Kimwood Machine Co., supra* page 114.

8. We have seen that in design cases most courts do not excuse product manufacturers who are justifiably ignorant of generic risks. *See*, Note Regarding the Foresight/Hindsight Distinction, *supra* page 141. Is there any logical justification for treating design and warning cases differently in this respect? Usually courts impose the duty to warn to promote safety, but some courts impose the duty to promote individual autonomy. *See* note 12 below. Should the answer vary depending on whether the warning case is based on safety or autonomy?

9. **Burden of proof**. Most courts adhering to the majority rule require plaintiff to prove that the manufacturer either knew or could have known about the risk to be warned about at the time of distribution. A small number of courts place the burden on the defendant to prove justifiable ignorance of risk. *E.g.*, Shanks v. Upjohn Co., 835 P.2d 1189 (Alaska 1992); Feldman v. Lederle Laboratories, 97 N.J. 429, 479 A.2d 374 (1984). In *Feldman* plaintiff developed gray teeth as a result of taking a tetracycline drug as an infant. She brought a products liability case against the manufacturer for failure to warn physicians of the drug's side effect, tooth discoloration. *Feldman* gives the following reasons for shifting the burden of proof:

> [A]s to warnings, generally conduct should be measured by knowledge at the time the manufacturer distributed the product. Did the defendant know, or should he have known, of the danger, given the scientific, technological, and other information available when the product was distributed; or, in other words, did he have actual or constructive knowledge of the danger? * * * Under this standard negligence and strict liability in warning cases may be deemed to be functional equivalents.

* * *

In strict liability warning cases, unlike negligence cases, however, the defendant should properly bear the burden of proving that the information was not reasonably available or obtainable and that it therefore lacked actual or constructive knowledge of the defect. Wade ["On the Effect in Product Liability of Knowledge Unavailable Prior to Marketing," 58 N.Y.U.L.Rev. 734, 76–61] (1983); *see* Pollock, "Liability of a Blood Bank or Hospital for a Hepatitis Associated Blood Transfusion in New Jersey," 2 Seton Hall L.Rev. 47, 60 (1970) ("burden of proof that hepatitis is not detectable and unremovable should rest on the defendant" blood bank or hospital). The defendant is in a superior position to know the technological material or data in the particular field or specialty. The defendant is the expert, often performing self-testing. It is the defendant that injected the product in the stream of commerce for its economic gain. As a matter of policy the burden of proving the status of knowledge in the field at the time of distribution is properly placed on the defendant.

10. In Beshada v. Johns–Manville Products Corp., 90 N.J. 191, 447 A.2d 539 (1982) plaintiffs sued asbestos manufacturers for failure to warn about the risks of exposure to asbestos. Some of the plaintiffs were exposed as early as the 1930's. Defendants claimed that the duty to warn arose only after the risks became scientifically knowable. The court rejected the argument, and held that defendants could be liable for failure to warn about significant risks without regard to whether they could have known about them. *Feldman* adopts the opposite approach with respect to the duty to warn about unknowable risks. *Feldman*, however, does not overrule *Beshada*. How can the cases be reconciled? Does *Feldman* apply to all products except asbestos? Or does *Beshada* apply to all products except drugs?

11. In those jurisdictions that treat negligence, products liability, and breach of warranty as imposing the same standard of liability for failure to warn, what purpose is served by recognizing more than one theory of recovery? In other words, why should such jurisdictions not impose liability for failure to warn on a negligence theory only?

12. **Autonomy vs. Safety.** In most cases the duty to warn is based on the notion that adequate warnings are necessary because they enhance the safety of the product. They do this by providing information that enables the user to minimize or avoid the risks associated with the product. When viewed in this sense, a warning is no different than any other proposed safety feature of a product. It is required only if necessary to make the product reasonably safe.

Should there be a duty to provide warnings that cannot materially enhance safety? Some authors argue that there should be if a reasonable person would want to have the information before choosing to use the product. Twerski, Weinstein, Donaher, Piehler, The Use and Abuse of Warnings in Products Liability—Design Defect Litigation Comes of Age, 61 Corn.L.Rev. 495, 519 (1976). The obligation to warn under such circumstances is based on notions of individual autonomy rather than on accident reduction. The authors cite Davis v. Wyeth Laboratories, Inc., 399 F.2d 121 (9th Cir.1968) as an example. There, an adult contracted polio from a dose of polio vaccine. The chances of this occurring were about one in one million.

The risk of contracting polio from a wild strain if the vaccine were not taken was approximately the same for adults. Under these circumstances, Mr. Davis could not reduce his risk of getting polio by declining to take the vaccine. The court found that the vaccine was unavoidably unsafe, and that there was no way to identify which users would contract the disease. In deciding to impose a duty to warn of the risk, the court stated:

> In such cases, then, the drug is fit and its danger is reasonable only if the balance is struck in favor of its use. Where the risk is otherwise known to the consumer, no problem is presented, since choice is available. Where not known, however, the drug can properly be marketed only in such fashion as to permit the striking of the balance; that is, by full disclosure of the existence and extent of the risk involved.
>
> As comment k recognizes, human experimentation is essential with new drugs if essential knowledge ever is to be gained. No person, however, should be obliged to submit himself to such experimentation. If he is to submit it must be by his voluntary and informed choice or a choice made on his behalf by his physician.
>
> In such cases, then, the drug is fit and its danger is reasonable only if the balance is struck in favor of its use. It can properly be marketed only in such fashion as to permit the striking of that balance; that is, by full disclosure of the existence and extent of the risk involved.

* * *

> There will, of course, be cases where the personal risk, although existent and known, is so trifling in comparison with the advantage to be gained as to be de minimis. Appellee so characterizes this case. It would approach the problem from a purely statistical point of view: less than one out [of] a million is just not unreasonable. This approach we reject. When, in a particular case, the risk qualitatively (e.g., of death or major disability) as well as quantitatively, on balance with the end sought to be achieved, is such as to call for a true choice judgment, medical or personal, the warning must be given.
>
> Appellee contends that even under such a test no true choice situation is presented here. It asserts that "common sense and knowledge of the mainstreams of human conduct would unavoidably bring one to the conclusion" that appellant would have chosen to take the risk. It says, "Simply stated that proposition is this: A man has less than one in a million chance of contracting the dreaded disease of polio if he takes the vaccine. If he does not take the vaccine his chances of contracting polio are abundantly increased."
>
> We do not so read the record. The Surgeon General's report of September, 1962, as we have quoted it, predicted that for the 1962 season only .9 persons over 20 years of age out of a million would contract polio from natural sources. While appellant was the father of two young children, he resided in an area that not only was not epidemic but whose immediate past history of incidence was extremely low. We have no way of knowing the extent to which either factor would affect the critical statistics. Thus appellant's risk of contracting the disease without immunization was about as great (or small) as his risk of

contracting it from the vaccine. Under these circumstances we cannot agree with appellee that the choice to take the vaccine was clear.

We may note further that where the end sought is prevention of disease (and the likelihood of contracting the disease from natural sources is a relevant factor) the situation is a different one from that in which the disease has already struck and the end sought is relief or cure. Risks are far more readily taken in the latter case.

We conclude that the facts of this case imposed on the manufacturer a duty to warn the consumer (or make adequate provision for his being warned) as to the risks involved, and that failure to meet this duty rendered the drug unfit in the sense that it was thereby rendered unreasonably dangerous. Strict liability, then, attached to its sale in absence of warning.

399 F.2d at 129–30.

13. Does the decision in *Davis v. Wyeth Laboratories, Inc.* represent good public policy? Is the decision likely to have an effect on the prevalence of polio in the United States?

14. What is the appropriate remedy for breach of a duty to warn based on autonomy rather than safety? The opinion in *Davis v. Wyeth Laboratories, Inc.* contemplates awarding compensation for harm caused by polio. Is that an appropriate remedy? Under the rationale of *Davis,* the fundamental harm to Mr. Davis was an interference with his dignitary interest in making fully informed decisions. There was no interference with his interest in avoiding physical illness because the failure to warn did not increase his risk of contracting polio. Why should compensation for interference with his dignitary interest be based on the magnitude of his physical injury? Would a more appropriate measure of damages be the sum of money necessary to repair the harm to his dignity?

15. Is the action for failure to give an autonomy-based warning limited to people, like Mr. Davis, who suffered a physical injury? Every person who took the Wyeth vaccine had their autonomy interfered with because of the failure to warn. Other torts, such as assault and battery, protect purely dignitary interests. Why not give each vaccinated person a cause of action that awards damages based on impairment of their dignitary interest?

16. Is the action for failure to give an autonomy-based warning limited to cases involving information about risks of physical harm? What about other information that reasonable people would want to take into account when deciding whether to buy a product? Suppose, for example, that a shoe manufacturer fails to disclose that it uses child labor in manufacturing its products. A customer purchases shoes without knowing that children made them, but he would not have bought the shoes if he had known. Should he have a cause of action against the manufacturer, for interference with his autonomy, because the manufacturer failed to warn him that the shoes were made by children? If not, why not? The customer's decision to buy the shoes is no more voluntary than was Mr. Davis' decision to use the vaccine.

17. For general treatments of liability for failure to warn, see Gershonowitz, The Strict Liability Duty To Warn, 44 Wash. & Lee L.Rev. 71 (1987); Henderson and Twerski, Doctrinal Collapse in Products Liability: The Emp-

ty Shell of Failure to Warn, 65 N.Y.U.L.Rev. 265 (1990); Madden, The Duty to Warn in Products Liability: Contours and Criticism, 89 W.Va.L.Rev. 221 (1987); Noel, Products Defective Because of Inadequate Directions or Warnings, 23 Sw.L.J. 256 (1969); Twerski, Weinstein, Donaher, Piehler, The Use and Abuse of Warnings in Products Liability—Design Defect Litigation Comes of Age, 61 Cornell L.Rev. 495 (1976); Sales, The Duty To Warn And Instruct For Safe Use In Strict Tort Liability, 13 St. Mary's L.J. 521 (1982).

DOSIER v. WILCOX & CRITTENDON CO.
Court of Appeals of California, First District, 1975.
45 Cal.App.3d 74, 119 Cal.Rptr. 135.

ARATA, ASSOCIATE JUSTICE.

Plaintiff–appellant Edward Dosier takes this appeal from a judgment for defendants Wilcox–Crittendon Company and North and Judd Manufacturing Company in a personal injury action based on strict liability. Plaintiff's complaint against these defendants as manufacturers of an alleged "hook" is framed in two causes of action; the first is based upon a claimed defect and the second is based upon a failure to warn. The evidence reveals that North and Judd are engaged principally in the manufacture of harness and saddlery hardware, belt buckles, shoe buckles, dog leads, handbag hardware, hooks and eyes for men's trousers and a line of plastics used for electrical fittings. Wilcox–Crittendon is a wholly-owned subsidiary of North and Judd. The "hook" involved in this case was manufactured by North and Judd, and bears the company's trademark. It is described in its catalog as a No. 333 snap. The snap, hereinafter referred to as "hook" is made of cast malleable iron * * *. It is manufactured principally to be used as a bull tie, stallion chain or cattle tie; it is distributed or marketed through wholesale hardware houses, and houses that sell harness and saddlery wares. The particular "hook" at issue in this case was purchased by a buyer for United Air Lines for its plant maintenance shop at San Francisco Airport for use in connection with a "safety rope around a workstand." It was bought from Keystone Brothers, a harness and saddlery wares outlet in San Francisco in 1964. At the time of the purchase the "hook" was selected by the buyer from a display board featuring harness equipment such as bridles, spurs and bits; there was no discussion as to intended use when the purchase was made. The buyer was familiar with this type of "hook" as a result of his earlier experience on a farm.

On March 28, 1968, the plaintiff, as an employee of United Air Lines, was working with a crew installing a grinding machine at its maintenance plant. As part of the rigging process, he attached the "hook" to a 1700 pound counterweight and lifted it to a point where it was suspended in the air. At this point plaintiff reached under the suspended counterweight in search of a missing bolt when suddenly the "hook" gave way and the counterweight fell on his arm causing the injuries for which he seeks damages. The "hook" was supplied to plaintiff by a plant foreman as part of a sling; there was no marking on the "hook" as to its content or lifting capacity.

Plaintiff–appellant states the issues on appeal as follows: "1. Whether the hook was defective because defendants failed to provide warnings of its proper use and capacity; and 2. Whether plaintiff's use of the hook for lifting was reasonably foreseeable by the manufacturer." An analysis of these two issues as stated reveals that there is one common element in both; *i.e., whether the "hook" was being used in a way intended by the manufacturer.* In order to invoke the doctrine of strict liability, the plaintiff must prove that the product was being used, at the time of injury, in a way the manufacturer intended it to be used. [Citations] In applying this rule our courts have held that it should not be narrowly applied and that even an "unusual use" which the manufacturer *is required to anticipate* should not relieve the manufacturer of liability in the absence of warnings against such use. [Citations] Just what a manufacturer is "required to anticipate" in connection with the use of a product is a question of reasonable foreseeability: [Citations] It has been repeatedly held that the foreseeability of the misuse of a product is a question for the trier of fact. [Citations]

One of plaintiff–appellant's main complaints on appeal is that the trial judge committed prejudicial error by receiving evidence concerning the circumstances surrounding the purchase of the "hook" and its use by United. We cannot agree. In deciding whether or not a product is being used in a way the manufacturer intended it to be used, the market for which it is produced is a most important consideration. This bears directly upon the issue of foreseeability. In commenting on this point in Helene Curtis Industries v. Pruitt (1967) 5 Cir., 385 F.2d 841, 860, the court said: "The intended marketing scheme is one basis for deciding which users can be foreseen." The importance and relevancy of the "marketing scheme" is recognized in Johnson v. Standard Brands Paint Co., *supra,* 274 Cal.App.2d 331 at p. 338, 79 Cal.Rptr. 194 at p. 198, where the court said: " * * * there was substantial evidence to support the jury's implied finding that the decedent was *within the ambit of those entitled to protection from the risk created by the distribution and sale of the defective ladder * * *.*" [Emphasis added.]

The logic of the conclusion that the marketing scheme of the manufacturer is relevant in cases involving strict liability was demonstrated at the time of the enunciation of the rule in Greenman v. Yuba Products, *supra,* 59 Cal.2d 57 at p. 63, 27 Cal.Rptr. 697, at p. 701, 377 P.2d 897, at p. 901: "The purpose of such liability is to insure that the costs of injuries resulting from defective products are borne by manufacturers that put such products on the market rather than by injured persons who are powerless to protect themselves." And, again, in Vandermark v. Ford Motor Co. (1964) 61 Cal.2d 256, 262, 37 Cal.Rptr. 896, 899, 391 P.2d 168, 171: "Retailers like manufacturers are engaged in the business of distributing goods to the public. They are an integral part of the overall producing and marketing enterprise that should bear the cost of injuries resulting from defective products." From the foregoing it should be evident that in order to distribute the cost, the manufacturer must be able to identify and anticipate the particular market. Therefore evidence of the method of distribution of the product is relevant.

* * *

In concluding, we analyze this case upon the issues as stated in plaintiff-appellant's opening brief: " * * * the main issues to be determined by the jury were: 1. Whether the hook was defective because defendants failed to provide warnings of its proper use and capacity; 2. Whether plaintiff's use of the hook for lifting was reasonably foreseeable to the manufacturer." It should be obvious that the second issue, foreseeability of the use, is the main issue in this case, because there is no duty to warn against a use that is not reasonably foreseeable. * * * Since the issue of foreseeability was a question of fact submitted to the jury on evidence * * * sufficient to support a finding of nonforeseeability, the general verdict in favor of defendants is conclusive against plaintiffs * * *.

For the foregoing reasons the judgment is affirmed.

DRAPER, P.J., and HAROLD C. BROWN, J., concur.

Notes

1. In risk-utility jurisdictions, misuse is relevant in failure to warn cases in the same way as in design cases. That is, courts require product manufacturers to guard against risks created by intended uses and foreseeable misuses of their products. Where it is not practical to design the product in such a way as to eliminate the risk created by foreseeable misuse and intervening causes, the manufacturer may still have to warn about the dangers. *E.g.,* Anderson v. Klix Chemical Co., 256 Or. 199, 472 P.2d 806 (1970) (manufacturer must warn that cleaning product should not be applied with a sprayer). As *Dosier* illustrates, if the misuse or intervening cause is unforeseeable, the product may not be defective at all.

2. What if the hook in *Dosier* had been sold in a hardware store?

2. ADEQUACY OF WARNING

In order for a warning to be adequate it must make the product reasonably safe for both its intended and its foreseeable uses. A warning achieves this objective if it has the following characteristics. First, it must be displayed in such a way as to reasonably catch the attention of the persons expected to use the product. Second, it must fairly apprise a reasonable user of the nature and extent of the danger. Third, it must instruct the user as to how to use the product in such a way as to avoid the danger. *See* Madden, The Duty to Warn in Products Liability: Contours and Criticism, 89 W.Va.L.Rev. 221, 310–320 (1987); Noel, Products Defective Because of Inadequate Directions or Warnings, 23 Sw.L.J. 256, 283–288 (1969).

The following cases illustrate the way courts apply these principles.

SPRUILL v. BOYLE–MIDWAY, INC.
United States Court of Appeals, Fourth Circuit, 1962.
308 F.2d 79.

J. Spencer Bell, Circuit Judge.

This is an appeal by the defendants, Boyle–Midway, Incorporated, and American Home Products Corporation, from a judgment of the District Court for the Eastern District of Virginia entered upon a jury verdict for the plaintiffs in a wrongful death action. The defendants having preserved their rights by proper motions throughout the trial now ask us to set aside the judgment and rule that the case ought properly not to have gone to the jury; or that if it was properly submitted to the jury that the evidence in the case does not support the verdict.

The defendants are manufacturers and distributors of a product identified as "Old English Red Oil Furniture Polish". The plaintiffs in the court below were the parents and siblings of a fourteen months old infant who died as a result of chemical pneumonia caused by the ingestion of a small quantity of the defendants' product.

The mother of the deceased stated that she had purchased the polish on the morning of November 13, 1959, and later in the day was using it in her home to polish furniture. While using it in the deceased's bedroom she noticed a catalog which her mother had asked to see. While still in the course of polishing the furniture, she left the room and took the catalog next door to her mother's home. She testified that she was out of the room for four or five minutes.

At the time she left the room the deceased was in his crib in one corner of the room which was near one end of a bureau. The child could reach the end of the bureau nearest the crib but could not reach articles beyond the very edge of the bureau. The mother placed the polish, prior to leaving the room, upon the end of the bureau that was out of the child's reach. When she returned she found that the child had pulled a cover-cloth which was on the bureau into the crib, and the bottles and other articles sitting on the cloth came into the crib with it. The child had removed the cap of the bottle and had consumed a small portion of the polish.

The child was admitted to a hospital that same day, and according to the testimony of Dr. Barclay ultimately died on November 15th from hydrocarbon pneumonia. This particular type of pneumonia is a form of chemical pneumonia which usually results from the ingestion or inhalation of a petroleum distillate.

Old English Red Oil Furniture Polish is a liquid of a bright cherry red color contained in a clear glass bottle which is about 6¾ tall and 2¼ in diameter. The bottle has a red metal cap. The evidence shows that there are one and one-half to two threads upon the neck of the bottle and the cap.

The ingredients of Old English Red Oil Furniture Polish are 98.2% mineral seal oil, 1.8% cedar oil, a trace of turpentine, and oil soluble red dye. Chemical analysis of the product states: "This preparation consists almost entirely of [a] petroleum distillate which is somewhat heavier than kerosene and commonly designated as Mineral Seal Oil, or 300 degree oil, as it distills near 300 degrees C."

The label consists of a piece of paper of deep red hue which passes completely around the bottle at its center. On the front part of the label appear the words "Old English Brand Red Oil Furniture Polish" in large letters; beneath this in small letters "An all purpose polish for furniture, woodwork, pianos, floors". The reverse side of the label, the background of which is white, contains the following printed matter: at the top in red letters about $\frac{1}{8}$th of an inch in height, all in capitals, "CAUTION COMBUSTIBLE MIXTURE". Immediately beneath this in red letters $\frac{1}{16}$ th of an inch high "Do not use near fire or flame"; several lines down, again in letters $\frac{1}{16}$th of an inch in height, in brown ink, all in capitals, the word "DIRECTIONS"; then follow seven lines of directions printed in brown ink in letters about $\frac{1}{32}$nd of an inch in height. On the eighth line in letters $\frac{1}{16}$th of an inch high in brown ink appear the words "Safety Note"; following this in letters approximately $\frac{1}{32}$nd of an inch in height:

> "Contains refined petroleum distillates. May be harmful if swallowed, especially by children."

Following this is the name of the manufacturer and various other information with which we are not here concerned.

There was testimony that mineral seal oil is a toxic substance, and that it is a petroleum distillate. The defendants' expert chemists testified that one teaspoonful of this product would kill a small child. There was uncontroverted evidence of several doctors that the child died of hydrocarbon pneumonia resulting from the ingestion of the defendants' polish. Dr. Julius Caplan, one of the doctors treating the deceased, attributed death to the nature of the polish, and stated that because of its toxic quality it was capable of penetrating the intestinal tract, thus getting into the blood stream and thereby setting up fatal lung damage. Dr. James Morgan, another treating physician, testified that this polish contained a hydrocarbon that was toxic and that such resulted in the death of the child.

The mother testified that she had no knowledge that the defendants' product would have caused injury or death to her child. She stated that she had read the statement at the top of the label in large colored letters "Caution Combustible", but did not read the directions because she knew how to use furniture polish.

At the trial the plaintiffs were allowed to put into evidence certain interrogatories they had served upon the defendants together with the defendants' answers and admissions which showed that the defendants had knowledge or notice of at least thirty-two cases of chemical pneumonia since 1953 resulting from the ingestion of this product. Ten of these thirty-two cases resulted in death. At least seven of these thirty-two cases were infants; four of these infants died as a result of chemical pneumonia. The defendants vigorously objected to the admission of this testimony, and on this appeal assigned its admission as error.

The jury in returning its verdict excluded the mother from sharing in any part of the judgment. The defendants made no request for a special verdict; therefore, the jury returned a general verdict. It was in favor of the plaintiffs other than the child's mother.

* * *

The defendants here have at no time raised the issue of lack of privity between themselves and the deceased and it appears that the point is conceded. In any event it is apparent that this case comes within the exception to the doctrine of Winterbottom v. Wright, 10 Mees & W. 109, 152 Eng.Reprint 402 (1842) which is made for inherently dangerous products. There can be no doubt but that this exception to that doctrine is well established in Virginia. General Bronze Corp. v. Kostopulos, 203 Va. 66, 122 S.E.2d 548 (1961); Norfolk Coca–Cola Bottling Works v. Krausse, 162 Va. 107, 173 S.E. 497 (1934); Robey v. Richmond Coca–Cola Bottling Works, 192 Va. 192, 64 S.E.2d 723 (1951). Indeed it is significant to note that the product involved in the leading case of Thomas v. Winchester, 6 N.Y. 397, 57 Am.Dec. 455 (1852), which firmly established the exception made for inherently dangerous products, was a poison.

Within the last year the courts of Virginia held that the test of whether a product is inherently dangerous is whether, "the danger of injury stems from the product itself, and not from any defect in it." General Bronze Corp. v. Kostopulos, supra. We hold that the danger of injury from the product stems from the product itself and not from any defect arising out of, or resulting from, negligence in the course of manufacture. It is therefore, an inherently dangerous product.

The defendants have contended throughout that they are liable only for injuries caused in the course of the intended use of their product. Since their product was not intended to be consumed, they say, there is no liability for death or injury resulting from consumption of it. We agree with the general principle but the application the defendants would have us make of it here is much too narrow. "Intended use" is but a convenient adaptation of the basic test of "reasonable foreseeability" framed to more specifically fit the factual situations out of which arise questions of a manufacturer's liability for negligence. "Intended use" is not an inflexible formula to be apodictically applied to every case. Normally a seller or manufacturer is entitled to anticipate that the product he deals in will be used only for the purposes for which it is manufactured and sold; thus he is expected to reasonably foresee only injuries arising in the course of such use.

However, he must also be expected to anticipate the environment which is normal for the use of his product and where, as here, that environment is the home, he must anticipate the reasonably foreseeable risks of the use of his product in such an environment. These are risks which are inherent in the proper use for which his product is manufactured. Thus where such a product is an inherently dangerous one, and its danger is not obvious to the average housewife from the appearance of the product itself, the manufacturer has an obligation to anticipate reasonably foreseeable risks and to warn of them, though such risks may be incidental to the actual use for which the product was intended. As the courts of Virginia have stated it,

> "The common law requires a higher degree of care and vigilance in dealing with a dangerous agency than is required in the ordinary affairs of life and business which involve small risk of injury." American Oil Co. v. Nicholas, 156 Va. 1, 157 S.E. 754, 757 (1931). See also Standard Oil Co. v. Wakefield, 102 Va. 824, 47 S.E. 830, 66 L.R.A. 792 (1904).

We have no doubt but that under the circumstances of its use the courts of Virginia would regard Old English Red Oil Furniture Polish as a dangerous agency. A very small quantity of it is lethal to children and extremely dangerous to adults, yet the product gives no indication by its appearance of its life endangering capacity. It appears as harmless as a bottle of soft drink, yet this product is sent daily into thousands of homes in which dwell persons incompetent to safely judge its capacity for harm. It goes there without any reasonable indication from its natural character of its death dealing power if improperly used. It would be quite reasonable to anticipate that in the process of using it for its intended purpose it would be placed in close proximity to children. *They* certainly cannot be expected to recognize it as a lethal poison. Under these circumstances we think that a reasonable jury could properly find that it was foreseeable that sooner or later some child would draw the fatal draught.

* * *

However, even though a reasonable manufacturer should have foreseen that the product would have been consumed by humans, that manufacturer may not be liable if it has adequately warned of the danger to be reasonably foreseen. But a mere indication of danger, in and of itself, does not accomplish an inevitable tergiversation of liability. If warning of the danger is given and this warning is of a character reasonably calculated to bring home to the reasonably prudent person the nature and extent of the danger, it is sufficient to shift the risk of harm from the manufacturer to the user. To be of such character the warning must embody two characteristics: first, it must be in such form that it could reasonably be expected to catch the attention of the reasonably prudent man in the circumstances of its use; secondly, the content of the warning must be of such a nature as to be comprehensible to the average user and to convey a fair indication of the nature and extent of the danger to the mind of a reasonably prudent person.

The only protection available to children living in homes where this product is used is the caution of their parents, who are incapable of recognizing this harmless looking product for the dangerous agency it is. Without additional warning these adults have not the knowledge to invoke their caution on behalf of their young.

Under such circumstances as these the Virginia Courts have imposed upon the manufacturer or seller of the product a duty to warn of the danger.

> "A person who knowingly sells or furnishes an article which, by reason of defective construction *or otherwise,* is eminently dangerous to life or property, *without notice or warning of the defect or danger,* is liable to third persons who suffer therefrom." (Emphasis added). McClanahan v. California Spray–Chemical Corp., [194 Va. 842, 75 S.E.2d 712 (1953)]; quoting with approval, 3 Cooley, Torts, § 498 at 467 (4th ed., 1932).

Where one is under a duty to warn another of danger and he fails to perform this duty by giving adequate warning, he is liable to the person to whom the duty is owed for injuries he suffers due to ignorance of the danger. Low Moor Iron Co. v. La Bianca, 106 Va. 83, 55 S.E. 532 (1906). The sufficiency of the warning is to be judged on the basis of the nature of the danger, and the degree of care required is "commensurate with the risk therefrom reasonably to be foreseen". Sadler v. Lynch, 192 Va. 344, 64 S.E.2d 664 (1951).

The duty to call attention to the danger is properly on defendant under the Virginia law. Moreover the question of the sufficiency of the warning is normally for the jury. McClanahan v. California Spray–Chemical Corp., supra; American Oil Co. v. Nicholas, supra; C.F. Maize v. Atlantic Refining Co., 352 Pa. 51, 41 A.2d 850, 160 A.L.R. 449 (1945) quoted with approval in McClanahan, supra. See generally Dillard and Hart, "Product Liability: Directions For Use And The Duty To Warn", 41 Va.L.Rev. 145, 177–78 (1955).

* * *

Keeping in mind the nature of the danger as described above we think reasonable men could properly differ as to the sufficiency of the notice here given, and that the finding of insufficiency of notice made by the jury in this case is amply supported by the evidence. The notice here given was not printed on the label in such a manner as to assure that a user's attention would be attracted thereto. Indeed, we think one might reasonably conclude that it was placed so as to conceal it from all but the most cautious users. It is located in the midst of a body of print of the same size and color, with nothing to attract special attention to it except the words "Safety Note".

Further, even if the user should happen to discover the warning it states only "contains refined petroleum distillates. May be harmful if swallowed especially by children". The first sentence could hardly be taken to convey any conception of the dangerous character of this product to the average user. The second sentence could be taken to indicate to the average person that harm is not certain but merely possible. The expert medical evidence in this case shows that "harm" will not be contingent but rather inevitable, to young and old alike. Moreover, the last phrase of the sentence hardly conveys the thought that a very small quantity of the polish is lethal to children.

There were two elements of danger inherent in this product, first, its character as a lethal poison, and second, its combustibility. We think that a reasonable jury could conclude that the greater danger in the environment of the modern home, and therefore the danger which due caution would require to be given the greater prominence on the label, was its poisonous character. Certainly a reasonable jury could conclude that this danger was required to be given a prominence at least *equal* to that arising from its combustible nature. A jury convinced that the poisonous character of this polish poses the greater danger could reasonably conclude that a manufacturer which hides its warning of the greater danger within its warning of the lesser is indulging its mercantile interests at the expense of the duty of due care it owes to the purchasing public.

The defendants contend, however, that,

> "The question of the sufficiency of the warning is alleviated by the mother's admission that she never read the label. Not having availed herself of the information contained on the bottle she cannot be permitted to ask for a more explanatory label."

The short answer to this is that where the manufacturer is obligated to give an adequate warning of danger the giving of an inadequate warning is as complete a violation of its duty as would be the failure to give any warning. In this case had the warning been in a form calculated to attract the user's attention, due to its position, size, and the coloring of its lettering, and had the words used therein been reasonably calculated to convey a conception of the true nature of the danger, this mother might not have left the product in the presence of her child. Indeed, she might not have purchased the product at all, a fact of which the manufacturer appears to be aware. Having deprived the mother of an adequate warning which might have prevented the injury, it cannot be permitted to rely upon a warning which was insufficient to prevent the injury. This is the reasoning behind the rule laid down by the courts of Virginia that, " * * * [A]n insufficient warning is in legal effect no warning". Sadler v. Lynch, 192 Va. 344, 347, 64 S.E.2d 664, 666 (1951); McClanahan v. California Spray–Chemical Corp., supra. The jury in this case could reasonably find that the warning given was insufficient both in form and in content, and did, in fact, so find. The warning being insufficient, defendants cannot be permitted to take aid and comfort from it to any extent.

* * *

Perceiving no error by the court below, we

Affirm.

Notes

1. *Spruill's* treatment of the adequacy of the warning is excellent and up to date. The requirement in *Spruill* that the product be "inherently dangerous" in order for there to be a duty to warn is a vestige of the past. This characterization is no longer necessary to avoid the rule that the parties be in privity of contract. Gardner v. Q.H.S., Inc., 448 F.2d 238, 242 (4th Cir.1971).

2. In some jurisdictions the "inherent danger" requirement produced an attempt to make a sharp distinction between negligent manufacturing of a flawed product and negligent failure to warn. A product was "inherently dangerous" if it was dangerous even though properly made. Liability arose for failure to warn about such dangers rather than for improper manufacture. If a product was not dangerous unless defectively manufactured, liability was for negligence in causing the defect, not for failure to warn. *See* Dillard and Hart, Product Liability: Directions for Use and the Duty to Warn, 41 Va.L.Rev. 145, 153 (1955).

3. Most courts no longer make this distinction. They recognize that even a defective product may sometimes safely be used for some purposes, but not for others. Such a product may often reasonably be marketed if it is accompanied by warnings against unsafe uses. *See* Restatement of Torts (Second) § 388 (1965). The modern statement of the rule is that there is a duty to warn against significant risks if the absence of the warning is likely to make the product unduly dangerous. Madden, The Duty to Warn in Products Liability: Contours and Criticism, 89 W.Va.L.Rev. 221, 234–235 (1987).

4. **Relationship Between Design and Warning Theories.** In many cases there is a very close relationship between product defect because of a failure to warn and product defect because of design. *See* Twerski, Weinstein, Donaher, Piehler, The Use and Abuse of Warnings in Products Liability—Design Defect Litigation Comes of Age, 61 Cornell L.Rev. 495, 500–505 (1976). In *Spruill*, for example, the warning was inadequate in large part because of the way the product was designed. Its red color made it more appealing to children than other polishes, and its formula made it much more poisonous to children than one would expect. The warning might have been sufficient if the polish had been far less toxic and a different color. One might even argue that the polish was defective and unreasonably dangerous because of its color and toxicity. If the jury found this to be true, then the product would be defective both in design and for a failure to warn. Another possibility is a finding that the design is reasonable, but only if an adequate warning is given. In this event, the polish would be defective because of a failure to warn only.

It is because of this close relationship between the two theories that plaintiffs frequently sue in the alternative, claiming that the product is defective both because of the way it is designed and because of a failure to warn. The warning theory is particularly appealing in such cases because it may be easier to persuade a jury that the manufacturer should change his warning than that he should change his design.

5. There are some products where the design is clearly unreasonable regardless of what warning is given. Should manufacturers of such products be able to escape liability by giving a sufficient warning? The Restatement (Third) of Torts: Products Liability § 2 Comment l says that the warning should not insulate the manufacturer from liability. Several courts agree. *See* Brownlee v. Louisville Varnish Co., 641 F.2d 397 (5th Cir.1981) (Alabama law; aerosol spray paint can without a relief valve to protect against explosion in the event that it is subjected to excessive heat); Heckman v. Federal Press Co., 587 F.2d 612 (3d Cir.1978) (Pennsylvania law; power press without a guard to protect the worker's hand from the ram); *contra*, Curcio v. Caterpillar, Inc., 344 S.C. 266, 543 S.E.2d 264 (2001) (track loader without an interlock safety device); *See*, Note, The Interrelationship Between Design Defects and Warnings in Products Liability Law: *Abbot v. American Cyanamid Co.*, 11 Geo.Mason U.L.Rev. 171 (1989). Should the answer depend on whether the court uses consumer expectations or risk-utility as the test of defect?

6. As *Spruill* indicates, manufacturers have a duty to warn against foreseeable misuse. This is now generally accepted. *See, e.g.,* Knowles v. Harnischfeger Corp., 36 Wash.App. 317, 674 P.2d 200 (1983) (using a crane to lift a person). Manufacturers also, of course, must warn against generic risks associated with the proper use of their products. *See, e.g.,* Borel v. Fibreboard Paper Products Corp., 493 F.2d 1076 (5th Cir.1973), cert. denied, 419 U.S. 869, 95 S.Ct. 127, 42 L.Ed.2d 107 (1974) (risk that inhaling asbestos can cause asbestosis and cancer).

EDWARDS v. CALIFORNIA CHEMICAL CO.
District Court of Appeal of Florida, Fourth District, 1971.
245 So.2d 259, cert. denied, 247 So.2d 440 (Fla.1971).

WALDEN, JUDGE.

This negligence case was terminated in the trial court by entry of summary judgment against the plaintiff. He appeals. We reverse because of the existence of genuine issues of material fact that preclude summary disposition.

A summary judgment review of the record reveals that plaintiff, an illiterate, labored at the Boca Raton Hotel and Country Club taking care of the golf course grounds. He became ill from arsenic poisoning following use of Ortho Standard Lead Arsenate. This product was manufactured by the defendant, California Chemical Co., and was sold and distributed by the defendant, Hector Supply Co.

Lead arsenate is highly toxic. It can be absorbed into the body by inhalation, contact with unbroken skin and digestion. To safely use the product the user must wear protective clothing and employ a respirator.

The gravamen of plaintiff's complaint and the crux of this appeal centers upon the defendant's failure to warn the plaintiff of the necessity for a user to employ a respirator and protective rubber or neoprene clothing. More particularly, we must decide if the warning contained upon the product's label was a sufficient warning as a matter of law so as to entitle defendants to summary judgment.

On one side of the bag containing the lead arsenate were printed lengthy and specific instructions for use as an insecticide as concerns its application to various agricultural crops including that of lawns and golf greens, as follows:

"ORTHO® STANDARD LEAD ARSENATE
READ ENTIRE LABEL. USE STRICTLY IN ACCORDANCE WITH CAUTIONS, WARNINGS AND DIRECTIONS, AND WITH APPLICABLE STATE AND FEDERAL REGULATIONS. USES, TIMING AND DOSAGE MAY VARY AS A CONSEQUENCE OF LOCAL WEATHER OR CONDITIONS; WE RECOMMEND REFERENCE TO LOCAL AGRICULTURAL AUTHORITIES CONCERNING SPECIFIC USAGE.

DIRECTIONS

Official recommendations for the use and dosage of Lead Arsenate vary in different sections. Use ORTHO Standard Lead Arsenate according to the standard practices in your locality for the control of those insects against which Lead Arsenate is effective. The following general directions are suggested as a guide for the use of this material.

APPLES, PEARS, QUINCES: Codling Moth, Leafrollers, Plum Curculio, Tent Caterpillars--Use 3 lbs. to 100 gals. water for Calyx and cover sprays. For Apple Maggot-Use 2 lbs. per 100 gals. Consult your ORTHO Fieldman or your local Agricultural Authority in regard to the number and dates of applications. Californis Oak Moth, Red Humped Caterpillar and Tent Caterpillar-Use 3 to 4 lbs. to 100 gals. water when insects first attack foliage.

CHERRIES (Eastern States): Cherry Maggot--2 1/2 lbs. to 100 gals. water. Apply according to local recommendations.

GRAPES: Achemon Sphinx Moth, Grape Root Worm, Grape Leaf Folder--Use 3 to 4 lbs. to 100 gals. water. (400 gals. diluted spray per acre) when insects first attack foliage. Do not apply after edible parts start to form.

WALNUTS: Codling Moth (California)--2 to 3 lbs. in 100 gals. water. (1500 gals. diluted spray per acre). Combine with 1/2 lb. safener, DELMO-Z Spray or ORTHO Spray Lime and 1/3 gal. ORTHOL-K Light Medium Flowable Emulsion plus 1/2 lb. ORTHO DDT 50 Wettable for first bloom spray usually early May. Under severe conditions a second application may be needed during late June. Do not apply to walnuts after the husks open.

POTATOES, TOMATOES: Colorado Potato Beetle, Armyworms, Tomato Fruitworm, Sphinx Moth--Use 4 to 6 lbs. either alone or with about 3 lbs. of ORTHO Spray Lime in 100 gals. water. Use no more than 200 gals. diluted spray per acre. For Small Quantity Dosage-Use 2 level teaspoonfuls to 1 qt. water (8 level teaspoonfuls (3 1/3 tablespoonfuls) to 1 gal. water). Tomato Fruitworm-Treat up to harvesting. For dusting Potatoes for above pests: Use this material as it comes from the package at the rate of 5 to 7 lbs. per acre, or mixed with from 3 to 5 times as much ORTHO Spray Lime.

LAWNS AND GOLF GREENS: Sod Webworm, Lawn Moth, Cutworms, White Grubs, Earthworms (Night Crawlers)-Use in accordance with the recommendations of local Agricultural Authorities. 5 lbs. per 1000 sq. ft. of turf is the usual rate of application. Japanese Beetle Larvae (Eastern States)--Use 10 lbs. per 1000 sq. ft. Keep children and pets off treated areas until this material has been washed into the soil.

TO MIX: Put water in spray tank slightly above agitator. Start the agitator. Slowly shake the required quantity of ORTHO Standard Lead Arsenate into the water, agitate until a uniform mixture is made, then fill tank with water. Keep the solution constantly agitated while spraying. When combining with ORTHO oil sprays, follow mixing directions on labels.

NOTE: When using on plants having tender foliage, always add from 8 to 10 lbs. ORTHO Spray Lime to each 100 gals. diluted spray. When used alone on plants with hardy, or reasonably hardy, foliage, the addition of Chemically Hydrated Lime in this way is a good practice also.

NOTICE ON CONDITIONS OF SALE: 1. Chevron Chemical Company (manufacturer) warrants that this material conforms to the chemical description on the label and is reasonably fit for use as directed hereon. Manufacturer neither makes, nor authorizes any agent or representative to make, any other warranty, guarantee or representation, express or implied, concerning this material.

2. Because critical, unforeseeable factors beyond the manufacturer's control prevent it from eliminating all risks in connection with the use of chemicals even though reasonably fit for such use, buyer and user acknowledge and assume all risks and liability (except those assumed by the manufacturer under 1 above) resulting from handling, storage, and use of this material. These risks include, but are not limited to, damage to plants, crops and animals to which the material is applied, failure to control pests, damage caused by drift to other plants or crops, and personal injury. Buyer and user accept and use this material on these conditions, whether or not such use is in accordance with directions.   FORM 6158-D"
[A3841]

The product was labeled on the other side, as concerns its warning of danger, as follows:

COLORED
SOLD AS AN INSECTICIDE

Active Ingredient   By Wt.
  Standard Lead Arsenate (PbHAsO4....................95%
Inert Ingredients.................................. 5%
  Lead expressed as Metallic................56.7%
  Arsenic expressed as Metallic.............20.5%
  Water soluble Arsenic expressed
    as Metallic, not more than............... 0.5%
[A3635]

POISON

ANTIDOTE: For Arsenic--Give a tablespoonful of salt in a glass of warm water and repeat until vomit fluid is clear. Then give two tablespoonfuls of Epsom Salt or Milk of Magnesia in water and plenty of milk and water. Have victim lie down and keep quiet. CALL A PHYSICIAN IMMEDIATELY.
DANGER:
    KEEP OUT OF REACH OF CHILDREN
DO NOT INHALE
DO NOT GET ON SKIN
DO NOT TAKE INTERNALLY

WARNING: Poisonous if swallowed. Avoid breathing dust or spray mist. Avoid contact with skin, eyes, or clothing. Wash thoroughly after using. Do not apply to fruits and vegetables except Tomatoes within 30 days of harvest unless otherwise specified. Wash sprayed fruit and vegetables at harvest. Avoid contamination of forage crops and pasture. Do not apply under conditions involving possible drift to food, forage or other plantings that might be damaged or the crops thereof rendered unfit for sale, use or consumption.

DIRECTIONS ON BACK

NET WEIGHT
4 POUNDS

Completely empty bag and dispose of waste pesticide by burying. Burn bag immediately and stay out of smoke. Residue and ashes from burned bags must also be buried.

As can be seen—this without dispute—there was no warning or indication upon the label that a respirator and protective clothing were required for safe use.

It is clear that manufacturers and sellers of inherently dangerous products have a duty to give users a fair and adequate warning of its dangerous potentialities. And clearly plaintiff was within a class who would foreseeably use the product and be harmed in the absence of adequate warning.

Turning to the warning label and the question of its adequacy, we believe that * * * [the adequacy of the warning label is] a question of fact properly to be decided by the jury.

* * *

In the instant case the labelings present an anomalous situation when viewed by a potential user. He is told how to use it as an insecticide but he is not told how to use it with safety.

On one side of the container the label tells him that the product may be used as an insecticide. He is furnished with a careful catalog of twenty-three insects that are controllable by the product. Ten crops are itemized as being amenable to treatment. He is given the exact proportion of arsenate and water that must be blended depending upon the particular insect to be eradicated. He is told with exactness at what stage of growth applications are to be made, depending upon the crop. Additives are prescribed in certain circumstances. He is told the amount of the product to be applied to a given area. He is given the amount of arsenate to be employed per 1000 square feet to be used for certain insects. He is instructed in detail as to how to mix, maintain in suspension, and spray the mixture. In sum, he is told with extreme particularity *how, where, when* and *for what purpose* to use the product as an insecticide.

On the other hand and side, we have the label warning of danger. It is red, and reflects a skull and cross-bones together with a large word, "Poison." The exact label is set forth above. Primarily it admonishes that the product is not to be inhaled, touched to the skin or taken internally. There is a total failure or omission of the defendants to tell or instruct the user as to *how* the product may be safely used. It does not prescribe, as earlier noted, that a respirator and protective clothing must be used.

As a matter of reason and everyday common sense the jury would be authorized, in light of these two labels, to believe that it would be difficult if not impossible, for a user to use the product in the fashions detailed by defendants without in some measure inhaling, touching or ingesting some of the product.

In light of the specific instructions in one area and the failure in the other and more important area to prescribe protective clothing and a respirator and to tell the user *how to safely use the product,* the jury would be warranted in believing that the label warning was inadequate. It could be inferred from the omission that the product was not sufficiently dangerous and virulent to require protective devices or else the label would have so stated and warned. In other words, the jury could determine that the duty to warn under these circumstances could only be fulfilled by putting the user on specific notice as to how the product might be safely used, in addition to its advices as to how it might be efficiently used.

From our survey we feel that only a jury could determine if plaintiff had been fairly and adequately warned. It would have to decide in the language of the Wait case, supra, if the defendants here fulfilled their duty to warn " * * * with a degree of intensity that would cause a reasonable man to exercise for his own safety the caution commensurate with the potential danger." And in the language of the Williams case, supra, " * * * was the degree of warning commensurately proportionate to the potential danger * * *?"

Having considered the complete appellate treatment and discussed the matters that we deem deserving, we reverse and remand for further proceedings consistent herewith.

Reversed and remanded.

REED, J., and WILLIAMS, ROBERT L., ASSOCIATE JUDGE, concur.

Notes

1. There is a distinction between instructions and warnings. A warning apprises the user of the risks associated with the product. Instructions explain how to use the product. As *Edwards* indicates, there is a duty to instruct in addition to a duty to warn when this is reasonably necessary.

Midgley v. S.S. Kresge Co., 55 Cal.App.3d 67, 127 Cal.Rptr. 217 (1976) provides another example. The manufacturer of a child's telescope provided a special filter to be attached to the eyepiece for viewing the sun. The instructions warned against looking at the sun without the filter, but they did not clearly show the proper method of attaching the filter. A 13 year old child bought the telescope. He understood from the warning that he had to use the filter when looking at the sun, but he did not understand how to attach it. He received eye damage because he viewed the sun with the filter improperly attached. The manufacturer was held liable for failing to provide adequate instructions for installation of the sun filter.

2. It is also true that instructions unaccompanied by a warning of the consequences of failing to follow the instructions will result in liability. This is true even if following the instructions would have prevented the accident. This is because the user may fail to understand the significance of failing to follow the instructions. He may, for example, regard the instructions as being concerned with the efficient use of the product, and having nothing to do with safety. Under these circumstances, he may not realize that failing to follow the instructions could lead to an accident. *See* Dillard & Hart, Product Liability: Directions for Use and the Duty to Warn, 41 Va.L.Rev. 145, 147–152 (1955); Noel, Products Defective Because of Inadequate Directions or Warnings, 23 Sw.L.J. 256, 263 (1969). This is illustrated by the following cases.

   A. In Hügel v. General Motors Corp., 190 Colo. 57, 544 P.2d 983 (1975), the rear wheels came off of plaintiff's motor home while it was being driven because the wheel studs sheared. This occurred because the wheel stud bolts were not tightened to the proper torque. The owner's manual stated the proper torque, and prescribed intervals when the torque should be checked. The manual did not explain the risks resulting from a failure to meet the torque requirements. Because of this deficiency, the duty to warn was not satisfied.

   B. In McLaughlin v. Mine Safety Appliances Co., 11 N.Y.2d 62, 226 N.Y.S.2d 407, 181 N.E.2d 430 (1962) defendant manufactured heat blocks designed to revive injured persons. The instructions said to wrap the blocks in insulating material before use. These instructions were inadequate because they did not say that serious burns could result if the insulation was not used.

3. Suppose a manufacturer equips its product with a safety device that adequately protects users from injury. Must it warn against the consequences of circumventing the device? *See* Miller v. Anetsberger Bros., 124 A.D.2d 1057, 508 N.Y.S.2d 954 (1986).

RHODES v. INTERSTATE BATTERY SYSTEM OF AMERICA, INC.

United States Court of Appeals, Eleventh Circuit, 1984.
722 F.2d 1517.

KRAVITCH, CIRCUIT JUDGE:

In this Georgia diversity action plaintiff-appellant Rhodes seeks damages for personal injuries suffered in an explosion occurring when he struck a match and loosened the vent caps on an automobile battery manufactured and distributed by defendant-appellees. Rhodes appeals an order of the district court dismissing his claim on summary judgment. We reverse and remand.

The battery was manufactured by Johnson Controls, Inc. ("Johnson") for distribution by Interstate Battery System of America, Inc. ("Interstate"), which sold the product under its own name. The plastic top of the battery contained two vent caps designed to cover six cell holes leading to the acid below. Permanently embossed into the vent caps is the following warning:

DANGER—EXPLOSIVE GASES

BATTERIES PRODUCE EXPLOSIVE GASES. KEEP SPARKS FLAME, CIGARETTES AWAY. VENTILATE WHEN CHARGING OR USING IN ENCLOSED SPACE. ALWAYS SHIELD EYES WHEN WORKING NEAR BATTERIES.

POISON—CAUSES SEVERE BURNS

CONTAINS SULFURIC ACID. AVOID CONTACT WITH SKIN, EYES OR CLOTHING. ANTIDOTE EXTERNAL—FLUSH WITH WATER. EYES—FLUSH WITH WATER FOR 15 MINUTES AND GET PROMPT MEDICAL ATTENTION. INTERNAL—DRINK LARGE AMOUNTS OF WATER OR MILK, FOLLOW WITH MILK OF MAGNESIA, BEATEN EGG OR VEG. OIL. CALL PHYSICIAN IMMEDIATELY. KEEP OUT OF REACH OF CHILDREN.

The first line in each paragraph of the warning appears in letters approximately twice as large as the remaining text.

Fifteen months prior to the date of Rhodes' injury, his wife purchased the battery and had it installed at a local service station. On the night of the accident, Rhodes stopped after work for two to three hours at a tavern, and when he emerged he discovered the battery was dead. To ascertain whether the battery was low on water, he struck a match to check the fluid level. When the flame was about twelve to fifteen inches from the battery, the battery exploded, covering Rhodes' face and eyes with sulfuric acid.

In his deposition, Rhodes admitted he had not read the warning label. In fact, although he had owned several cars over the years, he stated that he had never seen or read a warning label on an automobile battery.

Rhodes sought recovery in negligence and strict liability against both Johnson and Interstate for their failure to provide an adequate warning of the dangers associated with their product. The defendants maintained Rhodes was precluded from recovery as a matter of law because he failed to read the warning label, which fully and adequately described the inherent dangers of the battery. The district court agreed with the defendants and granted summary judgment on both the negligence and strict liability claims. Concluding that Rhodes' claims present genuine issues of fact as to the adequacy of the warning, we reverse the order of the district court.

I. NEGLIGENCE

Rhodes' negligence theory is predicated on the principle that a manufacturer or supplier is under a duty to inform potential users of the product of any facts making it dangerous. *Kicklighter v. Nails by Jannee, Inc.,* 616 F.2d 734, 740 n. 4 (5th Cir.1980);[1] *Reddick v. White Consolidated Indus., Inc.,* 295 F.Supp. 243, 245 (S.D.Ga.1969). This duty may be breached in either of two ways: (1) failure to take adequate measures to communicate the warning to the ultimate user, or (2) failure to provide a warning that, if communicated, was adequate to apprise the user of the product's potential risks. *Stapleton v. Kawasaki Heavy Indus., Ltd.,* 608 F.2d 571, 573 (1979), *modified on other grounds,* 612 F.2d 905 (5th Cir.1980). Both of these issues are uniformly held to be questions for the jury. *Id.* Nevertheless, the district court ordered summary judgment because under Georgia law Rhodes' failure to read the warning label constituted contributory negligence, thus barring plaintiff's recovery as a matter of law.

The district court relied upon three decisions of the Georgia Court of Appeals holding that any insufficiency in the adequacy of the warning label of a product cannot be the proximate cause of the injury when the plaintiff is contributorily negligent by failing to read the warning. *See Cobb Heating & Air Conditioning Co. v. Hertron Chemical Co.,* 139 Ga.App. 803, 229 S.E.2d 681 (1976); *Parzini v. Center Chemical Co.,* 129 Ga.App. 868, 201 S.E.2d 808 (1973), *rev'd on other grounds,* 234 Ga. 868, 218 S.E.2d 580 (1975); *McCleskey v. Olin Mathieson Chemical Corp.,* 127 Ga.App. 178, 193 S.E.2d 16 (1972). Although these cases do stand for the general proposition that failure to read a warning is contributory negligence, they do not necessarily preclude recovery in this case. The plaintiffs in *Cobb, Parzini* and *McCleskey* did not assert, as Rhodes does here, that the warning was not adequately communicated to the user. Rhodes does not maintain that the warning itself, if communicated, was inadequate to apprise him of the danger. He claims his failure to read the label resulted from the defendants' negligence in communicating the warning, i.e., that other, more effective ways of communicating the battery's dangers were available and should have been employed.[2] If the defendants did not take reasonable steps to communicate the warning to Rhodes, his failure to read it would not constitute contributory negligence. *See Stapleton,* 608 F.2d at 573.

* * *

Cobb, Parzini and *McCleskey* * * * hold only that an injured party cannot claim inadequacy of the contents of a warning if he never bothered to read the warning. They do not bar a claim, such as Rhodes', that an injury was caused by the manufacturer's failure to take appropri-

---

1. The Eleventh Circuit in *Bonner v. City of Prichard,* 661 F.2d 1206, 1209 (11th Cir.1981) (en banc), adopted as binding precedent decisions of the Fifth Circuit rendered prior to October 1, 1981.

2. Rhodes suggests alternative means of communication such as phosphorus paint that would be visible at night, advertising through the media, and verbal or written warnings issued by the seller.

ate measures to communicate the potential risks to the ultimate user. Unlike the plaintiffs in those three cases, Rhodes alleges he was not accustomed to handling this product and did not have the opportunity to view the battery and its accompanying warning under sufficient lighting. His claim is that an embossed warning on the top of the battery is not likely to warn a consumer in his position of the potential dangers and that the defendants were negligent in not attempting to convey the risks in a more effective manner.

Summary judgment is not appropriate unless the moving party demonstrates that there was no genuine issue of any material fact and that he is entitled to judgment as a matter of law. Fed.R.Civ.P. 56(c). Since we have determined that Rhodes is not prevented from asserting a claim based upon the defendants' negligent failure to provide a warning reasonably likely to apprise him of a battery's dangerous qualities, he should be allowed to attempt to persuade a jury to so find. A factual issue exists as to the adequacy of the defendants' adopted means of conveying the warning. It is for the jury to decide whether or not their chosen method was negligent. We therefore reverse the order of summary judgment on plaintiff's negligence claim.

II. Strict Liability

The district court dismissed Rhodes' strict liability claim against Interstate * * *.

The court * * * held "as a matter of law" that the language embossed on the vent caps was an adequate warning of the potential danger to the plaintiff and that the battery was therefore not defective. Its decision apparently was premised upon a number of factual determinations leading to a conclusion that the appropriate place for a warning on an automobile battery is on its cell cover.

It generally has been held that a jury is to determine whether a product is defective, whether the user was aware of the danger, and whether his use of the product in view of this knowledge was unreasonable. *Parzini v. Center Chemical Co.*, 136 Ga.App. 396, 221 S.E.2d 475 (1975). The doctrine of strict liability requires a manufacturer of a dangerous product to use reasonable efforts to bring the warning to the attention of the potential user. A product without such a warning is defective. *Center Chemical Co. v. Parzini*, 234 Ga. 868, 870, 218 S.E.2d 580, 582 (1975). Whether the warning in this case was adequate to apprise an automobile owner of the battery's inherent dangers is a question of fact. A jury could conclude that the danger posed by the emission of flammable gases was sufficiently great that the warning should have been presented in a more effective manner. *See Stapleton*, 608 F.2d at 573. The district court erred in deciding the issue as a matter of law, and its order of summary judgment on plaintiff's strict liability claim must be reversed.

Reversed and Remanded.

JAMES C. HILL, CIRCUIT JUDGE, dissenting:

* * *

The warning embossed on the battery involved in this case is set out in the majority opinion. It not only warned of danger; it cautioned users of the exact danger from which Rhodes' injuries flowed—*i.e.*, the warning importuned users that the battery contained explosive gases which would ignite if exposed to flame.

In order to submit himself to this danger, Rhodes had to remove the battery's vent caps, on which were embossed the explicit warnings. Rhodes admitted that he did not read the warning. Furthermore, in response to questions by the defendants, Rhodes testified:

Q. Have you ever looked at a car battery?

A. I don't mess with batteries.

Q. Well, you've looked at a battery before, haven't you?

A. I've looked at them, but even if there was a warning on it, I wouldn't have paid attention to it.

Q. You wouldn't have paid attention to it?

A. Well, it would have to be a big warning.

Q. What form would the warning have to take for you to pay attention to it?

A. I would say if it said "Warning" and it was in big enough letters, something that I could see, I may pay attention to it, I don't know if I would pay attention to it then.

(R. 21–22) It thus appears that any product manufacturer would have been hard pressed to bring its warning message home to Rhodes.

The law to be applied to these facts is clear. Without exception, the Georgia courts hold that, as a matter of law, a plaintiff's failure to read a warning printed on an injury-producing product constitutes contributory negligence and precludes plaintiff from recovering against the product manufacturer and distributor. *Cobb Heating and Air Conditioning Co. v. Hertron Chemical Co.*, 139 Ga.App. 803, 229 S.E.2d 681 (1976); *Parzini v. Center Chemical Co.*, 129 Ga.App. 868, 201 S.E.2d 808, *rev'd on other grounds*, 234 Ga. 868, 218 S.E.2d 580 (1975); *McCleskey v. Olin Mathieson Chemical Corp.*, 127 Ga.App. 178, 193 S.E.2d 16 (1972). Rhodes, having failed to read the warning embossed on the battery vent caps, is thus barred from recovering against the battery manufacturer and distributor.

In spite of the fact that Rhodes suggests some exotic methods whereby the warning might have been better forced upon him—*e.g.*, using letters printed with phosphorescent paint, etc.—the Georgia cases cited above do not require more of defendants than was done here.[3]

3. We need not decide whether phosphorescent paint on the vent caps of a battery confined in darkness beneath the closed hood of an automobile would absorb enough

Simply stated, the extent of a product manufacturer's exposure to strict liability is not, and can not be, limited only by the scope of a litigant's imagination.

For this very reason, the rule must be that product manufacturers are required to employ warnings that are "reasonably calculated" to reach potential users. *West v. Broderick & Bascom Rope Co.*, 197 N.W.2d 202, 212 (Iowa 1972); Noel, Products Defective Because of Inadequate Directions or Warnings, 23 Sw.L.J. 256, 281–85 (1969); Restatement (Second) of Torts § 388(c) (1965). In most cases, whether a warning is "reasonably calculated" to reach the product's users will present a factual issue precluding summary judgment. For such a determination "depends on the language used and the impression that it is calculated to make upon the mind of the average user of the product and involves questions of display, syntax and emphasis." *Stapleton v. Kawasaki Heavy Industries, Ltd.*, 608 F.2d 571, 573 n. 4 (5th Cir.1979), *modified on other grounds,* 612 F.2d 905 (1980), *quoting, D'Arienzo v. Clairol, Inc.*, 125 N.J.Super. 224, 230–31, 310 A.2d 106, 112 (1973).

However, summary judgment may be entered in any negligence action where the uncontested facts demonstrate that only one result could be supported and that one party is entitled to judgment as a matter of law. *Gross v. Southern Railway Co.*, 414 F.2d 292 (5th Cir.1969); *Atlantic Coast Line Rwy. v. Key,* 196 F.2d 64 (5th Cir.1952). Here, the undisputed facts establish that the battery carried a warning of its dangers, that the warning clearly appeared on the top of the battery (the portion exposed to anyone attempting to service the battery), and that the warning in no uncertain terms cautioned users to keep flame away from the battery. The district court, on these facts, was entitled to hold that, as a matter of law, this warning was "reasonably calculated" to reach potential users.

Under established Georgia law, this action should have ended with the district court granting summary judgment to defendants. * * *

If courts are to continue to function efficiently and to consider and resolve those serious disputes that are presented, they must be allowed to dispose of cases without substantial dispute by summary judgment. Certainly, courts should not be put to the task of conducting a trial each time a litigant suggests that, under some remotely conceivable set of facts, he could recover on his claim or maintain a satisfactory defense to the action. For if left to the fertile imaginations of those scrambling to avoid summary judgment, the standard governing a Rule 56 motion would soon prove to be insurmountable. Fearing that we are fast approaching that standard, I

Dissent.

---

radiated light to return it visibly in the dark of night. Rhodes probably does not suggest that battery manufacturers employ paint containing radium or other sources of self-illumination said to be carcinogenic.

Notes

1. How should a court decide the following case?

Plaintiff stopped to help a stranded motorist. It was evening and the visibility was poor. After discovering that the battery was dead plaintiff looked under the hood. He located the battery and observed the name of the manufacturer. He found the battery caps and removed one or two of them. He went to his car to look for a flashlight, but was unable to find one. He returned, leaned over the battery, lit a cigarette lighter, and the battery exploded. Plaintiff sued the battery manufacturer for failing to provide an adequate warning. A warning label was attached to the top of the battery at the time of the accident. Below is a photograph of the battery and label viewed from the front of the car:

Plaintiff claimed that he did not see the label. The jury found for defendant on the basis that the warning was adequate. Plaintiff appeals, claiming that the finding was against the weight of the evidence. Decide the case.

2. In cases where plaintiff did not read the warning, defendants frequently argue that the alleged inadequacy of the warning did not cause the injury. This causation issue is treated in Chapter 5, Section B. Does *Rhodes* present a causation problem?

3. A warning is not adequate if it minimizes the danger associated with the product. In Gardner v. Q.H.S., Inc., 448 F.2d 238 (4th Cir.1971), defendant manufactured plastic hair rollers filled with paraffin. They were designed to be boiled in water for fifteen minutes before use. The user put them in a pot of water on an electric stove which she set on high. She forgot

about them and the water boiled away. The melted paraffin caught on fire and produced an intense flame that billowed four or five feet above the pan. This caused extensive property damage. The rollers came with the following warning:

> Use plenty of water. Do not let water boil away. Cautionary note: Rollers may be inflammable only if left over flame in pan without water. Otherwise Q.H.S. Setting/Rollers are perfectly safe.

The court held that a jury could conclude that the warning was inadequate. The court said:

> [T]he jury could * * * conclude that the "cautionary note" was inadequate to inform the user to use the extraordinary degree of caution necessary to avoid the dangerous consequences of improper or extraordinary use of the product. It is true that the user was instructed to use plenty of water and not to let the water boil away. But if the user disobeyed these instructions, he was told only that the product "*may*" be inflammable if left over "*flame*" in pan without water; otherwise, the product was "*perfectly* safe." The user was not told that the rollers contained paraffin. Some users would certainly conclude that "flame" did not include electrical heat. The user was not told that there was a strong possibility that the paraffin would ignite if the water boiled away and that flames of a considerable height could erupt if the paraffin ignited. And what cautionary notice was given was in printing of the same size as the general instructions and unobtrusively made part of them.

448 F.2d at 243 (4th Cir.1971).

See also, Borel v. Fibreboard Paper Products Corp., 493 F.2d 1076 (5th Cir.1973), cert. denied, 419 U.S. 869, 95 S.Ct. 127, 42 L.Ed.2d 107 (1974). The manufacturer of an insulation product containing asbestos warned that "Inhalation of asbestos in excessive quantities over long periods of time may be harmful." The court held that this was not adequate to inform insulation workers of the substantial risk of contracting asbestosis and cancer.

4. A warning that is otherwise adequate will not exonerate the manufacturer if he undermines its effectiveness. For example, in Maize v. Atlantic Refining Co., 352 Pa. 51, 41 A.2d 850 (1945) plaintiff's decedent died as a result of inhaling the fumes of a poisonous cleaning fluid named "Safety-Kleen." The name of the product was printed on four sides of the container in large letters. The following warning was printed on the can in much smaller letters:

Caution

Do not inhale fumes. Use only in well ventilated place.

The court held that a jury could find that the warning was inadequate. The prominent display of the word "safety" could well make the cautionary note seem unimportant. It could even prevent the user from reading the entire label. *See also,* Incollingo v. Ewing, 444 Pa. 263, 444 Pa. 299, 282 A.2d 206 (1971) (a proper warning concerning a dangerous prescription drug can be nullified by overpromotion by the drug company's detail men).

BROUSSARD v. CONTINENTAL OIL CO.

Court of Appeal of Louisiana, Third Circuit, 1983.
433 So.2d 354, writ denied, 440 So.2d 726 (La.1983).

STOKER, JUDGE.

This is a personal injury suit by Mildredge T. Broussard against Black & Decker (U.S.), Inc. and The Home Insurance Company. Plaintiff-appellant (Broussard) was badly burned in an explosion of natural gas sparked by a Black & Decker hand drill. Broussard was using the drill while working at a Continental Oil Company (Conoco) plant at Grand Chenier, Louisiana. Plaintiff also sued Conoco and its plant supervisor but reached a settlement agreement with those defendants before trial. * * *

The verdict of the jury at trial was that Black & Decker was not at fault for failure to adequately warn in connection with the accident. Judgment was for the defendants and against plaintiff. * * * [Plaintiff appealed, claiming that the jury committed manifest error in finding that defendant was not at fault for failing to warn adequately.]

We find no error in the jury's verdict * * *. We affirm.

Background Facts

Plaintiff was directly employed by Crain Brothers Construction Company, and the trial court found he was the statutory employee of Conoco. On the day of the accident, plaintiff and four other men, including Sanders Miller, were in the process of building a sump box enclosure at the end of a natural gas vent line (pipe) at the Grand Chenier plant. Plaintiff was a carpenter's helper and Miller was a carpenter. Upon arriving at the site, both men noticed that natural gas could be heard and smelled coming from the vent line. Miller immediately notified Conoco's relief plant foreman about the escaping gas and asked if it could be shut off. The foreman refused to do so because the whole plant would have had to be shut down to prevent the gas from being vented at the location of the sump box. After Miller requested a shut down a second time, the foreman talked to Mr. Leeman, another Conoco employee and the plant supervisor. Miller was again told nothing could be done.

Miller testified that he recognized the danger of working around the flammable natural gas. The workers took what precautions they could to minimize the risk of igniting the natural gas fumes. Cigarettes, cigarette lighters and matches were left in the work vehicles. The vehicles were parked some distance away from the site. A gasoline powered electricity generator was placed at the end of two 50–foot extension cords. Miller warned the plaintiff to be careful not to cause a spark while hammering, especially when the fumes were heavy.

The explosion occurred as plaintiff was standing inside a plywood box loosely held together and being constructed as a concrete form. He was positioned inside the form to drill holes in its sides through which rods were to be inserted. It is not seriously contested that sparks from the drill plaintiff was using ignited the natural gas fumes coming from the vent line. Such sparks are normally emitted from this and similar type drills when the "brushes" inside the armature of the drill contact and slide along the inside surface of the rapidly spinning cylinder in which the brushes sit. There is no evidence, nor is the issue before this Court, that the design which allows the creation and emission of these sparks constitutes a design defect. Rather, the issues relate to the failure to warn on the part of the defendant manufacturer of the hazard of explosion.

Both the plaintiff Broussard and Sanders Miller testified that they were unaware at the time of the accident that sparks from electrical power drills could ignite gaseous atmospheres. Allen Nunez, the relief foreman, likewise testified that neither he nor anyone at the Conoco plant knew of the potential of explosion in a like situation before the accident occurred. However, a warning that would have informed the users of the drill of the precise cause and effect encountered appears in the owner's manual. Black & Decker claim that a copy of this manual is placed in every box containing one of their drills as it leaves the manufacturer's control. See Appendix, Item No. 18.

The owner's manual is not attached to the drill but is loosely placed in the box. Thus, unless the box with the owner's manual inside (or the owner's manual itself, with the safety warnings inside its folded pamphlet form) is kept with the drill, the warning is not available to users other than the buyer. In addition to the owner's manual warning, there is a small notice on the side of the drill which simply reads, "CAUTION: For Safe Operation See Owner's Manual." This notice is approximately one-eighth inch high and one inch long.

Sanders Miller received the drill at the office of the Crain Brothers Construction Company from the secretary who worked in the office. The secretary asked Miller if he wanted the box the drill came in. Miller replied he had no use for it, and the box was thrown away. Neither Miller nor the plaintiff saw the owner's manual.

Did Black & Decker Fail to Provide Adequate Warning?

With reference to adequacy of warning of the danger from the emission of sparks, Black & Decker contends item eighteen in the owner's manual was sufficient. Plaintiff Broussard contends that it was not. Broussard contends that Black & Decker was guilty of fault in not putting the warning on the drill itself. Item eighteen reads as follows:

> "18. DO NOT OPERATE portable electric tools in gaseous or explosive atmospheres. Motors in these tools normally spark, and the sparks might ignite fumes."

The warning set forth in these words is adequate; the question is whether it was sufficient to put it in the owner's manual or whether it was unreasonable under the circumstances not to put this warning on the drill itself. As noted above there was a warning on the drill which read, "CAUTION: For Safe Operation See Owner's Manual."

We are confronted here with the application of absolute liability of a manufacturer. The product, the drill, does not contain a defect in the ordinary sense of design or manufacturing defect, but ordinary use of the drill is dangerous under the factual circumstances which were present in this case, i.e., use in the presence of natural gas fumes. Unreasonable risk is a requirement of strict liability just as it is in negligence. *Entrevia v. Hood*, 427 So.2d 1146 (La.1983); *DeBattista v. Argonaut–Southwest Ins. Co.*, 403 So.2d 26 (La.1981); *Cobb v. Insured Lloyds*, 387 So.2d 13 (La.App.1980); *Hunt v. City Stores, Inc.*, 387 So.2d 585 (La.1980); *Chappuis v. Sears Roebuck & Company*, 358 So.2d 926 (La.1978); *Olsen v. Shell Oil Company*, 365 So.2d 1285 (La.1978) and *Loescher v. Parr*, 324 So.2d 441 (La.1976).

The judicial process involved in deciding whether a risk is unreasonable in strict liability is similar to that employed in determining whether a risk is unreasonable in a traditional negligence problem and in deciding the scope of duty or legal cause under the duty risk analysis. *Entrevia v. Hood*, supra, and *Hunt v. City Stores, Inc.*, supra. Strict liability and negligence are not identical in all respects. A major distinction between the two theories is that the inability of a defendant to know or prevent the risk is not a defense in a strict liability case but precludes a finding of negligence. *Entrevia v. Hood*, supra, and the cases cited therein. Knowledge of the risk is not a problem here for Black & Decker knew of the risk. The question is what was adequate warning.

In *Entrevia v. Hood*, the Supreme Court said:

"The unreasonable risk of harm criterion, however, is not a simple rule of law which may be applied mechanically to the facts of a case. [It is] to be determined after a study of the law and customs, a balancing of claims and interests, a weighing of the risk and the gravity of harm, and a consideration of individual and societal rights and obligations. * * *"

In approaching our decision in this case we accept at face value the assertions of Broussard and Sanders Miller that they were unaware that the drill in question would emit sparks when in operation. Building upon this assertion plaintiff relies heavily on the case of *Chappuis v. Sears Roebuck & Company*, supra, and especially the following pronouncement from that case:

"Absolute liability upon a manufacturer whose product is useful, traditional, but which might become dangerous in some circumstances must be distinguished from the obligation here involved. There may be many tools or other products which become dangerous for normal use in certain conditions. But when the danger is known to the manufacturer and cannot justifiably be expected to be within the knowledge of users generally, the manufacturer must take reasonable steps to warn the user."

In *Chappuis* the ordinary claw hammer, the subject of that case, did have a warning label on the handle. The Louisiana Supreme Court held that the warning was not adequate to put the user on notice of the particular risk involved. The particular risk was that once the steel hammer face became chipped, it is liable to chip again when used and a flying chip might physically injure someone.

The questions before us are:

1. Was adequate warning given through the general caution on Black & Decker's drill directing users to consult the owner's manual for safe operation?

2. If the general warning was not adequate, was it unreasonable for Black & Decker not to place on the drill itself the warning contained in item 18 of its safety rules contained in the owner's manual?

These questions must be tested together as they rest on the same practical considerations.

Plaintiff's own expert witness unwittingly pointed up the difficulty in putting warnings on the drill itself. This expert demonstrated the use of warnings through symbols as opposed to words. The expert devised a series of symbols of his own creation based on international symbols which he suggested could have been placed on the drill itself. The symbols purportedly represent ten of the eighteen warnings Black & Decker set forth in the owner's manual. Plaintiff relies on *Chappuis v. Sears Roebuck & Company,* supra, as support of his contention that such warnings should have been placed on the drill itself.

While we think the use of symbols as suggested by plaintiff's expert merits no consideration, we note that the expert deemed at least ten of the warnings represented by the symbols were worthy of being noted on the drill. The fact that numerous risks other than sparking explosions or fires merit notice is a significant factor. The suggested use of symbols is also significant because the reason for it is the recognition that the space on the drill is not large enough to contain extensive warnings and cautions in words. This factor will be discussed later, but at this point we will state our opinion relative to the efficacy symbols in lieu of words.

Plaintiff's expert testified that the symbols he proposed are neither standard nor easily recognizable by the general public. Further, the testimony indicates that the symbols are unclear and subject to different interpretations. The symbols fail in one aspect of sufficiency according to expert (as distinguished from legal) standards in that they do not inform why the activities are dangerous, just that they are dangerous. Above all, however, we are convinced that the use of symbols would require users of the drill to refer to an owner's manual or other written material to discover what the symbols meant. This would be no more efficacious than what Black & Decker did when it put a caution on the drill directing users to consult the owner's manual for safe operation.

We think counsel for plaintiff recognized lack of merit in the suggested use of symbols. On plaintiff's behalf Exhibit P-17 was introduced in evidence. On the side of this exhibit a label measuring approximately 2⅝ inches by 1¾ inches was affixed on which the following words were typed:

"Safety Rules

- Don't abuse cord
- Wear proper apparel
- Don't use in damp areas
- Use proper extension cords outdoors
- Don't touch metal parts when drilling near any electrical wiring
- Remove tightening key
- Unplug to change bits
- Use safety glasses
- Avoid gaseous areas
- Secure work

SEE MANUAL FOR COMPLETE TEXTS"

The whole of the above quoted material is typed in small letter characters in a slant-wise or diagonal fashion on the label in order to fit. It will be noted that the only reference to the risk of igniting gas from emission of sparks is contained in the three words, "Avoid gaseous areas."

We are not impressed with plaintiff's Exhibit P-17. The most important failing of the exhibit is that the mere words, "Avoid gaseous areas" does not meet the test of the *Chappuis* case because it does not explain or point out the precise risk of injury posed by use in gaseous areas. Moreover, this exhibit graphically illustrates the problem of attempting to put multiple warnings on a hand drill of the size and nature involved.

Defendant considers that more than ten warnings should be given. Nevertheless, if only ten are selected, deficiencies in any scheme for putting them all on the drill become apparent. As a practical matter, the effect of putting at least ten warnings on the drill would decrease the effectiveness of all of the warnings. A consumer would have a tendency to read none of the warnings if the surface of the drill became cluttered with the warnings. Unless we should elevate the one hazard of sparking to premier importance above all others, we fear that an effort to tell all about each hazard is not practical either from the point of view of availability of space or of effectiveness. We decline to say that one risk is more worthy of warning than another.

With the merits and demerits of the arguments urged by the parties in mind, we now decide whether Black & Decker exposed plaintiff to unreasonable risk. We follow the interest balancing procedure discussed in the jurisprudence and most recently in *Entrevia v. Hood,* supra. We conclude that defendant acted reasonably toward plaintiff and all persons who might use its hand drill. In view of the numerous risks which a manufacturer of a hand drill must explicitly describe in *Chappuis* terms, the most practical and effective thing which the manufacturer could do is to direct the user to the owner's manual as Black & Decker did.

For the reasons we have given we hold that the jury's finding of no fault on the part of Black & Decker was correct.

* * *

Decree

For the reasons assigned, the judgment of the trial court is affirmed. All costs of this appeal are to be paid by plaintiff.

Affirmed.

Notes

1. Decide the following case:

Plaintiff, age 14, was injured while riding as a passenger on a small motorcycle. He rode with his feet extending out away from the motorcycle because it had no rear foot rests. The motorcycle hit a bump and his leg bounced backward and was caught between the rear tire and the fender/muffler assembly. As a result his foot suffered burns and abrasions. The driver, also age 14, bought the motorcycle two weeks prior to the accident. Plaintiff sued the manufacturer of the motorcycle claiming that it failed to warn him adequately of the dangers of riding as a passenger on the motorcycle. The gas tank had two decals which read as follows:

WARNING—OPERATOR ONLY—NO PASSENGERS

Remember: Preserve Nature/Always Wear Helmet/Ride Safely/Read Owner's Manual Carefully Before Riding.

The following warning appeared on the inside front cover of the owner's manual:

<blockquote>

Important Notice.

OPERATOR ONLY.

NO PASSENGERS.

</blockquote>

This motorcycle is designed and constructed as an operator-only model. The seating configuration does not safely permit the carrying of a passenger.

Plaintiff understood that the motorcycle was built for only one rider. Neither he nor the owner read the owner's manual. Defendant moves for a summary judgment. How should the court rule?

2. Suppose the jury in *Broussard* had found in favor of the plaintiff, and defendant appealed on the basis that the warning was sufficient as a matter of law. How should the appellate court rule?

Perceptions of Risk and the Effect of Warnings

A. Some Findings from Psychology

A large and diverse body of research, primarily by psychologists, has explored the ways in which people understand and respond to risks. Part of this literature examines how individuals respond to warnings. Much of this research investigates ways in which individuals fail to behave as perfectly rational decision makers.

No one can afford to be perfectly rational in the sense that they catalogue and then appropriately weight every single piece of information bearing on their decision. At best we exhibit bounded rationality. *See,* Herbert Simon, Models of Bounded Rationality (1982). We frequently employ various decision making aids, sometimes called heuristics, to help solve problems. Psychological research has uncovered a number of ways in which such heuristics results in cognitive biases that may distort judgment. *See generally* Daniel Kahneman et al., Judgment Under Uncertainty: Heuristics and Biases (1982); Richard Nisbet & Lee Ross, Human Inference: Strategies and Shortcomings of Social Judgment (1980); Robin Hogarth & Melvin Reder (eds.) Rational Choice: the Contrast Between Economics and Psychology (1987).

A number of these biasing heuristics may play a role in assessing risks. The *availability heuristic* describes the tendency of individuals to ignore statistical background information in favor of particularly vivid, or easily "available" evidence that they can easily recall. If one has never fallen from a ladder, warnings about their danger may be assessed against the background of all the safe times one used the product. It is the availability heuristic that causes people to become relatively dismissive of warnings and instructions concerning products they have used safely for a long time. On the other hand, of course, one fall from a ladder may be so vivid that it overwhelms base-rate information about the probability of risk. For this individual, the same warning may "over-deter" in the sense that he will not use the ladder even in relatively safe situations.

Anchoring is a similar heuristic. When people assess a probability of some event they tend to do so against the background of some starting point, some "anchor." The anchor may come from many sources. One particularly relevant anchor may come from manufacturer advertising. If manufacturer representations create an "anchor" of relative safety, the warnings and instructions accompanying a product may be undervalued. This insight underlies part of Marshall Shapo's insightful representational theory of product liability. Shapo, A Representational Theory of Consumer Protection: Doctrine, Function and Legal Liability for Product Disappointment, 60 Va.L.Rev. 1109 (1974).

When people are informed of the biases that can sometimes result from using heuristics such as anchoring and availability they are able to adjust their decision making and engage in more systematic analysis. Indeed, a body of psychological research, called dual process theory, indicates that depending on the situation, everyone uses both systematic and heuristic decision making processes. *Systematic processing* (sometimes called rational processing) is relatively more analytic, logical, and abstract. *Heuristic processing* (sometimes called experiential processing) is more holistic, associative, and concrete and is more emotionally driven. *See* Shelly Chaiken and Yaacov Trope (eds.) Dual–Process Theories in Social Psychology (1999); Keith Stanovich, Who is Rational: Studies of Individual Differences in Reasoning (1999); Sunstein, Cognition and Cost–Benefit Analysis, 29 J. Legal Stud. 1059 (2000).

The effect of emotions on risk perceptions has been studied extensively by Paul Slovic and his colleagues. People perceive a situation or activity as riskier and in greater need of control when it produces a sense of dread. Dread is the product of a number of factors. People tend to dread risks that produce fatalities or feared diseases such as cancer. They also tend to dread risks that produce global consequences and has effects on future generations. People also perceive activities as riskier when they are perceived to be uncontrollable, not voluntarily encountered, and not well known. *See* Slovic, Fischhoff, & Lichtenstein, Facts and Fears: Understanding Perceived Risk, In Richard C. Schwing & Walter A. Albers, Jr. (eds.) Societal Risk Assessment: How Safe is Safe Enough? 181 (1980); Slovic, Perception of Risk, 236 Science 282 (1987); Slovic, Rational Actors and Rational Fools: The Influence of Affect on Judgment and Decision–Making, 6 Roger Williams U.L.Rev. 163 (2000).

The impact of control and voluntariness on perceptions of risk are connected to what is sometimes called an *optimism bias*. For example, ninety percent of drivers consider themselves to be above average and ninety-seven percent of individuals believe that they are at least average in their ability to avoid bicycle or power-mower accidents. As these examples suggest, optimism is correlated with the perception that a risk is preventable by individual action and the belief of most that one's self-protective actions are more extensive or effective than actions taken by others. Unfortunately, this bias is resistant to efforts to align perceptions to be more in line with actual risks. *See* Viscusi & Magat, Learning About Risk: Consumer and Worker Responses to Hazard Information 95 (1987); Weinstein, Unrealistic Optimism About Susceptibility to Health Problems, 5 J. Behav. Med. 441, 447 (1982); Weinstein, Optimistic Biases About Personal Risks, 246 Science 1232, 1232 (1989); Weinstein & Klein, Resistance of Personal Risk Perceptions to Debiasing Interventions, 14 Health Psychol. 132, 132 (1995).

Emotions also influence our *sensitivity to probability*. Responses to uncertain situations have an all or none characteristic that is sensitive to the possibility rather than the probability of strong positive or negative consequences. Very small probabilities tend to carry great weight. This helps us understand why societal concerns about hazards such as nuclear power and exposure to extremely small amounts of toxic chemicals do not diminish substantially in response to information about the very low probability that the hazard will produce adverse consequences. This also helps us to appreciate the relative advantage of a cheaper product that creates a 1 in 10,000 chance of injury and its competitor that has reduced the likelihood of injury to 1 in 1,000,000. *See* Kraus et al., Intuitive Toxicology: Expert and Lay Judgments of Chemical Risks, 12 Risk Analysis 215 (1992); Loewenstein et al., Risk as Feelings 127, Psychol. Bull. 267 (2001).

One additional finding relevant to warnings is that judgments of risks and benefits are negatively correlated. For many hazards the greater the perceived risk the lower the perceived benefit and vice versa. Smoking, and drinking alcoholic beverages tend to be perceived as relatively high in risk and relatively low in benefit. On the other hand, vaccines and x-rays are perceived to relatively high in benefit and low in risk. As Slovic notes, "This result implies that people base their judgments of an activity or a technology not only on what they think about it but also on what they feel about it. If they like an activity, they are moved to judge the risks as low and the benefits as high; if they dislike it, they tend to judge the opposite—high risk and low benefit." Slovic, Rational Actors and Rational Fools: The Influence of Affect on Judgment and Decision–Making, 6 Roger Williams U. L. Rev. 163, 181 (2000). These results suggest that advertising designed to produce a perception that a product is beneficial will have the effect of reducing perceptions of risk. On the other hand, warnings that point out the risks associated with a product may, if read, cause one to perceive less benefit to the product.

B. Scholarly Legal Response to the Psychological Literature

Several valuable law review articles have used this body of psychological research to suggest changes in products liability law. Professor Howard Latin has provided one of the more useful reviews of the psychological literature. Latin, "Good" Warnings, Bad Products, and Cognitive Limitations, 41 U.C.L.A.L.Rev. 1193 (1994). Latin argues that warning defect law is frequently premised on a Rational Risk Calculator model of individual behavior but that a better alternative would be a Mistake and Momentary Inattention model. The latter model focuses on ways in which people fail to behave as fully rational and attentive individuals. After reviewing a number of the cognitive biases discussed above, Latin draws our attention to other reasons why even when people are confronted with "good" warnings, i.e., warnings that are conspicuous and substantively sufficient to appraise people of risks and instruct them about how to use a product safely, they may nevertheless fail to act on the warnings in a way that minimizes risk. Many of these failures are the result of inadequate attention devoted to the warning. Some people may be illiterate, others simply inattentive or incompetent users. Young children often fit all three categories. It is not surprising, that courts encounter the most difficulty in warning defect cases when the plaintiff is a young child. In these cases, the warning discussion perforce must be with respect to a responsible adult if it is to have any meaning at all. *See Spruill v. Boyle–Midway, supra* page 250. The problem is especially acute when the product is likely to be used by a child. See Moss v. Crosman Corp., 136 F.3d 1169 (7th Cir.1998) (child killed by BB Gun).

Warnings fail for other reasons as well. Latin notes that people disregard warnings because they rely on explanations by others or their own general experience. *Id.* at 1209–1210. Given competing demands on a person's time, warnings may not always get one's full attention. In addition, the product may have been separated from some of the warnings and instructions about its use as in *Broussard, supra* page 270, or the warnings may not be accessible at the moment they are needed. This, in a sense, is the problem in *Rhodes, supra* page 262.

At the end of his article, Latin raises the possibility that limitations on consumers' ability to assess, comprehend and act on warnings might justify "true strict liability" whereby manufacturers would be liable for any injury proximately caused by their products. *Id.* at 1293. Recently, Hanson and Kysar have drawn on the same body of psychological research to propose that consumer inability to assess risks and the ability of sellers, through advertising, to exploit cognitive biases, argues for corrective legal devices such as enterprise liability, manufacturers' liability for all product-caused harm. Hanson & Kyser, Taking Behavioralism Seriously: The Problem of Market Manipulation, 74 N.Y.U.L.Rev. 630 (1999); Hanson & Kysar, Taking Behavioralism Seriously: Some Evidence of Market Manipulation, 112 Harv.L.Rev. 1420 (1999). The advantages and disadvantages of this type of liability and the degree to which the psychological research on human reaction to risk supports enterprise liability are debated in Henderson & Rachlinski, Product–Related Risk and Cognitive Biases: The Shortcomings of Enterprise Liability, 6 Roger Williams U.L.Rev. 213 (2000) and Hanson & Kysar, Taking Behavioralism Seriously: A Response to Market Manipulation, 6 Roger Williams U.L.Rev. 259 (2000). This entire issue of the Roger Williams Law Review is devoted to a series of valuable papers on the Implications of Psychology for Products Liability. In addition to articles cited above, *see* Fischoff, Need to Know: Analytical and Psychological Criteria, 6 Roger Williams U.L.Rev. 55 (2000).

3. OBVIOUS OR KNOWN DANGERS

BURKE v. SPARTANICS LTD.
United States Court of Appeals, Second Circuit, 2001.
252 F.3d 131.

CALABRESI, CIRCUIT JUDGE:

A metal shearing machine severed the fingers of plaintiff-appellant Alphonso Burke's right hand while he was at work. Burke brought suit in the United States District Court for the Eastern District of New York (Joanna Seybert, *Judge*), invoking the court's diversity jurisdiction. In his suit Burke asserted various New York State tort claims against the machine's manufacturer, defendant-appellee Spartanics Ltd. ("Spartanics"), which in turn impleaded Burke's employer, Metal Etching Company ("Metal Etching"), as a third-party defendant. The case proceeded to trial on Burke's claims, principally that the machine was defectively designed, and that Spartanics failed to provide adequate warnings of the dangers of using the machine. The jury returned a verdict against plaintiff on all counts. Burke now appeals from the judgment entered pursuant to that verdict and also from the district court's denial of his post-trial motion for judgment as a matter of law or for a new trial. We affirm.

Background

The Accident

The accident occurred while Burke was receiving instruction from a supervisor, Mr. O'Neill, on how to perform a particular job with the machine in question, which cuts sheets of metal with a shear. Believing that O'Neill had finished setting up the job, Burke went to the rear of the machine to clear out some cut pieces of metal. After being cut, the pieces of metal had fallen and accumulated in a ramp mounted behind the machine. As was the usual practice in Metal Etching's shop, in order to gain leverage while removing the metal with his left hand, Burke placed his right hand on the machine's cutting surface. Apparently unaware of what Burke was doing, O'Neill attempted to make a cut and, in doing so, severed Burke's fingers, which were in the cutting plane.

The ramp from which Burke was removing the metal when the accident occurred had been installed by Metal Etching. This ramp altered a feature of the machine as initially delivered by Spartanics. The original machine had another ramp with a conveyor belt that ran across the rear of the machine leading to a stacking bin at the machine's side. Metal Etching installed its own ramp above the conveyor system in order to catch the metal cuttings before they hit the conveyor. It did so allegedly to avoid a totally different hazard that the original ramp would supposedly have created. With the original conveyor system in place, however, there was no need for workers to clear cut material from the rear of the machine. But with the new ramp installed, employees not only had to remove the cut material but found that doing so required bracing themselves with one hand on the cutting surface.

By the time of the accident, Burke had been using the machine for about seven months. He fully understood how it worked, where the cutting plane was, and how dangerous it was to place one's hand in the plane while the machine was in operation. He was also aware of the warning label on the front of the machine that specifically warned against getting near the cutting mechanism. There was no warning label on the rear of the machine.

* * *

The Instruction on Duty to Warn

At the charging conference, plaintiff's counsel requested that the court's instructions on the manufacturer's duty to warn include the statement that "even if Mr. Burke was aware of a danger, that did not obviate the need of Spartanics to warn." Judge Seybert rejected this proposal, and, instead, instructed the jury that "[i]f you find that Alphonso Burke already knew of the danger or dangers associated with the Spartanics WL–2 metal shearing machine, you will find that the defendant had no duty to warn him of the dangers associated with the machine."

The Post–Trial Motions

After the jury returned its verdict finding for defendants on August 3, 1999, Burke moved for judgment as a matter of law. The district court reserved decision, received written motion papers several weeks later, and subsequently denied the motion on January 20, 2000. Burke now appeals from the judgment, entered immediately after trial, pursuant to the jury verdict and from the district court's disposition of his post-trial motion, which had raised issues similar to those now presented on appeal. * * *

Discussion

Burke argues * * * that the court incorrectly instructed the jury on the standard governing Spartanics' duty to warn. * * *

C. THE INSTRUCTION ON SPARTANICS' DUTY TO WARN

At trial, Burke objected to the district court's instruction to the jury that, if it found that "[1] Burke already knew of the danger or dangers associated with the Spartanics metal shearing machine, or [2] that the dangers associated with the machine were obvious, and generally known and recognized, you will find that the defendant Spartanics had no duty to warn Mr. Burke of the dangers associated with the metal shearing machine." Based on Burke's own requested instruction, his statements to the trial judge, and his briefing on appeal, we discern two discrete arguments put forward by appellant: first, that the court below erred in instructing the jury that Spartanics had no duty to warn of risks that were "obvious"; second, that the court erred in instructing the jury that Spartanics had no duty to warn of risks about which Burke himself was aware. For both propositions appellant relies on our recent decision in *Liriano v. Hobart Corp.*, 170 F.3d 264, 269 (2d Cir.1999) ("*Liriano III*"), in which we applied New York's failure-to-warn law as set forth by the New York Court of Appeals' in *Liriano v. Hobart Corp.*, 700 N.E.2d 303, 308 (N.Y.1998) ("*Liriano II*"), answering questions certified by *Liriano v. Hobart Corp.*, 132 F.3d 124 (2d Cir.1998) ("*Liriano I*").

The first of these arguments is plainly wrong. It is a well-established principle of New York law that "a limited class of hazards need not be warned of as a matter of law because they are patently dangerous or pose open and obvious risks." *Liriano II,* 700 N.E.2d 303, 308; *accord, e.g., Bazerman v. Gardall Safe Corp.*, 609 N.Y.S.2d 610, 611 (App. Div., 1st Dep't 1994). This is just another way of saying that a reasonable person would not warn of obvious dangers, *i.e.* those harms that most all people know about. As a result, as to these risks, it cannot be negligent to fail to warn.

Not only did the New York Court of Appeals in *Liriano II* reaffirm the "obviousness" exception to a manufacturer's duty to warn, *see Lauber v. Sears, Roebuck and Co.,* 709 N.Y.S.2d 325, 326 (App. Div., 4th Dep't 2000); *Brady v. Dunlop Tire Corp.,* 711 N.Y.S.2d 633, 634–35 (App. Div., 3d Dep't 2000), but nothing in our opinion in *Liriano III* suggests the contrary. The question in *Liriano III* was simply "obviousness of what?" The *Liriano* cases involved an employee who injured his hand in the course of using a meat grinder that was manufactured with a safety guard but from which the guard had been removed. In *Liriano III* we upheld the verdict for the plaintiff because the jury could have found that, absent an appropriate warning, it was not obvious "(a) that it is feasible to reduce the risk with safety guards, (b) that such guards are made available with the grinders, and (c) that the grinders should be used only with the guards." *Liriano III,* 170 F.3d at 271. Because the *existence of a safer method* of using the grinder was not obvious, a jury could have found that a duty to warn, *i.e.* to inform the plaintiff that the machine should not be used in the absence of that safer method, was violated. Accordingly, it was unnecessary in *Liriano III* to decide whether it was obvious that the method plaintiff actually used was dangerous.

* * *

At oral argument, Burke made clear that his contention is that Spartanics should have placed a warning, at the rear approach to the machine, about the dangers of placing one's hand in the cutting plane. His argument was *expressly not* that Spartanics should have warned that the (perhaps obvious) dangers associated with access to the machine from the back could be obviated by use of the original conveyor system, and that the machine should not be used without that conveyor system. Nor was this latter argument, an analogue to that upheld in *Liriano III,* put forward below. Accordingly, *Liriano III* is of no benefit to plaintiff, and the trial court was correct in charging the jury that there was no duty to warn if "the dangers associated with the machine were obvious, and generally known and recognized."

Burke's second argument—that *his own* knowledge of the machine's dangerousness did not negate Spartanics' duty to warn—is essentially correct, but for reasons that do not ultimately undermine our confidence in the jury verdict. The problem with the court's instruction lies in its conflation of two separate issues: (1) whether the manufacturer, considering the reasonably foreseeable uses to which its product might be put, had a duty to warn potential users in general about the machine's dangers; and (2) whether, in retrospect, giving a warning would have made any difference *to this particular plaintiff.* The first question concerns the "open and obvious risks" exception, which goes to the manufacturer's *duty.* The second question, in contrast, goes to the analytically distinct issue of whether a putative breach of that duty was a *cause* of this plaintiff's injury.

Whether a given risk is "obvious" depends in large part on what the mass of users knows and understands. Thus, "[a] manufacturer has a duty to warn against latent dangers resulting from *foreseeable uses* of its product of which it knew or should have known." *Liriano II,* 700 N.E.2d at 305 (emphasis added). Accordingly, "courts treat obvious danger as 'a condition that would ordinarily be seen and the danger of which would ordinarily be appreciated by *those who would be expected to use the product.*'" *Id.* at 308 (quoting Prosser and Keeton, *Torts* § 96, at 686–87 (5th ed.1984)) (emphasis added).

The class of reasonably foreseeable users will, of course, encompass a spectrum of persons with widely varying abilities and experience bearing on their perception of the hazards at hand. Some may be practiced and skilled operators, while others may be novices, or may use the machine in adverse conditions that, though atypical, are still foreseeable. *See id.* at 305 ("A manufacturer also has a duty to warn of the danger of unintended uses of a product provided these uses are reasonably foreseeable."); *id.* at 307 (duty to warn of dangers arising from foreseeable alterations to a product).

So long as the relevant risks are not obvious to *some* members of the class of foreseeable users, a reasonable manufacturer might well be expected to warn. And, as a result, a duty to warn will generally be said to exist. * * * *See id.* at 308 (the purpose of the "open and obvious" exception is to identify "dangers of which a user might not otherwise be aware," thereby enabling "consumers to adjust their behavior"). This is so, moreover, notwithstanding the fact that there may also be foreseeable users for whom the warning is superfluous. It is always possible that a particular plaintiff has a greater awareness of the risks in question than do other users who are or ought to be foreseeable to the manufacturer, and it is, therefore, error to instruct the jury, as was done here, that there is no duty to warn simply because *the particular plaintiff* was cognizant of the relevant hazards.[1]

But of course a defendant's *liability* will not arise from a breach of duty alone. Instead, the plaintiff must show, in addition, that "the failure to warn [was] a substantial cause of the events which produced the injury." *Billsborrow v. Dow Chem.,* 579 N.Y.S.2d 728, 733 (App. Div., 2d Dep't 1992). And "where the injured party was fully aware of the hazard through general knowledge, observation or common sense, or participated in the removal of the safety device whose purpose is obvious, lack of a warning about that danger may well obviate the failure to warn as a legal cause of an injury resulting from that danger." *Liriano II,* 700 N.E.2d at 308 * * *. Thus, it may well be the case that a given risk is not "obvious," in the sense of precluding any duty to warn, but that nevertheless, because the risk was well understood by the plaintiff, a

---

1. In assessing the manufacturer's duty, we ask, essentially, what it ought to have done when distributing its product * * *, a question that necessarily arises *before* the particular accident forming the basis for litigation. The content of this duty, therefore, cannot vary depending on who, among foreseeable users, ultimately happens to be injured by the product. * * *

warning would have made no difference. *See Brady,* 711 N.Y.S.2d at 634–36 (distinguishing issue of whether risk was "open and obvious" from issue of whether plaintiff had "actual knowledge of the hazard"). And the failure to warn was therefore not a cause of the harm.

There are sufficient similarities between the issues of (a) whether a hazard was sufficiently obvious to all *foreseeable users* to preclude any *duty to warn,* and (b) whether the danger was sufficiently well known to *the plaintiff* to preclude a showing of *causation*, that confusion between them is not surprising. This is especially so because the concrete experiences of individual plaintiffs understandably, and properly, provide an important reference point in assessing the range of knowledge among reasonably foreseeable users. *See Liriano III,* 170 F.3d at 268–69. Nonetheless, recognizing the difference between these questions is important.

If the distinction is not observed, manufacturers' duties may be diluted by cases in which the particular plaintiff happens to have had a greater appreciation of the risks than would the mass of other foreseeable users. Where such greater individual awareness of the risk means that a warning would not have prevented the injury, failure to distinguish *duty* from *cause* may lead to an (erroneous) finding of no duty to warn notwithstanding the fact that foreseeable users would in fact be significantly aided by a warning. And, as a result of such a holding, subsequent plaintiffs injured by the same instrumentality would be faced with a prior ruling establishing the absence of any duty to warn, even though their appreciation of the risk might well be low enough to establish causation. Conversely, the distinction protects manufacturers against suits by plaintiffs who, though sufficiently ignorant that a warning would have enabled them to avoid an accident, were so unforeseeable that the manufacturer had no duty to provide them with notice of what to foreseeable users would be obvious. *Cf. Liriano II,* 700 N.E.2d at 308 (noting that requiring warnings against obvious dangers would tend to "trivialize[ ] and undermine[ ] the entire purpose of the rule [by] drowning out cautions against latent dangers").

Harmless Error

The same fact—Burke's awareness of the risk of placing his hand in the cutting plane while removing metal from the ramp—that appellant urges (correctly) should not have been permitted to negate Spartanics' duty to warn *does,* however, fully negate any causal connection between the absence of a rear warning and his injuries. *See, e.g., Smith,* 490 N.E.2d at 842 (finding no causation because plaintiff must have known based on his "general knowledge of pools, his observations prior to the accident, and plain common sense ... that, if he dove into the pool, the area into which he dove contained shallow water"); *McMurry v. Inmont Corp.,* 694 N.Y.S.2d 157, 158–59 (App. Div., 2d Dep't 1999) (holding that, given plaintiff's experience and training, "a warning would not have added anything to the appreciation of this hazard"). The erroneous instruction was therefore harmless. * * *

In reaching this conclusion, we are cognizant that the essence of Burke's claim is that a warning on the rear of the machine would have *reminded* him of the danger of placing his hand near the cutting mechanism, not simply that a warning would have *informed* him of that danger. Warnings, of course, can serve to bring dangerous conditions to a user's attention, not merely to explain that they are dangerous. Thus, the mere fact that Burke already knew that it was dangerous to put his hand in the cutting plane (in the sense that, had he been asked whether it was dangerous, he would have answered that it was and would have understood why), is compatible with the notion that, had he seen a warning at the time he was choosing to put his hand there, such a warning might have prompted him to exercise greater care (whether by finding another source of leverage or by making sure that O'Neill knew not to engage the blade). *Cf. Liriano II,* 700 N.E.2d at 308 (noting that ultimate measure of need for warnings is whether they aid or hinder customers in adjusting their behavior to avoid accidents).

Nonetheless, on the facts presented here, we have no doubt that the lack of a warning on the rear of the machine was not a cause-in-fact of the accident. This is not a case in which a usually careful employee uncharacteristically forgot to take a safety precaution, nor one in which a plaintiff, though fully apprised of a machine's dangers, simply forgot to take care in the course of using the machine for the first time, or after a long hiatus. In such circumstances, it might be the case that a reminder could avert an accident. * * *

Here, instead, the method by which plaintiff removed cut metal from the ramp (*i.e.*, by bracing himself with one hand on the machine's cutting surface) was the routine manner in which this task was carried out at Metal Etching. Indeed, plaintiff testified that he had been trained to act in this way, that his supervisor acted in this way, and that he had never been instructed by his employer to clear out the machine in any other manner. Burke also testified that putting his hand near the blade "caused [him] concern" but that he never complained because he did not want to cause trouble, because it was the only way to accomplish the task, and because it was understood that, precisely to mitigate the maneuver's well-known dangers, one did not operate the machine while someone else was behind it retrieving materials.

If we assume—as we must—that the jury, based on the incorrect instruction, found that these facts concerning Burke's awareness of the machine's dangers precluded any duty on defendant to provide a rear warning, then we must also say, as a matter of law, that the same jury, properly instructed, would have found that Burke was sufficiently aware of the danger to preclude the required causal connection between the absence of a warning and the accident in question. In circumstances such as these, an erroneous instruction is harmless. * * *

Conclusion

We hold * * * that the jury charge on defendant's duty to warn, though in part erroneous, was harmless. Accordingly, and having considered and rejected all of appellant's other arguments, we AFFIRM

Notes

1. The majority position is that there is no duty to warn of obvious dangers. This position is reflected in Restatement (Third) of Torts: Products Liability, § 2, Comment *j*. The rule applies regardless of whether plaintiff seeks recovery on a negligence, products liability, or breach of warranty theory. As the *Burke* opinion notes, the obvious danger rule may be stated either as a duty question or a causal question. A failure to warn is not a cause of the harm if the person to be warned is already fully aware of the dangers that should have been warned against. *See, e.g.,* Stanback v. Parke, Davis & Co., 657 F.2d 642 (4th Cir.1981) (drug company's failure to warn about a risk associated with a vaccine did not cause the harm because the physician who administered it was fully aware of the risk). Where the risk is obvious or generally known, there is no duty to warn even if a given plaintiff lacks subjective knowledge of the danger. Pemberton v. American Distilled Spirits Co., 664 S.W.2d 690 (Tenn.1984).

2. In *Liriano III*, discussed frequently in *Burke*, Judge Calabresi affirmed a jury verdict for a plaintiff against his employer and the manufacturer of a meat grinder in whose product he badly injured his hand. The meat grinder was manufactured with a safety guard, but the guard had been removed by the employer. The manufacturer claimed it had no duty to warn Liriano of the obvious danger posed by the product. However, the Second Circuit argued that warnings may do more than exhort people to be careful. In addition, they may assist people in making choices by advising them of the existence of alternatives. *Liriano III,* at 270.

> Consequently, the instant case does not require us to decide the difficult question of whether New York would consider the risk posed by meat grinders to be obvious as a matter of law. A jury could reasonably find that there exist people who are employed as meat grinders and who do not know (a) that it is feasible to reduce the risk with safety guards, (b) that such guards are made available with the grinders, and (c) that the grinders should be used only with the guards. Moreover, a jury can also reasonably find that there are enough such people, and that warning them is sufficiently inexpensive, that a reasonable manufacturer would inform them that safety guards exist and that the grinder is meant to be used only with such guards. *Id.* at 271.

The causal question that proved decisive in *Burke* did not arise in *Liriano* because the plaintiff was an inexperienced 17 year old recent immigrant who had been on the job for only one week. Thus, it could less easily be said of him than of Mr. Burke that he actually knew of the danger posed by the machine.

3. Nevertheless, the final result of *Liriano* was that the plaintiff was assigned one-third of the responsibility for the accident, the employer 63.3% of the responsibility and the manufacturer 3.3% of the responsibility. Does this seem so out of line? Note, however, that New York is one of very few states that permit a defendant to implead the plaintiff's employer and obtain full contribution based on the employer's proportionate fault regardless of the level of worker's compensation benefits paid by the employer. *See* Dole v.

Dow Chemical Co., 30 N.Y.2d 143, 331 N.Y.S.2d 382, 282 N.E.2d 288 (N.Y. 1972). Most jurisdictions either permit no contribution or limit contribution up to an amount equal to the plaintiff's worker's compensation benefits. *See* Chapter 10, Section B 4 for a more complete discussion of this issue.

4. *Liriano III* is roundly criticized in Bowbeer and Killoran, Liriano v. Hobart Corp.: Obvious Dangers, the Duty to Warn of Safer Alternatives, and the Heeding Presumption, 65 Brook.L.Rev. 717 (1999). As to the duty to warn of ways to reduce risk, the authors argue:

> The fallacies of the Second Circuit's analysis become evident when one considers its ramifications for meat grinder manufacturers alone. First, any grinder manufacturer would have to conclude from this opinion that it should provide an on-product warning capable of informing even uneducated, inexperienced, non-English speaking users about the existence of every machine part that is capable of being removed (however forcibly) and the safety consequences (however obvious) of its absence. * * * Indeed, by the same rationale, the Liriano duty to warn should be extended to cover not only the removal but the potential modification of machine parts that could have safety consequences.
>
> * * *
>
> Consider, for example, the protective guard on the meat grinder in Liriano. It seems easy enough for the court to suggest a warning indicating that a guard is available and that the machine should only be used with the guard in place. Even if the user knows what is meant by a guard and could tell whether it was missing, what if the guard was not removed, but instead modified by enlarging the holes to accommodate a larger "stomper"? The warning that focuses solely on the presence of the guard rather than its performance characteristics might well lead to a false sense of security. Thus, the warning would have to caution against using the product with the guard removed or modified. But, the question arises: How will the user recognize whether the guard is in its original condition? Will the warning need to include a picture? A set of dimensions and specifications?

Id. at 737–38.

Do you agree? Does the *Liriano* analysis make the obvious danger rule unworkable? Is *Burke* a retreat from *Liriano*? For an influential law review article on the duty to warn, see Henderson and Twerski, Doctrinal Collapse in Products Liability: The Empty Shell of Failure to Warn, 65 N.Y.U .L.Rev. 265 (1990).

5. **Professional Users.** In deciding what kind of a warning to give, the manufacturer can take into consideration the knowledge and expertise of those who may reasonably be expected to use the product. If the product is marketed only to professionals, who are aware of its dangers and how to deal with them, it may reasonably give a much less detailed warning than it would have to give to members of the general public. *See, e.g.,* Martinez v. Dixie Carriers, Inc., 529 F.2d 457 (5th Cir.1976). A worker was overcome by dripolene fumes while cleaning out a barge. He was a member of a professional crew which was aware of the nature of the liquid and the dangers associated with handling it. The manufacturer of the dripolene gave a

warning, but not a detailed one. It was held not liable for failure to give a more adequate warning. *See also,* Loughan v. Firestone Tire & Rubber Co., 749 F.2d 1519 (11th Cir.1985) (Florida law; no duty to warn experienced mechanic about the risk of mismatching the component parts of a multi-piece rim-wheel assembly).

6. The obviousness of the danger has traditionally been decided by the judge as question of law. In recent years this has changed in many jurisdictions. In cases where the obviousness of the specific danger involved in the case is at all debatable, many courts tend to submit the question of obviousness to the jury. *See* Pardieck & Hulbert, Is the Danger Really Open and Obvious?, 19 Ind.L.Rev. 383 (1986).

Consider, for example, Laaperi v. Sears, Roebuck & Co., Inc., 787 F.2d 726 (1st Cir.1986). Defendant sold a smoke detector powered by house current. It failed to function in an electrical fire caused by a short circuit. The smoke detector was hooked up to the circuit that shorted out, and it could not function because it received no electricity after the circuit cut off. Plaintiff sued for negligent failure to warn that a short circuit that starts a fire could also incapacitate the smoke detector. Defendant argued that no warning was necessary because the risk was obvious to the average consumer. The court stated:

> Defendants ask us to declare that the risk that an electrical fire could incapacitate an AC-powered smoke detector is so obvious that the average consumer would not benefit from a warning. This is not a trivial argument; in earlier—some might say sounder—days, we might have accepted it. *Compare* Jamieson v. Woodward & Lothrop, 247 F.2d 23 (D.C.Cir.1957). Our sense of the current state of the tort law in Massachusetts and most other jurisdictions, however, leads us to conclude that, today, the matter before us poses a jury question; that "obviousness" in a situation such as this would be treated by the Massachusetts courts as presenting a question of fact, not of law. To be sure, it would be obvious to anyone that an electrical outage would cause this smoke detector to fail. But the average purchaser might not comprehend the specific danger that a fire-causing electrical problem can simultaneously knock out the circuit into which a smoke detector is wired, causing the detector to fail at the very moment it is needed. Thus, while the failure of a detector to function as the result of an electrical malfunction due, say, to a broken power line or a neighborhood power outage would, we think, be obvious as a matter of law, the failure that occurred here, being associated with the very risk—fire—for which the device was purchased, was not, or so a jury could find.

787 F.2d at 731.

7. For a discussion of liability for failure to warn about known and obvious dangers, *see* Madden, The Duty to Warn in Products Liability: Contours and Criticism, 89 W.Va.L.Rev. 221, 253–259 (1987); Noel, Products Defective Because of Inadequate Directions or Warnings, 23 Sw.L.J. 256, 272–274 (1969).

CAMPOS v. FIRESTONE TIRE & RUBBER CO.
Supreme Court of New Jersey, 1984.
98 N.J. 198, 485 A.2d 305.

The opinion of the Court was delivered by

SCHREIBER, J.

This failure-to-warn product liability case presents for consideration the effect of a foreseeable user's knowledge of a danger on a manufacturer's responsibility to distribute a product free from defect. Does that knowledge eliminate any duty to warn? Or is it a link to be considered on whether the failure to warn was a substantial factor in causing the accident and injuries?

Plaintiff Armando Campos was born and raised in Portugal. He emigrated to this country in 1971. Shortly after his arrival in the United States he obtained a job with Theurer Atlantic, Inc. (Theurer), a manufacturer of truck trailers.

In connection with its trailer operation Theurer placed new truck tires on rims before their installation on the trailers. Plaintiff's work was to assemble the tires. This involved placing a tire containing an inner tube on a three-piece rim assembly, putting the assembled tire into a steel safety cage designed to prevent injuries in case the assembled parts separated under pressure, and then inserting air into the tire by inflating the tube inside it. He generally worked a five-day, forty-hour week, and assembled about eight tires an hour. Plaintiff's employment continued in this manner until the accident on November 1, 1978.

About 9:30 a.m. on that day, plaintiff was readying a new Dunlop tire to be mounted on a trailer. He assembled the three-piece rim and tire, placed the tire in the cage, and clamped the air pressure hose into place so that air was being forced into the tire. He then noticed that a locking element on the rim components was opening. Fearing that there would "be a very big accident" if the pieces separated under pressure, he immediately tried to disengage the hose. He explained, "Because if I didn't, it could kill me and kill everybody that was around there." As he reached into the cage, the assembly exploded and plaintiff was severely injured.

Defendant, Firestone Tire & Rubber Company, had manufactured the rim assembly. We were advised at oral argument that Theurer, not defendant, had made the protective cage. Defendant had delivered manuals describing the proper method of preparing the tire to its customers, including Theurer. Defendant had also given Theurer a large chart prepared by the National Highway Traffic Safety Administration of the United States Department of Transportation. That chart was kept on the wall at the Theurer shop and contained instructions on safety precautions, including the following advice: "ALWAYS INFLATE TIRE IN SAFETY CAGE OR USE A PORTABLE LOCK RING GUARD. USE

A CLIP–ON TYPE AIR CHUCK[1] WITH REMOTE VALVE SO THAT OPERATOR CAN STAND CLEAR DURING TIRE INFLATION." However, Campos could not read or write Portuguese or English and these written warnings were therefore ineffective.

In addition to the written instructions, plaintiff had received some oral instructions from his supervisor. He had been told that a truck tire was to be placed in the cage before inflating it. Further, he had had a similar accident in July, 1972, when, to prevent a mishap, he had inserted his hand into the protective cage while air was being blown into the tire. The injuries that he received then were less severe than in this accident.

Plaintiff proceeded against defendant, Firestone Tire & Rubber Company, on two strict liability theories, improper design and failure to warn. His contention that the rim had been improperly designed because it should have consisted of one rather than three pieces was rejected by the jury. His second claim, which was accepted by the jury, was that defendant had not adequately warned him of the danger and that that failure to warn was a proximate cause of his injury. The jury returned a verdict of $255,000.

Defendant appealed. A divided Appellate Division reversed and entered judgment for the defendant. *See* 192 *N.J.Super.* 251, 469 *A.*2d 943 (1983). This Court granted plaintiff's petition for certification. 96 *N.J.* 310, 475 *A.*2d 600 (1984).

I

* * *

Plaintiff's expert suggested that defendant should have produced a graphic or symbolic warning against inserting one's hand in the protective cage during the inflation process. He thought that it would have been appropriate to have prepared a sign containing a symbol similar to the picture of a cigarette with a diagonal red line across that informs one not to smoke. He testified that the manufacturer should have anticipated that illiterate people would be exposed to these dangers and added, "we have to do things which will protect them as well."

Although plaintiff's similar accident six years earlier may have served as some warning against reaching into the cage while the tire was being inflated, plaintiff's expert stated that plaintiff's "instinctive" reaction was to try to stop the accident by inserting his hand into the cage. Plaintiff's expert responded as follows to a question regarding how symbols would have helped the plaintiff avoid the accident:

> A. Not very much. A little perhaps. That is, if there was a reminder in graphical form against putting his hands in telling him that explosive separations can take place, and he's instructed verbal-

---

[1] This is a device that clamps on the air hose so as to hold the air hose and valve in place when air is being injected into the tube within the tire. The worker is then free to stand clear while the tire is being inflated.

ly by somebody in his own native tongue as to what that symbol means. Then at least that amount of information has been provided to him.

I don't think it's going to be very effective beyond a certain point because this particular incident situationally starts before the tire even gets into the cage. It starts either on the assembly line or it starts when the man is assembling it and doesn't assemble it correctly. I certainly agree that the warning graphical which the man let's say understands is not—it's better than nothing, but not very much better.

Q. Is it better than the pain caused by a prior injury in terms of suppressing his instincts for putting his hands in the cage?

A. No.

The Appellate Division majority and dissenting opinions viewed the effect of this evidence differently. The majority relied on the proposition that "there is no duty to warn where the danger is obvious and the user knowledgeable." 192 N.J.Super. at 267, 469 A.2d 943. It concluded that this was such a case and held that there being no duty to warn this plaintiff, plaintiff's case necessarily failed. The dissent, acknowledging that the "fact that the danger may have been [objectively] obvious [could] affect the [manufacturer's] duty," *id.*, 192 N.J.Super. at 267, 469 A.2d 943, contended that the particular plaintiff's subjective knowledge is relevant on the issue of proximate cause rather than duty, *id.*, 192 N.J.Super. at 269, 469 A.2d 943. The dissent concluded that since the trial court's charge on proximate cause had consisted only of general principles without relating them to the factual circumstances, the cause should be remanded for a new trial. *Id.*, 192 N.J.Super. at 270–71, 469 A.2d 943.

The duty to warn in the strict liability cause of action is based on the notion that absent a warning or adequate warning, a product is defective, in that it is not reasonably fit, suitable, or safe for its intended purposes. *Freund v. Cellofilm Properties, Inc.*, 87 N.J. 229, 242, 432 A.2d 925 (1981). * * *

A manufacturer has a duty to warn * * * foreseeable users of all hidden or latent dangers that would arise out of a reasonably anticipated use of its product. As we have heretofore stated, the duty to warn embodies "the notion that the warning be sufficient to adequately protect any and all foreseeable users from hidden dangers presented by the product." *Freund, supra,* 87 N.J. at 243, 432 A.2d 925. That accords with the general view. * * *

We turn next to consider whether a duty to warn exists when the danger is obvious. Although some jurisdictions have adopted an "obvious danger rule" that would absolve a manufacturer of a duty to warn of dangers that are objectively apparent, *see* 2 R. Hursch & H. Bailey, *American Law of Products Liability* 2d § 8:15, at 181–84 (1974) (summarizing case law on the subject), in our state the obviousness of a danger, as distinguished from a plaintiff's subjective knowledge of a danger, is merely one element to be factored into the analysis to determine whether a duty to warn exists. A manufacturer is not automatically relieved of his duty to warn merely because the danger is patent. *See Schipper v. Levitt & Sons,* 44 *N.J.* 70, 81, 87, 207 *A.*2d 314 (1965) (suggesting that obviousness of danger should not necessarily preclude recovery in negligence against mass developer of homes); Marshall, "An Obvious Wrong Does Not Make a Right: Manufacturers' Liability for Patently Dangerous Product," 48 *N.Y.U.L.Rev.* 1065 (1973); Darling, "The Patent Danger Rule: An Analysis and a Survey of its Vitality," 29 *Mercer L.Rev.* 583 (1978). Rather, the general proposition is as stated in *Michalko v. Cooke Color & Chem. Corp.,* 91 *N.J.* 386, 403, 451 *A.*2d 179 (1982):

> [A] manufacturer is under a duty to warn owners and foreseeable users of the dangers of using a particular machine if, without such a warning, the machine is not reasonably safe. A manufacturer which does not caution against the dangers inherent in the use of its product should be held strictly liable for injuries resulting from the absence of such warnings. [*Id.,* 91 *N.J.* at 403, 451 *A.*2d 179 (footnote omitted).]

Whether a duty exists "involves a weighing of the relationship of the parties, the nature of the risk, and the public interest in the proposed solution." *Goldberg v. Housing Auth.,* 38 *N.J.* 578, 583, 186 *A.*2d 291 (1962). The additional cost of a warning will in most cases have but a slight impact on the risk-utility analysis, since such cost would generally have little, if any, effect on a product's utility. *Freund, supra,* 87 *N.J.* at 238 n. 1, 242, 432 *A.*2d 925; *see also Cepeda v. Cumberland Eng'g Co.,* 76 *N.J.* 152, 174, 386 *A.*2d 816 (1978) (listing risk-utility factors). More relevant questions in the warning context include the following. Is the lack of the warning consonant with the duty to place in the stream of commerce only products that are reasonably safe, suitable, and fit? Will the absence of a duty encourage manufacturers to eliminate warnings or to produce inadequate warnings? Is the danger so basic to the functioning or purpose of the product—for example, the fact that a match will burn—that a warning would serve no useful purpose?

We have no difficulty in holding that under the facts and circumstances of this case defendant had a duty to warn plaintiff of the danger of inserting his hand into the cage. Defendant has consistently argued that "[t]his case is not about objective knowledge" and that the "obvious danger rule," even if it were the law in New Jersey, is inapplicable. * * * Moreover, there was evidence that written warnings were insufficient and that pictorial warnings should have been used. *See Hubbard–Hall Chem. Co. v. Silverman,* 340 F.2d 402, 405 (1st Cir.1965). In view of the unskilled or semi-skilled nature of the work and the existence of many in the work force who do not read English, warnings in the form of symbols might have been appropriate, since the employee's "ability to take care of himself" was limited. *See Cepeda v. Cumberland Eng'g Co., supra,* 76 *N.J.* at 199, 386 *A.*2d 816 (Schreiber, J., concurring and dissenting).

II

Defendant has strongly urged that it should be exonerated as a matter of law, not because the danger was objectively obvious, but because plaintiff had actual knowledge of the danger. Because of that subjective knowledge, the defendant argued, a warning requirement was irrelevant.

A duty to warn is not automatically extinguished because the injured user or consumer perceived the danger. That preexisting knowledge, however, might negate a claim that the absence of a warning was a cause in fact of plaintiff's injury. We thus agree with the dissenting Appellate Division opinion that viewing the plaintiff's conduct subjectively, the fact finder might properly assess plaintiff's awareness of the danger in terms of causation rather than duty. As the dissent has commented:

> Since the duty is to place on the market a product free of defects, and this duty attaches at the time the product is introduced into the stream of commerce, a particular user's subjective knowledge of a danger does not and cannot modify the manufacturer's duty. Such subjective knowledge may be either relevant or decisive in determining whether, when the proximate cause of this defect is assessed, the manufacturer will be held liable, but it does not limit the manufacturer's duty to distribute only defect-free products into the market place. [192 *N.J.Super.* at 266–67, 469 *A.*2d 943.]

See also Michalko, supra, 91 *N.J.* at 402, 451 *A.*2d 179 ("The question whether the failure to warn proximately caused plaintiff's injury is a factual dispute that the jury should decide."); *accord Whitehead v. St. Joe Lead Co.,* 729 *F.*2d 238, 249 (3d Cir.1984).

We continue to adhere to the principle that "the defect [must have] *caused injury* to a reasonably foreseeable user." *Michalko, supra,* 91 *N.J.* at 394, 451 *A.*2d 179 (emphasis supplied). Professor, now United States District Court Judge, Dean Keeton stated the proposition in this manner:

> If the basis for recovery under strict liability is inadequacy of warnings or instruction about dangers, then plaintiff would be required to show that an adequate warning or instruction would have prevented the harm. [Keeton, "Products Liability—Inadequacy of Information," 48 *Tex.L.Rev.* 398, 414 (1970).]

Here the issue of causation was vigorously contested. Defendant claimed that a prior accident in which plaintiff had been injured by inserting his hand into the cage while a tire was being inflated had served as a dramatic warning and yet was of no avail. In addition, there was evidence that plaintiff's conduct in putting his hand into the cage was an instinctive reaction and that a pictorial warning therefore would not have prevented the accident. *See G. Calabresi, The Costs of Accidents: A Legal and Economic Analysis* 109 (1972) (noting that specific deterrence is not served in circumstances when individuals cannot control their acts). Indeed, plaintiff's own expert stated that a pictorial warning might have been of little help in preventing the accident. In view of the crucial role that causation played in the case, it was essential that an appropriate charge on that issue be given to the jury.

A strict liability charge to a jury "should be tailored to the factual situation to assist the jury in performing its fact finding responsibility." *Suter, supra,* 81 *N.J.* at 176, 406 *A.*2d 140, quoted in *Freund, supra,* 87 *N.J.* at 242, 432 *A.*2d 925. The instructions should set forth an understandable and clear exposition of the issues, and should cover all essential matters. These include proximate cause and its place in the liability scheme. * * * A proper jury charge is essential for a fair trial. * * *

The trial court charged only generally that plaintiff had the burden of proving that the failure to give adequate warnings was a proximate cause of the accident and injuries and that the failure was a substantial factor in bringing about the happening of the accident. No attempt was made to place this issue before the jury in the factual context of the case. * * * Indeed, plaintiff made little, if any, showing that with a proper warning the accident would not have occurred. Although there may be some question whether plaintiff sustained his burden of proving causation, *see Brown v. United States Stove Co., supra,* 98 *N.J.* 155, 484 *A.*2d 1234, we are of the opinion that the matter should be remanded for a new trial. *See also* Twerski, "Seizing the Middle Ground Between Rules and Standards in Design Defect Litigation: Advancing Directed Verdict Practice in the Law of Torts," 57 *N.Y.U.L.Rev.* 521, 562 (1982) (noting that in failure to warn products liability cases some courts have helped plaintiffs overcome the burden of proof by positing a rebuttable presumption that the warning would have been heeded if given).

Conclusion

The judgment of the Appellate Division entering a judgment in favor of the defendant is reversed; the plaintiff's cause of action predicated upon a failure to provide an adequate warning is remanded for a new trial. Costs to abide the event.

For reversal and remandment—CHIEF JUSTICE WILENTZ and JUSTICES CLIFFORD, SCHREIBER, HANDLER, POLLOCK, O'HERN and GARIBALDI—7.

For affirmance—None.

Notes

1. In similar cases, a number of other courts have held that there is no duty to warn as a matter of law because the risk of separation was common knowledge and known to the plaintiff. Bishop v. Firestone Tire & Rubber Co., 814 F.2d 437 (7th Cir.1987) (Indiana law); Tri–State Insurance Co. of Tulsa, Oklahoma v. Fidelity & Casualty Insurance Co. of New York, 364 So.2d 657 (La.App.1978), writ denied, 365 So.2d 248 (1978).

2. **Obvious Dangers.** A minority of courts agree with *Campos* that a defendant must sometimes warn about obvious dangers. In Olson v. A.W.

Chesterton Co., 256 N.W.2d 530 (N.D.1977), an employee was injured while applying belt dressing with a pour on applicator to the unguarded pinch point of a conveyor belt. Plaintiff's expert testified that the label on the belt dressing container should have warned of the dangers inherent in running conveyor belts, and should have advised the use of a product with an aerosol applicator with top-drive, power pulley systems. The manufacturer of the belt dressing was held liable for failure to warn. The court stated:

> There is no valid reason for automatic preclusion of liability based solely upon "obviousness" of danger in an action founded upon the risk-spreading concept of strict liability in tort which is intended to burden the manufacturers of defectively dangerous products with special responsibilities and potential financial liabilities for accidental injuries.

256 N.W.2d at 537.

3. In Vallillo v. Muskin Corp., 212 N.J.Super. 155, 514 A.2d 528 (1986), a very experienced adult swimmer was injured when he dove into a four and one-half foot, above-ground swimming pool while unsuccessfully attempting to make a shallow dive. He sued the manufacturer of the pool for failing to provide better warnings against this practice. The court held that the failure to warn was not a cause of the injury as a matter of law because the danger of diving into a shallow pool was in plaintiff's mind at the time he executed the dive. The court distinguished *Campos* as requiring warnings against known dangers only when necessary to jog a plaintiff's memory of the danger or to guard against instinctive actions. Is this distinction valid?

4. WHO TO WARN

(a) Users, Consumers, and Bystanders

HUMBLE SAND & GRAVEL, INC. v. GOMEZ
Supreme Court of Texas, 2004
146 S.W.3d 170

Justice HECHT delivered the opinion of the Court, in which Justice OWEN, Justice JEFFERSON, Justice SMITH, Justice WAINWRIGHT, and Justice BRISTER joined.

Generally, a product supplier must warn expected users of foreseeable risks that make the product unreasonably dangerous, but a supplier need not warn of risks that are common knowledge, and when the product is supplied through an intermediary, a supplier may sometimes rely on the intermediary to warn the actual product users. We must apply these basic principles to the circumstances presented in this case. Specifically, the issue is whether a supplier of flint used for abrasive blasting had a duty to warn its customers' employees that inhalation of silica dust can be fatal and that they should wear air-supplied protective hoods, given the customers' knowledge of those dangers.

If the flint supplier in this case had such a duty, it is only because all similarly situated flint suppliers have the same duty, not because of some peculiar aspect of this one defendant's situation. Therefore, to determine whether a general legal duty exists, we must look beyond the particular circumstances of the injury here complained of, just as the parties themselves have done, to the broader industrial setting in which that injury occurred. The record before us establishes that by the 1980s, the dangers of using flint in abrasive blasting had been well known throughout the abrasive blasting industry as well as to health and safety professionals and government regulators for most of the twentieth century, but that blasting workers themselves remained largely ignorant of those dangers, and their employers were careless in enforcing workplace conditions that would protect workers' safety. The record also reflects that federal regulations have been imposed on employers to improve working conditions but not on flint manufacturers to warn of dangers involved in the use of their product. While the parties here no longer dispute that such a warning by the defendant supplier would have prevented the plaintiff's injury, missing from this record is any evidence that, in general, warnings by flint suppliers could effectively reach their customers' employees actually engaged in abrasive blasting. Without such evidence, we are unable to determine whether a duty to warn should be imposed on flint suppliers. Consequently, we reverse the judgment of the court of appeals and, in the interest of justice, remand the case to the trial court for a new trial.

I

Raymond Gomez contracted silicosis while working at and around abrasive blasting * * * for about 6 1/2 years, from 1984–1987 [where he worked for Spincote Plastic Coating Co.] and again from 1991–1994 [where he worked for Sivalls, Inc.] * * * In 1995, Gomez filed suit in Jefferson County against more than twenty defendants, including four suppliers of flint used as the abrasive in the blasting work, two suppliers of blasting equipment, thirteen suppliers of protective gear worn by workers, and several jobsite owners. Gomez settled with all of the defendants except Humble Sand & Gravel Company, one of the flint suppliers, for a total of $389,200, and then following a jury trial obtained a judgment against Humble for [$2,053,058.76]. * * *

Gomez [was employed by Spincote to spray]* * * steel tubing with particles of flint shot through a nozzle with compressed air under pressures around 100 p.s.i. Flint is very hard stone composed mostly of crystalline silica (silica dioxide (SiO_2), commonly called quartz), which in its natural, undisturbed state is not at all dangerous. But when flint particles are blasted against metal at high pressure, they not only scour and abrade the surface, they shatter into an airborne dust of smaller particles. Some of this dust is coarse enough to rebound against workers, injuring exposed skin, and to hang in the air, obscuring visibility. But some particles of free silica are so fine—5 microns (or about 200 millionths of an inch) in diameter, something like 1/20th the diameter of a human hair—as to be invisible to the naked eye. The visible dust can clog the nose and mouth but is too coarse to be inhaled into the lungs and is relatively harmless. But the microscopic particles of free silica are both respirable and toxic. Inhaled over months or years, free silica particles cause silicosis, an incurable disease involving a fibrosis and scarring of the lungs and other complications that can eventually result in disability and death. Silicosis is caused only by inhaling free silica. Inhalation of free silica particles cannot be prevented by ordinary, loose-fitting, disposable paper masks; the particles are too small. People working around silica dust must wear air-fed hoods or respirators covering their heads or faces to protect themselves.

The parties here agree, and the record establishes, that the health risks from inhaling silica dust have been well known for a very long time [to the abrasive blasting industry]. * * *

* * *

Studies of the health hazards of abrasive blasting with flint also determined that such work could be done relatively safely if workers were required to use suitable air line respirators—devices that fit over the face or head with a clean air supply for workers to breathe. * * *

* * * The widespread knowledge of the dangers of silica dust produced by abrasive blasting and the necessity of wearing proper protective equipment was not often shared by the ordinary workers themselves or their supervisors and did not translate into safety in the workplace. It is undisputed on the record before us that the dangers of silicosis frequently went unheeded in practice. * * *

Humble, a relatively small, family-owned and-operated business with eight employees located in Picher, Oklahoma, began packaging and selling flint for abrasive blasting in 1982. Humble processed flint from chat (crushed rock) piles left over from World War II zinc-mining operations. Humble sold flint both in bulk and in 100–pound bags, and only to industrial customers. From the beginning, Ron Humble, who ran the business with his father, knew that breathing the silica dust generated by abrasive blasting could cause silicosis and that the disease could be fatal. He also knew that he should put some sort of warning label on the bags, and after making inquiries of OSHA and a trade organization that yielded him no useful information, he decided to copy the following label used by a competitor, Independent Gravel, who he understood had been in business for more than fifty years:

WARNING!

MAY BE INJURIOUS TO HEALTH IF PROPER PROTECTIVE EQUIPMENT IS NOT USED.

* * *

Dr. Bingham and Dr. Rose [testifying for plaintiff] * * * criticized the [warning] in the following two respects. First, the * * * warning understated the risk of inhaling silica dust by stating only that it "may be injurious to health" and not that it may result in disability and death. Second, the * * * warning did not specify that the only "proper protective equipment" was an air-fed hood, allowing the mistaken notion that other equipment, like disposable paper masks, would do as well.

* * *

Humble sold flint to Spincote for abrasive blasting[.] * * *

* * *

Abrasive blasting at Spincote's plants was done inside a building in an area called the blast house. Gomez was hired to work as an "end grinder", a job that did not involve blasting but was performed in the dusty environment of the building. Gomez was given only a disposable paper mask that was held against his face with rubber bands. After his first month, Gomez was moved to "end cutter", a job that did involve blasting. At that point, he was provided an air-fed hood in addition to the paper mask and was shown how to use the hood properly. * * *

However, Gomez and his former co-worker agreed that when blasting stopped for breaks during or at the end of a shift, employees had to remove their hoods to leave the blast house, even though the air was still dusty, because the hoses supplying air to the hoods would not reach past the immediate work area. Gomez also testified that he did not wear a hood when cleaning up the blast house, which involved shoveling back into the blasting machine's flint supply pot dust that had accumulated knee-and waist-deep. This activity stirred the dust, including free silica particles, back up into the air. * * * Spincote had twice been cited for excessive free silica particles in the work environment, and Gomez was exposed to them whenever he removed his hood and mask, even if the blasting had stopped.

[Gomez testified that when he worked for Sivalls, Inc. from 1991 to 1994 he also "always wore his hood and mask when blasting but not at other times when he was around dust."]

* * * Although Humble sold flint to some customers in bulk, the flint it sold to Spincote was always in 100–pound bags. Spincote also bought flint from other suppliers, some of which was in bags. Gomez testified that the first time he saw Humble's bags, he noticed the warning label and asked his foreman about it. His foreman replied that as long as he wore his hood and mask he would be all right. * * *

* * *

In November 1994, Gomez sought medical treatment for shortness of breath, and within a few days he was diagnosed as having subacute silicosis. A biopsy of his lung tissue confirmed that he had had a high exposure to silica dust. * * *

* * *

II

* * *

The jury found Humble liable under two separate legal theories: products liability and negligence. Although the jury's finding did not specify how Humble had been negligent, the only evidence of negligence that caused Gomez's injury was that Humble failed to adequately warn of the dangers of using flint in abrasive blasting. * * * Thus, the factual basis for liability under both theories was the same. * * *

It is firmly established in Texas that the existence and elements of a common law duty are ordinarily legal issues for the court to decide, whether the duty (for products liability) is not to distribute a defective product or (for negligence) to act with ordinary care. * * *

We have recognized, however, that in some instances these issues may turn on facts that cannot be determined as a matter of law and must instead be resolved by the factfinder[.] * * *

* * *

Humble's argument has two components: one, it had no duty to warn its customers of the risks of working around silica dust because those risks were common knowledge in the abrasive blasting industry long before 1984; and two, it had no duty to warn its customers' employees of those risks because its customers were in a better position to warn their own employees. If the risks of silica dust were not commonly known in the industry, then Humble had at least a duty to warn its customers, which Gomez argues Humble did not do. Even if the risks were commonly known, the question remains whether Humble still had a duty to warn its customers' employees. We consider each component of Humble's argument in turn.

III

A supplier has no duty to warn of risks involved in a product's use that are commonly known to foreseeable users, even if some users are not aware of them. "Commonly" does not mean universally. "Commonly known" means " 'beyond dispute' ". As we have said, "the inquiry whether a recognition of risk 'is within the ordinary knowledge common to the community' is an objective standard." * * *

With these principles in mind, we turn to the present case. * * * [T]he record before us in this case establishes, and the parties do not disagree, that as a matter of objective fact, the general dangers of inhaling silica dust, including disability and death, and of not wearing air-fed hoods to protect against inhalation, have been common knowledge among flint suppliers and abrasive blasting operators for decades and were certainly so in 1984 when Gomez went to work for Spincote. * * *

* * *

At the same time, it is equally well established on this record that the dangers of silica dust were not generally known to workers like Gomez employed in abrasive blasting operations.* * *

From this record we conclude that flint suppliers like Humble had no duty to warn its customers like Spincote and Sivalls, abrasive blasting operators, that inhaling silica dust can be disabling and fatal and that workers must wear air-fed hoods, because that information had long been commonly known throughout the industry. Blasting operators' disregard of the risks to their employees of inhaling silica dust was not for want of additional information that flint suppliers should have furnished, but for want of care. We turn, then, to the question whether Humble had a duty to warn its customers' employees, who were not generally aware of the risks.

IV

A

In *Alm v. Aluminum Co. of America,* we recognized that "a manufacturer or supplier may, in certain situations, depend on an intermediary to communicate a warning to the ultimate user of a product."[2] Alm claimed that an aluminum cap had popped off a soda bottle and struck him in the eye. Alcoa manufactured the machine that fastened the cap to the bottle top, and Alm claimed Alcoa should have warned him of the risk that a cap could pop off. But the machine Alcoa manufactured was owned and operated by an independent bottler. Alcoa did not control the bottling process or sell the bottled soft drink and had no practical way of reaching consumers with any warning. In that situation, we said, "Alcoa should be able to satisfy its duty to warn consumers by proving that its intermediary [the bottler] was adequately trained and warned, familiar with the propensities of the product, and capable of passing on a warning."[3] We analogized Alcoa's position to that of a bulk supplier of material that is repackaged and sold and who thus has no means of providing the ultimate consumer with a warning about risks of use.[4] In a different vein, we noted that other courts had held that a pharmaceutical manufacturer is not required to warn patients of the dangers of a prescription drug as long as physicians who prescribe the drug—"learned intermediaries"—have been adequately warned. In both situations, we said, it would be reasonable for the supplier to rely on the intermediary to warn the ultimate consumer. But we cautioned that—

> the mere presence of an intermediary does not excuse the manufacturer from warning those whom it should reasonably expect to be endangered by the use of its product. The issue in every case is whether the original manufacturer has a reasonable assurance that its warning will reach those endangered by the use of its product.[5]

We concluded that while Alcoa had no duty to warn Alm directly, it did have a duty to warn the bottler and had failed to do so adequately.

* * *

2. 717 S.W.2d 588, 591 (Tex.1986).
3. *Id.* at 592.
4. *Id.*
5. *Alm,* 717 S.W.2d at 591.

Alm cited but did not discuss section 388 of the *Restatement (Second) of Torts,* which sets out a rule similar to the one applied in *Alm:*

> One who supplies directly or through a third person a chattel for another to use is subject to liability to those whom the supplier should expect to use the chattel ... if the supplier
>
> (a) knows or has reason to know that the chattel is or is likely to be dangerous for the use for which it is supplied, and
>
> (b) has no reason to believe that those for whose use the chattel is supplied will realize its dangerous condition, and
>
> (c) fails to exercise reasonable care to inform them of its dangerous condition or of the facts which make it likely to be dangerous.

* * *

[The Court discusses Comment n to § 388 which elaborates on the considerations relevant to determining] whether one supplying a chattel for the use of others through a third person has satisfied his duty to those who are to use the chattel by informing the third person of the dangerous character of the chattel, or of the precautions which must be exercised in using it in order to make its use safe. * * *

* * *

Section 388 and comment n describe a duty of ordinary care that is mirrored in products liability law. Section 2(c) of the *Restatement (Third) of Torts: Products Liability* states that a product—

> is defective because of inadequate instructions or warnings when the foreseeable risks of harm posed by the product could have been reduced or avoided by the provision of reasonable instructions or warnings by the seller or other distributor, or a predecessor in the commercial chain of distribution, and the omission of the instructions or warnings renders the product not reasonably safe.

Were we to apply section 2(c) * * * literally * * *, then Humble would certainly be liable to Gomez because he would have avoided the foreseeable risk of silicosis had Humble warned that inhaling silica dust could result in death. Gomez's testimony, which the jury could and obviously did believe, establishes that he would have seen such a warning, just as he saw the warning that Humble did print on its bags, would have understood it, and would never have continued working as a blaster. But the comments to section 2, like those to section 388, show that the stated rule cannot be so mechanically applied. Comment i explains:

> There is no general rule as to whether one supplying a product for the use of others through an intermediary has a duty to warn the ultimate product user directly or may rely on the intermediary to relay warnings. The standard is one of reasonableness in the circumstances. Among the factors to be considered are the gravity of the risks posed by the product, the likelihood that the intermediary will

convey the information to the ultimate user, and the feasibility and effectiveness of giving a warning directly to the user. Thus, when the purchaser of machinery is the owner of a workplace who provides the machinery to employees for their use, and there is reason to doubt that the employer will pass warnings on to employees, the seller is required to reach the employees directly with necessary instructions and warnings if doing so is reasonably feasible.

Although comment i is much shorter than comment n, the reporters' notes indicate that no substantive difference was intended[.] * * *

Comment i distills down to three non-exclusive factors the considerations set out at length in comment n for determining when a warning to an intermediary is sufficient. A number of courts, beginning with the federal district court in *Goodbar v. Whitehead Bros.* in 1984,[6] a case involving silica products, have identified six non-exclusive factors in comment n:

> (1) the dangerous condition of the product; (2) the purpose for which the product is used; (3) the form of any warnings given; (4) the reliability of the third party as a conduit of necessary information about the product; (5) the magnitude of the risk involved; and (6) the burdens imposed on the supplier by requiring that he directly warn all users.[7]

We should point out that neither comment n, comment i, nor any of the cases applying them suggests that the scope of a supplier's duty to warn the ultimate users of its product can be determined simply by counting up the factors for and against allowing a warning to be given to an intermediary instead. Rather, the various considerations must be weighed against each other, the measure being reasonableness in the circumstances, as both comments state and as we said in *Alm*.

Gomez contends that it is never reasonable to excuse a supplier from warning ultimate users directly about product dangers whenever a warning is feasible. The determinative factor in *Alm*, Gomez argues, was that it was utterly impossible for a bottle capping machine manufacturer to warn soft drink consumers with whom it had no means of direct contact of the danger of exploding bottle caps. That, Gomez continues, is why *Alm* analogized Alcoa's position to a bulk supplier, who likewise has no packaging or other medium on which to place a warning that will reach the ultimate users of the product. But *Alm* cannot fairly be read so strictly. *Alm* also compared Alcoa's position to that of pharmaceutical manufacturers, who are not required to warn patients regarding usage of

---

6. 591 F.Supp. 552 (W.D.Va.1984), aff'd sub nom. *Beale v. Hardy*, 769 F.2d 213 (4th Cir.1985).

7. *Goodbar*, 591 F.Supp. at 557; see, e.g., *Smith v. Walter C. Best, Inc.*, 927 F.2d 736, 739–740 (3d Cir.1990); *Willis v. Raymark Indus., Inc.*, 905 F.2d 793, 796 (4th Cir. 1990); *Baker v. Monsanto Co.*, 962 F.Supp. 1143, 1151 (S.D.Ind.1997); *In re TMJ Implants Prods. Liab. Litig.*, 872 F.Supp. 1019, 1020 (D.Minn.1995); *Sara Lee Corp. v. Homasote Co.*, 719 F.Supp. 417, 421 (D.Md. 1989); *Eagle-Picher Indus., Inc. v. Balbos*, 326 Md. 179, 604 A.2d 445, 464 (1992); *Hoffman v. Houghton Chem. Corp.*, 434 Mass. 624, 751 N.E.2d 848, 856 (2001).

prescription drugs as long as physicians have been duly warned. The rationale for this "learned intermediary" rule is not that a direct warning from manufacturers to patients is infeasible, in the practical, physical sense of that word, but that it is better for the patient for the warning to come from his or her physician. We have never suggested, in *Alm* or elsewhere, that the sole factor in determining a product supplier's duty to warn is feasibility. The *Restatement* provisions we have quoted certainly do not do so.

Even if a product supplier's duty to warn the ultimate users does not depend solely on the feasibility of doing so, Gomez insists that it is never reasonable to depend on an employer to warn its employees. An employee cannot rely on an employer, Gomez argues, the way a patient relies on a physician. But the differences in the two relationships do not themselves dictate whether it is ever reasonable for a supplier to rely on an employer to warn its employees in the use of a product. A number of courts have found such reliance appropriate in various circumstances.[8] Based on these cases and the *Restatement* provisions we have cited, we think that the relationship between a supplier, an intermediary, and the ultimate user is but one factor to consider in deciding the scope of the supplier's duty to warn.

To the considerations derived from the *Restatement* provisions we add those which we have said inform any decision whether to recognize a common law duty, inasmuch as the decision whether to require a warning to ultimate users in addition to a warning to intermediaries is for us one of legal duty. * * * [T]he considerations in determining duty include "social, economic, and political questions", "the risk, foreseeability, and likelihood of injury", "the social utility of the actor's conduct, the magnitude of the burden of guarding against the injury," "the consequences of placing the burden on the defendant", and "whether one party would generally have superior knowledge of the risk or a right

---

8. *See, e.g., Duane v. Oklahoma Gas & Elec. Co.*, 833 P.2d 284, 287 (Okla.1992); *City of Jackson v. Ball*, 562 So.2d 1267, 1270 (Miss.1990); *Washington v. Dep't of Transp.*, 8 F.3d 296, 300–301 (5th Cir.1993) (holding under Louisiana law that the manufacturer of an industrial shop vacuum had no duty to warn its customers employees of the danger of using electrical equipment around acetone vapors); *Davis v. Avondale Indus., Inc.*, 975 F.2d 169, 172–173 (5th Cir.1992) (holding under Louisiana law that jury should have been instructed that a welding rod manufacturer had no duty to warn a sophisticated user's employee of the dangers of using the product); *Cook v. Branick Mfg., Inc.*, 736 F.2d 1442, 1446 (11th Cir.1984) (holding under Alabama law that tire rim manufacturer was not required to warn customer's employees to use safety pin); *Marshall v. H.K. Ferguson Co.*, 623 F.2d 882, 886–887 (4th Cir.1980) (stating that the defendant, who designed and constructed a brewery, had no duty to warn the employees of the owner and operator regarding the operation of the brewery); *Martinez v. Dixie Carriers, Inc.*, 529 F.2d 457, 466 (5th Cir.1976); *Jacobson v. Colorado Fuel & Iron Corp.*, 409 F.2d 1263, 1272–1273 (9th Cir.1969); *Byrd v. Brush Wellman, Inc.*, 753 F.Supp. 1403, 1405, 1413 (E.D.Tenn.1990); *Singleton v. Manitowoc Co.*, 727 F.Supp. 217, 225–226 (D.Md.1989); *Higgins v. E.I. DuPont de Nemours, Inc.*, 671 F.Supp. 1055, 1058–1059 (D.Md.1987); *Morsberger v. Uniking Conveyor Corp.*, 647 F.Supp. 1297, 1299 (W.D.Va.1986); *Goodbar v. Whitehead Bros.*, 591 F.Supp. 552, 559 (W.D.Va.1984), *aff'd sub nom. Beale v. Hardy*, 769 F.2d 213, 214 (4th Cir.1985); *see also* Joel Slawotsky, *The Learned Intermediary Doctrine: The Employer as Intermediary*, 30 Tort & Ins. L.J. 1059, 1060 (1995).

to control the actor who caused the harm."[9] We take all of these factors into account in determining the scope of Humble's duty to warn.

B

Based on all of the considerations that have been set out, whether a flint supplier had a duty to warn abrasive blasting operators' employees during the time frame that Gomez was employed that inhaling silica dust could result in disability and death and that an air-fed hood should be worn around silica dust at all times depends, we think, on the following factors. As we have already said, these factors must be applied to the abrasive blasting industry as a whole, not merely to Humble, Spincote, and Gomez individually.

1. The likelihood of serious injury from a supplier's failure to warn.

Silicosis, unquestionably a serious injury, is likely to result from working around silica dust without properly using protective equipment. Whether such injury was also likely to result from a supplier's failure to warn workers of the seriousness of silicosis and the importance of wearing an air-fed hood is far from clear on the record before us. For one thing, the record does not reflect whether flint was supplied mostly in bags or in bulk, or whether some operators purchased flint only in bags (Spincote purchased both in bags and in bulk). There is no evidence that it was feasible for bulk sellers to warn their customers' employees, and several courts have held that there is no duty to do so. None has held to the contrary. If in fact flint was supplied mostly in bulk, without warnings, then the likelihood of injury due to inadequate warnings on bags, as opposed to no warnings at all on bulk deliveries, may have been small. Furthermore, there is no evidence that any abrasive blasting worker other than Gomez ever saw a warning label on a bag of flint. Gomez's fellow employee did not testify whether he had ever seen such labels. The record is completely silent on whether it was common in the industry for blasting workers to handle bags. Thus, it is unclear whether warnings printed on bags could ordinarily have been expected to reach blasting workers. Even if blasting workers ordinarily saw bag labels, there is some suggestion at least that the warnings would have been ineffectual, that they would have continued on in their jobs out of economic necessity. Although Texas law presumes that an adequate warning will be followed, the presumption is rebuttable. There is no question, of course, that Gomez would have escaped injury had Humble's bags borne an adequate warning label; he so testified, and the jury believed him. But as we have already explained, the inquiry for purposes of determining duty must be an objective one with a view of the industry as a whole. A supplier with a duty to warn is liable for each injury caused by its failure to do so. Whether such a duty exists, however, depends in part on whether injury in general is likely to result from the absence of a warning.

9. *Praesel v. Johnson,* 967 S.W.2d 391, 397–398 (Tex.1998).

On the record before us, nothing more can be said than that *one* supplier's failure to warn *one* worker increased the likelihood of *his* injury. A legal duty resulting in enormous liability cannot be imposed on an entire industry on the basis of a fluke. It may be that, in general, a supplier's failure to print more specific warnings on bags of flint significantly increased the likelihood of serious injury, but there is nothing in the record either to support or contradict that proposition.

2. *The burden on a supplier of giving a warning.*

The record establishes that the burden on a supplier of flint in bags is either inconsequential or nonexistent.

3. *The feasibility and effectiveness of a supplier's warning.*

It was obviously feasible for suppliers to print warning labels on bags, but it is not clear from the record before us whether such labels would have reached blasting workers or would have reduced the risk of silicosis if they had. The feasibility of printing words on a bag is not in any doubt, but the feasibility of using that medium to communicate any meaningful warning effectively is. Gomez testified that he would never have worked as a blaster had he known the seriousness of the risks, but his expert testified that it is possible to avoid those risks by proper use of protective equipment. Gomez does not contend that flint suppliers could have provided adequate information regarding the proper use of safety equipment. The most a supplier should have done, according to Gomez and the expert witnesses who testified for him, was to warn that exposure to silica dust can be deadly and that an air-fed hood should always be worn. It is important to note that neither of the two 1974 studies cited by Gomez to show conditions in the abrasive blasting industry suggested that exposure to free silica was due to the lack or inadequacy of warnings by suppliers, or that better supplier warnings would have alleviated the problem. Both studies concluded that safe working conditions were up to employers. A warning that could not provide useful safety information was of limited utility.

4. *The reliability of operators to warn their own employees.*

Although abrasive blasting operators knew the dangers of working around silica dust, were in a far better position than flint suppliers to warn their own employees of those dangers, and could have reduced or eliminated altogether the risk of silicosis by following federal regulations, the record establishes that they routinely neglected safety measures and did not warn employees. There is no indication that the burden of such measures on operators was great. But while the evidence shows that operators often could not be relied upon to enforce safe conditions in the work place, there is no evidence that any government agency or industrial safety group ever considered that safety could be improved by suppliers' warnings.

5. *The existence and efficacy of other protections.*

The existence of a comprehensive regulatory scheme to protect against harm weighs against imposing a common law duty to accomplish the same result if the scheme affords significant protections. OSHA regulations prescribed standards for abrasive blasting that were legally enforceable against operators and that, if followed, would have provided safe working conditions. But the evidence is overwhelming that the regulations were widely disregarded and as a practical matter, afforded workers little protection.

6. *The social utility of requiring, or not requiring, suppliers to warn.*

Requiring suppliers to warn would avoid some injuries, including Gomez's, but shifting responsibility away from operators might lessen even further their incentives to provide a safe working environment, ultimately resulting in injuries to more workers than if warnings were not given.

On balance:

We cannot determine from this record that a duty should be imposed on flint suppliers like Humble to provide their customers' employees the limited warnings Gomez argues should have been given. "An ideal tort system should impose responsibility on the parties according to their abilities to prevent the harm."[10] If most of the harm to abrasive blasting workers was due to the use of flint supplied in bulk, it would be a perverse result if the responsibility for injury fell solely on those doing the least harm—suppliers who sold flint in bags. If abrasive blasting workers do not ordinarily see bag labels, it would do little good to require that the labels be more specific. And if abrasive blasting operators persistently require their employees to work in unsafe conditions, it is not clear that the purposes of imposing a duty to warn—encouraging care and protecting users—can be advanced by requiring flint suppliers to warn that those conditions are indeed unsafe. We say "if" because these matters remain in doubt based on the evidence before us.

By the same token, we cannot say from the record that a duty to warn should *not* be imposed on flint suppliers. We must determine what result is appropriate in such a case.

C

Courts have variously referred to the argument that a product supplier should not be required to warn knowledgeable customers or their employees of risks of use as the sophisticated user "doctrine" or "defense". While "doctrine" does not indicate whether the issue is one of duty or avoidance, "defense" implies the latter with the burden of proof on the supplier. As we have analyzed this case, we think the question presented is one of duty. Other courts have taken the same approach. As noted above, the burden of showing the existence and scope of a duty is ordinarily on the plaintiff.

At bottom, our principal concern with imposing a duty on Humble and other suppliers of flint in bags is that the warning Gomez contends should have been given would have been inefficacious for the several

---

10. *Duncan v. Cessna Aircraft Co.,* 665 S.W.2d 414, 425 (Tex.1984).

reasons we have explained. "The issue," as we said in *Alm,* "is whether the original manufacturer has a reasonable assurance that its warning will reach those endangered by the use of its product."[11] It is precisely this issue that cannot be resolved on the record in this case. We think the burden should have been on Humble to show that the warning Gomez contends flint suppliers should have given would not have been effectual. This is appropriate, even though proof of duty is usually the plaintiff's responsibility, for several reasons. First, in most circumstances a supplier's duty to warn is simply assumed; the availability of the warning to end users is not in question. Circumstances in which that assumption is not warranted, as when sales are in bulk or there is an intermediary who should have the duty to warn, seem more the exception than the rule. Indeed, in this case it is not apparent that a supplier's warning would *not* reach end users; it is just not apparent that it *would*. Second, the record in this case is sufficiently descriptive of the nature of the abrasive blasting injury for us to conclude that evidence regarding the efficacy or inefficacy of a supplier's warning in the blasting workplace, in general, is likely to be more readily available to a supplier than a worker. Of course, a worker would know first-hand, and therefore better than a flint supplier, the conditions in the environment in which he himself worked, but he could not be expected to have access to information about other workplaces. A supplier would have easier access to information from his customers than a stranger. As already stated, we do not suggest that a supplier has any duty to investigate his customers' operations to avoid liability. The issue here is only whether suppliers have better access to information about how their product is used among their customers than one customer's employee. Third, as we have said, other cases tend to treat the intermediary issue generally as defensive, and while they do not analyze why that should be the case, we think it is better to have a uniform rule on the issue. Thus, we conclude that the burden was on Humble to demonstrate that, based on the factors we have set out, the legal duty that a supplier ordinarily has to warn end users of product dangers should not be imposed on suppliers of flint in bags to warn abrasive blasters of two specific dangers: that air-fed hoods or respirators should be used around blasting areas at all times, and that the failure to do so can result in a disease that is fatal. As with all determinations of legal duty in Texas, the issue is one for the court unless the relevant facts are disputed.

The fact that a warning by Humble would have reached Gomez does not, by itself, in the context of the industry involved here, support an inference that all flint suppliers should have a legal duty to warn all abrasive blasters. By the same token, the silence of the record concerning the general efficacy of such warnings does not support an inference that imposition of a duty is not justified. Because the parties have not focused on the issue we think is crucial, we conclude that the interests of justice would be best served by a new trial. As we have explained, if the evidence relevant to this issue is undisputed, the trial court should

11. *Alm v. Aluminum Co. of Am.,* 717 S.W.2d 588, 591 (Tex.1986).

determine duty as a matter of law, but if the evidence is in conflict, that conflict should first be resolved by the finder of fact and then the duty issue determined.

* * *

For these reasons, the court of appeals' judgment is reversed and the case is remanded to the trial court for a new trial.

Justice O'NEILL filed a dissent, in which Justice SCHNEIDER joined. [Justice O'Neill's dissenting opinion is omitted.]

Notes

1. The manufacturer's obligation is to use reasonable care to protect the people who are likely to be injured by his goods. Manufacturers of consumer goods, which are individually packaged and sold, usually must warn the user or consumer. A warning given to a non-consuming purchaser, such as a retailer or wholesaler, will not satisfy the manufacturer's obligation. Thus, to be effective, the warning must often accompany the product. Whether it must be on the product itself is a different matter. *See Broussard, infra* page 270.

2. In Sills v. Massey–Ferguson, Inc., 296 F.Supp. 776 (N.D.Ind.1969), a bystander was injured when he was hit by an object thrown by the blade of a rotary-type lawnmower 150 feet away. He sued the manufacturer on negligence and products liability theories, claiming that defendant should have warned the general public to stay a safe distance from the mower. The court recognized that the manufacturer might be acting reasonably in warning the user only. This is because the user is in a position to protect bystanders, and warning the general public would be difficult. The court held that whether there is a duty to warn the general public is a jury question.

3. **Sophisticated Purchasers.** When products are sold in bulk to sophisticated industrial users for use in the manufacturing process, many courts have held that the supplier is not required to warn the purchaser's employees. The supplier can escape liability by adequately warning and training the purchaser. Rusin v. Glendale Optical Co., Inc., 805 F.2d 650 (6th Cir.1986) (Michigan law; protective glasses; warning required); Alm v. Aluminum Co. of America, 717 S.W.2d 588 (Tex.1986) (bottle capping machine; training the purchaser may be necessary). This is because of the difficulty of warning the individual employees, and because of the reasonableness of relying on the purchaser to protect his employees.

4. Is the sophisticated user defense determined as a question of fact or a question of law? The courts are split on this question. For an excellent analysis of the cases, *see* Note, Failures to Warn and the Sophisticated User Defense, 74 Va.L.Rev. 579 (1988).

5. Goodbar v. Whitehead Bros., 591 F.Supp. 552, 566 (W.D.Va. 1984), discussed in *Humble Sand & Gravel* stated:

> [A bulk] sand supplier to a large, knowledgeable foundry like the Lynchburg Foundry has no duty to warn the foundry employees about the occupational disease of silicosis and its causes when only the

Foundry is in a position to communicate effective warning and accordingly should be the one to shoulder any burden of effective warning. The difficulties that the sand suppliers face in attempting to warn the Foundry's employees of the hazards inherent in the use of sand in a foundry setting are numerous. These include (1) the identification of the users or those exposed to its products would require a constant monitoring by the suppliers in view of the constant turnover of the Foundry's large work force; (2) the manner in which the sand products are delivered in bulk (i.e. unpackaged railroad car lots or truck); (3) no written product warnings placed on the railroad cars would ever reach the workers involved in casting or those in the immediate vicinity due to the way the loose sand is unloaded, conveyed, and kept in storage bins until needed; (4) only the Foundry itself would be in a position to provide the good housekeeping measures, training and warnings to its workers on a continuous and systematic basis necessary to reduce the risk of silicosis; (5) the sand suppliers must rely on the Foundry to convey any safety information to its employees; (6) the confusion arising when twelve different suppliers and the Foundry each try to cope with the awesome task of instructing the Foundry workers; and (7) in a commercial setting, it would be totally unrealistic to assume that the suppliers would be able to exert pressure on a large, industrial customer such as the Foundry to allow the suppliers to come in and educate its workers about the hazards of silicosis.

6. Consider Oman v. Johns–Manville Corp., 764 F.2d 224 (4th Cir. 1985), cert. denied, 474 U.S. 970, 106 S.Ct. 351, 88 L.Ed.2d 319 (1985). Four shipyard workers were required to use products containing asbestos. They contracted asbestosis because of exposure to air-borne asbestos fibers which came from the products. They sued the manufacturers for failure to warn them about the risks associated with the products. The court discussed the duty to warn issue as follows:

The third and final issue presented for review concerns the sufficiency of the district court's charge to the jury regarding the defendants' duty to warn. The defendants argue that the district court should have charged the jury that the manufacturer's duty to warn the ultimate users, the employees, is satisfied if a sophisticated employer is aware of the dangers involved in the use of the product.

In Featherall v. Firestone Tire and Rubber Co., 219 Va. 949, 252 S.E.2d 358 (1979), the Supreme Court of Virginia adopted *Restatement (Second) of Torts* § 388 (1965) to govern a manufacturer's duty to warn about dangers associated with a product's use. *Featherall*, 219 Va. at 962, 252 S.E.2d at 366. Virginia law includes comment n of § 388, "Warnings given to third person." Jones v. Meat Packers Equipment Co., 723 F.2d 370, 373 (4th Cir.1983); Barnes v. Litton Indus. Products, Inc., 555 F.2d 1184, 1188 (4th Cir.1977); Goodbar v. Whitehead Bros., 591 F.Supp. 552, 557 (W.D.Va.1984).

Comment n discusses the various factors a court must balance to determine what precautions the manufacturer or supplier of a product must take to satisfy the requirement of reasonable care found in § 388(c). These factors include: (1) the dangerous condition of the product; (2) the purpose for which the product is used; (3) the form of any warnings given; (4) the reliability of the third party as a conduit of necessary information about the product; (5) the magnitude of the risk involved; and (6) the burdens imposed upon the supplier by requiring that he directly warn all users. These considerations must be balanced to determine if the manufacturer owes a duty to place a warning on his product.

In this case the product, because it contained asbestos fibers, was very dangerous. The burden on the manufacturers in placing a warning on the product was not great. The employer was unaware of the danger until 1964. Finally, once the employer became aware of the potential danger it failed to convey its knowledge to its employees. We cannot say that the district court erred in refusing to give the charge requested by the manufacturers under the set of facts involved in this case.

764 F.2d at 232–33. Note that the court which decided *Oman* also affirmed *Goodbar v. Whitehead Bros.* on appeal in a decision which adopted Judge Kiser's opinion as the opinion of the court. Beale v. Hardy, 769 F.2d 213 (4th Cir.1985). Both decisions were governed by the substantive law of the same state, and both opinions were written by the same judge. Can the two opinions be reconciled?

7. Some courts reject the sophisticated user doctrine. *See, e.g.,* Whitehead v. St. Joe Lead Co., 729 F.2d 238 (3d Cir.1984). An employee in a solder manufacturing plant suffered lead poisoning as a result of long term exposure to minute particles of airborne lead released by the manufacturing process. She sued the companies that supplied lead ingot to her employer on both products liability and negligence theories. She claimed that they should have warned her of the dangers associated with the use of lead. The court rejected defendants' argument that they had no duty to warn plaintiff because her employer (the purchaser) knew of the danger. The court concluded that under New Jersey law the sophisticated user doctrine did not apply to products liability actions. This is because the defendants had a nondelegable duty to make the product safe, and hindsight is used to impute knowledge to defendants that the employer would not adequately protect plaintiff. On the negligence theory, the court ruled that it was for the jury to determine whether defendants reasonably relied on the employer to protect plaintiff.

8. The sophisticated user doctrine is discussed in Madden, The Duty to Warn in Products Liability: Contours and Criticism, 89 W.Va.L.Rev. 221, 285–298 (1987); Goggin & Brophy, Toxic Torts: Workable Defenses Available to the Corporate Defendant, 28 Vill.L.Rev. 1208, 1268–1276 (1983); Comment, Duty to Warn and the Sophisticated User Defense in Products Liability Cases, 15 U.Balt.L.Rev. 276 (1986); Note, Failures to Warn and the Sophisticated User Defense, 74 Va.L.Rev. 579 (1988).

9. In 1993, Humble Sand & Gravel began using the following more extensive warning on its bags:

WARNING BREATHING DUST OF THIS PRODUCT CAUSES SILICOSIS, A SERIOUSLY DISABLING AND FATAL LUNG DISEASE. AN APPROVED AND WELL–MAINTAINED AIR–SUPPLIED ABRASIVE BLASTING HOOD MUST WORN AT ALL TIMES WHILE HANDLING AND USING THIS PRODUCT. FOLLOW ALL APPLICABLE OSHA STANDARDS.

Another manufacturer supplied the following warning on its bags:

WARNING: CONTAINS FREE SILICA. DO NOT BREATHE DUST. May Cause Delayed Lung Injury,(Silicosis). Follow OSHA Safety and Health Standards for Crystalline Silica (Quartz).

Are either of these warnings adequate? What if the bags of one of the manufacturers supplying flint to an employer contains an adequate warning? Can other manufacturers piggy back on this warning? What is the nature of their argument?

(b) Learned Intermediaries

PEREZ v. WYETH LABORATORIES INC.
Supreme Court of New Jersey, 1999.
161 N.J. 1, 734 A.2d 1245.

The opinion of the Court was delivered by

O'HERN, J.

Our medical-legal jurisprudence is based on images of health care that no longer exist. At an earlier time, medical advice was received in the doctor's office from a physician who most likely made house calls if needed. * * *

Pharmaceutical manufacturers never advertised their products to patients, but rather directed all sales efforts at physicians. In this comforting setting, the law created an exception to the traditional duty of manufacturers to warn consumers directly of risks associated with the product as long as they warned health-care providers of those risks.

For good or ill, that has all changed. * * * Drug manufacturers now directly advertise products to consumers on the radio, television, the Internet, billboards on public transportation, and in magazines. * * *

* * * We believe that when mass marketing of prescription drugs seeks to influence a patient's choice of a drug, a pharmaceutical manufacturer that makes direct claims to consumers for the efficacy of its product should not be unqualifiedly relieved of a duty to provide proper warnings of the dangers or side effects of the product.

I

THE NORPLANT SYSTEM (NORPLANT)

This appeal concerns Norplant, a Food and Drug Administration (FDA)-approved, reversible contraceptive that prevents pregnancy for up to five years. The Norplant contraceptive employs six thin, flexible, closed capsules that contain a synthetic hormone, levonorgestrel. The capsules are implanted under the skin of a woman's upper arm during an in-office surgical procedure characterized by the manufacturer as minor. A low, continuous dosage of the hormone diffuses through the capsule walls and into the bloodstream. Although the capsules are not usually visible under the skin, the outline of the fan-like pattern can be felt under the skin. Removal occurs during an in-office procedure, similar to the insertion process.

We have no doubt of the profound public interest in developing new products for reproductive services. We intend no disparagement of the product when we recite plaintiffs' claims concerning the efficacy of Norplant. The procedural posture that brings this case before us requires that we accept as true plaintiffs' version of the facts. The motion to dismiss was in the nature of a motion for judgment on the pleadings.

According to plaintiffs, Wyeth began a massive advertising campaign for Norplant in 1991, which it directed at women rather than at their doctors. Wyeth advertised on television and in women's magazines such as *Glamour, Mademoiselle* and *Cosmopolitan*. According to plaintiffs, none of the advertisements warned of any inherent danger posed by Norplant; rather, all praised its simplicity and convenience. None warned of side effects including pain and permanent scarring attendant to removal of the implants. Wyeth also sent a letter to physicians advising them that it was about to launch a national advertising program in magazines that the physicians' patients may read.

Plaintiffs cite several studies published in medical journals that have found Norplant removal to be difficult and painful. One study found that thirty-three percent of women had removal difficulty and forty percent experienced pain. Another study found that fifty-two percent of physicians reported complications during removal. Medical journals have catalogued the need for advanced medical technicians in addition to general surgeons for Norplant removal. Plaintiffs assert that none of this information was provided to consumers.

In 1995, plaintiffs began to file lawsuits in several New Jersey counties claiming injuries that resulted from their use of Norplant. Plaintiffs' principal claim alleged that Wyeth, distributors of Norplant in the United States, failed to warn adequately about side effects associated with the contraceptive. Side effects complained of by plaintiffs included weight gain, headaches, dizziness, nausea, diarrhea, acne, vomiting, fatigue, facial hair growth, numbness in the arms and legs, irregular menstruation, hair loss, leg cramps, anxiety and nervousness, vision problems, anemia, mood swings and depression, high blood pressure, and removal complications that resulted in scarring.

Class action certification was denied. All New Jersey Norplant cases were consolidated in Middlesex County. Eventually, twenty-five New Jersey Norplant cases involving approximately fifty Norplant users were pending in the Superior Court in Middlesex County.

After a case management conference, plaintiffs' counsel sought a determination of whether the learned intermediary doctrine applied. Pursuant to that conference, five bellwether plaintiffs were selected to challenge defendant's motion for summary judgment concerning the learned intermediary doctrine. *See Perez v. Wyeth Labs., Inc.*, 313 N.J.Super. 646, 650, 713 A.2d 588 (Law Div.1997). The trial court dismissed plaintiffs' complaints, concluding that * * * the learned intermediary doctrine applied. *Ibid.* * * *

Plaintiffs appealed. * * * The Appellate Division affirmed the trial court's grant of summary judgment in favor of defendants and its determination that the learned intermediary doctrine applied. 313 N.J.Super. 511, 713 A.2d 520 (1998). * * *

We granted plaintiffs' petition for certification. 156 *N.J.* 410, 719 A.2d 642 (1998).

II

In *Feldman v. Lederle Laboratories,* 97 *N.J.* 429, 479 A.2d 374, (1984) (*Feldman I*), we considered the relationship between principles of products liability law and pharmaceutical products. In *Feldman I*, we declined to "hold as a matter of law and policy that all prescription drugs that are unsafe are unavoidably so." *Id.* at 447, 479 A.2d 374. * * *

As explained in *Niemiera by Niemiera v. Schneider,* 114 *N.J.* 550, 559, 555 A.2d 1112 (1989):

> In New Jersey, as elsewhere, we accept the proposition that a pharmaceutical manufacturer generally discharges its duty to warn the ultimate user of prescription drugs by supplying physicians with information about the drug's dangerous propensities. *See, e.g., Bacardi v. Holzman,* 182 *N.J.Super.* 422, 442 A.2d 617 (App.Div.1981). This concept is known as the "learned intermediary" rule because the physician acts as the intermediary between the manufacturer and the consumer. The phrase appears to have been coined in the case of *Sterling Drug, Inc. v. Cornish,* 370 *F.*2d 82, 85 (8th Cir. 1966).

We observed that there were circumstances, such as in *Davis v. Wyeth Laboratories, Inc.,* 399 *F.*2d 121 (9th Cir.1968), in which the manufacturer should not be relieved of a duty to warn. *Niemiera, supra,* 114 *N.J.* at 559, 555 A.2d 1112. In *Davis,* the manufacturer of a polio vaccine was held to have an independent duty to warn the consumer because in mass immunization clinics such as where the plaintiff received a polio vaccine, there was "no physician present to weigh the risks and benefits of the drug therapy for each patient." *Ibid.* * * *

* * *

III

DIRECT-TO-CONSUMER ADVERTISING

It is paradoxical that so pedestrian a concern as male-pattern baldness should have signaled the beginning of direct-to-consumer marketing of prescription drugs. Upjohn Company became the first drug manufacturer to advertise directly to consumers when it advertised for Rogaine, a hair-loss treatment. Jon D. Hanson & Douglas A. Kysar, *Taking Behavioralism Seriously: Some Evidence of Market Manipulation,* 112 Harv. L.Rev. 1420, 1456 (1999). The ad targeted male consumers by posing the question, "Can an emerging bald spot ...

damage your ability to get along with others, influence your chance of obtaining a job or date or even interfere with your job performance?" *Ibid.* (footnotes omitted). A related ad featured an attractive woman asserting suggestively, "I know that a man who can afford Rogaine is a man who can afford me." *Ibid.* (footnote omitted).

Advertising for Rogaine was the tip of the iceberg. Since drug manufacturers began marketing directly to consumers for products such as prescription drugs in the 1980s, "almost all pharmaceutical companies have engaged in this direct marketing practice." *Ibid.* (footnote omitted).
* * *

These campaigns "bring to 'bear all the slick pressure of which Madison Avenue is capable'." Hanson & Kysar, *supra,* 112 Harv. L.Rev. at 1456 (footnote omitted).

Pressure on consumers is an integral part of drug manufacturers' marketing strategy. From 1995 to 1996, drug companies increased advertising directed to consumers by ninety percent. * * *

* * *

The difficulties that accompany this [type of advertising] practice are manifest. "The marketing gimmick used by the drug manufacturer often provides the consumer with a diluted variation of the risks associated with the drug product." Even without such manipulation, "[t]elevision spots lasting 30 or 60 seconds are not conducive to 'fair balance' [in presentation of risks]." Given such constraints, pharmaceutical ads often contain warnings of a general nature. However, "[r]esearch indicates that general warnings (for example, see your doctor) in [direct-to-consumer] advertisements do not give the consumer a sufficient understanding of the risks inherent in product use." Consumers often interpret such warnings as a "general reassurance" that their condition can be treated, rather than as a requirement that "specific vigilance" is needed to protect them from product risks.

[Hanson & Kysar, *supra,* 112 Harv. L.Rev. at 1456.]

IV

How Has the Law Responded to These Changes?

A. The new *Restatement (Third) of Torts* has left the issue to "developing case law."

Parallel to the developments in drug marketing, the American Law Institute was in the process of adopting the *Restatement (Third) of Torts: Products Liability* (1997). The comment to Section 6 explains that subsection (d)(1) sets forth the traditional rule of the learned intermediary that drug and medical device manufacturers are liable for failing to warn of a drug's risks only when the manufacturer fails to warn the health-care provider of risks attendant to a specific drug. *Restatement, supra,* § 6(d) comment a. That same comment also notes that subsection (d)(2) reflects decisional law and provides limited exceptions to the traditional rule by requiring manufacturers to warn patients in certain circumstances. *Ibid.* Because situations may exist when the health-care provider assumes a "much-diminished role as an evaluator or decision-maker," it is appropriate to impose a duty on the manufacturer to warn the patient directly. *Id.* at § 6d comment b. Despite the early effort to provide an exception to the doctrine in the case of direct marketing of pharmaceuticals to consumers, the drafters left the resolution of that issue to "developing case law." *Id.* at § 6d comment e. One commentator described the *Restatement's* approach as a "tepid endorsement" of the learned intermediary doctrine. Charles J. Walsh et al., *The Learned Intermediary Doctrine: The Correct Prescription for Drug Labeling*, 48 *Rutgers L.Rev.* 821, 869 (1994). Thus, under the new *Restatement*, "warnings may have to be provided to a health-care provider or even to the patient," depending on the circumstances. William A. Dreier, *The Restatement (Third) of Torts: Products Liability and the New Jersey Law—Not Quite Perfect Together*, 50 *Rutgers L.J.* 2059, 2097 (1998). This is an entirely appropriate resolution. * * *

B. The New Jersey Products Liability Act does not legislate the boundaries of the learned intermediary doctrine.

As noted, the New Jersey Products Liability Act provides:

> An adequate product warning or instruction is one that a reasonably prudent person in the same or similar circumstances would have provided with respect to the danger and that communicates adequate information on the dangers and safe use of the product, taking into account the characteristics of, and the ordinary knowledge common to, the persons by whom the product is intended to be used, or in the case of prescription drugs, taking into account the characteristics of, and the ordinary knowledge common to, the prescribing physician. If the warning or instruction given in connection with a drug or device or food or food additive has been approved or prescribed by the federal Food and Drug Administration under the "Federal Food, Drug, and Cosmetic Act," 52 *Stat.* 1040, 21 *U.S.C.* § 301 *et seq.*, . . . a rebuttable presumption shall arise that the warning or instruction is adequate. . . .

[*N.J.S.A.* 2A:58C–4.]

* * * Although the statute provides a physician-based standard for determining the adequacy of the warning due to a physician, the statute does not legislate the boundaries of the doctrine. For example, the Act does not purport to repeal a holding such as *Davis v. Wyeth Labs*, *supra*, which required that manufacturers directly warn patients in mass inoculation cases. * * * We believe that the part of the provision establishing "a presumption that a warning or instruction is adequate on drug or food products if the warning has been approved or prescribed by the Food and Drug Administration," *Committee Statement*, *supra*, will provide the benchmark for this decision.

* * *

C. Direct advertising of drugs to consumers alters the calculus of the learned intermediary doctrine.

In *Reyes, supra,* the respected Judge John Minor Wisdom explained the rationale behind the learned intermediary doctrine. His perspective reflects the then-prevalent attitude about doctor-patient relationships:

> This special standard for prescription drugs is an understandable exception to the Restatement's general rule that one who markets goods must warn foreseeable ultimate users of dangers inherent in [the] products.... Prescription drugs are likely to be complex medicines, esoteric in formula and varied in effect. As a medical expert, the prescribing physician can take into account the propensities of the drug, as well as the susceptibilities of [the] patient. [The physician's] task [is to weigh] the benefits of any medication against its potential dangers. The choice [the physician] makes is an informed one, an individualized medical judgment bottomed on a knowledge of both patient and palliative. Pharmaceutical companies then, who must warn ultimate purchasers of dangers inherent in patent drugs sold over the counter, in selling prescription drugs are required to warn only the prescribing physician, who acts as a "learned intermediary" between manufacturer and consumer.

[498 *F.*2d at 1276 (footnote and citation omitted).]

A more recent review summarized the theoretical bases for the doctrine as based on four considerations.

> First, courts do not wish to intrude upon the doctor-patient relationship. From this perspective, warnings that contradict information supplied by the physician will undermine the patient's trust in the physician's judgment. Second, physicians may be in a superior position to convey meaningful information to their patients, as they must do to satisfy their duty to secure informed consent. Third, drug manufacturers lack effective means to communicate directly with patients, making it necessary to rely on physicians to convey the relevant information. Unlike [over the counter products], pharmacists usually dispense prescription drugs from bulk containers rather than as unit-of-use packages in which the manufacturer may have enclosed labeling. Finally, because of the complexity of risk information about prescription drugs, comprehension problems would complicate any effort by manufacturers to translate physician labeling for lay patients. For this reason, even critics of the rule do not suggest that pharmaceutical companies should provide warnings only to patients and have no tort duty to warn physicians.

[Noah, *supra,* 32 *Ga. L.Rev.* at 157–59 (footnotes omitted).]

These premises: (1) reluctance to undermine the doctor patient-relationship; (2) absence in the era of "doctor knows best" of need for the patient's informed consent; (3) inability of drug manufacturer to communicate with patients; and (4) complexity of the subject; are all (with the possible exception of the last) absent in the direct-to-consumer advertising of prescription drugs.

First, with rare and wonderful exceptions, the " 'Norman Rockwell' image of the family doctor no longer exists." *Id.* at 180 n. 78 (citing Paul D. Rheingold, *The Expanding Liability of the Drug Manufacturer to the Consumer,* 40 *Food Drug Cosm. L.J.* 135, 136 (1985)). Informed consent requires a patient-based decision rather than the paternalistic approach of the 1970s. * * * The decision to take a drug is "not exclusively a matter for medical judgment." *See* Teresa Moran Schwartz, *Consumer-Directed Prescription Drug Advertising and the Learned Intermediary Rule,* 46 *Food Drug Cosm. L.J.* 829, 831 (1991) (citing Margaret Gilhooley, *Learned Intermediaries, Prescription Drugs, and Patient Information,* 30 *St. Louis. U. L.J.* 633, 652 (1986)).

Second, because managed care has reduced the time allotted per patient, physicians have considerably less time to inform patients of the risks and benefits of a drug. Sheryl Gay Stolberg, *Faulty Warning Labels Add to Risk in Prescription Drugs,* N.Y. Times, June 4, 1999, at A27. "In a 1997 survey of 1,000 patients, the F.D.A. found that only one-third had received information from their doctors about the dangerous side effects of drugs they were taking." *Ibid.*

Third, having spent $1.3 billion on advertising in 1998, *supra* at 12–13, 734 *A.*2d at 1251–52, drug manufacturers can hardly be said to "lack effective means to communicate directly with patients," Noah, *supra,* 32 *Ga. L.Rev.* at 158, when their advertising campaigns can pay off in close to billions in dividends.

Consumer-directed advertising of pharmaceuticals thus belies each of the premises on which the learned intermediary doctrine rests.

> First, the fact that manufacturers are advertising their drugs and devices to consumers suggests that consumers are active participants in their health care decisions, invalidating the concept that it is the doctor, not the patient, who decides whether a drug or device should be used. Second, it is illogical that requiring manufacturers to provide direct warnings to a consumer will undermine the patient-physician relationship, when, by its very nature, consumer-directed advertising encroaches on that relationship by encouraging consumers to ask for advertised products by name. Finally, consumer-directed advertising rebuts the notion that prescription drugs and devices and their potential adverse effects are too complex to be effectively communicated to lay consumers. Because the FDA requires that prescription drug and device advertising carry warnings, the consumer may reasonably presume that the advertiser guarantees the adequacy of its warnings. Thus, the common law duty to warn the ultimate consumer should apply.

[Susan A. Casey, Comment, *Laying an Old Doctrine to Rest: Challenging the Wisdom of the Learned Intermediary Doctrine,* 19 Wm. Mitchell L.Rev. 931, 956 (1993) (footnotes omitted).]

When all of its premises are absent, as when direct warnings to consumers are mandatory, the learned intermediary doctrine, "itself an exception to the manufacturer's traditional duty to warn consumers directly of the risk associated with any product, simply drops out of the calculus, leaving the duty of the manufacturer to be determined in accordance with general principles of tort law." *Edwards v. Basel Pharms.*, 116 *F.*3d 1341, 1343 (10th Cir.1997) (discussing question of adequacy of nicotine patch warning under Texas law certified in *Edwards v. Basel Pharms.*, 933 *P.*2d 298 (Okla.1997)). We acknowledge that the Fifth Circuit recently held that under Texas law, the learned intermediary doctrine does apply in the context of Norplant. *In re Norplant Contraceptive Products Liab. Litig.*, 165 *F.*3d 374, 379–80 (1999). Nonetheless, we agree with the Tenth Circuit's approach.

Concerns regarding patients' communication with and access to physicians are magnified in the context of medicines and medical devices furnished to women for reproductive decisions. In *MacDonald v. Ortho Pharmaceutical Corp.*, 394 Mass. 131, 475 *N.E.*2d 65, *cert. denied*, 474 *U.S.* 920, 106 *S.Ct.* 250, 88 *L.Ed.*2d 258 (1985), the plaintiff's use of oral contraceptives allegedly resulted in a stroke. The Massachusetts Supreme Court explained several reasons why contraceptives differ from other prescription drugs and thus "warrant the imposition of a common law duty on the manufacturer to warn users directly of associated risks." *Id.* at 136–37, 475 *N.E.*2d 65. For example, after the patient receives the prescription, she consults with the physician to receive a prescription annually, leaving her an infrequent opportunity to "explore her questions and concerns about the medication with the prescribing physician." *Id.* at 137, 475 *N.E.*2d 65. Consequently, the limited participation of the physician leads to a real possibility that their communication during the annual checkup is insufficient. *Id.* at 138, 475 *N.E.*2d 65. The court also explained that because oral contraceptives are drugs personally selected by the patient, a prescription is often not the result of a physician's skilled balancing of individual benefits and risks but originates, instead, as a product of patient choice. *Id.* at 137, 475 *N.E.*2d 65. Thus, "the physician is relegated to a ... passive role." *Ibid.*

* * * When a patient is the target of direct marketing, one would think, at a minimum, that the law would require that the patient not be misinformed about the product. It is one thing not to inform a patient about the potential side effects of a product; it is another thing to misinform the patient by deliberately withholding potential side effects while marketing the product as an efficacious solution to a serious health problem. Further, when one considers that many of these "life-style" drugs or elective treatments cause significant side effects without any curative effect, increased consumer protection becomes imperative, because these drugs are, by definition, not medically necessary.

* * *

Obviously, the learned intermediary doctrine applies when its predicates are present. "In New Jersey, as elsewhere, we accept the proposition that a pharmaceutical manufacturer generally discharges its duty to warn the ultimate users of prescription drugs by supplying physicians with information about the drug's dangerous propensities." *Niemiera, supra,* 114 *N.J.* at 559, 555 *A.*2d 1112. Had Wyeth done just that, simply supplied the physician with information about the product, and not advertised directly to the patients, plaintiffs would have no claim against Wyeth based on an independent duty to warn patients. The question is whether the absence of an independent duty to warn patients gives the manufacturer the right to misrepresent to the public the product's safety.

D. Prescription drug manufacturers that market their products directly to consumers should be subject to claims by consumers if their advertising fails to provide an adequate warning of the product's dangerous propensities.

In reaching the conclusion that the learned intermediary doctrine does not apply to the direct marketing of drugs to consumers, we must necessarily consider that when prescription drugs are marketed and labeled in accordance with FDA specifications, the pharmaceutical manufacturers should not have to confront "state tort liability premised on theories of design defect or warning inadequacy." Note, *A Question of Competence: The Judicial Role in the Regulation of Pharmaceuticals,* 103 *Harv. L.Rev.* 773, 773 (1990). We draw much of this summary concerning the specifics of FDA pharmaceutical regulation from the brief of *amicus curiae,* the Pharmaceutical Research and Manufacturers of America. Because such regulations may change from day to day, our commentary concerning the current regulations may soon become moot.

The FDA is authorized to regulate advertisements for prescription drugs pursuant to 21 *U.S.C.A.* Section 352(n) of the Food, Drug and Cosmetic Act, 21 *U.S.C.A.* Sections 301–397. Advertisements subject to Section 352(n) include "advertisements in published journals, magazines, other periodicals, and newspapers, and advertisements broadcast though media such as radio, television, and telephone communication systems." 21 *C.F.R.* § 202.1(*l*)(1). Although the FDA has regulated drug advertising since 1963, those regulations initially addressed only advertising directed at health-care providers. Noah, *supra,* 32 *Ga. L.Rev.* at 142–43. Aware of the potential threat to consumers when pharmaceutical companies first sought to advertise to non-health-care professionals, the FDA, in the early 1980s initially imposed a [voluntary] moratorium on such advertising so that it could study the issue more carefully; but, in 1985, it lifted the moratorium, content to apply its existing regulations to this new practice. Perhaps spurred by the rapid growth of direct consumer advertising and the inherent shortcomings of rules designed to control advertising to physicians, coupled with the emergence of brand new media such as the Internet for disseminating promotional messages, the Agency has now proposed to modify its approach. [*Id.* at 142–43.]

Section 352(n) of the Act contains the "brief summary requirement," which is a misnomer considering that the summary is anything but brief. Accordingly, all advertisements must include a description of "side effects, contraindications, and effectiveness as shall be required in regulations...." 21 *U.S.C.A.* § 352(n)(3). The regulations addressing prescription drugs also require that the brief summary provide "all the risk-related information in a product's approved package labeling," which is usually a package insert or product package insert. 62 *Fed.Reg.* 43,171 (Aug. 12, 1997) (citing 21 *C.F.R.* § 202.1(e)(1) and (e)(3)(iii)). As noted by *amicus curiae*, the FDA "[r]egulations are exhaustive, addressing issues as broad as the requirement that ads be fairly balanced (21 *C.F.R.* § 202.1(e)(6)) and as narrow as how graphs must be labeled (21 *C.F.R.* § 202.1(e)(7)(iv)) and the type size used to set forth a medicine's established name (21 *C.F.R.* § 202.1(b)(2))."

In August 1997, the FDA released a Draft Guidance, which specifically addresses consumer-directed broadcast advertisements such as radio, television and telephone communications. 21 *Fed.Reg.* 43,172 (Aug. 12, 1997). Broadcast advertisements must contain a "major statement" of the major risks of the drug. *Ibid.* Instead of presenting a brief summary with the broadcast, which is not as feasible as in the print media, the Guidance proposes an alternative requirement known as the "adequate provision" requirement. *Ibid.* That provision provides that the manufacturer "may make adequate provision for the dissemination of the approved package labeling in connection with the broadcast presentation (§ 202.1(e)(1))." *Ibid.* The Guidance explains that four components must be present to meet the "adequate provision" requirement in broadcasts—a toll-free number that provides information concerning where consumers might find information about package labeling; an alternative mechanism for obtaining package labeling information for consumers who do not have access to technology such as the Internet; a statement directing consumers to pharmacists and/or physicians; and an Internet web-page address. *See Guidance for Industry: Consumer–Directed Broadcast Advertisements* (visited June 14, 1999) <http://www.fda.gov/cder/guidance/index.htm>. Within two years of the release of the Guidance, the FDA "intends to evaluate the effects of the guidance...." 62 *Fed.Reg.* 43,172. These FDA actions indicate that the agency views direct-to-consumer advertising as a means of providing consumers with improved access to important information about prescription drugs.

FDA regulations are pertinent in determining the nature and extent of any duty of care that should be imposed on pharmaceutical manufacturers with respect to direct-to-consumer advertising. [Citation.] Presently, any duty to warn physicians about prescription drug dangers is presumptively met by compliance with federal labeling. [Citation.] That presumption is not absolute. [Citation.] Nevertheless, FDA regulations serve as compelling evidence that a manufacturer satisfied its duty to warn the physician about potentially harmful side effects of its product.

We believe that in the area of direct-to-consumer advertising of pharmaceuticals, the same rebuttable presumption should apply when a manufacturer complies with FDA advertising, labeling and warning requirements. That approach harmonizes the manufacturer's duty to doctors and to the public when it chooses to directly advertise its products, and simultaneously recognizes the public interest in informing patients about new pharmaceutical developments. Moreover, a rebuttable presumption that the duty to consumers is met by compliance with FDA regulations helps to ensure that manufacturers are not made guarantors against remotely possible, but not scientifically-verifiable, side-effects of prescription drugs, a result that could have a "significant anti-utilitarian effect." *See Feldman II, supra,* 125 *N.J.* at 162, 592 *A.*2d 1176 (Garibaldi, J., dissenting); *see also* Michael D. Green, *Statutory Compliance and Tort Liability: Examining the Strongest Case,* 30 *U. Mich. J.L. Ref.* 461, 466–67 (1997) (noting that over deterrence in drug advertising context could impede and delay manufacturers from research and development of new and effective drugs, force beneficial drugs from market, lead to shortages in supplies and suppliers of pharmaceuticals, and create unnecessary administrative costs).

We believe that this standard is fair and balanced. For all practical purposes, absent deliberate concealment or nondisclosure of after-acquired knowledge of harmful effects, compliance with FDA standards should be virtually dispositive of such claims. By definition, the advertising will have been "fairly balanced." This presumptive effect is in accordance with legislative intent that we discern from the punitive damages provision of the Products Liability Act. *See L.* 1987, *c.* 142, § 5(c). That provision prohibits, in the case of the sale of pharmaceutical products, an award of punitive damages if there has been compliance with FDA labeling and pre-marketing requirements, impliedly reserving compensatory damages for those rare cases when the presumption is overcome. *N.J.S.A.* 2A:58C–5(c).

V

The final issues in this case concern proximate cause, that is, whether misinformation actually affected these patients and, if so, whether the intervention of the physician (without whom the product may not reach the patient) breaks the chain of causation.

* * * We believe it best to resolve the threshold issue of whether the learned intermediary doctrine applies in the case of direct-to-consumer marketing of pharmaceutical goods and to remand the matter for further proceedings. The issue on remand will be whether, on a summary judgment motion, there is sufficient evidence for a reasonable jury to determine in the cases of the bellwether plaintiffs, or any remaining plaintiffs, that the absence of information or presence of misinformation in Norplant advertising was in violation of FDA requirements and whether such violations, if any, were a substantial factor in bringing about the harm suffered.

The more difficult question is whether the role of the physician breaks the chain of causation. Although the physician writes the prescription, the physician's role in deciding which prescription drug is selected has been altered. With the arrival of direct-to-consumer adver-

tising, patients now enter physicians' offices with "preconceived expectations about treatment because of information obtained from DTC [direct-to-consumer] advertisements." Tamar V. Terzian, *Direct-to-Consumer Prescription Drug Advertising*, 25 Am. J.L. & Med. 149, 157 (1999).
* * *

* * *

* * * In the case of direct marketing of drugs, we believe that neither the physician nor the manufacturer should be entirely relieved of their respective duties to warn. Pharmaceutical manufacturers may seek contribution, indemnity or exoneration because of the physician's deficient role in prescribing that drug. In each case, a jury must resolve the close questions of whether a breach of duty has been a proximate cause of harm, *Cowan v. Doering,* 111 *N.J.* 451, 545 *A.*2d 159 (1988), and how that causative harm, if found, may be apportioned among culpable defendants.* * *.

* * *

The judgment of the Appellate Division is reversed and the matter is remanded to the Law Division for further proceedings.

[The opinion of POLLOCK, J., dissenting is omitted.]

Notes

1. The history of the learned intermediary doctrine is traced in Comment, Pharmaceutical Manufacturers and Consumer–Directed Information—Enhancing the Safety of Prescription Drug Use, 34 Cath.U.L.Rev. 117, 122–29 (1984).

2. Under the doctrine the manufacturer has no duty to warn the patient directly. Whether or not the intermediary must warn the patient is governed by the law of informed consent. Under that rule, the doctor may sometimes be required to pass on some or all of the warnings to the patient. At other times, he may weigh the risks and benefits and make the decision to prescribe the drug without informing the patient. *See* Comment, Pharmaceutical Manufacturers and Consumer–Directed Information—Enhancing the Safety of Prescription Drug Use, 34 Cath.U.L.Rev. 117, 129 (1984).

3. The learned intermediary doctrine has been generally accepted. Some courts apply it to professional nurses as well as physicians. Walker v. Merck & Co., Inc., 648 F.Supp. 931 (M.D.Ga.1986). It has also been applied to warnings about the risks of treatment with potentially dangerous medical equipment. Kirsch v. Picker International, Inc., 753 F.2d 670 (8th Cir.1985) (X-ray machine); Terhune v. A.H. Robins Co., 90 Wash.2d 9, 577 P.2d 975 (1978) (intrauterine device).

4. The Restatement (Third) of Torts: Products Liability § 6 (d) provides:

> (d) A prescription drug or medical device is not reasonably safe due to inadequate instructions or warnings if reasonable instructions or warnings regarding foreseeable risks of harm are not provided to:

(1) prescribing and other health-care providers who are in a position to reduce the risks of harm in accordance with the instructions or warnings; or

(2) the patient when the manufacturer knows or has reason to know that health-care providers will not be in a position to reduce the risks of harm in accordance with the instructions or warnings.

5. The doctrine does not apply to non-prescription drugs. Here the manufacturer must warn the consumer directly. Torsiello v. Whitehall Laboratories, Division of Home Products Corp., 165 N.J.Super. 311, 398 A.2d 132 (1979), cert. denied, 81 N.J. 50, 404 A.2d 1150 (1979); Michael v. Warner/Chilcott, 91 N.M. 651, 579 P.2d 183 (1978), cert. denied, 91 N.M. 610, 577 P.2d 1256 (1978). May the manufacturer avoid liability by advising the consumer to see a doctor before using the product for more than ten days?

6. **Immunization Clinics.** In Davis v. Wyeth Laboratories, Inc., 399 F.2d 121 (9th Cir.1968), polio vaccine was distributed in a mass immunization program in which the drug manufacturer participated. The court required that warnings be given directly to the consumers because the drug "was dispensed to all comers at mass clinics without an individualized balancing by a physician of the risks involved." *Id.* at 131.

7. The courts are split over the question of how far to expand the exception to the learned intermediary doctrine. In Reyes v. Wyeth Laboratories, 498 F.2d 1264 (5th Cir.1974), cert. denied, 419 U.S. 1096, 95 S.Ct. 687, 42 L.Ed.2d 688 (1974), the court required that the consumer be warned directly even though she did not receive the vaccine as part in a mass immunization clinic. There, the polio vaccine was given to plaintiff at her parents request by a nurse at a public health clinic. The clinic dispensed the vaccine as a part of an ongoing program, and no doctor was present to make an individualized determination for plaintiff of the risks and benefits. The court held that the learned intermediary exception did not apply because the manufacturer could foresee that the vaccine would be routinely administered in this fashion.

8. Other courts disagree. *See* Walker v. Merck & Co., Inc., 648 F.Supp. 931 (M.D.Ga.1986), refusing to apply the exception where a mass immunization program was not involved. In *Walker*, a practical nurse administered measles vaccine to plaintiff in a local program designed to inoculate certain high school students. The court held that the manufacturer did not have to warn the students directly. It distinguished this program from those involving mass immunization clinics because of the difficulty involved in identifying and warning individual recipients.

9. **Individually Prescribed Drugs.** In Givens v. Lederle, 556 F.2d 1341 (5th Cir.1977), the Fifth Circuit expanded the exception to the learned intermediary doctrine to apply it in certain cases where the drug is prescribed by the patient's doctor. These are cases where the doctor prescribes the drug without having made an individualized determination of the risks and benefits of the drug on plaintiff's behalf. In *Givens*, polio vaccine was administered by the patient's doctor in his office. The doctor testified that the administration did not differ from that of a public health center. The court ruled that the rationale of *Reyes* applied because "the vaccine was

administered here in a manner more like that at a small county health clinic, as in *Reyes*, than by prescription." *Accord,* Samuels v. American Cyanamid Co., 130 Misc.2d 175, 495 N.Y.S.2d 1006 (1985) (vaccine routinely administered in company clinic to employee prior to overseas travel).

10. Most courts have refused to expand the exception this far. *See, e.g.,* Plummer v. Lederle Laboratories, Division of American Cyanamid Co., 819 F.2d 349 (2d Cir.1987) (the manufacturer of polio vaccine has no duty to warn the patient when the drug is prescribed by his physician).

11. **Birth Control Pills.** The courts are also split on the question of whether manufacturers of birth control pills must directly warn the consumer. The majority of courts hold that the duty is to warn the prescribing physician only. *E.g.,* Brochu v. Ortho Pharmaceutical Corp., 642 F.2d 652 (1st Cir.1981). *But see* MacDonald v. Ortho Pharmaceutical Corp., 394 Mass. 131, 475 N.E.2d 65 (1985), cert. denied, 474 U.S. 920, 106 S.Ct. 250, 88 L.Ed.2d 258 (1985) (discussed in *Perez,* imposing a duty). Two Federal District courts have reached a similar conclusion on the basis of their prediction of state law. Odgers v. Ortho Pharmaceutical Corp., 609 F.Supp. 867 (E.D.Mich.1985); Stephens v. G.D. Searle & Co., 602 F.Supp. 379 (E.D.Mich.1985).

12. A Food and Drug Administration regulation requires that a warning directly to the consumer accompany birth control pills. One court has held that violation of this regulation constitutes negligence *per se.* Lukaszewicz v. Ortho Pharmaceutical Corp., 510 F.Supp. 961 (E.D.Wis.1981), amended, 532 F.Supp. 211 (E.D.Wis.1981). On the other hand, MacDonald v. Ortho Pharmaceutical Corp., 394 Mass. 131, 475 N.E.2d 65 (1985), cert. denied, 474 U.S. 920, 106 S.Ct. 250, 88 L.Ed.2d 258 (1985) held that the regulation did not have conclusive effect. Either compliance or noncompliance with the regulation was admissible as evidence of the adequacy of the warning that was given, but was not controlling.

13. **Pharmacists' Liability**. The majority of the jurisdictions do not require pharmacists to warn their customers of the dangerous propensities of the drugs they sell. As long as a prescription is valid on its face, and there are no obvious discrepancies, a pharmacist will not be held liable for filling it in accordance with the physician's directions. There is no duty to warn about possible side-effects of a single drug, or of possible interactions of multiple drugs. *See e.g.,* West v. G.D. Searle & Company, 317 Ark. 525, 879 S.W.2d 412 (1994); Sanderson v. Eckerd Corp., 780 So.2d 930 (Fla.App.2001); Frye v. Medicare–Glaser Co., 153 Ill.2d 26, 605 N.E.2d 557, 178 Ill.Dec. 763 (1992). This rule is based on the policy of fostering the physician-patient relationship. Under the learned intermediary rule, patients are to receive all warnings from the physician, the person best able to determine what warnings are appropriate. Additional warnings by a pharmacist could cause the patient to discontinue taking an appropriate drug or to become confused. *See,* Note, From Pill–Counting to Patient Care: Pharmacists' Standard of Care in Negligence Law, 68 Fordham L.Rev. 165, 168–69 (1999). In recent years, however, a number of courts have imposed upon pharmacies at least a limited duty to warn. *See* Garbutt & Hofmann, Recent Developments in Pharmaceutical Products Liability Law: Failure to Warn, the Learned Intermediary Defense, and Other Issues in the New Millennium, 58 Food & Drug

J. 269 (2003); Marchitelli, Liability of Pharmacist Who Accurately Fills Prescription for Harm Resulting to User, 44 A.L.R.5th 393 *See*, Lasley v. Shrake's Country Club Pharmacy, Inc., 179 Ariz. 583, 880 P.2d 1129 (1994) (requiring pharmacist to give warnings that reasonable prudence dictates); Horner v. Spalitto, 1 S.W.3d 519 (Mo.App.1999) (negligent failure to warn about a fatal drug overdose prescribed by a Physician). Recent legislation requiring pharmacists to monitor patients' drug therapy has helped foster the minority rule. *See*, Comment, Pharmacist Liability: The Doors of Litigation Are Opening, 40 Santa Clara L.Rev. 907 (2000).

In Happel v. Wal–Mart Stores, Inc., 199 Ill.2d 179, 766 N.E.2d 1118, 262 Ill.Dec. 815 (2002), the pharmacy apparently knew or should have known that a drug prescribed for its patient was contraindicated for a person with the patient's allergies. According to one witness, the plaintiff had on earlier visits told the pharmacy workers about her aspirin allergy. If the plaintiff's allergy had been placed in the pharmacy computer, the computer screen would have flashed a "drug interaction" warning, and halted the prescription process, when the pharmacist attempted to process a prescription for Toradol. The pharmacy's standard procedure at this point was to call the physician and notify him of the contraindication. For whatever reason, the pharmacy failed to inform either the patient or her physician. The Illinois Supreme Court held that under these circumstances the pharmacy had a duty to warn either the patient or her physician and, therefore, the trial court should not have granted the defendant a summary judgment.

The *Happel* court noted that the pharmacy was under no legal obligation to collect any allergy information from its patients. Do you think this opinion will have a chilling effect on pharmacy willingness to collect such information? *See* Morgan v. Wal–Mart Stores, Inc., 30 S.W.3d 455 (Tex.App. 2000) (No duty to warn. Pharmacy did not have any special knowledge of its customers.). If the defendant in *Happel* is found responsible at trial, should it be entitled to indemnification from the physician who prescribed the drug?

14. For discussions of the learned intermediary doctrine, see Thompson, The Drug Manufacturer's Duty to Warn—To Whom Does it Extend? 13 Fla.St.U.L.Rev. 135 (1985); Comment, Pharmaceutical Manufacturers and Consumer–Directed Information—Enhancing The Safety of Prescription Drug Use, 34 Cath.U.L.Rev. 117 (1984); Comment, Products Liability: The Continued Viability of the Learned Intermediary Rule as it Applies to Product Warnings for Prescription Drugs, 20 Univ.Rich.L.Rev. 405 (1986); Imbroscio & Bell, Adequate Drug Warnings in the Face of Uncertain Causality: The Learned Intermediary Doctrine and the Need for Clarity, 107 W. Va. L. Rev. 847 (2005).

15. The *Perez* litigation involved the contraceptive, Norplant. *See* In re Norplant Contraceptive Products Liability Litigation, 215 F.Supp.2d 795 (E.D.Tex. 2002) for a useful recent summary of the status of the doctrine in all fifty states. According to this opinion, no other state has as yet adopted the New Jersey Court's position.

16. *Perez* sets out the New Jersey Products Liability Act which creates a rebuttable presumption that a warning is adequate if it has been approved or prescribed by the Food and Drug Administration. Does this presumption help defendants? Assume a defendant invokes the presumption by proving

its warning was approved by the FDA. What evidence must plaintiff offer to rebut the presumption? In the absence of the presumption, what evidence would plaintiff have to offer to make a submissible failure to warn case?

With respect to warnings and instructions directed to physicians, the FDA reviews and approves their exact wording. However, with respect to the direct-to-consumer warnings the FDA offers only general guidance concerning the content of the warnings. In this context, does the creation of a rebuttable presumption have any practical significance? Would it be easier or harder for a plaintiff to defeat the presumption in the broadcast advertising situation?

(c) *Allergies and Idiosyncratic Reactions*

KAEMPFE v. LEHN & FINK PRODUCTS CORP.
Supreme Court of New York, Appellate Division, First Department, 1964.
21 A.D.2d 197, 249 N.Y.S.2d 840.

EAGER, JUSTICE.

The plaintiff, in a suit against the manufacturer of the spray deodorant "Etiquet", has recovered judgment for a severe case of dermatitis resulting from an allergic reaction in the use of the product. The action was tried and submitted to the jury on the theory that the defendant-manufacturer was negligent in its alleged failure to give adequate warning to the very few persons who might possibly suffer some allergic reaction in the use of the product.

The plaintiff, a 19 year old woman, had purchased at a local drug store two containers of the product labeled "Etiquet Spray–On Deodorant", which was prepared, sold and used for the purpose of preventing body perspiration and odor. The label on the container read as follows: "Easy to use A quick squeeze—it sprays Stops underarm odor Checks perspiration Safe for normal skin Harmless to clothes." The container also was marked with the statement, "Contains Aluminum Sulphate".

Aluminum sulphate, the essential ingredient in the preparation, when applied to the skin, has the effect of closing the pores, stopping perspiration and eliminating odor. According to the testimony, practically all of the deodorants on the market contain aluminum sulphate.

After her purchase of the product, the plaintiff, following the directions thereon, applied the spray in the area of both armpits. Thereafter, during that day, she detected an itching sensation and observed an inflammation where the spray had been applied. Subsequently, a rash or dermatitis developed which spread to adjacent parts of her body. It was accompanied by burning, blistering and itching. Although permanent injury was not claimed, the sequelae persisted for sometime until it was fully healed. This was plaintiff's first allergic reaction to this or any other product.

The plaintiff's medical expert testified that the aluminum sulphate in the product was the cause of plaintiff's dermatitis. By his testimony, it was established that a few persons may be sensitive to products containing this particular ingredient. The doctor stated, however, that the chemical agent aluminum sulphate, which is used in almost all deodorants, is not normally harmful to skin; that it is in fact safe for "normal skin" as claimed.

This is the typical case where a peculiar reaction to a product in common use was due solely to an allergy possessed by the user. Plaintiff's medical expert testified that her rash was due to an allergy, and, in this connection, he described an allergy as "the reaction of the skin to a substance which, as a rule, does not bother normal people but which in people who are susceptible, sensitized, makes them react differently from normal people." The plaintiff is apparently one in a multitude of persons who has an allergy to the ingredient aluminum sulphate. Here, as measured by defendant's sales figures for this product for the year 1956 (the year in which plaintiff used this preparation) and the number of complaints it received therefrom, it appears that some sensitivity was experienced in the ratio of about one to 150,000 customers.

* * *

In the case of the non-poisonous and reasonably safe product in general use, the duty to warn depends upon whether or not it was reasonably foreseeable by the supplier that a substantial number of the population may be so allergic to the product as to sustain an injury of consequence from its use. (See Tentative Draft No. 7, Restatement of the Law of Torts, Second (April 16, 1963), § 402A, subd. (j), p. 5.) "If the danger of such an allergy is known or should be known to the maker, and if the consequences of the idiosyncrasy are serious enough, reasonable care may well require the taking of some precaution such as warning and instructions for making tests." (Harper and James, The Law of Torts, § 28.8, p. 1551.)

The fundamental test of negligence—reasonable foreseeability of harm and reasonable care to guard against same—is applicable in these cases. The manufacturer or seller may be held liable where he knows or with reasonable diligence should anticipate that the normal use of his product may result in substantial harm and where he fails to exercise reasonable care to warn of such danger. On the other hand, it is clear that the manufacturer or seller should not be held bound to anticipate and warn against a remote possibility of injury in an isolated and unusual case. The law requires a person to exercise reasonable care to guard against probabilities, not mere remote possibilities. A supplier of a product in daily use ought not to be placed in the position of an insurer. We have not yet reached the point where the manufacturer is under the absolute duty of making a product, useful to many, free from all possible harm to each and every individual; nor the point where the manufacturer is to be held under an absolute duty of giving special warning against a remote possibility of harm due to an unusual allergic reaction from use by a minuscule percentage of the potential customers. "Every substance, including food which is daily consumed by the public, occasionally becomes anathema to him peculiarly allergic to it. To require insurability against such an unforeseeable happenstance would weaken the structure of common sense, as well as present an unreasonable burden on the channels of trade." (Bennett v. Pilot Products Co., 120 Utah 474, 478, 235 P.2d 525, 527, 26 A.L.R.2d 958, 961; Gerkin v. Brown & Sehler Co., 177 Mich. 45, 143 N.W. 48.)

So, according to the prevailing authority, the existence of a duty on the part of a manufacturer to warn depends upon whether or not, to his actual or constructive knowledge, the product contains an ingredient "to which a substantial number of the population are allergic" (see Tentative Draft No. 7, Restatement of the Law, Torts, Second, supra), or an ingredient potentially dangerous to an identifiable class of an appreciable number of prospective customers. (See Merrill v. Beaute Vues Corporation, 235 F.2d 893 (Murrah, J., concurring at 898). See, also, Note, 46 Cornell L.Q. 465 (1961).) "If the allergy is one common to any substantial number of possible users, the seller may be required at least to give warning of the danger." (Prosser, Torts (2d ed.), § 84, p. 503.) On the other hand, "in the ordinary case, the maker may also assume a normal user; and he is not liable where the injury is due to some allergy or other personal idiosyncrasy of the consumer, found only in an insignificant percentage of the population." (Prosser, idem.)

Knowledge or constructive notice of an unreasonable danger to users of a particular product may impose upon the manufacturer a duty of warning. But, in the case of a useful and reasonably safe product, in general use, the supplier owes no special duty of warning to the unknown few who constitute a mere microscopic fraction of potential users who may suffer some allergic reaction not common to the ordinary or normal person. (See, further, Bish v. Employers Liability Assurance Corp., 5 Cir., 236 F.2d 62; Merrill v. Beaute Vues Corporation, supra; Bennett v. Pilot Products Co., supra; Casagrande v. F.W. Woolworth Co., 340 Mass. 552, 556, 165 N.E.2d 109, 112; Crotty v. Shartenberg's–New Haven, Inc., 147 Conn. 460, 162 A.2d 513, 516; Levi v. Colgate–Palmolive Proprietary Ltd., 41 New So W St 48, 58 New So W W N 63.)

In light of the foregoing, the plaintiff, as the basis for imposing upon defendant a special duty of warning, was bound at the very least to show (1) that she was one of a substantial number or of an identifiable class of persons who were allergic to the defendant's product, and (2) that defendant knew, or with reasonable diligence should have known of the existence of such number or class of persons. There was, however, a failure of proof as to both of these requirements. Furthermore, it does not appear that a special warning here would have been effective for any purpose.

Without question, aluminum sulphate is an ingredient generally used in all deodorant and anti-perspirants. These products, containing this particular sulphate, are considered safe for normal skin and are universally used without harm. The plaintiff was one of an unknown and very insignificant few, who, because of a state of hypersensitiveness to the sulphate, unknown even to herself, would acquire dermatitis on the application of the product to her skin. There was no proof of the precise nature of or the exact cause for her allergy. There was no showing that she was one of any identifiable class of an appreciable number of persons with a similar allergy. Her medical expert did say that there was a class or group of persons who are sensitive to aluminum sulphate but did not elaborate. It does not appear, however, that the members of such class or group were of consequential numbers or exposed to serious and unreasonable danger. The only evidence in this connection was that, in one year, the defendant, in connection with 600,000 sales of its products, had but four complaints of a sensitive reaction in the use of the same; and, for all that appears, the affliction in each case may have been differently caused or comparatively minor. Such evidence establishes no more than a remote possibility of allergic sensitivity in isolated cases to the defendant's product.

Furthermore, the defendant did give notice, by statement on the container, of the presence of aluminum sulphate in the deodorant. If, as further stated on the container, the product was "safe for normal skin"—and there was no credible evidence to the contrary—what special warning would the defendant, acting reasonably, be expected to give to the very exceptional few who, unknown even to themselves, might have an allergy to the aluminum sulphate expressly stated to be contained in the product. This is left solely to a matter of speculation because there is not one iota of evidence in the record as to any customary or adequate mode of warning or as to known or proper tests to be suggested for use by the unknown few who might possibly suffer an allergic reaction.

Of course, the statement that the product contained a particular sulphate was adequate to warn any and all persons who knew that they had an allergy with respect to the same. As to those persons, an additional express warning not to use the product would serve no purpose. Specific words of caution would be meaningless as to those, such as the plaintiff, who did not know of their allergy to the particular sulphate. The plaintiff's prior use of deodorants containing the particular ingredient did not yield any manifestations of sensitivity and she expected none when she applied the defendant's product. So, it is difficult to see that a special warning in general terms of danger to the infinitesimal few with an allergy would be of any help or have persuaded plaintiff here from the purchase and use of defendant's merchandise. Under the circumstances, the special warning would have been wholly ineffective. (See Merrill v. Beaute Vues Corporation, supra, 235 F.2d at 897.) And the defendant should not be held negligent in failing to give a warning which would have served no purpose.

The conclusion we reach is that the plaintiff failed as a matter of law to establish that the defendant was derelict in any duty of warning to plaintiff. This conclusion is supported by the reasoning underlying the decisions which have denied recovery in these cases on theory of breach of implied warranty. It has been universally held that a person, who sustains harm due solely to an unusual hypersensitiveness to a reasonably safe product, may not recover against the seller or manufacturer on such theory.

* * *

Since the plaintiff failed as a matter of law to establish negligence of the defendant, the defendant's motion to dismiss, made at the close of the case, should have been granted. Consequently, the order of the Appellate Term, affirming the judgment for plaintiff entered upon the verdict of the jury rendered in City Court, should be reversed on the law, with costs, the judgment for plaintiff vacated and the complaint dismissed, with costs, to defendant.

Determination unanimously reversed, on the law, with costs to the appellant in this Court and in the Appellate Term, the judgment for plaintiff vacated and the complaint dismissed.

All concur.

Notes

1. The rule stated in the main case has been adopted by a substantial number of courts. *E.g.,* Presbrey v. Gillette Co., 105 Ill.App.3d 1082, 61 Ill.Dec. 816, 435 N.E.2d 513 (1982) (deodorant; reaction extremely rare); Booker v. Revlon Realistic Professional Products, Inc., 433 So.2d 407 (La. App.1983) (hair care product; four of seven million users complained). The Restatement (Third) of Torts: Products Liability § 2 Comment k (1997) adopts this approach.

2. **Nature of Allergies.** Professor Noel gives the following description of the nature of allergic reactions:

> Medical descriptions of how allergic reactions occur are complicated and still developing. From a legal standpoint, the established and significant factor is that an allergic reaction is one suffered by only a minority of the persons exposed to a particular substance. In this connection, a "sensitizer" is to be distinguished from a "primary irritant," which is something that produces irritation on the skin of the majority of normal persons.
>
> The sensitizing capacity of various substances differs enormously. Sometimes many exposures are necessary to develop allergic reactions, and these reactions may be confined to a very few people. Where a "strong sensitizer" is involved, the allergic reaction develops within a very limited time of exposure in much larger numbers of people.

Noel, Products Defective Because of Inadequate Directions or Warnings, 23 Sw.L.J. 256, 289 (1969). *See also,* Schattman, A Cause of Action for the Allergic Consumer, 8 Hous.L.Rev. 827, 829–833 (1971). Virtually every chemical ingredient in every product can cause an allergic reaction in some persons. Mobilia, Allergic Reactions to Prescription Drugs: A Proposal for Compensation, 48 Alb.L.Rev. 343, 345 (1984).

3. Courts adhering to the requirement that a substantial class of persons be affected by the allergy before there is a duty to warn generally impose this requirement regardless of whether suit is brought on the theory

of negligence, products liability, or breach of implied warranty. Noel, Products Defective Because of Inadequate Directions or Warnings, 23 Sw.L.J. 256, 289–298 (1969).

4. The special rule imposing a duty to warn only if a substantial number of people are likely to be harmed by the ingredient only applies to true allergic reactions. In cases where plaintiff is harmed by a "primary irritant" in a product, the duty to warn is based on general principles of foresight and reasonableness, with no absolute requirement that a "substantial" group of potential victims be involved. This is true even though a given plaintiff may suffer an unusually severe reaction to a primary irritant because of a peculiar susceptibility. *See, e.g.,* Advance Chemical Co. v. Harter, 478 So.2d 444 (Fla.App.1985), review denied, 488 So.2d 829 (Fla. 1986) (ammonia).

5. The cases vary considerably on the question of how big the class must be in order to be considered substantial. Both the severity of the injury and its prevalence are factors. Comment, Strict Liability and Allergic Drug Reactions, 47 Miss.L.J. 526, 531 (1976). Courts are more willing to find a small group "substantial" if the harm is severe. For an excellent analysis of this issue, *see* Noel, Products Defective Because of Inadequate Directions or Warnings, 23 Sw.L.J. 256, 289–298 (1969).

6. **Express Warranty.** Many courts do not impose a "substantial" number requirement in express warranty cases involving allergic reactions. A manufacturer, for example, who warrants that the product is "absolutely safe!" will be liable to an allergic user even if the allergy is rare. Spiegel v. Saks 34th Street, 43 Misc.2d 1065, 252 N.Y.S.2d 852 (1964), affirmed, 26 A.D.2d 660, 272 N.Y.S.2d 972 (1966).

7. An important line of authority rejects the requirement that the allergy affect a substantial group of people. These cases permit a jury to find that a warning was reasonably necessary even if a substantial group were not affected. The leading case is Wright v. Carter Products, Inc., 244 F.2d 53 (2d Cir.1957), also involving an allergic reaction to aluminum sulfate in a deodorant. The evidence showed that the manufacturer received one complaint for approximately every 220,000 jars of deodorant sold. Defendant argued that it had no duty to warn because only a "minuscule" percentage of users were adversely affected. The court rejected a "quantitative standard," holding that foreseeability is the determinative factor.

8. Courts appear particularly apt to reject the substantial group requirement in cases involving prescription drugs. See Basko v. Sterling Drug, Inc., 416 F.2d 417 (2d Cir.1969); Crocker v. Winthrop Laboratories, Division of Sterling Drug, Inc., 514 S.W.2d 429 (Tex.1974).

9. Which line of authority states the better rule?

10. Why not apply "true" strict liability in allergy cases, and hold manufacturers liable for all harm caused by all allergic reactions regardless of foreseeability? *See* Henderson, Process Norms in Products Litigation: Liability for Allergic Reactions, 51 U.Pitt.L.Rev. 761 (1990).

(d) The Continuing Duty to Warn

COVER v. COHEN
Court of Appeals of New York, 1984.
61 N.Y.2d 261, 473 N.Y.S.2d 378, 461 N.E.2d 864.

MEYER, Judge.

[Plaintiff, a pedestrian, was seriously injured when he was hit by a runaway 1973 Chevrolet Malibu. The driver of the car was attempting to parallel park on a city street. He put the car in reverse, and started to back up. The accelerator spring caused the throttle to stick in the full open position, and the car shot backward at high speed, hitting plaintiff and crushing him against a wall. Plaintiff sued the driver, manufacturer, and dealer who sold the car. The jury found in plaintiff's favor against all three defendants. The manufacturer appealed.

Beginning with 1974 models the federal government required a "redundant and failsafe" accelerator control system which presumably would have prevented this accident. The trial judge admitted evidence of this subsequent design change on the question of whether the car was defective in design and for a failure to warn at the time of manufacture. The court reversed and remanded for retrial because such evidence was not admissible in strict liability actions in New York to prove defect.

The manufacturer also argued that the trial court improperly admitted a 1974 technical service bulletin issued by the manufacturer with respect to the carburetor spring of the 1973 Chevrolet Malibu.]

For the same reasons that govern the Federal standard, the technical service bulletin issued by General Motors some 13 months after delivery of the Cohen Chevrolet was not admissible on the design defect cause of action or the failure to warn cause of action insofar as it turned on the design and risk status of the vehicle at the time of delivery. A manufacturer or retailer may, however, incur liability for failing to warn concerning dangers in the use of a product which come to his attention after manufacture or sale, through advancements in the state of the art, with which he is expected to stay abreast, or through being made aware of later accidents involving dangers in the product of which warning should be given to users (see *Schumacher v. Richards Shear Co.*, 59 N.Y.2d 239, 247, 464 N.Y.S.2d 437, 451 N.E.2d 195; 1 N.Y.P.J.I.2d 364–365; 1A Frumer & Friedman, Products Liability, § 8.02). Because liability on the theory of negligent failure to warn was presented during trial of the instant action and can be expected to arise again during retrial and because it is a necessary predicate for determining admissibility of the technical service bulletin, we outline the governing law.

Although a product be reasonably safe when manufactured and sold and involve no then known risks of which warning need be given, risks thereafter revealed by user operation and brought to the attention of the manufacturer or vendor may impose upon one or both a duty to warn (Prosser, Torts [4th ed.], p. 647; Restatement, Torts 2d, § 388). Not entirely clear from the cases, however, is what constitutes sufficient notice to the manufacturer or vendor to require its issuance of a warning, whether the manufacturer satisfies its obligation by notifying the vendor or must notify the user as well, or what the obligation of the vendor who receives such notice is to the user.

What notice to a manufacturer or vendor of problems revealed by use of the product will trigger his postdelivery duty to warn appears to be a function of the degree of danger which the problem involves and the number of instances reported (*Comstock,* 358 Mich., at p. 176, 99 N.W.2d 627 [thousands of defective power brakes]; *Bottazzi,* 664 F.2d, at p. 52 [several instances of corrosion of propeller shaft of a helicopter]; *Braniff Airways,* 411 F.2d, at p. 453, cert. den. 396 U.S. 959, 90 S.Ct. 431, 24 L.Ed.2d 423 [instances of cylinder barrel separation in an aircraft engine]; Restatement, Torts 2d, § 388, Comment *i* ["part of a lot, some of which he has discovered to be so imperfect as to be dangerous"]). When a prima facie case on that issue has been made will, of course, depend upon the facts of each case. Where, as here, however, the manufacturer has issued and sent to the vendor a technical service bulletin acknowledging that "[s]ome 1973 passenger cars * * * may exhibit an erratic idle speed and slow return to idle", that acknowledgment, * * * together with testimony that erratic idle speed or slow return to idle or both may seriously impair control of the vehicle presents a question of fact.

The nature of the warning to be given and to whom it should be given likewise turn upon a number of factors, including the harm that may result from use of the product without notice, the reliability and any possible adverse interest of the person, if other than the user, to whom notice is given, the burden on the manufacturer or vendor involved in locating the persons to whom notice is required to be given, the attention which it can be expected a notice in the form given will receive from the recipient, the kind of product involved and the number manufactured or sold, and the steps taken, other than the giving of notice, to correct the problem (*McLaughlin v. Mine Safety Appliances Co.,* 11 N.Y.2d 62, 226 N.Y.S.2d 407, 181 N.E.2d 430; see Restatement, Torts 2d, § 388, Comment *n;* Prosser, *loc. cit.*). Germane also will be any governmental regulation dealing with notice. Generally, the issue will be one of fact for the jury (*Rekab, Inc.,* 261 Md., at p. 150, 274 A.2d 107) whose function will be to assess the reasonableness of the steps taken by the manufacturer or vendor in light of the evidence concerning the factors listed above presented in the particular case, as well as any expert testimony adduced on the question. The manufacturer and the vendor do not necessarily have the same obligation to warn concerning dangers learned of after delivery of the product, as the Trial Judge recognized by dismissing for insufficiency of evidence the cause of action against Kinney for negligent failure to warn. On trial of the case, therefore, the technical service bulletin will be admissible, * * * but the instructions to the jury on the duty to warn should outline the factors for them to consider under the evidence presented.

* * *

For the foregoing reasons, the order of the Appellate Division should be reversed, with costs, and a new trial granted * * *.

COOKE, C.J., and JASEN, JONES, WACHTLER and KAYE, JJ., concur.

SIMONS, J., taking no part.

Order reversed, with costs to defendant General Motors against plaintiffs, and a new trial granted * * *.

Notes

1. **Defective Products.** Where the product was defective at the time of sale because the manufacturer failed to guard against or warn about known or knowable risks, the question is whether a post-sale warning will cut off the liability that otherwise would result. Should such a warning ever absolve the manufacturer? In some cases the courts have held that it will. This is particularly likely to be true where, in addition to warning, the manufacturer offers to repair or replace the product at no charge, and the owner disregards the offer. *See, e.g.,* Balido v. Improved Machinery, Inc., 29 Cal.App.3d 633, 105 Cal.Rptr. 890 (1972).

2. **Dangers Not Discoverable at the Time of Sale.** If a product contains a scientifically unknowable generic risk at the time it is sold, a majority of courts hold that there is no liability for a failure to warn at the time of sale. These cases are discussed in the Note Regarding the Foresight/Hindsight Distinction, *supra* page 141. Once the risk is subsequently discovered, a number of courts impose a duty to warn at that time. This duty is less onerous than the duty arising at the time of sale because it is often harder to warn when the product is out of the manufacturer's control. *Cover v. Cohen* contains a good statement of the considerations pertinent to the question of whether reasonable care requires a post-sale warning.

3. Courts have shown a particular willingness to require post-sale warnings in the case of prescription drugs. *E.g.,* Davis v. Wyeth Laboratories, Inc., 399 F.2d 121 (9th Cir.1968); Wooderson v. Ortho Pharmaceutical Corp., 235 Kan. 387, 681 P.2d 1038 (1984), cert. denied, 469 U.S. 965, 105 S.Ct. 365, 83 L.Ed.2d 301 (1984). What explains this?

4. A minority of courts use a hindsight standard for determining what warnings are required. In such jurisdictions a product can be defective because of a failure to warn about risks that were unknowable at the time of manufacture. In such a jurisdiction, should a manufacturer who discovers a previously unknown risk associated with a product already on the market be able to escape liability by giving a post-sale warning? Suppose it issues an adequate post-sale warning, and plaintiff receives it prior to his injury? What if plaintiff does not receive it? What effect would all this have on the manufacturer's willingness to discover and warn about unknown risks?

5. **Changes in Technology.** Suppose a change in technology takes place that makes it possible to improve the safety of a product already in use.

Does the manufacturer have a duty to inform the owner of the change? Some courts have flatly said no, as long as the product was not defective at the time it was marketed. Jackson v. New Jersey Manufacturers Insurance Co., 166 N.J.Super. 448, 400 A.2d 81 (1979), cert. denied, 81 N.J. 330, 407 A.2d 1204 (1979). Other courts have held that a warning is sometimes required. In Kozlowski v. John E. Smith's Sons Co., 87 Wis.2d 882, 275 N.W.2d 915 (1979) a worker was killed when a sausage stuffing machine's 500 pound piston burst through the machine's safety ring. The machine was first marketed in 1938. In 1946 the manufacturer developed a by-pass safety valve that would have prevented the accident. The valve was first marketed as optional equipment. Later, in 1971, it was made a standard feature of new sausage stuffing machines. In discussing the post-sale duty to warn about the necessity for the by-pass valve, the court said:

> We do not in this decision hold that there is an absolute continuing duty, year after year, for all manufacturers to warn of a new safety device which eliminates potential hazards. A sausage stuffer and the nature of that industry bears no similarity to the realities of manufacturing and marketing household goods such as fans, snowblowers or lawn mowers which have become increasingly hazard proof with each succeeding model. It is beyond reason and good judgment to hold a manufacturer responsible for a duty of annually warning of safety hazards on household items, mass produced and used in every American home, when the product is 6 to 35 years old and outdated by some 20 newer models equipped with every imaginable safety innovation known in the state of the art. It would place an unreasonable duty upon these manufacturers if they were required to trace the ownership of each unit sold and warn annually of new safety improvements over a 35 year period.
>
> As noted, the sausage stuffer machine industry is far more limited in scope. Consequently, a jury in determining a manufacturer's duty in this restricted area must look to the nature of the industry, warnings given, the intended life of the machine, safety improvements, the number of units sold and reasonable marketing practices, combined with the consumer expectations inherent therein.

275 N.W.2d at 923–24.

6. Is there a justification for requiring a post-sale warning about generic risks but not requiring one for improvements in technology?

7. **Misuse.** Should the manufacturer be required to give post-sale warnings against subsequently discovered misuse that was unforeseeable at the time of sale? There are very few cases. Rodriguez v. Besser Co., 115 Ariz. 454, 565 P.2d 1315 (App.1977) held that there was no duty to warn about the risks of a dangerous product modification that the manufacturer learned about after the sale. *Contra*, McDaniel v. Bieffe USA, Inc., 35 F.Supp.2d 735 (D.Minn.1999) (misuse of motorcycle helmet). Should dangers from misuse be treated differently from generic risks with respect to imposing a post-sale obligation to warn?

In Bell Helicopter Co. v. Bradshaw, 594 S.W.2d 519 (Tex.Civ.App.1979), the defendant manufactured a 1961 helicopter with a tail rotor that could be used for only 600 hours, and that required detailed maintenance and inspection. At the time of manufacture, this rotor represented the most advanced technology available. Bell became aware of accidents caused by widespread disregard of its recommended maintenance and inspection procedures. In 1970 it developed an improved rotor that could be used for 2500 hours and that required much less maintenance and inspection. Between 1969 and 1973 the helicopter in question was owned by a Bell service station. Because of its relationship with the service station, Bell could have required it to replace the old rotor system with the new one. It did not require replacement, and the service station sold the helicopter in 1973 with the old rotor system. An accident occurred because it was not equipped with the new system. The court upheld a jury verdict for plaintiff. It held that Bell was required either to mandate replacement of the old system or to recommend to users in very strong language that the system be replaced.

8. The Restatement (Third) of Torts: Products Liability §§ 10 and 11 (1997) provide:

§ 10. Liability of Commercial Product Seller or Distributor for Harm Caused by Post-sale Failure to Warn

(a) One engaged in the business of selling or otherwise distributing products is subject to liability for harm to persons or property caused by the seller's failure to provide a warning after the time of sale or distribution of a product if a reasonable person in the seller's position would provide such a warning.

(b) A reasonable person in the seller's position would provide a warning after the time of sale if:

(1) the seller knows or reasonably should know that the product poses a substantial risk of harm to persons or property; and

(2) those to whom a warning might be provided can be identified and can reasonably be assumed to be unaware of the risk of harm; and

(3) a warning can be effectively communicated to and acted on by those to whom a warning might be provided; and

(4) the risk of harm is sufficiently great to justify the burden of providing a warning.

Comment:

b. When a reasonable person in the seller's position would provide a warning. The standard governing the liability of the seller is objective: whether a reasonable person in the seller's position would provide a warning. This is the standard traditionally applied in determining negligence. See Restatement, Second, Torts § 283, Comment c. In applying the reasonableness standard to members of the chain of distribution it is possible that one party's conduct may be reasonable and another's unreasonable. For example, a manufacturer may discover information under circumstances satisfying Subsection (b)(1) through (4) and thus be required to provide a post-sale warning. In contrast, a retailer is generally not in a position to know about the risk discovered by the manufacturer after sale and thus is not subject to liability because it neither knows nor should know of the risk. Once the retailer is made aware of the risk, however, whether the retailer is subject to liability for failing to issue a post-sale warning depends on whether a reasonable person in the retailer's position would warn under the criteria set forth in Subsection (b)(1) through (4).

§ 11. Liability of Commercial Product Seller or Distributor for Harm Caused by Post-sale Failure to Recall Product

One engaged in the business of selling or otherwise distributing products is subject to liability for harm to persons or property caused by the seller's failure to recall a product after the time of sale or distribution if:

(a) (1) a governmental directive issued pursuant to a statute or administrative regulation specifically requires the seller or distributor to recall the product; or

 (2) the seller or distributor, in the absence of a recall requirement under Subsection (a)(1), undertakes to recall the product; and

(b) the seller or distributor fails to act as a reasonable person in recalling the product.

Comment:

 c. When seller or other distributor voluntarily undertakes to recall. Some courts have held that, when a seller, under no statutory or regulatory obligation to undertake a recall, volunteers to do so, the seller is subject to liability for failing to act reasonably to recall the product. The rationale for this rule lies partly in the general rule that one who undertakes a rescue, and thus induces other would-be rescuers to forbear, must act reasonably in following through. In the context of products liability, courts appear to assume that voluntary recalls are typically undertaken in the anticipation that, if the seller does not recall voluntarily, it will be directed to do so by a governmental regulator. Having presumably forestalled the regulatory recall directive, the seller should be under a common-law duty to follow through on its commitment to recall. In some instances voluntary recalls are subject to regulation by governmental agencies. Whether product sellers are subject to, or protected from, liability for harm caused by noncompliance or compliance with the terms of such regulations is governed by Restatement, Second, of Torts §§ 286–288C. *See* § 4, Comment f.

9. The post-sale duty to warn of a successor corporation is discussed in Chapter 12, Section A (3), *infra* page 705.

10. The preceding notes reveal substantial restrictions on the post-sale obligations of manufacturers. The obligation is generally restricted to warning about the product's danger rather than fixing the product. Furthermore, the duty to warn may apply only to generic risk, and not to misuse or changes in technology. Yet, under the law of negligence, a person who innocently places another person in peril has an unrestricted duty to use reasonable care to rescue that person. The Restatement (Second) of Torts § 321, provides:

 (1) If the actor does an act, and subsequently realizes or should realize that it has created an unreasonable risk of causing physical harm to

another, he is under a duty to exercise reasonable care to prevent the risk from taking effect.

(2) The rule stated in Subsection (1) applies even though at the time of the act the actor has no reason to believe that it will involve such a risk.

Can a plaintiff in a products liability case circumvent the restrictions in §§ 10 and 11 of the Restatement (Third) by relying on § 321 of the Restatement (Second)? If not, why should the manufacturer's duty to rescue be more restricted than the duty of other actors that innocently endanger people?

11. *See generally* Allee, Post–Sale Obligations of Product Manufacturers, 12 Fordham Urban L.J. 625 (1983–84); Schwartz, The Post–Sale Duty to Warn: Two Unfortunate Forks in the Road to a Reasonable Doctrine, 58 N.Y.U.L.Rev. 892 (1983); Note, Efficient Accident Prevention as a Continuing Obligation: The Duty to Recall Defective Products, 42 Stan.L.Rev. 103 (1989); Note, Manufacturers of Inherently Dangerous Products: Should They Have a Continuing Duty to Make Their Previously Sold Products Conform to State of the Art Safety Features? 92 W.Va.L.Rev. 153 (1989); Richmond, Expanding Products Liability: Manufacturers' Post-sale Duties to Warn, Retrofit and Recall, 36 Idaho L. Rev. 7 (1999); Ross, Post-sale Duty to Warn: A Critical Cause of Action, 27 Wm. Mitchell L. Rev. 339 (2000).

Chapter 5

CAUSATION IN FACT

SECTION A. TESTS FOR DETERMINING CAUSATION[1]

To recover under product liability, a plaintiff must prove that the product's defect was a cause-in-fact of his injury. The plaintiff need not prove that the defect was the sole cause of his injury; injuries can have multiple causes. The plaintiff's burden is merely to prove that the product defect was *a* cause-in-fact of his injury.

Courts usually define cause-in-fact by the "but for" or "sine qua non" test, which requires the plaintiff to prove that his injury would not have occurred if the product defect had not existed. This test is sometimes difficult to apply because a court cannot be certain what would have happened had events been different than they actually were. In most cases, however, the "but for" test is not difficult to apply.[2] For example, a court can be relatively certain that a plaintiff who was cut by glass in a soft drink would not have been injured if there had been no glass.

The "but for" test of causation is inadequate in cases in which each of two or more independently sufficient causes produces an injury. If a victim ingests two drugs, either of which would have caused an injury, neither is a "but for" cause, because even without the ingestion of one drug, the victim would still have been injured.[3] The "but for" test may also be difficult to apply in cases where the victim is exposed to a toxic agent by multiple parties but it is impossible given the current state of medical knowledge to discover which exposure caused the injury in question. In such cases, courts often use the "substantial factor" test.

---

1. This note is adapted in part from W. Powers, Texas Products Liability Law, pp. 6–3—6–7 (1986).

2. For a useful discussion of "but for" causation and the use of counter-factual examples in causal reasoning *see* Spellman & Kincannon, The Relationship Between Counterfactual ("But For") and Causal Reasoning: Experimental Findings and Implications for Jurors' Decisions, 64: No. 4 Law & Contemp. Probs. 240 (2001).

3. *See* Restatement (Second) of Torts § 432(2) (1965); Basko v. Sterling Drug, Inc., 416 F.2d 417 (2d Cir.1969).

Under that test, a cause in fact is something that is a substantial factor in bringing about the injury. (Rest.2d Torts, § 431)[4]

Because what constitutes a "substantial factor" is rarely defined with any specificity, it can be difficult to apply. In *Saunders System Birmingham Co. v. Adams*,[5] for example, a driver rented an automobile with defective brakes. The court held that the defective brakes were not a cause of an ensuing accident because the driver failed to apply the brakes soon enough. Neither the defective brakes nor the driver's failure to apply them was a "but for" cause of the accident because the accident would have occurred in the absence of either one of them. Both seem to be independently sufficient causes, however, since either alone would have sufficed to cause the accident. Nevertheless, the court held that the defect in the brakes was not a cause of the accident. Although the court did not explain this distinction, the relative temporal proximity to the accident of each potential cause may explain it. Despite the difficulties in applying the "substantial factor" test, it at least provides a potential basis for a finding of cause-in-fact in cases involving independently sufficient causes that fail to meet the "but for" test.

Some courts have held that an independently sufficient cause subjects a defendant to liability under the "substantial factor" test only if the other independently sufficient cause was of human or culpable origin.[6] Under this approach, a fire that was caused independently by a railroad's defective spark arrester and by lightning would not establish liability for the manufacturer of the spark arrester. This distinction was rejected by the Restatement (Second) of Torts.[7] This remains the position in the proposed Third Restatement. However, the Third Restatement does recognize that the situation is not without difficulty.[8] Even the handful of courts that draw the distinction between natural and human causes usually place the burden of proving the natural origin of

---

4. Rutherford v. Owens–Illinois, Inc., 16 Cal.4th 953, 968, 941 P.2d 1203, 67 Cal. Rptr.2d 16 (1997). Some courts seem to treat the term "substantial factor" as if it were a synonym for the "but for" test. *See* Kramer v. Lewisville Memorial Hosp., 858 S.W.2d 397, 400 (Tex. 1993). ("As is true in other types of negligence cases, the ultimate standard of proof on the causation issue is whether, by a preponderance of the evidence, the negligent act or omission is shown to be a substantial factor in bringing about the harm and without which the harm would not have occurred.")

5. 217 Ala. 621, 117 So. 72 (1928).

6. *See, e.g.,* Cook v. Minneapolis, St. P. & S.S.M. Ry., 98 Wis. 624, 74 N.W. 561 (1898).

7. Restatement (Second) of Torts § 432, comment d (1965). *See also* Anderson v. Minneapolis, St. P. & S.S.M. Ry. Co., 146 Minn. 430, 440, 179 N.W. 45, 49 (1920).

8. Restatement (Third) of Torts: Liability for Physical Harm (Proposed Final Draft No. 1, 2005) § 27, comment *d.* notes, "When one of multiple sufficient causes is not tortious, the case for subjecting the tortious cause to liability is less persuasive than when both causes are tortious. See Comment *c*. Courts and commentators have debated the merits of whether liability should be imposed in this situation for many decades. Nevertheless, both of the first two Restatements and a significant majority of the courts since the Second Restatement have treated the tortious cause that concurs with an innocent cause as subject to liability, and so this Restatement continues that position. Moderating the force of this rule, however, is the fact that sometimes courts rely on intuition and conclude that the innocent cause preempted the tortious cause, see Comments *h* and *i* and therefore the party responsible for the tortious cause is not subject to liability."

the second cause on the defendant seeking to escape liability.[9] Nevertheless, some courts draw the distinction in negligence cases, suggesting that they might also do so in product liability.

The following materials deal with special problems of proof of causation-in-fact that arise in products liability cases.

SECTION B. PROOF OF CAUSATION

1. RELIANCE ON WARNINGS

Recall that in Burke v. Spartanics, Ltd., 252 F.3d 131 (2d Cir.2001), page 279 *supra*, Judge Calabresi noted that the question of whether a defendant must warn of obvious dangers often poses issues of both duty and causation. In the following case, the causation issue predominates.

ANDERSON v. F.J. LITTLE MACHINE CO.
United States Court of Appeals, Eighth Circuit, 1995.
68 F.3d 1113.

JOHN R. GIBSON, CIRCUIT JUDGE.

Ronald and Mary Anderson appeal from the district court's entry of summary judgment against them on their products liability claim against Allied Products Corporation. Ronald Anderson's hand was caught and injured in a machine manufactured by Allied's predecessor when he tried to clean a metal roller while the machine was operating. The Andersons asserted failure to warn and defective design claims sounding in both negligence and strict liability. The district court granted Allied summary judgment on the ground that the danger from the pinch roller was open and obvious and the Andersons had therefore not established a failure to warn case. The Andersons appeal, arguing that: (1) the court failed to consider their defective design claims; (2) the court erroneously used Ronald Anderson's contributory fault to bar his recovery when contributory fault can only be used to diminish damages; and (3) the court erred in entering summary judgment when there was an issue of fact as to whether Anderson was aware of "the nature and extent of the potential danger" the machine presented. We affirm in part and reverse in part.

Ronald Anderson was injured in February 1988 while working at American National Can. He was a "qualified mechanic" and had worked there twenty-one years at the time of the accident. He had worked in his department for eight years. Anderson was working with a metal straightening machine when he noticed that the rollers on the machine were scratching the metal sheets it was processing. Rather than turning off the straightening machine, Anderson leaned over the guard rail and tried to wipe the upper roller clean with a cloth while the machine was running. A sign was posted at the machine that read: "Danger. Hand Hazard. Watch Your Fingers." Anderson admitted that he knew "there was a safer way" to clean the machine, which was to shut the machine

---

9. *See, e.g.,* Kingston v. Chicago & N.W. Ry. Co., 191 Wis. 610, 211 N.W. 913 (1927).

down, but that cleaning the machine under power was "faster and easier." Anderson also knew of other people who had been hurt cleaning the rollers while the machine was under power. Moreover, even the Andersons' proposed expert conceded in his deposition that: "I'm sure given this man's experience, time that he's had in this plant, that he was well aware of the danger of an in-running nip."

Anderson's hand was pulled into the rollers, injuring his hand and fingers. He sued Allied, alleging products liability theories of negligence and strict liability. Mary Anderson sued for loss of consortium. Allied moved for summary judgment. The district court held that the Andersons made no showing of failure to warn, and that the warning Ronald Anderson received was "legally sufficient." The court held: "Plaintiff admits knowledge of the danger and concedes that it was open and obvious." The court entered summary judgment for Allied.

We review an entry of summary judgment de novo, *Glass v. Medtronic, Inc.,* 957 F.2d 605, 607 (8th Cir.1992), using the same standard applied by the district court. Summary judgment is appropriate only when the record, viewed in the light most favorable to the non-moving party, shows that there is no genuine issue of material fact and that the moving party is entitled to judgment as a matter of law. * * *

I.

The Andersons argue that there was an issue of fact as to whether Ronald Anderson knew of the danger from the pinch roller and that, therefore, the court should not have entered judgment for Allied on their failure to warn claim.

Under Missouri law, the causation element in failure to warn cases includes two separate requirements: First, the plaintiffs' injuries must be caused by the product from which the warning is missing.... Second, plaintiffs must show that a warning would have altered the behavior of the individuals involved in the accident.... The presumption that plaintiffs will heed a warning assumes that a reasonable person will act appropriately if given adequate information. Thus, a preliminary inquiry before applying the presumption is whether adequate information is available *absent* a warning. In [*Duke v. Gulf & Western Mfg. Co.,* 660 S.W.2d 404, 418–19 (Mo.Ct.App. 1983)], the court of appeals proceeded to recognize a presumption that a warning would be heeded only after finding that there was a legitimate jury question whether the plaintiff did not already know the danger. As causation is a required element of the plaintiffs' case, the burden is on plaintiffs to show that lack of knowledge. *Arnold v. Ingersoll–Rand Co.,* 834 S.W.2d 192, 194 (Mo.1992) (en banc) (citations omitted) (emphasis in original).

In *Arnold,* the testimony of those involved in the accident indicated they were aware that there was danger of an explosion if gas fumes accumulated in their shop, yet they permitted such an accumulation. The court held that the plaintiff did not establish that any warning by the defendant would have altered the course of events leading to the accident, and that the failure to warn case should not have been submitted to the jury. *Id.*

In this case, there was abundant evidence from Ronald Anderson's deposition that he knew touching the moving pinch rollers was dangerous. He admitted that it was not necessary to risk that danger because there was a "safer way to do what [he was] doing," that is, to turn the machine off. He was aware that other employees at American National Can had been hurt cleaning rollers when the machine was running. Even more to the point, Anderson admits there was a sign above the machine that read: "Danger. Hand Hazard. Watch Your Fingers."

This evidence of knowledge negates the causation element the Andersons must prove, since a warning would not have provided additional information that would have influenced Ronald Anderson's conduct. *See Arnold,* 834 S.W.2d at 194; *Campbell v. American Crane Corp.,* 60 F.3d 1329, 1333 (8th Cir.1995) (under Missouri law, reversing judgment for plaintiff on failure to warn claim because danger was open and obvious).

To rebut this evidence of knowledge, the Andersons make two points. First, Ronald Anderson said in his deposition that he did not think cleaning the roller while the machine was under power was a hazard. This statement comes in the midst of a series of admissions that he was aware of the hazard. Merely contradicting one's earlier testimony will not create an issue of fact to stave off summary judgment where there is no indication that the damaging testimony was the result of mistake or confusion. *See Camfield Tires, Inc. v. Michelin Tire Corp.,* 719 F.2d 1361, 1364–66 (8th Cir.1983); *Greiner v. City of Champlin,* 27 F.3d 1346, 1350 (8th Cir.1994).

Second, the Andersons argue that the warning should have been more specific. "Danger. Hand Hazard. Watch Your Fingers" warns of exactly the harm that happened to Anderson—a hand injury. The warning provided more than a "general awareness of danger," *Duke v. Gulf & Western Mfg. Co.,* 660 S.W.2d 404, 419 (Mo.Ct.App.1983), and is more than adequate under Missouri law. *See Arnold,* 834 S.W.2d at 194. The district court did not err in entering summary judgment for Allied on the failure to warn claim.

II.

The Andersons also contend that the district court implicitly ruled that their claim was barred by Ronald Anderson's contributory fault. This argument ignores the fact that the Andersons had the burden as plaintiffs to prove causation by showing Ronald Anderson would have behaved differently if there had been a different warning. *Arnold,* 834 S.W.2d at 194. Failure to make a prima facie case was the basis of the district court's ruling; it is beside the point that Anderson's behavior in ignoring the warning may also have constituted contributory fault.

III.

Finally, the Andersons point out that the district court entered summary judgment on all their claims, apparently without considering their strict liability and negligence defective design claims. While the district court did state in the last sentence of the order: "The straightener was not unreasonably dangerous and Allied is entitled to judgment as a matter of law," there is no analysis leading up to this conclusion except for the failure to warn analysis. We conclude that the district court's order does not adequately consider the defective design claims.

Allied argues that even if the district court did not reach the design claims, we should affirm because the evidence shows that the danger was open and obvious. Allied argues that the obviousness of the danger forecloses a defective design claim.

Allied cites *Morrison v. Kubota Tractor Corp.*, 891 S.W.2d 422 (Mo.Ct.App.1994), in arguing that, so long as the danger is open and obvious, there can be no design defect claim. *Morrison* does indeed support Allied's conclusion as to the Andersons' negligence claim. *Morrison* was a negligence suit based on lack of a roll bar (ROPS) on a tractor. *Morrison* states: "If the absence of a ROPS is to be regarded as a design defect, it is a defect that is patent beyond doubt. Such an open and obvious lack of this safety feature on the tractor ... is not actionable under the negligence law of Missouri as declared by our Supreme Court." *Id.* at 427–28. But *Morrison* specifically reserves the question of "whether the open and obvious nature of the peril ... may justify a directed verdict in a products liability case brought on a *strict liability* theory after Missouri's adoption (by statute) of comparative fault in such cases." *Id.* at 428 n. 5 (emphasis in original).

In our recent case of *Drabik v. Stanley–Bostitch, Inc.*, 997 F.2d 496 (8th Cir.1993), we considered this question and held that Missouri courts have not adopted the "consumer-expectation" test in strict liability cases based on section 402(A) of the Restatement (Second) of Torts (1965). *Drabik*, 997 F.2d at 506. The "consumer-expectation" test is named for language in comment i to section 402(A) of the Restatement (Second) of Torts, which states: "The article sold must be dangerous to an extent beyond that which would be contemplated by the ordinary consumer who purchases it, with the ordinary knowledge common to the community as to its characteristics." In *Drabik*, we held that the district court correctly submitted a defective design case to the jury, despite evidence that the plaintiff understood the danger the product posed: * * * 997 F.2d at 506. This reasoning forecloses Allied's argument that the obviousness of the danger entitles it to summary judgment.

However, Allied cites *Pree v. Brunswick Corp.*, 983 F.2d 863 (8th Cir.), *cert. denied*, 510 U.S. 815, 114 S.Ct. 65, 126 L.Ed.2d 35 (1993), in support of its argument that patent danger cannot form the basis for a defective design case. In *Pree*, the plaintiff's case failed both because the danger was patent and because the plaintiff failed to establish that there were other, safer designs that could have been used for the product. 983 F.2d at 866–67.

In this case, the Andersons produced the affidavit of a mechanical engineer who stated that he had inspected the machine that hurt Ronald Anderson. * * *

Allied argues that the mechanical engineer's testimony was not admissible under *Daubert v. Merrell Dow Pharmaceuticals, Inc.*, 509 U.S. 579, 113 S.Ct. 2786, 125 L.Ed.2d 469 (1993). Allied did not raise the *Daubert* issue in the district court, and therefore the district court did not rule on the issue. Under *Daubert,* the admissibility of scientific evidence is committed to the district court's discretion, within the boundaries set forth in that opinion, 509 U.S. at ___, 113 S.Ct. at 2799; see *Pestel v. Vermeer Mfg. Co.*, 64 F.3d 382 (8th Cir.1995). In *Pestel,* a products liability plaintiff presented a mechanical engineer expert who had designed a guard for use in a stump-cutting machine. The *Pestel* district court excluded the guard from evidence because it had not been tested and because the expert admitted the guard could not be used without further design modifications. *Id.* at 384. This court held that the district court did not abuse its discretion in excluding the guard. *Pestel* did not hold that the guard was inadmissible as a matter of law, but rather deferred to the district court's exercise of its discretion. The Andersons' case differs from *Pestel,* as there was evidence that someone installed guards on the straightening machine, indicating that the use of some type of guard was feasible.[1] We cannot say as a matter of law that such expert testimony could not be admitted.

* * * *Daubert* was not raised in the district court. Thus, the district court did not have an opportunity to consider the foundational issues outlined in *Daubert,* nor to give the parties an opportunity to squarely address those issues. We should not rule a *Daubert* issue on the limited record before us. If Allied raises *Daubert* on remand, the district court will undoubtedly allow the parties to develop this issue.

We therefore reverse the order of the district court insofar as it rules against the Andersons on their strict liability defective design claim. We affirm the district court's entry of summary judgment on the failure to warn claims and on the negligent design defect claim.

[Judge Gibson's opinion, concurring in part and dissenting in part is omitted.]

Notes

1. The majority position is that there is no duty to warn of obvious dangers. This position is reflected in Restatement (Third) of Torts: Products Liability, § 2, Comment *j*. A failure to warn is not a cause of the harm if the person to be warned is already fully aware of the dangers that should have

---

[1]. The question of whether post-accident improvements are themselves admissible is not before us; we merely observe that the improvement would be relevant to the district court's decision in ruling on the admissibility of the expert testimony.

been warned against. *See, e.g.,* Stanback v. Parke, Davis & Co., 657 F.2d 642 (4th Cir.1981) (drug company's failure to warn about a risk associated with a vaccine did not cause the harm because the physician who administered it was fully aware of the risk). For an influential law review article on the duty to warn, *see* Henderson and Twerski, Doctrinal Collapse in Products Liability: The Empty Shell of Failure to Warn, 65 N.Y.U.L.Rev. 265 (1990).

2. Should a woman who purchased coffee at a fast food restaurant, and who suffered second degree burns after she spilled coffee on herself while riding in an automobile, be able to get to a jury on a failure to warn claim? *See* Holowaty v. McDonald's Corp., 10 F.Supp.2d 1078 (D.Minn.1998). How about an 11 year old who was burned while a passenger in a car when he accidently spilled a cup of hot chocolate he had just purchased from a vending machine? *See* McCroy v. Coastal Mart, Inc., 207 F.Supp.2d 1265 (D. Kan.2002). If a sticker on the vending machine states, "Warning Hot Liquid Handle With Care," can the plaintiff claim the warning did not advise the consumer of the severity of injuries that might result if the liquid was spilled?

3. In Hiner v. Deere and Company, Inc. 340 F.3d 1190 (10th Cir. 2003), the plaintiff was injured when a round bale of hay rolled off a loader and fell on him. The farmer knew of the possibility of roll-down injuries, but did not know the loader could elevate on its own without operator input. On these facts, the Tenth Circuit concluded that the plaintiff's general knowledge of roll-down dangers did not preclude his self-raising warning-defect claim. Is it sensible for courts to require a warning to provide some specificity concerning *how* an injury might happen?

4. What of a person who dives into a shallow above ground pool and suffers head injuries and paralysis? Does it matter if the plaintiff does not understand "the laws of physics, biomechanics, and hydrodynamics [that] can transform a miscalculated shallow dive into a deep dive that is recognized as dangerous?" *See* Glittenberg v. Doughboy Recreational Industries, 441 Mich. 379, 491 N.W.2d 208 (1992).

5. As discussed in *Burke v. Spartanics*, regardless of whether a danger is obvious to a reasonable person, if the plaintiff actually knows of a risk most courts will bar recovery under a warning defect theory on causal grounds. Austin v. Will–Burt company, 361 F.3d 862 (5th Cir. 2004).

6. The *Anderson* court saved for a later day the question of whether the plaintiff's expert's testimony was admissible under the test developed in *Daubert*. Increasingly, plaintiffs in products liability cases must jump the *Daubert* hurdle before they are able to get to trial. *Daubert* and a number of additional admissibility decisions are discussed in Chapter 6, Section D, *infra*.

TOWN OF BRIDPORT v. STERLING CLARK LURTON CORP.
Supreme Court of Vermont, 1997.
166 Vt. 304, 693 A.2d 701.

JOHNSON, JUSTICE.

Plaintiff, the Town of Bridport, brought suit against defendant, Sterling Clark Lurton Corp., after its town hall was destroyed by a fire caused by the spontaneous combustion of products manufactured by defendant. Plaintiff appeals the trial court's grant of summary judgment in favor of defendant, arguing that (1) an inadequate warning may be a proximate cause of an injury even though the user did not read the warning given; and (2) a genuine issue of material fact exists as to the adequacy of the warnings given in this case. [ ] Defendant urges us to accept the court's conclusion that plaintiff failed to show proximate cause, and also argues that it had no duty to warn on these facts. We agree with the trial court that, as a matter of law, the warnings on defendant's products were adequate to alert a reasonable consumer to the risk of spontaneous combustion, and therefore affirm.

* * *

[T]he facts are as follows. With the help of grants, donations and volunteer labor, the Bridport Restoration Project Committee was gradually restoring the old town hall. Although plaintiff owned the hall, the Masonic Lodge leased the second floor of the building as a meeting room. In preparation for an upcoming dinner, several Masons decided to work on the floor, which was in poor condition as a result of the renovations.

One of the Masons, Robert Grant, volunteered to purchase the chemicals needed to prepare the floor. He bought two products, a gallon container of gum turps and a gallon container of boiled linseed oil, both manufactured by defendant. Grant stated in his deposition that he did not read the labels "to any extent" but that he thought he had "briefed the label" for application instructions. On the advice of a store clerk, he mixed the products using a 50/50 ratio.

Another volunteer, Gary Barkley, joined Grant at the hall. Barkley never looked at the product containers. The two men spread the mixture of linseed oil and gum turps on the floor and swept or mopped it up with sawdust that was provided by Margaret Sunderland, the Secretary of the Restoration Project Committee. When Barkley and Grant left the hall, they left behind the materials used to clean the floor, including a bucket containing the wet, oily sawdust, the product containers, and possibly a mop used to clean the floor. The building burst into flames the next day, and the fire was traced to the materials used to clean the floor.

The appearance and content of the warnings labels on the products are not in dispute. The front of the gum turps container stated "DANGER! FLAMMABLE. HARMFUL OR FATAL IF SWALLOWED. VAPOR HARMFUL. SKIN AND EYE IRRITANT. See other cautions on back panel." These capitalized warnings were set forth in large, bold print directly beneath the identifying product label. The back panel contained a box with several warnings regarding dangers from breathing, swallowing, and suffering skin or eye contact with the product, as well as an instruction to "Keep away from heat, sparks and flame." Under the box, a paragraph labeled "USES" noted "When mixed one part Gum Turpentine to two parts Boiled Linseed Oil it makes an excellent furniture polish. Be sure to wash and dispose of oily rags in a safe place to avoid spontaneous combustion."

Similarly, the front of the linseed oil container displayed a box measuring nearly 1" by 3", which stated "READ CAUTION ON BACK PANEL BEFORE USE." The back of the panel displayed a box about 1 "by 4", printed in two colors, which set forth this warning: "CAUTION: Oily cloths are subject to spontaneous combustion. All oily cloths should be spread to dry in airy spot or burned promptly after using."

Plaintiff alleged that these warnings were inadequate, and that the manufacturer's failure to provide adequate warnings was a proximate cause of the fire. Defendant moved for summary judgment, arguing that plaintiff could not show that inadequate warnings were a proximate cause of the fire where the users of the products did not read the warnings given. The trial court accepted this reasoning, and awarded summary judgment to defendant. Plaintiff moved for relief from judgment on the grounds that one factor in determining the adequacy of a warning is its conspicuousness on a label. The court rejected this argument, noting that plaintiff's failure to "present [ ] ... evidence of what a reasonable linseed oil warning should be.... [left] no triable question of fact for resolution by the jury," and holding that the warnings given were sufficient as a matter of law. This appeal followed.

II.

Plaintiff's claims are premised on a manufacturer's duty to warn of known product defects, which " 'arises when the product manufactured is dangerous to an extent beyond that which would be contemplated by the ordinary purchaser, *i.e.*, a consumer possessing the ordinary and common knowledge of the community as to the product's characteristics.' " *Ostrowski v. Hydra–Tool Corp.*, 144 Vt. 305, 308, 479 A.2d 126, 127 (1984) (quoting *Menard v. Newhall*, 135 Vt. 53, 55, 373 A.2d 505, 507 (1977)). In "failure to warn" cases, the plaintiff must show that the manufacturer had a duty to warn, that the failure to warn made the product unreasonably dangerous and therefore defective, and that the lack of a warning was a proximate cause of the injury. *Menard*, 135 Vt. at 54, 373 A.2d at 506. * * *

Proximate cause in these cases is typically shown by means of a presumption. If a plaintiff can demonstrate that the manufacturer had a duty to warn and failed to provide an adequate warning, a causal presumption arises that had an adequate warning been provided, the user would have read and heeded the warning and the accident would have been avoided. See *Menard*, 135 Vt. at 54–55, 373 A.2d at 506–07 (adopting "read and heed" presumption); Restatement (Second) of Torts § 402A cmt. j (1965).

A defendant may, of course, present evidence to overcome the presumption. See *Menard*, 135 Vt. at 55, 373 A.2d at 506–07 (where child ignored instructions given by father, presumption that warning would have been read and heeded disappeared). Defendant argues, relying on *Menard*, that the evidence in this case that the product users did not read the warnings on the containers rebuts the presumption, leaving no evidence of proximate cause.

Defendant reads our holding in *Menard* too broadly. In that case, a child playing with a BB gun shot and injured a friend. The plaintiffs argued that the manufacturer should have warned of this danger. The child's father, however, had instructed his son in the use of the weapon, including what kinds of things he could shoot. The child ignored those instructions when he shot at his playmate. Under those circumstances, the "read and heed" presumption disappears; if the user is cautioned of the risk and ignores that advice, there is no reasonable basis to assume that the user would have heeded a warning from the manufacturer. * * *

Here, Grant was not aware of the risk, nor did he read the warnings on the containers and then disregard them. Plaintiff's claim that inadequate warnings were a proximate cause of the accident does not fail as a matter of law merely because Grant did not read the warnings. To be adequate, a warning must be displayed so as to catch the eye of a reasonably prudent person. See, e.g., *Spruill v. Boyle–Midway, Inc.,* 308 F.2d 79, 85 (4th Cir.1962) (where manufacturer has duty to warn, warning must be in such form as to catch attention of reasonably prudent person)* * *. Although Grant did not look at the warnings, plaintiff still could show that inadequate warnings were a proximate cause of the fire by establishing that the warnings were not properly designed to draw the attention of a reasonably prudent person. * * *

Defendant points to several cases in which courts have held that a user's failure to read a warning removed any causal connection between the inadequacy of the warning and the accident. In those cases, however, the conspicuousness of the warning was not at issue. See, e.g., *Stanback v. Parke, Davis & Co.,* 657 F.2d 642, 645 (4th Cir.1981) (where physician testified that he already knew of risk associated with flu vaccine, and did not inform patients of warnings accompanying vaccines, manufacturer was not liable for failure to warn); *Bloxom v. Bloxom,* 512 So.2d 839, 850–51 (La.1987) (auto manufacturer had duty to warn of danger in manual, but as owner of car never looked at or read manual, manufacturer was insulated from liability for its failure to do so) * * *. Here, plaintiff squarely raised the conspicuousness of the warnings as an issue; in its memoranda opposing the motion for summary judgment plaintiff argued that the warnings were inadequate in both form and content.

III.

As an alternate ground in support of the court's decision, defendant argues that summary judgment was proper because no genuine issue of material fact exists with respect to the conspicuousness of the warning labels on the product containers. The trial court adopted this reasoning in its denial of plaintiff's motion for reconsideration. Defendant correctly notes, as did the court, that plaintiff did not produce evidence to support its allegation that the warnings were insufficiently prominent.

* * *

Under these facts, where the user did not read the warning given, plaintiff can show proximate cause only by showing that the warning should have been more conspicuous. Plaintiff could not survive summary judgment by claiming that adequacy was an issue for the jury without providing evidence that the warnings were in fact inadequate.

* * *

We recognize that, where a warning has been provided by the manufacturer, ordinarily the sufficiency of that warning is a question for the jury. * * * In a proper case, however, a court may conclude that the sufficiency of a warning is apparent as a matter of law. * * * The warnings at issue in this case were bold and prominent, and warned of the dangers of fire and spontaneous combustion. As plaintiff presented no evidence showing that the warnings were not sufficiently conspicuous, the court's grant of summary judgment was proper.

Affirmed.

Notes

1. In failure to warn cases, a number of courts use a presumption that a proper warning would have been followed. The leading case is Technical Chem. Co. v. Jacobs, 480 S.W.2d 602 (Tex.1972). That court found the origin of the presumption in Comment *j* to the Restatement (Second) of Torts § 402A which states "Where warning is given, the seller may reasonably assume that it will be read and heeded." The court stated:

> Such a presumption works in favor of the manufacturer when an adequate warning is present. Where there is no warning, as in this case, however, the presumption that the user would have read an adequate warning works in favor of the plaintiff user. In other words, the presumption is that Jacobs would have read an adequate warning. The presumption, may, however, be rebutted if the manufacturer comes forward with contrary evidence that the presumed fact did not exist. [Citations] Depending upon the individual facts, this may be accomplished by the manufacturer's producing evidence that the user was blind, illiterate, intoxicated at the time of the use, irresponsible or lax in judgment or by some other circumstance tending to show that the improper use was or would have been made regardless of the warning.

480 S.W.2d at 606.

2. In *Menard*, discussed in *Town of Bridport*, the court outlines the nature of the presumption created in failure-to-warn cases. The presumption "merely shifts the burden to the manufacturer to go forward with the evidence. * * * Under such circumstances, as far as the case at bar is concerned, Daisy was obligated to go forward with evidence that the defendant Newhall would have ignored any warning given and, after introduction of that evidence, the presumption disappears. As Chief Justice Powers stated in *Tyrrell v. Prudential Insurance Co. of America*, 109 Vt. 6, 23–24, 192 A. 184, 192 (1937):

"A presumption, of itself alone, contributes no evidence and has no probative quality. It takes the place of evidence, temporarily, at least, but if and when enough rebutting evidence is admitted to make a question for the jury on the fact involved, the presumption disappears and goes for naught. In such a case, the presumption does not have to be overcome by evidence; once it is confronted by evidence of the character referred to, it immediately quits the arena."

Menard, 373 A.2d at 506–07.

3. Should courts admit the self-serving testimony of the plaintiff as to whether he would have heeded an adequate warning? *Compare* Van Dike v. AMF, Inc., 146 Mich.App. 176, 379 N.W.2d 412, 415 (Mich.App.1985) (no) *with* Laaperi v. Sears, Roebuck & Co., Inc., 787 F.2d 726, 732 (1st Cir.1986) (yes).

4. The read and heed presumption may have real bite in some circumstances. In Tuttle v. Lorillard Tobacco Co., 377 F.3d 917 (8th Cir. 2004), former major League baseball player Bill Tuttle died of oral cancer allegedly caused by his long use of Beech–Nut smokeless tobacco. The court noted that in jurisdictions where a "heeding presumption" does exist, "the presumption operates to the benefit of the manufacturer where adequate warnings are provided because the manufacturer receives the benefit of the doubt that the warning provided is effective in alerting the user of the product's potential danger. Where no warning is given, the presumption operates in favor of the user by presuming the user would have read, understood, and heeded the warning. The practical effect of the presumption is to relieve a plaintiff of the burden of proving proximate cause." *Id.* At 925, n. 5. However, because the Court concluded that Minnesota state courts had not adopted the presumption and because Mr. Tuttle died before testifying that he would have read and heeded warnings had they been provided, the failure to warn claim failed for want of admissible proof of causation.

5. Some courts have held that a plaintiff who admittedly failed to read the warnings which the plaintiff alleges are inadequate may not recover on the theory that the issuance of adequate warnings would have prevented his injuries. *See* E.R. Squibb & Sons, Inc. v. Cox, 477 So.2d 963 (Ala.1985). Other jurisdictions have held that the manufacturer who issues insufficient warnings may not avoid liability solely on the basis that the plaintiff failed to read the warnings which were issued. *See* Johnson v. Johnson Chemical Co., Inc., 588 N.Y.S.2d 607, 183 A.D.2d 64 (1992). Much of the apparent contradiction disappears if we distinguish between warnings that are substantively inadequate and those that are inadequate in their presentation, e.g., are insufficiently inconspicuous or dramatic. *See* Rowson v. Kawasaki Heavy Industries, Ltd., 866 F.Supp. 1221 (N.D.Iowa 1994).

6. What of situations where there was no warning but it is almost certain that even if the plaintiff had read an adequate warning, the warning would not have altered her behavior? For example, a vaccine may have a rare side effect but failure to be vaccinated may expose one to a far greater risk of a serious illness. May the defendant simply present the statistics on the relative risks and argue that no rational person, even if appraised of the risk, would refuse to be vaccinated? *See* Restatement (Third) of Torts: Products Liability, § 2, Comment *i*.

7. Defendant manufacturer fails to put an important warning on its product label. The buyer uses the product without reading the label, and a bystander is injured by the hazard that was not warned against. The bystander sues defendant for failure to warn. What result? *See* Fischer, Causation in Fact in Omission Cases, 1992 Utah L.Rev. 1335.

2. ENHANCED INJURIES

TRULL v. VOLKSWAGEN OF AMERICA, INC.
Supreme Court of New Hampshire, 2000.
145 N.H. 259, 761 A.2d 477.

NADEAU, J.

The United States Court of Appeals for the First Circuit (*Coffin*, Senior Circuit Judge) has certified the following question of law, *see* Sup.Ct. R. 34:

> Under New Hampshire law, in a crashworthiness or enhanced injury case, does the plaintiff bear the burden of demonstrating the specific nature and extent of the injuries attributable to the manufacturer, or does the burden of apportionment fall on the defendant once the plaintiff has proved causation?

Trull v. Volkswagen of America, Inc., 187 F.3d 88, 103 (1st Cir.1999). We conclude that the defendants bear the burden of apportionment once the plaintiffs prove causation.

We adopt the court of appeals' recitation of the facts. In February 1991, the plaintiffs, David and Elizabeth Trull, and their two sons, Nathaniel and Benjamin, were traveling in New Hampshire when their Volkswagen Vanagon slid on black ice and collided with an oncoming car. *Id.* at 91. Both parties agree that Nathaniel and Benjamin were seated in the rear middle bench seat of the Vanagon, which was equipped with lap-only seatbelts, and were wearing the available lap belts. Benjamin died in the accident, and both Elizabeth and Nathaniel suffered severe brain injuries. *Id.*

In this diversity products liability action, the plaintiffs sought damages from the defendants "on the ground that defects in the design of the Vanagon made their injuries more severe than they otherwise would have been." *Id.* "Plaintiffs had two primary theories of recovery: (1) the Vanagon was defective because it was a forward control vehicle constructed in such a way that it lacked sufficient protection against a frontal impact, and (2) the Vanagon was defective because the rear bench seats, on which Nathaniel and Benjamin were seated, did not have shoulder safety belts as well as lap belts." *Id.* at 92. The plaintiffs contend that the defendants are liable in, *inter alia*, negligence and strict liability because the automobile was not crashworthy. * * *

The trial proceeded with Nathaniel's and Benjamin's claims, and the jury found for the defendants. * * *

The plaintiffs appealed to the United States Court of Appeals for the First Circuit, arguing, among other things, that the district court "improperly imposed on plaintiffs the burden of proving the nature and extent of the enhanced injuries attributable to the Vanagon's design." *Id.* at 92. Recognizing that the question "of who, under New Hampshire law, should bear the burden in a so-called 'crashworthiness' case, poses sophisticated questions of burden allocation involving not only a choice of appropriate precedent but also an important policy choice," the court of appeals granted the plaintiffs' motion to certify the question to this court. *Id.* at 92, 103.

The plaintiffs' theory of liability for defective design is commonly referred to as the "crashworthiness," "second collision," or "enhanced injury" doctrine. *See Caiazzo v. Volkswagenwerk A.G.*, 647 F.2d 241, 243 n. 2 (2d Cir.1981) (defining "crashworthiness" as "the protection that a passenger motor vehicle affords its passengers against personal injury or death as a result of a motor vehicle accident"); *Larsen v. General Motors Corporation*, 391 F.2d 495, 502 (8th Cir.1968) (defining "second collision" as that occurring between the passenger and the interior of the vehicle); *Smith v. Ariens Co.*, 375 Mass. 620, 377 N.E.2d 954, 956–57 (1978) (permitting recovery where design defect "enhanced injuries" plaintiff received in collision).

The crashworthiness doctrine "extends the scope of liability of a manufacturer to the situations in which the construction or design of its product has caused separate or enhanced injuries in the course of an initial accident brought about by an independent cause." *Bass v. General Motors Corp.*, 150 F.3d 842, 847 (8th Cir.1998) (quotation omitted). The doctrine is implicated, not because the design caused the accident, * * * but because, as a result of the second collision, the plaintiffs suffered either a more severe injury or an injury they otherwise would not have received due to the defective design, *see Lee v. Volkswagen of America, Inc.*, 688 P.2d 1283, 1286 (Okla.1984). Consequently, the plaintiffs seek damages from the defendants for at least a portion of their injuries.

* * *

While we do not hold that manufacturers are "insurers" for defectively designed vehicles, *see Price*, 142 N.H. at 390, 702 A.2d at 333, we do hold that in a crashworthiness case, a "manufacturer should be liable for that portion of the damage or injury caused by the defective design over and above the damage or injury that probably would have occurred as a result of the impact or collision absent the defective design." *Larsen*, 391 F.2d at 503.

Thus, in crashworthiness cases,

> where the injuries sustained are separate and divisible . . . , the burden of proof remains solely upon the plaintiff[s], including the burden of proving "enhancement," i.e., the plaintiff[s] must prove which of the several injuries are attributable to the manufacturer's defective product and the degree of "enhancement" occasioned by

the product as distinguished from the injuries flowing from the third party's acts of negligence.

Lee, 688 P.2d at 1288. The question of actual apportionment of damages among several causes is one of fact for the jury. * * * In essence, the normal principles of torts apply.

When, however, the plaintiffs receive injuries that are indivisible, courts are split as to whether the plaintiffs or the defendants bear the burden of segregating the injuries caused by the automobile's defect. * * * *Restatement (Third) of Torts: Products Liability* § 16 comment *d* at 243–53 (1998).

The defendants urge us to adopt the minority approach referred to as the "*Huddell-Caiazzo*" approach, which places the burden on the plaintiffs to prove the nature and extent of their enhanced injuries. See *Huddell v. Levin*, 537 F.2d 726, 737–38 (3d Cir.1976) (applying New Jersey law); *Caiazzo*, 647 F.2d at 250 (applying New York law).

Under the *Huddell-Caiazzo* approach,

[f]irst, in establishing that the design in question was defective, the plaintiff[s] must offer proof of an alternative safer design, practicable under the circumstances. Second, the plaintiff[s] must offer proof of what injuries, if any, would have resulted had the alternative, safer design been used. Third, the plaintiff[s] must offer some method of establishing the extent of enhanced injuries attributable to the defective design.

Caiazzo, 647 F.2d at 250 (ellipses and quotation omitted).

The plaintiffs, conversely, urge us to adopt the majority approach referred to as the "*Fox-Mitchell*" approach, derived from *Fox v. Ford Motor Co.*, 575 F.2d 774, 786–88 (10th Cir.1978) (applying Wyoming law), and *Mitchell*, 669 F.2d at 1206–08 (applying Minnesota law). See *Restatement (Third) of Torts: Products Liability* § 16 reporter's note at 244 (noting that *Fox-Mitchell* approach is adopted in majority of jurisdictions).

Under the *Fox-Mitchell* approach, the plaintiffs must "prove only that the design defect was a substantial factor in producing damages over and above those which were probably caused as a result of the original impact or collision." *Trull*, 187 F.3d at 101 (quotation omitted). This approach provides that once the plaintiffs carry the burden of proving that the defective design of the car was a substantial factor in causing the enhanced injury, the burden of proof shifts to the tortfeasors to apportion the damages between them.

* * *

In crashworthiness cases involving indivisible injuries, we conclude that the plaintiffs must prove that a "design defect was a substantial factor in producing damages over and above those which were probably caused as a result of the original impact or collision. Once the plaintiff[s] make [ ] that showing, the burden shifts to the defendant[s] to show which injuries were attributable to the initial collision and which to the defect." Trull, 187 F.3d at 101–02 (quotation and citation omitted).

* * *

In contrast, "[a]doption of the *Huddell*[-*Caiazzo*] position takes away the incentive of automobile manufacturers to design their products in a responsible fashion." *Polston*, 423 S.E.2d at 661. Furthermore, "application of the *Huddell*[-*Caiazzo*] standard might impair the promotion of 'safer products' design by weakening the deterrent value of products action." Id. at 661–62 (quotation and ellipsis omitted).

We agree with the *Mitchell* court's rejection of *Huddell* on the basis that a plaintiff would be "relegated to an almost hopeless state of never being able to succeed against a defective designer," *Mitchell*, 669 F.2d at 1204, and that the *Huddell-Caiazzo* approach "requires obvious speculation and proof of the impossible," id. at 1205. To hold otherwise would result in the implicit adoption of the view that

> it is better that a plaintiff, injured through no fault of his own, take nothing, than that a wrongdoer pay more than his theoretical share of the damages arising out of a situation which his wrong has helped to create. In other words, the rule is a result of a choice made as to where a loss due to failure of proof shall fall—on an innocent plaintiff or on defendants who are clearly proved to have been at fault.

Id. at 1208; see Restatement (Third) of Torts: Products Liability § 16 comment *d* * * *. We have adopted similar reasoning in holding that two or more tortfeasors may be jointly and severally liable where their negligence, through their independent acts, produces a single, indivisible injury. * * * Consequently, the defendants should bear the burden of apportioning their respective liability once the plaintiffs have made a *prima facie* showing that the defendants' conduct contributed as a proximate cause to the harm suffered.

* * *

In summary, the *Fox-Mitchell* approach and subsequent burden shifting is necessary only where the plaintiffs' injuries are indivisible. * * * Whether the plaintiffs' injuries are indivisible or divisible is a question of law for the trial judge. * * * If the plaintiffs' injuries are established or are stipulated to as indivisible, the plaintiffs must prove only "that a design defect was a substantial factor in producing damages over and above those which were probably caused as a result of the original impact or collision." *Polston*, 423 S.E.2d at 662. If the plaintiffs meet this burden, the burden of proof shifts to the defendants to apportion the damages between them. * * *

Remanded.

DALIANIS, J., concurred; GROFF, MANGONES, and MOHL, JJ., superior court justices, specially assigned under RSA 490:3, concurred.

RESTATEMENT (THIRD) OF TORTS: PRODUCTS LIABILITY (1997)

§ 16 Increased Harm Due to Product Defect

(a) When a product is defective at the time of commercial sale or other distribution and the defect is a substantial factor in increasing the Plaintiff's harm beyond that which would have resulted from other causes, the product seller is subject to liability for the increased harm.

(b) If proof supports a determination of the harm that would have resulted from other causes in the absence of the product defect, the product seller's liability is limited to the increased harm attributable solely to the product defect.

(c) If proof does not support a determination under Subsection (b) of the harm that would have resulted in the absence of the product defect, the product seller is liable for all of the plaintiff's harm attributable to the defect and other causes.

Comment d. *Extent of liability for increased harm when proof does not support determination of what harm would have resulted in the absence of product defect.* Subsection (c) provides that when the plaintiff has proved defect-caused increased harm, the product seller is subject to liability for all harm suffered by the plaintiff if proof does not support a determination of what harm would have resulted if the product had not been defective. The defendant, a wrongdoer who in fact has caused harm to the plaintiff, should not escape liability because the nature of the harm makes such a determination impossible. Compare § 433B(2) of the Restatement, Second, of Torts.

Notes

1. Following the New Hampshire Supreme Court opinion, the district court entered a judgment on the jury's verdict finding the manufacturer liable for negligence. The First Circuit affirmed. Trull v. Volkswagen of America, Inc., 320 F.3d 1 (1st Cir. 2002).

2. Is the division of burdens really as straightforward as the *Trull* court suggests? In some cases there is a very close relationship between proof of defect and proof of causation. Manufacturers must design products in such a way as to avoid the risk of unreasonably enhancing injuries in the event of an accident. In some cases it may not be possible to prove that the product's design creates an unreasonable risk of enhancing injuries without proving that it enhanced plaintiff's injuries. Huddell v. Levin, 537 F.2d 726 (3d Cir.1976), raises this problem. It is difficult to determine whether the design of a head restraint is unreasonable without knowing how much harm the design caused, and comparing this to the amount of harm that would have been caused by an alternative design. In such cases, shifting the burden of proof on the question of enhancement of injury may also have the practical effect of shifting the burden of proof on the question of defect. Lee v. Volkswagen of America, Inc., 688 P.2d 1283 (Okla.1984), is an example of an enhanced injury case that does not present this problem. In that case, the

plaintiffs claimed a defective door latch caused a door to come open during a crash, ejecting the plaintiffs. Presumably, one could determine whether the door latch was defective independently of whether plaintiff suffered enhanced injuries. How difficult will it be to separate the proof of defect and proof of causation in *Trull*?

3. The question of whether an injury is divisible is conceptually separate from the question of apportionment of responsibility under a comparative responsibility regime. When an injury is divisible and all the parties are legally responsible for the injury, how should we proceed? The Restatement (Third) of Torts: Apportionment of Liability § 26 gives primacy to causation. When damages for an injury can be divided by causation, the factfinder first separates them into their indivisible component parts and then separately apportions liability for each indivisible component part under the applicable comparative responsibility rules.

4. What role should plaintiff's fault play in crashworthiness cases? When the injury is indivisible? When it is divisible? *See* Dannenfelser v. Daimlerchrysler Corp. 370 F.Supp.2d 1091 (D.Hawai'i 2005).

3. LINKING THE DEFENDANT TO THE PRODUCT

MULCAHY v. ELI LILLY & CO.
Supreme Court of Iowa, 1986.
386 N.W.2d 67.

SCHULTZ, JUSTICE.

* * *

The plaintiffs Linda Mulcahy and Michael Mulcahy seek damages personally and as natural guardians for their two children. In 1949 Cleo Rorman was prescribed and ingested DES during her pregnancy with Linda Mulcahy. Plaintiffs allege Linda sustained injury by *in utero* exposure to DES. Further, they claim such exposure caused Linda to give birth prematurely to her two children in 1973 and 1976 and that they sustained injury as a result.

Plaintiffs commenced their action in the United States District Court for the Northern District of Iowa. They filed suit against 25 companies alleged to have manufactured and marketed DES at the time of the ingestion. Plaintiffs have set forth theories of recovery against the defendants based upon strict liability, negligence, misrepresentation, breach of warranties, alternate liability, enterprise liability, market share liability, and concert of action. The record reflects that only three defendants sold DES in Ames, Iowa, in 1949; however, plaintiffs request we assess industry-wide liability against all defendants.

All defendants filed motions for summary judgment in federal district court arguing that there was no evidence as to which defendant marketed or manufactured the DES which Mrs. Rorman ingested. The federal district court reserved ruling on the motions of the three companies that had sales in Ames, Iowa, but held that summary judgment in favor of the remaining defendants would be appropriate "unless Iowa law permits imposition of liability on a defendant without evidence that the defendant manufactured or marketed the particular product that is alleged to have caused the injury." Pursuant to Iowa Code chapter 684A and Iowa Rules of Appellate Procedure 451–61, the federal district court certified [the following] questions of law to us * * *.

a. In a DES product liability case when a product has been ingested by a user and when, after exhaustive discovery, and through no fault of any party, the manufacturer or seller of the ingested product cannot be positively identified, will Iowa law recognize any of the following theories of liability:

(1) Market share liability;

(2) Alternative liability; and

(3) Enterprise liability?

b. If Iowa law will recognize any of these theories of recovery when the product ingested and its manufacturer or seller cannot be positively identified,

(1) What must the plaintiff prove before the burden of proof and/or production shifts to the defendant manufacturers or sellers; and

(2) What must a manufacturer or seller demonstrate to exculpate itself from liability?

We note preliminarily that a plaintiff in a products liability action must ordinarily prove that a manufacturer or supplier produced, provided or was in some way responsible for the particular product that caused the injury. *See Osborn v. Massey–Ferguson, Inc.*, 290 N.W.2d 893, 901 (Iowa 1980); *see also* Restatement (Second) of Torts §§ 402A, 433B (1965); W. Prosser, *The Law of Torts* § 98 (4th ed. 1971). In the present action plaintiffs rely on theories which would be exceptions to the rule that a plaintiff must show a causal connection between the defendant's product and plaintiff's injury. Such theories advanced by plaintiffs would allow recovery without proof of which drug company actually manufactured or supplied the DES ingested by Mrs. Rorman.

We proceed to the federal court's question "a" and to the three theories specified there, considering them in reverse order. In addressing the questions posed, we restrict our answers to the facts provided with the certified questions or referred to in our answers. We neither suggest nor foreclose adoption of any of these theories under other circumstances.

I. *Enterprise liability.* Enterprise liability, also termed "industry-wide liability," *see, e.g., Starling v. Seaboard Coast Line Railroad*, 533 F.Supp. 183, 187 (S.D.Ga.1982); *Zafft v. Eli Lilly & Co.*, 676 S.W.2d 241, 245 (Mo.1984), was first advanced in *Hall v. E.I. Du Pont De Nemours & Co.*, 345 F.Supp. 353 (E.D.N.Y.1972). *Hall* was summarized as follows in *Morton v. Abbott Laboratories*, 538 F.Supp. 593, 598 (M.D.Fla.1982):

Like concert of action, plaintiff's second theory—enterprise liability—would impose liability on each DES manufacturer on the basis of their group conduct. The concept of enterprise, or industry-wide, liability derives from Judge Weinstein's opinion in *Hall v. Du Pont De Nemours & Co.,* 345 F.Supp. 353 (E.D.N.Y.1972). In that case, 13 children sued six blasting cap manufacturers alleging that they had been injured in explosions of the caps. Although the six defendants were not the only possible sources of blasting caps, they did comprise virtually the entire blasting cap industry in this country. Plaintiffs based their claim on the practices of that industry in failing to take reasonable safety precautions and make reasonable warnings. They alleged that members of the industry had adhered to industry-wide safety standards and had delegated substantial safety investigation and design functions to their trade association.

The *Hall* court focused on the joint conduct of the defendants, finding that their joint control of the risk presented by their industry warranted the imposition of joint liability. *Id.* at 371–76. The facts in this DES case in no way suggest application of *Hall's* theory of joint liability. In *Hall* there were six manufacturers in the industry; here there were 149. Judge Weinstein limited his holding in *Hall* by warning against its application to a "decentralized" industry with many individual members. There was no industry-wide delegation of safety functions to a drug manufacturers' trade association; indeed, if there was any body responsible for safety in the drug industry it was the Food and Drug Administration.

A Pennsylvania court recently summarized the criteria necessary to establish enterprise liability in *Burnside v. Abbott Laboratories,* [351] Pa.Super. [264], [285], 505 A.2d 973, 984 (1985):

(1) The injury-causing product was manufactured by one of a small number of defendants in an industry; (2) the defendants had joint knowledge of the risks inherent in the product and possessed a joint capacity to reduce those risks; and (3) each of them failed to take steps to reduce the risk but, rather, delegated this responsibility to a trade association.

Were we to accept an enterprise theory of liability, the theory would not apply here. The first criteria in *Burnside,* that the product was manufactured by a small number of defendants in the industry, is not satisfied. Plaintiffs' petition names 25 companies as defendants because they allegedly manufactured and sold DES in 1949. We believe this is not a small number. The number of manufacturers and sellers named, however, may be conservative as revealed by the case law which refers to the DES industry between 1947 and 1971. *See Martin v. Abbott Laboratories,* 102 Wash.2d 581, 589, 689 P.2d 368, 374 (1984) ("The number of firms marketing DES has fluctuated considerably over the years. Estimates are that up to 200 or 300 companies manufactured and marketed DES between 1947 and 1971."); *see also Sindell v. Abbott Laboratories,* 26 Cal.3d 588, 609, 607 P.2d 924, 935, 163 Cal.Rptr. 132, 143 (1980) ("at least 200 manufacturers produced DES"); *Zafft,* 676 S.W.2d at 245 ("reject industry-wide liability in DES cases because of the large number of drug manufacturers involved"); *Collins v. Eli Lilly Company,* 116 Wis.2d 166, 186, 342 N.W.2d 37, 47 (1984) ("involves perhaps hundreds of potential defendant drug companies"). Based on the large number of manufacturers, the assumption underlying the enterprise concept—that defendants jointly control the risk—becomes "necessarily weak." *Collins,* 116 Wis.2d at 186, 342 N.W.2d at 47. The overall number of DES manufacturers mitigates against group conduct requiring imposition of liability on all for the acts of the unidentified wrongdoer.

Under the statement of facts provided us in this case, we are unable to decide whether the other criteria enumerated in *Burnside* have been satisfied. We note, however, that other courts have rejected enterprise liability in DES cases because these other criteria were not met. Unlike the blasting cap industry, DES manufacturers did not control their conduct by jointly imposed safety standards. *Burnside,* [351] Pa.Super. at [286], 505 A.2d at 985. Members of the DES industry did not delegate control or responsibility for safety functions to a trade association. *Id.* at [286], 505 A.2d at 985; *Morton,* 538 F.Supp. at 598; *Zafft,* 676 S.W.2d at 245. Instead, the Food and Drug Administration exercised pervasive regulation and control. *Sindell,* 26 Cal.3d at 609, 607 P.2d at 935, 163 Cal.Rptr. at 143; *Morton,* 538 F.Supp. at 598; *Zafft,* 676 S.W.2d at 245.

The enterprise liability theory avoids the legal causation problem that arises from an inability to identify the manufacturer of the specific injury-causing product. It does so by shifting responsibility to the industry for causing the injury because of the concert of action by manufacturers of such products through their trade associations or their collective action.

We agree with the court in *Martin* that "enterprise liability as described in *Hall* is predicated upon industry-wide cooperation of a much greater degree than occurred among DES manufacturers." 102 Wash.2d at 599, 689 P.2d at 380. We also agree with the following statement in *Morton,* 538 F.Supp. at 598:

> Accordingly, like the many other courts that have considered the question, this Court finds that the enterprise liability theory espoused in *Hall* cannot support liability in this DES case. *See, e.g., Ryan, supra* at 1017; *Namm v. Charles E. Frosst & Co.,* 178 N.J.Super. 19, 427 A.2d 1121, 1129 (N.J.App.Div.1981); *Sindell, supra,* 26 Cal.3d 588, 163 Cal.Rptr. at 141–42, 607 P.2d at 933–35.

We hold that the facts certified by the federal court in this proceeding are inappropriate for application of enterprise liability in any event.

II. *Alternative liability.* In contrast to the enterprise theory, "alternative liability" does address the problem of causation with respect to the making or the providing of the DES which brought about the injury. Although "alternate liability" also involves wrongful conduct by more than one party, the conduct of one of the parties must have caused the injury to plaintiff. Under this theory the burden of proof as to which actor caused the harm shifts to the defendants because there is uncertainty as to which of them caused the injury. *Morton,* 538 F.Supp. at 598 (citing Restatement (Second) of Torts § 433B(3) (1965)).

The general rule in Iowa, as elsewhere, is that a plaintiff has the burden of proving by a preponderance of the evidence that the defendant caused the complained of harm or injury. Iowa R.App.P. 14(f)(8); Restatement (Second) of Torts § 433B(1) (1965). Causation is an essential element in a tort action. *Iowa Electric Light & Power Co. v. General Electric Co.,* 352 N.W.2d 231, 234 (Iowa 1984). In a negligence action the causation requirement entails proof of a "causal connection between the defendant's alleged negligence and the injury." *Sponsler v. Clarke Electric Cooperative, Inc.,* 329 N.W.2d 663, 665 (Iowa 1983). In strict liability, plaintiff must establish inter alia "(1) manufacture of a product by defendant * * * [and] (6) said defect was the proximate cause of personal injuries." *Osborn,* 290 N.W.2d at 901.

The causation requirement necessarily involves two links in a case of this kind: first, that the defendant manufactured the DES ingested by the mother in question, and second, that the DES brought about injuries. *See* Prosser, *The Fall of the Citadel (Strict Liability to the Consumer),* 50 Minn.L.Rev. 791, 840 (1966). We are only concerned here with the first link, the "identification" requirement. *Payton v. Abbott Labs,* 386 Mass. 540, 571, 437 N.E.2d 171, 188 (1982); *cf. McElhaney v. Eli Lilly & Co.,* 564 F.Supp. 265, 268 (D.S.D.1983) (In distinguishing the two elements: "Causation goes to the question of what instrumentality or mechanism caused the plaintiff's injury * * * whereas the issue here is the identity of the source of that instrumentality.").

The identification requirement is summarized thus in an annotation in 51 A.L.R.3d 1344, 1349 (1973):

> Regardless of the theory which liability is predicated upon * * * it is obvious that to hold a producer, manufacturer, or seller liable for injury caused by a particular product, there must first be proof that the defendant produced, manufactured, sold or was in some way responsible for the product. * * *

The "alternative liability" theory has been frequently proposed as a means of avoiding the identification problem. *E.g., Morton,* 538 F.Supp. at 595; *Ryan v. Eli Lilly & Co.,* 514 F.Supp. 1004, 1016 (D.S.C.1981); *Sindell,* 26 Cal.3d at 598, 607 P.2d at 928, 163 Cal.Rptr. at 136; *Abel v. Eli Lilly & Co.,* 418 Mich. 311, 325, 343 N.W.2d 164, 170 (1984); *Zafft,* 676 S.W.2d at 244. The American Law Institute succinctly states the theory in section 433B(3) of the Restatement (Second) of Torts (1965):

> Where the conduct of two or more actors is tortious, and it is proved that harm has been caused to the plaintiff by only one of them, but there is uncertainty as to which one has caused it, the burden is upon each such actor to prove that he has not caused the harm.

The basis for this exception is said to be

the injustice of permitting proved wrongdoers, who among them have inflicted an injury upon the entirely innocent plaintiff, to escape liability merely because the nature of their conduct and the resulting harm has made it difficult or impossible to prove which of them has caused the harm.

Restatement (Second) of Torts § 433B(3) comment f. The theory has its roots in *Summers v. Tice,* 33 Cal.2d 80, 199 P.2d 1 (1948). The facts of *Summers* were summarized as follows in *Namm v. Charles E. Frosst & Co.,* 178 N.J.Super. 19, 32, 427 A.2d 1121, 1127–28 (App.Div.1981):

> [P]laintiff went hunting with the two defendants and specifically cautioned them to stay in line and be careful. However, when a bird was flushed, both defendants fired at it even though plaintiff Summers was directly in the line of fire and clearly visible. Summers was hit once in the eye and once in the lip. It was determined that both defendant hunters were negligent in firing their guns in the direction of plaintiff and that plaintiff could not identify which of the negligent defendants' shots hit him. The court shifted the burden of proof as to whose shot actually hit plaintiff to the two admittedly negligent hunters, the only possible tortfeasors.

See also Restatement (Second) of Torts § 433B(3) illustration 9.

Summers has generally been distinguished from the DES cases. *See, e.g., Sindell,* 26 Cal.3d at 602–03, 607 P.2d at 931, 163 Cal.Rptr. at 139; *Payton,* 386 Mass. at 572, 437 N.E.2d at 189; *Zafft,* 676 P.2d at 244; *Collins,* 116 Wis.2d at 183, 342 N.W.2d at 46. We agree with the majority of courts holding the "pure" alternative liability theory embodied in section 433B(3) "does not present a viable theory for DES cases." *Collins,* 116 Wis.2d at 183, 342 N.W.2d at 46; *accord, Martin,* 102 Wash. at 595, 689 P.2d at 377. *See also Morton,* 538 F.Supp. at 598–99; *Ryan,* 514 F.Supp. at 1016; *Namm,* 178 N.J.Super. at 34, 427 A.2d at 1128; *Zafft,* 676 S.W.2d at 244. (We note that a contrary result was reached in *Ferrigno v. Eli Lilly & Co.,* 175 N.J.Super. 551, 420 A.2d 1305 (Law Div.1980). *Namm* expressly disagrees with *Ferrigno. Namm,* 178 N.J.Super. at 32, 427 A.2d at 1127 n. 3.)

An element of the alternative liability theory, the conduct of one of the parties caused the injury, is absent in the facts given to us. In the parent case of *Summers,* two defendants were in fact present and both discharged their guns in the plaintiff's direction. An analogous DES case might exist—a question we do not decide—if a plaintiff established that only two manufacturers' DES products were sold at a certain pharmacy, and the mother bought her DES only at that pharmacy but cannot identify which brand she purchased.

Plaintiffs argue that alternative liability is applicable here because they have limited the field to three defendants—Eli Lilly, Abbott, and Upjohn. They rely on "evidence that DES manufactured by Eli Lilly & Co. was available in at least one pharmacy in Ames, Iowa in 1949" and on their assertion that DES manufactured by Abbott and Upjohn "may have been available in one Ames, Iowa pharmacy in 1949." Assuming arguendo that plaintiffs have substantial evidence that DES from Lilly, Abbott, and Upjohn was marketed in Ames, Iowa, plaintiffs' *Summers* problem is that they do not possess evidence to negate marketing of DES in Ames by other manufacturers. To say that the three named companies constitute the only possible manufacturers of the DES Mrs. Rorman ingested is sheer speculation; any number of other manufacturers may have supplied DES to the Ames market. As stated in *Namm*, 178 N.J.Super. at 33, 427 A.2d at 1128:

> The application of the principle of alternative liability to any one or all of the [named] defendants herein would impose liability without fault upon any one who manufactured a product manufactured by others as well. It would result in the taking of the property of all the named defendants in order to pay for harm which may have been caused by only one of the defendants, or even by one who is not a party to the lawsuit, who is unknown to the defendants, over whom they have no control or even any meaningful contact.

A decision frequently cited as applying the alternative liability theory in the DES context is *Abel v. Eli Lilly & Co.*, 418 Mich. 311, 343 N.W.2d 164 (1984). On a motion to dismiss, the Michigan Supreme Court held that the plaintiffs stated a cause of action based on the theory of alternative liability. *Id.* at 339, 343 N.W.2d at 177. The court noted several significant differences between *Summers* and the factual situation involving DES. Despite these differences, the court fashioned a "DES-modified alternative liability" theory "to accommodate the unique facts of this unusual litigation." *Id.* at 329, 343 N.W.2d at 172. The *Abel* court's version still requires plaintiffs to prove they have been harmed by the conduct of one of the defendants—requiring plaintiffs to "bring before the court all the actors who may have caused the injury in fact." *Id.* at 331, 343 N.W.2d at 173. Plaintiffs also have the burden of showing that all the defendants have acted tortiously, and that plaintiffs, through no fault of their own, are unable to identify which actor caused the injury. *Id.* For the reasons we have stated regarding the inapplicability of the alternative liability theory to this case, we decline to follow *Abel*.

We hold that alternative liability is inapplicable under the facts presented to us.

III. *Market share liability*. Some courts have structured new theories to overcome one of the problems encountered in applying alternative liability in DES cases—failure to have all possible producers before the court. *See, e.g., Sindell v. Abbott Laboratories*, 26 Cal.3d 588, 607 P.2d 924, 163 Cal.Rptr. 132 (1980); *Martin v. Abbott Laboratories*, 102 Wash.2d 581, 689 P.2d 368 (1984); *Collins v. Eli Lilly Co.*, 116 Wis.2d 166, 342 N.W.2d 37 (1984).

The California Supreme Court in *Sindell* discussed the need for a cause of action for injured plaintiffs:

> In our contemporary complex industrialized society, advances in science and technology create fungible goods which may harm consumers and which cannot be traced to any specific producer. The

response of the courts can be either to adhere rigidly to prior doctrine, denying recovery to those injured by such products, or to fashion remedies to meet these changing needs.

26 Cal.3d at 610, 607 P.2d at 936, 163 Cal.Rptr. at 144.

The court cited the "most persuasive" policy reason supporting a remedy was that "as between an innocent plaintiff and negligent defendants, the latter should bear the cost of the injury." *Id.* at 610–11, 607 P.2d at 936, 163 Cal.Rptr. at 144. Further, the court relied on a "broader policy standpoint" that "defendants are better able to bear the cost of injury resulting from the manufacture of a defective product." *Id.* at 611, 607 P.2d at 936, 163 Cal.Rptr. at 144.

The "market share" theory, fashioned in *Sindell,* apportions liability among defendants based on their respective shares of the "relevant" market. The plaintiff must first join "the manufacturers of a substantial share of the DES which her mother might have taken," and also meet her burden as to all other elements. *Id.* at 612, 607 P.2d at 937, 163 Cal.Rptr. at 145. The burden of proof then shifts to the defendants to demonstrate they could not have manufactured the DES that caused the plaintiff's injuries. *Id.* If a defendant fails to meet this burden, the court fashions a "market share" theory to apportion damages according to the likelihood that any of defendants supplied the product by holding each defendant liable "for the proportion of the judgment represented by its share of that market." *Id.* The intended result under this approach is that "each manufacturer's liability for an injury would be approximately equivalent to the damage caused by the DES it manufactured." *Id.* at 613, 607 P.2d at 938, 163 Cal.Rptr. at 146. The market share theory was approved by a federal district court as expressing South Dakota law, in *McElhaney v. Eli Lilly & Co.,* 564 F.Supp. 265, 271 (D.S.D.1983). *See also Zafft,* 676 S.W.2d at 247 (Gunn, J., dissenting).

The Washington and Wisconsin Supreme Courts also advocate a modification of alternative liability based on substantially the same policy considerations. *Martin,* 102 Wash.2d at 603, 689 P.2d at 381; *Collins,* 116 Wis.2d at 189, 342 N.W.2d at 48. They add that all manufacturers and distributors of DES "contributed to the *risk* of injury to the public and, consequently the risk of injury to individual plaintiffs," and therefore share a degree of culpability. *Collins,* 116 Wis.2d at 191, 342 N.W.2d at 49; *accord Martin,* 102 Wash.2d 604, 689 P.2d 382. The approaches of these two jurisdictions differ from the *Sindell* market share theory only in the apportionment of damages.

The Washington court, finding the *Sindell* theory distorts liability because only a substantial share of likely defendants share all of the damages, developed an approach termed the "market-share alternate liability." *Martin,* 102 Wash.2d at 602, 689 P.2d at 381. Application of this theory permits a plaintiff to commence an action against only one defendant and requires the plaintiff to establish by a preponderance of the evidence that the defendant produced or marketed the type of DES ingested by the plaintiff's mother. *Id.* at 604, 689 P.2d at 382. A defendant may bring in other defendants. Damages are allocated initially by presuming that each defendant has an equal share. Defendants are entitled to rebut this presumption by establishing their respective market share in plaintiff's geographic area, thus reducing their potential liability. *Id.* at 605–06, 689 P.2d at 383. If the defendants are able to establish their market share, they are only liable for that percentage of the total judgment. Other defendants who fail to establish their relevant market share are liable for a readjusted, equal share of the remaining damages. *Id.* at 606, 689 P.2d at 383. *See also McCormack v. Abbott,* 617 F.Supp. 1521 (D.Mass.1985) (adopting *Martin* approach which the federal court held was consistent with Massachusetts court's guidelines in *Payton v. Abbott,* 386 Mass. 540, 437 N.E.2d 171 (1982)).

The Wisconsin court, finding that "unalloyed market share theory does not constitute the most desirable course to follow in DES cases because the theory, while conceptually attractive, is limited in practical applicability," fashioned what is frequently termed the "risk contribution theory." *Collins,* 116 Wis.2d at 189, 342 N.W.2d at 48. Under this theory, as in *Martin,* the plaintiff is only required to sue one defendant and to allege the defendant produced or marketed the type of DES taken by the plaintiff's mother. If only one defendant is sued and no others are impleaded by the defendant, that defendant is liable for all of the damages. *Id.* at 193, 342 N.W.2d at 50. If more than one defendant is joined or impleaded, damages are determined according to the jury's assignment of liability under Wisconsin's comparative negligence statute. *Id.* at 199, 342 N.W.2d at 52–53. The court lists several factors that the jury should consider in apportioning damages among the defendants. *Id.* at 200, 342 N.W.2d at 53.

We reject the market share liability theory on a broad policy basis. We acknowledge that plaintiff in a DES case with an unidentified product manufacturer presents an appealing claim for relief. Endeavoring to provide relief, courts have developed theories which in one way or another provided plaintiffs recovery of loss by a kind of court-constructed insurance plan. The result is that manufacturers are required to pay or contribute to payment for injuries which their product may not have caused.

This may or may not be a desirable result. We believe, however, that awarding damages to an admitted innocent party by means of a court-constructed device that places liability on manufacturers who were not proved to have caused the injury involves social engineering more appropriately within the legislative domain. In order to reach such a determination, three broad policy questions must be answered. One is whether the burden of damages for these injuries should be transferred in a constitutional manner to the industry irrespective of an individual manufacturer's connection with the particular injury. If so, the second question relates to the principles and procedures by which the burden would be transferred. Finally, how do we ascertain the extent of damages to be assessed against each manufacturer? As to the latter, we note a wide divergency of solutions advanced by courts in fashioning relief without the benefit of legislation.

Our General Assembly has not entered this field, and we in the judicial branch adhere to our established principles of legal cause. *Starling v. Seaboard Coast Line Railroad,* 533 F.Supp. 183, 190 (S.D.Ga. 1982); *Zafft v. Eli Lilly & Co.,* 676 S.W.2d 241, 247 (Mo.1984). *Cf. Mizell v. Eli Lilly & Co.,* 526 F.Supp. 589 (D.S.C.1981) (relying on *Ryan,* 514 F.Supp. 1004, court rejects *Sindell* market share theory as choice of law because it violates public policy of the forum). A commentator in the field of negligence has stated, "Proof of negligence in the air, so to speak, will not do." F. Pollock, *The Law of Torts* 455 (11th ed. 1920). Plaintiffs request that we make a substantial departure from our fundamental negligence requirement of proving causation, without previous warning or guidelines. The imposition of liability upon a manufacturer for harm that it may not have caused is the very legal legerdemain, at least by our long held traditional standards, that we believe the courts should avoid unless prior warnings remain unheeded. It is an act more closely identified as a function assigned to the legislature under its power to enact laws.

We hold correspondingly that under Iowa common law a plaintiff in a products liability case must prove that the injury-causing product was a product manufactured or supplied by the defendant. We reserve for later consideration the case which involves actual concert of action by the defendants and the case which is genuinely factually analogous to *Summers v. Tice,* 33 Cal.2d 80, 199 P.2d 1 (1948). This proceeding does not present such facts.

We thus answer certified question "a" in the negative. Certified question "b" requires no answer.

Certified Question Answered.

All Justices concur except LAVORATO, J., who takes no part.

Notes

1. McCormack v. Abbott Laboratories, 617 F.Supp. 1521 (D.Mass. 1985), predicted that Massachusetts would adopt the form of market share liability fashioned in Martin v. Abbott Laboratories, 102 Wash.2d 581, 689 P.2d 368 (1984). The court offered the following justification for the doctrine:

> Lack of identification evidence in DES cases is rarely attributable to any fault on the part of the plaintiff. Rather, it results from the fact that DES was, for the most part, produced in a "generic" form which lacked any identifying markings. DES was a fungible drug produced by as many as 300 drug companies from a chemically identical formula. Secondly, courts have suggested that pharmacies and drug companies have contributed to the dearth of identification evidence by not keeping or not being able to locate pertinent records. Lastly, the very fact that DES is a drug whose effects are delayed for many years has played a

significant role in the unavailability of proof. *See, e.g.,* Sindell v. Abbott Laboratories, 1980, 26 Cal.3d 588, 163 Cal.Rptr. 132, 607 P.2d 924; Martin v. Abbott Laboratories, 1984, 102 Wash.2d 581, 689 P.2d 368.

Additionally, one of the functions of the identification requirement—separating wrongdoers from innocent actors—is of minor importance in the situation before this court. By producing and marketing an allegedly defective drug, all the defendants contributed to the risk of injury to the public and consequently, the risk of injury to individual plaintiffs. Under the market-share theory, a plaintiff must still prove that the defendants were negligent before the court may proceed to apportion damages on the basis of market share. Thus, none of the defendants can be considered truly innocent actors. Although the defendants may not have caused the actual injury of a given plaintiff, each may be shown to share, in some measure, a degree of culpability in producing and marketing DES. Furthermore, the court, while recognizing that the identification requirement also serves to protect defendants from being held liable for more harm than they have caused, believes that a market-share theory of liability, if properly fashioned, will not subject a particular defendant to liability for more harm than it statistically could have caused in the relevant market.

Finally, the magnitude of the physical and psychological injuries which are at issue in DES cases counsels toward permitting a remedy under some form of a market-share theory of liability. As between the injured plaintiff and the possibly responsible drug company, the latter is in a better position to absorb the cost of the injury. The company can insure itself against liability, absorb the damage award, or distribute it among the public as a cost of doing business, thereby spreading the cost over all consumers. In many cases, the only alternative will be to place the burden solely on the injured plaintiff. Comment, Market Share Liability: An Answer to the DES Causation Problem, 94 Harv.L.Rev. 668 (1981).

617 F.Supp. at 1525–26.

2. In George v. Parke–Davis, 107 Wash.2d 584, 733 P.2d 507 (1987), the Washington Supreme Court, in response to a request from a federal district court, answered a series of certified questions concerning the practical problems of apportionment that surround the application of the market share approach. Among the questions it discussed are the following:

A. Should shares be based on nationwide data or sales in the local market, i.e. the particular pharmacy or pharmacies from which the plaintiff made her purchases? The court opted for a local market calculation but if this proves to be impossible, the trial court may permit the introduction and use of county-wide, statewide or perhaps even nationwide data insofar as they tend to establish an accurate approximation of the defendants' local market share. In extreme cases, where it is impossible to determine market share, the defendants who cannot establish their share of the market must pay a pro rata share of the judgment.

B. Should liability be joint and several or only several? This question becomes important when some companies who sold DES in the plaintiff's market cannot be sued or are insolvent. The court concluded that liability is only several, casting the burden of judgment proof defendants on the plaintiff. If, however, a defendant cannot establish its own market share, and impleads a third party defendant who for whatever reason is not amenable to suit, then the impleading defendant has the burden of establishing the market share of the impleaded defendant. If it can do so, then the defendant will not be responsible for this percentage of the plaintiff's damages. If it cannot do so, the damages of the impleading defendant will not be reduced. In an attempt to explain how this complex rule would work, the court offered the following example:

> Assume a plaintiff, who has suffered $100,000 worth of damages, sues two viable drug companies, A and B. A can establish its actual market share was 20 percent, while B cannot establish its actual market share and must rely on the pro rata presumptions established in *Martin*. In order to reduce its liability, B impleads third party drug manufacturers C, D and E. C is a viable company which cannot establish its actual market share and which must rely on the pro rata presumption of *Martin*. D is not amenable to suit, but it is established that its actual market share is 10 percent. E is not amenable to suit and its actual market share *cannot* be calculated. The following chart represents the liabilities of the various parties:

Drug Company	Percent Liable	Total Liability	Plaintiff's Recovery
A	20	$20,000	$20,000
B	35	35,000	35,000
C	35	35,000	35,000
D	10	10,000	0
E	0	(not a proper defendant)	

TOTAL PLAINTIFF RECOVERY $90,000

> A is liable for 20 percent on the basis of its actual market share. D is liable for 10 percent on the basis of its actual market share, but because it is judgment proof, the plaintiff cannot collect the $10,000. B and C are presumptively liable for the remaining $70,000, and must split this liability pro rata so that they are each liable for $35,000. E is not a proper defendant, both because it is unamenable to suit and because its actual market share cannot be calculated. The plaintiff will recover only $90,000 of her damages, because she cannot recover the $10,000 judgment against drug company D.

C. Should bulk suppliers of the basic ingredient from which DES was manufactured be liable for contribution or indemnity claims by defendants who actually sold DES tablets? The court concluded that raw diethylstilbestrol is not inherently harmful and moreover the FDA assigns the tasks of testing drugs and warning users to drug manufacturers, not bulk suppliers. Therefore, there is no vertical liability in DES cases.

D. What is the effect of a settlement with some defendants? The court adopted the defendant's solution. Each non-settler is severally liable. The settler is liable only for the amount of the settlement, regardless of the market share assigned to the settler at trial.

3. *See* Murphy v. E.R. Squibb & Sons, Inc., 40 Cal.3d 672, 221 Cal.Rptr. 447, 710 P.2d 247 (1985) (ten percent of the nationwide market of DES sold is not a substantial share); Brown v. Superior Court (Abbott Laboratories), 44 Cal.3d 1049, 245 Cal.Rptr. 412, 751 P.2d 470 (1988) (rejecting joint liability in market share liability cases; each defendant is severally liable for the proportion of the judgment represented by its market share).

4. Hymowitz v. Eli Lilly and Co., 73 N.Y.2d 487, 541 N.Y.S.2d 941, 539 N.E.2d 1069 (1989), adopted a version of market share liability that holds defendants severally liable; mandates use of a national market in all cases; and holds defendants, who could not have sold the DES that plaintiff's mother ingested, liable as long as they participated in the marketing of DES for pregnancy use. Is this version of market share liability superior to the California approach? *See* Fischer, Products Liability—An Analysis of Market Share Liability, 34 Vand.L.Rev. 1623, 1642–1650 (1981).

5. Should courts that accept market share liability apply the theory in the following cases?

    A. Plaintiff's decedent died from cancer caused by exposure to asbestos used in various products. Plaintiff brings suit against all manufacturers who could have supplied the products to which he was exposed. The products had widely divergent toxicities, some creating a much higher risk of harm than others.

    B. A bystander in a service garage was injured when a multi-piece tire and rim assembly exploded while being inflated. After the accident, the service garage operator remounted the assembly and placed it in the stream of commerce without observing the brand name on the assembly. The manufacturer cannot now be identified. Plaintiff sues twelve manufacturers of truck wheels and rims.

    C. Plaintiff contracted encephalitis as a result of being inoculated with a defective dose of Salk anti-polio vaccine. Being unable to identify the manufacturer of the vaccine, plaintiff brought an action against all the drug companies that manufactured the vaccine at the time of her inoculation.

6. Most courts that have addressed the issue have declined to apply market-share liability in areas other than DES cases. In Shackil v. Lederle Labs., 116 N.J. 155, 561 A.2d 511 (1989), a child and her parents filed suit against manufacturers of combined diphtheria-pertussis-tetanus vaccine, after the child who was inoculated allegedly suffered from a seizure disorder that resulted in chronic encephalopathy and severe retardation. The court held that market-share liability would not be adopted in the DPT vaccine manufacturing context, stating that the imposition of a theory of market share liability "would frustrate overarching public-policy and public-health considerations by threatening the continued availability of needed drugs and impairing the prospects of the development of safer vaccines."

RUTHERFORD v. OWENS–ILLINOIS, INC.
Supreme Court of California, 1997.
16 Cal.4th 953, 941 P.2d 1203, 67 Cal.Rptr.2d 16.

BAXTER, Justice.

I. Introduction.

In this consolidated action for asbestos-related personal injuries and wrongful death brought and tried in Solano County, defendant Owens–Illinois, Inc. (Owens–Illinois) contends the trial court erred in instructing the liability phase jury pursuant to Solano County Complex Asbestos Litigation General Order No. 21.00. This instruction shifts the burden of proof to defendants in asbestos cases tried on a products liability theory to prove that their products were *not* a legal cause of the plaintiff's injuries, provided the plaintiff first establishes certain predicate facts, chief among them that the defendant manufactured or sold defective asbestos-containing products to which plaintiff was exposed, and that plaintiff's exposure to asbestos fibers generally was a legal cause of plaintiff's injury. The Court of Appeal concluded the trial court erred in giving the burden-shifting instruction.

* * *

We conclude the Court of Appeal correctly determined that the burdenshifting instruction should not have been given in this case. For reasons to be explained, we hold that in cases of asbestos-related cancer, a jury instruction shifting the burden of proof to asbestos defendants on the element of causation is generally unnecessary and incorrect under settled statewide principles of tort law. Proof of causation in such cases will always present inherent practical difficulties, given the long latency period of asbestos-related disease, and the occupational settings that commonly exposed the worker to multiple forms and brands of asbestos products with varying degrees of toxicity. In general, however, no insuperable barriers prevent an asbestos-related cancer plaintiff from demonstrating that exposure to the defendant's asbestos products was, in reasonable medical probability, a substantial factor in causing or contributing to his risk of developing cancer. We conclude that plaintiffs are required to prove no more than this. In particular, they need *not* prove with medical exactitude that fibers from a particular defendant's asbestos-containing products were those, or among those, that actually began the cellular process of malignancy. Instruction on the limits of the plaintiff's burden of proof of causation, together with the standardized instructions defining cause-in-fact causation under the substantial factor test (BAJI No. 3.76) and the doctrine of concurrent proximate legal causation (BAJI No. 3.77) will adequately apprise the jury of the elements required to establish causation. No burden-shifting instruction is necessary on the matter of proof of causation, and in the absence of such necessity, there is no justification or basis for shifting part of the plaintiff's burden of proof to the defendant to prove that it was not a legal cause of plaintiff's asbestos-related disease or injuries. (See *Summers v. Tice* (1948) 33 Cal.2d 80, 86, 199 P.2d 1 (*Summers*) [burden shift justified because without it all tortfeasors might escape liability and the injured plaintiff be left "remediless."].) However, as will be explained, the giving of the burden-shifting instruction in this case was harmless.

Ultimately, the sufficiency of the evidence of causation will depend on the factual circumstances of each case. Although the plaintiff must, in accordance with traditional tort principles, demonstrate to a reasonable medical probability that a product or products supplied by the defendant, to which he became exposed, were a substantial factor in causing his disease or risk of injuries, he is free to further establish that his particular asbestos disease is cumulative in nature, with many separate exposures each having constituted a "substantial factor" (BAJI No. 3.76) that contributed to his risk of injury. And although a defendant cannot escape *liability* simply because it cannot be determined with medical exactitude the precise contribution that exposure to fibers from defendant's products made to plaintiff's ultimate contraction of asbestos-related disease, all joint tortfeasors found liable as named defendants will remain entitled to limit *damages* ultimately assessed against them in accordance with established comparative fault and apportionment principles.

II. FACTUAL AND PROCEDURAL BACKGROUND.

Charles Rutherford (Rutherford) was in the Air Force from 1935 to 1940, after which he became an apprentice sheet metal worker at the Mare Island Naval Shipyard (Mare Island). He worked in the sheet metal shop for several years, and then became an engineering technician working with ventilation before retiring from Mare Island after 40 years. * * *

In January 1988, three months before his death, Rutherford filed an asbestos-related personal injury action in Solano County Superior Court naming as defendants nineteen manufacturers and/or distributors of asbestos products, including the sole defendant in this appeal, Owens-Illinois. The original complaint alleged Rutherford had contracted lung cancer as a result of his exposure to defendants' asbestos products while on the job at Mare Island, and alleged causes of action for products liability, negligent and intentional infliction of emotional distress, and loss of consortium. After Rutherford died of lung cancer in April 1988, the complaint was amended to allege a wrongful death action * * *.

Plaintiffs' case was consolidated for trial with four other actions presenting the similar claims of various other plaintiffs * * *.

Under procedures adopted by the Solano County Superior Court for general use in complex asbestos litigation within that county, trial of these consolidated cases was bifurcated into "damages" and "liability" phases (heard by separate juries). In the first damages phase of trial, the jury was to determine, as to each plaintiff, whether exposure to asbestos was a proximate cause of injury (i.e., whether plaintiff was suffering from asbestos-related disease or, as here, plaintiffs' decedent had died from asbestos-related disease) and, if so, the total amount of resulting damages.

Plaintiffs presented medical evidence that Rutherford had died of asbestos-related lung cancer. He had worked aboard ships around asbestos insulators at Mare Island starting in 1940. Although Rutherford's answers to interrogatories reflected he had never himself worked as an installer of asbestos insulation, he nevertheless had been exposed to respirable asbestos dust on a daily basis during periods of his employment at Mare Island. * * * Evidence was also presented that Rutherford had smoked approximately a pack of cigarettes a day over a period of 30 or more years until he quit smoking in 1977. As will be explained, this evidence took on heightened relevance at the second "liability" phase of trial.

At the end of the first phase of trial, the jury answered the question, "Did the decedent, Charles Rutherford, have lung cancer legally caused by his inhalation of asbestos fibers?" in the affirmative. The jury returned a verdict finding that a total of $278,510 in economic damages had been incurred by plaintiffs, and $280,000 in noneconomic damages suffered by plaintiffs as a result of decedent's death. Owens–Illinois has not challenged the damages phase jury's verdict finding Rutherford's injuries and death were proximately caused by his exposure to asbestos, nor has it challenged the plaintiffs' total award of economic and noneconomic damages.

Between the first and second phases of trial, nearly all the defendants except Owens–Illinois settled with plaintiffs.[1] The second liability phase thus involved only issues of Owens–Illinois's percentage of fault and apportionment of damages. At this phase of trial, the Rutherford plaintiffs elected to proceed under the burden-shifting instruction authorized, once again, under the procedures adopted by the Solano County Superior Court for general use in complex asbestos litigation within that county. * * * Briefly, the instruction, available in asbestos personal injury actions tried on a products liability theory, provides that if the plaintiff has proved that a particular asbestos supplier's product was "defective," that the plaintiff's injuries or death were legally caused by asbestos exposure *generally,* and that he was exposed to asbestos fibers from the defendant's product, the burden then shifts to the defendant to prove, if it can, that its product was not a legal cause of the plaintiff's injuries or death.

* * *

---

1. The record reflects that before his death, Rutherford identified three additional asbestos manufacturers to whose products he believed he had been exposed: Johns–Manville, Unarco and Amatex. The parties suggest those manufacturers were not named as defendants because they were bankrupt. Owens–Illinois further states in its brief that of the 19 named defendants in the Rutherford action, "[o]nly one of these entities—Owens–Illinois—remained through trial, because the rest of them settled with, or were dismissed by plaintiffs. Thus ... it was a case in which almost every defendant implicitly acknowledged its potential for liability."

Medical testimony was also presented to establish that the plaintiffs' asbestos-related disease was "dose-related"—i.e., that the risk of developing asbestos-related cancer increased as the total occupational dose of inhaled asbestos fibers increased. Dr. Allan Smith, a professor of epidemiology, testified that asbestos-related lung cancers are dose-related diseases, and that all occupational exposures through the latency period can contribute to the risk of contracting the diseases. Owens–Illinois's own medical expert, Dr. Elliot Hinckes, testified that asbestos-related cancers are dose responsive, and that if a worker had occupational exposure to many different asbestos-containing products, each such exposure would contribute to the degree of risk of contracting asbestos-related lung cancer, although he testified further that a very light or brief exposure could be considered "insignificant or at least nearly so" in the "context" of other, very heavy exposures. There was no evidence in this case that Rutherford had been exposed predominantly to any one kind or brand of asbestos product. All of the evidence regarding Rutherford's asbestos exposure was specifically related to industrial-occupational exposure, i.e., exposure to asbestos products while they were being installed or removed at Mare Island.

Owens–Illinois was allowed to establish that other asbestos manufacturers, and the plaintiffs' various employers, shared comparative fault for the plaintiffs' long-term exposure to asbestos. Owens–Illinois was also permitted to present evidence that smoking was a "negligent" contributing factor to each plaintiff's condition. Undisputed evidence indicated that smoking sharply increases the risk of lung disease, including lung cancer, and works "synergistically" with asbestos exposure to enhance the severity of resulting damage to the lungs. The trial court's instructions made clear that each plaintiff's entire recovery must be reduced to the extent of his own comparative "negligence" contributing to his condition, because each had continued to smoke tobacco long after he had notice that smoking was hazardous to health, and that the long-term consumption of tobacco products could be a contributing cause of lung disease.

* * *

The liability phase jury was instructed to assign percentages of fault for each injury, adding up to a total of 100 percent, among (1) the plaintiff himself (here, plaintiffs' decedent); (2) Owens–Illinois; (3) other manufacturers of asbestos to which the plaintiff or decedent was exposed; and (4) each employer that contributed to the exposure. In Rutherford's case, the jury apportioned fault as follows: 1.2 percent to Owens–Illinois, 2.5 percent to Rutherford himself, and 96.3 percent to the remaining entities to which the jury was allowed to assign fault. After further adjustment for pretrial settlements, the Rutherford plaintiffs recovered a net judgment of $177,047 in economic damages and $2,160 in noneconomic damages against defendant Owens–Illinois.*

---

* Ed Note. Proposition 51, adopted by the voters in 1986, provides that in a tort action governed by principles of comparative fault, a defendant shall not be jointly liable for

Owens–Illinois appealed. In its Court of Appeal briefs, Owens–Illinois asserted as trial error * * * the giving of the burden-shifting instruction, and several other unrelated evidentiary issues of no direct concern to us on review.

* * *

The Court of Appeal * * * resolved * * * that the * * * burden-shifting instruction was "erroneous" * * *.

We conclude the Court of Appeal correctly determined plaintiffs should not have been permitted to elect to proceed under the * * * burden-shifting instruction. We also find, however, that defendant has not demonstrated prejudice from the instructional error. Accordingly, we shall reverse the judgment of the Court of Appeal * * *.

III. Discussion.

1. *Preliminary Considerations; Solano County Superior Court's Local Rulemaking Authority in Complex Asbestos Litigation.*

Owens–Illinois urged the Court of Appeal to reverse the liability (second phase of trial) verdicts on the ground that the trial court improperly shifted the burden to defendant to prove that its products were not a legal cause of Rutherford's injuries and death. * * *

Upon plaintiffs' election, the trial court instructed the jury at the second liability phase of trial * * *. [A]t the commencement of the liability phase of an asbestos products liability action (tried under either the consumer expectation or risk/benefit theories of product liability), the plaintiff "shall elect whether to request that all defendants carry the burden of proof regarding the legal cause of the plaintiff's or plaintiff's decedent's injury as to each said defendant. [¶] The plaintiff so requesting [the burden-shifting instruction] must, as to each defendant, prove by a preponderance of the evidence each of the following: [¶] a) That the asbestos product manufactured or distributed by said defendant was defective; [¶] b) That plaintiff's or plaintiff's decedent's injury was legally caused by his exposure to or contact with asbestos fibers, or products containing asbestos, and [¶] c) That plaintiff's exposure to or contact with asbestos fibers, or products containing asbestos, included exposure to or contact with such fibers or products manufactured or distributed by said defendant. [¶] The burden shall then shift to each defendant to prove by a preponderance of the evidence that this product was not a legal cause of the plaintiff's or plaintiff's decedent's injury. * * *

the plaintiff's *noneconomic* damages, but shall only be severally liable for such damages "in direct proportion to that defendant's percentage of fault." (Civ.Code, § 1431.2, subd. (a).)

2. *Alternative Liability and Burden Shifting.*

We are in basic agreement with Owens–Illinois and those courts that have concluded asbestos plaintiffs can meet their burden of proving legal causation under traditional tort principles, without the need for an "alternative liability" burden-shifting instruction. Indeed, the burden-shifting instruction offered * * * appears in conflict with certain aspects of these basic tort principles, and with standardized instructions on which the liability phase jury in this case was also instructed.

Generally, the burden falls on the plaintiff to establish causation. (*Sindell v. Abbott Laboratories* (1980) 26 Cal.3d 588, 597, 163 Cal.Rptr. 132, 607 P.2d 924 (*Sindell*).) Most asbestos personal injury actions are tried on a products liability theory. In the context of products liability actions, the plaintiff must prove that the defective products supplied by the defendant were a substantial factor in bringing about his or her injury. (*Cronin v. J.B.E. Olson Corp.* (1972) 8 Cal.3d 121, 127, 104 Cal.Rptr. 433, 501 P.2d 1153 * * *.

California has definitively adopted the substantial factor test of the Restatement Second of Torts for cause-in-fact determinations. (*Mitchell v. Gonzales* (1991) 54 Cal.3d 1041, 1044, fn. 2, 1052, fn. 7, 1 Cal.Rptr.2d 913, 819 P.2d 872.) Under that standard, a cause in fact is something that is a substantial factor in bringing about the injury. * * * Rest.2d Torts, § 431, subd. (a), p. 428; BAJI No. 3.76 (8th ed.1994).) The substantial factor standard generally produces the same results as does the "but for" rule of causation which states that a defendant's conduct is a cause of the injury if the injury would not have occurred "but for" that conduct. * * * Prosser & Keeton on Torts (5th ed.1984) § 41, p. 266.) The substantial factor standard, however, has been embraced as a clearer rule of causation—one which subsumes the "but for" test while reaching beyond it to satisfactorily address other situations, such as those involving independent or concurrent causes in fact.

The term "substantial factor" has not been judicially defined with specificity, and indeed it has been observed that it is "neither possible nor desirable to reduce it to any lower terms." (Prosser & Keeton on Torts, supra, § 41, p. 267.) This court has suggested that a force which plays only an "infinitesimal" or "theoretical" part in bringing about injury, damage, or loss is not a substantial factor. Undue emphasis should not be placed on the term "substantial." For example, the substantial factor standard, formulated to aid plaintiffs as a broader rule of causality than the "but for" test, has been invoked by defendants whose conduct is clearly a "but for" cause of plaintiff's injury but is nevertheless urged as an insubstantial contribution to the injury. (Prosser & Keeton on Torts (5th ed., 1988 supp.) § 41, pp. 43–44.) Misused in this way, the substantial factor test "undermines the principles of comparative negligence, under which a party is responsible for his or her share of negligence and the harm caused thereby." (*Mitchell v. Gonzales, supra,* 54 Cal.3d at p. 1053, 1 Cal.Rptr.2d 913, 819 P.2d 872.)

An instruction shifting the burden of proof on causation constitutes a fundamental departure from these principles, and can only be justified on a showing of necessity for application of the specific theory of causation—alternative liability—first approved by this court in the celebrated case of *Summers, supra,* 33 Cal.2d 80, 199 P.2d 1. * * *

Summers involved a hunting accident in which two quail hunters negligently fired their shotguns in the direction of the plaintiff at about the same time. A single birdshot pellet struck plaintiff in the eye, causing serious injury. It was impossible to determine which of the negligent hunters had fired the single pellet, but it was clear only one of them had to have directly caused the injury. This court concluded both hunters could be found jointly and severally liable for plaintiff's injuries. We observed that each defendant was a wrongdoer who had acted negligently toward an innocent plaintiff, and that together the two had brought about a situation in which the negligence of one of them had injured the plaintiff. Under the then applicable traditional proximate cause standards, the plaintiff would have been unable to establish which defendant had caused his eye injury. To remedy this problem, the lower court shifted to each defendant the burden of proving, if he could, that he was *not* the cause of plaintiff's injury. We approved of the procedure.

A number of important factors present in *Summers* thus combined to lead this court to conclude that it would be fair and just to apply the theory of alternative liability and its concomitant burden-shifting rule. First, all the tortfeasors were named as defendants and before the court—the two hunters. In certainty one of them had caused the plaintiff's eye injury; there were no other potential tortfeasors. Second, it was established in *Summers* that each hunter was a wrongdoer who had acted negligently in firing his shotgun in the direction of the plaintiff at about the same time. Nor were there any facts to distinguish the nature or extent of the negligent conduct of each defendant; they were coequals from the standpoint of fault. Third, the plaintiff's injury was instantaneous and indivisible (as opposed to a latent, progressively deteriorating injury). Fourth, there was no contributing or concurrent causation—one of the hunters was the cause-in-fact of the entirety of plaintiff's injury resulting from a single shotgun pellet lodging in his eye. There was no factual basis on which to *apportion* "fault" or liability for the injury. Finally, given the nature of the injury, the plaintiff in *Summers* was without any evidentiary means whatsoever to prove from which hunter's shotgun the injurious single pellet had been fired. In short, given the facts of *Summers,* without the burden-shifting instruction the tortfeasors would have escaped liability, leaving the injured plaintiff without the legal means to seek redress for his negligently inflicted injuries.

The *Summers* alternative liability theory was incorporated in the Restatement Second of Torts, section 433B, subdivision (3) pages 441–44 (Section 433B(3)), which provides: "Where the conduct of two or more actors is tortious, and it is proved that harm has been caused to plaintiff by only one of them, but there is uncertainty as to which one has caused it, the burden is upon each actor to prove that he has not caused the harm."

The express language of Section 433B(3) therefore envisions the theory of alternative liability to be applicable as between two or more defendants only where all have been shown to be tortfeasors in the first instance, and where the conduct of only one of them caused the harm. The comments to Section 433B(3) are in accord. Comment g to Section 433B(3), at page 446, states that the burden shifts to the defendant only if the plaintiff can demonstrate that all defendants "acted tortiously and that the harm resulted from the conduct of ... one of them." And comment h indicates that the theory of alternative liability is generally limited to cases where the defendants' conduct creates a substantially similar risk of harm ("The cases thus far decided in which the rule stated in Subsection (3) has been applied have all been cases in which all of the actors involved have been joined as defendants. All of these cases have involved conduct simultaneous in time, or substantially so, and all of them have involved conduct of substantially the same character, creating substantially the same risk of harm, on the part of each actor...."). (*Ibid.*)

The majority of courts have refused to extend the doctrine of alternative liability and its burden-shifting rule to asbestos-related latent personal injury actions brought against multiple suppliers of asbestos products. These cases have found the factors which support application of *Summers* alternative liability and burden shifting readily distinguishable from the facts typically involved in complex asbestos litigation.

For example, in *Goldman v. Johns–Manville Sales Corp.* (Ohio 1987) 33 Ohio St.3d 40, 514 N.E.2d 691 (*Goldman*), the Supreme Court of Ohio rejected application of *Summers* alternative liability/burden shifting to asbestos personal injury actions, concluding that given the nature of such litigation, it is often the case that the culpable party or parties will not be before the court, making a *Summers*-type burden shift unfair to the named defendants standing trial. The *Goldman* court observed that "[i]n asbestos litigation, it is often uncertain that the culpable party is before the court * * *."

The *Goldman* court also observed that the wide variation in form and toxicity of asbestos products further distinguishes asbestos cases from the facts of *Summers*, making the burden-shifting rule inappropriate in such cases. "Asbestos-containing products do not create similar risks of harm because there are several varieties of asbestos fibers, and they are used in various quantities, even in the same class of product." (*Goldman, supra,* 514 N.E.2d at p. 697.)

* * *

In *Sindell, supra,* 26 Cal.3d 588, 163 Cal.Rptr. 132, 607 P.2d 924, this court too *rejected* application of a pure *Summers* alternative liability theory—in the case that went on to establish an important variation of that doctrine, "market share liability"—under circumstances where all potential tortfeasors that may have actually caused plaintiff's injuries were not before the court as named defendants in the lawsuit.

* * *

Although many of the above cited cases focus on the fact that not all potential tortfeasors may be before the court to ensure that the *actual* tortfeasor will be held liable if it cannot disprove its role in causing plaintiff's injuries, or that different toxicities and brands of asbestos products and their differing effects on different asbestos-related diseases make it inappropriate to apply a *Summers* alternative liability/burden-shifting rule to asbestos cases, we believe the most fundamental reason why a burden-shifting instruction is unnecessary to proving an asbestos-related cancer latent injury case becomes clear when the limits on the plaintiff's burden of proof on causation are properly understood. A fuller analysis of the medical problems and uncertainties accompanying factual proof of causation in an asbestos cancer case will serve to illustrate the point.

At the most fundamental level, there is scientific uncertainty regarding the biological mechanisms by which inhalation of certain microscopic fibers of asbestos leads to lung cancer and mesothelioma. Although in some cases medical experts have testified that asbestos-related cancer is the final result of the fibrosis (scarring) process (see *Armstrong World Industries, Inc. v. Aetna Casualty & Surety Co.* (1996) 45 Cal.App.4th 1, 37–39, 52 Cal.Rptr.2d 690), a general reference on the subject describes the link between fibrosis and carcinogenesis as "a debated issue for which further extensive analysis is needed." (1 Encyclopedia of Human Biology (1991) Asbestos, p. 423.) An answer to this biological question would be legally relevant, because if each episode of scarring contributes cumulatively to the formation of a tumor or the conditions allowing such formation, each significant exposure by the plaintiff to asbestos fibers would be deemed a cause of the plaintiff's cancer; if, on the other hand, only one fiber or group of fibers actually causes the formation of a tumor, the others would not be legal causes of the plaintiff's injuries.

If, moreover, the question were answered in favor of the latter (single cause) theory, another question–apparently unanswerable–would arise: *which* particular fiber or fibers actually caused the cancer to begin forming. Because of the irreducible uncertainty of the answer, asbestos-related cancer would, under the single-fiber theory of carcinogenesis, be an example of alternative causation, i.e., a result produced by a single but indeterminable member of a group of possible causes. The disease would thus be analogous to the facts of the hunting accident in *Summers, supra,* 33 Cal.2d 80, 199 P.2d 1.

Apart from the uncertainty of the causation, at a much more concrete level uncertainty frequently exists whether the plaintiff was even exposed to dangerous fibers from a product produced, distributed or installed by a particular defendant. The long latency periods of asbestos-related cancers mean that memories are often dim and records missing or incomplete regarding the use and distribution of specific products. In some industries, many different asbestos-containing products have been used, often including several similar products at the same time periods and worksites. Not uncommonly, plaintiffs have been unable to prove direct exposure to a given defendant's product. * * *

Finally, at a level of abstraction somewhere between the historical question of exposure and the unknown biology of carcinogenesis, the question arises whether the risk of cancer created by a plaintiff's exposure to a particular asbestos-containing product was significant enough to be considered a legal cause of the disease. Taking into account the length, frequency, proximity and intensity of exposure, the peculiar properties of the individual product, any other potential causes to which the disease could be attributed (e.g., other asbestos products, cigarette smoking), and perhaps other factors affecting the assessment of comparative risk, should inhalation of fibers from the particular product be deemed a "substantial factor" in causing the cancer? * * *

The burden of proof as to exposure is not disputed in this case. Even with the jury instruction at issue, plaintiffs bore the burden of proof on the issue of exposure to the defendant's product; plaintiffs do not complain of that burden, which is properly theirs under California law. Only in one circumstance have we relieved toxic tort plaintiffs of the burden of showing exposure to the defendant's product: where hundreds of producers had made the same drug from an identical formula, practically precluding patients from identifying the makers of the drugs they took. (*Sindell, supra,* 26 Cal.3d at pp. 610–613, 163 Cal.Rptr. 132, 607 P.2d 924.) Plaintiffs do not here argue that a comparable situation exists with asbestos makers justifying adoption of a market-share liability theory. * * *

Nor is the burden of proof as to the mechanism of carcinogenesis disputed here; defendant *concedes* that plaintiff does not bear such a burden to "connect the manufacturer and the fibers." Asbestos plaintiffs, Owens–Illinois acknowledges, "are *not* required to identify the manufacturer of specific fibers" that caused the cancer. We agree: Plaintiffs cannot be expected to prove the scientifically unknown details of carcinogenesis, or trace the unknowable path of a given asbestos fiber. But the impossibility of such proof does not dictate use of a burden shift. Instead, we can bridge this gap in the humanly knowable by holding that plaintiffs may prove causation in asbestos-related cancer cases by demonstrating that the plaintiff's exposure to defendant's asbestos-containing product in reasonable medical probability was a substantial factor in contributing to the aggregate *dose* of asbestos the plaintiff or decedent inhaled or ingested, and hence to the *risk* of developing asbestos-related cancer, without the need to demonstrate that fibers from the defendant's particular product were the ones, or among the ones, that *actually* produced the malignant growth.

In refining the concept of legal cause we must also ensure that the triers of fact in asbestos-related cancer cases know the precise contours of the plaintiff's burden. The generally applicable standard instructions on causation are insufficient for this purpose. Those instructions tell the jury that every "substantial factor in bringing about an injury" is a legal cause (BAJI No. 3.76), even when more than one such factor "contributes concurrently as a cause of the injury" (BAJI No. 3.77). They say nothing, however, to inform the jury that, in asbestos-related cancer cases, a particular asbestos-containing product is deemed to be a substantial factor in bringing about the injury if its contribution to the plaintiff or decedent's *risk* or *probability* of developing cancer was substantial.

Without such guidance, a juror might well conclude that the plaintiff needed to prove that fibers from the defendant's product were a substantial factor *actually contributing* to the development of the plaintiff's or decedent's cancer. In many cases, such a burden will be medically impossible to sustain, even with the greatest possible effort by the plaintiff, because of irreducible uncertainty regarding the cellular formation of an asbestos-related cancer. We therefore hold that, in the trial of an asbestos-related cancer case, although no instruction "shifting the burden of proof as to causation" to defendant is warranted, the jury should be told that the plaintiff's or decedent's exposure to a particular product was a substantial factor in causing or bringing about the disease if in reasonable medical probability it was a substantial factor contributing to plaintiff's or decedent's *risk* of developing cancer.

We turn, finally, to the aspect of uncertainty about causation that *is* directly disputed by the parties here—the question of which exposures to asbestos-containing products contributed significantly enough to the total occupational dose to be considered "substantial factors" in causing the disease. Who should bear the burden of proof, including the risk of nonpersuasion, on that question? On this point, we agree with defendant: in the absence of a compelling need for shifting the burden, it should remain with the plaintiff. The fundamental justification for a *Summers*-type shift of the burden is that without it all defendants might escape liability and the plaintiff be left "remediless." (*Summers, supra,* 33 Cal.2d at p. 86, 199 P.2d 1.) On the issue of which exposures to asbestos were substantial factors increasing the risk of cancer, the difficulties of proof do not in general appear so severe as to justify a shift in the burden of proof. The substantial factor standard is a relatively broad one, requiring only that the contribution of the individual cause be more than negligible or theoretical. A standard instruction (BAJI No. 3.77) tells juries that each of several actors or forces acting concurrently to cause an injury is a legal cause of the injury "regardless of the extent to which each contributes to the injury." A plaintiff who suffers from an asbestos-related cancer and has proven exposure to inhalable asbestos fibers from several products will not, generally speaking, face insuperable difficulties in convincing a jury that a particular one of these product exposures, or several of them, were substantial factors in creating the risk of asbestos disease or latent injury. No burden-shifting instruction is therefore necessary on this question, and in the absence of necessity the justification for shifting part of the plaintiff's ordinary burden of proof onto a defendant also disappears.

While the above analysis provides fully adequate grounds for rejecting use of a burden-shifting instruction in the asbestos-related cancer context, we also note that, in other respects as well, asbestos-related cancer cases do not fit easily into the alternative liability model represented by *Summers*. As courts in California and other jurisdictions have observed, unlike the situation in *Summers,* asbestos cases often have less than the complete set of possible tortfeasors before the court, and do not display the same symmetry of "comparative fault" or "indivisible injury" as was the factual case in *Summers*.

* * *

In conclusion, our general holding is as follows. In the context of a cause of action for asbestos-related latent injuries, the plaintiff must first establish some threshold *exposure* to the defendant's defective asbestos-containing products, *and* must further establish in reasonable medical probability that a particular exposure or series of exposures was a "legal cause" of his injury, i.e., a *substantial factor* in bringing about the injury. In an asbestos-related cancer case, the plaintiff need *not* prove that fibers from the defendant's product were the ones, or among the ones, that actually began the process of malignant cellular growth. Instead, the plaintiff may meet the burden of proving that exposure to defendant's product was a substantial factor causing the illness by showing that in reasonable medical probability it was a substantial factor contributing to the plaintiff's or decedent's risk of developing cancer. The jury should be so instructed.* * *

3. *Prejudice.*

Lastly, we face the question of prejudice from the giving of the erroneous burden-shifting instruction in this case. Owens–Illinois asserts that the instruction deprived it of its jury trial right on causation and "[t]he verdict must be reversed on this basis alone." We have, however, recently considered and rejected precisely this theory of inherent prejudice from instructional error in civil cases. (*Soule v. General Motors Corp.* (1994) 8 Cal.4th 548, 573–580, 34 Cal.Rptr.2d 607, 882 P.2d 298.) Instead, we held, instructional error requires reversal only " 'where it seems probable' that the error 'prejudicially affected the verdict' " (*Id.* at p. 580, 34 Cal.Rptr.2d 607, 882 P.2d 298.) The reviewing court should consider not only the nature of the error, "including its natural and probable effect on a party's ability to place his full case before the jury," but the likelihood of actual prejudice as reflected in the individual trial record, taking into account "(1) the state of the evidence, (2) the effect of other instructions, (3) the effect of counsel's arguments, and (4) any indications by the jury itself that it was misled." (*Id.* at pp. 580–581, 34 Cal.Rptr.2d 607, 882 P.2d 298.) Applying this analysis, we conclude defendant has failed to demonstrate a miscarriage of justice arose from the erroneous instruction.

* * *

Finally, the record does not contain any indications the jury was actually misled. To the contrary, the jury's verdict suggests that, regardless of the burden shift, it accepted much of the defense's *factual* theory, concluding that exposure to Kaylo contributed a relatively small amount to decedent's cancer risk, but rejected defendant's argument that such a small contribution should be considered insubstantial. Thus the jury found inhalation of fibers from Kaylo was a substantial causative factor, but allocated only 1.2 percent of the total legal cause to defendant's comparative fault. (2.5 percent of the total cause was allocated to the decedent's own fault, 25 percent to that of decedent's employer, and the remainder, divided by type of product, to makers of other asbestos-containing products used at the shipyard.) From the jury's low estimate of defendant's share of causation, it appears they resolved most of the factual uncertainty in defendant's favor despite the burden-shifting instruction. In the absence of any instruction or evidence that a small amount was necessarily insubstantial, and guided by BAJI No. 3.77's command that every contributing cause was a legal cause regardless of the degree of its contribution, the jury concluded even 1.2 percent of the cause was, on the facts of this case, substantial. A different result seems unlikely to have ensued had they been correctly instructed plaintiffs bore the burden of showing exposure to Kaylo was a substantial factor increasing the decedent's risk of developing lung cancer.

We are, for these reasons, unconvinced the instructional error was prejudicial.

IV. CONCLUSION.

Although the Court of Appeal correctly determined Solano County General Order No. 21.00 should not have been given in this case, no miscarriage of justice has been shown to have resulted from the trial court's error in giving the burden-shifting instruction. * * *

GEORGE, C.J., and KENNARD, WERDEGAR, CHIN and BROWN, JJ., concur.

Notes

1. In a dissenting opinion, Justice Mosk argued that:

Without a burden-shifting instruction, if each defendant argues that its product was only a small part of a plaintiff's total exposure, and that it therefore could not have been a substantial factor in causing his injury, there is a risk that a jury might find that *no* one manufacturer was responsible for the injury, even though all of the manufacturers together caused the harm. This is particularly true in light of the exceptionally long latency periods from initial exposure to the onset of asbestos-related disease and the nature of the typical industrial environment, involving multiple exposures to various asbestos products over a period of time.

Without the burden-shifting instruction, it would appear that many innocent plaintiffs who were unknowingly exposed to products such as Kaylo in the workplace would face serious, even insurmountable, difficulties in establishing that exposure to a specific defendant's defective product was a substantial cause of injury.

Do you think this is a very realistic concern? *See* Lindstrom v. A–C Product Liability Trust, 424 F.3d 488 (6th Cir. 2005).

2. And how should we define "substantial factor"? Two lower court opinions pose interesting issues concerning the definition of this term.

In Cropper v. Owens–Corning Fiberglas Corp., 34 Phila.Co.Rptr. 359 (Pa.Com.Pl. 1997) the jury asked the trial judge for a definition of the term. The court provided a definition from Webster's dictionary, which defined the term as "considerable in quantity, significantly large." *Id.* at 372. The plaintiff objected to this definition. The court concluded however that in the absence of a countervailing definition in either statutory or case law, the use of dictionary definitions is generally approved in Pennsylvania. Does this definition comport with that provided in *Rutherford*?

In Grahn v. Dillingham Construction, Inc., 2004 WL 2075570 (Cal.App. 2004), the court was asked to choose between definitions offered by the plaintiff and the defendant in light of *Rutherford*. Plaintiff's definition was as follows:

"A person's exposure to a particular asbestos product is a substantial factor in causing or bringing about an asbestos-related disease if, in reasonable medical probability the exposure contributed to the person's risk of developing that asbestos-related disease."

The defendant's definition varied slightly from this.

"A person's exposure to an asbestos-containing product is a substantial factor in causing or bringing about an asbestos-related disease if in reasonable medical probability the exposure was a *substantial factor* contributing to the person's risk of developing that asbestos-related disease." (Italics added.)

Which definition more nearly captures the spirit of *Rutherford*?

3. As noted at the beginning of this chapter, the Restatement (Third) of Torts: Liability for Physical Harm (Proposed Final Draft No. 1, 2005) § 26 rejects the substantial factor test for a "but for" test. "Conduct is a factual cause of harm when the harm would not have occurred absent the conduct." As Comment *e* of § 26 notes, a hallmark of the "but for" test is the need for a counterfactual inquiry. "One must ask what would have occurred if the actor had not engaged in the tortious conduct."

Comment *j* has this to say concerning the substantial factor test:

j. Substantial factor. The "substantial-factor" test as the routine standard for factual cause originated in the Restatement of Torts §§ 431–432 and was replicated in the Restatement Second of Torts §§ 431–432. Its primary function was to permit the factfinder to decide that factual cause existed when there were overdetermined causes—each of two separate causal chains sufficient to bring about the plaintiff's harm, thereby rendering neither a but-for cause. See § 27. The substantial-factor test has not, however, withstood the test of time, as it has proved confusing and been misused.

The "substantial factor" rubric is employed alternately to impose a more rigorous standard for factual cause or to provide a more lenient standard. Thus, for example, comparative-responsibility jurisdictions improperly employ the substantial-factor test to suggest to a jury that it should find the plaintiff's "substantial" contributory negligence, rather than the defendant's tortious conduct, to be "the" cause of harm. Conversely, some courts have accepted the proposition that, although the plaintiff cannot show the defendant's tortious conduct was a but-for cause of harm by a preponderance of the evidence, the plaintiff may still prevail by showing that the tortious conduct was a substantial factor in causing the harm. That proposition is inconsistent with the substantial-factor standard adopted in Restatement Second of Torts § 431, Comment *a*, and is inconsistent with this Section as well. To be sure, courts may decide, based on the availability of evidence and on policy grounds, to modify or shift the burden of proof for factual cause, as they have when multiple tortfeasors act negligently toward another but only one causes the harm. See § 28(b). Courts may, for similar reasons, decide to permit recovery for unconventional types of harm, such as a lost opportunity to avoid an adverse outcome. Nevertheless, the substantial-factor rubric tends to obscure, rather than to assist, explanation and clarification of the basis of these decisions. The element that must be established by whatever standard of proof is the but-for or necessary-condition standard of this Section. Section 27 provides a rule for finding each of two acts that are elements of sufficient competing causal sets to be factual causes without employing the substantial-factor language of the prior Torts Restatements. There is no question of degree for either of these concepts.

4. If one is to reject the substantial factor test, how is one to deal with cases such as *Rutherford*? Section 27 of the Third Restatement states an exception to the "but for" test adopted in § 26.

If multiple acts exist, each of which alone would have been a factual cause under § 26 of the physical harm at the same time, each act is regarded as a factual cause of the harm.

Comments *f* and *g* address fact pattern such as that arising in *Rutherford*

f. Multiple sufficient causal sets. In some cases, tortious conduct by one actor is insufficient, even with other background causes, to cause the plaintiff's harm. Nevertheless, when combined with conduct by other persons, the conduct overdetermines the harm, i.e., is more than sufficient to cause the harm. This circumstance thus creates the multiple sufficient causal set situation addressed in this Comment. The fact that an actor's conduct requires other conduct to be sufficient to cause another's harm does not obviate the applicability of this Section.* * * Moreover, the fact that the other person's conduct is sufficient to cause the harm does not prevent the actor's conduct from being a factual cause of harm pursuant to this Section, if the actor's conduct is necessary to at least one causal set. For example, one actor's contribution may be sufficient to bring about the harm while another actor's contribution is only sufficient when combined with some portion of the first actor's contribution. Whether the second actor's contribution can be so combined into a sufficient causal set is a matter on which this Restatement takes no position and leaves to future development in the courts. See Comment *i*.

g. Toxic substances and disease. Since the publication of the Restatement Second of Torts, the situation addressed in Comment *f* has occurred most frequently in cases in which persons have been exposed to multiple doses of a toxic agent. When a person contracts a disease such as cancer, and sues multiple actors claiming that each provided some dose of a toxic substance that caused the disease, the question of the causal role of each defendant's toxic substance arises. Assuming that there is some threshold dose sufficient to cause the disease, the person may have been exposed to doses in excess of the threshold before contracting the disease. Thus, some of the person's exposures may not have been a but-for cause of the disease. Nevertheless, each of the exposures prior to the person contracting the disease (or the time at which the person's contracting the disease was determined, see § 26, Comment *k*) is a factual cause of the person's disease under the rule in this Section. Whether there are some exposures that are sufficiently de minimis that the actor should not be held liable is a matter not of factual causation, but rather of policy, and is addressed in § 36.

The relevant portion of Comment *i* referred to in Comment *f* states:

Comment *f* addresses cases in which three candidates for cause combine to bring about a result, and any two would have been sufficient. In this situation, no candidate is a but-for cause, and none is a sufficient cause. Nevertheless, Comment *f* provides that each is a factual cause under the rule stated in this Section. Comment *g* addresses this issue in the context of combined doses of toxic substances. The situation is more complicated, however, if two of the three candidates for cause—or doses in a toxic-substances case—come from the same defendant or source. In that case, one of the defendants' conduct or toxic substance would have been sufficient, whereas the other defendant's conduct or toxic substance would not. Intuition might suggest that the latter is not a cause, especially if the latter is small in comparison to the former. This intuition may simply be an example of a de minimis contribution, already discussed and addressed in § 36, Comment *b*, but it may also be based on other factors, including notions of preemption. Moreover, and significantly, it may not be widely shared. In a case addressed by Comment *f*, in which three actors each provide one-half of a sufficient toxic dose, why should the result change if one actor provides two doses and another actor provides one? And should it matter if the two doses come combined from the source or in two discrete contributions? * * *

The black letter of Section 36 states:

When an actor's negligent conduct constitutes only a trivial contribution to a causal set that is a factual cause of physical

harm under § 27, the harm is not within the scope of the actor's liability.

At the end of the day, do you believe the Third Restatement provides a more coherent way of dealing with cases like *Rutherford* than the Second Restatement's reliance on a substantial factor test of causation?

5. The causal difficulties posed by toxic exposures are not unique to the United States, nor are judicial attempts to respond to them. In *Fairchild v. Glenhaven Funeral Services Ltd.*, [2003] 1 A.C. 32, the House of Lords dealt with the cases of individuals who contracted mesothelioma after being exposed to asbestos produced by a number of defendants. Following are some excerpts from Lord Bingham of Cornhill's speech:

> **2** The essential question underlying the appeals may be accurately expressed in this way. If (1) C was employed at different times and for differing periods by both A and B, and (2) A and B were both subject to a duty to take reasonable care or to take all practicable measures to prevent C inhaling asbestos dust because of the known risk that asbestos dust (if inhaled) might cause a mesothelioma, and (3) both A and B were in breach of that duty in relation to C during the periods of C's employment by each of them with the result that during both periods C inhaled excessive quantities of asbestos dust, and (4) C is found to be suffering from a mesothelioma, and (5) any cause of C's mesothelioma other than the inhalation of asbestos dust at work can be effectively discounted, but (6) C cannot (because of the current limits of human science) prove, on the balance of probabilities, that his mesothelioma was the result of his inhaling asbestos dust during his employment by A or during his employment by B or during his employment by A and B taken together, is C entitled to recover damages against either A or B or against both A and B? To this question (not formulated in these terms) the Court of Appeal (Brooke, Latham and Kay LJJ), in a reserved judgment of the court reported at [2002] 1 WLR 1052, gave a negative answer. It did so because, applying the conventional "but for" test of tortious liability, it could not be held that C had proved against A that his mesothelioma would probably not have occurred but for the breach of duty by A, nor against B that his mesothelioma would probably not have occurred but for the breach of duty by B, nor against A and B that his mesothelioma would probably not have occurred but for the breach of duty by both A and B together. So C failed against both A and B. The crucial issue on appeal is whether, in the special circumstances of such a case, principle, authority or policy requires or justifies a modified approach to proof of causation.

* * *

> **7** From about the 1960s, it became widely known that exposure to asbestos dust and fibres could give rise not only to asbestosis and other pulmonary diseases, but also to the risk of developing a mesothelioma. This is a malignant tumour, usually of the pleura, sometimes of the peritoneum. In the absence of occupational exposure to asbestos dust it is a very rare tumour indeed, afflicting no more than about one person in a million per year. But the incidence of the tumour among those

occupationally exposed to asbestos dust is about 1,000 times greater than in the general population, and there are some 1,500 cases reported annually. It is a condition which may be latent for many years, usually for 30–40 years or more; development of the condition may take as short a period as ten years, but it is thought that that is the period which elapses between the mutation of the first cell and the manifestation of symptoms of the condition. It is invariably fatal, and death usually occurs within one to two years of the condition being diagnosed. The mechanism by which a normal mesothelial cell is transformed into a mesothelioma cell is not known. It is believed by the best medical opinion to involve a multi-stage process, in which six or seven genetic changes occur in a normal cell to render it malignant. Asbestos acts in at least one of those stages and may (but this is uncertain) act in more than one. It is not known what level of exposure to asbestos dust and fibre can be tolerated without significant risk of developing a mesothelioma, but it is known that those living in urban environments (although without occupational exposure) inhale large numbers of asbestos fibres without developing a mesothelioma. It is accepted that the risk of developing a mesothelioma increases in proportion to the quantity of asbestos dust and fibres inhaled: the greater the quantity of dust and fibre inhaled, the greater the risk. But the condition may be caused by a single fibre, or a few fibres, or many fibres: medical opinion holds none of these possibilities to be more probable than any other, and the condition once caused is not aggravated by further exposure. So if C is employed successively by A and B and is exposed to asbestos dust and fibres during each employment and develops a mesothelioma, the very strong probability is that this will have been caused by inhalation of asbestos dust containing fibres. But C could have inhaled a single fibre giving rise to his condition during employment by A, in which case his exposure by B will have had no effect on his condition; or he could have inhaled a single fibre giving rise to his condition during his employment by B, in which case his exposure by A will have had no effect on his condition; or he could have inhaled fibres during his employment by A and B which together gave rise to his condition; but medical science cannot support the suggestion that any of these possibilities is to be regarded as more probable than any other. There is no way of identifying, even on a balance of probabilities, the source of the fibre or fibres which initiated the genetic process which culminated in the malignant tumour. It is on this rock of uncertainty, reflecting the point to which medical science has so far advanced, that the three claims were rejected by the Court of Appeal and by two of the three trial judges.

* * *

9 The issue in these appeals does not concern the general validity and applicability of [the "but for"] requirement, which is not in question, but is whether in special circumstances such as those in these cases there should be any variation or relaxation of it. The overall object of tort law is to define cases in which the law may justly hold one party liable to compensate another. Are these such cases?

* * *

Conclusion

34 To the question posed in paragraph 2 of this opinion I would answer that where conditions (1)-(6) are satisfied C is entitled to recover against both A and B. That conclusion is in my opinion consistent with principle, and also with authority (properly understood). Where those conditions are satisfied, it seems to me just and in accordance with common sense to treat the conduct of A and B in exposing C to a risk to which he should not have been exposed as making a material contribution to the contracting by C of a condition against which it was the duty of A and B to protect him. I consider that this conclusion is fortified by the wider jurisprudence reviewed above. Policy considerations weigh in favour of such a conclusion. It is a conclusion which follows even if either A or B is not before the court. It was not suggested in argument that C's entitlement against either A or B should be for any sum less than the full compensation to which C is entitled, although A and B could of course seek contribution against each other or any other employer liable in respect of the same damage in the ordinary way. No argument on apportionment was addressed to the House. I would in conclusion emphasise that my opinion is directed to cases in which each of the conditions specified in (1)-(6) of paragraph 2 above is satisfied and to no other case. It would be unrealistic to suppose that the principle here affirmed will not over time be the subject of incremental and analogical development. Cases seeking to develop the principle must be decided when and as they arise. For the present, I think it unwise to decide more than is necessary to resolve these three appeals which, for all the foregoing reasons, I concluded should be allowed.

6. The *Fairchild* opinion has a useful discussion of how a number of European and Commonwealth countries approach the problem presented in the case. In Germany, this type of case is covered by the second sentence (to which emphasis has been added) of BGB § 830.1 which provides:

> If several persons have caused damage by an unlawful act committed in common each is responsible for the damage. *The same rule applies if it cannot be discovered which of several participants has caused the damage by his act.*

Article 926 of the Greek Civil Code, entitled "Damage caused by several persons" provides:

> If damage has occurred as a result of the joint action of several persons, or if several persons are concurrently responsible for the same damage, they are all jointly and severally implicated. The same applies if several persons have acted simultaneously or in succession and it is not possible to determine which person's act caused the damage.

A similar provision exists in the Austrian Civil Code:

> 1302. In such a case, if the injury is inadvertent, and it is possible to determine the portions thereof, each person is responsible only for the injuries caused by his mistake. If, however, the injury was intentional, or if the portions of the individuals in the injury cannot be determined, all are liable for one and one for all; however, the individual who has

paid damages is granted the right to claim reimbursement from the others.

7. How, if at all, does the House of Lord's approach differ from that in *Rutherford*? From the position of the Third Restatement?

8. Does the House of Lord's approach depend on a certain theory of how asbestos exposure causes mesothelioma? Does the *Rutherford* approach depend on a certain theory of how asbestos exposure causes cancer? Would either court adopt a different approach if it were known that there was or was not a strong dose-response relationship between exposure an the likelihood of developing the disease? If in fact we do not know whether the relationship between exposure and development of a given disease follows a single hit or a cumulative dose model, should the law adopt a default model for purposes of litigation? If your answer is yes, which model is preferable?

9. In a part of the *Rutherford* opinion not reproduced above, the court refused to permit the defendants to join the tobacco companies who sold cigarettes to the plaintiffs. What are the arguments for and against this position?

10. Both the *Mulcahy* and the *Rutherford* opinions discuss *Summers v. Tice* and its burden shifting, alternative liability approach to indeterminate defendant problems. The *Summers* rule is reflected in Restatement (Third) of Torts: Liability for Physical Harm (Proposed Final Draft No. 1, 2005).

§ 28. Burden Of Proof

(a) Subject to Subsection (b), the plaintiff has the burden to prove that the defendant's tortious conduct was a factual cause of the plaintiff's physical harm.

(b) When the plaintiff sues all of multiple actors and proves that each engaged in tortious conduct that exposed the plaintiff to a risk of physical harm and that the tortious conduct of one or more of them caused the plaintiff's harm but the plaintiff cannot reasonably be expected to prove which actor caused the harm, the burden of proof, including both production and persuasion, on factual causation is shifted to the defendants.

The Restatement's requirement that the plaintiff sue *all* the entities whose tortious acts exposed the plaintiff to a risk of harm reflects the position of the great majority of courts that have adopted this approach. *See* § 28, Comment *g*.

Chapter 6

PROOF OF DEFECT AND CAUSATION

SECTION A. INDUSTRY STANDARD AND CUSTOM

BRUCE v. MARTIN–MARIETTA CORP.
United States Court of Appeals, Tenth Circuit, 1976.
544 F.2d 442.

BREITENSTEIN, CIRCUIT JUDGE.

These consolidated appeals relate to a product liability case arising out of an airplane crash. Plaintiffs-appellants are persons injured, and representatives of persons killed, in the crash. Defendant-appellee Martin–Marietta Corporation manufactured the plane. Defendant-appellee Ozark Airlines was an intermediate owner and seller of the plane. Jurisdiction is based on diversity. The district court gave summary judgment for the defendants. We affirm.

The airplane, a Martin 404, was chartered to carry the Wichita State University team and some of its supporters to a football game in Logan, Utah. On October 2, 1970, the plane crashed into a mountain west of Silver Plume, Colorado. The plane first struck trees at an altitude of approximately 10,800 ft. and then traveled 425 ft. before coming to rest. Seats in the passenger cabin broke loose from their floor attachments, were thrown forward against the bulkhead of the plane, and blocked exit. A fire then developed. Of the 40 persons on the plane, 32 died in the crash.

Martin manufactured the plane and sold it to Eastern Airlines in March, 1952. Eastern used the plane about ten years and in 1962 sold it to Mohawk Airlines which used it about three years and sold it to Ozark Airlines in 1965.

In 1967, Ozark sold the plane to Fairchild–Hiller Corporation, a manufacturer of aircraft. The plane was in storage until sometime in 1970 when it was sold to Jack Richards Aircraft Company. Golden Eagle Aviation contracted with Wichita State University to provide transportation for its football games away from home. Golden Eagle supplied the crew and used the Richards aircraft. Eastern, Mohawk and Ozark are all carriers providing scheduled services under pertinent federal aviation regulations. The defendants in the instant suit are Martin and Ozark.

On these appeals the plaintiffs do not contend that any action of either defendant caused the plane to crash. Their claims are that the defendants' failures to design, manufacture, or maintain the plane in crashworthy condition caused the deaths, or enhanced the injuries, of the passengers. The alleged defects are the inadequacy of the seat fastenings and the lack of protection against fire. Plaintiffs seek recovery on theories of negligence, implied warranty, and strict liability in tort.

* * *

I.

LIABILITY OF MARTIN

Martin was the manufacturer and original seller of the plane. Martin does not claim any change in the condition of the plane. As to strict liability, the question is whether the plane was sold "in a defective condition unreasonably dangerous to the user." The negligence question is whether Martin exercised reasonable care. See *Volkswagen of America, Inc. v. Young,* 272 Md. 201, 321 A.2d 737.

* * *

The question is whether there is any genuine issue as to any material fact. Plaintiffs claim that the plane was not equipped with crashworthy design characteristics in two particulars: (1) the seats and seat fastenings were not designed or manufactured to withstand a crash and, (2) the aircraft was not designed so as to minimize the possibility of fire occurring after a crash.

* * *

[P]laintiffs presented the affidavit of an aircraft accident investigator whose qualifications are not questioned. He said:

"My studies thus far indicate that there were airline passenger seats in common use on October 2, 1970, which, if installed in the subject Martin 404 aircraft, would have remained in place throughout this otherwise survivable accident and would not have trapped the occupants in the burning aircraft. An occupant in this crash should not have had his escape from the burning aircraft impeded by seat failures. In the crash in question the seat failures constituted an unreasonable dangerous condition to the passengers because the seat failures prevented them from exiting the burning aircraft."

* * *

The plaintiffs' specific allegations relate to the fire hazard and the adequacy of the seat fastenings. * * * The only fact shown by plaintiffs with regard to the seats is that in 1970, 18 years after Martin made and sold the plane, airplane passenger seats, which would have withstood the crash, were in use. The record establishes that when the plane was made and first sold, its design was within the state of the art. The plaintiffs' affidavit that 18 years after the manufacture and sale of the plane safer passenger seats were in use is not relevant to the determination of whether Martin, by satisfying the 1952 state-of-art requirements, exercised reasonable care and, hence, was not negligent.

Plaintiffs say that state-of-art evidence is not material when the claim is based on strict liability. They argue that a showing of a design defective in 1970 establishes that the plane was defective in 1952, the time of the original sale, absent a subsequent alteration of the plane. For support of their position, plaintiffs rely on *Pryor v. Lee C. Moore Corp.*, 10 Cir., 262 F.2d 673, and *Mickle v. Blackmon*, 252 S.C. 202, 166 S.E.2d 173. These cases hold that prolonged safe use of a product is evidence of lack of defect but is not conclusive. We have no quarrel with the rule but have no need to apply it here.

There is authority that state-of-art evidence is not relevant to a strict liability claim. *Cunningham v. MacNeal Memorial Hospital*, 47 Ill.2d 443, 266 N.E.2d 897, 902, 904; and *Gelsumino v. E.W. Bliss Co.*, 10 Ill.App.3d 604, 295 N.E.2d 110, 113. The basic reasoning is that the principles noted in § 402A(1) are, by subsection (a), made applicable although "the seller has exercised all possible care in the preparation and sale of his product." To our knowledge, none of the states whose laws might apply to the instant case have adopted the Illinois rule. We respectfully reject it.

The crucial words in § 402A are "defective condition" and "unreasonably dangerous." A majority of the courts have required a plaintiff to prove both. See e.g. *Kleve v. General Motors Corp.*, Iowa, 210 N.W.2d 568; *Brown v. Western Farmers Ass'n*, Or., 521 P.2d 537; and *Jagmin v. Simonds Abrasive Co.*, 61 Wis.2d 60, 211 N.W.2d 810. Some courts have eliminated the "unreasonably dangerous" requirement. See *Anderson v. Fairchild Hiller Corp.*, D.Alas., 358 F.Supp. 976; *Cronin v. J.B.E. Olson Corp.*, 8 Cal.3d 121, 104 Cal.Rptr. 433, 501 P.2d 1153; and *Glass v. Ford Motor Co.*, 123 N.J.Super. 599, 304 A.2d 562. Other courts have eliminated the "defective condition" requirement. See *Ross v. Up–Right, Inc.*, 5 Cir., 402 F.2d 943; and *Seattle–First National Bank v. Tabert*, 86 Wash.2d 145, 542 P.2d 774. We proceed on the basis that both requirements must be satisfied.

With regard to "defective condition" Comment g to § 402A Restatement of Torts 2d at 351, says:

> "The rule stated in this Section applies only where the product is, at the time it leaves the seller's hands, in a condition not contemplated by the ultimate consumer, which will be unreasonably dangerous to him."

With regard to "unreasonably dangerous" Comment I says, Ibid. at 352:

"The article sold must be dangerous to an extent beyond that which would be contemplated by the ordinary consumer who purchases it, with the ordinary knowledge common in the community as to its characteristics."

Whether concern is with one or both of the requirements, there is "general" agreement that to prove liability under § 402A the plaintiff must show that the product was dangerous beyond the expectation of the ordinary customer. State-of-art evidence helps to determine the expectation of the ordinary consumer. A consumer would not expect a Model T to have the safety features which are incorporated in automobiles made today. The same expectation applies to airplanes. Plaintiffs have not shown that the ordinary consumer would expect a plane made in 1952 to have the safety features of one made in 1970. State-of-art evidence was properly received and considered by the trial court.

* * *

[The court's discussion of liability of defendant Ozark is omitted].

The judgments in favor of Martin and Ozark are severally affirmed.

Notes

1. Other courts have disagreed, and held that industry custom and standards are not admissible on the question of consumer expectations. *See* Lenhardt v. Ford Motor Co., 102 Wash.2d 208, 683 P.2d 1097 (1984), noted in 60 Wash.L.Rev. 195 (1984).

2. What other evidence is admissible to prove that the expectations of the ordinary consumer were frustrated? Is expert testimony admissible? May plaintiff testify that he did not realize that the product was dangerous?

3. *Bruce* is a useful poster-child for the problems courts in the 1970s were encountering when they attempted to apply a consumer expectations test of defectiveness to failures of complex products. Following the logic of this test, state-of-the-art evidence helps to determine the expectations of the ordinary consumer. Based on this and other evidence, the jury in *Bruce* would be asked to determine whether the airplane was dangerous beyond the expectations of an ordinary consumer in 1952. Is this an intelligible project? What expectations, beyond a vague hope that one will arrive alive, does the ordinary consumer have about the safety of aircraft?

4. Nevertheless, some states continue to use a consumer expectation test. In Austin v. Will–Burt Co., 361 F.3d 862 (5th Cir. 2004) the court quoted language in Mississippi's products liability statute that precludes recovery under a design defect theory unless the product "failed to function as expected" and that this requirement is to be applied as of "the time the product left the control of the manufacturer." *Id.* at 872. The court held that this provision reinstates for design defect cases a frequently expressed requirement of the consumer expectations test. *Id.* at 873. The plaintiff was electrocuted when a retractable mast mounted on top of a news van came in contact with a power line as it was being raised. The plaintiff argued that the mast should have been insulated or should have contained a proximity

warning device which stops the mast from rising when it nears a power line. The court noted that almost no masts contained these safety features in 1982 when the mast was manufactured. Moreover, even in 1997 when the plaintiff was killed very few masts had such features. This industry custom is strong evidence that the mast did not "fail to function as expected." Would the court come to a different conclusion if the evidence indicated that proximity warning devices were customary on masts built after 1990?

5. "And what about 'state of the art'? 'State of the art' is a chameleon-like term, referring to everything from ordinary customs of the trade to the objective existence of technological information to economic feasibility. Its meanings are so diverse and so easily confused that the wise course of action, I think, is to eschew its use completely." Wade, On the Effect in Product Liability of Knowledge Unavailable Prior to Marketing, 58 N.Y.U.L.Rev. 734, 750–51 (1983).

The courts, of course, failed to take Dean Wade's advice. The different meanings of the term are reviewed below in Potter v. Chicago Pneumatic Tool Co., 241 Conn. 199, 694 A.2d 1319 (Conn. 1997).

> Several courts have defined state-of-the-art evidence in terms of industry custom; see, e.g., *Smith v. Minster Machine Co.*, 669 F.2d 628, 633 (10th Cir.1982) (viewing proper meaning of "state of the art . . . to mean simply the custom and practice in an industry"); *Sturm, Ruger & Co. v. Day*, 594 P.2d 38, 44 (Alaska 1979), cert. denied, 454 U.S. 894, 102 S.Ct. 391, 70 L.Ed.2d 209 (1981) ("[g]enerally speaking, 'state of the art' refers to customary practice in the industry"); *Suter v. San Angelo Foundry & Machine Co.*, 81 N.J. 150, 172, 406 A.2d 140 (1979) (state of the art includes common practice and industry standards); or in terms of compliance with then existing statutes or governmental regulations. See, e.g., *Frazier v. Kysor Industrial Corp.*, 43 Colo.App. 287, 293, 607 P.2d 1296 (1979) (noting absence of statutes or regulations to determine state of the art); *Rucker v. Norfolk & Western Railway Co.*, 64 Ill.App.3d 770, 781–82, 21 Ill.Dec. 388, 381 N.E.2d 715 (1978)(characterizing evidence of compliance with federally mandated design specifications as state-of-the-art defense), rev'd on other grounds, 77 Ill.2d 434, 33 Ill.Dec. 145, 396 N.E.2d 534 (1979).
>
> The majority of courts, however, have defined state-of-the-art evidence as the level of relevant scientific, technological and safety knowledge existing and reasonably feasible at the time of design. See, e.g., *Carter v. Massey–Ferguson, Inc.*, 716 F.2d 344, 347 (5th Cir.1983) (" 'state of the art' refers to the technological environment, that is, what *can* be done" [emphasis in original]); *Gosewisch v. American Honda Motor Co.*, 153 Ariz. 389, 394, 737 P.2d 365 (App.1985) ("state of the art refers to what feasibly could have been done"); *Montgomery Ward & Co. v. Gregg*, 554 N.E.2d 1145, 1155–56 (Ind.App.1990) (defining state of the art as technological advancement, not as industry custom or practice); *Chown v. USM Corp.*, 297 N.W.2d 218, 222 (Iowa 1980) (defining state of the art as technological and practical feasibility); *O'Brien v. Muskin Corp.*, 94 N.J. 169, 182, 463 A.2d 298 (1983) (defining state of the art as "existing level of technological expertise and scientific knowledge relevant to a particular industry at the time a product is designed");

Boatland of Houston, Inc. v. Bailey, 609 S.W.2d 743, 748 (Tex.1980) ("[state-of-the-art] includes the scientific knowledge, economic feasibility, and the practicalities of implementation when the product was manufactured").

Potter, 694 A.2d at 1345–46. State-of-the-art in this latter sense is addressed in Chapter 4, *supra.*

UNION SUPPLY CO. v. PUST
Supreme Court of Colorado, En Banc, 1978.
196 Colo. 162, 583 P.2d 276.

[Plaintiff was a sugar beet refinery worker whose arm was caught in an unguarded "nip point" of a conveyor as he was cleaning pulp off of the conveyor. As a result of the accident his arm and part of his shoulder were amputated. He brought an action based on strict liability and breach of implied warranty against the manufacturer of the conveyor. He alleged that the conveyor was defective in design because it should have had safety guards and an automatic cleaning device. He also alleged that the product was defective because of a failure to warn of the hazards of working at the "nip point."]

At the close of all the evidence, the district court granted Union Supply's motion to dismiss the complaint. On appeal, the court of appeals reversed the judgment dismissing Pust's complaint, and held that jury questions had been presented on the issues of strict liability and implied warranty. * * *

B. INDUSTRY SAFETY STANDARDS

Union Supply argues that the trial court erred in permitting Pust to introduce parts of two sets of nongovernmental conveyor safety codes. Safety Code B20.1 of the American Standards Association has been approved by the Conveyor Equipment Manufacturer's Association (CEMA) and the American Society of Mechanical Engineers (ASME). The National Safety Council Data Sheets 569 and 570 were drafted by an engineering committee of the National Safety Council, and have been approved by many groups, including CEMA and ASME. Thus, they are consensus standards of safety for conveyor systems, approved by the conveyor manufacturers. They were in effect at the time of Pust's injury.

The trial court ruled that these standards were admissible on the issue of whether the conveyor was in a "defective condition unreasonably dangerous." The court specified that they were to be introduced by an expert witness and must be shown to be recognized standards of safety in the conveyor manufacturing field.

The principal objections raised by Union Supply to the use of the safety standards in this case are that they are irrelevant and that they are inadmissible hearsay. We note initially that the parts introduced from Safety Code B20.1 and Data Sheets 569 and 570 do *not* presume to assess who has the duty to provide safety features. Thus, they do not raise extraneous issues of negligence. *Cf. Murphy v. L & J Press Corp.*, 558 F.2d 407 (8th Cir.).

In our view, these safety standards are relevant, especially in design defect cases. In cases of defects in manufacture, the jury is frequently able to judge the defective item by comparing it to others similarly produced by the manufacturer. However, as the California Supreme Court has noted: " * * * A design defect, by contrast, cannot be identified simply by comparing the injury-producing product with the manufacturer's plans or with other units of the same product line, since by definition the plans and all such units will reflect the same design." *Barker v. Lull Engineering Co., Inc.*, 20 Cal.3d 413, 143 Cal.Rptr. 225, 573 P.2d 443. By reason of the nature of the case, the trier of fact is greatly dependent on expert evidence and industry standards in deciding whether a defect is present.

In the case of *Wallner v. Kitchens of Sara Lee, Inc.*, 419 F.2d 1028 (7th Cir.), an employee's hand was injured when it was caught in the unguarded moving parts of a conveyor. The trial court admitted a conveyor industry safety code into evidence on the strict liability cause of action because it was: "sufficiently relevant to the questions of the dangerousness of the conveyor when it left Thiele's manufacturing plant to make its admission proper."

Union Supply appropriately points out that these safety codes fit within the classical definition of hearsay as out-of-court statements being offered into evidence to prove the truth of the matter asserted therein. However, since these industry safety standards contain sufficient indicia of reliability, we hold that they may be introduced as substantive evidence.

These codes were formulated by groups of experts in the conveyor designing and manufacturing field, and were approved by many organizations. They are likely to be more probative than a single learned treatise or an expert opinion, as they represent the consensus of an entire industry. There is no motive for the formulators to falsify, and there is no danger that the standards will be subsequently altered or incorrectly remembered by a witness. Finally, since we require that the safety standards be introduced through an expert witness, the adverse party will have a fair opportunity to cross-examine the expert on any inconsistencies, misrepresentations or other limitations of the standards. Given these guarantees of trustworthiness, we approve the admission of industry safety codes as substantive evidence on the strict liability issue of whether a product is in a "defective condition unreasonably dangerous." *Accord, Murphy v. L & J Press Corp.*, 558 F.2d 407 (8th Cir.); *Dorsey v. Yoder Co.*, 331 F.Supp. 753 (E.D.Pa.); *Price v. Buckingham Manufacturing Co., Inc.*, 110 N.J.Super. 462, 266 A.2d 140.

The trial court correctly ruled that these standards must be introduced through an expert and must be authenticated as reliable and bona fide industry-wide safety codes. This was carefully done here by the expert testimony of Dr. Youngdahl, who participated in the formulation of each of the standards. Finally, we require that sufficient advance notice of the intended use of such standards be given to the adverse party so that he will have sufficient time to prepare to meet the evidence.

* * *

IV. CONCLUSION

In sum, we hold that this case should have been submitted to the jury on the strict liability and implied warranty causes of action. We affirm the judgment of the court of appeals.

ERICKSON and CARRIGAN, JJ., do not participate.

Notes

1. Industry custom and standards has always been admissible in negligence cases. *See* Restatement (Second) of Torts § 295A; Restatement (Third) of Torts: Liability for Physical Harm (Proposed Final Draft No. 1, 2005) § 13.

2. In product liability cases there is a split of authority. Some courts are in accord with the principal case, and admit the evidence. *E.g.,* Thibault v. Sears, Roebuck & Co., 118 N.H. 802, 395 A.2d 843 (1978) (the evidence is admissible and relevant to the question of whether the design is reasonable, but it is not binding on the jury); Brooks v. Beech Aircraft Corp., 120 N.M. 372, 902 P.2d 54 (1995) (industry custom and evidence of compliance with applicable regulations is relevant but not conclusive as to product defectiveness). Other courts disagree, and hold that the evidence is not admissible. *E.g.,* Matthews v. Stewart Warner Corp., 20 Ill.App.3d 470, 314 N.E.2d 683 (1974). Courts that refuse to permit defendants to introduce customary evidence usually justify their decision on the grounds that such testimony would deflect the jury's attention away from the product to the reasonableness of the defendant's actions. It, therefore, introduces negligence concepts not appropriate in actions alleging products liability under Restatement (Second) of Torts § 402A. *See* Lenhardt v. Ford Motor Co., 102 Wash.2d 208, 683 P.2d 1097, 1099 (1984); Lewis v. Coffing Hoist Division, Duff–Norton Co., Inc., 515 Pa. 334, 528 A.2d 590, 594 (1987).

3. The Restatement (Third) of Torts: Products Liability adopts a reasonableness standard to assess both design and warning defect claims and, therefore, it sees a role for evidence of industry custom in assessing these claims. For example, § 2, Comment *d* (discussing design defects) states:

> Assessment of a product design in most instances requires a comparison between an alternative design and the product design that caused the injury, undertaken from the viewpoint of a reasonable person. That approach is also used in administering the traditional reasonableness standard in negligence. See Restatement, Second, Torts § 283, Comment c. The policy reasons that support use of a reasonable-person perspective in connection with the general negligence standard also support its use in the products liability context.

How the defendant's design compares with other, competing designs in actual use is relevant to the issue of whether the defendant's design is defective. Defendants often seek to defend their product designs on the ground that the designs conform to the "state of the art." The term "state of the art" has been variously defined to mean that the product design conforms to industry custom, that it reflects the safest and most advanced technology developed and in commercial use, or that it reflects technology at the cutting edge of scientific knowledge. The confusion brought about by these various definitions is unfortunate. This Section states that a design is defective if the product could have been made safer by the adoption of a reasonable alternative design. If such a design could have been practically adopted at time of sale and if the omission of such a design rendered the product not reasonably safe, the plaintiff establishes defect under Subsection (b). When a defendant demonstrates that its product design was the safest in use at the time of sale, it may be difficult for the plaintiff to prove that an alternative design could have been practically adopted. The defendant is thus allowed to introduce evidence with regard to industry practice that bears on whether an alternative design was practicable. Industry practice may also be relevant to whether the omission of an alternative design rendered the product not reasonably safe. While such evidence is admissible, it is not necessarily dispositive. If the plaintiff introduces expert testimony to establish that a reasonable alternative design could practically have been adopted, a trier of fact may conclude that the product was defective notwithstanding that such a design was not adopted by any manufacturer, or even considered for commercial use, at the time of sale.

4. Some opinions distinguish between custom evidence introduced by plaintiff and custom evidence introduced by defendant. *See* Rexrode v. American Laundry Press Co., 674 F.2d 826, 831 (10th Cir.1982), cert. denied, 459 U.S. 862, 103 S.Ct. 137, 74 L.Ed.2d 117 (1982) (plaintiff may introduce evidence of violation of safety standards to show defect, but defendant may not introduce evidence of compliance with safety standards to show no defect).

5. Plaintiff is burned by hot coffee and claims that it is defective because it was too hot. May defendant introduce evidence of the temperature at which coffee is usually served by restaurants? *See* Huppe v. Twenty–First Century Restaurants of Am., Inc., 130 Misc.2d 736, 497 N.Y.S.2d 306 (1985).

6. *See generally,* Spradley, Defensive Use of State of the Art Evidence in Strict Products Liability, 67 Minn.L.Rev. 343, 350–367 (1982); Comment, Custom's Proper Role in Strict Product Liability Actions Based on Design Defect, 38 U.C.L.A. L.Rev. 439 (1990).

ALEVROMAGIROS v. HECHINGER CO.
United States Court of Appeals, Fourth Circuit, 1993.
993 F.2d 417.

RESTANI, JUDGE:

This is a products liability case, brought by an injured individual against the manufacturer and seller of a ladder allegedly containing a design defect. At trial, the expert witness for plaintiff testified that the ladder did not conform to advisory industry standards, although he had never tested or examined an undamaged model of the ladder. At the close of plaintiff's case, the court granted defendants' motion for a directed verdict on the ground that plaintiff had not established the violation of any standard. We affirm the district court's decision, holding that a directed verdict in a products liability case is appropriate where an expert witness fails to prove that advisory industry standards have been violated or that those standards fall below an acceptable level.

I

Plaintiff-appellant Theodore Alevromagiros is the owner of a chain of eating establishments called Fantastic Family Restaurants, which offer Greek and American cuisine. In the summer of 1989, while conducting repairs on his restaurant in Herndon, Virginia, Alevromagiros directed a contractor to buy a ladder from defendant-appellee Hechinger Company ("Hechinger"). On behalf of Alevromagiros, the contractor purchased a six-foot high stepladder manufactured by defendant-appellee White Metal Rolling and Stamping Corporation of Atlanta, Georgia ("White Metal"). No accident occurred when the ladder was used at that time.

Several months later in December 1989, Alevromagiros climbed on the ladder to reset some ceiling tiles. While resetting the tiles, Alevromagiros felt "some bending or something" in the ladder. He then fell to the floor, severely fracturing his arm. Two eye-witnesses to the incident confirmed that the ladder twisted, causing Alevromagiros to fall backwards.

The only expert witness to testify at trial was Stanley Kalin, called to the stand by plaintiff-appellant Alevromagiros. The district court found that Kalin, who received a bachelor's degree in industrial engineering from Johns Hopkins University, was qualified to be an expert witness. On direct examination, Kalin drew the judge's and jury's attention to the bent and twisted appearance of the ladder from which Alevromagiros fell. In particular, he noted the buckling of the spreader bars, which connected the front and rear portions of the ladder. The front part of the ladder was also not aligned with the rear part. Kalin continued on to point out the absence of safety features such as triangular bracing, better designed spreaders, and stiffeners.

Alevromagiros did not seek to introduce into evidence an undamaged ladder otherwise exactly like the one involved in the accident. After discovering that local Hechinger stores no longer carried that particular model, Alevromagiros stopped searching. Therefore, Kalin never conducted a physical examination of an identical but undamaged ladder to determine its safe or unsafe design. During Kalin's testimony, Alevromagiros sought to introduce a competitor's ladder containing safety features not present in the ladder sold by Hechinger to Alevromagiros. The district judge refused to admit the competitor's ladder on the grounds that "I don't believe that the expert can bring in one ladder from a competitor and attempt to make a standard out of that." The judge also sustained an objection to Kalin's testimony about the safety features of other ladders because "[t]he question is not what other ladders have."

On cross-examination, Kalin acknowledged that there were advisory industry standards promulgated by the American National Standards Institute (ANSI) and Underwriters Laboratories (UL). Kalin also admitted the existence of a UL acceptance file, indicating that the ladder at issue in the case complied with UL standards. He did not agree that the ladder conformed to ANSI standard 14.2, which requires a metal spreader or locking device of sufficient size and strength to securely hold the front and back sections of a ladder in the open position. Although Kalin failed to perform the recommended ANSI tests on an identical but undamaged ladder, he maintained that the construction of the ladder was not in accordance with the literal wording of the standard. He also stated that, "tragically," the ANSI and UL standards did not require triangular braces on the rear portion of a ladder.

After Alevromagiros had presented all of his evidence, Hechinger and White Metal moved for a directed verdict. In discussing the motion, the district judge noted that Kalin "didn't testify to any standards" and "no tests * * * have been performed." The judge inquired of the parties,

> Don't we have to have more than just somebody saying, I am an industrial engineer and I have looked at this ladder, it is the only one I have really looked at for this purpose, but I don't like it, there ought to be something else done to it? Doesn't there have to be more than that to make out a case of defective design?

The district judge ultimately granted defendants' motion for directed verdict, from which plaintiff Alevromagiros now appeals.

II

* * *

There are two issues presented by this appeal: 1) whether plaintiff introduced sufficient evidence to withstand a motion for directed verdict; and 2) whether the judge erred in refusing to admit physical or testimonial evidence regarding a competing product.

A

To prevail in a products liability case under Virginia law, the plaintiff must prove that the product contained a defect which rendered it unreasonably dangerous for ordinary or foreseeable use. In addition, the plaintiff must establish that the defect existed when it left the defendant's hands and that the defect actually caused the plaintiff's injury. * * * The product need not incorporate the best or most highly-advanced safety devices. * * *

In determining what constitutes an unreasonably dangerous defect, a court will consider safety standards promulgated by the government or the relevant industry, as well as the reasonable expectations of consumers. Consumer expectations, which may differ from government or industry standards, can be established through "evidence of actual industry practices, * * * published literature, and from direct evidence of what reasonable purchasers considered defective." *Id.*[1]

"Absent an established norm in the industry," a court is constrained to rely on the opinion testimony of experts to ascertain the applicable safety standard. * * * The credibility of competing experts is a question for the jury only if the party with the burden of proof has offered enough evidence to sustain a verdict in its favor. * * *

The cases that plaintiff-appellant cites are distinguishable either on the law or on the facts. In Carney v. Sears, Roebuck & Co., the Fourth Circuit reversed a decision made in favor of a store that sold a ladder which subsequently broke, thereby injuring plaintiff. 309 F.2d 300, 306 (4th Cir.1962). The legal significance of *Carney*, which has no application here, is that a judge may not release a defendant from liability for a manufacturing defect solely because the product has been in the possession of plaintiff for fifteen months. *Id.* at 305.

Bartholomew, relied upon heavily by Alevromagiros, presents a markedly different factual situation. *Bartholomew* involved the design of a car whose dashboard instruments indicated the car was in park when the gear shift lever was not fully in the park position. 224 Va. at 427, 297 S.E.2d at 678. The court found that the automobile industry had not yet promulgated safety standards relating to this particular problem. Consequently, the court admitted the opinion of plaintiff's expert that the car's design was unreasonably dangerous, based on information published by the National Highway Traffic Safety Administration, consultation with other experts, and experiments with transmission systems in at least three types of cars. *Id.* at 430, 297 S.E.2d at 679. In the case at bar, there is neither an absence of industry standards, nor an expert opinion based on extensive testing and published reports.

In the case before us, Kalin concededly never performed the recommended physical tests to determine whether the ladder sold by Hechinger to Alevromagiros conformed to the published industry standards. He testified to no customs of the trade, referred to no literature in the field, and did not identify the reasonable expectations of consumers. His comment that the advisory industry standards "tragically" did not require the use of triangular braces does not constitute proof that industry standards are inadequate. It is merely another example of his own subjective opinion. Like the Fifth Circuit, we are unprepared to agree that "it is so if an expert says it is so." Viterbo v. Dow Chemical Co., 826 F.2d 420, 421 (5th Cir.1987).

1. We recognize that conformity with industry custom does not automatically absolve a manufacturer or seller of a product from liability. Nevertheless, a product's compliance with industry custom "may be conclusive when there is no evidence to show that it was not reasonably safe." *Turner v. Manning, Maxwell & Moore, Inc.*, 216 Va. 245, 251, 217 S.E.2d 863, 868 (1975).

Viewing the evidence in the light most favorable to the non-movant, this court finds that Alevromagiros had not proven that the ladder was unreasonably dangerous and therefore no reasonable jury could have concluded that he was entitled to judgment. The district judge's grant of a directed verdict for the defendants-appellees Hechinger and White Metal is affirmed.

B

Alevromagiros argues that his case was stymied by his inability to introduce into evidence a competing ladder with more safety features than the ladder he purchased from Hechinger. The district judge refused to admit the competing ladder or any testimony about it, saying "[s]imply because certain manufacturers put certain features on ladders, that is not the test." The judge later remarked, "bringing in one particular competitor's ladder * * * and making that an industry standard, that is terribly misleading."

Both parties rely on Eighth Circuit cases which have directly addressed the issue of admitting samples of competitive merchandise in a products liability case. Hoppe v. Midwest Conveyor Co. found that the comparative design of a competing product was relevant in a case concerning a "highly complicated piece of machinery." 485 F.2d 1196, 1202 (8th Cir.1973). The later case of Kontz v. K–Mart Corp. refused to apply Hoppe to a fact situation involving a simple folding lawn chair. 712 F.2d 1302, 1304 (8th Cir.1983). As in *Kontz*, the jury in the case currently being appealed did not need to see examples of competing products in order to understand the nature of the product at issue. The jurors easily could have been misled or confused by the assumption that one competing product represented the relevant industry-wide standard. Therefore, the judge did not abuse his discretion in refusing to admit the competing product into evidence.

III

In conclusion, a plaintiff may not prevail in a products liability case by relying on the opinion of an expert unsupported by any evidence such as test data or relevant literature in the field. Such a plaintiff may not introduce a single example of a competing product and purport to make it a standard for the industry. He or she must establish the violation of industry or government standards, or prove that consumer expectations have risen above such standards. Because we find insufficient evidence to withstand a motion for directed verdict, the judgment of the district court is therefore

AFFIRMED.

Notes

1. *Accord*, Owens v. Allis–Chalmers Corp., 414 Mich. 413, 326 N.W.2d 372 (1982); Sexton v. Bell Helmets, Inc., 926 F.2d 331 (4th Cir.1991).

2. Should compliance with design standards such as those promulgated by ANSI or ASME protect a defendant from liability, irrespective of other

evidence? Does it matter in this regard whether the plaintiff's claim was that a different design would be safer without creating new, competing risks (such as a stronger axle on a tractor) or that a different design would represent a better trade-off between competing risks (such as a door on a tractor that might prevent intrusions in some situations but might trap the occupant in other situations)? In the latter case, would a defendant's failure to follow standards such as those promulgated by ASME not be powerful evidence of defect? Does this put the manufacturer in an untenable position?

3. Today, the defendant might well have challenged the admissibility of the plaintiff's expert's testimony under Federal Rule of Evidence 702. We discuss this issue in Section D, *infra*.

SECTION B. POST–ACCIDENT REMEDIAL MEASURES

FIRST PREMIER BANK v. KOLCRAFT ENTERPRISES, INC.

Supreme Court of South Dakota, 2004.
686 N.W.2d 430.

KONENKAMP, JUSTICE.

* * *

BACKGROUND

On January 12, 1992, Daniel Boone, age ten months, was severely burned while he was sleeping in a playpen in the children's bedroom at his parents' apartment. Defendant Kolcraft Enterprises manufactured the pads for its "Playard" playpens using two types of polyurethane foam. For customers in California, polyurethane treated with a fire retardant was used, as required by law. For all other customers, non-treated foam was used. After this incident, Kolcraft began using treated foam in all the pads it manufactured.

Peggy Boone first sued her landlord for her child's injuries. That matter settled. Plaintiff, First Premier Bank, was later appointed the child's guardian *ad litem* to pursue further legal action on the child's behalf. Its complaint alleged that the playpen was (1) defective and unreasonably dangerous in its design, or (2) defective and unreasonably dangerous because of a failure to warn. Kolcraft moved for summary judgment before trial and a directed verdict at the close of the evidence, arguing that as a matter of law plaintiff could not prove that Kolcraft's Playard proximately caused Daniel's injuries. The trial court denied both motions.

Before trial, both sides sought to exclude certain evidence by motions *in limine*. The judge declined to rule on the motions until the parties were ready to offer evidence during trial. In opening statements, with the court's indulgence, both sides mentioned topics subject to these motions. In other rulings, the court allowed testimony about the smoking habits of Daniel's parents and their non-functioning smoke detector, and permitted the defense to introduce the mother's earlier statement that a blanket was the origin of the fire. The court, however, did not allow plaintiff to introduce evidence that Kolcraft began using fire retardant foam in all its playpen pads after the incident here.

After a three-week trial, the jury found against plaintiff. The trial court denied plaintiff's motion for a new trial. On appeal, plaintiff advances manifold assignments of error with multiple subparts. Because not all these issues merit discussion, we address the following: * * * (6) Whether the trial court erred in excluding evidence of Kolcraft's subsequent remedial measures on the ground that this evidence would "unduly delay" the trial. * * *

VI.

SUBSEQUENT REMEDIAL MEASURES

To show that the product was defective at the time Daniel was burned in 1992, plaintiff offered evidence that Kolcraft began using fire retardant treated foam in all its Playard pads in 1993 or 1994.[2] The trial court disallowed this evidence on the ground that it would cause "undue delay" under SDCL 19–12–3 (Rule 403). Plaintiff believes that the trial court abused its discretion in excluding evidence of these remedial measures. To plaintiff, this type of evidence is "highly probative" and should only be excluded under narrow circumstances not present here. SDCL 19–12–9 (Rule 407) provides:

> When, after an event, measures are taken which, if taken previously, would have made the event less likely to occur, evidence of the subsequent measures is not admissible to prove negligence or culpable conduct in connection with the event. This section does not require the exclusion of evidence of subsequent measures when offered for another purpose, such as proving ownership, control, or feasibility of precautionary measures, if controverted, or impeachment.

In sum, the general rule is that subsequent remedial measures are not admissible as evidence. This Court has nonetheless allowed evidence of subsequent remedial measures in strict products liability actions. *Shaffer v. Honeywell, Inc.*, 249 N.W.2d 251, 257 n. 7 (S.D.1976) (drawing distinction between negligence actions and strict liability actions). A prefederal rules case, *Shaffer* deduced that while proof of such measures is not permitted in negligence actions, post-accident safety measures are admissible as evidence in strict liability cases. The issue arose again after the Federal Rules of Evidence had been adopted in South Dakota. Yet, without even mentioning Rule 407, the Court in *Klug v. Keller Industries, Inc.* 328 N.W.2d 847, 852 (S.D.1982), reaffirmed the *Shaffer* rationale, finding "no compelling reason" to alter its prior holding.

---

2. Peggy purchased the Playard in 1991 at the Half Price Store in Sioux Falls.

Since *Shaffer* and *Klug*, the force of authority has swung decidedly against admitting subsequent remedial measures in strict products liability actions. There are two reasons for this. In 1997, Congress amended FRE 407 specifically to clarify that strict liability actions are included in its prohibition.³ The pertinent part of the amended version now provides that "evidence of the subsequent measures is not admissible to prove negligence, culpable conduct, *a defect in a product, a defect in a product's design, or a need for a warning or instruction.*" See FRE 407 as amended (new language in italics). South Dakota never adopted the 1997 amendment and that would perhaps end our analysis but for the fact that this Court has never interpreted SDCL 19–12–9 (Rule 407) in this type of case. * * *

Long before the 1997 amendment, however, most federal courts, in interpreting Rule 407 as originally drafted, had come to the conclusion that admitting evidence of subsequent remedial measures in strict products liability cases while excluding it in negligence actions inserts an unwarranted breach in the rule through which "extremely damaging" and "highly prejudicial" evidence can enter. *Cann v. Ford Motor Co.*, 658 F.2d 54, 60 (2d Cir.1981), *cert. denied*, 456 U.S. 960, 102 S.Ct. 2036, 72 L.Ed.2d 484 (1982) (citations omitted). See * * * *Flaminio v. Honda Motor Co.*, 733 F.2d 463, 468–72 (7th Cir.1984) * * *. Only the Eighth and Tenth Circuits followed a contrary interpretation before the 1997 amendment. * * *

Likewise, those states adopting some form of FRE 407 also paralleled federal jurisprudence, interpreting their rules to exclude subsequent remedial measures in both negligence and strict products liability cases. * * * *See generally* Annotation, *Admissibility of Evidence of Subsequent Repairs or Other Remedial Measures in Products Liability Cases*, 74 A.L.R.3d 1001.

Rule 407 was designed to ensure that the threat of legal liability would not discourage remedial measures to improve products. Thus, the rule seeks to motivate manufacturers to make improvements without fearing the legal ramifications of their remedial acts. The rule accomplishes this by removing the threat that product improvements will be used as evidence against manufacturers. *Duchess v. Langston Corp.*, 564 Pa. 529, 769 A.2d 1131, 1143 (2001) (continual process of improvement and innovation in the marketplace favors broader application of evidentiary exclusion). This purpose would seem to apply equally to negligence and strict liability actions, so we find it difficult to comprehend why the public policy behind Rule 407 should be construed differently in cases based on strict liability. From the viewpoint of manufacturers, it is the fact that the evidence will be used against them that inhibits subsequent

---

3. According to the Advisory Committee notes, Rule 407 has been amended to provide that evidence of subsequent remedial measures may not be used to prove "a defect in a product or its design, or that a warning or instruction should have accompanied a product. This amendment adopts the view of a majority of the circuits that have interpreted Rule 407 to apply to products liability actions."

repairs or improvements. For them, what difference does it make under which theory the evidence might be admitted?

As Judge Posner explained in *Flaminio,* the attempted distinction between negligence and strict liability in relation to Rule 407 is "purely semantic." 733 F.2d at 469.

> The analysis is not fundamentally affected by whether the basis of liability is the defendant's negligence or his product's defectiveness or inherent dangerousness. In either case, if evidence of subsequent remedial measures is admissible to prove liability, the incentive to take such measures will be reduced.

Id. (citing *Birchfield v. Int'l Harvester Co.,* 726 F.2d 1131, 1139 (6thCir.1984)) (citations omitted).

Introducing evidence of subsequent remedial measures tends to divert the jury's attention from whether the product was defective at the time it was manufactured and sold to some later time. South Dakota's statutory language governing products liability supports the conclusion that SDCL 19-12-9 (Rule 407) applies to strict products liability actions. The point of time for assessing liability for the defective product in question is the time the product was "first sold." SDCL 20-9-10.1.[4] If the time of product sale is the point for deciding liability in strict liability cases, then product knowledge acquired after that point becomes irrelevant.

We find the distinction conceived in *Shaffer* and *Klug* between negligence and strict liability to be indiscernible in relation to Rule 407 and overrule those two cases to the extent that they hold to the contrary. The general prohibition against admitting evidence of subsequent remedial measures embodied in SDCL 19-12-9 (Rule 407) precludes use of subsequent design changes as substantive evidence of a product defect in a strict products liability case.

Although not arguing that any relevant exception to Rule 407 applies, plaintiff contends that probative value is not in question here because the trial court refused to admit the evidence based on undue delay of the proceedings. We think policy considerations in Rule 407 favor the general rule of exclusion, but we cannot say, in view of the state of the law at the time of trial, that it was an abuse of discretion to invoke the "undue delay" language in Rule 403 to preclude this evidence. Certainly, lack of sufficient probative value or unfair prejudice can be advanced as independent grounds for the general exclusion of

---

4. SDCL 20-9-10.1 provides:

Product liability—Action on negligence or strict liability—Standard of care—Consideration of conformity at time of manufacture.

In any product liability action based upon negligence or strict liability, whether the design, manufacture, inspection, testing, packaging, warning, or labeling was in conformity with the generally recognized and prevailing state of the art existing *at the time the specific product involved was first sold* to any person not engaged in the business of selling such a product, *may be considered* in determining the standard of care, whether the standard of care was breached or whether the product was in a defective condition or unreasonably dangerous to the user. (Emphasis supplied.)

subsequent remedial evidence under Rule 403. *Luda Foster v. Ford Motor Co.,* 621 F.2d 715, 721 (5th Cir.1980); FRE 407 advisory committee note. We find no abuse of discretion.

* * *

Affirmed in part, reversed in part, and remanded for a new trial.

Notes

1. Not every court has been persuaded that Rule 407 should apply to product liability cases. Forma Scientific, Inc. v. BioSera, Inc., 960 P.2d 108 (Colo. 1998) interpreted the Colorado rule. Colorado, like South Dakota, has not revised its state version of Rule 407 to conform with the new wording of the federal rule. When Rule 407 was adopted in Colorado in 1979 the committee overseeing the adoption of the rules added the following comment: "The phrase 'culpable conduct' is not deemed to include proof of liability in a 'strict liability' case based on defect, where subsequent measures are properly admitted as evidence of the original defect." The court agreed, arguing that "manufacturer's conduct, whether culpable or negligent, is not germane in a strict liability action." In a dissenting opinion, Justice Vollack noted that whatever the state of design defect "strict liability" in 1979, by the time this case was decided in Colorado "design defect and negligence cases are analytically similar." *See* Camacho v. Honda Motor Co., 741 P.2d 1240 (Colo. 1987).

Which side has the best of it on the question of whether design defect cases involve a question of "culpable conduct?" Would your answer be the same in a jurisdiction that has stuck with Restatement (Second) of Torts § 402A and in a jurisdiction that has adopted Restatement (Third) of Torts: Products Liability §2?

2. The *Forma Scientific* opinion also disagreed with *First Premier Bank* that permitting evidence of subsequent remedial measures would deter firms from taking such measures.

> [T]he public policy rationale underlying CRE 407—not to discourage entities from taking safety precautions—is largely inapplicable in the context of today's mass manufacturers. It is unreasonable to presume that a mass manufacturer of goods takes its cue from evidentiary rules rather than considerations of consumer safety and/or the safety of consumer property. Even taking a less rosy view, recognizing that not all manufacturers necessarily place the best interests of their consumers at the forefront, market forces generally operate to compel manufacturers to improve their products. This is amply demonstrated by the actions taken here by Forma to protect its consumers' property interests by lessening the risk of inadvertent shut offs of its ultra-cold temperature freezers. * * * Clearly, Forma was not deterred from making changes even though Forma already knew the trial court's position that such evidence would be admissible in this case.

Which court has the best of this argument? Regardless of the merits of the *Forma Scientific* hypothesis concerning whether admitting such evidence will deter, what is wrong with the court's logic in the quoted paragraph?

3. The *Forma Scientific* court left open the question of whether Rule 407 should apply in a products case based on an alleged failure to warn. *Compare* DeLuryea v. Winthrop Laboratories, Div. of Sterling Drugs, Inc., 697 F.2d 222, 228–29 (8th Cir.1983) *with* Unterburger v. Snow Co., 630 F.2d 599, 603 (8th Cir.1980).

4. Most circuits hold that Federal Rule of Evidence 407 rather than the corresponding state rule applies to diversity cases in federal courts. For an especially good analysis of this issue, see Wellborn, The Federal Rules of Evidence and the Application of State Law in Federal Courts, 55 Tex.L.Rev. 371 (1977).

5. In Texas, the original Rule 407 expressly provided that post-accident remedial measures were admissible in products liability cases based on "strict liability." Following the amendment of FRE 407, the Texas legislature directed the state Supreme Court to amend Texas Rule 407 "to conform that rule to Rule 407, Federal Rules of Evidence." The two rules are now identical. Under the old rule, should evidence of post-accident remedial measures be admissible in a product case based on negligence?

6. The trial judge in *First Premier Bank* excluded the defendant's subsequent remedial measures on Rule 403 grounds, citing the "undue delay" provision in that rule. A separate provision in Rule 403 permits evidence to be excluded if it's probative value is substantially outweighed by a danger of confusion or prejudice. Is a concern that the prejudicial effect of subsequent remedial measures evidence will outweigh its probative value one of the rationales underlying Rule 407?

7. Should post-accident changes in warnings, notifications of defect to consumers, and recall letters be admissible to prove defectiveness? Do any of the possible underlying rationales of Rule 407 apply differently to this type of evidence? *See* Stahl v. Novartis Pharmaceuticals Corp., 283 F.3d 254 (5th Cir. 2002).

8. What of a design change made subsequent to sale but before plaintiff's injury? *See* Huffman v. Caterpillar Tractor Co., 908 F.2d 1470 (10th Cir.1990). What of a manufacturer's pre-injury decision to change a design that had not yet been implemented before the plaintiff's injury. *See* Dewick v. Maytag Corp., 296 F.Supp.2d 905 (N.D.Ill. 2003).

9. It is generally held that design changes implemented by someone other than the defendant, e.g., the plaintiff's employer, are admissible. *See* Couch v. Astec Industries, Inc. 132 N.M. 631, 53 P.3d 398 (2002); Diehl v. Blaw–Knox, 360 F.3d 426 (3d Cir. 2004). What are the arguments for and against this position?

10. Since it is universally held that a plaintiff may introduce subsequent remedial measure evidence to rebut a defense that the plaintiff's alternative design is not feasible, is Rule 407 really that important in design defect litigation? How likely is it that the defendant will forego this defense in order to keep such evidence from the jury?

SECTION C. EXPERT WITNESSES

DAUBERT v. MERRELL DOW PHARM., INC.
Supreme Court of the United States, 1993.
509 U.S. 579, 113 S.Ct. 2786, 125 L.Ed.2d 469.

JUSTICE BLACKMUN delivered the opinion of the Court.

In this case we are called upon to determine the standard for admitting expert scientific testimony in a federal trial.

Petitioners Jason Daubert and Eric Schuller are minor children born with serious birth defects. They and their parents sued respondent in California state court, alleging that the birth defects had been caused by the mothers' ingestion of Bendectin, a prescription anti-nausea drug marketed by respondent. Respondent removed the suits to federal court on diversity grounds.

After extensive discovery, respondent moved for summary judgment, contending that Bendectin does not cause birth defects in humans and that petitioners would be unable to come forward with any admissible evidence that it does. In support of its motion, respondent submitted an affidavit of Steven H. Lamm, physician and epidemiologist, who is a well-credentialed expert on the risks from exposure to various chemical substances. Doctor Lamm stated that he had reviewed all the literature on Bendectin and human birth defects—more than 30 published studies involving over 130,000 patients. No study had found Bendectin to be a human teratogen (i.e., a substance capable of causing malformations in fetuses). On the basis of this review, Doctor Lamm concluded that maternal use of Bendectin during the first trimester of pregnancy has not been shown to be a risk factor for human birth defects.

Petitioners did not (and do not) contest this characterization of the published record regarding Bendectin. Instead, they responded to respondent's motion with the testimony of eight experts of their own, each of whom also possessed impressive credentials. These experts had concluded that Bendectin can cause birth defects. Their conclusions were based upon "in vitro" (test tube) and "in vivo" (live) animal studies that found a link between Bendectin and malformations; pharmacological studies of the chemical structure of Bendectin that purported to show similarities between the structure of the drug and that of other substances known to cause birth defects; and the "reanalysis" of previously published epidemiological (human statistical) studies.

The District Court granted respondent's motion for summary judgment. The court stated that scientific evidence is admissible only if the principle upon which it is based is " 'sufficiently established to have general acceptance in the field to which it belongs.' " * * * quoting *United States v. Kilgus*, 571 F.2d 508, 510 (C.A.9 1978). The court concluded that petitioners' evidence did not meet this standard. Given the vast body of epidemiological data concerning Bendectin, the court

held, expert opinion which is not based on epidemiological evidence is not admissible to establish causation. * * * Thus, the animal-cell studies, live-animal studies, and chemical-structure analyses on which petitioners had relied could not raise by themselves a reasonably disputable jury issue regarding causation. * * * Petitioners' epidemiological analyses, based as they were on recalculations of data in previously published studies that had found no causal link between the drug and birth defects, were ruled to be inadmissible because they had not been published or subjected to peer review. * * *

The United States Court of Appeals for the Ninth Circuit affirmed. 951 F.2d 1128 (1991). Citing *Frye v. United States*, 54 App.D.C. 46, 47, 293 F. 1013, 1014 (1923), the court stated that expert opinion based on a scientific technique is inadmissible unless the technique is "generally accepted" as reliable in the relevant scientific community. * * * The court declared that expert opinion based on a methodology that diverges "significantly from the procedures accepted by recognized authorities in the field ... cannot be shown to be 'generally accepted as a reliable technique.'" * * * quoting United States v. Solomon, 753 F.2d 1522, 1526 (C.A.9 1985).

We granted certiorari * * * in light of sharp divisions among the courts regarding the proper standard for the admission of expert testimony. Compare, *e.g., United States v. Shorter*, 257 U.S.App.D.C. 358, 363–364, 809 F.2d 54, 59–60 (applying the "general acceptance" standard), cert. denied, 484 U.S. 817, 108 S.Ct. 71, 98 L.Ed.2d 35 (1987), with *DeLuca v. Merrell Dow Pharmaceuticals, Inc.*, 911 F.2d 941, 955 (C.A.3 1990) (rejecting the "general acceptance" standard).

II

A

In the 70 years since its formulation in the *Frye* case, the "general acceptance" test has been the dominant standard for determining the admissibility of novel scientific evidence at trial. * * * Although under increasing attack of late, the rule continues to be followed by a majority of courts, including the Ninth Circuit.

The *Frye* test has its origin in a short and citation-free 1923 decision concerning the admissibility of evidence derived from a systolic blood pressure deception test, a crude precursor to the polygraph machine. In what has become a famous (perhaps infamous) passage, the then Court of Appeals for the District of Columbia described the device and its operation and declared:

"Just when a scientific principle or discovery crosses the line between the experimental and demonstrable stages is difficult to define. Somewhere in this twilight zone the evidential force of the principle must be recognized, and while courts will go a long way in admitting expert testimony deduced from a well-recognized scientific principle or discovery, *the thing from which the deduction is made* *must be sufficiently established to have gained general acceptance in the particular field in which it belongs."* * * *

Because the deception test had "not yet gained such standing and scientific recognition among physiological and psychological authorities as would justify the courts in admitting expert testimony deduced from the discovery, development, and experiments thus far made," evidence of its results was ruled inadmissible. * * *

The merits of the *Frye* test have been much debated, and scholarship on its proper scope and application is legion. Petitioners' primary attack, however, is not on the content but on the continuing authority of the rule. They contend that the *Frye* test was superseded by the adoption of the Federal Rules of Evidence. We agree.

We interpret the legislatively-enacted Federal Rules of Evidence as we would any statute. *Beech Aircraft Corp. v. Rainey*, 488 U.S. 153, 163, 109 S.Ct. 439, 446, 102 L.Ed.2d 445 (1988). Rule 402 provides the baseline:

> "All relevant evidence is admissible, except as otherwise provided by the Constitution of the United States, by Act of Congress, by these rules, or by other rules prescribed by the Supreme Court pursuant to statutory authority. Evidence which is not relevant is not admissible."

"Relevant evidence" is defined as that which has "any tendency to make the existence of any fact that is of consequence to the determination of the action more probable or less probable than it would be without the evidence." Rule 401. The Rule's basic standard of relevance thus is a liberal one.

Frye, of course, predated the Rules by half a century. In *United States v. Abel*, 469 U.S. 45, 105 S.Ct. 465, 83 L.Ed.2d 450 (1984), we considered the pertinence of background common law in interpreting the Rules of Evidence. We noted that the Rules occupy the field, * * * but, quoting Professor Cleary, the Reporter, explained that the common law nevertheless could serve as an aid to their application:

> "In principle, under the Federal Rules no common law of evidence remains. 'All relevant evidence is admissible, except as otherwise provided. * * *' In reality, of course, the body of common law knowledge continues to exist, though in the somewhat altered form of a source of guidance in the exercise of delegated powers." * * *

We found the common-law precept at issue in the *Abel* case entirely consistent with Rule 402's general requirement of admissibility, and considered it unlikely that the drafters had intended to change the rule. In *Bourjaily v. United States*, 483 U.S. 171, 107 S.Ct. 2775, 97 L.Ed.2d 144 (1987), on the other hand, the Court was unable to find a particular common-law doctrine in the Rules, and so held it superseded.

Here there is a specific Rule that speaks to the contested issue. Rule 702, governing expert testimony, provides:

"If scientific, technical, or other specialized knowledge will assist the trier of fact to understand the evidence or to determine a fact in issue, a witness qualified as an expert by knowledge, skill, experience, training, or education, may testify thereto in the form of an opinion or otherwise."

Nothing in the text of this Rule establishes "general acceptance" as an absolute prerequisite to admissibility. Nor does respondent present any clear indication that Rule 702 or the Rules as a whole were intended to incorporate a "general acceptance" standard. The drafting history makes no mention of Frye, and a rigid "general acceptance" requirement would be at odds with the "liberal thrust" of the Federal Rules and their "general approach of relaxing the traditional barriers to 'opinion' testimony." *Beech Aircraft Corp. v. Rainey*, 488 U.S., at 169, 109 S.Ct., at 450 (citing Rules 701 to 705). * * * Given the Rules' permissive backdrop and their inclusion of a specific rule on expert testimony that does not mention "general acceptance," the assertion that the Rules somehow assimilated Frye is unconvincing. Frye made "general acceptance" the exclusive test for admitting expert scientific testimony. That austere standard, absent from and incompatible with the Federal Rules of Evidence, should not be applied in federal trials.

B

That the *Frye* test was displaced by the Rules of Evidence does not mean, however, that the Rules themselves place no limits on the admissibility of purportedly scientific evidence. Nor is the trial judge disabled from screening such evidence. To the contrary, under the Rules the trial judge must ensure that any and all scientific testimony or evidence admitted is not only relevant, but reliable.

The primary locus of this obligation is Rule 702, which clearly contemplates some degree of regulation of the subjects and theories about which an expert may testify. "If scientific, technical, or other specialized knowledge will assist the trier of fact to understand the evidence or to determine a fact in issue" an expert "may testify thereto." The subject of an expert's testimony must be "scientific * * * knowledge."[1] The adjective "scientific" implies a grounding in the methods and procedures of science. Similarly, the word "knowledge" connotes more than subjective belief or unsupported speculation. The term "applies to any body of known facts or to any body of ideas inferred from such facts or accepted as truths on good grounds." Webster's Third New International Dictionary 1252 (1986). Of course, it would be unreasonable to conclude that the subject of scientific testimony must be "known" to a certainty; arguably, there are no certainties in science. See, *e.g.*, Brief for Nicolaas Bloembergen et al. as *Amici Curiae* 9 ("Indeed, scientists do not assert that they know what is immutably 'true'—they are committed to searching for new, temporary theories to

---

1. Rule 702 also applies to "technical, or other specialized knowledge." Our discussion is limited to the scientific context because that is the nature of the expertise offered here.

explain, as best they can, phenomena"); Brief for American Association for the Advancement of Science and the National Academy of Sciences as Amici Curiae 7–8 ("Science is not an encyclopedic body of knowledge about the universe. Instead, it represents a process for proposing and refining theoretical explanations about the world that are subject to further testing and refinement") (emphasis in original). But, in order to qualify as "scientific knowledge," an inference or assertion must be derived by the scientific method. Proposed testimony must be supported by appropriate validation—i.e., "good grounds," based on what is known. In short, the requirement that an expert's testimony pertain to "scientific knowledge" establishes a standard of evidentiary reliability.[2]

Rule 702 further requires that the evidence or testimony "assist the trier of fact to understand the evidence or to determine a fact in issue." This condition goes primarily to relevance. "Expert testimony which does not relate to any issue in the case is not relevant and, ergo, non-helpful." 3 Weinstein & Berger P 702[02], p. 702–18. * * * The consideration has been aptly described by Judge Becker as one of "fit." [United States v. Downing, 753 F.2d 1224, 1242 (3d Cir.1985)]. "Fit" is not always obvious, and scientific validity for one purpose is not necessarily scientific validity for other, unrelated purposes. * * * The study of the phases of the moon, for example, may provide valid scientific "knowledge" about whether a certain night was dark, and if darkness is a fact in issue, the knowledge will assist the trier of fact. However (absent creditable grounds supporting such a link), evidence that the moon was full on a certain night will not assist the trier of fact in determining whether an individual was unusually likely to have behaved irrationally on that night. Rule 702's "helpfulness" standard requires a valid scientific connection to the pertinent inquiry as a precondition to admissibility.

That these requirements are embodied in Rule 702 is not surprising. Unlike an ordinary witness, see Rule 701, an expert is permitted wide latitude to offer opinions, including those that are not based on first-hand knowledge or observation. See Rules 702 and 703. Presumably, this relaxation of the usual requirement of first-hand knowledge—a rule which represents "a 'most pervasive manifestation' of the common law insistence upon 'the most reliable sources of information,'"Advisory Committee's Notes on Fed.Rule Evid. 602 (citation omitted)—is premised on an assumption that the expert's opinion will have a reliable basis in the knowledge and experience of his discipline.

C

Faced with a proffer of expert scientific testimony, then, the trial judge must determine at the outset, pursuant to Rule 104(a), whether the expert is proposing to testify to (1) scientific knowledge that (2) will

---

2. We note that scientists typically distinguish between "validity" (does the principle support what it purports to show?) and "reliability" (does application of the principle produce consistent results?). * * * [O]ur reference here is to evidentiary reliability—that is, trustworthiness. * * * In a case involving scientific evidence, evidentiary reliability will be based upon scientific validity.

assist the trier of fact to understand or determine a fact in issue.³ This entails a preliminary assessment of whether the reasoning or methodology underlying the testimony is scientifically valid and of whether that reasoning or methodology properly can be applied to the facts in issue. We are confident that federal judges possess the capacity to undertake this review. Many factors will bear on the inquiry, and we do not presume to set out a definitive checklist or test. But some general observations are appropriate.

Ordinarily, a key question to be answered in determining whether a theory or technique is scientific knowledge that will assist the trier of fact will be whether it can be (and has been) tested. "Scientific methodology today is based on generating hypotheses and testing them to see if they can be falsified; indeed, this methodology is what distinguishes science from other fields of human inquiry." Green [Expert Witnesses and Sufficiency of Evidence in Toxic Substance Litigation: The Legacy of *Agent Orange* and Bendectin Litigation, 86 N.W.U.L.Rev. 643, 645 (1992).]. See also C. Hempel, Philosophy of Natural Science 49 (1966) ("[T]he statements constituting a scientific explanation must be capable of empirical test"); K. Popper, Conjectures and Refutations: The Growth of Scientific Knowledge 37 (5th ed. 1989) ("[T]he criterion of the scientific status of a theory is its falsifiability, or refutability, or testability").

Another pertinent consideration is whether the theory or technique has been subjected to peer review and publication. Publication (which is but one element of peer review) is not a *sine qua non* of admissibility; it does not necessarily correlate with reliability, and in some instances well-grounded but innovative theories will not have been published. * * * Some propositions, moreover, are too particular, too new, or of too limited interest to be published. But submission to the scrutiny of the scientific community is a component of "good science," in part because it increases the likelihood that substantive flaws in methodology will be detected. * * * The fact of publication (or lack thereof) in a peer-reviewed journal thus will be a relevant, though not dispositive, consideration in assessing the scientific validity of a particular technique or methodology on which an opinion is premised.

Additionally, in the case of a particular scientific technique, the court ordinarily should consider the known or potential rate of error, * * * and the existence and maintenance of standards controlling the technique's operation. * * *

Finally, "general acceptance" can yet have a bearing on the inquiry. A "reliability assessment does not require, although it does permit, explicit identification of a relevant scientific community and an express

---

3. Although the *Frye* decision itself focused exclusively on "novel" scientific techniques, we do not read the requirements of Rule 702 to apply especially or exclusively to unconventional evidence. Of course, well-established propositions are less likely to be challenged than those that are novel, and they are more handily defended. Indeed, theories that are so firmly established as to have attained the status of scientific law, such as the laws of thermodynamics, properly are subject to judicial notice under Fed. Rule Evid. 201.

determination of a particular degree of acceptance within that community." *United States v. Downing*, 753 F.2d, at 1238. Widespread acceptance can be an important factor in ruling particular evidence admissible, and "a known technique that has been able to attract only minimal support within the community," *Downing*, supra, at 1238, may properly be viewed with skepticism.

The inquiry envisioned by Rule 702 is, we emphasize, a flexible one. Its overarching subject is the scientific validity—and thus the evidentiary relevance and reliability—of the principles that underlie a proposed submission. The focus, of course, must be solely on principles and methodology, not on the conclusions that they generate.

Throughout, a judge assessing a proffer of expert scientific testimony under Rule 702 should also be mindful of other applicable rules. Rule 703 provides that expert opinions based on otherwise inadmissible hearsay are to be admitted only if the facts or data are "of a type reasonably relied upon by experts in the particular field in forming opinions or inferences upon the subject." Rule 706 allows the court at its discretion to procure the assistance of an expert of its own choosing. Finally, Rule 403 permits the exclusion of relevant evidence "if its probative value is substantially outweighed by the danger of unfair prejudice, confusion of the issues, or misleading the jury. * * *" Judge Weinstein has explained: "Expert evidence can be both powerful and quite misleading because of the difficulty in evaluating it. Because of this risk, the judge in weighing possible prejudice against probative force under Rule 403 of the present rules exercises more control over experts than over lay witnesses." Weinstein, 138 F.R.D., at 632.

III

We conclude by briefly addressing what appear to be two underlying concerns of the parties and amici in this case. Respondent expresses apprehension that abandonment of "general acceptance" as the exclusive requirement for admission will result in a "free-for-all" in which befuddled juries are confounded by absurd and irrational pseudoscientific assertions. In this regard respondent seems to us to be overly pessimistic about the capabilities of the jury, and of the adversary system generally. Vigorous cross-examination, presentation of contrary evidence, and careful instruction on the burden of proof are the traditional and appropriate means of attacking shaky but admissible evidence. * * * Additionally, in the event the trial court concludes that the scintilla of evidence presented supporting a position is insufficient to allow a reasonable juror to conclude that the position more likely than not is true, the court remains free to direct a judgment, Fed.Rule Civ.Proc. 50(a), and likewise to grant summary judgment, Fed.Rule Civ.Proc. 56. * * * These conventional devices, rather than wholesale exclusion under an uncompromising "general acceptance" test, are the appropriate safeguards where the basis of scientific testimony meets the standards of Rule 702.

Petitioners and, to a greater extent, their amici exhibit a different concern. They suggest that recognition of a screening role for the judge that allows for the exclusion of "invalid" evidence will sanction a stifling and repressive scientific orthodoxy and will be inimical to the search for truth. * * * It is true that open debate is an essential part of both legal and scientific analyses. Yet there are important differences between the quest for truth in the courtroom and the quest for truth in the laboratory. Scientific conclusions are subject to perpetual revision. Law, on the other hand, must resolve disputes finally and quickly. The scientific project is advanced by broad and wide-ranging consideration of a multitude of hypotheses, for those that are incorrect will eventually be shown to be so, and that in itself is an advance. Conjectures that are probably wrong are of little use, however, in the project of reaching a quick, final, and binding legal judgment—often of great consequence—about a particular set of events in the past. We recognize that in practice, a gatekeeping role for the judge, no matter how flexible, inevitably on occasion will prevent the jury from learning of authentic insights and innovations. That, nevertheless, is the balance that is struck by Rules of Evidence designed not for the exhaustive search for cosmic understanding but for the particularized resolution of legal disputes.

IV

To summarize: "general acceptance" is not a necessary precondition to the admissibility of scientific evidence under the Federal Rules of Evidence, but the Rules of Evidence—especially Rule 702—do assign to the trial judge the task of ensuring that an expert's testimony both rests on a reliable foundation and is relevant to the task at hand. Pertinent evidence based on scientifically valid principles will satisfy those demands.

The inquiries of the District Court and the Court of Appeals focused almost exclusively on "general acceptance," as gauged by publication and the decisions of other courts. Accordingly, the judgment of the Court of Appeals is vacated and the case is remanded for further proceedings consistent with this opinion.

It is so ordered.

Daubert and other toxic tort cases involve a complex body of scientific research and methods of data analysis that may be unfamiliar to many law students. Following is a brief discussion of the types of scientific evidence presented in the Bendectin litigation. With minor alterations, similar types of data and data analysis underlie the assessment of the relationship between other toxic agents and other disease outcomes such as cancer.

SANDERS, BENDECTIN ON TRIAL: A STUDY OF MASS TORT LITIGATION 45–60 (1998)

CHAPTER 3

The Science

Causation is a key element of tort liability. Unless the plaintiff can prove that some actionable behavior on the part of the defendant caused the plaintiff's injury there can be no recovery. * * *

Bendectin is one of a number of mass exposure cases which over the last decade or so have created a renewed interest in the causal question. These cases involve injuries allegedly caused by exposure to substances such as Agent Orange, asbestos, Bendectin, benzene, DES, Dioxin, MER/29, PCBs, and Thalidomide. New substances are constantly being added to the list, including the drugs Halcion and Prozac and exposure to electromagnetic fields, cathode ray tubes, and breast implants. Some substances are clearly harmful, either because their effect is so powerful, as is the case with Thalidomide, or because they produce signature diseases, such as asbestosis or mesothelioma, two diseases closely linked with asbestos exposure. The effects of other agents, including Halcion, Prozac, breast implants, electromagnetic fields, CRTs, and Bendectin are less clear.

The most difficult cases involve agents that fall into the latter category. All of these substances or forces share three defining characteristics: They do not produce a signature disease; there is no generally accepted biological theory about how they produce their alleged effect; and there is at best only a weak correlation between the substance or force and the injury. These products pose a special set of problems because a plaintiff's proof of causation must be based primarily on analyses of the chemical and physical attributes of the agent and on the agent's effect on animal and human subjects.

The first part of this chapter reviews the types of scientific evidence presented in the Bendectin cases. * * *

The Types Of Scientific Evidence.

There are five general categories of scientific evidence concerning Bendectin: structure-activity, in vitro, in vivo (animal studies), epidemiology, and aggregate time trend data. The first, structure-activity, is an argument by analogy. Toxicologists attempt to draw inferences about the biological activity of a drug by examining its chemical structure and comparing this structure to that of drugs whose biological activity is well understood. * * * For example, the most suspect ingredient in Bendectin has always been the antihistamine, doxylamine succinate. There is some evidence that some antihistamines are teratogens. In the Bendectin cases, plaintiff experts have argued that this structural similarity constitutes evidence that Bendectin causes defects.[1] The structure-activity analogy, by itself is weak evidence as to whether a chemical will be a teratogen. Molecules with minor structural differences can produce very different biological effects. * * *

In vitro studies test teratogenicity by exposing single cells, organs, culture-maintained embryos, or limb buds to a suspect substance and examine the biochemical events. * * * Organ cultures of embryonic limb buds are the most frequent subjects of in vitro studies testing for teratogenicity. Experiments indicate that embryonic mouse limbs developing in a culture exhibit pathological responses to several teratogens similar to those developing in vivo. * * * Cost is an important advantage of in vitro studies. * * * There also is an as yet unrealized longer term advantage: by using animal and human cell cultures, in vitro studies allow direct comparisons across species of the effects of cell and organ exposure to drugs. Ultimately, such comparisons may enable us to make better cross-species extrapolations of in vivo study results. At present, however, extrapolation of in vitro results to live animals, not to mention humans, is difficult. Impediments to extrapolation include the following factors: a chemical may not be absorbed by living organisms; the chemical is distributed in a living organism such that more (or less) reaches specific locations than would be predicted based on its absorption; and the chemical is rapidly metabolized into a metabolite that has a different profile of activity than the parent agent. * * *

In vivo studies examine the effects of a drug and other agents on various animal species thought to be similar to humans in their response to certain drugs. * * * The choice of a species for comparison is not an easy one. As Schardein notes, "testing in animals demonstrates quite convincingly that with respect to the few proven human teratogens, no one species of laboratory animal has been clearly demonstrated to everyone's satisfaction to be the one of choice to the exclusion of all others".[2]

Different protocols are employed depending on the type(s) of injuries for which one is testing. Today, the protocols for teratogenic testing are fairly well standardized. Because species choice is difficult, the protocols call for tests on at least two species at three dose levels. The recommended number of animals per group is twenty rodents and at least twelve to fifteen rabbits. Better laboratories may replicate the treatment groups to increase statistical power. The litter, not the fetus, is the unit of analysis. * * * By the mid-1980s approximately 2800 chemicals (mostly drugs) had been tested for teratogenic effects. Of those tested, approximately 38 percent had shown some teratogenic effect in some animal species. * * *

1. DeLuca v. Merrell Dow Pharm., 911 F.2d 941, 946 n. 8 (3d Cir.1990); Richardson v. Richardson–Merrell, Inc., 857 F.2d 823, 829 (D.C. Cir. 1988), cert. denied, 493 U.S. 882 (1989).

2. JAMES L. SCHARDEIN, CHEMICALLY INDUCED BIRTH DEFECTS 19 (1985).

Epidemiological studies involve human subjects. The beginnings of modern epidemiology are traced to John Snow, a London general practitioner who developed a hypothesis that cholera was spread through contaminated drinking water and conducted a set of tests to verify his theory. For example, he compared the incidence of the disease in a community drawing its water from the Thames upstream from London and a community drawing its water downstream from the city. He then attempted to control for other variables by looking at a single London region that was supplied drinking water by two different companies, and observed significant differences in the incidence of the disease in subdistricts supplied by each firm. Finally, he conducted what is known today as a case-control study by going to the homes of each cholera fatality, discovering who supplied the drinking water and comparing this to the total number of houses supplied by each company. The results, confirming the connection between the disease and the source of drinking water, were published in 1849. * * *

Studies on the teratogenic effects of drugs compare the incidence of birth defects among those exposed and those not exposed to a drug. There are two general ways of making such comparisons: cohort studies and case-control studies. Cohort studies compare the incidence of defects in groups of persons exposed to the drug to the incidence in groups of persons not exposed. Case-control studies compare a group of persons who have the defect in question ("cases") with another group that do not have it ("controls"). The two groups then are compared with regard to the frequency of exposure to the drug. * * *

Epidemiological studies typically measure risk by using the concepts of prevalence rate, relative risk, attributable risk, and odds ratio. * * * The prevalence rate is the number of persons with an injury divided by the total number of people in a group. The prevalence of birth defects in newborns is five to seven percent. The relative risk is a ratio that divides the prevalence of injury among people exposed to a risk factor by the prevalence if injury among those who were not exposed. For example, imagine that in a certain area there were 5,000 newborns and the mothers of 1,000 of these children took Bendectin during pregnancy. Among the 1,000 children whose mothers took Bendectin, 60 have a birth defect and 940 do not. Among the 4,000 children whose mothers did not take Bendectin we find that 160 have a birth defect and 3840 do not. The prevalence among the exposed children is $60/(60+940) = .06$. The prevalence rate among non-exposed children is $160/(160+3840) = .04$. The relative risk is $.06/.04 = 1.5$. The attributable risk indicates the differences in the risks between exposed and unexposed groups. In our example, the unexposed risk is .04 and the exposed risk is .06. Thus the risk attributable to Bendectin, *if* Bendectin use were the only difference between exposed and unexposed children, is .02. Sometimes researchers will report an attributable risk ratio, which is the percentage of the risk due to the substance. In the previous example, the attributable risk ratio is $(.02/.06) \times 100 = 33$ percent. Finally, there is the odds ratio. In case-control studies prevalence rates are not available because we do not know the denominator. The odds ratio does not require this information. The odds ratio is the cross product in a 2 by 2 table. In a cohort study comparing exposed to unexposed individuals, it is the ratio of the odds of injury if the person was exposed to the odds of injury if the person was not exposed.

Odds Ratio in a Cohort Study

	Injured	Not Injured
Exposed	a	b
Not Exposed	c	d

$$\text{Odds Ratio} = \frac{a/b}{c/d} = \frac{a*d}{b*c}$$

For example, using the data from above, the odds ratio would be $(60*3840)/(940*160) = 1.53$.

In a case control study comparing a group of cases (people with the injury in question) to a group of controls (people without the injury), the odds ratio is the ratio of the odds that the cases were exposed to the odds that the controls were exposed.

Odds Ratio in a Case–Control Study

	Cases (Injury)	Controls (No Injury)
History of Exposure	a	b
No History of Exposure	c	d

Note that cohort and case-control studies differ in how they are conducted, but not in how the odds ratio is computed. The odds ratio is a good approximation to relative risk when, with respect to their history of exposure, both the cases and controls are representative of the population from which they are drawn and when the disease or defect is rare in the population * * *.[3] Case-control studies are also called retrospective studies because the logic of the study is to look backward from injury to see if there was exposure. On the other hand cohort studies are sometimes called prospective studies because the logic of the study is to look forward from exposure to see if there is injury. In point of fact, some cohort studies are done retrospectively. The data is collected after both exposure and injury have occurred.

---

3. The two values are similar when the injury is rare because then b is a good approximation of a+b and d is a good approximation of c+d. Thus in our example, because the injury is rare the odds ratio and relative risk are quite close. Consider, however, a situation where the prevalence of injury in the exposed population is 60% and in the unexposed population is 40%. Using the previous example, the relative risk is still 1.5 $[600/(600 + 400)/1600/(1600 + 2400) = 1.5]$. However the odds ratio is $(600*2400)/(1600*400) = 2.25$.

A final type of data introduced in the Bendectin cases is aggregate time trend data. In several Bendectin cases this was called secular trend data. This type of data has been used to trace the spread of epidemics or the cyclical pattern of influenza outbreaks. * * * In the case of Bendectin, researchers compare the annual incidence of birth defects with annual Bendectin sales. They wish to ascertain whether the rapid increase in Bendectin prescriptions in the 1970s or the precipitous drop in prescriptions in the early 1980s matched similar increases or decreases in birth defects.

Causal Inference.

The cause-in-fact issue in mass exposure cases such as Bendectin is usefully thought of as two separate issues: general causation and specific causation. General causation asks whether exposure to a substance causes harm to anyone. Specific causation asks whether exposure to a substance caused a particular plaintiff's injury. Under traditional tort theory, a successful plaintiff must prevail by a preponderance of the evidence on both issues. The plaintiff must not only show that the substance causes the injury in question, but that it is more likely than not that the plaintiff's specific injury was caused by the substance. * * *

General Causation.

One of the fundamental objectives of science is to make causal assertions. Such assertions are typically based on some set of empirical observations. However, these observations may mislead us. The causal conclusions we draw from the observations may be invalid. There are a number of fundamental threats to the validity of causal assertions that must be considered before concluding that a causal relationship does or does not exist.

Cook and Campbell[4] have identified four basic types of validity: statistical conclusion validity, internal validity, construct validity, and external validity. Each may be threatened to various degrees and in a number of ways.

Statistical Conclusion Validity.

Most of the scientific evidence on whether Bendectin causes birth defects involves the interpretation of correlations between the drug and injury. When researchers observe a correlation between two variables, they may wish to conclude that the variables are causally related. Statistics help quantify threats to valid conclusions based on quantitative data.

Animal, epidemiological, and aggregate time trend studies may be thought of as samples from an underlying population. Statistics allow us to quantify the element of random chance involved in making inferences about population parameters from sample data. Typically, statistical analyses of Bendectin data involve testing the hypothesis that there is no

---

4. THOMAS D. COOK AND DONALD T. CAMPBELL. QUASI-EXPERIMENTATION: DESIGN AND ANALYSIS ISSUES FOR FIELD TESTING (1979).

relationship between exposure and birth defects. The hypothesis that there is no relationship is called the null hypothesis (H_0).[5] In animal studies the null hypothesis is that the offspring of mothers given the drug had the same frequency of defects as the offspring of mothers not given the drug. Likewise, in epidemiological studies the null hypothesis is that the relative risk, or odds ratio is equal to 1, indicating that children of mothers exposed to the drug have a defect rate equal to the defect rate of children of mothers who were not exposed. The null hypothesis is tested against an alternative hypothesis (H_1). Typically the alternative hypothesis is simply that there are differences between exposed and unexposed offspring, that is the odds ratio is not equal to one.

A test statistic can assist the investigator in deciding whether to accept or reject the null hypothesis by quantifying the likelihood that a difference as big or bigger than the one observed between exposed and unexposed samples could have occurred by chance if the null hypothesis is correct.

Given the existence of a null hypothesis and an alternative hypothesis, the investigator may choose whether to accept the null hypothesis or reject it. This choice can be either correct or incorrect. Figure 4 presents the possible decisions and errors. If one rejects the null hypothesis and in fact there is a relationship between Bendectin and birth defects then there is no error. This is a true positive. Similarly, if one accepts the null hypothesis and in fact there is no relationship, again there is no error. This is a true negative. There are two threats to statistical conclusions, two ways for a decision to be in error, called Type I and Type II.

A Type I error is the error of saying there is a relationship when in fact there is no relationship. Tests of statistical significance guard against making Type I errors. They assist the researcher in distinguishing between results that are likely to be due to chance and, therefore, consistent with the null hypothesis (non-significant results) and results that suggest the null hypothesis is not true (statistically significant results). * * * Scientists, being conservative, generally try to minimize Type I errors; that is, they decline to declare a causal relationship unless it is quite unlikely that the observed results occurred by chance. The Greek letter Alpha (α) is by custom used to designate this criterion. Traditionally and typically, the null hypothesis will not be rejected unless the results of the study would occur less than one time in twenty if the true case is that there is no relationship. Alpha must be less than .05. There is nothing magic about an Alpha of .05, however. Under varying circumstances an Alpha of .10 is not inappropriate, nor is an Alpha of .01. As Green notes, statistical significance measures only false-positive, not false-negative error.[6]

---

5. The null hypothesis got its name because typically the hypothesis to be tested is the absence of a relationship between two populations (here the populations of those exposed and those unexposed to the drug). However, the null hypothesis does not have to posit the absence of a relationship, i.e., an odds ratio of one. * * *

6. Michael Green, "Expert Witnesses and Sufficiency of Evidence in Toxic Sub-

The opposite of a Type I error is a Type II error, concluding there is no relationship when a relationship exists. We would commit a Type II error if we concluded that Bendectin does not have a teratogenic effect when in fact it does. Obviously, we would also like to minimize the probability of this error, by custom designated as Beta (β). The probability of rejecting the null hypothesis when some specific alternative hypothesis is true is called the power of the test, and is equal to 1 minus Beta. Power is a function of the study's sample size, the size of the effect one wishes to detect, and the significance level used to guard against Type I error. * * * Because power is a function of, among other things, the Alpha chosen to guard against Type I errors, all things being equal, minimizing the probability of one type of error can be done only by increasing the probability of making the other. In contingency table analyses typical of epidemiological research, the power of a study is also a function of the frequency of exposure in the population (e.g., percentage of pregnant women using Bendectin) and the incidence of the effect (e.g., frequency of limb reductions) * * *.[7] Because the power of any test is reduced by the decreasing incidence of an effect, Type II threats to causal conclusions are particularly relevant with respect to rare events such as limb reduction birth defects.

Figure 4. Possible Decisions and Errors

	Population Reality	
	H_0 true	H_1 true
D_1: Reject H_0 Decision based on Sample Data	False Positive Type I Error [α = Probability of Committing Type I Error]	True Positive No Error
D_0: Accept H_0	True Negative No Error	False Negative Type II Error [β = Probability of Committing Type II Error]

Two other threats to statistical conclusion validity deserve special mention. First, there is the error rate problem. Researchers engaged in a fishing expedition, sifting through a large number of correlations in search of significant relationships, will inevitably find some. A .05 significance test means that if the null hypothesis of no relationship is

---

stances Litigation: The Legacy of Agent Orange and Bendectin Litigation," 86 Nw. U.L.Rev. 643, 683 (1992).

7. See Powell, "How To Tell The Truth With Statistics: A New Statistical Approach to Analyzing The Bendectin Epidemiological Data In The Aftermath of *Daubert v. Merrell Dow Pharmaceuticals*," 31 Hou. L.Rev. 1241 (1994) * * *.

true, there is only one chance in twenty that we would get a relationship as strong as or stronger than the relationship found in the study. By definition, therefore, one time in twenty we should observe a relationship this strong even when the null hypothesis is true. For example, if one made sixty comparisons, we would expect there would be three significant correlations, even if no true causal relationships exist.

The unreliability of measurement techniques pose the second threat. Epidemiological research depends on determining whether individuals have or have not been exposed to a toxic substance and whether or not they suffer from some adverse effect. Coding errors occur when researchers treat individuals who were not exposed as having been exposed and those exposed as not exposed, or the researchers misdiagnose individuals. Unreliable coding threatens validity by inflating error variance and attenuating true relationships. With respect to the Bendectin research, epidemiological results are threatened by the inability to pinpoint precisely when an expectant mother took the drug. This is important because many teratogenic injuries are most likely to occur during organogenesis, when cells and tissues migrate and associate to form organ rudiments. During this period, the fetus is most vulnerable to structural defects. If women who took Bendectin at some later time in their pregnancy are counted among the "exposed" group, the study may underestimate any effect that might exist. * * *

Internal Validity

Statistical conclusion validity presents a special case of internal validity, which Cook and Campbell define as "the approximate validation with which we infer that a relationship between two variables is causal or that the absence of a relationship implies the absence of cause."[8] Threats to internal validity usually can be thought of as specification errors. Specification errors occur when the researcher fails to consider a factor that mediates the observed effect between two variables, either because it explains changes in both the "cause" and the "effect" or intervenes between the "cause" and the "effect" and acts independently on the "effect." * * *

Cook and Campbell discuss a number of threats to internal validity. A *history threat* is the threat that an observed effect may be due to an event that takes place between two points of measurement when this event is not the treatment under investigation. For example, Merrell typically introduces evidence indicating that a measurable decrease in birth defects did not accompany rapid withdrawal of the drug from the market between 1981 and 1983. Discovery of a new teratogenic substance, introduced into the environment over this same period, would constitute a history threat to the validity of the conclusion that Bendectin does not cause birth defects as would a rapid rise in Unisom sales among pregnant women looking for a cheap substitute for Bendectin.

8. Cook and Campbell, *supra* note 4 at 37.

A *testing threat* occurs when an effect is caused in part by the number of times responses are measured. For example, the ability of a mother to recall drug use during pregnancy may be affected by the number of times she is asked.

A *selection threat* exists when there is a possibility that the groups being compared are composed of different types of individuals, and, therefore, that observed differences are due to factors other than the treatment or exposure under investigation. For example, in a study of the effect of drinking on heart ailments the results may be threatened by the fact that drinkers are more likely than non-drinkers to also be smokers. Selection effects take many different forms and often interact with other threats to internal validity. One example of a potential selection effect in Bendectin research derives from the fact that morning sickness is a weak indicator that the fetus is healthy. Thus, women who took Bendectin would be more likely to have a healthy baby than women who did not. On the other hand, one study suggests that the relationship is reversed with respect to limb reduction defects. Kricker, et al. report that vomiting during pregnancy was associated with an increased risk of limb reduction defects.[9] If so, women who took Bendectin would be more likely to have children with this particular injury regardless of the effect of the drug.

If they are known, selection threats may be controlled for statistically or by the design of a study. For example, epidemiological case-control studies may match cases and controls in an attempt to control for factors that might affect the outcome. A study on birth defects may match cases and controls on factors such as maternal age or maternal smoking and drinking behavior, all of which are known to be associated with the incidence of some types of birth defects. * * *

A basic advantage of experimental research is its ability to control for many selection effects by randomly assigning individuals to treatments. However, even experimental designs cannot control for all threats to internal validity. For example, experiments cannot entirely control for differential mortality in treatment groups. Differential mortality obscures the interpretation of other results because the remaining individuals in the two groups may no longer be comparable on average. * * * This difference may be attributable to the treatment itself, such as when animals die from very large doses of a substance. See, for example, Tyl, et al. where rats given very large doses of Bendectin suffered high rates of maternal mortality.[10]

Construct Validity

The third broad type of validity is construct validity. What one investigator may interpret as evidence of a causal relationship between constructs A and B, another investigator may interpret as a relationship

---

9. Kricker, et al. "Congenital Limb Deficiencies: Maternal Factors in Pregnancy," 26 Australia–New Zealand Journal of Obstetrics and Gynecology 272 (1986).

10. Tyl et al., "Developmental Toxicity Evaluation of Bendectin in CD Rats," 37 Teratology 539 (1988).

between constructs X and B or even X and Y. * * * There are several sources of construct invalidity. One, experimenter expectancy, occurs when the experimenter anticipates a certain outcome. Another, evaluation apprehension, arises when the subject wishes to please the investigator. Hypothesis-guessing may threaten construct validity when the subject attempts to guess the hypothesis being tested and adjust his or her answers accordingly. Drug testing experiments often present construct validity concerns because any observed effect between the drug and a therapeutic effect may not be due to the chemical action of the drug, but rather to the psychological expectation that the drug will have a beneficial effect. In an effort to increase construct validity, scientists have designed methods such as placebo controls and double blind designs. In a double blind design, neither the subject nor the researcher knows who is receiving the treatment and who is receiving the placebo. * * *

Epidemiological case control studies are subject to a construct validity threat due to the existence of recall bias. Women whose offspring have suffered some injury are more likely to recall taking substances during pregnancy (including Bendectin) than women whose children are uninjured. Observed differences in outcome may, therefore, be measuring differential memory rather than the effect of the drug, i.e. the effect of X on B, not A on B. The result of recall bias is that the effects of a drug are overestimated.

Another source of construct invalidity is the confounding of constructs and levels of constructs. * * * One might conclude that A does not cause B when the test involves very low levels of A. At higher levels of A, however, the researcher might uncover a relationship. The requirement that laboratory animal studies routinely expose animals to suspect drugs at more than one dose level is an effort to avoid this construct validity threat.

A similar threat arises whenever one has but a single operationalization of the cause or the effect: a mono-operation bias. Early animal studies failed to detect the teratogenic effects of Thalidomide, in part because they used species unaffected by the drug.[11] Even when there are multiple operationalizations, the use of a single method to measure a relationship threatens validity. Wherever possible, researchers should employ multiple methods.

Assessing construct validity is frequently a question of convergence and divergence across measures. One is much more likely to believe that a cause and effect relationship exists when different measurements and methods converge to produce the same result (convergent validity). Similarly, researchers are more likely to believe that a cause and effect relationship of a particular type exists if there is a divergence between

---

11. Sherman and Strauss, "Thalidomide: A Twenty-Five Year Perspective," 41 Food, Drug & Cosmetics L.J. 458, 161 (1986), note that Thalidomide is not a teratogen in rats, mice or hamsters.

measures and manipulations of related but distinct constructs (discriminant validity).

External Validity

Finally, there is external validity. Just as statistical conclusion validity is a special type of internal validity, construct validity is a type of external validity. External validity involves the ability to generalize conclusions to *particular* persons, settings and times and to *types* of persons, settings and times. * * * Cook and Campbell list two basic threats to external validity, each of which can be expressed in terms of an interaction between a treatment and some other factor. First, the potential interaction between selection and treatment poses a threat to external validity. If a study uncovers a cause and effect relationship, the researcher must determine to which categories of individuals the relationship can be generalized. For example, if a study includes only men as subjects, the researcher must determine whether the results can be generalized to women. Other examples involve the ability to generalize across race, ethnicity, and class.

External validity threats are particularly significant in non-epidemiological research. Perhaps the central issue with respect to in vivo teratology studies is the degree to which the results can be extrapolated from animals to humans. * * * Unfortunately, there is no uniformly accepted formula for the extrapolation across species. Two common formulas respectively compare either the body weight or the surface area of the animal with the corresponding human measurement. The use of these different scaling factors can lead to divergent estimates of effects on humans. * * * Compounding this calculation is again the problem of different metabolic processing of a chemical in the animal species and in humans. "Differences among animal species, or even among strains of the same species, in metabolic handling of a chemical, are not uncommon and can account for toxicity differences."[12] Because humans are generally more sensitive to chemical exposures than are other species * * *, it is customary to assume that in the absence of information about the effects of exposure to humans, animal effects are potentially predictive of at least some human effects. However, the case for a human effect is much stronger if there are significant effects in several animal species and strains of laboratory animals. * * *

Other, more subtle threats to generalization caused by an interaction between selection and treatment pose special problems in the courtroom. For instance, jurors may rely upon the persuasiveness of experts as an indicator of the merits of their position. Litigants select testifying experts in part for their persuasiveness and, therefore, the assumption that a causal relationship exists between persuasiveness and correctness may be unwarranted for the type of expert that appears as a witness in court. * * *

---

12. National Research Council, Committee on Risk Assessment of Hazardous Air Pollutants, Science and Judgment in Risk Assessment 59 (1995).

The interaction between setting and treatment creates a second external threat to validity. A researcher may not be able to generalize studies done in one setting to other settings. All laboratory studies are vulnerable to this threat. Even well crafted experiments that do their best to increase external validity cannot insure that their results can be transferred from the laboratory. Some laboratory studies suffer from multiple threats to external validity. Laboratory animal studies encounter difficulty in this regard due to dose rate differences. Because many substances produce an adverse effect in only a small percentage of organisms when ingested at a rate similar to that encountered in the environment or prescribed by a physician, it takes a large number of animal subjects to detect a substance's effects with any reliability. Smaller samples would generate an unacceptably large number of false negatives (failure to detect an effect when it exists), a threat to internal validity. Thus, animals are generally administered high doses of the drug in hopes of maximizing the incidence of effects. * * * If there is a positive result, toxicologists must then extrapolate a predicted incidence at a more realistic lower rate. Unfortunately, there are a number of ways in which high dose toxicity testing differs from lower dose effects: there may be limits to the solubility of the compound; enzymes may become saturated at high doses, limiting absorption; detoxification mechanisms in the liver and elsewhere may be saturated; and metabolites may cause toxicity that would not occur with lower doses. All of these factors produce non-linear effects. * * * Because of these differences, there is no single agreed upon extrapolation model for dose-rate effects, and competing models generate widely differing predictions at low dose rates. * * * Extrapolation is particularly difficult in the case of teratogenic effects, in part because the basic unit of the experiment is not really one organism, but two, the mother and her offspring. * * *

Because of external validity problems, the methodologies typically used in in vivo research are better suited to regulatory questions than the questions that arise in individual tort litigation. When testing a new drug, the critical question is whether there might be a teratogenic effect in humans even though no effect is detected in test animals. The use of multiple species, and high dose rates decreases the chances that a drug will somehow slip through the in vivo screen, something that apparently happened with Thalidomide. This strategy works in the sense that all but one known human teratogen also produces positive results in at least one animal species and 80% are teratogenic in more than one species. * * * There have been no known new drug-induced epidemics of birth defects since the implementation of laws requiring animal testing.

When we move from the laboratory to the courtroom in a tort case, however, the question being asked of animal studies changes subtly. In the courtroom a central question is whether a positive effect in a test animal is persuasive evidence that the substance is a teratogen in humans. The answer depends in part on the animal species in question. According to one FDA study, of 165 compounds for which no human teratologic effects had been reported only 28 percent appeared negative in all animal species tested, and 50 percent appeared negative in multiple species. On the other hand, over 41 percent of the compounds appeared to be positive in more than one animal species. * * * In a species-by-species analysis, the FDA found that a negative response to substances for which human teratologic effects have not been reported was observed only 35 percent of the time in mice and hamsters, 50 percent in rats, 70 percent in rabbits, and 80 percent in monkeys. * * *

The lack of a strong relationship between humans and animals is related, of course, to dose rates. One reason we may fail to find an effect among humans is that relatively rare events are difficult to detect. Studies may fail to detect an effect because they lack sufficient power to uncover an uncommon result of a rarely encountered exposure. This does not mean, however, that if we only did bigger and better studies in humans we could find the same effect that is found in the laboratory. At the dose rates routinely experienced by humans, a substance simply may not be teratogenic. As Shepard notes:

> Most teratologists accept the principle that any agent can be shown to be teratogenic in an animal providing enough is given at the right time. For instance both sodium chloride and sucrose have been shown to produce animal teratogenicity.[13]

If the question is whether a finding that a substance is teratogenic in mice constitutes strong evidence it is teratogenic in humans, the answer is no. This does not mean, however, that the results of animal tests are completely irrelevant to the question of human teratogenicity. A strong, multi-species effect at relatively low dose rates substantially increases the likelihood that a substance causes harm to humans at normal dose levels. Questions concerning the relationship between animal and human studies, * * * the use of statistical evidence to prove causation, * * * and the allocation of damages among multiple causes and multiple defendants, * * * have generated a large body of commentary.

Summary

This brief review of validity's different facets indicates some of the ways in which conclusions about causation may be in error. Statistical conclusion validity and other types of internal validity concentrate on the danger of Type I or Type II errors, drawing false positive or false negative conclusions about causation. Statistical conclusion validity deals with threats to internal validity caused by random error, the possibility that an observed relationship could be due to chance. Other threats to internal validity are due to the possible existence of bias through factors that systematically affect the value of the means of variables. * * * Construct validity and other types of external validity address the dangers of generalization. The principal threat stems from the possible existence of an undetected interaction. * * * With respect to construct validity the danger is that an effect can be obtained using one measure, such as individual recall of drug ingestion, and a different effect using a

---

13. Shepard, "Human Teratogenicity," 33 Advances in Pediatrics 225, 227 (1986).

different measure, such as hospital prescription records. The risk of undetected interaction effects is even easier to see with respect to other threats to external validity, such as the interaction between selection and treatment. In each case, a relationship observed in one circumstance may not apply in a different circumstance.

Because careful research designs may minimize, but cannot eliminate all threats to validity, researchers have developed a number of criteria that should be used in assessing whether a relationship is causal. One of the most well known is a set of nine criteria originally developed by Sir Austin Bradford Hill.[14]

1. Is the temporal relationship correct? Does the "effect" follow the "cause?"

2. Is there evidence from true experiments in humans? Because experiments randomly assign people to treatments, they control for many unknown systematic threats to validity. Ceteris paribus, experimental data is more persuasive than other types of data.

3. Is the association a strong one? The stronger the statistical association (usually measured by relative risk or the odds ratio) and the greater the level of statistical significance (usually measured by a chi square test) the more likely the relationship is causal. Both the level of statistical significance and the strength of the relationship are important. With very large samples a relationship may be statistically significant but not very strong. A relative risk of 1.2 is not significant with an N of 200, but may be highly significant with an N of 20,000.

4. Is the association consistent from study to study? If one study reveals a statistically significant relationship, can the result be replicated in a later study? If so, the argument for a causal relationship is greatly strengthened.

5. Is there a dose-response gradient? In animal studies, especially, the causal argument is strengthened if higher doses of a substance produce more injury.

6. Is the association specific? For example, exposure to asbestos produces the specific disease asbestosis. Most researchers believe that human teratogens produce a specific pattern of injuries. The existence of such a pattern strengthens the causal argument.

7. Does the association make biological sense? For example, if a drug such as Bendectin is to cause harm to the fetus it must be shown that it can cross the placental barrier, which in fact it can.

8. Does the association make epidemiological sense?

14. A.B. Hill, A Short Textbook of Medical Statistics. 285–296 (1977); Andrew C. Harper and Laurie J. Lambert, The Health of Populations: An Introduction. 92–95 (1994).

9. Is there appropriate analogy to other known causal relationships? For example, the antihistamine component of Bendectin is more suspect because some other antihistamines are known teratogens.

Specific Causation.

Even if we were to conclude that maternal exposure to Bendectin causes birth defects in children, this alone would not allow us to conclude that the injury suffered by any given plaintiff was caused by Bendectin. Unless the plaintiff can show that it is more likely than not that this specific injury was caused by Bendectin, legally he has not carried the burden of proof on the causal question. There is no known way to distinguish between birth defects caused by Bendectin and defects from other causes. Therefore, the plaintiff is forced to fall back on the same scientific evidence used to prove general causation: the in vitro, in vivo, an epidemiological research. With respect to specific causation, the epidemiological findings are particularly relevant. Theoretically, a plaintiff can prove specific causation by a preponderance of the evidence by providing epidemiological evidence that indicates a relative risk greater than 2.0; that is, people exposed to the substance suffer injuries at least more than twice as frequently as those not exposed. The plaintiff can then argue that it is more likely than not that the substance caused this particular injury. For example, if the background risk of a certain type of cancer is one in one thousand, and the risk among those exposed to some product is three in one thousand, plaintiffs exposed to the substance who have this type of cancer can argue that more likely than not—two chances out of three—their cancer was caused by the product.

Whether a plaintiff should ever prevail with a relative risk less than 2.0 is controversial. Some cases allow recovery if the plaintiff can also provide evidence eliminating some of the other possible causes of injury. The New Jersey Supreme Court allowed a plaintiff to attempt such a proof in an asbestos exposure case.[15] By this logic, plaintiffs should sometimes lose even when the relative risk exceeds 2.0, if the defendant is able to attribute the injury to some other particular cause.

Some commentators have proposed eliminating the preponderance of the evidence requirement for the specific causation element of mass torts, instead suggesting that damages be reduced by a proportional amount. * * * For example, if the relative risk associated with a product were 1.5, then a plaintiff should recover one-third of the damages because the odds are 2 to 1 that the injury was due to some other cause. Carried to its logical conclusion, this proposal should cause the plaintiff to recover only a percentage of his damages in any case where the correlation between exposure and injury is less than one. For example, even in a situation where the relative risk is three, the plaintiff should recover two thirds of his damages.

---

15. Landrigan v. Celotex Corp., 127 N.J. 404, 605 A.2d 1079 (1992).

As Abraham notes, however, these alternatives require a body of epidemiological evidence sufficient to provide reliable "probabilistic measures of causation."[16] * * * In many situations, this body of evidence simply does not exist. Thus far, with one or two narrow exceptions, courts have refused to adopt this course of action.[17] In all of the Bendectin trials the plaintiff was legally required to show specific causation by a preponderance of the evidence.

Notes

1. In a separate opinion in *Daubert*, Chief Justice Rehnquist, joined by Justice Stevens, agrees that the *Frye* test did not survive the adoption of the Federal Rules. However, he dissents from the Court's "general observations" on evidentiary reliability and scientific admissibility.

> I defer to no one in my confidence in federal judges; but I am at a loss to know what is meant when it is said that the scientific status of a theory depends on its "falsifiability," and I suspect some of them will be, too.
>
> I do not doubt that Rule 702 confides to the judge some gatekeeping responsibility in deciding questions of the admissibility of proffered expert testimony. But I do not think it imposes on them either the obligation or the authority to become amateur scientists in order to perform that role. I think the Court would be far better advised in this case to decide only the questions presented, and to leave the further development of this important area of the law to future cases.

Does *Daubert* force judges to become amateur scientists? From the preceding discussion of the science in the Bendectin litigation, do you think they are up to the task?

2. After *Daubert*, circuit courts disagreed as to the proper standard of review of trial court admissibility decisions. In General Electric Co. v. Joiner, 522 U.S. 136, 118 S.Ct. 512, 139 L.Ed.2d 508 (1997), the Supreme court held that the proper standard is abuse of discretion. In *Joiner*, the plaintiff, who had a history of cigarette smoking and a family history of lung cancer, developed small-cell lung cancer at age thirty-seven. He alleged the cancer was "promoted" by exposure to polychlorinated biphenyls (PCBs) at his worksite. The district court excluded plaintiff expert testimony on causation under *Daubert*. The Eleventh Circuit reversed, holding that because the Federal Rules display a preference for admissibility appellate courts should "apply a particularly stringent standard of review to the trial judge's exclusion of expert testimony." 78 F.3d 524, 529 (11th Cir.1996). The Supreme Court reversed, held that the appropriate test is abuse of discretion and found that the trial court had not abused its discretion.

The Supreme Court also addressed the plaintiff's claim that the district court merely disagreed with his experts conclusions, violating *Daubert's*

---

16. Abraham, "Individual Action and Collective Responsibility: The Dilemma of Mass Tort Reform," 73 Vir.L.Rev. 845, 867 (1987).

17. *See* Herskovits v. Group Health Coop., 99 Wash.2d 609, 612–19, 664 P.2d 474, 476–79 (1983).

mandate that when making admissibility determinations trial courts should focus on principles and methodology, not on the conclusions that they generate. Most appellate courts had downplayed the Supreme Court's methodology-conclusion distinction. For example, in an opinion following *Daubert,* Judge Becker said "we think that [the distinction between principles and methods versus conclusions] has only limited practical import ... a challenge to 'fit' is very close to a challenge to the expert's ultimate conclusion about the particular case, and yet it is part of the judge's admissibility calculus under Daubert." *In re Paoli*, 35 F.3d 717, 746 (3d Cir.1994) In *Joiner*, the Supreme Court ratified Judge Becker's view. "[N]othing in either Daubert or the Federal Rules of Evidence requires a district court to admit opinion evidence which is connected to existing data only by the *ipse dixit* of the expert. A court may conclude that there is simply too great an analytical gap between the data and the opinion proffered. That is what the District Court did here and we hold that it did not abuse its discretion in so doing." 552 U.S. at 146.

3. The Bendectin litigation was frequently cited as an example of the evils of junk science. See Michael Green, Bendectin and Birth Defects: The Challenges of Mass Toxic Substances Litigation (1996); Joseph Sanders, Bendectin on Trial: A Study of Mass Tort Litigation (1998). The use of "junk" science or "innovative" science (depending on one's point of view) has sparked a heated debate in the academic and popular presses. The most outspoken critique of "junk" science has been Peter Huber. *See* Peter Huber, Galileo's Revenge: Junk Science in the Courtroom (1991). There is a vast literature on both sides of the debate. *See, e.g.* Bernstein, Out of the Fryeing Pan and Into the Fire: The Expert Witness Problem in Toxic Tort Litigation, 10 Rev.Litig. 117 (1990); Black et al., Science and the Law in the Wake of *Daubert*: A New Search for Scientific Knowledge, 72 Tex.L.Rev. 715 (1994); Chesebro, Galileo's Retort: Peter Huber's Junk Scholarship, 42 Amer. U. L. Rev. 1637 (1993). Faigman et al., Check Your Crystal Ball at the Courthouse Door, Please: Exploring the Past, Understanding the Present, and Worrying About the Future of Scientific Evidence, 15 Cardozo L.Rev. 179 (1994); Gianelli, The Admissibility of Novel Scientific Evidence: *Frye v. United States* A Half–Century Later, 80 Colum.L.Rev. 1197 (1980); Green, Expert Witnesses and Sufficiency of Evidence in Toxic Substances Litigation: The Legacy of Agent Orange and Bendectin Litigation, 86 Nw.U.L.Rev. 643 (1992); Gross, Expert Evidence, 1991 Wis.L.Rev. 1113 (1991); Milich, Controversial Science in the Courtroom: Daubert and the Law's Hubris, 43 Emory L.J. 913 (1994); Poulter, *Daubert* and Scientific Evidence: Assessing Evidentiary Reliability in Toxic Tort Litigation, 1993 Utah L.Rev. 1307 (1993); Sanders, From Science to Evidence: The Testimony on Causation in the Bendectin Cases, 46 Stan.L.Rev. 1 (1993); Schuck, Multi–Culturalism Redux: Science, Law, and Politics, 11 Yale L. & Pol'y Rev. 1 (1993).

4. Silicone implants are another mass tort that were the subject of substantial controversy. *See* Marcia Angell. Science On Trial: The Clash of Medical Evidence and the Law in the Breast Implant Case (1966); David E. Bernstein, The Breast Implant Fiasco, 87 Cal.L.Rev. 457 (1999). Plaintiffs enjoyed some early success, e.g. Hopkins v. Dow Corning Corp., 33 F.3d 1116 (9th Cir. 1994). As in the case of Bendectin, discovery was consolidated under the Multi-district Litigation Act, 28 U.S.C. § 1407(a) (1991). (See

Chapter 13, *infra*, for a discussion of the role of the MDL Act in products liability litigation.). Judge Pointer, who oversaw the MDL proceedings, appointed a panel of experts under Federal Rule of Evidence 706. In December, 1998 the panel issued its report, which concluded that there is little evidence linking silicone implants to systemic diseases. The report may be found at <http://www.fjc.gov/ BREIMLIT/SCIENCE/report.htm>. Two reports developed outside the context of litigation reached similar conclusions. An independent review group in the United Kingdom issued a report on the adverse health effects of silicone implants in July of 1998. The panel found little support for a causal connection between implants and autoimmune disease or cancer. In the early summer of 1999 the Institute of Medicine issued its report on the safety of silicone Breast Implants. Bondurant, Ernster, and Herdman, (eds.) Committee on the Safety of Silicone Breast Implants, Institute of Medicine, Safety of Silicone Breast Implants. (1999). The Committee concluded that local and perioperative complications associated with implants "occur frequently enough to be a cause for concern and to justify the conclusion that they are the primary safety issue with silicone breast implants. Among others, these include overall re-operations, ruptures or deflations, contractures, infections, hematomas and pain." *Id.* at 4. It was far less concerned that implants cause systemic ailments. For example, with respect to the question of whether implants cause a novel disease the Committee said, "there does not appear to be even suggestive evidence for the existence of a novel syndrome in women with breast implants. In fact, epidemiological evidence suggests that there is no novel syndrome." *Id.* at 5.

Following the reports, plaintiffs alleging that implants caused connective tissue or autoimmune diseases have enjoyed very little success. For example, Allison v. McGhan Medical Corp., 184 F.3d 1300 (11th Cir. 1999) referred to the MDL panel in ruling the plaintiff's experts' testimony inadmissible because it failed each of the *Daubert* factors and there was too great an analytical gap between the experts' conclusions and the evidence upon which they based those conclusions. Clearly the silicone implant litigation involving connective tissue and autoimmune diseases is rapidly winding down as plaintiffs are unable to get their experts past the *Daubert* gate. *See* Norris v. Baxter Healthcare Corp., 397 F.3d 878 (10th Cir. 2005). In large part this is the result of the MDL panel and other scientific reviews of the evidence. Whatever their potential drawbacks, scientific panels do offer the potential of shortening the life-cycle of some mass torts. *See* Walker and Monahan, Scientific Authority: The Breast Implant Litigation and Beyond, 86 Va. L.Rev. 801 (2000) for a valuable discussion of how the results of such groups should be brought into the litigation arena.

Not surprisingly, experts prepared to testify about implant induced local injuries have enjoyed a more favorable reception in the courts, especially when the plaintiff's implants have ruptured. *See* Toole v. Baxter Healthcare Corp., 235 F.3d 1307 (11th Cir.2000).

5. Like Chief Justice Rehnquist, the *Allison* court expressed some doubt as to the ability of trial judges to act as "amateur scientists" in complex cases involving epidemiological, toxicological and statistical questions of causation. A number of resources exist to help judges with this task. *See* Federal Judicial Center, Reference Manual on Scientific Evidence (2d ed.

2000); Faigman, Kaye, Saks & Sanders (eds); Modern Scientific Evidence (2005–2006 edition).

KUMHO TIRE CO., LTD. v. CARMICHAEL
Supreme Court of the United States, 1999.
526 U.S. 137, 119 S.Ct. 1167, 143 L.Ed.2d 238.

JUSTICE BREYER delivered the opinion of the Court.

In *Daubert v. Merrell Dow Pharmaceuticals, Inc.*, * * * this Court focused upon the admissibility of scientific expert testimony. It pointed out that such testimony is admissible only if it is both relevant and reliable. And it held that the Federal Rules of Evidence "assign to the trial judge the task of ensuring that an expert's testimony both rests on a reliable foundation and is relevant to the task at hand." * * * The Court also discussed certain more specific factors, such as testing, peer review, error rates, and "acceptability" in the relevant scientific community, some or all of which might prove helpful in determining the reliability of a particular scientific "theory or technique." * * *

This case requires us to decide how *Daubert* applies to the testimony of engineers and other experts who are not scientists. We conclude that *Daubert's* general holding—setting forth the trial judge's general "gatekeeping" obligation—applies not only to testimony based on "scientific" knowledge, but also to testimony based on "technical" and "other specialized" knowledge. See Fed. Rule Evid. 702. We also conclude that a trial court *may* consider one or more of the more specific factors that *Daubert* mentioned when doing so will help determine that testimony's reliability. But, as the Court stated in *Daubert,* the test of reliability is "flexible," and *Daubert's* list of specific factors neither necessarily nor exclusively applies to all experts or in every case. Rather, the law grants a district court the same broad latitude when it decides *how* to determine reliability as it enjoys in respect to its ultimate reliability determination. * * * Applying these standards, we determine that the District Court's decision in this case—not to admit certain expert testimony—was within its discretion and therefore lawful.

I

On July 6, 1993, the right rear tire of a minivan driven by Patrick Carmichael blew out. In the accident that followed, one of the passengers died, and others were severely injured. In October 1993, the Carmichaels brought this diversity suit against the tire's maker and its distributor, whom we refer to collectively as Kumho Tire, claiming that the tire was defective. The plaintiffs rested their case in significant part upon deposition testimony provided by an expert in tire failure analysis, Dennis Carlson, Jr., who intended to testify in support of their conclusion.

Carlson's depositions relied upon certain features of tire technology that are not in dispute. A steel-belted radial tire like the Carmichaels' is made up of a "carcass" containing many layers of flexible cords, called "plies," along which (between the cords and the outer tread) are laid steel strips called "belts." Steel wire loops, called "beads," hold the cords together at the plies' bottom edges. An outer layer, called the "tread," encases the carcass, and the entire tire is bound together in rubber, through the application of heat and various chemicals. * * * The bead of the tire sits upon a "bead seat," which is part of the wheel assembly. That assembly contains a "rim flange," which extends over the bead and rests against the side of the tire. * * *

Carlson's testimony also accepted certain background facts about the tire in question. He assumed that before the blowout the tire had traveled far. (The tire was made in 1988 and had been installed some time before the Carmichaels bought the used minivan in March 1993; the Carmichaels had driven the van approximately 7,000 additional miles in the two months they had owned it.) Carlson noted that the tire's tread depth, which was 11/32 of an inch when new, * * * had been worn down to depths that ranged from 3/32 of an inch along some parts of the tire, to nothing at all along others. * * * He conceded that the tire tread had at least two punctures which had been inadequately repaired. * * *

Despite the tire's age and history, Carlson concluded that a defect in its manufacture or design caused the blow-out. He rested this conclusion in part upon three premises which, for present purposes, we must assume are not in dispute: First, a tire's carcass should stay bound to the inner side of the tread for a significant period of time after its tread depth has worn away. * * * Second, the tread of the tire at issue had separated from its inner steel-belted carcass prior to the accident. * * * Third, this "separation" caused the blowout. * * *

Carlson's conclusion that a defect caused the separation, however, rested upon certain other propositions, several of which the defendants strongly dispute. First, Carlson said that if a separation is *not* caused by a certain kind of tire misuse called "overdeflection" (which consists of under inflating the tire or causing it to carry too much weight, thereby generating heat that can undo the chemical tread/carcass bond), then, ordinarily, its cause is a tire defect. * * * Second, he said that if a tire has been subject to sufficient overdeflection to cause a separation, it should reveal certain physical symptoms. These symptoms include (a) tread wear on the tire's shoulder that is greater than the tread wear along the tire's center; * * * (b) signs of a "bead groove," where the beads have been pushed too hard against the bead seat on the inside of the tire's rim; * * * (c) sidewalls of the tire with physical signs of deterioration, such as discoloration; * * * and/or (d) marks on the tire's rim flange. * * * Third, Carlson said that where he does not find *at least two* of the four physical signs just mentioned (and presumably where there is no reason to suspect a less common cause of separation), he concludes that a manufacturing or design defect caused the separation. * * *

Carlson added that he had inspected the tire in question. He conceded that the tire to a limited degree showed greater wear on the shoulder than in the center, some signs of "bead groove," some discoloration, a few marks on the rim flange, and inadequately filled puncture holes (which can also cause heat that might lead to separation). * * * But, in each instance, he testified that the symptoms were not significant, and he explained why he believed that they did not reveal overdeflection. For example, the extra shoulder wear, he said, appeared primarily on one shoulder, whereas an overdeflected tire would reveal equally abnormal wear on both shoulders. * * * Carlson concluded that the tire did not bear at least two of the four overdeflection symptoms, nor was there any less obvious cause of separation; and since neither overdeflection nor the punctures caused the blowout, a defect must have done so.

Kumho Tire moved the District Court to exclude Carlson's testimony on the ground that his methodology failed Rule 702's reliability requirement. The court agreed with Kumho that it should act as a *Daubert*-type reliability "gatekeeper," even though one might consider Carlson's testimony as "technical," rather than "scientific." * * * The court then examined Carlson's methodology in light of the reliability-related factors that *Daubert* mentioned, such as a theory's testability, whether it "has been a subject of peer review or publication," the "known or potential rate of error," and the "degree of acceptance ... within the relevant scientific community." * * * The District Court found that all those factors argued against the reliability of Carlson's methods, and it granted the motion to exclude the testimony (as well as the defendants' accompanying motion for summary judgment).

The plaintiffs, arguing that the court's application of the *Daubert* factors was too "inflexible," asked for reconsideration. And the Court granted that motion. * * * After reconsidering the matter, the court agreed with the plaintiffs that *Daubert* should be applied flexibly, that its four factors were simply illustrative, and that other factors could argue in favor of admissibility. It conceded that there may be widespread acceptance of a "visual-inspection method" for some relevant purposes. But the court found insufficient indications of the reliability of

> "the component of Carlson's tire failure analysis which most concerned the Court, namely, the methodology employed by the expert in analyzing the data obtained in the visual inspection, and the scientific basis, if any, for such an analysis." * * *

It consequently affirmed its earlier order declaring Carlson's testimony inadmissable and granting the defendants' motion for summary judgment.

The Eleventh Circuit reversed. See *Carmichael v. Samyang Tire, Inc.*, 131 F.3d 1433 (1997). It "review[ed] ... de novo" the "district court's legal decision to apply *Daubert*." * * * It noted that "the Supreme Court in *Daubert* explicitly limited its holding to cover only the 'scientific context,'" adding that "a *Daubert* analysis" applies only where an expert relies "on the application of scientific principles," rather than "on skill-or experience-based observation." * * * It concluded that Carlson's testimony, which it viewed as relying on experience, "falls outside the scope of *Daubert*," that "the district court erred as a matter of law by applying *Daubert* in this case," and that the case must be remanded for further (non-*Daubert*-type) consideration under Rule 702. * * *

We granted certiorari in light of uncertainty among the lower courts about whether, or how, *Daubert* applies to expert testimony that might be characterized as based not upon "scientific" knowledge, but rather upon "technical" or "other specialized" knowledge. Fed. Rule Evid. 702; compare, *e.g., Watkins v. Telsmith, Inc.,* 121 F.3d 984, 990–991 (C.A.5 1997), with, *e.g., Compton v. Subaru of America, Inc.,* 82 F.3d 1513, 1518–1519 (C.A.10), cert. denied, 519 U.S. 1042, 117 S.Ct. 611, 136 L.Ed.2d 536 (1996).

II

A

In *Daubert,* this Court held that Federal Rule of Evidence 702 imposes a special obligation upon a trial judge to "ensure that any and all scientific testimony . . . is not only relevant, but reliable." 509 U.S., at 589, 113 S.Ct. 2786. The initial question before us is whether this basic gatekeeping obligation applies only to "scientific" testimony or to all expert testimony. We, like the parties, believe that it applies to all expert testimony. * * *

For one thing, Rule 702 itself says:

> "If scientific, technical, or other specialized knowledge will assist the trier of fact to understand the evidence or to determine a fact in issue, a witness qualified as an expert by knowledge, skill, experience, training, or education, may testify thereto in the form of an opinion or otherwise."

This language makes no relevant distinction between "scientific" knowledge and "technical" or "other specialized" knowledge. It makes clear that any such knowledge might become the subject of expert testimony. In *Daubert,* the Court specified that it is the Rule's word "knowledge," not the words (like "scientific") that modify that word, that "establishes a standard of evidentiary reliability." * * * Hence, as a matter of language, the Rule applies its reliability standard to all "scientific," "technical," or "other specialized" matters within its scope. We concede that the Court in *Daubert* referred only to "scientific" knowledge. But as the Court there said, it referred to "scientific" testimony "because that [wa]s the nature of the expertise" at issue. * * *

Neither is the evidentiary rationale that underlay the Court's basic *Daubert* "gatekeeping" determination limited to "scientific" knowledge. *Daubert* pointed out that Federal Rules 702 and 703 grant expert witnesses testimonial latitude unavailable to other witnesses on the "assumption that the expert's opinion will have a reliable basis in the knowledge and experience of his discipline." * * * (pointing out that experts may testify to opinions, including those that are not based on firsthand knowledge or observation). The Rules grant that latitude to all experts, not just to "scientific" ones.

Finally, it would prove difficult, if not impossible, for judges to administer evidentiary rules under which a gatekeeping obligation depended upon a distinction between "scientific" knowledge and "technical" or "other specialized" knowledge. There is no clear line that divides the one from the others. Disciplines such as engineering rest upon scientific knowledge. Pure scientific theory itself may depend for its development upon observation and properly engineered machinery. And conceptual efforts to distinguish the two are unlikely to produce clear legal lines capable of application in particular cases. * * *

Neither is there a convincing need to make such distinctions. Experts of all kinds tie observations to conclusions through the use of what Judge Learned Hand called "general truths derived from ... specialized experience." Hand, Historical and Practical Considerations Regarding Expert Testimony, 15 Harv. L.Rev. 40, 54 (1901). And whether the specific expert testimony focuses upon specialized observations, the specialized translation of those observations into theory, a specialized theory itself, or the application of such a theory in a particular case, the expert's testimony often will rest "upon an experience confessedly foreign in kind to [the jury's] own." * * * The trial judge's effort to assure that the specialized testimony is reliable and relevant can help the jury evaluate that foreign experience, whether the testimony reflects scientific, technical, or other specialized knowledge.

We conclude that *Daubert's* general principles apply to the expert matters described in Rule 702. * * *

B

The petitioners ask more specifically whether a trial judge determining the "admissibility of an engineering expert's testimony" *may* consider several more specific factors that *Daubert* said might "bear on" a judge's gate-keeping determination. These factors include:

— Whether a "theory or technique ... can be (and has been) tested";

— Whether it "has been subjected to peer review and publication";

— Whether, in respect to a particular technique, there is a high "known or potential rate of error" and whether there are "standards controlling the technique's operation"; and

— Whether the theory or technique enjoys "general acceptance" within a "relevant scientific community." * * *

Emphasizing the word "may" in the question, we answer that question yes.

Engineering testimony rests upon scientific foundations, the reliability of which will be at issue in some cases. * * * In other cases, the relevant reliability concerns may focus upon personal knowledge or experience. As the Solicitor General points out, there are many different kinds of experts, and many different kinds of expertise. * * * (citing cases involving experts in drug terms, handwriting analysis, criminal *modus operandi,* land valuation, agricultural practices, railroad procedures, attorney's fee valuation, and others). Our emphasis on the word "may" thus reflects *Daubert's* description of the Rule 702 inquiry as "a flexible one." * * * *Daubert* makes clear that the factors it mentions do *not* constitute a "definitive checklist or test." * * * And *Daubert* adds that the gatekeeping inquiry must be " 'tied to the facts' " of a particular "case." * * * The conclusion, in our view, is that we can neither rule out, nor rule in, for all cases and for all time the applicability of the factors mentioned in *Daubert,* nor can we now do so for subsets of cases categorized by category of expert or by kind of evidence. Too much depends upon the particular circumstances of the particular case at issue.

Daubert itself is not to the contrary. It made clear that its list of factors was meant to be helpful, not definitive. Indeed, those factors do not all necessarily apply even in every instance in which the reliability of scientific testimony is challenged. It might not be surprising in a particular case, for example, that a claim made by a scientific witness has never been the subject of peer review, for the particular application at issue may never previously have interested any scientist. Nor, on the other hand, does the presence of *Daubert's* general acceptance factor help show that an expert's testimony is reliable where the discipline itself lacks reliability, as, for example, do theories grounded in any so-called generally accepted principles of astrology or necromancy.

At the same time, and contrary to the Court of Appeals' view, some of *Daubert's* questions can help to evaluate the reliability even of experience-based testimony. In certain cases, it will be appropriate for the trial judge to ask, for example, how often an engineering expert's experience-based methodology has produced erroneous results, or whether such a method is generally accepted in the relevant engineering community. Likewise, it will at times be useful to ask even of a witness whose expertise is based purely on experience, say, a perfume tester able to distinguish among 140 odors at a sniff, whether his preparation is of a kind that others in the field would recognize as acceptable.

We must therefore disagree with the Eleventh Circuit's holding that a trial judge may ask questions of the sort *Daubert* mentioned only where an expert "relies on the application of scientific principles," but not where an expert relies "on skill-or experience-based observation." * * * We do not believe that Rule 702 creates a schematism that segregates expertise by type while mapping certain kinds of questions to certain kinds of experts. Life and the legal cases that it generates are too complex to warrant so definitive a match.

To say this is not to deny the importance of *Daubert's* gatekeeping requirement. The objective of that requirement is to ensure the reliability and relevancy of expert testimony. It is to make certain that an expert, whether basing testimony upon professional studies or personal experience, employs in the courtroom the same level of intellectual rigor that characterizes the practice of an expert in the relevant field. Nor do we deny that, as stated in *Daubert,* the particular questions that it mentioned will often be appropriate for use in determining the reliability of challenged expert testimony. Rather, we conclude that the trial judge must have considerable leeway in deciding in a particular case how to go about determining whether particular expert testimony is reliable. That is to say, a trial court should consider the specific factors identified in *Daubert* where they are reasonable measures of the reliability of expert testimony.

C

The trial court must have the same kind of latitude in deciding *how* to test an expert's reliability, and to decide whether or when special briefing or other proceedings are needed to investigate reliability, as it enjoys when it decides *whether or not* that expert's relevant testimony is reliable. Our opinion in *Joiner* makes clear that a court of appeals is to apply an abuse-of-discretion standard when it "review[s] a trial court's decision to admit or exclude expert testimony." * * * That standard applies as much to the trial court's decisions about how to determine reliability as to its ultimate conclusion. Otherwise, the trial judge would lack the discretionary authority needed both to avoid unnecessary "reliability" proceedings in ordinary cases where the reliability of an expert's methods is properly taken for granted, and to require appropriate proceedings in the less usual or more complex cases where cause for questioning the expert's reliability arises. Indeed, the Rules seek to avoid "unjustifiable expense and delay" as part of their search for "truth" and the "jus[t] determination" of proceedings. Fed. Rule Evid. 102. Thus, whether *Daubert's* specific factors are, or are not, reasonable measures of reliability in a particular case is a matter that the law grants the trial judge broad latitude to determine. * * *

III

We further explain the way in which a trial judge "may" consider *Daubert's* factors by applying these considerations to the case at hand, a matter that has been briefed exhaustively by the parties and their 19 *amici.* The District Court did not doubt Carlson's qualifications, which included a masters degree in mechanical engineering, 10 years' work at Michelin America, Inc., and testimony as a tire failure consultant in other tort cases. Rather, it excluded the testimony because, despite those qualifications, it initially doubted, and then found unreliable, "the methodology employed by the expert in analyzing the data obtained in the visual inspection, and the scientific basis, if any, for such an analysis." * * * In our view, the doubts that triggered the District Court's initial inquiry here were reasonable, as was the court's ultimate conclusion.

For one thing, and contrary to respondents' suggestion, the specific issue before the court was not the reasonableness *in general* of a tire expert's use of a visual and tactile inspection to determine whether overdeflection had caused the tire's tread to separate from its steel-belted carcass. Rather, it was the reasonableness of using such an approach, along with Carlson's particular method of analyzing the data thereby obtained, to draw a conclusion regarding *the particular matter to which the expert testimony was directly relevant.* That matter concerned the likelihood that a defect in the tire at issue caused its tread to separate from its carcass. The tire in question, the expert conceded, had traveled far enough so that some of the tread had been worn bald; it should have been taken out of service; it had been repaired (inadequately) for punctures; and it bore some of the very marks that the expert said indicated, not a defect, but abuse through overdeflection. * * * The relevant issue was whether the expert could reliably determine the cause of *this* tire's separation.

Nor was the basis for Carlson's conclusion simply the general theory that, in the absence of evidence of abuse, a defect will normally have caused a tire's separation. Rather, the expert employed a more specific theory to establish the existence (or absence) of such abuse. Carlson testified precisely that in the absence of *at least two* of four signs of abuse (proportionately greater tread wear on the shoulder; signs of grooves caused by the beads; discolored sidewalls; marks on the rim flange) he concludes that a defect caused the separation. And his analysis depended upon acceptance of a further implicit proposition, namely, that his visual and tactile inspection could determine that the tire before him had not been abused despite some evidence of the presence of the very signs for which he looked (and two punctures).

For another thing, the transcripts of Carlson's depositions support both the trial court's initial uncertainty and its final conclusion. Those transcripts cast considerable doubt upon the reliability of both the explicit theory (about the need for two signs of abuse) and the implicit proposition (about the significance of visual inspection in this case). Among other things, the expert could not say whether the tire had traveled more than 10, or 20, or 30, or 40, or 50 thousand miles, adding that 6,000 miles was "about how far" he could "say with any certainty." * * * The court could reasonably have wondered about the reliability of a method of visual and tactile inspection sufficiently precise to ascertain with some certainty the abuse-related significance of minute shoulder/center relative tread wear differences, but insufficiently precise to tell "with any certainty" from the tread wear whether a tire had traveled less than 10,000 or more than 50,000 miles. And these concerns might have been augmented by Carlson's repeated reliance on the "subjective[ness]" of his mode of analysis in response to questions seeking specific information regarding how he could differentiate between a tire that actually had been overdeflected and a tire that merely looked as though it had been. * * * They would have been further augmented by the fact that Carlson said he had inspected the tire itself for the first time the morning of his first deposition, and then only for a few hours. (His initial conclusions were based on photographs.) * * *

[T]he court, after looking for a defense of Carlson's methodology as applied in these circumstances, found no convincing defense. Rather, it found (1) that "none" of the *Daubert* factors, including that of "general acceptance" in the relevant expert community, indicated that Carlson's testimony was reliable; * * * (2) that its own analysis "revealed no countervailing factors operating in favor of admissibility which could outweigh those identified in Daubert" * * *; and (3) that the "parties identified no such factors in their briefs." * * * For these three reasons *taken together,* it concluded that Carlson's testimony was unreliable.

Respondents now argue to us, as they did to the District Court, that a method of tire failure analysis that employs a visual/tactile inspection is a reliable method, and they point both to its use by other experts and to Carlson's long experience working for Michelin as sufficient indication that that is so. But no one denies that an expert might draw a conclusion from a set of observations based on extensive and specialized experience. Nor does anyone deny that, as a general matter, tire abuse may often be identified by qualified experts through visual or tactile inspection of the tire. * * * As we said before, * * * the question before the trial court was specific, not general. The trial court had to decide whether this particular expert had sufficient specialized knowledge to assist the jurors "in deciding the particular issues in the case." * * *

The particular issue in this case concerned the use of Carlson's two-factor test and his related use of visual/tactile inspection to draw conclusions on the basis of what seemed small observational differences. We have found no indication in the record that other experts in the industry use Carlson's two-factor test or that tire experts such as Carlson normally make the very fine distinctions about, say, the symmetry of comparatively greater shoulder tread wear that were necessary, on Carlson's own theory, to support his conclusions. Nor, despite the prevalence of tire testing, does anyone refer to any articles or papers that validate Carlson's approach. * * * Indeed, no one has argued that Carlson himself, were he still working for Michelin, would have concluded in a report to his employer that a similar tire was similarly defective on grounds identical to those upon which he rested his conclusion here. Of course, Carlson himself claimed that his method was accurate, but, as we pointed out in *Joiner,* "nothing in either *Daubert* or the Federal Rules of Evidence requires a district court to admit opinion evidence that is connected to existing data only by the *ipse dixit* of the expert." * * *

Respondents additionally argue that the District Court too rigidly applied *Daubert's* criteria. They read its opinion to hold that a failure to satisfy any one of those criteria automatically renders expert testimony inadmissible. The District Court's initial opinion might have been vulnerable to a form of this argument. There, the court, after rejecting respondents' claim that Carlson's testimony was "exempted from *Daubert*-style scrutiny" because it was "technical analysis" rather than "scientific evidence," simply added that "none of the four admissibility criteria outlined by the *Daubert* court are satisfied." * * * Subsequently, however, the court granted respondents' motion for reconsideration. It then explicitly recognized that the relevant reliability inquiry "should be 'flexible,'" that its "'overarching subject [should be] . . . validity' and reliability," and that "*Daubert* was intended neither to be exhaustive nor to apply in every case." * * * And the court ultimately based its decision upon Carlson's failure to satisfy either *Daubert's* factors *or any other* set of reasonable reliability criteria. In light of the record as developed by the parties, that conclusion was within the District Court's lawful discretion.

In sum, Rule 702 grants the district judge the discretionary authority, reviewable for its abuse, to determine reliability in light of the particular facts and circumstances of the particular case. The District Court did not abuse its discretionary authority in this case. Hence, the judgment of the Court of Appeals is

Reversed.

Notes

1. Justice Scalia, joined by Justices O'Connor and Thomas, concurred, but with the following addenda:

> I join the opinion of the Court, which makes clear that the discretion it endorses—trial-court discretion in choosing the manner of testing expert reliability—is not discretion to abandon the gatekeeping function. I think it worth adding that it is not discretion to perform the function inadequately. Rather, it is discretion to choose among *reasonable* means of excluding expertise that is *fausse* and science that is junky. Though, as the Court makes clear today, the *Daubert* factors are not holy writ, in a particular case the failure to apply one or another of them may be unreasonable, and hence an abuse of discretion.

2. Must a trial court hold a F.R.E. § 104(a) "Daubert" hearing when assessing the admissibility of an expert's testimony? Most courts have said no. *See* Goebel v. Denver & Rio Grande Western R.R. Co., 215 F.3d 1083 (10th Cir.2000); Nelson v. Tennessee Gas Pipeline Co., 243 F.3d 244 (6th Cir.2001). In Padillas v. Stork–Gamco, Inc., 186 F.3d 412 (3d Cir.1999), the court reversed a district court decision to exclude plaintiff's expert testimony on design defect because the trial judge failed to hold an *in limine* hearing.

> An in limine hearing will obviously not be required whenever a Daubert objection is raised to a proffer of expert evidence. Whether to hold one rests in the sound discretion of the district court. But when the ruling on admissibility turns on factual issues, as it does here, at least in the summary judgment context, failure to hold such a hearing may be an abuse of discretion. *Id.* at 418

On the other hand, in Oddi v. Ford Motor Co., 234 F.3d 136 (3d Cir.2000), the court rejected plaintiffs claim that he was entitled to an *in limine* hearing. Distinguishing *Padillas*, the court noted that here the trial court had before it extensive depositions and affidavits of the plaintiff's expert. It noted that in *Padillas* absent a hearing the court "could not determine what methodology the expert used, and the reliability of the expert's conclusion could therefore not be established ... However, here [the expert] did explain how he arrived at his opinion, and he did it in as much detail as possible given the nature of his 'inquiry.' " *Id.* at 154.

3. Justice Stevens dissented from part III of the court's opinion, believing that the case should have been sent back to the appellate court for its assessment of whether the trial judge abused his discretion. In Weisgram v. Marley Co., 528 U.S. 440, 120 S.Ct. 1011, 145 L.Ed.2d 958 (2000) the district court entered a judgment on a jury verdict for plaintiff and denied defendant's motion for judgment as a matter of law or a new trial. The Eighth Circuit vacated and directed entry of judgment as a matter of law for manufacturer after concluding the trial court had erred in admitting expert testimony. The plaintiff appealed, arguing the appellate court abused its discretion when it failed to remand the case to the trial court. The Supreme Court affirmed and held that appellate courts may direct entry of judgment as a matter of law for verdict loser, upon determining that after the exclusion there is no longer sufficient evidence to sustain the verdict.

JAUREQUI v. CARTER MANUFACTURING CO., INC.
United States Court of Appeals, Eighth Circuit, 1999.
173 F.3d 1076.

HANSEN, CIRCUIT JUDGE.

Juan Jaurequi brought this diversity action against John Deere Company and Deere & Company (collectively "Deere"), alleging that design and warning defects associated with a Deere corn head proximately caused an accident in which Jaurequi's legs were amputated. Shortly before trial, Deere moved for the exclusion of Jaurequi's proffered expert testimony and for summary judgment. The district court granted both motions, and Jaurequi appeals. We affirm.

I.

Deere manufactures mobile combines which harvest and process various crops, including corn, beans, and milo. Although the same combine may be used for all of these crops, each crop requires the use of a different "head" to gather the standing crop and convey it into the combine for processing. For example, when harvesting corn, a corn head must be attached to the front of the combine. This case involves a 1974 Model 343 Deere three row corn head. The corn head contains several moving parts which draw the corn stalks in and separate the ears of corn from the stalks as the combine moves down the rows of corn. A cross auger then moves the separated ears to the rear center of the head where the ears are deposited at the throat of the combine and are then taken up into the bowels of the combine where they are husked and shelled. A corn head is intended to be used only for corn, and only while the combine is moving through a field harvesting standing corn.

The corn head at issue in this case was manufactured and sold by Deere in Moline, Illinois, in 1974. In 1986, Carter Manufacturing (Carter) acquired the already used corn head on behalf of Texas Triumph Seed Company (Texas Triumph). Texas Triumph, a specialty seed company, required a unit specially suited for harvesting small test plots of corn. Carter constructed this specialty unit out of a 1961 Massey–Harris combine and the Deere corn head. Both components were significantly modified so that they could work together and so that they could accomplish Texas Triumph's needs. This new combination unit was suitable only for research plot use and was named the "Carter Plot Combine." Deere was never informed or consulted regarding the modifications made to its corn head.

When Carter purchased the corn head, all of the original warnings Deere had placed on it had been obliterated with green paint by a previous owner. Rather than replacing the warnings with updated ones available from a Deere dealer, or uncovering the original warnings, Carter again painted over the entire corn head, including the already painted over warnings, with red paint to match the red Massey combine.

The plaintiff, Juan Jaurequi, was an employee of Texas Triumph when the injuries giving rise to this suit occurred. On the day he was injured, Jaurequi, together with other Texas Triumph employees, was using the Carter Plot Combine to harvest milo, also known as sorghum. The Carter Plot Combine had not been constructed with this use in mind, and the unit was in fact incapable of harvesting standing milo. However, it was possible to place hand-picked milo heads directly on the cross auger at a point well behind the corn head's dangerous crop gathering parts where it would then be transported to the throat of the combine. This is what Jaurequi and his coworkers were doing on the date of the accident. The workers hand-picked the standing milo and brought this milo in bags to the stationary but operating combine. The workers, standing to the side and near the rear of the corn head, then dumped the bags of milo onto the cross auger at the rear of the corn head at a point behind the corn head's uselessly churning snapping rolls and gathering chains and hooks. This process was necessary because Texas Triumph had neglected to bring its milo harvester to the Missouri test plots.

On the day before the accident, when the machine had been used to harvest corn, Jaurequi was warned by a coworker, Jerry Anquiano, that he should never go in front of the corn head, because the machine's dangerous moving parts would pull him into the corn head. Additionally, on the day of the accident, Jaurequi was twice warned by Ronald Terrell, another coworker, that he should not feed the corn head from the front because he risked being pulled in by the moving parts. Terrell instructed Jaurequi to stand to the side of the corn head when feeding the machine. However, Jaurequi persisted in feeding the machine from the front. On one occasion, Jaurequi moved too close to the corn head's moving parts which gather the stalks and snap off the ears. His legs became enmeshed in the machinery, and he sustained severe injuries to both legs which have left him a double amputee. * * *

Jaurequi later brought this products liability action against Deere, alleging that Deere was both strictly liable and liable in negligence for failures to warn and for design defects associated with the corn head. Central to Jaurequi's case was the proffered "expert" testimony of Terrence Willis and Harold Wakely.

Terrence Willis, a mechanical engineer, was prepared to testify that Jaurequi "was not provided the necessary detail which would identify where the hazard zone ended and the safety region began," and that "[s]uch specific information cannot be determined visually ... because of the speed at which the gathering chains suddenly emerge from under the snout...." * * * It was Willis's opinion that although "the motion of the gathering chains in the immediate vicinity of the snapping rolls is open and obvious," the risk is not obvious at the point at which the gathering chains emerge, which is closer to the tips of the snouts. * * * At the point of emergence, Willis stated that the gathering hooks are invisible because they are moving so fast. Willis admitted, however, that he had never observed the corn head at issue while it was running * * * and that he had never seen any corn head in operation except from the roadside during his various trips through the Illinois countryside. * * * When asked for the basis of his opinion that the gathering hooks are invisible when they emerge from under the snout, Willis stated, "I guess as an engineer, I know what it looks like in the running mode." * * *

Willis believed that the corn head should have been equipped with "larger and more prominent warnings." * * * In particular, Willis proposed "a plastic covered snout area colored with black and yellow stripes." * * * Willis speculated in his affidavit that, had the warnings been designed as he suggests, they would not have been painted over. * * * However, he admitted in his deposition that he had no basis for this belief.* * *

In his affidavit, Willis stated that Jaurequi was not warned of the "specifics of this hazard zone." * * * In his deposition, however, Willis admitted that he had not evaluated Jaurequi's behavior and had focused his analysis only on the question of whether the mechanical design of the corn head was defective. * * * He admitted that he did not actually know what Jaurequi knew or did not know. * * *

Willis further opined that Deere should have incorporated "awareness barriers" into its corn head. * * * Specifically, Willis opined that awareness barriers would foster safety and would not interfere with the operation of the machine. * * * Willis admitted, however, that he had not studied the feasibility of this idea, much less designed and tested it. * * * He additionally admitted that he was unaware of any studies indicating the effectiveness of awareness barriers, * * * and that he had never before designed an awareness barrier of any kind. * * * Finally, Willis admitted that he was aware of no manufacturer of corn heads which had ever put awareness barriers in front of the gathering chains as he proposed should be done. * * *

Jaurequi also proffered the expert testimony of Harold Wakely, a human factors engineer who holds a doctorate in experimental psychology. Wakely was prepared to testify that the corn head was defective because the original warning signs were too small, too far from the point of danger, and oriented at an angle which made them difficult to read. Additionally, Wakely was prepared to testify that the warning did not emphasize the precise point at which the danger was concentrated. Wakely admitted, however, that he had never read the original warnings on the corn head and did not know what these warnings actually said. * * *

Wakely felt that alternative warnings were necessary because the gathering hook on the gathering chain "is not visible at the time of danger but only after the greatest hazard is passed as it moves away from the subject." * * * Wakely stated in his affidavit that although Jaurequi had been warned by his coworkers of general dangers associated with the combine, Jaurequi was not aware of "the exact location of the danger," i.e., the gathering hooks at the point of emergence under the snouts. * * * This statement contradicts Wakely's deposition testimony that "I don't know what kind of warning was given to Mr. Jaurequi." * * *

Wakely admitted that he has found no product of any vintage which employed the types of warnings, stripes, and chevrons that he was advocating. * * * Wakely speculated in his deposition that John Deere could have made the snouts out of plastic and that this might have made it difficult to paint over any chevrons. * * * When pressed, however, Wakely admitted that he had no basis for saying "how long or if paint would stay on the plastic." * * *

Shortly before trial, Deere moved to exclude the testimony of Willis and Wakely, and for summary judgment on all claims. The district court granted both motions, and this appeal followed.

II.

A. *Exclusion of Expert Testimony*

Jaurequi contests the district court's decision to exclude the testimony of Willis and Wakely. We review the district court's exclusion of expert testimony for abuse of discretion. * * *

In excluding the testimony of Willis and Wakely, the district court relied on Daubert v. Merrell Dow Pharm., Inc. * * * Jaurequi contends that such reliance was improper, arguing that the proffered testimony of Willis and Wakely was not scientific but rather technical and does not fall within the scope of Daubert.

* * * [R]ecently, however, the Court has squarely held that Daubert applies to all expert testimony. Kumho Tire Co., Ltd. v. Carmichael, * * * The Court reaffirmed that we are to test the district court's evidentiary ruling excluding expert testimony under an abuse of discretion standard recognizing "that the law grants the trial judge broad latitude to determine" whether the Daubert factors "are, or are not, reasonable measures of reliability in a particular case." * * *

CASES APPLYING DAUBERT

While this court has never attempted to map the exact boundaries within which a Daubert-type analysis is appropriate, several of our post-Daubert, pre-Kumho cases have applied the Daubert reliability factors to proffered expert testimony very similar to that of Willis and Wakely in this case. See Dancy v. Hyster Co., 127 F.3d 649, 652 (8th Cir.1997) (district court properly looked to Daubert reliability factors for guidance regarding the admissibility of proffered expert testimony in alternative design case) * * *; Peitzmeier [v. Hennessy Indus., Inc., 97 F.3d 293, 296–97 (8th Cir. 1997)] (same); Pestel v. Vermeer Mfg. Co., 64 F.3d 382, 384 (8th Cir.1995) (same).

Our decision in Peitzmeier is particularly instructive. There the plaintiff objected to the district court's invocation of Daubert, arguing that Daubert is inapplicable to "opinions founded on basic engineering principles." Peitzmeier, 97 F.3d at 297. We disagreed, writing that the Supreme Court's discussion in Daubert is relevant not only to "novel scientific testimony," but also to engineering testimony regarding alternative designs in products liability cases. * * * Because the expert's proposed safety mechanisms had been neither designed nor tested, because his ideas had not been subjected to peer review, and because the expert presented no evidence regarding his theory's rate of error or its general acceptance, we upheld the trial court's exclusion of the proffered expert testimony. * * *

In Pestel, another alternative design case, we similarly upheld the district court's exclusion of proffered engineering testimony, again citing relevant Daubert factors. We pointed out that the proposed safety device had not been tested or even developed. * * * With regard to peer review, we noted that the expert had not consulted others in the industry or subjected the concept to any manufacturers, engineers, or professors for scrutiny. * * * We also noted that the plaintiff had presented no evidence regarding general acceptance. * * * We expressly declined to consider the fourth Daubert factor—potential rate of error—because this factor did not appear to be relevant to our inquiry. * * *

In Robertson v. Norton Co., 148 F.3d 905, 907–08 (8th Cir.1998), we held that a district court abused its Daubert discretion in admitting expert opinion concerning the adequacy of product warnings which accompanied a heavy duty sander/grinder because, among other reasons, the expert had not even reviewed the warnings accompanying the grinder. Similarly, in this case the witness Wakely did not know what the original Deere warnings said, and in fact testified that he did not care what they had said. * * *

As these cases illustrate, it is clearly established in this circuit that when engineers are brought in to suggest that a product should have been designed differently, the district court does not err in looking to Daubert for guidance as to whether such testimony should be admitted or excluded. Of course, the Daubert reliability factors should only be relied upon to the extent that they are relevant, * * * and the district court must customize its inquiry to fit the facts of each particular case, * * *. In short, although

> [n]ot every guidepost outlined in Daubert will necessarily apply to expert testimony based on engineering principles and practical experience, ... the district court's "preliminary assessment of whether the reasoning or methodology underlying the testimony is scientifically valid and of whether that reasoning or methodology properly can be applied to the facts in issue" is no less important.

Watkins v. Telsmith, Inc., 121 F.3d 984, 990–91 (5th Cir.1997) (quoting Daubert, 509 U.S. at 592–93, 113 S.Ct. 2786) * * *.

Our Daubert approach to expert testimony is fully in accord with the Supreme Court's decision in Kumho. * * * The specific factors identified in Daubert must be considered by the trial judge when they reasonably measure the reliability of the expert's testimony. * * *

Application to Proffered Expert Testimony

In the case at hand, Willis was prepared to testify that the corn head was unreasonably dangerous because it lacked awareness barriers. However, Willis has not attempted to construct or even draw the suggested device, much less test its utility as a safety device or its compatibility with the corn head's proper function. Nor has he pointed to any manufacturer that incorporates awareness barriers into corn heads or similar farming machinery. In short, he has provided no basis for us to believe that his opinions are anything more than unabashed speculation. We therefore hold that the district court did not abuse its broad discretion in concluding that the proffered testimony regarding the lack of awareness barriers flunked the reliability prong of Daubert.

The remainder of the expert testimony proffered by Jaurequi dealt with the sufficiency of the warnings on the corn head. As summarized above, Willis and Wakely felt that the warnings were deficient in placement, design, orientation, and content. However, this testimony also appears unreliable. Neither Willis nor Wakely had created or even designed a warning device which would have been more appropriate, much less tested its effectiveness. In fact, as indicated above, Wakely admitted that he had never even read the warnings which Deere did employ (and which had been painted over before Carter acquired the corn head) and that he was unaware of their content. Finally, neither Willis nor Wakely pointed in their deposition testimony to other manufacturers of farm machinery who were employing chevrons or pictorial warnings in 1974. The reliability of their testimony is therefore extremely questionable.

* * * Our close review of the district court's consideration of the expert testimony convinces us that it analyzed the proffered testimony in exactly the same way the Supreme Court said the inquiry may be done under Daubert and Rule 702 * * * and that its decision to exclude the testimony of both experts was not only well within its broad discretion as to such matters, but also correct.

That said, the more serious problem with the proffered expert testimony on the failure-to-warn issue is one of relevance. It is undisputed that the corn head's warnings had twice been painted over by persons other than Deere. Neither expert had any basis for concluding that the warnings they proposed would have escaped either painter's brush. Thus, the alleged inadequacies of the content of these warnings cannot be considered a cause in fact of Jaurequi's injuries. * * * Deere cannot be held responsible for the deliberate obliteration by others of Deere's warnings years after the product was sold.

Furthermore, Jaurequi admitted to four different people on eight separate occasions that he had persisted in loading milo from the front of the corn head even after he had been warned of how dangerous this behavior was. Two coworkers had instructed Jaurequi not to load milo from the front because doing so brought him into close proximity with the dangerous moving parts of the corn head. The last of these warnings came shortly before Jaurequi walked into the moving parts of the corn head and lost his legs. We have held that where, " 'despite deficient warnings by the manufacturer, a user is fully aware of the danger which a warning would alert him or her of, then the lack of warning is not the proximate cause of the injury.' " Peitzmeier, 97 F.3d at 300 * * * Such was clearly the case with Jaurequi.

These breaks in the causal chain render any insufficiencies in the painted-over Deere warning signs irrelevant. We therefore find no abuse of discretion in the district court's exclusion of the proffered expert testimony on the failure to warn issue.

B. SUMMARY JUDGMENT
* * *

The district court was * * * correct in granting Deere's motion for summary judgment.

III.

Accordingly, we affirm the judgment of the district court.

Notes

1. *Jaurequi* is one of a growing number of opinions addressing the admissibility of expert opinion in "traditional" design defect and warning defect cases. As in *Jaurequi*, the design defect cases frequently turn on the extent to which the expert has tested the feasibility of the proffered alternative design. *See* Rogers v. Ford Motor Co., 952 F.Supp. 606 (N.D.Ind.1997) (expert testimony excluded because he failed to demonstrate by testing or other analysis that alternative design of seat belt would produce fewer injuries); Blevins v. New Holland North America, Inc. 128 F.Supp.2d 952 (W.D.Va.2001) (expert testimony that manufacturer should have equipped hay baler with emergency stop system admissible); Smith v. Ingersoll–Rand Co., 214 F.3d 1235 (10th Cir.2000) (human factors engineer testimony that lack of visibility around machine used to remove pavement prior to resurfac-

ing a road made it defective held to be admissible); Bourelle v. Crown Equipment Corp., 220 F.3d 532 (7th Cir.2000) (expert's testimony regarding alternative design for forklift unreliable and inadmissible); Oddi v. Ford Motor Co., 234 F.3d 136 (3d Cir.2000) (expert testimony asserting that truck was not crashworthy due to defective design of front bumper properly excluded under *Daubert*); White v. Ford Motor Co., 312 F.3d 998 (9th Cir. 2002) (expert's opinion as to cause of parking brake failure admissible); Guy v. Crown Equipment Corp., 394 F.3d 320 (5th Cir. 2004) (expert testimony proposing alternative design to forklift properly excluded); Zaremba v. General Motors Corp., 360 F.3d 355 (2d Cir. 2004) (expert testimony on alternative roof design for automobile failed to meet any of the *Daubert* factors).

2. Another group of cases address the adequacy of the expert's causal analysis when it is uncertain whether a product defect caused the injury. *See* Pride v. BIC Corp., 218 F.3d 566 (6th Cir.2000) (plaintiff's experts' testimony that defect in lighter caused fire was unreliable and therefore inadmissible); Oglesby v. General Motors Corp., 190 F.3d 244 (4th Cir.1999) (expert testimony that manufacturing defect in hose connector caused accident was inadmissible); Ford Motor Co. v. Ridgway, 135 S.W.3d 598 (Tex. 2004) (source of truck fire undetermined).

WESTBERRY v. GISLAVED GUMMI AB
United States Court of Appeals, Fourth Circuit, 1999.
178 F.3d 257.

WILKINS, CIRCUIT JUDGE:

James Curtis and Connie Rena Westberry brought this action against Gislaved Gummi AB (GGAB), claiming that GGAB was liable under South Carolina law for damages the Westberrys suffered as a result of the company's failure to warn of the danger of the talcum powder (talc) lubricant GGAB placed on rubber gaskets it manufactured. GGAB presently appeals the judgment against it following a jury verdict in favor of the Westberrys, and Mrs. Westberry cross appeals the refusal of the district court to grant an additur or a new trial on the issue of her damages. We affirm.

I.

GGAB manufactured rubber products, including rubber gaskets used in window frames. Westberry's employer purchased gaskets produced by GGAB for use in manufacturing skylights and windows in the Greenwood, South Carolina plant where Westberry was employed. Because the rubber gaskets were difficult to handle without a protective lubricant, GGAB applied a coating of talc to the gaskets prior to shipping.

Westberry's first duties in the plant involved working on a production line adjacent to the area where the GGAB gaskets were cut. In January 1994, he changed to the position of gasket cutter, which required him to remove the gaskets from their boxes and to place them in the cutting machine. Although the evidence was conflicting, Westberry testified that these duties brought him into contact with high concentrations of airborne talc. Westberry received no warning that talc could be dangerous, and he wore no protective gear when performing his duties as a gasket cutter.

Following his change to the position of gasket cutter, Westberry began to experience unrelenting sinus problems. He was hospitalized for four days in July 1994 with a severe sinus infection and was treated with antibiotics by his physician, Dr. W. David Isenhower, Jr. Beginning in September 1994, Westberry underwent several sinus surgeries in an attempt to alleviate his sinus pain, including a procedure in which his frontal sinuses were obliterated.

Westberry brought the present action against GGAB, claiming that its failure to warn him of the dangers of breathing airborne talc proximately caused the aggravation of his pre-existing sinus condition. He alleged causes of action sounding in strict liability, breach of warranty, and negligence. Following a trial at which Westberry's treating physician, Dr. Isenhower, provided the principal evidence of causation, the jury returned a verdict in favor of Westberry. Although GGAB challenges the judgment on a number of grounds, the only one warranting extended discussion is its contention that the district court abused its discretion in admitting the opinion testimony of Dr. Isenhower concerning the cause of Westberry's sinus problems.

II.

* * *

A district court considering the admissibility of expert testimony exercises a gate keeping function to assess whether the proffered evidence is sufficiently reliable and relevant. * * * The inquiry to be undertaken by the district court is "a flexible one" focusing on the "principles and methodology" employed by the expert, not on the conclusions reached. *Daubert,* 509 U.S. at 594–95, 113 S.Ct. 2786. In making its initial determination of whether proffered testimony is sufficiently reliable, the court has broad latitude to consider whatever factors bearing on validity that the court finds to be useful; the particular factors will depend upon the unique circumstances of the expert testimony involved. *See Kumho Tire Co.,* 119 S.Ct. at 1175–76. * * * The court, however, should be conscious of two guiding, and sometimes competing, principles. On the one hand, the court should be mindful that Rule 702 was intended to liberalize the introduction of relevant expert evidence. *See Cavallo v. Star Enter.,* 100 F.3d 1150, 1158–59 (4th Cir.1996). And, the court need not determine that the expert testimony a litigant seeks to offer into evidence is irrefutable or certainly correct. *See id.* As with all other admissible evidence, expert testimony is subject to being tested by "[v]igorous cross-examination, presentation of contrary evidence, and careful instruction on the burden of proof." *Daubert,* 509 U.S. at 596, 113 S.Ct. 2786. On the other hand, the court must recognize that due to the difficulty of evaluating their testimony, expert witnesses have the potential to "be both powerful and quite misleading." *Id.* at 595, 113

S.Ct. 2786 (internal quotation marks omitted). And, given the potential persuasiveness of expert testimony, proffered evidence that has a greater potential to mislead than to enlighten should be excluded. *See United States v. Dorsey,* 45 F.3d 809, 815–16 (4th Cir.1995).

This court reviews the decision of a district court to admit or exclude evidence for an abuse of discretion. * * *

A.

GGAB argues that the district court erred in failing to undertake a determination of the reliability and relevance of the evidence as required by Rule 702 because it believed such an analysis was applicable only to novel scientific opinions. We agree. As the Supreme Court recently made clear, the obligation of a district court to determine whether expert testimony is reliable and relevant prior to admission applies to all expert testimony. *See Kumho Tire Co.,* 119 S.Ct. at 1174. Nevertheless, because we can affirm the evidentiary ruling of the district court on a ground different from that employed below, we consider whether Dr. Isenhower's testimony was sufficiently reliable and relevant to warrant admission. * * *

B.

GGAB contends that Dr. Isenhower's testimony was inadmissible because it was not based on reliable scientific methodology. This is so, it argues, because Dr. Isenhower had no epidemiological studies, no peer-reviewed published studies, no animal studies, and no laboratory data to support a conclusion that the inhalation of talc caused Westberry's sinus disease. Further, GGAB continues, Dr. Isenhower did not have any tissue samples indicating that talc was found in Westberry's sinuses, nor did he have studies showing that talc, at any threshold level, causes sinus disease. Instead, Dr. Isenhower merely relied on a differential diagnosis—supported in part by the temporal relationship between Westberry's exposure to talc and the problems he experienced with his sinuses—in reaching the conclusion that Westberry's sinus problems were caused by his exposure to talc from GGAB's gaskets. GGAB maintains that neither a differential diagnosis nor a temporal relationship between exposure and onset or worsening of symptoms is sufficient to establish the reliability of Dr. Isenhower's opinion. We disagree.

Differential diagnosis, or differential etiology, is a standard scientific technique of identifying the cause of a medical problem by eliminating the likely causes until the most probable one is isolated. * * * A reliable differential diagnosis typically, though not invariably, is performed after "physical examinations, the taking of medical histories, and the review of clinical tests, including laboratory tests," and generally is accomplished by determining the possible causes for the patient's symptoms and then eliminating each of these potential causes until reaching one that cannot be ruled out or determining which of those that cannot be excluded is the most likely. *Kannankeril v. Terminix Int'l, Inc.,* 128 F.3d 802, 807 (3d Cir.1997) (explaining that "[d]ifferential diagnosis is defined for physicians as 'the determination of which of two or more diseases with similar symptoms is the one from which the patient is suffering, by a systematic comparison and contrasting of the clinical findings' ") (quoting *Stedman's Medical Dictionary* 428 (25th ed.1990)); *see McCullock v. H.B. Fuller Co.,* 61 F.3d 1038, 1044 (2d Cir.1995) (describing differential etiology as an analysis "which requires listing possible causes, then eliminating all causes but one"); *Glaser v. Thompson Med. Co.,* 32 F.3d 969, 978 (6th Cir.1994) (recognizing that differential diagnosis is "a standard diagnostic tool used by medical professionals to diagnose the most likely cause or causes of illness, injury and disease"). * * *

We previously have upheld the admission of an expert opinion on causation based upon a differential diagnosis. *See Benedi v. McNeil-P.P.C., Inc.,* 66 F.3d 1378, 1383–85 (4th Cir.1995) (holding that expert testimony by treating physician concerning cause of plaintiff's liver failure—acetaminophen combined with alcohol—was admissible despite the lack of epidemiological data). And, the overwhelming majority of the courts of appeals that have addressed the issue have held that a medical opinion on causation based upon a reliable differential diagnosis is sufficiently valid to satisfy the first prong of the Rule 702 inquiry. *Compare Heller,* 167 F.3d at 154, 156–57 (concluding that a proper differential diagnosis is adequate to support expert medical opinion on causation), *Kennedy v. Collagen Corp.,* 161 F.3d 1226, 1228–30 (9th Cir.1998) (holding district court abused its discretion in excluding an expert opinion on causation based upon a reliable differential diagnosis), *cert. denied,* 526 U.S. 1099, 119 S.Ct. 1577, 143 L.Ed.2d 672 (1999), *Baker,* 156 F.3d at 252–53 (determining that a differential diagnosis rendered expert opinion on causation sufficiently reliable for admission), *Zuchowicz v. United States,* 140 F.3d 381, 385–87 (2d Cir.1998) (upholding determination that expert opinion was reliable in part based on differential diagnosis), *and Ambrosini v. Labarraque,* 101 F.3d 129, 140–41 (D.C.Cir.1996) (holding that because expert opinion was based on differential diagnosis, district court abused its discretion in refusing to admit it), *with Moore v. Ashland Chem. Inc.,* 151 F.3d 269, 277–79 (5th Cir.1998) (en banc) (concluding that district court did not abuse its discretion in rejecting expert opinion on causation without discussing why differential diagnosis was insufficient to support admission of opinion into evidence), *cert. denied,* 526 U.S. 1064, 119 S.Ct. 1454, 143 L.Ed.2d 541 (1999). Thus, we hold that a reliable differential diagnosis provides a valid foundation for an expert opinion.

C.

GGAB next maintains that, assuming a differential diagnosis may provide a trustworthy foundation for an opinion on causation, Dr. Isenhower's differential diagnosis did not. According to GGAB, Dr. Isenhower's differential diagnosis was unreliable because he could not "rule in" talc as a possible cause of sinus disease. *See Raynor v. Merrell Pharms. Inc.,* 104 F.3d 1371, 1374–76 (D.C.Cir.1997) (holding that expert opinion that exposure to Bendectin caused birth defects based in part on differential diagnosis was not admissible in light of "overwhelming body of contradictory epidemiological evidence" (internal quotation marks omitted)). Further, GGAB contends that Dr. Isenhower's differential diagnosis was not reliable because he failed to "rule out" all other possible causes.

GGAB asserts that Dr. Isenhower could not "rule in" talc because he had no means of accurately assessing what level of exposure was adequate to produce the sinus irritation Westberry experienced. In order to carry the burden of proving a plaintiff's injury was caused by exposure to a specified substance, the "plaintiff must demonstrate 'the levels of exposure that are hazardous to human beings generally as well as the plaintiff's actual level of exposure.'" *Mitchell v. Gencorp Inc.,* 165 F.3d 778, 781 (10th Cir.1999) (quoting *Wright v. Willamette Indus., Inc.,* 91 F.3d 1105, 1106 (8th Cir.1996)); *see Allen v. Pennsylvania Eng'g Corp.,* 102 F.3d 194, 199 (5th Cir.1996) (concluding that "[s]cientific knowledge of the harmful level of exposure to a chemical, plus knowledge that the plaintiff was exposed to such quantities, are minimal facts necessary to sustain the plaintiffs' burden in a toxic tort case"); *cf. Black v. Food Lion, Inc.,* 171 F.3d 308, 314 (5th Cir.1999) (explaining that "[t]he underlying predicates of any cause-and-effect medical testimony are that medical science understands the physiological process by which a particular disease or syndrome develops and knows what factors cause the process to occur"). But, it must also be recognized that

> [o]nly rarely are humans exposed to chemicals in a manner that permits a quantitative determination of adverse outcomes.... Human exposure occurs most frequently in occupational settings where workers are exposed to industrial chemicals like lead or asbestos; however, even under these circumstances, it is usually difficult, if not impossible, to quantify the amount of exposure.

Federal Judicial Center, *Reference Manual on Scientific Evidence* 187 (1994). Consequently, while precise information concerning the exposure necessary to cause specific harm to humans and exact details pertaining to the plaintiff's exposure are beneficial, such evidence is not always available, or necessary, to demonstrate that a substance is toxic to humans given substantial exposure and need not invariably provide the basis for an expert's opinion on causation. *See Heller,* 167 F.3d at 157 (noting "that even absent hard evidence of the level of exposure to the chemical in question, a medical expert could offer an opinion that the chemical caused plaintiff's illness").

Although GGAB is correct that Dr. Isenhower had no scientific literature on which to rely to "rule in" talc as a possible basis for Westberry's sinus condition, it was undisputed that inhalation of high levels of talc irritates mucous membranes. * * * The Material Safety Data Sheet (MSDS) for talc provided by GGAB for Dr. Isenhower's examination provided that "[i]nhalation of dust in high concentrations irritates mucous membranes," J.A. 659, and it is undisputed that sinuses are mucous membranes. Further, although Dr. Isenhower did not point to Westberry's exposure to a specific level of airborne talc, there was evidence of a substantial exposure. Westberry testified that he was exposed to very high levels of airborne talc throughout his workday. According to his testimony, when he removed the gaskets from the box in which they had been shipped, the gaskets, which were black, had so much talc on them that they appeared to be white or gray. And, talc was released into the air as the gaskets went through the cutting machines. Westberry testified that the talc that settled from the air around his work area was so thick that one could see footprints in it on the floor. He further stated that he worked in clouds of talc and that it covered him and his clothes. Moreover, at the close of his workday Westberry was required to blow off his work area and machinery with a blower, stirring up all of the talc that had fallen. This testimony concerning the level of airborne talc was adequate to permit a factfinder to conclude that Westberry was exposed to high concentrations of airborne talc, and there was no dispute that exposure to high concentrations of airborne talc could cause irritation to mucous membranes. Indeed, GGAB's expert conceded on cross-examination that if the levels of airborne talc were those testified to by Westberry (and relied upon by Dr. Isenhower), his own opinion that talc did not cause Westberry's sinus problems would change. Thus, this clearly is not a case in which the plaintiff was unable to establish any substantial exposure to the allegedly defective product. *Cf. Wintz v. Northrop Corp.,* 110 F.3d 508, 512–14 (7th Cir.1997) (holding that expert opinion was not reliable when expert formed opinion that in utero exposure to bromide caused birth defects, but expert had no information concerning the mother's work environment or her exposure to bromide); *Allen,* 102 F.3d at 199 (concluding that expert opinion that plaintiff's brain cancer was caused by exposure to ethylene oxide in his hospital workplace was not sufficiently reliable to support admissibility when "experts' background information concerning [plaintiff's] exposure to [chemical was] so sadly lacking as to be mere guesswork").

Additionally, Dr. Isenhower testified that he relied in part on the temporal proximity of Westberry's exposure to talc in his workplace to the onset and worsening of Westberry's sinus problems to conclude that talc was the cause. GGAB makes no serious argument that a strong temporal relationship between Westberry's exposure to talc and his sinus disease did not exist, but contends that the temporal relationship between Westberry's exposure to talc and his sinus problems was not a proper basis for an expert opinion on causation. Again, we disagree.

Of course, the mere fact that two events correspond in time does not mean that the two necessarily are related in any causative fashion. *See Heller,* 167 F.3d at 154. But, depending on the circumstances, a temporal relationship between exposure to a substance and the onset of a disease or a worsening of symptoms can provide compelling evidence of causation. *See id.; Zuchowicz,* 140 F.3d at 385, 390; *Cavallo v. Star Enter.,* 892 F.Supp. 756, 774 (E.D.Va.1995) (explaining that "there may be instances where the temporal connection between exposure to a given chemical and subsequent injury is so compelling as to dispense with the need for reliance on standard methods of toxicology," for example, if one were exposed to a substantial amount of "chemical X and immediately thereafter developed symptom Y"); *see also* 2 Stephen A. Saltzburg et al., *Federal Rules of Evidence Manual* 1233–34 (7th ed.1998). *But see Moore,* 151 F.3d at 278 (holding that "[i]n the absence of an established scientific connection between exposure and illness, or compelling circumstances such as those discussed in *Cavallo,* the temporal connection between exposure to chemicals and an onset of symptoms, standing alone, is entitled to little weight").

Here, Dr. Isenhower testified that Westberry's sinus disease began shortly after Westberry began working as a gasket cutter. Furthermore, during the time he was treating Westberry, Dr. Isenhower experimented with keeping Westberry out of work and noticed that his sinus condition improved when he was not working but worsened when he returned. Under these circumstances, we conclude that the temporal relationship between Westberry's exposure and the onset and worsening of his sinus disease provided support for Dr. Isenhower's opinion that talc was the source of the problem.

GGAB also argues that Dr. Isenhower's differential diagnosis was unreliable because he failed to "rule out" all potential causes other than talc because he did not explain why a cold Westberry developed in May 1994 and water skiing he did over the summer of 1994 could not have accounted for his sinus problems. A differential diagnosis that fails to take serious account of other potential causes may be so lacking that it cannot provide a reliable basis for an opinion on causation. *See In re Paoli R.R. Yard PCB Litig.,* 35 F.3d at 758–61. However, "[a] medical expert's causation conclusion should not be excluded because he or she has failed to rule out every possible alternative cause of a plaintiff's illness." *Heller,* 167 F.3d at 156. The alternative causes suggested by a defendant "affect the weight that the jury should give the expert's testimony and not the admissibility of that testimony," *id.* at 157, unless the expert can offer *"no* explanation for why she has concluded [an alternative cause offered by the opposing party] was not the sole cause," *id.* at 156. *See also Kannankeril,* 128 F.3d at 808 (explaining that "[i]n attacking the differential diagnosis performed by the plaintiff's expert, the defendant may point to a plausible cause of the plaintiff's illness other than the defendant's actions" and "[i]t then becomes necessary for the plaintiff's experts to offer a good explanation as to why his or her conclusion remains reliable") * * *.

Dr. Isenhower's testimony made clear that he considered and excluded other potential causes for Westberry's sinus disease. Furthermore, on cross-examination Dr. Isenhower explained why he did not believe that the cold Westberry developed in 1994 or the waterskiing he did over that summer accounted for his sinus problems. Accordingly, Dr. Isenhower's alleged failure to account for all possible alternative causes for Westberry's sinus problems did not prohibit the admissibility of his opinion as to causation.

III.

In sum, we reject GGAB's contention that Dr. Isenhower's testimony was invalid and untrustworthy. A reliable differential diagnosis provides a valid basis for an expert opinion on causation. And, Dr. Isenhower's differential diagnosis was sufficiently reliable. Because Dr. Isenhower's testimony satisfied the reliability and relevance standards of Rule 702, the district court properly admitted this testimony. * * *

AFFIRMED

Notes

1. In Cavallo v. Star Enterprise differential diagnosis is defined as "[A] process whereby medical doctors experienced in diagnostic techniques provide testimony countering other possible causes ... of the injuries at issue." 892 F.Supp. 756, 771 n. 31 (E.D.Va.1995) Unfortunately, the term is not used this way in medical discourse. Medical dictionaries define differential diagnosis as "diagnosis based on comparison of symptoms of two or more similar diseases to determine which the patient is suffering from." Taber's Cyclopedic Medical Dictionary 404 (14th ed.1981). Some courts do recognize that legal usage is contrary to medical usage and employ the more appropriate term "differential etiology" (the study of the causes of disease).

At one level, the confusion in terminology is only semantic. However, at another level the confusion can mislead. It is often said that physicians are well trained in the process of differential diagnosis and that they devote considerable attention in medical school to learning clinical reasoning. But training in the process of deducing *disease* based on a set of symptoms and laboratory tests and deducing the *cause* of an ailment, are not the same thing. Many physicians may have far less training in the latter task. As the district court in *Wynacht v. Beckman Instruments, Inc.*, notes

> [T]here is a fundamental distinction between Dr. Ziem's ability to render a medical diagnosis based on clinical experience and her ability to render an opinion on causation of Wynacht's injuries. Beckman apparently does not dispute, and the Court does not question, that Dr. Ziem is an experienced physician, qualified to diagnose medical conditions and treat patients. The ability to diagnose medical conditions is not remotely the same, however, as the ability to deduce, delineate, and describe, in a scientifically reliable manner, the causes of these medical conditions.

113 F.Supp.2d 1205, 1209 (E.D.Tenn.2000).

2. What is the role of differential diagnosis testimony? Consider the comment of the trial judge in *Cavallo*

> The process of differential diagnosis is undoubtedly important to the question of "specific causation." If other possible causes of an injury cannot be ruled out, or at least the probability of their contribution to causation minimized, then the "more likely than not" threshold for proving causation may not be met. But, it is also important to recognize that a fundamental assumption underlying this method is that the final suspected "cause" remaining after this process of elimination must actually be capable of causing the injury. That is, the expert must "rule

in" the suspected cause as well as "rule out" other possible causes. And, of course, expert opinion on this issue of "general causation" must be derived from a scientifically valid methodology.

892 F.Supp. 756, 771 (E.D.Va.1995).

The "rule in before ruling out" position of *Cavallo* presumes that at least in toxic tort cases a differential diagnosis, no matter how well done, can rarely, by itself, prove general causation. The *Cavallo* position has been repeated in numerous cases. *See* Ambrosini v. Labarraque, 101 F.3d 129, 138–39 (D.C.Cir.1996); Grimes v. Hoffmann–LaRoche, Inc., 907 F.Supp. 33, 38 (D.N.H.1995); Hall v. Baxter Healthcare Corp., 947 F.Supp. 1387, 1413 (D.Ore.1996); In re Breast Implant Litigation, 11 F.Supp.2d 1217, 1230 (D.Colo.1998); National Bank of Commerce v. Associated Milk Producers, Inc., 22 F.Supp.2d 942, 963 (E.D.Ark.1998), affirmed, 191 F.3d 858 (8th Cir.1999); Meister v. Medical Engineering Corp., 267 F.3d 1123 (D.C.Cir. 2001); Siharath v. Sandoz Pharmaceuticals Corp. 131 F.Supp.2d 1347, 1362 (N.D.Ga. 2001) aff'd Rider v. Sandoz Pharm. Corp., 295 F.3d 1194, 1201 (11th Cir. 2002); Clausen v. M/V New Carissa, 339 F.3d 1049, 1057–58 (9th Cir. 2003); McClain v. Metabolife International, Inc., 401 F.3d 1233, 1253 (11th Cir. 2005); Norris v. Baxter Healthcare Corp. 397 F.3d 878 (10th Cir. 2005).

As occurred in *Westberry*, the "rule in" requirement sometimes is presented as a question of dosage. *See* Mancuso v. Consolidated Edison, 56 F.Supp.2d 391, 403 (S.D.N.Y.1999); Mitchell v. Gencorp Inc., 165 F.3d 778, 781 (10th Cir.1999); Newton v. Roche Laboratories, Inc., 243 F.Supp.2d 672, 683 (W.D.Tex. 2002); Swallow v. Emergency Medicine of Idaho, P.A., 138 Idaho 589, 67 P.3d 68, 74 (2003); Christian v. Gray, 65 P.3d 591 (Okla. 2003); Burleson v. Texas Department of Criminal Justice, 393 F.3d 577, 587 (5th Cir. 2004); *Wills v. Amerada Hess Corp.*, 379 F.3d 32, 49 (2d Cir. 2004); Parker v. Mobil Oil Corp., 16 A.D.3d 648, 793 N.Y.S.2d 434 (2005). *But see* Becker v. National Health Products, Inc., 896 F.Supp. 100, 102 (N.D.N.Y. 1995); Kannankeril v. Terminix International, Inc., 128 F.3d 802 (3d Cir. 1997).

3. Most courts refuse to permit an expert to testify that a causal relationship exists solely on the basis of temporal order, i.e. the illness followed the exposure. Statements to this effect may be found in a number of swine flu cases from the early 1980s. *See* Hasler v. United States, 718 F.2d 202, 205 (6th Cir.1983). Post-*Daubert* opinions frequently take the position that such testimony should be excluded for lack of reliability. The judge's comments in Whiting v. Boston Edison Co., 891 F.Supp. 12 (D.Mass.1995) are typical:

> Dr. Winters (and Dr. Shalat) propound the argument that because [acute lymphocytic leukemia] is extremely rare in adult males, and because Gary Whiting was exposed to radiation before he contracted ALL, his ALL must have been caused by radiation exposure. This is a classic illustration of the logical fallacy post hoc ergo propter hoc. It ignores the fact that ALL can occur (and most often does) in adult males who have no history of occupational exposure to radiation, as well as the fact that adult males who are exposed to radiation at levels similar to

Gary Whiting's have no higher incidence of ALL than do unexposed adult males.

Whiting, 891 F.Supp. at 23 n. 52. *See also* Schmaltz v. Norfolk & Western Ry. Co., 878 F.Supp. 1119, 1122 (N.D.Ill.1995); Kelly v. American Heyer–Schulte Corp., 957 F.Supp. 873, 882 (W.D.Tex.1997); Nelson v. Am. Home Prods. Corp., 92 F.Supp.2d 954, 971 (W.D.Mo.2000); Schafersman v. Agland Coop., 262 Neb. 215, 631 N.W.2d 862 (2001); Swallow v. Emergency Medicine of Idaho, P.A., 138 Idaho 589, 67 P.3d 68, 74 (2003); Praytor v. Ford Motor Co., 97 S.W.3d 237 (Tex.App. 2002). *But see* Kannankeril v. Terminix International, Inc., 128 F.3d 802 (3d Cir.1997). For recent discussions of the differential diagnosis cases *see* Eggen, Clinical Medical Evidence of Causation in Toxic Tort Cases: Into the Crucible of *Daubert*, 38 Hou.L.Rev. 369 (2001); Sanders and Machal–Fulks, The Admissibility of Differential Diagnosis Testimony to Prove Causation in Toxic Tort Cases: The Interplay of Adjective and Substantive Law, 64, No.4 L. & Contemp.Probs. 107 (2001).

4. When a body of epidemiological evidence indicates a relative risk substantially less than 2.0, the plaintiff may not be able to show that it is more likely than not that the exposure caused her injury. Numerous writers have advocated the use of proportional liability in such cases. *See, e.g.*, Estep, Radiation Injuries and Statistics: The Need for a New Approach to Injury Litigation, 59 Mich.L.Rev. 259 (1960); Farber, Toxic Causation, 71 Minn. L.Rev. 1219 (1987); Makdisi, Proportional Liability: A Comprehensive Rule to Apportion Tort Damages Based on Probability, 67 N.C. L.Rev. 1063 (1989); Landes and Posner, Tort Law as a Regulatory Regime for Catastrophic Personal Injuries, 13 J. Legal Stud. 417 (1984); Robinson, Probabilistic Causation and Compensation for Tortious Risk, 14 J. Legal Stud. 779 (1985); Rosenberg, The Causal Connection in Mass Exposure Cases: A "Public Law" Vision of the Tort System, 97 Harv.L.Rev. 849 (1984). While these proposals for proportional liability take many forms, they may be divided into three major categories:

> The [first] category would permit plaintiff to recover a portion of her damages only after she has suffered the injury or acquired the disease. Thus, if defendant created a twenty percent probability of having caused the harm, an injured plaintiff would recover twenty percent of her damages. If defendant created a sixty percent probability of having caused the harm, plaintiff would recover sixty percent of her damages. [Under this category plaintiffs would sue after the harm manifests itself.]
>
> [The second] category would permit plaintiff to recover a portion of her prospective damages before she has been injured or made ill. Thus, if defendant exposed ten persons to a toxin that created a ten percent risk of causing a certain disease in the future, each exposed person would recover ten percent of her prospective damages in advance.
>
> Under the third category * * * plaintiffs also would sue before injury. A judgment for plaintiff would require the tortfeasor either to set aside an amount equal to the exposure victims' prospective damages in an insurance fund or to buy insurance. Money from the fund, or proceeds from the insurance policy, would later go to those exposed persons who actually contracted the illness or injury.

Fischer, Proportional Liability: Statistical Evidence and the Probability Paradox, 46 Vand.L.Rev. 1201, 1202 (1993).

5. The courts have yet to adopt proportional liability in such cases. Should they? For a criticism of the theory, *see* Fischer, Proportional Liability: Statistical Evidence and the Probability Paradox, 46 Vand.L.Rev. 1201 (1993).

6. In the post-*Daubert* world, many toxic cases with questionable causation never reach the jury. The trial judge excludes the plaintiff's causal experts on reliability grounds and then enters a summary judgment because the plaintiff is no longer able to present a prima facie case on causation. *See, e.g.,* Heller v. Shaw Industries, Inc., 167 F.3d 146 (3d Cir.1999). Four of the five main cases in this section follow this path. One should not be mislead, however, into believing that this is the modal outcome when expert admissibility is challenged. On the contrary, most cases result in a decision to admit. A number of factors conspire to skew the distribution of published opinions. First, expert testimony often goes unchallenged. Second, even when challenged, a decision to admit is less likely to lead to a published district court opinion. Third, decisions to admit (as well as many decisions to exclude parts of an expert's testimony) are interlocutory and, therefore, not immediately appealable. Intervening events, including settlement and favorable trial outcome, may render the admissibility determination moot.

7. On December 1, 2000 amended Federal Rules of Evidence 702 and 703 became effective. Rule 702 now states:

> If scientific, technical, or other specialized knowledge will assist the trier of fact to understand the evidence or to determine a fact in issue, a witness qualified as an expert by knowledge, skill, experience, training, or education, may testify thereto in the form of an opinion or otherwise, if (1) the testimony is based upon sufficient facts or data, (2) the testimony is the product of reliable principles and methods, and (3) the witness has applied the principles and methods reliably to the facts of the case.

One early case interpreting the new provision, the court in *Rudd v. General Motors Corp.*, 127 F.Supp.2d 1330, 1335–1337 (M.D. Ala. E.D. 2001) had this to say:

> According to the advisory committee notes, Rule 702 was amended, effective December 1, 2000, in order expressly to endorse the gatekeeping model of the trial judge envisioned by the Supreme Court in *Daubert.* * * *
>
> [T]he advisory committee notes for Rule 702 explain that the 2000 amendment, while intended as an endorsement of the *Daubert* conception of the trial judge as gatekeeper, was not intended to "codify" the specific factors mentioned in *Daubert.*
>
> In *Kumho,* an automobile-products liability case, the Supreme Court clarified that the trial court's Rule 702 gatekeeping responsibilities obtain equally for all expert testimony, not just scientific testimony. * * *
>
> The advisory committee notes for Rule 702, as amended effective December 1, 2000, comment that the amended rule was formulated in

part to affirm Kumho's holding that the trial judge's gatekeeper function applies to all expert testimony. But the newly-expanded rule goes further than *Kumho* to "provide [ ] some general standards that the trial court *must* use to assess the reliability and helpfulness of proffered expert testimony." Id. (emphasis added). While there is a dearth of case law interpreting the new reliability standards set forth in Rule 702 (that "(1) the testimony is based upon sufficient facts or data, (2) the testimony is the product of reliable principles and methods, and (3) the witness has applied the principles and methods reliably to the facts of the case"), * * * the advisory committee notes provide some guidance, remarking that

> "Nothing in this amendment is intended to suggest that experience alone—or experience in conjunction with other knowledge, skill, training or education—may not provide a sufficient foundation for expert testimony.... If the witness is relying solely or primarily on experience, then the witness must explain how that experience leads to the conclusion reached, why that experience is a sufficient basis for the opinion, and how that experience is reliably applied to the facts. The trial court's gatekeeping function requires more than simply taking the expert's word for it."

Id. (internal citations and quotations omitted).

While the inquiry into "reliable principles and methods" has been a familiar feature of admissibility analysis under *Daubert,* the new Rule 702 appears to require a trial judge to make an evaluation that delves more into the facts than was recommended in *Daubert,* including as the rule does an inquiry into the sufficiency of the testimony's basis ("the testimony is based upon sufficient facts or data") and an inquiry into the application of a methodology to the facts ("the witness has applied the principles and methods reliably to the facts of the case"). * * * Neither of these two latter questions that are now mandatory under the new rule—the inquiries into the sufficiency of the testimony's basis and the reliability of the methodology's application—were expressly part of the formal admissibility analysis under *Daubert.*

However, while this court can find no case law precisely implementing these kinds of analyses, the amended rule's reliability-of-application inquiry was at least foreshadowed in *General Electric Co. v. Joiner,* * * * where the Supreme Court suggested that *Daubert*'s distinction between factual conclusions and methodology might be too sharply-drawn. * * *

Going beyond the permissive language of *Joiner,* the plain language of new Rule 702, as well as the advisory committee notes to the new Rule, makes it clear that this court is now *obliged* to screen expert testimony to ensure it stems from, not just a reliable methodology, but also a sufficient factual basis and reliable application of the methodology to the facts. Despite this express provision for judicial evaluation of such factually-entwined matters, however, the advisory committee notes caution that the trial judge must still avoid usurping the role of the trier of fact:

"[The revised rule] is not intended to authorize a trial court to exclude an expert's testimony on the ground that the court believes one version of the facts and not the other.... [T]he rejection of expert testimony is the exception rather than the rule. *Daubert* did not work a seachange over federal evidence law, and the trial court's role as gatekeeper is not intended to serve as a replacement for the adversary system. Vigorous cross-examination, presentation of contrary evidence, and careful instruction on the burden of proof are the traditional and appropriate means of attacking shaky but admissible evidence."

Fed.R.Evid. 702, advisory committee notes, 2000 amendment (internal citations and quotations omitted).

8. To what extent is the entire admissibility debate really about the jury system? *See* Green, Expert Witnesses and Sufficiency of Evidence in Toxic Substances Litigation: The Legacy of Agent Orange and Bendectin Litigation, 86 Nw.U.L.Rev. 643 (1992); Sanders, From Science to Evidence: The Testimony on Causation in the Bendectin Cases, 46 Stan.L.Rev. 1 (1993); Lunney, Protecting Juries from Themselves: Restricting the Admission of Expert Testimony in Toxic Tort Cases, 48 S.M.U. L.Rev. 103 (1994); Sanders, The Merits of the Paternalistic Justification for Restrictions on the Admissibility of Expert Evidence, 33 Seton Hall L.Rev. 881 (2003). For all of the rhetoric about how well juries perform in assessing expert testimony, there is surprisingly little empirical research on point. For a review of what we do know, *see* Vidmar, The Performance of the American Civil Jury: An Empirical Perspective, 40 Ariz.L.Rev. 849 (1998).

WHERE THE STATES ARE

Daubert and its progeny apply only to the federal courts. In the wake of *Daubert* a majority of states have adopted Daubert or a rule quite similar to Daubert. However, a substantial number of states have chosen not to adopt Daubert. Most of these states have chosen to stay with some version of the Frye test. Following is a recent decision in North Carolina adopting this course.

HOWERTON V. ARAI HELMET, LTD.
Supreme Court of North Carolina, 2004.
358 N.C. 440, 597 S.E.2d 674.

WAINWRIGHT, JUSTICE.

On 5 October 1996, plaintiff, W. Bruce Howerton, Jr., D.D.S. ("Howerton"), suffered a devastating motorcycle accident while riding his off-road motorcycle at a motocross practice track in western North Carolina. * * * The motocross track on which Howerton rode the day of the accident was a winding dirt course with numerous jumps and obstacles. Howerton wore typical motocross safety gear, including riding boots, knee braces, gloves, and an Arai "MX/a" motorcycle helmet. While jumping a course obstacle known as a "table top," Howerton landed atop another motorcycle rider who had entered the landing area of the jump perpendicular to Howerton's line of travel. The two motorcycles became entangled on impact, causing Howerton's motorcycle to stop abruptly and launching Howerton into an airborne somersault over the handlebars of his motorcycle. Howerton landed upside down on the back of his helmeted head, breaking the chin guard attached to his helmet and forcing his chin downward into his chest. As he landed, Howerton experienced what he described as severe popping, crunching, and pain in his neck. Lying in the dirt, Howerton struggled to breathe and was unable to move his legs; he immediately recognized the severity of his injuries. Paramedics were summoned and Howerton was transported to the hospital by helicopter. As a result of his accident, Howerton sustained debilitating cervical vertebral fractures at the C5/C6 level that left him a quadriplegic, permanently paralyzed from the neck down.

On 4 October 1999, Howerton brought actions against the other motorcycle rider, the owners of the motocross track, and Arai Helmet, Ltd., the manufacturer of the motorcycle helmet Howerton was wearing when the accident occurred. Our review of this matter concerns only Howerton's claims against Arai.

* * *

Howerton alleged, among other things, that Arai negligently designed, manufactured, and promoted a helmet that was unreasonably dangerous under ordinary usage and that such negligence was the direct and proximate cause of his quadriplegia. * * *

The Arai "MX/a" helmet worn by Howerton on the day of his accident was equipped with a flexible, removable guard across the chin and mouth that was secured to the helmet on each side by nylon screws. By comparison, many other helmets are designed with a rigid, integral chin bar that is structurally molded into the helmet. In addition to protecting the motorcyclist's mouth and nose area from debris, some of these rigid guards are purportedly designed to increase the strength and stability of the motorcyclist's neck upon impact by preventing the neck from rotating too far forward. Such a chin guard limits the forward rotation of the head by stopping against the motorcyclist's chest, protecting the head and neck from extreme forward rotation.

The purpose of the guard on the specific Arai "MX/a" helmet worn by Howerton on the day of his accident is subject to conflicting characterizations which lie at the heart of this litigation. Howerton complains that the chin guard on his Arai helmet should have restricted the movement of his neck like a rigid chin guard and cushioned his head on impact so as to prevent the catastrophic spinal injury which he suffered. Howerton alleges that when the nylon screws securing the chin guard to his helmet broke on impact, his head was allowed to rotate too far forward, beyond its normal anatomical range, resulting in a "hyperflexion" of his neck which caused the resulting cervical fractures and paralysis. * * *

According to Arai, however, "[t]he intended function of the mouth guard on the MX/a helmet is to prevent pebbles, dirt and small branches from contacting that part of the rider's face behind the mouth guard while riding off-road or in wooded areas." Arai insists that its breakaway rock guard was never designed "to function as an integral part of a full face helmet and was never intended to offer the same degree of facial protection ... in the full range of possible motorcycle accidents." Rather, Arai contends that the chin guard on its helmet was intentionally designed to bend or break away on impact so as to minimize excessive and dangerous torquing of the neck.

To prove the alleged defectiveness of his Arai helmet and its causal connection to his injuries, Howerton offered the opinion testimony of * * * key expert witnesses:*

(1) Professor Hugh H. Hurt, Jr. is an expert in motorcycle accidents and motorcycle helmets. Professor Hurt is President of the Head Protection Research Laboratory of Southern California and Professor Emeritus of Safety Science at the University of Southern California. Professor Hurt has researched and published extensively in the field of motorcycle accidents and motorcycle helmet safety for more than twenty-five years. Based upon Professor Hurt's extensive credentials, Arai stipulated that he is qualified as an expert pursuant to North Carolina Rule of Evidence 702. Professor Hurt's opinion was that the flexible chin guard on Howerton's Arai helmet was defectively designed and manufactured such that it broke loose on impact and failed to limit the forward rotation of Howerton's head. Instead of stopping the chin against the sternum, as a rigid chin guard would do, Professor Hurt opined that the flexible chin guard on Howerton's Arai helmet broke on impact, allowing Howerton's neck to flex towards the chest, beyond its normal range of movement. Finding the chin guard on the Arai helmet to be "flexible and weak."

* * *

(4) Charles Edward Rawlings, III, M.D. is a board certified neurosurgeon. With more than ten years of neurosurgical experience, Dr. Rawlings has conducted numerous spinal surgeries on patients with cervical fractures similar to the one sustained by Howerton. Although Dr. Rawlings was not Howerton's treating neurosurgeon, Dr. Rawlings reviewed Howerton's medical records and opined that Howerton suffered a flexion-compression injury that was the cause of his paralysis.

On 7 January 2002, Arai filed its "Omnibus Motion for Summary Judgment on All Claims and Motion to Exclude Testimony of Plaintiff's Experts on the Issue of Causation." In this motion, Arai argued that:

> Plaintiff must prove that his injuries were caused by the product at issue. In this complex product liability case, Plaintiff cannot meet

---

* [Ed note: The plaintiff proffered the opinion of four experts.]

this burden absent admissible expert testimony on the issue of causation. * * * None of [plaintiff's] experts have performed testing relevant to the causation issues in this case. None have undertaken independent research to support their hypotheses or subjected their hypotheses to peer-review via publication. Each has relied on inadequate or non-existent data that renders their opinions subject to an unreasonably high rate of error. Finally, none of these expert[s] have been able to demonstrate that their opinions are generally accepted within their own fields. In fact, many of the opinions expressed by these experts are contrary to the existing body of medical or biomechanical research. In some cases, the opinions expressed by these experts are in conflict with one another, or in conflict with their own previously published opinions. Accordingly, the Arai Defendants move that the opinions of Plaintiff's experts be held inadmissible at trial pursuant to Rule 104 and Rule 702 of the North Carolina Rules of Evidence and the related authorities of the North Carolina courts and United States Supreme Court. Further, that the Court award the Arai Defendants summary judgment on all claims based on the inability of Plaintiff to offer admissible evidence of causation.

On 29 January 2002, the trial court conducted a brief hearing on the matter, considering arguments from counsel, discovery materials, and pleadings. The trial court did not, however, hear live voir dire testimony from the experts.

On 1 March 2002, the trial court granted Arai's motion to exclude the testimony of Howerton's experts on the issue of causation. With respect to each of Howerton's four experts, the trial court made the following findings of fact:

Professor Hugh H. Hurt, Jr.

16. Professor Hugh Hurt is a helmet expert from California. He opined that a full-face helmet equipped with an integrated chin bar would have prevented plaintiff's injury.

17. Professor Hurt's opinion was based on the assertion that he had noticed red "u" or "v" shaped marks on the chests of three motorcycle riders who were involved in motorcycle accidents while wearing full-face helmets. The necks of the three riders were not broken, however, two of these riders were killed in the accidents at issue. Professor Hurt deduced that these marks were caused by the rigid integrated chin bars on the riders' full-face helmets striking their chests during the accident, and concluded that this may have prevented a neck injury.

18. Professor Hurt explained the basis of his opinion that the marks on the chests of three riders proves that rigid chin bars prevent neck injuries as follows: "like Bo knows baseball, Hurt knows motorcycle accidents."

19. Professor Hurt could not quantify the extent to which a full-face helmet would prevent forward flexion of the head and neck.

20. Professor Hurt did not test or perform independent research on his hypothesis that full-face helmets equipped with rigid chin bars prevent neck injuries. He did not subject his hypothesis to peer review by publishing it to his peers.

21. Professor Hurt did not report his hypothesis to the United States government, for whom he conducted extensive studies that included work on motorcycle helmet safety.

22. Professor Hurt was not able to identify any published work by any author that expressly supported his hypothesis and, thus, did not present any evidence other than his unsupported assertions that his hypothesis is generally accepted in his field.

23. Indeed, Professor Hurt's published work did not support—and in fact tends to contradict—his hypothesis that full-face helmets prevent neck injuries. In a University of Southern California report published in 1981, Professor Hurt published data indicating that serious neck injuries occurred more frequently in riders wearing full-face helmets than in riders wearing full coverage helmets (i.e., open-face helmets that were not equipped with chin bars.).

24. Professor Hurt also opined that the MX/a design provided superior head protection, and that open-face helmets, that is, helmets without chin bars, are not defective.

25. Professor Hurt's opinion that a full-face helmet would have prevented plaintiff's injury is speculative and based on inadequate data.

26. Professor Hurt's opinion that a full-face helmet would have prevented plaintiff's injury is not reliable. Professor Hurt's opinion was not developed through sound scientific or engineering methods. Professor Hurt has not performed relevant testing or independent research and has not subjected his hypothesis that full face helmets prevent neck injuries to peer-review by publishing that claim. Further, he was unable to demonstrate that his hypothesis is generally accepted in his field by pointing to any published support for his claim. Finally, to the extent that his methods represent a technique, it is clear that this technique is subject to an unacceptably high risk of error.

* * *

Dr. Charles Rawlings

33. Dr. Charles Rawlings is a neurosurgeon. Dr. Rawlings currently is attending law school and has not actively practiced neurosurgery on a full time basis since at least January of 2000.

34. Dr. Rawlings has never performed independent research or testing on the mechanisms of cervical fractures. He has never published any medical article on the mechanisms of cervical fracture. He has never published on hyperflexion neck injuries.

35. Dr. Rawlings opined that plaintiff suffered no injuries, including his paralysis, prior to the time his head rotated forward beyond the normal range of motion.

36. When deposed Dr. Rawlings admitted that the medical literature does identify a "hyperflexion" injury of the cervical spine. Dr. Rawlings conceded that the hallmark features of hyperflexion injuries include bilateral or unilateral locked facets. He further conceded that plaintiff's injury did not involve bilateral or unilateral locked facets.

37. Due to the absence of these features, Dr. Rawlings defined plaintiff's injury as a flexion-compression injury. Dr. Rawlings nevertheless opined that eighty percent of all compression-flexion injuries involve hyperflexion. However, Dr. Rawlings was unable to identify any published medical literature that supports this claim.

38. Dr. Rawlings never examined plaintiff and reviewed only a selected portion of his medical records. Although Dr. Rawlings offered opinions based on efforts to compare plaintiff's accident to the accidents experienced by patients in his practice, he did not have adequate data to make such a comparison. To the extent that this represented a medical technique, if at all, it incorporated an unacceptably high potential for error.

39. Dr. Rawlings also opined based on plaintiff's radiology films that plaintiff's head rotated ten to twenty degrees beyond his normal anatomical range. However, he conceded that he has never published his claimed ability to draw such conclusions from radiology films. Nor could he cite any published authority supporting the conclusion that such an estimate can be accurately derived from medical records or radiology films. Dr. Rawlings further testified that a body of scientific literature may exist that addresses head rotation with respect to neck injury, but conceded that he had made no effort to research this literature.

40. Dr. Rawlings made no attempt to validate his hypothesis that plaintiff's head rotated ten to twenty degrees beyond his normal anatomical range. He could not point to any tests, measurements or literature supporting his opinion on this point.

41. Dr. Rawlings was unable to offer any medically reliable opinion on the extent to which plaintiff's head may have been rotated forward at impact. He conceded that unless the amount of force is known, it is impossible to distinguish one degree and forty-five degrees of flexion based on radiology films. Dr. Rawlings

conceded that he did not know the amount of force involved in this accident. Dr. Rawlings acknowledged that he had no medical basis to opine about whether plaintiff's head was rotated forward in flexion five degrees or forty-five degrees at impact.

42. Even though he did not know the force involved in the accident and could not accurately identify the position of plaintiff's head at impact, Dr. Rawlings opined that plaintiff would not have been paralyzed but for his head rotating forward beyond the normal anatomical range of motion. He admitted, however, that there are no objective criteria that can be used to confirm this hypothesis. Nor could he point to any medical literature indicating that it is possible to state whether a particular patient would be paralyzed based on a given set of variables.

43. Dr. Rawlings opinioned that plaintiff experienced an anterior teardrop fracture of C5 and that this feature was indicative of a hyperflexion mechanism. This opinion was generally inconsistent with the testimony of the treating neurosurgeon who used the anterior face of C5 as a site to attach a metal plate to fuse plaintiff's vertebra and was in a superior position to judge its condition. Dr. Rawlings' claim that C5 was the only possible source of the bone fragment at issue is contrary to the report of the attending radiologist. In any event, the Arai defendants presented evidence that even if a teardrop fracture occurred, fractures of this type are not specific to hyperflexion injury mechanisms.

44. Dr. Rawlings' opinion that plaintiff's injury was caused by hyperflexion is speculative and based on inadequate data.

45. Dr. Rawlings' opinion that plaintiff's injury was caused by hyperflexion is not reliable. Dr. Rawlings' opinion was not based on sound scientific or medical methods. He has not performed independent research or testing on cervical injury mechanisms or on hyperflexion. He has never subjected his related hypotheses to peer-review by publication. Moreover, the hypotheses underlying Dr. Rawlings' opinion are not generally accepted. Finally, to the extent that his methods represent a technique, it is clear that his potential for error is inappropriately high.

* * *

Based upon these findings of fact, the trial court excluded the testimony of all of Howerton's causation experts, ruling in relevant part that:

1. North Carolina has adopted *Daubert v. Merrell Dow Pharmaceuticals, Inc.,* 509 U.S. 579, 113 S.Ct. 2786, 125 L.Ed.2d 469 (1993). *See State v. Goode,* 341 N.C. 513, 527, 461 S.E.2d 631, 639 (1995); *see also State v. Bates,* 140 N.C.App. 743, 748, 538 S.E.2d 597, 600 (2000).

2. Even before the issuance of the *Daubert* decision, North Carolina courts adopted "reliability" as the touchstone of admissibility for expert opinion testimony as demonstrated in *State v. Pennington,* 327 N.C. 89, 98, 393 S.E.2d 847, 852 (1990). The indicia of reliability identified by the North Carolina Supreme Court in *Pennington* are consistent with the indicia of reliability found in *Daubert*. The opinions expressed by plaintiff's experts fail under either analysis.

3. The inquiry of the Court is not limited to the qualifications of the experts. Implicit in Rule 702 of the North Carolina Rules of Evidence is the precondition that the matters or data upon which an expert bases his opinion be recognized in the scientific community as sufficiently reliable and relevant. * * * The test of reliability involves a preliminary assessment of whether the reasoning or methods at issue are sufficiently valid. *Goode,* 341 N.C. at 527, 461 S.E.2d at 639 (citing *Daubert*).

4. The Court, in its discretion, has concluded that Professor Hurt's opinion that a full-face helmet design would have prevented plaintiff's injury is unreliable and inadmissible.

* * *

6. The Court, in its discretion, has concluded that Dr. Rawlings' opinion that plaintiff's injuries were caused by hyperflexion is unreliable and inadmissible.

* * *

8. After reviewing all of the relevant materials submitted by the parties, and based on the preceding findings of fact and conclusions of law, the Court, in its discretion, concludes that the above-cited opinions of Professor Hurt, Mr. Hooper, Dr. Rawlings and Dr. Hutton, should be excluded from the trial of this matter.

With the testimony of each of his causation experts excluded * * * Howerton was without any admissible evidence to establish a prima facie case that his injuries were caused by Arai's allegedly defective helmet. Thus, the trial court granted summary judgment in favor of Arai * * *.

On 5 March 2002, Howerton gave Notice of Appeal to the North Carolina Court of Appeals, arguing, among other things, that: (1) the trial court erred in its reliance upon and application of *Daubert* to exclude the expert testimony advanced by Howerton; * * *

The North Carolina Court of Appeals rejected all of Howerton's assignments of error and affirmed the order of the trial court in its entirety. *Howerton v. Arai Helmet, Ltd.,* 158 N.C.App. 316, 581 S.E.2d 816 (2003). * * *

Applying an abuse of discretion standard of review, the Court of Appeals evaluated the causation testimony of each of Howerton's four experts under the basic *Daubert* criteria and held that the trial court's decision to exclude all such testimony was neither arbitrary nor an abuse of discretion.

* * *

On 21 August 2003, this Court allowed Howerton's petition for discretionary review. * * *

This case initially presents us with the question of whether North Carolina has adopted the federal standard under *Daubert v. Merrell Dow Pharmaceuticals* for ruling on the admissibility of expert testimony under North Carolina Rule of Evidence 702. The Court of Appeals held that we have impliedly done so and Arai argues that we should now expressly do so. For the reasons stated below, we reject both of these contentions.

* * *

North Carolina Rule of Evidence 702 reads, in pertinent part:

> (a) If scientific, technical or other specialized knowledge will assist the trier of fact to understand the evidence or to determine a fact in issue, a witness qualified as an expert by knowledge, skill, experience, training, or education, may testify thereto in the form of an opinion.

It is well-established that trial courts must decide preliminary questions concerning the qualifications of experts to testify or the admissibility of expert testimony. N.C.G.S. § 8C–1, Rule 104(a) (2003). When making such determinations, trial courts are not bound by the rules of evidence. *Id*. In this capacity, trial courts are afforded "wide latitude of discretion when making a determination about the admissibility of expert testimony." *State v. Bullard,* 312 N.C. 129, 140, 322 S.E.2d 370, 376 (1984). Given such latitude, it follows that a trial court's ruling on the qualifications of an expert or the admissibility of an expert's opinion will not be reversed on appeal absent a showing of abuse of discretion. * * *

The most recent North Carolina case from this Court to comprehensively address the admissibility of expert testimony under Rule 702 is *State v. Goode,* which set forth a three-step inquiry for evaluating the admissibility of expert testimony: (1) Is the expert's proffered method of proof sufficiently reliable as an area for expert testimony? (2) Is the witness testifying at trial qualified as an expert in that area of testimony? (3) Is the expert's testimony relevant?

In the first step of the *Goode* analysis, the trial court must determine whether the expert's method of proof is sufficiently reliable as an area for expert testimony. * * *

Under *Goode,* to determine whether an expert's area of testimony is considered sufficiently reliable, "a court may look to testimony by an expert specifically relating to the reliability, may take judicial notice, or may use a combination of the two." 341 N.C. at 530, 461 S.E.2d at 641. Initially, the trial court should look to precedent for guidance in determining whether the theoretical or technical methodology underlying an expert's opinion is reliable. Although North Carolina does not exclusively adhere to the *Frye* "general acceptance" test, *Pennington,* when specific precedent justifies recognition of an established scientific theory or technique advanced by an expert, the trial court should favor its admissibility, provided the other requirements of admissibility are likewise satisfied. *See, e.g., State v. Williams,* 355 N.C. 501, 553–54, 565 S.E.2d 609, 640 (2002) (recognizing the admissibility of DNA evidence and upholding its use as the basis of an opinion by a properly qualified expert in forensic DNA analysis), *cert. denied,* 537 U.S. 1125, 123 S.Ct. 894, 154 L.Ed.2d 808 (2003); *Goode,* (reliability of bloodstain pattern interpretation supported in part by prior appellate acceptance of such technique in North Carolina and other jurisdictions); * * *

Conversely, there are those scientific theories and techniques that have been recognized by this Court as inherently unreliable and thus generally inadmissible as evidence. *See, e.g.,* * * * *State v. Grier,* 307 N.C. 628, 645, 300 S.E.2d 351, 361 (1983) (holding that polygraphs are inadmissible in any trial, even if otherwise stipulated to by the parties).

Where, however, the trial court is without precedential guidance or faced with novel scientific theories, unestablished techniques, or compelling new perspectives on otherwise settled theories or techniques, a different approach is required. Here, the trial court should generally focus on the following nonexclusive "indices of reliability" to determine whether the expert's proffered scientific or technical method of proof is sufficiently reliable: "the expert's use of established techniques, the expert's professional background in the field, the use of visual aids before the jury so that the jury is not asked 'to sacrifice its independence by accepting [the] scientific hypotheses on faith,' and independent research conducted by the expert." *Pennington,* 327 N.C. at 98, 393 S.E.2d at 852–53 (quoting *Bullard,* 312 N.C. at 150–51, 322 S.E.2d at 382) * * *.

Within this general framework, reliability is thus a preliminary, foundational inquiry into the basic methodological adequacy of an area of expert testimony. This assessment does not, however, go so far as to require the expert's testimony to be proven conclusively reliable or indisputably valid before it can be admitted into evidence. In this regard, we emphasize the fundamental distinction between the admissibility of evidence and its weight, the latter of which is a matter traditionally reserved for the jury. * * *

Therefore, once the trial court makes a preliminary determination that the scientific or technical area underlying a qualified expert's opinion is sufficiently reliable (and, of course, relevant), any lingering questions or controversy concerning the quality of the expert's conclusions go to the weight of the testimony rather than its admissibility. *See, e.g.,* * * * *McLean v. McLean,* 323 N.C. 543, 556, 374 S.E.2d 376, 384 (1988) (concluding that deficiencies in the expert's methodology were relevant in considering the expert's credibility and the weight to be given his testimony, but that they did not render his opinion inadmissible). Here, we agree with the United States Supreme Court that "[v]igorous cross-examination, presentation of contrary evidence, and careful instruction on the burden of proof are the traditional and appropriate means of attacking shaky but admissible evidence." *Daubert,* 509 U.S. at 596, 113 S.Ct. at 2798, 125 L.Ed.2d at 484 * * *.

In the second step of analysis under *Goode,* the trial court must determine whether the witness is qualified as an expert in the subject area about which that individual intends to testify * * *.

As pertains to the sufficiency of an expert's qualifications, we discern no qualitative difference between credentials based on formal, academic training and those acquired through practical experience. In either instance, the trial court must be satisfied that the expert possesses "scientific, technical or other specialized knowledge [that] will assist the trier of fact to understand the evidence or to determine a fact in issue."

* * *

The third and final step under *Goode* concerns the relevancy of the expert's testimony. The trial court must always be satisfied that the expert's testimony is relevant. To this end, we defer to the traditional definition of relevancy set forth in the North Carolina Rules of Evidence: "'Relevant evidence' means evidence having any tendency to make the existence of any fact that is of consequence to the determination of the action more probable or less probable than it would be without the evidence." N.C.G.S. § 8C–1, Rule 401 (2003).

* * *

Based on our review of these well-settled principles of North Carolina law governing the admissibility of expert testimony under North Carolina Rule of Evidence 702, we are satisfied that our own approach is distinct from that adopted by the federal courts. * * *

While * * * North Carolina cases share obvious similarities with the principles underlying *Daubert,* application of the North Carolina approach is decidedly less mechanistic and rigorous than the "exacting standards of reliability" demanded by the federal approach. *See Weisgram,* 528 U.S. at 455, 120 S.Ct. at 1021, 145 L.Ed.2d at 972. Moreover, had we ever intended to adopt *Daubert* and supercede this established body of North Carolina case law, we would certainly have referenced the basic *Daubert* factors that have come to define the federal standard. But we did not.

We did not do so because we are not satisfied that the federal approach offers the most workable solution to the intractable challenge of separating reliable expert opinions from their unreliable counterparts, of distinguishing science from pseudoscience, or of discerning where in this "twilight zone" a "scientific principle or discovery crosses the line between the experimental and demonstrable stages." *Frye,* 293 F. at

1014. Obviously, there are no easy solutions to the inherent difficulties of determining the legal reliability of scientific and technical hypotheses. While the law works towards conclusiveness and finality, science operates on an evolving continuum of probabilities and likelihoods that, in many instances, is not consonant with the legal paradigm. In light of this dilemma, our challenge is to define a standard of admissibility that does not create more problems than it solves and that does not raise more questions than it answers.

One of the most troublesome aspects of the *Daubert* "gatekeeping" approach is that it places trial courts in the onerous and impractical position of passing judgment on the substantive merits of the scientific or technical theories undergirding an expert's opinion. We have great confidence in the skillfulness of the trial courts of this State. However, we are unwilling to impose upon them an obligation to expend the human resources required to delve into complex scientific and technical issues at the level of understanding necessary to generate with any meaningfulness the conclusions required under *Daubert*. * * *

When the United States Supreme Court jettisoned the "rigid 'general acceptance' requirement" of *Frye,* it did so in order to further the "liberal thrust of the Federal Rules and their 'general approach of relaxing the traditional barriers to "opinion" testimony.'" *Daubert,* 509 U.S. at 588, 113 S.Ct. at 2794, 125 L.Ed.2d at 480. We believe that in practice, however, application of the "flexible" *Daubert* standard has been anything but liberal or relaxed and that trial courts, such as the one in the present case, have often been reluctant to stray far from the original *Daubert* factors in their analysis of the reliability of expert testimony. * * *

As a consequence of these stringent threshold standards for admitting expert testimony, we are concerned with the case-dispositive nature of *Daubert* proceedings, whereby parties in civil actions may use pre-trial motions to exclude expert testimony under *Daubert* to bootstrap motions for summary judgment that otherwise would not likely succeed. As expressed in dicta by one federal trial court,

> This court notes that inherently, the judge's role in a *Daubert* determination [is] fraught with conflict. In most cases, if the court bars the testimony of one party's expert witness or witnesses, that party is unable to present an essential element of his or her claim, or to proffer a defense. Accordingly, judges are aware that applying *Daubert* heavy-handedly has the effect of lightening one's caseload, as a party stripped of its expert often must dismiss the claims or settle the lawsuit.

Brasher v. Sandoz Pharms. Corp., 160 F.Supp.2d 1291, 1295 n. 12 (N.D.Ala.2001); *see also* Lloyd Dixon & Brian Gill, RAND Institute for Civil Justice, *Changes in the Standards for Admitting Expert Evidence in Federal Civil Cases Since the* Daubert *Decision* 62 (2001) ("Challenges to expert evidence increasingly resulted in summary judgment after *Daubert.*").

Procedurally, this imbalance may be explained because trial courts apply different evidentiary standards when ruling on motions to exclude expert testimony and motions for summary judgment. In a motion for summary judgment, the evidence presented to the trial court must be admissible at trial, N.C.G.S. § 1A–1, Rule 56(e) (2003), and must be viewed in a light most favorable to the non-moving party. * * *

Not so in the case of preliminary motions to exclude expert testimony under *Daubert,* which are resolved under Rule of Evidence 104(a). Here, trial courts are not bound by the rules of evidence, are not required to view the evidence in a light favorable to the non-movant, and may preliminarily resolve conflicting issues of fact relevant to the *Daubert* admissibility ruling. N.C.G.S. § 8C–1, Rule 104(a). * * *

[W]e are concerned that trial courts asserting sweeping pre-trial "gatekeeping" authority under *Daubert* may unnecessarily encroach upon the constitutionally-mandated function of the jury to decide issues of fact and to assess the weight of the evidence. See * * * *Logerquist v. McVey,* 196 Ariz. 470, 488, 1 P.3d 113, 131 (2000) ("The *Daubert/Joiner/ Kumho* trilogy of cases ... puts the judge in the position of passing on the weight or credibility of the expert's testimony, something we believe crosses the line between the legal task of ruling on the foundation and relevance of evidence and the jury's function of whom to believe and why, whose testimony to accept, and on what basis."); *Bunting v. Jamieson,* 984 P.2d 467, 472 (Wyo.1999) (adopting *Daubert,* but nonetheless expressing concern that "application of the *Daubert* approach to exclude evidence has been criticized as a misappropriation of the jury's responsibilities.... '[I]t is imperative that the jury retain its fact-finding function.'" (citations omitted)).

Although our criticism of *Daubert* is largely anecdotal and by no means exhaustive, given the serious implications of these concerns, we believe that on balance the North Carolina law which has coalesced in *Goode* establishes a more workable framework for ruling on the admissibility of expert testimony under North Carolina Rule of Evidence 702. * * * We therefore expressly reject the federal *Daubert* standard upon which both the trial court and the Court of Appeals erroneously based their respective rulings. North Carolina is not, nor has it ever been, a *Daubert* jurisdiction.

* * *

Accordingly, we hereby vacate the judgment of the trial court on this issue and reverse the opinion of the Court of Appeals affirming that judgment. The matter is remanded to the trial court for further proceedings not inconsistent with this opinion.

* * *

In summary, for the reasons stated above, we hereby reverse the opinion of the Court of Appeals in its entirety and vacate the judgment of the trial court in its entirety. The case is remanded to the Court of

Appeals with instructions to remand to the trial court for further proceedings not inconsistent with this Court's opinion.

REVERSED AND REMANDED.

Justice BRADY did not participate in the consideration or decision of this case.

Justice PARKER concurring in part and dissenting in part.

I concur in the majority's holding that this Court has not adopted the federal test for admissibility of expert testimony enunciated in Daubert v. Merrell Dow Pharmaceuticals, Inc. and in the decision not to adopt the *Daubert* factors as the test for determining admissibility of expert testimony under Rule 702 of the North Carolina Rules of Evidence but to continue to adhere to the test enunciated in our prior case law.

However, I am constrained to dissent respectfully from the holding of the majority reversing the opinion of the Court of Appeals and vacating the trial court's order allowing defendant's motion to exclude testimony of plaintiff's experts and the trial court's order allowing defendants' omnibus motion for summary judgment. In my view plaintiff's experts' testimony failed to satisfy the first prong of the three-part analysis set forth in the majority opinion based on this Court's decision in *State v. Goode*, namely, whether "the expert's proffered method of proof [is] sufficiently reliable as an area for expert testimony." As revealed in the careful analysis of the evidence in the trial court's findings, none of plaintiff's expert witnesses had done independent research or used established techniques to substantiate their respective proffered hypotheses as to (i) how the injury occurred, and (ii) whether the injury would have been prevented had plaintiff's helmet had a rigid mouth guard rather than a flexible one. *See State v. Pennington* (stating nonexclusive indices of reliability).

The trial court relied on both *Daubert* and *Pennington* in exercising its discretion to exclude the experts' testimony as to causation. Given this Court's jurisprudence governing the admissibility of expert testimony, the trial court's use of the *Daubert* factors does not in my opinion render the trial court's ruling fatally defective. *See Shore v. Brown*, 324 N.C. 427, 428, 378 S.E.2d 778, 779 (1989) (stating that "[i]f the correct result has been reached, the judgment will not be disturbed even though the trial court may not have assigned the correct reason for the judgment entered")

* * *

Notes

1. Other states that have rejected Daubert include California: *See* People v. Leahy, 8 Cal.4th 587, 34 Cal.Rptr.2d 663, 882 P.2d 321 (Cal. 1994); New York: People v. Wesley, 83 N.Y.2d 417, 611 N.Y.S.2d 97, 633 N.E.2d 451 (N.Y. 1994); Florida: Brim v. State, 695 So.2d 268 (Fla.1997); Kansas: Kuhn

v. Sandoz Pharm. Corp., 270 Kan. 443, 14 P.3d 1170 (2000); and Minnesota: Goeb v. Tharaldson, 615 N.W.2d 800 (Minn.2000). *See* Hamilton, The Movement from Frye to Daubert: Where Do the States Stand?, 38 Jurimetrics J. L. Sci. & Tech. 201 (1999); Bernstein, Frye, Frye, Again: The Past, Present, and Future of the General Acceptance Test, 4 Jurimetrics J. L. Sci. & Tech. 385 (2001); Conley and Gaylord, Scientific Evidence in the State Courts, 44 No. 4 Judges' J. 6 (2005).

2. The *Howerton* opinion suggests that if prior opinions have ruled on the admissibility of expert testimony a court should simply follow the earlier decisions rather than making an independent assessment of reliability. What is the federal position on this issue? As a practical matter, what is a court likely to do when addressing a frequently litigated issue such as the admissibility of DNA evidence?

3. The *Howerton* opinion also seems to suggest that if a general technique or theory is admissible all questions concerning the application of the technique or theory in a particular case should go to weight. On this point consider the comments of Judge Becker in In re Paoli R.R. Yard PCB Litigation, 35 F.3d 717, 745 (3d Cir. 1994).

> In *Paoli I* we suggested that so long as any deviation the expert made from a reliable method merely constituted a change in the *application* of that method, the expert's testimony remained based on a reliable scientific method. We though [sic] that ferreting out misapplication fell within the province of the jury, and that only if the expert so altered a reliable methodology as to skew it would the reliability inquiry of *Downing* be applicable to the altered methodology. * * *
>
> However, after *Daubert,* we no longer think that the distinction between a methodology and its application is viable. To begin with, it is extremely elusive to attempt to ascertain which of an expert's steps constitute parts of a "basic" methodology and which constitute changes from that methodology. If a laboratory consistently fails to use certain quality controls so that its results are rendered unreliable, attempting to ascertain whether the lack of quality controls constitutes a failure of methodology or a failure of application of methodology may be an exercise in metaphysics. Moreover, any misapplication of a methodology that is significant enough to render it unreliable is likely to also be significant enough to skew the methodology.
>
> As suggested, *Daubert* inters any need for us to make such a distinction, for *Daubert's* requirement that the expert testify to scientific knowledge—conclusions supported by good grounds for each step in the analysis—means that *any* step that renders the analysis unreliable under the *Daubert factors renders the expert's testimony inadmissible. This is true whether the step completely changes a reliable methodology or merely misapplies that methodology.*

What are the pros and cons of these two positions?

4. The *Howerton* court makes the interesting point that judges may be influenced in their admissibility ruling by the realization that if they rule all of the plaintiff's causation evidence inadmissible they will be in a position to grant the defendant a summary judgement and thereby lighten their caseload. Is this a realistic concern? If so, how might it be addressed?

5. The RAND study authored by Dixon and Gill that is cited in *Howerton* is one of the most complete studies of the impact of *Daubert* conducted to date. One key finding in the study is that over time the federal courts have been increasingly less likely to rule in favor of the party challenging expert evidence. The authors offer two possible reasons for this change: 1) Judges have relaxed admissibility criteria, and 2) The quality of proffered evidence has improved over the years. The methodology of the RAND study made it impossible to assess the relative importance of these two explanations.

6. The *Logerquist* case cited in *Howerton* not only refused to abandon *Frye* and adopt *Daubert* it apparently rejected any reliability filter for observation and experience-based expert testimony about human behavior for the purpose of explaining that behavior. In *Logerquist* the testimony in question was that of a clinical psychiatrist that the plaintiff had true repressed memories of childhood sexual abuse. The *Logerquist* opinion was criticized by numerous authors in Volume 33 of the Arizona State Law Journal.

7. As is obvious from the *Howerton* opinion, many states are not simply either *Frye* jurisdictions or *Daubert* jurisdictions, but rather are complex admixtures of both. For example, in Castillo v. E.I Du Pont De Nemours & Co., 854 So.2d 1264 (Fla. 2003) the Florida Supreme Court reaffirmed that the state has incorporated the *Daubert* factors into its admissibility jurisprudence, but has refused to incorporate the *Daubert* and *Kumho Tire* fit analysis.

Chapter 7

PROXIMATE CAUSE

SECTION A. INTRODUCTION[1]

In negligence cases, courts recognized the necessity of restricting liability for harm caused by careless acts in order to avoid unduly discouraging socially useful conduct. This is particularly important because the predominant test for determining causation in fact—the "but for" test—can carry liability forward to an almost infinite extent. Courts devised rules concerning proximate cause, intervening cause, and duty as tools for limiting liability. These rules will collectively be referred to as "proximate cause doctrines." The policy behind these doctrines is also important in strict product liability cases. Regardless of whether the primary justification for strict liability is loss spreading, deterrence, or easing the plaintiff's burden of proof, no one seriously contends that absolute liability for all harm caused by all products is desirable. To keep the scope of products liability within proper bounds, many courts apply proximate cause doctrines borrowed from the law of negligence.

You will recall from your first year torts course that the proximate cause doctrines impose three basic types of limits that restrict the scope of liability. One restriction relates to the type of harm that occurred; a court might decline to hold a defendant liable for fire damage unless the risk of a fire was a foreseeable result of the negligent act. Another restriction relates to the manner of harm; a court might decline to hold defendant liable unless the accident came about in a foreseeable way. A third restriction relates to the class of persons that may recover; some courts restrict liability to plaintiffs who were foreseeable victims of the negligent act. In products liability cases, not all courts use all three restrictions, but many commonly employ more than one of these limits.

Type of Harm. In Products liability cases some courts use foresight of harm as the criterion for limiting liability in strict product liability cases. These cases impose liability where the harm is foreseeable, but not where it is unforeseeable. Thus, in Oehler v. Davis,[2] the defendant sold a

---

1. This section is adapted from Fischer, Products Liability—Proximate Cause, Intervening Cause, and Duty, 52 Mo.L.Rev. 547, 547–73 (1987).

2. 223 Pa.Super. 333, 298 A.2d 895 (1972).

dog collar ring that was defective because it contained a physical flaw.[3] The ring broke because of the defect, allowing a dog to escape. The dog escaped and injured the plaintiff through excessive playfulness. The court held that the defendant was not liable because the risk of harm through playfulness was unforeseeable. The defendant would have been liable if the plaintiff had been injured by a foreseeable risk, such as an attack by a vicious dog.

In strict liability cases "foreseeability" of risk is often used in a different sense than in negligence cases. A risk associated with a product could be unforeseeable for a variety of reasons. For example, ignorance of any of the following matters can render a risk unforeseeable: physical flaws in the product, generic risks associated with the product, product misuse, intervening causes, and the identity of persons affected by the product. In negligence cases ignorance of any of these matters is sufficient to exonerate the defendant if they cause the risk to be unforeseeable. In strict liability cases ignorance of some of these matters will exonerate the defendant, but ignorance of others will not.

The restricted sense in which "foreseeability" is used in strict product liability cases is clearly illustrated by cases involving unintended physical flaws. In *Oehler v. Davis*, for example, if the manufacturer of the dog collar ring had been justifiably ignorant of the flaw in its product it could not have "foreseen" any risk of harm, and therefore, would not have been negligent. We have seen in Chapter 4 Section B, however, that a manufacturer's inability to discover the flaw is not an excuse in a strict liability case. Therefore, "foreseeability" of harm in strict liability cases involving manufacturing defects (products not in the condition that the manufacturer intended) is necessarily determined by imputing knowledge of the flaw to the hypothetical reasonable manufacturer and asking what kinds of accidents the defect is likely to cause.[4] Thus, an element of "hindsight" is used to determine which risks are "foreseeable," and in this respect the scope of liability is broader in strict liability cases than in negligence cases.

In Chapter 4, Sections C and D, we saw that an injury can also be unforeseeable because of ignorance of a generic risk associated with a product, such as the side-effect of a drug. These are risks common to all products in the line. If products containing generic risks are defective, it is because of the way they are designed or because of a failure to warn. Manufacturers must design products so as to minimize risks associated

---

3. *Id.* at 339, 298 A.2d at 899 (Cercone, J., dissenting) (the ring was defective because of improper casting and improper composition).

4. *E.g.*, Feldman v. Lederle Laboratories, 97 N.J. 429, 450, 479 A.2d 374, 385 (1984):

This difference between strict liability and negligence is commonly expressed by stating that in a strict liability analysis, the defendant is assumed to know of the dangerous propensity of the product, whereas in a negligence case, the plaintiff must prove that the defendant knew or should have known of the danger.... This distinction is particularly pertinent in a manufacturing defect context.

Id.

with products, and they must warn against nonobvious risks that cannot feasibly be eliminated. Some courts refuse to impute knowledge of scientifically unknowable risks to manufacturers in cases involving products that allegedly are defective because of a failure to warn,[5] and others refuse to impute such knowledge in cases where the product is allegedly improperly designed.[6] This is the position of the Products Liability Restatement.[7] In such jurisdictions the scope of liability is the same whether the case is brought on a negligence or a strict liability theory;[8] there is no liability for unforeseeable risks. Other courts impose a broader scope of liability in strict liability cases by imputing knowledge of the risk to the manufacturer.[9] In such jurisdictions foreseeability is used in the same restricted sense in design and warning cases as it is in manufacturing defect cases. That is, these courts first impute knowledge of the danger to the hypothetical reasonable manufacturer for purposes of determining whether the product is defective.[10] After determining that the product is defective, they determine proximate cause by asking what kinds of accidents a reasonable manufacturer with such knowledge is likely to anticipate.[11]

Manner of Harm. Some courts reject the requirement that the type of harm be foreseeable in strict product liability cases. Instead, they require that the use to which the product was put be foreseeable,[12] or that any intervening causes be foreseeable. For example, in Baker v. International Harvester Co.[13] plaintiff's decedent was a hunter who boarded the ladder of a moving combine without the knowledge of the operator in order to hunt from the combine. He was killed when he fell off the ladder and was run over by the combine. The appellate court affirmed the trial court's dismissal of the case because the decedent's use of the combine for hunting was unforeseeable as a matter of law. The court said, "Strict liability focuses on foreseeable or reasonably anticipated use of the combine, rather than on the reasonably anticipated harm the combine may cause."[14]

The distinction between misuse and intervening cause is merely a matter of terminology. An intervening cause is an actively operating force that comes on the scene after the defendant's tortious conduct has taken place. If the relevant intervening act is done by the user of the

5. Note Regarding the Foresight/Hindsight Distinction, *supra* page 141.

6. Note Regarding the Foresight/Hindsight Distinction, *supra* page 141.

7. Restatement (Third) of Torts: Products Liability § 2 (1997).

8. *E.g.*, Jones v. Hutchinson Mfg., 502 S.W.2d 66 (Ky.Ct.App.1973).

9. *E.g.*, Phillips v. Kimwood Mach. Co., *supra* page 114.

10. *E.g.*, Barker v. Lull Engineering Co. *supra*, page 134 (California design defect case; under the risk-utility branch of the California two-part test, courts use hindsight to determine whether the danger inherent in the challenged design outweighs the benefits of the design).

11. Bigbee v. Pacific Tel. & Tel. Co., 34 Cal.3d 49, 192 Cal.Rptr. 857, 665 P.2d 947 (En Banc, 1983).

12. *See, e.g.*, Eshbach v. W.T. Grant's & Co., 481 F.2d 940 (3d Cir.1973); Brown v. United States Stove Co., 98 N.J. 155, 166, 484 A.2d 1234, 1240 (1984); Newman v. Utility Trailer & Equip. Co., 278 Or. 395, 564 P.2d 674 (1977).

13. 660 S.W.2d 21 (Mo.Ct.App.1983).

14. 660 S.W.2d 21, 22 (Mo.Ct.App. 1983).

product, courts often label the conduct as misuse rather than as an intervening cause, but the effect is clearly the same regardless of the label.[15] Both intervening causes and acts of misuse are judged by the same foreseeability standard.[16]

A great many products liability cases involve either misuse or intervening causes. Defendant's tortious conduct must be complete when the product leaves its hands because the law requires the product to be defective at that time.[17] Accidents cannot happen unless someone subsequently acts, and these acts are intervening causes. Liability frequently turns on a determination of whether these acts cut off the manufacturer's liability.

Often in product liability cases, the defectiveness of the product turns on the question of whether the intervening cause or misuse is foreseeable. This is because manufacturers must design products to be reasonably safe in light of anticipated misuse and intervening causes. Cases of this sort are treated in Chapter 4, Section C 2 (b) and Section D 1.

This Section focuses on a distinctly different problem, cases where the product is clearly defective, but the intervening cause or misuse may nevertheless cut off liability. One situation where this occurs is where the product is independently defective, but an unforeseeable intervening cause produces a different type of harm than was foreseeable. In Ventricelli v. Kinney Sys. Rent A Car, Inc.[18] defendant rented a car to plaintiff with a defective trunk that would not stay closed. This created a foreseeable risk that the trunk lid would fly open while the car was being driven and cause an accident by obstructing the driver's vision. Instead of this occurring, the driver was hit by another car as he was standing behind his car, in a parking space in the street, trying to close the trunk lid. The court held that the unforeseeable intervening cause, the negligence of the other driver, cut off the liability of the car renter because it produced a different kind of accident than the renter could foresee.[19]

A somewhat different situation is where the type of harm is foreseeable but the manner of harm is not. Some courts impose liability.[20] In

---

15. Kuisis v. Baldwin–Lima–Hamilton Corp., 457 Pa. 321, 331 n. 13, 319 A.2d 914, 920 n. 13 (1974) (intervening cause and abnormal use are equivalent); Pegg v. General Motors Corp., 258 Pa.Super. 59, 78, 391 A.2d 1074, 1083 (1978).

16. *E.g.,* Pegg v. General Motors Corp., 258 Pa.Super. 59, 78, 391 A.2d 1074, 1083 (1978); Keeton, Products Liability and Defenses—Intervening Misconduct, 15 Forum 109, 112–113 (1978).

17. Restatement (Second) of Torts § 402A(1), Comment g (1966).

18. 45 N.Y.2d 950, 411 N.Y.S.2d 555, 383 N.E.2d 1149 (1978).

19. In determining whether an intervening cause is "foreseeable," some courts use hindsight rather than foresight. That is, they look back on the whole sequence of events and rule that the intervening cause is unforeseeable if the sequence of events appears extraordinary. *See* Griggs v. Firestone Tire & Rubber Co., 513 F.2d 851, 861 (8th Cir.1975), cert. denied, 423 U.S. 865, 96 S.Ct. 124, 46 L.Ed.2d 93 (1975); Eshbach v. W.T. Grant's & Co., 481 F.2d 940, 945 (3d Cir.1973); Young v. Tide Craft, Inc., 270 S.C. 453, 465–66, 242 S.E.2d 671, 677 (1978).

20. Pust v. Union Supply Co., 38 Colo. App. 435, 561 P.2d 355 (1976), affirmed, 196 Colo. 162, 583 P.2d 276 (1978) (strict liability); Noonan v. Buick Co., 211 So.2d 54 (Fla.App.1968), cert. denied, 219 So.2d 698

Tucci v. Bossert[21] a manufacturer sold a can of drain cleaner without warning of the risk of explosion in the event that water was added to the container. Some children found a partially filled container of the drain cleaner in the trash, added water to it, and were injured in the ensuing explosion. The court held the manufacturer liable, even though the conduct of the children was unforeseeable, because the type of harm (explosion caused by water) was foreseeable. Other courts disagree. They require foreseeability of the manner of harm in such cases.[22]

In one particular type of case most courts require foreseeability of the manner of harm. Where a third party discovers the defect and either continues to use it himself or fails to warn others who will use it, courts generally impose liability only where the third person's conduct was foreseeable. For example, in Peck v. Ford Motor Co.,[23] a strict liability case, a Ford truck stalled in the middle of a heavily traveled lane of traffic due to a defect. The driver put out inadequate warning markers and left the scene without notifying the police. Three hours later plaintiff's vehicle crashed into the truck. The court held that Ford's duty terminated shortly after the truck stalled because the driver's negligence was unforeseeable. Likewise, Mull v. Ford Motor Co.,[24] was a suit brought on negligence and implied warranty theories. A taxicab stalled in a busy street because of a defect. The driver attempted to "buck" it to the curb by using the starter. The hood popped up and completely obscured the driver's vision. He, nevertheless, continued to "buck" the cab, and ran into plaintiff, severely injuring him. The court held that it was unforeseeable as a matter of law that the driver would proceed after the hood flew up.

Class of Persons. Another limitation on the scope of liability is that the defendant must foresee a risk of harm to the class of persons to which the plaintiff belongs. This limitation is often stated as an aspect of duty rather than proximate cause. You learned about this limitation in your torts class when you studied the famous case of Palsgraf v. Long Island R.R.[25] As you probably recall, Mrs. Palsgraf was a bystander on a railroad platform. Some distance away a conductor knocked a package out of a passenger's hand. Although the conductor did not know it, the package contained fireworks. They exploded upon impact with the ground, and the explosion allegedly knocked a large scale onto Mrs. Palsgraf. The court held that the railroad breached no duty to Mrs. Palsgraf because any negligence on the part of the conductor did not

(1968) (negligence); Moran v. Faberge, Inc., 273 Md. 538, 332 A.2d 11 (1975) (negligence); American Laundry Mach. Indus. v. Horan, 45 Md.App. 97, 412 A.2d 407 (1980) (negligence); Haberly v. Reardon Co., 319 S.W.2d 859 (Mo.1958) (negligence); Libbey–Owens Ford Glass Co. v. L & M Paper Co., 189 Neb. 792, 205 N.W.2d 523 (1973) (negligence).

21. 53 A.D.2d 291, 385 N.Y.S.2d 328 (1976).

22. Dyer v. Best Pharmacal, 118 Ariz. 465, 577 P.2d 1084 (App.1978) (strict liability; negligence); Mohrdieck v. Morton Grove, 94 Ill.App.3d 1021, 50 Ill.Dec. 409, 419 N.E.2d 517 (1981) (negligence); Ritter v. Narragansett Elec. Co., 109 R.I. 176, 283 A.2d 255 (1971) (negligence, strict liability).

23. 603 F.2d 1240 (7th Cir.1979).

24. 368 F.2d 713 (2d Cir.1966).

25. 248 N.Y. 339, 162 N.E. 99 (1928).

create a foreseeable risk to her. The degree to which this limitation will be accepted in negligence cases is as yet unsettled.[26] It is, however, a well-established requirement in products liability cases.

In a line of authority that is closely analogous to *Palsgraf*, products liability cases generally limit recovery to foreseeable plaintiffs. The leading case is Winnett v. Winnett.[27] A four year old child was injured when she got her fingers caught in the holes of a moving conveyor belt on a forage wagon. The court held that the plaintiff could not recover because it was unforeseeable that she would be permitted to approach the equipment while it was operating and place her hands on the moving conveyor.

In its inception, products liability only extended to users or consumers of defective products.[28] Later, courts expanded the scope of liability by permitting bystanders to recover.[29] The distinction between these various classes of persons is now of little practical importance because the basic test of liability is the same regardless of the classification.[30] Both users and consumers[31] and bystanders[32] can recover only if the manufacturer can foresee that they will be injured by the defective product.

Some parties cannot readily be classified as either users, consumers or bystanders. Cases involving rescuers are an example. One approach to cases of this kind is to apply the same foreseeability test that is used with other classes of plaintiffs.[33] Other courts decide these cases under hard and fast rules. New York, for example, permits rescuers to recover even if they are unforeseeable.[34] Missouri grants recovery to rescuers of persons but denies recovery to rescuers of property.[35]

26. H. Hart & A. Honore, Causation in the Law 245–48 (1959); W. Prosser & W. Keeton, The Law of Torts 285 (5th ed. 1984).

27. 57 Ill.2d 7, 310 N.E.2d 1 (1974).

28. Restatement (Second) of Torts § 402A (1966).

29. *E.g.*, Elmore v. American Motors Corp., 70 Cal.2d 578, 451 P.2d 84, 75 Cal. Rptr. 652 (1969).

30. Winnett v. Winnett, 57 Ill.2d 7, 11, 310 N.E.2d 1, 4 (1974).

31. DeSantis v. Parker Feeders, Inc., 547 F.2d 357 (7th Cir.1976); Helene Curtis Indus. v. Pruitt, 385 F.2d 841 (5th Cir. 1967), cert. denied, 391 U.S. 913, 88 S.Ct. 1806, 20 L.Ed.2d 652 (1968); Klimas v. International Tel. & Tel. Corp., 297 F.Supp. 937 (D.R.I.1969); Magee v. Wyeth Laboratories, Inc., 214 Cal.App.2d 340, 29 Cal.Rptr. 322 (1963).

32. Passwaters v. General Motors Corp., 454 F.2d 1270 (8th Cir.1972); Elmore v. American Motors Corp., 70 Cal.2d 578, 451 P.2d 84, 75 Cal.Rptr. 652 (1969); Mitchell v. Miller, 26 Conn.Supp. 142, 214 A.2d 694 (1965); Winnett v. Winnett, 57 Ill.2d 7, 310 N.E.2d 1 (1974); Barr v. Rivinius, Inc., 58 Ill.App.3d 121, 15 Ill.Dec. 591, 373 N.E.2d 1063 (1978); Gilbert v. Stone City Constr. Co., 171 Ind.App. 418, 357 N.E.2d 738 (1976); Chrysler Corp. v. Alumbaugh, 168 Ind.App. 363, 342 N.E.2d 908, modified on petition for reh'g, 168 Ind.App. 363, 348 N.E.2d 654 (1976); Embs v. Pepsi–Cola Bottling Co., 528 S.W.2d 703 (Ky.1975); Lamendola v. Mizell, 115 N.J.Super. 514, 280 A.2d 241 (1971). *Contra* Howes v. Hansen, 56 Wis.2d 247, 201 N.W.2d 825 (1972).

33. Court v. Grzelinski, 72 Ill.2d 141, 19 Ill.Dec. 617, 379 N.E.2d 281 (1978) (fireman injured in attempt to put out fire caused by a defective product can recover if jury finds him foreseeable); Bobka v. Cook County Hosp., 97 Ill.App.3d 351, 52 Ill.Dec. 790, 422 N.E.2d 999 (1981) (sister who donated skin to brother injured by defective product could not recover because she was not foreseeable).

34. Guarino v. Mine Safety Appliance Co., 25 N.Y.2d 460, 255 N.E.2d 173, 306 N.Y.S.2d 942 (1969) (breach of warranty) (citing with approval Wagner v. International Ry., 232 N.Y. 176, 133 N.E. 437 (1921)).

35. Welch v. Hesston Corp., 540 S.W.2d 127 (Mo.Ct.App.1976).

Relationship of policy limits to one another. The basic policy limits—type of harm, manner of harm, and class of persons—are not always three mutually exclusive and distinct categories, but can be related to each another. That is, there are some situations where one type of policy limit yields the same result as another; they just amount to different ways of saying the same thing. In other cases the different approaches yield distinctly different results.

A prime example is the close relationship between the requirement that plaintiff fall within a foreseeable class of persons and the requirement that the type of harm be foreseeable. Frequently, the plaintiff is unforeseeable only because the type of harm is unforeseeable. An understanding of this relationship is particularly useful in jurisdictions requiring that the plaintiff be foreseeable, but rejecting foreseeability of the type of harm. In such situations, a defendant can seek to achieve the same result by using the alternative characterization that the plaintiff was unforeseeable.

In many cases the plaintiff is foreseeable only because the type of harm is foreseeable.[36] A fire fighter, injured in the course of putting out a fire caused by a defective product, is a foreseeable plaintiff only if the defect creates a risk of fire or explosion.[37] Likewise, a bystander is a foreseeable victim of a defective product only if the defect poses the risk of creating the kind of accident that can harm a bystander. Examples include vehicles containing defects that impair the operator's view of the road[38] or create the risk of loss of control.[39] Vehicles not containing such defects do not foreseeably jeopardize bystanders.[40] In such cases the plaintiff is unforeseeable because the type of harm is unforeseeable.

For general discussions of proximate cause in strict liability cases, *see* H. Hart and A. Honore, Causation in the Law (1959); R. Keeton, Legal Cause in the Law of Torts (1963); Fischer, Products Liability—Proximate Cause, Intervening Cause, and Duty, 52 Mo.L.Rev. 547 (1987); Harper, Liability Without Fault and Proximate Cause, 30 Mich. L.Rev. 1001 (1932); Polelle, The Foreseeability Concept and Strict Products Liability: The Odd Couple of Tort Law, 8 Rut.-Cam.L.J. 101 (1976); Twerski, The Many Faces of Misuse: An Inquiry into the Emerging Doctrine of Comparative Causation, 29 Mercer L.Rev. 403 (1978); Note, Torts—Proximate Cause in Strict Liability Cases, 50 N.C.L.Rev. 714 (1972).

The next section deals with an important proximate cause problem that is unique to products liability cases. This is the problem of altera-

---

36. R. Keeton, Legal Cause in the Law of Torts 85 (1963).

37. *See* Court v. Grzelinski, 72 Ill.2d 141, 19 Ill.Dec. 617, 379 N.E.2d 281 (1978).

38. Gilbert v. Stone City Constr. Co., 171 Ind.App. 418, 357 N.E.2d 738 (1976).

39. Lamendola v. Mizell, 115 N.J.Super. 514, 280 A.2d 241 (1971).

40. *See* Barr v. Rivinius, Inc., 58 Ill. App.3d 121, 15 Ill.Dec. 591, 373 N.E.2d 1063 (1978).

tions to the product that take place after the product is placed in the stream of commerce.

SECTION B. PRODUCT ALTERATION

ROBINSON v. REED–PRENTICE DIV. OF PACKAGE MACH. CO.
Court of Appeals of New York, 1980.
49 N.Y.2d 471, 426 N.Y.S.2d 717, 403 N.E.2d 440.

Opinion of the Court

COOKE, CHIEF JUDGE.

We hold that a manufacturer of a product may not be cast in damages, either on a strict products liability or negligence cause of action, where, after the product leaves the possession and control of the manufacturer, there is a subsequent modification which substantially alters the product and is the proximate cause of plaintiff's injuries.

Plaintiff Gerald Robinson, then 17, was employed as a plastic molding machine operator by third-party defendant Plastic Jewel Parts Co. A recent arrival to New York from South Carolina where he had been an itinerant farm worker, Robinson had been employed by Plastic Jewel for approximately three weeks. On October 15, 1971, plaintiff suffered severe injuries when his hand was caught between the molds of a plastic molding machine manufactured by defendant Reed–Prentice and sold to Plastic Jewel in 1965, some six and one-half years prior to the accident.

Plaintiff commenced this action against Reed–Prentice which impleaded third-party defendant Plastic Jewel. At the close of proof, causes of action in strict products liability and negligence in the design and manufacture of the machine were submitted to the jury. A sizeable general verdict was returned in favor of plaintiff, the jury apportioning 40% of the liability against Reed–Prentice, the remainder against Plastic Jewel. On appeal, the Appellate Division reversed and ordered a new trial limited to the issue of damages unless plaintiff stipulated to a reduced verdict. Plaintiff so stipulated and the judgment, as amended and reduced, was affirmed. This court then granted Reed–Prentice and Plastic Jewel leave to appeal (CPLR 5602, subd. [a], par. 1, cl. [ii]). We now reverse.

The plastic injection molding machine is designed to melt pelletized plastic inside a heating chamber. From the heating chamber, the liquefied plastic is forced into the mold area by means of a plunger. The mold area itself is composed of two rectangular platens on which the plastic molds are attached. One of the platens moves horizontally to open and close the mold; the other remains stationary. When the operating cycle is begun, hydraulic pressure causes the movable platen to be brought up against the stationary platen, thus forming a completed mold into which the heated plastic is pumped. After the plastic is cured, the movable platen returns to its original position, thereby permitting the operator to manually remove the finished product from its mold.

To protect the operator from the mold area, Reed–Prentice equipped the machine with a safety gate mounted on rollers and connecting interlocks in conformity with the State Industrial Code (12 N.Y.C.R.R. 19.34). Completely covering the mold area, the metal safety gate contained a Plexiglas window allowing the operator to monitor the molding process. Since the gate shielded the mold area, access to the platens was impossible while the machine was operating. Only when the molding sequence was completed could the operator roll the safety gate to the open position, allowing him to reach into the mold area to remove the finished product. The interlocks were connected to electrical switches which activated the hydraulic pump. When the safety gate was closed, the interlocks complete a circuit that activates the hydraulic pump, thereby causing the movable platen to close upon its stationary counterpart. When the safety gate was opened, however, this essential circuit would not be completed and hence the machine would not be activated.

After the machine was delivered by Reed–Prentice, Plastic Jewel discovered that its design did not comport with its production requirements. Plastic Jewel purchased the machine in order to mold beads directly onto a nylon cord. The cord was stored in spools at the back of the machine and fed through the mold where the beads were molded around it. After each molding cycle, the beads were pulled out of the mold and the nylon cord was reset in the mold for the next cycle. To allow the beads to be molded on a continuous line, Plastic Jewel determined that it was necessary to cut a hole of approximately 6 by 14 inches in the Plexiglas portion of the safety gate. The machine, as designed, contracted for and delivered, made no provision for such an aperture. At the end of each cycle, the now corded beads would be pulled through the opening in the gate, the nylon cord would be restrung, and the next cycle would be started by opening and then closing the safety gate without breaking the continuous line of beads. While modification of the safety gate served Plastic Jewel's production needs, it also destroyed the practical utility of the safety features incorporated into the design of the machine for it permitted access into the molding area while the interlocking circuits were completed. Although the record is unclear on this point, plaintiff's hand somehow went through the opening cut into the safety gate and was drawn into the molding area while the interlocks were engaged. The machine went through the molding cycle, causing plaintiff serious injury.

The record contains evidence that Reed–Prentice knew, or should have known, the particular safety gate designed for the machine made it impossible to manufacture beads on strings. During the period immediately prior to the purchase of the machine, Reed–Prentice representatives visited the Plastic Jewel plant and observed two identical machines with holes cut in the Plexiglas portion of their safety gates. At that meeting, Plastic Jewel's plant manager discussed the problem with a Reed–Prentice salesman and asked whether a safety gate compatible with its product needs could be designed. Moreover, a letter sent by Reed–Prentice to Plastic Jewel establishes that the manufacturer knew precisely what its customer was doing to the safety gate and refused to modify its design. However, the letter pointed out that the purchaser had "completely flaunted the safeties built into this machine by removing part of the safety window", and that it had not "held up your end of the purchase when you use the machine differently from its design" and the manufacturer stated "[a]s concerns changes, we will make none in our safety setup or design of safety gates". At trial, plaintiff's expert indicated that there were two modifications to the safety gate which could have been made that would have made it possible to mold beads on a string without rendering the machine unreasonably dangerous. Neither of these modifications were made, or even contemplated, by Reed–Prentice.

Defendants maintain that a manufacturer may not be held to answer in damages where the purchaser of its product deliberately destroys the functional utility of that product's safety features and, as a result of that intentional act, a third party is injured. Once a product which is not defective is injected into the stream of commerce, they argue, the responsibility of the manufacturer is at an end. Thus, having delivered to Plastic Jewel a plastic injection molding machine which was free from defect and in conformity with State promulgated safety regulations, Reed–Prentice fully discharged any legal duty it may have owed to Plastic Jewel and its employees. Plaintiff asserts that a manufacturer's duty is tempered by principles of foreseeability. Thus, if a manufacturer knows or has reason to know that its product would be used in an unreasonably dangerous manner, for example by cutting a hole in a legally required safety guard, it may not evade responsibility by simply maintaining that the product was safe at the time of sale.

A cause of action in strict products liability lies where a manufacturer places on the market a product which has a defect that causes injury (*Codling v. Paglia*, 32 N.Y.2d 330, 342, 345 N.Y.S.2d 461, 469, 298 N.E.2d 622, 628). As the law has developed thus far, a defect in a product may consist of one of three elements: mistake in manufacturing (*Victorson v. Bock Laundry Mach. Co.*, 37 N.Y.2d 395, 373 N.Y.S.2d 39, 335 N.E.2d 275; *Codling v. Paglia, supra*), improper design (*Micallef v. Miehle Co., Div. of Miehle–Goss Dexter*, 39 N.Y.2d 376, 384 N.Y.S.2d 115, 348 N.E.2d 571; *Bolm v. Triumph Corp.*, 33 N.Y.2d 151, 350 N.Y.S.2d 644, 305 N.E.2d 769), or by the inadequacy or absence of warnings for the use of the product (*Torrogrossa v. Towmotor Co.*, 44 N.Y.2d 709, 405 N.Y.S.2d 448, 376 N.E.2d 920). Plaintiff maintains that the safety gate of the molding machine was improperly designed for its intended purpose.

Where a product presents an unreasonable risk of harm, notwithstanding that it was meticulously made according to detailed plans and specifications, it is said to be defectively designed. This rule, however, is tempered by the realization that some products, for example knives, must by their very nature be dangerous in order to be functional. Thus, a defectively designed product is one which, at the time it leaves the seller's hands, is in a condition not reasonably contemplated by the ultimate consumer and is unreasonably dangerous for its intended use; that is one whose utility does not outweigh the danger inherent in its introduction into the stream of commerce (Restatement, Torts 2d, § 402A). Design defects, then, unlike manufacturing defects, involve products made in the precise manner intended by the manufacturer (2 Frumer & Friedman, Products Liability, § 16A[4][f][iv]). Since no product may be completely accident proof, the ultimate question in determining whether an article is defectively designed involves a balancing of the likelihood of harm against the burden of taking precaution against that harm (*Micallef v. Miehle Co., supra,* 39 N.Y.2d p. 386, 384 N.Y.S.2d p. 121, 348 N.E.2d p. 577; 2 Harper and James, Torts, § 28.4).

But no manufacturer may be automatically held liable for all accidents caused or occasioned by the use of its product (see Wade, A Conspectus of Manufacturers' Liability for Products, 10 Ind.L.Rev. 755, 768). While the manufacturer is under a nondelegable duty to design and produce a product that is not defective, that responsibility is gauged as of the time the product leaves the manufacturer's hands (Restatement, Torts 2d, § 402A, Comments *g, p; Hanlon v. Cyril Bath Co.,* 541 F.2d 343, 345 (3d Cir.); *Santiago v. Package Mach. Co.,* 123 Ill.App.2d 305, 312, 260 N.E.2d 89; *Temple v. Wean United,* 50 Ohio St.2d 317, 322–323, 364 N.E.2d 267). Substantial modifications of a product from its original condition by a third party which render a safe product defective are not the responsibility of the manufacturer (*Keet v. Service Mach. Co.,* 472 F.2d 138, 140; *Hardy v. Hull Corp.,* 446 F.2d 34, 35–36 (9th Cir.); *Coleman v. Verson Allsteel Press Co.,* 64 Ill.App.3d 974, 21 Ill.Dec. 742, 382 N.E.2d 36; Ariz.Rev.Stat.Ann., § 12–683, subd. 2; R.I.Gen.Laws, § 9–1–32; Proposed Uniform Product Liability Act, § 112, subd. [D], 44 Fed.Reg. 62737).

At the time Reed–Prentice sold the molding machine, it was not defective. Had the machine been left intact, the safety gate and connecting interlocks would have rendered this tragic industrial accident an impossibility. On closer analysis, then, plaintiff does not seek to premise liability on any defect in the design or manufacture of the machine but on the independent, and presumably foreseeable, act of Plastic Jewel in destroying the functional utility of the safety gate. Principles of foreseeability, however, are inapposite where a third party affirmatively abuses a product by consciously bypassing built-in safety features. While it may be foreseeable that an employer will abuse a product to meet its own self-imposed production needs, responsibility for that willful choice may not fall on the manufacturer. Absent any showing that there was some defect in the design of the safety gate at the time the machine left the practical control of Reed–Prentice (and there has been none here), Reed–Prentice may not be cast in damages for strict products liability.

Nor does the record disclose any basis for a finding of negligence on the part of Reed–Prentice in the design of the machine. Well settled it is that a manufacturer is under a duty to use reasonable care in designing his product when "used in the manner for which the product was intended * * * as well as an unintended yet reasonably foreseeable use" (*Micallef v. Miehle, supra,* 39 N.Y.2d pp. 385–386, 384 N.Y.S.2d p. 121, 348 N.E.2d p. 577). Many products may safely and reasonably be used for purposes other than the one for which they were specifically designed. For example, the manufacturer of a screwdriver must foresee that a consumer will use his product to pry open the lid of a can and is thus under a corresponding duty to design the shank of the product with sufficient strength to accomplish that task. In such a situation, the manufacturer is in a superior position to anticipate the reasonable use to which his product may be put and is obliged to assure that no harm will befall those who use the product in such a manner. It is the manufacturer who must bear the responsibility if its purposeful design choice presents an unreasonable danger to users. A cause of action in negligence will lie where it can be shown that a manufacturer was responsible for a defect that caused injury, and that the manufacturer could have foreseen the injury. Control of the instrumentality at the time of the accident in such a case is irrelevant since the defect arose while the product was in the possession of the manufacturer.

The manufacturer's duty, however, does not extend to designing a product that is impossible to abuse or one whose safety features may not be circumvented. A manufacturer need not incorporate safety features into its product so as to guarantee that no harm will come to every user no matter how careless or even reckless (cf. *Aetna Ins. Co. v. Loveland Gas & Elec. Co.,* 369 F.2d 648 (6th Cir.); *Drazen v. Otis Elevator Co.,* 96 R.I. 114, 189 A.2d 693). Nor must he trace his product through every link in the chain of distribution to insure that users will not adapt the product to suit their own unique purposes. The duty of a manufacturer, therefore, is not an open-ended one. It extends to the design and manufacture of a finished product which is safe at the time of sale. Material alterations at the hands of a third party which work a substantial change in the condition in which the product was sold by destroying the functional utility of a key safety feature, however foreseeable that modification may have been, are not within the ambit of a manufacturer's responsibility. Acceptance of plaintiff's concept of duty would expand the scope of a manufacturer's duty beyond all reasonable bounds and would be tantamount to imposing absolute liability on manufacturers for all product-related injuries (see Henderson, Judicial Review of Manufacturers' Conscious Design Choices: The Limits of Adjudication, 73 Col. L.Rev. 1531).

Unfortunately, as this case bears out, it may often be that an injured party, because of the exclusivity of workers' compensation, is barred from commencing an action against the one who exposes him to unreasonable peril by affirmatively rendering a safe product dangerous. However, that an employee may have no remedy in tort against his employer gives the courts no license to thrust upon a third-party manufacturer a duty to insure that its product will not be abused or that its safety features will be callously altered by a purchaser (cf. *McLaughlin v. Mine Safety Appliances Co.,* 11 N.Y.2d 62, 71–72, 226 N.Y.S.2d 407, 413–414,

181 N.E.2d 430, 435). Where the product is marketed in a condition safe for the purposes for which it is intended or could reasonably be intended, the manufacturer has satisfied its duty.

Accordingly, the judgment appealed from and the order of the Appellate Division brought up for review should be reversed, with costs, and the complaint and third-party complaint dismissed.

[The dissenting opinion of FUSCHBERG, J., is omitted]

JASEN, GABRIELLI, JONES, WACHTLER and MEYER, JJ., concur with COOKE, C.J.

FUCHSBERG, J., dissents and votes to affirm in a separate opinion.

Judgment appealed from and order of the Appellate Division brought up for review reversed, etc.

Notes

1. The Restatement of Torts (Second) § 402A(1)(b) (1965) states that the seller of a defective product that causes physical harm is liable if the product is "expected to and does reach the user or consumer without substantial change in the condition in which it is sold." Section 2 of the Third Restatement of Products Liability repeats this idea because it assesses defect "at the time of sale or distribution." When the Second Restatement was promulgated, the Institute took no position on whether the seller is liable if he does expect his product to undergo a substantial change. Restatement of Torts (Second) § 402A Caveat (2); Comment p. It also took no position on the liability of a seller of component parts. *Id.* at Caveat (3); Comment q. The Second Restatement terms provide a basis for exonerating the manufacturer only if a substantial change occurs *before* the product reaches the consumer. This clearly includes raw materials and components that are incorporated into a final product. The liability of manufacturers of such products is discussed in Chapter 4 Section C. 2. (c), *supra* pages 192–198.

2. *Robinson v. Reed–Prentice* involves the situation where the change occurs *after* the product reaches the consumer. Some courts hold that the "substantial change" language in the Restatement does not apply in this situation. They resolve the issue by other doctrines, such as the law of causation. *See* Dennis v. Ford Motor Co., 471 F.2d 733 (3d Cir.1973). Other courts interpret the Restatement as applying to modifications made after purchase. *See, e.g.,* Saupitty v. Yazoo Mfg. Co., 726 F.2d 657 (10th Cir.1984); Davis v. Berwind Corp., 547 Pa. 260, 690 A.2d 186 (Pa. 1997). A majority of these courts hold that subsequent changes exonerate the manufacturer only if they are unforeseeable. *See, e.g.,* Sheldon v. West Bend Equip. Corp., 718 F.2d 603 (3d Cir.1983) (a modification is not "substantial" if it is foreseeable).

3. While some courts talk in terms of intervening cause or misuse and others talk in terms of substantial change, a majority of courts hold the seller liable if the alteration was foreseeable. *E.g.*, Thompson v. Package Mach. Co., 22 Cal.App.3d 188, 99 Cal.Rptr. 281 (1971) (strict liability, design; alteration of safety gate on plastic molding machine); Soler v. Castmaster,

Div. of H.P.M. Corp., 98 N.J. 137, 484 A.2d 1225 (1984) (strict liability; die-casting machine defective because it did not contain an interlock; subsequent conversion of machine from manual operation to continuous operation made the machine more dangerous; the combination of both defects caused the accident); D'Antona v. Hampton Grinding Wheel Co., 225 Pa.Super. 120, 310 A.2d 307 (1973) (strict liability, warranty, negligence; substitution of different grinding wheel on a grinding machine; alleged defect in machine caused wheel to explode). *Accord*, Restatement (Third) of Torts: Products Liability § 2, cmt. p and § 15, cmt. b (1997) (not requiring proof of the absence of a substantial change; rather, treating product alteration as a form of misuse). There are some limitations on this doctrine. Even an unforeseeable alteration will not cut off the manufacturer's liability if it is not a cause in fact of the harm. Saupitty v. Yazoo Mfg. Co., 726 F.2d 657 (10th Cir.1984) (strict liability; design defect; removal of brakes and belt guard from lawn mower; absence of these safety features played no role in the accident).

4. One common type of case involves the removal of a safety device. The utility or necessity of removing the device has a bearing on whether its removal is foreseeable. *E.g.*, Kuziw v. Lake Eng'g. Co., 586 F.2d 33 (7th Cir.1978) (Illinois law; foreseeable that safety guard would be removed because this was the only way to clean the machine).

5. While *Robinson v. Reed–Prentice* represents a minority view, there are a significant number of other cases in which courts have refused to impose liability even though the modification was foreseeable. *E.g.*, Latimer v. General Motors Corp., 535 F.2d 1020 (7th Cir.1976) (strict liability, implied warranty, negligence; removal of cotter key permitted drive shaft to come loose and tear brake lines; manufacturer had no duty to install a guard to protect the brake lines even if removal of cotter key was foreseeable); Union Carbide Corp. v. Holton, 136 Ga.App. 726, 222 S.E.2d 105 (1975) (negligence; plaintiff was injured when a disposable cylinder originally containing pressurized gas exploded because it was refilled; manufacturer of the cylinder was not liable for failure to make it impossible to refill or for failure to warn against refilling even if refilling was foreseeable). *See also*, Smith v. Louis Berkman Co., 894 F.Supp. 1084 (W.D.Ky.1995) (interpreting conflicting statutes).

6. In Hill v. General Motors Corp., 637 S.W.2d 382 (Mo.App.1982), the owners of a Chevrolet Blazer installed oversize wheels and tires, and modified its suspension system by installing lifts. The vehicle overturned because these changes altered its center of gravity. A passenger, injured in the accident, brought an action against Chevrolet for negligent failure to warn of the risk of making such modifications. Relying on *Robinson v. Reed–Prentice*, the court dismissed the claim. It held that there was no "duty to warn in anticipation that a user will alter its product so as to make it dangerous" even if the modification is foreseeable. *Compare* Griggs v. Firestone Tire & Rubber Co., 513 F.2d 851 (8th Cir.1975), cert. denied, 423 U.S. 865, 96 S.Ct. 124, 46 L.Ed.2d 93 (1975). A truck tire mounted on a multi-piece rim exploded and injured plaintiff. The explosion occurred because the components of the rim assembly were mismatched by a prior owner of the truck. One component was manufactured in 1945 and the other in 1957. Both components were manufactured by Firestone, but they were not compatible. Applying Missouri law, the court held Firestone liable for

failure to give an adequate warning against mismatching the components. Is the case consistent with *Hill v. General Motors Corp.?* Would the result have been different if only one of the rim components had been manufactured by Firestone?

7. In Lopez v. Precision Papers, Inc., 107 A.D.2d 667, 484 N.Y.S.2d 585 (1985), affirmed, 67 N.Y.2d 871, 501 N.Y.S.2d 798, 492 N.E.2d 1214 (1986), plaintiff was using a forklift in a warehouse to unload a wooden pallet of paper rolls stacked on top of other merchandise. He had to lift the fork blades over his head in order to insert them into the pallet. After the pallet was raised, a roll of paper fell off and injured plaintiff. The forklift was originally equipped with an overhead guard that would have protected plaintiff. The guard was removable so that it could be driven into low clearance areas, such as trucks, to unload merchandise. The guard was unnecessary when the forklift was being used in confined spaces because the operator could not lift the load above his head in such places. Plaintiff's employer removed the guard so that it could be used to unload trucks. At the time of the accident plaintiff was violating a company policy that prohibited use of forklifts without overhead guards in the warehouse. Plaintiff alleged that the manufacturer could foresee that the forklift would sometimes be used in open spaces without the guard; therefore, it was defective because it was not equipped with a safety interlock mechanism that would have prevented the lift from being raised above the operator's head if the guard was not in place. The court held that plaintiff stated a cause of action against the manufacturer. Is this holding consistent with *Robinson v. Reed–Prentice?*

8. **Duty to warn.** In Liriano v. Hobart Corp., 92 N.Y.2d 232, 700 N.E.2d 303, 677 N.Y.S.2d 764 (1998) defendant sold a meat grinder with a safety guard. The purchaser removed the guard, and the purchaser's employee was injured when he got his hand caught in the 'worm' gear while feeding meat into the grinder. The court recognized that because of *Robinson v. Reed–Prentice*, the defendant could not be liable to the employee under a design defect theory. The court held, however, that defendant—having learned that purchasers of the meat grinder were removing the guard—could be liable for failure to give a post-sale warning about the risk of using the machine without a guard.

SOUTHWIRE CO. v. BELOIT EASTERN CORP.
United States District Court, E.D. Pennsylvania, 1974.
370 F.Supp. 842.

[The court noted the paucity of cases concerning the burden of proof on the issue of whether a product has undergone substantial change. It stated:]

* * *

In view of the plethora of cases which have been brought under § 402A, it is surprising that so little has been written on the subject of § 402A(1)(b), which deals with substantial changes in the condition of the product. It seems to us that one essential element of a plaintiff's case under § 402A is proof that the product is expected to and does reach the user and consumer without substantial change in the condition in which it is sold. While no reported case that we can find contains any discussion of the point of burden of proof (or, more precisely, risk of nonpersuasion), there are several cases which mention it in passing. Judge Spaulding, in dissent in the case of Kuisis v. Baldwin–Lima Hamilton Co., 224 Pa.Super. 65, 301 A.2d 911 (1973), wrote that it is the plaintiff's burden to show that there was no substantial change in the defective part of the product between the time it was sold and the time of the accident.[1] Assuming that plaintiff had the burden of negating all reasonable causes for the malfunction except for the manufacturing defect relied on in a § 402A suit, Judge Staley, in Greco v. Bucciconi Engineering Co., 407 F.2d 87 (3d Cir.1969), spoke of the substantial change concept in terms of intervening superseding cause.[2] And, in an opinion just filed, Judge Weis wrote:

> Thus the plaintiff failed to prove a critical prerequisite that the product was in the same condition, so far as was relevant, on the day of the accident as it was at the time Bethlehem acquired possession.

Schreffler v. Birdsboro Corporation, 490 F.2d 1148, at 1153 (3d Cir.1974) (footnotes omitted). In effect, these cases imply that plaintiffs' failure to negate substantial changes is the same as saying that they failed to

---

1. Judge Spaulding cited Burbage v. Boiler Engineering & Supply Co., *supra*, as authority. While we agree with Judge Spaulding's statement of the law, we note that in *Burbage* the Pennsylvania Supreme Court merely upheld the jury's finding that the changes in question did not cause the defect; the court did not confront the burden of proof question.

2. Intervening superseding cause is a concept used in negligence cases and may be defined as an act of another person or force which by its intervention prevents the defendant from being liable for harm to another which his antecedent negligence is a substantial factor in bringing about. Restatement (Second) of Torts §§ 440–53 (1965). See also 27 P.L.E. § 80 at pp. 152–53 (1960).

We are not unmindful of the fact that the notion of "substantial change" is difficult to define, except perhaps on an *ad hoc* basis. A substantial change which negates § 402A liability may well be posited as something less significant than an intervening superseding ca[u]se. The rationale behind this argument is as follows. Since a defendant in a § 402A action can be held liable without proof of any fault on his part, this broad liability should not be imposed on a faultless defendant unless the plaintiff can prove a chain of causation linking the defendant's defective product to plaintiff's injury without substantial changes that may be less significant than intervening superseding causes needed to negate the liability of a negligent defendant. On the other hand, since § 402A liability is designed to be broader than negligence liability, it would be consistent with the intent of § 402A to require that, for a substantial change to negate § 402A liability, it must be at least as significant a break in the chain of causation as an intervening superseding cause is in negligence law. One could even argue that substantial change should be defined as the sole proximate cause before negating the § 402A liability of a defendant with a defective and unreasonably dangerous product. In the case at bar, we do not need to adopt any of these approaches, since we have found: (1) that plaintiffs failed to prove that the casting was a defective and unreasonably dangerous product which would have broken had there been no welding or undue stress; and (2) that the defendant has proved, although it did not have to, that a substantial change (i.e., the counterweight welding) was a cause of the accident. In this case then, plaintiffs failed to prove both causation in fact and proximate cause, since they failed to establish an unbroken chain of causation (or repair a broken one) between an originally defective casting and the ultimate injury.

prove proximate cause, since they failed to negate the break in the causal connection between the original defect and the ultimate injury.

Rarely do judges comment, except in charges to the jury, on who has the burden of proving proximate cause, since it is such a fundamental element of plaintiff's case that it is assumed *sub silentio* to be within plaintiff's burden of proof. *See* Restatement of Torts (Second) § 433B (1965). Similarly, we believe that plaintiffs have the burden of proving no substantial change in order to prevail under § 402A(1)(b), although, as indicated above, we can find no case that directly reaches this holding. The plaintiffs' brief suggests that the question of proving substantial changes is an affirmative defense. They cite no case or commentator to support their proposition, and we have not found any authority or persuasive reason for their conclusion. To be sure, there are reasons for requiring the defendant to carry the burden of coming forward and alleging a substantial change. In many cases, the alleged substantial change is perceived only by the defendant who should, therefore, have to allege it and maintain the burden of going forward with the evidence on the point. The plaintiff is accordingly put on notice to try to prove no substantial changes were made. And as a general rule, rather than requiring a plaintiff to negate an infinite number of possible changes, it seems more reasonable and in keeping with our adversary process to expect the defendant to allege the substantial changes he expects a plaintiff to try to disprove. But once the defendant has come forward, we believe that the burden of proof (or again, more precisely, the risk of non-persuasion) must remain with the plaintiff; if the scales remain in equilibrium on the point, plaintiff is the loser.

To impose on the plaintiff the burden of proving both proximate cause and no substantial change is consistent with the underlying concept of § 402A. In the seminal case of Greenman v. Yuba Power Products, 59 Cal.2d 57, 27 Cal.Rptr. 697, 377 P.2d 897 (1963), Chief Justice Traynor articulated the rationale behind § 402A as follows:

> The purpose of [strict] liability is to insure that the costs of injuries resulting from defective products are borne by the manufacturers who put them on the market rather than by the injured persons who are powerless to protect themselves.[3]

While § 402A is meant to require manufacturers and sellers to bear much of the responsibility and cost of injuries to consumers resulting from their defective products, it is not meant to impose upon each manufacturer and seller an absolute liability as insurer for all injuries to consumers, regardless of the relation of plaintiff's injuries to the particular defendant's product.

In the instant case, we have found that plaintiffs failed to negate the substantial change alleged by Beloit and similarly failed to demonstrate

---

3. In addition to Judge Traynor's reason, Dean Prosser notes that permitting a plaintiff to sue the manufacturer directly on a theory of strict liability avoids a series of actions which would accomplish the same result, after an otherwise time-consuming and wasteful process. *See* Prosser, Law of Torts 674 (3d ed. 1964).

the proximate cause element necessary for recovery. Indeed, we have found that Beloit proved (although it had no such burden) that the casting failed, not as a self-contained component part with a defect unreasonably dangerous at the time it left Beloit, but due to the changes that were made in it by the counterweight welding. Accordingly, plaintiffs cannot recover.

* * *

Note

On the subject of substantial change, *see* Comment, Substantial Change: Alteration of a Product as a Bar to a Manufacturer's Strict Liability, 80 Dick.L.Rev. 245 (1976); Note, Product Modification: The Effect of Foreseeability, 42 U.Pitt.L.Rev. 431 (1981); Products Liability: Alteration of Product After it Leaves Hands of Manufacturer or Seller as Affecting Liability for Product–Caused Harm, 41 A.L.R.3d 1251 (1972).

SECTION C. EFFECT OF APPORTIONMENT OF FAULT ON SUPERSEDING CAUSE

BARRY v. QUALITY STEEL PRODUCTS, INC.

Supreme Court of Connecticut, 2003.
263 Conn. 424, 820 A.2d 258.

NORCOTT, J.

* * *

The plaintiffs [Neil Barry and Bernard Cohade, who were employed by DeLucaConstruction Company (DeLuca),] brought this product liability action[1] pursuant to Statutes § 52–572m et seq. against Quality Steel

---

1. Our conclusion that the defendants were not entitled to a superseding cause instruction is premised solely on a common-law analysis of the law of proximate and superseding causes, because that is the way this case was tried to a jury and argued on appeal regarding the law of causation. We note, however, that this was a products liability case, which is governed by General Statutes §§ 52–572m through 52–572q. General Statutes § 52–572o, entitled "[c]omparative responsibility," and General Statutes § 52–572p, entitled "[l]imitation of liability of product seller," incorporate notions of apportionment of responsibility and damages and misuse of a product, respectively, and arguably may affect how the principles we articulate herein should apply on retrial.

More specifically, subsections (a), (b) and (c) of § 52–572o set forth principles of comparative responsibility, and subsection (d) sets forth principles of joint and several liability. Subsection (e) of § 52–572o sets forth principles of contribution. To the extent that these provisions are based on principles of comparative fault, they are consistent with the principles that we articulate in this opinion. Furthermore, § 52–572p sets forth principles regarding alteration or modification of a product, which may be consistent or inconsistent with the claims of the defendants regarding the use of their product. Finally, any of these provisions, to the extent applicable to the facts of this case, may be consistent or inconsistent with the exclusivity of remedy principles of the Worker's Compensation Act. We refer to these statutory provisions because, as the case was argued and briefed in this court, and apparently as presented to the jury in the trial court, none of these provision were discussed, and it may be that they will apply to some extent to the facts of the case in the ensuing retrial.

alleging that it had designed and manufactured a defective product, namely, roof brackets, which were utilized by the plaintiffs in the hanging of shingles, and against Ring's End, the seller of the brackets. Thereafter, the plaintiffs filed a motion in limine asking the trial court to exclude evidence of any alleged negligence on the part of DeLuca, and to deny the defendants' request to charge the jury on the doctrine of superseding cause. The court denied the motion and, at the end of the testimony, the trial court instructed the jury on the doctrine of superseding cause. After answering a set of special interrogatories, the jury returned a verdict in favor of the defendants on all counts. The trial court denied the plaintiffs' motion to set aside the verdict and rendered judgment for the defendants. This appeal followed.

The jury reasonably could have found the following facts. The plaintiffs were employed as carpenters by DeLuca. On February 26, 1998, the plaintiffs were putting shingles on the roof of [a building] when the platform staging on which they were working collapsed, causing the plaintiffs to fall to the ground and sustain severe injuries. Immediately prior to the collapse, the plaintiffs were working on a wooden plank attached to the roof by roof brackets designed and manufactured by Quality Steel and purchased from Ring's End.

The roof brackets were used as part of a structure that created a platform on which the plaintiffs could work. To install the brackets, the plaintiffs nailed them to the roof through three slots on the bracket. After the brackets were attached to the roof, a plank was placed on top of the brackets, which then provided a surface on which the plaintiffs could stand in order to shingle the roof. * * *

* * * [While working on the planks,] the planking suddenly fell out from under them and they fell to the ground. Almost immediately after the plaintiffs fell, Gene Marini, the general superintendent at DeLuca, discovered one of the roof brackets used by the plaintiffs in a distorted condition on the ground near where they fell.

Quality Steel's instruction label on the roof brackets suggests that the user attach the brackets to the roof using sixteenpenny nails. The defendants introduced evidence that some of the brackets were installed by another DeLuca employee, Nate Manizza, using [smaller] eightpenny nails. The plaintiffs both testified that when they installed roof brackets they used larger, twelvepenny nails. Neither the plaintiffs nor Manizza could remember if they had installed the specific brackets that had collapsed causing the plaintiffs to fall. Cohade testified, however, that he saw Manizza installing the brackets in the general area where the plaintiffs fell. There was also testimony from both the plaintiffs' and the defendants' experts that the use of a twelvepenny nail would be sufficient to hold the bracket to the roof and would not be causative of the collapse of the planking that occurred in this case.

The defendants also introduced evidence * * * that DeLuca had violated the federal Occupational Safety and Health Administration (OSHA) regulations by failing to provide additional fall protection for the plaintiffs while they were working on the New Canaan Nature Center roof. * * *

The jury also reasonably could have found that the roof bracket designed and manufactured by Quality Steel and used by the plaintiffs before the platform collapsed was undersized in comparison to the manufacturing specifications. Specifically, both the plaintiffs' and the defendants' experts testified that the platform arm of the roof bracket was thinner than required by Quality Steel's own specifications. Additionally, the jury, through their special interrogatories, found that Quality Steel's product was defective and unreasonably dangerous at the time it was manufactured and sold by the defendants, and that the defective condition of the product was a proximate cause of the plaintiffs' accident. * * *

I

The plaintiffs claim that the trial court improperly instructed the jury on the doctrine of superseding cause because: (1) the plaintiffs' injuries were not outside the scope of the risk created by the defendants' misconduct in manufacturing and selling a defective product; and (2) any negligence on the part of DeLuca was not the sole proximate cause of the plaintiffs' injuries. The defendants claim, in response, that the combined negligence of the plaintiffs, DeLuca and Manizza, constituted sufficient evidence of a superseding cause, thereby exonerating the defendants from the plaintiffs' product liability claim. * * *

We begin our analysis with an examination of the relationship among proximate cause, concurrent cause and superseding cause. "Proximate cause results from a sequence of events unbroken by a superseding cause, so that its causal viability continued until the moment of injury or at least until the advent of the immediate injurious force." *Coburn v. Lenox Homes, Inc.,* 186 Conn. 370, 383, 441 A.2d 620 (1982). "[T]he test of proximate cause is whether the defendant's conduct is a substantial factor in bringing about the plaintiff's injuries." (Internal quotation marks omitted.) *Paige v. St. Andrew's Roman Catholic Church Corp.,* 250 Conn. 14, 25, 734 A.2d 85 (1999). A concurrent cause is one that is "contemporaneous and coexistent with the defendant's wrongful conduct and actively cooperates with the defendant's conduct to bring about the injury." *Wagner v. Clark Equipment Co.,* 243 Conn. 168, 183, 700 A.2d 38 (1997). Finally, "[a] superseding cause is an act of a third person or other force which by its intervention prevents the actor from being liable for harm to another which his antecedent negligence is a substantial factor in bringing about."[2] (Internal quotation marks omitted.) Id., at 179, 700 A.2d 38.

2. Although we discuss the concept of superseding cause herein in relation to "antecedent negligence," we recognize that the present case is not based on negligence but on product liability. Nonetheless, the relationship between the concept of superseding cause and proximate cause, and the lack of continuing viability of the doctrine of superseding cause, which we discuss herein, apply equally to injuries proximately caused by a defective product, as well as injuries proximately caused by negligent conduct.

"The function of the doctrine of superseding cause * * * is to define the circumstances under which responsibility *may be shifted entirely* from the shoulders of one person, who is determined to be negligent, to the shoulders of another person, who may also be determined to be negligent, or to some other force." (Emphasis added; internal quotation marks omitted.) Id. * * *

* * *

In the present case, the jury's interrogatories reveal two possible sources of a superseding cause. The first possible superseding cause of the plaintiffs' injuries was DeLuca's failure to provide additional fall protection for the plaintiffs. The second possible superseding cause was Manizza's use of eightpenny nails to attach the roof brackets to the roof.

We * * * conclude that the doctrine of superseding cause no longer serves a useful purpose in our jurisprudence when a defendant claims that a subsequent negligent act by a third party cuts off its own liability for the plaintiff's injuries. We conclude that under those circumstances, superseding cause instructions serve to complicate what is fundamentally a proximate cause analysis. Specifically, we conclude that, because our statutes allow for apportionment among negligent defendants; see General Statutes § 52–572h; and because Connecticut is a comparative negligence jurisdiction; General Statutes § 52–572o; the simpler and less confusing approach to cases, such as the present one, where the jury must determine which, among many, causes contributed to the plaintiffs' injury, is to couch the analysis in proximate cause rather than allowing the defendants to raise a defense of superseding cause.[3]

[Some legal] * * * treatises support the view that the doctrine of superseding cause is merely a more complicated analysis of whether the defendant's actions were the proximate cause of the plaintiff's injuries. For example, one treatise states: "[Superseding] cause is merely proximate cause flowing from a source not connected with the party sought to be charged. While the term may have some descriptive value, unduly elaborate discussion of [superseding] cause as such tends to becloud

---

Thus, our references herein to antecedent negligence in the context of proximate and superseding causes, necessarily includes the manufacture and sale of a defective product. Both references, therefore, are to antecedent *tortious* conduct—in this case, the manufacture and sale of a defective product.

3. Our conclusion that the doctrine of superseding cause no longer serves a useful purpose is limited to the situation in cases, such as the one presently before us, wherein a defendant claims that its tortious conduct is superseded by a subsequent negligent act or there are multiple acts of negligence. Our conclusion does not necessarily affect those cases where the defendant claims that an unforeseeable intentional tort, force of nature, or criminal event supersedes its tortious conduct. See *Doe v. Manheimer*, 212 Conn. 748, 761, 563 A.2d 699 (1989) (concluding that criminal attack on plaintiff was superseding cause of plaintiff's injuries notwithstanding plaintiff's claim that defendant's allowed overgrowth of vegetation on property where attack occurred was substantial factor in both occurrence and duration of attack), overruled in part on other grounds, *Stewart v. Federated Dept. Stores, Inc.*, 234 Conn. 597, 608, 662 A.2d 753 (1995). Nor does our conclusion necessarily affect the doctrine of superseding cause in the area of criminal law. See *State v. Munoz*, 233 Conn. 106, 124–25, 659 A.2d 683 (1995). We leave those questions to cases that squarely present them.

rather than clarify the relatively simple idea of causal connection. *When it is determined that a defendant is relieved of liability by reason of [superseding] cause, it would appear to mean simply that the negligent conduct of someone else-and not that of the defendant-is the proximate cause of the event.*" (Emphasis added.) 1 T. Shearman & A. Redfield, Negligence (Rev. Ed.1941) § 37, pp. 99–100.

Under this latter approach, the fact finder need only determine whether the allegedly negligent conduct of any actor was a proximate cause, specifically, whether the conduct was a substantial factor in contributing to the plaintiff's injuries. If such conduct is found to be a proximate cause of the plaintiff's foreseeable injury, each actor will pay his or her proportionate share pursuant to our apportionment statute, regardless of whether another's conduct also contributed to the plaintiff's injury. Put differently, the term superseding cause merely describes more fully the concept of proximate cause when there is more than one alleged act of negligence, and is not functionally distinct from the determination of whether an act is a proximate cause of the injury suffered by the plaintiff. We find this latter approach, that the doctrine of superseding cause is, in essence, a determination regarding proximate cause or causes, persuasive and hereby adopt it in our case law.

Thus, the doctrine of superseding cause no longer serves a useful purpose in our negligence jurisprudence. Historically, the doctrine reflects the courts' attempt to limit the defendants' liability to foreseeable and reasonable bounds. See W. Prosser & W. Keeton, supra, § 44, at p. 302. In this regard, the doctrine of superseding cause involves a question of policy and foreseeability regarding the actions for which a court will hold a defendant accountable. This aspect of superseding cause is already incorporated in our law regarding proximate causation.[4] As some commentators have noted, however, the doctrine was also shaped in response to the harshness of contributory negligence and joint and several liability. See T. Christlieb, "Why Superseding Cause Analysis Should Be Abandoned," 72 Tex. L.Rev. 161, 165–66 (1993). Under this reasoning, in order to avoid what some courts determined was an undue burden on the plaintiff under contributory negligence regimes, courts developed certain ameliorative doctrines, which identified some aspect of the defendant's negligent act that served as a basis for shifting the plaintiff's

---

4. This court has, in prior opinions, outlined our proximate cause jurisprudence. "The second component of legal cause is proximate cause, which we have defined as [a]n actual cause that is a substantial factor in the resulting harm.... The proximate cause requirement tempers the expansive view of causation [in fact] ... by the pragmatic ... shaping [of] rules which are feasible to administer, and yield a workable degree of certainty.... Remote or trivial [actual] causes are generally rejected because the determination of the responsibility for another's injury is much too important to be distracted by explorations for obscure consequences or inconsequential causes.... In determining proximate cause, the point beyond which the law declines to trace a series of events that exist along a chain signifying actual causation is a matter of fair judgment and a rough sense of justice." (Citations omitted; internal quotation marks omitted.) *Paige v. St. Andrew's Roman Catholic Church Corp.,* supra, 250 Conn. at 25, 734 A.2d 85. This definition of proximate cause implicitly includes one of the stated purposes of the doctrine of superseding cause, namely, to limit the defendant's liability to foreseeable bounds.

negligence to the defendant so that the plaintiff could recover for his losses. Id., at 165. Thus, the courts sometimes labeled a defendant's negligence as an intervening act that cut off any contributory negligence of the plaintiff, which, had it not been superseded by the defendant's negligence, would have constituted a total bar to recovery. Id.

We conclude that this aspect of the doctrine of superseding cause has no place in our modern system of comparative fault and apportionment. We agree with the author of the previously cited note that it is inconsistent to conclude simultaneously that all negligent parties should pay in proportion to their fault, as § 52–572h requires, but that one negligent party does not have to pay its share because its negligence was somehow "superseded" by a subsequent negligent act. See id., at 181. We also find persuasive the author's criticism of the Restatement (Second) method; see 2 Restatement (Second), Torts §§ 442 through 453, pp. 467–91 (1965); which looks to the nature of the subsequent negligent act to determine whether it somehow supersedes the previous act. T. Christlieb, supra, at 72 Tex. L.Rev. 184. This approach gives undue prominence to the temporal order of the allegedly negligent acts. As the author aptly notes, causal contributions do not operate in neat temporal sequences; rather, most events, such as the events giving rise to the plaintiff's injury in the present case, result from a convergence of many conditions. Id., at 185. The Restatement (Second) approach, then, has the potential of misleading the fact finder regarding the determination of whether each allegedly tortious act is a proximate cause of the plaintiff's injury by placing too much emphasis on the timing of the acts.

Moreover, it is no longer necessary to utilize doctrines that aid fact finders in making policy decisions regarding how to assign liability among various defendants and the plaintiff because those decisions already are inherent in our modern scheme of comparative negligence and apportionment. Thus, under the approach we adopt herein, the question to be answered by the fact finder is whether the various actors' allegedly negligent conduct was a cause in fact and a proximate cause of the plaintiff's injury in light of all the relevant circumstances. If found to be both, each actor will be liable for his or her proportionate share of the plaintiff's damages.[5]

---

5. A similar approach, namely, that modern definitions of proximate cause, along with the advent of comparative fault regimes, render the doctrine of superseding cause unnecessary, has been followed in other texts. See M. Green, "The Unanticipated Ripples of Comparative Negligence: Superseding Cause in Products Liability and Beyond," 53 S.C. L.Rev. 1103, 1107–1108 (2002). Green notes that the predominant approach to superseding cause requires that the harm for which a plaintiff seeks to recover be one of the harms whose risk made the defendant's conduct tortious. Id., at 1120. Put differently, "[t]he defendant's liability extends to harms that came to fruition as a result of the risks that made the defendant's failure to take greater care negligent." Id. Thus, in the author's opinion, which we find persuasive, the doctrine of superseding cause is already incorporated into the test for proximate cause. Repeating the test for superseding cause, then, merely adds confusion to an already confusing subject, and serves no meaningful purpose in a jurisdiction, such as ours, wherein a defendant will be liable only for his or her proportion of the plaintiff's damages.

At least two other states also have addressed the issue of whether the doctrine of superseding cause continues to play a useful role in their negligence jurisprudence after the advent of comparative fault and apportionment regimes. Because these cases illustrate aspects of the approach we adopt here today, we discuss them in detail.

In *Torres v. El Paso Electric Co.*, 127 N.M. 729, 732, 987 P.2d 386 (1999), the plaintiff was injured when he came into contact with a power line while replacing the roof of his employer's building. In the negligence action brought by the plaintiff against the electric company, the defendant claimed that the actions of the plaintiff, the plaintiff's employer and various other electrical contractors, constituted a superseding cause of the plaintiff's injuries that relieved the defendant of any liability. Id., at 734, 987 P.2d 386. The jury ultimately determined that, although the defendant was negligent, its negligence was not the proximate cause of the plaintiff's injuries. Id., at 733, 987 P.2d 386.

The New Mexico Supreme Court, in *Torres,* began its analysis of the plaintiff's appeal by explaining that New Mexico previously had adopted a pure comparative negligence system and, as a natural corollary, subsequently had abolished joint and several liability. Id., at 734–35, 987 P.2d 386. The court went on to explain that, prior to the adoption of comparative negligence, courts had used the doctrine of superseding cause to avoid the contributory negligence bar that some deemed to be unfair. Id., at 735–36, 987 P.2d 386. The court determined that this application of the doctrine of superseding cause was inconsistent with New Mexico's comparative fault laws. Id., at 736, 987 P.2d 386. Moreover, when analyzing the doctrine, the court appropriately stated: "A finding of an independent [superseding] cause represents a finding against the plaintiff on proximate cause or, in other words, a finding that the defendant's act or omission did not, in a natural and continuous sequence, produce the injury." Id. Thus, the court determined that, the doctrine was no longer appropriate in cases where the defendant alleged that the plaintiff's negligence superseded its own liability, because the use of the doctrine created an unacceptable risk that the jury would inadvertently apply the common-law rule of contributory negligence. Id.

* * *

In *Control Techniques, Inc. v. Johnson*, 762 N.E.2d 104 (Ind.2002), the Indiana Supreme Court analyzed the relationship between that state's comparative fault act and the doctrine of superseding cause. In *Control Techniques, Inc.,* the plaintiff sustained serious injuries while measuring the voltage of a circuit breaker. Id., at 106. The jury allocated 5 percent of the fault to the defendant. Id. On appeal, the defendant contended that the negligence of another company that had installed the circuit breaker constituted a superseding cause of the accident and foreclosed any liability on its part for defective design and manufacture. Id., at 107.

After an analysis of that state's common-law doctrine of superseding cause, the court in *Control Techniques, Inc.,* concluded that the doctrines of causation and foreseeability impose the same limitations on liability as the superseding cause doctrine. Id., at 108. As the court aptly noted: "Causation limits a negligent actor's liability to foreseeable consequences. A superseding cause is, by definition, one that is not reasonably foreseeable. As a result, the doctrine in today's world adds nothing to the requirement of foreseeability that is not already inherent in the requirement of causation." Id. Ultimately, the Indiana Supreme Court concluded that it was proper for the trial court to instruct only on proximate causation because the substance of the doctrine of superseding cause was fully explained in the instruction on proximate cause. Id., at 110.

We find these two cases persuasive and conclude that the rationale supporting the abandonment of the doctrine of superseding cause outweighs any of the doctrine's remaining usefulness in our modern system of torts. Specifically, as the New Mexico Supreme Court determined, we believe that the instruction on superseding cause complicates what is essentially a proximate cause analysis and risks jury confusion. The doctrine also no longer serves a useful purpose in our tort jurisprudence, especially considering our system of comparative negligence and apportionment, where defendants are responsible solely for their proportionate share of the injury suffered by the plaintiff. Thus, it is no longer appropriate to give an instruction of the doctrine of superseding cause in cases involving multiple acts of negligence. Instead, under the approach we adopt herein, if the defendant was both the cause in fact and a proximate cause of the plaintiff's injury, the defendant will be liable for his or her proportionate share of the damages, notwithstanding other acts of negligence that also may have contributed to the plaintiff's injury.

This analysis leads to the conclusion that the doctrine of superseding cause should not have been presented to the jury in the present case. Upon retrial, therefore, the fact finder must determine if the manufacture and sale of a defective product was a cause in fact and a proximate cause of the plaintiffs' injuries, without reference to the doctrine of superseding cause. See also footnote [1] [this is not 1 in current version, it's 4] of this opinion.

* * *

The judgment for the defendants is reversed and the case is remanded for a new trial * * *.

In this opinion the other justices concurred.

Notes

1. The foreseeability of risk test is emerging as the predominate test of proximate cause in American tort cases. For the reasons stated in *Barry,* there is increasing recognition that in foreseeability jurisdictions superseding cause analysis adds little but confusion to the proximate cause issue. *See, e.g.,* David G. Owen, Products Liability Law § 12.3 at 789–90 (2005); Victor E. Schwartz, Comparative Negligence 93–95 (3d ed. 1994); Restatement

(Third) of Torts: Liability for Physical Harm § 34, Comment c (Proposed Final Draft No. 1, 2005); Michael D. Green, The Unanticipated Ripples of Comparative Negligence: Superseding Cause in Products Liability and Beyond, 53 S.C.L.Rev. 1103 (2002); David W. Robertson, Love and Fury: Recent Radical Revisions to the Law of Comparative Fault, 59 La.L.Rev. 175, 190–91 (1998); Terry Christlieb, Note, Why Superseding Cause Analysis Should be Abandoned, 72 Tex.L.Rev. 161, 181 (1993). If the intervening cause (including misuse) is foreseeable, the defendant will be required to protect against it in its design or warning, but only if reasonable prudence so requires. If the intervening cause is unforeseeable it is superseding (and cuts off liability) only if it creates a different kind of accident than was foreseeable to a reasonable product manufacturer. Under these circumstances superseding cause analysis is superfluous because there is no proximate cause under the foreseeability test.

2. In strict products liability cases courts often require plaintiff to prove, as an element of her case, that plaintiff's injury resulted from a use of the product that was reasonably foreseeable to defendant. *See,* e.g., California Jury Instruction BAJI 9.00.3, *supra* page 88. If California were to follow the holding in *Barry*, would it have to change its jury instruction?

3. In footnote 3, *Barry* reserves judgement on the whether its abolition of superseding cause analysis applies to intentional or criminal intervening causes. When an unforeseeable intentional or criminal intervening cause produces a foreseeable type of harm, should the non-criminal tortfeasor ever be exempt form liability? Consider cases like *Mull v. Ford Motor Co., supra* page 484, where a third party deliberately continues to use the product after discovering the defect, and injures a bystander because of the defect. Should such unforeseeable deliberate misuse cut off the liability of the product manufacturer? Should the answer to this question depend on whether the jurisdiction allows a comparison of the fault of intentional tortfeasors with the fault of nonintentional tortfeasors? *See,* Michael D. Green, The Unanticipated Ripples of Comparative Negligence: Superseding Cause in Products Liability and Beyond, 53 S.C.L.Rev. 1103, 1132 (2002) ("The best circumstances for eschewing any role for superseding cause in cases involving intentional or criminal intervention is in jurisdictions with several liability that permit apportionment of liability among intentional and nonintentional tortfeasors.").

4. As the Introduction to this Chapter points out, the trend toward adopting the foreseeability test of proximate cause in products liability cases is far from universal. As the discussion in the Introduction indicates, superseding cause analysis remains an important tool for limiting the scope of liability in jurisdictions rejecting the foreseeability test.

5. The Supreme Court in Exxon Co., U.S.A. v. Sofec, Inc., 517 U.S. 830, 116 S.Ct. 1813, 135 L.Ed.2d 113 (1996) adopted a rule in which superseding cause would play a significant independent role, contrary to *Barry*. In *Sofec*, an admiralty case, the defendant negligently created a risk to plaintiff's ship and its crew during a storm by allowing a connection to break as the ship was pumping oil. After half an hour, an assisting ship removed a broken hose that had been attached to the ship and that had been impairing its maneuverability. For the next half hour, the ship's captain maneuvered the

ship out to sea—to avoid the dangers of being stranded in shallow water. After that point, the captain was negligent in a variety of ways, leading to hitting a reef with the ship being a total loss. The Court unanimously affirmed the trial judge's decision not to compare the two faults. The trial judge, sitting as finder of fact, had found that the decisions of the captain were "made calmly, deliberately and without the pressure of an imminent peril." Superseding cause law survives the adoption of comparative principles for apportionment of liability, according to the Court, because superseding cause is not "internally inconsistent" with comparative negligence.

6. Does *Barry* itself actually use the foreseeability test of proximate cause? Footnote 4 states that a purpose of the court's definition of proximate cause is "to limit the defendant's liability to foreseeable bounds." But the actual tests of proximate cause *Barry* describes speak only in terms of such concepts as *unbroken sequences of events* and *substantial factors* rather than in terms of foreseeability.

Chapter 8

THE EFFECT OF STATUTES AND REGULATIONS

SECTION A. RELEVANCE OF STATUTES

LORENZ v. CELOTEX CORP.
United States Court of Appeals, Fifth Circuit, 1990.
896 F.2d 148.

On Appeal from the United States District Court for the Northern District of Texas.

Before GEE, JONES, and SMITH, CIRCUIT JUDGES:

EDITH H. JONES, CIRCUIT JUDGE:

Plaintiff Janice Grafton Lorenz brought this products liability action, alleging that her husband died of lung cancer as a result of his exposure to asbestos products manufactured by defendant, the Celotex Corporation. After a jury trial, the jury returned a verdict in favor of Celotex. Lorenz appeals, claiming that the district court erroneously instructed the jury that compliance with government safety standards constitutes strong and substantial evidence that a product is not defective. We affirm.

BACKGROUND

Paul Lorenz died of lung cancer in 1981. His widow, Janice Grafton Lorenz, alleges that his illness was the result of his exposure to asbestos insulation products while he served as a boiler technician aboard a United States Navy vessel from 1966 to 1968. As a boiler technician, Lorenz periodically removed and replaced the asbestos insulation on the pipes and valves in the boiler room. He also occasionally installed asbestos millboard around the boilers. At least some of the insulation and millboard used was manufactured by the Philip Carey Company, predecessor-in-interest of defendant Celotex.

Seeking to recover damages for her husband's wrongful death, Mrs. Lorenz filed this action against thirteen different asbestos manufacturers. Mrs. Lorenz sought recovery on both negligence and strict liability grounds based on the manufacturers' failure to warn of the hazards of working with asbestos. All the defendants except Celotex settled or were dismissed prior to trial.

On January 9, 1989 the case proceeded to trial, with Celotex as the sole defendant. Plaintiff offered the testimony of expert witnesses who indicated that asbestos was a substantial factor in her husband's illness, and presented evidence that Celotex had failed to warn of any such danger. Celotex attempted to establish that its products were not defective or unreasonably dangerous by presenting evidence that use of its insulation products produced asbestos dust counts below the maximum level established by the official and unofficial safety standards in place at the time of Lorenz's exposure. At the close of the evidence, the district court, upon Celotex's request, instructed the jury that:

> Compliance with government safety standards constitutes strong and substantial evidence that a product is not defective.

The jury returned a verdict in favor of Celotex on both the strict liability and negligence claims, and the district court entered judgment for Celotex. Lorenz appeals, contending that the district court erred by giving the instruction on compliance with government standards because (1) the instruction was substantively incorrect, and (2) there was no evidence to support the instruction.

DISCUSSION

A. *Substantive Correctness*

The language of the challenged instruction comes directly from this court's opinions in *Gideon v. Johns–Manville Sales Corp.*, 761 F.2d 1129, 1144 (5th Cir.1985), and *Dartez v. Fibreboard Corp.*, 765 F.2d 456, 471 (5th Cir.1985) (quoting *Gideon*). In *Gideon*, a plaintiff who had contracted asbestosis sought to recover damages from several asbestos manufacturers, including Raymark Industries, Inc. The jury determined that Raymark's asbestos textile products were defective and held the company liable for the plaintiff's injuries. On appeal, the court reversed the judgment against Raymark because there was insufficient evidence to support the findings against it. *Gideon*, 761 F.2d at 1143–45. In reaching its decision, the court placed great weight on the fact that Raymark's products complied with the applicable government safety standards. *Id.* at 1144. The court noted that "[c]ompliance with such government safety standards constitutes strong and substantial evidence that a product is not defective." *Id.* Similarly, in *Dartez* the court reversed another judgment against Raymark Industries on insufficiency of evidence grounds. *Dartez*, 765 F.2d at 470–71. Once again the court relied heavily on the fact that Raymark's products complied with applicable government standards, quoting *Gideon* for the proposition that such compliance is strong and substantial evidence that a product is not defective. *Id.* at 471.

Despite the fact that the district court took its instruction from *Gideon* and *Dartez*, Lorenz contends that the instruction was substantively incorrect for several reasons. First, she argues that the language in those opinions was intended merely as a comment on the weight of the particular evidence in those cases, not as a general rule of law. Even a casual reading of *Gideon* and *Dartez* belies Lorenz's interpretation. In each case the court states the rule as a general proposition, without qualifying the statement to the particular facts of the case. *Gideon*, 761 F.2d at 1144; *Dartez*, 765 F.2d at 471. In addition, each opinion cites authority to support the proposition.[1] We cannot agree with Lorenz that the language in *Gideon* and *Dartez* was not intended to state a general rule of law.

Lorenz next argues that the instruction is substantively incorrect because it is unsupported by Texas law. Lorenz correctly points out that in diversity cases, jury instructions must accurately describe the applicable state substantive law. *Turlington v. Phillips Petroleum Co.*, 795 F.2d 434, 441 (5th Cir.1986). It appears that no Texas case has expressly stated that compliance with government standards constitutes strong and substantial evidence that a product is not defective. However, * * * Lorenz has not cited, and the court has not found, any Texas cases establishing a rule that compliance with government standards is less than strong and substantial evidence.[2] See 59 TEX.JUR.3d *Products Liability* § 67 (1988) (reporting that the rule in Texas is that "[e]vidence of compliance with government safety standards does constitute strong and substantial evidence that a product is not defective * * * "). In the absence of controverting Texas authority, the district court and this court are bound by the interpretation of Texas law expressed in *Gideon* and *Dartez*. [Citation] Accordingly, we conclude that the district court's instruction was substantively correct.

B. No Evidence

Lorenz also contends that the district court erred by giving the instruction because Celotex did not present any evidence that its products complied with an applicable government standard. A district court may not instruct a jury on a legal theory on which no evidence is presented. [Citation] However, in this case, Celotex introduced sufficient

---

1. *Gideon* relies on *Simien v. S.S. Kresge Co.*, 566 F.2d 551, 557 (5th Cir.1978). In *Simien*, the defendant argued that a jacket it manufactured was not defective because it complied with government flammability standards. The court noted that such testimony was "evidence, indeed substantial evidence, that the jacket was not unreasonably dangerous." *Simien*, 566 F.2d at 557.

2. Lorenz relies on *Bristol–Meyers Co. v. Gonzales*, 561 S.W.2d 801 (Tex.1978); *Golden Villa Nursing Home, Inc. v. Smith*, 674 S.W.2d 343 (Tex.App.—Houston [14th Dist.] 1984, writ ref'd n.r.e.); and *Rumsey v. Freeway Manor Minimax*, 423 S.W.2d 387 (Tex.Civ.App.—Houston [1st Dist.] 1968, no writ), but none of those cases supports Lorenz's argument that compliance with government safety standards is less than strong and substantial evidence. Rather, those cases stand for the general proposition that compliance with government standards usually does not insulate a defendant or automatically preclude a finding of liability. *E.g., Bristol–Meyers Co. v. Gonzales*, 561 S.W.2d at 804 (compliance with F.D.A. warning requirements did not preclude liability for inadequate warning); *see also Simien v. S.S. Kresge Co.*, 566 F.2d 551, 557 (5th Cir.1978) (while evidence of compliance with government standards was strong and substantial evidence, it was not conclusive on the issue of liability).

evidence to permit the court to instruct the jury that compliance with government safety standards constitutes strong and substantial evidence that a product is not defective.

Lorenz first argues that Celotex failed to present evidence of a government standard applicable to this case. We disagree. At trial, Celotex presented evidence that until the end of the 1960's, exposure to asbestos dust counts below five million particles per cubic foot was generally considered safe. This standard was first proposed in a 1938 Surgeon General's Report, known as the Dressen Report after its principal author. The American Conference of Governmental Industrial Hygienists, a "quasi-official body responsible for making recommendations concerning industrial hygiene," *Borel v. Fibreboard Paper Products Corp.*, 493 F.2d 1076, 1084 (5th Cir.1973), cert. denied, 419 U.S. 869, 95 S.Ct. 127, 42 L.Ed.2d 107 (1974), adopted the five million particle per cubic foot standard as the threshold limit for safe exposure to asbestos in 1946, and reaffirmed the standard in 1961 and 1964. State governments also adopted the five million particle per cubic foot standard. In 1945, the state of New York, where Lorenz resided at the time of his death, adopted the five million standard. Ohio, where Philip Carey had its headquarters and principal insulation plant, adopted the standard in 1947. Most importantly, the state of Texas, whose law governs this case, adopted the five million particles per cubic foot standard in 1958. It was not until after the period of Paul Lorenz's exposure that governments began to reduce the acceptable asbestos dust count.

Lorenz contends that none of the government standards offered by Celotex should apply in this case because none of those standards applies to the *labeling* of asbestos products. This argument cannot withstand analysis. To establish Celotex's liability for failure to warn of the dangers of using its products, Lorenz had to prove that Celotex "knew or should have known of such dangers at the time the products were marketed." *Gideon v. Johns–Manville Sales Corp.*, 761 F.2d 1129, 1145 (5th Cir.1985). Evidence of compliance with government safety standards (here, evidence that use of Celotex's insulation products produced dust counts below the threshold limit) constitutes strong and substantial evidence that a product is not defective. *See Id.* at 1144. Thus, evidence that use of Celotex's products produced dust counts below the threshold limit is, logically, strong and substantial evidence that Celotex did not know or should not have known that its products were so dangerous or defective that they required a warning. Accordingly, we conclude that Celotex presented evidence of an applicable government standard.

Likewise, Celotex presented sufficient evidence that it complied with the applicable standards. First, Celotex introduced the results of several studies of asbestos exposure among insulation workers. In each case, the study concluded that exposure levels were below the five million particles per cubic foot threshold. Second, Celotex offered uncontroverted evidence that to the extent that its products differed from those being used in the studies it introduced, Celotex's insulation was less *dusty*. Arthur Mueller, a former research and development worker at Philip Carey, testified that Philip Carey's products contained a smaller percentage of asbestos than the competition's. He also testified that Philip Carey's insulation was designed to be cut with a knife rather than a saw, came with preformed fittings, and used an asbestos-free cement. Taken together, the evidence that asbestos counts for insulation workers in general were below the safety standard and that Celotex's products were less dusty than the typical insulation product constitutes evidence that Celotex's products complied with the five million particles per cubic foot standard.

Conclusion

The trial court did not err by instructing the jury that compliance with government safety standards constitutes strong and substantial evidence that a product is not defective. The instruction was substantively correct and was supported by the evidence. Therefore, the judgment of the district court is AFFIRMED.

Notes

1. **Compliance with statute, ordinance or regulation.** In negligence cases, compliance is relevant to the question of reasonableness, but it is not controlling. The theory is that the jury should be free to conclude that reasonable care under the circumstances requires more than the statutory minimum. This rule is embodied in the Restatement (Third) of Torts: Liability for Physical Harm § 16 (Proposed Final Draft No. 1, 2005), which provides:

> (A) An actor's compliance with a pertinent statute, while evidence of non-negligence, does not preclude a finding that the actor is negligent * * * for failing to adopt precautions in addition those mandated by the statute.
>
> (b) If the actor's adoption of a precaution would require the actor to violate a statute, the actor cannot be found negligent for failing to adopt that precaution.

2. What effect should such compliance have in a strict liability case? Most courts have adopted the negligence rule, holding that the evidence is admissible but not conclusive. *E.g.,* Brech v. J.C. Penney Co., Inc., 698 F.2d 332 (8th Cir.1983); Wilson v. Piper Aircraft Corp., 282 Or. 61, 577 P.2d 1322 (1978); *see also* Restatement (Third) of Torts: Products Liability § 4(b) (compliance is "properly considered" but does not prevent finding product defective). *Lorenz v. Celotex Corp.* takes a somewhat stronger position by ruling that compliance with statute or regulation is strong and substantial evidence that a product is not defective.

3. Few decisions explain in detail how the evidence of compliance with statute or regulation is relevant to the question of defect in strict liability actions. In a concurring opinion in Wilson v. Piper Aircraft Corp., 282 Or. 61, 79, 577 P.2d 1322, 1332 (1978), Justice Linde offered the following views as to both the relevancy and the effect of FAA approval of an aircraft design:

It is true that compliance with government safety standards will generally not be held to negate a claim of "dangerously defective" design, but it would equally be an oversimplification to say that it can never do so. The role of such compliance should logically depend on whether the goal to be achieved by the particular government standards, the balance struck between safety and its costs, has been set higher or lower than that set by the rules governing the producer's civil liability. It may well be that when government intervenes in the product market to set safety standards, it often confines itself to demanding only minimum safeguards against the most flagrant hazards, well below the contemporary standards for civil liability. But that was not necessarily the case when the first safety standards were legislated, and it is not necessarily so for all products today.

In the design of aircraft, government regulation obviously places a much greater weight on the side of safety than it does for most products. The FAA not only sets detailed performance standards for the operational aspects of the design, it also requires that the design be tested for compliance with these standards by the producer and ultimately by the agency itself before a certificate is issued. This does not mean that an aircraft design, to be certified, must be the safest that could be built at any cost in money, speed, or carrying capacity. No doubt the FAA does not demand for small, single-engined recreational aircraft the redundant circuits and fail-safe systems expected in commercial airliners, not to mention the space program. It does mean, however, that FAA certification of a design represents a more deliberate, technically intensive program to set and control a given level of safety in priority to competing considerations than is true of many run-of-the-mill safety regulations.

The question remains how this policy assigned to the FAA compares with Oregon's standards of products liability for design defects. In two decisions in 1974, this court quoted a series of factors suggested by Professor Wade as posing the preliminary issue for a court whether a claim of "defect" crosses the legal threshold for submission to the jury. The difficulty in the present case springs from the fact that most of these factors—briefly summarized, the safety risks, the availability of safer design, the financial and other costs of the safer alternative, and the user's awareness of and ability to avoid the risks—are at least very similar to the factors that are presumably meant to enter into the FAA's judgment whether an aircraft design is safe enough.

It must be kept in mind that this aircraft is alleged to be defective not because it fell short of the safety standards set for its type, but on the ground that these standards provide insufficient safety for the whole series. But once the common-law premise of liability is expressed as a balance of social utility so closely the same as the judgment made in administering safety legislation, it becomes very problematic to assume that one or a sequence of law courts and juries are to repeat that underlying social judgment de novo as each sees fit. Rather, when the design of a product is subject not only to prescribed performance standards but to government supervised testing and specific approval or disapproval on safety grounds, no further balance whether the product design is "unreasonably dangerous" for its intended or foreseeable use under the conditions for which it is approved needs to be struck by a court or a jury *unless* one of two things can be shown: either that the standards of safety and utility assigned to the regulatory scheme are less inclusive or demanding than the premises of the law of products liability, or that the regulatory agency did not address the allegedly defective element of the design or in some way fell short of its assigned task.

It is these two questions, rather than a de novo evaluation of the safety of a design and the technological feasibility and costs of an even safer alternative, that properly become the issues for preliminary determination by a trial court in deciding whether a "design defect" claim against a product specifically tested and approved under government safety regulations should nevertheless go to a jury. In other words, it should be defendant's burden to show that a governmental agency has undertaken the responsibility of making substantially the same judgment that the court would otherwise be called on to make; and if so, it should then be plaintiff's burden to show that the responsible agency has not in fact made that judgment with respect to the particular "defect" at issue. When the product has been tested and approved by a federal agency, these issues can normally be decided simply by examining the statutory assignment of the agency (including relevant legislative history), the further standards adopted by the agency itself, and the records and reports underlying its approval of the product. In the case of a state agency, the documentation may be less extensive but other evidence of the actual process may be more accessible to a state court.

With respect to the present case, the cited sources seem likely to show that the FAA's goals and standards match this court's criteria for a "duly safe" design, at least as far as an aircraft's airworthiness is concerned. * * * It is not inconceivable that the answers might prove to come out one way with respect to FAA criteria and tests for aircraft engines and differently with respect to seat belts, or instrument knobs, or entry and exit steps, or other features whose risks are less central to airworthiness. Of course we do not know all that the parties might be able to show in this regard.

I repeat that this need to examine the precise standards and findings of the governing safety program results not from legislative preemption of common-law standards of liability, absent indications to that effect, but rather from these standards themselves when they are identical with those underlying the regulatory scheme. It may be that the tension between the policies embodied in intensive safety regulation and licensing and in case-by-case civil liability premised on "dangerously defective" design cannot remain unresolved, especially with respect to goods federally approved for a national market. A choice may have to be made between a theory of recovery premised on the need to compensate victims of product-caused injuries and one premised on liability for "faulty" products, no matter how attenuated the "fault" has become.

282 Or. at 81–86, 577 P.2d at 1333–35.

4. Should compliance with government mandates be given greater effect than courts presently give? If so, should the effect be conclusive, or should an intermediate position be adopted? Should the answer depend on the type of defect alleged and the type of regulation involved? The various possibilities are analyzed in Green, Statutory Compliance and Tort Liability: Examining the Strongest Case, 20 U. Mich.J.L.Ref. 461 (1997); Schwartz, The Role of Federal Safety Regulations in Products Liability Actions, 41 Vand.L.Rev. 1121 (1988); Note, The Role of Regulatory Compliance in Tort Actions, 26 Harv.J.Legis. 175 (1989); Symposium, Regulatory Compliance as a Defense to Products Liability, 88 Geo.L.J. 2049 (2000).

5. Some state legislatures have adopted an intermediate position. E.g., Ind.Code § 34–20–5–1. Colo.Rev.Stat. § 13–21–403 provides:

(1) In any product liability action, it shall be rebuttably presumed that the product which caused the injury, death, or property damage was not defective and that the manufacturer or seller thereof was not negligent if the product:

* * *

(b) Complied with, at the time of sale by the manufacturer, any applicable code, standard, or regulation adopted or promulgated by the United States or by this state, or by any agency of the United States or of this state.

(2) In like manner, noncompliance with a government code, standard, or regulation existing and in effect at the time of sale of the product by the manufacturer which contributed to the claim or injury shall create a rebuttable presumption that the product was defective or negligently manufactured.

How does the presumption provided in this statute affect the evidence that a plaintiff must provide to meet her burden of proof? Might the statute play any other role in a case? See McClain v. Chem–Lube Corp., 759 N.E.2d 1096 (Ind.Ct.App.2001)(discussing role of presumption and trial court's error in granting summary judgment based on statutory presumption without consideration of plaintiff's evidence).

6. **Violation of Statute.** The majority of courts agree that violation of safety statutes, ordinances, and regulations designed to protect plaintiff from the type of harm plaintiff suffered is negligence *per se*. For example, in Stanton v. Astra Pharmaceutical Prod., Inc., 718 F.2d 553 (3d Cir.1983) an eight-month old child suffered an adverse reaction to Xylocaine, a local anesthetic, and experienced cardiac and respiratory arrest, resulting in severe and irreversible brain damage. The drug manufacturer was held liable on a negligence *per se* theory because it failed to file annual reports and unexpected-adverse-reaction reports with the FDA, as required by 21 C.F.R. § 130.35(e) and (f) (1972).

7. For a recent general treatment of negligence *per se*, see Seidelson, The Appropriate Judicial Response to Evidence of the Violation of a Criminal Statute in a Negligence Action, 30 Duq.L.Rev. 1 (1991). The Restatement (Third) of Torts: Liability for Physical Harm (Proposed Final Draft No. 1,

2005) gives the following statement of the general rule pertaining to negligence *per se*:

§ 14. Statutory Violations as Negligence Per Se

An actor is negligent if, without excuse, the actor violates a statute that is designed to protect against the type of accident the actor's conduct causes, and if the accident victim is within the class of persons the statute is designed to protect.

§ 15. Excused Violations

An actor's excused violation of a statute is not negligence. A violation is excused when:

(a) the violation is reasonable because of the actor's childhood, physical disability, or physical incapacitation;

(b) the actor exercises reasonable care in attempting to comply with the statute;

(c) the actor neither knows nor should know of the factual circumstances that render the statute applicable;

(d) the actor's violation of the statute is due to the confusing way in which the requirements of the statute are presented to the public; or

(e) the actor's compliance with the statute would involve a greater risk of physical harm to that person or to others than noncompliance.

The Restatement (Third) of Torts: Products Liability § 4(a) is in accord:

In connection with liability for defective design or inadequate instructions or warnings:

(a) a product's noncompliance with an applicable product safety statute or administrative regulation renders the product defective with respect to the risks sought to be reduced by the statute or regulation.

8. A minority of courts treat violation of statutes, ordinances, and regulations as evidence of negligence, which is relevant, but not conclusive. MacDonald v. Ortho Pharmaceutical Corp., 394 Mass. 131, 475 N.E.2d 65 (1985), cert. denied, 474 U.S. 920, 106 S.Ct. 250, 88 L.Ed.2d 258 (1985) (FDA mandated warning on birth control pills).

9. A theory related to negligence *per se* is the creation by implication of statutory causes of action. Professor Sherman analyzes implied actions under federal statutes in Sherman, Use of Federal Statutes in State Negligence Per Se Actions, 13 Whittier L.Rev. 831 (1992). In the article he also analyzes the relationship between negligence *per se*, federal preemption, and the creation by implication of federal statutory causes of action.

SECTION B. REGULATION

In addition to statutes, there are a number of federal (and state) administrative agencies charged with protecting against accidental injury in a variety of spheres. The Environmental Protection Agency had jurisdiction over asbestos and ultimately banned its use in 1989 (although a court decision struck down the ban and some uses remain permitted today). The Food and Drug Administration regulates the safety of food, cosmetics and drugs representing approximately 25 percent of all retail purchases. The Consumer Product Safety Commission is another regulatory agency with jurisdiction over many products that are also the subject of products liability suits. As you read the next case, consider the respective roles of regulation and tort law in providing socially optimal deterrence. What other goals exist and how well do each of these different legal regimes further them? Should one or the other be given greater authority over the sorts of problems that we have confronted so far? Why?

SOUTHLAND MOWER CO. v. CONSUMER PRODUCT SAFETY COMMISSION

United States Court of Appeals, Fifth Circuit, 1980.
619 F.2d 499.

GEE, CIRCUIT JUDGE:

Approximately 77,000 people are injured each year in the United States by contacting the blades of walk-behind power mowers.[1] Of these injuries, an estimated 9,900 involve the amputation of at least one finger or toe, 11,400 involve fractures, 2,400 involve avulsions (the tearing of flesh or a body part), 2,300 involve contusions, and 51,400 involve lacerations. The annual economic cost inflicted by the 77,000 yearly blade-contact injuries has been estimated to be about $253 million. This figure does not include monetary compensation for pain and suffering or for the lost use of amputated fingers and toes.

To reduce these blade-contact injuries, the Consumer Product Safety Commission ("CPSC" or "the Commission") promulgated[2] a Safety

---

1. 44 Fed. Reg. 9990, 10030 (1979). The estimates are based on 1977 data.

2. The gestation period for the safety standard was long and complex. The administrative process was initiated on August 15, 1973, when, pursuant to § 10 of the CPSA, 15 U.S.C. § 2059, the Outdoor Power Equipment Institute, Inc. (OPEI) petitioned the CPSC to begin a proceeding to develop a consumer product safety standard addressing the hazards of power lawn mowers and asked the Commission to adopt a voluntary standard, ANSI B71.1–1972, "Safety Specifications for Power Lawn Mowers, Lawn & Garden Tractors, & Lawn Tractors," approved by the American National Standards Institute, Inc. as the proposed consumer product safety standard. On November 16, 1973, the Commission, after considering information about injuries associated with power lawn mowers, granted that portion of OPEI's petition that requested a proceeding to develop the power lawn mower safety standard. The Commission denied OPEI's request to publish ANSI B71.1–1972, with amendments, as a proposed consumer product safety standard, however.

Instead, the Commission solicited offers to develop a standard pursuant to § 7(b) of the CPSA, 15 U.S.C. § 2056(b). Subsequently, the Commission selected Consumers Union of United States, Inc. (CU) to develop the safety standard. See 39 Fed. Reg. 37803 (1974). As the offeror, CU gave representatives of industry, consumers, and other interests the opportunity to participate in developing the standard. It submitted the resulting proposal to the Commission on July 17, 1975. The recommended standard comprehensively addressed all types of lawn mowers and lawn mower inju-

Standard for Walk–Behind Power Lawn Mowers, 16 C.F.R. Part 1205 (1979), 44 Fed. Reg. 9990–10031 (Feb. 15, 1979), pursuant to section 7 of the Consumer Product Safety Act ("CPSA" or "the Act"), 15 U.S.C. § 2056 (1976).[3] In the present case we consider petitions by the Outdoor Power Equipment Institute ("OPEI"), manufacturers of power lawn mowers, and an interested consumer to review the Safety Standard for Walk–Behind Power Lawn Mowers.

The standard consists of three principal provisions: a requirement that rotary walk-behind power mowers pass a foot-probe test, 16 C.F.R. § 1205.4, 44 Fed. Reg. 10025–26, a requirement that rotary machines have a blade-control system that will stop the mower blade within three seconds after the operator's hands leave their normal operating position, 16 C.F.R. § 1205.5(a), 44 Fed. Reg. 10029, and a requirement, applicable to both rotary and reel-type mowers, that the product have a label of specified design to warn of the danger of blade contact, 16 C.F.R. § 1205.6, 44 Fed. Reg. 10029–30. The standards also contain additional directives that are intended to increase the effectiveness of the primary regulations. Thus, because the foot-probe provision can be satisfied by shielding the blade area, the standard mandates tests to assure that shields have a certain minimum strength, 16 C.F.R. § 1205.4(a)(2), 44 Fed. Reg. 10026–28, and that a shielded mower can traverse obstructions. 16 C.F.R. § 1205.4(a)(3), 44 Fed. Reg. 10028–29. The standard also

ries and contained requirements relating to blade-contact and thrown-object injuries, as well as injuries resulting from lawn mowers' slipping, rolling, overturning, or failing to steer or brake, injuries caused by burns from direct contact with exposed heated surfaces of mowers or from fires ignited by lawn mower ignition fluids, and injuries caused by electric shock from electrically powered lawn mowers or electric ignition systems.

After analyzing the recommended CU standard, on May 5, 1977, the Commission published a proposed comprehensive power lawn mower safety standard for public comment. 42 Fed. Reg. 23052 (1977). The proposal elicited more than 100 initial comments, and the Commission solicited and received further comments on these already submitted comments. 42 Fed. Reg. 34892 (1977). On June 7, 1978, the Commission published a notice that it would issue requirements addressing injuries from blade contact with walk-behind power mowers before issuing separate standards dealing with injuries associated with thrown objects, fuel and electrical hazards, and riding mowers. 43 Fed. Reg. 24697 (1978). In November 1978, the Commission requested additional comments on the safety and reliability of brake-clutch mechanisms. 43 Fed. Reg. 51638 (1978). On February 26, 1979, Part 1205 Safety Standard for Walk–Behind Power Lawn Mowers, applying only to blade-contact injuries from walk-behind power lawn mowers, was issued, to become effective December 31, 1981.

3. 15 U.S.C. § 2056(a) (1976) provides:

(a) The Commission may by rule, in accordance with this section and section 2058 of this title, promulgate consumer product safety standards. A consumer product safety standard shall consist of one or more of any of the following types of requirements:

(1) Requirements as to performance, composition, contents, design, construction, finish, or packaging of a consumer product.

(2) Requirements that a consumer product be marked with or accompanied by clear and adequate warnings or instructions, or requirements respecting the form of warnings or instructions.

Any requirement of such a standard shall be reasonably necessary to prevent or reduce an unreasonable risk of injury associated with such product. The requirements of such a standard (other than requirements relating to labeling, warnings, or instructions) shall, whenever feasible, be expressed in terms of performance requirements.

stipulates that shields that move to permit attachment of auxiliary equipment must either automatically return to their normal position when the supplemental equipment is not attached or prevent blade operation unless the shield is manually returned to its normal position when the added equipment is not used. 16 C.F.R. § 1205.4(c). Similarly, the three-second blade-stop requirement is supported by ancillary instructions that mowers employing engine cutoff to halt the blade have power restart mechanisms, 16 C.F.R. § 1205.5(a)(iv), and that all mowers have a control that must be activated before the blade can resume operation in order to prevent the blade from accidentally restarting. 16 C.F.R. § 1205.5(a)(2).

* * *

* * * OPEI * * * argues that substantial evidence on the record as a whole does not support the Commission's determination that the foot-probe and shielding requirements "are reasonably necessary to reduce or eliminate an unreasonable risk of injury" associated with walk-behind power lawn mowers. In addition, OPEI attacks the blade-stop requirement on the grounds that it is a design restriction rather than a performance requirement, imposes criteria that can only be satisfied by technology that is currently unsafe and unreliable, and mandates a three-second blade-stopping time that is not justified by substantial record evidence. * * *

* * *

Foot-Probe and Shielding Requirements

The standard mandates that walk-behind power rotary mowers pass a foot-probe test designed to assure that the machine guards the operator's feet against injuries caused by contact with the moving blade. The test requires that a probe simulating a human foot be inserted along the rear 120 degrees of the mower and at the discharge chute without coming into contact with the blade when inserted. 16 C.F.R. § 1205.4, 44 Fed. Reg. 10025–26. See also Fed. Reg. 10001–10002. Mowers meet the foot-probe test by having shields that prevent the probe from entering the blade's path. 16 C.F.R. § 1205(a)(1), 44 Fed. Reg. 10025.

OPEI does not deny that a foot-probe test for the rear area of the mower is reasonably necessary to reduce injuries. Rather, it asserts that application of the test to the discharge chute is not supported by substantial record evidence. It alleges that the injury data does not show that foot injuries occur at that location and that it would be theoretically impossible for an operator to suffer a foot injury at the discharge chute while holding the "deadman's" blade-control[4] switch on the mower handle.

4. A deadman control refers to a device on the mower handle that requires continuous pressure to sustain rotation of the mower blades. Only if the operator can reach the discharge chute with his foot while holding the mower handle can he suffer blade-contact injuries at the discharge chute by mowers meeting the blade-stop requirement. Discharge-chute foot injuries suffered after the operator has re-

The Act requires that safety standards be supported by "substantial evidence on the record as a whole." 15 U.S.C. § 2060(c). The foot-probe provision can be sustained only if the record contains " 'such relevant evidence as a reasonable mind might accept as adequate to support a conclusion' " that an unreasonable risk of foot injury exists from blade-contact at the discharge chute, that the foot-probe test will ameliorate it, and that the benefits of this proposed reform make it reasonable in light of the burdens it imposes on product manufacturers and consumers. *Aqua Slide 'N' Dive v. Consumer Product Safety Commission*, 569 F.2d 831, 838–40 (5th Cir.1978) (hereinafter cited as *Aqua Slide*) (quoting *Consolidated Edison Co. v. NLRB*, 305 U.S. 197, 229, 59 S.Ct. 206, 216, 83 L.Ed. 126 (1938)).

The determination of whether an unreasonable risk of discharge-chute injury exists involves "a balancing test like that familiar in tort law: The regulation may issue if the severity of the injury that may result from the product, factored by the likelihood of the injury, offsets the harm the regulation imposes upon manufacturers and consumers." *Aqua Slide*, 569 F.2d at 839 (quoting *Forester v. Consumer Product Safety Commission*, 559 F.2d 774, 789 (D.C.Cir.1977) (defining "unreasonable risk" in case brought under the Federal Hazardous Substances Act, 15 U.S.C. §§ 1261–74 (1976), and referring to "similar language" and legislative history of CPSA for support)). [Citations] Thus, under the unreasonable risk balancing test, even a very remote possibility that a product would inflict an extremely severe injury could pose an "unreasonable risk of injury" if the proposed safety standard promised to reduce the risk effectively without unduly increasing the product's price or decreasing its availability or usefulness. *Aqua Slide*, 569 F.2d at 839–40. Conversely, if the potential injury is less severe, its occurrence must be proven more likely in order to render the risk unreasonable and the safety standard warranted.

In the present case, the discharge-chute probe is intended to reduce the risk of such injuries as amputation of toes, fractures of bones in the feet or toes, avulsions, deep lacerations, and contusions. While the seriousness of these injuries cannot be gainsaid, it does not rise to the level of gravity that would render almost any risk, however remote, unreasonable if the risk could be reduced effectively by the proposed regulation.[5] Substantial evidence that such injury is significantly likely to occur is therefore necessary to sustain this portion of the lawn mower safety standard.

Our examination of the record has failed to reveal substantial evidence that injury at the discharge chute was sufficiently probable that

leased the mower handle and deadman's controls are addressed in the standard's blade-stop provision.

5. Cf. *Aqua Slide*, 569 F.2d at 840 (remote risk of paraplegia could be unreasonable under CPSA); Bunny Bear, Inc. v. Peterson, 473 F.2d at 1006–07 (harm of burns or smoke inhalation, including death, from crib fires was sufficiently great to justify requirement that crib mattress pass a "cigarette test" by not igniting when touched with cigarette, when possibility existed that adult attending child might drop lighted cigarette on mattress).

it made the risk addressed by the foot probe of this area unreasonable. In a study of 36 blade-contact foot injuries conducted for the CPSC by the National Electronic Injury Surveillance System (NEISS),[6] one injury occurred when the operator inserted his foot into the blade path at the discharge chute while holding the mower handle. This injury represented almost three percent of the blade-contact foot injuries in the sample. However, the study did not involve a random sample, and it is not possible to extrapolate the percentage of total blade-contact injuries represented by discharge-chute incidents involving the operator's feet from the limited information furnished in the record. In any event, trustworthy statistical inferences cannot be drawn from a single incident of discharge-chute injury. Without reliable evidence of the likely number of injuries that would be addressed by application of the foot-probe test to the discharge chute, we are unable to agree that this provision is reasonably necessary to reduce or prevent an unreasonable risk of injury. *See D. D. Bean & Sons Co. v. Consumer Product Safety Commission*, 574 F.2d 643, 650–51 (1st Cir.1978) (hereinafter D. D. Bean) (holding that absence of relevant injury data associated with particular hazards renders requirements of safety standard addressed to them invalid and observing that "a single injury ... is not substantial evidence of an 'unreasonable risk of injury.'"). It must be remembered that "(t)he statutory term 'unreasonable risk' presupposes that a real, and not a speculative, risk be found to exist and that the Commission bear the burden of demonstrating the existence of such a risk before proceeding to regulate." *Id.* at 651.

Our conclusion that substantial evidence fails to justify this provision is not altered by the fact that the industry's voluntary standard, ANSI B71.1–1972 § 1968, and ANSI 71.1b–1977 § 11.8, requires probing of the discharge chute. See 44 Fed. Reg. at 10003. A private industry safety standard cannot, by itself, provide sufficient support for a Commission regulation. "'While such private standards may tend to show the reasonableness of similar Commission standards, they do not prove the need for such provisions.'" *Aqua Slide*, 569 F.2d at 844 (quoting *Forester v. Consumer Product Safety Commission*, 559 F.2d at 793 (emphasis in original)). We therefore vacate that part of the standard requiring the discharge-chute area of power lawn mowers to pass a foot-probe test.

6. NEISS collects data from selected hospitals and reports them to the CPSC. The system, which has been operational since July 1, 1972, was designed to develop statistically valid, rationally representative product-related injury data. It employs a computer-based network of 119 statistically selected hospital emergency rooms located throughout the country. 15 U.S.C. §§ 2054, 2055. See "Draft Hazard Analysis of Power Mower Related Injuries & Analysis of Proposed Power Mower Standard," U.S. CPSC, Bureau of Epidemiology (March 1977), at pp. 3–5. The Commission also obtains injury information from in-depth investigations (IDI's) of particular accidents reported through the NEISS network. IDI's conducted by the Commission, unlike basic NEISS accident data, are not statistically representative of all injuries in a particular product category. IDI's do, however, provide details concerning the sequence of events involved in the injury not available from NEISS surveillance information. *Id.* at 5. To overcome this deficiency, the Commission weighted IDI cases involving specified types of injuries to derive an adjusted IDI sample that conforms to NEISS data.

OPEI also attacks certain aspects of the shielding requirements that supplement the foot-probe test as devoid of substantial evidentiary support. The standard directs that shielding must pass a shield-strength test in order to assure that shields maintain their structural integrity and remain attached under conditions of use and provide the intended protection. 16 C.F.R. § 1205.4(a)(2). Similarly, the standard requires that shielded mowers undergo an obstruction test, 16 C.F.R. § 1205.4(b)(2), which simulates surface irregularities that the mower may encounter in normal use. The test is designed to ascertain that the shielding will not interfere with mower performance by catching on obstructions and stopping the mower. It is also intended to prevent the shields themselves from contributing to lawn mower hazards, either by lifting the mower excessively when it meets an obstruction and thus exposing the blade or by suddenly halting the mower and causing it to lift and/or the operator to stumble on it.

The Commission estimates that the foot-probe/shielding requirements, including the supporting strength and obstruction tests, will reduce blade-contact foot injuries by 13,000 incidents each year. It did not apportion this injury reduction among the respective foot-probe shielding requirements on the ground that this was impossible because they are interrelated. The Commission estimates that the shield provisions will cost about $4 per mower, primarily for redesigning shields. Little expense is believed to result from the shield-strength test, since it is similar to a requirement in the existing voluntary industry standard, ANSI B71.1–1972 §§ 11.5, 11.15; ANSI B71.1b–1977, §§ 11.5, 13.2.1, which receives almost universal compliance.

OPEI readily admits that shielding is necessary to protect operators against blade-contact foot injuries at the rear of the mower. It contends, however, that the shield-strength test is invalid because few injuries have been shown to be caused by inadequately strong shields. OPEI also argues that the possibility that users might remove the protective shielding if it interfered with mower utility by catching on surface irregularities cannot justify the obstruction test and asserts that the test has not been proven necessary to guard against injuries caused by the mower's sudden stopping when it catches on obstacles.

We find that OPEI's approach to the shield-strength test is misconceived. It is true that were this requirement viewed in isolation as intended to address a risk of injury from mower shields falling off or cracking and exposing the operator's foot to the blade, independent of the standard's requirement that mowers be equipped with foot-probe shields, the record would not contain sufficient evidence that such injuries are so numerous that they support the regulation.[7] But the shield-strength test is mandated as an ancillary feature of the foot-probe

---

7. The record contains an in-depth CPSC investigation of 102 blade-contact injuries that revealed only two incidents in which the operator's foot was hurt by the blade at the rear of a mower that had a broken or missing shield. It also contains a few letters from consumers complaining of shields that did not remain attached to their mowers.

and shielding requirements that in turn are concededly necessary to reduce an unreasonable risk of operator blade-contact foot injuries. The shield-strength provision is not to be understood as a discrete measure addressing a distinct type of operator foot injury but as part of the Commission's effort to make the shielding remedy itself effective and safe. Since an unreasonable risk of operator foot injury from blade contact has been established, the shields are reasonably necessary to prevent access to the blade, and the "curative effect" of the shield-strength requirement in preventing blade exposure from inadequate shielding is "patent," we "do not think that the Commission had to cite empirical data in support of its finding that the particular (shield strength) requirement (was) likely to reduce the risk of injury." *D. D. Bean*, 574 F.2d at 649.

* * *

For similar reasons we reject OPEI's challenge to the obstruction test requirement and find that it is reasonably necessary to guard against intentional consumer defeat of the shielding safety device and to prevent shielding from interfering with mower utility. Although OPEI does not dispute the likelihood that consumers will remove shields if they interfere with mower performance[8] or contest the feasibility of the obstruction test, it does contend that the possibility that consumers may remove protective shielding if it hampers mower utility by catching on surface obstructions does not present the kind of unreasonable risk of injury that the Commission has authority to regulate. In essence, OPEI argues that the risk of injury from consumer defeat of safety shielding is not "unreasonable" because consumers would have chosen to incur the risk, and their judgment must be respected.

However, Congress intended for injuries resulting from foreseeable misuse of a product to be counted in assessing risk. *Aqua Slide*, 569 F.2d at 841. See S. Rep. No. 92–749, 92d Cong., 2d Sess. 14, 92 Cong. Rec. 36198 (1972) (remarks of Sen. Moss) (risk of injury "associated with" consumer products, 15 U.S.C. § 2052(a)(3), to be regulated by CPSC includes risks of injury resulting from "exposure to or reasonably foreseeable misuse of a consumer product"); Kimber, Federal Consumer Product Safety Act § 94 at 109 (1975). *Cf. Pacific Legal Foundation v. Department of Transportation*, 593 F.2d 1338, 1345 (D.C.Cir.1979) (Secretary of Transportation required to consider probable public reaction to passive automobile restraints, including possibility of attempts to deactivate them, in promulgating safety standard under National Traffic & Motor Vehicle Safety Act of 1966, 15 U.S.C. §§ 1381 et seq. (1976)). This principle, and not the tort liability concept of "assumption of risk," governs the Commission's authority to treat consumers' foreseeable

---

8. The experience of massive consumer resistance to ignition lock-seat belt systems is instructive as to the possibility that consumers will defeat safety devices they find inconvenient to use despite the loss of safety benefits such avoidance entails. See *Pacific Legal Foundation v. Department of Transportation*, 593 F.2d 1338, 1340–42 (D.C.Cir.1979); "Safety Belt Interlock System Usage Survey" (August 1976) (reporting high percentage of drivers defeated seat belt system).

action of removing safety shields as creating an unreasonable risk of injury and to issue rules addressing that danger. *See United States v. General Motors Corp.*, 518 F.2d 420, 434–35 (D.C.Cir.1975) ("(d)eterminations of fault or liability relevant to the award of damages ... are not controlling on the interpretation of the" meaning of product "defect" in prophylactic defect notification legislation of National Traffic & Motor Vehicle Act of 1966). Of course, a fully informed choice on the part of consumers to employ a dangerous product may provide information that is relevant to the Commission's assessment of the reasonableness of a risk of injury. For example, consumers' decisions to use sharp knives may pose a reasonable risk of injury because duller knives, while safe, would be useless for cutting purposes, and the Commission could reasonably find that consumers have accurate information of the severity and likelihood of injury posed by sharp knives. *See Aqua Slide*, 569 F.2d at 839; S. Rep. No. 92–749, *supra* at 6–7. In the present case, however, there is no evidence that consumers accurately appreciate the nature of the risk of blade-contact injuries and that their presumed willingness to defeat protective measures is reasonable.

* * *

Blade-Control System

The second key element of the standard requires a blade-control system that (1) will prevent the blade from rotating unless the operator activates a control, (2) allows the blade to be driven only if the operator remains in continuous contact with the "deadman's" control, and (3) causes the blade to stop moving within three seconds after the deadman's control is released. 16 C.F.R. § 1205.5. In addition, the standard directs that engine-powered mowers with only manual starting controls must have a blade-control system that stops the blade without turning off the engine. This requirement is intended to reduce the temptation for consumers to disable the blade-control mechanism in order to avoid the inconvenience of having to restart the engine manually each time the deadman's switch is released. Also, all walk-behind rotary power mowers must have a separate restart mechanism as well as an initial ignition device in order to prevent inadvertent starting of the blade by accidental activation of the primary ignition control. The controls must be located in an "operator control zone" at the rear of the mower so that during normal use, including starting efforts, the operator generally will be behind the mower handle. *Id.*

The blade-control system is intended to protect the operator against blade-contact injuries to both hands and feet by stopping the blade before the operator can contact it after he or she leaves the normal operating position and thus releases the deadman's control. The Commission estimates that the blade-control provisions will eliminate approximately 46,500 operator blade-contact injuries a year. This figure represents approximately 60 percent of all blade-contact injuries and nearly 80 percent of all injuries claimed to be reduced by the standard. As OPEI acknowledges, the blade-contact requirements thus are the "centerpiece" of the Commission's strategy for reducing blade-control injuries.

Perhaps as befits its importance in the regulatory scheme promulgated by the Commission, the blade-control system is vigorously attacked by both OPEI and consumer proponents of stricter safety requirements. OPEI asserts that the blade-control system provision is expressed as a design requirement, rather than as a performance requirement, in violation of the Act. It argues that a number of alternative requirements are available that are less design restrictive and more performance oriented than the blade-stop criterion and that the Commission therefore erred in adopting the blade-stop approach. OPEI further contends that the standard is unreasonable because it requires the use of mechanisms that allegedly are not safe or reliable. And, OPEI claims, the three-second stopping time is unreasonably short. In contrast, consumer advocate John O. Hayward maintains that the three-second blade-stopping time is too lax and that substantial evidence demonstrates that only a two-second or shorter blade-stopping time is justified.

The CPSA directs that a safety standard's provisions "shall, whenever feasible, be expressed in terms of performance requirements." 15 U.S.C. § 2056(a). The statutory preference[9] for performance requirements is rooted in the belief that this mode of regulation stimulates product innovation, promotes the search for cost-effective means of compliance, and fosters competition by offering consumers a range of choices in the marketplace, while design-restrictive rules tend to freeze technology, stifle research aimed at better and cheaper compliance measures, and deprive consumers of the opportunity to choose among competing designs. [Citations]

Although only a limited number of designs can satisfy the blade-stop provision, we find this part of the standard is nonetheless a performance requirement. While the standard mandates that mower blades stop within a specified time period, it does not dictate a specific means of fulfilling this condition. Manufacturers are neither formally nor practically restricted to employing a particular design, since two existing mechanisms, a blade-disengagement system employing a brake-clutch device and an engine-stop system, are capable of passing the blade-stop test. *See, e. g., D. D. Bean*, 574 F.2d at 652. Moreover, the existence of many different designs for brake-clutch apparatus preserves manufacturer discretion in building mowers. And manufacturers remain free to develop new forms of technology that will meet the blade-stop criterion. The statutory direction that safety standards are to be framed as performance requirements when feasible does not mean that the Commission must develop standards that are so general that they can be satisfied by every possible means for achieving an acceptable level of safety. Indeed, a performance requirement may be quite design restrictive in its practical import. *See, e. g., Pacific Legal Foundation v.*

---

9. While the statute favors performance requirements when feasible, it does not prohibit design standards when they are appropriate. * * *

Department of Transportation, 593 F.2d 1338, 1340–41 & n. 6 (D.C.Cir.), cert. denied, 444 U.S. 830, 100 S.Ct. 57, 62 L.Ed.2d 38 (1979) (upholding, under National Traffic & Motor Vehicle Safety Act of 1966, safety requirement that court characterized as "performance standard" and that could be satisfied by only two currently available systems, automatic passive seat belts and air bags); *Paccar, Inc. v. National Highway Traffic Safety Administration*, 573 F.2d 632, 639 & n. 26 (9th Cir.), cert. denied, 439 U.S. 862, 99 S.Ct. 184, 58 L.Ed.2d 172 (1978) (evaluating "performance requirement" issued under NTMVSA that as a practical matter required employment of a particular device). *Chrysler Corp. v. Department of Transportation*, 472 F.2d 659, 664 & n. 4 (6th Cir.1972) (holding that performance requirement could establish minimum conditions that could be met by few systems since industry not foreclosed from developing other ways of complying). The blade-stop provisions therefore qualify as performance requirements.

* * *

After studying the proposed alternative requirements, the Commission concluded that research time and money exceeding the Commission's resources[10] would be necessary in order to develop adequate tests, if they could be designed, to submit the alternative safety standards for public comment, and to issue a final standard that included the additional safety provisions. In its judgment, delaying the promulgation of the lawn mower safety standard until such an effort was completed was not justifiable because the heavy annual toll of serious injuries inflicted by mowers could be reduced immediately by implementation of the blade-stop requirement. Both sound policy and substantial record evidence support the Commission's decision.

* * *

We turn now to the issue of whether substantial evidence supports the selection of three seconds as the time limit within which blades must stop. The Commission based the three-second blade-stop time limit primarily upon four time-motion studies of operator-blade access time. These experiments were designed to measure the interval between the moment the operator released the deadman's control and the instant he or she reached the mower blade. One study of operator-blade access data collected at the University of Iowa in 1971 and analyzed by the National Bureau of Standards in 1975 showed that operators reached the blade hazard point after moving directly to it from the mower's rear in times ranging from 2.0 to 3.5 seconds.[11] A second operator-blade access study,

---

10. The Commission estimated that the development of the alternative safety requirements would take approximately five Commission staff years and cost $500,000 in research funds.

11. In eight trials, as analyzed in 1975, operators reached the blade in the following times (in seconds): 2, 3, 3, 2.5, 3.5, 2, 2.5, 3. (An earlier analysis performed by the NBS in 1974 and revised by the 1975 analysis had found that the access time ranged from 2.5 to 7.0 seconds. More accurate measurement methods used in the later study appear to account for the discrepancy.) It was recognized that the Iowa study was of limited value, however, because it employed machines that did not conform to the industry's voluntary standard in that they had

using 100 subjects ranging in age from 16–62 with a mean age of 35, was conducted by Consumer's Union at Eckerd College in St. Petersburg, Florida, on March 5–7, 1975. The participants were tested using a reaction-time device designed to simulate a walk-behind power lawn mower. Each participant underwent 25 trials, for a total of 2,500 time-motion incidents. A December 7, 1976, summary of this Eckerd College Study reported that operator access time ranged from 1.66 to 4.90 seconds for normal, as opposed to intentionally fast, movements. This summary cited data from trials using 12 and 15 subjects, aged 18–21. The Final Report on the Eckerd College Study, issued in May 1977, shows operator access time for the 100 participants as ranging from .6 to 3.3 seconds. The discrepancy is not explained. A third blade-access study using five subjects was conducted by the Office of the Medical Director (OMD) of the CPSC. In this experiment, direct, "casual" approach time ranged from 2.35 to 3.3 seconds, with an average time of 2.81 seconds.[12] OMD also recorded intentionally fast direct access times. These ranged from 1.26 to 2.5 seconds, with an average access time of 1.79 seconds. In addition, OMD tested subjects' access times when they approached the discharge chute blade area by going around the opposite side and front of the mower. The access time in the indirect, casual approach test ranged from 3.64 to 4.70 seconds, with an average time of 4.25 seconds.[13] Operator-access time in the indirect, hurried approach test fell between 2.48 and 3.68 seconds, with an average of 2.98 seconds.[14] The record contains only preliminary findings from the fourth empirical examination of operator blade-access times. This study was undertaken by the National Bureau of Standards. "(A) superficial examination of the limited observational data" was reported to show an average blade-access time of under three seconds.

In setting the blade-stop time, the Commission considered not only the time in which an operator could reach the blade after releasing the deadman's control but also the incremental cost of successively faster blade-stop times. The record contains substantial evidence that the cost of blade-stop mechanisms varies inversely with the length of time in which the device stops the blade,[15] so that a three-second blade-stop

shorter discharge chutes than the ANSI code now permits for current models. As a result, these blade-access times may have been shorter than access to the blades of current mower models. It should be noted, however, that figures derived from the other studies are in reasonable agreement with those of the University of Iowa test and that the test was not without some evidentiary value.

12. Blade-access times for the direct, casual approach test were: for subject A, 2.89 and 2.75 seconds; for subject B, 3.14 and 2.95 seconds; for subject C, 2.43 and 2.95 seconds; for subject D, 2.60 and 2.35 seconds; and for subject E, 2.90 and 3.30 seconds.

13. In this test, subject A had access times of 3.64 and 3.88 seconds; subject B, 4.52 and 4.18 seconds; subject C, 4.39 seconds; subject D, no recorded time; and subject E, 4.42 and 4.70 seconds.

14. Here access times were 2.60 and 2.48 for subject A; none recorded for subject B; 3.45 and 3.02 for subject C; 2.63 for subject D; and 3.68 for subject E.

15. A report by the Stanford Research Institute (SRI), "An Economic Analysis of the Proposed Consumers Union Power Mower Safety Standard" (April 1975), stated that the projected cost increases for walk-behind power mowers attributable to the blade-stop requirement would be $90–115 if the stop time were 3.0–4.9 seconds but only $75–100 per mower if the stop time were 5.0–6.0 seconds. In another 1977

requirement will be cheaper to implement than a one-or two-second time limit.

We find that the three-second blade-stop requirement is not too lax, contrary to petitioner Hayward's claim. The three-second measure will protect consumers against many, although certainly not all, blade-contact injuries. While the Commission may not rely upon mere "common sense" or speculation to establish the existence of an unreasonable risk of injury, it may exercise considerable discretion in determining an appropriate remedy. The Commission was entitled to consider the incremental cost of requiring a shorter blade-stop time in rejecting a one-or two-second blade-stop solution. The standard need not guarantee protection for all consumers; it is sufficient that it promises greater safety for consumers and is reasonably necessary to reduce the risk of blade-contact injuries.

Correspondingly, we find no merit in OPEI's contention that the requirement of a three-second stopping time is unreasonably demanding. OPEI strenuously urges that the empirical studies cannot support a three-second blade-stop limit because they unrealistically fail to account for such psychological factors as a person's fear of a noisily operating machine and resulting reluctance to approach it. OPEI argues that these conditions would tend to make the operator stay away from the blade area for a longer time than was recorded in the artificial tests and perhaps until all noise and vibration from a moving blade ceases. OPEI also argues that the three-second requirement is not reasonable because a blade that is not moving under power would be decelerating and thus would inflict less damage than a fully powered blade.

The Commission properly rejected these contentions. The record contained neither suggestions for devising a test to measure psychological factors nor evidence indicating that in more "realistic" circumstances operator access to blades would be slower than registered in the time-motion studies. No deceleration curve information was cited to substantiate the claim that between three and seven seconds after power shutoff a blade would be coasting slowly, and no available test can accurately determine the blade velocity at which a risk of injury is reasonable.

We are also unpersuaded by OPEI's contention that current technology is inadequate safely to achieve a three-second blade-stop time. OPEI asserts that this requirement can only be met by using brake-clutch

study, SRI estimated that a 3–second blade-stop requirement would cost $16.50 more per mower than a 5–second test for manual start rotary mowers and $10.50 more per mower for electric start mowers. The Consumers Union Economic Support Study estimated roughly that the marginal per mower cost of a mechanism would be $10, while a 5–second blade-stop requirement would permit a $2 per mower savings over a 3–second blade clutch. OPEI submitted comparative incremental retail costs in September 1977 that stated that, for gas-powered rotary mowers with electric start mechanisms, a 7–second stop requirement would cost $5 per mower without "easy restart," and a 3–second brake-clutch device would cost $13.50 per mower. For gas-powered rotary mowers with manual starts, OPEI's cost estimate was $10 for a mower meeting a 7–second stop requirement, $15 for a mower having 5–second engine kill with easy restart, and $34.50 for a 3–second brake-clutch system.

systems, which it alleges are unreliable and unsafe. The record does contain some evidence of unsatisfactory blade-clutch performance. For example, one lawn mower manufacturer provided test data on 19 mower units using five different brake-clutch designs that revealed that none of the mowers functioned successfully for 250 hours of testing, the period suggested as necessary to establish machine-life reliability. However, the manufacturer of the brake-clutch mechanisms employed in this test analyzed these results and concluded that the problem arose because the mowers' engines ran at a lower speed than engines for which the clutch was designed. The clutch manufacturer explained that while its standard clutches would not perform satisfactorily on low-speed engines, most lawn mowers had engines with faster speeds. It also expressed confidence that its standard clutches could be modified to perform well on low-speed engines. Moreover, other evidence in the record suggested that different types of clutches from those used in this experiment have been used successfully with low-speed motors.

Extensive evidence that available brake-clutch technology can produce lawn mowers capable of three-second blade stops overcomes the doubt expressed by some commentators as to their ability to provide a safe and reliable three-second blade-stop mechanism. One clutch manufacturer introduced empirical data showing that its brake-clutch mechanism was durable and reliable. In actual mowing tests, three of its units successfully completed over 250 field test hours, and in laboratory testing, several mower units completed 250 hours of operation without blade-stop failure and without increased wear on the engine or crankshaft. The General Services Administration subjected another brake-clutch design to fairly extensive field testing in 1977. The GSA used 50 mowers under varied conditions in ten locations for four months and reported no brake-clutch failures during the trial. This test was continued in 1978, and it was reported that the mowers were continuing to perform well, with complete reliability and safety. While some commentators criticized current mechanisms for being vulnerable to clutch slippage under heavy mowing conditions, the GSA report did not suggest that clutch slippage was a major source of dissatisfaction.

Most convincing proof that safe and reliable three-second blade-stop mowers are currently feasible is the fact that, at the time the standard was issued, at least two mower manufacturers were currently producing and marketing mowers that had a brake-clutch mechanism complying with the standard. As one of these manufacturers declared, that such mowers are offered for sale demonstrates their manufacturer's belief in the safety and reliability of this type of brake-clutch mechanism. In addition, the evidence established that a brake clutch is basically a simple device that is widely used with safety and reliability in the production of automobiles and other types of machinery, such as chainsaws. The technology associated with brake clutches is therefore highly developed, and comments presented to the Commission made clear that potential difficulties with the particular application of various types of brake-clutch devices to power lawn mowers can be identified and resolved with present technical knowledge.

This evidence provides substantial support for the Commission's judgment that technology is available to design, produce, and assemble brake-clutch power lawn mowers that are unlikely to fail in an unsafe manner. While the precise means of stopping the blade within the mandated time must be developed for each model of mower and requires engineering analysis and testing of a lawn mower's entire system to assure that the brake clutch is compatible with other components of the mower, the record establishes that existing technology can be refined and applied to power lawn mowers to bring them into successful compliance with the requirements of the standard. The three-second blade-stop time is therefore valid. *See, e. g., ASG Industries, Inc. v. Consumer Product Safety Commission*, 593 F.2d at 1333–34 (CPSC has "authority to employ technology forcing standards" so that, even when "the required technology (to remedy a risk) is not now available," the Commission may "predicate a finding of unreasonable risk on the projection of technological advance (if the agency has) some basis in its records ... supporting the projection as meaningful and reasonable, as contrasted with mere speculative desire"). *Cf. Pacific Legal Foundation v. Department of Transportation*, 593 F.2d at 1344 & n.44 (Motor Vehicle Safety Act of 1966 "authorizes safety standards that push the automobile industry beyond present engineering capabilities"); *Chrysler Corp. v. Department of Transportation*, 472 F.2d 659, 673 (6th Cir.1972) ("the Agency is empowered to issue safety standards which require improvements in existing technology or which require the development of new technology, and it is not limited to issuing standards based solely on devices already fully developed").

* * *

Finding of Reasonable Necessity and Public Interest

In the preceding discussion, we have examined the petitioners' challenges to specific provisions of the standard and have found several of the complaints unfounded. However, OPEI also contends that the standard as a whole is not supported by substantial record evidence. It claims that the Commission based its determination that the standard was "reasonably necessary" and would produce a net benefit to society upon a document, "Economic Impact of Blade Contact Requirements for Power Mowers" ("the economic report"), which was unreliable because its methodology was fatally flawed, and its findings had never been exposed to public scrutiny in the administrative rulemaking process. Petitioner Hayward also criticizes the Commission's evaluation of the standard's net social benefit. He argues that the CPSC undervalued the safety benefits of the standard by erroneously failing to place a monetary value on the pain and suffering inflicted by the injuries that the rule was expected to reduce.

The Commission seeks to counter OPEI's broad attack on the standard by defending the final economic report's data and methodology and by asserting that the report was, in essence, merely a revision of earlier cost-benefit analyses of shielding and blade-stop requirements in light of additional evidence introduced into the record by OPEI. The Commission further contends that it adequately considered pain and suffering in evaluating the standard's benefits and that it was not required to quantify these aspects of the cost of lawn mower accidents.

We have carefully scrutinized the record and find the substantial evidence supports the conclusion that the safety benefits expected from the standard bear a reasonable relationship to its costs and make the standard reasonably necessary and in the public interest. The cost-benefit analysis contained in the final economic report and adopted by the standard, 44 Fed.Reg. at 10020–21, 10030, is not methodologically flawed. The Commission estimated that the regulations would raise the retail price of a complying lawn mower $35, costing the consumer $4.40 per year over the projected eight-year life of the mower. Total yearly compliance costs were believed to be $189 million for 5.4 million mower units (1978 production estimate). Blade-contact injuries were calculated to cost $253 million annually, exclusive of pain and suffering. Since, as we have noted, there are approximately 77,000 blade-contact injuries from walk-behind power mowers each year, each injury costs about $3,300, without counting the cost of pain and suffering. Currently there are some 40 million mowers in use by consumers, so that a consumer has about one chance in 500 (1/520) of incurring an injury costing $3,300, exclusive of pain and suffering. The standard's injury cost associated with each mower without the safety features is thus $6.35 per year. The Commission anticipated that implementation of the standard would reduce this injury cost by 83 percent, for an annual savings of $5.30 per mower, exclusive of the savings of pain and suffering costs. Because the standard would result in a net benefit of $.90, a mower meeting the standard's safety requirements would represent a worthwhile investment for the consumer, and the standard's implementation is in the best interests of society.

OPEI questions this analysis by asserting that, given an eight-year mower life, full compliance with the standard will take eight years because only one-eighth of all mowers will be replaced each year. As a result, only one-eighth of the total 83 percent estimated injury cost reduction attributed to the standard will be achieved after the standard's first year, with an additional one-eighth of the projected savings being achieved for each succeeding year until full compliance is had. From this observation, OPEI reasons that a complying mower will reduce injury costs by a mere $.70 after one year and not by the $5.30 projected by the Commission in justifying the standard. OPEI derived the $.70 per mower savings figure by reducing both the number of annual injuries and their total costs by one-eighth in determining a $5.65 per mower injury costs after one year, rather than the Commission's estimated annual injury cost of $6.35 per mower. OPEI then subtracted the $5.65 from the $6.35

to ascertain the savings in per mower injury cost after one year. On the basis of this calculation, OPEI claims that after one year a consumer will have paid $4.40 to reduce his mower injury costs by only $.70 and that the standard thus imposes an unreasonable expense on the consumer.

OPEI's attack on the cost-benefit analysis underpinning the standard is misconceived. It fails to recognize that only purchasers of complying mowers will pay the $4.40 annual cost for the standard's safety features and that these owners will receive the full benefit of the standard's anticipated effectiveness in reducing their injury costs for each year of the mower's life. OPEI's cost-benefit assessment thereby erroneously substitutes a figure representing the injury savings per mower in use, whether complying or not, for the amount of injury savings for owners of complying mowers, which is the relevant calculation. The correct analysis employed by the Commission to support the standard demonstrates its reasonable necessity in reducing the risk of blade-contact accidents. Because the economic findings establish that the standard is in the public interest even absent reliance upon the costs of pain and suffering, we need not determine whether the Commission must assign a dollar value to these aspects of the cost of accidents when precise calculation of their cost is not crucial for determining whether a standard is reasonably necessary and in the public interest. The methodology of the standard's supporting findings as to the costs and benefits of its requirements is sustained.

We also find that the evidence in the 1979 final economic report supporting the standard's cost effectiveness is reliable. In this report the Commission ultimately found that the standard would cost $189 million annually to implement, would prevent $211 million in yearly injury costs when full compliance was achieved, and would save $26.4 million after one year, assuming that the costs of accidents remained constant. The Commission's final economic analysis of the standard used data from fiscal year 1977 to compute an annual blade-contact injury cost of $253 million, exclusive of pain and suffering costs, caused by an estimated 77,000 injuries.

* * *

In summary, the standard's scope and its requirements that mowers pass a rear foot-probe test, shield-strength and obstruction tests, satisfy a three-second blade-stop criterion, and carry a prescribed warning label are upheld. The Commission's conclusion that the standard is reasonably necessary and in the public interest is also valid. The standard's requirement that mowers pass a discharge chute foot-probe test is not justified by substantial evidence on the record as a whole and is therefore vacated.

AFFIRMED IN PART, VACATED IN PART.

Notes

1. Assume that the foot-shielding and blade-control requirements added approximately $100 (in current dollars) to the cost of a new lawnmower

and that you were on the verge of buying a new lawnmower just as the CPSC regulation was to become final. Would you hurry out and buy an existing mower or wait until the new mowers with the safety devices became available? If there was sufficient consumer demand for these safety devices, why is regulation necessary? If there isn't, what justifies imposing these costs on unwilling consumers?

2. How persuasive is the court's justification for upholding the shield-strength requirement? If the CPSC had mandated a shield-strength standard equivalent to the safe at Ft. Knox would the court have had to uphold it on the same rationale? Shouldn't each marginal requirement have to satisfy the "reasonably necessary to prevent or reduce an unreasonable risk of injury" statutory language?

3. What are the respective advantages and disadvantages of tort law and regulation in obtaining an appropriate level of safety in consumer products? In whom would you have greater confidence to get the risk-benefit analysis correct: the Consumer Product Safety Commission in the rule making process described in *Southland* or a jury? Why? What are the implications of your answer for the respective role of tort law and regulation in providing appropriate incentives for safety? *See* Krier & Gillette, Risk, Courts and Agencies, 138 U.Pa.L.Rev. 1027 (1990).

4. Note that there was a seven-year period from the time the CPSC began its efforts to promulgate safety standards for lawn mowers and the Fifth Circuit's affirmance of those standards. How much do you suppose that single regulatory effort cost the federal government?

SECTION C. PREEMPTION

Federal regulation or legislation may provide the exclusive source of standards for products liability cases either because state law adopts federal standards, as in Section A when courts employ safety statutes as negligence per se, or when the federal standard itself displaces state law. This displacement, enabled by the Supremacy clause of the United States Constitution, is known as preemption.

BATES v. DOW AGROSCIENCES LLC
Supreme Court of the United States, 2005.
544 U.S. 431, 125 S.Ct. 1788, 161 L.Ed.2d 687.

JUSTICE STEVENS delivered the opinion of the Court.

Petitioners are 29 Texas peanut farmers who allege that in the 2000 growing season their crops were severely damaged by the application of respondent's newly marketed pesticide named "Strongarm." The question presented is whether the Federal Insecticide, Fungicide, and Rodenticide Act (FIFRA), 7 U.S.C. § 136 *et seq.* (2000 ed. and Supp. II), preempts their state-law claims for damages.

I

Pursuant to its authority under FIFRA, the Environmental Protection Agency (EPA) conditionally registered Strongarm on March 8, 2000, thereby granting respondent (Dow) permission to sell this pesticide—a weed killer—in the United States. Dow obtained this registration in time to market Strongarm to Texas farmers, who normally plant their peanut crops around May 1. According to petitioners—whose version of the facts we assume to be true at this stage—Dow knew, or should have known, that Strongarm would stunt the growth of peanuts in soils with pH levels of 7.0 or greater. Nevertheless, Strongarm's label stated, "Use of Strongarm is recommended in all areas where peanuts are grown," and Dow's agents made equivalent representations in their sales pitches to petitioners. When petitioners applied Strongarm on their farms—whose soils have pH levels of 7.2 or higher, as is typical in western Texas—the pesticide severely damaged their peanut crops * * *.

Meanwhile, Dow reregistered its Strongarm label with EPA prior to the 2001 growing season. EPA approved a "supplemental" label that was for "[d]istribution and [u]se [o]nly in the states of New Mexico, Oklahoma and Texas," the three States in which peanut farmers experienced crop damage. This new label contained the following warning: "Do not apply Strongarm to soils with a pH of 7.2 or greater."

After unsuccessful negotiations with Dow, petitioners gave Dow notice of their intent to bring suit as required by the Texas Deceptive Trade Practices–Consumer Protection Act (hereinafter Texas DTPA). In response, Dow filed a declaratory judgment action in Federal District Court, asserting that petitioners' claims were expressly or impliedly pre-empted by FIFRA. Petitioners, in turn, brought counterclaims, including tort claims sounding in strict liability and negligence. They also alleged fraud, breach of warranty, and violation of the Texas DTPA. The District Court granted Dow's motion for summary judgment, rejecting one claim on state-law grounds and dismissing the remainder as expressly pre-empted by 7 U.S.C. § 136v(b), which provides that States "shall not impose or continue in effect any requirements for labeling or packaging in addition to or different from those required under this subchapter."

The Court of Appeals affirmed. It read § 136v(b) to pre-empt any state-law claim in which "a judgment against Dow would induce it to alter its product label." The court held that because petitioners' fraud, warranty, and deceptive trade practices claims focused on oral statements by Dow's agents that did not differ from statements made on the product's label, success on those claims would give Dow a "strong incentive" to change its label. Those claims were thus pre-empted. The court also found that petitioners' strict liability claim alleging defective design was essentially a "disguised" failure-to-warn claim and therefore pre-empted. It reasoned: "One cannot escape the heart of the farmers' grievance: Strongarm is dangerous to peanut crops in soil with a pH level over 7.0, and that was not disclosed to them.... It is inescapable that success on this claim would again necessarily induce Dow to alter the Strongarm label." The court employed similar reasoning to find the negligent testing and negligent manufacture claims pre-empted as well.

This decision was consistent with those of a majority of the Courts of Appeals, as well of several state high courts,[1] but conflicted with the decisions of other courts[2] and with the views of the EPA set forth in an *amicus curiae* brief filed with the California Supreme Court in 2000.[3] We granted certiorari to resolve this conflict.

II

* * *

In 1972, spurred by growing environmental and safety concerns, Congress adopted the extensive amendments that "transformed FIFRA from a labeling law into a comprehensive regulatory statute." *Ruckelshaus v. Monsanto Co.*, 467 U.S. 986, 991, 104 S.Ct. 2862, 81 L.Ed.2d 815 (1984). "As amended, FIFRA regulated the use, as well as the sale and labeling, of pesticides; regulated pesticides produced and sold in both intrastate and interstate commerce; provided for review, cancellation, and suspension of registration; and gave EPA greater enforcement authority." * * *

Under FIFRA as it currently stands, a manufacturer seeking to register a pesticide must submit a proposed label to EPA as well as certain supporting data. The agency will register the pesticide if it determines that the pesticide is efficacious (with the caveat discussed below), that it will not cause unreasonable adverse effects on humans and the environment, and that its label complies with the statute's prohibition on misbranding. A pesticide is "misbranded" if its label contains a statement that is "false or misleading in any particular," including a false or misleading statement concerning the efficacy of the pesticide. A pesticide is also misbranded if its label does not contain adequate instructions for use, or if its label omits necessary warnings or cautionary statements.

Because it is unlawful under the statute to sell a pesticide that is registered but nevertheless misbranded, manufacturers have a continuing obligation to adhere to FIFRA's labeling requirements. § 136j(a)(1)(E); see also § 136a(f)(2) (registration is prima facie evidence that the pesticide and its labeling comply with the statute's requirements, but registration does not provide a defense to the violation of the statute); § 136a(f)(1) (a manufacturer may seek approval to amend its label). * * *

Section 136v, which was added in the 1972 amendments, addresses the States' continuing role in pesticide regulation. As currently codified, § 136v provides:

---

1. See, *e.g.*, *Etcheverry v. Tri-Ag Service, Inc.*, 22 Cal.4th 316, 93 Cal.Rptr.2d 36, 993 P.2d 366 (2000).

2. See, *e.g.*, *Ferebee v. Chevron Chemical Co.*, 736 F.2d 1529 (C.A.D.C.1984); *American Cyanamid Co. v. Geye*, 79 S.W.3d 21 (Tex.2002).

3. See Brief *Amicus Curiae* for United States in *Etcheverry v. Tri-Ag Serv., Inc.*, No. S072524 (Cal.Sup.Ct.) (hereinafter Brief *Amicus Curiae* for United States in *Etcheverry*). The Solicitor General has since adopted a contrary position. See Brief for United States as *Amicus Curiae* 20.

(a) In general

A State may regulate the sale or use of any federally registered pesticide or device in the State, but only if and to the extent the regulation does not permit any sale or use prohibited by this subchapter.

(b) Uniformity

Such State shall not impose or continue in effect any requirements for labeling or packaging in addition to or different from those required under this subchapter.

* * *

In 1978, Congress once again amended FIFRA, this time in response to EPA's concern that its evaluation of pesticide efficacy during the registration process diverted too many resources from its task of assessing the environmental and health dangers posed by pesticides. Congress addressed this problem by authorizing EPA to waive data requirements pertaining to efficacy, thus permitting the agency to register a pesticide without confirming the efficacy claims made on its label. In 1979, EPA invoked this grant of permission and issued a general waiver of efficacy review, with only limited qualifications not applicable here. In a notice published years later in 1996, EPA confirmed that it had "stopped evaluating pesticide efficacy for routine label approvals almost two decades ago," and clarified that "EPA's approval of a pesticide label does not reflect any determination on the part of EPA that the pesticide will be efficacious or will not damage crops or cause other property damage." The notice also referred to an earlier statement in which EPA observed that " 'pesticide producers are aware that they are potentially subject to damage suits by the user community if their products prove ineffective in actual use.'" This general waiver was in place at the time of Strongarm's registration; thus, the EPA never passed on the accuracy of the statement in Strongarm's original label recommending the product's use "in all areas where peanuts are grown."

Although the modern version of FIFRA was enacted over three decades ago, this Court has never addressed whether that statute preempts tort and other common-law claims arising under state law. Courts entertained tort litigation against pesticide manufacturers since well before the passage of FIFRA in 1947, and such litigation was a common feature of the legal landscape at the time of the 1972 amendments. Indeed, for at least a decade after those amendments, arguments that such tort suits were pre-empted by § 136v(b) either were not advanced or were unsuccessful. *See, e.g., Ferebee v. Chevron Chemical Co.,* 736 F.2d 1529 (C.A.D.C.1984). It was only after 1992 when we held in *Cipollone v. Liggett Group, Inc.,* 505 U.S. 504, 112 S. Ct. 2608, 120 L. Ed.2d 407, that the term "requirement or prohibition" in the Public Health Cigarette Smoking Act of 1969 included common-law duties, and therefore pre-empted certain tort claims against cigarette companies, that a groundswell of federal and state decisions emerged holding that § 136v(b) pre-empted claims like those advanced in this litigation.

This Court has addressed FIFRA pre-emption in a different context. In *Wisconsin Public Intervenor v. Mortier,* 501 U.S. 597, 111 S. Ct. 2476, 115 L. Ed.2d 532 (1991), we considered a claim that § 136v(b) pre-empted a small town's ordinance requiring a special permit for the aerial application of pesticides. Although the ordinance imposed restrictions not required by FIFRA or any EPA regulation, we unanimously rejected the pre-emption claim. In our opinion we noted that FIFRA was not "a sufficiently comprehensive statute to justify an inference that Congress had occupied the field to the exclusion of the States." "To the contrary, the statute leaves ample room for States and localities to supplement federal efforts even absent the express regulatory authorization of § 136v(a)."

As a part of their supplementary role, States have ample authority to review pesticide labels to ensure that they comply with both federal and state labeling requirements. Nothing in the text of FIFRA would prevent a State from making the violation of a federal labeling or packaging requirement a state offense, thereby imposing its own sanctions on pesticide manufacturers who violate federal law. The imposition of state sanctions for violating state rules that merely duplicate federal requirements is equally consistent with the text of § 136v.

III

Against this background, we consider whether petitioners' claims[4] are pre-empted by § 136v(b), which, again, reads as follows: "Such State shall not impose or continue in effect any requirements for labeling or packaging in addition to or different from those required under this subchapter."

* * *

The prohibitions in § 136v(b) apply only to "requirements." An occurrence that merely motivates an optional decision does not qualify as a requirement. The Court of Appeals was therefore quite wrong when it assumed that any event, such as a jury verdict, that might "induce" a pesticide manufacturer to change its label should be viewed as a requirement. The Court of Appeals did, however, correctly hold that the term "requirements" in § 136v(b) reaches beyond positive enactments, such as statutes and regulations, to embrace common-law duties. Our decision in *Cipollone* supports this conclusion. See 505 U.S., at 521, 112 S.Ct. 2608 (plurality opinion) ("The phrase '[n]o requirement or prohibition'

---

4. The briefing and the record leave some confusion as to what precise claims are at issue. In light of the posture of this case, we find it appropriate to address the following claims: breach of express warranty, fraud, violation of the Texas DTPA, strict liability (including defective design and defective manufacture), and negligent testing. We will also address negligent failure to warn, since the Court of Appeals read petitioners' allegations to support such a claim. But because petitioners do not press such a claim here, we leave it to the court below to determine whether they may proceed on such a claim on remand. * * *

sweeps broadly and suggests no distinction between positive enactments and common law; to the contrary, those words easily encompass obligations that take the form of common-law rules"). While the use of "requirements" in a pre-emption clause may not invariably carry this meaning, we think this is the best reading of § 136v(b).

That § 136v(b) may pre-empt judge-made rules, as well as statutes and regulations, says nothing about the *scope* of that pre-emption. For a particular state rule to be pre-empted, it must satisfy two conditions. First, it must be a requirement *"for labeling or packaging"*; rules governing the design of a product, for example, are not pre-empted. Second, it must impose a labeling or packaging requirement that is *"in addition to or different from* those required under this subchapter." A state regulation requiring the word "poison" to appear in red letters, for instance, would not be pre-empted if an EPA regulation imposed the same requirement.

It is perfectly clear that many of the common-law rules upon which petitioners rely do not satisfy the first condition. Rules that require manufacturers to design reasonably safe products, to use due care in conducting appropriate testing of their products, to market products free of manufacturing defects, and to honor their express warranties or other contractual commitments plainly do not qualify as requirements for "labeling or packaging." None of these common-law rules requires that manufacturers label or package their products in any particular way. Thus, petitioners' claims for defective design, defective manufacture, negligent testing, and breach of express warranty are not pre-empted.

To be sure, Dow's express warranty was located on Strongarm's label.[6] But a cause of action on an express warranty asks only that a manufacturer make good on the contractual commitment that it voluntarily undertook by placing that warranty on its product. Because this common-law rule does not require the manufacturer to make an express warranty, or in the event that the manufacturer elects to do so, to say anything in particular in that warranty, the rule does not impose a requirement "for labeling or packaging."

In arriving at a different conclusion, the court below reasoned that a finding of liability on these claims would "induce Dow to alter [its] label." This effects-based test finds no support in the text of § 136v(b), which speaks only of "requirements." A requirement is a rule of law that must be obeyed; an event, such as a jury verdict, that merely motivates an optional decision is not a requirement. The proper inquiry calls for an examination of the elements of the common-law duty at issue, see *Cipollone,* 505 U.S., at 524, 112 S.Ct. 2608; it does not call for speculation as to whether a jury verdict will prompt the manufacturer to take any particular action (a question, in any event, that will depend on a

---

6. The label stated: "Dow AgroSciences warrants that this product * * * is reasonably fit for the purposes stated on the label when used in strict accordance with the directions, subject to the inherent risks set forth below." [Citations]

variety of cost/benefit calculations best left to the manufacturer's accountants).

The inducement test is unquestionably overbroad because it would impeach many "genuine" design defect claims that Dow concedes are not pre-empted. A design defect claim, if successful, would surely induce a manufacturer to alter its label to reflect a change in the list of ingredients or a change in the instructions for use necessitated by the improvement in the product's design. Moreover, the inducement test is not entirely consistent with § 136v(a), which confirms the State's broad authority to regulate the sale and use of pesticides. Under § 136v(a), a state agency may ban the sale of a pesticide if it finds, for instance, that one of the pesticide's label-approved uses is unsafe. This ban might well induce the manufacturer to change its label to warn against this questioned use. Under the inducement test, however, such a restriction would anomalously qualify as a "labeling" requirement. It is highly unlikely that Congress endeavored to draw a line between the type of indirect pressure caused by a State's power to impose sales and use restrictions and the even more attenuated pressure exerted by common-law suits. The inducement test is not supported by either the text or the structure of the statute.

Unlike their other claims, petitioners' fraud and negligent-failure-to-warn claims are premised on common-law rules that qualify as "requirements for labeling or packaging." These rules set a standard for a product's labeling that the Strongarm label is alleged to have violated by containing false statements and inadequate warnings. While the courts of appeal have rightly found guidance in *Cipollone's* interpretation of "requirements," some of those courts too quickly concluded that failure-to-warn claims were pre-empted under FIFRA, as they were in *Cipollone*, without paying attention to the rather obvious textual differences between the two pre-emption clauses.

Unlike the pre-emption clause at issue in *Cipollone*,[7] § 136v(b) prohibits only state-law labeling and packaging requirements that are "*in addition to or different from*" the labeling and packaging requirements under FIFRA. Thus, a state-law labeling requirement is not pre-empted by § 136v(b) if it is equivalent to, and fully consistent with, FIFRA's misbranding provisions. Petitioners argue that their claims based on fraud and failure-to-warn are not pre-empted because these common-law duties are equivalent to FIFRA's requirements that a pesticide label not contain "false or misleading" statements, § 136(q)(1)(A), or inadequate instructions or warnings. §§ 136(q)(1)(F), (G). We agree with petitioners insofar as we hold that state law need not explicitly incorporate FIFRA's standards as an element of a cause of action in order to survive pre-emption. As we will discuss below, however, we leave it to the Court of Appeals to decide in the first instance

---

7. "No requirement or prohibition based on smoking and health shall be imposed under State law with respect to the advertising or promotion of any cigarettes the packages of which are labeled in conformity with the provisions of this [Act]."

whether these particular common-law duties are equivalent to FIFRA's misbranding standards.

The "parallel requirements" reading of § 136v(b) that we adopt today finds strong support in *Medtronic, Inc. v. Lohr,* 518 U.S. 470, 116 S.Ct. 2240, 135 L.Ed.2d 700 (1996). In addressing a similarly worded preemption provision in a statute regulating medical devices, we found that "[n]othing in [21 U.S.C.] § 360k denies Florida the right to provide a traditional damages remedy for violations of common-law duties when those duties parallel federal requirements." * * * Accordingly, although FIFRA does not provide a federal remedy to farmers and others who are injured as a result of a manufacturer's violation of FIFRA's labeling requirements, nothing in § 136v(b) precludes States from providing such a remedy.

Dow, joined by the United States as *amicus curiae,* argues that the "parallel requirements" reading of § 136v(b) would "give juries in 50 States the authority to give content to FIFRA's misbranding prohibition, establishing a crazy-quilt of anti-misbranding requirements different from the one defined by FIFRA itself and intended by Congress to be interpreted authoritatively by EPA." Brief for Respondent 16; see also Brief for United States as *Amicus Curiae* 25–27. In our view, however, the clear text of § 136v(b) and the authority of *Medtronic* cannot be so easily avoided. Conspicuously absent from the submissions by Dow and the United States is any plausible alternative interpretation of "in addition to or different from" that would give that phrase meaning. Instead, they appear to favor reading those words out of the statute, which would leave the following: "Such State shall not impose or continue in effect any requirements for labeling or packaging." This amputated version of § 136v(b) would no doubt have clearly and succinctly commanded the pre-emption of *all* state requirements concerning labeling. That Congress added the remainder of the provision is evidence of its intent to draw a distinction between state labeling requirements that are pre-empted and those that are not.

Even if Dow had offered us a plausible alternative reading of § 136v(b)—indeed, even if its alternative were just as plausible as our reading of that text—we would nevertheless have a duty to accept the reading that disfavors pre-emption. "[B]ecause the States are independent sovereigns in our federal system, we have long presumed that Congress does not cavalierly pre-empt state-law causes of action." *Medtronic,* 518 U.S. at 485, 116 S.Ct. 2240. In areas of traditional state regulation, we assume that a federal statute has not supplanted state law unless Congress has made such an intention " 'clear and manifest.' " Our reading is at once the only one that makes sense of each phrase in § 136v(b) and the one favored by our canons of interpretation. The notion that FIFRA contains a nonambiguous command to pre-empt the types of tort claims that parallel FIFRA's misbranding requirements is particularly dubious given that just five years ago the United States advocated the interpretation that we adopt today.[8]

The long history of tort litigation against manufacturers of poisonous substances adds force to the basic presumption against pre-emption. If Congress had intended to deprive injured parties of a long available form of compensation, it surely would have expressed that intent more clearly.[9] Moreover, this history emphasizes the importance of providing an incentive to manufacturers to use the utmost care in the business of distributing inherently dangerous items. See *Mortier,* 501 U.S., at 613, 111 S.Ct. 2476 (stating that the 1972 amendments' goal was to "strengthen existing labeling requirements and ensure that these requirements were followed in practice"). Particularly given that Congress amended FIFRA to allow EPA to waive efficacy review of newly registered pesticides (and in the course of those amendments made technical changes to § 136v(b)), it seems unlikely that Congress considered a relatively obscure provision like § 136v(b) to give pesticide manufacturers virtual immunity from certain forms of tort liability. Overenforcement of FIFRA's misbranding prohibition creates a risk of imposing unnecessary financial burdens on manufacturers; under-enforcement creates not only financial risks for consumers, but risks that affect their safety and the environment as well.

Finally, we find the policy objections raised against our reading of § 136v(b) to be unpersuasive. Dow and the United States greatly overstate the degree of uniformity and centralization that characterizes FIFRA. In fact, the statute authorizes a relatively decentralized scheme that preserves a broad role for state regulation. Most significantly, States may ban or restrict the uses of pesticides that EPA has approved, § 136v(a); they may also register, subject to certain restrictions, pesticides for uses beyond those approved by EPA, § 136v(c). See also § 136w-1 (authorizing EPA to grant States primary enforcement responsibility for use violations). A literal reading of § 136v(b) is fully consistent with the concurrent authority of the Federal and State Governments in this sphere.

Private remedies that enforce federal misbranding requirements would seem to aid, rather than hinder, the functioning of FIFRA. Unlike the cigarette labeling law at issue in *Cipollone,* which prescribed certain immutable warning statements, FIFRA contemplates that pesticide labels will evolve over time, as manufacturers gain more information about their products' performance in diverse settings. As one court explained, tort suits can serve as a catalyst in this process:

> By encouraging plaintiffs to bring suit for injuries not previously recognized as traceable to pesticides such as [the pesticide there at

---

8. Brief *Amicus Curiae* for United States in *Etcheverry* 33–35. See also Brief for United States as *Amicus Curiae* 20 (explaining its subsequent change in view).

9. It is no answer that, even if all label-related claims are pre-empted under Dow's reading, other non-label-related tort claims would remain intact. Given the inherently dangerous nature of pesticides, most safety gains are achieved not through modifying a pesticide's design, but by improving the warnings and instructions contained on its label. See Brief for American Chemistry Council as *Amicus Curiae* 3.

issue], a state tort action of the kind under review may aid in the exposure of new dangers associated with pesticides. Successful actions of this sort may lead manufacturers to petition EPA to allow more detailed labelling of their products; alternatively, EPA itself may decide that revised labels are required in light of the new information that has been brought to its attention through common law suits. In addition, the specter of damage actions may provide manufacturers with added dynamic incentives to continue to keep abreast of all possible injuries stemming from use of their product so as to forestall such actions through product improvement.

Ferebee, 736 F.2d, at 1541–1542.

Dow and the United States exaggerate the disruptive effects of using common-law suits to enforce the prohibition on misbranding. FIFRA has prohibited inaccurate representations and inadequate warnings since its enactment in 1947, while tort suits alleging failure-to-warn claims were common well before that date and continued beyond the 1972 amendments. We have been pointed to no evidence that such tort suits led to a "crazy-quilt" of FIFRA standards or otherwise created any real hardship for manufacturers or for EPA. Indeed, for much of this period EPA appears to have welcomed these tort suits. While it is true that properly instructed juries might on occasion reach contrary conclusions on a similar issue of misbranding, there is no reason to think such occurrences would be frequent or that they would result in difficulties beyond those regularly experienced by manufacturers of other products that everyday bear the risk of conflicting jury verdicts. Moreover, it bears noting that lay juries are in no sense anathema to FIFRA's scheme: In criminal prosecutions for violation of FIFRA's provisions, see § 1361(b), juries necessarily pass on allegations of misbranding.

In sum, under our interpretation, § 136v(b) retains a narrow, but still important, role. In the main, it pre-empts competing state labeling standards—imagine 50 different labeling regimes prescribing the color, font size, and wording of warnings—that would create significant inefficiencies for manufacturers. The provision also pre-empts any statutory or common-law rule that would impose a labeling requirement that diverges from those set out in FIFRA and its implementing regulations. It does not, however, pre-empt any state rules that are fully consistent with federal requirements.

Having settled on our interpretation of § 136v(b), it still remains to be decided whether that provision pre-empts petitioners' fraud and failure-to-warn claims. Because we have not received sufficient briefing on this issue, which involves questions of Texas law, we remand it to the Court of Appeals. We emphasize that a state-law labeling requirement must in fact be equivalent to a requirement under FIFRA in order to survive pre-emption. For example, were the Court of Appeals to determine that the element of falsity in Texas' common-law definition of fraud imposed a broader obligation than FIFRA's requirement that labels not contain "false or misleading statements," that state-law cause of action would be pre-empted by § 136v(b) to the extent of that difference. State-law requirements must also be measured against any relevant EPA regulations that give content to FIFRA's misbranding standards. For example, a failure-to-warn claim alleging that a given pesticide's label should have stated "DANGER" instead of the more subdued "CAUTION" would be pre-empted because it is inconsistent with 40 CFR § 156.64 (2004), which specifically assigns these warnings to particular classes of pesticides based on their toxicity.[10]

In undertaking a pre-emption analysis at the pleadings stage of a case, a court should bear in mind the concept of equivalence. To survive pre-emption, the state-law requirement need not be phrased in the *identical* language as its corresponding FIFRA requirement; indeed, it would be surprising if a common-law requirement used the same phraseology as FIFRA. If a case proceeds to trial, the court's jury instructions must ensure that nominally equivalent labeling requirements are *genuinely* equivalent. If a defendant so requests, a court should instruct the jury on the relevant FIFRA misbranding standards, as well as any regulations that add content to those standards. For a manufacturer should not be held liable under a state labeling requirement subject to § 136v(b) unless the manufacturer is also liable for misbranding as defined by FIFRA.

The judgment of the Court of Appeals is vacated, and the case is remanded for further proceedings consistent with this opinion.

It is so ordered.

    JUSTICE BREYER, concurring in the judgment.

* * *

    JUSTICE THOMAS, with whom JUSTICE SCALIA joins, concurring in the judgment in part and dissenting in part.

* * *

[T]he majority omits a step in its reasoning that should be made explicit: A state-law cause of action, even if not specific to labeling, nevertheless imposes a labeling requirement "in addition to or different from" FIFRA's when it attaches liability to statements on the label that do not produce liability under FIFRA. The state-law cause of action then adds some supplemental requirement of truthfulness to FIFRA's requirement that labeling statements not be "false or misleading." That is why the fraud claims here are properly remanded to determine whether the state and federal standards for liability-incurring statements are, in their application to this case, the same.

Under that reasoning, the majority mistreats two sets of petitioners' claims. First, petitioners' breach-of-warranty claims should be remanded

---

10. At present, there appear to be relatively few regulations that refine or elaborate upon FIFRA's broadly phrased misbranding standards. To the extent that EPA promulgates such regulations in the future, they will necessarily affect the scope of pre-emption under § 136v(b).

for pre-emption analysis, contrary to the majority's disposition, see *ante*, at 1798. To the extent that Texas' law of warranty imposes liability for statements on the label where FIFRA would not, Texas' law is pre-empted. Second, the majority holds that petitioners' claim under the Texas Deceptive Trade Practices–Consumer Protection Act (DTPA) is not pre-empted to the extent it is a breach-of-warranty claim. However, the DTPA claim is also (and, in fact, perhaps exclusively) a claim for false or misleading representations on the label. Therefore, all aspects of the DTPA claim should be remanded. The DTPA claim, like petitioners' fraud claims, should be pre-empted insofar as it imposes liability for label content where FIFRA would not.

* * * The ordinary meaning of § 136v(b)'s terms makes plain that some of petitioners' state-law causes of action may be pre-empted. Yet the majority advances several arguments designed to tip the scales in favor of the States and against the Federal Government. These arguments, in addition to being unnecessary, are unpersuasive. For instance, the majority states that the presumption against pre-emption requires choosing the interpretation of § 136v(b) that disfavors pre-emption. That presumption does not apply, however, when Congress has included within a statute an express pre-emption provision. See *Cipollone v. Liggett Group, Inc., supra*, at 545–546, 112 S.Ct. 2608 (SCALIA, J., concurring in judgment in part and dissenting in part). Section 136v(b) is an explicit statement that FIFRA pre-empts some state-law claims. Thus, our task is to determine which state-law claims § 136v(b) pre-empts, without slanting the inquiry in favor of either the Federal Government or the States.

* * *

Because we need only determine the ordinary meaning of § 136v(b), the majority rightly declines to address respondent's argument that petitioners' claims are subject to other types of pre-emption. Brief for Respondent 36–37. For instance, the majority does not ask whether FIFRA's regulatory scheme is "so pervasive," and the federal interest in labeling "so dominant," that there is no room for States to provide additional remedies. Nor does the majority ask whether enforcement of state-law labeling claims would "stan[d] as an obstacle to the accomplishment and execution of the full purposes and objectives of Congress" in enacting FIFRA.

Today's decision thus comports with this Court's increasing reluctance to expand federal statutes beyond their terms through doctrines of implied pre-emption. See *Camps Newfound/Owatonna, Inc. v. Town of Harrison*, 520 U.S. 564, 617, 117 S.Ct. 1590, 137 L.Ed.2d 852 (1997) (THOMAS, J., dissenting). This reluctance reflects that pre-emption analysis is not "[a] freewheeling judicial inquiry into whether a state statute is in tension with federal objectives," *Gade v. National Solid Wastes Management Assn.*, 505 U.S. 88, 111, 112 S.Ct. 2374, 120 L.Ed.2d 73 (1992) (KENNEDY, J., concurring in part and concurring in judgment), but an inquiry into whether the ordinary meanings of state and federal law conflict.

Notes

1. In several decisions since 1992, the Supreme Court has addressed the preemptive effect of federal legislation or regulation on state products liability claims. As the *Bates* Court notes, *Cipollone v. Liggett Group,* which found products claims challenging the sufficiency of warnings in cigarette promotion and advertising were explicitly preempted by language in the 1969 amendments to the Federal Cigarette Labeling and Advertising Act, was the first in this line of cases. Since *Cipollone*, the Supreme Court and lower courts have addressed the preemptive effect of a number of federal statutes on state products liability suits.

2. **Express Preemption and Implied Preemption.** In both *Bates* and *Cipollone,* the Court addressed the preemptive effect of language contained in the federal statute. By contrast with this express preemption, implied preemption may exist when state law could defeat the aims of Congress, when Congress enacts federal legislation that completely occupies the field, when compliance with both federal and state requirements would be impossible, or when state law stands as an obstacle to federal objectives contained in a federal legislation. In *Cipollone*, the Court declared that when Congress includes an express preemption provision, there arises a presumption that any preemption is limited to the language in the statute and that no additional implied preemption exists. Within three years of *Cipollone,* the Court watered down that pronouncement. In Freightliner v. Myrick, 514 U.S. 280, 115 S.Ct. 1483, 131 L.Ed.2d 385 (1995), the Court declared that *Cipollone* stood for nothing more than that an express preemption clause justified an inference that Congress did not intend any implied preemption. And in Geier v. American Honda Motor Co., 529 U.S. 861, 120 S.Ct. 1913, 146 L.Ed.2d 914 (2000), the Court held that the express preemption clause in National Traffic and Motor Vehicle Safety Act of 1966 had to be read narrowly in light of a clause that expressly preserved state tort claims, but then proceeded to hold that plaintiffs' tort claim was impliedly preempted because the plaintiffs' claim conflicted with federal regulations, which permitted defendant to design its 1987 cars without passenger-side airbags. See Raeker–Jordan, the Pre-emption Presumption that Never Was: Pre-emption Doctrine Swallows the Rule, 40 Ariz.L.Rev. 1379 (1998).

3. **Statutory Language.** The more typical effect of preemption is to limit states in their positive enactments. In *Cipollone*, the Court found that the 1969 amendments, which barred states from imposing a "requirement or prohibition" about smoking in cigarette advertising or promotion included not only state legislation but also common law suits. A year after *Cipollone,* in CSX Transportation, Inc. v. Easterwood, 507 U.S. 658, 113 S.Ct. 1732, 123 L.Ed.2d 387 (1993), the Court found that express preemption of any state "law, rule, regulation, order, or standard relating to railroad safety" contained in the Federal Railroad Safety Act of 1970, 45 U.S.C. §§ 421–447, preempted a negligence claim that a train was traveling at an excessive speed, where its speed complied with a federal regulation prescribing maximum train speeds. Referring to *Cipollone*, the Court found the breadth of

the preemption language sufficient to encompass common law tort claims, as well as positive enactments.

In Medtronic v. Lohr, 518 U.S. 470, 116 S.Ct. 2240, 135 L.Ed.2d 700 (1996), the Court decided the preemptive scope of language in the Medical Device Amendments of 1976, (codified in scattered sections of 21 U.S.C.) ("MDA"). That language barred states from establishing "any requirement which is different from, or in addition to" any requirement imposed by the MDA that relates to the safety of medical devices. Quite understandably, in light of *Cipollone*, the defendant argued that the term "requirement" included all state common-law tort actions. Four members of the Court, in an opinion by Justice Stevens, rejected that argument, claiming that the term only encompassed state statutes and regulations. Later in the opinion, Justice Stevens appeared to retreat from this position by contemplating that at least some state tort actions might be preempted by the MDA. The approach by Justice Stevens suggested that interpretation of statutory preemption language depends on its context within the specific statutory scheme rather than on prior precedent. Four Justices accepted the defendant's argument. Justice Breyer, the fifth vote, agreed in principle that "requirement" included state tort actions but concluded that preemption only existed when a state tort claim challenged the adequacy of a specific requirement for a device, such as a specification that a kidney dialysis machine be grounded with a three-prong plug, by claiming that such a machine was defective for failing to be powered by a low-voltage battery.

In *Geier*, the Court was confronted with a statute that preempted "any safety standard" established by a state for motor vehicles that was not identical to any federal safety standard promulgated pursuant to the National Traffic and Motor Vehicle Safety Act of 1966, 15 U.S.C. § 1381 et seq. The Court declined to interpret "standard" to include state tort actions but in doing so relied on a savings clause in the statute that provided that compliance with a federal safety standard did not prevent a defendant from being liable in a common law tort action. Otherwise, the Court opined, state tort law might constitute a "safety standard." The effect of *Geier* is to preempt tort claims that automobiles should have been equipped with air bags when federal law made them optional.

Does *Bates* clarify the proper interpretation of "requirement" when it is included in an express preemption provision?

4. **Fraud on a Federal Agency.** In Buckman Co. v. Plaintiffs' Legal Committee, 531 U.S. 341, 121 S.Ct. 1012, 148 L.Ed.2d 854 (2001), the Court held that a state law claim that a manufacturer committed fraud in obtaining approval for its medical device was impliedly preempted. Enforcement for noncompliance with the regulatory processes is for the federal agency involved, and the Court expressed concern that permitting such state claims might interfere with the efficient functioning of the agency. Since the decision was based on implied preemption, it would be applicable to other federal regulatory schemes. Why is *Buckman* (which was not cited by the Court in *Bates*) not relevant to the question of state law warnings claims that are co-extensive with the misbranding prohibition in FIFRA?

5. In what way might state fraud or failure-to-warn tort claims impose a broader obligation than the misbranding prohibition contained in FIFRA?

Might the decision in *Bates* encourage pesticide manufacturers to provide less in labeling on their products?

6. The Court concludes that plaintiffs' negligent testing claim is not preempted. If plaintiffs are successful with their negligent testing claim, how would they demonstrate a causal relationship between that negligent testing and their harm?

7. The Court concludes that state law claims such as a design defect that might induce the manufacturer to change its labeling are not preempted because they are not requirements. Why, then, isn't that reasoning applicable to warnings claims? If a manufacturer suffers an adverse jury verdict in a warnings case, isn't it free to pay the judgment and continue to employ the language it has in place? For an argument along these lines, see Justice Blackmun's concurring opinion in *Cipollone*.

8. The dissent argues that plaintiffs' breach of warranty and deceptive trade practices claims should be preempted if they would impose liability for conduct that would not violate FIFRA, consistent with the majority's observation that the "in addition to or different from" language does not preempt warnings claims that are consistent with FIFRA requirements. On what basis did the majority find that plaintiffs' warranty and trade practices claims were not preempted?

9. In *Bates*, the gravamen of the plaintiffs' warning claim is that Dow failed to warn at all of a serious risk. In many FIFRA preemption cases, the plaintiff complains not that there was no warning but that the warning was substantively inadequate. *See* Netland v. Hess & Clark, Inc., 284 F.3d 895 (8th Cir.2002) (cited in footnote four of the *Bates* opinion). How does *Bates* apply to these situations?

10. **Medical Devices.** The lower courts have been divided since *Lohr* on whether a medical device that goes through the MDA pre-market approval process (which does not have any specific requirements relating to the design or labeling of a device) is subject to a state tort claim challenging its design or labeling. *Compare, e.g.,* Horn v. Thoratec Corp., 376 F.3d 163 (3d Cir.2004) and Brooks v. Howmedica, Inc., 273 F.3d 785 (8th Cir.2001) *with* Goodlin v. Medtronic, Inc., 167 F.3d 1367 (11th Cir.1999); *see* Kemp v. Medtronic, Inc., 231 F.3d 216, 224 (6th Cir.2000) ("The various courts of appeals that have confronted issues of preemption arising under the MDA have struggled mightily with *Lohr's* language in the effort to discern its holding."). *See generally* Grey, Make Congress Speak Clearly: Federal Preemption of State Tort Remedies, 77 B.U.L.Rev. 557 (1997); Leflar & Adler, the Preemption Pentad: Federal Preemption of Products Liability Claims After *Medtronic*, 64 Tenn.L.Rev. 691 (1997).

11. **Federal Motor Vehicle Safety Standards.** *Geier* plainly preempts tort claims that manufacturers should have provided airbags when federal regulations provided an option as to the form of passive restraints employed. Since *Geier* courts have been confronted with the question of whether federal automobile safety standards provide merely a minimum standard, in which case tort claims are not preempted, or are designed to provide a mandatory provision. *See* Harris v. Great Dane Trailers, Inc., 234 F.3d 398 (8th Cir.2000) (safety regulation regarding lighting and reflective tape to make trailers visible to other motorists does not preempt tort

claims); Fisher v. Ford Motor Co., 224 F.3d 570 (6th Cir.2000) (tort claim that language different from that mandated by federal regulation should have been employed to warn of dangers of airbags preempted).

12. **Preemption as Tort Reform.** As the Court explains in footnotes 3 and 8 and in the text accompanying note 8, the United States submitted an amicus brief on behalf of Dow and its theory of the broader preemptive effect of FIFRA. That position reversed course for the United States, which had, years before, argued for a narrow interpretation of the FIFRA preemption provision. This change has occurred in other areas as well, most notably in the area of prescription drugs, in which the government has submitted amicus briefs in support of preemption based on the Federal Food Drug and Cosmetic Act, which provides the basis for FDA regulation of drugs. Compare Witczak v. Pfizer, Inc., 377 F.Supp.2d 726 (D.Minn.2005) (rejecting preemption) with Needleman v. Pfizer Inc., 2004 WL 1773697 (N.D.Tex. 2004) (finding preemption). The Bush administration has candidly admitted that it has taken strong pro preemption positions as an alternative means to attain tort reform. What weight should the Court give to an administrative agency's opinion about the scope of a preemption clause in a statute it is empowered to implement? *See* Sprietsma v. Mercury Marine, 537 U.S. 51, 123 S.Ct. 518, 154 L.Ed.2d 466 (2002); Geier v. American Honda Motor Co., 529 U.S. 861, 120 S.Ct. 1913, 146 L.Ed.2d 914 (2000). For an argument against preemption for prescription drugs, see Vladeck, Preemption and Regulatory Failure, 33 Pepperdine L.Rev. 95, 122–26 (2005).

13. Other federal statutes that arguably preempt common law product liability actions include: the Federal Communications Act, 47 U.S.C. § 151 et seq. (cellphones); the Federal Hazardous Substances Act, 15 U.S.C.A. § 1261 et seq.; the Federal Boat Safety Act, 46 U.S.C. §§ 4301–11; the Federal Virus–Serum–Toxin Act, 21 U.S.C. §§ 151–59 (regulating animal vaccines); the Federal Locomotive Boiler Inspection Act, 49 U.S.C. §§ 20301–20306 & 20701–20903 (railroad locomotives); and the Federal Flammable Fabrics Act, 15 U.S.C. §§ 1191–1204.

Chapter 9

DAMAGES

SECTION A. IN GENERAL

Damages in products liability cases are governed by the same general principles that apply to all tort cases. Compensatory damages are intended to return the plaintiff, insofar as money can do so, back to the position that existed prior to the defendant's tortious conduct.[1] Compensatory damages are often divided into special damages and general damages also known respectively as pecuniary and non-pecuniary damages. Special damages are damages that are peculiar to the plaintiff and are more amenable to objective measurement. They include such things as the value of lost property, past and future medical expenses, and past and future lost earnings capacity. General damages such as pain and suffering and mental anguish, are presumed to flow from the tort and are difficult to measure objectively.

Even within categories of special damages, calculating the proper level of compensation can be quite difficult. For example, as you will recall from your torts course, plaintiffs are entitled to compensation for lost earnings *capacity*, not actual lost earnings. Measurement of earnings capacity is never simple and can become quite difficult in situations where the plaintiff has voluntarily chosen to withdraw from the labor force for some period of time, as might be the case for a mother after the birth of a child.

Assessing damages may also be complicated by the existence of preexisting injuries or the occurrence of subsequent injuries. Ample authority exists for the position that the defendant is responsible only for the damages caused by the defendant's wrongful conduct. However, in practice apportionment of damages can be quite difficult.

A similar problem arises in toxic tort cases where there is no biological marker that would allow us to determine the cause of the plaintiff's injury and, therefore, forces us to rely on epidemiological evidence. For example, in asbestos cases where courts have admitted

---

1. When the victim of the defendant's tort dies, damages are governed by the relevant Wrongful Death and Survival Statutes. *See* Dobbs, The Law of Torts, Ch. 19 (2000).

evidence that the plaintiff smoked cigarettes and, based on that evidence, have permitted the jury to apportion lung cancer damages into those caused by smoking and those caused by asbestos, apportionment is complicated by the fact that the joint effect of asbestos exposure and cigarette smoking on developing lung cancer is multiplicative rather than additive. Cigarette smoking creates a ten-fold increase in lung cancer, asbestos exposure produces a five-fold increase, but compared to the non-smoking, non-asbestos exposed individual, asbestos exposed smokers experience a 53–fold increased risk of developing lung cancer.[2] One logical apportionment would be to assign 2/3 of the damages to cigarette smoking and 1/3 to asbestos use, implicitly comparing the ten-fold increase due to smoking with the five-fold increase due to asbestos. However, as Gerald Boston points out, other apportionments are defensible.[3] One might argue, for example, that in a suit against an asbestos manufacturer a smoking plaintiff should only be responsible for the ten-fold cigarette smoking increase, not the multiplicative effect of asbestos x cigarettes. Thus, he should be assigned 1/5th of the liability. Conversely, one could argue the defendant only caused a five-fold increase and should be responsible for only 1/10th of the damages.

General damages such as pain and suffering and the loss of enjoyment of life are even more indeterminate. As the court in McDougald v. Garber notes:

> An economic loss can be compensated in kind by an economic gain; but recovery for non-economic losses such as pain and suffering and loss of enjoyment of life rests on 'the legal fiction that money damages can compensate for a victim's injury.' * * * We accept this fiction, knowing that although money will neither ease the pain nor restore the victim's abilities, this device is as close as the law can come in its effort to right the wrong. We have no hope of evaluating what has been lost, but a monetary award may provide a measure of solace for the condition created.

73 N.Y.2d 246, 254, 538 N.Y.S.2d 937, 536 N.E.2d 372 (1989).

Over the years, general damages have often been criticized, in part because of their indeterminacy.[4] Another line of criticism argues that pain and suffering damages serve no compensatory function especially in cases where the plaintiff has not suffered a serious, permanent injury.[5]

2. Mustacchi, Lung Cancer Latency and Asbestos Liability, 17 J. Legal Medicine, 277, 297 (1996).

3. Boston, Toxic Apportionment: A Causation and Risk Contribution Model, 25 Envtl.L. 549, 576 (1995).

4. For useful discussions of how well juries do in assessing damages *see* Bovbjerg, Sloan & Blumstein, Valuing Life and Limb in Tort: Scheduling "Pain and Suffering," 83 Nw.U.L.Rev. 908 (1989); Wissler, Hart & Saks, Decisionmaking About General Damages: A Comparison of Jurors, Judges, and Lawyers, 98 Mich.L.Rev. 751 (1999); Schkade, Sunstein & Kahneman, Deliberating About Dollars: The Severity Shift, 100 Colum.L.Rev. 1139 (2000); Green & Bornstein, Precious Little Guidance: Jury Instruction on Damage Awards, 6 Psychol. Pub. Pol'y & L. 743 (2000).

5. *See* Schwartz, Proposals for Products Liability Reform: A Theoretical Synthesis, 97 Yale L.J. 353 (1988); Abel, A Critique of Torts, 37 U.C.L.A. L.Rev. 785 (1990); Pryor, The Tort Law Debate, Efficiency, and the Kingdom of the Ill: A Critique of the Insur-

Do you agree? What other objectives of tort law might general damages serve?

As a practical matter, in a tort regime that follows the "American Rule" whereby each party pays its own attorney fees and that compensates plaintiff lawyers through contingency fees, pain and suffering damages provide the resources to pay the attorney and fully compensate plaintiffs for their special damages. Is this a sufficient justification for such damages?

The 1970s and 1980s witnessed several waves of tort reform designed to rein in perceived excesses in the tort system.[6] Many of the specific reforms were intended to limit damages. A large number of jurisdictions have legislated caps on non-pecuniary damages, frequently in the range of $250,000 to $500,000. These statutes have been met with mixed judicial reviews. In several jurisdictions, these statutes have been declared to be unconstitutional.[7] A second reform involved the "collateral source rule." Under this rule, a plaintiff's recovery against the defendant is not diminished by the fact that the plaintiff has received compensation for the same injury from a third source such as an insurance policy. Theoretically, the collateral source rule allows some injured plaintiffs to be overcompensated. In practice, overcompensation is less likely because the terms of insurance policies give the insurer a right of subrogation. Nevertheless, a number of jurisdictions have modified or abolished the collateral source rule at least in situations where there is no right of subrogation.[8]

The remainder of this chapter focuses on damage issues that frequently arise in the context of products liability litigation.

SECTION B. PECUNIARY LOSS AND HARM TO PROPERTY

ALLOWAY v. GENERAL MARINE INDUSTRIES
Supreme Court of New Jersey, 1997.
149 N.J. 620, 695 A.2d 264.

POLLOCK, J.

The primary issue is whether New Hampshire Insurance Co. ("New Hampshire") and its insured, Samuel P. Alloway III ("Alloway") (jointly described as "plaintiffs") may recover from General Marine Industries, Inc. ("GMI") in negligence and strict liability for economic loss caused

---

ance Theory of Compensation, 79 Va.L.Rev. 91 (1993); Croley & Hanson, The Nonpecuniary Costs of Accidents: Pain-and-Suffering Damages in Tort Law, 108 Harv.L.Rev. 1787 (1995).

6. *See* Sanders & Joyce, "Off to the Races": The 1980s Tort Crisis and the Law Reform Process, 27 Hous.L.Rev. 207 (1990); Saks, Do We Really Know Anything About the Behavior of the Tort Litigation System—And Why Not?, 140 U.Pa.L.Rev. 1147 (1992).

7. *See* Dobbs, The Law of Torts § 384 (2000).

8. *See* Fla. Stat. Ann. § 768.76; N.J. Stat. Ann. 2A: 15–97.

by a defect in a power boat purchased by Alloway and insured by New Hampshire. Alloway purchased the boat from Mullica River Boat Basin ("Mullica"), a retail boat dealer, and insured it with New Hampshire under a comprehensive general insurance policy. Mullica had purchased the boat from Century Boats ("Century"), an unincorporated division of Glasstream Boats, Inc. ("Glasstream"), the manufacturer. Subsequently, Glasstream went bankrupt, and GMI, formerly known as GAC Partners, P.L. ("GAC"), purchased Glasstream's assets.

Allegedly because of a defective seam in the swimming platform, water seeped into the boat, which sank while docked. New Hampshire paid Alloway under the policy. Alloway then subrogated New Hampshire to his rights, subject to Alloway's claim for the deductible portion of his loss.

Plaintiffs instituted this action to recover for their respective economic losses. The Law Division granted GMI's motion to dismiss, holding that plaintiffs could not recover for economic loss resulting from damage to the boat itself. It held that plaintiffs' only claim was for breach-of-warranty under the Uniform Commercial Code ("U.C.C."), a claim barred by 11 U.S.C.A. § 363 ("§ 363") of the Bankruptcy Code. The Appellate Division reversed, holding that plaintiffs could recover in tort for the economic loss and that the Bankruptcy Code did not bar recovery. 288 *N.J.Super.* 479, 672 A.2d 1177 (1996). We granted certification, 145 *N.J.* 372, 678 A.2d 713 (1996). We reverse the judgment of the Appellate Division and reinstate that of the Law Division.

I.

From the limited record, the following facts emerge. In October 1989, Glasstream filed a voluntary petition in bankruptcy. Five months later, the Bankruptcy Court directed Glasstream to sell substantially all of its assets to GMI "free and clear of any interest in such property." At some unspecified time, Glasstream made the boat and sold it to Mullica.

On July 14, 1990, Alloway purchased the boat, a new thirty-three foot Century Grande XL ("Grande") boat from Mullica. The purchase price was $61,070. Century expressly warranted for twelve months from the date of purchase that the boat was "free from defects in material and workmanship under normal use and when operated according to instructions." Alloway obtained from New Hampshire a comprehensive general insurance policy on the boat.

Three months later, while docked at the Bayview Marina in Manahawkin, New Jersey, the Grande sank. No other property was damaged, and no one sustained personal injuries.

Alloway filed a claim with New Hampshire, which spent $40,106.63 to repair the boat. * * *

Thereafter, Alloway filed a three-count complaint against Mullica and GMI, seeking recovery for his economic loss. In count one, Alloway sought to recover for Mullica's breach of "the manufacturer's warranty" for "repair or replacement of any part found to be defective." Count two alleged a strict-liability claim asserting that Century had manufactured a defective boat for which GMI was liable as Century's successor. Count three alleged that Glasstream, "negligently manufactured and inspected the boat," that GMI was liable to Century's successor, and that Mullica had failed to discover the defect.

Alloway then assigned his claims to New Hampshire * * *.

The Law Division granted GMI's motion to dismiss for failure to state a cause of action. It relied on *Spring Motors Distribs. v. Ford Motor Co.*, 98 *N.J.* 555, 489 *A.*2d 660 (1985), which held that a purchaser could not maintain an action in strict liability for economic loss. It also relied on *D'Angelo v. Miller Yacht Sales*, 261 *N.J.Super.* 683, 619 *A.*2d 689 (1993), in which the Appellate Division held that a consumer who had purchased a yacht that was not as represented could sue the manufacturer under the U.C.C. for breach of warranty, but not in strict liability. According to the *D'Angelo* court, the U.C.C. provides a consumer with the exclusive remedy for economic loss resulting from the breach of express or implied warranties. *Id.* at 688, 619 *A.*2d 689. The Law Division reasoned that because plaintiffs sought to recover for economic loss to the boat itself, GMI was not liable as Glasstream's successor.

Because Mullica's insurer was insolvent, New Hampshire dismissed its subrogation claim against Mullica. See *N.J.S.A.* 17:30 A–5,–8 (denying subrogation claims against insured of insolvent insurer). Alloway then settled his claim against Mullica, thereby extinguishing plaintiffs' claims for breach of warranty. Thus, Alloway has already received payment from New Hampshire for the cost of repairs, less the $2,500 deductible under his policy, and an undisclosed sum in settlement of his claim against Mullica.

The Appellate Division reversed, relying on *Santor v. A & M Karagheusian, Inc.*, 44 *N.J.* 52, 207 *A.*2d 305 (1965), which recognized that a consumer could maintain a strict-liability claim against a manufacturer for loss of value of a defective carpet. According to the Appellate Division, *Spring Motors* precluded a commercial purchaser, but not a consumer, from recovering in strict liability. 288 *N.J.Super.* at 486–87, 672 *A.*2d 1177. Observing that *Spring Motors* declined to reconsider *Santor*, the Appellate Division concluded that "[s]ince *Santor* has not been overruled, we must follow it." *Id.* at 488, 672 *A.*2d 1177. In so holding, the court rejected the Appellate Division's holding in *D'Angelo*, *supra*, 261 *N.J.Super.* 683, 619 *A.*2d 689.

The Appellate Division also concluded that plaintiffs could recover against GMI as the successor to Glasstream. The court relied on *Ramirez v. Amsted Industries, Inc.*, 86 *N.J.* 332, 431 *A.*2d 811 (1981), which permitted a worker who was injured by a defective power press to maintain a strict-liability action against a defendant that had purchased the assets of the manufacturer of the press.[1] * * * Essentially, the Appellate Division held that GMI, as the successor to Glasstream, was

---

[1] Ed. Note: In *Ramirez*, the court adopted a product line theory of successor liability. See Chapter 12 for a discussion of successor liability.

liable to plaintiffs in negligence and strict liability for economic loss caused by the sinking of the boat.

II.

The threshold issue is whether plaintiffs may rely on theories of strict liability and negligence to recover damages for economic loss resulting from a defect that caused injury only to the boat itself. Plaintiffs seek damages for the cost of repair and for the boat's lost value on trade-in. They do not allege that other property was damaged or that anyone sustained personal injuries. The question reduces to whether plaintiffs may use tort theories to recover the lost benefit of their bargain from the purchaser of the manufacturer's assets, GMI.

Preliminarily, economic loss encompasses actions for the recovery of damages for costs of repair, replacement of defective goods, inadequate value, and consequential loss of profits. *See* James J. White & Robert S. Summers, *Uniform Commercial Code* 534–44 (3d ed.1988) * * *.

Allocation of economic loss between a manufacturer and a consumer involves assessment of tort and contract principles in the determination of claims arising out of the manufacture, distribution, and sale of defective products. Generally speaking, tort principles are better suited to resolve claims for personal injuries or damage to other property. *See Spring Motors Distribs., supra,* 98 *N.J.* at 579–80, 489 *A.*2d 660; *East River S.S. v. Transamerica Delaval,* 476 *U.S.* 858, 871–72, 106 *S.Ct.* 2295, 2302–03, 90 *L.Ed.*2d 865 (1986); *Seely v. White Motor Co.,* 63 *Cal.*2d 9, 45 *Cal.Rptr.* 17, 403 *P.*2d 145, 149–51 (1965); *Bocre Leasing Corp. v. General Motors Corp.,* 84 *N.Y.*2d 685, 621 *N.Y.S.*2d 497, 499, 645 *N.E.*2d 1195, 1197 (1995). Contract principles more readily respond to claims for economic loss caused by damage to the product itself. *See Spring Motors, supra,* 98 *N.J.* at 580, 489 *A.*2d 660; *East River, supra,* 476 *U.S.* at 871–72, 106 *S.Ct.* at 2302, 90 *L.Ed.*2d 865; *Seely, supra,* 45 *Cal.Rptr.* 17, 403 *P.*2d at 149–51; *Lewinter v. Genmar Indus.,* 26 *Cal. App.*4th 1214, 32 *Cal.Rptr.*2d 305, 309 (1994); *Florida Power & Light Co. v. Westinghouse Elec. Corp.,* 510 *So.*2d 899, 901–02 (Fla.1987); *Oceanside At Pine Point v. Peachtree Doors, Inc.,* 659 *A.*2d 267, 270 (Me.1995); *Bocre Leasing, supra,* 621 *N.Y.S.*2d at 501, 645 *N.E.*2d at 1199.

Various considerations support the distinction. Tort principles more adequately address the creation of an unreasonable risk of harm when a person or other property sustains accidental or unexpected injury. * * * When, however, a product fails to fulfill a purchaser's economic expectations, contract principles, particularly as implemented by the U.C.C., provide a more appropriate analytical framework. *See* * * * *Casa Clara v. Charley Toppino & Sons,* 620 *So.*2d 1244, 1247 (Fla.1993) * * *. Implicit in the distinction is the doctrine that a tort duty of care protects against the risk of accidental harm and a contractual duty preserves the satisfaction of consensual obligations. * * *

Relevant to the distinction are "the relative bargaining power of the parties and the allocation of the loss to the better risk-bearer in a modern marketing system." Spring Motors, supra, 98 *N.J.* at 575, 489 A.2d 660 * * *. Perfect parity is not required for a finding of substantially equal bargaining power. * * * Although a manufacturer may be in a better position to absorb the risk of loss from physical injury or property damage, a purchaser may be better situated to absorb the "risk of economic loss caused by the purchase of a defective product." *Ibid.*

In the present case, nothing indicates that Alloway was at a disadvantage when bargaining for the purchase of the boat. Moreover, a thirty-three foot luxury boat with a swimming platform is not a necessity. Additionally, Alloway prudently protected himself against the risk of loss by obtaining an insurance policy that distributed that risk to his insurer, New Hampshire. To this extent, the question becomes whether GMI, which acquired the assets of the bankrupt manufacturer, or New Hampshire, which is in the business of insuring against the risk of harm caused by defective products, can better bear the risk of loss from damage to the boat. * * *

Also involved is an appreciation of the relative roles of the legislative and judicial branches in defining rights and duties in commercial transactions. Absent legislation, courts possess greater latitude in determining those rights and duties. Once the Legislature acts, respect for it as a coequal branch of government requires courts to consider the legislation in determining the limits of judicial action. * * * By enacting the U.C.C., the Legislature adopted a comprehensive system for compensating consumers for economic loss arising from the purchase of defective products. * * * The U.C.C. represents the Legislature's attempt to strike the proper balance in the allocation of the risk of loss between manufacturers and purchasers for economic loss arising from injury to a defective product. *See generally* James J. White & Robert S. Summers, 1 *Uniform Commercial Code* 582 (4th ed.1995) * * *.

Consequently, the U.C.C. provides for express warranties regarding the quality of goods, *N.J.S.A.* 12A:2–313, as well as an implied warranty of merchantability, *N.J.S.A.* 12A:2–314, and an implied warranty of fitness for a particular purpose, *N.J.S.A.* 12A:2–315. When a seller delivers goods that are not as warranted, the buyer may recover the difference between the value of the defective goods and their value if they had been as warranted. Furthermore, a provision in a merchant's form is not binding on a consumer unless the consumer has signed the form. *N.J.S.A.* 12A:2–209(2). A consumer, moreover, may recover incidental and consequential damages. *N.J.S.A.* 12A:2–715(1), (2); *N.J.S.A.* 12A:2–714. In addition, the Legislature has directed courts to construe the U.C.C. liberally and to promote the U.C.C.'s underlying purposes and policies. *N.J.S.A.* 12A:1–102(1).

As a counterbalance, the U.C.C. allows manufacturers to limit their liability through disclaimers, except for personal injuries. *N.J.S.A.* 12A:2–316. Further, the U.C.C. allows parties to modify or limit damages by agreement. *N.J.S.A.* 12A:2–719. Finally, the U.C.C. provides a four-year statute of limitations to institute an action under its provisions.

N.J.S.A. 12A:2–725. This comprehensive scheme offers significant protection to consumers while insuring that merchants are not saddled with substantial and uncertain liability. * * *

Over thirty years ago, before the U.C.C. took effect, this Court ruled that strict liability in tort provided more suitable relief than an action for breach of an implied warranty of merchantability. *Santor, supra,* 44 N.J. at 53, 207 A.2d 305. The Court reached this unprecedented result notwithstanding that an action for breach of implied warranty, like one in strict liability, did not require privity between the purchaser and the manufacturer. * * *

Disagreement with *Santor* was not long in coming. In *Seely, supra,* 63 *Cal.*2d 9, 45 *Cal.Rptr.* 17, 403 *P.*2d 145, which was decided four months after *Santor,* the purchaser of a defective truck sued for damage to the truck and lost profits from his inability to use it in his hauling business. Writing for the California Supreme Court, Chief Justice Roger Traynor recognized the purchaser's claim for breach of an express warranty, but rejected his claim in strict liability. In reaching that result, Chief Justice Traynor reasoned that absent personal injury or property damage, strict liability in tort was not designed "to undermine the warranty provisions of the ... Uniform Commercial Code but, rather, to govern the distinct problem of physical injuries." *Id.*, 45 *Cal.Rptr.* at 21, 403 *P.*2d at 149.

Twenty years later, we addressed "the rights of a commercial buyer to recover for economic loss caused by the purchase of defective goods." *Spring Motors, supra,* 98 *N.J.* at 560, 489 A.2d 660. In that case, Spring Motors Distributors ("Spring Motors"), a commercial lessor of vehicles, bought a fleet of trucks from Ford Motor Co. ("Ford") * * *. Pursuant to the sales, Ford issued an express warranty on transmissions manufactured by Clark Equipment Co. ("Clark"), which had issued express warranties to Ford. Spring Motors' lessee experienced difficulties with the transmissions. * * * Consequently, Spring Motors suffered economic losses, which included costs of repair, lost profits, and a decrease in the market value of the trucks. * * * Thereafter, Spring Motors sued Ford under theories of negligence, strict liability and breach of warranty. * * * The basic issue was whether the applicable statute of limitations was the four-year statute in the U.C.C., *N.J.S.A.* 12A:2–725, or the six-year statute of limitations pertaining to tort actions for property damage, *N.J.S.A.* 2A:14–1. We held that Spring Motors had a cause of action against both Ford and Clark for breach of warranty and that the U.C.C.'s four-year period of limitations determined the time for the commencement of the action.

When the harm suffered is to the product itself, unaccompanied by personal injury or property damage, we concluded that principles of contract, rather than of tort law, were better suited to resolve the purchaser's claim. * * * Consequently, we held that the U.C.C. provided the appropriate period of limitations. * * * Because the action was between commercial parties, we did not address the issue raised by

Santor, whether a consumer could maintain an action for both breach of warranty and strict liability.

One year after we decided *Spring Motors*, the United States Supreme Court reviewed the roles of tort and contract law in a case involving economic loss caused by the defective design and manufacture of turbines in supertankers. *See East River, supra*, 476 U.S. 858, 106 S.Ct. 2295, 90 L.Ed.2d 865. In a unanimous opinion, the Court began, "[i]n this admiralty case, we must decide whether a cause of action in tort is stated when a defective product purchased in a commercial transaction malfunctions, injuring only the product itself and causing purely economic loss." *Id.* at 859, 106 S.Ct. at 2296, 90 L.Ed.2d 865. The Court continued, "charting a course between products liability and contract law, we must determine whether injury to a product itself is the kind of harm that should be protected by products liability or left entirely to the law of contracts." *Ibid.*

After analyzing relevant state court decisions, including *Santor, Seely,* and *Spring Motors,* the Court concluded "that a manufacturer in a commercial transaction has no duty under negligence or strict products-liability theory to prevent a product from injuring itself." *Id.* at 871, 106 S.Ct. at 2302, 90 L.Ed.2d 865. In an action for economic loss, the reasons for imposing a tort duty are weak while "those for leaving the party to its contractual remedies are strong." *Ibid.* For example, injury to a product itself neither implicates the safety concerns of tort law, *ibid.*, nor justifies "[t]he increased cost to the public that would result from holding the manufacturer liable in tort." *Id.* at 872, 106 S.Ct. at 2302, 90 L.Ed. 2d 865. Allowing recovery for all foreseeable damages in claims seeking purely economic loss, could subject a manufacturer to liability for vast sums arising from the expectations of parties downstream in the chain of distribution. * * *

Subsequently, state and federal courts, when exercising admiralty jurisdiction, have recognized that *East River*'s bar of strict-liability claims extends to actions brought by consumers. * * *

The vast majority of courts across the country likewise have concluded that purchasers of personal property, whether commercial entities or consumers, should be limited to recovery under contract principles. *See, e.g., Arkwright–Boston Mfgs. Mutual Ins. Co. v. Westinghouse Elec. Corp.*, 844 F.2d 1174, 1178 (5th Cir.1988) (holding that Texas law did not permit recovery of economic loss resulting from damage to product itself); *Aloe Coal Co. v. Clark Equip. Co.*, 816 F.2d 110, 118 (3d Cir.1987) (holding that, under Pennsylvania law, fire damage to product itself was not recoverable from manufacturer on theory of negligence, but buyer's remedies limited to law of warranty); *Purvis v. Consolidated Energy Prods. Co.*, 674 F.2d 217, 222–23 (4th Cir.1982) (finding that losses resulting from ineffective equipment were recoverable under law of contracts and not strict liability); *East Mississippi Power Assoc. v. Porcelain Prods. Co.*, 729 F.Supp. 512, 517–19 (S.D.Miss.1990) (holding that Mississippi law does not allow electric company to recover economic loss from manufacturer of defective insulation); *Public Serv. Co. v. Westinghouse Elec. Corp.*, 685 F.Supp. 1281, 1285 (D.N.H.1988) (holding that, under New Hampshire law, manufacturer of steam turbine electric generator could not be held strictly liable when allegedly defective product injured only itself); * * * *Wellcraft Marine v. Zarzour*, 577 So.2d 414, 418 (Ala.1991) (finding that purchaser of defective motor boat could not recover under state products liability statute because damage was only to boat) * * *.

Only a handful of jurisdictions have followed *Santor*. *See* White & Summers, *supra*, § 10–5 at 580 (criticizing *Santor* and stating "courts seem to have grown more willing in the last decade to label loss as economic, thus not recoverable in tort than before"); *see, e.g., Sharon Steel Corp. v. Lakeshore, Inc.*, 753 F.2d 851, 855–56 (10th Cir.1985) (allowing plaintiff to recover damages for economic loss under New Mexico law when plaintiff was subjected to unreasonable risk of injury) * * *.

Scholars likewise have criticized the extension of strict liability to include claims for purely economic loss. *See, e.g.*, White & Summers, *supra*, § 10–5; O'Donnell, Weiss & Kaplan, *On Differences Between Blood and Red Ink: A Second Look At The Policy Arguments For The Abrogation Of The Economic Loss Rule In Consumer Litigation*, 19 Nova L.Rev. 923, 926 (1995) (urging courts to prohibit strict-liability actions for pure economic injury, even when the potential plaintiff is not a commercial entity); Franklin, *When Worlds Collide: Liability Theories and Disclaimers in Defective Product Cases*, 18 Stan.L.Rev. 974, 989–90 (1966) (criticizing courts as unaware of relevance of sales law to products-liability law) * * *.

Following the majority rule, the American Law Institute's proposed *Restatement (Third) of Torts: Products Liability* § 21 (Proposed Final Draft April 1, 1997), defines "economic loss" to exclude recovery under tort theories for damage to a product itself. Section 21, comment d, states that "[w]hen a product defect results in harm to the product itself, the law governing commercial transactions sets forth a comprehensive scheme governing the rights of the buyer and seller." *Id*. at comment d. According to the Restatement, "*Santor* . . . appears today to stand alone in allowing a products liability action when a product did not create an unreasonable risk of harm but merely caused economic loss when it failed to meet performance expectations." *Id*. at Reporters Note to Comment d.

Recently, several state courts have confined consumers to contract principles in actions for economic loss. In a case that involved a pleasure boat with a defective hull, the Alabama Supreme Court declined to recognize a tort action against the manufacturer when the boat took on water after striking a submerged object. *Wellcraft Marine, supra*, 577 So.2d 414. The purchaser sued the manufacturer and others for breach of implied warranties and under the Alabama Extended Manufacturer's Liability Doctrine. In rejecting the latter claim, the Court said that the

Doctrine did not apply when the damage was to the product itself. *Id.* at 418. Declining to distinguish between purchasers who were consumers or commercial buyers, the Court held that the "rule remains the same, regardless of the nature of the consumer." *Ibid.*

In *Casa Clara, supra,* 620 *So.*2d 1244, the Florida Supreme Court rejected the contention of homeowners that they should be allowed to recover in tort for economic loss. Consequently, the Court held that the homeowners could not maintain a tort action to recover the costs of repair and lost value in their homes. * * *

Other jurisdictions also have rejected homeowners' reliance on tort law to recover economic loss arising out of construction defects. *See, e.g., Oceanside, supra,* 659 *A.*2d at 270 (rejecting association's and individual homeowners' tort claims of economic loss caused by water damage around windows); *Morris v. Osmose Wood Preserving,* 99 *Md.App.* 646, 639 *A.*2d 147, 152 (1994) (rejecting homeowners' tort claims against plywood manufacturer for gradual deterioration of plywood in roofs because such damage constituted economic loss), *modified,* 340 *Md.* 519, 667 *A.*2d 624 (1995); *Lempke v. Dagenais,* 130 *N.H.* 782, 547 *A.*2d 290, 291 (1988) (rejecting property owners' tort claims for economic loss resulting from defective construction of garage); *Waggoner, supra,* 808 *P.*2d at 650, 653 (rejecting mobile home purchasers' tort actions against manufacturer for costs of repair and lost value resulting from defective roof design when damage was to only the mobile home itself, and holding that claim would be more properly made in warranty action). *Cf. Aronsohn v. Mandara,* 98 *N.J.* 92, 107, 484 *A.*2d 675 (1984) (declining "to decide the validity of plaintiff's negligence claim, since ... the contractor's negligence would constitute a breach of the contractor's implied promise to construct the patio in a workmanlike manner").

An unresolved issue is whether the U.C.C. or tort law should apply when a defective product poses a serious risk to other property or persons, but has caused only economic loss to the product itself. In the present case, plaintiffs have not alleged that the defective seam in the boat posed such a risk. Hence, we do not resolve the issue.

In *East River,* the United States Supreme Court rejected cases that adopted intermediate positions, which attempted "to differentiate between 'the disappointed users ... and the endangered ones' ... and permit only the latter to sue in tort." 476 *U.S.* at 869–70, 106 *S.Ct.* at 2301, 90 *L.Ed.*2d 865 (quoting *Russell v. Ford Motor Co.,* 281 *Or.* 587, 575 *P.*2d 1383, 1387 (1978)). The Court stated:

> [T]he intermediate positions, which essentially turn on the degree of risk, are too indeterminate to enable manufacturers easily to structure their business behavior. Nor do we find persuasive a distinction that rests on the manner in which the product is injured. We realize that the damage may be qualitative, occurring through gradual deterioration or internal breakage. Or it may be calamitous. But either way, since by definition no person or other property is damaged, the resulting loss is purely economic. Even when the harm

to the product itself occurs through an abrupt, accident-like event, the resulting loss due to repair costs, decreased value, and lost profits is essentially the failure of the purchaser to receive the benefit of its bargain—traditionally the core concern of contract law.

[*Id.* at 871, 106 *S.Ct.* at 2301–02, 90 *L. Ed.*2d 865 (citations omitted).]

The *Restatement* implicitly adopts *East River,* but states "[a] plausible argument can be made that products that are dangerous in these respects [i.e. discovery of the defect prevented harm from occurring or the only harm was to the product itself, but not to persons or property] rather than merely ineffectual, should be governed by the rules governing products liability law." *Restatement, supra,* at § 21, comment d.

As previously indicated, in this case we do not resolve the issue whether tort or contract law applies to a product that poses a risk of causing personal injuries or property damage but has caused only economic loss to the product itself. *See Spring Motors, supra,* 98 *N.J.* at 578, 489 *A.*2d 660 (distinguishing "cases involving claims for actual or potential personal injuries"). Similarly, we do not reach the issue of the preclusion of a strict-liability claim when the parties are of unequal bargaining power, the product is a necessity, no alternative source for the product is readily available, and the purchaser cannot reasonably insure against consequential damages.

* * *

III.

Here, plaintiffs seek the lost value on trade-in and the costs of repairing the boat under theories of negligence and strict liability. Thus, this action raises the question whether a consumer and his insurer can maintain an action in tort for economic loss only.

Alloway insured against the risk that gave rise to his economic loss. In a sense, the question becomes whether the better risk bearer is his insurer, New Hampshire, or GMI, the purchaser of the assets of the bankrupt boat manufacturer. To impose liability on GMI is to impose on it, in addition to the price it paid for Glasstream's assets in the bankruptcy proceeding, the added cost of the loss of a boat that it never owned. The imposition of that cost would dislocate the allocation of responsibility in the U.C.C. and impose the cost of an uncertain liability on one that did not agree to assume that cost. Alloway, on the other hand, relied not on any warranty or other contractual undertaking from GMI, but on the warranties issued by the boat dealer, Mullica, and the New Hampshire policy. Under both the warranties and the insurance policy, Alloway has been reimbursed.

By providing for express and implied warranties, the U.C.C. amply protects all buyers–commercial purchasers and consumers alike–from economic loss arising out of the purchase of a defective product. In addition, many buyers insure against the risk of the purchase of defective goods either directly through the purchase of an insurance policy, such as Alloway's purchase of the New Hampshire policy, or through insurance provided indirectly through many credit card purchases. Under the U.C.C. as construed by this Court, moreover, the absence of privity no longer bars a buyer from reaching through the chain of distribution to the manufacturer. *See Spring Motors, supra,* 98 *N.J.* at 582, 586–87, 489 *A.*2d 660; *Santor, supra,* 44 *N.J.* at 63, 207 *A.*2d 305. In addition, the United States Supreme Court, the overwhelming majority of state courts, and legal scholars have recognized the unfairness of imposing on a seller tort liability for economic loss. Accordingly, we hold that plaintiffs' tort claims are barred.

* * *

The judgment of the Appellate Division is reversed, and the judgment of the Law Division dismissing the complaint is reinstated.

[Judge Handler's concurring opinion is omitted.]

Notes

1. In a case of first impression, the North Dakota Supreme Court cited *Alloway* and agreed that the economic loss doctrine applies to consumer purchases as well as commercial transactions. Clarys v. Ford Motor Co., 592 N.W.2d 573 (1999). *Alloway* was applied with the same result in Flowers v. Viking Yacht Co., 366 N.J.Super. 49, 840 A.2d 291 (Law Div. 2003). It remains to be seen whether the *Santor* rule will survive in New Jersey in cases where the consumer is purchasing a "necessity" rather than a luxury good.

2. As noted in *Alloway*, some jurisdictions have created a "sudden and calamitous" exception to the economic loss rule. Under this exception, "if property damage results from a sudden or dangerous occurrence, then tort theory may provide recovery. If the loss relates to a purchaser's disappointed expectations due to deterioration, internal breakdown, or non-accidental cause, then the remedy lies in contract." Bagel v. American Honda Motor Co., Inc., 132 Ill.App.3d 82, 87 Ill.Dec. 453, 477 N.E.2d 54, 57–58 (1985). Do you think the New Jersey Supreme Court in *Alloway* rejected the "sudden and calamitous" exception to the economic loss rule? For an "Erie Guess" on this question, *see* Naporano Iron & Metal Co. v. American Crane Corp., 79 F.Supp.2d 494 (D.N.J.1999).

3. Cases in which there is a physical injury to a person clearly fall on the tort side of the tort-contract line. More difficult are those cases where there is physical injury to "other property." Sometime it is difficult to ascertain where the "product itself" ends and "other property" begins. What result, for example, when a component part of a complex product fails, destroying the entire product, or the roof of a new house leaks, causing damage to the rest of the structure? In both of these situations, most courts apply the economic loss rule. *See* Northern Power & Engineering Corp. v. Caterpillar Tractor Co., 623 P.2d 324, 330 (Alaska 1981); Calloway v. City of Reno, 116 Nev. 250, 993 P.2d 1259 (2000). *But see* Saratoga Fishing Co. v. J.M. Martinac & Co., 520 U.S. 875, 117 S.Ct. 1783, 138 L.Ed.2d 76 (1997).

4. How much damage to other property must occur for the plaintiff to get out from under the economic loss rule? Most courts apply a *de minimus* rule. *See* Rich Products Corp. v. Kemutec, Inc., 66 F.Supp.2d 937, 971 (E.D.Wis.1999). As Judge Posner noted in Miller v. United States Steel Corp., 902 F.2d 573, 574 (7th Cir.1990), "Incidental property damage, however, will not take a commercial dispute outside the economic loss doctrine * * *; the tail will not be allowed to wag the dog."

5. Some courts refuse to permit one to advance tort claims when the failure of a product leads to "disappointed expectations," even when the disappointment involved damage to other property. What result in a case where the defendant's defective milk substitute lead to illness and death for some of plaintiff's calves? Are the calves "other property" or is their illness simply a "disappointed expectation"? *See* Grams v. Milk Products, Inc., 283 Wis.2d 511, 699 N.W.2d 167 (2005).

6. What if the loss to the product is the result of fraud on the part of the defendant? Does this undo the rationale for the economic loss rule? Does it matter if the fraud related to the quality of the goods? *See* Werwinski v. Ford Motor Co., 286 F.3d 661 (3d Cir. 2002).

7. Does a strict liability action lie against the product manufacturer in the following cases?

A. A grain storage silo is destroyed by a tornado. Plaintiff claims it is defective because it was not "tornado-proof."

B. A defective burglar alarm malfunctions, and property is stolen by a burglar.

C. A defective burglar alarm malfunctions, and the homeowner is attacked by a burglar.

D. A defective smoke detector fails to sound an alarm in a fire. The resulting delay in calling the fire department enhances the fire damage to plaintiff's home.

E. A defective humidifier system in a home puts excessive amounts of moisture into the air. This causes wet carpets, sticking doors, squeaking steps, warped studs, cracked sheet rock, swollen paneling, rusted fixtures, and furniture damage.

F. Defective bull semen causes genetic problems in calves of artificially inseminated cattle.

SECTION C. MENTAL DISTRESS

GNIRK v. FORD MOTOR CO.
United States District Court, District of South Dakota, 1983.
572 F.Supp. 1201.

Memorandum Opinion

Donald J. Porter, District Judge.

I

Plaintiff Wilma Gnirk seeks compensatory damages against The Ford Motor Company (Ford) for emotional distress inflicted upon her while witnessing the death of her child, a passenger in a Ford car. Ford moves for summary judgment, contending that plaintiff, as a "bystander" cannot recover for emotional distress because (1) it was not intentionally inflicted upon her by Ford; and (2) since she sustained no "accompanying physical injury, i.e., a physical impact and attendant, contemporaneous physical injury", even if Ford's legal liability for her child's death were assumed, she may not recover. Ford further contends that all damages incident to the child's death must be sought under the South Dakota wrongful death act, SDCL 21–5–7 which act does not allow recovery for emotional distress. For the reasons following, Ford's motion for summary judgment is denied.

II

Plaintiff alleges that on November 20, 1980 she and her thirteen month old son were traveling in a 1976 Ford L.T.D. car. She co-owned and was then driving the car. In order to open a fence gate she stopped the car, shifted the gear selector into park, and left the engine running. She got out on the driver's side, leaving her son in the front seat with a seat belt fastened around him. While she was opening the gate the car gear shifted from park to reverse and the car backed up, struck a post, and then went forward a distance into a stock dam. From the time the car first moved, plaintiff chased it and tried unsuccessfully several times to get into the moving car to stop it. When it finally stopped, the car was completely submerged in the stock dam. The child was in the car alone. Plaintiff, a non-swimmer, entered the water but could not locate the car. She then walked a mile and a half to the nearest farmhouse for help.

The event above described, plaintiff alleges, caused her great depression, insomnia, permanent psychological injury, and physical illness.

Plaintiff's claim is analyzed under 402A. This is not to say it is the only theory which will survive defendant's motion. Essentially the same principles apply to an action under 402A as to an action for breach of implied warranty. *Pearson v. Franklin Laboratories, Inc.*, 254 N.W.2d 133, 138–39 (S.D.1977).

III

Upon the facts here, it is appropriate to view plaintiff in the role of a user of Ford's product, rather than as a "bystander".[1] Bystander cases are typically void of any product liability implications running from the defendant tort-feasor to the bystander-plaintiff.[2] Having no connection

---

1. See Note, Emotional Distress In Products Liability: Distinguishing Users from Bystanders, 50 Fordham L.Rev. 291 (1981); Note, The Negligent Infliction of Mental Distress: The Scope of Duty and Foreseeability of Injury, 57 N.D. L.Rev. 577, 599–602 (1981).

2. See generally Annot., 29 A.L.R.3d 1337 (1970). A minority of courts adhere to the "impact rule" which precludes recovery unless the plaintiff-bystander suffered some contemporaneous physical injury or impact from the tortious acts of defendant committed against a third party. See, e.g., *Champion v. Gray*, 420 So.2d 348 (Fla.Dist.Ct.App. 1982); *Little v. Williamson*, 441 N.E.2d 974 (Ind.Ct.App.1982). A second level of courts, following the lead of New York's highest court in *Tobin v. Grossman*, 24 N.Y.2d 609, 249 N.E.2d 419, 301 N.Y.S.2d 554 (1969),

with the tort-feasor, or his negligent tort, the only part played by the bystander is to serve as the unwilling eyewitness to the death or injury of the victim by the tort-feasor. Thus, the bystander has nowhere to look but to the common law rules of negligence, if she [he] is to find a legal duty upon the tort-feasor not to inflict emotional distress upon her by negligently killing or injuring the victim in her presence.

Plaintiff here has a legal connection with Ford which goes to the heart of the case, making it unnecessary for her, or for this court, to look beyond the Restatement (Second) of Torts § 402A (1965) [hereinafter cited as 402A]. By virtue of her status as the user of the Ford car involved, at the time involved, Ford under 402A owed to plaintiff an independent legal duty not to harm her. *Engberg v. Ford Motor Co.,* 87 S.D. 196, 205 N.W.2d 104 (1973); *Shaffer v. Honeywell, Inc.,* 249 N.W.2d 251 (S.D.1976). Moreover, Ford's duty to plaintiff under *Engberg* stems not from the South Dakota wrongful death act but rather from 402A. Ford's legal duty to plaintiff under 402A endures even if the victim does not survive.

IV

In 1918 the South Dakota Supreme Court considered an issue pertinent to the damage issue here. In *Sternhagen v. Kozel,* 40 S.D. 396, 167 N.W. 398 (1918) it was plaintiff's claim that, owing to an alleged tort "she suffered a severe fright and through such fright received a severe mental and physical shock." The Court saw the question presented as whether or not "one, who, through a tort committed against him, suffers a fright—which fright is not the result of an accompanying physical injury, but is itself the proximate cause of a physical injury—can recover

deny recovery unless the plaintiff-bystander was in the "zone of danger"—meaning that in order to recover, plaintiff must have actually feared for her own safety as a result of the defendant's acts. *See, e.g. Rickey v. Chicago Transit Authority,* 98 Ill.2d 546, 75 Ill.Dec. 211, 457 N.E.2d 1 (Ill.1983) (available on Westlaw, All States library); *Stadler v. Cross,* 295 N.W.2d 552 (Minn.1980); *Keck v. Jackson,* 122 Ariz. 114, 593 P.2d 668 (1979); *Shelton v. Russell Pipe & Foundry Co.,* 570 S.W.2d 861 (Tenn.1978); *Towns v. Anderson,* 195 Colo. 517, 579 P.2d 1163 (1978); *Whetham v. Bismarck Hospital,* 197 N.W.2d 678 (N.D.1972); *Guilmette v. Alexander,* 128 Vt. 116, 259 A.2d 12 (1969); *Klassa v. Milwaukee Gas Light Co.,* 273 Wis. 176, 77 N.W.2d 397 (1956). *See also* Restatement (Second) of Torts § 313(2) comment d. (1965) (adopting zone of danger rule); Still, an approximately equal number of courts have abolished the impact rule and the zone of danger rule in favor of a broader "foreseeability test." Under this test, if the plaintiff-bystander's emotional distress is reasonably foreseeable to the defendant-tort-feasor—considering on a case by case basis such factors as the relationship between the plaintiff and the third party-victim, the proximity of the plaintiff to the scene of the accident, and the method by which the plaintiff is made aware of the accident—then recovery is allowed. *See, e.g., Dillon v. Legg,* 68 Cal.2d 728, 441 P.2d 912, 69 Cal.Rptr. 72 (1968) (landmark); *Haught v. Maceluch,* 681 F.2d 291 (5th Cir.1982) (applying Texas law); *Paugh v. Hanks,* 6 Ohio St.3d 72, 451 N.E.2d 759 (1983); *Culbert v. Sampson's Supermarkets, Inc.,* 444 A.2d 433 (Me.1982); *Barnhill v. Davis,* 300 N.W.2d 104 (Iowa 1981); *Walker v. Clark Equipment,* 320 N.W.2d 561 (Iowa 1982); *Portee v. Jaffee,* 84 N.J. 88, 417 A.2d 521 (1980); *Corso v. Merrill,* 119 N.H. 647, 406 A.2d 300 (1979); *Sinn v. Burd,* 486 Pa. 146, 404 A.2d 672 (1979); *Dziokonski v. Babineau,* 375 Mass. 555, 380 N.E.2d 1295 (1978); *D'Ambra v. United States,* 114 R.I. 643, 338 A.2d 524 (1975); *Leong v. Takasaki,* 55 Hawai'i 398, 520 P.2d 758 (1974); *Hughes v. Moore,* 214 Va. 27, 197 S.E.2d 214 (1973).

damages for such fright and the resulting physical injury." The Court answered as follows:

> "Without determining whether one could recover for fright alone, such fright not accompanying physical injury either as its result or cause we are of the opinion that: When physical injury accompanies a fright as its effect, the injured party may recover for the fright, for the physical injury, and for any mental injury accompanying such fright and physical injury, exactly as one can recover where the fright is the result of a physical injury."

* * *

The *Sternhagen* court did not indicate what physical phenomena or manifestation is sufficient to constitute the "physical injury" referred to in the quotation from the case, *supra* [167 N.W. at 399]. That issue has not yet been addressed by the state Supreme Court. In the absence of a controlling statute or decision of the highest court of the state, this court, exercising diversity jurisdiction, 28 U.S.C. § 1332, must apply the rule it believes the Supreme Court of South Dakota would adopt. *McElhaney v. Eli Lilly & Co.,* 564 F.Supp. 265, 268 (D.S.D.1983).

In recent years, [due to increased understanding of the relationship between physical and psychic injury] courts have realistically construed the term "physical injury". *See, e.g., Haught v. Maceluch,* 681 F.2d 291, 299 n. 9 (5th Cir.1982) (applying Texas law; depression, nervousness, weight gain, and nightmares are equivalent to physical injury); *D'Ambra v. United States,* 396 F.Supp. 1180, 1183–84 (D.R.I.1973) ("psychoneurosis" or acute depression constitutes physical injury); *Corso v. Merrill,* 119 N.H. 647, 658, 406 A.2d 300, 307 (1979) (depression constitutes a physical injury); *Mobaldi v. Board of Regents,* 55 Cal.App.3d 573, 578, 127 Cal.Rptr. 720, 723 (1976) (depression and weight loss constitute physical injury), *overruled on other grounds, Baxter v. Superior Court,* 19 Cal.3d 461, 466 n. 4, 563 P.2d 871, 874 n. 4, 138 Cal.Rptr. 315, 318 n. 4 (1977); *Hughes v. Moore,* 214 Va. 27, 29, 35, 197 S.E.2d 214, 216, 220 (1973) (anxiety reaction, phobia and hysteria constitute physical injury); *Daley v. LaCroix,* 384 Mich. 4, 15–16, 179 N.W.2d 390, 396 (1970) (weight loss and nervousness constitute physical injury); *Toms v. McConnell,* 45 Mich.App. 647, 657, 207 N.W.2d 140, 145 (1973) (depression constitutes physical injury).[3]

There is no fine line distinguishing physical from emotional injury. *D'Ambra v. United States,* 396 F.Supp. 1180, 1184 (D.R.I.1973) (quoting from *Sloane v. Southern Cal. Ry. Co.,* 111 Cal. 668, 680, 44 P. 320, 322 (1896)); *Molien,* 27 Cal.3d at 929, 616 P.2d at 820–21, 167 Cal.Rptr. at 838–39. The Restatement acknowledges this much:

---

3. An increasing number of courts have dispensed with the requirement that plaintiff's emotional distress must have manifested itself in some form of physical injury in order to be recoverable. *See Paugh v. Hanks,* 6 Ohio St.3d 72, 451 N.E.2d 759 (1983); *Culbert v. Sampson's Supermarkets, Inc.,* 444 A.2d 433, (Me.1982); *Barnhill v. Davis,* 300 N.W.2d 104, (Iowa 1981); *Molien v. Kaiser Foundation Hospitals,* 27 Cal.3d 916, 616 P.2d 813, 167 Cal.Rptr. 831 (1980); *Sinn v. Burd,* 486 Pa. 146, 404 A.2d 672 (1979); *Leong v. Takasaki,* 55 Hawai'i 398, 520 P.2d 758 (1974).

[Emotional distress] accompanied by transitory, non-recurring physical phenomena, harmless in themselves, such as dizziness, vomiting, and the like, does not make the actor liable where such phenomena are in themselves inconsequential and do not amount to any substantial bodily harm. On the other hand, long continued nausea or headaches may amount to physical illness, which is bodily harm; and even long continued mental disturbance, as for example in the case of repeated hysterical attacks, or mental aberration, may be classified by the courts as illness, notwithstanding their mental character.

Restatement (Second) of Torts, § 436A comment c (1965).

Comment c, above quoted, is a reasonable rule or guide for trial of the issue of whether plaintiff sustained bodily injury proximately caused by alleged emotional disturbance inflicted by Ford. If plaintiff makes out a case for the jury on the issue, and if the jury find for her on the issue she is entitled to recover damages for emotional distress suffered during the event in which her son drowned, for physical injury proximately caused, and for any mental injury accompanying such emotional distress and physical injury, *Sternhagen, supra,* 167 N.W. 398, 399.

* * *

The court concludes that a genuine issue of fact exists concerning whether the event in which her son lost his life inflicted great depression, insomnia, and permanent psychological injury upon plaintiff, which injury proximately caused bodily injury to plaintiff. * * * [T]he Ford motion must be overruled * * *.

Notes

1. Except where mental distress is intentionally inflicted, courts traditionally refuse to allow recovery unless the mental distress resulted in a physical harm. See Meracle v. Children's Service Society of Wisconsin, 149 Wis.2d 19, 437 N.W.2d 532 (1989). As *Gnirk v. Ford Motor Co.* indicates, many courts have liberalized this rule by adopting a very broad definition of physical harm. *E.g.,* Ellington v. Coca Cola Bottling Co., 717 P.2d 109 (Okla.1986). Other courts have rejected the rule outright, and grant recovery for serious mental distress without physical harm. *E.g.,* Folz v. State, 110 N.M. 457, 797 P.2d 246 (1990); Jeannelle v. Thompson Medical Co., 613 F.Supp. 346 (E.D.Mo.1985); Kately v. Wilkinson, 148 Cal.App.3d 576, 195 Cal.Rptr. 902 (1983).

2. Traditionally, courts also refused recovery unless the mental distress was caused by a physical impact. However, this requirement has slowly eroded. Some courts allowed plaintiffs who were in the "zone of danger" to recover even though they did not suffer a physical impact. *See* Rickey v. Chicago Transit Authority, 98 Ill.2d 546, 75 Ill.Dec. 211, 457 N.E.2d 1 (1983), noted in 60 Chi.-Kent L.Rev. 735; 17 J.Mar.L.Rev. 563; 15 Loy.U.Chi. L.J. 453; 1984 S.Ill.U.L.J. 497; Lee v. State Farm Mutual Insurance Co., 272 Ga. 583, 533 S.E.2d 82 (2000).

3. **Bystanders.** Many courts have further eroded the impact rule by adopting the approach in Dillon v. Legg, 68 Cal.2d 728, 69 Cal.Rptr. 72, 441 P.2d 912 (1968), to permit individuals to recover for mental distress resulting from concern about another person who has been injured. In order to prevail under *Dillon*, the plaintiff must show that 1) the plaintiff is closely related to the injured party (usually a parent, child, or spouse), 2) the plaintiff was sufficiently near the scene of the accident, and 3) the plaintiff contemporaneously observed the accident. *See* Shepard v. Superior Court, 76 Cal.App.3d 16, 142 Cal.Rptr. 612 (1977) (strict liability, warranty); Walker v. Clark Equipment Co., 320 N.W.2d 561 (Iowa 1982), noted in 68 Iowa L.Rev. 853 (strict liability, warranty); Pasquale v. Speed Products Engineering, 166 Ill.2d 337, 211 Ill.Dec. 314, 654 N.E.2d 1365 (1995) (strict liability); Culbert v. Sampson's Supermarkets, Inc., 444 A.2d 433 (Me.1982), noted in 21 Duq.L.Rev. 797 (negligence).

4. *Gnirk v. Ford Motor Co.* avoids the application of these hard and fast rules by characterizing plaintiff as a product user rather than a bystander. A few other courts have followed this approach. Kately v. Wilkinson, 148 Cal.App.3d 576, 195 Cal.Rptr. 902 (1983); Bray v. Marathon Corp., 356 S.C. 111, 588 S.E.2d 93 (2003) (worker observed co-worker being crushed to death while both were operating a trash compactor). *But see* Straub v. Fisher and Paykel Health Care, 990 P.2d 384 (Utah 1999). *See* Silverman, Recovery for Emotional Distress in Strict Products Liability, 61 Chi.-Kent L.Rev. 545 (1985).

5. In addition to the articles previously cited, *see* Note, The Merger of Emotional Distress and Strict Liability in Tort, 19 New England L.Rev. 403 (1983–1984).

6. Consider the following problem:

Julia Hassler, a respiratory therapist, worked at a local hospital. One of her patients was Jane Armstrong. The machine Julia used is an open or "blow by" respiratory system. This system uses a ventilator to generate and regulate the flow of oxygen to the patient. In a "blow by" system, an oxygen/air mixture is delivered to the patient through a long, flexible delivery tube, one end of which is attached to the ventilator. As the delivery tube reaches the patient, it is connected to one prong of a "Y" attachment, through which the oxygen/air mixture is delivered directly to the patient. The other prong of the "Y" attachment provides an opening enabling the patient to exhale.

Gulf Breeze Corp. manufactures a humidifier that warms and humidifies the oxygen/air mixture. The humidifier consists of a small plastic chamber that rests on top if a heating unit. The oxygen/air mixture supplied by the ventilator is delivered to the humidifier through a tube connected to an opening in the plastic chamber where the mixture is warmed and humidified. It then exits the chamber through another tube that delivers the warmed mixture to the patient through the "Y" attachment described above. The humidifier does not change the pressure or rate of flow of the oxygen/air mixture. Gulf Breeze manufactures only the humidifier, not the ventilator, the delivery tubes, or the "Y" attachment.

On January 15, 1997, Julia disconnected the delivery tube from the hospital ventilator and connected it to a portable oxygen source so that Mrs. Armstrong could move around the room. Mrs. Armstrong experienced difficulty breathing and began to gurgle from lung secretions. To suction Mrs. Armstrong's secretions, Julia disconnected the delivery tube from the portable oxygen source and reconnected it to the humidifier and hospital ventilator, but failed to install the "Y" attachment, without which Mrs. Armstrong could not exhale. As a result, Mrs. Armstrong suffered barotrauma, respiratory and cardiac arrest, and died. Julia claims that as a result of witnessing Mrs. Armstrong's death, she suffered severe emotional distress that caused termination of her employment, dissolution of her marriage, and her incarceration after attempting to shoot her husband.

She sues Gulf Breeze, arguing that the humidifier was defective because it did not have a pressure release valve that would prevent the type of injury suffered by Mrs. Armstrong and failed to warn of the humidifier's dangerousness without such a valve. Assess the merits of the claim in a jurisdiction that has adopted *Gnirk*. For purposes of your answer you may assume the humidifier is defective.

BURNS v. JAQUAYS MINING CORP.
Court of Appeals of Arizona, 1987.
156 Ariz. 375, 752 P.2d 28.

HOWARD, PRESIDING JUDGE.

This is an appeal from the granting of a summary judgment.[1] The main issue in this case is whether subclinical asbestos-related injury is sufficient to constitute the actual loss or damage required to support a cause of action. We hold that it is not.

Jaquays owned land in Gila County upon which it operated an asbestos mill and had a tailings pile. In 1973, the City of Globe approved the creation of a mobile home subdivision, Mountain View Mobile Home Estates, on adjacent land. The plaintiffs were all at one time residents of the trailer park. Asbestos fiber was blown from the mill and tailings pile into the trailer park. In 1979, the plaintiffs learned the asbestos was dangerous and life threatening. In December 1979, the governor declared the trailer park a disaster area. Steps were taken to clean up the contamination and, in 1983, the state began to relocate the residents who stayed on the premises. It was not until September 16, 1985, that the asbestos hazard was finally contained.

The first lawsuits were filed in 1980 and 1981. Other suits were filed in 1982 and 1983.[2] Plaintiffs seek damages for personal injuries and property damage based on negligence, gross negligence, strict liability

---

1. The defendants who were awarded the summary judgment are Jaquays Mining Corporation, D.W. Jaquays Mining and Contractors Equipment Co., D.W. Jaquays and Ethelyn (sic) Jaquays (hereinafter referred to collectively as "Jaquays"), Mr. and Mrs. Larry M. Schwartz, Gila County, Pinal–Gila Counties Air Quality Control District, City of Globe, State of Arizona, Mr. and Mrs. Rex Town and Neal Beaver.

2. Fifty-six plaintiffs remain in this case.

and nuisance. They also claim damages for the increased risk of developing cancer or other asbestos-related diseases, the need for life-long medical surveillance to monitor the development of those diseases and emotional distress caused by the knowledge and fear of these impending developments. The trial court granted summary judgment on all counts except the count for damages to property.

We view the facts in the light most favorable to the plaintiffs. * * * According to the plaintiffs' expert witnesses, the residents of the trailer park were exposed to substantial and cumulative quantities of asbestos fiber. Their cumulative exposure was comparable to and greater than the exposure experienced by workers in asbestos mines, milling and manufacturing industries. They all have asbestos fibers in their lungs which are causing changes in the lung tissue. Sooner or later some of the residents, if they live long enough, will suffer from asbestosis and other asbestos-related diseases. Some of the children who have been exposed will die of asbestos-related diseases and some will become seriously handicapped.

It is clear from the record that none of the plaintiffs has been diagnosed as having asbestosis. Some of the plaintiffs claim to be suffering from mental anguish as a result of their exposure to asbestos, but there is no competent evidence of any physical impairment or harm caused by this exposure. "The threat of future harm, not yet realized, is not enough." Prosser and Keeton on the Law of Torts § 30 at 165 (5th ed. 1984). [Citations] We believe the following quote from *Schweitzer v. Consolidated Rail Corp. (Conrail)*, 758 F.2d 936, 942 (3d Cir.1985), cert. denied, 474 U.S. 864, 106 S.Ct. 183, 88 L.Ed.2d 152, is applicable here:

> "It is true that the possible existence of subclinical asbestos-related injury prior to manifestation may be of interest to a histologist. [citations omitted.] Likewise, the existence of such injury may be of vital concern to insurers and their insureds who have bargained for liability coverage triggered by 'bodily injury.' [citation omitted.] We believe, however, that subclinical injury resulting from exposure to asbestos is insufficient to constitute the actual loss or damage to a plaintiff's interest required to sustain a cause of action under generally applicable principles of tort law.
>
> Moreover, we are persuaded that a contrary rule would be undesirable as applied in the asbestos-related tort context. If mere exposure to asbestos were sufficient to give rise to a F.E.L.A. cause of action, countless seemingly healthy railroad workers, workers who might never manifest injury, would have tort claims cognizable in federal court. It is obvious that proof of damages in such cases would be highly speculative, likely resulting in windfalls for those who never take ill and insufficient compensation for those who do. Requiring manifest injury as a necessary element of an asbestos-related tort action avoids these problems and best serves the underlying purpose of tort law: the compensation of victims who have suffered. There-

fore we hold that, as a matter of federal law, F.E.L.A. actions for asbestos-related injury do not exist before manifestation of injury."

The reasoning in *Schweitzer* was approved in *Jackson v. Johns–Manville Sales Corp. (Jackson III)*, 781 F.2d 394, 412 n. 22 (5th Cir.1986), cert. denied, 478 U.S. 1022, 106 S.Ct. 3339, 92 L.Ed.2d 743. See also *Urie v. Thompson*, 337 U.S. 163, 69 S.Ct. 1018, 93 L.Ed. 1282 (1949) (cause of action for silicosis accrues when the disease manifests itself); *Clutter v. Johns–Manville Sales Corp.*, 646 F.2d 1151 (6th Cir.1981) (a cause of action under Ohio law for asbestosis accrues when the disease manifests itself); *Bendix Corp. v. Stagg*, 486 A.2d 1150 (Del.1984) (statute of limitations for injuries arising from inhalation of asbestos fiber began to run when harmful effect of asbestosis first manifested itself and became physically ascertainable, and not at time of exposure or time scar tissue began to form).

Arizona follows the "discovery rule" as far as the statute of limitations for personal injuries is concerned. * * * The statute of limitations does not begin to run until there is a manifestation of disease or physical injury. The purpose of the discovery rule, in the context of a latent disease, is to protect a plaintiff who, through no fault of his own, discovers only belatedly that he has the disease. Allowing plaintiffs to sue for injuries when the disease is still subclinical would be an abrogation of the discovery rule in asbestos cases and mandate the commencement of a suit as soon as the contact with the asbestos fiber occurs, hardly a desirable result.

We agree with the observations made by the court in *Schweitzer v. Consolidated Rail Corp. (Conrail)*, supra. Justice would not be done either to the plaintiffs or the defendants by allowing a suit prior to manifestation of any physical injuries or disease. In addition to the reasons given by the federal court, we also note that until the asbestosis manifests itself one can only speculate as to the debilitating effects the plaintiff will suffer. Not all asbestosis is one hundred percent debilitating. We see no reason to depart from traditional tort concepts and allow recovery for injuries before any disease becomes manifest. The statute of limitations does not begin to run until there is a manifestation of physical injuries or disease.

In order to overcome the lack of manifestation of any asbestos-related diseases and to supply the necessary physical harm required for a claim of damages for enhanced risk of cancer and emotional distress, the plaintiffs point to the affidavit of one of their experts, Dr. Michael Gray, who did not conduct a physical examination of all the residents. He states that many of the residents have suffered severe and clinically significant mental distress as a consequence of the asbestos situation. He did not specifically identify any of the plaintiffs as being in this class. He also stated that the emotional distress manifested itself "in a variety of disorders affecting normal sleep patterns, normal gastrointestinal functions, alterations in the ability to cope with other life stress, manifestations of anger, headaches, personality disorders, sexual dysfunction, and other adverse health effects which in no fashion could be termed trivial, insignificant, or of only minor or temporary inconvenience for these people." In addition to the fact that the affidavit fails to link any of the plaintiffs with these so-called physical manifestations, there is another reason why plaintiffs' claims for enhanced risk of cancer and for emotional distress are insufficient. There can be no claim for damages for the fear of contracting asbestos-related diseases in the future without the manifestation of a bodily injury. * * * We agree with the New Jersey Supreme Court in *Ayers v. Township of Jackson*, 106 N.J. 557, 525 A.2d 287 (1987), that neither the single controversy rule, nor the statute of limitations will preclude a timely filed cause of action for damages prompted by the future discovery of a disease or injury related to the exposure to a toxic substance, even though there has been prior litigation between the parties on different claims based on the same tortious conduct.

The psychosomatic injuries diagnosed by Dr. Gray consist of headaches, acid indigestion, weeping, muscle spasms, depression and insomnia. There is no evidence that these were other than transitory physical phenomena. They were not linked to any specific plaintiff, and they are not the type of bodily harm which would sustain a cause of action for emotional distress. Comment c to the Restatement (Second) of Torts § 436(A) (1965) is applicable here:

> "The rule [preventing recovery for emotional disturbance alone] applies to all forms of emotional disturbance, including temporary fright, nervous shock, nausea, grief, rage, and humiliation. The fact that these are accompanied by transitory, non-recurring physical phenomena, harmless in themselves, such as dizziness, vomiting, and the like, does not make the actor liable where such phenomena are in themselves inconsequential and do not amount to any substantial bodily harm. On the other hand, long continued nausea or headaches may amount to physical illness, which is bodily harm; and even long continued mental disturbance, as for example in the case of repeated hysterical attacks, or mental aberration, may be classified by the courts as illness, notwithstanding their mental character." * * *

The complaints in this case also alleged a private and public nuisance as follows:

> "As a direct and proximate result of the continued maintenance of a nuisance on said property Plaintiffs were caused to become sick, ill and disabled and were prevented from attending to their usual duties and occupation and were compelled to secure medical care and attention in an effort to heal and/or alleviate said injuries and illnesses and will, in the future, be continuously exposed to risk of grave illnesses and harm and may be compelled to secure additional medical care and attention in an effort to heal their said injuries, to their damage. As a further direct and proximate result of the

exposure to carcinogenic asbestos the plaintiffs have incurred psychological and emotional trauma and distress."

Restatement (Second) of Torts § 929 sets forth the damages one can recover as a result of a nuisance:

"(1) If one is entitled to a judgment for harm to land resulting from a past invasion and not amounting to a total destruction of value, the damages include compensation for (a) the difference between the value of the land before the harm and the value after the harm, or at his election in an appropriate case, the cost of restoration that has been or may be reasonably incurred, (b) the loss of use of the land, and (c) discomfort and annoyance to him as an occupant."

The Comment on Subsection (1), Clause (c) states:

"(e) *Discomfort and other bodily and mental harms.* Discomfort and annoyance to an occupant of the land and to the members of the household are distinct grounds of compensation for which in ordinary cases the person in possession is allowed to recover in addition to the harm to his proprietary interests. He is also allowed to recover for his own serious sickness or other substantial bodily harm but is not allowed to recover for serious harm to other members of the household, except so far as he maintains an action as a spouse or parent, under the rules stated in §§ 693 and 703. The owner of land who is not an occupant is not entitled to recover for these harms except as they may have affected the rental value of his land."

Those damages that are recoverable are those for the disruption and inconvenience resulting from, in this case, the contamination by asbestos. See *Ayers v. Township of Jackson*, supra. While some of the damages prayed for in plaintiffs' nuisance counts are not recoverable, the counts do set forth a claim for damages for inconvenience, discomfort and annoyance and for property damage, all of which is within the permissible ambit of § 929 of the Restatement. We conclude that the trial court erred in dismissing the nuisance counts.

The last issue is the plaintiffs' claim for recovery of damages to institute a medical surveillance. Dr. Gray testified that as of 1981, all of the adults of ages 65 or under are at greatly advanced risk of asbestos-related lung cancers, mesothelioma, gastrointestinal cancers and asbestosis. Some of the children will die from these diseases and some will become severely handicapped. Dr. Gray also testified that because of the risk, all of the residents should be provided with present and future medical surveillance in order to minimize, detect and treat the diseases as they arise. He described the type of surveillance that should be available, which included physical exams, blood and urine laboratory work-up, electro-cardiograms, periodic chest x-rays, CT scanning techniques and/or magnetic resonance imaging and pulmonary function testing. For individuals over 40 years of age and/or individuals who are 20 years from their initial exposures to asbestos, periodic rectal examinations and gastrointestinal consultation was required as well as additional testing when respiratory disease was apparent. He believed that the frequency of the medical surveillance would, in substantial measure, be influenced by the nature and prevalence of various asbestos-related abnormalities detected on the population as a whole and in each individual. He recommended that the testing be conducted approximately every other year, with the frequency increased as time progresses because the probability of asbestos-related disease increases directly as a latency period increases. He suggested that radiologic chest assessments, if utilized, should occur approximately every five years.

We believe, under the facts of this case and despite the absence of physical manifestation of any asbestos-related diseases, that the plaintiffs should be entitled to such regular medical testing and evaluation as is reasonably necessary and consistent with contemporary scientific principles applied by physicians experienced in the diagnosis and treatment of these types of injuries. We agree with the court in *Ayers v. Township of Jackson*, supra 525 A.2d at 312, that when the evidence shows "through reliable expert testimony predicated on the significance and extent of exposure * * * the toxicity of [the contaminant], the seriousness of the diseases for which the individuals are at risk, the relative increase in the chance of onset of the disease in those exposed and the value of early diagnosis, * * * surveillance to monitor the effects of exposure to toxic chemicals is reasonable and necessary," and its cost is a compensable item of damages. As the New Jersey Supreme Court said at 525 A.2d 311:

> "Compensation for reasonable and necessary medical expenses is consistent with well accepted legal principles. [citation omitted.] It is also consistent with the important public health interest in fostering access to medical testing for individuals whose exposure to toxic chemicals creates an enhanced risk of disease. The value of early diagnosis and treatment for cancer patients is well documented. [citation omitted.]"

The New Jersey court gave another cogent reason for its ruling:

> "Recognition of pre-symptom claims for medical surveillance serves other important public interests. The difficulty of proving causation, where the disease is manifested years after exposure, has caused many commentators to suggest that tort law has no capacity to deter polluters, because the costs of proper disposal are often viewed by polluters as exceeding the risk of tort liability. [citations omitted.] However, permitting recovery for reasonable pre-symptom, medical-surveillance expenses subjects polluters to significant liability when proof of the causal connection between the tortious conduct and the plaintiffs' exposure to chemicals is likely to be most readily available. The availability of a substantial remedy before the consequences of the plaintiffs' exposure are manifest may also have the beneficial effect of preventing or mitigating serious future illnesses and thus reduce the overall costs of the responsible parties. Other considerations compel recognition of a pre-symptom medical surveillance claim. It is inequitable for any individual, wrongfully exposed

to dangerous toxic chemicals but unable to prove that disease is likely, to have to pay his own expenses when medical intervention is clearly reasonable and necessary."

The next question is whether the plaintiffs are entitled to a lump sum award for this medical surveillance or whether a court-supervised fund should be utilized. We believe that the latter approach is proper. As the court said in *Ayers*, 525 A.2d at 314:

"In our view, the use of a court-supervised fund to administer medical-surveillance payments in mass exposure cases, * * * is a highly appropriate exercise of the Court's equitable powers. [citation omitted.] * * * Such a mechanism offers significant advantages over a lump-sum verdict * * *. In addition, a fund would serve to limit the liability of defendants to the amount of expenses actually incurred. A lump-sum verdict attempts to estimate future expenses, but cannot predict the amounts that actually will be expended for medical purposes. Although conventional damage awards do not restrict plaintiffs in the use of money paid as compensatory damages, mass-exposure toxic-tort cases involve public interests not present in conventional tort litigation. The public health interest is served by a fund mechanism that encourages regular medical monitoring for victims of toxic exposure. Where public entities are defendants, a limitation of liability to amounts actually expended for medical surveillance tends to reduce insurance costs and taxes, * * *. Although there may be administrative and procedural questions in the establishment and operation of such a fund, we encourage its use by trial courts in managing mass-exposure cases. In litigation involving public-entity defendants, we conclude that the use of a fund to administer medical-surveillance payments should be the general rule, in the absence of factors that render it impractical or inappropriate. [footnote omitted.] This will insure that in future mass-exposure litigation against public entities, medical-surveillance damages will be paid only to compensate for medical examinations and tests actually administered, and will encourage plaintiffs to safeguard their health by not allowing them the option of spending the money for other purposes. * * * *"

The judgment below is reversed as to plaintiffs' claims for damages based on nuisance and for medical surveillance, and it is affirmed in all other respects.

Notes

1. When a plaintiff is exposed to a toxic substance that increases his risk of contracting cancer, but he shows no signs of illness, can he recover for the mental distress resulting from his fear of getting the disease? Most courts have said no. *See* Mead, Recovery for Psychic Harm in Strict Products Liability: Has the Interest in Psychic Equilibrium Come the Final Mile?, 59 St.John's L.Rev. 457, 520–526 (1985); Reina, Recovery for Fear of Cancer and Increased Risk of Cancer: Problems With Gideon and a Proposed

Solution, 7 Rev.Litig. 39 (1987); Note, Predicting the Future: Present Mental Anguish for Fear of Developing Cancer in the Future as a Result of Past Asbestos Exposure, 23 Mem.St.U.L.Rev. 337 (1993). *See also* Edwards & Ringleb, Exposure to Hazardous Substances and the Mental Distress Tort: Trends, Applications, and a Proposed Reform, 11 Colum.J.Envtl.L. 119 (1986).

2. In Metro–North Commuter R.R. Co. v. Buckley, 521 U.S. 424, 117 S.Ct. 2113, 138 L.Ed.2d 560 (1997), the Supreme Court held that a plaintiff who was exposed to asbestos dust on the job but who suffered from no asbestos-related disease and exhibited no physical symptoms of exposure could not recover under the Federal Employers' Liability Act (FELA) for mental distress and medical monitoring costs. Mere exposure to the asbestos dust was not the type of "physical impact" necessary to support an emotional distress claim. The *Metro-North* holding parallels that of most state courts. See Capital Holding Corp. v. Bailey, 873 S.W.2d 187 (Ky.1994); Payton v. Abbott Labs, 386 Mass. 540, 437 N.E.2d 171 (1982); Simmons v. Pacor, Inc. 543 Pa. 664, 674 A.2d 232 (1996). In *Simmons*, the court held that plaintiffs who suffered from asymptomatic pleural thickening due to asbestos exposure have not suffered a compensable injury nor could they recover for emotional distress caused by fear of a future cancer. *Id.* at 237–38. *See also* Potter v. Firestone Tire & Rubber Co., 6 Cal.4th 965, 25 Cal.Rptr.2d 550, 863 P.2d 795 (1993) (en banc)(no recovery for fear of cancer in negligence action unless plaintiff is "more likely than not" going to develop cancer); Parker v. Brush Wellman, Inc., 377 F.Supp.2d 1290 (N.D. Ga. 2005) (plaintiffs who suffered only "sub-clinical, cellular, and sub-cellular damage" from alleged exposure to beryllium contained in manufacturers' aircraft component products did not sustain an actionable physical "injury" under Georgia law and the absence of any cognizable injury foreclosed recovery for negligently inflicted emotional distress). *See* Henderson & Twerski, Asbestos Litigation Gone Mad: Exposure–Based Recovery For Increased Risk, Mental Distress, and Medical Monitoring, 53 S.C.L.Rev. 815 (2002).

3. A number of courts have begun to recognize a cause of action for medical monitoring expenses. *See* Askey v. Occidental Chemical Corp., 102 A.D.2d 130, 477 N.Y.S.2d 242, 247 (1984); Ayers v. Jackson Township, 106 N.J. 557, 525 A.2d 287 (1987); Hansen v. Mountain Fuel Supply, 858 P.2d 970 (Utah 1993); Potter v. Firestone Tire & Rubber Co., 6 Cal.4th 965, 25 Cal.Rptr.2d 550, 863 P.2d 795 (1993). The *Hansen* opinion established the following elements the plaintiff must prove to establish a monitoring claim: (I) exposure (ii) to a toxic substance (iii) where exposure was caused by the defendant's negligence (iv) resulting in an increased risk (v) of a serious disease, illness or injury (vi) for which a medical test for early detection exists (vii) and for which early detection is beneficial, meaning that a treatment exists that can alter the course of the illness, and (viii) the test has been prescribed by a qualified physician according to contemporary scientific principles. 858 P.2d at 979. Unlike "fear of disease" claims, most courts have not required the plaintiff to show that it is more likely than not they will ultimately develop a disease. However, the full parameters of this cause of action are still uncertain and a number of recent opinions have refused to recognize medical monitoring as a cause of action in the absence

of some injury. *See* Wood v. Wyeth–Ayerst Labs., 82 S.W.3d 849, 856 (Ky.2002) (cause of action for medical monitoring damages following negligent exposure to a potentially dangerous substance required a showing of actual physical injury); Hinton v. Monsanto Co., 813 So.2d 827, 830–31 (Ala.2001) (same); Badillo v. Am. Brands, Inc., 117 Nev. 34, 16 P.3d 435, 438–39 (2001) (medical monitoring recognized as a remedy but not as a separate cause of action); Trimble v. Asarco, Inc., 232 F.3d 946, 963 (8th Cir.2000) (Nevada does not recognize a medical monitoring cause of action). *See* Bourne, Medical Monitoring Without Physical Injury: The Least Justice Can Do For Those Industry Has Terrorized With Poisonous Products, 58 S.M.U.L.Rev. 251 (2005); Maskin, et al., Medical Monitoring: A Viable Remedy for Deserving Plaintiffs or Tort Law's Most Expensive Consolation Prize? 27 Wm. Mitchell L. Rev. 521 (2000); McCarter, Medical Sue–Veillance, A History and Critique of the Medical Monitoring Remedy in Toxic Tort Litigation, 45 Rutgers L.Rev. 227 (1993); Schwartz, et al., Medical Monitoring: The Right Way And The Wrong Way, 70 Mo.L.Rev. 349 (2005).

4. The problem posed by plaintiffs who are not yet seriously injured continues to plague the asbestos litigation. These plaintiffs clog the system and potentially siphon off resources that could compensate those who are currently suffering a serious injury. One solution to this problem is to triage cases by requiring those who do not as yet exhibit any physical manifestations of a disease to delay their lawsuit until such time as they do become ill. *See* Tex. Civ. Prac. & Rem. Code, Chapter 90, Claims Involving Asbestos and Silica.

SECTION D. PUNITIVE DAMAGES

ACOSTA v. HONDA MOTOR CO., LTD.
United States Court of Appeals, Third Circuit, 1983.
717 F.2d 828.

BECKER, CIRCUIT JUDGE.

[Plaintiff was injured in an accident which occurred when the rear wheel of his motorcycle collapsed. He sued the manufacturer of the motorcycle (Honda Motor Co., Ltd., "Honda"), the company responsible for manufacturing and assembling the rear wheel of the motorcycle (Daido Kogyo, Co., Ltd.), and the motorcycle's distributor (American Honda Motor Co., Inc., "American Honda"). The jury found the defendants strictly liable and assessed plaintiff $175,000 in compensatory damages. It also awarded punitive damages of $210,000 against each defendant. Defendants subsequently moved for judgment n.o.v. The trial judge granted American Honda's motion and denied the motions of the other defendants. Plaintiff appealed from the grant of judgment n.o.v. for American Honda, and defendants Honda and Daido Kogyo cross-appealed from the denial of their motions.]

* * *

III.

Defendants' principal contention on appeal is that the evidence was insufficient as a matter of law to sustain the award of punitive damages and that the district court erred in submitting the issue to the jury in the first place. Before turning to that question, however, we first must address their argument that punitive damages are unavailable in this case because, no matter what the evidence, punitive damages are fundamentally inconsistent with a regime of strict products liability in general, and with section 402A in particular.

A. THE AVAILABILITY OF PUNITIVE DAMAGES IN THE STRICT LIABILITY CONTEXT

Although this question is one of first impression in the Virgin Islands, we do not lack guidance. Many courts, both state and federal, have already considered the issue, and the overwhelming majority have concluded

> that there is no theoretical problem in a jury finding that a defendant is liable because of the defectiveness of a product and then judging the conduct of the defendant in order to determine whether punitive damages should be awarded on the basis of 'outrageous conduct' in light of the injuries sustained by the plaintiff. *Hoffman v. Sterling Drug, Inc.*, 485 F.2d 132, 144–47 (3d Cir.1973); *Thomas v. American Cystoscope Makers, Inc.*, 414 F.Supp. 255, 263–267 (E.D.Pa.1976). Punitive damage awards provide a useful function in punishing the wrongdoer and deterring product suppliers from making economic decisions not to remedy the defects of the product.

Neal v. Carey Canadian Mines, Ltd., 548 F.Supp. 357 (E.D.Pa.1982) (Bechtle, J.) (construing Pennsylvania law).

* * *

[A]s long as a plaintiff can carry his burden of proof under section 402A, there is no inconsistency in his also being permitted to offer proof regarding the nature of the manufacturer's conduct.

The Restatement (Second) of Torts does include a generally applicable provision regarding punitive damages. Section 908(2) declares:

> Punitive damages may be awarded for conduct that is outrageous, because of the defendant's evil motive or his reckless indifference to the rights of others. In assessing punitive damages, the trier of fact can properly consider the character of the defendant's act, the nature and extent of the harm to the plaintiff that the defendant caused or intended to cause and the wealth of the defendant.

Nowhere in that section or the comments did the drafters suggest that these principles should not apply to strict products liability, and we concur with the considered opinion of the Court of Appeals for the Fifth Circuit that "[p]unishment and deterrence, the basis for punitive damages * * *, are no less appropriate with respect to a product manufacturer who knowingly ignores safety deficiencies in its product that may endanger human life" than in other cases in which "the defendant's conduct shows wantonness or recklessness or reckless indifference to the rights of others." *Dorsey v. Honda Motor Co.*, 655 F.2d 650, 658 (5th Cir.1981) (construing Florida law), *opinion modified on rehearing*, 670

F.2d 21 (5th Cir.), *cert. denied,* [459] U.S. [880], 103 S.Ct. 177, 74 L.Ed.2d 145 (1982).

* * *

B. Standard of Proof

Although we reject each of the various arguments against awarding punitive damages in the strict liability context, we agree with Judge Friendly's observation in [*Roginsky v. Richardson–Merrell, Inc.,* 378 F.2d 832 (2d Cir.1967)], that "the consequences of imposing punitive damages in a case like the present are so serious" that "particularly careful scrutiny" is warranted. 378 F.2d at 852 (denying petition for rehearing); cf. Comment, *Criminal Safeguards and the Punitive Damages Defendant,* 34 U.Chi.L.Rev. 408, 417 (1967) ("If one accepts the proposition that the consequences of punitive damages can be 'momentous and serious,' then justice requires increasing the burden of persuasion of the plaintiff in a punitive damages action.") We therefore hold under Virgin Islands law that a plaintiff seeking punitive damages, at least in an action in which liability is predicated on section 402A, must prove the requisite "outrageous" conduct by clear and convincing proof.[1] Accord Wangen v. Ford Motor Co., [97 Wis.2d 260, 294 N.W.2d 437, 446 (1980)]; Model Uniform Product Liability Act § 120(A), 44 Fed.Reg. 62748 (1979).[2]

C. The Standard Applied

Applying the "clear and convincing" standard to the facts of this case, we conclude that the district court should have entered judgments n.o.v. on the punitive damages issue for all three defendants, and not just for American Honda. We recognize, of course, that we are bound to "view all the evidence and the inferences reasonably drawn therefrom" in plaintiff's favor, see *Chuy v. Philadelphia Eagles Football Club,* 595 F.2d 1265, 1273 (3d Cir.1979) (in banc), and that "[o]ur limited function at this point is to ascertain from a review of the record whether there is sufficient evidence to sustain the verdict of the jury on this issue," *id.* It nevertheless appears to us that the record "is critically deficient of that minimum quantum of evidence from which a jury might reasonably afford relief." *Denneny v. Siegel,* 407 F.2d 433, 439 (3d Cir.1969).

Plaintiff's evidence allegedly supporting his claim for punitive damages essentially consisted of the following:

    1. The rear wheel of his motorcycle collapsed from a thirty-five mile per hour impact with a ditch four inches deep;

---

1. Even with such proof, however, a plaintiff is not entitled to recover such damages as a matter of right. Rather the Restatement is quite clear that the award is discretionary with the trier of fact. See § 908 comment d.

2. Section 120(A) provides:

Punitive damages may be awarded to the claimant if the claimant proves by clear and convincing evidence that the harm suffered was the result of the product seller's reckless disregard for the safety of product users, consumers, or others who might be harmed by the product.

2. The particular wheel of plaintiff's motorcycle suffered from an inherent lack of strength as evidenced by the fact that it weighed sixteen percent less than several other randomly sampled rear wheels of motorcycles of the same model;

3. The owner's manual represented the CB750 as a high-speed touring motorcycle but provided no warning that the rear wheel might collapse upon the type of impact that occurred in this case;

4. Although the owner's manual instructed users to set and maintain the tension of the motorcycle's shock absorbers and wheel spokes, the manual did not warn that the failure to do so might result in the collapse of the wheel;

5. Defendants merely spot-checked rear wheels during the assembly process and did not crush test or weigh each wheel;

6. Plaintiff's expert witness testified that the above evidence constituted defective manufacture and a failure adequately to inspect or to warn; and

7. Plaintiff's expert concluded that defendant's conduct manifested a "colossal disregard for the safety of the users of the motor vehicle," App. II at 125–26.

Plaintiff contends that the jury was entitled to infer from this evidence that defendants recklessly disregarded his rights and safety as a user of the motorcycle. We cannot agree. As we have suggested above, section 908 of the *Restatement* declares that reckless or outrageous conduct on the part of the defendant is the touchstone of punitive damages. See *Berroyer v. Hertz,* 672 F.2d 334 (3d Cir.1982); *Chuy v. Philadelphia Eagles, supra,* 595 F.2d at 1277. Although section 908 does not elaborate on the kind of conduct for which punitive damages are appropriate, comment b refers to section 500, which in turn provides:

> The actor's conduct is in reckless disregard of the safety of another if he does an act or intentionally fails to do an act which it is his duty to the other to do, knowing or having reason to know of facts which would lead a reasonable man to realize, not only that his conduct creates an unreasonable risk of physical harm to another but also that such risk is substantially greater than that which is necessary to make his conduct negligent.

The commentary accompanying section 500 explains further:

> Recklessness may consist of either of two different types of conduct. In one the actor knows, or has reason to know * * * of facts which create a high degree of risk of physical harm to another, and deliberately proceeds to act, or to fail to act, in conscious disregard of, or indifference to, that risk. In the other the actor has such knowledge, or reason to know, of the facts, but does not realize or appreciate the high degree of risk involved, although a reasonable man in his position would do so. An objective standard is applied to him and he is held to the realization of the aggravated risk which a

reasonable man in his place would have, although he does not himself have it.

* * *

For either type of conduct, to be reckless it must be unreasonable; but to be reckless, it must be something more than negligent. It must not only be unreasonable, but it must involve a risk of harm to others substantially in excess of that necessary to make the conduct negligent. It must involve an easily perceptible danger of death or substantial physical harm, and the probability that it will so result must be substantially greater than is required for ordinary negligence.

We have examined the evidence; viewed in the light most favorable to plaintiff, it does not show that the conduct of any defendant was outrageous or reckless. Indeed we discern no basis upon which the jury could have concluded that defendants knew or had reason to know that the rear wheel of Acosta's motorcycle was defective in design or manufacture and that they decided not to remedy the defect in conscious disregard of or indifference to the risk thereby created. Although the wheel had been used in over 275,000 motorcycles, and the model first offered in 1970 (six years before plaintiff's accident), there was no evidence of previous consumer complaints or lawsuits that might have called to defendants' attention that there might be a problem. Moreover, plaintiff offered no proof that defendants developed or failed to modify the engineering designs for the rear wheel of the CB750 with any knowledge or reason to know of its alleged lack of safety.[3] Such matters would have been admissible on the punitive damages issues.

In short, a jury could not have reasonably concluded that the evidence by the clear and convincing standard showed defendants to have acted with reckless disregard for the safety of users of the CB750.[4] Accordingly, we hold that the district court should have granted defendants' motions for directed verdicts on the punitive damage claim and that it was error to deny the subsequent motions for judgment n.o.v. on behalf of Honda and Daido Kogyo.

VI. Conclusion

For the foregoing reasons, we will reverse the judgment of the district court denying Honda's and Daido Kogyo's motions for judgment

---

3. In fact, defendants adduced evidence, which was not contradicted, that pre-production testing followed standard procedures, including on-the-road testing and laboratory testing (including wheel crushing to determine durability), and that samples from each production run of completed motorcycles were subjected to final dynamometer tests before shipping.

4. The clear and convincing standard of proof we announce today pertains to the degree of proof needed to be found by the trier of fact before it assesses punitive damages. The standard is not applicable to an appellate court in reviewing the determination of the trier of fact that there was or was not clear and convincing evidence of outrageous conduct. Rather the applicable standard of review on appeal is whether the record "is critically deficient of that minimum quantum of evidence from which a jury might reasonably afford relief." *Denneny v. Siegel,* 407 F.2d 433, 439 (3d Cir. 1969).

n.o.v. on the award of punitive damages and the district court will be directed to enter judgment for Honda and Daido Kogyo on that claim. [The court also vacated an award of attorney's fees under a Virgin Island's statute and remanded the case to the district court for reconsideration of that award in light of its disposition of the punitive damages issue.] In all other respects, the judgment of the district court will be affirmed.

OWEN, PROBLEMS IN ASSESSING PUNITIVE DAMAGES AGAINST MANUFACTURERS OF DEFECTIVE PRODUCTS
49 U.Chi.L.Rev. 1, 15–25 (1982).

C. Problems with Punishing a Manufacturing Entity

Punitive damages were developed largely as a punishment and deterrent for trespassers, oxen thieves and other such human malefactors. When the device is transferred to the complex bureaucracy of a modern manufacturing concern, the fit is awkward in many respects. Final "decisions" concerning a complex product are often the result of a splintered, bureaucratic process involving a complicated combination of human judgments made by scores of persons at different levels in the hierarchy who pass on different aspects of the problem at different times. Various engineers may have to rely upon the work of research chemists, physicists, and other scientists; input from the financial and marketing arms of the enterprise must be factored in along the way. The entire process may take years. Each of these human actors makes decisions based on his own motives and on different types and amounts of information, and even the responsible executive at the end of the decisional line can possess only a small bit of the total information involved. Moreover, the corporate owners of the enterprise are usually far removed from most decisions of even the top executives.

This is not to say that institutional safety procedures cannot be put in place and monitored to ensure that safety gets its day in the manufacturer's decisional court, and the modern company without procedures of this type should be held to some account. Yet we must remember that the concepts of moral responsibility, punishment, and deterrence can mean vastly different things when judging the "conduct" of an institution rather than of a human being.

The serious difficulty of attempting to apply human standards of culpability to manufacturers in this context is highlighted by the problem of defining the proscribed misconduct * * *. The problem in capsule form is simply this: humans are clearly culpable when they act to gain a minor advantage in a way they know will be likely to kill or injure others. Thus, we usually punish a person who deliberately or recklessly kills or maims another without good reason. Yet manufacturers of hazardous products such as automobiles (which kill and maim thousands every year) must design them in many different ways they know with virtual certainty will result in harm or death at some time to a certain number of unfortunate, statistical persons. In a sense, facturers always act "intentionally" in derogation of surely punishment is inappropriate for simply being in making high speed machines.

* * *

Virtually all important actions involve some risks t and responsible individuals and institutions give careful c such risks before they act. It is fundamental to life in a (..... world with an unpredictable future that one must proceed to act, notwithstanding the presence of some foreseeable risks, provided that the benefits of the contemplated action (or inaction) appear at the time to exceed the risks. If this basic tenet of risk-benefit analysis were not virtually the universal rule, life would grind nearly to a halt. Everyone employs this process hundreds of times each day, ticking off the balance of advantages versus disadvantages (which may affect other persons adversely) of one choice after another, often in only fractions of a second. The rules of negligence law provide that an actor generally will not be liable even for compensatory damages unless the balance of trade-offs was a bad one—that is, one in which the costs exceeded the benefits, thus making the action on balance cost-*in*effective. Punishment for such decisions usually can be justified only when the actor not only made the wrong decision but also made a deliberate choice to advance his good over what he knew to be the greater good of others.

* * *

Cost-benefit analysis is fundamental to the design engineer's trade. The depth of the rubber on an automobile's bumper forever may be increased by another one-tenth inch. One more crossbeam always may be added to protect the occupants in certain types of collisions. The configuration of crossbeams may be changed to increase their strength; thicker or harder steel may be used in the beams; perhaps they may be made of another metal, or perhaps even of a form of plastic. Many hundreds of such choices are made by design engineers in the production of a single complex product, and each such decision involves a range of trade-offs between cost, weight, appearance, performance capabilities (for separate functions in varying environments), and safety in one type of accident versus another. A steel beam that protects an occupant in one type of accident may endanger him in another, as by rendering that portion of the vehicle less energy absorbent, and may endanger pedestrians and the occupants of other vehicles as well. Although much of this decision making involves the application of proven scientific principles, much is art, and some by its nature can be little more than trial and error.

Notes

1. If Professor Owen is correct that cost-benefit analysis is fundamental to the design engineer's trade and that explicit cost-benefit analyses

should be encouraged, a recent article by Professor Kip Viscusi raises serious questions about whether the legal system is sending mixed messages to corporate defendants. Viscusi, Corporate Risk Analysis: A Reckless Act?, 52 Stan.L.Rev. 547 (2000). Viscusi conducted an experiment in which some "jurors" heard that the defendant had done a cost-benefit analysis when assessing whether to add a safety feature while other "jurors" were told that the company did no analysis. Overall, jurors who were told the company did conduct a cost-benefit analysis were slightly more likely to assess punitive damages and awarded substantially greater amounts. This is the case even when the cost-benefit analysis suggested that under a *Carroll Towing* analysis of negligence, it was not negligent to fail to make the automobile safer. *Id.* at 554–558. *See also* Viscusi, Jurors, Judges, and the Mistreatment of Risk by the Courts, 30 J. Legal Stud. 107 (2001). In light of these results, if you are a defense counsel for a corporation accused of manufacturing a product with a design defect, what would you advise with respect to the use of cost-benefit analyses at trial?

2. Professor Viscusi is a critic of punitive damages. In another recent article he compares various health and safety statistics in states with and without punitive damages and concludes punitive damages do not produce a deterrent effect. Viscusi, The Social Costs of Punitive Damages Against Corporations in Environmental and Safety Torts, 87 Geo.L.J. 285 (1998). Viscusi's analysis is critiqued in Luban, A Flawed Case Against Punitive Damages, 87 Geo. L. J. 359 (1998), with a surrebuttal by Viscusi, Why There is No Defense of Punitive Damages, 87 Geo.L.J. 381 (1998).

3. Another area of debate is the size, frequency, and rationality of punitive damages. *See* Rustad, In Defense of Punitive Damages in Products Liability: Testing Tort Anecdotes with Empirical Data, 78 Iowa L.Rev. 1 (1992); Eisenberg et al., The Predictability of Punitive Damages, 26 J. Legal Stud. 623 (1997); Polinsky, Are Punitive Damages Really Predictable and Rational? A Comment on Eisenberg et al., 26 J. Legal Stud. 663 (1997). For different approaches to understanding punitive damages see, Galanter & Luban, Poetic Justice: Punitive Damages and Legal Pluralism, 26 Am. U.L.Rev. 1393 (1993); Polinsky & Shavell, Punitive Damages: An Economic Analysis, 111 Harv.L.Rev. 869, 950–51 (1998); Sunstein, Kahneman & Schkade, Assessing Punitive Damages (With Notes on Cognition and Valuation in Law), 107 Yale L.J. 2071 (1998); Hastie & Viscusi, What Juries Can't Do Well: The Jury's Performance as a Risk Manager, 40 Ariz.L.Rev. 901 (1998); Lempert, Juries, Hindsight, and Punitive Damage Awards: Failures of a Social Science Case for Change, 48 DePaul L.Rev. 867 (1999); MacCoun, The Costs and Benefits of Letting Juries Punish Corporations: Comment on Viscusi, 52 Stan.L.Rev. 1821 (2000); Schkade et al., Deliberating About Dollars: The Severity Shift, 100 Colum.L.Rev. 1139 (2000); Viscusi, The Challenge of Punitive Damages Mathematics, 30 J. Legal Stud. 313 (2001). *See generally* Ausness, Retribution and Deterrence: The Role of Punitive Damages in Products Liability Litigation, 74 Ky.L.J. 1 (1985/1986); Ghiardi & Kircher, Punitive Damages Recovery in Products Liability Cases, 65 Marq.L.Rev. 1 (1981); Owen, Punitive Damages in Products Liability Litigation, 74 Mich.L.Rev. 1257 (1976); Owen, Problems in Assessing Punitive Damages Against Manufacturers of Defective Products, 49 U.Chi.L.Rev. 1 (1982).

4. **Standard of Liability.** Courts generally agree that a showing of simple negligence is not enough to justify an award of punitive damages. One basis for imposing punitive damages is intentional or malicious desire to harm the plaintiff. Most courts also authorize punitive damages upon a showing of such states of mind as "recklessness" or "conscious disregard" of plaintiff's rights. E.g., Wangen v. Ford Motor Co., 97 Wis.2d 260, 275, 294 N.W.2d 437, 446 (1980) (malice, vindictiveness, ill-will, or wanton, willful or reckless disregard of plaintiff's rights). Most punitive damage claims in products liability cases involve allegations of "recklessness" or "conscious disregard" because intent to harm is almost never present in such cases.

5. Courts vary considerably in the definition of the kind of conduct that qualifies as "recklessness" or "conscious disregard." A good many courts have adopted the Restatement of Torts (Second) § 500 definition of recklessness. Consider some of the other formulations courts have used:

A. Reckless disregard is "conscious indifference to the safety of persons or entities that might be harmed by a product." Model Uniform Product Liability Act, § 102(J).

B. A manufacturer must act in:

reckless disregard for the public safety. To meet this standard the manufacturer must either be aware of, or culpably indifferent to, an unnecessary risk of injury. Awareness should be imputed to a company to the extent that its employee(s) possess such information. Knowing of this risk, the manufacturer must also fail to determine the gravity of the danger or fail to reduce the risk to an acceptable minimal level. 'Disregard for the public safety' reflects a basic disrespect for the interests of others.

Thiry v. Armstrong World Industries, 661 P.2d 515, 518 (Okla. 1983).

C. Malice is conduct done in conscious disregard of the probability of injury to members of the consuming public. Grimshaw v. Ford Motor Co., 119 Cal.App.3d 757, 174 Cal.Rptr. 348 (1981). See Owens–Illinois v. Zenobia, 325 Md. 420, 601 A.2d 633, 652 (Md.App. 1992) ("In non-intentional tort action, the trier of facts may not award punitive damages unless the plaintiff has established that the defendant's conduct was characterized by evil motive, intent to injure, ill will, or fraud, *i.e.* 'actual malice.' ")

D. Fischer v. Johns–Manville Corp., 103 N.J. 643, 512 A.2d 466 (1986) adopted the following standard:

[P]unitive damages are available in failure-to-warn, strict products liability actions when a manufacturer is (1) aware of or culpably indifferent to an unnecessary risk of injury, and (2) refuses to take steps to reduce that danger to an acceptable level. This standard can be met by a showing of "a deliberate act or omission with knowledge of a high degree of probability of harm and reckless indifference to consequences."

Do any of these definitions adequately identify the kind of behavior that is deserving of punishment? *See* Owen, Problems in Assessing Punitive Damages Against Manufacturers of Defective Products, 49 U.Chi.L.Rev. 1, 20–28 (1982).

5. Several courts have adopted as the standard of liability the requirement that defendant's conduct reflect flagrant indifference to public safety. Moore v. Remington Arms Co., Inc., 100 Ill.App.3d 1102, 1115, 56 Ill.Dec. 413, 422, 427 N.E.2d 608, 617 (1981); Leichtamer v. American Motors Corp., 67 Ohio St.2d 456, 472, 424 N.E.2d 568, 580 (1981), noted in 11 Cap. U.L.Rev. 363 (1981). This standard was suggested by Professor Owen. *See* Owen, Punitive Damages in Products Liability Litigation, 74 Mich.L.Rev. 1257, 1366–1371 (1976).

6. A five year old child put a cotton swab inside his ear canal in an attempt to clean his ear. The swab tore his tympanic membrane (ear drum) and dislocated the bones of his inner ear causing tinnitus and disequilibrium. In the ten years prior to the injury, the manufacturer received approximately forty complaints regarding ear injuries from using its cotton swabs. Over this same ten year period it sold 36 billion cotton swabs. The manufacturer sold the swabs without an adequate warning. Plaintiff sues the manufacturer, seeking actual and punitive damages. State law permits the imposition of punitive damages where defendant "intentionally acts knowing that its conduct involves a high degree of probability that substantial harm will result." Is defendant liable to plaintiff for punitive damages?

7. Should compliance with government regulations be a defense to punitive damage claims? *See* Schwartz, Punitive Damages and Regulated Products, 42 Am.U.L.Rev. 1335 (1993).

8. As a part of tort reform, and partly in response to United States Supreme Court opinions on the constitutionality of punitive damages (discussed below) many states have codified punitive damages. These statutes have established the standard of conduct required before punitives are justified and a number of them have placed caps on punitives. For example, the Mississippi statute defines the standard of conduct as follows:

(1) In any action in which punitive damages are sought:

(a) Punitive damages may not be awarded if the claimant does not prove by clear and convincing evidence that the defendant against whom punitive damages are sought acted with actual malice, gross negligence which evidences a willful, wanton or reckless disregard for the safety of others, or committed actual fraud.

Miss. Code Ann. § 11–1–65

The requirement for clear and convincing evidence is now the majority position. *See* Owens–Illinois v. Zenobia, 325 Md. 420, 601 A.2d 633, 656 (Md.App.1992).

Imposition of damage caps is illustrated by the Texas statute, which contains the following provision:

(a) In an action in which a claimant seeks recovery of exemplary damages, the trier of fact shall determine the amount of economic damages separately from the amount of other compensatory damages.

(b) Exemplary damages awarded against a defendant may not exceed an amount equal to the greater of:

(1)(A) two times the amount of economic damages; plus (B) an amount equal to any noneconomic damages found by the jury, not to exceed $750,000; or

(2) $200,000.

Tex. Civ. Prac. & Rem.Code § 41.008. The Texas statute also provides for bifurcated trials upon the defendant's motion. § 41.009.

9. **Factors to consider when awarding punitive damages.** Many statutes also set forth a set of factors to be considered when assessing the size of a punitive damage award. The Kansas statute lists the following set of factors:

(b) At a proceeding to determine the amount of exemplary or punitive damages to be awarded under this section, the court may consider:

(1) The likelihood at the time of the alleged misconduct that serious harm would arise from the defendant's misconduct;

(2) the degree of the defendant's awareness of that likelihood;

(3) the profitability of the defendant's misconduct;

(4) the duration of the misconduct and any intentional concealment of it;

(5) the attitude and conduct of the defendant upon discovery of the misconduct;

(6) the financial condition of the defendant; and

(7) the total deterrent effect of other damages and punishment imposed upon the defendant as a result of the misconduct, including, but not limited to, compensatory, exemplary and punitive damage awards to persons in situations similar to those of the claimant and the severity of the criminal penalties to which the defendant has been or may be subjected.

Kan. Stat. Ann. § 60–3702 (2000); *see also* Ky. Rev. Stat. § 411.186 (Baldwin 2000); Tex. Civ. Prac. & Rem.Code § 41.011 (West 1999). Some jurisdictions have creates similar lists through court opinions. *See* Green Oil Co. v. Hornsby, 539 So.2d 218 (Ala.1989); Management Computer Services v. Hawkins, Ash, Baptie & Co., 206 Wis.2d 158, 557 N.W.2d 67 (1996); *see* Restatement (Second) of Torts § 908, Comment *e*. *See generally* Allowance of Punitive Damages in Products Liability Case, 13 A.L.R. 4th 52 (2001).

ROMO v. FORD MOTOR CO.
Court of Appeal, Fifth District, California, 2003.
113 Cal.App.4th 738, 6 Cal.Rptr.3d 793.

OPINION

VARTABEDIAN, Acting P.J.

In the wake of its decision in *State Farm Mut. Automobile Ins. Co. v. Campbell* (2003) 538 U.S. 408, 123 S.Ct. 1513, 155 L.Ed.2d 585 (hereafter *State Farm*), the United States Supreme Court granted certiorari in the present case. The court summarily vacated the judgment and remanded the case to us for reconsideration in light of *State Farm*. We have received and considered further briefing from the parties and from amici curiae and we now conditionally affirm the punitive damages portion of the judgment before us, conditioned upon plaintiffs' acceptance of reduction of the punitive damages portion of the judgment to $23,723,287. If plaintiffs timely consent to the reduction, then the judgment shall be modified accordingly and, as modified, affirmed.

I. BACKGROUND

A. *The Roll-over*

In *Romo v. Ford Motor Co.* (2002) 99 Cal.App.4th 1115, 122 Cal. Rptr.2d 139, we were presented with an appeal from the judgment in a personal injury and wrongful death case arising from a rollover accident. * * *

The Romo family was riding in their 1978 Ford Bronco when it rolled over as plaintiff Juan Ramon Romo was trying to avoid a car that had swerved in front of him. Ramon, Salustia, and Ramiro Romo were killed in the accident when the steel portion of the Bronco's roof collapsed and the fiberglass portion shattered. Juan, Evangelina, and Maria Romo were injured.

B. *The Trial*

In a products liability action brought by the surviving Romos individually and on behalf of the estates of the deceased family members, the jury awarded compensatory damages from Ford Motor Company (Ford) (after adjustments by the trial court) of nearly $5 million. In addition, the jury awarded the Romos punitive damages from Ford in the amount of $290 million. (Ford did not move for bifurcation of the punitive damages portion; as a result, there was a unified trial and the jury returned a single verdict on all issues.) After the trial court granted Ford's motion for new trial of the punitive damages issues based on jury misconduct, both sides appealed.

C. *The First Appeal*

Ford raised numerous issues concerning both the compensatory damages aspect and the punitive damages aspect of the case. We concluded all of Ford's contentions were without merit. The Romos appealed from the order granting a new trial on punitive damages. We determined that the record rebutted any presumption of prejudicial juror misconduct and that the new trial motion was granted in error. The net result of the appeal was that the judgment was reinstated and affirmed.

After the California Supreme Court denied Ford's petition for review on all issues, Ford filed a petition for certiorari in the United States Supreme Court. * * *

II. DISCUSSION

Our effort to comply with the instructions from the United States Supreme Court has required us to reexamine the purpose and nature of punitive damages and to revisit certain pivotal California appellate cases, chief among them *Grimshaw v. Ford Motor Co.* (1981) 119 Cal.App.3d 757, 174 Cal.Rptr. 348 (*Grimshaw*). * * *

A. *The Statute: "[F]or the Sake of Example and by Way of Punish[ment]"*

Civil Code section 3294, subdivision (a), provides: "In an action for the breach of an obligation not arising from contract, where it is proven by clear and convincing evidence that the defendant has been guilty of oppression, fraud, or malice, the plaintiff, in addition to the actual damages, may recover damages for the sake of example and by way of punishing the defendant." Civil Code section 3295, subdivision (a), with certain restrictions, permits introduction of evidence in a punitive damages case of "[t]he profits the defendant has gained by virtue of the wrongful course of conduct of the nature and type shown by the evidence" and of "the financial condition of the defendant."

B. *Punishment and Deterrence*

"The purpose of punitive damages is to punish wrongdoers and thereby deter the commission of wrongful acts." (*Neal v. Farmers Ins. Exchange* (1978) 21 Cal.3d 910, 928, fn. 13, 148 Cal.Rptr. 389, 582 P.2d 980.) Of course, there are degrees of punishment and deterrence. One way to deter parking meter violations would be forfeiture of the cars of parking offenders. The law does not do that, but the law does seek to deter drug traffickers through forfeiture of cars used to transport drugs. * * *

In the case of punitive damages, the degree of punishment and deterrence that can be exacted under state law is subject to limits arising from the due process clause of the Fourteenth Amendment. (*State Farm, supra,* 538 U.S. at p. 412, 123 S.Ct. at p. 1517.) In reconsidering the present case in light of *State Farm,* we believe the inquiry profitably and initially may focus on two questions: first, *what* is sought to be "punished and deterred"? and, second, *how* is that action to be "punished and deterred"? While at first glance the answer to these questions seems straightforward (i.e., malicious conduct, money), consideration of California punitive damages precedent in light of the restrictions articulated in *State Farm* seems to us to require a more nuanced consideration of those answers.

1. *What* **Is to Be Deterred: Punishment of Private Wrongs**

There is a fundamental difference between parking fines and drug forfeitures, on the one hand, and punitive damages, on the other. In the former case, the exactions arise from "public" wrongs—that is, wrongs against society. In the case of punitive damages, the exaction arises from a "private" wrong: if there is no wrong resulting in compensable injury to *this* plaintiff, there can be no exaction of punitive damages. * * *

Moreover, in the case of "private" wrongs, our common law tradition does not seek to "punish and deter" ordinary private wrongs: normally, the sole purpose of a damages award in tort is to compensate a wrongfully injured party for injury to person or property. (See Prosser & Keeton on Torts (5th ed.1984)) § 1, p. 6 (hereafter Prosser & Keeton) * * *.

For more than two centuries, common law courts have recognized that certain wrongful acts constitute an affront to honor and dignity, and that this affront is not a loss that the common law normally compensates with a damages award. Perhaps in recognition that offenses to honor were particularly likely to result in extrajudicial retribution if not sufficiently compensated within the judicial system, common law courts permitted an award of exemplary or punitive damages in certain cases of outrageous behavior without any pretext that the award was compensating the victim for some otherwise compensable loss. (See generally Colby, *Beyond the Multiple Punishment Problem: Punitive Damages as Punishment for Individual, Private Wrongs* (2003) 87 Minn. L.Rev. 583, 614–616 [hereafter *Private Wrongs*].) "Such damages are given to the plaintiff over and above the full compensation for the injuries, for the purpose of punishing the defendant, of teaching the defendant not to do it again, and of deterring others from following the defendant's example." (Prosser & Keeton, *supra*, § 2, p. 9.) Even though the resulting award sought to punish the defendant rather than to compensate the plaintiff, cases recognized that the punishment was for the *particular* affront to the plaintiff, not a broader sanction for an affront to society at large. Consequently, from an early date it was required that the punitive damages award bear some "reasonable relationship" to the individual injury and the compensatory damages awarded in the action. (*Id.*, at p. 639.)

2. *What* Is to Be Deterred: Punishment of Quasi–Public Wrongs

The idea of awarding punitive damages based purely on a conception of torts as private wrongs lost favor in the era of products liability litigation. In cases of mass-produced consumer goods or company-wide practices of large insurers, outrageous or malicious wrongdoing was no longer simply an affront to the dignity of a single victim. Instead, the affront was to all affected by the goods or services or, given the reach of the misconduct, the affront was viewed as one to society as a whole. In this view, because the "wrong" was directed beyond the immediate plaintiff, punitive damages awards needed to be based on the overall scope of the wrong in order to punish and deter the mass torts. (See *Private Wrongs, supra,* 87 Minn.L.Rev. at p. 603) [describing such punitive damages as "total harm" damages] * * *. As the issue became less the inadequacy of common law measures of damages as a satisfactory substitute for self-help and more a question of preventing outrageous large-scale wrongdoing, it was thought that, in order to be effective, punitive damages had to render the overall conduct unprofitable or prohibitively costly.

The issue was presented to the Court of Appeal in *Grimshaw,* 119 Cal.App.3d 757, 174 Cal.Rptr. 348, the products liability action involving the Ford Pinto. There, Ford argued, as phrased by the court, "that the Legislature was thinking in terms of traditional intentional torts, such as, libel, slander, assault and battery, malicious prosecution, trespass, etc., and could not have intended [Civil Code section 3294] to be applied to a products liability case arising out of a design defect in a mass produced automobile because neither strict products liability nor mass produced automobiles were known [when the law was enacted] in 1872." (*Id.* at p. 809, 174 Cal.Rptr. 348.) The court rejected this narrow view of the purpose of the punitive damages statute. The court stated: * * * "Governmental safety standards and the criminal law have failed to provide adequate consumer protection against the manufacture and distribution of defective products. [Citations.] Punitive damages thus remain as the most effective remedy for consumer protection against defectively designed mass produced articles." (*Ibid.*) Thus, the goal of punitive damages came to be seen largely as actual deterrence of a broad course of conduct through sanctions imposed in individual litigation.

3. *How* to Punish and Deter: California's Broad View

In addition to its broad view of the goal of punitive damages, the *Grimshaw* court also adopted the broad view of the measure of punitive damages: "Unlike malicious conduct directed toward a single specific individual, Ford's tortious conduct endangered the lives of thousands of Pinto purchasers. Weighed against the factor of reprehensibility, the punitive damage award ... was not excessive." (*Grimshaw, supra,* 119 Cal.App.3d at pp. 819–820, 174 Cal.Rptr. 348.) Further, the *Grimshaw* court stated: "An award which is so small that it can be simply written off as a part of the cost of doing business would have no deterrent effect. An award which affects the company's pricing of its product and thereby affects its competitive advantage would serve as a deterrent." (*Id.* at p. 820, 174 Cal.Rptr. 348.)[1] (In *Grimshaw* itself there was no issue of the maximum amount of punitive damages that could be awarded: the punitive damage award by the trial court was 1.4 times the compensatory damages. (119 Cal.App.3d at pp. 820, 822–823, 174 Cal.Rptr. 348.))

In keeping with familiar rules of stare decisis, we applied the broad standards for punitive damages established by California case law in our original opinion in this case. To be sure, such standards were subject to limitations or "guideposts" established in *BMW of North America, Inc. v. Gore* (1996) 517 U.S. 559, 116 S.Ct. 1589, 134 L.Ed.2d 809. But, as evidenced in our original opinion, we applied these guideposts in light of the broad purposes and broad measure of punitive damages, in which courts undertook to *actually* deter a practice or course of conduct by

---

1. We also note the Legislature seems to have shared this broad view of punitive damages. In enacting restrictions on the timing of presentation of punitive damages evidence to the jury in 1979, the Legislature viewed the scope of such evidence to include the "profits the defendant has gained by virtue of the wrongful course of conduct of the nature and type shown by the evidence." (Civ.Code, § 3295, subd. (a)(1).)

depriving the wrongdoer of profit from the course of conduct or making such conduct so expensive it put the wrongdoer at a competitive disadvantage. (See *Grimshaw, supra,* 119 Cal.App.3d at p. 820, 174 Cal.Rptr. 348.) "Punishment and deterrence" in this view is far along a scale that might be viewed as increasing from mere admonition toward direct incapacitation.

4. Punishment and Deterrence in *State Farm:* The Narrow View Reasserted

State Farm, in our view, impliedly disapproved this broad view of the goal and measure of punitive damages. Instead, as a matter of due process under the federal Constitution, the court adopted the more limited, historically based view of punitive damages. * * * In doing so, the court in *State Farm* went beyond the "guideposts" established in *Gore* and articulated a constitutional due process limitation on both the goal and the measure of punitive damages. Further, the result is a punitive damages analysis that focuses primarily on what defendant did to the present plaintiff, rather than the defendant's wealth or general incorrigibility. * * *

5. *What* Is to Be Punished, Revisited

Thus, the *State Farm* court first limited the goal that the states are permitted to reach through punitive damages: "Due process does not permit courts, in the calculation of punitive damages, to adjudicate the merits of other parties' hypothetical claims against a defendant under the guise of the reprehensibility analysis...." (*State Farm, supra,* 538 U.S. at p. 423, 123 S.Ct. at p. 1523.) "Punishment on the [basis that harm is minor to the individual but massive in the aggregate] creates the possibility of multiple punitive damages awards for the same conduct; for in the usual case nonparties are not bound by the judgment some other plaintiff obtains." (*Ibid.*) "While States enjoy considerable discretion in deducing when punitive damages are warranted, each award must comport with the principles set forth in *Gore.* Here the argument that State Farm will be punished in only the rare case, coupled with reference to its assets ... had little to do with the actual harm sustained by the Campbells." (*Id.* at p. 427 [123 S.Ct. at p. 1525].) As we read *State Farm,* then, the legitimate state goal that punitive damages may seek to achieve is the "condemnation of such conduct" as has resulted in "outrage and humiliation" to the plaintiffs before the court (*ibid.*); it is not a permissible goal to punish a defendant for everything else it may have done wrong.[2]

---

2. This is not to say that evidence of similar conduct is not relevant and admissible. Whether civilly or criminally, a state is permitted to punish recidivist conduct more severely than an individual instance of malfeasance. (*State Farm, supra,* 538 U.S. at p. 423, 123 S.Ct. at p. 1523.) However, "in the context of civil actions courts must ensure the conduct in question replicates the prior transgressions." (*Ibid.*)

6. *How* to Punish and Deter, Revisited

In addition to limiting the goal to be reached through punitive damages, the court's rejection of the broad view of punitive damages—as established in California by *Grimshaw*—also must result in a reconsideration of the standard of constitutional excessiveness by which punitive damages are constrained. As we demonstrated in our prior opinion in this case, the broad view of punitive damages fully supported the $290 million punitive damages award in the present case. That massive award, however, was justified only as a means to actually punish and deter an entire course of conduct that harmed not only plaintiffs but, potentially, untold others. In *State Farm,* the court made it clear that the permissible punishment is for the harm inflicted on the present plaintiffs. "A defendant should be punished for the conduct that harmed the plaintiff, not for being an unsavory individual or business." (*State Farm, supra,* 538 U.S. at p. 423, 123 S.Ct. at p. 1523; see also *id.* at pp. 424–426, 123 S.Ct. at pp. 1524–1525.) Deterrence, in this view, arises as a natural result of imposing damages over and above traditional compensatory damages, not from the imposition of sanctions in an individual case that are actually disabling to the defendant.

The issue for the *State Farm* court, by contrast with the *Grimshaw* view (for example), is not whether a particular punitive damages award is sufficient actually and in fact to dissuade the course of conduct but, instead, whether such award punishes and deters to an extent found sufficient historically. (*State Farm, supra,* 538 U.S. at p. 425, 123 S.Ct. at p. 1524.) Accordingly, the court used as a guide to the proper level of punishment and deterrence the "long legislative history, dating back over 700 years and going forward to today, providing for sanctions of double, treble, or quadruple damages to deter and punish." (*Ibid.*) The court found that these multipliers "demonstrate what should be obvious: Single-digit multipliers are more likely to comport with due process, while still achieving the state's goals of deterrence and retribution...." (*Ibid.*) When considered in light of products liability actions against large corporate defendants for which single-digit multipliers may simply be a cost of doing business (see *Grimshaw, supra,* 119 Cal.App.3d at p. 820, 174 Cal.Rptr. 348), the court's conclusion is far from "obvious." However, in the light of the historical goal and measure of punitive damages, the obviousness appears, to a certain extent.

7. *Which* Single Digit Sufficiently Punishes and Deters?

Although the need to limit most punitive damages awards to a single-digit multiplier was obvious to the Supreme Court, there was not a *particular* single digit that appeared appropriate in all cases, according to the court. (*State Farm, supra,* 538 U.S. at p. 425, 123 S.Ct. at p. 1524.) * * *

The court reiterated that reprehensibility of the defendant's conduct is the most important consideration in determining the reasonableness of a punitive damages award. (*State Farm, supra,* 538 U.S. at p. 419, 123

S.Ct. at p. 1521.) As discussed above, however, the court newly emphasized that the conduct directed toward the plaintiff was the focus of this inquiry. * * * "Due process does not permit courts, in the calculation of punitive damages, to adjudicate the merits of other parties' hypothetical claims against a defendant under the guise of the reprehensibility analysis." (*Ibid.*)

In its treatment of the second *Gore* factor, the reasonable relationship requirement, the *State Farm* court gave this additional guidance: While a higher single-digit multiplier might be appropriate where non-economic harm is difficult to detect or to value under traditional compensatory damages standards, the "converse is also true.... When compensatory damages are substantial, then a lesser ratio, perhaps only equal to compensatory damages, can reach the outermost limit of the due process guarantee." (*State Farm, supra,* 538 U.S. at p. 425, 123 S.Ct. at p. 1524.) Further, the court instructed that we must look at the *nature* of the compensatory damages award, with the result that a lower multiplier will be appropriate if the compensatory damages award for the particular tort already compensates for the "outrage and humiliation" that punitive damages are primarily intended to condemn. (*Id.* at p. 426, 123 S.Ct. at p. 1525.)

* * *

C. *The Jury Instructions in This Case in Light of* State Farm

Now that we have set forth our understanding of *State Farm,* we come to the task of applying that opinion as part of our independent review of the punitive damages award. (*Cooper Industries, Inc. v. Leatherman Tool Group, Inc.* (2001) 532 U.S. 424, 431–433, 121 S.Ct. 1678, 149 L.Ed.2d 674.)

First, we conclude *State Farm* 's constitutionalization of the historical, pre-*Grimshaw* punitive damages doctrines as part of federal due process means that the jury was fundamentally misinstructed concerning the *amount* of punitive damages it could award in the present case. In particular, under BAJI No. 14.71, the jury in this case was instructed that, in addition to other factors, it should consider in arriving at an award of punitive damages "[t]he amount of punitive damages which will have a deterrent effect on the defendant in the light of defendant's financial condition." * * * [T]his view of "actual" deterrence, while clearly supported by California law under *Grimshaw,* fails to restrict the jury to punishment and deterrence based solely on the harm to the plaintiffs, as apparently required by federal due process.

Other portions of the instruction required that the jury find malice "in the conduct on which you base your finding of liability." This requirement established a threshold for the imposition of punitive damages, but it did not restrict the amount of the award. Accordingly, plaintiffs' counsel argued that the award should be large enough to force Ford to recall all remaining 1978–1979 Broncos still on the road and "crush them to dust." Counsel argued that $1 billion was the appropriate award, based on the profit Ford made on all 1978–1979 Broncos, factored to reflect Ford's use of that money over the next 20 years. Finally, counsel requested $1 billion so that the resulting publicity would reach all remaining owners of this model Bronco so they would know how dangerous the vehicle was. These considerations are impermissible under *State Farm* and plaintiffs' argument served to magnify the impact of the misinstruction.

While the underlying facts supporting a punitive damages award are for the jury to decide, the amount of punitive damages must be independently reviewed on appeal. (*Cooper Industries, Inc. v. Leatherman Tool Group, Inc., supra,* 532 U.S. at pp. 436–437, 121 S.Ct. 1678.) In conducting such review, we remove any prejudice accruing to the defendant as a result of misinstruction concerning the amount of such award; we do so by modifying the judgment to reflect a level of punitive damages below which we believe no properly instructed jury was reasonably likely to go. (*People v. Watson* (1956) 46 Cal.2d 818, 836, 299 P.2d 243.) Accordingly, our reduction of the award satisfies the due process interests of defendant.

* * *

D. *Constitutional Excessiveness in Light of State Farm*

* * *

1. Reprehensibility

Substantial evidence supports the jury's implicit conclusion that Ford acted with malicious conduct under aggravated circumstances; such a set of facts propels this situation toward the higher end of the reprehensibility scale. * * *

Defendant's conduct was highly reprehensible under *Gore* based on the following: defendant caused a high degree of physical harm, including deathly harm, to the victims of the instant accident; the nonaccidental, malicious conduct in placing the defective 1978–1979 model Ford Bronco with consumers, including these victims, while not intentionally causing the present deaths and injuries, reflected, in a nonisolated manner, a reckless disregard of consumers' safety and lives; and the victims were financially vulnerable relative to defendant's financial resources.

* * *

2. The Relationship Between Compensatory and Punitive Damages

Because of the nature of the causes of action in the present case and the jury's peculiar allocation of compensatory damages, application of the second *Gore* factor (see *State Farm, supra,* 538 U.S. at p. 427, 123 S.Ct. at p. 1525) is rather complex. Nevertheless, it is possible on the present record to reach certain conclusions about the relationship between compensatory damages and a reasonable award of punitive damages.

* * *

[N]o one would deny that a *decedent* has lost something valuable when he or she loses life. Yet there was no award whatsoever in the original verdict—and no possibility of such an award under the instructions—reflecting the "outrage" to the deceased family members themselves, occasioned by their loss of the opportunity for the personal satisfactions, large and small, that make life worth living.

Such loss to the decedent is not a proper subject of compensatory damages for the estate or the heirs. Plaintiffs as individuals and as heirs of the deceased family members were adequately compensated for their losses, as such losses are recognized by statute and in our common law tradition. The decedents were not—and could not be—adequately compensated for the loss of their lives.

Compensation, however, is not the issue. Punitive damages are not intended to compensate; instead they are intended to punish and make an example of the defendant as a result of defendant's malicious conduct. In this context of malicious conduct, as opposed to ordinary negligence actions, public policy and legitimate interests of the state in the protection of its people require a mechanism to punish and deter conduct that kills people. It would be unacceptable public policy to establish a system in which it is less expensive for a defendant's malicious conduct to kill rather than injure a victim. (Cf. *Grimshaw, supra,* 119 Cal.App.3d at p. 833, 174 Cal.Rptr. 348.) Thus, the state has an extremely strong interest in being able to impose sufficiently high punitive damages in malicious-conduct wrongful death actions to deter a "cheaper to kill them" mindset, while still maintaining limits on wrongful death compensation in cases of ordinary negligence. We do not perceive that due process considerations of proportionality between compensatory and punitive damages require a state to establish a system that inadequately punishes and deters malicious conduct that, with reasonable foreseeability, may cause death; we hold that death actions present an example of the type of extraordinary case contemplated by *State Farm* (see *State Farm, supra,* 538 U.S. at p. 425, 123 S.Ct. at p. 1524) in which a single-digit multiplier does not necessarily form an appropriate limitation upon a punitive damages award.

This is not to say that all standards are thrown out in cases brought by personal representatives of the estates of deceased victims. Even among instances of malicious conduct that causes death, some of such conduct will be more or less reprehensible than other instances. We conclude, however, that the proportionality factor has less weight in the context of malicious conduct causing death. * * *

Further, the legal standard for the award of compensatory damages in [wrongful death] actions ensures that there is no "punitive" component in the compensatory damages award in such actions; as a result there is no danger of duplicative damages in a punitive damages award * * *, as there was in the context of the emotional distress compensatory award in *State Farm*. (See *State Farm, supra,* 538 U.S. at p. 426, 123 S.Ct. at 1525.) * * *

By contrast, in the case of the individual plaintiffs' personal injury claims, a large portion of the compensatory damages award was for noneconomic damages. Because some component of this award, particularly as related to plaintiffs' emotional distress claims, likely involved considerations similar to the punitive damages award, a somewhat lesser multiplier is appropriate as to those damages. (See *State Farm, supra,* 538 U.S. at p. 426, 123 S.Ct. at p. 1525.)

* * *

3. Comparable Civil and Criminal Punishments

We turn to the third *Gore* factor, disparity between criminal and civil penalties for similar conduct and the size of the award in the present case. (*State Farm, supra,* 538 U.S. at p. 428, 123 S.Ct. at p. 1526.) Willful and conscious disregard of danger resulting in loss of life can constitute involuntary manslaughter. By the same token, the failure of prosecutors to seek criminal convictions in cases of the present sort does not permit an enhancement of the punitive damages award in a civil case. (*State Farm, supra,* 538 U.S. at p. 428, 123 S.Ct. at p. 1526.) We conclude the third *Gore* factor requires neither a higher nor lower ratio between the compensatory and punitive damages award.

4. Conclusion: The Point at Which "the State's Legitimate Objectives" Are Satisfied

Our independent review in this case convinces us that the extreme reprehensibility of defendant's actions and the undercompensation of plaintiffs' individual losses outweigh the punitive element already contained to some extent in the individual compensatory damages awards. As a result, we consider that a punitive damages award of triple the compensatory award to the individual plaintiffs would be constitutionally reasonable. An award of three times the compensatory damages of $4,574,429, or a total of $13,723,287, to the individual plaintiffs jointly, is not more than a properly instructed jury likely would award and would not be constitutionally unreasonable.

Considerations of reprehensibility and the nature of damages in [wrongful death] actions, as well as the public policy consideration that malicious conduct resulting in death should not be encouraged by making it less expensive for a defendant to kill than to injure, all lead us to conclude that an award of punitive damages to the estate of each deceased parent of $5 million is constitutionally reasonable. An award of punitive damages to Juan Romo as administrator of the estates in the total amount of $10 million is not more than a properly instructed jury likely would award and would not be constitutionally unreasonable.

For reasons described above, we do not believe that the deathly harm component of the punitive award in the present case is strictly constrained by the single-digit multiplier set forth in *State Farm*. Nevertheless, we note the overall punitive damages award we find appropriate after independent review, $23,723,287, is approximately five times the total compensatory damages awarded in this case.

III. DISPOSITION

In the event plaintiffs elect to remit all of the punitive damages judgment save and except for the total sum of $23,723,287, the punitive damages judgment shall be modified and affirmed in that amount. In the event plaintiffs decline remittitur, the punitive damages judgment is reversed and the matter is remanded for a new trial on the amount of punitive damages only. The parties shall bear their own costs on appeal.

WE CONCUR: BUCKLEY and CORNELL, JJ.

Notes

1. In Johnson v. Ford Motor Co., 35 Cal.4th 1191, 113 P.3d 82, 29 Cal.Rptr.3d 401 (2005), the California Supreme Court refused to adopt the full *Romo* analysis. "The *Romo* court's analysis does not convince us that the United States Supreme Court, in *State Farm* adopted wholesale the historical view of punitive damages * * * as a constitutional rule binding on the states." 113 P.3d at 92. "[T]he United States Supreme Court's analysis in [*BMW* and *State Farm*] makes clear that due process does not prohibit state courts, in awarding or reviewing punitive damages from considering the defendant's illegal or wrongful conduct toward others that was similar to the tortious conduct that injured the plaintiff or plaintiffs. We therefore join numerous courts holding that a civil defendant's recidivism remains pertinent to an assessment of culpability." *Id.* at 90–91.

2. Note that in *State Farm*, the wrongful behavior of the defendant involved its unreasonable refusal to accept a good faith settlement offer within policy limits and then, after a verdict substantially in excess of policy limits, initially refusing to pay the excess. At one point after the verdict, defendant told the insured, "You may want to put a for sale sign on your property to get things moving." Apparently, the plaintiffs were unable to point to any other incidents involving third party automobile insurance in which under similar circumstances the defendant attempted to avoid paying damages beyond policy limits. Much of the allegedly bad behavior of the defendant introduced at trial concerned its low-ball settlement policies with respect to first party insurance. In at least some states these practices were legal. Clearly, this conduct did not "replicate" the conduct at issue in the State Farm litigation. In *Romo*, however, the plaintiffs presented evidence of similar rollover accidents that arguably do "replicate" the defendant's conduct, i.e., the design of the Bronco, in their case.

3. **Multiple awards for the same conduct.** Although the *Johnson* court refused to adopt the "historical" or "narrow" view of punitive damages laid out in *Romo*, neither was it willing to return to what the *Romo* court called the "broad" view. In *Johnson,* a case involving the resale of

automobiles without disclosing that they had undergone transmission repairs and replacements, the court refused to adopt the plaintiff's position that a proper measure of damages would be the disgorgement of aggregate profits from all similar conduct in California. The court agreed with *State Farm* that permitting such a recovery creates the possibility of multiple punitive damages awards for the same conduct.

With respect to the plaintiff's argument that this problem can be avoided by permitting a defendant to present evidence of past punitive awards for the same conduct, the court noted:

> But the exact basis for a prior punitive damages award will not always be clear, and even where it is proven that the defendant has already been punished severely for a course of conduct that included harm to the current plaintiff, there is no guarantee the jury or court will agree to deny the plaintiff before them recovery of punitive damages simply because another plaintiff, in another court, has already recovered. * * * Permitting an aggregate recovery followed by credits in future cases could, moreover, unfairly deprive subsequent claimants of their own recoveries, as well as present a problem of "successive prosecution" in which a defendant that loses a single case would also lose the benefit of all previous victories against the same claim of misconduct. * * *
>
> Finally, and most pertinent to this case, an individual plaintiff resting his or her claim for a large punitive damages award on profits earned from transactions with a large class of similar claimants, but proceeding without the formalities of a class action, can hope to recover without ever proving the specifics of those "hypothetical claims." * * * Here, the Johnsons, as individual plaintiffs, proved only the facts of Ford's tortious transaction with them, yet they sought and obtained disgorgement of Ford's estimated earnings on a thousand or more other transactions without proof that each of the others was also tortious. 113 P.3d at 94–95.

4. **Evidence of prior awards.** In Owens–Corning Fiberglas Corp. v. Malone, 972 S.W.2d 35, 54 (Tex.1998) the court adopted the path rejected in *Johnson*: "We hold in *Malone* that evidence about the profitability of a defendant's misconduct and about past settlements that specify amounts for punitive damages or about other paid punitive damage awards for the same course of conduct is relevant and admissible for the factfinder to consider when the defendant offers such evidence in mitigation of punitive damages." *Malone* notes that one problem with the jury instruction solution to the problems of multiple punitive damages is that prior awards may have occurred in another state and thus there may be pressure not to deny an award to the residents of the trial state in favor of citizens of another jurisdiction. Presumably, an appellate court could reduce a jury award in post-verdict proceedings if it felt that the award was too large in light of earlier awards, but the same pressures may work to limit the willingness of state judges to reduce awards to their citizens.

With respect to the problems of punitive damages in mass tort cases, see Forde, Punitive Damages in Mass Tort Cases: Recovery on Behalf of a Class, 15 Loy.U.Chi.L.J. 397 (1984); Seltzer, Punitive Damages in Mass Tort Litigation: Addressing the Problems of Fairness, Efficiency and Control, 52

Fordham L.Rev. 37 (1983); Pace, Recalibrating the Scales of Justice Through National Punitive Damage Reform, 46 Am.U.L.Rev. 1573 (1997); Owen, A Punitive Damages Overview: Functions, Problems and Reform, 39 Vill. L.Rev. 363 (1994); Phillips, Multiple Punitive Damage Awards, 39 Vill.L.Rev. 433 (1994); Garber, Product Liability, Punitive Damages, Business Decisions and Economic Outcomes, 1998 Wis.L.Rev. 237 (1998).

5. **Bifurcation.** As noted in *Romo*, a number of states permit the defendant to elect a bifurcated trial. When the defendant makes this election, the jury considers the question of punitive damages only after reaching a verdict in favor of the plaintiff and assessing compensatory damages. In some states, the jury only decides the amount of punitive damages in the second trial. Why do you think the defendant did not elect this option in *Romo*? *See* Landsman et al., Be Careful What You Wish For: The Paradoxical Effects of Bifurcating Claims for Punitive Damages, 1998 Wis.L.Rev. 297.

Chapter 10

APPORTIONMENT OF LIABILITY AMONG MULTIPLE PARTIES

We begin this Chapter with affirmative defenses based on the plaintiff's conduct. These defenses traditionally did not invoke apportionment among the parties to the suit but were, if successful, complete bars to recovery. Although some vestiges of this complete bar rule still exist, the modern trend, reflected in the remainder of this Chapter, is toward apportioning liability both between culpable plaintiffs and defendants, among culpable defendants, sometimes even to culpable nonparties, and across different bases for liability, including negligence, products liability, and, even, intentional torts. To accord with the breadth of apportioning liability and the recent Restatement (Third) of Torts: Apportionment of Liability, we use the term "comparative responsibility," rather than "comparative negligence" or "comparative fault".

SECTION A. CONSUMER CONDUCT DEFENSES AND COMPARATIVE RESPONSIBILITY

You should already be familiar with two defenses that are based on the plaintiff's own conduct—contributory negligence and assumption of risk—as these defenses are applicable to negligence actions and were addressed in your first-year torts course. A third defense—product misuse—is new.

The application of these defenses to modern products liability litigation initially raised two sets of issues. First, courts had to determine whether a specific defense was applicable to the various theories of liability (tort theories and warranty) and whether the contours of the defenses were the same in the context of products liability bases on restatement section 402A as in the context of negligence.

With the advent of comparative responsibility, courts had to both rethink what defenses might be asserted and determine the effect of those that were cognizable. Specifically, courts that had previously decided contributory negligence was not a defense were faced with whether to permit a plaintiff's contributory negligence to reduce recovery in a strict products liability claim. The latter issue arose for assumption of risk as well, which had for the most part been a complete bar to recovery in all tort claims. If a court adopts a comparative scheme, it must also determine the specific contours of the scheme, such as whether a plaintiff who is more than 50% responsible can still recover.

1. CONTRIBUTORY NEGLIGENCE

You should recall from your first-year torts course that contributory negligence consists of a plaintiff failing to exercise reasonable care for his or her own safety. (In some cases, the same conduct that constitutes contributory negligence may also create risks for others; this occurs most frequently in driving automobiles.) In a normal negligence case, the defense of contributory negligence can involve all of the intricate issues associated with proving the defendant's negligence. Thus, for the plaintiff's contributory negligence to affect the plaintiff's recovery—either as a total bar or as a percentage reduction—the defendant must establish (1) that the plaintiff had a duty to use reasonable care, (2) that the plaintiff breached this duty by failing to use reasonable care, (3) that the plaintiff's failure to use reasonable care factually caused all or some of the plaintiff's injuries, and (4) that the plaintiff's failure was a proximate cause of the injuries.

The basic test of contributory negligence is whether the plaintiff created a foreseeable, unreasonable risk to his own safety. Whether or not the plaintiff was a child, had a physical handicap, faced an emergency not of his own making, violated a statute, and so on, are factors that affect a determination of the plaintiff's contributory negligence in the same way that they would affect a determination of the defendant's negligence. These issues will not be rehearsed in this chapter; the principal concern here is whether and how contributory negligence affects products liability litigation.

In a product case based on negligence, the plaintiff's contributory negligence has the same effect as it does in an ordinary action for negligence. The basic contours of the defense are not affected merely because a product was the cause of a plaintiff's injuries. Nevertheless, some issues that arise in products cases and nonproducts cases alike can be especially acute in products cases.

Even in nonproduct cases, several courts have held that a plaintiff's contributory negligence does not affect his recovery when the defendant's own negligence consisted of violating a statute that was itself designed to protect people like the plaintiff from their own carelessness. *See, e.g.,* Zerby v. Warren, 297 Minn. 134, 210 N.W.2d 58 (1973) (defendant sold glue to minor in violation of statute). Similarly, it is not unusual in a product case for a manufacturer's own negligence to be its failure to design a product that guards against the consumer's occasional carelessness. Permitting the defendant to benefit from the plaintiff's contributory negligence in such a case would frustrate the very purpose of finding the manufacturer negligent in the first place, and some courts have declined to do so. For example, recall that in Bexiga v. Havir Mfg. Corp., 60 N.J. 402, 290 A.2d 281 (1972), reproduced in Chapter 4 at page 181, the manufacturer of a punch press was negligent for not installing a safety device that would have prevented a user from putting his hand under the press. The court noted that the plaintiff's own contributory negligence in placing his hand under the press was the very danger a safety device would have prevented. Consequently, the court held that this particular version of contributory negligence did not affect the plaintiff's recovery.

The applicability of contributory negligence as a defense in breach of warranty cases is more complex. Article 2 of the Uniform Commercial Code does not expressly cover contributory negligence, but some of its provisions and official comments tangentially address the plaintiff's conduct in the guise of proximate causation. Comment 13 to section 2–314 (which deals with an implied warranty of merchantability) provides that "[a]ction by the buyer following an examination of the goods which ought to have indicated the defect complained of can be shown as a matter bearing on whether the breach itself was the cause of the injury."

Section 2–316(3)(b), which deals with disclaimers, provides that when a buyer has inspected goods or refuses to inspect them, no implied warranty exists with regard to defects that the inspection should have revealed. Comment 8 to section 2–316 elaborates: "[I]f the buyer discovers the defect and uses the goods anyway, or if he unreasonably fails to examine the goods before he uses them, resulting injuries may be found to result from his own action rather than proximately from the breach of warranty."

Section 2–715(2)(b) provides that the plaintiff can recover consequential damages for breach of warranty including "injury to person or property proximately resulting from any breach of warranty." Comment 5 to section 2–715 provides that

> [w]here the injury involved follows the use of goods without discovery of the defect causing the damage, the question of "proximate" cause turns on whether it was reasonable for the buyer to use the goods without such inspection as would have revealed the defects. If it was not reasonable for him to do so, or if he did in fact discover the defect prior to his use, the injury would not proximately result from the breach of warranty.

Often without referring to these code provisions, several courts have held that contributory negligence constitutes a defense in an action for breach of warranty. For example, in Signal Oil and Gas Co. v. Universal Oil Products, 572 S.W.2d 320 (Tex.1978), the court held that a plaintiff's contributory negligence constitutes a comparative defense (and consequently reduces rather than bars the plaintiff's recovery) in an action for breach of an implied warranty of merchantability. In Erdman v. Johnson Bros. Radio & Television Co., 260 Md. 190, 271 A.2d 744 (1970), the court held that the plaintiff's contributory negligence is a complete bar to recovery for breach of an implied warranty of merchantability. The plaintiff in *Erdman* apparently was actually aware of the defect, so the court may have been applying a more limited defense of assumption of risk. *See also* Torres v. Northwest Engineering Co., 86 Hawai'i 383, 949 P.2d 1004 (1997) (express warranty claim governed by pure comparative negligence principles where plaintiff was killed when the defendant's crane toppled over). Other courts, however, have held that contributory negligence is not a defense to an action of breach of warranty (at least where the plaintiff was not actually aware of the defect). Many of these cases dealt with express warranties. *See, e.g.,* Holt v. Stihl, Inc., 449 F.Supp. 693 (E.D.Tenn.1977) (applying Tennessee law); Shields v. Morton Chemical Co., 95 Idaho 674, 518 P.2d 857 (1974); Shaffer v. Debbas, 17 Cal.App.4th 33, 21 Cal.Rptr.2d 110, 114 (1993) (stating that "comparative negligence is not a defense to a breach of express warranty action").

In an action for fraud or for innocent misrepresentation under section 402B of the Restatement (Second) of Torts, the plaintiff's conduct may affect his or her recovery under the rationale that the plaintiff's reliance on the representation was not "justifiable." The plaintiff has no duty to investigate facts that are the subject of the misrepresentation, so a mere failure to inspect goods is unlikely to affect recovery. If the plaintiff does inspect the goods and fails to discover a defect, however, reliance on the representation might not be justifiable. But at least for an action for fraud, section 545A of the Restatement (Second) of Torts provides that the plaintiff's contributory negligence as such is not a defense.

For an action for negligent misrepresentation, section 552A of the Restatement (Second) of Torts provides that the plaintiff's contributory negligence in relying on the representation is a defense. Comment a to section 552A provides that in determining whether the plaintiff was negligent, "the plaintiff is held to the standard of care, knowledge, intelligence and judgment of a reasonable man, even though he does not possess the qualities necessary to enable him to conform to that standard." This standard differs from justifiable reliance in cases involving fraud, in which a plaintiff with idiosyncratic mental characteristics might justifiably rely on a representation, even though a reasonable person would not do so.

Most jurisdictions apply comparative principles to cases involving negligent misrepresentations. *See* Gilchrist Timber Co. v. ITT Rayonier, Inc., 696 So.2d 334 (Fla.1997) (reviewing the law in various jurisdictions); Williams Ford, Inc. v. Hartford Courant Co., 232 Conn. 559, 575, 657 A.2d 212 (1995). There is very little authority as to whether comparative responsibility rules apply to section 402B claims. *See* Phillips v. Duro–Last Roofing, Inc., 806 P.2d 834 (Wyo. 1991) (comparative responsibility defense not available).

The most common issue involving contributory negligence in the context of product liability litigation has been whether contributory negligence is a defense in a products liability action.

2. CONTRIBUTORY NEGLIGENCE UNDER 402A

At the time Restatement (Second) of Torts Section 402A was promulgated most American jurisdictions still followed the old contributory negligence rule under which any negligence on the part of the plaintiff acted as a total bar to recovery. It is against this backdrop that the ALI adopted Comment *n*.

RESTATEMENT (SECOND) OF TORTS

§ 402A, Comment n. *Contributory negligence.* Since the liability with which this Section deals is not based upon negligence of the seller, but is strict liability, the rule applied to strict liability cases (see § 524) applies. Contributory negligence of the plaintiff is not a defense when such negligence consists merely in a failure to discover the defect in the product, or to guard against the possibility of its existence. On the other hand the form of contributory negligence which consists in voluntarily and unreasonably proceeding to encounter a known danger, and commonly passes under the name of assumption of risk, is a defense under this Section as in other cases of strict liability. If the user or consumer discovers the defect and is aware of the danger, and nevertheless proceeds unreasonably to make use of the product and is injured by it, he is barred from recovery.

McCOWN v. INTERNATIONAL HARVESTER CO.
Supreme Court of Pennsylvania, 1975.
463 Pa. 13, 342 A.2d 381.

JONES, CHIEF JUSTICE.

Appellant, manufacturer of large over-the-road tractors, was held liable under Section 402A of Restatement (Second) of Torts (1965) for the injuries sustained by the appellee in a one-vehicle accident. The Superior Court affirmed and we granted allocatur limited to the issue of the availability of contributory negligence as a defense to a 402A action.

Appellee was injured while driving a tractor manufactured by appellant. The design of the steering mechanism of the tractor made the vehicle unusually difficult to maneuver. Specifically, twelve to fifteen percent more mechanical effort than that normally expended had to be applied to the steering wheel to accomplish any given turn. Appellee, after driving the vehicle for several hours, stopped for an equipment check on the blacktopped shoulder of the Pennsylvania Turnpike. After completing the inspection the appellee proceeded to reenter the Turnpike.

Unrelated to any steering difficulty appellee struck a guardrail adjoining the shoulder with the right front tire of the tractor. This collision caused the steering wheel to spin rapidly in the direction opposite to the turn. The spokes of the spinning steering wheel struck appellee's right arm, fracturing his wrist and forearm. Evidence adduced at trial indicated that the force and speed of the steering wheel's counterrotation were directly related to the design of the steering mechanism.

For the purposes of this appeal appellant concedes the defect in the steering system's design, but argues that appellee's contributory negligence in colliding with the guardrail should at least be considered in determining appellee's recovery. We disagree and affirm.

In *Webb v. Zern,* 422 Pa. 424, 220 A.2d 853 (1966), this Court adopted Section 402A of the Restatement and in *Ferraro v. Ford Motor Co.,* 423 Pa. 324, 223 A.2d 746 (1966), permitted the assertion of assumption of the risk as a defense to a 402A action, citing with approval comment *n* to Section 402A. Today, we complete our acceptance of the principles delineated in comment *n* by rejecting contributory negligence as an available defense in 402A cases.

Appellant's position that contributory negligence should affect 402A liability could have two possible applications. Either contributory negligence should serve to diminish any recovery in an amount adjudged equal to a plaintiff's lack of care or, as in most other tort actions, contributory negligence should be available as a complete defense to liability.

Acceptance of the appellant's first alternative would create a system of comparative assessment of damages for 402A actions. Neither the General Assembly by statute nor this Court by case law has established such a scheme of comparative negligence in other areas of tort law. Without considering the relative merits of comparative negligence, we think it unwise to embrace the theory in the context of an appeal involving Section 402A.

Adoption of contributory negligence as a complete defense in 402A actions would defeat one theoretical basis for our acceptance of Section 402A. "Our courts have determined that a manufacturer by marketing and advertising his products impliedly represents that it is safe for its intended use." *Salvador v. Atlantic Steel Boiler Co.,* 457 Pa. 24, 32, 319 A.2d 903, 907 (1974). Based on that implied representation is the consumer's assumption that a manufacturer's goods are safe. Recognition of consumer negligence as a defense to a 402A action would contradict this normal expectation of product safety. One does not inspect a product for defects or guard against the possibility of product defects when one assumes the item to be safe. The law should not require such inspection or caution when it has accepted as reasonable the consumer's anticipation of safety. We reject contributory negligence as a defense to actions grounded in Section 402A.

Judgment affirmed.

MR. JUSTICE ROBERTS did not participate in the consideration or decision of this case.

MR. JUSTICE POMEROY filed a concurring opinion.

POMEROY, JUSTICE (concurring).

* * *

Contrary to what the opinion of the Court seems to suggest, the answer to the question presented by this appeal is not to be found altogether in the language of comment [*n*] to Section 402A. Comment *n* provides, on the one hand, that the negligent failure to discover a defect in a product or to guard against the possibility of its existence is not defense to a strict liability action, and, on the other hand, that assumption of risk is a defense. But the conduct of John McCown, the appellee, fits into neither of the above categories. His negligence, if any, was the manner of his operation of an International Harvester tractor. Although comment *n* is silent with regard to the consequences of negligent use of a product, it points to a resolution of the issue by referring to Section 524 of the Restatement (Second) of Torts. That section provides that in general "the contributory negligence of the plaintiff is not a defense to the strict liability of one who carries on an abnormally dangerous activity." Neither the Comments to Section 524 nor comment *n* to Section 402A offer a rationale for the application of this rule in products liability cases, but I am satisfied that the elimination of the defense of plaintiff's negligence is in accord not only with the weight of authority in other jurisdictions but also with the policy which underlies the concept of strict liability in tort.

The strict liability of Section 402A is founded in part upon the belief that as between the sellers of products and those who use them, the former are the better able to bear the losses caused by defects in the products involved. * * * This greater loss-bearing capacity is unrelated to negligence in the manufacture or marketing of products. Indeed, retail and wholesale sellers of chattels are themselves often in no position to discover or avoid defects in their inventories, even by the exercise of a high degree of care. Thus, defendants in Section 402A actions are subjected to liability without regard to fault. It is a proper corollary to this principle that the lesser loss-bearing capacity of product users exists independently of their negligence or lack of it. It follows that such negligence should not ordinarily or necessarily operate to preclude recovery in a strict liability case. On the other hand, where assumption of risk is involved, the "loss-bearing" policy underlying Section 402A is outweighed by a countervailing policy, one which refuses recovery to persons who consciously expose themselves to known dangers. This policy is deemed stronger than the one, reflected in the normal law of contributory negligence, which denies recovery to individuals whose conduct is merely lacking in due care under the circumstances.

This is not to say, however, that evidence of ordinary negligence on the part of a plaintiff is never relevant in a Section 402A action; such evidence may bear directly upon the determination of whether the plaintiff has proved all the elements necessary to make out a cause of action. Thus, negligence in the use of a product may tend to show that the plaintiff caused a defect and therefore that the product was not defective when sold. See Comment g to Section 402A. Again, if the negligent use of a product amounts to abnormal use, it may be inferred that the product was not defective if it is safe for normal handling and use. See Comment h to Section 402A. Similarly, negligence in the use of a product may have a bearing on the question whether a defect in a product was the legal cause of the plaintiff's injury. See Restatement (Second) of Torts §§ 5 and 9 and the Comments to these sections.

What has been said is not intended as an exhaustive listing of the purposes for which evidence of the plaintiff's negligence may be relevant in Section 402A cases. It is intended merely to indicate that, although such negligence is not per se a bar to recovery, it may nevertheless have that effect in a proper case where it negates an essential element of the cause of action. I do not read the opinion of the Court as suggesting anything to the contrary.

Notes

1. As Justice Pomeroy's concurrence points out, the result in *McCown* was not compelled by the language of Comment *n*, since the plaintiff's negligence was more than a mere failure to discover or guard against possibility of a defect. Many courts followed the *McCown* approach. By declining to distinguish between negligent failure to discover or guard against the possibility of a defect and other forms of contributory negligence, *McCown* held that no version of contributory negligence is applicable to strict tort liability.

2. The first sentence of Comment *n* suggests that the irrelevance of the defendant's negligence in strict tort liability implies that the plaintiff's negligence should also be irrelevant. Justice Pomeroy suggests the same point in *McCown* when he says that it is "a proper corollary" of the principle that defendants are subjected to liability without fault "that the lesser loss-bearing capacity of product users exists independently of their negligence or lack of it." Is this a sound argument? In this regard, how does contributory negligence differ from assumption of risk, which Justice Pomeroy believes is consistent with section 402A because of a "countervailing policy"?

3. Do the policies underlying strict tort liability support or undermine the application of contributory negligence to strict tort liability actions?

3. ASSUMPTION OF RISK

You should recall the basic defense of assumption of risk from your study of negligence. Assumption of risk has two distinct versions: express or contractual assumption of risk and implied assumption of risk. Express or contractual assumption of risk involves an actual agreement between the parties that one party rather than the other will bear the risk of injury, even if it is caused by the other party's negligence. A limit on liability—such as a shipping company limiting its liability for damage to a specific dollar amount—is a version of express assumption of risk for damages above the limit.

As long as a contractual assumption of risk is not unconscionable, it will be honored as a defense to an action for negligence. In actions for breach of warranty, express assumptions of risk are usually in the form of warranty disclaimers or limitations on damages. Disclaimers are governed by section 2–316 of the Uniform Commercial Code, and limitations on damages are governed by section 2–719. Both forms are permitted, but they are subject to important exceptions and formal requirements that are addressed in Chapters 2 and 4.

Express assumption of risk can affect a cause of action for misrepresentation under the rubric of justifiable reliance. A consumer who has expressly agreed to assume a risk might not have justifiably relied on a representation that the product would not impose the risk. Conversely, the representation and the express assumption of risk, being contrary to each other, might be interpreted in a way that negates the express assumption of risk.

Express, contractual assumption of risk as a defense to strict tort liability is a bit more complex. As in the case of breach of warranty, a general express assumption of risk as a defense to strict tort liability, is, in effect, a disclaimer. Since a disclaimer is not valid as a defense to strict tort liability, a general express assumption of risk is likewise invalid. *See* Restatement (Third) of Torts: Products Liability § 18:

> Disclaimers and limitations of remedies by product sellers or other distributors, waivers by products purchasers, and other similar contractual exculpations, oral or written, do not bar or reduce otherwise valid products liability claims against sellers or other distributors of new products for harm to persons.

As we shall see in the material on implied assumption of risk that follows, however, an express assumption of risk that demonstrates the plaintiff was actually aware of a specific risk imposed by the product might be a defense in strict tort liability.

Implied assumption of risk is a more common topic of litigation than is express assumption of risk. In its basic form, implied assumption of risk involves a plaintiff who voluntarily encounters a risk that he subjectively knows and appreciates, even though the parties have not expressly allocated the risk by oral or written agreement. It is not sufficient that the plaintiff *should* have known about the risk; she must *actually* be aware of and appreciate the nature of the risk, and she must voluntarily subject herself to it. Much litigation about assumption of risk as a defense in negligence cases addresses the questions of whether the plaintiff was actually aware of the risk and whether she voluntarily encountered it.

Under the traditional form of implied assumption of risk, the defendant is not required to prove that the plaintiff acted unreasonably by subjecting himself to the risk. Several courts, especially after the advent of comparative negligence schemes, have altered the traditional rule, holding that assumption of risk is applicable only when the plaintiff voluntarily encounters a known and appreciated risk that, under the circumstances, is an unreasonable risk to encounter. This change renders the defense of assumption of risk nothing more than a specific type of contributory negligence. Thus, some courts have appropriately characterized this change as an abandonment of assumption of risk as an independent defense in negligence actions. Regardless of the nomenclature, jurisdictions that use comparative negligence schemes typically include assumption of risk along with contributory negligence in a single percentage finding by the jury. Even in these jurisdictions, however, an express, contractual assumption of risk continues to be an absolute bar, according to its terms.

Courts often use the nomenclature *"volenti non fit injuria"* to refer to the defense of assumption of risk. Some courts distinguish in their nomenclature between parties who have a contractual relationship (such as an employment relationship) and parties who are strangers, using the term "assumption of risk" in the former situation and *"volenti non fit injuria"* in the latter. Even if different nomenclature is used, however, the contours of the defense remain the same.

The effect of implied assumption of risk is somewhat unclear in actions for breach of warranty. Some courts have held that implied assumption of risk is a separate defense, just as it is in a negligence action. *See, e.g.,* Pritchard v. Liggett & Myers Tobacco Co., 350 F.2d 479 (3d Cir.1965); Phillips v. Allen, 427 F.Supp. 876 (W.D.Pa.1977); Duncan v. Cessna Aircraft Co., 665 S.W.2d 414 (Tex.1984). But the Uniform Commercial Code does not itself establish such a defense.

Language in the Uniform Commercial Code and its comments suggests that a plaintiff's actual knowledge of a risk might negate the warranty itself or affect a determination of whether breach of the warranty was a proximate cause of the plaintiff's injuries. Comment 13 to section 2–314 (which deals with implied warranties of merchantability) provides that "[a]ction by the buyer following an examination of the goods which ought to have indicated the defect complained of can be shown as a matter bearing on whether the breach itself was the cause of the injury." Presumably, action after an inspection that actually reveals a defect will have the same effect.

Comment 8 to section 2–316 (which deals with disclaimers) states that "if the buyer discovers the defect and uses the goods anyway, * * * the resulting injuries may be found to result from his own action rather than proximately from a breach of warranty."

Several courts have used the rubric of proximate causation suggested by the comments to the Code rather than hold that implied assumption of risk is an independent defense. *See, e.g.,* Hensley v. Sherman Car Wash Equipment Co., 33 Colo.App. 279, 520 P.2d 146 (1974). In jurisdictions that have adopted comparative schemes for breach of warranty cases, the difference in approach might determine whether conduct that amounts to an assumption of risk is an absolute bar to recovery or merely a percentage reduction. The difference in approach might also affect a decision whether an assumption of risk by one person affects recovery by another person who is injured. If such conduct affects the scope of the warranty or proximate causation, it is difficult to limit the effect of the conduct to the person who engaged in it, or to use it merely to reduce the plaintiff's recovery under a comparative scheme.

In actions for misrepresentation, conduct that would constitute assumption of risk undermines the plaintiff's claim that he justifiably relied on the representation. *See, e.g.,* Klages v. General Ordnance Equipment Corp., 240 Pa.Super. 356, 367 A.2d 304 (1976); *cf.* Kolb v. Texas Employers' Ins. Ass'n, 585 S.W.2d 870, 872–73 (Tex.App. 1979).

Recall that Comment *n* to section 402A clearly states that implied voluntary assumption of risk is a defense to an action for strict tort liability, but requires that the plaintiff do so "unreasonably." From the beginning of strict tort liability, courts have uniformly recognized implied assumption of risk as a defense, either as an absolute bar or as a percentage reduction under a comparative scheme. The main issues have been whether the details of the defense are the same for strict tort liability as for negligence—for example, whether the defense applies only to unreasonable risks—and whether special issues arise in the context of products liability litigation concerning the plaintiff's actual awareness of the risk.

HEIL CO. v. GRANT
Court of Civil Appeals of Texas, 1976.
534 S.W.2d 916.

DUNAGAN, CHIEF JUSTICE.

This is a products liability case which involves the doctrines of assumption of risk and misuse. * * * Valmarie Grant and her children sued for the death of James Grant (hereinafter referred to as Decedent), their husband and father respectively. The defendant-appellant is the Heil Company, a major manufacturer of hydraulic hoists.

* * *

Decedent and Vernon [Grant] were working beneath the raised bed [of a dump truck] when it somehow descended. Vernon jumped away but Decedent did not. Heil Company's engineer found no malfunction in the hoist mechanism and concluded that the pullout cable had been tripped. Immediately before the accident, Vernon told Decedent that if he hit the pullout cable, the bed would come down.

* * *

Plaintiffs sued the Heil Company under a theory of strict liability for defective design of the hoist mechanism and for failure to warn of the hazard.

* * *

The Heil Company pleaded, offered evidence of and requested Special Issues on the defenses of assumption of risk and misuse. The trial court, applying the Dead Man's Statute, excluded that portion of Vernon Grant's testimony which related to those defenses and refused to submit Special Issues thereon since there was no other evidence to support such issues. Heil Company's primary contention before this court is that the exclusion of Vernon Grant's testimony was harmful error because that testimony was admissible and established or raised fact issues of those defenses.

* * *

Plaintiffs contend that Vernon Grant's warning to Decedent ("I stated * * * that if he hit the cable, the bed would come down") did not constitute evidence that Decedent "knew" of the risk. Plaintiffs argue that Decedent might not have heard, understood or remembered the warning and that Vernon Grant's testimony was merely evidence that Decedent *could* have known of the risk.

An injured person's knowledge of a dangerous condition or defect is measured subjectively; i.e., by that person's actual, conscious knowledge. *Massman–Johnson v. Gundolf,* 484 S.W.2d 555, 557 (Tex.1972). The fact that the injured person *should have known* of the danger will not support the assumption of risk defense. *Halepeska v. Callihan Interests, Inc.,* [371 S.W.2d 368 (Tex.1963)]. Sometimes, however, that person may know such facts as to be charged with knowledge of the danger. *Halepeska v. Callihan Interests, Inc.,* supra. This standard would be applied when it was difficult or impossible to determine the state of the injured person's mind; as it was in the instant case of a fatal injury. The "actual knowledge or charged knowledge" test has been applied in determining the strict liability of a supplier of defective products. See *Rourke v. Garza,* 530 S.W.2d 794 (Tex.1975).

* * *

Whether an injured person actually knew of the danger is peculiarly within the province of the jury. *Hillman–Kelley v. Pittman,* 489 S.W.2d 689, 692 (Tex.Civ.App.—El Paso 1972, n.w.h.). Here, there was some evidence from which the jury could have found that Decedent "knew" of the danger, to-wit: the fact that he had been told of the effect of hitting the pullout cable. Although the jury could also have found that Decedent did not know of the danger because he did not hear, understand or remember the warning, we are not able to say, as a matter of law, that he did not know of that danger.

Plaintiffs argue that even if Decedent had knowledge of some danger, there is no evidence that he knew of the specific defect involved. Knowledge of the general hazard involved in operating a punch-press machine will not support the assumption of risk defense. *Rhoads v. Service Machine Co.,* 329 F.Supp. 367 (E.D.Ark.1971). The general hazard in the instant case was working beneath the raised bed of the dump truck. Vernon Grant and Heil Company's engineer both concluded that the bed descended because the pullout cable was tripped. This evidence indicates that the specific danger was that striking the pullout cable would cause the bed to descend. The jury, upon consideration of Vernon Grant's testimony, could have found that Decedent knew of this specific hazard. Plaintiffs also contend that the requisite knowledge must be of a "defect" and that "knowledge that a phenomenon will occur in a product * * * is not knowledge that the product is dangerously defective." [Henderson v. Ford Motor Co., 519 S.W.2d 87, 89 (Tex. 1974)] * * * It is clear, however, that the assumption of risk defense is premised upon knowledge of the dangerous condition of a product rather than recognition of its defectiveness.

* * *

Plaintiffs argue that even if Decedent knew of the danger of the pullout cable, there is no evidence that he knew of the other dangerous defects, to-wit: the defectively designed control valve; the failure to supply a support brace; and the failure to instruct as to proper bracing procedures. These defects may well have been producing or proximate causes of the death in that (1) but for the defects, the death might not have occurred, and (2) the death was a foreseeable result of the defects. * * * In our opinion, however, all of the above producing causes were part of the same danger. The assumption of risk defense is based upon the injured person's awareness of the danger of injury rather than an awareness of the producing causes of the injury. Since there was some evidence that Decedent knew of the specific danger in hitting the pullout cable, plaintiffs' argument is without merit.

The danger encountered must be both known and appreciated to raise the assumption of risk defense. * * * Again, the test is subjective. * * * We look for some evidence that Decedent actually appreciated the risk or was in possession of facts from which he would be legally charged with appreciation of the danger. *Halepeska v. Callihan Interests, Inc.,* supra, 371 S.W.2d at 379. If by reason of age, or lack of information, experience, intelligence or judgment, Decedent did not understand the risk involved, he will not be taken to have assumed that risk. Restatement (Second) of Torts, Section 496D, comment c.

* * *

There is some evidence that Decedent might not have appreciated the danger of hitting the pullout cable. However, by reason of Decedent's information, age and experience, we conclude that there was some evidence of probative force that he did appreciate that danger. Thus, an issue for the jury exists.

Plaintiffs' final point in support of their contention of no evidence of the necessary elements of the assumption of risk defense is that Decedent's encounter of the risk was not shown to have been voluntary. A voluntary encounter means by free and intelligent choice. * * * We have thoroughly considered each of these arguments and find them to be without merit. We conclude that there was some evidence that would support a jury finding that Decedent's encounter with the risk was by free and intelligent choice.

Plaintiffs' second contention under * * * Point I is that any error in excluding the testimony of Vernon Grant which related to assumption of risk was harmless because that defense is inapplicable when strict liability is based upon a failure to warn of a dangerous condition. Plaintiffs rely upon statements to the effect that when there is a breach of the duty to warn, there is no assumption of the risk. * * * These statements were made in situations in which no warning had been given to the injured person. The function of the warning is to give that person knowledge and an opportunity to appreciate the danger. * * * The supplier of a defective product is usually in the best position to supply this warning but there is no reason why the warning cannot come from another source. "One who voluntarily chooses to use a chattel with a complete realization, *regardless of how it was acquired,* of the risks to which he thus exposes himself voluntarily assumes such risks * * *" 1 Hursh & Bailey, *American Law of Products Liability 2d,* sec. 2:107 (Emphasis added.)

* * *

Plaintiffs' final argument * * * is that any error in excluding evidence of assumption of risk was harmless because that defense is inapplicable when strict liability is based upon the defective design of a product being used in a manner reasonably foreseeable to the supplier. Plaintiffs argue that the supplier is in the best position to discover a design defect and should not be permitted to avoid liability on the ground that the injured person made a foolish judgment to encounter the danger. The thrust of this argument is that assumption of risk *should* not be applicable in any case when strict liability is based upon the defective design of a product. The defense of assumption of risk was held available in such a case in *Rourke v. Garza,* supra, 530 S.W.2d 794. Plaintiffs' contention is overruled.

Notes

1. Do the policies underlying products liability support or undermine the application of assumption of risk? In this regard, does assumption of risk differ from contributory negligence?

2. Note that without Vernon Grant's testimony, assumption of risk was not an issue for the jury, which meant that the plaintiff could recover. Implicit in this aspect of the case is that the defendant has the burden of proof on assumption of risk.

3. What was the *risk* that James Grant assumed? If one decides to "assume the risk" and play Russian roulette with a gun that has six chambers, would the risk assumed include that a second bullet had been secretly placed in one of the chambers by another participant?

4. Some courts have characterized the risk, for purposes of this defense, quite narrowly. Consider Haugen v. Minnesota Mining & Mfg. Co., 15 Wash.App. 379, 550 P.2d 71 (1976), in which plaintiff was blinded in one eye after the grinding wheel at which he was working exploded and propelled a

piece into his eye. Plaintiff was not wearing safety goggles that had been provided for him by his employer. The trial judge instructed the jury that for assumption of risk to exist, the defendant had to prove that the plaintiff "actually knew, appreciated, and voluntarily and unreasonably exposed himself to the specific defect and danger which caused his injuries." The court of appeals affirmed:

> If plaintiff assumed any risk at all, it is the risk of having dust or small particles of wood or metal lodged in his eye during the grinding process. He was obviously not aware of the latent defect in the structural integrity of the disc itself and the danger posed by that defect. This latent defect was not and probably could not have been known by the plaintiff. Plaintiff, therefore, could not have assumed the risk engendered by the defect.

Id. at 75. The Pennsylvania courts also have insisted on greater specificity in characterizing the risk for assumption of risk purposes. "For assumption of risk to apply, a plaintiff needn't understand the mechanical process but must be subjectively aware of the nature, character, and extent of the danger posed *by the specific attribute* which is allegedly defective; this requires more than a general awareness that the product is somehow dangerous." Mackowick v. Westinghouse Elec. Corp., 373 Pa.Super. 434, 541 A.2d 749 (1988); *see also* Lonon v. Pep Boys, Manny, Moe & Jack, 371 Pa.Super. 291, 538 A.2d 22 (1988); Warner Fruehauf Trailer Co., Inc. v. Boston, 654 A.2d 1272 (D.C. 1995).

5. As we shall see in the materials that follow, as courts moved toward away from contributory negligence and toward comparative responsibility assumption of the risk played a far less significant role in products liability actions. The Restatement (Third) of Torts: Apportionment of Liability § 2, Comment *i* treats implied assumption of risk as an element of comparative responsibility, thereby requiring a finding that the plaintiff's conduct was unreasonable and making the effect of such a finding that it would reduce, rather than bar, recovery. Many states have also abolished implied assumption of risk as a separate defense, either by court opinion or legislation. *See* Hornbeck v. Western States Fire Apparatus, Inc., 280 Or. 647, 572 P.2d 620, 622 (1977); Larsen v. Pacesetter Sys., Inc., 74 Haw. 1, 837 P.2d 1273 (1992) (calling assumption of risk bar, "absurd" in products liability setting, merged into comparative fault); Perez v. McConkey, 872 S.W.2d 897 (Tenn. 1994); Blackburn v. Dorta, 348 So.2d 287, 292–93 (Fla. 1977). With this merger of assumption of risk and contributory negligence does it make any difference whether the plaintiff actually has subjective knowledge of the defect and proceeds unreasonably, or merely "should have known of the danger" and then proceeds unreasonably?

4. COMPARATIVE RESPONSIBILITY

DALY v. GENERAL MOTORS CORP.
Supreme Court of California, 1978.
20 Cal.3d 725, 144 Cal.Rptr. 380, 575 P.2d 1162.

RICHARDSON, JUSTICE.

The most important of several problems which we consider is whether the principles of comparative negligence expressed by us in *Li v.*

Yellow Cab Co. (1975) 13 Cal.3d 804, 119 Cal.Rptr. 858, 532 P.2d 1226, apply to actions founded on strict products liability. We will conclude that they do.

* * *

In the early hours of October 31, 1970, decedent Kirk Daly, a 36–year–old attorney, was driving his Opel southbound on the Harbor Freeway in Los Angeles. The vehicle, while traveling at a speed of 50–70 miles per hour, collided with and damaged 50 feet of metal divider fence. After the initial impact between the left side of the vehicle and the fence the Opel spun counterclockwise, the driver's door was thrown open, and Daly was forcibly ejected from the car and sustained fatal head injuries. It was equally undisputed that had the deceased remained in the Opel his injuries, in all probability, would have been relatively minor.

* * * The sole theory of plaintiffs' complaint was strict liability for damages allegedly caused by a defective product, namely, an improperly designed door latch claimed to have been activated by the impact. It was further asserted that, but for the faulty latch, decedent would have been restrained in the vehicle and, although perhaps injured, would not have been killed. Thus, the case involves a so-called "second collision" in which the "defect" did not contribute to the original impact, but only to the "enhancement" of injury.

* * *

Over plaintiffs' objections, defendants were permitted to introduce evidence indicating that: (1) the Opel was equipped with a seat belt-shoulder harness system, and a door lock, either of which if used, it was contended, would have prevented Daly's ejection from the vehicle; (2) Daly used neither the harness system nor the lock; (3) the 1970 Opel owner's manual contained warnings that seat belts should be worn and doors locked when the car was in motion for "accident security"; and (4) Daly was intoxicated at the time of collision, which evidence the jury was advised was admitted for the limited purpose of determining whether decedent had used the vehicle's safety equipment. After relatively brief deliberations the jury returned a verdict favoring all defendants, and plaintiffs appeal from the ensuing adverse judgment.

Strict Products Liability and Comparative Fault

In response to plaintiffs' assertion that the "intoxication-nonuse" evidence was improperly admitted, defendants contend that the deceased's own conduct contributed to his death. Because plaintiffs' case rests upon strict products liability based on improper design of the door latch and because defendants assert a failure in decedent's conduct, namely, his alleged intoxication and nonuse of safety equipment, without which the accident and ensuing death would not have occurred, there is thereby posed the overriding issue in the case, should comparative principles apply in strict products liability actions?

* * *

[In Li v. Yellow Cab Co., 13 Cal.3d 804, 119 Cal.Rptr. 858, 532 P.2d 1226 (1975), we adopted] a "pure" form of comparative negligence which, when present, reduced but did not prevent plaintiff's recovery. * * * We held that the defense of assumption of risk, insofar as it is no more than a variant of contributory negligence, was merged into the assessment of liability in proportion to fault. * * * Within the broad guidelines therein announced, we left to trial courts discretion in the particular implementation of the new doctrine.

* * *

Those counseling against the recognition of comparative fault principles in strict products liability cases vigorously stress, perhaps equally, not only the conceptual, but also the semantic difficulties incident to such a course. The task of merging the two concepts is said to be impossible, that "apples and oranges" cannot be compared, that "oil and water" do not mix, and that strict liability, which is not founded on negligence or fault, is inhospitable to comparative principles. The syllogism runs, contributory negligence was only a defense to negligence, comparative negligence only affects contributory negligence, therefore comparative negligence cannot be a defense to strict liability. * * * While fully recognizing the theoretical and semantic distinctions between the twin principles of strict products liability and traditional negligence, we think they can be blended or accommodated.

The inherent difficulty in the "apples and oranges" argument is its insistence on fixed and precise definitional treatment of legal concepts. In the evolving areas of both products liability and tort defenses, however, there has developed much conceptual overlapping and interweaving in order to attain substantial justice. The concept of strict liability itself, as we have noted, arose from dissatisfaction with the wooden formalisms of traditional tort and contract principles in order to protect the consumer of manufactured goods. Similarly, increasing social awareness of its harsh "all or nothing" consequences led us in *Li* to moderate the impact of traditional contributory negligence in order to accomplish a fairer and more balanced result. We acknowledged an intermixing of defenses of contributory negligence and assumption of risk and formally effected a type of merger.

* * *

Furthermore, the "apples and oranges" argument may be conceptually suspect. It has been suggested that the term "contributory negligence," one of the vital building blocks upon which much of the argument is based, may indeed itself be a misnomer since it lacks the first element of the classical negligence formula, namely, a duty of care owing to another. A highly respected torts authority, Dean William Prosser, has noted this fact by observing, "It is perhaps unfortunate that contributory negligence is called negligence at all. 'Contributory fault' would be a more descriptive term. Negligence as it is commonly understood is conduct which creates an undue risk of harm to others. Contributory negligence is conduct which involves an undue risk of harm to the actor himself. Negligence requires a duty, an obligation of conduct to another person. Contributory negligence involves no duty, unless we are to be so ingenious as to say that the plaintiff is under an obligation to protect the defendant against liability for the consequences of his own negligence." (Prosser, Law of Torts, *supra*, § 65, p. 418.)

We think, accordingly, the conclusion may fairly be drawn that the terms "comparative negligence," "contributory negligence" and "assumption of risk" do not, standing alone, lend themselves to the exact measurements of a micrometer-caliper, or to such precise definition as to divert us from otherwise strong and consistent countervailing policy considerations. Fixed semantic consistency at this point is less important than the attainment of a just and equitable result. The interweaving of concept and terminology in this area suggests a judicial posture that is flexible rather than doctrinaire.

We pause at this point to observe that where, as here, a consumer or user sues the manufacturer or designer alone, technically, neither fault nor conduct is really compared functionally. The conduct of one party in combination with the product of another, or perhaps the placing of a defective article in the stream of projected and anticipated use, may produce the ultimate injury. In such a case, as in the situation before us, we think the term "equitable apportionment or allocation of loss" may be more descriptive than "comparative fault."

Given all of the foregoing, we are, in the wake of *Li*, disinclined to resolve the important issue before us by the simple expedient of matching linguistic labels which have evolved either for convenience or by custom. Rather, we consider it more useful to examine the foundational reasons underlying the creation of strict products liability in California to ascertain whether the purposes of the doctrine would be defeated or diluted by adoption of comparative principles. We imposed strict liability against the manufacturer and in favor of the user or consumer in order to relieve injured consumers "from *problems of proof* inherent in pursuing negligence * * * and warranty * * * remedies, * * *." (*Cronin v. J.B.E. Olson Corp., supra*, 8 Cal.3d at p. 133, 104 Cal.Rptr. at p. 442, 501 P.2d at p. 1162, italics added; *Greenman v. Yuba Power Products, Inc., supra*, 59 Cal.2d at p. 63, 27 Cal.Rptr. 697, 377 P.2d 897; *Escola v. Coca Cola Bottling Co.* (1944) 24 Cal.2d 453, 461–462, 150 P.2d 436 (conc. opn. by Traynor, J.).) As we have noted, we sought to place the burden of loss on manufacturers rather than " * * * injured persons *who are powerless to protect themselves * * *.*" (*Greenman, supra*, 59 Cal.2d at p. 63, 27 Cal.Rptr. at p. 701, 377 P.2d at p. 901, italics added; see *Escola, supra*, 24 Cal.2d at p. 462, 150 P.2d 436; *Price v. Shell Oil Co.* (1970) 2 Cal.3d 245, 251, 85 Cal.Rptr. 178, 182, 466 P.2d 722, 726 ["*protection of otherwise defenseless victims* of manufacturing defects and the spreading throughout society of the cost of compensating them"] (italics added).)

The foregoing goals, we think, will not be frustrated by the adoption of comparative principles. Plaintiffs will continue to be relieved of proving that the manufacturer or distributor was negligent in the production, design, or dissemination of the article in question. Defendant's liability for injuries caused by a defective product remains strict. The principle of protecting the defenseless is likewise preserved, for plaintiff's recovery will be reduced *only* to the extent that his own lack of reasonable care contributed to his injury. The cost of compensating the victim of a defective product, albeit proportionately reduced, remains on defendant manufacturer, and will, through him, be "spread among society." However, we do not permit plaintiff's own conduct relative to the product to escape unexamined, and as to that share of plaintiff's damages which flows from his own fault we discern no reason of policy why it should, following *Li,* be borne by others. Such a result would directly contravene the principle announced in *Li,* that loss should be assessed equitably in proportion to fault.

* * *

A second objection to the application of comparative principles in strict products liability cases is that a manufacturer's incentive to produce safe products will thereby be reduced or removed. While we fully recognize this concern we think, for several reasons, that the problem is more shadow than substance. First, of course, the manufacturer cannot avoid its continuing liability for a defective product even when the plaintiff's own conduct has contributed to his injury. The manufacturer's liability, and therefore its incentive to avoid and correct product defects, remains; its exposure will be lessened only to the extent that the trier finds that the victim's conduct contributed to his injury. Second, as a practical matter a manufacturer, in a particular case, cannot assume that the user of a defective product upon whom an injury is visited will be blameworthy. Doubtless, many users are free of fault, and a defect is at least as likely as not to be exposed by an entirely innocent plaintiff who will obtain full recovery. In such cases the manufacturer's incentive toward safety both in design and production is wholly unaffected. Finally, we must observe that under the present law, which recognizes assumption of risk as a complete defense to products liability, the curious and cynical message is that it profits the manufacturer to make his product so defective that in the event of injury he can argue that the user had to be aware of its patent defects. To that extent the incentives are inverted. We conclude, accordingly, that no substantial or significant impairment of the safety incentives of defendants will occur by the adoption of comparative principles.

In passing, we note one important and felicitous result if we apply comparative principles to strict products liability. This arises from the fact that under present law when plaintiff sues in negligence his own contributory negligence, however denominated, may diminish but cannot wholly defeat his recovery. When he sues in strict products liability, however, his "assumption of risk" *completely bars* his recovery. Under *Li,* as we have noted, "assumption of risk" is merged into comparative principles. (13 Cal.3d at p. 825, 119 Cal.Rptr. 858, 532 P.2d 1226.) The consequence is that after *Li* in a negligence action, plaintiff's conduct which amounts to "negligent" assumption of risk no longer defeats plaintiff's recovery. Identical conduct, however, in a strict liability case acts as a complete bar under rules heretofore applicable. Thus, strict products liability, which was developed to free injured consumers from the constraints imposed by traditional negligence and warranty theories, places a consumer plaintiff in a worse position than would be the case were his claim founded on simple negligence. This, in turn, rewards adroit pleading and selection of theories. The application of comparative principles to strict liability obviates this bizarre anomaly by treating alike the defenses to both negligence and strict products liability actions. In each instance the defense, if established, will reduce but not bar plaintiff's claim.

A third objection to the merger of strict liability and comparative fault focuses on the claim that, as a practical matter, triers of fact, particularly jurors, cannot assess, measure, or compare plaintiff's negligence with defendant's strict liability. We are unpersuaded by the argument and are convinced that jurors are able to undertake a fair apportionment of liability.

* * *

We note that the majority of our sister states which have addressed the problem, either by statute or judicial decree, have extended comparative principles to strict products liability.

* * *

Moreover, we are further encouraged in our decision herein by noting that the apparent majority of scholarly commentators has urged adoption of the rule which we announce herein.

* * *

Having examined the principal objections and finding them not insurmountable, and persuaded by logic, justice, and fundamental fairness, we conclude that a system of comparative fault should be and it is hereby extended to actions founded on strict products liability. In such cases the separate defense of "assumption of risk," to the extent that it is a form of contributory negligence, is abolished. While, as we have suggested, on the particular facts before us, the term "equitable apportionment of loss" is more accurately descriptive of the process, nonetheless, the term "comparative fault" has gained such wide acceptance by courts and in the literature that we adopt its use herein.

[The court then held that its decision would not be applied retroactively, not even to the case before it. Under the law existing at the time of trial, evidence of the plaintiff's intoxication and failure to use a seat belt should have been excluded.]

The judgment is reversed.

TOBRINER, CLARK and MANUEL, JJ., concur.

* * *

JEFFERSON, JUSTICE, concurring and dissenting.

* * * The majority * * * does not consider it significant that it is unable to determine what labels should be given to the new comparative principles—whether the new doctrine should be known as comparative fault, equitable apportionment of loss, or equitable allocation of loss. This inability to give the new doctrine an appropriate label is some indication of the shaky ground upon which the majority has decided to tread.

The majority rejects what I consider to be a sound criticism of its holding—that it is illogical and illusory to compare elements or factors that are not reasonably subject to comparison. The majority states that it is convinced that jurors will be able to compare the noncomparables—plaintiff's negligence with defendant's strict liability for a defective product—and still reach a fair apportionment of liability.

I consider the majority conclusion a case of wishful thinking and an application of an impractical, ivory-tower approach. The majority's assumption that a jury is capable of making a fair apportionment between a plaintiff's negligent conduct and a defendant's defective product is no more logical or convincing than if a jury were to be instructed that it should add a quart of milk (representing plaintiff's negligence) and a metal bar three feet in length (representing defendant's strict liability for a defective product), and that the two added together equal 100 percent-the total fault for plaintiff's injuries; that plaintiff's quart of milk is then to be assigned its percentage of the 100 percent * * *.

* * *

What the majority envisions as a fair apportionment of liability to be undertaken by the jury will constitute nothing more than an *unfair reduction* in the plaintiff's total damages suffered, resulting from a jury process that necessarily is predicated on speculation, conjecture and guesswork. Because the legal concept of negligence is so utterly different from the legal concept of a product defective by reason of manufacture or design, a plaintiff's negligence is no more capable of being rationally compared with a defendant's defective product to determine what percentage each contributes to plaintiff's total damages than is the quart of milk with the metal bar-posed in the above illustration.

* * *

The guessing game that will be imposed on juries by the application of comparative negligence principles to defective product liability cases will be further enhanced in those cases in which several defendants are joined in an action-some being sued on a negligence theory and others on the defective product theory and where there are several plaintiffs whose conduct may range from no negligence at all to varying degrees of negligence. The jury will be required to determine percentages of fault with respect to all the parties (and perhaps some nonparties) by seeking to compare and evaluate the *conduct* of certain parties with the *product* of other parties to produce 100 percent of fault as the necessary starting point in order to calculate a reduction in the damages suffered by each plaintiff found to be negligent. I cannot agree with the majority that such a process is reasonably workable or that it will produce an equitable result to injured plaintiffs. If a just or fair result is reached by a jury under the majority's holding, it will be strictly accidental and accomplished by pure happenstance.

* * *

There is no common denominator by which factors such as pounds, circles, quarts, triangles, inches, and squares can be added together for a total so that a determination can be made of the percentage contribution of each to the total.

* * *

BIRD, C.J., concurs.

MOSK, JUSTICE, dissenting.

I dissent.

This will be remembered as the dark day when this court, which heroically took the lead in originating the doctrine of products liability (*Greenman v. Yuba Power Products, Inc.* (1963) 59 Cal.2d 57, 27 Cal. Rptr. 697, 377 P.2d 897) and steadfastly resisted efforts to inject concepts of negligence into the newly designed tort (*Cronin v. J.B.E. Olson Corp.* (1972) 8 Cal.3d 121, 104 Cal.Rptr. 433, 501 P.2d 1153), inexplicably turned 180 degrees and beat a hasty retreat almost back to square one. The pure concept of products liability so pridefully fashioned and nurtured by this court for the past decade and a half is reduced to a shambles.

The majority inject a foreign object—the tort of negligence—into the tort of products liability by the simple expedient of calling negligence something else: on some pages their opinion speaks of "comparative fault," on others reference is to "comparative principles," and elsewhere the term "equitable apportionment" is employed, although this is clearly not a proceeding in equity. But a rose is a rose and negligence is negligence; thus the majority find that despite semantic camouflage they must rely on *Li v. Yellow Cab Co.* (1975) 13 Cal.3d 804, 119 Cal.Rptr. 858, 532 P.2d 1226, even though *Li* is purely and simply a negligence case which merely rejects contributory negligence and substitutes therefor comparative negligence.

* * *

The defective product is comparable to a time bomb ready to explode; it maims its victims indiscriminately, the righteous and the evil, the careful and the careless. Thus when a faulty design or otherwise defective product is involved, the litigation should not be diverted to consideration of the negligence of the plaintiff. The liability issues are simple: was the product or its design faulty, did the defendant inject the defective product into the stream of commerce, and did the defect cause the injury? The conduct of the ultimate consumer-victim who used the product in the contemplated or foreseeable manner is wholly irrelevant to those issues.

The majority devote considerable effort to rationalizing what has been described as a mixture of apples and oranges. Their point might be persuasive if there were some authority recognizing a defense of contributory products liability, for which they are now substituting comparative products liability. However, all our research to discover such apples and oranges has been fruitless. The conclusion is inescapable that the majority, in avoiding approval of comparative negligence in name as a defense to products liability, are thereby originating a new defense that can only be described as comparative products liability.

* * *

The majority deny their opinion diminishes the therapeutic effect of products liability upon producers of defective products. It seems self-evident that procedures which evaluate the injured consumer's conduct in each instance, and thus eliminate or reduce the award against the producer or distributor of a defective product, are not designed as an effective incentive to maximum responsibility to consumers. The converse is more accurate: the motivation to avoid polluting the stream of commerce with defective products increases in direct relation to the size of potential damage awards.

In sum, I am convinced that since the negligence of the defendant is irrelevant in products liability cases, the negligence—call it contributory or comparative—of the plaintiff is also irrelevant.

Notes

1. Justice Mosk's opinion in *Daly* reflects a common objection to applying comparative responsibility principles to products liability cases. In addition to applying comparative principles, the court also recognizes the plaintiff's negligence as a defense. Why is it that Mosk thinks an analysis of the plaintiff's negligence is intrinsically incompatible with the theory of strict tort liability? Does *Daly* suggest that originally the real objection to contributory negligence as a defense to products liability cases was the draconian, all-or-nothing effect of contributory negligence? Note that the advent of comparative responsibility affected the *content*, not just the *effect*, of the defenses in some jurisdictions. Courts are much more likely to recognize a defense when its effect is to reduce a plaintiff's recovery than when its effect is to bar a plaintiff's recovery.

2. Following the advent of comparative responsibility, many states faced the problem of determining whether to apply their comparative responsibility scheme or a similar comparative "allocation" scheme to products liability and breach of warranty actions. As the opinion in *Daly* indicates,

most states that have comparative responsibility schemes have applied some type of comparative scheme to strict tort liability.

3. Justice Jefferson's opinion in *Daly* reflects a common objection to the application of comparative fault principles to products liability: asking a jury to compare the product's defectiveness with the plaintiff's conduct is like asking it to compare apples and oranges (or, in his colorful terms, a quart of milk and a three foot metal bar). Is this really a problem? Don't we compare seemingly "noncomparable" items all the time, such as when we decide how much money to spend on food versus education? Is Justice Jefferson's analogy of a comparison between quarts and feet an apt one? Aren't there ways to compare apples and oranges? How might a court compare a product's defectiveness with the plaintiff's conduct? Consider the Restatement (Third) of Torts: Apportionment of Liability § 8, Comment a:

> Of course, it is not possible to precisely compare conduct that falls into different categories, such as intentional conduct, negligent conduct, and conduct governed by strict liability, because the various theories of recovery are incommensurate. However, courts routinely compare seemingly incommensurate values, such as when they balance safety and productivity in negligence or products liability law. "Assigning shares of responsibility" may be a less confusing phrase because it suggests that the factfinder, after considering the relevant factors, *assigns* shares of comparative responsibility rather than *compares* incommensurate quantifies. Nevertheless, the term "comparative responsibility" is used pervasively by courts and legislatures to describe percentage-allocation systems.

Does "assigning" rather than "comparing" help in apportioning liability between plaintiff and defendants?

4. What precisely should be compared in cases like *Daly*, and how should the jury be instructed to make this comparison? There is a declaration in Murray v. Fairbanks Morse, 610 F.2d 149 (3d Cir.1979)(Virgin Islands) that, in strict products liability actions, the comparison should be on the basis of causal contribution to the injuries, and not on the basis of fault. Texas briefly adopted a comparative causation approach in Duncan v. Cessna Aircraft Co., 665 S.W.2d 414 (Tex. 1984); *See also,* Mauch v. Manufacturers Sales & Serv., 345 N.W.2d 338 (N.D.1984); Webb v. Navistar Intern. Transp. Corp., 166 Vt. 119, 692 A.2d 343 (1996). Is this task any easier than comparing fault? The Restatement (Third) of Torts: Apportionment of Liability uses the term "comparative responsibility," explaining:

> 'Responsibility' is a general and neutral term. Assigning shares of 'fault' or 'negligence' can be misleading because some causes of action are not based on negligence or fault. Assigning shares of 'causation' wrongly suggests that indivisible injuries jointly caused by two or more actors can be divided on the basis of causation. Assigning shares of 'culpability' could be misleading if it were not made clear that 'culpability' refers to 'legal culpability,' which may include strict liability.

Id. § 8, Comment a. Can you imagine situations where the different tests might lead to different comparative responsibility conclusions? See the discussion on apportioning on the basis of causation *and* responsibility in Section B of this Chapter, page 650 *infra*.

5. In Sandford v. Chevrolet Division of General Motors, 292 Or. 590, 642 P.2d 624 (1982), the Oregon Supreme Court grappled with the problem of what is to be compared in a comparative allocation scheme applied to strict tort liability. Justice Linde's analysis of the possibilities is instructive. Notice that his analysis must account for the Oregon statute. Many states have adopted comparative responsibility by statute, so their application of a comparative scheme to strict tort liability must account for the statute's provisions:

> A second problem posed by the statute is the question exactly what is to be assessed in determining the "percentage of fault attributable to the person" seeking recovery, and whether that person's fault was "greater than the combined fault of the person or persons against whom recovery is sought." The question has puzzled commentators as well as courts. At least three views are possible.
>
> A. *Quantifying "fault."* The first is that the formula calls upon the factfinder to assess the relative magnitude of the parties' respective "fault." As stated by a leading textbook on these laws: "The process is *not* allocation of physical causation, which could be scientifically apportioned, but rather of allocating *fault,* which cannot be scientifically measured." Schwartz, Comparative Negligence 276 (1974). It has been recognized that fault is an evaluation that does not lend itself to quantification, so that a comparison of fault magnifies the subjective elements already intrinsic to the ordinary judgment of negligence. This is true even in assigning proportions to two or more distinct types of negligence, but critics have found a greater theoretical obstacle when the responsibility of one party is grounded in fault other than negligence, or in no fault at all. The obstacle is greater where strict products liability is explained as a device for spreading losses from economic activity regardless of fault, but this court early disavowed that explanation, at least in the absence of legislation.
>
> * * *
>
> B. *"Comparative causation."* Some courts, applying comparative responsibility law to products liability under statutes different from ours or under no statute, have tried to escape the difficulty by stating that the allocation of damages is to reflect relative causation, that is to say, an assessment of the proportion in which the plaintiff's injuries were caused by the product defect on the one hand and by plaintiff's own negligence on the other. * * * They have done so in the belief that this is conceptually more logical or pragmatically easier than to compare the defect of a product with the negligence of one whom it has injured.
>
> * * * With due respect to these courts, however, we are not persuaded that the concept of "comparative causation" is more cogent or meaningful than comparative fault, if by "causation" is meant some relation of cause and effect in the physical world rather than the very attribution of responsibility for which "causation" is to serve as the premise.

Both the defect and the plaintiff's fault must in fact be causes of one injury before a question of apportionment of fault arises.

* * *

The concept of apportioning causation must be tested on the assumption that both causes had to join to produce the injury for which damages are to be allocated. There are cases in which it may be possible to segregate the harm done by one cause from different or incremental harm done by a second cause, so as to apply proportional allocation to the additional harm only. * * * Once it is assumed, however, that two or more distinct causes had to occur to produce an indivisible injury, we doubt that the purpose of the proportional fault concept is to subject the combined causation to some kind of vector analysis, even in the rare case of simultaneous, physically commensurable forces. In most cases, it would be a vain exercise to search for a common physical measure for the causative effect of a product defect and of the injured party's negligent conduct.

C. *Mixing "fault" with "proximate" causation.* A third view considers it futile to attempt to explain what is to be compared, because it is equally illogical to compare strict liability with negligence and to quantify the relative causative effect of either when it would have caused no harm in the absence of the other. Thus [Professor] Twerski, in the cited article, describes the technical problems of making the comparison as a "red herring": "The short answer to the dilemma of how one can compare strict liability and negligence is that one must simply close one's eyes and accomplish the task." 10 Ind.L.Rev. 796, 806–808.

* * *

In part this * * * view rests on the assumption that rational analysis in tort cases dissolves in the collegial judgment of juries. That is probably an unwarranted generalization; ability and effort to decide in accordance with law can be expected to differ from one jury to the next with such variables as the makeup of the particular jury, with the quality of evidence and advocacy, and not least with the rationality of the legal formulations in which the court explains the jury's task to it.

In any event, the assumption does not let us escape the need to state coherent rules of liability. Some tort cases are tried to the court without a jury * * *. Trial judges must know on what findings an apportionment of damages depends, whether these are to be made by the judge or by a jury. Our system of appeal as well as trial predicates that jurors will conscientiously attempt to apply the law if it is explained in comprehensible terms. * * * A juror who wants to know how to treat cause and how to treat fault is entitled to an answer, whatever comes of it in a collective decision. Counsel need to know whether to address the relative gravity of the parties' fault or to seek expert testimony on the relative impact of their respective fault in causing the asserted harm. We cannot dismiss the question as a distinction without a difference.

* * *

D. *Proportionate fault under ORS 18.470.* ORS 18.470, *supra,* by its terms applies whenever "the fault attributable to the person seeking recovery was not greater than the combined fault of the person or persons against whom recovery is sought." If there was such fault, "any damages allowed shall be diminished in the proportion to the percentage of fault attributable to the person recovering."

* * *

ORS 18.470 falls within the first of the different approaches that we have reviewed. It calls upon the factfinder to assess and quantify fault. If the plaintiff's conduct is not faultless, the assessment has two purposes: to determine whether her fault is "not greater than" that of defendants, and if it is not, then to reduce the plaintiff's recovery of damages "in the proportion to the percentage of fault attributable to" the plaintiff. The question remains against what standard this "percentage of fault" introduced by the 1975 amendment is to be measured.

The answer is implicit in the two steps found in the statute, one in the amended ORS 18.470 and the second in section 2 of the act, codified in ORS 18.480. First, if the plaintiff's behavior which was one cause of the injury is alleged to have been negligent or otherwise "fault," it is to be measured against behavior that would have been faultless under the circumstances. The factfinder is to determine the degree to which the plaintiff's behavior fell short of that norm and express this deficit as a numerical percentage, which then is applied to diminish the recoverable damages. There necessarily must be some comparable assessment of the fault attributable to defendants as a departure from the norm invoked against them (which, in products liability, will involve the magnitude of the defect rather than negligence or moral "blameworthiness") in order to determine which is greater. In this comparison, the benchmark for assessing a defendant's fault for marketing a product which is dangerously defective in design, manufacture, or warning is what the product should have been without the defect. The benchmark for the injured claimant's fault is conduct which would not be unlawful or careless in any relevant respect.

* * *

If the claimant's fault in this sense is greater than the fault of defendants, recovery is barred. Thereafter, ORS 18.470 standing alone does not seem to assign any further role to the magnitude of defendants' fault in calculating the percentage of plaintiff's damages that she may recover. Section 2 of the 1975 act, however, added directions for the second step. ORS 18.480 provides:

"(1) When requested by any party the trier of fact shall answer special questions indicating:

"(a) The amount of damages to which a party seeking recovery would be entitled, assuming that party not to be at fault;

"(b) The degree of each party's fault expressed as a percentage of the total fault attributable to all parties represented in the action.

"(2) A jury shall be informed of the legal effect of its answer to the questions listed in subsection (1) of this section."

Accordingly, after determining whether and how far each party's conduct was at fault, measured against the norm governing that party's conduct, these respective degrees of fault are to be converted into a percentage which will be applied to the plaintiff's total damages to determine his actual recovery.

To summarize: When an injured claimant's misconduct is a cause in fact of the injury, it can defeat a products liability claim if the claimant's fault is "greater than" the defendants' combined fault involved in marketing the defective product. If it is not greater, plaintiff's fault proportionately reduces her recoverable damages. "Fault" includes contributory negligence except for such unobservant, inattentive, ignorant, or awkward failure of the injured party to discover the defect or to guard against it as is taken into account in finding the particular product dangerously defective.

* * *

6. As in Oregon, most jurisdictions have adopted comparative fault principles in products liability cases through legislation. *See* Smith v. Ingersoll–Rand Co., 14 P.3d 990 (Alaska 2000) (interpreting the 1986 Alaska tort reform act). Webb v. Navistar Intern. Transp. Corp., 166 Vt. 119, 692 A.2d 343 (1996) contains a useful summary of the movement to comparative responsibility in many jurisdictions.

7. A few jurisdictions have refused to adopt comparative responsibility in products cases, often because the state comparative negligence statute is limited to negligence cases. In Bowling v. Heil Co., 31 Ohio St.3d 277, 511 N.E.2d 373 (1987), following Ohio Rev.Code § 2315.19, the Ohio Supreme Court refused to inject a plaintiff's negligence into the law of products liability.

8. Section 17 of the Restatement (Third) of Torts: Products Liability reflects the majority position and applies comparative responsibility to all types of consumer misconduct.

Apportionment Of Responsibility Between Or Among Plaintiff, Sellers And Distributors Of Defective Products, And Others

(a) A plaintiff's recovery of damages for harm caused by a product defect may be reduced if the conduct of the plaintiff combines with the product defect to cause the harm and the plaintiff's conduct fails to conform to generally applicable rules establishing appropriate standards of care.

(b) The manner and extent of the reduction under Subsection (a) and the apportionment of plaintiff's recovery among multiple defendants are governed by generally applicable rules apportioning responsibility.

9. A few states, even while adopting comparative fault principles for products liability cases, continue to hold that mere failure to discover a defect is not negligence as a matter of law. *See* Sandford v. Chevrolet Div. General Motors, 292 Or. 590, 642 P.2d 624 (1982); General Motors v.

Sanchez, 997 S.W.2d 584 (Tex. 1999). How frequently would the failure to discover a defect be negligent?

10. *Daly* involved the application of comparative fault to strict products liability. What about breach of warranty and innocent representation under section 402B? Is there any reason to apply comparative fault to strict tort liability but not to these other causes of action? What should be compared if the defendant has breached an express warranty or innocently misrepresented the product? How will liability be apportioned in a case in which a plaintiff includes claims based on warranty, misrepresentation, negligence and products liability?

11. For discussions of comparative fault in products liability cases,, see Fischer, Products Liability—Applicability of Comparative Negligence, 43 Mo.L.Rev. 431 (1978); Levine, Strict Products Liability and Comparative Negligence: The Collision of Fault and No Fault, 14 San Diego L.Rev. 337 (1978); Twerski, The Use and Abuse of Comparative Negligence in Products Liability, 10 Ind.L.Rev. 796 (1977); Davis, Individual and Institutional Responsibility: A Vision for Comparative Fault in Products Liability, 39 Villanova L.Rev. 281 (1994); McNichols, The Relevance of the Plaintiff's Misconduct in Strict Tort Products Liability, The Advent of Comparative Responsibility and the Proposed Restatement (Third) of Torts, 47 Okla.L.Rev. 201 (1994); Owen, Products Liability: User Misconduct Defenses, 52 S.C.L.Rev. 1 (2000).

5. PRODUCT MISUSE

Comment h of Restatement section 402A provides that a product is not defective when it is safe for normal handling and that an injury resulting from abnormal handling, e.g. a bottled beverage knocked against a radiator to remove the cap, the seller is not liable. This language parallels Justice Traynor's position in *Greenman* that the maker of the defendant was liable for a defect in it products only if the plaintiff "was injured while using the Shopsmith in a way it was intended to be used * * *." These provisions reflect the common law rule that misuse is a defense in products cases.

As is the case with assumption of the risk, the role of misuse is diminished in the comparative fault world. A substantial majority of states now apply comparative fault principles to products cases and most of these courts do not limit comparative fault to instances of product misuse or assumption of risk. *See* Smith v. Ingersoll–Rand Co., 14 P.3d 990 (Alaska 2000) (all forms of plaintiff misconduct now relevant in products cases). However, this defense is far from dead. Misuse lives along side of comparative fault in some states and other states continue to hold that ordinary negligence is not a defense in product cases, thereby restricting plaintiffs to misuse and assumption of risk arguments.

JIMENEZ v. SEARS, ROEBUCK & CO.
Supreme Court of Arizona, In Banc, 1995.
183 Ariz. 399, 904 P.2d 861.

FELDMAN, CHIEF JUSTICE.

Richard and Amanda Jimenez (Plaintiffs) brought this products liability action against Sears, Roebuck & Co. (Defendant), alleging it sold them a defective and unreasonably dangerous power tool. Defendant asserted the defense of product misuse and asked the trial court to instruct the jury according to the principles of comparative fault contained in A.R.S. §§ 12–2501 to 12–2509, the Uniform Contribution Among Tortfeasors Act (UCATA), so that Plaintiffs' damages could be reduced in proportion to their degree of fault. The trial court refused to so instruct. On review, we must decide whether the 1987 version of UCATA changes misuse from an all-or-nothing defense to one of comparative fault, thus permitting reduction in damages. * * *

FACTS AND PROCEDURAL HISTORY

Richard Jimenez bought a hand-held electric disc grinder from Defendant. Before operating it, Richard read the owner's manual, checked that the disc was tightly attached, connected the power cord, and briefly tested the grinder to see that it ran properly. He then used the tool to smooth down a steel weld on the top, flat part of a trailer tongue, stopping every several minutes to avoid overheating the machine. After about 45 minutes' use, the disc shattered, sending fragments into Richard's body and causing serious injury.

Plaintiffs filed a tort action, alleging that the grinder Defendant sold was defective and unreasonably dangerous and proximately caused Richard's injury and Amanda's loss of consortium. Defendant argued that Richard misused the grinder by failing to wear a protective apron while operating the tool, as recommended in the owner's manual, and by positioning the grinder so that the safety guard did not fully shield his body from the spinning grinding disc.

* * *

While grinding a welding spot on the trailer, Richard used the grinder in several different positions. Defendant claims that Richard used the tool improperly by reaching too far across the trailer tongue and turning the safety guard away from him. Richard denies that he held the grinder too far from his body for proper control and claims that the guard was partially facing him when the disc exploded.

Upon submitting the case to the jury, the trial judge instructed the jury on the defense of product misuse. In pertinent part, the instructions read:

Defendant is not at fault if defendant proves the following:

(1) The product was used ... for a purpose, in a manner or in an activity not reasonably foreseeable by defendant, or contrary to any express and adequate instructions or warnings appearing on or attached to the product, or on its original container or wrapping, and plaintiff knew, or with the exercise of reasonable and diligent care should have known, of the warnings or instructions; and

(2) *Such use ... was the only cause of plaintiff's injury.*

(Emphasis added.) This instruction followed our interpretation of A.R.S. § 12-683(3).[1] *See Gosewisch v. American Honda Motor Co.*, 153 Ariz. 400, 407, 737 P.2d 376, 383 (1987). It entitled Defendant to a verdict if Richard's misuse was the *sole cause* of the injury and allowed Plaintiffs full recovery of their damages if Richard's alleged misuse of the grinder was only a concurrent cause. The trial judge denied Defendant's request to give comparative fault instructions and a form of verdict that tracked UCATA and would have allowed the jury to allocate a percentage of fault to Richard—and the judge to then reduce Plaintiffs' damages—if the jury found that Richard's misuse was a concurrent cause of his injuries.

The jury awarded Plaintiffs $112,000 in total damages. After the trial court denied its motion for a new trial, Defendant appealed, arguing, *inter alia*, that the trial judge erred by failing to give the comparative fault instructions .. Relying on the dissent in *Gibbs v. O'Malley Lumber Co.*, 177 Ariz. 342, 348, 868 P.2d 355, 361 (App.1994), the court of appeals agreed with Defendant, reversed the judgment, and remanded for a new trial. *Jimenez v. Sears, Roebuck & Co.*, 180 Ariz. 432, 885 P.2d 120 (App.1994). Plaintiffs petitioned for review, raising the following issue:

Whether comparative fault principles are applicable to the misuse defense in a strict products liability action.

We granted review because the court of appeals' opinions in *Gibbs* and the present case conflict on this important issue of law. * * *

DISCUSSION

A. Does comparative negligence apply when Defendant raises the defense of misuse in a products liability action?

We first consider whether applying the rules of comparative fault to product misuse confuses that defense with a form of contributory negligence or whether the misuse defense is a different "species." We begin

---

1. A.R.S. § 12-683(3) was enacted in 1978 and is part of a group of statutes dealing with product liability. See A.R.S. Title 12, ch. 6, art. 9, which reads as follows:

In any product liability action, a defendant shall not be liable if the defendant proves that any of the following apply:

.....

3. The proximate cause of the incident giving rise to the action was a use or consumption of the product which was for a purpose, in a manner or in an activity other than that which was reasonably foreseeable or was contrary to any express and adequate instructions or warnings appearing on or attached to the product or on its original container or wrapping, if the injured person knew or with the exercise of reasonable and diligent care should have known of such instructions or warnings.

by distinguishing misuse from contributory negligence and assumption of the risk, defenses that have been subject to the rules of comparative fault since UCATA's original enactment in 1984.

1. Misuse, contributory negligence, and assumption of risk

Arizona adopted the doctrine of strict products liability to address the problem of consumer injury caused by unreasonably dangerous products, allocating the risk of loss to the manufacturers and sellers of these products. A prima facie case of strict products liability is established by showing that when the product left the defendant's control, it was in a defective condition that made it unreasonably dangerous and the defect was *a* proximate cause of plaintiff's injuries. *Gosewisch,* 153 Ariz. at 403, 737 P.2d at 379; *see also O.S. Stapley Co. v. Miller,* 103 Ariz. 556, 559–60, 447 P.2d 248, 251–52 (1968) (adopting strict liability rule of RESTATEMENT (SECOND) OF TORTS § 402A (1965), hereinafter RESTATEMENT).

We have recognized two affirmative defenses in products liability that, if proven, bar a plaintiff's recovery: assumption of risk and product misuse. However, along with most if not all other courts, we have rejected contributory negligence as a products liability defense. In *O.S. Stapley* we explained the differences between contributory negligence, assumption of risk, and misuse: (1) "[F]ailure to discover a defect in the product which the plaintiff should, if he was reasonably diligent, have discovered" is contributory negligence; (2) "notwithstanding the discovery of such a defect, [if] the plaintiff nevertheless uses the article" it is assumption of risk; and (3) the plaintiff's use of the product "for certain purposes or in a manner not reasonably foreseen by the manufacturer" is misuse. 103 Ariz. at 561, 447 P.2d at 253.

Contributory negligence is not applicable to strict liability because, under the doctrine of strict liability, "no duty rests upon the ultimate consumer or user to search for or guard against the possibility of product defects." *Id.* On the other hand, a plaintiff who voluntarily and unreasonably encounters a known danger has assumed the risk and cannot recover on a strict liability claim. *Id.* (quoting RESTATEMENT § 402A cmt. n). Misuse differs from assumption of risk in that knowledge of a product's defect is not necessary to establish misuse but is essential for assumption of risk. Randy R. Koenders, Annotation, *Products Liability: Product Misuse Defense,* 65 A.L.R.4TH 263 § 33, at 333 (1988). Misuse has been variously referred to as use for a purpose or in a manner that, from the manufacturer or seller's view, was unintended, unforeseeable, unanticipated, unexpected, non-customary, or abnormal. These concepts distinguish misuse from contributory negligence, which involves careless use for a proper purpose.

At common law, misuse was intervening conduct so rare and unusual, and thus unforeseeable, that it was treated as a superseding cause to the product defect. W. PAGE KEETON, ET AL., PROSSER & KEETON ON THE LAW OF TORTS § 102, at 711 (5th ed.1984). Because of the extraordinary nature of such conduct, courts tended to view unforeseeable misuse as breaking the chain of causation between the defect and injury. * * * As with assumption of the risk, misuse was an absolute defense to liability.

In 1978, the legislature codified the common-law defense of misuse under A.R.S. § 12–683(3). In pertinent part, § 12–683(3) provides that a *"defendant shall not be liable"* when *"the proximate cause"* of the accident *"was a use ... of the product which was for a purpose, in a manner or in an activity other than that which was reasonably foreseeable."* (Emphasis added.) The text of this statute—using the term "the proximate cause"—arguably preserved the common-law all-or-nothing consequence of misuse and its essential common-law character, in the sense of use for a purpose or in a manner or for an activity neither intended nor reasonably foreseeable by the manufacturer.

In *Gosewisch,* we held that under § 12–683(3) misuse is a complete defense only if (1) the plaintiff misused the product and (2) misuse was the sole proximate cause of the injury. 153 Ariz. at 407, 737 P.2d at 383. We construed *"[t]he proximate cause"* language of § 12–683(3) to mean "the sole proximate cause" rather than "a" proximate or contributing cause of the incident that gave rise to the action. Thus, under our interpretation of § 12–683(3) in *Gosewisch,* if there was evidence of misuse, it would have been correct to instruct the jury, as in the present case, that misuse bars recovery if it was the sole cause of the plaintiff's injury.

Under the comparative fault rules of the 1987 version of UCATA, however, a jury can reduce a plaintiff's damages in an amount proportionate to the relative degree of the plaintiff's fault that proximately caused the injury. A.R.S. § 12–2505(A). If applicable to product liability cases, this of course recognizes the misuse defense in cases in which it is a contributing cause rather than the sole cause of injury. Thus, the jury would be instructed to determine whether the plaintiff's misuse contributed to the plaintiff's injuries and, if so, to compare the plaintiff's share of misuse-causation with the causal contribution of the product's defect. The judge would then reduce the plaintiff's damage recovery by the percentage of cause the jury attributed to the plaintiff. We turn next, therefore, to the question of whether our comparative fault statutes encompass the defense of product misuse.

2. Does the statute contemplate applying comparative fault to misuse?

The 1987 UCATA amendments both abolished joint-and-several liability and apparently broadened the scope of torts subject to the rules of comparative fault. Section 12–2506(F)(2) was added to define apportionable fault:

> *"Fault" means an* actionable breach of legal duty, *act or omission proximately causing or contributing to injury* or damages sustained by a person seeking recovery, *including* negligence in all of its degrees, contributory negligence, assumption of risk, strict liability,

breach of express or implied warranty of a product, *products liability and misuse, modification or abuse of a product.*

(Emphasis added.) Defendant claims that the inclusion of the emphasized language in the 1987 UCATA definition of fault is a clear legislative mandate to make misuse as described in § 12–683(3) a comparative defense, even if it falls short of the sole cause of the accident. Thus, Defendant argues, § 12–2506 requires that the jury be instructed on comparative fault in a products liability case in which misuse is a factual issue.

* * *

Gosewisch did not consider the pending amendments to § 12–2506 and interpreted § 12–683(3) in light of the 1984 UCATA version then in effect. The legislature is free, of course, to rewrite statutes. By later including misuse as a category of fault to be apportioned in a products liability case and by abolishing joint-and-several liability, the legislature made misuse a species of comparative fault as surely as it had made contributory negligence and assumption of the risk subject to comparative fault when it included those defenses in the 1984 version of the same act.

Moreover, § 12–2505(A), the comparative negligence statute, does not limit the application of comparative fault principles to negligence theories. This section instead instructs that "*[i]n an action for personal injury,* ... liability of the person who caused the injury shall be allocated ... in direct proportion to that person's percentage of fault." (Emphasis added.) When read together, § 12–683(3) and UCATA §§ 12–2505 and 12–2506 require a factual determination of the plaintiff's misuse as a relative degree of fault in allocating causal responsibility in a strict products liability claim.

Such an interpretation furthers the general legislative goal embodied in UCATA of allocating fault and thus arguably promoting a tort system fair to both plaintiffs and defendants. Under § 12–2506 as it now stands, each tortfeasor responsible for causing injury to the plaintiff is liable only for its causal contribution "and no more." *Dietz,* 169 Ariz. at 510, 821 P.2d at 171. This does not interfere with the objectives of the strict products liability theory because the harm attributable to the product defect continues to be allocated to those who market the product and the cost of compensation is spread among all consumers. We therefore interpret the present version of § 12–2506(F)(2) to encompass product misuse in the jury's allocation of comparative fault. * * *

In so concluding, we are supported by substantial authority. Our state is not alone in applying comparative fault principles to strict liability defenses. The drafters of the third revision of the RESTATEMENT OF TORTS recommend that defenses against product liability plaintiffs be subject to the apportionment rules in jurisdictions that have adopted the comparative responsibility rules. Restatement (Third) of Torts § 10, at 261, and § 12, at 300 (Tentative Draft No. 2, 1995). * * *

[M]any courts have used comparative fault in strict products liability cases. *See* Restatement § 12, Reporters' Note at 304–08; Romualdo P. Eclavea, Annotation, *Applicability of Comparative Negligence Doctrine to Actions Based on Strict Liability in Tort,* 9 A.L.R.4th 633 (1988 & Supp.1994) * * *.

* * *

C. Under the facts of this case, did the trial court err in refusing a comparative fault instruction?

If the facts did not warrant an instruction on comparative fault, then, of course, refusing that instruction would not have been error. As indicated earlier, we believe * * * that there is a difference between contributory negligence, which is not a defense in a strict product liability action, and misuse, which is a defense. Whether theoretically correct or internally contradictory, the misuse doctrine was based on the concept that the purpose to which the product was put was not only unforeseeable but broke the chain of causation. Obviously, therefore, not every improper use of a product will constitute misuse rather than contributory negligence. Careless and thus improper handling or operation of the product is negligent use but not misuse. Contrary to the statement made in the last sentence of Justice Martone's special concurrence, we do *not* hold that foreseeable misuse or contributory negligence is a defense in a strict products case. The facts in this case may not qualify as misuse. We note, however, that until we asked for supplemental briefs on this issue, Plaintiffs did not object to the misuse instruction on the theory that it was unwarranted by the facts but only on the statutory interpretation grounds discussed in part A(2) above. We therefore believe that the issue is not before us and, for purposes of this appeal, assume that the instruction was factually warranted.

CONCLUSION

* * * On this record, therefore, the trial court erred in refusing to give the jury comparative fault instructions on the statutory defense of product misuse.

We vacate that part of the court of appeals' opinion addressing the issues considered in this opinion and remand to the superior court for further action consistent with this opinion.

MOELLER, V.C.J., and CORCORAN, J., concur.

[The concurring opinion of Justice Zlaket is omitted.]

MARTONE, JUSTICE, concurring in the judgment.

Because the issues of misuse and contributory negligence are conceptually difficult, and the majority's opinion is contradictory,[2] I write to

---

2. *Compare ante,* at 403, 904 P.2d at 865 ("this of course recognizes the misuse defense in cases in which it is a contributing cause rather than the sole cause of injury") *with ante,* at 408, 904 P.2d at 870 ("we do *not* hold that foreseeable misuse or contributory negligence is a defense in a strict products case.") If the latter is true, to what does the opinion apply?

express my understanding of what we have done and why, where I agree and where I disagree.

Even before *Gosewisch v. American Honda Motor Company,* 153 Ariz. 400, 737 P.2d 376 (1987), misuse occurred when the plaintiff used a product in a way that was unforeseeable. Thus, by definition, whenever there is misuse, the defendant can never proximately cause the injury because it is unforeseeable. *Gosewisch* only made this concept explicit when it said that the misuse statute bars recovery only if misuse is "the only proximate cause." 153 Ariz. at 407, 737 P.2d at 383. Thus, conduct that is genuinely misuse will, by definition, always be the sole proximate cause. It is for this reason that misuse is an all or nothing defense. Because misuse is the sole proximate cause, the product's defect plays no role in causation and therefore, "a defendant shall not be liable." A.R.S. § 12–683.

Let me illustrate. Suppose a handgun has a defect in it. Suppose further that plaintiff uses the handgun as a hammer to drive a nail rather than for the purpose for which it was intended. As the handle of the weapon strikes the nail, it fires and the plaintiff is injured. This is product misuse. This is not contributory negligence. Under these facts, the defendant is not liable as a matter of law. On the other hand, suppose plaintiff mishandles the gun at a firing range. He is not careful about where he points it but the safety is on. Suppose further that because of a product defect, the safety does not work and he is injured. Plaintiff's conduct is contributory negligence, which is not a defense to a strict liability case. Up to this point, there is both conceptual and doctrinal clarity.

The problem arises because misuse is included within the definition of "fault" under A.R.S. § 12–2506(F)(2). Thus comparative principles apply. Yet, if misuse still means the sole proximate cause, comparative principles cannot apply. Therefore, the legislature must mean something other than misuse. But it cannot mean contributory negligence if that is not a defense to a products case. What then is this new species of misuse? Under the court's opinion, this kind of misuse occurs when "it is a contributing cause rather than the sole cause of injury." *Ante,* at 403, 904 P.2d at 865. But as we have seen, this is not misuse at all. But if it is not misuse, and it is not contributory negligence, what is it? Neither the court's opinion nor the other concurring opinion answers this. I do not know how misuse can be less than the sole contributing cause of an injury and not at the same time be contributory negligence. Thus, I believe that our opinion makes some contributory negligence (where a product is not used properly and that improper use is a concurring cause) a defense to a products case * * *.

Consider the case before us. This is simply not a case of misuse. Jimenez was using the grinder for the purpose for which it was intended. The defendant argued that he "misused the grinder by failing to wear a protective apron while operating the tool." *Ante,* at 401, 904 P.2d at 863.

But this would be contributory negligence, not misuse of the product. To be sure, a grinder could be misused. For example, if the plaintiff used the grinder as a substitute submergible bilge pump for his boat and electrocuted himself, the grinder would have been misused, and would have been the sole cause of the injury.

Because I do not see how a *foreseeable* misuse (and thus a concurring cause) could be anything other than contributory negligence, if today's decision is to have any practical effect, it means that some form of contributory negligence is a comparative defense to a strict products liability case. This would be compatible with A.R.S. § 12–683(3), because it gives two meanings to the word "misuse." The first is its true meaning, ("The proximate cause of the incident giving rise to the action was a use or consumption of the product which was for a purpose, in a manner or in an activity other than that which was reasonably foreseeable"). But the second is a species of contributory negligence ("or was contrary to any express and adequate instructions or warnings appearing on or attached to the product or on its original container or wrapping, if the injured person knew or with the exercise of reasonable and diligent care should have known of such instructions or warnings").

While all of this may muddy up the conceptual clarity of the former distinction between misuse and contributory negligence, it may well be that the practical effect will be beneficial. For example, Prosser & Keaton note that "[p]erhaps if comparative negligence had preceded the development of strict liability, contributory negligence would have been recognized as a defense." W. Page Keeton et al., *Prosser and Keeton on the Law of Torts* § 102, at 712 (5th ed. 1984).

To summarize, true misuse (unforeseeable, sole cause) continues to be an all or nothing defense under § 12–683. Foreseeable misuse (concurring cause) is really contributory negligence, and is now a comparative defense to a products case.

Notes

1. In his concurring opinion, Justice Martone argues that Mr. Jimenez's use of the grinder did not constitute misuse. The majority refuses to express an opinion on this question. Do you believe this was a misuse under A.R.S.§ 12–683(3)?

2. The most common formulation of the misuse rule is that the misuse must be unforseeable. Defendants are responsible for harm from product uses which are reasonably foreseeable. Using a screwdriver to open a can of paint is not a misuse. However, interpreted most liberally, the unforseeability requirement would appear to exclude all but the most extreme forms of misuse. Therefore, many states attempt to give the defense a greater scope by modifying it in some way. For example, many states require that the use be "reasonably foreseeable" or "objectively foreseeable." *See* Jeld–Wen, Inc. v. Gamble, 256 Va. 144, 501 S.E.2d 393, 397 (1998) (finding that use not "reasonably foreseeable" as a matter of law); Jurado v. Western Gear Works,

131 N.J. 375, 619 A.2d 1312, 1319 (1993) (articulating "objectively" foreseeable standard).

In Barnard v. Saturn Corp., 790 N.E.2d 1023 (Ind. App. 2003) the plaintiff disregarded numerous instructions and warning when he crawled under his automobile that he had raised with the jack provided with the car. In affirming a directed verdict for the defendant, the court noted:

> Although it is unlikely, in light of the nature and purpose of a car jack, that General Motors and Seeburn could not have reasonably foreseen a user ever deciding to get underneath a vehicle supported solely by a jack, Mark deployed this particular jack in direct contravention of its reasonably expected permitted use. Thus, we believe Mark misused the jack.

The court added the following footnote:

> If a manufacturer could not foresee a particular use, they would not know to warn against it. Thus, we believe the term "reasonably expected use" must include the manufacturer's reasonably expected permitted use. If not, the moment a seller or manufacturer provided a specific warning against a particular use, they would have admitted to foreseeing use of the product in that proscribed manner.

3. Courts have had a difficult time determining precisely how to account in strict tort liability for an unforeseeable product use. Comment h addresses misuse in terms of product defectiveness, and the court in *Romito*, page 144 *supra* treats it as a matter of duty. *Jimenez* treats unforeseeable use as an affirmative defense, similar to contributory negligence and assumption of risk, while denying that contributory negligence is a defense in a strict liability case. Misuse also might be considered under the rubric of proximate causation, as the *Jimenez* court states. Can you modify the facts in *Jimenez* so that proximate cause is an issue? So that duty is an issue?

The difference in these approaches can have a substantial effect on a case. One effect is that, if a plaintiff's unforeseeable use of a product negates a claim of defectiveness or proximate causation, the plaintiff would be unable to obtain any recovery. If, on the other hand, unforeseeable misuse is treated as a defense, a court that otherwise uses a comparative scheme might merely reduce the plaintiff's recovery.

A second effect is that the rubric a court uses might affect the burden of proof. The plaintiff has the burden of proof on defectiveness and causation. *See, e.g.*, Rogers v. Toro Mfg. Co., 522 S.W.2d 632 (Mo.App.1975) (plaintiff has burden to prove proper use). The defendant has the burden on affirmative defenses.

A third effect is that, as a defense similar to contributory negligence or assumption of risk, unforeseeable misuse might bar or reduce the plaintiff's recovery only if the plaintiff was the one who misused the product. If the unusual use negates defectiveness or proximate causation, it should affect recovery by third persons as well.

Finally, if misuse is to be treated as a matter of duty, the issue becomes one for the court rather than the jury.

Consider a plaintiff who is injured by a windshield that shatters when he drives a car through a closed gate to escape attackers. Should the plaintiff's unusual use of the car affect the plaintiff's recovery as a (possibly comparative) defense, as a matter of proximate causation, or as a matter of the car's defectiveness? Should the defendant be permitted to use this aspect of the case in all three ways? Should it have no effect on the plaintiff's recovery? Ultimately, we are best served if we take the advice of Restatement (Third) of Torts: Products Liability, Comment *p* and recognize that misuse is not a discrete legal issue. Rather it is an aspect of the concepts of defect, causation, and plaintiff's fault.

4. In Colvin v. Red Steel Co., 682 S.W.2d 243 (Tex.1984), the plaintiff was injured when he lost his balance and fell at a construction site. As he was falling, he grabbed a loose I-beam to stabilize himself. The I-beam was shorter than prescribed by the specifications. Consequently, it was lighter than it should have been, and it failed to support him.

The court held that the I-beam was not defective. Since it was shorter than prescribed by the specifications, however, it might be argued that it was "flawed." Should the court have held that the product was misused? Should it have held that the flaw, if any, was not a proximate cause of the injury? What difference does the choice make to this case or other cases involving these I-beams? What if the building collapsed because the I-beams were too short?

5. If a product's only risks are manifested when it is used in an unusual manner, it might not be defective at all. Unusual injuries that are caused by a product that is defective because it also imposes risks in non-unusual situations could be analyzed as an issue of proximate or legal causation. If so, is there any reason to have an independent "defense" of misuse? For further discussion of the relationship between misuse and defectiveness, see Jurado v. Western Gear Works, 131 N.J. 375, 619 A.2d 1312 (1993); Dosier v. Wilcox & Crittendon Co., 45 Cal.App.3d 74, 119 Cal.Rptr. 135 (1975). For a discussion of the relationship between misuse and proximate or legal causation, see Chapter 7.

6. You should appreciate how the rejection of contributory negligence as a defense by the courts adopting strict liability created a great deal of pressure on other affirmative defenses, misuse and assumption of risk, to expand to accommodate foolish, culpable, or downright stupid plaintiff conduct. Perhaps if the reform to comparative responsibility had preceded the development of strict liability, the doctrinal shell game over affirmative defenses might have been avoided.

7. General Motors Corp. v. Hopkins, 548 S.W.2d 344 (Tex.1977) was an early case applying comparative principles to misuse. The court held that misuse *by the plaintiff* is a defense that reduces the plaintiff's recovery by the percentage "causation" assigned to the plaintiff by the jury if the misuse was a proximate cause of the plaintiff's injury. In addition to applying comparative principles to misuse, *Hopkins* presents an interesting application of the misuse defense itself.

The plaintiff was injured when the carburetor on his car stuck in the open position, causing the car to go out of control. Prior to the accident, the plaintiff noticed a problem with the carburetor and replaced it with one he had obtained himself. Later, he reinstalled the original carburetor, which caused the accident. The court stated that plaintiff's conduct constituted a misuse, and that the "misuse may bear upon the issue of whether the product was defective when it left the hands of the supplier or the misuse may bear on the issue of what caused the harm."

It is unclear whether the court in *Hopkins* really thought it is unforeseeable that car owners will occasionally repair or replace the carburetor. It is also unclear whether the court thought the facts that the plaintiff noticed a problem with the carburetor, replaced it, and then reinstalled it constituted a voluntary assumption of a known and appreciated risk. Maybe the court suspected that the plaintiff botched the job. If so, maybe the carburetor was not defective at all when it left the manufacturer, but in that case, the plaintiff should have lost, not merely had his recovery reduced. Is it possible that the court was using misuse to cover conduct that was actually contributory negligence, which at the time *Hopkins* was decided was not nominally a defense to strict tort liability in Texas? Fudging misuse to cover conduct that is actually contributory negligence is more palatable when it only reduces the plaintiff's recovery rather than bars it.

As *Hopkins* and *Jimenez* indicate, the defense of misuse has been used to cover a variety of issues. When you encounter a case involving misuse, you should be careful to ascertain precisely how the court is using the defense.

8. Unforeseeable misuse is also a "defense" to an action for breach of warranty. *See* Singer v. Walker, 39 A.D.2d 90, 331 N.Y.S.2d 823 (1972). Again, the test is whether the manufacturer should have foreseen the use, not whether the manufacturer intended the product to be used in the manner that the plaintiff used it. Many courts analyze misuse as an issue of the scope of the warranty or an issue of proximate causation. *See, e.g.,* Hardman v. Helene Curtis Ind., Inc., 48 Ill.App.2d 42, 198 N.E.2d 681 (1964); Chisholm v. J.R. Simplot Co., 94 Idaho 628, 495 P.2d 1113 (1972). Moreover, an implied warranty of merchantability under section 2–314 applies only to products that are used for their ordinary purposes.

9. Conduct that would constitute unforeseeable product misuse would probably defeat recovery in an action for negligence under the rubric of proximate causation. *See* Chapter 7; Restatement (Second) of Torts § 395, Comments j and k.

10. Do the policies underlying strict tort liability support unforeseeable misuse as a defense to strict tort liability? Do they suggest that unforeseeable misuse should be a percentage reduction or an absolute bar?

SECTION B. APPORTIONING LIABILITY AMONG DEFENDANTS AND THE SPECIAL ROLE OF EMPLOYERS: CONTRIBUTION AND INDEMNITY

In many situations a plaintiff has the option of suing one of several tortfeasors to recover the entire amount of his damages. Sometimes this is because various sellers in the chain of a product's distribution are each liable. Sometimes it is because joint tortfeasors are independently liable to the plaintiff under the doctrine of joint and several liability. If one of several tortfeasors is required to pay the plaintiff's entire damages, that tortfeasor may be able to recover contribution or indemnity from one or more of the other tortfeasors. If one tortfeasor settles with the plaintiff, the settlement may affect the liability of other tortfeasors.

The basic rules of joint and several liability, contribution, indemnity, and settlement were developed primarily in cases involving ordinary negligence. You should be familiar with these basic doctrines from your first-year torts class. Consequently, this Chapter does not contain a comprehensive treatment of contribution and indemnity. Instead, it focuses primarily on special problems that arise in the context of product cases.

The doctrine of joint and several liability provides that when a plaintiff's injury has been caused by two or more tortfeasors, the plaintiff can recover for the injury in its entirety from any of the joint tortfeasors. The plaintiff can actually collect only once; if he collects an entire judgment or settlement from one joint tortfeasor, the judgment is "satisfied," and he cannot thereafter collect or obtain a judgment against the other joint tortfeasors. But until the claim is satisfied, the plaintiff can obtain judgments against all jointly and severally liable tortfeasors for the entire harm. Joint and several liability thus has two primary consequences: 1) it imposes on defendants the burden of joining, by way of a contribution or indemnity claim, additional persons who may be liable to the plaintiff; 2) it also imposes the risk that one or more of the defendants is insolvent, and therefore unable to pay its share of plaintiff's damages, on the other jointly and severally defendants. Despite the first consequence, most plaintiffs find it tactically advantageous to join all potentially liable parties and not to sue simply one defendant who is jointly and severally liable.

There are two ways in which joint and several liability may not be applicable when multiple tortfeasors cause the plaintiff's injuries. If different tortfeasors cause distinct injuries, each tortfeasor is normally liable only for the harm that that tortfeasor in fact caused. Only tortfeasors who have jointly caused an indivisible injury are jointly and severally liable.* In cases involving divisible injuries, the plaintiff normally has the burden to prove which defendant caused what harm. Be careful about the concept of "indivisibility." An injury is indivisible in two respects: First, when all tortfeasors are a cause of the entirety of the injury, it is indivisible, at least based on causal grounds. Thus, if two cars negligently driven collide and a wheel flies off of one and fractures the plaintiff's skull, both drivers are liable for the "indivisible" fractured skull.

The second way in which an injury may be indivisible involves injuries that are theoretically divisible but practically indivisible in the sense that proof does not exist to permit determining what injuries were

---

* Multiple tortfeasors who cause separate injuries can be liable for each other's separate injuries under vicarious liability or concerted action.

caused by which defendants. In this situation, most courts shift the burden to the defendants to sort out who caused what portion of the injury. If defendants cannot satisfy this burden of proof, these courts treat the injury as though it were indivisible, holding each tortfeasor jointly and severally liable. *See, e.g.,* Landers v. East Texas Salt Water Disposal Co., 151 Tex. 251, 248 S.W.2d 731 (1952). Other courts have developed special doctrines—such as the market share theory adopted in Sindell v. Abbott Laboratories, 26 Cal.3d 588, 163 Cal.Rptr. 132, 607 P.2d 924 (1980), cert. denied, 449 U.S. 912, 101 S.Ct. 285, 66 L.Ed.2d 140 (1980)—to help plaintiffs meet their burden of proof when they cannot reasonably be expected to sort out ambiguous or confusing causal connections.

Divisible and indivisible injuries can occur in the same accident. For example, a plaintiff might suffer two separate injuries, one of which was caused by two tortfeasors and the other of which was caused solely by one of the tortfeasors. Problems involving causation are addressed in detail in Chapter 5. The point here is that you should be very careful to sort out who caused what portions of an injury before applying the rules of joint and several liability.

In many states, the adoption of comparative fault and tort reform legislation has limited the availability of joint and several liability, even in indivisible injury cases. A significant number of states, approximately 15, have simply abolished joint and several liability for independent tortfeasors. Each defendant is only severally liable for its comparative share of the plaintiff's damages. How does this change affect the burdens identified above that are imposed by joint and several liability?

A substantial number of states have "hybrid" systems, consisting of a blend of several and joint and several liability. There is, however, considerable variation among these hybrid jurisdictions. *See generally* Restatement (Third) of Torts: Apportionment of Liability § 17. Some states, such as California, employ several liability for noneconomic damages, such as pain and suffering, but permit joint and several liability for economic damages, such as lost wages and medical expenses. Other states limit joint and several liability to defendants whose percentage of comparative responsibility is greater than the plaintiff's or above a specified threshold percentage. Some states combine these two measures, imposing joint and several liability only for economic damages on those above a threshold. Other systems exist, and many states' laws contain specific exceptions or qualifications to the primary scheme. Thus, lawyers must be keenly aware of the particular system that governs a given case. As with many other features of joint and several liability, contribution, and indemnity, these limitations on joint and several liability often apply to tort cases generally, not just products liability cases.

A tortfeasor who is jointly and severally liable for an entire injury can recover *contribution* (a portion of the damages) or sometimes can recover *indemnity* (the entire damages) from the other tortfeasors.

Before the advent of comparative responsibility, contribution shares were determined on a *pro rata* basis, but in jurisdictions that use comparative responsibility schemes, contribution shares are now determined according to the percentages assigned by the jury to each defendant. Regardless of which method is used, in many states a tortfeasor is not required to pay contribution beyond its own *pro rata* or percentage share. Thus, if one of the tortfeasors is insolvent, the tortfeasor who originally paid the plaintiff bears all of the excess liability. *But see* Restatement (Third) of Torts: Apportionment of Liability § 23, Comment g (permitting contribution recovery from all defendants for their proportional share of any insolvent party's share of liability).

A major issue concerning contribution and indemnity is determining when indemnity rather than contribution is appropriate. Courts have taken a variety of approaches to this distinction, but all agree that indemnity rather than contribution is appropriate: (1) if the parties have entered into an express contract for indemnity; (2) if the party seeking indemnity is liable solely on the basis of vicarious liability for a tort actually committed by the party from whom indemnity is sought; and (3) when an innocent product seller (such as a retailer) is held liable for a defective product that was supplied to it by a seller higher in the chain of distribution (such as a manufacturer). Some courts also allow indemnity rather than contribution when the party seeking indemnity is qualitatively less culpable than the party from whom indemnity is sought.

1. APPORTIONMENT WITHIN THE DISTRIBUTIVE CHAIN: INDEMNITY

TROMZA v. TECUMSEH PRODUCTS CO.
United States Court of Appeals, Third Circuit, 1967.
378 F.2d 601.

KALODNER, CIRCUIT JUDGE.

In the instant personal injury action the jury awarded damages to the plaintiff John Tromza against the defendants Tecumseh Products Company ('Tecumseh') and Marquette Corporation ('Marquette'), and the District Court found against Marquette in its cross-claim for indemnity against Tecumseh.

The District Court entered judgment in favor of the plaintiff against Tecumseh and Marquette pursuant to the jury's verdict, following its denial of their respective motions for judgment n.o.v., and Marquette's additional motion for a new trial. It also entered judgment in favor of Tecumseh against Marquette after denying Marquette's motion for judgment n.o.v. as to the cross-claim. This appeal by Marquette followed.

* * *

Tecumseh manufactured and sold to Marquette a sealed compressor refrigeration unit which Marquette incorporated in a refrigerator which it manufactured. The compressor unit was enclosed in a steel casing or shell, whose two halves were welded by Tecumseh. The refrigerator manufactured by Marquette carried a plate which stated that the factory test pressure of the refrigeration unit was 195 pounds.

The casing or shell of the compressor unit exploded when the plaintiff, a repair man, submitted the refrigerator to a pressure of 170 pounds in proceeding to repair a gas leak in its refrigeration system. The plaintiff was seriously injured by the explosion.

* * *

The case was submitted to the jury on the plaintiff's theory that Tecumseh was negligent both in its manufacture of the compressor unit and in failing to discover the defect by a proper inspection, and that Marquette was negligent in failing to make a proper test or inspection of the unit. We agree with the District Court that the evidence clearly supported the jury's finding that both Tecumseh and Marquette were negligent. As to Marquette, it need only be pointed out that there was undisputed evidence that the customary industry practice was to submit an assembled refrigerator to a pressure test of 235–250 pounds while Marquette made only a 195 pound pressure test.

Coming now to Marquette's contention that the District Court erred in entering judgment in favor of Tecumseh on Marquette's cross-claim [for indemnity]:

The sum of Marquette's contentions on this score is (1) it was only "secondarily liable" and Tecumseh was "primarily liable," and therefore it is entitled to recover indemnity from Tecumseh; and (2) it is entitled to recovery for breach of an implied warranty by Tecumseh.

In reply, Tecumseh contends that the principle of primary-secondary liability in tort does not apply generally to an indemnity claim between manufacturers.

It must here be noted that the District Court, in its opinion reported at 253 F.Supp. 26, 27 (E.D.Pa.1966), premised its ruling in favor of Tecumseh on the cross-claim on its following stated reasoning:

> "Since the identical negligence (failure to make proper inspection) was charged against each defendant, in the light of the jury's verdict the defendants must be found to be joint or concurrent tort-feasors rather than as occupying a relationship of primary and secondary liability. There was no legal relationship between them, such as master and servant, which is ordinarily the basis for distinction of primary and secondary liability [citations]."

The District Court's determination, in its opinion, that Marquette and Tecumseh were charged with "identical negligence (failure to make proper inspection)" thereby making them "joint or concurrent tort-feasors rather than as occupying a relationship of primary and secondary liability," is at variance with its own prior statement that "the only negligence alleged against defendant Marquette was failure to make a proper test or inspection at the time of assembly; whereas defendant

Tecumseh was charged with a two-pronged negligence, both in the welding process and in failure to find the defect by a proper inspection," and its further statement that "The Court remains of opinion that the evidence and the jury's verdict, on the two-fold grounds above stated, clearly support plaintiff's verdict against defendant Tecumseh." 253 F.Supp. 26, 27.

Since the District Court premised its determination that Marquette and Tecumseh "must be found to be joint or concurrent tort-feasors rather than as occupying a relationship of primary and secondary liability" on its view that they were both charged with "identical negligence (failure to make proper inspection)," the circumstance that the negligence charged against the defendants was not "identical," renders the categorization of the defendants as "joint or concurrent tort-feasors" clear error.

Further, the District Court erred in its view that under Pennsylvania law, applicable here, a "legal relationship * * * such as master and servant * * * is ordinarily the basis for distinction of primary and secondary liability." *Pittsburgh Steel Company* [404 Pa. 53, 171 A.2d 185 (1961)] and *Builders Supply Co.* [366 Pa. 322, 77 A.2d 368 (1951)] which it cites, afford no nourishment to its view, since they specifically do not limit application of the primary-secondary liability doctrine to cases where a legal relationship exists between the party primarily liable and the party secondarily liable.

That that is so is clearly evident from the following quotation from the Pennsylvania Supreme Court's opinion in Builders Supply Co. at 366 Pa. 327–328, 77 A.2d 371:

"Without multiplying instances, it is clear that the right of a person vicariously or secondarily liable for a tort to recover from one primarily liable has been universally recognized. But the important point to be noted in all the cases is that secondary as distinguished from primary liability rests upon a fault that is imputed or constructive only, being based on some legal relation between the parties, *or* arising from some positive rule of common or statutory law *or* because of a failure to discover or correct a defect or remedy a dangerous condition caused by the act of the one primarily responsible." (emphasis supplied)

The foregoing quotation was preceded by this statement at 366 Pa. 325–326, 77 A.2d 370:

"The right of *indemnity* rests upon a difference between the primary and the secondary liability of two persons each of whom is made responsible by the law to an injured party. It is a right which enures to a person who, without active fault on his own part, has been compelled, by reason of some legal obligation, to pay damages occasioned by the initial negligence of another, and for which he himself is only secondarily liable. The difference between primary and secondary liability is not based on a difference in *degrees* of negligence or on any doctrine of *comparative* negligence, a doctrine which, indeed, is not recognized by the common law. See Fidelity & Casualty Co. of New York v. Federal Express, Inc., 6 Cir., 136 F.2d 35, 40. It depends on a difference in the *character* or *kind* of the wrongs which cause the injury and in the nature of the legal obligation owed by each of the wrongdoers to the injured person."

The principles stated in *Builders Supply Co.* were succinctly epitomized in the leading case of Union Stock Yards Co. of Omaha v. Chicago B. & Q.R.R. Co., 196 U.S. 217, 228, 25 S.Ct. 226, 229, 49 L.Ed. 453 (1905), as follows:

> "In all these cases [where indemnity was sought] the wrongful act of the one held finally liable created the unsafe or dangerous condition from which the injury resulted. The principal and moving cause, resulting in the injury sustained, was the act of the first wrongdoer, and the other has been held liable to third persons for failing to discover or correct the defect caused by the positive act of the other."

* * *

Applying the principles stated to Marquette's cross-claim against Tecumseh, we are of the opinion that Marquette was entitled to judgment against Tecumseh. The latter was primarily responsible for manufacturing a defective compressor unit and failing to detect the defect by a proper inspection. Since Marquette's liability arose "because of a failure to discover or correct a defect or remedy a dangerous condition caused by the act of the one [Tecumseh] primarily responsible," its liability is secondary.

For the reasons stated the judgment entered pursuant to the jury's verdict in favor of Tromza against Tecumseh and Marquette will be affirmed, and the judgment entered in favor of Tecumseh against Marquette on Marquette's cross-claim will be vacated with directions to the District Court to enter judgment on the cross-claim in favor of Marquette and against Tecumseh.

Notes

1. Given the jury's finding that Marquette was negligent in its own right for failing to test and inspect the compressor unit, how can the court conclude, in light of the controlling *Builders Supply* case, that Marquette's liability "is imputed or constructive only"? What practical difference did the question of whether indemnity was available in this pre-comparative responsibility case make?

2. Jurisdictions that have adopted comparative responsibility and comparative contribution schemes have typically abandoned the distinction between primary and secondary liability, holding that indemnity is appropriate only: (1) when the parties have a contract for indemnity, (2) when the party seeking indemnity is merely vicariously liable, and (3) when an "innocent" product seller seeks indemnity from a manufacturer or seller

higher in the chain of distribution. In other situations, different degrees of culpability merely affect the percentages assigned to each defendant by the jury, and thereby affect the contribution shares of each defendant. *See* Restatement (Third) of Torts: Apportionment of Liability § 22.

3. At early common law, contribution was not permitted at all, on the ground that the law should not aid a wrongdoer, who, after all, had paid for no more than the damages he had caused. Many courts still deny contribution to intentional tortfeasors, but most have abrogated the no-contribution rule for non-intentional tortfeasors, either by statute or judicial decision.

4. You should pay special attention to a specific jurisdiction's rules about contribution and indemnity and the impact of comparative responsibility. The history of these issues in California is more complex than usual, but it illustrates the types of issues that can arise. That history was described in a non-products context by Justice Tobriner in American Motorcycle Ass'n v. Superior Court, 20 Cal.3d 578, 146 Cal.Rptr. 182, 578 P.2d 899 (1978). The plaintiff was seriously injured in a motorcycle race. He alleged that the American Motorcycle Association [AMA] and a local motorcycle club were negligent in designing the course and conducting the race. AMA filed a cross-complaint against the plaintiff's parents seeking indemnity. AMA argued that its negligence, if any, was passive, whereas the parents' negligence was active in that they helped their child enter the race and negligently failed to supervise him. Tracing the convoluted history of indemnity and contribution in California, Justice Tobriner wrote:

> Three years ago, in Li v. Yellow Cab Co. (1975) 13 Cal.3d 804, 119 Cal.Rptr. 858, 532 P.2d 1226, we concluded that the harsh and much criticized contributory negligence doctrine, which totally barred an injured person from recovering damages whenever his own negligence had contributed in any degree to the injury, should be replaced in this state by a rule of comparative negligence, under which an injured individual's recovery is simply proportionately diminished, rather than completely eliminated, when he is partially responsible for the injury.

* * *

> In California, as in most other American jurisdictions, the allocation of damages among multiple tortfeasors has historically been analyzed in terms of two, ostensibly mutually exclusive, doctrines: contribution and indemnification. In traditional terms, the apportionment of loss between multiple tortfeasors has been thought to present a question of contribution; indemnity, by contrast, has traditionally been viewed as concerned solely with whether a loss should be entirely shifted from one tortfeasor to another, rather than whether the loss should be shared between the two.

* * *

> Although early common law decisions established the broad rule that a tortfeasor was never entitled to contribution, it was not long before situations arose in which the obvious injustice of requiring one tortfeasor to bear an entire loss while another more culpable tortfeasor escaped with impunity led common law courts to develop an equitable

exception to the no contribution rule. (See generally Leflar, Contribution and Indemnity Between Tortfeasors (1932) 81 U.Pa.L.Rev. 140, 146–158.) As Chief Justice Gibson observed in Peters v. City & County of San Francisco (1953) 41 Cal.2d 419, 431, 260 P.2d 55, 62: "[T]he rule against contribution between joint tort-feasors admits of some exceptions, and a right of indemnification may arise as a result of contract *or equitable considerations* and is not restricted to situations involving a wholly vicarious liability, such as where a master has paid a judgment for damages resulting from the voluntary act of his servant." (Emphasis added.)

* * *

[T]he equitable indemnity doctrine originated in the common sense proposition that when two individuals are responsible for a loss, but one of the two is more culpable than the other, it is only fair that the more culpable party should bear a greater share of the loss. Of course, at the time the doctrine developed, common law precepts precluded any attempt to ascertain comparative fault; as a consequence, equitable indemnity, like the contributory negligence doctrine, developed as an all-or-nothing proposition.

Because of the all-or-nothing nature of the equitable indemnity rule, courts were, from the beginning, understandably reluctant to shift the entire loss to a party who was simply slightly more culpable than another. As a consequence, throughout the long history of the equitable indemnity doctrine courts have struggled to find some linguistic formulation that would provide an appropriate test for determining when the relative culpability of the parties is sufficiently disparate to warrant placing the entire loss on one party and completely absolving the other.

* * *

As one Court of Appeal has charitably stated: "The cases are not always helpful in determining whether equitable indemnity lies. The test[s] utilized in applying the doctrine are vague. Some authorities characterize the negligence of the indemnitor as 'active,' 'primary,' or 'positive,' and the negligence of the indemnitee as 'passive,' 'secondary,' or 'negative.' [Citations.] Other authorities indicate that the application of the doctrine depends on whether the claimant's liability is 'primary,' 'secondary,' 'constructive,' or 'derivative.' [Citations.] These formulations have been criticized as being artificial and as lacking the objective criteria desirable for predictability in the law. [Citations.]" (*Atchison, T. & S.F. Ry. Co. v. Franco, supra,* 267 Cal.App.2d 881, 886, 73 Cal.Rptr. 660, 664.)

* * *

If the fundamental problem with the equitable indemnity doctrine as it has developed in this state were simply a matter of an unduly vague or imprecise linguistic standard, the remedy would be simply to attempt to devise a more definite verbal formulation. In our view, however, the principal difficulty with the current equitable indemnity doctrine rests not simply on a question of terminology, but lies instead in the all-or-nothing nature of the doctrine itself.

* * *

[T]he New York Court of Appeals, in the celebrated decision of *Dole v. Dow Chemical Co., supra,* 30 N.Y.2d 143, 331 N.Y.S.2d 382, 282 N.E.2d 288, modified that state's traditional all-or-nothing indemnity doctrine to permit a tortfeasor to obtain "partial indemnification" from another tortfeasor on the basis of comparative fault. The *Dole* court, after noting that the previously existing "active-passive" indemnification test "has in practice proven elusive and difficult of fair application," went on to observe: "But the policy problem involves more than terminology. If indemnification is allowed at all among joint-tortfeasors, the important resulting question is how ultimate responsibility should be distributed. There are situations when the facts would in fairness warrant what [the named defendant] here seeks—passing on to [a concurrent tortfeasor] all responsibility that may be imposed on [the named defendant] for negligence, a traditional full indemnification. There are circumstances where the facts would not, by the same test of fairness, warrant passing on to a third party any of the liability imposed. There are circumstances which would justify apportionment of responsibility between third-party plaintiff and third-party defendant, in effect a partial indemnification." (331 N.Y.S.2d at p. 386, 282 N.E.2d at p. 291.)

Concluding that the all-or-nothing common law indemnity doctrine did not, in many situations, produce the equitable allocation of loss to which it aimed, the *Dole* court proceeded to modify the doctrine, holding that the "[r]ight to apportionment of liability or to full indemnity, * * * as among parties involved together in causing damage by negligence, should rest on relative responsibility * * *." (331 N.Y.S.2d at pp. 391–392, 282 N.E.2d at p. 295.) The *Dole* court was undeterred from undertaking this modification of the prior common law indemnity doctrine either by the existence of a contribution statute which, like that currently in force in California, provided joint tortfeasors with a right of pro rata contribution in limited circumstances, or by the fact that at that time New York still adhered to the all-or-nothing contributory negligence doctrine.

* * *

None of the parties to the instant proceeding, and none of the numerous amici who have filed briefs, seriously takes issue with our conclusion that a rule of comparative partial indemnity is more consistent with the principles underlying *Li* than the prior "all-or-nothing" indemnity doctrine. The principal argument raised in opposition to the recognition of a common law comparative indemnity rule is the claim that California's existing contribution statutes, section 875 et seq. of the Code of Civil Procedure,* preclude such a judicial development. As we explain, we reject the contention on a number of grounds.

---

* [Editors' note: Section 875 provides in pertinent part: "Where a money judgment has been rendered jointly against two or more defendants in a tort action there shall

First, as we have already noted, the New York Court of Appeals adopted a similar partial indemnity rule in *Dole v. Dow Chemical Co., supra,* 331 N.Y.S.2d 382, 282 N.E.2d 288, despite the existence of a closely comparable statutory contribution scheme.

* * *

We believe that a similar conclusion must be reached with respect to the pertinent California legislation. The legislative history of the 1957 contribution statute quite clearly demonstrates that the purpose of the legislation was simply "to lessen the harshness" of the then prevailing common law no contribution rule. Nothing in the legislative history suggests that the Legislature intended by the enactment to preempt the field or to foreclose future judicial developments which further the act's principal purpose of ameliorating the harshness and inequity of the old no contribution rule. Under these circumstances, we see no reason to interpret the legislation as establishing a bar to judicial innovation.

* * *

Several amici argue alternatively that even if the contribution statute was not intended to preclude the development of a common law comparative indemnity doctrine, our court should decline to adopt such a doctrine because it would assertedly undermine the strong public policy in favor of encouraging settlement of litigation embodied in section 877 of the Code of Civil Procedure, one of the provisions of the current, statutory contribution scheme.

* * *

Although section 877* reflects a strong public policy in favor of settlement, this statutory policy does not in any way conflict with the recognition of a common law partial indemnity doctrine but rather can, and should, be preserved as an integral part of the partial indemnity doctrine that we adopt today. Thus, while we recognize that section 877, by its terms, releases a settling tortfeasor only from liability for contribution and not partial indemnity, we conclude that from a realistic perspective the legislative policy underlying the provision dictates that a tortfeasor who has entered into a "good faith" settlement (see *River Garden Farms, Inc. v. Superior Court, supra,* 26 Cal.App.3d 986, 103 Cal.Rptr. 498) with the plaintiff must also be discharged from any claim for partial or comparative indemnity that may be pressed by a concurrent tortfeasor.

* * *

Accordingly, we conclude that Code of Civil Procedure section 875 et seq. do not preclude the development of new common law principles in this area, and we hold that under the common law of this state a

---

be a right of contribution among them as hereinafter provided."]

*[Editors' note: Section 877 provides that settlement with one tortfeasor does not discharge other tortfeasor from liability but does release the settling party from any contribution claim by other tortfeasors. See pages ___-___ *infra*].

concurrent tortfeasor may seek partial indemnity from another concurrent tortfeasor on a comparative fault basis.

5. How should courts treat claims for indemnity or contribution against those with immunity from a plaintiff's tort claim? Should the manufacturer of a defective automobile be able to obtain contribution from the victim's negligent spouse in a jurisdiction that still recognizes spousal immunity? Should a manufacturer be able to obtain contribution from a negligent but immune governmental unit? The most prevalent and serious of these problems occur when an employee sues a product manufacturer and the manufacturer seeks contribution or indemnity from the plaintiff's employer, who is immune from liability to the employee because of the exclusive remedy bar of workers' compensation statutes. This issue is addressed *infra* in subsection 4.

6. Procedurally, an action for indemnity or contribution can be brought in the principal action—by impleading the party from whom contribution or indemnity is sought as a third party defendant—or, in most states, it can be brought as an independent action, at least if the other tortfeasor is not already a party to the principal lawsuit.

2. APPORTIONMENT OUTSIDE THE DISTRIBUTIVE CHAIN: CONTRIBUTION

By contrast with *Tromza* and the question of indemnity among those in the distribution chain, apportioning liability among defendants who are liable to the plaintiff based on different tort theories raises the question of contribution. Thus, consider a case in which a negligent driver causes an automobile accident that results in the death of a passenger in another automobile. The manufacturer of the automobile is also liable because of a defect making the car uncrashworthy (for now, we assume that both the driver and defect caused the same harm). If joint and several liability is applicable, either the negligent driver or manufacturer may be required to pay more than its "share" of plaintiff's damages. Contribution is the claim that one of those defendants would assert against the other if required (or in anticipation of being required) to pay more than its share. Do you appreciate why the modification of joint and several liability explained at the outset of this section has lessened the need for contribution?

The adoption of comparative responsibility principles in products liability cases illustrated in the *Daly* case, page 613 *supra*, was extended to contribution claims. Thus, instead of a pro rata apportionment among defendants, comparative responsibility shares would be employed to determine the respective shares of all defendants and contribution would be available when a defendant was required to pay more than its comparative share of responsibility to the defendant.

The essence of a comparative responsibility scheme is that the tortious conduct of all of the parties is reduced to a single set of percentages that allocate the loss among the multiple parties. The scheme governs both the reduction of the plaintiff's recovery and contribution among multiple defendants. Such a unified scheme is very difficult to administer, however, if different rules apply to different causes of action and/or different parties. For example, how can a court allocate damages in a single system governing negligence, strict tort liability, and breach of warranty if the rules governing what counts as the plaintiff's contributory negligence are different under these three theories of recovery?

The Texas Supreme Court confronted this problem in Duncan v. Cessna Aircraft Co., 665 S.W.2d 414 (Tex. 1984), which is reproduced below in the next subsection. *Duncan* involved the crash of a small airplane that killed the student pilot and his instructor. Cessna sought contribution from the estate of the instructor, which had settled with the student's estate. Texas had two statutes providing for contribution: the comparative negligence statute permitted comparative contribution in negligence cases and another statute provided for pro rata contribution in other tort cases. This created a problem, as the *Duncan* court recognized, because both negligence and strict liability claims had been asserted by the plaintiff. Having different apportionment rules apply to different claims against the same defendant or to claims against or between different defendants would be confusing and difficult to administer. After recognizing the trend toward employing comparative responsibility principles and rehearsing much of the analysis of the court in *Daly v. General Motors Corp.*, page 613 *supra*, the court adopted a comparative scheme for all claims in cases with any strict products liability claim, including breach of warranty, which would also apply to contribution claims between defendants.

Loss allocation becomes more complicated when, as suggested above, defendants are not a cause of the same injury to the plaintiff. Consider a driver who was injured in a collision with a negligent motorist. Suppose that: (1) the original impact caused injury to the plaintiff's back, (2) a defective steering wheel shattered and caused injury to his hand, and (3) a doctor then negligently administered a drug to treat the plaintiff's hand, and the drug caused a rash. The negligent motorist was a cause-in-fact of all the plaintiff's injuries. The steering wheel manufacturer was a cause-in-fact only of the injured hand and the rash. The doctor was a cause-in-fact only of the rash. The plaintiff's negligent driving, of course, was a cause-in-fact of all three injuries.

Since the back injury was caused only by the negligent motorist, she alone should be liable for it, along with the plaintiff. Since the hand injury was caused by both the negligent motorist and the steering wheel manufacturer, the hand injury should be allocated among them and the plaintiff according to comparative fault. Since the rash was caused jointly by all three defendants, liability for it should be allocated among all of the parties according to comparative responsibility.

But how will all of this be submitted to the jury? Will the jury be asked to segregate the three separate injuries according to cause-in-fact (*i.e.*, the back, the hand, and the rash) and *then* apportion each injury, according to fault, among the parties who caused each? Doing so would require three separate strings of percentages, each totaling 100, because different sets of defendants caused each injury. This approach, however, would be very difficult to implement in many cases. Injuries are not always so easy to divide as are a back injury, a hand injury, and a rash. Maybe the doctor's malpractice aggravated the hand injury or caused more pain to the plaintiff's back. If so, the trial court could not simply ask the jury to ascertain comparative fault findings for each injury identified by the court in advance. The jury itself would have to resolve fact questions about how to divide the injuries on the basis of cause-in-fact. It would *then* somehow have to compare the fault of each defendant who caused each separate injury. This, to say the least, would be cumbersome.

All of this could be avoided by asking the jury to perform both operations—division by cause-in-fact and allocation according to fault—in one step. The jury's percentage findings could reflect, under proper instruction, a determination of each party's responsibility for the plaintiff's injuries, taking into account *both* cause-in-fact and fault. Thus, in the example above, the jury could assign percentages to the motorist, the steering wheel manufacturer, and the doctor by taking into account *both* the relative *fault* of the parties *and* the facts that the doctor had no *causal* connection with the back injury or the hand injury and that the steering wheel manufacturer had no *causal* connection with the back injury.

A difficulty arises, however, if a court takes this approach *and* retains joint and several liability. Again referring to the example above, suppose the jury assigns 10% responsibility to the plaintiff, 60% responsibility to the other motorist, 20% responsibility to the steering wheel manufacturer, and 10% responsibility to the doctor. If the other motorist were insolvent, the steering wheel manufacturer and the doctor would be required to pay for the other motorist's 60% share. But this share includes liability for the back injury, which the steering wheel manufacturer and the doctor did not cause! This creates a problem as joint and several liability has not been used to make a defendant pay for an injury that it did not cause.

Even in jurisdictions that have modified joint and several liability, a party's relative culpability may not have any relationship to the harm caused. When the harm is very difficult to apportion causally, such as in crashworthiness cases, employing the one-step allocation of liability described above might mean skewed liability with the more culpable parties paying for more than the harm caused by them.

For these reasons, the Restatement (Third) of Torts: Apportionment of Liability in § 26 urges a two-step process for apportionment of liability. First, liability should be apportioned based on cause-in-fact among the parties who were causally responsible for each segment of harm. Then, if there are different parties causally responsible for different segments of harm, as in the illustration above, separate percentages of comparative responsibility should be assigned to the parties liable for each segment of harm. However, recognizing that in some cases in which causal apportionment among multiple parties is difficult, this two-step apportionment process might be too complicated to be feasible, a one-step process combining cause and fault might be employed.

In ordinary negligence actions, some courts have distinguished among three types of conduct by a plaintiff. First, a plaintiff's substandard care might occur before an accident and be a proximate cause of the accident, such as when a plaintiff negligently runs a red light and hits a car passing through the intersection. This is ordinary contributory negligence. Second, a plaintiff's substandard care might occur after an injury and be a proximate cause of an aggravation to the injury, such as when an injured plaintiff fails to follow his doctor's orders and, in doing so, aggravates his condition. Many courts label this type of conduct as failure to mitigate damages, although section 918 of the Restatement (Second) of Torts calls this type of conduct "avoidable consequences." Third, a plaintiff's substandard conduct might occur before the injury-producing accident and be a proximate cause of a portion of the plaintiff's injuries, but not a proximate cause of the accident itself. A plaintiff's failure to wear a seat belt is an example. Some courts label this type of conduct "avoidable consequences," although section 918 uses this term to refer to post-accident plaintiff conduct. You must be very careful about the nomenclature in your jurisdiction.

For courts that draw these distinctions at all, mitigation of damages and avoidable consequences (as we have used the terms) are not absolute bars to recovery. Failure to mitigate damages merely reduces the plaintiff's damages by precluding recovery for the aggravated damage caused by the failure to mitigate. The same result could be reached simply by holding that such conduct is a form of contributory negligence, but that contributory negligence is an absolute bar to recovery only for the injuries it proximately causes. Nevertheless, the rubric of mitigation of damages is sometimes used rather than the rubric of contributory negligence.

The doctrine of avoidable consequences is more complex. Some jurisdictions have enacted statutes prohibiting the admissibility of evidence of seatbelt use in tort cases. See, e.g., Conn.Gen.Stat. § 14–100a(c). Independent of statutory provisions, some courts have held that failure to wear a seatbelt or a motorcycle helmet is not a defense. See Dare v. Sobule, 674 P.2d 960 (Colo.1984) (helmet); Fischer v. Moore, 183 Colo. 392, 517 P.2d 458 (1973) (seatbelt).

If the cases apply only to these specific behaviors there is effectively nothing more than a selective "no duty" rule concerning seat belts or helmets. If they are applicable to all types of "avoidable consequences" conduct, they would exclude a broad range of contributory negligence from consideration.

Whatever approach a specific jurisdiction uses in ordinary negligence cases, two important issues arise in the context of products liability litigation. First, do the details developed in negligence cases also apply to strict tort liability? For example, after *McCown* should the Pennsylvania Supreme Court nevertheless consider failure to mitigate damages as a defense to strict tort liability, on the ground that it is not a form of "contributory negligence"? Or should a court that follows Comment n nevertheless decline to count against a plaintiff his or her failure to wear a seatbelt?

Second, to what extent would a shift away from contributory negligence as an absolute bar in favor of comparative negligence affect these distinctions, even in ordinary negligence cases? For example, would mitigation of damages continue to be an absolute bar for the appropriate portion of the damages, or would it be part of the comparative percentages? And if such a shift affects these distinctions in negligence, does it have the same effect in strict tort liability?

3. PARTIAL SETTLEMENTS

DUNCAN v. CESSNA AIRCRAFT CO.
Supreme Court of Texas, 1984.
665 S.W.2d 414.

[James Parker and Benjamin Smithson were killed when a Cessna 150, in which Smithson was giving Parker a flying lesson, crashed. Duncan, Parker's wife, sued Smithson's estate and Smithson's employer for negligence, but she settled with them before trial. She and Smithson's wife then sued Cessna, alleging that "design and manufacturing defects in the legs of the cockpit seats caused the legs to break during the crash, causing the deaths of their husbands."

Cessna counterclaimed against Smithson's estate for contribution for any damages recovered from Cessna by Duncan, alleging that Smithson was negligent. Cessna also claimed that any recovery by Duncan should be reduced by one-half, based on her settlement with Smithson's estate and his employer. In response to the suit by Smithson's estate, Cessna asserted that Smithson's own contributory negligence should bar or reduce his recovery.]

Cessna argues that it is entitled to contribution from Smithson's estate for part of Duncan's damages because Smithson's pilot negligence proximately caused the fatal crash. The court of appeals agreed and remanded the cause for a partial retrial to allow Cessna to adduce proof of Smithson's negligence. [The court decided, as explained in the prior section, to adopt uniform comparative principles to apportion liability among all parties, regardless of the type of claim. The court chose to call the apportionment scheme it adopted "comparative causation." The court explained: "We choose comparative *causation* instead because it is conceptually accurate in cases based on strict liability and breach of warranty theories in which the defendant's 'fault,' in the traditional sense of culpability, is not at issue." The court then confronted the effect of plaintiff's settlement with the estate of the instructor.]

D. The Effect of Partial Settlements

We must also address the question of how a settlement with one tortfeasor affects the remaining defendants' liability and the plaintiff's recovery. We hold that in multiple defendant cases in which grounds of recovery other than negligence are established, the non-settling defendants' liability and the plaintiff's recovery shall be reduced by the percent share of causation assigned to the settling tortfeasor by the trier of fact.

The effect of a partial settlement in cases involving negligent tortfeasors was addressed by this court in *Palestine Contractors, Inc. v. Perkins,* 386 S.W.2d 764 (Tex.1964). In *Palestine* the court was faced with a choice between allowing a dollar credit or a pro rata credit and chose the latter. This court approved a pro rata credit because the rule allowed finality of settlement without prejudicing the non-settling defendants' rights. A pro rata credit reduces the non-settling defendants' liability by an amount equal to the number of settling tortfeasors divided by the total number of tortfeasors. Allowing a pro rata credit removes the incentive for collusive settlements because the plaintiff bears the risk of accepting an inadequate settlement. The court considered it fair to impose this risk on plaintiffs inasmuch as plaintiffs may avoid the risk entirely by rejecting the settlement offers. *Id.* at 771–73.

A dollar credit reduces the liability of the non-settling defendants, pro tanto, by the dollar amount of any settlement. The defendant's liability thus may fluctuate depending on the amount of a settlement to which he was not a party. This fluctuation cannot be reconciled with the policy of apportioning liability in relation to each party's responsibility, the conceptual basis of comparative causation. A dollar credit also encourages collusion by shielding plaintiffs from the effect of bad settlements while denying them the benefit of good settlements. Allowing a dollar credit does, however, ensure one recovery. *Id.*

Even though the reasoning in *Palestine Contractors* remains sound, we do not consider pro rata credit to be suitable in a comparative causation system. Pro rata allocation merely divides the damages by the number of defendants without considering their relative roles in causing the injuries. In the twenty years since *Palestine,* the law has advanced from crude head counting to a more refined percent allocation of liability based on the relative harm caused by each defendant. *Compare* Art. 2212, *with* Art. 2212a. Accordingly, we hold that a settlement with one tortfeasor will reduce the liability of the nonsettling defendants by the percentage of causation allocated to the settling tortfeasor rather than by a pro rata share. The term "tortfeasor" includes those whose liability is based on strict products liability, breach of warranty, and negligence.

A percent credit necessarily means that settling plaintiffs may recover more than the amount of damages ultimately determined, but they also may recover less. Plaintiffs bear the risk of poor settlements; logic and equity dictate that the benefit of good settlements should also be theirs. One objection to giving plaintiffs this benefit is that doing so would violate the one recovery rule of *Bradshaw v. Baylor University,* 126 Tex. 99, 84 S.W.2d 703 (1935). This case thus requires that we answer a question expressly left open in *Cypress Creek v. Muller,* 640 S.W.2d 860 (Tex.1982)—how does the *Bradshaw* one recovery rule apply in cases not controlled by Art. 2212a?

* * *

The reasoning behind the one recovery rule no longer applies. The system of comparative causation we adopt allows allocation of liability between the parties, even when the injury itself is indivisible. *Cf.* Art. 2212a (apportioning liability in negligence cases). Because each defendant's share can now be determined, it logically follows that each may settle just that portion of the plaintiff's suit. The settlement does not affect the amount of harm caused by the remaining defendants and likewise should not affect their liability.

An additional rationale supporting the one recovery rule was that it prevented unjust enrichment; however, any enrichment of plaintiffs under the new system of comparative causation is not unjust, for the simple reason that no one is harmed. The settling defendant cannot complain, because he agreed to pay. The non-settling defendant has no right to complain, because he was not a party to and is not affected by the settlement.

* * *

For the reasons stated, we hold that the one recovery rule does not prevent our adopting a system that reduces the plaintiff's recovery and the non-settling defendants' liability by the percentage of causation assigned to any tortfeasor with whom plaintiff has settled. We hereby adopt a percent credit rule, which will leave defendants unaffected by settlements in which they do not participate. Each party's share of liability will be that determined by the jury. Plaintiffs will benefit from good settlements and bear the risk of bad ones, just as they do in single-tortfeasor cases. Allowing plaintiffs to keep the excess from good settlements may violate the one recovery rule, but no one is harmed. Accordingly, to the extent it conflicts with this opinion, we overrule *Bradshaw v. Baylor University.*

* * *

Notes

1. As the court indicates, settling defendants were treated differently under *Duncan* than under Texas' comparative negligence scheme. Is there any reason for doing this?

2. Implicit in the court's opinion is that Cessna's contribution claim against the instructor's estate is barred once the estate settled with the plaintiff. Without such a bar, there would be little incentive to settle, as the settling tortfeasor could still remain subject to liability through the contribu-

tion claim. Some clever lawyers managed to solve this problem themselves by having the plaintiff agree to indemnify the settling tortfeasor for any contribution liability. *See* Pierringer v. Hoger, 21 Wis.2d 182, 124 N.W.2d 106 (1963), which spawned use of *Pierringer* releases. However, almost all states today bar a contribution claim against a settling tortfeasor so as to facilitate settlements, especially when the lawyers are not as clever (or diligent) as those in the *Pierringer* case. Hence, since the remaining defendants lose their contribution claim, the question addressed in *Duncan* arises: What credit should nonsettling tortfeasors receive against any judgment for the comparative responsibility of the settling tortfeasor?

3. In choosing among the different crediting schemes, the court selects a credit based on the comparative share of the settling defendant. How is the comparative share of that party to be determined? Remember, the settling defendant wants to be free from the suit and has no interest in remaining involved (and continuing to incur litigation costs) after the settlement. How will the factfinder determine the comparative share of the settling defendant with that defendant dismissed from the case? What interests and concerns do the plaintiff and remaining defendants have with regard to this determination? *See* Restatement (Third) of Torts: Apportionment of Liability § 16. The Apportionment Restatement, like *Duncan,* adopts a comparative share credit for nonsettling defendants. The Uniform Apportionment of Tort Responsibility Act, 5 ULA 12 (Supp.2005) was promulgated in 2003 by the Commissioners on Uniform State Laws, and intended to address the handful of remaining jurisdictions that have not yet adopted comparative responsibility. In § 8, it also adopts a comparative share credit when jointly and severally liable defendants settle. Interestingly, the Texas legislature eventually adopted a comparative share approach for all tort claims, but in 2005 it amended the proportionate responsibility statute to reinstate the pro tanto approach in most cases. *See* Tex.Civ.Prac. & Rem. Code § 33.012. Why do you think it made this change?

4. In assessing the respective merits of a comparative share and pro tanto credit, consider the following hypothetical version of the *Duncan* case. Assume the instructor was a young pilot trying to build his flying hours through instruction in the hope of securing a commercial pilot position. He had little money and only $100,000 of liability insurance for any aviation accident. After the crash, his insurer offers to settle with the plaintiff for the policy limits of $100,000, after appreciating that the damages will be at least an order of magnitude higher than that. Assume you are the lawyer for the student pilot's widow, and you satisfy yourself there are no other available assets from the instructor's estate or insurance. Would you advise her to accept the settlement? If your answer is no (it should be), what does this suggest about the desirability of a comparative share credit? Is there any way to address this serious deficiency of the comparative share credit? The Restatement (Third) of Torts: Apportionment of Liability § 16, Comment g, recommends a procedure that would entail a pretrial determination of partial insolvency when a plaintiff seeks to settle with a defendant who is partially insolvent, as in the hypothetical above. If the court determines that the defendant has no further available assets, then the credit for nonsettling defendants would be the amount of assets available to satisfy any judgment, thereby preserving for plaintiffs the benefit of joint and several liability.

5. Consider a jurisdiction in which joint and several liability has been abolished and defendants are only severally liable for their comparative share of the plaintiff's damages. In the absence of joint and several liability, no defendant can be held liable for more than that defendant's share and hence there is no basis for a contribution claim. With no contribution claim, there is no credit against the judgment for nonsettling defendants, but the net result, in terms of what those nonsettling defendants pay, is the same as a comparative share credit in a joint and several liability jurisdiction.

6. Sometimes a settlement is structured so that the settling tortfeasor obtains a financial interest in the plaintiff's recovery from the other tortfeasors. For example, the settling tortfeasor might be paid a percentage of the plaintiff's recovery in excess of a specific amount. This type of settlement is called a "Mary Carter" agreement, after the case of Booth v. Mary Carter Paint Co., 202 So.2d 8 (Fla.App.1967). Other arrangements, such as a "loan" from a defendant to a plaintiff to be repaid from any recovery from other tortfeasors, are employed. While the details vary, the common characteristic is that a defendant who formerly was adverse is now aligned with the plaintiff. The early use of these types of settlements typically involved keeping them secret and contemplated that the settling defendant would testify at trial. Do you see why?

A few courts have barred all such agreements. *See, e.g.,* Lum v. Stinnett, 87 Nev. 402, 488 P.2d 347 (1971); Trampe v. Wisconsin Telephone Co., 214 Wis. 210, 252 N.W. 675 (1934). Other courts have permitted "Mary Carter" and similar agreements but permit the nonsettling defendants to discover the terms of the settlement and disclose its existence to the jury. *See, e.g.,* Hemet Dodge v. Gryder, 23 Ariz.App. 523, 534 P.2d 454 (1975); Ward v. Ochoa, 284 So.2d 385 (Fla.1973); Gatto v. Walgreen Drug Co., 61 Ill.2d 513, 337 N.E.2d 23 (1975); Grillo v. Burke's Paint Co., Inc., 275 Or. 421, 551 P.2d 449 (1976); see generally Restatement (Third) of Torts: Apportionment of Liability § 24, Comment i.

In a jurisdiction that gives nonsettling defendants a pro tanto credit for a settlement, how should the value of a "Mary Carter" settlement be determined?

4. THE SPECIAL CASE OF EMPLOYERS

Recall that, because of the workers compensation system, as explained in note 2 following the *Bexiga* case in Chapter 4, employers are immune from a tort suit by an employee for an accidental occupational injury. The quid pro quo for this immunity is that the employee recovers workers compensation from the employer, regardless of fault. In addition, the employee may sue a "third-party" tortfeasor who also is responsible for the employee's injury. The predominant such "third party" is a product manufacturer. The incentive for the employee to pursue such a claim is that tort damages are considerably more generous than workers compensation benefits, which are typically something like one-third or less than the damages available in tort for the same injury.

Under joint and several liability, the third party is liable for all of the employee's damages in tort due to the occupational injury. In most jurisdictions, the employer has a subrogation lien against any such tort recovery by the employee for the amount of workers compensation benefits paid, less the costs, such as attorney's fees, of obtaining the tort recovery. Thus, the employee must pay back to the employer the workers compensation benefits previously provided.

Before reading the *Lambertson* case, make sure that you understand how the loss associated with an occupational injury is distributed among an employee, employer and third-party tortfeasor. One additional piece that you need is that in most jurisdictions, third parties are not permitted to assert a contribution claim against the employer because the employer is not jointly liable in tort to the employee with the third party.

Is this distribution of the costs of an occupational injury fair? Does it promote workplace safety? What other values might inform the question of how to apportion liability for a workplace injury among an employee, employer, and third-party tortfeasor?

LAMBERTSON v. CINCINNATI WELDING CORP.
Supreme Court of Minnesota, 1977.
312 Minn. 114, 257 N.W.2d 679.

SHERAN, Chief Justice.

Cincinnati Corporation, defendant and third-party plaintiff in a personal injury/product liability action, appeals from a judgment of the district court which awarded a worker $34,000 in damages but denied defendant manufacturer contribution from an employer which was partly at fault for the accident. We reverse in part and remand with instructions.

Cincinnati is the manufacturer of a press brake, a large machine used for bending metal. The brake has a large vertical ram which moves up and down. Dies are placed on the ram and on the bed of the machine, and metal to be bent is placed between the ram and the bed. When the ram comes down onto the metal, a bend, or brake, is made in the metal at the point where the die on the ram matches the die in the bed. The movement of the ram is controlled by the operator by means of a single foot pedal at the base of the machine.

Cincinnati sold a press brake to Hutchinson Manufacturing and Sales, Inc., plaintiff's employer. On April 25, 1972, plaintiff was assisting a coemployee in the operation of the press brake. The coemployee was controlling the foot pedal, and plaintiff was placing long metal strips between the ram and the bed and removing them after they had been bent. As the ram was being raised after one cycle, a piece of metal which had been bent fell to the side of the bed opposite to the side where plaintiff was working. Plaintiff reached through the jaws of the machine to retrieve the piece of metal, but his coemployee had kept his foot on the pedal, thus permitting the ram to descend again, crushing plaintiff's arm between the ram and the bed.

After recovering workers' compensation from Hutchinson, plaintiff brought this action against Cincinnati. Plaintiff testified that he had never operated the press brake before and did not know it was capable of double cycling, i. e., continuing through another cycle without the ram's stopping at the top. He testified that he knew he should not have put his arm between the jaws, but that he did not know that his coemployee still had his foot on the pedal or that the ram would descend again before he could retrieve the piece of metal.

Plaintiff introduced expert testimony and safety rules and regulations from which the jury could have found that certain safety devices and features could have been installed on the press brake at the time of its manufacture and sale to Hutchinson in 1967, and that such devices would have prevented the accident. * * *

In 1969, after representatives of Cincinnati viewed the particular uses to which the press brake was put at Hutchinson, Cincinnati offered to Hutchinson (at Hutchinson's expense) two changes in the machine: (1) Operation by two or more palm buttons or foot switches; (2) automatic stoppage of the ram at the top of the cycle i. e., no double cycling. These changes apparently were declined. In 1971, Cincinnati sent out a sales pamphlet to all owners of its press brakes describing a Waveguard safety device, an electronic sensing device designed to detect foreign matter in the press and stop the press if such matter were present. Hutchinson did not order or install such a device. * * *

* * *

The case was submitted to the jury on special verdict on a theory of negligence. The jury found all parties causally negligent and apportioned their comparative negligence as follows: Plaintiff 15 percent; Cincinnati 25 percent; Hutchinson 60 percent. The jury found damages of $40,000. The trial court ordered judgment against Cincinnati for $34,000, the full amount of the verdict less 15 percent for plaintiff's negligence, and denied Cincinnati's claim for contribution or indemnity from Hutchinson.

* * *

The * * * most important issue in this case concerns the claim of Cincinnati, a third-party tortfeasor, for indemnity or contribution from Hutchinson, plaintiff's employer. This issue is a troublesome one and has generated a substantial amount of debate in the bench and bar of this and other states. Arthur Larson, a leading commentator on workmen's compensation law, has called the controversy surrounding indemnity and contribution against employers in third-party actions "(p)erhaps the most evenly-balanced controversy in all of compensation law." 2A Larson, Workmen's Compensation Law, § 76.10. The essence of the controversy is this: If contribution or indemnity is allowed, the employer may be forced to pay his employee through the conduit of the third-party tortfeasor an amount in excess of his statutory workers' compensation liability. This arguably thwarts the central concept behind workers' compensation, i. e., that the employer and employee receive the benefits of a guaranteed, fixed-schedule, nonfault recovery system, which then constitutes the exclusive liability of the employer to his employee. See, Minn.St. 176.031. If contribution or indemnity is not allowed, a third-party stranger to the workers' compensation system is made to bear the burden of a full common-law judgment despite possibly greater fault on the part of the employer. This obvious inequity is further exacerbated by the right of the employer to recover directly or indirectly from the third party the amount he has paid in compensation regardless of the employer's own negligence. [Citations] Thus, the third party is forced to subsidize a workers' compensation system in a proportion greater than his own fault and at a financial level far in excess of the workers' compensation schedule.

The even balance in this controversy results from conflicts among the policies underlying workers' compensation, contribution/indemnity, and comparative negligence and the fault concept of tort recovery. Workers' compensation, a creature of Minnesota law since 1913, subjects almost all employers and employees to an essentially nonfault recovery system for accidents arising out of and in the course of employment. In exchange for guaranteed compensation for injury regardless of his own fault or the solvency of at-fault fellow employees, the employee is limited to a fixed schedule of recovery and gives up any right to a common-law action against the employer. See, Minn.St. 176.021, 176.031. This court has indicated on many occasions that the purpose of workers' compensation is broadly remedial and that workers' compensation laws are to be construed to favor employee recovery of benefits. [Citations]

Despite its essential nonfault character, the workers' compensation system retains an important common-law aspect—the third-party action. See, Minn.St. 176.061. The employee, and in some instances the employer, is allowed to bring an action against a third party who is legally responsible for the employee's injury. Such an action accomplishes two beneficial results for the workers' compensation system: (1) The at-fault third party is made to reimburse the employer who has been forced to bear the cost of the third party's activity; and (2) the employee obtains a full common-law recovery against the third party, who is not subject to the benefits and burdens of the workers' compensation system. While some states have placed the former result first in importance and have decreed that the employer must be reimbursed for all compensation benefits before the employee receives anything from a third-party judgment (see, 2A Larson, Workmen's Compensation Law, § 74.31), Minnesota has given paramount importance to the latter object in mandating that the employee receive a third of the judgment after litigation expenses are paid and before the employer can collect compensation paid. * * *

In summary, the interests of the respective parties in the workers' compensation system are therefore as follows: The employer has a primary interest in limiting his payment for employee injury to the workers' compensation schedule and a secondary interest in receiving reimbursement when a third party has caused him to incur obligations to his employee. See, *Nyquist v. Batcher,* supra. The employee has a primary interest in receiving full workers' compensation benefits and, to the extent a third party has caused him injury, a common-law recovery from that third party.

In contrast, the third party's interest is that of any other cotortfeasor to limit its liability to no more than its established fault. This interest is vindicated through contribution or indemnity. Contribution and indemnity are variant common-law remedies used to secure restitution and fair apportionment of loss among those whose activities combine to produce injury. * * * When one tortfeasor has paid or is about to pay more than his equitable share of damages to an injured party, he has an interest in obtaining indemnity or contribution from his fellow tortfeasors.

Comparative negligence, which is embodied in Minn.St. 604.01 and was substantially borrowed from our sister state of Wisconsin in 1969, introduces yet another dimension to the third-party tortfeasor's predicament. By abolishing the defense of contributory negligence in cases where plaintiff's percentage of total causal negligence is less than defendant's, it permits an injured workman to recover against the third party more frequently. In addition, Minn.St. 604.01, subd. 1, specifies a rule for contribution:

> "* * * When there are two or more persons who are jointly liable, contributions to awards shall be in proportion to the percentage of negligence attributable to each, provided, however, that each shall remain jointly and severally liable for the whole award."

Thus, a jointly liable tortfeasor has an interest, at least where the other tortfeasors are solvent and otherwise available for contribution, in contributing no more to the plaintiff's recovery than the percentage of negligence attributable to him.

* * *

* * * In *Hendrickson v. Minnesota Power & Light Co.,* 258 Minn. 368, 104 N.W.2d 843 (1960), this court denied recovery to a third-party tortfeasor seeking contribution or indemnity from a negligent employer. The court held: (1) There was no right of contribution because there was no common liability to the employee, i. e., the employer was not liable in tort to the employee because of the exclusive-remedy provision of our workers' compensation law * * *.

* * *

Cincinnati initially seeks indemnity from Hutchinson chiefly on the ground that it offered safety devices to Hutchinson which, if installed on the press brake, could have prevented the accident. The difficulty with this argument lies in the jury's unchallenged finding that Cincinnati was 25–percent negligent in the first instance, when it placed its press brake in the stream of commerce without certain kinds of safety devices. Since the independent acts of negligent manufacture and sale by Cincinnati and refusal of safety devices by Hutchinson combined to produce plaintiff's injury, liability should be apportioned between them, not shifted entirely to one or the other. Therefore, if Cincinnati is entitled to any remedy, that remedy is contribution.

Cincinnati's claim for contribution, however, confronts two further problems: (1) Our holding in *Hendrickson v. Minnesota Power & Light Co.,* 258 Minn. 368, 104 N.W.2d 843 (1960), that contribution is not available because of the absence of a common liability; and (2) the policy interest of the employer in paying no more than his workers' compensation liability because of an employee injury and the other conflicting policies and statutes discussed earlier in this opinion.

Considering the first of these problems, we cannot find any continuing persuasive force in the reasoning of the court in *Hendrickson.* * * *

While there is no common liability to the employee in tort, both the employer and the third party are nonetheless liable to the employee for his injuries; the employer through the fixed no-fault workers' compensation system and the third party through the variable recovery available in a common law tort action. Contribution is a flexible, equitable remedy designed to accomplish a fair allocation of loss among parties. Such a remedy should be utilized to achieve fairness on particular facts, unfettered by outworn technical concepts like common liability.

The second problem confronting Cincinnati's claim is a more formidable one. The equitable merit in Cincinnati's claim is plain: It has been forced to bear the entire burden of plaintiff's recovery despite the fact that it was only 25–percent negligent and has a 60–percent-negligent employer joined in the action and available for contribution. In contrast, granting contribution would result in substantial employer participation in its employee's common-law recovery despite the exclusive-remedy clause. This problem is, in large part, a legislative one which demands a comprehensive solution in statutory form. * * *

While the opinions of other jurisdictions must be read with caution on this issue because of different statutes and concepts of recovery in negligence cases, we have found direction in the approach taken by the Pennsylvania Supreme Court. That court has allowed contribution from the employer up to the amount of the workers' compensation benefits. *Maio v. Fahs*, 339 Pa. 180, 14 A.2d 105 (1940); *Brown v. Dickey*, 397 Pa. 454, 155 A.2d 836 (1959). See, also, *Stark v. Posh Construction Co.*, 192 Pa.Super. 409, 162 A.2d 9 (1960). This approach allows the third party to obtain limited contribution, but substantially preserves the employer's interest in not paying more than workers' compensation liability. While this approach may not allow full contribution recovery to the third party in all cases, it is the solution we consider most consistent with fairness and the various statutory schemes before us. If further reform is to be accomplished, it must be effected by legislative changes in workers'-compensation-third-party law.

For the reasons expressed above, the judgment is reversed and the case is remanded with instructions to grant contribution against Hutchinson in an amount proportional to its percentage of negligence, but not to exceed its total workers' compensation liability to plaintiff.

Affirmed in part, reversed in part and remanded with instructions.

Notes

1. *Lambertson* notwithstanding, most jurisdictions that retain joint and several liability do not permit any contribution claim by a third party against the employer. Indeed, in those jurisdictions an employer may not be joined in the suit and may not have a percentage of comparative responsibility assigned to it, as occurred in *Lambertson. See, e.g.,* Outboard Marine Corp. v. Schupbach, 93 Nev. 158, 561 P.2d 450 (1977); Hefferin v. Stempkowski, 247 Pa.Super. 366, 372 A.2d 869 (1977). In such jurisdictions, the employer's role in the accident may nevertheless be relevant as a superseding cause. *See* Chapter 7. Illinois permits limited contribution claims against employers similar to that provided in *Lambertson. See* Kotecki v. Cyclops Welding Corp., 146 Ill.2d 155, 585 N.E.2d 1023 (1991). New York is perhaps the only state that permits full contribution from responsible employees, and in 1996, the legislature limited such contribution claims to employees who have suffered "grave injury." *See* N.Y.C.P.L.R. §§ 1601–02.

2. Consider the impact of the employer's subrogation rights on efforts to settle the tort suit. Most settlements involve compromise by both sides to reach common ground. Do you see why the employer (more accurately, the employer's workers compensation insurer) would be less willing to compromise its subrogation claim in order to facilitate a settlement? Under what circumstances would this effect be most pronounced?

3. Consider how *Lambertson* modifies the apportionment of liability for workplace injuries. The workers compensation scheme might be conceptualized as an implicit settlement of any tort claim that the employee might have against the employer in exchange for workers compensation benefits. *See* Dix & Associates Pipeline Contractors, Inc. v. Key, 799 S.W.2d 24, 29 (Ky.1990) ("As a practical matter, workers compensation coverage constitutes a settlement between the employee and the employer whereby the employee settles his tort claim for the amount he will receive as compensation."). In that view, would any of the parties have a legitimate complaint about how liability is apportioned under a *Lambertson* scheme?

4. The adoption of several liability in a number of jurisdictions modifies the apportionment calculus. In most jurisdictions with several liability, non-parties, including the employer, may be apportioned comparative responsibility in order to determine the several share of defendants. Thus, even if contribution claims are barred against employers (and with several liability, contribution claims largely disappear), comparative responsibility can be assigned to non-party employers. Consider how this affects the apportionment of liability for workplace injuries. Is this apportionment preferable to that adopted in *Lambertson* or in jurisdictions described in note 1?

How should the employer's subrogation claim be treated in a jurisdiction with several liability when the non-party employer is assigned some percentage of comparative responsibility? Consider the Texas solution. Defendants in a products liability or other tort claim may join an employer as a "responsible third party." When the employer is so joined the jury is instructed that it may assign a percentage of the responsibility for the injury to the employer. Tex.Civ.Prac. & Rem. Code § 33.004. Even if the jury assigns a percentage of responsibility to the employer, the employee is restricted to her workers compensation remedy. Nor can other defendants obtain contributions from the employer. However, the inclusion of the employer in the comparative responsibility calculation may reduce the percentage of responsibility assigned to other defendants and in some cases this may push their percentage below the fifty percent threshold required for joint and several liability. Moreover, the employer's insurance company's subrogation rights are reduced by the comparative share of responsibility the trier of fact assigns to the employer. Tex. Labor Code § 417.001. How would the Texas scheme apportion liability in *Lambertson? See also* Restatement (Third) of Torts: Apportionment of Liability § B19, Comment l.

5. Proposals for reform in apportioning liability for occupational injuries have been numerous. *See* II American Law Institute, Reporters' Study, Enterprise Responsibility for Personal Injury 191–92 (1991) (proposing that subrogation claims be barred and third-party tortfeasors be credited with the amount of workers compensation benefits); Department of Commerce, Model Uniform Product Liability Act § 114 (1979) (same); Klein, Apportionment of Liability in Workplace Injury Cases, 26 Berkeley J.Emp. & Lab.L. 65 (2005) (advocating workers compensation be treated as if it were a settlement of employer's tort obligation to employee, each third-party defendant pay its comparative share of plaintiff's damages, and employer's subrogation claim be nullified); O'Connell, Bargaining for Waivers of Third–Party Tort Claims: An Answer to Product Liability Woes for Employers and Their Employees and Suppliers, 1976 U.Ill.L.F. 435 (advocating increasing workers compensation benefits and making them the exclusive remedy for occupational injuries).

Chapter 11

STATUTES OF LIMITATION AND REPOSE

RAYMOND v. ELI LILLY & CO.
Supreme Court of New Hampshire, 1977.
117 N.H. 164, 371 A.2d 170.

KENISON, CHIEF JUSTICE.

The facts of this case are detailed in *Raymond v. Eli Lilly & Co.,* 412 F.Supp. 1392 (D.N.H.1976), and need not be repeated in full here. For the present purposes the relevant facts are as follows: On February 26, 1975, Patricia Raymond brought suit in Hillsborough County Superior Court alleging that C–Quens, an oral contraceptive manufactured and distributed by the defendant, caused hemorrhages in her optic nerves causing her to become legally blind. Arthur Raymond, the plaintiff's husband, sued the defendant for consequential damages resulting from his wife's blindness. The defendant removed the action to the United States District Court for the District of New Hampshire based upon diversity of citizenship of the parties and moved for summary judgment in both actions on the ground that the New Hampshire six year statute of limitations for personal actions, RSA 508:4 (Supp. 1975), barred the claims.

The federal district court denied the motions for summary judgment applying principles underlying the so-called "*Shillady* rule" that "actions for malpractice based on the leaving of a foreign object in a patient's body do not accrue until the patient learns or in the exercise of reasonable care and diligence should have learned of its presence." *Shillady v. Elliot Community Hosp.,* 114 N.H. 321, 324, 320 A.2d 637, 639 (1974). Based upon Mrs. Raymond's testimony, depositions and medical records, the district court found that, although the plaintiff was injured in 1968, she did not know, nor had any reason to know of her potential claim against the defendant until "[s]ometime in 1970 or 1971," *Raymond v. Eli Lilly & Co.,* 412 F.Supp. at 1396, 1402, and held that her cause of action did not accrue until then.

[Rather than proceed to trial on the merits, the defendant made an interlocutory appeal to the United States Court of Appeals for the First

Circuit. The Court of Appeals then certified the question of interpreting New Hampshire's statute of limitations to the New Hampshire Supreme Court.]

The statute of limitations applicable in this case provides that "personal actions may be brought within six years after the cause of action accrued, and not afterwards." RSA 508:4 (Supp. 1975). The statute does not define the word "accrued." In the absence of a statutory definition, the time of accrual is left to judicial determination. * * * There are at least four points at which a tort cause of action may accrue: (1) When the defendant breaches his duty; (2) when the plaintiff suffers harm; (3) when the plaintiff becomes aware of his injury; and (4) when the plaintiff discovers the causal relationship between his harm and the defendant's misconduct. *See* 3 R. Hursh & Bailey, American Law of Products Liability 2d § 17:9–10 (1975), *Developments in the Law–Statute of Limitations,* 63 Harv.L.Rev. 1177, 1200–01 (1950); Annot., 80 A.L.R.2d 368, 373 (1961). In many tort cases the above events occur simultaneously and the moment of accrual is clear. However, in some cases there may be a delay between the breach of duty and the injury, * * * or between the injury and the plaintiff's discovery of the cause of his injury, * * * or there may be a delay between each of the four events. * * * Where any such delay exists, the choice of accrual becomes complex. * * *

White v. Schnoebelen, 91 N.H. 273, 18 A.2d 185 (1941) involved a delay between the defendant's negligence and the plaintiff's injury. The defendant negligently installed a lightning rod in 1930. As a result, a lightning fire destroyed the plaintiff's house in 1937. The plaintiff filed suit in 1938. The defendant claimed that the limitations period began to run in 1930 when he allegedly breached his duty of care. The plaintiff argued that the cause of action did not accrue until 1937 when he suffered the damage to his property. We held that the suit was not barred by the six-year statute of limitations because injury is an element of a cause of action for negligence and the action could not accrue until all the elements, including injury, were present.

* * *

White did not involve, as this case does, the problem of accrual when there is a delay between the date of injury and the date upon which the plaintiff discovers the causal relationship between the injury and the wrongdoing. In fact, if anything, the *White* rule assumes that the plaintiff knows of the cause of his injury at the moment he suffers harm. With obvious reference to *White v. Schnoebelen,* we have stated that "[i]n the usual tort case some physical impact would serve to notify the plaintiff of the violation of her rights and there is no reason why the time within which her action for the resulting damages must be brought should not start to run from that date." *Shillady v. Elliot Community Hosp.,* 114 N.H. at 323, 320 A.2d at 638 * * *.

Because *White* did not address the question in this case, it is erroneous to assume that under the *White* rule Mrs. Raymond's cause of action would be barred.

On two occasions we have dealt with the problem of accrual where, as in this case, a person was harmed but did not discover that he had a claim against the tortfeasor until a later date. In a case in which the defendant fraudulently concealed facts necessary to put the injured person on notice of his claim, we held that the cause of action accrued not when the injury occurred, but rather when the plaintiff discovered or in the exercise of reasonable diligence should have discovered the concealed facts. *Lakeman v. LaFrance*, 102 N.H. 300, 303, 156 A.2d 123, 126 (1959). Similarly, in a case in which a surgeon left a foreign object in a patient's body, and the patient was ignorant of that fact, although the object did cause him pain, we held that his cause of action did not accrue until he learned or in the exercise of reasonable care and diligence should have learned of the presence of the object in his body. *Shillady v. Elliot Community Hosp.*, 114 N.H. at 324, 320 A.2d at 639. A substantial number of other states have reached the same conclusions in fraudulent concealment cases * * *.

The concept that a cause of action does not accrue until the plaintiff knows or should reasonably know of the causal connection between his injury and the defendant's wrongdoing has been called the discovery rule. *Lopez v. Swyer*, 62 N.J. at 272, 300 A.2d at 565 (1973). Those jurisdictions that have adopted the rule do not regard its application as violating the policies behind the limitations statute. *Wyler v. Tripi*, 25 Ohio St.2d 164, 170, 267 N.E.2d 419, 422–23 (1971). "A primary consideration underlying the statute of limitations is fairness to the defendant." 9 Suff.U.L.Rev. at 1455. "There comes a time when [the defendant] ought to be secure in his reasonable expectation that the slate has been wiped clean of ancient obligations, and he ought not to be called on to resist a claim when 'evidence has been lost, memories have faded, and witnesses have disappeared.'" *Developments, supra* at 1185. However, a person cannot be said to have been "sleeping on his rights" when he does not know and reasonably could not have known he had such rights. *Wyler v. Tripi, supra* at 178, 267 N.E.2d at 427. By employing the discovery rule we avoid the harsh and illogical consequences of interpreting the statute in a manner that outlaws the plaintiff's claim before he was or should have been aware of its existence. *Shillady v. Elliot Community Hosp.*, 114 N.H. at 324, 320 A.2d at 639.

The discovery rule is based upon equitable considerations; in determining whether and how the rule should be applied we must identify, evaluate and weigh the interests of the opposing parties. *Shillady v. Elliot Community Hosp.*, 114 N.H. at 325, 320 A.2d at 639; *Lopez v. Swyer*, 62 N.J. at 274, 300 A.2d at 567. The federal district court has undertaken this task pursuant to *Shillady* and has concluded that the defendant's interests have not changed or been prejudiced in any way by the delay in this case. *Raymond v. Eli Lilly & Co.*, 412 F.Supp. at 1403. Before we independently weigh the equities, we will explain our understanding of what the rule means and then review the extent to which courts have adopted the rule in product liability cases.

One might read several discovery rule cases and conclude that the courts are applying two substantively distinct rules. In most cases the courts frame the rule in terms of the plaintiff's discovery of the causal relationship between his injury and the defendant's conduct. In some cases, including *Shillady,* a court will state simply that, under the discovery rule, a cause of action accrues when the plaintiff discovers or should have discovered his injury. Still other courts use both statements of the rule within the same case. The reason for these apparent differences is that in most cases in which the court states the rule in terms of the discovery of the injury, the injury is the kind that puts the plaintiff on notice that his rights have been violated. Thus, there is no reason for the court to express the rule in terms of the discovery of the causal connection between the harm and the defendant's conduct. In a case, such as the one before us, in which the injury and the discovery of the causal relationship do not occur simultaneously, it is important to articulate exactly what the discovery rule means. We believe that the proper formulation of the rule and the one that will cause the least confusion is the one adopted by the majority of the courts: A cause of action will not accrue under the discovery rule until the plaintiff discovers or in the exercise of reasonable diligence should have discovered not only that he has been injured but also that his injury may have been caused by the defendant's conduct.

One of the first product liability cases in which the discovery rule was applied was *R.J. Reynolds Tobacco Company v. Hudson,* 314 F.2d 776 (5th Cir.1963). Mr. Hudson smoked cigarettes from 1924 to 1957. He experienced severe trouble breathing two years before his suit. The tobacco company argued that Mr. Hudson's suit was barred by the one-year limitations statute because he knew of his injury more than one year prior to suit. The court rejected this contention holding that the cause of action accrued when Mr. Hudson learned or should have learned that his acute respiratory distress and diseased larynx were caused by smoking. 77 Harv.L.Rev. 1343 (1964). In *Breaux v. Aetna Casualty & Surety Company,* 272 F.Supp. 668 (E.D.La.1967), the plaintiff alleged that his consumption of a drug called Kantrex manufactured by Bristol Laboratories, Inc., caused him to go deaf and that the company negligently failed to warn him of the harmful propensities of the drug. The court cited *Hudson* for the proposition that the discovery rule applied in products liability cases and held that under Louisiana law the statute of limitations did not begin to run until the plaintiff knew or, as a reasonable person under the circumstances, should have known that there was a causal nexus between his deafness and the administration of the drug Kantrex.

* * *

The defendant argues that three cases in particular support its view that Mrs. Raymond's cause of action accrued when she first experienced difficulties with her vision, not when she discovered that the drugs may have caused the injury.

* * *

Having reviewed the case law, we now consider whether adopting the discovery rule in a drug-products liability case would be equitable. *Shillady v. Elliot Community Hosp.*, 114 N.H. at 325, 320 A.2d at 639. We must focus on the defendant's reasonable expectation of the duration of its exposure to liability and the extent to which the defendant might be prejudiced by the loss of evidence due to the passage of time. *Developments, supra* at 1185. With respect to their expectations of repose, drug companies are unique among most potential tortfeasors. The harmful propensities of drugs are often not fully known at the time the drugs are marketed. These companies know or at least should expect that some time may pass before the harmful effects of their products manifest themselves in drug users and that there may be another lapse of time before the injured person is able to discover the causal connection between his injury and the drug he consumed. * * * Given these unique circumstances and the fact that the scope of a drug manufacturer's liability is substantial and seems to expand continually through the growth of substantive tort and warranty doctrines. * * *

[W]e do not think the drug company can reasonably expect to be immune to suit before its customer has a fair opportunity to discover the company's tortious conduct.

With respect to the problem of lost or inaccurate evidence due to the passage of time, several reasons exist why the potential for prejudice to the defendant is not significant in a drug case of this kind. Most of the evidence necessary to prove or defend against liability is likely to be documentary in nature. It is not the kind of evidence that is lost or becomes unreliable as time passes. Companies generally compile and maintain research records that document the extent of their knowledge of the harmful propensities of their drugs. Certainly, doctors and hospitals meticulously maintain and store records of patient treatments. * * * Additionally, unlike the situation in most cases, the passage of time in a drug case is likely to increase both the amount and the accuracy of the evidence—in this case the scientific community's knowledge of the causal relationship between certain drugs and injury or disease. Finally, we note that manufacturers are in a superior position to control the discovery of the hazards of their products. "Through the processes of design, testing, inspection and collection of data on product safety performance in the field, the manufacturer has virtually exclusive access to much of the information necessary for effective control of dangers facing product consumers. Indeed, the strict principles of modern products liability law evolved in part to motivate manufacturers to use this information to help combat the massive problem of product accidents." Owen, *Punitive Damages in Products Liability Litigation*, 74 Mich.L.Rev. 1258, 1258 (1976). We do not think that in suits such as the instant one "the passage of time would increase problems of proof or entail the danger of false, fraudulent, frivolous, speculative or uncertain claims." *Wigginton v. Reichold Chemicals, Inc.*, 133 Ill.App.2d 776, 779, 274 N.E.2d 118, 120 (1971). It is manifestly unrealistic and unfair to bar a tort suit before the injured party has an opportunity to discover that he has a cause of action, *Lipsey v. Michael Reese Hosp.*, 46 Ill.2d 32, 41, 262 N.E.2d 450, 455 (1970), at least in a case in which the defendant has not demonstrated that the delay itself has been prejudicial to him. In conclusion, the equities clearly support application of the discovery rule in this case.

One of the principal justifications for applying the discovery rule in medical malpractice cases is that it provides protection against substandard medical care. * * * Protection against the manufacture and distribution of harmful drugs is also desirable and necessary. The additional burdens placed upon the defendant by the discovery rule are justified if they cause the defendant to conform to a higher standard of care.

* * *

In a final attempt to prevent an affirmative answer to the certified question, the defendant argues that Mrs. Raymond's action should be barred because, even after she discovered her cause of action, she still had a reasonable amount of time within which to sue. The defendant takes the position that the discovery rule should apply only where the plaintiff discovers his claim after the statutory time has already expired or the time left within which to sue is unreasonably short. In so arguing, the defendant fundamentally misconceives the issue before us. Our task is to determine when a cause of action accrues. It is at that point that the limitation period commences. From that date the plaintiff is statutorily entitled to no less than six years within which to file his claim. If we adopted the defendant's position, Mrs. Raymond would have only three or four years from the date of accrual within which to sue, contrary to the explicit wording of the statute. A simple example further exposes the weakness of the defendant's argument. If a person injured in 1977 discovers his cause of action in 1980, he has, under the defendant's proposal, three more years or until 1983 to sue. If another person is injured on the same day in 1977 but discovers his cause of action six or more years after his injury, say in 1984, he has six more years or until 1990 to sue. This reasoning puts the late discovering plaintiff in a more favorable position than the person who discovers his claim relatively early. We cannot permit an interpretation of the word "accrual" to produce such illogical results.

Analysis of the case law and the equitable considerations cause us to answer "Yes" to the certified question.

So ordered.

DOUGLAS, J., did not sit; the others concurred.

Notes

1. Recognize that, at least since the advent of asbestos litigation in the mid–1980s, a host of toxic substances cases has arisen in which there is a long latency period from exposure to disease manifestation. In many of these cases, the latency period is several decades. The opinion in *Raymond* examines several policies underlying statutes of limitation. Do you agree that the discovery rule adopted by the Court in *Raymond* does not substantially undermine these policies? In addition to evidentiary problems, does a manufacturer or its insurer also have an interest in "closing the books" after a specified period of time? Is your answer affected by the fact that insurers must hold "reserves" to cover potential liability?

2. Note the observation by the *Raymond* court that very frequently in drug (and other toxic substances) cases there is one very significant issue for which the evidence *improves* with time–scientific evidence of causation. Is the benefit of this passage of time for accurate decision making outbalanced by the degradation of evidence about other issues in the case?

3. The *Raymond* court suggests that discovery requires both knowledge of the injury and of the cause of the injury. Suppose that a plaintiff knows that she has an injury and that it was caused by a drug but does not know that the manufacturer's conduct was wrongful. For example, the plaintiff does not find out until some later time that the manufacturer failed adequately to warn about the adverse effect she suffered. Several times in its opinion, the *Raymond* court uses language that suggests this distinction between knowledge that the drug caused the injury and knowledge that tortious conduct by the defendant caused the injury. Should accrual of a cause of action be delayed until the plaintiff knows she has a cause of action against the defendant? *Compare* Nolan v. Johns–Manville Asbestos, 85 Ill.2d 161, 52 Ill.Dec. 1, 421 N.E.2d 864 (1981) *with* Berardi v. Johns–Manville Corp., 334 Pa.Super. 36, 482 A.2d 1067 (1984); *see also* Rose v. A.C. & S., Inc., 796 F.2d 294 (9th Cir.1986) (under Washington law, plaintiff must know the facts that comprise her cause of action, including that an unreasonably dangerous product caused the harm).

Whatever the plaintiff must know, how sure must she about it? Suppose a plaintiff takes five drugs during her pregnancy and bears a child with birth defects. Upon inquiry to her physician about what might have been responsible, the physician responds that, "one of the drugs might have been the cause, but none has been tested for teratogenicity in humans." Suppose that there are a couple of case reports of women who took one of the drugs during pregnancy and bore children with birth defects? Suppose the *National Enquirer* runs an expose of one of the drugs, claiming that it is a teratogen and only through a cover-up by the FDA and the manufacturer has this information been suppressed? *Cf.* Urland v. Merrell–Dow Pharmaceuticals, Inc., 822 F.2d 1268 (3d Cir.1987) (plaintiff barred by statute of limitations; discovery by plaintiff established in part by interview with reporter for the *National Enquirer*, which published a sensationalized article about drug and its teratogenicity).

Recall the heightened scrutiny of expert witnesses testifying to causation addressed in Chapter 6. Does it make any sense to set the standard for knowledge of causation for accrual purposes to be different from the standard for admissible testimony for an expert? On the other hand, doesn't delaying accrual until there is adequate evidence of causation provide no statute of limitations protection to manufacturers?

4. In a wrongful death claim based on products liability, should the statute of limitation begin to run when the decedent knew or should have known of the underlying products liability claim, or should it begin to run only when the decedent dies? In Cowgill v. Raymark Industries, Inc., 780 F.2d 324 (3d Cir.1985), the court held that because a wrongful death claim is derivative of the decedent's underlying claim, the statute of limitation for the wrongful death claim begins to run at the time of accrual of the decedent's underlying claim, not at the time of the decedent's death. *Contra* White v. Johns–Manville Corp., 103 Wash.2d 344, 693 P.2d 687 (1985).

In *Cowgill,* the plaintiff was the decedent's wife. Suppose she tried to get her husband to sue before his death, but was not successful? Should her rights be cut off by her husband's refusal to sue? Should the result be the same if the plaintiff was the decedent's minor child for whom the statute of limitation would normally be tolled until majority?

5. In a claim for contribution or indemnity, the statute of limitations generally starts to run from the time the contribution or indemnity claimant's cause of action accrued, which is when the claimant pays more than its share of the judgment or settles the plaintiff's claim. *See* Morrissette v. Sears, Roebuck & Co., 114 N.H. 384, 322 A.2d 7 (1974).

HEATH v. SEARS, ROEBUCK & CO.
Supreme Court of New Hampshire, 1983.
123 N.H. 512, 464 A.2d 288.

[Nine separate cases were consolidated for appeal to the New Hampshire Supreme Court. Each case involved the application of New Hampshire's twelve-year statute of repose and two of New Hampshire's statutes of limitation to products liability claims. The plaintiffs argued that the statutes violated the "open courts" and equal protection provisions of the New Hampshire constitution.]

DOUGLAS, JUSTICE.

* * *

The constitutional challenges in these cases focus principally upon the twelve-year "statute of repose" in RSA 507–D:2, II(a) (Supp.1979) and the three-year limitation provision of RSA 507–D:2, I (Supp.1979). Generally, both federal and State courts recognize the power of legislative bodies to enact statutes of limitations which prescribe a reasonable time within which a party is permitted to bring suit for the recovery of his rights. The United States Supreme Court has stated:

> "It may be properly conceded that all statutes of limitation[s] must proceed on the idea that the party has full opportunity afforded him to try his rights in the courts. A statute could not bar the existing rights of claimants without affording this opportunity; if it should do

so, it would not be a statute of limitations, but an unlawful attempt to extinguish rights arbitrarily, whatever might be the purport of its provisions."

Wilson v. Iseminger, 185 U.S. 55, 62, 22 S.Ct. 573, 575, 46 L.Ed. 804 (1902).

The concept of allowing a reasonable period of time for suit to be brought after the cause of action arises is not new in our law, for along with "substantive rights, the first settlers brought over the incidental rights of adequate remedy and convenient procedure." *State v. Saunders,* 66 N.H. 39, 74, 25 A. 588, 589 (1889). Thus, the "right to an adequate remedy [exists] for the infringement of a right derived from the unwritten law." *Id.,* 25 A. at 589. When it came time to establish a post-revolution form of government, the first part of our Constitution was devoted to chronicling our inherent rights. Part one, article fourteen of the New Hampshire Constitution provides:

"Every subject of this state is *entitled to a certain remedy,* by having recourse to the laws, for *all injuries he may receive* in his person, property, or character; to obtain right and justice freely, without being obliged to purchase it; completely, and without any denial; promptly, and without delay; conformably to the laws."

(Emphasis added.)

In an effort to facilitate the vindication of tort victims' rights, legislatures and courts have developed the "discovery" rule, under which a cause of action does not accrue until the plaintiff discovers or, in the exercise of reasonable diligence, should have discovered both the fact of his injury and the cause thereof. *Raymond v. Eli Lilly & Co.,* 117 N.H. 164, 171, 371 A.2d 170, 174 (1977); *see United States v. Kubrick,* 444 U.S. 111, 117–25, 100 S.Ct. 352, 356–60, 62 L.Ed.2d 259 (1979). The rule is premised on "the manifest unfairness of foreclosing an injured person's cause of action before he has had even a reasonable opportunity to discover its existence." *Brown v. Mary Hitchcock Memorial Hosp.,* 117 N.H. 739, 741–42, 378 A.2d 1138, 1139–40 (1977).

Although the legislature's power is broad in determining how long a plaintiff may have to initiate a cause of action and when that limitation period begins to run, this power may not be exercised in an unconstitutional manner. In *Carson v. Maurer,* 120 N.H. 925, 424 A.2d 825 (1980), we held that, although not a fundamental right, "the right to recover for personal injuries is * * * an important substantive right." *Id.* at 931–32, 424 A.2d at 830. Thus, the classifications there at issue were required to be "reasonable" and to "rest upon some ground of difference having a fair and substantial relation to the object of the legislation * * *." *Id.* at 932, 424 A.2d at 831.

In *Carson,* we ruled that the legislature's extension of the discovery rule to some medical injury plaintiffs, while denying its applicability to others, constituted an impermissible discrimination between classes of plaintiffs. We therefore held that RSA chapter 507–C (Supp.1979) violated the equal protection provisions of our Constitution to the extent that it limited application of the rule to only a narrow class of medical-malpractice plaintiffs. *Id.* at 936, 424 A.2d at 833.

More recently, in *Henderson Clay Products, Inc. v. Edgar Wood & Associates, Inc.,* 122 N.H. 800, 451 A.2d 174 (1982), we struck down RSA 508:4–b insofar as it precluded application of the discovery rule against architects, but allowed its application against materialmen and suppliers of labor. Relying upon *Carson,* we concluded:

> "It is difficult to rationally permit a situation to exist whereby the supplier of labor and material has a liability exposure for a period of six years after the injury has been discovered or, in the exercise of due care, should have been discovered when, at the same time, the designers of the premises can be immunized from the liability before the cause of action even accrues or can be factually asserted."

Id. at 801–02, 451 A.2d at 175; *see* 26 ATLA L.Rep. 152–53 (1983).

Here, too, our standard of review is whether the statute-of-limitations provisions contained in RSA 507–D:2 (Supp.1979) are reasonable and are substantially related to the legislative objective of reducing products liability insurance rates.

RSA 507–D:2, II(a) (Supp.1979), the twelve-year "statute of repose," requires a products liability action to be brought not "later than 12 years after the manufacturer of the final product parted with its possession and control or sold it, whichever occurred last." The effect of this absolute limitation on suits against manufacturers is to nullify some causes of actions before they even arise. As compared with nonproducts liability causes of action, which generally must be brought within six years after they accrue, *whenever* that may be, *see* RSA 508:4 (Supp. 1981), we hold that the twelve-year bar imposed by RSA 507–D:2, II(a) (Supp.1979) is neither reasonable nor substantially related to the object of the legislation.

The twelve-year limit is unreasonable because the mere purchase of pills produced by a drug manufacturer in California, or of a defective automobile made in Michigan, does not place the consumer on notice of a hidden defect injurious to his health or safety. When product defects lead to injury, our law has long provided for recovery without regard to *when* the substance or object was made or placed into the national or international stream of commerce. This is particularly important in cases where the injuries may not clearly manifest themselves until years later, such as the clear-cell adenocarcinomas found in the daughters of mothers who twenty or more years previously took a female estrogen pill commonly known as DES (diethylstilbestrol). *See, e.g., Bichler v. Eli Lilly and Co.,* 55 N.Y.2d 571, 577–78, 436 N.E.2d 182, 184, 450 N.Y.S.2d 776, 778 (1982).

The unreasonableness inherent in a statute which eliminates a plaintiff's cause of action before the wrong may reasonably be discovered was noted by Judge Frank in his dissent in *Dincher v. Marlin Firearms*

Co., 198 F.2d 821, 823 (2d Cir.1952), in which he condemned the "Alice in Wonderland" effect of such a result:

> "Except in topsy-turvy land, you can't die before you are conceived, or be divorced before ever you marry, or harvest a crop never planted, or burn down a house never built, or miss a train running on a non-existent railroad. For substantially similar reasons, it has always heretofore been accepted, as a sort of logical 'axiom,' that a statute of limitations does not begin to run against a cause of action before that cause of action exists, *i.e.,* before a judicial remedy is available to a plaintiff."

(Footnotes omitted.)

Nor do we think that the twelve-year "statute of repose" is substantially related to a legitimate legislative object. As previously noted, the crisis in products liability insurance had abated nationwide independent of RSA chapter 507–D (Supp.1979). Nonetheless, persons injured by defective products are deprived arbitrarily of a right to sue the manufacturers responsible for those defective products by virtue of a statute that has become entirely divorced from its underlying purpose. *Cf. Boucher v. Sayeed,* 459 A.2d 87, 92–93 (R.I.1983) (medical malpractice crisis existing at time of enactment but not at time of suit was insufficient basis to uphold statute against equal protection challenge). We do not believe that the legislature may constitutionally bar suits against manufacturers by products liability plaintiffs, as a class, twelve years after the manufacturer sold or parted with control of the product, while allowing other plaintiffs to recover for personal injuries not related to a defective product, at any time within six years after the cause of action accrues.

Our sister States of Alabama, Florida, and North Carolina have come to the same conclusion under similar provisions of their State Constitutions. [citations]

The plaintiffs also challenge the three-year statute of limitations established in RSA 507–D:2, I (Supp.1979). This three-year period begins to run from the "time the injury is, or should, in the exercise of reasonable diligence, have been discovered by the plaintiff." As previously mentioned, personal actions generally must be brought within six years of the time they accrue, with the exception of libel or slander actions, to which a three-year limit applies. RSA 508:4 (Supp.1981). We do not think that merely because a manufactured product causes the injury, or because the cause of action is legislatively defined as a "product liability action," *see* RSA 507–D:1, I (Supp.1979), a plaintiff's injury is therefore different from any other injury.

For instance, in the context of an automobile collision case, it makes no sense to say that for that part of an injury caused by another driver's alleged negligence a six-year statute applies while a product defect that may have been a factor in causing the harm to the plaintiff is subject to a three-year statute. Libel and slander were and are separate common-law torts which may reasonably be distinguished for statute of limitations purposes; however, there is no tort called "products liability."

For the reasons stated in our analysis of the twelve-year "statute of repose," we hold that RSA 507–D:2, I (Supp.1979) also denies products liability plaintiffs equal protection of the laws. This is not to say that the legislature could not constitutionally establish a statute of limitations of three years for *all* personal injury actions if it so desired. However, it may not constitutionally discriminate against one class of plaintiffs for the purpose of protecting manufacturers by means of a statute of limitations which is neither reasonable nor substantially related to a legitimate legislative object.

The last statute-of-limitations provision under attack in these cases, RSA 507–D:2, III (Supp.1979), requires third-party claims in products liability cases to be initiated within ninety days of the end of the time periods set forth in paragraphs I and II of that section. To the extent that the statute of limitations for third-party actions is dependent upon RSA 507–D:2, I and II(a) (Supp.1979), which we have already ruled invalid, we further hold that RSA 507–D:2, III (Supp.1979) is unconstitutional.

Notes

1. Several other courts have held that statutes of repose in product cases are unconstitutional, either under an "open courts" provision similar to Part 1, Article 14, of the New Hampshire Constitution or under an equal protection provision of the state or federal constitution. *See, e.g.,* Perkins v. Northeastern Log Homes, 808 S.W.2d 809 (Ky.1991) (construction) ("discrimination"); Berry By and Through Berry v. Beech Aircraft Corp., 717 P.2d 670 (Utah 1985) (open courts); Lankford v. Sullivan, Long & Hagerty, 416 So.2d 996 (Ala.1982) (open courts); Diamond v. E.R. Squibb & Sons, Inc., 397 So.2d 671 (Fla.1981) (open courts); Kennedy v. Cumberland Engineering Co., Inc., 471 A.2d 195 (R.I.1984) (open courts); Nelson v. Krusen, 678 S.W.2d 918 (Tex.1984) (medical malpractice; open courts); Shibuya v. Architects Hawaii Ltd., 65 Hawai'i 26, 647 P.2d 276 (1982) (architects and builders statute of repose; equal protection); Kallas Millwork Corp. v. Square D Co., 66 Wis.2d 382, 225 N.W.2d 454 (1975) (architects, engineers, and designers statute of repose; equal protection).

Not all courts have agreed, however. *See, e.g.,* Thornton v. Mono Mfg. Co., 99 Ill.App.3d 722, 54 Ill.Dec. 657, 425 N.E.2d 522 (1981) (open courts); Dague v. Piper Aircraft Corp., 275 Ind. 520, 418 N.E.2d 207 (1981) (open courts); Tetterton v. Long Mfg. Co., Inc. 314 N.C. 44, 332 S.E.2d 67 (1985) (open courts); Davis v. Whiting Corp., 66 Or.App. 541, 674 P.2d 1194 (1984) (open courts). *But cf.* Best v. Taylor Machine Works, 179 Ill.2d 367, 228 Ill.Dec. 636, 689 N.E.2d 1057 (1997) (finding several other provisions in tort reform act unconstitutional and concluding they could not be severed from other provisions from act, including statute of repose, thereby rendering entire act invalid).

2. What, precisely, was wrong with the New Hampshire statute of repose? Would it have been upheld if it had applied to all personal injury causes of action, not just products liability claims?

3. Is the Court's reasoning in *Heath* consistent with the fact that special liability rules are applicable to products liability claims? In this regard, is strict tort liability itself subject to an equal protection attack?

4. Section 2–725 of the Uniform Commercial Code provides:

(1) An action for breach of any contract for sale must be commenced within four years after the cause of action has accrued. By the original agreement the parties may reduce the period of limitation to not less than one year but may not extend it.

(2) A cause of action accrues when the breach occurs, regardless of the aggrieved party's lack of knowledge of the breach. A breach of warranty occurs when tender of delivery is made, except that where a warranty explicitly extends to future performance of the goods and discovery of the breach must await the time of such performance the cause of action accrues when the breach is or should have been discovered.

(3) Where an action commenced within the time limited by subsection (1) is so terminated as to leave available a remedy by another action for the same breach such other action may be commenced after the expiration of the time limited and within six months after the termination of the first action unless the termination resulted from voluntary discontinuance or from dismissal for failure or neglect to prosecute.

(4) This section does not alter the law on tolling of the statute of limitations nor does it apply to causes of action which have accrued before this Act becomes effective.

Under what circumstances might a plaintiff, whose tort claims is barred by the applicable statute of limitations, be able to pursue a breach of warranty claim? Would this section be constitutional under the analysis in *Heath* if the plaintiff does not file suit until after the four year period has expired?

5. In the General Aviation Revitalization Act of 1994 ("GARA"), 49 U.S.C. § 40101, Congress enacted a federal statute of repose for general aviation aircraft, the first statute providing federal law for state products liability actions. The statute of repose, subject to a few exceptions, for claims of design or manufacturing defect is 18 years (small private planes are frequently kept in service for several decades; it is not unusual to find planes built in the 1960s and 1970s in use). GARA was enacted when domestic aviation manufacturers were foundering; several were in bankruptcy proceedings. GARA is widely, but not universally, credited with contributing to the revival of the domestic general aviation industry. See Anton, A Critical Evaluation of the General Aviation Revitalization Act of 1994, 63 J.AirL. & Com. 759 (1998); Steggerda, GARA's Achilles: The Problematic Application of the Knowing Misrepresentation Exception, 24 Transp.L.J. 191 (1997).

6. Shortened statutes of limitation and statutes of repose are examples of "tort reform" legislation, much of which is directed at products liability litigation. (Medical malpractice litigation is the other common target.) Common reform provisions include abrogation or reduction of joint and several liability, caps on damages generally, caps on non-economic damages (such as pain and suffering), and caps on punitive damages. Do these provisions violate an "open courts" provision such as Part 1, Article 14, of the New

Hampshire Constitution? If they were applied only to products liability claims, would they violate equal protection?

7. *See generally* McGovern, The Variety, Policy and Constitutionality of Product Liability Statutes of Repose, 30 Am.U.L.Rev. 579 (1980); Phillips, An Analysis of Proposed Reform of Products Liability Statutes of Limitations, 56 N.C.L.Rev. 663 (1978).

PUSTEJOVSKY v. RAPID–AMERICAN CORP.
Supreme Court of Texas, 2000.
35 S.W.3d 643.

JUSTICE GONZALES delivered the opinion of the Court.

This case raises the question whether a plaintiff may bring separate actions for separate latent occupational diseases caused by exposure to asbestos. Specifically, we must decide whether the single action rule or the statute of limitations bars Henry Pustejovsky, who settled an asbestosis suit with one defendant in 1982, from bringing suit against different defendants twelve years later for asbestos-related cancer. The trial court granted summary judgment for the defendants based on limitations. The court of appeals affirmed, holding that under the single action rule, Pustejovsky's cause of action for cancer accrued, and limitations began to run, when he knew of the asbestosis. 980 S.W.2d 828, 833. We conclude, however, that neither the single action rule nor the statute of limitations bars Pustejovsky's later claim for asbestos-related cancer. Accordingly, we reverse the court of appeals' judgment and remand this case to the trial court for further proceedings consistent with this opinion.

I

Henry J. Pustejovsky, Jr. was exposed to asbestos from 1954 to 1979 while employed as a metal pourer with Alcoa Aluminum in Rockdale, Texas. In the late 1970s or early 1980s, Pustejovsky learned from co-workers that exposure to asbestos could be harmful. In 1982, Pustejovsky consulted an attorney, who arranged for a doctor to examine Pustejovsky to determine whether exposure to asbestos fibers at work had affected his health. The doctor found scarring on Pustejovsky's lungs and diagnosed him with asbestosis, a nonmalignant disease caused by inhaling asbestos fibers. The doctor also informed him that the asbestosis resulted from his years of working around asbestos products. In 1982, Pustejovsky sued Johns–Manville Corporation, an asbestos supplier, for damages related to his asbestosis. That suit was promptly settled out of court for approximately $25,000.

In 1994, when Pustejovsky was 59 years old, he began experiencing shortness of breath, cold-like symptoms, and fatigue. In September of that year, a doctor examined Pustejovsky and diagnosed him with malignant pleural mesothelioma, a cancerous tumor of the lung lining. Two months later, Pustejovsky joined with three other plaintiffs and sued Rapid American Corporation, Owens Corning Fiberglas Corporation

(Owens Corning), Pittsburgh Corning Corporation, and other suppliers of asbestos products. These four plaintiffs sought damages for their injuries caused by exposure to asbestos. In May 1995, [Rapid–American] filed a motion for summary judgment, asserting that Pustejovsky's claim is barred by the statute of limitations, which began to run for all asbestos-related claims, including mesothelioma, when Pustejovsky was diagnosed with asbestosis in 1982. * * *

Pustejovsky contested the motions with undisputed expert medical evidence that mesothelioma and asbestosis are separate conditions resulting from distinct disease processes. Because the conditions are distinct, Pustejovsky argued, limitations for mesothelioma was not triggered by the diagnosis of his asbestosis in 1982. The trial court granted defendants' motions for summary judgment and severed Pustejovsky's claim against defendants on the grounds that the statute of limitations began to run in 1982, when Pustejovsky discovered his asbestosis. The court of appeals affirmed the summary judgment, holding that Pustejovsky's second action was barred by the single action rule and the statute of limitations. 980 S.W.2d at 829. The court determined that asbestosis and mesothelioma are but different damages resulting from the same injury by exposure to asbestos. The court concluded that Pustejovsky could not sue for mesothelioma after settling his asbestosis claim without violating the single action rule's prohibition against claim splitting. Although the court of appeals acknowledged that other jurisdictions had rejected the single action rule as a bar to latent disease claims, it held that any decision to do so here should be by our Court. 980 S.W.2d at 831–33.

* * *

II

The applicable standard of review is whether Rapid American, as the summary-judgment movant, established that there is no genuine issue of material fact and that it is entitled to judgement as a matter of law on the grounds it set forth in its motion. *See* Tex.R.Civ.P. 166a(c); *Cathey v. Booth,* 900 S.W.2d 339, 341 (Tex.1995); *Nixon v. Mr. Property Management Co.,* 690 S.W.2d 546, 548–49 (Tex.1985). A defendant moving for summary judgment on the affirmative defense of limitations must prove conclusively the elements of that defense. *Velsicol Chem. Corp. v. Winograd,* 956 S.W.2d 529, 530 (Tex.1997). When, as here, the plaintiff pleads the discovery rule as an exception to limitations, the defendant has the burden of negating that exception as well. *Id.*

Pustejovsky pleaded the discovery rule, supported by the affidavit testimony of an expert on the subject of mesothelioma, Dr. James Robb, as well as Pustejovsky's affidavit and medical records. As Dr. Robb testified, asbestosis is a non-malignant disease caused by inhaling asbestos dust. When inhaled, asbestos fibers may begin a scarring process that destroys air sacs in the lung where oxygen is transferred into the blood. The condition is marked by decreased pulmonary function and lung capacity. Symptoms include shortness of breath, a dry and unproductive cough, and in some cases, weight loss and chest pain. The scarring is progressive and incurable, but it is not always fatal. According to Dr. Robb, the latency period between toxic exposure and manifestation of asbestosis is typically fifteen to twenty-five years.

Dr. Robb testified further that mesothelioma is a malignant tumor in the membranes lining the lungs, abdomen, and chest. The cancer is a very painful and severely debilitating disease that almost always causes the victim's death within seven to fifteen months of diagnosis. The latency period for mesothelioma is generally over fifteen years, averages thirty to forty years, and in some cases can extend as long as seventy years.

Dr. Robb explained that mesothelioma does not have any causal connection to asbestosis. While both diseases are associated with exposure to asbestos, mesothelioma is not dependant on a precondition of asbestosis, and asbestosis does not necessarily develop into, or cause the development of, mesothelioma. According to Dr. Robb, approximately fifteen percent of asbestosis victims also contract mesothelioma. *See* 980 S.W.2d at 829.

In his summary judgment response, Pustejovsky argued that because the diseases are separate, distinct conditions, his asbestosis diagnosis could not trigger limitations for a disease that would not manifest for another twelve years. Because he brought suit for mesothelioma in less than a year of its diagnosis, Pustejovsky contends that limitations does not bar his present suit.

The defendants did not offer medical evidence controverting Dr. Robb's testimony. Rather, Rapid American argues that the fact that asbestosis and mesothelioma are distinct diseases does not matter because both diseases were caused by the same course of exposure to asbestos. Rapid American contends that the single action rule requires that the statute of limitations for all causes of action based on asbestos exposure began to run from the 1982 diagnosis of asbestosis. Therefore, it argues, Pustejovsky's present claim for mesothelioma is time-barred as a matter of law. Accordingly, we first consider existing jurisprudence about our single action rule.

III

The single action rule, also known as the rule against splitting claims, provides a plaintiff one indivisible cause of action for all damages arising from a defendant's single breach of a legal duty. *See Gideon v. Johns–Manville Sales Corp.*, 761 F.2d 1129, 1136–37 (5th Cir.1985). Our jurisprudence "was designed to prevent more than one suit growing out of the same subject-matter of litigation; and our decisions from the first have steadily fostered this policy." *Galveston, H. & S.A. Ry. Co. v. Dowe*, 70 Tex. 5, 7 S.W. 368, 371 (1888). As one court has explained:

> The reason for the rule lies in the necessity for preventing vexatious and oppressive litigation, and its purpose is accomplished by forbid-

ding the division of a single cause of action so as to maintain several suits when a single suit will suffice.

Eastland County v. Davisson, 13 S.W.2d 673, 676 (Tex. Comm'n App.1929, judgm't adopted). This equitable doctrine is a species of res judicata that prohibits splitting a single cause of action and subsequently asserting claims that could have been litigated in the first instance. *See Jeanes v. Henderson,* 688 S.W.2d 100, 103 (Tex.1985); *Pierce v. Reynolds,* 160 Tex. 198, 329 S.W.2d 76, 78 (1959). In a recent accounting malpractice case, we reiterated a corollary rule about the accrual of a cause of action:

> [A] cause of action accrues when the plaintiff knows or reasonably should know that he had been legally injured by the alleged wrong, however slightly. The fact that the plaintiff's actual damages may not be fully known until much later does not affect the determination of the accrual date....

Murphy v. Campbell, 964 S.W.2d 265, 273 (Tex.1997).

Rapid–American contends that Texas courts have already applied the single action rule and the principles reiterated in *Murphy* in asbestos-related cases to bar any second suits. In *Pecorino v. Raymark Indus., Inc.,* the plaintiff filed suit after he was diagnosed with mesothelioma, even though he had previously settled a lawsuit with the same defendant for asbestosis. 763 S.W.2d 561, 562–63 (Tex.App.—Beaumont 1989, writ denied). The defendant moved for summary judgment on the grounds that the plaintiff had signed a release in the first suit, and that the limitations period for the second suit had run. The court held that the plaintiff's first suit and the release conclusively demonstrated that the plaintiff knew at the time of his asbestosis diagnosis that he had suffered a serious, severe legal injury as a result of his asbestos exposure. *Id.* at 569. The court rejected adopting a "separate action" rule, and explained: "Texas law is now well settled that a plaintiff has but one cause of action for the losses, injuries and damages arising from a single breach of duty, a single causal connection, being a single cause of action." *Id.* (citing *Tennessee Gas Transmission Co. v. Fromme,* 153 Tex. 352, 269 S.W.2d 336, 337–38 (1954)). The court further stated that the limitations period for the plaintiff's one cause of action began to run upon his discovery that he had been harmed, even if he had not yet suffered the full extent of that harm:

> The several pleadings of the [plaintiff] are based upon the same exposure and the same years of exposure to asbestos and asbestos-containing products. Under the decisional precedents of our state, one cause of action arose. Hence, this cause of action could not be split for the purpose of recovering additional monetary damages. *Id.* at 571.

The Fifth Circuit Court of Appeals also has considered the single action rule in the context of asbestos litigation. In *Gideon v. Johns–Manville Sales Corp.,* the Fifth Circuit rejected a challenge admitting the plaintiff's evidence that he had a greater than fifty percent chance of developing asbestos-related cancer. 761 F.2d 1129 (5th Cir.1985). There, the court found that the evidence was admissible because Texas law not only entitles, but requires plaintiffs to recover all of the damages arising out of a single wrong as part of a single cause of action:

> [The plaintiff's] injury is ... the inhalation of fibers and the invasion of his body by those fibers, thus causing him physical damage. Under Texas law, therefore, [the plaintiff] has but one cause of action for all the damages caused by the defendants' legal wrong; the diseases that have developed and will in probability develop are included within this cause of action, for they are but part of the sequence of harms resulting from the alleged breach of legal duty. [He] could not split his cause of action and recover damages for asbestosis, then later sue for damages caused by such other pulmonary disease as might develop, then still later sue for cancer should cancer appear.

Id. at 1137 (footnotes omitted). As the court explained, under Texas law the cause of action arises from the wrongful act itself, and not from the harm it may cause: "The cause of action 'inheres in the causative aspects of a breach of legal duty, the wrongful act itself, and not in the various forms of harm which result therefrom....' [A plaintiff] does not have a discrete cause of action for each harm." *Id.* at 1136–37.

* * *

Our court has not considered the effect of the single action rule on multiple asbestos-related injuries. Rapid–American argues that we should adopt the reasoning from the federal and state courts of appeals, and apply them to preclude Pustejovsky's current action. It argues that Pustejovsky was entitled to one cause of action for the defendants' single breach of duty. Thus, it contends that Pustejovsky's single action accrued in 1982 because Pustejovsky's asbestosis put him on notice that he had suffered a work-related injury. Furthermore, relying on *Murphy*, Rapid American argues that Pustejovsky's lack of knowledge of the scope of his damages from his exposure to asbestos does not affect the accrual of his cause of action. Following these general rules, Rapid American contends, Pustejovsky's claims for damages related to mesothelioma accrued in 1982, and therefore, limitations bars his current action.

IV

For several decades, courts have grappled with the problem of applying limitations to toxic exposure diseases with protracted latency periods, particularly when the exposure can cause more than one disease with different latency periods. *See generally, Maskin, et al., Overview and Update of Emerging Damage Theories in Toxic Tort Litigation,* C837 ALI ABA 629, 642–50 (1993). Like the courts in *Pecorino, Gideon,* and *Graffagnino* [*v. Fibreboard Corp.,* 776 F.2d 1307 (5th Cir.1985)], some courts consider the single action rule to be unmalleable and have applied the rule to different diseases caused by the same exposure. *See e.g., Howell v. Celotex Corp.,* 904 F.2d 3, 4–5 (3d Cir.1990) (applying Pennsylvania law). But other courts and commentators have recognized that the single action rule is a catch 22 for victims of multiple latent diseases, if applied to them the same as traditionally applied to victims of traumatic injuries. *See Sopha v. Owens–Corning Fiberglass Corp.*, 230 Wis.2d 212, 601 N.W.2d 627, 634–35 (1999); *Devlin v. Johns–Manville Corp.*, 202 N.J.Super. 556, 495 A.2d 495, 502 (N.J.Super.Ct.Law Div. 1985); *see generally* Green, *The Paradox of Statutes of Limitations in Toxic Substances Litigation*, 76 CAL. L. REV. 965, 1002 (1988); Note, *Claim Preclusion in Modern Latent Disease Cases: A Proposal for Allowing Second Suits*, 103 HARV.L.REV. 1989, 1989–97 (1990). A plaintiff who sues for asbestosis is precluded from any recovery for a later-developing lethal mesothelioma. But the discovery rule would preclude a plaintiff with asbestosis from waiting to see if an asbestosis-related cancer later develops if, as Rapid American contends, all damages for exposure to asbestosis must be brought in a single suit.

A plaintiff suing for asbestosis could join that claim with a claim for the prospect of developing cancer in the future. But the plaintiff can only recover future damages for injury that the plaintiff has a reasonable medical probability of developing. *See Insurance Co. of N. Am. v. Myers*, 411 S.W.2d 710, 713–14 (Tex.1966). According to the expert testimony here, only fifteen percent of asbestosis victims ever develop mesothelioma. If so, then no asbestosis plaintiff could establish future damages with the requisite certainty. Rapid American's position means for the asbestosis victim that any later-developing terminal condition must go unredressed.

In part because of the harshness of its application of the single action rule, the court in *Dartez v. Fibreboard Corp.*, opined that Texas courts would permit recovery for the fear of developing cancer in the future. *Dartez*, 765 F.2d 456, 467 (5th Cir.1985). Other courts have likewise recognized a cause of action for fear of cancer. *See Herber v. Johns–Manville Corp.*, 785 F.2d 79 (3d Cir.1986); *In re Moorenovich*, 634 F.Supp. 634, 637 (D.Me.1986); *Giovanetti v. Johns–Manville Corp.*, 372 Pa.Super.431, 539 A.2d 871, 874 (1988); *Eagle–Picher Indus., Inc. v. Cox*, 481 So. 2d 517, 523 (Fla.Dist.Ct.App.1985), *rev. denied*, 492 So. 2d 1331 (Fla.1986). *See generally,* Renia, *Recovery for Fear of Cancer and Increased Risk of Cancer: Problems with* Gideon *and a Proposed Solution*, 7 REV. LITIG. 39, 40–42 (1987). Additionally, some courts have allowed recovery for an increased risk of cancer on proof of less than a reasonable probability that the plaintiff will actually get cancer. *See, e.g., Brafford v. Susquehanna Corp.*, 586 F.Supp. 14, 17–18 (D.Colo.1984); *Boryla v. Pash*, 960 P.2d 123, 127 (Colo.1998); *United States v. Anderson*, 669 A.2d 73, 78 (Del.1995).

Most jurisdictions that have considered the question, however, allow separate actions for separate diseases arising from the same exposure to asbestos. An early case to treat distinct asbestos diseases separately is *Wilson v. Johns–Manville Sales Corp.*, 684 F.2d 111 (D.C.Cir.1982). In that case, an employee who developed mesothelioma several years after being diagnosed with asbestosis died without ever filing suit. When his widow sued, his employer asserted that the suit was untimely because limitations began to run upon the asbestosis diagnosis. The controlling issue was whether manifestation of any asbestos-related disease triggered limitations for all separate and distinct diseases. Speaking for the court, Judge Ruth Bader Ginsberg commented:

> In latent disease cases, [the] community interest would be significantly undermined by a judge-made rule that upon manifestation of any harm, the injured party must then, if ever, sue for all harms the same exposure may (or may not) occasion some time in the future.

Id. at 119. The court concluded in that case that the plaintiff's asbestosis diagnosis did not start limitations to run on later developing mesothelioma. *Id.* at 119–20.

* * *

V

Since the 1980s, when the federal court of appeals in *Gideon, Dartez,* and *Graffagnino,* and the state court of appeals in *Pecorino* prognosticated how we might rule on applying the single action rule to asbestos litigation, we have considered pertinent issues in two cases that inform our analysis in this case. Most recently, in *Temple-Inland v. Carter,* we held that an individual who has been exposed to asbestos, but has not developed an asbestos-related disease, could not recover mental anguish damages for the reasonable fear of possible future asbestos-related diseases. 993 S.W.2d 88, 89 (Tex.1999). We noted that the existence of a physical injury may not be sufficient for recovery of mental anguish damages when the injury has not produced disease despite a reasonable fear that such disease will develop. *Id.* at 92. We explained that while the law generally allows recovery of mental anguish damages in personal injury cases, allowing recovery for fear of a disease when the plaintiff has no symptoms results in systematic under-compensation of those who actually contract the disease, and a windfall for those who do not. *Id.* at 93. We expressly did not decide in *Temple-Inland* whether "a plaintiff who has developed an asbestos-related disease may recover mental anguish damages for a reasonable fear of developing other asbestos-related diseases." *Id.* at 94 (discussing Dartez v. *Fibreboard Corp.,* 765 F.2d 456 (5th Cir.1985)). While we do not resolve that question here either, the same concerns about under-compensation in some cases, and windfalls in other cases, militate against a cause of action for fear of cancer as an acceptable substitute for a cause of action for existing cancer.

In *Childs v. Haussecker,* we held for the first time that the discovery rule applies to claims for latent occupational diseases. 974 S.W.2d 31, 37–8 (Tex.1998). We held that accrual of the limitations period is deferred in such cases until "a plaintiff's symptoms manifest themselves to a degree or for a duration that would put a reasonable person on notice that he or she suffers from some injury and he or she knows, or in the exercise of reasonable diligence should have known, that the injury is likely work-related." *Id.* at 33. In *Childs,* we balanced the principles underlying the statute of limitations, including the benefit of repose, judicial economy, and the injustice to plaintiffs caused by strictly applying the statute of limitations. *Id.* at 38. We recognized the important protective purposes the statute of limitations serves, and held that deferring accrual in latent disease cases until an innocent plaintiff discovers his or her injuries does not betray those purposes. *Id.* We expressly held open the question whether limitations should run for separate diseases from the same exposure that manifest at different times. *Id.* at 41.

VI

Pustejovsky asks our court to follow those jurisdictions that treat claims for distinct asbestis diseases as separate causes of action and hold that Pustejovsky's asbestosis settlement does not bar his suit for mesothelioma. In considering Pustejovsky's arguments, we begin by noting, as we did in *Childs,* that it is the Court's responsibility to determine the accrual date for Pustejovsky's cause of action for mesothelioma for limitations purposes. *Childs,* 974 S.W.2d at 36. The statute of limitations applicable to Pustejovsky's claims provides that an action to recover damages for injuries to the person shall be commenced within two years after the day the cause of action accrues. *See* Tex. Civ. Prac. & Rem. Code 16.003(a). The statute does not define the accrual date, and thus it falls to the courts to establish when such claims accrue. *Childs,* 974 S.W.2d at 36. Also, we note that the single action rule is a judicially-created doctrine. Consequently, it is appropriate for us to consider whether allowing a suit for mesothelioma here significantly undermines the interests the single action rule and res judicata represent.

As we noted earlier, the single action rule is a species of res judicata. Strictly speaking, res judicata's policy concerns about protecting a defendant from multiple litigation are not present here because none of the parties Pustejovsky sued for his mesothelioma were parties to the suit and settlement of his asbestosis claim with Johns Manville Corporation. Res judicata does not apply without an identity of parties or those in privity with them. *See Amstadt v. U.S. Brass Corp.,* 919 S.W.2d 644, 652 (Tex.1996). But res judicata is implicated here because it informs what should constitute a single cause of action.

A single action rule for separate latent occupational diseases in this context would be incompatible with the "transactional" approach for res judicata that we established in *Barr v. Resolution Trust Corp.,* 837 S.W.2d 627, 631 (Tex.1992). Under that approach, the subject matter of a suit is based on the factual matters that make up the gist of the complaint. *Id.* at 630. Any claim that arises out of those facts should be litigated in the same lawsuit. *Id.* But the transactional approach set out in *Barr* does not necessarily penalize a plaintiff for not bringing a claim arising out of the same facts that nonetheless could not have been litigated in the initial action. *See Id.* at 631 (stating that "A subsequent suit will be barred if it arises out of the same subject matter of a previous suit and which through the exercise of diligence, *could have been litigated* in a prior suit.") (emphasis added).

We have held that a cause of action generally accrues upon injury even if the fact of injury is not known, or not all of the resulting damages have yet occurred. *Murphy,* 964 S.W.2d at 270. Rapid–American contends that the single action rule must be applied even if it means the loss of a recovery for damages that could not have been litigated in the prior suit. Generally, the single action rule and the transactional approach to res judicata are not in tension. In cases in which the injury is progressive, a plaintiff exercising due diligence will normally be able to discover the full extent of injury and recover for reasonably certain future damages. Also, we have made occasional exceptions to the accrual rule, known as the discovery rule, in cases in which "the nature of the injury incurred is inherently undiscoverable and the evidence of injury is objectively verifiable." *Id.,* (quoting *Computer Assoc. Int'l, Inc. v. Altai, Inc.,* 918 S.W.2d 453, 456 (Tex.1996)). We said in *S.V. v. R.V.,* "An injury is inherently undiscoverable if it is by nature unlikely to be discovered within the prescribed limitations period despite due diligence." 933 S.W.2d 1, 7 (Tex.1996).

In the typical case involving progressive injuries, the single action rule may occasionally result in uncompensated damages, in order to vindicate other competing interests. But in asbestos-related cases, in which multiple, latent injuries may manifest years or even decades apart, the rule would produce much more erratic results. The summary judgment record reveals that no amount of due diligence would have allowed Pustejovsky to recover for mesothelioma when he brought his suit for asbestosis. It is our long-established rule that a plaintiff may recover damages for a disease that may develop in future years only if the person establishes that there is a reasonable medical probability that the disease will appear. *See Insurance Co. of N. Am. v. Myers,* 411 S.W.2d 710, 713–14 (Tex.1966); *Fisher v. Coastal Transp. Co.,* 149 Tex. 224, 230 S.W.2d 522, 523–525 (1950); *Dartez v. Fibreboard Corp.,* 765 F.2d 456, 466 (5th Cir.1985). Courts have interpreted this test to mean that the plaintiff must demonstrate a greater than fifty percent chance of incurring the future damages. *See Fibreboard Corp. v. Pool,* 813 S.W.2d 658, 681 (Tex.App.—Texarkana 1991, writ denied), *cert. denied,* 508 U.S. 909, 113 S.Ct. 2339, 124 L.Ed.2d 250 (1993); *Brookshire Bros., Inc. v. Wagnon,* 979 S.W.2d 343, 353 (Tex.App.—Tyler 1998, pet. denied). Under this rule, a plaintiff who has been injured by exposure to asbestos must demonstrate a greater than fifty percent chance of developing cancer to recover future damages related to the cancer. * * *

* * * But nothing in this record demonstrates that Pustejovsky had a greater than fifty percent chance of developing cancer at the time of his first suit. As with many similarly situated asbestosis sufferers, it is unlikely that Pustejovsky could have adduced evidence at the time of his first suit that would have allowed him to recover for his future risk of cancer. [Citations.] We conclude that applying a single accrual rule under these circumstances would be inconsistent with the transactional

approach to res judicata, further supporting Pustejovsky's argument that we should adopt a separate accrual rule in this case.

Next, the concerns that warranted the particularized discovery rule for latent occupational diseases in *Childs* are similar to the concerns here that militate for applying a separate injury rule for each distinct disease process. In *Childs,* we observed that, unlike the typical tort for traumatic injury, the prolonged latency period for some occupational diseases prevents a plaintiff from knowing immediately upon exposure whether they will contract the associated disease. *Childs,* 974 S.W.2d at 38. Likewise, because asbestosis and mesothelioma have different latency periods, a plaintiff who suffers from asbestosis may not manifest mesothelioma for several more decades, if at all. Permitting limitations to run on terminal injuries before the plaintiff knows of them is unjust. If applying the single action rule forbids a second suit, the plaintiff with asbestosis has little choice but to attempt to recover for all possible future conditions. As we noted in *Childs,* "premature litigation of speculative claims is neither efficient nor desirable." *Id.*

Allowing separate limitations for separate disease processes does not betray the purposes that limitations and the single action rule serve. Like statutes of limitations, the single action rule is intended to discourage stale and fraudulent claims. *See Id.* at 38–39. But evidence about the litigation's crucial issue, whether the plaintiff actually has mesothelioma, only improves as the disease progresses from asymptomatic to diagnosable. *See Id.* If limitations for an asbestos-related malignancy runs from the discovery of the cancer then damages are tried for an existing, diagnosable disease instead of for the risk or fear of cancer.

The single action rule, like limitations and res judicata, serves the purpose of giving defendants a point of repose. However, a defendant is in no different position with respect to an asbestosis plaintiff who may develop mesothelioma in the future than with an individual who contracts mesothelioma without ever suffering asbestosis. And the defendant's need for repose must be balanced against the plaintiff's need of an opportunity to seek redress for the gravest injuries, those culminating in wrongful death.

An additional policy reason for the single action rule is the need to protect defendants from vexatious, piecemeal litigation and provide judicial economy. But having to defend against the potential for cancer in every asbestosis case, if we were to allow such a claim, is arguably more vexatious and judicially inefficient than allowing a separate action for actual cancer cases.

VII

After considering the interests underlying the statute of limitations, the discovery rule, and the single action rule, we conclude that the prior asbestosis settlement does not bar Pustejovsky's suit for mesothelioma. We hold that a person who sues on or settles a claim for a non-malignant asbestos-related disease with one defendant is not precluded from a subsequent action against another defendant for a distinct malignant asbestos-related condition. The diagnosis of a malignant asbestos-related condition creates a new cause of action, and the statute of limitations governing the malignant asbestos-related condition begins when a plaintiff's symptoms manifest themselves to a degree or for a duration that would put a reasonable person on notice that he or she suffers from some injury and he or she knows, or with reasonable diligence should know, that the malignant asbestos-related condition is likely work-related. We decline to follow *Gideon, Dartez,* and *Graffagnino* here, and we disapprove of *Pecorino* to the extent it holds to the contrary.

We limit our holding to asbestos-related diseases resulting from workplace exposure for several reasons. We have considered on other occasions arguments that established doctrine and procedures must change to accommodate asbestos litigation, and on some occasions made those changes. [Citations.] We are unaware of any other toxic-exposure torts currently in litigation that present these circumstances.

For these reasons, we conclude that Pustejovsky's evidence created a question of fact precluding summary judgment on the grounds of limitations. Accordingly, we reverse the court of appeals' judgment and remand the cause to the trial court for further proceedings.

Notes

1. As *Pustejovsky* states, most jurisdictions are in accord. *See, e.g.,* Hamilton v. Asbestos Corp., 22 Cal.4th 1127, 95 Cal.Rptr.2d 701, 998 P.2d 403 (2000); Wilber v. Owens–Corning Fiberglas Corp., 476 N.W.2d 74 (Iowa 1991); Sopha v. Owens–Corning Fiberglas Corp., 230 Wis.2d 212, 601 N.W.2d 627 (1999) *Contra* Joyce v. A.C. & S., Inc., 785 F.2d 1200 (4th Cir.1986); Matthews v. Celotex Corp., 569 F.Supp. 1539 (D.N.D.1983).

2. The critical issue in the *Pustejovsky* decision is the single action rule. Because plaintiff had previously sued based on his exposure to asbestos and that suit had been finally resolved, the single action rule would normally bar any new action for damage arising from the exposure. The single action rule can produce substantial unfairness, as it did in a very old English case in which the plaintiff sued for battery and recovered £11 for a bruise. After the suit was resolved, the plaintiff brought a second suit because, "part of his skull ... came out of his head" after the first suit was resolved. The court dismissed the second action, suggesting the plaintiff acted hastily and should have waited to file suit. Fetter v. Beal, 1 Ld. Raymond 339, 91 Eng.Rep. 1122 (King's Bench 1697). What if the skull injury didn't occur until after the statute of limitations ran? *See generally* Restatement (Second) of Judgments § 24, Comment h.

Once the *Pustejovsky* court decided to relax the single action rule, resolution of when the claim for mesothelioma accrues for statute of limitations purposes follows logically. It would make no sense to permit the plaintiff to assert two claims for asbestotic injury but hold that the claims both accrue when the plaintiff first discovers any injury. Had the plaintiff not brought the first action, only the statute of limitations issue would have been posed.

3. Actually, the single action rule was inapplicable in the *Pustejovsky* case. Res judicata or claim preclusion, and its derivative, the single action rule, only operate with regard to the defendants sued in the first action, and Pustejovsky sued entirely different parties in the second suit. No mandatory joinder rule requires a plaintiff to sue all defendants in a single action who might be liable for the plaintiff's injury. *See* 7 Charles Alan Wright, Arthur R. Miller & Mary Kay Kane, Federal Practice and Procedure: Civil 2d § 1623 (1986). *But see* Albertson v. Volkswagenwerk Aktiengesellschaft, 230 Kan. 368, 634 P.2d 1127 (1981) (imposing mandatory joinder requirement based on adoption of comparative fault). Did the *Pustejovsky* court simply err in this aspect of its opinion or did it appreciate that it was reaching out to make law that would apply to the large body of asbestos cases that still exist?

4. Why exactly is an asbestos victim like Mr. Pustejovsky different from the victim in *Fetter v. Beal*?

5. The court goes to some efforts to limit its decision to asbestos cases. Why would it not apply to a cigarette victim who first contracted emphysema, a non-malignant lung disease that also affects a victim's ability to obtain and circulate adequate oxygen, and later contracted lung cancer?

6. A distinct, but related question, is when can a plaintiff exposed to asbestos (or another toxic agent) first file suit? Legally cognizable injury is required before a plaintiff has a valid tort claim. Suppose a plaintiff is diagnosed with pleural plaque, an asbestos-caused shadow shown on x-rays of the lungs of its victims but which does not cause any clinical symptoms? Of course, if pleural plaque is a legally cognizable injury and an individual is diagnosed with it, the statute of limitation accrues and the clock begins to tick. That may explain why the plaintiff in Adams v. Johns–Manville, 727 F.2d 533 (5th Cir.1984) brought suit, after his doctor found abnormalities consistent with asbestos exposure in x-rays, even though he had lost no wages, incurred no medical expenses, and had no symptoms of asbestotic disease. A plaintiff like Adams may seek to recover for two other items of damages mentioned by the *Pustejovksy* court and one not mentioned: 1) emotional distress from exposure and concern about the risk of future disease; 2) the greater risk of developing future disease; and 3) medical monitoring to ensure an early diagnosis of any disease that does develop. *See Burns v. Jaquays Mining Corp., supra* pp. 567–575. In response to cases like *Adams,* California enacted a statute of limitations providing asbestos victims one year after they suffer sufficient injury that they lose time from work and discover the connection between the injury and asbestos exposure in which to file suit. Cal. Code Civ. Proc. § 340.2.

7. Plaintiffs who for whatever reasons sue at the first signs of disease pose a threat to other, more seriously injured individuals who at best may find that their case is delayed by the backlog of other asbestos cases and at worst may find that by the time they get to the head of the queue the defendant has insufficient funds remaining to pay their claim. *See* Henderson & Twerski, Asbestos Litigation Gone Mad: Exposure–Based Recovery for Increased Risk, Mental Distress and Medical Monitoring, 53 S.C.L.Rev. 815 (2002). In response to this problem a few states have passed

legislation that attempts to triage claims by forcing those who wish to bring a suit to go through a mandated procedure to determine the extend of their injury. Individuals with less serious injury and an absence of physical symptoms may be required to forego their lawsuit until they manifest a more serious harm. *See* Tex.Civ.Prac. & Rem. Code §§ 90.001 et seq. What are the merits of this approach?

8. *See generally* Green, The Paradox of Statutes of Limitations in Toxic Substances Litigation, 76 Calif. L. Rev. 965 (1988).

Chapter 12

PARTIES AND TRANSACTIONS GOVERNED BY STRICT LIABILITY

SECTION A. PARTIES WHO CAN BE SUED

1. RETAILERS, WHOLESALERS, AND DISTRIBUTORS

VANDERMARK v. FORD MOTOR CO.
Supreme Court of California, 1964.
61 Cal.2d 256, 37 Cal.Rptr. 896, 391 P.2d 168.

[Plaintiff was injured when he lost control of his automobile and collided with a light post. He sued the manufacturer, Ford Motor Company, and the retailer from whom he had purchased the car, Maywood Bell Ford. After considering several issues concerning the liability of Ford, the court addressed the application of strict tort liability to Maywood Bell Ford.]

TRAYNOR, J.

* * *

Plaintiffs contend that Maywood Bell is also strictly liable in tort for the injuries caused by the defect in the car and that therefore the trial court erred in directing a verdict for Maywood Bell on the warranty causes of action. Maywood Bell contends that the rule of strict liability in the Greenman case applies only to actions against manufacturers brought by injured parties with whom the manufacturers did not deal. It contends that it validly disclaimed warranty liability for personal injuries in its contract with Vandermark[1] (see Civ.Code, § 1791; Burr v. Sherwin

---

1. The warranty clause of the contract provided:

"Dealer warrants to Purchaser (except as hereinafter provided) each part of each Ford Motor Company product sold by Dealer to Purchaser to be free under normal use and service from defects in material and workmanship for a period of ninety (90) days from the date of delivery of such product to Purchaser, or until such product has been driven, used or operated for a distance of four thousand (4,000) miles, whichever event first shall occur. Dealer makes no warranty whatso-

Williams Co., 42 Cal.2d 682, 693, 268 P.2d 1041), and that in any event neither plaintiff gave it timely notice of breach of warranty. (Civ.Code, § 1769.)

Retailers like manufacturers are engaged in the business of distributing goods to the public. They are an integral part of the overall producing and marketing enterprise that should bear the cost of injuries resulting from defective products. (See Greenman v. Yuba Power Products, Inc., 59 Cal.2d 57, 63, 27 Cal.Rptr. 697, 377 P.2d 897.) In some cases the retailer may be the only member of that enterprise reasonably available to the injured plaintiff. In other cases the retailer himself may play a substantial part in insuring that the product is safe or may be in a position to exert pressure on the manufacturer to that end; the retailer's strict liability thus serves as an added incentive to safety. Strict liability on the manufacturer and retailer alike affords maximum protection to the injured plaintiff and works no injustice to the defendants, for they can adjust the costs of such protection between them in the course of their continuing business relationship. Accordingly, as a retailer engaged in the business of distributing goods to the public, Maywood Bell is strictly liable in tort for personal injuries caused by defects in cars sold by it. (See Greenberg v. Lorenz, 9 N.Y.2d 195, 200, 213 N.Y.S.2d 39, 173 N.E.2d 773; McBurnette v. Playground Equipment Corp., Fla., 137 So.2d 563, 566–567; Graham v. Butterfield's Inc., 176 Kan. 68, 269 P.2d 413, 418; Henningsen v. Bloomfield Motors, Inc., 32 N.J. 358, 406, 161 A.2d 69, 75 A.L.R.2d 1; State Farm Mut. Auto. Ins. Co. v. Anderson–Weber, Inc., 252 Iowa 1289, 110 N.W.2d 449, 450, 455–456; Rest.2d Torts (Tent.Draft No. 7), § 402A, com. f.)

Since Maywood Bell is strictly liable in tort, the fact that it restricted its contractual liability to Vandermark is immaterial. Regardless of the obligations it assumed by contract, it is subject to strict liability in tort because it is in the business of selling automobiles, one of which proved to be defective and caused injury to human beings. The requirement of timely notice of breach of warranty (Civ.Code, § 1769) is not applicable to such tort liability just as it is not applicable to tort liability based on negligence (Greenman v. Yuba Power Products, Inc., 59 Cal.2d 57, 60–62, 27 Cal.Rptr. 697, 377 P.2d 897; see Rest.2d Torts (Tent.Draft No. 7), § 402A, com. m).

* * *

[T]he judgment in favor of Maywood Bell Ford is reversed.

ever with respect to tires or tubes. Dealer's obligation under this warranty is limited to replacement, without charge to Purchaser, of such parts as shall be returned to Dealer and as shall be acknowledged by Dealer to be defective. This warranty shall not apply to any Ford Motor Company product that has been subject to misuse, negligence, or accident, or in which parts not made or supplied by Ford Motor Company shall have been used if, in the determination of Dealer, such use shall have affected its performance, stability, or reliability, or which shall have been altered or repaired outside of Dealer's place of business in a manner which, in the determination of Dealer, shall have affected its performance, stability, or reliability. This warranty is expressly in lieu of all other warranties, express or implied, and of all other obligations on the part of Dealer."

GIBSON, C.J., and SCHAUER, McCOMB, PETERS, TOBRINER and PEEK, JJ., concur.

Notes

1. As noted in *Vandermark*, Comment *f* of Restatement (Second) of Torts section 402 is in accord. The overwhelming majority of courts have followed the position taken in *Vandermark* and Comment *f* by applying strict tort liability to retailers, as well as wholesalers, distributors, and others in the chain of distribution. *See, e.g.*, Pittsburg Coca–Cola Bottling Works v. Ponder, 443 S.W.2d 546 (Tex.1969); Keener v. Dayton Electric Manufacturing Co., 445 S.W.2d 362 (Mo.1969); Cooley v. Quick Supply Co., 221 N.W.2d 763 (Iowa 1974); Mettinger v. Globe Slicing Mach. Co., Inc., 153 N.J. 371, 709 A.2d 779 (1998); Simeone ex rel. Estate Of Albert Francis Simeone, Jr. v. Bombardier–Rotax GmbH, 360 F.Supp.2d 665 (E.D.Pa. 2005). *But see* Sam Shainberg Co. of Jackson v. Barlow, 258 So.2d 242 (Miss.1972) (court refused to impose liability on either the retailer or the wholesaler of a defective pair of shoes).

2. Comment *e* to Restatement (Third) of Torts: Products Liability § 1 also reflects the majority position.

> The rule stated in this Section provides that all commercial sellers and distributors of products, including nonmanufacturing sellers and distributors such as wholesalers and retailers, are subject to liability for selling products that are defective. Liability attaches even when such nonmanufacturing sellers or distributors do not themselves render the products defective and regardless of whether they are in a position to prevent defects from occurring. * * * Legislation has been enacted in many jurisdictions that, to some extent, immunizes nonmanufacturing sellers or distributors from strict liability. The legislation is premised on the belief that bringing nonmanufacturing sellers or distributors into products liability litigation generates wasteful legal costs. Although liability in most cases is ultimately passed on to the manufacturer who is responsible for creating the product defect, nonmanufacturing sellers or distributors must devote resources to protect their interests. In most situations, therefore, immunizing nonmanufacturers from strict liability saves those resources without jeopardizing the plaintiff's interests. To assure plaintiffs access to a responsible and solvent product seller or distributor, the statutes generally provide that the nonmanufacturing seller or distributor is immunized from strict liability only if: (1) the manufacturer is subject to the jurisdiction of the court of plaintiff's domicile; and (2) the manufacturer is not, nor is likely to become, insolvent.

3. As noted in Comment *c,* an *innocent* (in the sense of nonnegligent) retailer or wholesaler who is held liable for selling a defective product can obtain indemnity from the manufacturer or other intermediate sellers in the chain of distribution. *See* Chapter 10. Consequently, the effect of applying liability to a retailer or wholesaler is to place responsibility on the retailer or wholesaler to seek recovery from the manufacturer or other sellers in the chain of distribution. In many jurisdictions, this responsibility is not free of

cost for the retailer or wholesaler, however. The retailer or wholesaler who is liable in the first instance faces litigation costs in seeking indemnity, and it bears the risk of the manufacturer being insolvent. To recover indemnity from a manufacturer, a retailer or wholesaler must prove that the defect existed at the time the product left the manufacturer's control. Thus, the application of liability to a retailer or wholesaler places the burden of tracing the defect back to the manufacturer on the retailer or wholesaler rather than on the consumer, who nevertheless must demonstrate that the defect existed at the time of sale by any defendant in the chain of distribution.

Some state indemnity statutes relieve the nonmanufacturers of this burden. For example, the Texas products liability statute contains an indemnification provision that states that if innocent nonmanufacturers give reasonable notice to the manufacturer that they have been sued with respect to an alleged defect in the manufacturer's product, they may "recover from the manufacturer court costs and other reasonable expenses, reasonable attorney fees, and any reasonable damages incurred by the seller to enforce the seller's right to indemnification ..." Tex.Civ.Prac. & Rem. Code § 82.002. For useful discussions of this indemnity provision and statutory provisions in other states see O'Rourke, A Manufacturer's Duty to Indemnify a Retailer–Indemnification or Abnegation? An Analysis of the Scope and Effect of Section 82.002 of the Texas Products Liability Act,. 33 Tex. Tech L. Rev. 241 (2001); Sachs, Product Liability Reform and Seller Liability: A Proposal for Change, 55 Baylor L.Rev. 1031 (2003).

4. If the manufacturer is solvent and amenable to suit, what purpose is served by imposing liability on others in the chain of distribution? Some state legislatures have enacted statutes that protect retailers from liability. Most of these are conditioned on the solvency of the manufacturer and its amenability to suit in the jurisdiction. *See, e.g.,* Del. Code Ann. tit. 18 § 7001; Ky.Rev.Stat. § 411.340; Tex.Civ.Prac. & Rem. Code § 82.003. Some insulate nonmanufacturers from strict liability without qualification. *See, e.g.,* Ga. Code Ann. § 5–1–11.1. Some are less protective than a complete exemption but more restrictive than the Delaware and Kentucky statutes. *See, e.g.,* Colo.Rev.Stat. § 13–21–402(1) & (2) (liability only applicable to "principal distributor" of manufacturer over whom jurisdiction cannot be obtained). How should liability be apportioned when multiple defendants in the chain of distribution are sued, but the manufacturer is insolvent or otherwise unavailable? *See* Promaulayko v. Johns Manville Sales Corp., 116 N.J. 505, 562 A.2d 202 (1989).

5. Of course, retailers and wholesalers may be liable for their negligence. Retailers who negligently assemble a product or who, have some reason to foresee that a product may be dangerous and negligently fail to take appropriate action may be held liable for their own conduct. These parties may also be liable if they introduce a defect into the product, even if they do so innocently. *See* Restatement (Third) of Torts: Products Liability § 2, Illustration 2.

6. The Products Liability Restatement retains the requirement from § 402A that the seller be one who is "engaged in the business of selling or otherwise distributing the type of product that harmed the plaintiff." Section 1, Comment c. Thus, occasional sellers, including consumers, who sell

used goods, are not subject to strict tort liability. Occasionally, courts confront sellers who are close to the line. Thus, in Galindo v. Precision American Corp., 754 F.2d 1212 (5th Cir.1985), the plaintiff sued, among others, Georgia–Pacific, which had purchased a sawmill for use in its manufacturing operations and subsequently sold it before the plaintiff was injured by it. While Georgia–Pacific was plainly a commercial seller of products, the question was whether it was a commercial seller of *sawmills* where its only sales were of equipment that it had used in for production purposes. Anticipating defendants like car rental companies that are also engaged in the business of selling used cars, the court decided that a factual inquiry into the quantity and quality of Georgia Pacific's sales of sawmills was required. By contrast, courts have held that a single sale, even by a commercial seller, is insufficient for strict liability. See, e.g., Santiago v. E.W. Bliss Division, 201 N.J.Super. 205, 492 A.2d 1089 (App.Div.1985); see also McGraw v. Furon Co., 812 So.2d 273 (Ala.2001) (used rubber processor that sold an "unspecified" number of used machines was an occasional seller and not in the business of selling rubber processing machines).

7. As we saw in Chapter 4, as a result of the learned intermediary doctrine a drug manufacturer generally has no duty to warn the consumer of the drug. The duty to warn runs only to the appropriate medical personnel. What, however, of pharmacies? The traditional common law rule is that pharmacies have no independent duty to warn consumers. As long as the pharmacy faithfully fills the physician's prescription it need not warn of such things as adverse interactions with other drugs for which the customer has a prescription. As we noted in Chapter 4, however page 324 *infra*, in recent years a number of courts have imposed upon pharmacies at least a limited duty to warn.

8. The applicability of the three warranties under Article 2 of the U.C.C. to various sellers in the chain of distribution depends on the type of warranty. An express warranty or an implied warranty of fitness for a particular purpose is applicable only to sellers whose words or conduct creates them. An implied warranty of merchantability is automatically applicable to all sellers in the chain of distribution who are merchants. These points are addressed in more detail in Chapter 2.

2. GOVERNMENT CONTRACTORS

BOYLE v. UNITED TECHNOLOGIES CORP.
Supreme Court of the United States, 1988.
487 U.S. 500, 108 S.Ct. 2510, 101 L.Ed.2d 442.

SCALIA, J., delivered the opinion of the Court, in which REHNQUIST, C.J., and WHITE, O'CONNOR, and KENNEDY, JJ., joined. BRENNAN, J., filed a dissenting opinion, in which MARSHALL and BLACKMUN, JJ., joined. STEVENS, J., filed a dissenting opinion.

JUSTICE SCALIA delivered the opinion of the Court.

This case requires us to decide when a contractor providing military equipment to the Federal Government can be held liable under state tort law for injury caused by a design defect.

I

On April 27, 1983, David A. Boyle, a United States Marine helicopter copilot, was killed when the CH–53d helicopter in which he was flying crashed off the coast of Virginia Beach, Virginia, during a training exercise. Although Boyle survived the impact of the crash, he was unable to escape from the helicopter and drowned. Boyle's father, petitioner here, brought this diversity action in Federal District Court against the Sikorsky Division of United Technologies Corporation (Sikorsky), which built the helicopter for the United States.

At trial, * * * petitioner alleged [under Virginia tort law] that Sikorsky had defectively designed the copilot's emergency escape system: the escape hatch opened out instead of in (and was therefore ineffective in a submerged craft because of water pressure), and access to the escape hatch handle was obstructed by other equipment. The jury returned a general verdict in favor of petitioner and awarded him $725,000. The District Court denied Sikorsky's motion for judgment notwithstanding the verdict.

The Court of Appeals reversed and remanded with directions that judgment be entered for Sikorsky. 792 F.2d 413 (C.A.4 1986). It found, * * * as a matter of federal law, that Sikorsky could not be held liable for the allegedly defective design of the escape hatch because, on the evidence presented, it satisfied the requirements of the "military contractor defense," which the court had recognized the same day in *Tozer v. LTV Corp.*, 792 F.2d 403 (C.A.4 1986). 792 F.2d, at 414–415.

Petitioner sought review here, challenging the Court of Appeals' decision on three levels: First, petitioner contends that there is no justification in federal law for shielding government contractors from liability for design defects in military equipment. Second, he argues in the alternative that even if such a defense should exist, the Court of Appeals' formulation of the conditions for its application is inappropriate. Finally, petitioner contends that the Court of Appeals erred in not remanding for a jury determination of whether the elements of the defense were met in this case. We granted certiorari, 479 U.S. 1029, 107 S.Ct. 872, 93 L.Ed.2d 827 (1986).

II

Petitioner's broadest contention is that, in the absence of legislation specifically immunizing Government contractors from liability for design defects, there is no basis for judicial recognition of such a defense. We disagree. In most fields of activity, to be sure, this Court has refused to find federal pre-emption of state law in the absence of either a clear statutory prescription, or a direct conflict between federal and state law. But we have held that a few areas, involving "uniquely federal interests," *Texas Industries, Inc. v. Radcliff Materials, Inc.*, 451 U.S. 630, 640, 101 S.Ct. 2061, 2067, 68 L.Ed.2d 500 (1981), are so committed by the Constitution and laws of the United States to federal control that state law is pre-empted and replaced, where necessary, by federal law of a content prescribed (absent explicit statutory directive) by the courts—so-called "federal common law."

The dispute in the present case borders upon two areas that we have found to involve such "uniquely federal interests." We have held that obligations to and rights of the United States under its contracts are governed exclusively by federal law. The present case does not involve an obligation to the United States under its contract, but rather liability to third persons. That liability may be styled one in tort, but it arises out of performance of the contract—and traditionally has been regarded as sufficiently related to the contract that until 1962 Virginia would generally allow design defect suits only by the purchaser and those in privity with the seller.

Another area that we have found to be of peculiarly federal concern, warranting the displacement of state law, is the civil liability of federal officials for actions taken in the course of their duty. We have held in many contexts that the scope of that liability is controlled by federal law. The present case involves an independent contractor performing its obligation under a procurement contract, rather than an official performing his duty as a federal employee, but there is obviously implicated the same interest in getting the Government's work done.[1]

We think the reasons for considering these closely related areas to be of "uniquely federal" interest apply as well to the civil liabilities arising out of the performance of federal procurement contracts. We have come close to holding as much. In *Yearsley v. W.A. Ross Construction Co.*, 309 U.S. 18, 60 S.Ct. 413, 84 L.Ed. 554 (1940), we rejected an attempt by a landowner to hold a construction contractor liable under state law for the erosion of 95 acres caused by the contractor's work in constructing dikes for the Government. We said that "if (the) authority to carry out the project was validly conferred, that is, if what was done was within the constitutional power of Congress, there is no liability on the part of the contractor for executing its will." *Id.*, at 20–21, [60 S.Ct., at 414.] The federal interest justifying this holding surely exists as much in procurement contracts as in performance contracts; we see no basis for a distinction.

Moreover, it is plain that the Federal Government's interest in the procurement of equipment is implicated by suits such as the present one—even though the dispute is one between private parties. It is true that where "litigation is purely between private parties and does not touch the rights and duties of the United States," *Bank of American Nat. Trust & Sav. Assn. v. Parnell*, 352 U.S. 29, 33, 77 S.Ct. 119, 121, 1 L.Ed.2d 93 (1956), federal law does not govern. Thus, for example, in *Miree v. DeKalb County*, 433 U.S. 25, 30, 97 S.Ct. 2490, 2494, 53 L.Ed.2d

---

1. [The] dissent misreads our discussion here to "intimat(e) that the immunity (of federal officials) * * * might extend * * * to nongovernment employees" such as a government contractor. * * * But we do not address this issue, as it is not before us. We cite these cases merely to demonstrate that the liability of independent contractors performing work for the Federal Government, like the liability of federal officials, is an area of uniquely federal interest.

557 (1977), which involved the question whether certain private parties could sue as third-party beneficiaries to an agreement between a municipality and the Federal Aviation Administration, we found that state law was not displaced because "the operations of the United States in connection with FAA grants such as these * * * would (not) be burdened" by allowing state law to determine whether third-party beneficiaries could sue, *id.*, at 30, [97 S.Ct., at 2494], and because "any federal interest in the outcome of the [dispute] before us '[was] far too speculative, far too remote a possibility to justify the application of federal law to transactions essentially of local concern.'" *Id.*, at 32–33, 97 S.Ct., at 2495, quoting *Parnell, supra*, 352 U.S., at 33–34, 77 S.Ct., at 121; see also *Wallis v. Pan American Petroleum Corp.*, 384 U.S. 63, 69, 86 S.Ct. 1301, 1304, 16 L.Ed.2d 369 (1966). But the same is not true here. The imposition of liability on Government contractors will directly affect the terms of Government contracts: either the contractor will decline to manufacture the design specified by the Government, or it will raise its price. Either way, the interests of the United States will be directly affected.

That the procurement of equipment by the United States is an area of uniquely federal interest does not, however, end the inquiry. That merely establishes a necessary, not a sufficient, condition for the displacement of state law. Displacement will occur only where, as we have variously described, a "significant conflict" exists between an identifiable "federal policy or interest and the (operation) of state law," *Wallis, supra*, at 68, [86 S.Ct., at 1304,] or the application of state law would "frustrate specific objectives" of federal legislation, [*United States v. Kimbell Foods, Inc.*, 440 U.S. 715, 728, 99 S.Ct. 1448, 1458, 59 L.Ed.2d 711 (1979)]. The conflict with federal policy need not be as sharp as that which must exist for ordinary pre-emption when Congress legislates "in a field which the States have traditionally occupied." *Rice v. Santa Fe Elevator Corp.*, [331 U.S. 218, 231, 67 S.Ct. 1146, 1152, 91 L.Ed. 1447 (1947)]. Or to put the point differently, the fact that the area in question is one of unique federal concern changes what would otherwise be a conflict that cannot produce pre-emption into one that can. But conflict there must be. In some cases, for example where the federal interest requires a uniform rule, the entire body of state law applicable to the area conflicts and is replaced by federal rules. *See, e.g., Clearfield Trust* [*Co. v. United States*, 318 U.S. 363, 366–67, 63 S.Ct. 573, 574–75, 87 L.Ed. 838 (1943)], (rights and obligations of United States with respect to commercial paper must be governed by uniform federal rule). In others, the conflict is more narrow, and only particular elements of state law are superseded. See, *e.g.*, [*United States v. Little Lake Misere Land Co.*, 412 U.S. 580, 595, 93 S.Ct. 2389, 2398, 37 L.Ed.2d 187 (1973)] (even assuming state law should generally govern federal land acquisitions, particular state law at issue may not); *Howard v. Lyons*, [360 U.S. 593, 597, 79 S.Ct. 1331, 1333, 3 L.Ed.2d 1454 (1959)] (state defamation law generally applicable to federal official, but federal privilege governs for statements made in the course of federal official's duties).

In *Miree, supra,* the suit was not seeking to impose upon the person contracting with the Government a duty contrary to the duty imposed by the Government contract. Rather, it was the contractual duty *itself* that the private plaintiff (as third party beneficiary) sought to enforce. Between *Miree* and the present case, it is easy to conceive of an intermediate situation, in which the duty sought to be imposed on the contractor is not identical to one assumed under the contract, but is also not contrary to any assumed. If, for example, the United States contracts for the purchase and installation of an air conditioning unit, specifying the cooling capacity but not the precise manner of construction, a state law imposing upon the manufacturer of such units a duty of care to include a certain safety feature would not be a duty identical to anything promised the Government, but neither would it be contrary. The contractor could comply with both its contractual obligations and the state-prescribed duty of care. No one suggests that state law would generally be pre-empted in this context.

The present case, however, is at the opposite extreme from *Miree.* Here the state-imposed duty of care that is the asserted basis of the contractor's liability (specifically, the duty to equip helicopters with the sort of escape-hatch mechanism petitioner claims was necessary) is precisely contrary to the duty imposed by the Government contract (the duty to manufacture and deliver helicopters with the sort of escape-hatch mechanism shown by the specifications). Even in this sort of situation, it would be unreasonable to say that there is always a "significant conflict" between the state law and a federal policy or interest. If, for example, a federal procurement officer orders, by model number, a quantity of stock helicopters that happen to be equipped with escape hatches opening outward, it is impossible to say that the Government has a significant interest in that particular feature. That would be scarcely more reasonable than saying that a private individual who orders such a craft by model number cannot sue for the manufacturer's negligence because he got precisely what he ordered.

In its search for the limiting principle to identify those situations in which a "significant conflict" with federal policy or interests does arise, the Court of Appeals, in the lead case upon which its opinion here relied, identified as the source of the conflict the *Feres* doctrine, under which the Federal Tort Claims Act does not cover injuries to armed service personnel in the course of military service. See *Feres v. United States*, 340 U.S. 135, 71 S.Ct. 153, 95 L.Ed. 152 (1950). Military contractor liability would conflict with this doctrine, the Fourth Circuit reasoned, since the increased cost of the contractor's tort liability would be added to the price of the contract, and "(s)uch pass-through costs would * * * defeat the purpose of the immunity for military accidents conferred upon the government itself." *Tozer*, 792 F.2d, at 408. Other courts upholding the defense have embraced similar reasoning. See, *e.g., Bynum v. FMC Corp.*, 770 F.2d 556, 565–566 (C.A.5 1985); *Tillett v. J.I. Case Co.*, 756 F.2d 591, 596–597 (C.A.7 1985); *McKay v. Rockwell Int'l Corp.*, 704 F.2d 444, 449 (C.A.9 1983), cert. denied, 464 U.S. 1043, 104 S.Ct. 711, 79

L.Ed.2d 175 (1984). We do not adopt this analysis because it seems to us that the *Feres* doctrine, in its application to the present problem, logically produces results that are in some respects too broad and in some respects too narrow. Too broad, because if the Government contractor defense is to prohibit suit against the manufacturer whenever *Feres* would prevent suit against the Government, then even injuries caused to military personnel by a helicopter purchased from stock (in our example above), or by any standard equipment purchased by the Government, would be covered. Since *Feres* prohibits all service-related tort claims against the Government, a contractor defense that rests upon it should prohibit all service-related tort claims against the manufacturer—making inexplicable the three limiting criteria for contractor immunity (which we will discuss presently) that the Court of Appeals adopted. On the other hand, reliance on *Feres* produces (or logically should produce) results that are in another respect too narrow. Since that doctrine covers only service-related injuries, and not injuries caused by the military to civilians, it could not be invoked to prevent, for example, a civilian's suit against the manufacturer of fighter planes, based on a state tort theory, claiming harm from what is alleged to be needlessly high levels of noise produced by the jet engines. Yet we think that the character of the jet engines the Government orders for its fighter planes cannot be regulated by state tort law, no more in suits by civilians than in suits by members of the Armed Services.

There is, however, a statutory provision that demonstrates the potential for, and suggests the outlines of, "significant conflict" between federal interests and state law in the context of government procurement. In the [Federal Tort Claims Act] FTCA, Congress authorized damages to be recovered against the United States for harm caused by the negligent or wrongful conduct of Government employees, to the extent that a private person would be liable under the law of the place where the conduct occurred. 28 U.S.C. § 1346(b). It excepted from this consent to suit, however,

> "(a)ny claim * * * based upon the exercise or performance or the failure to exercise or perform a discretionary function or duty on the part of a federal agency or an employee of the Government, whether or not the discretion involved be abused." 28 U.S.C. § 2680(a).

We think that the selection of the appropriate design for military equipment to be used by our Armed Forces is assuredly a discretionary function within the meaning of this provision. It often involves not merely engineering analysis but judgment as to the balancing of many technical, military, and even social considerations, including specifically the trade-off between greater safety and greater combat effectiveness. And we are further of the view that permitting "second-guessing" of these judgments, see *United States v. Varig Airlines*, 467 U.S. 797, 814, 104 S.Ct. 2755, 2765, 81 L.Ed.2d 660 (1984), through state tort suits against contractors would produce the same effect sought to be avoided by the FTCA exemption. The financial burden of judgments against the contractors would ultimately be passed through, substantially if not totally, to the United States itself, since defense contractors will predictably raise their prices to cover, or to insure against, contingent liability for the Government-ordered designs. To put the point differently: It makes little sense to insulate the Government against financial liability for the judgment that a particular feature of military equipment is necessary when the Government produces the equipment itself, but not when it contracts for the production. In sum, we are of the view that state law which holds Government contractors liable for design defects in military equipment does in some circumstances present a "significant conflict" with federal policy and must be displaced.

We agree with the scope of displacement adopted by the Fourth Circuit here, which is also that adopted by the Ninth Circuit, see *McKay v. Rockwell Int'l Corp., supra,* at 451. Liability for design defects in military equipment cannot be imposed, pursuant to state law, when (1) the United States approved reasonably precise specifications; (2) the equipment conformed to those specifications; and (3) the supplier warned the United States about the dangers in the use of the equipment that were known to the supplier but not to the United States. The first two of these conditions assure that the suit is within the area where the policy of the "discretionary function" would be frustrated—*i.e.*, they assure that the design feature in question was considered by a Government officer, and not merely by the contractor itself. The third condition is necessary because, in its absence, the displacement of state tort law would create some incentive for the manufacturer to withhold knowledge of risks, since conveying that knowledge might disrupt the contract but withholding it would produce no liability. We adopt this provision lest our effort to protect discretionary functions perversely impede them by cutting off information highly relevant to the discretionary decision.

We have considered the alternative formulation of the Government contractor defense, urged upon us by petitioner, which was adopted by the Eleventh Circuit in *Shaw v. Grumman Aerospace Corp.,* 778 F.2d 736, 746 (1985), cert. pending, No. 85–1529. That would preclude suit only if (1) the contractor did not participate, or participated only minimally, in the design of the defective equipment; *or* (2) the contractor timely warned the Government of the risks of the design and notified it of alternative designs reasonably known by it, *and* the Government, although forewarned, clearly authorized the contractor to proceed with the dangerous design. While this formulation may represent a perfectly reasonable tort rule, it is not a rule designed to protect the federal interest embodied in the "discretionary function" exemption. The design ultimately selected may well reflect a significant policy judgment by Government officials whether or not the contractor rather than those officials developed the design. In addition, it does not seem to us sound policy to penalize, and thus deter, active contractor participation in the design process, placing the contractor at risk unless it identifies all design defects.

III

Petitioner raises two arguments regarding the Court of Appeals' application of the Government contractor defense to the facts of this case. First, he argues that since the formulation of the defense adopted by the Court of Appeals differed from the instructions given by the District Court to the jury, the Seventh Amendment guarantee of jury trial required a remand for trial on the new theory. We disagree. If the evidence presented in the first trial would not suffice, as a matter of law, to support a jury verdict under the properly formulated defense, judgment could properly be entered for the respondent at once, without a new trial. And that is so even though (as petitioner claims) respondent failed to object to jury instructions that expressed the defense differently, and in a fashion that would support a verdict.

It is somewhat unclear from the Court of Appeals' opinion, however, whether it was in fact deciding that no reasonable jury could, under the properly formulated defense, have found for the petitioner on the facts presented, or rather was assessing on its own whether the defense had been established. The latter, which is what petitioner asserts occurred, would be error, since whether the facts establish the conditions for the defense is a question for the jury. The critical language in the Court of Appeals' opinion was that "(b)ecause Sikorsky has satisfied the requirements of the military contractor defense, it can incur no liability for * * * the allegedly defective design of the escape hatch." 792 F.2d, at 415. Although it seems to us doubtful that the Court of Appeals was conducting the factual evaluation that petitioner suggests, we cannot be certain from this language, and so we remand for clarification of this point. If the Court of Appeals was saying that no reasonable jury could find, under the principles it had announced and on the basis of the evidence presented, that the Government contractor defense was inapplicable, its judgment shall stand, since petitioner did not seek from us, nor did we grant, review of the sufficiency-of-the-evidence determination. If the Court of Appeals was not saying that, it should now undertake the proper sufficiency inquiry.

Accordingly, the judgment is vacated and the case is remanded. *So ordered.*

[The dissenting opinions of BRENNAN, J., and STEVENS, J., are omitted.]

Notes

1. **Warning Defects.** *Boyle* itself involves a design defect. Does the defense apply to other types of defects? Most courts have concluded that the defense does apply to warnings when criteria similar to the criteria in *Boyle* are met: 1) The government exercised its discretion and control and approved the warnings and directions accompanying the product 2) the contractor provided warnings that conformed to the approved warnings; and 3) the contractor warned the government of dangers known to it but not the

government. *See* Densberger v. United Technologies Corp., 297 F.3d 66, 75 (2d Cir. 2002); Tate v. Boeing Helicoptors, 140 F.3d 654, 656–57 (6th Cir. 1998).

2. **Manufacturing Defects.** On its face, the government contractor defense would not seem to apply to manufacturing defects. After all, the second prong of the defense, that the product is manufactured in conformity with government design specifications, would seem to argue that products that fail to conform because of an error in manufacturing lie outside the scope of *Boyle*. Some courts have adopted this straightforward position. *See* Mitchell v. Lone Star Ammunition, Inc., 913 F.2d 242 (5th Cir. 1990) (defective mortar shell); McGonigal v. Gearhart Industries, Inc., 851 F.2d 774 (5th Cir. 1988) (defective fuse in grenade). Things, however, are not always so simple. A number of courts agree with Bailey v. McDonnell Douglas Corp., 989 F.2d 794 (5th Cir.1993), that "whether the defense will apply cannot be determined by the label attached to the claim. Strict adherence to the three *Boyle* conditions specifically tailored for the purpose will ensure that the defense is limited to appropriate claims." Thus, whether the defense applies to a claim based on an alleged manufacturing defect depends on whether the particular product at issue was to be manufactured in conformity with reasonably precise specifications approved by the government. *Id* at 801–02. *See* Snell v. Bell Helicopter Textron, Inc., 107 F.3d 744, 749 (9th Cir. 1997); Roll v. Tracor, Inc., 102 F.Supp.2d 1200 (D. Nev. 2000). Does the defense apply to contractors who have a service contract to maintain equipment? *See* Kerstetter v. Pacific Scientific Co., 210 F.3d 431 (5th Cir. 2000); Hudgens v. Bwell Helicopters/Textron, 328 F.3d 1329 (11th Cir. 2003).

3. **Non-military Contractors.** Should the government contractor defense apply to civilian products manufactured for the government? The courts are split on this issue. *Compare* Nielsen v. George Diamond Vogel Paint Co., 892 F.2d 1450 (9th Cir.1990) (paint for dam; the defense does not apply to civilian products) *with* Carley v. Wheeled Coach, 991 F.2d 1117 (3d Cir.1993) (ambulance; the defense applies to nonmilitary contractors); Silverstein v. Northrop Grumman Corp., 367 N.J.Super. 361, 842 A.2d 881 (2004) (postal vehicle). *See* Ausness, Surrogate Immunity: The Government Contract Defense and Products Liability, 47 Ohio St.L.J. 985, 1014–1018 (1986).

4. Suppose the government approves reasonably precise specifications, but the design feature challenged by the plaintiff was nowhere contained within the specifications? *See* Lewis v. Babcock Indus., 985 F.2d 83 (2d Cir.1993).

5. If a government contractor is able to present a colorable government contractor defense, it is entitled to removal to federal court under the Federal Officer Removal Statute, 28 USC § 1442. *See* Malsch v. Vertex Aerospace, LLC, 361 F.Supp.2d 583 (S.D.Miss. 2005).

6. A substantial literature followed *Boyle*, much of it critical. *See* Cass and Gillette, The Government Contractor Defense: Contractual Allocation of Public Risk, 77 Va.L.Rev. 257 (1991); Green and Matasar, The Supreme Court and the Products Liability Crisis: Lessons From *Boyle's* Government Contractor Defense, 63 S.Cal.L.Rev. 637 (1990). Notes include: 39 Am.

U.L.Rev. 391 (1990); 70 B.U.L.Rev. 691 (1990); 22 Conn.L.Rev. 239 (1989); 39 DePaul L.Rev. 825 (1990)77; 40 Mercer L.Rev. 753 (1989); 67 N.C.L.Rev. 1172 (1989); 42 Okla.L.Rev. 359 (1989); 20 St.Mary's L.J. 993 (1989); 57 UMKC L.Rev. 655 (1989); and 24 Wake Forest L.Rev. 745 (1989).

Problem

The United States Forest Service has decided to buy several large earthmoving–fire fighting machines. The procurement officer assigned to this project prepares performance specifications that describe what the Forest Service needs in terms of function and performance: speed, size, capacity to move earth and uproot trees, quantity of water it can pump per hour, etc. After a request for proposals is published and bids obtained, Paterkillar Industries, Inc., emerges as the successful bidder. The contract requires Paterkillar to prepare design specifications to be approved by the Forest Service and to build a to-be-specified number of the machines that it designs.

After several months, Paterkillar develops plans for a machine that it tells the Forest Service will do the job nicely. The Forest Service procurement officer says great and requests that Paterkillar produce 47 machines over the next 5 years. Paterkillar responds that it is willing to give the Forest Service a significant discount—only $1million per machine—but it will take 10 years, rather than 5, to produce 47 machines.

The procurement officer inquires: "Can't you make these machines a bit faster than that? How can we speed it up—we want to avoid another disaster like Yellowstone, summer of '88."

Paterkillar responds, "We could do quality control on a sampling basis instead of inspecting every one. That way we get 98% of the bugs, but we can't guarantee them all. That would enable us to produce 47 machines in just over 6 years." The procurement officer consults with the Secretary of the Interior who, upon being appraised of the situation, says, "Go for it!"

Ten years later, during a terrible forest fire in the Grand Canyon, Army reservists are brought in to assist in fighting the fire. During the course of fire fighting operations, a reservist, while wielding a shovel, is run over by a Paterkillar machine, while the machine is being backed up. The reservist brings a products liability action against Paterkillar, asserting three different theories:

> 1) The machine was defectively designed, because it didn't have an automatic warning sound whenever it was placed in reverse so that those in proximity would be notified it was about to back up.
>
> 2) The manufacturer failed adequately to warn of the dangers of backing up given the blind spot behind the machine that the driver could not see, even with the rear-view mirror provided.
>
> 3) The machine had a manufacturing flaw in its brake system that delayed the driver's ability to bring it to a halt once the driver

realized through shouts of others on the scene that the reservist was in his path.

Paterkillar seeks summary judgment based on *Boyle*. It introduces in support of its motion a copy of the blueprints for the machine with the notation: "Approved" and signed, "Peter Procurement Officer, United States Forest Service." The blueprints state nothing whatsoever about the existence of an automatic warning system for backing up. What outcome and why?

3. SUCCESSOR CORPORATIONS

SAVAGE ARMS, INC. v. WESTERN AUTO SUPPLY CO.
Supreme Court of Alaska, 2001.
18 P.3d 49.

EASTAUGH, JUSTICE.

I. *INTRODUCTION*

Can a corporation that purchases assets of the manufacturer of a rifle sold in Alaska be held liable for personal injury caused in Alaska by a defect in the rifle? The superior court held that it could, and we agree. But we reverse and remand for application of the pertinent successor liability doctrines discussed below. * * *

II. *FACTS AND PROCEEDINGS*

The relevant facts are few. Jack Taylor's minor son suffered personal injuries when a defective .22 caliber rifle discharged during target shooting near Nikiski. Savage Industries, Inc. manufactured the rifle, and Western Auto Supply Company, which claimed to have acquired the rifle from the manufacturer, sold it to a retail store in Maine; the rifle was eventually resold to Jack Taylor in Alaska. Taylor sued Savage Industries in 1990 for his son's injuries; in an amended complaint, he also sought recovery from Western Auto.

Western Auto filed a third-party complaint in its name seeking indemnity from Savage Arms, Inc., which had purchased assets from Savage Industries in 1989. Western Auto settled with the Taylors in May 1995, and its insurers paid the entire settlement amount.

At issue here are three superior court orders. The first held that Alaska law governs the issue of successor liability. The second granted Western Auto summary judgment against Savage Arms, holding Savage Arms liable as "the legal successor to Savage Industries, Inc." The third denied Savage Arms' motion to substitute Western Auto's insurers for Western Auto as the real parties in interest, but required the insurers to ratify the litigation.

* * *

III. DISCUSSION

* * *

B. Choice of Law

[Initially, the court was confronted with whether it should apply Texas law, because the asset sale between Savage Arms and Savage Industries had taken place there or Alaska law, where the injury occurred. The court first inquired whether the issue was one of corporate and contract law or tort law. Although the core of the transaction was an asset sale pursuant to a contract and governed by corporate law, the court decided the issue was properly characterized as one of tort law. Parties who enter into a contract should not be permitted to undermine products liability policies when a defective product causes harm. Once tort law governed the successor liability issue, applying the law of the place of the accident and the residence of the injured victim led the court to conclude that Alaska law governed the question of Savage Arms' successor liability.]

C. Successor Liability

Savage Arms challenges Western Auto's summary judgment on the issue of successor liability. It argues that it should not be held liable even if Alaska law applies. This argument raises issues of first impression in Alaska.

Generally, when one company sells all its assets to another, the acquiring corporation is not liable for the debts and liabilities of the selling company. Courts have traditionally recognized four exceptions to this rule of non-liability, where (1) the purchaser expressly or implicitly agrees to assume liability, (2) the asset purchase amounts to a consolidation or merger, (3) the purchasing corporation is a "mere continuation" of the selling corporation, or (4) the transfer amounts to little more than a "sham" transaction to avoid liabilities. More recently, some courts have recognized three additional "modern" exceptions to the rule of non-liability: the "continuity of enterprise," "product line," and "duty-to-warn" exceptions.

Western Auto argues that we should adopt any one of three different successor liability doctrines in this case: the traditional "mere continuation" exception and the modern "continuity of enterprise" and "product line" exceptions. We first identify which exceptions are available under Alaska law, and then remand for the factual analysis necessary to ascertain whether successor liability is proper in this case under any of the approved exceptions. The superior court did not specify which exception justified its imposition of successor liability against Savage Arms.

1. The traditional "mere continuation" exception

Courts have traditionally imposed liability on successor corporations where the successor corporation is "merely a continuation" of the selling corporation. The primary elements of the "mere continuation" exception include use by the buyer of the seller's name, location, and employees, and a common identity of stockholders and directors.[1] This well-established exception stems from judicial refusal to honor a transaction which is "little more than a shuffling of corporate forms, lacking any fundamental change with independent significance." [Citation]

The "mere continuation" exception is available to claimants seeking to impose liability on a successor corporation for products manufactured by a predecessor. Although Savage Arms argues that we should not adopt this exception, we disagree, because this is a well-recognized exception, and we see no reason to reject its application here. We therefore hold that it is available under Alaska law.

2. *The modern "continuity of enterprise" exception*

Western Auto also asks us to adopt the modern "continuity of enterprise" and "product line" exceptions. We conclude that the facts in this case are ill-suited to the "product line" exception, and we therefore decline to consider it at this time.[2] We do, however, adopt the "continuity of enterprise" exception, for the reasons explained below.

The "continuity of enterprise" exception is an outgrowth of the traditional "mere continuation" theory of liability.[3] Under this exception, a successor corporation may be held liable for injuries caused by its predecessor's products where the totality of the transaction between the successor and the predecessor demonstrates a basic continuity of the predecessor enterprise. The successor may be held liable even though the sale of assets is for cash and there is no continuity of shareholders.[4]

Thus, whereas the traditional "mere continuation" exception depends on the existence of identical shareholders, the "continuity of enterprise" looks beyond that formal requirement and considers the substance of the underlying transaction. The key factors under the "continuity of enterprise" exception, first articulated in *Turner v. Bituminous Casualty Co.*, are: (1) continuity of key personnel, assets, and business operations; (2) speedy dissolution of the predecessor corpora-

---

1. *See* David W. Pollak, *Successor Liability in Asset Acquisitions*, 1126 PLI/Corp. 85, 107–12 (1999) (discussing different jurisdictions' approaches to choice-of-law issues for successor liability claims); *see also* Phillip I. Blumberg, *The Continuity of the Enterprise Doctrine: Corporate Successorship in United States Law*, 10 Fla. J. Int'l L. 365, 371 (1996) ("The doctrine ... is applicable only where the successor has the same stockholders as the predecessor and conducts the same business with the same management, facilities, employees, products, and trade names.").

2. Under the "product line" exception, a successor will be liable if it acquires substantially all of the predecessor's assets and undertakes essentially the same manufacturing operation of the same or similar products. *See Ray v. Alad Corp.*, 19 Cal.3d 22, 136 Cal.Rptr. 574, 560 P.2d 3, 8–11 (1977); 63 Am.Jur.2d *Products Liability* § 133 (1997); Pollak, *supra* note 15, at 104–16. Because the facts in this case seem ill-suited to this exception, we decline to evaluate the wisdom of adopting the "product line" theory at this time. Our decision today does not preclude further consideration of this exception in an appropriate case.

3. *See* Richard L. Cupp, Jr., *Redesigning Successor Liability*, 1999 U. Ill. L.Rev. 845, 848 & n.16 (1999).

4. *See Turner v. Bituminous Cas. Co.*, 397 Mich. 406, 244 N.W.2d 873, 883–84 (1976); Cupp, *supra* note 26, at 848–49.

tion; (3) assumption by the successor of those predecessor liabilities and obligations necessary for continuation of normal business operations; and (4) continuation of corporate identity. This is a limited exception that looks past the identity of shareholders and directors, and focuses on whether the business itself has been transferred as an ongoing concern.

Only a minority of courts have thus far adopted the "continuity of enterprise" exception.[5] And the American Law Institute recently declined to adopt both this exception and the "product line" exception for the Restatement (Third) of Torts.[6] The Third Restatement's commentary indicates that the vast majority of courts considering these modern exceptions have rejected them. Although there is some dispute about exactly how many jurisdictions have decided the issue, it is clear that a majority of jurisdictions have not adopted the "continuity of enterprise" exception.

Critics of the modern exceptions (such as "continuity of enterprise") argue primarily that expanding liability harms the overall economy by making it more difficult for companies to reorganize or sell their assets without destroying the value of the ongoing business enterprise. For example, they assert that a buyer interested in purchasing substantially all of the assets of a corporation will, in some cases, decline to make the purchase if it will be forced to assume liability for past product defects as well. As a result, some corporations will be unable to find purchasers, and will instead be forced to sell off the corporate assets on a piecemeal basis, squandering any accumulated goodwill. Such a piecemeal sale would give a corporation certain economic advantages: the seller's shareholders would be able to receive full value for the remaining assets, and successor liability would not flow to the purchasers under any of the traditional or modern theories. But a piecemeal sale would cause an ongoing business to be lost to society, and potential claimants would be no better off.

This argument, although compelling in theory, seems to paint an incomplete picture of the economic realities. If successor liability is expanded to include the "continuity of enterprise" exception, some companies indeed might be unable to find buyers for their ongoing businesses. But we have not been referred to any evidence that adopting this modern "continuity of enterprise" exception (or the marginally more popular "product line" exception) has in fact increased the number of corporate liquidations or piecemeal breakups, or that rejecting the modern exceptions has in fact decreased liquidations or piecemeal sales. And our research has not disclosed studies that have so concluded.

We also note that permitting successor liability under the "continuity of enterprise" exception will not discourage large-scale transfers so long as anticipated successor liabilities do not exceed the value of the corporation's accumulated goodwill. Presumably, many corporations will

---

5. *See* Restatement (Third) of Torts: Products Liability § 12, Reporters' Note at 315–19 (1998).

6. *See id.* § 12 cmt. B at 210 & Reporters' Note at 215–19.

continue to engage in efficient and productive transfers, with the purchasing firm merely factoring into the purchase price the cost of those successor liabilities. When firms contract for an asset transfer where the basic enterprise is to be continued, they negotiate to a price that reflects the fair market value of the transfer, taking heed of the risk of future claims. The purchasing firm will value any potential successor liability claims at least at the incremental cost of obtaining insurance coverage against successor liability for them. Where that insurance is too expensive or is unavailable, negotiations could collapse, and the firm will either continue to exist (and be subject to liability claims) or liquidate (and future victims will receive no recovery). But in many cases, we would expect selling and purchasing firms simply to negotiate to a rational price that takes account of these potential claims. The posited negative effects on the overall economy are too indeterminate and speculative to outweigh the policy of compensating persons injured by product defects.

The same reasoning applies to the Restatement authors' concerns regarding potential "windfalls." In many cases, a predecessor manufacturing company will be purchased by a larger, more financially-sound corporation. The rule we adopt here does not limit injured plaintiffs' recovery to the value of the assets purchased by the successor corporation, so there could conceivably be situations in which product defect victims would receive a larger recovery than they conceivably could have received had the predecessor company remained an ongoing concern, and been bankrupted by the total claims. The Restatement authors view the added recovery potential as an "injustice" to the successor corporation. But we think the Restatement analysis defeats the assumptions behind tort law. We assume that meritorious claims will be paid; that they are sometimes not paid due to insolvency does not change that underlying assumption. To characterize as a "windfall" full recovery for losses caused by product defects unjustly challenges the legitimacy of the injuries suffered. And once again, purchasing corporations can attempt to account for this risk of loss in the purchase price.

The other objections to expanded successor liability rules are also not dispositive. Successor liability potentially conflicts with maximizing the value received for bankrupt estates.[7] But we see no persuasive reason to favor corporate creditors over claimants later injured by the seller corporation's products. Also, some courts have argued that the modern exceptions impose liability on entities having no causal relationship with the harm. But basic to the "continuity of enterprise" exception is the preservation of a substantial portion of the goodwill of the predecessor corporation; the successor is fundamentally the same enterprise as the predecessor. When a firm negotiates to purchase another corporation, keeping the "enterprise" intact, it must anticipate any potential successor liabilities and negotiate an appropriate price. To permit the succes-

---

7. *See* Michelle M. Morgan, *The Denial of Future Tort Claims in In Re Piper Aircraft: Will the Court's Quick-Fix Solution Keep the Debtor Flying High or Bring it Crashing Down?*, 27 Loy. U. Chi. L.J. 27, 36–37 (1995).

sor, which presumably negotiated a discount for potential successor liabilities when dickering over the purchase price, to avoid liability based on lack of causation would give the successor an unwarranted windfall.

Finally, this new rule will also have the effect of encouraging existing corporations to produce safer products, in keeping with the public policy goals that underlie product liability law generally. Corporations are currently motivated to correct defects to reduce their own exposure to liability, but the traditional successor liability regime undermines that incentive by giving the manufacturing corporation another option: offering itself for sale to a new investor. Without successor liability, the original shareholders can receive full compensation for the current value of the firm, without sharing the burden caused by any defective products manufactured before the sale. The rule we announce today will give manufacturing corporations additional incentives to market non-defective products, in order to maximize the corporations' market value in event of sale.

Some commentators, including the Restatement authors, reason that legislatures are better situated than courts to define the parameters of successor liability. But we think this is an appropriate subject for judicial decision because it is directly related to products liability law, a doctrinal road long traveled by courts. For example, the four traditional exceptions were created by the courts. There is also some suggestion that legislation in other states has failed to address these problems. We see no reason to await legislation before addressing this issue.

We therefore adopt the "continuity of enterprise" exception to the general rule of nonliability for corporate successors.

3. *Propriety of the summary judgment order*

Although we here approve the "mere continuation" and "continuity of enterprise" exceptions, it is nonetheless necessary to reverse Western Auto's summary judgment order for two reasons. First, material factual disputes remain unresolved. Many key facts are uncontested, but certain important facts (such as the percentage of stock former shareholders in Savage Industries own in Savage Arms) are not established by the record. Second, the uncertainty regarding the proper legal standard governing successor liability appears to have prevented the parties from developing the record to address the applicable legal tests. We consequently remand for consideration of the "mere continuation" and "continuity of enterprise" exceptions in the context of this case.

We also note that Savage Arms is not shielded from liability by the fact that it purchased Savage Industries' assets through a bankruptcy proceeding. The First Circuit ruled in a related aspect of this case[8] that

---

8. In April 1992 Western Auto filed a third-party complaint against Savage Arms for indemnification or apportionment of damages. Savage Arms contended that Western Auto's claims were barred by the terms of Savage Industries' bankruptcy. The First Circuit Court of Appeals ultimately resolved the issue in Western Auto's favor in December 1994. *See Western Auto Supply Co. v. Savage Arms, Inc. (In re Savage Indus., Inc.)*, 43 F.3d 714, 723 (1st Cir.1994).

Western Auto and Taylor were not "afforded appropriate notice of the material terms of the all-asset transfer, nor of the chapter 11 plan" and therefore that the parties to the transfer, Savage Industries and Savage Arms, "are not entitled to rely on the protective jurisdiction of the bankruptcy court." The failure to give proper notice and to seek approval of the plan from the bankruptcy court "precluded a legitimate basis for enjoining the Alaska state court action."

* * *

IV. *CONCLUSION*

We * * * VACATE the orders imposing successor liability on Savage Arms, and REMAND for application of the doctrines adopted today and for further proceedings.

Notes

1. Is the question of whether Savage Arms (the successor) is a "continuity of enterprise" of Savage Industries (the predecessor) a question of fact for the jury or one for the trial court after the factual record is developed?

2. As the court explains, after an early expansion of successor liability beyond the traditional four exceptions by courts in a few states, the vast majority of courts rejected this liberalization of successor liability. Indeed, one commentator in the mid-1990s declared that the movement to expand successor liability for products liability plaintiffs was a dead letter. *See* Green, Successors and CERCLA: the Imperfect Analogy to Products Liability and An Alternative Proposal, 87 Nw. U.L. Rev. 897, 909–10 (1993). As *Savage Arms* reveals, that commentator was wrong.

3. Frequently the question arises: why not sue the predecessor? The *Savage Arms* case arises in the unusual context of a sale of the entire assets of a company that had filed for bankruptcy. The proceeds of the sale of the predecessor's assets had already been distributed to its creditors through the bankruptcy proceedings, and hence there was no predecessor nor assets to pursue. More typically, when a solvent company sells all of its assets to a successor, the company distributes the proceeds of the sale to its shareholders and then dissolves under state law. After a period of a few years, most state dissolution laws bar suits against the dissolved company, which no longer has assets in any case. While suit against the shareholders might be possible in theory, as a practical matter it is not feasible if there is any significant number of them. Hence, absent successor liability or a company like Western Auto in the chain of distribution, traditional corporate law rules leave an injured plaintiff without a remedy if the product was sold prior to liquidation but the injury occurred after liquidation.

4. The court adopts a rationale that the successor can discount the price it pays for the assets of the predecessor. This, then, puts the liability where it belongs—on the predecessor who manufactured and sold a defective product and employs successor liability to make the successor a "conduit" to pass the costs of defective products on to the manufacturer responsible for them.

The sale of assets by Savage Industries to Savage Arms took place in Texas some undisclosed time before the plaintiff's child was shot. At the time, Texas law was unsympathetic to expanded successor liability. How could Savage Arms discount the price it would pay to Savage Industries based on a future decision by the Alaska Supreme Court that Alaska law should apply to accidents occurring there and that successor liability should be expanded to include asset sales?

What other impediments exist to a successor serving as a conduit to make the predecessor bear these costs? Are there other reasons, nevertheless, to expand successor liability and impose the loss on the successor?

For proposals to effectuate having successors serve as "conduits" to channel liability to the predecessor by discounting the price paid in an asset sale, see Green, Successor Liability: The Superiority of Statutory Reform to Protect Products Liability Claimants, 72 Cornell L.Rev. 17 (1986) (advocating modification of state dissolution laws to require consideration of future claims); Note, Successor Liability, Mass Tort, and Mandatory–Litigation Class Action, 118 Harv.L.Rev. 2357 (2005) (proposing non-opt-out class action encompassing current and future claims that might be made based on predecessor's products).

5. The court mentions, but does not discuss, the failure-to-warn theory by which successors have been found liable for defects in a predecessor's product. The Restatement (Third) of Torts: Products Liability includes this basis for successor liability:

§ 13. Liability of Successor for Harm Caused by Successor's Own Post-sale Failure to Warn

(a) A successor corporation or other business entity that acquires assets of a predecessor corporation or other business entity, whether or not liable under the rule stated in § 12 [the traditional four exceptions], is subject to liability for harm to persons or property caused by the successor's failure to warn of a risk created by a product sold or distributed by the predecessor if:

(1) the successor undertakes or agrees to provide services for maintenance or repair of the product or enters into a similar relationship with purchasers of the predecessor's products giving rise to actual or potential economic advantage to the successor, and

(2) a reasonable person in the position of the successor would provide a warning.

(b) A reasonable person in the position of the successor would provide a warning if:

(1) the successor knows or reasonably should know that the product poses a substantial risk of harm to persons or property; and

(2) those to whom a warning might be provided can be identified and can reasonably be assumed to be unaware of the risk of harm; and

(3) a warning can be effectively communicated to and acted upon by those to whom a warning might be provided; and

(4) the risk of harm is sufficiently great to justify the burden of providing a warning.

By contrast with the successor liability adopted in *Savage Arms*, liability based on failure-to-warn is based on the successor's acts or omissions, rather than the predecessor's. What justifies imposing this liability on the successor, qua successor, rather as a conduit to the predecessor? Recall that tort law generally does not impose a duty to rescue. Can this obligation be justified by the exception to the no-duty-to-rescue rule based on negligence in undertaking to provide services to someone? *See* Restatement (Third) of Torts: Liability for Physical Harm § 42 (Proposed Final Draft No. 1, 2005). Non-successor companies providing maintenance services are not subject to products liability for failure to warn. Is there any principled basis for making this distinction between successor repairers and non-successor repairers?

6. The *Savage Arms* case is also unusual in that it had a retailer suing the successor for indemnity. Thus, this case does not present the more sympathetic occasion where the plaintiff has been injured by a defective product and has no one to sue. Accepting the desirability of expanding successor liability for such plaintiffs, is it also desirable to impose liability on successors as opposed to retailers or others in the chain of distribution who actually sold the product? *See also* Simmons v. Mark Lift Indus., Inc., 366 S.C. 308, 622 S.E.2d 213 (2005) (holding that whatever successor liability claims exist are unaffected by existence of a retailer who also had been sued).

Suppose that, instead of selling all of its assets to Savage Arms in a bankruptcy proceeding, Savage Industries had liquidated its assets in piecemeal fashion? Isn't that precisely the reason for holding retailers and others in the chain of distribution strictly liable?

7. **The Effect of Federal Bankruptcy Law.** As footnote 8 in *Savage Arms* indicates, there is a question whether a purchaser of assets in a bankruptcy can be subject to successor liability claims. The First Circuit Court of Appeals decided that the failure to notify distributors such as Western Auto of the bankruptcy proceeding and sale precluded barring their post-bankruptcy claims against the purchaser based on a state successor liability theory. In a much broader ruling, the Seventh Circuit Court of Appeals concluded that federal bankruptcy courts do not have the authority to "cleanse" asset sales from future claims made against the purchaser:

This possibility [of successor claims] will depress the price of the bankrupt's assets, to the prejudice of creditors. All this is true, but proves too much. It implies, what no one believes, that by virtue of the arising-under jurisdiction a bankruptcy court enjoys a blanket power to enjoin all future lawsuits against a buyer at a bankruptcy sale in order to maximize the sale price: more, that the court could in effect immunize such buyers from all state and federal laws that might reduce the value of the assets bought from the bankrupt; in effect, that it could discharge the debts of nondebtors (like [the purchaser-successor]) as well as of debtors even if the creditors did not consent; that it could allow the parties to bankruptcy sales to extinguish the rights of third parties, here future tort claimants, without notice to them or (as notice might well be infeasible) any consideration of their interests. If the court could do all these nice things the result would indeed be to make the property of bankrupts more valuable than other property—more valuable to the creditors, of course, but also to the debtor's shareholders and managers to the extent that the strategic position of the debtor in possession in a reorganization enables the debtor's owners and managers to benefit from bankruptcy. But the result would not only be harm to third parties, such as the injured persons pursuing a successor liability claim, but also a further incentive to enter bankruptcy for reasons that have nothing to do with the purposes of bankruptcy law.

Zerand–Bernal Group, Inc. v. Cox, 23 F.3d 159, 163 (7th Cir.1994). *But see* In re White Motor Credit Corp., 75 B.R. 944 (Bankr. N.D. Ohio 1987).

8. The product line exception adopted by the California Supreme Court in *Ray v. Alad* was the first expansion of successor liability. Why do you suppose the *Savage Arms* court concluded, *see* footnote 2, that "the facts in this case seem ill-suited to this exception"? What does that say about the ability of the product line exception to serve the "conduit" function contemplated by the Alaska Supreme Court? Is the continuity-of-enterprise theory better suited to accomplish this goal?

9. Most of the cases dealing with successor corporate liability have involved obligations other than tort liability for defective products. Are there special considerations in the area of products liability that would support different rules in this area, irrespective of a state's position (either through case law or statute) on successor liability outside the area of products liability? Are these special considerations limited to cases in which the successor corporation continues the predecessor corporation's product line?

SECTION B. TRANSACTIONS COVERED BY PRODUCT LIABILITY AND WARRANTY

Section 1 of the Restatement (Third) of Torts: Products Liability refers to one who is "engaged in the business of selling or otherwise distributing products who sells or distributes a defective product * * *." Although the Restatement is not a statute, and should not be treated as such, it is clear that, on this issue, its language reflects a clear consensus among courts that product liability applies to "product sales" or other methods of "distribution" that are sufficiently analogous to sales.

The warranties created by Article 2 of the Commercial Code are similarly limited in their application. The warranty provisions themselves (sections 2–313, 2–314, and 2–315) refer to a "seller," and section 2–102 provides that Article 2 "applies to transactions in goods."

The material in this section addresses the applicability of products liability (and to a lesser extent the Article 2 warranties) to transactions that are not technically product sales but that nevertheless evoke many of the policies underlying products liability. The first group of cases—dealing with leases and bailments—focus on the problem of identifying transactions sufficiently analogous to sales to warrant the application of products liability. The second group—dealing with franchises, used products, real estate, and services—focus on the problem of whether the subject of the transaction is sufficiently similar to a normal "product" to justify the application of products liability. Cases involving services are especially difficult to analyze because they often involve products that have not technically been sold.

It is important to distinguish between cases involving the scope of products liability or common law warranties on the one hand and those involving Article 2 on the other. Although some courts have analyzed the application of product liability and an Article 2 warranty to a specific transaction interchangeably, other courts have used different analyses for these two theories. A court has considerably more leeway defining the scope of product liability than it does interpreting the legislative mandate of the Commercial Code. Although precedents involving the scope of one theory might be useful in defining the scope of the other, you should exercise caution before crossing the boundary between these two theories.

Even if a transaction is governed by some form of product liability, it is important to determine whether product liability, breach of warranty, or both are applicable, because the details of each theory differ. For example, pure economic damages are recoverable under an Article 2 warranty but normally are not recoverable under product liability. Conversely, a manufacturer can disclaim an implied warranty of merchantability but not product liability.

As was indicated at the outset of this chapter, these cases involving the scope of product liability have a dual importance. They have practical importance in their own right, and they again raise the issue of why product sales should be governed by special rules of tort liability. Although all boundary problems create some degree of ambiguity, a coherent theory of product liability should at least identify the factors that distinguish between transactions that fall within its scope and those that do not. As you study these cases, ask yourself whether the policies courts and commentators have used to justify product liability help in determining whether borderline cases fall within its scope of application.

1. LEASES AND BAILMENTS

MARTIN v. RYDER TRUCK RENTAL, INC.
Supreme Court of Delaware, 1976.
353 A.2d 581.

HERRMANN, CHIEF JUSTICE.

We hold today that a bailment-lease of a motor vehicle, entered into in the regular course of a truck rental business, is subject to application of the doctrine of strict tort liability in favor of an injured bystander.

I.

According to the plaintiffs in this case:

A truck was leased by the defendant, Ryder Truck Rental, Inc., to Gagliardi Brothers, Inc., in the regular course of Ryder's truck rental business. The truck, operated by a Gagliardi employee, was involved in an intersectional collision. Due to a failure of its braking system, the truck did not stop for a traffic light and struck the rear of an automobile which had stopped for the signal, causing that automobile to collide with the vehicle driven by the plaintiff, Dorothy Martin. As a result, she was injured, her car was damaged, and this suit was brought by her and her husband against Ryder.

The plaintiffs base their cause of action solely upon the doctrine of strict tort liability, *i.e.,* tort liability without proof of negligence. The Superior Court granted summary judgment in favor of Ryder, holding that the doctrine is not applicable to the factual situation here presented. We disagree.

II.

* * *

The defendant contends that if the Legislature intended to create a strict liability for bailments for hire, it would have done so in the UCC. Thus, the threshold question in the instant case is whether, by the enactment of the UCC and the limitation of its strict warranty provisions to sales, the Legislature has preempted this field of the law of products liability; or whether, the UCC notwithstanding, the courts are free to provide for bailments and leases the alternate, but somewhat conflicting, remedy of strict tort liability.

The warranty provisions of Article 2 of the UCC, §§ 2–313 (express) and 2–315 (implied), are clearly limited to the sales of goods; the Statute is "neutral" as to other types of relationships.[10] Manifestly, the Legislature has not preempted the field as to bailments and leases by enactment of the UCC.[11] Silence on the subject may not be deemed to be such preemption.

Hence, we are free, in the common law tradition, to apply the doctrine of strict tort liability to a bailment-lease. The question is whether that course should be adopted; and for that decision, consideration of the nature and evolution of the doctrine is important:

III.

* * *

10. The A.L.I. Official Comment to § 2–313 reads:

"Although this section is limited in its scope and direct purpose to warranties made by the seller to the buyer as part of a contract for sale, the warranty sections of this Article are not designed in any way to disturb those lines of case law growth which have recognized that warranties need not be confined either to sales contracts or to the direct parties to such a contract. They may arise in other appropriate circumstances such as in the case of bailments for hire * * *. [T]he matter is left to the case law with the intention that the policies of this Act may offer useful guidance in dealing with further cases as they arise."

11. Reserved for another day is the question of whether the Legislature has preempted the field as to direct sales cases and whether the warranty provisions of the UCC are, therefore, the exclusive source of strict liability in such cases.

A.

In *Cintrone v. Hertz Truck Leasing, etc.,* 45 N.J. 434, 212 A.2d 769 (1965), the New Jersey Supreme Court applied strict liability in tort to a motor vehicle bailment situation because "[a] bailor for hire, such as a person in the U-drive-it business, puts motor vehicles in the stream of commerce in a fashion not unlike a manufacturer or retailer"; subjects such a leased vehicle "to more sustained use on the highways than most ordinary car purchasers"; and by the very nature of his business, exposes "the bailee, his employees, passengers and the traveling public * * * to a greater *quantum* of potential danger of harm from defective vehicles than usually arises out of sales by the manufacturer." 212 A.2d at 777.

The California Supreme Court endorsed the *Cintrone* "step" in *Price v. Shell Oil Company,* 2 Cal.3d 245, 85 Cal.Rptr. 178, 466 P.2d 722 (1970):

> " * * * [A] broad philosophy evolves naturally from the purpose of imposing strict liability which 'is to insure that the costs of injuries resulting from defective products are borne by the manufacturers that put such products on the market rather than by the injured persons who are powerless to protect themselves.' [Citing *Yuba*]. Essentially the paramount policy to be promoted by the rule is the protection of otherwise defenseless victims of manufacturing defects and the spreading throughout society of the cost of compensating them. * * *

> " * * * [W]e can perceive no substantial difference between *sellers* of personal property and *non-sellers,* such as bailors and lessors. In each instance, the seller or non-seller 'places [an article] on the market, knowing that it is to be used without inspection for defects, * * *.' [Citing *Yuba*] In the light of the policy to be subserved, it should make no difference that the party distributing the article has retained title to it. Nor can we see how the risk of harm associated with the use of the chattel can vary with the legal form under which it is held. Having in mind the market realities and the widespread use of the lease of personalty in today's business world, we think it makes good sense to impose on the lessors of chattels the same liability for physical harm which has been imposed on the manufacturers and retailers. The former, like the latter, are able to bear the cost of compensating for injuries resulting from defects by spreading the loss through an adjustment of the rental." 85 Cal.Rptr. at 181, 466 P.2d at 725–26.

The extension of the doctrine of strict tort liability to bailors-lessors has been limited, however, to leases made in the regular course of a rental business, the doctrine being applicable only in a commercial setting by its very nature. *Price, supra,* 85 Cal.Rptr. at 183–84, 466 P.2d at 727–28; *Cintrone, supra,* 212 A.2d at 777. Strict tort liability has been found "peculiarly applicable" to the lessor of motor vehicles in "today's society with 'the growth of the business of renting motor vehicles, trucks and pleasure cars' * * * and the persistent advertising efforts to put one 'in the driver's seat.'" *Price, supra,* 85 Cal.Rptr. at 183, 466 P.2d at 727, quoting from *Cintrone, supra,* 212 A.2d at 776, 777.

For the reasons so well stated by the leading authorities in this field, we are of the opinion that, since the General Assembly has not preempted this area of the field, the common law must grow to fulfill the requirements of justice as dictated by changing times and conditions.

The present-day magnitude of the motor vehicle rental business, and the trade practices which have developed therein, require maximum protection for the victims of defective rentals. This translates into the imposition of strict tort liability upon the lessor. The public policy considerations which appeared in the development of the doctrine during the past decade, are especially relevant where, as in the instant case, the bailor-lessor retains exclusive control and supervision over the maintenance and repair of the motor vehicle it places in circulation upon the highways. All of the societal policy reasons leading to the expansion of strict tort liability in sales cases are equally applicable in this motor vehicle rental case: (1) the concept that the cost of compensating for injuries and damages arising from the use of a defective motor vehicle should be borne by the party who placed it in circulation, who is best able to prevent distribution of a defective product, and who can spread the cost as a risk and expense of the business enterprise; (2) the concept that the defective motor vehicle was placed on the highways in violation of a representation of fitness by the lessor implied by law from the circumstances and trade practices of the business; and (3) the concept that the imposition upon the lessor of liability without fault will result in general risk-reduction by arousing in the lessor an additional impetus to furnish safer vehicles.

Accordingly, we hold that the doctrine of strict tort liability is applicable to Ryder in the instant case. *Accord, Stang v. Hertz Corporation,* 83 N.M. 730, 497 P.2d 732 (1972); *Stewart v. Budget Rent–A–Car Corporation,* 52 Haw. 71, 470 P.2d 240 (1970); *Coleman v. Hertz Corporation,* Okl.App., 534 P.2d 940 (1975); *Galuccio v. Hertz Corporation,* 1 Ill.App.3d 272, 274 N.E.2d 178 (1971); *see Bachner v. Pearson,* Alaska, 479 P.2d 319 (1970); *Rourke v. Garza,* Tex.Civ.App., 511 S.W.2d 331 (1974).

* * *

IV.

Ryder contends that the imposition of any new measure of liability in this field (1) should be left to the Legislature, citing *Bona v. Graefe,* 264 Md. 69, 285 A.2d 607 (1972); or (2) should be made effective prospectively only. As to the first point: where, as here, the Legislature has not preempted the field the common law must be kept abreast of the time and must grow to fulfill the demands of justice. As to the second point: these plaintiffs may not be deprived of the benefits of the development of the law they have prompted by their perseverance in this litigation; to do so would render this opinion pure *dictum*. See *Great Northern Ry. Co. v. Sunburst Oil & Refining Co.*, 287 U.S. 358, 53 S.Ct. 145, 77 L.Ed. 360 (1932); Schaefer, *The Control of "Sunbursts"; Techniques of Prospective Overruling*, 42 N.Y.U.L.Rev. 631 (1967). We decline to limit the rulings herein to prospective application.

* * *

The judgment below is reversed and the cause remanded for further proceedings consistent herewith.

[The concurring opinion of JUSTICE DUFFY is omitted.]

Notes

1. As *Martin* indicates, a lease is governed by product liability only if the lessor is in the business of leasing products of that type, just as a sale is governed by product liability only if the seller is in the business of selling products of that type. *See* Brescia v. Great Road Realty Trust, 117 N.H. 154, 373 A.2d 1310 (1977).

2. Is there any reason to treat product leases differently than product sales?

3. In Garcia v. Halsett, 3 Cal.App.3d 319, 82 Cal.Rptr. 420 (1970), the court held that a laundromat owner was strictly liable to a boy whose arm became entangled in a defective washing machine. The court characterized the transaction as a "license."

Suppose a child fell while riding the defendant's merry-go-round? Would it make a difference whether the accident was caused by a defect in the wooden horse or by the operator starting the merry-go-round before the patrons were ready? Do the policies underlying products liability apply with equal force to these two situations?

4. Section 20 (b) of the Restatement (Third) of Torts: Products Liability applies product liability to lessors and bailors who "in a commercial transaction * * * [provide a] product to another either for use or consumption or as a preliminary step leading to ultimate use or consumption." The comments elaborate:

Comment:

  c. *Commercial product leases.* A commercial lessor of new and like-new products is generally subject to the rules governing new product sellers. When an individual rents a new or an almost-new used product on a short-term basis, with the lessee having no opportunity to inspect the product or adequately to assess its condition, and the product unit is drawn from a pool of rental units that includes new and almost-new used units with no attempt by the leasing agent to distinguish among units on the basis of age and condition, the lessor is subject to liability as if it were the retail seller of a new product. When the rental units are in obviously used condition, liability of the lessor depends on the rules stated in § 8.

* * *

f. Other means of commercial distribution: product bailments. Bailments typically involve short-term transfers of possession. Several categories of cases are fairly clear. When the defendant is in the business of selling the same type of product as is the subject of the bailment, the seller/bailor is subject to strict liability for harm caused by defects. Thus, an automobile dealer who allows a prospective customer to test-drive a demonstrator will be treated the same as a seller of the demonstrator car. Even when sale of a product is not contemplated, the commercial bailor is subject to strict liability if a charge is imposed as a condition of the bailment. Thus, a laundromat is subject to strict liability for a defective clothes dryer, and a roller rink that rents skates is treated similarly. When products are made available as a convenience to customers who are on the defendant's premises primarily for different, although related purposes, and no separate charge is made, strict liability is not imposed. Thus, bowling alleys that supply bowling balls for customer use and markets that supply shopping carts are not subject to strict products liability for harm caused by defects in those items. Similarly, doctors who use medical devices while treating patients are not considered distributors of those products.

5. By their own terms, sections 2–313, 2–314, and 2–315 of the Commercial Code apply to a "seller." Section 2–314 also refers to "a contract for * * * sale." Section 2–106(1) provides that a " '[c]ontract for sale' includes both a present sale of goods and a contract to sell goods at a future time. A 'sale' consists in the passing of title from the seller to the buyer for a price." Consequently, the Article 2 warranties seem not to apply to leases. Nevertheless, a few courts have applied an Article 2 warranty to a lease. *See, e.g.,* Owens v. Patent Scaffolding Co., 77 Misc.2d 992, 354 N.Y.S.2d 778 (1974); Hawkins Const. Co. v. Matthews Co., Inc., 190 Neb. 546, 209 N.W.2d 643 (1973). Of course, a court might also create a common law warranty to cover leases.

ARMSTRONG RUBBER CO. v. URQUIDEZ
Supreme Court of Texas, 1978.
570 S.W.2d 374.

McGee, Justice.

This appeal involves the question whether the doctrine of strict liability in tort applies where the product has not entered the stream of commerce and where there has been no sale of the product by the manufacturer but a bailment for mutual benefit. The widow and son of test driver Clemente Urquidez brought suit against Armstrong Rubber Company. The plaintiffs pled that Urquidez was killed as the result of a blowout of a tire alleged to be defective in design and manufacture. The trial court rendered judgment on the jury's determination that the tire was defective in its design or manufacture and that the defect was the producing cause of the accident. The widow was awarded $75,000 and the son $12,000 with the award subject to the subrogation rights of the intervening worker's compensation carrier. The Court of Civil Appeals affirmed. 560 S.W.2d 781. We reverse the judgments below and render judgment that the plaintiffs take nothing.

Automotive Proving Grounds, Inc. owns and operates a tire-testing facility near Pecos. On January 1, 1970, Automotive contracted to provide testing facilities to the defendant, Armstrong, on a part-time basis for a period of ten years. Under the contract Armstrong agreed to provide and maintain all trucks and vehicles required for its testing. It was Automotive's responsibility to maintain the track and buildings comprising the testing facility, to provide drivers, mechanics, and other personnel necessary for testing purposes and to promulgate safety rules and driver qualifications.

The deceased, Clemente Urquidez, was employed by Automotive as a test driver. At the time of the accident, he was driving a tractor/trailer rig owned by Armstrong. Urquidez was performing a standard test at 60 m.p.h. on the oval test track when the left front tire of the tractor blew out. Urquidez decelerated the truck into the infield area of the oval track where he encountered soft sand, overturned and was killed. The tire that blew out was an Allstate Express Cargo Nylon 12–ply non-interest spare manufactured by Armstrong. Both front tires on the tractor were non-interest spares. A "non-interest spare" is a term applied to a tire mounted on the test truck along with the tires being tested, but which is not itself being tested. The tire in question had never been sold by Armstrong. It was new when received at the Pecos facility. The tire was never tested at the Pecos facility but was manufactured and provided for use only as a non-interest spare on Armstrong's trucks. The tire was of the same quality as tires manufactured by Armstrong and sold across the nation.

The doctrine of strict liability as enunciated in the Restatement (Second) of Torts § 402A has been adopted as the rule in Texas. * * * Although phrased in terms of sellers, it is not necessary that the defendant actually sell the product, but only that he be engaged in the business of introducing the product into channels of commerce.

* * *

Armstrong initially questions the application of the doctrine of strict liability to the tire in question. Armstrong contends that the tire was provided for the industrial purpose of testing other tires and that the accident occurred in its "testing laboratory." Armstrong argues that the defective tire was neither manufactured for market nor placed in the stream of commerce. We agree that the tire never entered the stream of commerce.

In extending the doctrine of strict liability to the present bailment, the Court of Civil Appeals emphasized that tires of the same design and manufacture were "regularly sold by Armstrong in regular channels of commerce." We do not believe it sufficient, however, that the seller merely introduce products of similar design and manufacture into the stream of commerce. To invoke the doctrine of strict liability in tort the product producing injury or damage must enter the stream of commerce. In *General Motors Corp. v. Hopkins*, 548 S.W.2d 344, 351 (Tex.1977) we said that liability rests on the defendant "placing into the stream of commerce a product which is demonstrated at trial to have been dangerous."

The Court of Civil Appeals further emphasized that Urquidez was not employed to test non-interest spares. In that court's opinion the dual policy considerations of "loss distribution" and "injury reduction" might best be served by extending the doctrine of strict liability to the present bailment transaction. Armstrong, on the other hand, urges that the policy considerations underlying the doctrine of strict liability in tort should not be advanced as the basis for the doctrine's protection where the essential elements of the doctrine have not been satisfied. Clemente Urquidez was employed to test tires. It was in part his job to provide safe tires for the public. Armstrong therefore argues that he was not the ordinary user or consumer entitled to the protection afforded by strict liability in tort.

While we agree that Clemente Urquidez was not hired to test the non-interest spare, we would not extend the doctrine of strict liability in tort on that basis. Although the defective tire was not itself the subject of the test, it was manufactured and provided for the limited purpose of testing other tires. The non-interest spare was never sold and, more importantly, never entered the stream of commerce. We recognize that application of strict liability in tort does not depend upon a sale of the product, nevertheless the product must be released in some manner to the consuming public. *See, Rourke v. Garza, supra; McKisson v. Sales Affiliates, Inc., supra.* The Restatement does not make a manufacturer an insurer of every person who is injured by one of its products. *Martinez v. Dixie Carriers, Inc.*, 529 F.2d 457 (5th Cir.1976).

As this is a case of first impression, the plaintiffs direct our attention to several cases originating in other jurisdictions which extend the doctrine of strict liability in tort to bailment transactions. *Cf. Whitfield v. Cooper*, 30 Conn.Sup. 47, 298 A.2d 50 (1972); *Nowakowski v. Hoppe Tire Co.*, 39 Ill.App.3d 155, 349 N.E.2d 578 (5th Dist.1974); *Bainter v. Lamoine LP Gas Co.*, 24 Ill.App.3d 913, 321 N.E.2d 744 (3d Dist.1974); *Ful[l]bright v. Klamath Gas Co.*, 271 Or. 449, 533 P.2d 316 (1975). We have reviewed these authorities, but do not find them persuasive as each bailment arose in a transaction essentially commercial in character. In *Whitfield*, the defendant bailed its customer a defective car for use while defendant repaired the customer's car. In *Ful[l]bright*, the defendant provided a defective potato vine burner to its customer in connection with defendant's sale of gas. In *Bainter*, the defendant loaned a defective gas tank in which its customer stored gas purchased from defendant. In *Nowakowski*, the defendant substituted a defective wheel assembly from its own stock in the course of repairing its customer's truck. An employee of the customer was subsequently injured while mounting a tire on the defective wheel assembly provided by defendant. In each case cited, the bailment for mutual benefit accompanied a sale of goods or services. In each instance the manufacturer, supplier or retailer released the product to its customer. Accordingly, the product provided was in the stream of commerce. These cases are clearly distinguishable from our present facts where Armstrong pursuant to its contract with Automotive provided non-interest spares for the purpose of testing new or experimental tires.

Armstrong never released the non-interest spare to an ordinary user or consumer within the meaning of the Restatement. The defective tire, although not itself the subject of the test, always remained within the industrial, testing process. Accordingly, the tire never entered the stream of commerce. The lower courts, therefore, inappropriately applied the doctrine of strict liability to the present industrial transaction.

The judgments of the Court of Civil Appeals and the trial court are reversed and judgment is here rendered that the plaintiffs take nothing.

Notes

1. How would *Urquidez* be resolved under § 20 of the Products Liability Restatement set out in note 4, *supra* page 719?

2. The suggestion in *Urquidez*—that a bailment is governed by product liability only if the bailment is incidental to a sale of another product or service—was used to preclude the application of products liability in Thate v. Texas & Pacific Railway Co., 595 S.W.2d 591 (Tex.App. 1980): The plaintiff was injured while loading his employer's trucks onto a railroad car supplied by the defendant. The court held that the defendant had not placed the railroad car into the stream of commerce. It distinguished the stream-of-commerce test for product liability from a similar test to determine whether goods are in interstate commerce. The court also interpreted *Urquidez* to exclude from product liability bailments that are not incidental to a sale of a product or a service. Moreover, the court relied, as did the court in *Urquidez*, on the plaintiff's status as an employee of an industrial entity as opposed to that of an ordinary consumer.

Notwithstanding the language of *Urquidez* and *Thate,* bailment cases cannot be resolved by identifying one or two factors. Commercial consumers can recover for product liability in appropriate circumstances, and the mere association of a defective product with the sale of another product or service does not necessarily trigger product liability. For example, a defendant who merely uses a defective product while selling another product or service is not necessarily subject to product liability. A doctor who uses a defective needle is probably not subject to product liability, even though the needle is clearly a product and is used in association with the sale of service. See Ethicon, Inc. v. Parten, 520 S.W.2d 527 (Tex.App.1975). In Thomas v. St. Joseph Hospital, 618 S.W.2d 791 (Tex.App.1981), however, a hospital was held strictly liable for supplying a patient with a flammable gown. The distinction between the needle and the gown cannot be explained merely on the basis of their association with another product or service. The distinction seems to rest on the extent to which the plaintiff controlled the product.

Even when the plaintiff has control of a product, the defendant has not necessarily placed it into the stream of commerce. *Thate* is one example. Keen v. Dominick's Finer Foods, Inc., 49 Ill.App.3d 480, 7 Ill.Dec. 341, 364 N.E.2d 502 (1977), an Illinois case involving a supermarket customer who was injured by a defective shopping cart, is another. The bailment of the cart was associated with the sale of other products, and the customer had temporary control of the cart, but the court held that the supermarket was not subject to product liability. Although the case might have been decided differently in another state, it demonstrates the difficulty of drawing clear lines for determining whether or not a product has been placed in the stream of commerce. The difficulty is further illustrated by considering that even if a court were to hold that a shopping-cart injury is governed by product liability, it might nevertheless hold that an injury caused by a drinking fountain in a defendant's store is not. A distinction between the shopping-cart and the drinking fountain does not seem to be implausible, even though the plaintiff temporarily controlled each product, and each product was associated with the sale of other products in the defendant's store. The extent of the plaintiff's control of the product, the association of the product with the sale or lease of other products or services, and the industrial or consumer aspects of the transaction all seem to be factors in determining whether a defendant has placed a product in the stream of commerce. No single factor seems to be determinative, and no clear rule has emerged to determine whether a defendant has placed a product in the stream of commerce. Courts are likely to use an *ad hoc* approach that depends heavily on the facts of each case.

3. If one defendant escapes product liability because it has not placed a product in the stream of commerce, the plaintiff might still recover under product liability from another seller in the chain of distribution. For example, even though a doctor using a defective needle is probably not liable to the patient, the manufacturer who sold the needle to the doctor is subject to product liability. The fact that the manufacturer did not sell the needle to the plaintiff is of course irrelevant.

4. Several courts have applied product liability to product demonstrations even though a sale had not taken place. *See* First National Bank v. Cessna Aircraft Co., 365 So.2d 966 (Ala.1978) (airplane demonstration); Delaney v. Towmotor Corp., 339 F.2d 4 (2d Cir.1964) (forklift demonstration). In McKisson v. Sales Affiliates, Inc., 416 S.W.2d 787 (Tex.1967), the court applied product liability to a free sample given to a prospective customer.

5. Does products liability apply to products while they are being manufactured? In O'Malley v. American LaFrance, Inc., 2002 WL 32068354 (E.D.N.Y. Dec. 30, 2002) plaintiff was a firefighter whose employer ordered a custom-built fire truck from defendant (LTI). The employer sent plaintiff to defendant's factory to inspect the truck halfway through its construction. The truck had a storage compartment on its top deck. Plaintiff was injured in a fall when the door on top of the compartment gave way while plaintiff stood on the door. The door collapsed because it was not designed to bear weight. Defendant usually attached "no-step" warning labels on such doors, but it had not attached the labels at this stage of construction. The trial judge denied motions for summary judgment. In an unpublished opinion, the judge ruled that products liability can apply to incomplete products, but not if plaintiff's injury resulted from "the product's incompleteness." The court stated:

[I]f after the mid-inspection LTI simply had to add a red paint job, hoses and ladders, and a dalmatian, its product would have been sufficiently complete for products liability to attach at the moment of Mr. O'Malley's injury. No substantial changes would have altered the compartment doors, the alleged proximate cause of his ills. However, if LTI had planned to perform substantial work on the fire truck, including work that would have altered the compartment doors and perhaps made them safe, then it cannot be held accountable in products liability for an injury occurring midway through the construction process. By the evidence contained in the pleadings, the court cannot say which scenario is more accurate and therefore cannot grant LTI's motion on the strict products liability claim. * * * Mr. O'Malley asserts in his deposition testimony that the * * * storage compartment did not change in form from the time of his injury to the time when the truck was shipped to [his employer]. If this statement is true, indicating that LTI had no plans to alter the door's design or manufacture, the policies undergirding the doctrine of products liability would support a finding that plaintiffs could recover under a products liability theory. In contrast, Mr. Andrew's deposition testimony indicates that LTI planned to do additional work on the door; at the minimum, the company planned to add a "no-step" sticker. The court refuses to speculate what changes LTI planned or could have effected at the fire department's request following the mid-inspection.

6. What is the gravamen of the plaintiff's claim in *O'Malley*? Is he making a design defect or a warning defect claim? Does it matter?

7. Should a grocer be strictly liable for a soft drink bottle that explodes before the customer pays for the bottle at the checkout counter? Do any of the policies underlying product liability apply differently depending on whether the customer has paid at the time of the explosion? Would it make a difference if the bottle exploded on the shelf and injured a passing customer who had no intention of buying the soft drink? If the customer slipped on the floor after the bottle exploded and spilled? If the customer slipped on the floor because a tomato had been dropped by a sales clerk?

Do the policies underlying product liability help determine whether product liability should be applicable in these situations?

8. Several cases involving bailments have involved reusable containers. In Bainter v. Lamoine LP Gas Co., 24 Ill.App.3d 913, 321 N.E.2d 744 (1974), discussed in *Urquidez,* the court applied products liability to a gas supplier for an injury caused by a defective returnable gas container supplied to the plaintiff without charge. *See also,* Fulbright v. Klamath Gas Co., 271 Or. 449, 533 P.2d 316 (1975). Should product liability apply to a defective returnable soft drink bottle?

9. As in the case of leases, the language of sections 2–313, 2–314, and 2–315 seems to preclude the application of the Article 2 warranty to bailments. Sections 2–313, 2–314, and 2–315 each refer to a "seller," and section 2–314 also refers to a "contract for * * * sale." Section 2–106(1) defines a "sale" as "the passing of title from the seller to the buyer for a price." *See e.g.,* Garfield v. Furniture Fair–Hanover, 113 N.J.Super. 509, 274 A.2d 325 (Law Div. 1971).

2. FRANCHISES AND TRADEMARK LICENSES

KOSTERS v. SEVEN–UP CO.
United States Court of Appeals, Sixth Circuit, 1979.
595 F.2d 347.

MERRITT, CIRCUIT JUDGE.

During the past two decades, franchising has become a common means of marketing products and services, but our legal system has not yet settled the principles that define the liabilities of franchisors for injuries sustained by customers of their franchisees. This diversity case requires us to interpret the theories of tort and contract liability which Michigan law allows a jury to consider when deciding whether an injured purchaser is entitled to recover against the franchisor of a product.

I. STATEMENT OF THE CASE

The defendant, the Seven–Up Company, appeals from a $150,000 jury verdict awarded for injuries caused by an exploding 7–Up bottle. The plaintiff removed a cardboard carton containing six bottles of 7–Up from a grocery shelf, put it under her arm and headed for the check-out counter of the grocery store. She was blinded in one eye when a bottle slipped out of the carton, fell on the floor and exploded, causing a piece of glass to strike her eye as she looked down. The 7–Up carton was a so-called "over-the-crown" or "neck-thru" carton designed to be held from the top and made without a strip on the sides of the carton which would prevent a bottle from slipping out if held underneath.

The carton was designed and manufactured by Olinkraft, Inc. Olinkraft sold it to the Brooks Bottling Company, a franchisee of the defendant, Seven–Up Company. Seven–Up retains the right to approve the design of articles used by the bottler, including cartons. The franchise agreement between Seven–Up and the Brooks Bottling Company requires that "cases, bottles, and crowns used for 7–Up will be of a type * * * and design approved by the 7–Up Company," and "any advertising * * * material * * * must be approved by the 7–Up Company before its use by the bottler."

Using an extract provided by Seven–Up, Brooks produced the beverage and poured it into bottles. After securing Seven–Up's approval of the design under the franchise agreement, Brooks packaged the bottles in cartons selected and purchased by Brooks from various carton manufacturers, including Olinkraft. Brooks then sold cartons of 7–Up to stores in some 52 Michigan counties, including Meijers Thrifty Acres Store in Holland, Michigan, where the plaintiff picked up the carton and carried it under her arm toward the checkout counter. Plaintiff settled her claims against the bottler, the carton manufacturer and the grocer for $30,000.

Seven–Up denied liability, insisting its approval of the cartons was only of the "graphics" and for the purpose of assuring that its trademark was properly displayed.

* * *

The District Judge submitted the case to the jury on five related theories of product liability—a negligence theory, three strict liability theories and one contract theory * * *.

* * * We do not know which of these theories the jury accepted because it returned a general verdict. On appeal, Seven–Up argues that all of the theories are wrong except negligence. We begin our consideration of this diversity case by acknowledging that the views of an experienced District Judge on questions concerning the law of the state in which he sits are entitled to great respect.

* * *

Michigan appellate courts have not had the occasion to consider these principles in the context of franchising. It appears to be a new question not generally considered in other jurisdictions.[1] The franchise system is a method of selling products and services identified by a particular trade name which may be associated with a patent, a trade secret, a particular product design or management expertise. The franchisee usually purchases some products from the franchisor—in this case, the 7–Up syrup—and makes royalty payments on the basis of units sold, in exchange for the right to offer products for sale under the trademark. The franchise agreement establishes the relationship between the parties and usually regulates the quality of the product, sales territory, the advertising and other details; and it usually requires that certain supplies be purchased from the franchisor.

Seven–Up Company concedes that a franchisor, like a manufacturer or supplier, may be liable to the consumer for its own negligence, without regard to privity, under the doctrine of *MacPherson v. Buick Motor Co.*[, 217 N.Y. 382, 111 N.E. 1050 (1916)]. Seven–Up contends, however, that it does not carry the liabilities of a supplier when it did not supply the product and that other theories of strict tort liability do not apply. Liability may not be laid on the basis of implied warranty, it says, when the franchisor did not manufacture, handle, design or require the use of the particular product. The precise question before us here is whether Michigan's principles of "strict accountability" for breach of implied warranty extend to a franchisor who retains the right of control over the product (the carton) and specifically consents to its distribution

---

1. *But see City of Hartford v. Associated Constr. Co.*, 34 Conn.Supp. 204, 384 A.2d 390 (1978) (trademark licensor held liable under principles of strict liability for property damage caused by defective roofing base product mixed, sold and applied by trademark licensee); *Kasel v. Remington Arms Co., Inc.*, 24 Cal.App.3d 711, 101 Cal. Rptr. 314 (1972) (trademark licensor held liable under principles of strict liability in tort for personal injuries caused by defective shell manufactured by its trademark licensee). See also *Carter v. Bancroft & Sons Co.*, 360 F.Supp. 1103 (E.D.Pa.1973) (trademark licensor a "seller" within meaning of Pennsylvania law).

in the form sold but does not actually manufacture, sell, handle, ship or require the use of the product.

Different questions may arise in other franchising contexts. In some instances, the franchisor may not retain the right of control or may not actually approve the form of the product. The franchisee may sell a product contrary to the instructions or without the knowledge of the franchisor. The consumer may attempt to hold the franchisor liable for the conduct of the franchisee under the agency doctrines of *respondeat superior* or apparent authority. We do not deal with these questions here.

In this case, the Seven–Up Company not only floated its franchisee and the bottles of its carbonated soft drink into the so-called "stream of commerce." The Company also assumed and exercised a degree of control over the "type, style, size and design" of the carton in which its product was to be marketed. The carton was submitted to Seven–Up for inspection. With knowledge of its design, Seven–Up consented to the entry in commerce of the carton from which the bottle fell, causing the injury. The franchisor's sponsorship, management and control of the system for distributing 7–Up, plus its specific consent to the use of the carton, in our view, places the franchisor in the position of a supplier of the product for purposes of tort liability.

We are not saying that the Seven–Up Company is absolutely liable as an insurer of the safety of the carton under the theory of implied warranty, simply by virtue of its status as a franchisor. In the first place, under Michigan's theory of implied warranty of fitness, the carton must be found to be "defective," or as the District Judge more accurately put it, "not reasonably safe." It must be harmful or unsafe because something is wrong with it, and the jury must so find. Moreover, here the franchisor inspected the carton and approved it. Thus, we need not reach the question whether the franchisor would carry the liabilities of a supplier if it had not been made aware of the product and given the opportunity to assess the risks.

When a franchisor consents to the distribution of a defective product bearing its name, the obligation of the franchisor to compensate the injured consumer for breach of implied warranty, we think, arises from several factors in combination: (1) the risk created by approving for distribution an unsafe product likely to cause injury, (2) the franchisor's ability and opportunity to eliminate the unsafe character of the product and prevent the loss, (3) the consumer's lack of knowledge of the danger, and (4) the consumer's reliance on the trade name which gives the intended impression that the franchisor is responsible for and stands behind the product. Liability is based on the franchisor's control and the public's assumption, induced by the franchisor's conduct, that it does in fact control and vouch for the product.

These are factors Michigan courts have relied on in the past in determining who may be held liable for breach of implied warranty of fitness in other products liability situations. We believe Michigan courts would apply these principles in the franchising situation presented by this case, and we therefore conclude that the case was correctly submitted to the jury to assess liability for breach of implied warranty.

[The court then held that three other theories upon which the case was submitted to the jury were erroneous. Because the jury returned with a general verdict for the plaintiff, the court reversed and remanded for a new trial.]

Notes

1. As the opinion in *Kosters* indicates, only a few courts have considered the applicability of product liability or breach of warranty to franchisors. In addition to the cases cited in note 11 of the opinion, *see* Connelly v. Uniroyal, Inc., 75 Ill.2d 393, 27 Ill.Dec. 343, 389 N.E.2d 155 (1979) (holding a trademark licensor subject to product liability); Scheuler v. Aamco Transmissions, Inc., 1 Kan.App.2d 525, 571 P.2d 48 (1977) (holding a franchisor liable for breach of express warranty).

2. Section 14 of the Restatement (Third) of Torts: Products Liability provides:

§ 14. Selling or Distributing as One's Own a Product Manufactured by Another

One engaged in the business of selling or otherwise distributing products who sells or distributes as its own a product manufactured by another is subject to the same liability as though the seller or distributor were the product's manufacturer.

Comment:

d. Liability of trademark licensors. The rule stated in this Section does not, by its terms, apply to the owner of a trademark who licenses a manufacturer to place the licensor's trademark or logo on the manufacturer's product and distribute it as though manufactured by the licensor. In such a case, even if purchasers of the product might assume that the trademark owner was the manufacturer, the licensor does not "sell or distribute as its own a product manufactured by another." Thus, the manufacturer may be liable under §§ 1–4, but the licensor, who does not sell or otherwise distribute products, is not liable under this Section of this Restatement.

Trademark licensors are liable for harm caused by defective products distributed under the licensor's trademark or logo when they participate substantially in the design, manufacture, or distribution of the licensee's products. In these circumstances they are treated as sellers of the products bearing their trademarks.

3. Section 14 of the Restatement imposes liability on what could be called an "apparent manufacturer", i.e., who "sells or distributes another manufacturer's product as its own." But it does not impose liability on a trademark holder who authorizes a product manufacturer to place the trademark on its product. Here the trademark holder is also an "apparent manufacturer" upon whose reputation the purchasing public relies. Why

exempt the trademark holder from liability in the latter circumstances? Does any policy justify the exemption?

4. Kennedy v. Guess, Inc., 806 N.E.2d 776 (Ind. 2004) rejected the Restatement distinction. Plaintiff was injured by an allegedly negligently manufactured umbrella bearing the Guess logo. Guess licensed others to sell the umbrella, but Guess did not play a role as a seller, manufacturer or distributor. The court held that Guess could be liable on a negligence theory. The court believed liability was necessary to give the trademark holder an incentive to oversee "the design and manufacturing of products bearing the mark." Id. at 786. The court believed the Restatement rule creates the opposite incentive. Under the Restatement approach, the risk of liability diminishes as the amount of oversight diminishes. The court imposed several liability under the following scheme:

> Indiana common law should treat trademark licensors as having responsibility for defective products placed in the stream of commerce bearing their marks, but only so much of the liability for those defects as their relative role in the larger scheme of design, advertising, manufacturing, and distribution warrants. Consumers rightly expect that products bearing logos like "Guess" have been subject to some oversight by those who put their name on the product, but those same consumers can well imagine that in modern commerce the products they buy may have actually been manufactured by someone else.
>
> The process of sorting out comparative fault in such settings can well be left to juries.

806 N.E.2d at 786.

5. How does the *Kennedy v. Guess* apportionment scheme work? In adopting its negligence theory, the court cited with approval the negligence rationale set forth in Dudley Sports Co. v. Schmitt, 151 Ind.App. 217, 279 N.E.2d 266 (1972). *Dudley* stated that "a vendor is liable not only for his own negligence but also for any negligence on the part of the actual manufacturer, even though the vendor could not reasonably discover the defect." Id. at 273. Is *Kennedy v. Guess'* apportionment scheme compatible *Dudley's* negligence rationale? In apportioning liability between Guess and the umbrella manufacturer, would the court impute all of the manufacturer's fault to Guess because Guess is vicariously liable for the manufacturer's fault? Would that result in Guess getting 100% of the fault. Or, would the court attribute the manufacturer's fault to both Guess and the manufacturer, resulting in the fault of both parties adding up to more than 100%? Alternatively, would the court attribute none of the manufacturer's fault to Guess for purposes of allocating fault to those two parties? If the court adopted this latter approach, would any fault be attributable to Guess? Assuming Guess contracted with a reputable umbrella manufacturer, how could Guess be found negligent for failing to supervise the design and manufacture of the umbrellas?

3. PUBLICATIONS

WINTER v. G.P. PUTNAM'S SONS
United States Court of Appeals, Ninth Circuit, 1991.
938 F.2d 1033.

Before SNEED, TANG and THOMPSON, CIRCUIT JUDGES.

SNEED, CIRCUIT JUDGE:

Plaintiffs are mushroom enthusiasts who became severely ill from picking and eating mushrooms after relying on information in *The Encyclopedia of Mushrooms,* a book published by the defendant. Plaintiffs sued the publisher and sought damages under various theories. The district court granted summary judgment for the defendant. We affirm.

I.
FACTS AND PROCEEDINGS BELOW

The Encyclopedia of Mushrooms is a reference guide containing information on the habitat, collection, and cooking of mushrooms. It was written by two British authors and originally published by a British publishing company. Defendant Putnam, an American book publisher, purchased copies of the book from the British publisher and distributed the finished product in the United States. Putnam neither wrote nor edited the book.

Plaintiffs purchased the book to help them collect and eat wild mushrooms. In 1988, plaintiffs went mushroom hunting and relied on the descriptions in the book in determining which mushrooms were safe to eat. After cooking and eating their harvest, plaintiffs became critically ill. Both have required liver transplants.

Plaintiffs allege that the book contained erroneous and misleading information concerning the identification of the most deadly species of mushrooms. In their suit against the book publisher, plaintiffs allege liability based on products liability, breach of warranty, negligence, negligent misrepresentation, and false representations. Defendant moved for summary judgment asserting that plaintiffs' claims failed as a matter of law because 1) the information contained in a book is not a product for the purposes of strict liability under products liability law; and 2) defendant is not liable under any remaining theories because a publisher does not have a duty to investigate the accuracy of the text it publishes. The district court granted summary judgment for the defendant. Plaintiffs appeal. We affirm.

II.
DISCUSSION

A book containing Shakespeare's sonnets consists of two parts, the material and print therein, and the ideas and expression thereof. The first may be a product, but the second is not. The latter, were Shakespeare alive, would be governed by copyright laws; the laws of libel, to the extent consistent with the First Amendment; and the laws of misrepresentation, negligent misrepresentation, negligence, and mistake. These doctrines applicable to the second part are aimed at the delicate issues that arise with respect to intangibles such as ideas and expression. Products liability law is geared to the tangible world.

A. *Products Liability*

The language of products liability law reflects its focus on tangible items. In describing the scope of products liability law, the Restatement (Second) of Torts lists examples of items that are covered. All of these are tangible items, such as tires, automobiles, and insecticides. The American Law Institute clearly was concerned with including all physical items but gave no indication that the doctrine should be expanded beyond that area.

The purposes served by products liability law also are focused on the tangible world and do not take into consideration the unique characteristics of ideas and expression. Under products liability law, strict liability is imposed on the theory that "[t]he costs of damaging events due to defectively dangerous products can best be borne by the enterprisers who make and sell these products." *Prosser & Keeton on The Law of Torts*, § 98, at 692–93 (W. Keeton ed. 5th ed. 1984). Strict liability principles have been adopted to further the "cause of accident prevention ... [by] the elimination of the necessity of proving negligence." *Id.* at 693. Additionally, because of the difficulty of establishing fault or negligence in products liability cases, strict liability is the appropriate legal theory to hold manufacturers liable for defective products. *Id.* Thus, the seller is subject to liability "even though he has exercised all possible care in the preparation and sale of the product." Restatement § 402A comment a. It is not a question of fault but simply a determination of how society wishes to assess certain costs that arise from the creation and distribution of products in a complex technological society in which the consumer thereof is unable to protect himself against certain product defects.

Although there is always some appeal to the involuntary spreading of costs of injuries in any area, the costs in any comprehensive cost/benefit analysis would be quite different were strict liability concepts applied to words and ideas. We place a high priority on the unfettered exchange of ideas. We accept the risk that words and ideas have wings we cannot clip and which carry them we know not where. The threat of liability without fault (financial responsibility for our words and ideas in the absence of fault or a special undertaking or responsibility) could seriously inhibit those who wish to share thoughts and theories. As a New York court commented, with the specter of strict liability, "[w]ould any author wish to be exposed ... for writing on a topic which might result in physical injury? e.g. How to cut trees; How to keep bees?" *Walter v. Bauer*, 109 Misc.2d 189, 191, 439 N.Y.S.2d 821, 823 (Sup.Ct.1981) (student injured doing science project described in textbook; court held that the book was not a product for purposes of products liability law), *aff'd in part & rev'd in part on other grounds,* 88 A.D.2d 787, 451 N.Y.S.2d 533 (1982). One might add: "Would anyone undertake to guide by ideas expressed in words either a discrete group, a nation, or humanity in general?"

Strict liability principles even when applied to products are not without their costs. Innovation may be inhibited. We tolerate these losses. They are much less disturbing than the prospect that we might be deprived of the latest ideas and theories.

Plaintiffs suggest, however, that our fears would be groundless were strict liability rules applied only to books that give instruction on how to accomplish a physical activity and that are intended to be used as part of an activity that is inherently dangerous. We find such a limitation illusory. Ideas are often intimately linked with proposed action, and it would be difficult to draw such a bright line. While "How To" books are a special genre, we decline to attempt to draw a line that puts "How To Live A Good Life" books beyond the reach of strict liability while leaving "How To Exercise Properly" books within its reach.

Plaintiffs' argument is stronger when they assert that *The Encyclopedia of Mushrooms* should be analogized to aeronautical charts. Several jurisdictions have held that charts which graphically depict geographic features or instrument approach information for airplanes are "products" for the purpose of products liability law. *See Brocklesby v. United States,* 767 F.2d 1288, 1294–95 (9th Cir.1985) (applying Restatement for the purpose of California law), *cert. denied,* 474 U.S. 1101, 106 S.Ct. 882, 88 L.Ed.2d 918 (1986); *Saloomey v. Jeppesen & Co.,* 707 F.2d 671, 676–77 (2d Cir.1983) (applying Restatement for the purpose of Colorado Law); *Aetna Casualty & Surety Co. v. Jeppesen & Co.,* 642 F.2d 339, 342–43 (9th Cir.1981) (applying Nevada law); *Fluor Corp. v. Jeppesen & Co.,* 170 Cal.App.3d 468, 475, 216 Cal.Rptr. 68, 71 (1985) (applying California law). Plaintiffs suggest that *The Encyclopedia of Mushrooms* can be compared to aeronautical charts because both items contain representations of natural features and both are intended to be used while engaging in a hazardous activity. We are not persuaded.

Aeronautical charts are highly technical tools. They are graphic depictions of technical, mechanical data. The best analogy to an aeronautical chart is a compass. Both may be used to guide an individual who is engaged in an activity requiring certain knowledge of natural features. Computer software that fails to yield the result for which it was designed may be another. In contrast, *The Encyclopedia of Mushrooms* is like a book on how to *use* a compass or an aeronautical chart. The chart itself is like a physical "product" while the "How to Use" book is pure thought and expression.

Given these considerations, we decline to expand products liability law to embrace the ideas and expression in a book. We know of no court that has chosen the path to which the plaintiffs point.[1]

---

1. *See Jones v. J.B. Lippincott Co.,* 694 F.Supp. 1216, 1217–18 (D.Md.1988) (nursing student injured treating self with constipation remedy listed in nursing textbook;

B. The Remaining Theories

As discussed above, plaintiffs must look to the doctrines of copyright, libel, misrepresentation, negligent misrepresentation, negligence, and mistake to form the basis of a claim against the defendant publisher. Unless it is assumed that the publisher is a guarantor of the accuracy of an author's statements of fact, plaintiffs have made no case under any of these theories other than possibly negligence. Guided by the First Amendment and the values embodied therein, we decline to extend liability under this theory to the ideas and expression contained in a book.

In order for negligence to be actionable, there must be a legal duty to exercise due care. 6 B. Witkin, *Summary of California Law,* Torts § 732 (9th ed. 1988). The plaintiffs urge this court that the publisher had a duty to investigate the accuracy of *The Encyclopedia of Mushrooms'* contents. We conclude that the defendants have no duty to investigate the accuracy of the contents of the books it publishes. A publisher may of course assume such a burden, but there is nothing inherent in the role of publisher or the surrounding legal doctrines to suggest that such a duty should be imposed on publishers. Indeed the cases uniformly refuse to impose such a duty.[2] Were we tempted to

---

court held that Restatement § 402A does not extend to dissemination of an idea of knowledge); *Herceg v. Hustler Magazine, Inc.,* 565 F.Supp. 802, 803–04 (S.D.Tex. 1983) (person died after imitating "autoerotic asphyxiation" described in magazine article; court held that contents of magazines are not within meaning of Restatement § 402A); *Walter v. Bauer,* 109 Misc.2d 189, 190–91, 439 N.Y.S.2d 821, 822–23 (Sup.Ct.1981) (student injured doing science project described in textbook; court held that the book was not a defective product for purposes of products liability law because the intended use of a book is reading and the plaintiff was not injured by reading), *aff'd in part & rev'd in part on other grounds,* 88 A.D.2d 787, 451 N.Y.S.2d 533 (1982); *Smith v. Linn,* 386 Pa.Super. 392, 398, 563 A.2d 123, 126 (1989) (reader of *Last Chance Diet* book died from diet complications; court held that book is not a product under Restatement § 402A), *aff'd,* 587 A.2d 309 (1991); *cf. Cardozo v. True,* 342 So.2d 1053, 1056–57 (Fla.Dist.Ct.App.) (transmission of words is not the same as selling items with physical properties so that where a bookseller merely passes on a book without inspection, the thoughts and ideas within the book do not constitute a "good" for the purposes of a breach of implied warranty claim under the UCC), *cert. denied,* 353 So.2d 674 (1977).

2. *See First Equity Corp. v. Standard & Poor's Corp.,* 869 F.2d 175, 179–80 (2d Cir. 1989) (investors who relied on inaccurate financial publications to their detriment may not recover their losses); *Jones v. J.B. Lippincott Co.,* 694 F.Supp. 1216, 1216–17 (D.Md.1988) (publisher not liable to nursing student injured in treating self with remedy described in nursing textbook); *Lewin v. McCreight,* 655 F.Supp. 282, 283–84 (E.D.Mich.1987) (publisher not liable to plaintiffs injured in explosion while mixing a mordant according to a book on metalsmithing); *Alm v. Van Nostrand Reinhold Co.,* 134 Ill.App.3d 716, 721, 89 Ill.Dec. 520, 524, 480 N.E.2d 1263, 1267 (1985) (publisher not liable to plaintiff injured following instructions in book on how to make tools); *Roman v. City of New York,* 110 Misc.2d 799, 802, 442 N.Y.S.2d 945, 948 (Sup.Ct. 1981) (Planned Parenthood not liable for misstatement in contraceptive pamphlet); *Gutter v. Dow Jones, Inc.,* 22 Ohio St.3d 286, 291, 490 N.E.2d 898, 902 (1986) (Wall Street Journal not liable for inaccurate description of certain corporate bonds); *Smith v. Linn,* 386 Pa.Super. 392, 396, 563 A.2d 123, 126 (1989) (publisher of diet book not liable for death caused by complications arising from the diet), *aff'd,* 587 A.2d 309 (1991); *see also Herceg v. Hustler Magazine, Inc.,* 565 F.Supp. 802, 803 (S.D.Tex.1983) (finding magazine publisher not liable to family of youth who died emulating "autoerotic asphyxiation" as described in arti-

create this duty, the gentle tug of the First Amendment and the values embodied therein would remind us of the social costs.[3]

Finally, plaintiffs ask us to find that a publisher should be required to give a warning 1) that the information in the book is not complete and that the consumer may not fully rely on it or 2) that this publisher has not investigated the text and cannot guarantee its accuracy. With respect to the first, a publisher would not know what warnings, if any, were required without engaging in a detailed analysis of the factual contents of the book. This would force the publisher to do exactly what we have said he has no duty to do—that is, independently investigate the accuracy of the text. We will not introduce a duty we have just rejected by renaming it a "mere" warning label. With respect to the second, such a warning is unnecessary given that *no* publisher has a duty as a guarantor.

For the reasons outlined above, the decision of the district court is AFFIRMED.

Notes

1. Suppose that a grocer sold "elephant ears" to its customers along with extensive, but defective, instructions for their preparation. Would the transaction be governed by product liability?

2. Do the policies underlying the adoption of product liability help determine whether to apply the doctrine in cases of this type?

3. In Braun v. Soldier of Fortune Magazine, Inc., 968 F.2d 1110 (11th Cir.1992) the children of a murder victim brought a wrongful death action against a magazine, alleging that defendant negligently published the following advertisement through which plaintiffs' father's business partner hired an assassin to kill him:

> GUN FOR HIRE: 37 year old professional mercenary desires jobs. Vietnam Veteran. Discrete [sic] and very private. Body guard, courier, and other special skills. All jobs considered. Phone (615) 436–9785 (days) or (615) 436–4335 (nights), or write: Rt. 2, Box 682 Village Loop Road, Gatlinburg, TN 37738.

The court affirmed a jury verdict for plaintiffs on the basis that the jury could find that the "ad 'on its face' would convey to a reasonable publisher that the ad created a 'clearly identifiable unreasonable risk' of harm to the

cle but granting leave to amend incitement claim); cf. *Libertelli v. Hoffman–La Roche,* 7 Media L.Rptr. (BNA) 1734, 1736 (S.D.N.Y. 1981) (publisher of Physician's Desk Reference not liable for failure to include drug warning because the work was like a published advertisement of products rather than a reference work); *Yuhas v. Mudge,* 129 N.J.Super. 207, 209–10, 322 A.2d 824, 825 (1974) (magazine publisher not liable for injury caused by advertised product); *Beasock v. Dioguardi Enters., Inc.,* 130 Misc.2d 25, 30–31, 494 N.Y.S.2d 974, 979 (Sup.Ct.1985) (truck association not liable for injuries caused by products manufactured in adherence to industry standards adopted, approved and published by association).

3. A stronger argument might be made by a plaintiff alleging libel or fraudulent, intentional, or malicious misrepresentation, but such is not contended in this case. *Gutter v. Dow Jones, Inc.,* 490 N.E.2d at 902 n. 4.

public." *Id.* at 1116. The court emphasized that the magazine had no duty to investigate the ad. *Compare*, Eimann v. Soldier of Fortune Magazine, Inc., 880 F.2d 830 (5th Cir.1989) (no liability if the indication of illegal intent is ambiguous).

4. A few courts have addressed the issue of liability on the part of product certifiers, such as Good Housekeeping and Underwriters Laboratories. The cases have generally held that such a defendant who *negligently* makes representation about a product's quality can be held liable, but no court has applied product liability or an implied warranty of merchantability to a product certifier. *See* Hempstead v. General Fire Extinguisher Corp., 269 F.Supp. 109 (D.Del.1967); Hanberry v. Hearst Corp., 276 Cal.App.2d 680, 81 Cal.Rptr. 519 (1969).

5. As the *Winter* opinion notes, a few courts have applied products liability or an implied warranty of merchantability to air and sea navigational charts. *See* Fluor Corp. v. Jeppesen & Co., 170 Cal.App.3d 468, 216 Cal.Rptr. 68 (1985) (products liability); Saloomey v. Jeppesen & Co., 707 F.2d 671 (2d Cir.1983) (products liability); Times Mirror Co. v. Sisk, 122 Ariz. 174, 593 P.2d 924 (App.1978) (jury question on product liability, innocent misrepresentation under section 402B, and implied warranty). *Cf.* De Bardeleben Marine Corp. v. United States, 451 F.2d 140 (5th Cir.1971) (negligent misrepresentation; no liability for government). In In re Korean Air Lines Disaster of Sept. 1, 1983, 597 F.Supp. 619 (D.D.C.1984), the court held that a navigational chart was not defective solely for failing to warn aircraft that they might be shot if they entered Soviet airspace. *See*, Schultz, Application of Strict Product Liability to Aeronautical Chart Publishers, 64 J. Air L. & Com. 431 (1999).

Should it matter whether the "defect" in a navigational chart is a result of faulty surveying or faulty printing?

6. *See generally*, Ausness, The Application of Product Liability Principles to Publishers of Violent or Sexually Explicit Material, 52 Fla.L.Rev. 603 (2000); Day, Publications That Incite, Solicit, or Instruct: Publisher Responsibility or Caveat Emptor? 36 Santa Clara L.Rev. 73 (1995); Noah, Authors, Publishers, and Products Liability: Remedies for Defective Information in Books, 77 Or.L.Rev. 1195 (1998); Wolfson, Express Warranties and Published Information Content under Article 2b: Does the Shoe Fit?, 16 J. Marshall J. Computer & Info. L. 337 (1997); Myers, Note, Read at Your Own Risk: Publisher Liability for Defective How-to-Books. (Case Note), 45 Ark.L.Rev. 699 (1992).

4. USED PRODUCTS

TILLMAN v. VANCE EQUIPMENT CO.
Supreme Court of Oregon, 1979.
286 Or. 747, 596 P.2d 1299.

DENECKE, CHIEF JUSTICE.

Plaintiff brought this action based upon the theory of strict liability in tort to recover for personal injuries caused by a 24–year–old crane sold by defendant, a used equipment dealer, to plaintiff's employer, Durametal. The court tried the case without a jury and found for the defendant. The plaintiff appeals and we affirm.

Durametal asked the defendant to locate a crane for purchase by Durametal. Defendant found one that looked suitable; Durametal inspected and approved it. The defendant purchased the crane and immediately resold it to Durametal. Defendant prepared documents making the sale "as is."

Durametal assigned plaintiff to operate the crane, including greasing it. Plaintiff believed the greasing of the gears could not be done properly without removing the gear cover and applying the grease while the gears were moving. While he was so greasing the gears, plaintiff's hand was drawn into them and he was injured.

Plaintiff alleged the defendant seller was liable because the crane was defectively designed in that it could not be properly greased without removing the protective gear covering and for failing to provide warnings of the danger. The trial court found for the defendant because the crane was a used piece of equipment and sold "as is."

The parties disagree about the effect of the "as is" disclaimer in the documents of sale. The issues raised include whether that disclaimer has any effect in an action of strict liability in tort, and whether, if so, it is effective to disclaim liability for a design defect as distinguished from a defect in the condition of the individual product. We do not answer these questions because we conclude that the trial court was correct in holding that a seller of used goods is not strictly liable in tort for a defect in a used crane when that defect was created by the manufacturer.

* * *

In order to determine whether the defendant seller may be held liable we are required to re-examine why we arrived at the decision that a seller "who is free from fault in the usual legal sense" should be held strictly liable for a defective product. *Wights v. Staff Jennings,* 241 Or. 301, 306, 405 P.2d 624, 626 (1965).

"* * * Usually liability has been predicated on a breach of an implied warranty without explaining why the warranty was judicially implied. When the action was brought by the buyer against his immediate seller, it seemed enough that the plaintiff and defendant were parties to a contract, the warranty being born in some mysterious way out of the contractual relationship even in the absence of any promise express or implied in fact made by the seller. * * *." *Wights v. Staff Jennings, supra,* at 306, 405 P.2d at 626–27.

Because of the impediments accompanying a contractual remedy, including the requirement of privity, we evolved the tort of strict liability. *Redfield v. Mead, Johnson & Co.,* 266 Or. 273, 285, 512 P.2d 776 (1973) (specially concurring). Strict liability could be imposed upon a party with whom the plaintiff was not in privity. For this reason the manufacturer who created the defect could be sued directly. The injured party could usually obtain personal jurisdiction over the manufacturer by the use of the long-arm statutes. Because of the circumstances, there was no longer any urgent necessity to continue a cause of action against the seller who had not created the defect.

Nevertheless, courts did impose strict liability on the nonmanufacturer sellers of new goods * * *.

* * *

As Mr. Justice Traynor said in *Vandermark v. Ford Motor Company*, 61 Cal.2d 256, 37 Cal.Rptr. 896, 899, 391 P.2d 168, 171 (1964):

"Retailers like manufacturers are engaged in the business of distributing goods to the public. They are an integral part of the overall producing and marketing enterprise that should bear the cost of injuries resulting from defective products. (See *Greenman v. Yuba Power Products, Inc.*, 59 Cal.2d 57, 63, 27 Cal.Rptr. 697, 377 P.2d 897). In some cases the retailer may be the only member of that enterprise reasonably available to the injured plaintiff. In other cases the retailer himself may play a substantial part in insuring that the product is safe or may be in a position to exert pressure on the manufacturer to that end; the retailer's strict liability thus serves as an added incentive to safety. * * *."

Mr. Justice Schaefer stated in *Dunham v. Vaughan & Bushnell Mfg. Co.*, 42 Ill.2d 339, 247 N.E.2d 401, 404 (1969): "The strict liability of a retailer arises from his integral role in the overall producing and marketing enterprise and affords an additional incentive to safety."

Moreover, if a jurisdiction has adopted the principle of strict liability on the basis of enterprise liability, the liability of the seller of either a new or used product would logically follow.

* * *

This court has never been willing to rely on enterprise liability alone as a justification for strict liability for defective products. See *Markle v. Mulholland's, Inc., supra,* 265 Or. at 265, 509 P.2d 529. Instead, we have identified three justifications for the doctrine:

" * * * [C]ompensation (ability to spread the risk), satisfaction of the reasonable expectations of the purchaser or user (implied representational aspect), and over-all risk reduction (the impetus to manufacture a better product) * * *." *Fulbright v. Klamath Gas Co.*, 271 Or. 449, 460, 533 P.2d 316, 321 (1975).

While dealers in used goods are, as a class, capable like other businesses of providing for the compensation of injured parties and the allocation of the cost of injuries caused by the products they sell, we are not convinced that the other two considerations identified in *Fulbright* weigh sufficiently in this class of cases to justify imposing strict liability on sellers of used goods generally.

Our opinions have discussed, on other occasions, what we called in *Fulbright* the "implied representational aspect" of the justification for strict products liability. In *Heaton v. Ford Motor Co.*, 248 Or. 467, 435 P.2d 806 (1967), both the majority and the dissent indicated that at least in some cases it was for the jury to decide what degree of safety the average consumer of a product expects. However, in *Markle v. Mulholland's, Inc., supra,* 265 Or. 259, 509 P.2d 529, a majority of the court agreed that the question was not solely a factual one.

* * *

We consider, then, whether the trier of fact may infer any representation as to safety from the sale of a used product.

We conclude that holding every dealer in used goods responsible regardless of fault for injuries caused by defects in his goods would not only affect the prices of used goods; it would work a significant change in the very nature of used goods markets. Those markets, generally speaking, operate on the apparent understanding that the seller, even though he is in the business of selling such goods, makes no particular representation about their quality simply by offering them for sale. If a buyer wants some assurance of quality, he typically either bargains for it in the specific transaction or seeks out a dealer who routinely offers it (by, for example, providing a guarantee, limiting his stock of goods to those of a particular quality, advertising that his used goods are specially selected, or in some other fashion). The flexibility of this kind of market appears to serve legitimate interests of buyers as well as sellers.

We are of the opinion that the sale of a used product, without more, may not be found to generate the kind of expectations of safety that the courts have held are justifiably created by the introduction of a new product into the stream of commerce.

As to the risk-reduction aspect of strict products liability, the position of the used-goods dealer is normally entirely outside the original chain of distribution of the product. As a consequence, we conclude, any risk reduction which would be accomplished by imposing strict liability on the dealer in used goods would not be significant enough to justify our taking that step. The dealer in used goods generally has no direct relationship with either manufacturers or distributors. Thus, there is no ready channel of communication by which the dealer and the manufacturer can exchange information about possible dangerous defects in particular product lines or about actual and potential liability claims.

In theory, a dealer in used goods who is held liable for injuries caused by a design defect or manufacturing flaw could obtain indemnity from the manufacturer. This possibility supports the argument that permitting strict liability claims against dealers in used goods will add to the financial incentive for manufacturers to design and build safe products. We believe, however, that the influence of this possibility as a practical factor in risk prevention is considerably diluted where used goods are involved due to such problems as statutes of limitation and the increasing difficulty as time passes of locating a still existing and solvent manufacturer.

Both of these considerations, of course, are also obstacles to injured parties attempting to recover directly from the manufacturer. However, although the provision of an adequate remedy for persons injured by defective products has been the major impetus to the development of strict product liability, it cannot provide the sole justification for imposing liability without fault on a particular class of defendants.

For the reasons we have discussed, we have concluded that the relevant policy considerations do not justify imposing strict liability for defective products on dealers in used goods, at least in the absence of some representation of quality beyond the sale itself or of a special position vis-a-vis the original manufacturer or others in the chain of original distribution. Accord: *Rix v. Reeves,* 23 Ariz.App. 243, 532 P.2d 185 (1975).

We have suggested, although we have never had occasion to rule on the question, that those who are in the business of leasing products to others may be strictly liable for injuries caused by defective products on the same basis as sellers of new products. *Fulbright v. Klamath Gas Co., supra,* 271 Or. at 455–458, 459, 533 P.2d 316. It has been urged that recognizing such a liability on the part of lessors while refusing to hold sellers of used goods liable would be logically inconsistent, because most leased goods are used when they reach the lessee. *Hovenden v. Tenbush, supra,* 529 S.W.2d at 310. We see no such inconsistency when the focus of analysis is not on the status of the product but on that of the potential defendant. The lessor chooses the products which he offers in a significantly different way than does the typical dealer in used goods; the fact that he offers them repeatedly to different users as products he has selected may constitute a representation as to their quality; and it may well be that he has purchased them, either new or used, from a dealer who is directly related to the original distribution chain. Our rationale in the present case leaves the question of a lessor's strict liability an open one in this jurisdiction.

* * *

Affirmed.

Lent, J., did not participate in the decision in this matter.

Notes

1. Most courts have held that products liability is not applicable to the sale of used products. *See* Bruce v. Martin–Marietta Corp., 544 F.2d 442 (10th Cir.1976); Sell v. Bertsch & Co., 577 F.Supp. 1393 (D.Kan.1984); Rix v. Reeves, 23 Ariz.App. 243, 532 P.2d 185 (1975); LaRosa v. Superior Court, Santa Clara County, 122 Cal.App.3d 741, 176 Cal.Rptr. 224 (1981); Tauber–Arons Auctioneers Co. v. Superior Court, 101 Cal.App.3d 268, 161 Cal.Rptr. 789 (1980); Peterson v. Lou Bachrodt Chevrolet Co., 61 Ill.2d 17, 329 N.E.2d 785 (1975); Pridgett v. Jackson Iron & Metal Co., 253 So.2d 837, 841, 844 (Miss.1971); Crandell v. Larkin and Jones Appliance Co., Inc., 334 N.W.2d 31 (S.D.1983); ; King v. Damiron Corp., 113 F.3d 93 (7th Cir. 1997) (Applying

Connecticut law). *But see* Stanton v. Carlson Sales, Inc. 45 Conn.Supp. 531, 728 A.2d 534 (1998). (The opinion has a nice review of the law in a number of jurisdictions.); Frey v. Harley Davidson Motor Co., Inc., 734 A.2d 1 (Pa.Super. 1999).

A fairly large minority of courts, however, have applied product liability to a sale of used products. *See,* e.g., Jordan v. Sunnyslope Appliance Propane & Plumbing Supplies Co., 135 Ariz. 309, 660 P.2d 1236 (App.1983) imposing product liability on the seller of a used propane tank. The court reasoned that buyers of used products did expect them to be safe, and that used product sellers could insure against losses and could shift losses and distribute costs. Furthermore, liability would provide the seller with an incentive to increase maintenance and inspection of their products. In addition, sellers are protected against excessive liability because Arizona only imposes liability if products are both defective and "unreasonably dangerous." This standard "allows inquiry into matters such as age and condition of a used product, specific representations made, and sophistication of the buyer". Id at 1241. *See also,* Stanton v. Carlson Sales, Inc., 45 Conn.Supp. 531, 728 A.2d 534 (1998); Turner v. International Harvester Co., 133 N.J.Super. 277, 336 A.2d 62 (Law Div. 1975); Frey v. Harley Davidson Motor Co., Inc., 1999 Pa.Super 130, 734 A.2d 1 (1999); Hovenden v. Tenbush, 529 S.W.2d 302 (Tex.App. 1975); Galindo v. Precision American Corp., 754 F.2d 1212 (5th Cir.1985); Nelson v. Nelson Hardware, Inc., 160 Wis.2d 689, 467 N.W.2d 518 (1991).

2. Some minority-rule courts have suggested that a seller of used products should be permitted to disclaim products liability in some situations, even if a seller of new products cannot. In Turner v. International Harvester Co., 133 N.J.Super. 277, 336 A.2d 62 (1975), the court declined to hold that a sale of a used product is automatically beyond the scope of products liability. It then addressed the issue of whether the seller could disclaim liability:

> Should a simple "as is" disclaimer effectively insulate the dealer from a claim of strict liability in tort following an accident resulting from a *safety* defect present in the vehicle when it was in the control of the dealer? When selling to the ordinary consumer, the answer must be No. Bargaining power and ability to protect one's interests are generally disproportionate as between the buyer of used goods and one in the business of selling them. While freedom to contract need not be impaired if a buyer wishes to contract away his right to protection, an unequivocal waiver of safety defects must be shown (see the discussion with respect to waiver of tort claims under section III of this opinion, infra). Otherwise, when the additional indirect costs will be borne by the public through insurance costs, a decent regard for the public safety requires the thumb of the State to be on the buyer's side of the scale. Cf. Henningsen v. Bloomfield Motors, Inc., 32 N.J. 358, 161 A.2d 69 (1960).
>
> The third question also raises a jury issue. It may be found that the buyer in this case was (or represented himself to be) knowledgeable about this product because of his background or experience. This will not necessarily result from the transaction being denominated "commercial" [citation]. Also, the effect upon plaintiff and her family, and

upon injured persons in general, is no less because the injury occurred in a nonconsumer atmosphere. In fact, the pleadings and affidavits submitted here suggest that plaintiff's decedent may have been personally familiar with the particular truck he bought. The goods should be viewed, not in the abstract, but as they affect a particular seller, purchaser or user, and the circumstances of the sale.

* * *

Looking at the used automobile situation, one can readily envision an antique car buff or "hot rod" enthusiast purchasing a car which is defective in many respects and where the relationship between the buyer and seller is such that both reasonably expect that all aspects of the automobile will be separately appraised and all defects corrected by the purchaser. In this connection see Greenman v. Yuba Power Products, Inc., 59 Cal.2d 57, 62, 27 Cal.Rptr. 697, 700, 377 P.2d 897, 900 (1963), in which Justice Traynor stated that a manufacturer "is strictly liable in tort when an article he places on the market, *knowing* that it is to be used without inspection for defects, proves to have a defect that causes injury to a human being."

Even with respect to the sale of a truck, the actual situation of the parties to the contract may present a question. A used truck purchased by a large trucking company known by both buyer and seller to have extensive repair facilities might be expected to undergo great scrutiny only by the buyer, while a similar truck purchased by a merchant to make his retail deliveries might not reasonably be expected to be so examined unless special circumstances exist. Thus, in some circumstances the relationship of the parties and apparent sophistication of the purchaser might indicate the defect did not present an unreasonable danger to the particular purchaser as user of the product. In others the purchaser's conduct in not discovering or correcting a defect which a reasonable person of his background and experience should have corrected might warrant a finding that the defect was not unreasonably dangerous. * * *

3. Note also from the language of *Turner,* a decision about defectiveness may be different when a used product is sold. Certainly consumer expectations differ concerning a used product. Does the fact that a product is used affect a risk-utility balance?

4. Would it make any difference if a seller of a used product refurbished or reconditioned it? Some courts impose liability on remanufacturers. *See* Anderson v. Olmsted Utility Equipment, Inc., 60 Ohio St.3d 124, 573 N.E.2d 626 (1991) (seller who remanufactured and sold cherry picker is strictly liable for harm caused by a manufacturing defect in a component part); Stillie v. AM Intern., Inc., 850 F.Supp. 960, 962 (D.Kan.1994) ("[R]emanufacturers and sellers in the chain of distribution after remanufacture are subject to strict liability.").

5. Distinguish an action against a seller of a used product and an action against the original manufacturer or retailer by a subsequent purchaser who bought the product used from an intermediate seller. *See* Gibbs

v. General Motors Corp., 450 S.W.2d 827 (Tex.1970). What issues are likely to arise in such a case?

6. The Restatement (Third) of Torts: Products Liability addresses liability for the sale of used products:

§ 8. Liability of Commercial Seller or Distributor of Defective Used Products

One engaged in the business of selling or otherwise distributing used products who sells or distributes a defective used product is subject to liability for harm to persons or property caused by the defect if the defect:

(a) arises from the seller's failure to exercise reasonable care; or

(b) is a manufacturing defect under § 2(a) or a defect that may be inferred under § 3 and the seller's marketing of the product would cause a reasonable person in the position of the buyer to expect the used product to present no greater risk of defect than if the product were new; or

(c) is a defect under § 2 or § 3 in a used product remanufactured by the seller or a predecessor in the commercial chain of distribution of the used product; or

(d) arises from a used product's noncompliance under § 4 with a product safety statute or regulation applicable to the used product.

A used product is a product that, prior to the time of sale or other distribution referred to in this Section, is commercially sold or otherwise distributed to a buyer not in the commercial chain of distribution and used for some period of time.

Comment:

a. History. American courts have struggled with the question of whether to hold commercial sellers of used products to the same legal standards of responsibility for defects as commercial sellers of new products. Judicial responses have varied. Some courts hold used-product sellers strictly liable for harm caused by product defects existing at the time of sale. A greater number of courts hold commercial sellers of used products to lesser standards of responsibility. Liability rules applicable to used-product sellers are less stringent than those applicable to new-product sellers due to the wide variations in the type and condition of used products. For example, even in the minority of jurisdictions that generally hold commercial used-product sellers strictly liable for defects, disclaimers of liability may more readily be given effect in connection with sales of used products than in connection with sales of new products. Even in jurisdictions that generally apply more relaxed standards of responsibility for used products, factors that tend to raise a buyer's expectations regarding product quality, such as a seller's advertising a used product as "re-built" or "re-conditioned," correspondingly tend to raise the level of the sellers' responsibilities for product defects. The liability rules in this Section seek to accommodate these variations.

b. Rationale. Subsection (a) imposes liability on a commercial used-product seller for harm caused by a used product resulting from the seller's failure to exercise reasonable care. * * *

Subsections (b) and (c) subject commercial sellers of used products to liability without fault only under special circumstances. Consumers of most used products sold in obviously used condition typically do not, and should not, expect those products to perform as safely, with respect to the possibility of mechanical defects, as when those products were new. * * *

When a used product is sold commercially under circumstances in which a reasonable buyer would expect the risk of defect to be substantially the same as with a new product, a different judicial response is justified. Thus, under the circumstances described in Subsection (b), many of the same rationales that support strict liability for harm caused by mechanical defects in new products support strict liability for mechanical defects in like-new used products. This section does not adopt the "consumer expectations test" as the governing standard for defining product defect. * * * The question addressed in this Section is under what circumstances a plaintiff may hold the seller of a used product to the liability standard applicable to sellers of new products. When dealing with this more limited question, Subsection (b) takes the position that, when the seller's marketing of the product would lead a reasonable consumer to expect the product to present no greater risk of defect than if the product were new, the law may treat the used-product sale as the functional equivalent of the sale of a new product.

* * *

k. Effects of disclaimers on used-product seller's liability. A used-product seller's disclaimer of liability for harm caused by product defects may be given conclusive legal effect under applicable state law, depending on the nature of the harm caused by the defects. See, e.g., § 21, Comment f, dealing with recovery of economic loss. Whether a used-product seller's disclaimer of liability for harm to persons is legally conclusive is more problematic, but many courts give such disclaimers conclusive effect. In any event, disclaimer language is relevant in an inquiry into reasonable expectations under Subsection (b). That is, a disclaimer may diminish reasonable expectations as to the safety of a used product. This is especially likely when disclaimer language either reminds the buyer that the product is used or warns the buyer of the increased risk of defect.

7. Section 8 (c) of the Restatement imposes liability on a remanufacturers who sell a product for design, warning, and manufacturing defects in the product. Plaintiffs can make a strong case for holding remanufacturers liable for failing to discover and eliminate manufacturing flaws. After all, an import part of the remanufacturing process is to discover and replace bad parts. But is it good policy to require remanufacturers to redesign a used machine that may be decades old? For a discussion of this issue, *see,* David G. Owen, Products Liability Law § 16.4 (2005).

8. Comment 3 to section 2–314 of the Commercial Code states that an implied warranty of merchantability attaches to a sale of used goods, and most courts have held that the Article 2 warranties are applicable to a sale of used goods. *See, e.g.,* Roupp v. Acor, 253 Pa.Super. 46, 384 A.2d 968 (1978). *But see* Valley Datsun v. Martinez, 578 S.W.2d 485 (Tex.App. 1979).

5. REAL ESTATE

KRIEGLER v. EICHLER HOMES, INC.
Court of Appeals of California, First District, 1969.
269 Cal.App.2d 224, 74 Cal.Rptr. 749.

TAYLOR, JUSTICE.

Respondent Kriegler filed this action for physical damage sustained as the result of the failure of a radiant heating system in a home constructed by appellants, Eichler Homes, Inc. and Joseph L. Eichler (hereafter Eichler), who cross-complained against the supplier, respondent, General Motors Corporation (hereafter General Motors) and the heating contractors, respondents, Anderson and Rother, individually and doing business as Arro Company (hereafter collectively referred to as Arro). Eichler appeals from the judgment in favor of Kriegler on the complaint and in favor of General Motors and Arro on the cross-complaint.

The questions presented are: 1) whether Eichler was liable to Kriegler on the theory of strict liability * * *.

The basic facts are not in dispute. In April 1957 Kriegler purchased a home in Palo Alto that had been constructed by Eichler in the last quarter of 1951 and sold to Kriegler's predecessors, the Resings, in January 1952. Eichler employed Arro as the heating contractor. Because of a copper shortage caused by the Korean war, Arro obtained terne coated steel tubing from General Motors. In the fall of 1951, Arro installed this steel tubing in the Kriegler home and guaranteed the radiant heating system in writing. Arro installed steel tubing radiant heating systems in at least 4,000 homes for Eichler.

* * *

In November 1959, as a result of the corrosion of the steel tubing, the radiant heating system of the Kriegler home failed. The emergency and final repairs required removal and storage of furniture, as well as the temporary acquisition by Kriegler and his family of other shelter.

* * *

Eichler concedes that the doctrine of strict liability in tort applies to physical harm to property (Gherna v. Ford Motor Co., 246 Cal.App.2d 639, 649, 55 Cal.Rptr. 94) but argues that the doctrine cannot be applied to homes or builders. We do not agree. As set forth in Greenman v. Yuba Power Products, Inc., 59 Cal.2d 57, 27 Cal.Rptr. 697, 377 P.2d 897, 13 A.L.R.3d 1049, and Vandermark v. Ford Motor Co., 61 Cal.2d 256, 37

Cal.Rptr. 896, 391 P.2d 168, the strict liability doctrine applies when the plaintiff proves that he was injured while using the instrumentality in a way it was intended to be used as a result of a defect in design and manufacture of which plaintiff was not aware and which made the instrumentality unsafe for its intended use. So far, it has been applied in this state only to manufacturers, retailers and suppliers of personal property and rejected as to sales of real estate (Conolley v. Bull, 258 A.C.A. 254, 265, 65 Cal.Rptr. 689). We recently pointed out in Barth v. B.F. Goodrich Tire Co., 265 A.C.A. 253 at 278, 71 Cal.Rptr. 306, that the reasoning behind the doctrine applies to any case of injury resulting from the risk-creating conduct of a seller in any stage of the production and distribution of goods.

We think, in terms of today's society, there are no meaningful distinctions between Eichler's mass production and sale of homes and the mass production and sale of automobiles and that the pertinent overriding policy considerations are the same. Law, as an instrument of justice, has infinite capacity for growth to meet changing needs and mores. Nowhere is this better illustrated than in the recent developments in the field of products liability. The law should be based on current concepts of what is right and just and the judiciary should be alert to the never-ending need for keeping legal principles abreast of the times. Ancient distinctions that make no sense in today's society and that tend to discredit the law should be readily rejected as they were step by step in Greenman and Vandermark.

We find support in our view in the comments of our most eminent authority in the law of torts (see Prosser, Strict Liability to the Consumer in California, 18 Hastings L.J., 9, 20), and the exceptionally able and well-thought out opinion of the Supreme Court of New Jersey, in a case almost on all fours with the instant one (Schipper v. Levitt & Sons, Inc. (1965) 44 N.J. 70, 207 A.2d 314). In Schipper, the purchaser of a mass-produced home sued the builder-vendor for injuries sustained by the child of a lessee. The child was injured by excessively hot water drawn from a faucet in a hot water system that had been installed without a mixing valve, a defect as latent as the incorrect positioning of the pipes in the instant case. In reversing a judgment of nonsuit, the Supreme Court held that the builder-vendor was liable to the purchaser on the basis of strict liability. In language equally applicable here, the court said: "When a vendee buys a development house from an advertised model, as in a Levitt or in a comparable project, he clearly relies on the skill of the developer and on its implied representation that the house will be erected in reasonably workmanlike manner and will be reasonably fit for habitation. He has no architect or other professional adviser of his own, he has no real competency to inspect on his own, his actual examination is, in the nature of things, largely superficial, and his opportunity for obtaining meaningful protective changes in the conveyancing documents prepared by the builder vendor is negligible. If there is improper construction such as a defective heating system or a defective ceiling, stairway and the like, the well-being of the vendee and others is seriously endangered and serious injury is foreseeable. The public interest dictates that if such injury does result from the defective construction, its cost should be borne by the responsible developer who created the danger and who is in the better economic position to bear the loss rather than by the injured party who justifiably relied on the developer's skill and implied representation." (Pp. 325–326.)

"Buyers of mass produced development homes are not on an equal footing with the builder vendors and are no more able to protect themselves in the deed than are automobile purchasers in a position to protect themselves in the bill of sale." (P. 326.) The court then pointed out that the imposition of strict liability principles on builders and developers would not make them insurers of the safety of all who thereafter came on the premises. In determining whether the house was defective, the test would be one of reasonableness rather than perfection.

As it cannot be disputed that Kriegler here relied on the skill of Eichler in producing a home with a heating system that was reasonably fit for its intended purpose, the trial court properly concluded that Eichler was liable to Kriegler on the basis of strict liability, and the judgment in favor of Kriegler must be affirmed on that ground alone.

* * *

Affirmed.

SHOEMAKER, P.J., and AGEE, J., concur.

Hearing denied; MOSK, J., did not participate.

Notes

1. It is quite clear that the Article 2 warranties do not apply to real estate. *See, e.g.,* G–W–L, Inc. v. Robichaux, 643 S.W.2d 392 (Tex.1982). Section 2–102 states that Article 2 applies to transactions in "goods." Section 2–105 defines "goods" as "all things * * * which are *movable* at the time of identification * * *"(emphasis added). Nevertheless, several courts have adopted common law warranties to apply to real estate sales. *See, e.g.,* Humber v. Morton, 426 S.W.2d 554 (Tex.1968).

2. Section 19 of the Restatement treats real property as a product if the "context of [its] distribution and use is sufficiently analogous to the distribution and use of tangible personal property that it is appropriate to apply the rules stated in this Restatement." Comment e describes those contexts:

> e. *Real property.* Traditionally, courts have been reluctant to impose products liability on sellers of improved real property in that such property does not constitute goods or personalty. A housing contractor, building and selling one house at a time, does not fit the pattern of a mass producer of manufactured products, nor is such a builder perceived to be more capable than are purchasers of controlling or insuring against risks presented by weather conditions or earth movements. More recently, courts have treated sellers of improved real property as

product sellers in a number of contexts. When a building contractor sells a building that contains a variety of appliances or other manufactured equipment, the builder, together with the equipment manufacturer and other distributors, are held as product sellers with respect to such equipment notwithstanding the fact that the built-in equipment may have become, for other legal purposes, attachments to and thus part of the underlying real property. Moreover, the builder may be treated as a product seller even with respect to the building itself when the building has been prefabricated—and thus manufactured—and later assembled on-or off-site. Finally, courts impose strict liability for defects in construction when dwellings are built, even if on-site, on a major scale, as in a large housing project.

3. Most courts do not apply products liability to real property. *See,* Martens v. MCL Construction Corp., 347 Ill.App.3d 303, 320, 807 N.E.2d 480, 493 (2004) ("buildings and indivisible component parts of the building structure itself, such as bricks, supporting beams and railings, are not deemed products for the purpose of strict liability in tort."). But when a builder sells a house containing defective appliances or equipment, the builder is subject to products liability along with the manufacturer and other distributors of the defective product even if the product is attached to the building. *See,* Trent v. Brasch Manufacturing Co., Inc., 132 Ill.App.3d 586, 477 N.E.2d 1312 (1985) (defective heating and air conditioning system).

4. Should it make any difference whether the alleged defect is in a product installed in the home, such as a water heater, or in the house's overall design? Do the policies underlying product liability apply with different force to houses that contain defective products and houses that are themselves defectively designed or constructed?

5. As the opinion in *Kriegler* indicates, the seminal case applying products liability to real property sales was Schipper v. Levitt & Sons, Inc., 44 N.J. 70, 207 A.2d 314 (1965). Both *Kriegler* and *Schipper* involved a builder-vendor of mass-produced houses. The Products Liability Restatement, quoted above, limits the application of products liability to such cases by declining to apply the doctrine to custom built homes. Why is the sale of a mass produced home "sufficiently analogous to the distribution and use of tangible personal property that it is appropriate to apply" products liability, but the sale of a custom built home is not sufficiently analogous? Does it matter whether the custom built home is defective because of its design or because it incorporates a defectively manufactured I beam purchased from a steel manufacturer?

6. Some courts have declined to apply product liability to real estate transactions but have instead applied a common law implied warranty of habitability to certain home sales. *See, e.g.,* Humber v. Morton, 426 S.W.2d 554 (Tex.1968). Other courts have applied both product liability and a common law implied warranty of habitability to certain home sales. *See* Bednarski v. Hideout Homes & Realty Inc., 711 F.Supp. 823 (M.D.Pa. 1989). One potential difference between the two theories is that warranties normally can be disclaimed. *See* O'Mara v. Dykema, 328 Ark. 310, 942 S.W.2d 854, 859 (1997); Greeves v. Rosenbaum, 965 P.2d 669, 673 (Wyo.1998); Centex Homes v. Buecher, 95 S.W.3d 266 (Tex.2002) (Texas, like a number of states,

has two warranties, a warranty of good workmanship, similar to a warranty of merchantability, that applies to new home builder conduct and a warranty of merchantability that requires the builder to provide a house that is safe, sanitary, and otherwise fit for human habitation. The *Centex Homes* court concluded that the former may be disclaimed, but not the latter. Is having two warranties a good idea?).

7. Courts that have applied a common law warranty of habitability to home sales have given different definitions to the term. *Compare* Kamarath v. Bennett, 568 S.W.2d 658, 661 (Tex. 1978) ("In order to constitute a breach of implied warranty of habitability the defect must be of a nature which will render the premises unsafe, or unsanitary, or otherwise unfit for living therein.") *with* Petersen v. Hubschman Const. Co., Inc., 76 Ill.2d 31, 389 N.E.2d 1154, 27 Ill.Dec. 746 (1979) Ill., 1979. ("The mere fact that the house is capable of being inhabited does not satisfy the implied warranty. The use of the term "habitability" is perhaps unfortunate. Because of its imprecise meaning it is susceptible of misconstruction. It would more accurately convey the meaning of the warranty as used in this context if it were to be phrased in language similar to that used in the Uniform Commercial Code, warranty of merchantability, or warranty of fitness for a particular purpose." 389 N.E.2d at 1157) and R.N. Thompson & Associates, Inc. v. Wickes Lumber Co., 687 N.E.2d 617, 620 (Ind.App.1997) ("A warranty of habitability warrants that the home will be free from defects which substantially impair the use and enjoyment of the house.")

8. It is still unclear in many jurisdictions whether products liability or a common law implied warranty of merchantability applies to real estate transactions other than the sale of a new house by a builder-vendor. Some courts have extended coverage to sales of used houses. *See, e.g.,* Gupta v. Ritter Homes, Inc., 646 S.W.2d 168 (Tex.1983).

Sales other than those of new houses by a builder-vendor raise a variety of issues that courts have not sorted out. First, product liability and breach of warranty might not apply to the sale of a used house on the ground that these theories do not cover the sale of used goods. *See* subsection 4, *supra*.

Second, a purchaser of a used home who sues the original builder-vendor might face problems of privity. Normally, privity is not required in product liability, and a builder should be able to foresee future resales of its houses. Privity under the Uniform Commercial Code depends on the version of section 2–318 a state adopts. Privity under a common law implied warranty depends on a particular court's decision on the issue.

Third, a court might decide that a seller other than a builder-vendor (or even mass builder-vendor) is not the right type of defendant to be governed by product liability or breach of warranty. Normally, the standard under product liability would be whether the defendant is in the business of selling homes, and under the Uniform Commercial Code it is whether the defendant is a merchant. A court would have more flexibility under an implied, common-law warranty.

9. Some courts have refused to apply any form of product liability to the sale of houses. In Bruce Farms, Inc. v. Coupe, 219 Va. 287, 247 S.E.2d 400 (1978), the court declined to apply product liability to the sale of a house largely on the ground that doing so would raise questions about the types of

house sales that should be covered, and that these line-drawing issues are better left to the legislature. Are these line-drawing issues intrinsically any more difficult than determining the scope of products liability in other types of transactions? Nevertheless, can a case be made that the policies underlying product liability do not apply as forcefully to real estate, even the sale of a new house by a builder-vendor?

10. Is a mobile home a product? *See* Dewberry v. LaFollette, 598 P.2d 241 (Okla.1979); Stanley v. Schiavi Mobile Homes, Inc., 462 A.2d 1144 (Me. 1983).

PETERSON v. SUPERIOR COURT
Supreme Court of California, 1995.
10 Cal.4th 1185, 899 P.2d 905, 43 Cal.Rptr.2d 836.

GEORGE, JUSTICE.

In *Becker v. IRM Corp.* (1985) 38 Cal.3d 454, 213 Cal.Rptr. 213, 698 P.2d 116 (hereafter *Becker*), this court concluded that under California's products liability doctrine (which provides generally that manufacturers, retailers, and others in the marketing chain of a product are strictly liable in tort for personal injuries caused by a defective product), a residential landlord may be held strictly liable for an injury to its tenant caused by a defect in a leased dwelling. We granted review in the present case to decide whether *Becker* was wrongly decided and should be overruled, or, if *Becker* is not overruled, whether the principles underlying that decision apply outside the landlord-tenant context and warrant the imposition of strict products liability upon the proprietor of a hotel for an injury to its guest caused by a defect in the hotel premises.

* * *

In an amended complaint * * * plaintiff Nadine L. Peterson alleged that, while a guest at the Palm Springs Marquis Hotel, she slipped and fell in the bathtub while taking a shower, sustaining serious head injuries. Plaintiff alleged that the bottom surface of the bathtub was "extremely slick and slippery" and that the bathtub had no "safety measures" such as "anti-skid surfaces, grab rails, rubber mats, or the like." Plaintiff named as defendants, among others, the owners of the hotel, Banque Paribas and Palm Springs Marquis, Inc., the operator of the hotel, Harbaugh Hotel Management Corporation * * *. In addition to a cause of action for negligence, plaintiff brought a cause of action for "strict liability in tort," asserting the bathtub was a "defective product" because the bathtub "was so smooth, slippery, and slick as to have provided no friction or slip resistance whatsoever...."

* * *

II

The sole issue in the case before us is whether the trial court erred in granting defendants' *in limine* motion to preclude plaintiff from arguing that, pursuant to our decision in *Becker*, the proprietor of a hotel is strictly liable under the doctrine of products liability for injuries to hotel guests caused by defects in the premises. For the reasons that follow, we conclude, upon reconsideration, that the decision in *Becker* constitutes an unwarranted extension of the doctrine of products liability and should be overruled. As we explain, the circumstance that landlords and hotel proprietors lease residential dwellings and rent hotel rooms to the public does not bring them within the class of persons who properly may be held strictly liable under the doctrine of products liability.

* * *

Our decision in *Becker* drastically altered established rules governing a landlord's liability for injuries caused by defects in leased premises. "At common law, the landlord was under no general duty to keep the premises in safe condition after transfer of possession ... , and was ordinarily not liable for injuries to a tenant or his invitees, or to strangers, resulting from the defective condition of the premises, even though by the exercise of reasonable diligence he might have discovered the defects. [Citations.]" (4 Witkin, Summary of Cal.Law (9th ed. 1987) Real Property, § 595, pp. 773–774.)

In *Rowland v. Christian* (1968) 69 Cal.2d 108, 70 Cal.Rptr. 97, 443 P.2d 561, we recognized a trend in the law " 'towards imposing on owners and occupiers a single duty of reasonable care in all the circumstances.' " (Fns. omitted.) [Citations.] (Id. at p. 116, 70 Cal.Rptr. 97, 443 P.2d 561.) The decision in Rowland abandoned, in favor of applying "ordinary principles of negligence," the common law rule that a possessor of land owed a greater duty to avoid injury to an invitee than to a trespasser and licensee or social guest. (Id. at p. 118, 70 Cal.Rptr. 97, 443 P.2d 561.) Recognizing that "the basic policy of this state ... is that everyone is responsible for an injury caused to another by his want of ordinary care or skill in the management of his property" (id. at p. 119, 70 Cal.Rptr. 97, 443 P.2d 561), we held: "The proper test to be applied to the liability of the possessor of land ... is whether in the management of his property he has acted as a reasonable man in view of the probability of injury to others...." (Ibid.)

In *Brennan v. Cockrell Investments, Inc.* (1973) 35 Cal.App.3d 796, 111 Cal.Rptr. 122, the Court of Appeal, applying our decision in Rowland to an action against a landlord brought by a tenant who had been injured by a defective condition of the leased premises, held that we had abolished the common law rule that (subject to specified exceptions) a landlord is not liable for injuries to a tenant caused by a defect in leased premises: "Possession and degree of control over the premises are significant factors to be weighed in determining whether or not the landlord failed to meet the statutory standard of care. Indeed, these considerations go to the very essence of the negligence issue. But it is impossible to perceive any legitimate public interest that would be promoted by the creation of a landlord immunity exception.... That a landlord must act toward his tenant as a reasonable person under all of the circumstances ... seems a sound proposition and one that expresses well the principles of justice and reasonableness upon which the law of torts is based." (Id. at pp. 800–801, 111 Cal.Rptr. 122.)

In addition to discussing strict liability, the decision in *Becker*, as previously noted, considered the plaintiff's cause of action for negligence, expanding upon the standard enunciated in *Brennan v. Cockrell Investments, Inc., supra*: "[A] landlord in caring for his property must act toward his tenant as a reasonable person under all of the circumstances including the likelihood of injury, the probable seriousness of injury, the burden of reducing or avoiding the risk, and his degree of control over the risk-creating defect. [Citations.]" (*Becker, supra,* 38 Cal.3d 454, 468, 213 Cal.Rptr. 213, 698 P.2d 116.) The decision in *Becker* further held that a landlord has a duty to inspect rental premises "to determine whether they meet bare living standards, including whether they are safe," both when purchasing the rental property and when leasing the premises to a tenant. (Ibid.) This court distinguished those cases in which injuries were caused by defects that "developed after purchase of the building by the defendant and while the apartment was in possession of the tenant," observing that "[t]he duty to inspect should charge the defendant only with those matters which would have been disclosed by a reasonable inspection." (Id. at p. 469, 213 Cal.Rptr. 213, 698 P.2d 116.)

In the portion of the opinion addressing the products liability doctrine, however, the decision in *Becker* went far beyond holding landlords liable for injuries caused by their own fault, and imposed liability for injuries caused by defects that the landlord had not created, that would not have been disclosed by a reasonable inspection, and of which the landlord had no knowledge. As noted above, *Becker* applied principles of products liability and held "that a landlord engaged in the business of leasing dwellings is strictly liable in tort for injuries resulting from a latent defect in the premises when the defect existed at the time the premises were let to the tenant. [Fn. omitted.]" (*Becker, supra,* 38 Cal.3d 454, 464, 213 Cal.Rptr. 213, 698 P.2d 116.)

The effect of imposing upon landlords liability without fault is to compel them to insure the safety of their tenants in situations in which injury is caused by a defect of which the landlord neither knew nor should have known. As noted above, every other jurisdiction that has considered this issue expressly has rejected the approach followed by *Becker*. * * *

Justifying its significant and unprecedented expansion of a landlord's liability for injuries to tenants by applying the law of products liability to the relationship between landlord and tenant, *Becker* reasoned that an apartment itself should be considered a "product" that a landlord places into the stream of commerce. *Becker*'s reasoning in reaching that conclusion, however, is flawed in several respects.

As noted in *Becker*, this court held in *Greenman v. Yuba Power Products, Inc., supra,* 59 Cal.2d 57, 62, 27 Cal.Rptr. 697, 377 P.2d 897, that "[a] manufacturer is strictly liable in tort when an article he places on the market, knowing that it is to be used without inspection for defects, proves to have a defect that causes injury to a human being." In *Vandermark v. Ford Motor Co., supra*, 61 Cal.2d 256, 262–263, 37 Cal.Rptr. 896, 391 P.2d 168, we held that a retailer of manufactured goods also is strictly liable in tort: "Retailers like manufacturers are engaged in the business of distributing goods to the public. They are an integral part of the overall producing and marketing enterprise that should bear the cost of injuries resulting from defective products. [Citation.] In some cases the retailer may be the only member of that enterprise reasonably available to the injured plaintiff. In other cases the retailer himself may play a substantial part in insuring that the product is safe or may be in a position to exert pressure on the manufacturer to that end; the retailer's strict liability thus serves as an added incentive to safety. Strict liability on the manufacturer and retailer alike affords maximum protection to the injured plaintiff and works no injustice to the defendants, for they can adjust the costs of such protection between them in the course of their continuing business relationship."

Most of the preceding reasons for imposing strict liability upon a retailer of a defective product do not apply to landlords or hotel proprietors who rent residential premises. A landlord or hotel owner, unlike a retailer, often cannot exert pressure upon the manufacturer to make the product safe and cannot share with the manufacturer the costs of insuring the safety of the tenant, because a landlord or hotel owner generally has no "continuing business relationship" with the manufacturer of the defective product. As one commentator has observed: "If the objective of the application of the stream of commerce approach is to distribute the risk of providing a product to society by allowing an injured plaintiff to find a remedy for injury along the chain of distribution, it will probably fail in the landlord/tenant situation. The cost of insuring risk will not be distributed along the chain of commerce but will probably be absorbed by tenants who will pay increased rents. One could argue that this was not the effect sought by the court in earlier cases which anticipated that the cost of risk would be distributed vertically in the stream of commerce." (Note, *Becker v. IRM Corporation: Strict Liability in Tort for Residential Landlords, supra,* 16 Golden Gate L.Rev. 349, 360.)

In the present case, for example, plaintiff's products liability claim is premised upon the assertion that the bathtub in her hotel room was defective because its surface was too slippery. But a hotel owner is not a part of the chain of distribution of a bathtub that is installed in a hotel room, just as a restaurant owner is not the equivalent of a retailer of toilets simply because the restaurant provides restroom facilities to its patrons, and just as an owner of a business is not the equivalent of a retailer of ceiling fans simply because one is installed on the premises to promote the comfort of customers of the business. In such circumstances, the bathtub, toilets, and ceiling fans left the stream of commerce when they were purchased and installed in the premises of the various businesses. The mere circumstance that it was contemplated customers of these businesses would use the products in question or be benefited by them does not transform the owners of the businesses into the equivalent of retailers of the products. [Citation]

We need not, and do not, decide whether different considerations would apply in the event the landlord or hotel owner had participated in the construction of the building. [Citation] But in such circumstances strict liability would attach, if at all, based upon the landlord's status as a builder who is engaged in the business of constructing (i.e. manufacturing) rental properties. [Citations]

The record before us in the present case does not disclose whether defendants constructed the hotel. Plaintiff did not argue in the courts below, or in the briefs filed in this court, that strict liability applies because defendants had constructed the hotel. Accordingly, neither the trial court nor the Court of Appeal ruled upon this issue. Thus, we express no opinion regarding whether, or under what circumstances, strict liability might be imposed upon a landlord or hotel proprietor who participated in the construction of the building or otherwise created the defective product that caused the injury. On remand, plaintiff may seek leave from the superior court to raise such issues.

The conclusion that a landlord or hotel proprietor, unlike a retailer, is not strictly liable in tort is supported by those cases holding that a seller of used machinery is not strictly liable in tort, unless the seller rebuilds or reconditions the product and thus assumes a role analogous to that of a manufacturer. In *Wilkinson v. Hicks* (1981) 126 Cal.App.3d 515, 179 Cal.Rptr. 5, the plaintiff's hand was crushed while operating a punch press which the defendant, a dealer in used machinery, had sold to the plaintiff's employer. Evidence was introduced that a safety device that was part of the machine when it was built more than 50 years earlier apparently had been removed by a previous owner. Prior to the sale, the defendant had seen the machine in operation and observed that it was in good operating condition. The previous owner had experienced no malfunctions. The defendant sold the machine to the plaintiff's employer "as is" and, although the defendant's employees "tried out" the machine prior to delivering it, they made no adjustments or modifications to the machine.

The Court of Appeal held that a seller of used machinery such as the defendant is not strictly liable in tort for injuries caused by a defective product: "To impose such liability would as a practical matter require all dealers in used goods routinely to dismantle, inspect for latent defects, and repair or recondition their products.... It would in effect render used goods dealers as insurers against defects which came into existence after the original chain of distribution and while the product was under the control of previous consumers. [Citations.]" Wilkinson v. Hicks, *supra*, 126 Cal.App.3d at p. 521, 179 Cal.Rptr. 5; [Citation]

* * *

This reasoning applies with even greater force to a landlord or hotel owner who purchases an apartment building or hotel. Defects in such a structure may have been created by the builder, a subcontractor, a manufacturer of building supplies or fixtures, a previous owner of the building, or a previous tenant of the apartment or guest of the hotel. Because the landlord or hotel owner generally has no continuing business relationship, or other ready channel of communication, with any of these persons or entities, only in rare cases would the imposition of strict liability upon the landlord or hotel owner create an impetus to manufacture safer products. As one commentator has recognized: "Unlike other suppliers ... , landlords' ability to improve their products' safety is rather limited. Landlords cannot redesign the products or switch manufacturer; they can only repair the defects they know about. While imposing strict landlord liability will encourage landlords to make such repairs, it provides no greater safety incentive than imposing negligence liability." (Comment, *California's Approach to Landlord Liability for Tenant Injuries: Strict Liability Reexamined, supra,* 26 U.C.Davis L.Rev. 367, 405, fns. omitted.)

As to the second justification for the imposition of strict liability—an implied representation of safety—the decision in *Tauber-Arons* again quotes the decision in *Tillman:* " '[T]he sale of a used product, without more, may not be found to generate the kind of expectations of safety that the courts have held are justifiably created by the introduction of a new product into the stream of commerce.' " (*Tauber-Arons Auctioneers Co. v. Superior Court, supra,* 101 Cal.App.3d 268, 281, 161 Cal.Rptr. 789.)

This court in *Becker* held, to the contrary, that a tenant renting a dwelling has an expectation of safety similar to that of a consumer purchasing a new product, even if the building is not new. This conclusion was based upon the implied warranty of habitability contained in a residential lease, recognized in *Green v. Superior Court* (1974) 10 Cal.3d 616, 111 Cal.Rptr. 704, 517 P.2d 1168—a warranty that the court in *Becker* viewed as constituting an "implied assurance of safety made by the landlord." (*Becker, supra,* 38 Cal.3d at p. 465, 213 Cal.Rptr. 213, 698 P.2d 116.) The conclusion reached in *Becker*, however, overstates the effect of the implied warranty recognized in *Green*.

Our decision in *Green* reflected a national trend to replace the outmoded common law doctrine that a landlord was under no duty to maintain leased dwellings in a habitable condition during the term of the lease, with a rule more in line with the modern reality that every lease of a dwelling contains an implied warranty of habitability. [Citation] The rationale behind judicial recognition of an implied warranty of habitability in residential leases has been explained by one commentator as follows: "In the 1960s and 1970s nearly all states imposed on landlords an obligation to maintain the habitability of leased premises. One of many reasons for the adoption of this obligation was that economic changes had rendered the old rule of caveat emptor inappropriate.... The doctrine [of caveat emptor] arose out of an agrarian economy in which landlords and tenants typically had equal skills in inspecting and repairing property. Because leases largely covered farmland, the value of the structures on the land was of secondary importance. In the opinion of early courts, a lease was viewed most accurately as a conveyance of property from one party to another. Today, by contrast, a residential lease typically involves a bundle of goods and services and envisions a continuing relationship between the landlord and tenant. For the typical tenant, the apartment or house being leased is far more important than the land.

"A second reason for the new warranty was the typical inequality in bargaining positions of the landlord and tenant.... In the view of many, the law needed to respond to this inequality and restore the parties to a reasonable balance.

"A third reason ... was that landlords were usually better positioned to make needed repairs. In multi-unit structures, tenants often had no access to the central elements of the building such as water, electrical, heating, and cooling systems.... As short-term leases became the norm, tenants had insufficient financial incentive to make major structural repairs.

"Tenant expectations also played an important role.... Tenants leased homes, and they expected to be able to move into their homes without undue trouble or expense. They expected toilets to flush and furnaces to heat. To an increasing extent, they leased appliances as well as space, and they expected the appliances to function properly. Repairs with a long useful life, they believed, were the proper province of the landlord. Just as the tenant had an obligation to pay rent every month, the landlord had a continuing obligation to provide good shelter month by month....

"Perhaps the prime motive behind the new habitability duty, however, was the public policy concern over the quality of the nation's housing stock. Dilapidated housing was a public as well as a private concern. Substandard housing created filth that spread to the streets. It bred disease if not crime. It was an eyesore and a public disgrace.... Housing codes attempted to address this problem, but their enforcement was dramatically inadequate. Private enforcement seemed necessary, and the new habitability duty seemed to be a useful enforcement tool." (Freyfogle, *The Installment Land Contract as Lease: Habitability Protections and the Low-income Purchaser* (1987) 62 N.Y.U.L.Rev. 293, 297–299, fns. omitted.)

The implied warranty of habitability recognizes "the realities of the modern urban landlord-tenant relationship" and imposes upon the landlord the obligation to maintain leased dwellings in a habitable condition throughout the term of the lease. (*Green v. Superior Court, supra*, 10 Cal.3d 616, 619, 111 Cal.Rptr. 704, 517 P.2d 1168.) But deriving from this implied warranty an obligation on the part of the landlord to insure the safety of leased premises by imposing strict liability for injuries to tenants caused by defects in the premises goes far beyond this laudable goal. Rather than restore the parties to a reasonable balance, the doctrine of strict liability places an undue burden upon the landlord—

regardless of fault or ability to avoid injury. Rather than obligate the landlord to promptly repair defects of which the landlord knows or should know, the doctrine often will impose an onerous burden to discover and correct defects that would not be disclosed by a reasonable inspection. Rather than obligate the landlord to comply with applicable housing codes[1] and maintain the dwelling in a habitable condition, application of the products liability doctrine imposes strict liability upon the landlord, even when the landlord has taken all reasonable steps to render the dwelling safe.

The reasoning in *Becker* is flawed because recognition of the implied warranty of habitability does not lead to the conclusion that a landlord is strictly liable for injuries to tenants caused by defects in the premises.[2] Although, as noted above, nearly all states have recognized an implied warranty of habitability in residential leases, only California (by judicial decision) and Louisiana (by statute) hold landlords strictly liable for injuries to tenants caused by defects in the premises. One commentator has explained this trend as follows: "Gradually, ... courts are realizing that the implied warranty is actually a covenant rather than a warranty, which means that breaches need not give rise to excessive tort liability. The landlord's repair covenant is (or at least should be) breached only if the landlord fails to fix a problem within a reasonable period after notice. It is the landlord's inaction—the landlord's negligence—that gives rise to liability." (Freyfogle, *The Installment Land Contract as Lease: Habitability Protections and the Low-income Purchaser, supra*, 62 N.Y.U.L.Rev. 293, 302, fns. omitted.) One advantage to the approach of viewing the implied warranty as a covenant is that it applies equally to all landlords, whether or not they are "in the business of leasing dwellings." (*Becker, supra*, 38 Cal.3d at p. 464, 213 Cal.Rptr. 213, 698 P.2d 116; *Vaerst v. Tanzman, supra*, 222 Cal.App.3d at p. 1540, 272 Cal.Rptr. 503 [a landlord "who leased his own family residence to the tenants on a temporary basis ... is not within the purview of *Becker*...."].)

The implied warranty of habitability recognized in *Green* gives a tenant a reasonable expectation that the landlord has inspected the rental dwelling and corrected any defects disclosed by that inspection that would render the dwelling uninhabitable. The tenant further reasonably can expect that the landlord will maintain the property in a habitable condition by repairing promptly any conditions, of which the landlord has actual or constructive notice, that arise during the tenancy and render the dwelling uninhabitable.[3] A tenant injured by a defect in

---

1. The failure of a landlord, or a hotel proprietor, to comply with applicable statutes and ordinances may constitute negligence per se. * * *

2. Section 17.6 of the Restatement Second of Property provides that a landlord's liability is governed by a negligence standard when an injury results from the landlord's breach of an implied warranty of habitability * * *.

3. "The product to which the *Green* court referred seems to be the 'package of goods and services' performed by the landlord, such as the supplying of adequate heat, light, and ventilation, serviceable plumbing facilities, secure windows and doors, proper sanitation and proper mainte-

the premises, therefore, may bring a negligence action if the landlord breached its duty to exercise reasonable care. But a tenant cannot reasonably expect that the landlord will have eliminated defects in a rented dwelling of which the landlord was unaware and which would not have been disclosed by a reasonable inspection. The implied warranty of habitability, therefore, does not support an action for strict liability.

Even before the advent of the implied warranty of habitability applicable to residential leases, it was recognized that hotel proprietors have a special relationship with their guests that gives rise to a duty similar to that owed by common carriers "to protect them against unreasonable risk of physical harm." (Rest.2d Torts, § 314A.) "The duty in each case is only one to exercise reasonable care under the circumstances. The defendant is not liable where he neither knows nor should know of the unreasonable risk...." (Id., com. e, at p. 120.) We have recognized that an innkeeper, like a common carrier, is not an insurer of the safety of its guests. [Citations]

A hotel guest reasonably can expect that the hotel owner diligently will inspect the hotel room for defects and will correct any defects discovered. But the guest cannot reasonably expect that the owner will correct defects of which the owner is unaware and that cannot be discerned by a reasonable inspection. The duty of an innkeeper, therefore, like the duty of a landlord, does not support an action for strict liability.

The remaining justification for the imposition of strict liability discussed in *Tauber-Arons* is loss spreading. *Becker* relied upon this factor almost exclusively in distinguishing the rule, announced in *Tauber-Arons* and its progeny, that strict liability should not be imposed upon sellers of used merchandise: "The paramount policy of the strict products liability rule remains the spreading throughout society of the cost of compensating otherwise defenseless victims of manufacturing defects. [Citations.]" (*Becker, supra*, 38 Cal.3d at p. 466, 213 Cal.Rptr. 213, 698 P.2d 116.) But the court in *Tauber-Arons*, quoting a similar statement from this court's decision in *Price v. Shell Oil Co., supra*, 2 Cal.3d 245, 251, 85 Cal.Rptr. 178, 466 P.2d 722, that loss spreading was a "paramount policy" of products liability law, correctly observed that

nance. In *Green*, the 'product'—this package of goods and services—was found to be 'defective' only after the landlord had been given notice of and an opportunity to correct the conditions rendering the dwelling uninhabitable." (Note, *A Bird in the Hand: California Imposes Strict Liability on Landlords in Becker v. IRM Corp., supra*, 20 Loyola L.A.L.Rev. 323, 350, fns. omitted.)

We stated in *Green*: "Under the implied warranty which we recognize, a residential landlord covenants that premises he leases for living quarters *will be maintained* in a habitable state for the duration of the lease. This implied warranty of habitability does not require that a landlord ensure that leased premises are in perfect, aesthetically pleasing condition, but it does mean that 'bare living requirements' must be *maintained*. (Fn. omitted.) In most cases substantial compliance with those applicable building and housing code standards which materially affect health and safety will suffice to meet the landlord's obligations under the common law implied warranty of habitability we now recognize. (Fn. omitted.)" (*Green v. Superior Court, supra*, 10 Cal.3d 616, 637, 111 Cal.Rptr. 704, 517 P.2d 1168, italics added.)

this court in *Price* "did not, however, abandon all other considerations." (*Tauber-Arons Auctioneers Co. v. Superior Court, supra*, 101 Cal.App.3d 268, 283, 161 Cal.Rptr. 789.) Instead, the decision in *Price* states: "In *Vandermark* we again emphasized the necessity for a continuous course of business as a condition to application of the rule," observing that, under such circumstances, the imposition of strict liability "works no injustice to the defendants." *(Price v. Shell Oil Co., supra*, 2 Cal.3d 245, 253–254, 85 Cal.Rptr. 178, 466 P.2d 722.)

In many instances, it would be unjust to hold a landlord strictly liable for an injury to a tenant caused by a defect of which the landlord had no knowledge and which would not have been disclosed by a reasonable inspection. One commentator posed a hypothetical situation in which a tenant was injured by a construction defect, the landlord was held strictly liable, and the resulting judgment exceeded the limits of the landlord's insurance coverage. Noting the "potential for harsh results" inherent in *Becker*'s rule of strict liability, the commentator observed: "When latent defects injure tenants, both landlords and tenants are innocent of any wrongdoing. The primary justification for shifting accident costs from innocent tenants to equally innocent landlords is 'loss-spreading.' The landlord has access to liability insurance, and thus, in theory, can spread the costs of injuries that would financially devastate an individual. In reality, however, insurance policies have limits, and, as in the hypothetical, holding landlords strictly liable sometimes substitutes one innocent victim for another." (Comment, *California's Approach to Landlord Liability for Tenant Injuries: Strict Liability Reexamined, supra,* 26 U.C.Davis L.Rev. 367, 371.)

For the same reasons, it often would be unjust to hold a hotel proprietor strictly liable for an injury to a hotel guest caused by a defect in the premises, of which the hotel proprietor was unaware, and which would not have been disclosed by a reasonable inspection. The economic consequences could be particularly onerous for the operators of small establishments, such as small motels or bed and breakfast inns, who, through no fault of their own, could be rendered financially insolvent if a grievous injury to a guest caused by an unknown defect in the premises resulted in a judgment that exceeded available insurance coverage.

Subsequent to the decision in *Becker*, this court reaffirmed in *Brown v. Superior Court* (1988) 44 Cal.3d 1049, 245 Cal.Rptr. 412, 751 P.2d 470 that loss spreading is not the sole consideration in determining whether to impose strict liability for injuries resulting from a defective product. * * * [A problem] with relying exclusively upon the doctrine of loss spreading to justify the imposition of liability without fault is that the same reasoning could be used to impose strict liability in any situation in which the defendant is in a superior position economically to bear or distribute the loss suffered by the plaintiff. As one commentator has observed: "Spreading the cost of injury throughout society amounts to no more than a judicially imposed insurance system. To use this rationale for imposing strict liability in isolation of other rationales is to write a judicial ticket to impose strict liability in any area of law where there are injured plaintiffs who may not be compensated." (Note, *A Bird in the Hand: California Imposes Strict Liability on Landlords in Becker v. IRM Corp., supra,* 20 Loyola L.A.L.Rev. 323, 370.)

As the foregoing discussion demonstrates, the reasons for not applying the doctrine of strict products liability to sellers of used goods support, as well, the conclusion that landlords and hotel owners should not be held strictly liable in tort for injuries to tenants and hotel guests caused by defects in the premises. A landlord or hotel owner who rents dwellings or hotel rooms differs significantly from a manufacturer or retailer of a product. Manufacturers and retailers can be expected to possess expert knowledge concerning the product being produced or sold, but the same is not necessarily true of a landlord or hotel owner. As one commentator has observed: "[I]t is one thing to say that a landlord is an expert at leasing rental dwellings. It is quite another to say that a landlord possesses expert knowledge of the myriad of components which comprise the leased dwelling. Because of the practical impossibility of obtaining expert knowledge of all the components of an apartment, landlords must rely on others for their safe manufacture, installation and repair. In this respect, landlords are in no better position to know of defects than are tenants, yet they are held to the ultimate standard." (Note, *A Bird in the Hand: California Imposes Strict Liability on Landlords in Becker v. IRM Corp., supra,* 20 Loyola L.A.L.Rev. 323, 356, fns. omitted.)

Another concern arising from *Becker*'s imposition of strict liability upon landlords stems from the rule that a manufacturer may defend a products liability action by establishing that "the benefits of the challenged design outweigh the risk of danger inherent in such design." (*Barker v. Lull Engineering Co.* (1978) 20 Cal.3d 413, 432, 143 Cal.Rptr. 225, 573 P.2d 443.) Among the factors the finder of fact may consider in making this determination are "the gravity of the danger posed by the challenged design, the likelihood that such danger would occur, the mechanical feasibility of a safer alternative design, the financial cost of an improved design, and the adverse consequences to the product and to the consumer that would result from an alternative design. [Citations.]" (Id. at p. 431, 143 Cal.Rptr. 225, 573 P.2d 443.)

This court has recognized that most of these factors "involve technical matters peculiarly within the knowledge of the manufacturer." (*Barker v. Lull Engineering Co., supra,* 20 Cal.3d at p. 431, 143 Cal.Rptr. 225, 573 P.2d 443.) A landlord or hotel proprietor frequently is in no position to mount such a defense. As one commentator has noted: "[W]ill a defendant landlord, faced with an unavailable manufacturer—a situation which the majority [in *Becker*] concludes is a proper reason for extending liability—be expected to defend the technical advantages of a product without access to information or experts describing the origin and formulation of a particular design? * * * " (Note, *Let the Landlord Beware: California Imposes Strict Liability on Lessors of Rental Housing, supra,* 51 Mo.L.Rev. 899, 908, italics in original, fns. omitted.)

For all of the foregoing reasons, we conclude that the decision in *Becker v. IRM Corp., supra*, 38 Cal.3d 454, 213 Cal.Rptr. 213, 698 P.2d 116, was incorrect in holding that a landlord is strictly liable on the basis of products liability for injuries to a tenant caused by a defect in a leased dwelling. To the extent it so holds, the decision in *Becker* is overruled. For these same reasons, we further hold that the proprietor of a hotel should not be held strictly liable on the basis of products liability for injuries to a guest caused by a defect in the premises.

* * *

III

The judgment of the Court of Appeal is reversed to the extent it directs the superior court to permit plaintiff to proceed against defendants hotel owner and operator upon the theory of strict products liability; in all other respects, the judgment of the Court of Appeal is affirmed.

LUCAS, C.J., and MOSK, KENNARD, ARABIAN, BAXTER and WERDEGAR, JJ., concur.

Notes

1. In Armstrong v. Cione, 69 Hawai'i 176, 738 P.2d 79 (1987), the Hawaii Supreme Court declined to apply products liability to a landlord for defects in residential rental property. The court reasoned that several purposes underlying product liability are not applicable to leased residential property. Specifically, the plaintiff has no unique problems of proof, the landlord cannot pass the cost of liability up the chain of distribution to the manufacturer, and the landlord is not in a good position to make specific products in the rental property safer.

2. Some courts have applied a common law warranty of habitability to permit a lessee to recover for defects in the rented premises. *See, e.g.,* Pines v. Perssion, 14 Wis.2d 590, 111 N.W.2d 409 (1961); Kamarath v. Bennett, 568 S.W.2d 658 (Tex.1978) (superseded by Tex.Rev.Stat.Ann. 5236f (Vernon 1979)).

6. SERVICES

Cases involving services raise two related but distinct issues: (1) whether to apply product liability to pure services and (2) if pure services are not governed by product liability, how to distinguish between products and services in hybrid transactions involving both products and services. Although these two issues are distinct, they are also related: distinguishing between products and services in hybrid cases should be resolved consistently with the reasons for treating products and services differently in the first place.

Courts have relied on various forms of analysis to determine whether individual hybrid sales-service cases are governed by products liability, but they have failed to develop a comprehensive approach. One impediment to a comprehensive approach is that the so-called "sales-service" problem actually consists of four distinct problems that courts often conflate.

The first problem, which is the primary focus of this section, is whether pure services are governed by products liability and, if they are not, how "products" and "services" are to be distinguished. For example, a plumber who installs a water heater might be dealing in a product (an installed water heater) or a service (installation).

A second issue is whether a transaction that involves a product involves a "sale" of the product. This issue, which was considered in the sections dealing with leases and bailments, is a common one in cases involving services because service providers often use products while rendering their services. For example, a permanent wave solution is clearly a product, but it is unclear whether a beauty salon that has applied it to a customer has sold it or merely used it while performing a service. Similarly, defective hypodermic needles and hospital gowns are clearly products, but has a doctor who has used the needles or a hospital that has issued the gowns sold them to the patients?

A third issue is whether defendants engaged in a profession merit special treatment. Many of the sales-service cases have arisen in situations involving professional services, especially health care services, and it is often unclear whether a court's analysis applies equally to nonprofessional services.

A final issue is whether the sales-service distinction in cases relying on products liability is the same as the sales-service distinction in cases relying on the warranty provisions of Article 2 of the Uniform Commercial Code.

Each of these issues is important in its own right. The primary purpose of this section is to examine the first issue: whether pure services are governed by product liability and, if they are not, the distinction between products and services. Nevertheless, the other three issues are relevant because courts have intertwined all four issues in cases involving hybrid sales-service transactions. Because most sales-service cases involve more than one of the four issues, it is often difficult to determine what a particular case holds for any one of them, especially since courts have not always distinguished carefully among them.

Courts must disentangle these related but distinct issues before progress can be made toward a comprehensive approach to the sales-service distinction. While the focus of this section is on the distinction between products and services in product liability, it is important to understand that a court's apparent position on this issue may be influenced by the court's failure to disentangle it from one or more of the other three issues.

Even if courts separate the product-service distinction from these other issues, the distinction itself poses problems that have a dual significance. In addition to impeding the resolution of specific cases, the failure to develop a comprehensive approach in the product-service distinction reveals a latent general problem of products liability. A premise of products liability is that product injuries constitute a discrete, integral problem that merits special treatment. Otherwise, it would be inappropriate to distinguish product injuries from other personal injuries, liability for which is governed by negligence. But courts have not always clearly articulated the features of a product case and the policies they evoke that distinguish product injuries from other personal injuries. Without a clear understanding of *why* products cases are distinct, it has been difficult to ascertain *what* constitutes a products case in borderline situations presented by hybrid product-service transactions.

Both the proponents and opponents of products liability have relied on various general arguments to support their respective positions. Many of the arguments on both sides, however, do not distinguish between product injuries and other personal injuries; they apply equally to all personal injury cases. Consequently, they do not explain the selective use of liability in products liability cases, and they do not help identify "products cases" in borderline situations. The difficulty courts have encountered in defining the boundaries of products liability in the hybrid product-service cases reflects this underlying confusion about the values that products liability purports to embody. *See generally,* Powers, Distinguishing Between Products and Services in Strict Liability, 62 N.C.L.Rev. 415 (1984).

HOFFMAN v. SIMPLOT AVIATION, INC.
Supreme Court of Idaho, 1975.
97 Idaho 32, 539 P.2d 584.

SHEPARD, JUSTICE.

This is an appeal from a judgment in favor of plaintiffs-respondents following trial and jury verdict in an action resulting from an airplane accident. The principal questions presented are: 1) whether the rule of strict liability in tort in the field of products liability as adopted by this Court in *Shields v. Morton Chemical Co.*, 95 Idaho 674, 518 P.2d 857 (1974) should be extended beyond sales and into the area of personal services, and, 2) the application of the doctrine of implied warranty to personal services and availability of the defenses of fault or negligence. We decline to so extend the rule of strict liability and hold that the jury was erroneously instructed as to the doctrine of implied warranty. We reverse and remand for a new trial.

The facts giving rise to this action, while lengthy in recitation, are not particularly complex or involved nor are they essentially in dispute between the parties. The case is remarkable in this respect, however, that a structural part of an early vintage single engine airplane failed during flight causing its crash and the pilot is alive to prosecute this action.

[Hoffman alleged that the accident was caused by failure of a bolt, and that after repairing the airplane due to unrelated problems, Simplot returned the airplane to Hoffman with the bolt in a rusted condition.]

It is apparently conceded by all that none of the repair work performed by the Simplot employees was a causative factor in the crash of the aircraft. Similarly no part or product placed upon the aircraft by the Simplot employees was a causative factor. While the Simplot employees were repairing the damage to the left landing gear which was occasioned by the first accident, they were working in close proximity to the clevis bolt which attached the left wing strut to the fuselage.

The principal factual dispute relates to the condition of the clevis bolt at the time that the Simplot employees had completed the repairs and made the visual inspection of the aircraft. There was testimony to the effect that the bolt showed signs of rust and therefore failure could have been anticipated. However, the Simplot employees denied that the rust was visible to them as they worked on and inspected the aircraft and that because of the age and condition of the aircraft rust had no significance.

* * *

In *Shields v. Morton Chemical Company,* 95 Idaho 674, 518 P.2d 857 (1974) this court adopted the rule of strict liability in tort as set forth in the Restatement of the Law, Torts 2nd, § 402(A) (1965). The Restatement deals specifically and only with the sale of a product. Neither this court nor, with one exception, any other court has adopted strict liability in tort absent fault in the context of personal services. We decline to extend the rule of *Shields* to cases involving personal services. We find no consideration of such extension of the rule of strict liability in either the Uniform Commercial Code or the Restatement of Torts, 2nd. Almost uniformly any such extension of the rule has been consistently and expressly rejected. *See Gagne v. Bertran,* 43 Cal.2d 481, 275 P.2d 15 (1954); *Shepard v. Alexian Bros. Hospital,* 33 Cal.App.3d 606, 109 Cal.Rptr. 132 (1973); *Hoover v. Montgomery Ward & Co., Inc.,* 528 P.2d 76 (Or.1974); *Pepsi Cola Bottling Co. v. Superior Burner Service Co.,* 427 P.2d 833 (Alaska 1967). We find *Broyles v. Brown Engineering Co.,* 275 Ala. 35, 151 So.2d 767 (1963) to be unpersuasive. *See also* Prosser, Law of Torts, 679 (4th ed. 1971), 2 R. Hursh & H. Bailey, American Law Products Liability, 2nd § [§] 6–15, 6–18 (1974).

It would serve no purpose herein to extensively review the policy considerations which militate against the extension of the strict liability rule to cases involving personal service. The rationale has been thoroughly explored in the authorities and commentators set forth above and reiteration herein would serve no purpose. It is sufficient to say that as contrasted with the sales of products, personal services do not involve mass production with the difficulty, if not inability, of the obtention of proof of negligence. The consumer in the personal service context usually comes into direct contact with the one offering service and is aware or can determine what work was performed and who performed it.

* * *

It is clear that in a sales transaction an implied warranty may be imposed upon the seller to the effect that the goods are merchantable or are fit for the particular purpose for which purchased. I.C. §§ 28–2–314, 315. In circumstances involving personal services, however, the warranty is implied that the services will be performed in a workmanlike manner. The standard imposed may vary depending upon the expertise of the actor, either possessed or represented to be possessed, the nature of the services and the known resultant danger to others from the actor's negligence or failure to perform.

However, as stated in the landmark case of *Gagne v. Bertran,* 43 Cal.2d 481, 275 P.2d 15 (1954):

> "The services of experts are sought because of their special skill. They have a duty to exercise the ordinary skill and competence of members of their profession, and a failure to discharge that duty will subject them to liability for negligence. *Those who hire such persons are not justified in expecting infallibility, but can expect only reasonable care and competence. They purchase service, not insurance.*" (Emphasis supplied) 275 P.2d at 21.

See American Law of Products Liability 2nd, Hursh & Bailey, § 6–15 and Restatement of Torts, 2nd § 404.

The more vexing problem of theory is the distinction, if any between the doctrines of implied warranty and negligence in circumstances involving the rendering of personal services. Although such causes of action are generally thought to be independent of each other, in the instant circumstances they merge into one cause of action. A fundamental component in a negligence action is the existence of a duty (most often to refrain) toward another and a breach thereof. In circumstances involving the rendition of personal services the duty upon the actor is to perform the services in a workmanlike manner. *Pepsi Cola Bottling Co. v. Superior Burner Service,* 427 P.2d 833 (Alaska 1967) is remarkably similar in its problems of theory and doctrine to the case at bar. Justice Rabinowitz there concluded that in the area of personal services there is a duty upon the actor to perform in a workmanlike manner and there is an implied warranty that the services will so be provided. However, it was there stated:

> "Whether the tort standard of care is considered, or the duty of care imposed by an implied warranty of workmanlike performance is taken as the applicable standard, in our view the resultant standard of care required of appellee's employees in the circumstances of this case is identical. In both instances the standard of care is imposed by law and under either theory there is no difference in the standard of care required of the party rendering the personal services.

> "Characterization of the gist, of gravamen, of appellant's cause of action in the factual context of this case is not free of difficulties. Whether an action is one in contract or tort may have significant procedural and substantive ramifications. In the case at bar appellant's central argument in support of its contention that it was

entitled to go to the jury on both a tort cause of action and breach-of-an-implied-warranty-of-workmanlike-quality cause of action is that *contributory negligence would not be a bar to recovery under the latter."* (Emphasis supplied) 427 P.2d at 840–841.

* * *

* * * We hold that under the circumstances of the case at bar the implied warranty theory of plaintiffs should have been submitted to the jury with proper instructions. *Contra: Pepsi Cola Bottling Co. v. Superior Burner Service, supra.* The jury should have been instructed that plaintiffs were entitled to have defendants' services rendered in a workmanlike manner. The standard of care so imposed on the defendants should be determined in light of relevant factors such as: The inherent danger posed by an aircraft; the expertise possessed, or represented as possessed, by the defendants; the knowledge of the defendants' intended use of the aircraft, and the contributory negligence of or assumption of the risk by the plaintiffs, if any, in consideration of factors such as the age of the aircraft, its previous status and record of repair and maintenance and the previous accident.

* * *

In summary we hold that plaintiffs-respondents were entitled to have their theory of implied warranty submitted to the jury. Since the case involved the rendition of personal service, a cause of action does not exist for breach of implied warranty in the absence of fault on the part of the actor. The jury should be instructed also that the defenses of contributory negligence or assumption of the risk are available to defendants-appellants.

Appellants also assert that the special verdict forms returned by the jury were inherently contradictory to one another, therefore fatally defective and should have been rejected by the trial court. That contention does not merit discussion or treatment here since we have held *supra* that the trial court's instructions on the theory of strict liability were error and on retrial, hopefully, the possibility of contradictory special verdicts will not exist.

Reversed and remanded for a new trial consistent with this opinion. Costs to appellants.

McQUADE, C.J., and DONALDSON and BAKES, JJ., and SCOGGIN, DISTRICT JUDGE (Retired), concur.

Notes

1. The passage from *Gagne v. Bertran* quoted in *Hoffman* is quoted in nearly every opinion rejecting the application of products liability to pure service transactions. Does it help the analysis? We could just as easily say:

> Those who hire such persons to build their *products* are not justified in expecting infallibility, but can expect only reasonable care and competence. They purchase a *product,* not insurance.

2. The opinion in *Hoffman* suggests that the standards of strict liability (at least in the warranty version) and negligence are in fact the same. In Lewis v. Big Powderhorn Mountain Ski Corp., 69 Mich.App. 437, 245 N.W.2d 81 (1976), the court made a similar argument by asserting that since a judgment about the defectiveness of a service necessarily evaluates the defendant's *conduct,* rather than a *product,* it is equivalent to a judgment about the defendant's negligence. Is this correct?

3. The opinion in *Hoffman* also relies on the argument that one of the rationales underlying product liability—the difficulty of proving specific acts of negligence—is not as powerful in cases involving services. What of the other rationales supporting product liability? Are they any less powerful when applied to commercial service transactions?

4. Section 2–102 of the Uniform Commercial Code provides that the Article 2 warranties apply to "transactions in goods."

5. Broyles v. Brown Engineering Co., 275 Ala. 35, 151 So.2d 767 (1963) (per curiam), applied strict liability, under the rubric of a common law implied warranty, to a pure service transaction. Some commentators have also argued that services should be governed by strict liability. *See, e.g.,* Greenfield, Consumer Protection in Service Transactions–Implied Warranties and Strict Liability in Tort, 1974 Utah L.Rev. 661; Comment, Guidelines for Extending Implied Warranties to Service Markets, 125 U.Pa.L.Rev., 365 (1976); Note, Continuing the Common Law Response to the New Industrial State: The Extension of Enterprise Liability to Consumer Services, 22 U.C.L.A.L.Rev. 401 (1974).

HOOVER v. MONTGOMERY WARD & CO., INC.
Supreme Court of Oregon, 1974.
270 Or. 498, 528 P.2d 76.

HOWELL, JUSTICE.

* * *

[Hoover purchased tires from Montgomery Ward, who installed them. Hoover was then injured in a one-car accident and alleged that the tires were improperly installed.]

The trial court refused to submit the issue of strict liability to the jury, and the jury returned a verdict for the defendants on the issue of negligence. The plaintiff appeals.

* * * This case presents the question of whether the definition of "dangerously defective product" should be expanded to include within the scope of strict liability the negligent installation of a nondefective product. We have found no court which has stretched the doctrine of strict liability in tort to this extreme, and we decline to do so.

Plaintiff has directed the court's attention to a series of cases from other jurisdictions holding that, in a commercial transaction, the supplier of a product could be held liable under a theory of either strict liability in tort or breach of warranty, although the transaction did not fall within the traditional "sale" concept. However, these sale-service hybrid cases are inapposite to the case at hand.

In Newmark v. Gimbel's Incorporated, 54 N.J. 585, 258 A.2d 697 (1969), the New Jersey Supreme Court held a beauty shop strictly liable under an implied warranty of fitness when defective permanent wave lotion was applied to a patron's hair. The court reasoned that if the lotion had been sold over the counter there would have been strict liability. There was no logical reason to hold otherwise merely because the defective lotion was applied in a service context, especially when the cost of the service included the price of the lotion.

In *Newmark,* as in all sale-service hybrid cases, it is clear that the product, as opposed to the service, was defective. *See e.g.,* Friend v. Childs Dining Hall Co., 231 Mass. 65, 120 N.E. 407 (1918) (restaurant supplied tainted food); State Stove Manufacturing Company v. Hodges, 189 So.2d 113 (Miss.1966) cert. denied 386 U.S. 912, 87 S.Ct. 860, 17 L.Ed.2d 784 (1967) (contractor supplied defective hot water heater); Worrell v. Barnes, 87 Nev. 204, 484 P.2d 573 (1971) (redecorator of house supplied defective gas pipe fittings); and Carpenter v. Best's Apparel, Inc., 4 Wash.App. 439, 481 P.2d 924 (1971) (beauty shop supplied defective permanent wave lotion). In the case at hand, as stated above, there was no allegation that the tire was defective.

As one author notes:

> "When the contract between plaintiff and defendant is commercial in character, the courts are willing to extend liability without fault to the hybrid sale-service transaction, *provided that a defective product is supplied to the plaintiff* or used by the defendant in the course of performing the service. * * * "(Emphasis added; footnote omitted.) Note, Products and the Professional: Strict Liability in the Sale–Service Hybrid Transaction, 24 Hastings J. 111, 116 (1972).

See also, Phipps, When Does a "Service" Become a "Sale"?, 39 Ins. Counsel J. 274 (1972).

In cases other than the sale-service hybrid transaction courts have also been reluctant to extend the definition of "product" beyond the article actually manufactured or supplied. *See* Flippo v. Mode O'Day Frock Shops of Hollywood, 248 Ark. 1, 449 S.W.2d 692 (1970).

In the instant case it is obvious that the product sold to plaintiff was not dangerously defective. Even if we accepted plaintiff's version of the cause of the accident, it was not a dangerously defective tire which caused plaintiff's injuries, but rather the installation of the wheel on the hub and axle of the auto. In such case it might be said that plaintiff's auto became dangerously defective, but certainly not the tire. Plaintiff herself must have recognized this feature, because in her complaint she does not allege that the tire was an unreasonably dangerous product but that "the automobile was unreasonably dangerous for its intended use * * *."

It is clear that this was not a proper case for strict liability in tort and the trial court correctly refused to submit that issue to the jury.

We have carefully considered the plaintiff's other assignments of error and find that they are either without merit or were not properly preserved at trial. The jury obviously relied on defendants' disinterested witnesses and believed that the cause of the accident was plaintiff's manner of driving rather than negligence in the installation of the wheel on the hub and axle.

Affirmed.

Notes

1. The court in *Hoover* distinguished between the installation of a defective tire and the defective installation of a tire. What policies underlying product tort liability support this distinction? Consider the reasoning used by the court in *Hoffman* to conclude that pure services are not governed by product liability. Does this reasoning support the distinction suggested in *Hoover?*

2. Suppose the plaintiff claimed that the defendant defectively installed a defective tire. Would the first claim be governed by negligence and the second claim be governed by product liability?

3. In cases involving Article 2 warranties, several courts have applied the "essence of the transaction" test to determine whether a hybrid product-service transaction is a "transaction in goods" and therefore governed by Article 2 of the Uniform Commercial Code. Under this test, the court examines the entire transaction to determine whether it *essentially* involves a service or a good. *See, e.g.,* G–W–L, Inc. v. Robichaux, 643 S.W.2d 392 (Tex.1982). This approach seems to rule out the possibility suggested by *Hoover* that part of a transaction is governed by product liability while another part is not.

Some courts have used the essence of the transaction test for Article 2 warranties but a different approach for product liability. *Compare* G–W–L, Inc. v. Robichaux, 643 S.W.2d 392 (Tex.1982) *with* Barbee v. Rogers, 425 S.W.2d 342 (Tex.1968).

4. In Newmark v. Gimbel's, Inc., 102 N.J.Super. 279, 246 A.2d 11 (App. Div. 1968), affirmed, 54 N.J. 585, 258 A.2d 697 (1969), which is discussed in *Hoover,* a New Jersey court applied product liability to a beauty parlor that applied a permanent wave solution to the injured plaintiff. This case is often compared to another New Jersey case, Magrine v. Krasnica, 94 N.J.Super. 228, 227 A.2d 539 (Law. Div. 1967), affirmed *sub nom.* Magrine v. Spector, 100 N.J.Super. 223, 241 A.2d 637 (App. Div. 1968), affirmed 53 N.J. 259, 250 A.2d 129 (1969). In *Magrine* the plaintiff was injured when a defective needle being used by her dentist broke off in her gum. The court held that the dentist's services were not governed by product liability. In addition to involving a professional, an issue which is raised in *Barbee v. Rogers* which follows, *Magrine* is an example of a common class of cases in which a service provider *uses* a defective product in rendering the service. This may distinguish the case from *Newmark,* in which the defective wave

solution was "sold" to the plaintiff in the sense that it was used up. But would the result in *Magrine* have been different if the needle had been disposable? Maybe the distinction is that the defendant in *Newmark* was intended to take some of the wave solution away with her (on her hair). But would the result have been different if the case had involved shampoo, which was intended to be totally washed from the hair?

Cases involving the *use* of defective products by service providers—as distinguished from cases like *Hoover* in which the service provider also sells a product—have caused courts a great deal of difficulty. *Newmark* demonstrates the difficulty courts face in categorizing a transaction as one type or the other. Do the policies underlying product liability or underlying the decision not to apply product liability to pure services help sort out these types of cases?

Remember that in a case like *Magrine*, the plaintiff can sue the needle manufacturer under product liability. The manufacturer clearly sold a product, and the plaintiff's status as a "bystander" (that is, she did not herself purchase the product) does not defeat liability.

5. *Hoover, Magrine,* and *Newmark* involve transactions that are truly "hybrid," that is, the transactions have a component that is clearly a service. Other cases do not involve a complex transaction of this sort but nevertheless are difficult to classify as a product or a service. For example, is the delivery of a utility, such as electricity, natural gas, or water, a product or a service?

Several courts have considered two types of cases involving the sale of electricity. One type involves a plaintiff who touches an overhead line with a ladder or antenna. Nearly all courts have held that in such a case the plaintiff must prove negligence and cannot rely on product liability, either because electricity is not a product or because it has not yet entered the stream of commerce. *See, e.g.,* United Pacific Insurance Co. v. Southern California Edison Co., 163 Cal.App.3d 700, 209 Cal.Rptr. 819 (1985); Genaust v. Illinois Power Co., 62 Ill.2d 456, 343 N.E.2d 465 (1976); Kemp v. Wisconsin Electric Power Co., 44 Wis.2d 571, 172 N.W.2d 161 (1969); Hedges v. Public Service Co. of Indiana, Inc., 396 N.E.2d 933 (Ind.App.1979); Pilkington v. Hendricks County Rural Electric, 460 N.E.2d 1000 (Ind.App. 1984); Petroski v. Northern Indiana Public Service Co., 171 Ind.App. 14, 354 N.E.2d 736 (1976); Williams v. Detroit Edison Co., 63 Mich.App. 559, 234 N.W.2d 702 (1975) (warranty); Farina v. Niagara Mohawk Power Corp., 81 A.D.2d 700, 438 N.Y.S.2d 645 (1981); Wirth v. Mayrath Industries, Inc., 278 N.W.2d 789 (N.D.1979); Cratsley v. Commonwealth Edison Co., 38 Ill.App.3d 55, 347 N.E.2d 496 (1976); Wood v. Public Service Co. of New Hampshire, 114 N.H. 182, 317 A.2d 576 (1974); Smith v. Home Light and Power Co., 695 P.2d 788 (Colo.App.1984); Kentucky Utilities Co. v. Auto Crane Co., 674 S.W.2d 15 (Ky.App.1983).

A second type of case involves a power surge through the plaintiff's meter that causes a fire or other damage. Several courts have permitted plaintiffs to recover under product liability in this type of case. *See, e.g.,* Pierce v. Pacific Gas & Electric Co., 166 Cal.App.3d 68, 212 Cal.Rptr. 283 (1985); Ransome v. Wisconsin Electric Power Co., 87 Wis.2d 605, 275 N.W.2d 641 (1979).

Pierce and *United Pacific Insurance* contain especially good analyses. In *Pierce,* a California Court of Appeals surveyed the policies underlying product liability and concluded that they support the application of product liability to a power surge caused by a faulty transformer. The surge caused a fire in plaintiff's house. In *United Pacific Insurance,* another California Court of Appeals surveyed these policies and concluded that they do not support the application of product liability to a plaintiff who touched an overhead line. How would you analyze the difference between these two types of cases?

Elgin Airport Inn, Inc. v. Commonwealth Edison Co., 89 Ill.2d 138, 59 Ill.Dec. 675, 432 N.E.2d 259 (1982), presents an interesting variant of a "power surge" case. Power delivered at the wrong voltage burned out a piece of plaintiff's equipment. The court reasoned that unlike most "power-surge" cases, here the plaintiff could have easily protected itself by installing a protective device, and that its susceptibility to injury was greater than most consumers of electricity. Consequently, the defendant was not in a better position to prevent the injury, and spreading the loss to other rate payers would not have been fair.

Should product liability or an implied warranty of merchantability apply to the delivery of gas-laden water? *See* Moody v. Galveston, 524 S.W.2d 583 (Tex.App. 1975).

6. In Chubb Group v. C.F. Murphy & Associates, Inc., 656 S.W.2d 766 (Mo.App.1983), the court held that product liability was not applicable to the designer of the Kemper Arena in Kansas City, which had collapsed. Similarly, in Hunt v. Guarantee Electrical Co., 667 S.W.2d 9 (Mo.App.1984), the court declined to apply product liability to a defendant who provided and installed an electrical timer in an industrial production process. The timer had been installed to solve a specific problem with the process, and the alleged defect was the overall design of the process and the timer's part in that design. There was no allegation that the timer itself was defective.

But in Worrell v. Barnes, 87 Nev. 204, 484 P.2d 573 (1971), the court applied product liability and an implied warranty of merchantability to a defendant who installed a leaky gas fitting while remodeling the plaintiff's home. In Thomas v. Bove, 687 P.2d 534 (Colo.App.1984), the court applied an implied warranty of merchantability and an implied warranty of fitness to a defendant who installed a faulty heating system in a home. And in O'Laughlin v. Minnesota Natural Gas Co., 253 N.W.2d 826 (Minn.1977), the court applied product liability and an implied warranty of merchantability to a supplier and installer of a home heating system.

Do the policies underlying product liability or liability for breach of warranty support a conclusion, as in *Chubb,* that product liability should not be applied to the designer or builder of an entire building, so long as the alleged defect is in the design, not in a faulty component? If so, should there be a different result when, as in *Thomas, O'Laughlin,* and *Worrell,* the defendant installs a defective component in a building, such as a heating system? Are the cases distinguishable even if the alleged defect in the component is a design defect?

7. Section 19 of the Restatement (Third) of Torts: Products Liability provides that services are not products for purposes of the Restatement.

Comment d to § 20 describes the Restatement approach to sales-service hybrids:

> *d. Sales-service combinations.* When the same person provides both products and services in a commercial transaction, whether a product has been sold may be difficult to determine. When the product and service components are kept separate by the parties to the transaction, as when a lawn-care firm bills separately for fertilizer applied to a customer's lawn or when a machinery repairer replaces a component part and bills separately for it, the firm will be held to be the seller of the product. This is especially true when the parties to the transaction explicitly characterize the property aspect as a sale.
>
> When the parties do not clearly separate the product and service components, courts differ in their treatment of these so-called "sale-service hybrid transactions." These transactions tend to fall into two categories. In the first, the product component is consumed in the course of providing the service, as when a hair dye is used in treating a customer's hair in a salon. Even when the service provider does not charge the customer separately for the dye, the transaction ordinarily is treated as a sale of the material that is consumed in providing the service. When the product component in the sale-service transaction is not consumed or permanently transferred to the customer—as when defective scissors are used in the hair salon—the transaction ordinarily is treated as one not involving a sale of the product to the customer. But while the salon is not a seller, all commercial sellers in the chain of distribution of the scissors, from the manufacturer through the retailer who sold them to the salon, are clearly sellers of the scissors and are subject to liability to the salon customer under the rules of this Restatement. It should be noted that, in a strong majority of jurisdictions, hospitals are held not to be sellers of products they supply in connection with the provision of medical care, regardless of the circumstances.

BARBEE v. ROGERS
Supreme Court of Texas, 1968.
425 S.W.2d 342.

STEAKLEY, JUSTICE.

Petitioner sued N. Jay Rogers and S.J. Rogers, doing business as Texas State Optical, Respondents, and Texas State Optical, Inc., for damages. He alleged that he purchased contact lenses from them which were improperly fitted and that he was given improper prescriptions and instructions for their use.

* * *

Petitioner attacks the holding of the intermediate court upon three points of error * * *. These points assert in substance that the court erred in holding that Respondents were not liable upon the theory of strict liability in tort or for breach of a contractual implied warranty of fitness; and that the court erred in recognizing a professional relationship between Petitioner and Respondents. [The court held that, under the circumstances, the plaintiff had not established a claim of breach of warranty.] The question is thus narrowed to whether the doctrine of strict liability, which is tortious and not contractual, will be extended to the prescription, fitting and sale of contact lenses under the circumstances here shown.

Respondent, Dr. N. Jay Rogers, testified that he and his brother are licensed optometrists and compose a partnership operating eighty-four offices throughout Texas. They employ approximately one hundred twenty-five licensed optometrists and promote the sale of contact lenses by newspaper, television and radio advertisements. The contact lenses are sold for the same price regardless of the difficulty or the simplicity of the eye problems and the number of subsequent examinations which may be required. The charge is made for the product and not for the time of the optometrist. Respondents warrant to those responding to their advertisements of contact lenses that they will be properly cared for and fitted, subject to the qualification of care and use in accordance with specific instructions.

Petitioner's eyes were examined by a licensed optometrist in one of the offices of Respondents in May, 1959, and contact lenses were prescribed and subsequently fitted for him. They were unsatisfactory to Petitioner, and there followed a series of examinations and corrections by optometrists in the employ of Respondents at offices of Respondents in the Houston area. Petitioner testified that he suffered pain and discomfort when he wore the lenses and that he ceased using them approximately sixteen months later. He subsequently moved to California where he was examined by Dr. Robert E. Christensen, a medical doctor of Ophthalmology. Dr. Christensen testified by deposition that it was his opinion that the contact lenses worn by Petitioner were of a flatter curve than the corneal curve; that he found unusual scarring in Petitioner's eyes and that "it would be logical to relate the corneal scars to the contact lenses." A contact lens manufacturer, Jack R. Case, testified that "in checking the lenses on Mr. Barbee we found that the lenses, in our opinion, would be too large and too thick."

Article 4552 defines the practice of optometry as follows:

[The court quoted from the relevant statutes regulating optometrists.]

The licensed optometrist, such as Respondents and their employees, is thus enjoined by statute from treatment of the eyes and from the administration or prescription of drugs. The service he renders is the prescription and fitting of corrective devices for visual defects. It is shown by the evidence that the optometrist performs this service by means of mechanical instruments in the use of which he has special training. * * * It further appears from the evidence that there are two methods of fitting contact lenses, and there is no way to predetermine whether a particular contact lens curve or size will be easily adapted to the patient or can ever be adapted to him. The acts of prescription and fitting are described as an art with many variables and call for an exercise of judgment by the practitioner.

It is apparent that the activities of Respondents fall between those ordinarily associated with the practice of a profession and those characteristic of a merchandising concern. A professional relationship is present in the facts that contact lenses are prescribed and fitted by a licensed optometrist after examination of the eyes and in the exercise of his judgment. A merchandising relationship is suggested by the multiple offices of Respondents throughout the State; by their advertising and sales techniques designed to promote the sale of contact lenses at a predetermined and advertised price; and by their standardization of procedures and methods. Petitioner argues that the latter in effect destroys the statutory distinction between the professional act of fitting lenses or prisms to correct or remedy visual defects and the merchandising act of selling corrective eye devices. Respondents, on the other hand, point to this statutory distinction as making clear that the licensed optometrist is not considered a mere merchant.

In McKisson v. Sales Affiliates, Inc., [416 S.W.2d 787 (Tex.1967)], we extended the rule of strict liability applicable to foodstuffs for human consumption, Decker and Sons, Inc. v. Capps, 139 Tex. 609, 164 S.W.2d 828, 142 A.L.R. 1479 (1942), to defective products which cause physical harm to persons. In so doing, we adopted the rule of the Torts Restatement. It is to be noted that the jury findings here closely parallel those in *McKisson*. In our opinion, however, and we so hold, the rule of strict liability is inapplicable. Respondents and the licensed optometrists in their employ exercise skill and judgment in the examination, prescription and fitting process whereby it is sought to remedy visual abnormalities by the use of curved lenses or prisms. The failure here is not attributable to the product itself, i.e., the contact lenses, but to the professional and statutorily authorized act of "measuring the powers of vision" of Petitioner's eyes and "fitting lenses * * * to correct or remedy * * * [his] defect or abnormal condition of vision." This is not the act of one selling a "product in a defective condition unreasonably dangerous to the user" in the terms of the Torts Restatement. It is the act of one deemed in law to have the competence to remedy a visual defect by furnishing particularly prescribed contact lenses. Apart, then, from Respondents way of practicing optometry, the fact remains that the contact lenses sold to Petitioner were designed in the light of his particular physical requirements and to meet his particular needs. Presumably, and insofar as this record shows, they were not in existence when Petitioner sought the services of Respondents. They were not a finished product offered to the general public in regular channels of trade. The considerations supporting the rule of strict liability are not present. Petitioner cites no case authority for so extending the rule, and we have found none in our research. In addition to the disqualifying factor of the professional relationship, Petitioner's claim for application of the rule is not premised on any defect in the lenses as such, nor was it contemplated that Petitioner would use them without changes or adjustments to fit his needs. The miscarriage, if such there was, rests in the professional acts of Respondents and not in the commodity they prescribed, fitted and sold. As to this, the jury found that the negligence of Respondents in failing to properly fit the natural curvature of Petitioner's eyes was not the proximate cause of his injury.

The judgment of the Court of Civil Appeals is affirmed.

Notes

1. Do any of the policies supporting products liability support a distinction between professional defendants and other defendants? Does it matter that a defendant is engaged in an activity that allegedly is already subject to regulation from an external source or through internal norms? Does this rationale suggest that other "industries" that are heavily regulated, such as the drug industry, should be given special treatment?

2. Aside from defendant's status as a professional, can *Barbee* be explained solely under the rationale of *Hoover,* that is, that "[t]he miscarriage, if such there was, rests in the professional acts of respondents and not in the commodity they prescribed, fitted and sold"? Would the plaintiff have been able to recover if the lens had been made from toxic material that the optometrist bought from a supplier?

Like many cases involving services, the multiplicity of issues in *Barbee* makes it difficult to know with certainty what the court's position is with respect to any one of them.

3. Should a pharmacist be strictly liable for a drug sold pursuant to a doctor's prescription? Should it matter whether the alleged defect was (a) a failure to warn of side effects, (b) improper labeling by the pharmacist, (c) an impurity in the drug due to the pharmacist's handling, (d) an impurity inserted by the manufacturer, or (e) an unforeseen danger with the drug itself? Should it matter that the pharmacist dispensed a drug without a prescription, for example by refilling a prescription when the doctor had not authorized doing so? In addition to accounting for the professional status of a pharmacist, what issues are raised by imposing product liability on a pharmacist?

On the liability of pharmacists for failure to warn, *see* note 13, *supra* page 13. On their liability in other situations, *see* Stafford v. Nipp, 502 So.2d 702 (Ala.1987) (possible warranty liability for unauthorized refill); Murphy v. E.R. Squibb & Sons, Inc., 40 Cal.3d 672, 221 Cal.Rptr. 447, 710 P.2d 247 (1985) (no product liability for injuries caused by DES if drug prescribed by physician); Vandall, Applying Strict Liability to Pharmacists, 18 Toledo L.Rev. 1 (1986).

In cases such as *Murphy,* why should the physician's prescription shield the pharmacist, but not the drug manufacturer? Can this, in turn, be reconciled with the ordinary application of product liability to retailers?

4. In Ethicon, Inc. v. Parten, 520 S.W.2d 527 (Tex.App. 1975), the court held that a doctor was not strictly liable for an injury caused by a defective needle used during treatment. In Thomas v. St. Joseph Hospital,

618 S.W.2d 791 (Tex.App. 1981), a hospital was held strictly liable for supplying a patient with a flammable gown. In Providence Hospital v. Truly, 611 S.W.2d 127 (Tex.App. 1980), a hospital was held strictly liable for providing a patient with a defective drug. Can these cases be reconciled with each other and with *Barbee*? In addition to the issue of professional services, what other issues do they raise?

Chapter 13

COMPLEX LITIGATION

Complex litigation has become a staple in the products liability arena. Mass distribution of products, design defects, the emergence of toxic substances litigation, huge discovery and informational needs, and the growth of a sophisticated, well-financed plaintiffs' bar have all contributed to this development.

With many plaintiffs harmed by the same product, means to resolve those cases in a more efficient manner become critical. Rather than individual treatment for discovery, pre-trial pleading and motions, and trial, this Chapter addresses the means for treating those cases in an *aggregative* way at each of the steps in litigation.

Notes

1. In addition to the formal legal aggregation devices surveyed in this Chapter, there are a number of informal mechanisms as well. Often, counsel who are first to develop expertise in a particular type of products liability case will represent many plaintiffs both through marketing and referrals from other lawyers. At the next stage, multiple lawyers may exchange information or even agree to work together in pursuing their claims against a product manufacturer. The American Trial Lawyers Association facilitates the exchange of information among plaintiffs' lawyers pursuing similar cases. Defense lawyers representing multiple defendants in complex litigation, such as asbestos, may enter into agreements to coordinate their efforts. The most formal of these efforts was the formation of the Center for Claims Resolution, a consortium of 20 asbestos manufacturers who pooled their efforts in defending asbestos cases against any of the members of the Center. For further elaboration of these informal efforts, see Erichson, Informal Aggregation: Procedural and Ethical Implications of Coordination Among Counsel in Related Litigation, 50 Duke L.J. 381, 386–408 (2000). The seminal coordination effort among multiple counsel occurred in the MER/29 litigation, perhaps the first mass drug products liability case, in the 1960s. Rheingold, the MER/29 Story—An Instance of Successful Mass Disaster Litigation, 56 Cal.L.Rev. 116 (1968).

2. Another informal mechanism that has attracted attention is aggregate settlements in which a lawyer for a number of similar claimants will

settle all of their cases for a lump sum. This has been most prevalent in asbestos litigation, where the judge who is presiding over the federal multi-district litigation stated: "Group settlements were and are critical to the movement of these cases." In re Joint E. & S. Dists. Asbestos Litig., 237 F.Supp.2d 297, 306 (E.D.N.Y. & S.D.N.Y. 2002) (quoting letter authored by Judge Charles Weiner). The ethical issues raised by aggregate settlements are addressed in Restatement (Third) of the Law Governing Lawyers § 128, Comment (d)(i); Silver & Baker, Mass Lawsuits and the Aggregate Settlement Rule, 32 Wake Forest L.Rev. 733 (1997). For an explanation of the reasons for and variety of aggregate settlements, see Erichson, A Typology of Aggregate Settlements, 80 Notre Dame L.Rev. 1769 (2005).

A. ISSUE PRECLUSION/COLLATERAL ESTOPPEL

Issue preclusion or collateral estoppel's potential to play a significant role in complex litigation became possible with the Supreme Court's decision in Parklane Hosiery Co. v. Shore, 439 U.S. 322, 99 S.Ct. 645, 58 L.Ed.2d 552 (1979), which sanctioned the offensive use of nonmutual collateral estoppel. This meant that plaintiffs, who were not parties to prior litigation (hence "nonmutuality" of estoppel because defendants would be unable to invoke estoppel against plaintiffs who had never previously been a party and lost) in which the defendant litigated and lost on an issue, could bar the defendant from relitigating that issue. Recall that for collateral estoppel to be invoked, regardless of mutuality, requires that: 1) the party to be estopped previously litigated and lost on the identical issue; 2) a final judgment was entered against the party; and 3) resolution of that issue was necessary to the judgment against the party. *See* Restatement (Second) of Judgments § 27.

HARDY v. JOHNS–MANVILLE SALES CORP.
United States Court of Appeals, Fifth Circuit, 1982.
681 F.2d 334.

GEE, CIRCUIT JUDGE:

This appeal arises out of a diversity action brought by various plaintiffs-insulators, pipefitters, carpenters, and other factory workers-against various manufacturers, sellers, and distributors of asbestos-containing products. * * *

Defendants' interlocutory appeal under 28 U.S.C. § 1292(b) is directed instead at the district court's amended omnibus order dated March 13, 1981, which applies collateral estoppel to this mass tort. The omnibus order is, in effect, a partial summary judgment for plaintiffs based on nonmutual offensive collateral estoppel and judicial notice derived from this court's opinion in *Borel v. Fibreboard Paper Products Corp.*, 493 F.2d 1076 (5th Cir.1973), cert. denied, 419 U.S. 869, 95 S.Ct. 127, 42 L.Ed.2d 107 (1974) (henceforth *Borel*). *Borel* was a diversity lawsuit in which manufacturers of insulation products containing asbestos were held strictly liable to an insulation worker who developed asbestosis and mesothelioma and ultimately died. The trial court construed *Borel* as establishing as a matter of law and/or of fact that: (1) insulation products containing asbestos as a generic ingredient are "unavoidably unsafe products," (2) asbestos is a competent producing cause of mesothelioma and asbestosis, (3) no warnings were issued by any asbestos insulation manufacturers prior to 1964, and (4) the "warning standard" was not met by the *Borel* defendants in the period from 1964 through 1969. * * *

In *Flatt v. Johns–Manville Sales Corp.*, 488 F. Supp. 836 (E.D.Tex. 1980), the same court outlined the elements of proof for plaintiffs in asbestos-related cases. There the court stated that the plaintiff must prove by a preponderance of the evidence that

1. Defendants manufactured, marketed, sold, distributed, or placed in the stream of commerce products containing asbestos.
2. Products containing asbestos are unreasonably dangerous.
3. Asbestos dust is a competent producing cause of mesothelioma.
4. Decedent was exposed to defendant's products.
5. The exposure was sufficient to be a producing cause of mesothelioma.
6. Decedent contracted mesothelioma.
7. Plaintiffs suffered damages.

Id. at 838, *citing Restatement (Second) of Torts* § 402A(1) (1965). The parties agree that the effect of the trial court's collateral estoppel order in this case is to foreclose elements 2 and 3 above. Under the terms of the omnibus order, both parties are precluded from presenting evidence on the "state of the art"—evidence that, under Texas law of strict liability, is considered by a jury along with other evidence in order to determine whether as of a given time warning should have been given of the dangers associated with a product placed in the stream of commerce. Under the terms of the order, the plaintiffs need not prove that the defendants either knew or should have known of the dangerous propensities of their products and therefore should have warned consumers of these dangers, defendants being precluded from showing otherwise. On appeal, the defendants contend that the order violates their rights to due process and to trial by jury. Because we conclude that the trial court abused its discretion in applying collateral estoppel and judicial notice, we reverse.

[The court concluded that federal rather than state law governs the application of collateral estoppel in this case, in which jurisdiction is based on diversity of citizenship and thus, state law provides the substantive law to be applied.]

* * *

Having determined that federal law of collateral estoppel governs, we next turn to an examination of just what that law is. In *Parklane Hosiery Co. v. Shore*, 439 U.S. 322, 99 S.Ct. 645, 58 L.Ed.2d 552 (1979), the Supreme Court was asked to determine "whether a party who has had issues of fact adjudicated adversely to it in an equitable action may be collaterally estopped from relitigating the same issues before a jury in a subsequent legal action brought against it by a new party." Id. at 324, 99 S.Ct. at 648. The Court responded affirmatively, noting offensive collateral estoppel's "dual purpose of protecting litigants from the burden of relitigating an identical issue with the same party or his privy and of promoting judicial economy by preventing needless litigation." Id. at 326, 99 S.Ct. at 649. The Court reiterated that mutuality is not necessary to proper invocation of collateral estoppel under federal law, citing *Blonder-Tongue Laboratories, Inc. v. University of Illinois Foundation*, 402 U.S. 313, 91 S.Ct. 1434, 28 L.Ed.2d 788 (1971), and further held that the use of offensive collateral estoppel does not violate a defendant's seventh amendment right to a jury trial. To avoid problems with the use of the doctrine, the Court adopted a general rule of fairness, stating "that in cases where plaintiff could easily have joined in the earlier action or where ... for other reasons, the application of offensive collateral estoppel would be unfair to a defendant, a trial judge should not allow the use of offensive collateral estoppel." [Citations]

[The court concluded that due process prohibited the use of collateral estoppel against defendants who either were not parties in *Borel* or had settled before trial in *Borel* and therefore had not been subject to an adverse judgment in that case.]

THE *BOREL* DEFENDANTS

The propriety of estopping the six defendants in this case who were parties to Borel poses more difficult questions. In ascertaining the precise preclusive effect of a prior judgment on a particular issue, we have often referred to the requirements set out, *inter alia*, in *International Association of Machinists & Aerospace Workers v. Nix*, 512 F.2d 125, 132 (5th Cir.1975), and cases cited therein. The party asserting the estoppel must show that: (1) the issue to be concluded is identical to that involved in the prior action; (2) in the prior action the issue was "actually litigated"; and (3) the determination made of the issue in the prior action must have been necessary and essential to the resulting judgment. If it appears that a judgment may have been based on more than one of several distinctive matters in litigation and there is no indication which issue it was based on or which issue was fully litigated, such judgment will not preclude, under the doctrine of collateral estoppel, relitigation of any of the issues. [Citations]

Appellants argue that *Borel* did not necessarily decide that asbestos-containing insulation products were unreasonably dangerous because of failure to warn. According to appellants, the general *Borel* verdict, based on general instructions and special interrogatories, permitted the jury to ground strict liability on the bases of failures to test, of unsafeness for intended use, of failures to inspect, or of unsafeness of the product. Strict liability on the basis of failure to warn, although argued to the jury by trial counsel for the plaintiff in *Borel*, was, in the view of the appellants, never formally presented in the jury instructions and therefore was not essential to the *Borel* jury verdict.

Appellants' view has some plausibility. The special interrogatories answered by the *Borel* jury were general and not specifically directed to failure to warn.[1] Indeed, as we discussed at length in our review of the *Borel* judgment, the jury was instructed in terms of "breach of warranty." 493 F.2d at 1091. Although the jury was accurately instructed as to "strict liability in tort" as defined in section 402A of the *Restatement (Second) of Torts*, that phrase was never specifically mentioned in the jury's interrogatories. It is also true that the general instructions to the *Borel* jury on the plaintiff's causes of action did not charge on failure to warn, except in connection with negligence.[2] Yet appellants' argument in its broadest form must ultimately fail. We concluded in *Borel*:

1. SPECIAL INTERROGATORY NO. 1: Do you find from a preponderance of the evidence that any of the Defendants listed below was negligent in any of the respects contended by Plaintiff, which negligence was a proximate cause of the injuries and death of the deceased? Answer "Yes" or "No" opposite the named defendant. (The jury answered "No" as to Pittsburgh and Armstrong and "Yes" as to the other four defendants.)

SPECIAL INTERROGATORY NO. 2: (This interrogatory submitted the question whether any of the six defendants were guilty of an act or acts of gross negligence, and the jury found that no defendant was guilty of gross negligence.)

SPECIAL INTERROGATORY NO. 3: Do you find from a preponderance of the evidence that the deceased was guilty of contributory negligence and that such negligence was a proximate cause of the injuries and death of the deceased? (The jury answered "Yes.")

SPECIAL INTERROGATORY NO. 4: Do you find from a preponderance of the evidence that the warranties as contended for by the Plaintiff were violated by any of the Defendants listed below, which breach of warranty was a proximate cause of the injuries and death of the deceased? (The jury answered "Yes" as to each defendant.)

SPECIAL INTERROGATORY NO. 5: What amount of money, if paid now in cash, would fairly and reasonably compensate the Plaintiff, Freida Borel, for the damages she sustained by virtue of the death of her husband? ANSWER: Actual damages $68,000. Damages for gross negligence "None."

2. The jury was instructed, *inter alia*, as follows:

Mrs. Borel, as the plaintiff, alleges that the defendants, each and all of them, were guilty of negligence, which negligence was the proximate cause. Now, the plaintiff contends that the defendants knew or in the exercise of ordinary or reasonable care ought to have known that the insulation they so prepared and manufactured and distributed were deleterious, poisonous and highly harmful to the deceased's body, lungs, respiratory system, skin and health, and that therefore the defendants were negligent in failing to take any reasonable precaution or exercise reasonable care to warn the deceased of the danger and the harm to which he was exposed while handling the defendants' asbestos product as an insulator.

Further, they allege that the defendants were negligent in failing and omitting to provide the deceased with the knowledge as to what would be reasonably safe and sufficient wearing apparel and proper protective equipment and appliances or method of handling or using said products so as to protect the deceased from being disabled and resulting in his death. Further, they contend that the defendants should have tested their products, especially those containing asbestos, to ascertain the safe or dangerous nature of such products before offering them for sale, that the defendants should have removed such product from the market upon ascertaining that such products would cause asbestosis. Now those are the specific acts of negligence contended for by the plaintiff.

The jury found that the unreasonably dangerous condition of the defendants' product was the proximate cause of Borel's injury. This necessarily included a finding that, had adequate warnings been provided, Borel would have chosen to avoid the danger.

493 F.2d at 1093. As the appellants at times concede in their briefs, "if *Borel* stands for any rule at all, it is that defendants have a duty to warn the users of their products of the long-term dangers attendant upon its use, including the danger of an occupational disease." Indeed, the first sentence in our *Borel* opinion states that that case involved "the scope of an asbestos manufacturer's duty to warn industrial insulation workers of dangers associated with the use of asbestos." *Id.* at 1081. See also 493 F.2d at 1105 (on rehearing). Our conclusion in *Borel* was grounded in that trial court's jury instructions concerning proximate cause and defective product, which we again set forth in the margin.[3] Close reading

Now, in this connection it is necessary for the Court to give you certain instructions in regard to the warning. As you know, one of the acts of negligence contended for by the plaintiff and perhaps the principle act of negligence is that the manufacturer should have given a warning or a proper warning to the use of its product. The Court would instruct you that a manufacturer of goods has a duty to give reasonable warning as to the dangers inherent or reasonably foreseeable in using his product. The defendants are under an obligation and duty to give reasonable warning as to the danger of their products, even if the product or products is not being used in a specific manner, so long as the use to which the product was put was a use that the manufacturer could reasonably foresee.

Also in connection with the manner of warning, the Court would instruct you that the defendants are under no duty to warn of any danger in the use of their products unless and until the state of the medical and technical knowledge was such that a reasonabl(y) prudent manufacturer would have been aware of the danger and the necessity of giving warning. Further, the defendant cannot be held responsible for failure to give warnings unless it is first established by a preponderance of the evidence that the state of the medical and technical knowledge was such that the defendants, manufacturers of the products, involved knew or in the ordinary exercise of care should have known that the manner in which their products was being handled, used and installed by insulator workers rendered them unreasonably dangerous to the user or consumer or those engaged in the installing of the product.

Now, keeping these specific acts of negligence in mind, the Court would instruct you that if you find from a preponderance of the evidence that the defendants or any one of them was guilty of any one act or omission of negligence contended for by the plaintiff and that such act of negligence was a proximate cause of the injuries and death of Mr. Borel, then you would find for the plaintiff, unless you should find for the defendant or defendants under some further instruction of the Court. The Court would further instruct you that you need not find that all of the acts or omissions of negligence as contended for by the plaintiff exist. You only have to find that some one act or omission of negligence existed from a preponderance of the evidence and which single act or omission of negligence was the proximate cause....

3. The *Borel* trial court had stated in part:

Now, turning our attention to the matter of the defenses of the defendants in connection with the implied warranty or strict liability, you are charged that if there is any unreasonable risk or danger from using defendants' products containing asbestos, which risk or danger must be the risk or danger beyond that which would be contemplated by insulation contractor or insulator with the knowledge available to them as to characteristics of the product, such unreasonable risk or danger from using defendants' product must have been reasonably foreseen by the manufacturer. Therefore, if you find from a preponderance of the evidence that Mr. Borel came in contact with the defendants' product and developed asbestosis thereafter and at such time of contact, the product containing asbestos

of these instructions convinced our panel in *Borel* that a failure to warn was necessarily implicit in the jury's verdict. While the parties invite us to reconsider our holding in *Borel* that failure to warn grounded the jury's strict liability finding in that case, we cannot, even if we were so inclined, displace a prior decision of this court absent reconsideration en banc. * * * Nonetheless, we must ultimately conclude that the judgment in *Borel* cannot estop even the *Borel* defendants in this case for three interrelated reasons.

First, after review of the issues decided in *Borel*, we conclude that *Borel*, while conclusive as to the general matter of a duty to warn on the part of manufacturers of asbestos-containing insulation products, is ultimately ambiguous as to certain key issues. As the authors of the *Restatement (Second) Judgments* § 29, comment g (1982), have noted, collateral estoppel is inappropriate where the prior judgment is ambivalent:

> The circumstances attending the determination of an issue in the first action may indicate that it could reasonably have been resolved otherwise if those circumstances were absent. Resolution of the issue in question may have entailed reference to such matters as the intention, knowledge, or comparative responsibility of the parties in relation to each other.... In these and similar situations, taking the prior determination at face value for purposes of the second action would extend the effects of imperfections in the adjudicative process beyond the limits of the first adjudication, within which they are accepted only because of the practical necessity of achieving finality.

The *Borel* jury decided that Borel, an industrial insulation worker who was exposed to fibers from his employer's insulation products over a 33-year period (from 1936 to 1969), was entitled to have been given fair

---

manufactured by the defendant and that the danger of the use of the said asbestos products by Mr. Borel could not have been reasonably foreseen by the manufacturer, then there could be no proximate cause and your verdict would be for the defendants. In other words, there would be no proximate cause of the breach of the warranty or strict liability that would justify your finding in favor of the plaintiff, but you would have to find for the defendants. Also, in connection with the implied warranty theory, you are instructed that the burden of proof is on the plaintiff in this case. Before they are entitled to recover any damages against any of the defendants to establish by a preponderance of the evidence that the product sold by the particular defendant or defendants was defective at the time it was sold. Before a product can be found to be defective it must establish that it was unreasonably dangerous to the user o(r) consumer at the time it was sold. You are further instructed that the burden of proof is on the plaintiff to establish also by a preponderance of the evidence not only that the product was defective but also that the defect in the product was a proximate cause of the death of Clarence Borel. By the term DEFECTIVE as used in this charge is meant a condition not contemplated by the insulator, contractor or ultimate user. Accordingly, you are instructed that in the event plaintiff has failed to prove by a preponderance of the evidence the existence of a defect in the product at which time the product was sold and that such defect was the proximate cause of the death of Clarence Borel, then you cannot find for the plaintiff on the theory of breach of implied warranty or strict liability and you must return a verdict against the plaintiff and in favor of the defendants. 493 F.2d at 1090 n.26 (emphasis added).

warning that asbestos dust may lead to asbestosis, mesothelioma, and other cancers. The jury dismissed the argument that the danger was obvious and regarded as conclusive the fact that Borel testified that he did not know that inhaling asbestos dust could cause serious injuries until his doctor so advised him in 1969. The jury necessarily found "that, had adequate warnings been provided, Borel would have chosen to avoid the danger." 493 F.2d at 1093. In *Borel*, the evidence was that the industry as a whole issued no warnings at all concerning its insulation products prior to 1964, that Johns–Manville placed a warnings label on packages of its products in 1964, and that Fibreboard and Rubberoid placed warnings on their products in 1966. *Id.* at 1104.

Given these facts, it is impossible to determine what the *Borel* jury decided about *when* a duty to warn attached. Did the jury find the defendants liable because their warnings after 1966, when they acknowledged that they knew the dangers of asbestosis, were insufficiently explicit as to the grave risks involved? If so, as appellants here point out, the jury may have accepted the state of the art arguments provided by the defendants in *Borel*—i.e., that the defendants were not aware of the danger of asbestosis until the 1960's. Even under this view, there is a second ambiguity: was strict liability grounded on the fact that the warnings issued, while otherwise sufficient, never reached the insulator in the field? If so, perhaps the warnings, while insufficient as to insulation workers like Borel, were sufficient to alert workers further down the production line who may have seen the warnings—such as the carpenters and pipefitters in this case. Alternatively, even if the *Borel* jury decided that failure to warn before 1966 grounded strict liability, did the duty attach in the 1930's when the "hazard of asbestosis as a pneumoconiotic dust was universally accepted," *id.* at 1083, or in 1965, when documentary evidence was presented of the hazard of asbestos insulation products to the installers of these products?

As we noted in *Borel*, strict liability because of failure to warn is based on a determination of the manufacturer's reasonable knowledge:

> [I]n cases such as the instant case, the manufacturer is held to the knowledge and skill of an expert. This is relevant in determining (1) whether the manufacturer knew or should have known the danger, and (2) whether the manufacturer was negligent in failing to communicate this superior knowledge to the user or consumer of its product.... The manufacturer's status as expert means that at a minimum he must keep abreast of scientific knowledge, discoveries, and advances and is presumed to know what is imparted thereby.

493 F.2d at 1089. Thus, the trial judge in *Borel* instructed the jury that the danger "must have been reasonably foreseen by the manufacturer." *Id.* at 1090. As both this instruction and the ambiguities in the *Borel* verdict demonstrate, a determination that a particular product is so unreasonably hazardous as to require a warning of its dangers is not an absolute. Such a determination is necessarily relative to the scientific knowledge generally known or available to the manufacturer at the time

the product in question was sold or otherwise placed in the stream of commerce.

Not all the plaintiffs in this case were exposed to asbestos-containing insulation products over the same 30–year period as plaintiff Borel. Not all plaintiffs here are insulation workers isolated from the warnings issued by some of the defendants in 1964 and 1966. Some of the products may be different from those involved in *Borel*. Our opinion in *Borel*, "limited to determining whether there (was) a conflict in substantial evidence sufficient to create a jury question," did not resolve that as a matter of fact all manufacturers of asbestos-containing insulation products had a duty to warn as of 1936, and all failed to warn adequately after 1964. Although we determined that the jury must have found a violation of the manufacturers' duty to warn, we held only that the jury could have grounded strict liability on the absence of a warning prior to 1964 or "could have concluded that the (post–1964 and post–1966) 'cautions' were not warnings in the sense that they adequately communicated to Borel and other insulation workers knowledge of the dangers to which they were exposed so as to give them a choice of working or not working with a dangerous product." 493 F.2d at 1104. As we have already had occasion to point out in *Migues v. Fibreboard Corp.*, 662 F.2d at 1188–89, * * *:

> The *only* determination made by this court in *Borel* was that, based upon the evidence in that case, the jury's findings could not be said to be incorrect as a matter of law. But this Court certainly did not decide that every jury presented with the same facts would be compelled to reach the conclusion reached by the *Borel* jury: that asbestos was unreasonably dangerous. Such a holding would have been not only unnecessary, it would also have been unwarranted.

* * *

In *Borel*, this Court said: "the jury was *entitled* to find that the danger to Borel and other insulation workers from inhaling asbestos dust was foreseeable to the defendants at the time the products causing Borel's injuries were sold," 493 F.2d at 1093 (emphasis added).... This Court did not say that, as a matter of law, the danger of asbestos inhalation was so hidden from every asbestos worker in every situation as to create a duty to warn on the part of all asbestos manufacturers. * * *. This Court did not state that every jury would be required, as a matter of law, to find such warnings inadequate.

* * *

[Citation] Like *stare decisis*, collateral estoppel applies only to issues of fact or law necessarily decided by a prior court. Since we cannot say that *Borel* necessarily decided, as a matter of fact, that all manufacturers of asbestos-containing insulation products knew or should have known of the dangers of their particular products at all relevant times, we cannot justify the trial court's collaterally estopping the defendants from presenting evidence as to the state of the art.

Even if we are wrong as to the ambiguities of the *Borel* judgment, there is a second, equally important, reason to deny collateral estoppel effect to it: the presence of inconsistent verdicts. In *Parklane Hosiery v. Shore*, 439 U.S. at 330–31, the Court noted that collateral estoppel is improper and "unfair" to a defendant "if the judgment relied upon as a basis for the estoppel is itself inconsistent with one or more previous judgments in favor of the defendant." *Id.* at 330. Accord *Restatement (Second) Judgments* § 29(4) (1982).[4] Not only does issue preclusion in such cases appear arbitrary to a defendant who has had favorable judgments on the same issue, it also undermines the premise that different juries reach equally valid verdicts. See *Restatement (Second) Judgments* § 29, comment f (1982). One jury's determination should not, merely because it comes later in time, bind another jury's determination of an issue over which there are equally reasonable resolutions of doubt.

The trial court was aware of the problem and referred to *Flatt v. Johns–Manville Sales Corp.*, 488 F. Supp. at 841, a prior opinion by the same court. In *Flatt* the court admitted that Johns–Manville had "successfully defended several asbestos lawsuits in the recent past" but stated that "lawsuits in which Johns–Manville has prevailed have been decided on the basis that there was insufficient exposure to asbestos dust, or alternatively, the plaintiff, or decedent, did not contract asbestosis or mesothelioma." *Id.* Given the information made available to us in this appeal, we must conclude that the trial court in *Flatt* and in the proceeding below was inadequately informed about the nature of former asbestos litigation. On appeal, the parties inform us that there have been approximately 70 similar asbestos cases thus far tried around the country. Approximately half of these seem to have been decided in favor of the defendants. A court able to say that the approximately 35 suits decided in favor of asbestos manufacturers were all decided on the basis of insufficient exposure on the part of the plaintiff or failure to demonstrate an asbestos-related disease would be clairvoyant. Indeed, the appellants inform us of several products liability cases in which the state of the art question was fully litigated, yet the asbestos manufacturers were found not liable. Although it is usually not possible to say with certainty what these juries based their verdicts on, in at least some of the cases the verdict for the defendant was not based on failure to prove exposure or failure to show an asbestos-related disease. In *Starnes v. Johns–Manville Corp.*, No. 2075–122 (E.D.Tenn.1977), one of the cases cited in *Flatt v. Johns–Manville Sales Corp., supra*, the court's charge to the jury stated that it was "undisputed that as a result of inhaling materials containing asbestos, Mr. Starnes contracted the disease known

---

4. The injustice of applying collateral estoppel in cases involving mass torts is especially obvious. Thus, in *Parklane* the Court cited Prof. Currie's "familiar example": "A railroad collision injures 50 passengers all of whom bring separate actions against the railroad. After the railroad wins the first 25 suits, a plaintiff wins in suit 26.

Professor Currie argues that offensive use of collateral estoppel should not be applied so as to allow plaintiffs 27 through 50 automatically to recover." 439 U.S. at 331 n.14, 99 S.Ct. at 651 n.14, *citing* Currie, *Mutuality of Estoppel: Limits of the Bernhard Doctrine*, 9 Stan.L.Rev. 281, 304 (1957).

as asbestosis." The verdict for the defendant in Starnes must mean, *inter alia*, that the jury found the insulation products involved in that case not unreasonably dangerous. This court takes judicial notice of these inconsistent or ambiguous verdicts pursuant to Fed.R.Evid. 201(d). We conclude that the court erred in arbitrarily choosing one of these verdicts, that in *Borel*, as the bellwether.

Finally, we conclude that even if the *Borel* verdict had been unambiguous and the sole verdict issued on point, application of collateral estoppel would still be unfair with regard to the *Borel* defendants because it is very doubtful that these defendants could have foreseen that their $68,000 liability to plaintiff Borel would foreshadow multimillion dollar asbestos liability. As noted in *Parklane,* it would be unfair to apply collateral estoppel "if a defendant in the first action is sued for small or nominal damages (since) he may have little incentive to defend vigorously, particularly if future lawsuits are not foreseeable." 439 U.S. at 330, 99 S.Ct. at 651. * * * The reason the district court here applied collateral estoppel is precisely because early cases like *Borel* have opened the floodgates to an enormous, unprecedented volume of asbestos litigation. According to a recent estimate, there are over 3,000 asbestos plaintiffs in the Eastern District of Texas alone and between 7,500 and 10,000 asbestos cases pending in United States District Courts around the country. The omnibus order here involves 58 pending cases, and the many plaintiffs involved in this case are each seeking.$2.5 million in damages. Such a staggering potential liability could not have been foreseen by the *Borel* defendants. [Citation]

* * *

Like the court in *Migues*, we too sympathize with the district court's efforts to streamline the enormous asbestos caseload it faces. None of what we say here is meant to cast doubt on any possible alternative ways to avoid reinventing the asbestos liability wheel. We reiterate the *Migues* court's invitation to district courts to attempt innovative methods for trying these cases. We hold today only that courts cannot read *Borel* to stand for the proposition that, as matters of fact, asbestos products are unreasonably dangerous or that asbestos as a generic element is in all products a competent producing cause of cancer. To do otherwise would be to elevate judicial expedience over considerations of justice and fair play.

REVERSED.

Notes

1. The *Hardy* court provides three reasons why collateral estoppel was improperly imposed on the *Borel* defendants and an additional reason why it was improperly applied to the non-*Borel* defendants. Do you suppose the trial judge failed to appreciate the problems with his estoppel order in *Hardy*?

2. Does the $68,000 damage award in *Borel* for a worker who suffered from asbestosis before dying from mesothelioma suggest that the outcome

may have been the result of a jury compromise? Does this undermine the legitimacy of employing collateral estoppel in future cases, aside from the problems noted by the *Hardy* court? *See* Taylor v. Hawkinson, 47 Cal.2d 893, 306 P.2d 797 (1957). Given the bar on inquiring into what went on during jury deliberations, how can courts even determine if a verdict was a compromise, much less consider whether a compromise should affect the future availability of estoppel? *Cf.* Mekdeci v. Merrell National Labs., 711 F.2d 1510 (11th Cir.1983).

3. How persuasive is the *Hardy* court's claim that defendants in *Borel* could not have foreseen substantial future asbestos litigation? *Borel* was the second asbestos case brought, and after a $68,000 damage award, defendants appealed to the Fifth Circuit Court of Appeals, petitioned for rehearing en banc, and ultimately sought certiorari from the United States Supreme Court, in a case that involved errors on state law matters, posing a very unlikely situation for the Supreme Court to grant discretionary review. Given the timing of *Parklane Hosiery*, is there a stronger claim that the *Borel* defendants could not have anticipated that they might be collaterally estopped based on that judgment in future cases? If so, should it matter?

4. What strategical considerations are created by the fact that, if plaintiff is successful in obtaining a final judgment, the potential cost to the defendant goes far beyond the actual amount of the judgment. This occurs both through the risk of future collateral estoppel as well as that the judgment may signal to other potential claimants and their lawyers that pursuing their claims may be fruitful. How would you expect the first plaintiff and defendant to respond to these considerations? For a particularly tawdry response, which involved a plaintiff's agreement to "tank" at trial and thereby suffer an adverse jury verdict in exchange for a side payment, see Potter v. Eli Lilly & Co., 926 S.W.2d 449 (Ky.1996).

5. The difficulty in finding common issues among asbestos cases serves as a caution about commonality for other aggregative procedural devices. Keep this in mind as you proceed through the remainder of the materials in this Chapter.

6. Given the decisions contrary to *Borel* referred to by the *Hardy* court, is there any hope for collateral estoppel to assist in resolving the glut of asbestos cases that choked the federal and some state courts? Or are other procedural and/or substantive rules required? How about a federal asbestos compensation scheme? *See* Trangsrud, Joinder Alternatives in Mass Tort Cases, 70 Cornell L. Rev. 779, 815 (1985) ("while offensive collateral estoppel may contribute to the fair and efficient adjudication of some cases, its limited utility in most mass tort cases makes it unsuitable as a primary technique for the management of mass tort litigations").

7. Our evaluation of the fairness of aggregative devices for resolving recurring issues in complex litigation is surely informed by our confidence that these devices provide "correct" resolutions of the disputed issues. Consider what the outcome of the trial described below tells us about finding accurate or reliable outcomes.

GREEN, THE INABILITY OF OFFENSIVE COLLATERAL ESTOPPEL TO FULFILL ITS PROMISE: AN EXAMINATION OF ESTOPPEL IN ASBESTOS LITIGATION
70 Iowa L. Rev. 141, 221–23 (1984).

An unusual trial conducted two years ago in the United States District Court for the Eastern District of Texas provides striking corroboration of the inconsistencies generated when juries are faced with the difficult, indeterminate legal standards governing asbestos cases. Five plaintiffs' cases were consolidated for trial against a total of twelve defendants. Five separate juries were impaneled, one assigned to each plaintiff's case. Each jury was present in the courtroom for all proceedings. Only questions common to all cases were tried. These included: (1) whether each of 102 products manufactured by the defendants was unreasonably dangerous by reason of design or for failure to warn; (2) whether an adequate warning was provided for any of the products; (3) the date on which the defendants should have been aware of the danger of serious illness from occupational exposure to insulation products; and (4) whether one defendant, Johns–Manville, had actual knowledge of the danger, and, if so, when, and whether continued marketing of its products in light of that knowledge constituted gross negligence.

None of the case-specific factors recognized by collateral estoppel doctrine as bearing on the reliability of the first action was present; only common questions bearing on liability were tried by the same attorneys using the same evidence in one courtroom. The judge instructed the five juries simultaneously. Each jury was given eight identical special interrogatories to answer. Four juries were given three more uniform special interrogatories bearing on Johns–Manville's liability for punitive damages. Each of the juries also had a list of the products manufactured by all defendants in that jury's case.

Despite the procedural uniformity, the juries' findings on the evaluative issues were strikingly divergent. An extensive analysis of the inconsistencies is beyond the constraints of this Article, but a brief summary is instructive. The full range of the differences (and similarities)[1] is displayed [below]. Answers to the question inquiring when an asbestos manufacturer should have had knowledge of the danger ranged from 1935 to 1965, with 1946 and two 1964's the other three findings. Three juries decided whether nine Nicolet products were defective in design; one jury found all nine were defective in design at some time, while two juries found none of the products was defective in design. Although all of the juries found at least some products were marketed at some time without adequate warnings, there was substantial disagree-

---

[1]. The one interrogatory that all five juries answered identically, not surprisingly, was whether exposure to asbestos could cause asbestosis, mesothelioma, and lung cancer. However, when the more uncertain matter of whether asbestos exposure was the sole cause of lung cancer or mesothelioma, ... was posed, divergence reappeared. Two juries found asbestos exposure was not the sole cause of lung cancer or mesothelioma; three juries found that it was....

ment as to which products required warnings, whether a subsequently provided warning was adequate, and, most significantly, the evaluative determination of whether the failure to provide an adequate warning rendered those products defective. Two juries found that all Celotex products marketed without an adequate warning were defective, one jury found that only some of the products marketed without adequate warnings were defective, and one jury found that none so marketed were defective.

The attempt to resolve the asbestos backlog in the Eastern District of Texas by conducting five simultaneous test trials failed. But the quintuplet trial did demonstrate concretely what academic speculation cannot—the vagaries and unreliability of jury determinations of the difficult evaluative issues endemic in asbestos litigation.

Jury Interrogatories	Jury 1	Jury 2	Jury 3	Jury 4	Jury 5
1. Can occupational exposure to asbestos cause:					
(a) Asbestosis	(a) Yes	(a) Yes	(a) Yes	(a) Yes	(a) Yes
(b) Mesothelioma	(b) Yes	(b) Yes	(b) Yes	(b) Yes	(b) Yes
(c) Lung Cancer?	(c) Yes	(c) Yes	(c) Yes	(c) Yes	(c) Yes
2. Is occupational exposure to asbestos the sole cause of:					
(a) Asbestosis	(a) Yes	(a) Yes	(a) Yes	(a) Yes	(a) Yes
(b) Mesothelioma	(b) Yes	(b) Yes	(b) Yes	(b) Yes	(b) Yes
(c) Lung Cancer?	(c) Yes	(c) Yes	(c) Yes	(c) Yes	(c) Yes
3. Products unreasonably dangerous due to design.	All of the products	None of the products	No answer given	Some of the products[2]	Some of the products[1]
4. Date on which the defendant should have reasonably foreseen the dangers associated with occupational exposure to asbestos products.	1946	1965	1935	1964	Jan. 1965
5. Products marketed without adequate warnings.	All of the products	Some of the products	All of the products	Some of the products[2]	Some of the products[2]
6. Did failure to provide adequate warning make the product unreasonably dangerous?	All of the products	None of the products	All of the products	Some of the products[3]	Some of the products[3]
7. Was Johns–Manville grossly negligent?	N/A	No	Yes	No	Yes

[1] Of the 102 products, Jury 4 and 5 found consistently with regard to 38 and disagreed on the remaining 64.

[2] Of the 102 products, Jury 4 and Jury 5 found consistently with regard to 13 and disagreed on the remaining 89.

[3] Because of a number of "no" answers to interrogatory number 5, Jury 5 only answered this interrogatory for 12 products; Jury 4 and Jury 5 agreed on 11 of the 12 products that they both made findings on.

B. MULTIDISTRICT LITIGATION

28 U.S.C. § 1407

§ 1407. Multidistrict litigation

(a) When civil actions involving one or more common questions of fact are pending in different districts, such actions may be transferred to any district for coordinated or consolidated pretrial proceedings. Such transfers shall be made by the judicial panel on multidistrict litigation authorized by this section upon its determination that transfers for such proceedings will be for the convenience of parties and witnesses and will promote the just and efficient conduct of such actions. Each action so transferred shall be remanded by the panel at or before the conclusion of such pretrial proceedings to the district from which it was transferred unless it shall have been previously terminated: Provided, however, that the panel may separate any claim, cross-claim, counter-claim, or third-party claim and remand any of such claims before the remainder of the action is remanded.

(b) Such coordinated or consolidated pretrial proceedings shall be conducted by a judge or judges to whom such actions are assigned by the judicial panel on multidistrict litigation. * * *

(c) Proceedings for the transfer of an action under this section may be initiated by—

(i) the judicial panel on multidistrict litigation upon its own initiative, or

(ii) motion filed with the panel by a party in any action in which transfer for coordinated or consolidated pretrial proceedings under this section may be appropriate. * * *

* * *

IN RE SILICONE GEL BREAST IMPLANTS PRODUCTS LIABILITY LITIGATION

Judicial Panel on Multidistrict Litigation, 1992.
793 F.Supp. 1098.

OPINION AND ORDER

The record before us suggests that more than a million women have received silicone gel breast implants. Since the Food and Drug Administration held highly publicized hearings a few months ago about the safety of this product, a rush to the courthouse has ensued, although some litigation concerning the product has periodically been filed in the federal courts in the last several years.

This litigation presently consists of * * * 78 actions * * * pending in 33 federal districts * * *.*

Before the Panel are four separate motions pursuant to 28 U.S.C. § 1407: 1) motion of plaintiffs in three Northern District of California actions to centralize all actions in the Northern District of California or any other appropriate transferee forum (these plaintiffs now favor centralization in the Southern District of Ohio); 2) motion of plaintiffs in one Northern District of California action to centralize all actions in that

---

* Four federal districts, in Florida, California, Colorado, and New York, accounted for 33 of the actions. No other district had as many as 5 suits, and there were none in the Northern District of Alabama.–Eds.

district; 3) motion of plaintiffs in seven actions to centralize all actions in either the Northern District of California or the District of Kansas; and 4) motion of plaintiffs in the Eastern District of Virginia action (*Schiavone*) to centralize in that district the medical monitoring claims that are presented in seven purported class actions.[1]

The overwhelming majority of the more than 200 responses received by the Panel supports transfer. The major issue presented in the responses is selection of the transferee forum, with two large groups of parties aligned in favor of opposing views. The first large group of parties favors selection of either the Northern District of California (Judge Thelton E. Henderson or Judge Marilyn H. Patel) or the District of Kansas (Judge Patrick F. Kelly). This group includes 1) plaintiffs in at least 65 of the 78 actions before the Panel; 2) plaintiffs in at least 69 potential tag-along actions; and 3) approximately 250 attorneys who are purportedly investigating claims of more than 2,000 potential plaintiffs. The second large group of parties favors selection of the Southern District of Ohio (Judge Carl B. Rubin). This group includes 1) plaintiffs in nine of the 78 actions before the Panel; 2) plaintiffs in at least nine potential tag-along actions; 3) approximately 75 law firms that purport to represent 4,000 actual and potential plaintiffs; and 4) sixteen defendants, including major silicone gel breast implant manufacturers Dow Corning Corporation (Dow Corning), Baxter Healthcare Corporation, McGhan Medical Corporation (McGhan), Bristol-Meyers Squibb Company and Mentor Corporation (Mentor).

Miscellaneous responses received by the Panel include i) opposition of plaintiff in one Colorado action to transfer of her action (*Reid*), ii) opposition of defendant General Electric Company to transfer of the four actions in which it is a party, iii) opposition of plaintiffs in four potential tag-along actions to transfer of their actions, and iv) support of plaintiffs in one action for the motion of the *Schiavone* plaintiffs.

On the basis of the papers filed and the hearing held, the Panel finds that the actions in this litigation involve common questions of fact and that centralization under Section 1407 in the Northern District of Alabama before Chief Judge Sam C. Pointer, Jr., will best serve the convenience of the parties and witnesses and promote the just and efficient conduct of this litigation. The actions present complex common questions of fact, as nearly all responding parties have acknowledged, on the issue of liability for allegedly defective silicone gel breast implants. Centralization under Section 1407 is thus necessary in order to avoid duplication of discovery, prevent inconsistent pretrial rulings, and conserve the resources of the parties, their counsel and the judiciary.

---

1. The Section 1407 motions before the Panel included [several] additional actions that are not appropriate for inclusion in centralized pretrial proceedings. * * * One Northern District of Illinois action—*Mindy Saperstein, etc. v. Bristol-Meyers Company, et al.*, C.A. No. 92-C-0743-has been remanded to state court. Two Northern District of California actions—*Maria Stern v. Dow Corning*, C.A. No. C-83-2348-MHP; and *Mariann Hopkins v. Dow Corning Corporation, et al.*, C.A. No. C-88-4703-TEH, 1991 WL 328043—have already been tried.

We are not persuaded by various parties' requests for exclusion of certain actions or claims or for creation of a separate multidistrict litigation to handle medical monitoring claims. We point out that transfer under Section 1407 has the salutary effect of placing all actions in this docket before a single judge who can formulate a pretrial program that: 1) allows discovery with respect to any non-common issues to proceed concurrently with discovery on common issues, *In re Multi–Piece Rim Products Liability Litigation*, 464 F.Supp. 969, 974 (J.P.M.L. 1979); and 2) ensures that pretrial proceedings will be conducted in a manner leading to the just and expeditious resolution of all actions to the overall benefit of the parties. It may be, on further refinement of the issues and close scrutiny by the transferee judge, that some claims or actions can be remanded in advance of the other actions in the transferee district. But we are unwilling, on the basis of the record before us, to make such a determination at this time. Should the transferee judge deem remand of any claims or actions appropriate, procedures are available whereby this may be accomplished with a minimum of delay. *See* Rule 14, R.P.J.P.M.L., 120 F.R.D. 251, 259–61 (1988).

Selection of the transferee court and judge for this litigation has been a challenging task. The parties' arguments in their briefs and at the Panel hearing in this matter have focused primarily on the relative merits of the suggested California and Ohio forums. Proponents of the California forum stress that i) both Judge Henderson and Judge Patel have tried breast implant actions and are thus very familiar with the issues raised in this docket, ii) several implant manufacturers, including McGhan and Mentor, have their principal places of business in California, and iii) California is presumptively the state with the largest number of actual and potential claimants in the breast implant litigation. Meanwhile, proponents of the Ohio forum emphasize Judge Rubin's familiarity with the litigation, gained by presiding over the consolidated breast implant action (*Dante*) in his district since January 1992. During that time, Judge Rubin has conditionally certified a nationwide, opt-out class of breast implant recipients; established a document depository; appointed a Plaintiffs' Lead Counsel Committee consisting of seven members; scheduled trial on common issues for June 1993; and initiated the dissemination of notice to class members.

We observe that either the Northern District of California or the Southern District of Ohio could be an appropriate forum for this docket and certainly the judges referred to are experienced and well-qualified to handle this litigation. We are troubled, however, by the volume and tone of the negative arguments with which opposing counsel have sought to denigrate each other's forum choices, litigation strategies and underlying motives. A brief recitation of a few of these arguments sufficiently conveys their flavor. For example, various parties argue that 1) parties in the Ohio forum have engendered a flurry of pretrial activity in an effort to dictate our decision on selection of the transferee court; 2) the class in the Southern District of Ohio was certified in a precipitous fashion, without according adequate notice or opportunity to be heard to interested parties nationwide; 3) defendants oppose the California forum only because the two trials there resulted in substantial verdicts against one of them; and 4) the plaintiffs who favor the California forum are forum shopping for a judge who has tried a breast implant action in which plaintiffs prevailed.

Essentially, these arguments are fueled by an acrimonious dispute among counsel, relating to control of the litigation as well as to how it should proceed (class versus individual treatment). It is neither our function nor our inclination to take sides in this dispute. But we are indeed persuaded that the level of acrimony has caused the parties and counsel on each side to harbor a perception that they would be unfairly affected by selection of any of the suggested forums. This perception of "unfairness" is unwarranted, because this Panel believes that all of the federal judges involved in these 78 actions would conduct these proceedings in a fair and impartial manner. Nevertheless, we recognize that in a mega-tort docket of this nature, involving claimants who may be experiencing litigation for the first time, such a perception could become a dark cloud over these proceedings and threaten their just and efficient conduct.

In light of these considerations, we have determined to look beyond the preferences of the parties in our search for a transferee judge with the ability and temperament to steer this complex litigation on a steady course that will be sensitive to the concerns of all parties. Because no single location stands out as the geographic focal point for this nationwide docket, the scope of our search embraced the universe of federal district judges. By selecting Chief Judge Pointer, a former member of our Panel, Chairman of the Board of Editors of the Manual for Complex Litigation, Chairman of the Judicial Conference's Advisory Committee on Civil Rules, and an experienced multidistrict transferee judge, we are confident that we are entrusting this important and challenging assignment to a distinguished jurist. We urge all parties and counsel to work cooperatively with one another and with Judge Pointer toward the goal of a just, efficient and expeditious resolution of the litigation.

IT IS THEREFORE ORDERED that, pursuant to 28 U.S.C. § 1407, the actions listed on the following Schedule A be, and the same hereby are, transferred to the Northern District of Alabama and, with the consent of that court, assigned to the Honorable Sam C. Pointer, Jr., for coordinated or consolidated pretrial proceedings.

* * *

Notes

1. Why might a "bit" defendant like General Electric oppose consolidation of the four cases in which it was involved in the multidistrict proceeding?

2. If consolidated discovery is to take place, some decision will have to be made as to who, among the various plaintiffs' counsel, will conduct

various aspects of discovery. Normally the transferee judge appoints a lead and liaison counsel; often a plaintiffs' steering committee is appointed as well, as the Panel mentions had already occurred in the class action certified in the Southern District of Ohio. If the cases are then returned to the transferor districts where they began, how will lead and liaison counsel be paid for their work on consolidated discovery? *See* Federal Judicial Center, Manual for Complex Litigation § 22.927, at 461–63 (4th ed.2004). Is the dispute referred to by the Panel over whether the litigation should proceed through class or individual treatment relevant to this question?

3. Despite the admonition in § 1407 that, when pretrial is completed, cases shall be returned to their home districts for trial, many transferree courts employed the statutory forum non conveniens statute, 28 U.S.C § 1404, to transfer all multidistrict cases from their home districts to the transferree district for all purposes, including trial. The Supreme Court put a stop to that practice in Lexecon Inc. v. Milberg Weiss Bershad Hynes & Lerach, 523 U.S. 26, 118 S.Ct. 956, 140 L.Ed.2d 62 (1998), holding that the transferree court may not invoke § 1404(a) to transfer the cases to itself for trial. Nevertheless, final resolution of multidistrict cases may occur before they are transferred for trial by pretrial motion, such as by summary judgment, or settlement.

4. Section 1407 obviously cannot provide universal pretrial procedures for all related cases because it does not include state court cases. Cases filed in state court that are not removable, either because the plaintiff and the manufacturer are not diverse or, as occurs when plaintiff wants to keep the case in state court, a local defendant, such as a retailer or physician, is joined as a defendant, remain outside the ambit of § 1407. Nevertheless, beginning with asbestos litigation, state and federal MDL judges have developed a number of informal cooperative strategies, including even sitting jointly to hear motions that are common to both the state and federal cases. *See* Federal Judicial Center, National Center for State Courts & State Justice Institute, Manual for Cooperation Between State and Federal Courts (1997); McGovern, Toward a Cooperative Strategy for Federal and State Judges in Mass Tort Litigation, 148 U.Pa.L.Rev. 1867 (2000).

In 2002, the federal Multiparty, Multiforum Trial Jurisdiction Act of 2002 (MMTJA), 28 U.S.C. § 1369 was enacted. The MMTJA expands federal jurisdiction in a narrow class of mass accident cases. A condition for federal jurisdiction pursuant to the Act is that 75 persons die in an an accident that occurs in a discrete location. Because of the requirement of 75 deaths in a single accident, the Act is likely to be limited to a small of group of accidents such as commercial air crashes. Litigation over a tragic fire in a nightclub in Rhode Island known as The Station spawned the most extensive consideration of the scope of MMTJA's jurisdictional provisions to date. See Passa v. Derderian, 308 F.Supp.2d 43 (D.R.I.2004).

C. CLASS ACTIONS

When the modern class action rules were written in 1966, they were conceived of as a device for effectuating litigation. Small claims, that were not individually viable because the costs of litigating them would not justify the small or modest stakes, were the target, at least for Rule 23(b)(3) class actions. Rule 23 reveals a clear preference for individual litigation, except where there are good reasons for deviating. In addition to favoring individual litigation, the Advisory Committee comments in 1966 reveal that the class action device was thought unsuitable for mass torts:

> A "mass accident" resulting in injuries to numerous persons is ordinarily not appropriate for a class action because of the likelihood that significant questions, not only of damages but of liability and defenses of liability, would be present, affecting the individuals in different ways. In these circumstances an action conducted nominally as a class action would degenerate in practice into multiple lawsuits separately tried.

Fed. R. Civ. P. 23 advisory committee notes (1966).

Notwithstanding the advisory committee's view, the quantity of cases in a number of mass torts and the efforts of a number of plaintiffs' attorneys, beginning with the Beverly Hills Supper Club litigation, In re Beverly Hills Fire Litigation, 695 F.2d 207 (6th Cir.1982), has caused a rethinking of the propriety of class action treatment of large-scale products liability litigation.

Rule 23. Class Actions

(a) Prerequisites to a Class Action. One or more members of a class may sue or be sued as representative parties on behalf of all only if

> (1) the class is so numerous that joinder of all members is impracticable,
>
> (2) there are questions of law or fact common to the class,
>
> (3) the claims or defenses of the representative parties are typical of the claims or defenses of the class, and
>
> (4) the representative parties will fairly and adequately protect the interests of the class.

(b) Class Actions Maintainable. An action may be maintained as a class action if the prerequisites of subdivision (a) are satisfied, and in addition:

> (1) the prosecution of separate actions by or against individual members of the class would create a risk of
>
>> (A) inconsistent or varying adjudications with respect to individual members of the class which would establish incompatible standards of conduct for the party opposing the class, or
>>
>> (B) adjudications with respect to individual members of the class which would as a practical matter be dispositive of the interests of the other members not parties to the adjudications or substantially impair or impede their ability to protect their interests; or
>
> (2) the party opposing the class has acted or refused to act on grounds generally applicable to the class, thereby making appro-

priate final injunctive relief or corresponding declaratory relief with respect to the class as a whole; or

(3) the court finds that the questions of law or fact common to the members of the class predominate over any questions affecting only individual members, and that a class action is superior to other available methods for the fair and efficient adjudication of the controversy. The matters pertinent to the findings include: (A) the interest of members of the class in individually controlling the prosecution or defense of separate actions; (B) the extent and nature of any litigation concerning the controversy already commenced by or against members of the class; (C) the desirability or undesirability of concentrating the litigation of the claims in the particular forum; (D) the difficulties likely to be encountered in the management of a class action.

(c) Determining by Order Whether to Certify a Class Action; Appointing Class Counsel; Notice and Membership in Class; Judgment; Multiple Classes and Subclasses.

(1) (A) When a person sues or is sued as a representative of a class, the court must—at an early practicable time—determine by order whether to certify the action as a class action.

(B) An order certifying a class action must define the class and the class claims, issues, or defenses, and must appoint class counsel under Rule 23(g).

(C) An order under Rule 23(c)(1) may be altered or amended before final judgment.

(2) (A) For any class certified under Rule 23(b)(1) or (2), the court may direct appropriate notice to the class.

(B) For any class certified under Rule 23(b)(3), the court must direct to class members the best notice practicable under the circumstances, including individual notice to all members who can be identified through reasonable effort. The notice must concisely and clearly state in plain, easily understood language:

- the nature of the action,
- the definition of the class certified,
- the class claims, issues, or defenses,
- that a class member may enter an appearance through counsel if the member so desires,
- that the court will exclude from the class any member who requests exclusion, stating when and how members may elect to be excluded, and
- the binding effect of a class judgment on class members under Rule 23(c)(3).

(3) The judgment in an action maintained as a class action under subdivision (b)(1) or (b)(2), whether or not favorable to the class,

shall include and describe those whom the court finds to be members of the class. The judgment in an action maintained as a class action under subdivision (b)(3), whether or not favorable to the class, shall include and specify or describe those to whom the notice provided in subdivision (c)(2) was directed, and who have not requested exclusion, and whom the court finds to be members of the class.

(4) When appropriate (A) an action may be brought or maintained as a class action with respect to particular issues, or (B) a class may be divided into subclasses and each subclass treated as a class, and the provisions of this rule shall then be construed and applied accordingly.

(d) Orders in Conduct of Actions. In the conduct of actions to which this rule applies, the court may make appropriate orders: (1) determining the course of proceedings or prescribing measures to prevent undue repetition or complication in the presentation of evidence or argument; (2) requiring, for the protection of the members of the class or otherwise for the fair conduct of the action, that notice be given in such manner as the court may direct to some or all of the members of any step in the action, or of the proposed extent of the judgment, or of the opportunity of members to signify whether they consider the representation fair and adequate, to intervene and present claims or defenses, or otherwise to come into the action; (3) imposing conditions on the representative parties or on intervenors; (4) requiring that the pleadings be amended to eliminate therefrom allegations as to representation of absent persons, and that the action proceed accordingly; (5) dealing with similar procedural matters. The orders may be combined with an order under Rule 16, and may be altered or amended as may be desirable from time to time.

(e) Settlement, Voluntary Dismissal, or Compromise.

(1) (A) The court must approve any settlement, voluntary dismissal, or compromise of the claims, issues, or defenses of a certified class.

(B) The court must direct notice in a reasonable manner to all class members who would be bound by a proposed settlement, voluntary dismissal, or compromise.

(C) The court may approve a settlement, voluntary dismissal, or compromise that would bind class members only after a hearing and on finding that the settlement, voluntary dismissal, or compromise is fair, reasonable, and adequate.

(2) The parties seeking approval of a settlement, voluntary dismissal, or compromise under Rule 23(e)(1) must file a statement identifying any agreement made in connection with the proposed settlement, voluntary dismissal, or compromise.

(3) In an action previously certified as a class action under Rule 23(b)(3), the court may refuse to approve a settlement unless it affords a new opportunity to request exclusion to individual class

members who had an earlier opportunity to request exclusion but did not do so.

(4) (A) Any class member may object to a proposed settlement, voluntary dismissal, or compromise that requires court approval under Rule 23(e)(1)(A).

(B) An objection made under Rule 23(e)(4)(A) may be withdrawn only with the court's approval.

(f) Appeals. A court of appeals may in its discretion permit an appeal from an order of a district court granting or denying class action certification under this rule if application is made to it within ten days after entry of the order. An appeal does not stay proceedings in the district court unless the district judge or the court of appeals so orders.

(g) Class Counsel.

(1) Appointing Class Counsel.

(A) Unless a statute provides otherwise, a court that certifies a class must appoint class counsel.

(B) An attorney appointed to serve as class counsel must fairly and adequately represent the interests of the class.

(C) In appointing class counsel, the court

(i) must consider:

- the work counsel has done in identifying or investigating potential claims in the action,
- counsel's experience in handling class actions, other complex litigation, and claims of the type asserted in the action,
- counsel's knowledge of the applicable law, and
- the resources counsel will commit to representing the class;

(ii) may consider any other matter pertinent to counsel's ability to fairly and adequately represent the interests of the class;

(iii) may direct potential class counsel to provide information on any subject pertinent to the appointment and to propose terms for attorney fees and nontaxable costs; and

(iv) may make further orders in connection with the appointment.

(2) Appointment Procedure.

(A) The court may designate interim counsel to act on behalf of the putative class before determining whether to certify the action as a class action.

(B) When there is one applicant for appointment as class counsel, the court may appoint that applicant only if the applicant is adequate under Rule 23(g)(1)(B) and (C). If more than one adequate applicant seeks appointment as class counsel, the court must appoint the applicant best able to represent the interests of the class.

(C) The order appointing class counsel may include provisions about the award of attorney fees or nontaxable costs under Rule 23(h).

(h) *Attorney Fees Award.* In an action certified as a class action, the court may award reasonable attorney fees and nontaxable costs authorized by law or by agreement of the parties as follows:

(1) *Motion for Award of Attorney Fees.* A claim for an award of attorney fees and nontaxable costs must be made by motion under Rule 54(d)(2), subject to the provisions of this subdivision, at a time set by the court. Notice of the motion must be served on all parties and, for motions by class counsel, directed to class members in a reasonable manner.

(2) *Objections to Motion.* A class member, or a party from whom payment is sought, may object to the motion.

(3) *Hearing and Findings.* The court may hold a hearing and must find the facts and state its conclusions of law on the motion under Rule 52(a).

(4) *Reference to Special Master or Magistrate Judge.* The court may refer issues related to the amount of the award to a special master or to a magistrate judge as provided in Rule 54(d)(2)(D).

Note

1. In Eisen v. Carlisle & Jacquelin, 417 U.S. 156, 94 S.Ct. 2140, 40 L.Ed.2d 732 (1974), a securities fraud case, the Court reversed the decision of the trial judge to impose 90 percent of the cost of providing notice to class members required by Rule 23(c)(2) on defendants. The trial court entered the order after making a preliminary determination that plaintiffs were likely to prevail on the merits. The Supreme Court explained that courts were not to consider the merits of the claims made by a class action plaintiff in deciding whether to certify the class:

> We find nothing in either the language or history of Rule 23 that gives a court any authority to conduct a preliminary inquiry into the merits of a suit in order to determine whether it may be maintained as a class action. Indeed, such a procedure contravenes the Rule by allowing a representative plaintiff to secure the benefits of a class action without first satisfying the requirements for it. He is thereby allowed to obtain a determination on the merits of the claims advanced on behalf of the class without any assurance that a class action may be maintained. This procedure is directly contrary to the command of subdivision (c)(1) that the court determine whether a suit denominated a class action may be maintained as such "as soon as practicable after the commencement of [the] action...." In short, we agree with Judge Wisdom's conclusion in Miller v. Mackey International, 452 F.2d 424 (C.A.5 1971), where the court rejected a preliminary inquiry into the merits of a proposed class action:
>
>> "In determining the propriety of a class action, the question is not whether the plaintiff or plaintiffs have stated a cause of action or

will prevail on the merits, but rather whether the requirements of Rule 23 are met."

417 U.S. at 177, 94 S. Ct. at 2152, 40 L. Ed.2d at 748.

Does *Eisen's* insistence that trial judges blind themselves to the merits of the underlying claim make good sense? What are the consequences of such a rule? For critiques of *Eisen*, see Bone & Evans, Class Certification and the Substantive Merits, 51 Duke L.J. 1251 (2002); McGuire, The Death Knell for *Eisen:* Why the Class Action Analysis Should Include an Assessment of the Merits, 168 F.R.D. 366 (1996).

VALENTINO v. CARTER–WALLACE, INC.

United States Court of Appeals, Ninth Circuit, 1996.
97 F.3d 1227.

SCHROEDER, CIRCUIT JUDGE:

This is an interlocutory appeal from a district court order under Fed.R.Civ.P. 23 conditionally certifying a nationwide plaintiff class and subclass in a products liability case against the manufacturer of a drug used for the treatment of epilepsy. The jurisdiction of the district court was grounded on diversity, and our jurisdiction is pursuant to certification under 28 U.S.C. § 1292(b).

The drug in question, known as Felbatol, is manufactured by defendants Carter–Wallace, Inc. and Wallace Laboratories (Carter–Wallace). Carter–Wallace began marketing the drug in August 1993 without giving any special warning of serious side effects. Between January 1994 and July 1994, Carter–Wallace received reports that some patients had developed aplastic anemia following use of the drug.[1] In August 1994, Carter–Wallace mailed letters to the physician community warning them of this risk. By September 1994, Carter–Wallace had also received reports of liver failure in connection with use of the drug. Again, Carter–Wallace mailed letters to the physician community warning them of this risk.

The district court determined that the prerequisites of Fed.R.Civ.P. 23(a) had been met. The district court conditionally certified a plaintiff class consisting of "all persons who began using Felbatol prior to August 1, 1994." The district court also certified a "serious injury" subclass, defined as "all persons within the Felbatol user class who have developed or will develop aplastic anemia or liver failure, as a result of using Felbatol."

Pursuant to Fed.R.Civ.P. 23(c)(4)(A), the district court limited class certification to the issues of strict liability, negligence, failure to warn, breach of implied and express warranty, causation in fact, and liability for punitive damages. The district court stated that "with respect to these particular issues, common questions of law and/or fact predominate over any questions affecting only individual members and a class

---

[1]. Aplastic anemia is a disease which interferes with the bone marrow's ability to produce blood cells, resulting in a decrease in blood cell counts.

action is superior to other available methods for adjudication of the controversy." The court's order thus echoed the preponderance and superiority requirements of Fed.R.Civ.P. 23(b)(3). The court specifically excluded the individual issues of proximate causation, compensatory damages, and the amount of punitive damages from certification.

In its certification order, the court did not discuss whether the adjudication of the certified issues would significantly advance the resolution of the underlying case, thereby achieving judicial economy and efficiency. Nor did the court discuss any alternative methods for adjudicating these claims.

According to the named plaintiffs, during the brief period involved in this litigation the drug was prescribed to over 100,000 patients, who were told that the drug was unlike other anti-epilepsy drugs in that this one had few adverse side effects. Plaintiffs claim that over 3,000 people have reported some adverse reactions from the drug to the United States Food & Drug Administration, and there have been over seventy reported cases of aplastic anemia or liver damage, including nearly twenty reported deaths. Withdrawal from the drug has also been difficult for many patients.

Plaintiffs contend, with considerable justification, that because the case involves only one manufacturer, only one product, only one marketing program, and a relatively short period of time, the case is more manageable for class action purposes than cases that involve multiple manufacturers, multiple products, multiple marketing programs, and a long period of time. It appears undisputed that the claims of all members of the class will raise some common issues concerning the knowledge and conduct of Carter–Wallace. Apparently, in recognition of these common issues, the Judicial Panel on Multidistrict Litigation (JPML) has consolidated pretrial proceedings in all federal Felbatol cases and transferred them to the Northern District of California.

Carter–Wallace argues, with at least equal justification, that the existence of common issues of law or fact is a necessary but not the sole requirement for class certification, and that the class certified here does not meet other Rule 23 requirements. Carter–Wallace places particular stress on the Rule 23(b)(3) requirements that the common issues of fact predominate over individual issues and that the class action be superior to other methods of adjudicating the claims. Specifically, Carter–Wallace contends that the numerous adverse reactions of each plaintiff are intertwined with the certified liability issues, and that the law on each liability theory varies widely from state to state. Additionally, Carter–Wallace notes that the problems with the numerous adverse reactions affect the Rule 23(a) prerequisites of typicality and adequacy of representation in that the drug has had a variety of different effects on different people and further, that the class does not contain any representative who has allegedly developed aplastic anemia from taking the drug. Carter–Wallace also contends that class adjudication will be unmanageable and inefficient and that alternative, superior methods of adjudication exist.

Carter–Wallace's threshold contention in this appeal is, however, even more sweeping. It is that, regardless of any specific problems with this particular certification, class certification is never appropriate for multi-state plaintiffs asserting personal injury claims against manufacturers of drugs and medical devices. Carter–Wallace cites this circuit's opinion in *In re Northern Dist. of California, Dalkon Shield IUD Prods. Liab. Litig. (Dalkon Shield)*, 693 F.2d 847, 854–55 (9th Cir.1982), *cert. denied*, 459 U.S. 1171, 103 S.Ct. 817, 74 L.Ed.2d 1015 (1983), and recent cases from other circuits to support its broadside attack. [Citations] Our review of the record suggests that a principal reason why the district court entered twin certifications, first to create class litigation, and then to secure appellate review of that creation, was to obtain a ruling from this court on whether the law of this circuit supports Carter–Wallace's threshold position.

We hold that the law of this circuit, and more specifically our leading decision in Dalkon Shield, does not create any absolute bar to the certification of a multi-state plaintiff class action in the medical products liability context. We decline to hold, at least at this early stage of the litigation, that there can never be a plaintiff class certification in this particular case. We do hold, however, on the basis of the record before us, that we must vacate this class certification order, because there has been no demonstration of how this class satisfies important Rule 23 requirements, including the predominance of common issues over individual issues and the superiority of class adjudication over other litigation alternatives.

ANALYSIS

I. CLASS ACTIONS IN PRODUCTS LIABILITY LITIGATION

* * * The lead decision in this circuit was handed down in 1982 and vacated a nationwide punitive damages class and a statewide compensatory liability class of persons who had used allegedly defective intrauterine contraceptive devices. *In re Northern Dist. of California, Dalkon Shield IUD Prods. Liab. Litig.*, 693 F.2d 847 (9th Cir.1982), *cert. denied*, 459 U.S. 1171, 103 S.Ct. 817, 74 L.Ed.2d 1015 (1983).

In rejecting the nationwide class certification under Rule 23(b)(1)(B), we were clearly troubled in Dalkon Shield by the problems that would arise in endeavoring to apply the varying punitive damage standards of fifty different jurisdictions. We did not, however, hold this commonality obstacle fatal. *Id.* at 850. There was in *Dalkon Shield* the added problem that no plaintiff, and no plaintiff's lawyer, had agreed to represent the class so that the requirements of typicality and adequacy of representation could not be satisfied. *Id.* at 850–51.

In considering the certification of the California liability class under Rule 23(b)(3), we commented in *Dalkon Shield* on the problems presented by products liability actions where, unlike the mass tort involving a single catastrophic event such as an airplane crash or cruise ship food poisoning, "no single happening or accident occurs to cause similar types of physical harm or property damage." *Id.* at 853. We also discussed the inherent difficulties of proving proximate cause and a breach of a duty of care under a negligence theory, where there are different types of injuries and multiple defendants. *Id.* at 854–55. We were further troubled by the requirement that common issues predominate over individual issues in a certification of an entire case for class treatment; it appeared that only the underlying facts raised a common nucleus of issues, while the liability questions included highly individualized issues of damages and proximate cause. *Id.* at 856. Finally, we held that class adjudication would not be superior to individualized litigation given: first, the lack of any showing that class adjudication would save time or expense, and second, the management difficulties caused by the complexity and multiplicity of issues as well as the plaintiffs' hostility to the class action. *Id.*

We were careful in *Dalkon Shield*, however, not to preclude the future certification of more limited classes or subclasses pursuant to Rule 23(b)(3), or to rule out the possibility of broader class action certification in other products liability cases. *See id.* at 852–54, 856. Although *Dalkon Shield* pointed out many of the problems common to products liability litigation in meeting Rule 23's class certification requirements, we cannot conclude that *Dalkon Shield* creates an absolute bar to such certification in this circuit. As leading commentators have pointed out, the case was unusual in that there was simply no plaintiff or plaintiff's counsel ready, willing, and able to represent the class. [Citation] In addition, *Dalkon Shield* involved multiple defendants and multiple marketing schemes, unlike the present case where a single manufacturer marketed one drug over a limited period of time. *Compare Dalkon Shield*, 693 F.2d at 856 (holding district court erroneously certified class where manufacturer advertised in various medical journals and trade-show advertisements to different doctors), *with In re Copley Pharmaceutical*, 158 F.R.D. 485, 487, 491–93 (D.Wyo.1994) (certifying class where one manufacturer marketed four contaminated batches of one prescription drug).

The leading cases in other circuits in which class certifications have been approved are the "Agent Orange" litigation in the Second Circuit and the "School Asbestos" litigation in the Third Circuit. *See In re "Agent Orange" Prods. Liab. Litig.*, 818 F.2d 145 (2d Cir.1987), *cert. denied*, 484 U.S. 1004, 108 S.Ct. 695, 98 L.Ed.2d 648 (1988); *In re School Asbestos Litig.*, 789 F.2d 996 (3d Cir.), *cert. denied*, 479 U.S. 852, 107 S.Ct. 182, 93 L.Ed.2d 117, and *cert. denied*, 479 U.S. 915, 107 S.Ct. 318, 93 L.Ed.2d 291 (1986). Those cases also had some unique features.

In *Agent Orange*, the Second Circuit made it quite clear that the common issue in that case that caused class litigation to be both appropriate and superior to other forms of litigation was the common existence of a government contractor defense.

In our view, class certification was justified under Rule 23(b)(3) due to the centrality of the military contractor defense. First, this defense is common to all of the plaintiffs' cases, and thus satisfies the commonality requirement of Rule 23(a)(2). Second, because the military contractor defense is of central importance ... this issue is governed by federal law, and a class trial in a federal court is a method of adjudication superior to the alternatives. If the defense succeeds, the entire litigation is disposed of. If it fails, it will not be an issue in the subsequent individual trials. In that event, moreover, the ground for its rejection, such as a failure to warn the government of a known hazard, might well be dispositive of relevant factual issues in those trials.

Agent Orange, 818 F.2d at 166–67 (citations omitted).

In *School Asbestos*, the plaintiffs were school districts seeking compensation for property damages, not for personal injuries. The Third Circuit viewed that class action as much more manageable than a personal injury case would have been because, in essence, the effect of asbestos in different buildings is the same and the effect of asbestos on different people is not. *See School Asbestos*, 789 F.2d at 1010–11.

A leading decision in the Seventh Circuit has recently cast a pall on the future of class action certifications in products liability cases in that circuit. *See In re Rhone–Poulenc Rorer, Inc.*, 51 F.3d 1293 (7th Cir.), *cert. denied*, 133 L.Ed.2d 122, 116 S.Ct. 184 (1995); see also Castano v. American Tobacco Co., 84 F.3d 734 (5th Cir.1996) (decertifying national class of all nicotine-dependent persons, and expressing approval of *Rhone-Poulenc*). The Seventh Circuit in *Rhone-Poulenc* issued a writ of mandamus ordering the district court to decertify a class of plaintiff hemophiliacs who were allegedly infected by the human immunodeficiency virus (HIV) as a result of using blood solids manufactured by the defendants. The Seventh Circuit majority was heavily influenced by at least three factors. [The court discussed the three objections raised by the *Rhone-Poulenc* opinion, which is provided later in this Chapter. The objections included that the merits of the substantive claims being asserted were weak, that despite the insubstantiality of the claims, the potential damages if the class were successful would be so enormous as to impose enormous pressure on the defendants to settle, the difficulties of crafting instructions and trying a case with the law of different states applicable, and the Seventh Amendment right to jury trial problems with trying common issues before one jury and individual issues that overlap with those common issues in subsequent individual issues trials before a different jury. Nevertheless, the court was unpersuaded that these concerns required a flat ban on all class actions in mass products liability cases.]

We are more sympathetic to the approach taken by the Sixth Circuit in *In re American Medical Sys.*, 75 F.3d 1069 (6th Cir.1996). *American Medical* rejected class certification involving ten different models of penile implants that were implanted over a twenty-two year period. The court granted mandamus to decertify a nationwide class where the district court failed to identify common issues, explain why common issues predominate over individual issues, or make a finding of superiority. The court held that district courts must conduct a "rigorous analysis" into whether the prerequisites of Rule 23 are met before certifying a class. *See id.* at 1078–79. The Sixth Circuit has also recognized, however, that in the mass tort context, class adjudication of certain issues may be more efficient and expeditious than individualized litigation. *See Sterling v. Velsicol Chem. Co.*, 855 F.2d 1188 (6th Cir.1988).

Our reluctance to close the door on class action litigation in products liability cases is reinforced by current legal developments that could make class litigation more manageable. There has, for example, been discussion of federal class action legislation. *See, e.g.*, Thomas D. Rowe, Jr., *Beyond the Class Action Rule: An Inventory of Statutory Possibilities to Improve the Federal Class Action*, 71 N.Y.U.L.Rev. 186 (1996) (discussing several areas in which legislation might enhance federal class actions); William W. Schwarzer et al., *Judicial Federalism: A Proposal to Amend the Multidistrict Litigation Statute to Permit Discovery Coordination of Large–Scale Litigation Pending in State and Federal Courts*, 73 Tex.L.Rev. 1529 (1995) (proposing amendments to the multidistrict litigation statute, 28 U.S.C. § 1407(a), to include state court cases). Further, the American Law Institute is now concluding its work on products liability in the Restatement of the Law of Torts. *See* Restatement (Third) of Torts: Products Liability (Tent. Draft No. 3, 1996); *see also* Henderson, Jr. et al., *Optimal Issue Separation in Modern Products Liability Litigation*, 73 Tex.L.Rev. 1653, 1661–67 (1995) (discussing new Restatement as a reflection of current state of products liability law).

* * *

For these reasons, we reject Carter–Wallace's position that the law of this circuit should prohibit any class certifications in products liability litigation. We therefore turn to the appropriateness of this particular certification order.

II. The Class Certification Order in This Case

This court reviews a district court's decision to grant class certification for abuse of discretion. *See Six (6) Mexican Workers v. Arizona Citrus Growers*, 904 F.2d 1301, 1304 (9th Cir.1990). In order for a class action to be certified, the plaintiffs must establish the four prerequisites of Fed.R.Civ.P. 23(a) and at least one of the alternative requirements of Fed.R.Civ.P. 23(b). *See* Fed.R.Civ.P. 23(b). An action may be maintained as a class action if the court finds that: (1) common questions of law and fact predominate over questions affecting individual members, and (2) a class action is superior to other available methods for the fair and efficient adjudication of the controversy. Fed.R.Civ.P. 23(b)(3); *Dalkon Shield*, 693 F.2d at 855–56.

The certification order which we review is brief and conclusory. The record reflects that it was entered with the express hope on the part of the district judge of encouraging settlement, and to trigger a ruling from this court on the more general issue of the viability of class certification in this circuit. The order is provisional and contemplates the possibility of future modifications, additions, or refinements of subclasses. The order was entered at an early stage in the proceedings, and the record simply does not reflect any basis for us to conclude that some key requirements of Rule 23 have been satisfied.

It is not clear that Plaintiffs have met either the typicality or adequacy of representation requirement. See Fed.R.Civ.P. 23(a)(3) and (4). The plaintiff-class representatives include two individuals who have had difficulty withdrawing from Felbatol and returning to prior medications, one alleging liver failure and one some unspecified type of liver damage. No named plaintiff has experienced aplastic anemia as a result of taking the drug, even though this condition is one of the most serious of the alleged adverse consequences. The named plaintiffs thus may not be able to provide adequate representation for those who have suffered different injuries. See *Dalkon Shield*, 693 F.2d at 854–55.

Additionally, notice may be problematic. The number of known users who have reportedly suffered actual injuries from the drug is relatively small in comparison with all the users of the drug, so that many potential members of the classes cannot yet know if they are part of the class. We therefore have serious due process concerns about whether adequate notice under Rule 23(c)(2) can be given to all class members to enable them to make an intelligent choice as to whether to opt out. [Citation]

The first requirement of Rule 23(b)(3) is predominance of common questions over individual ones. Implicit in the satisfaction of the predominance test is the notion that the adjudication of common issues will help achieve judicial economy. [Citation] Even if the common questions do not predominate over the individual questions so that class certification of the entire action is warranted, Rule 23 authorizes the district court in appropriate cases to isolate the common issues under Rule 23(c)(4)(A) and proceed with class treatment of these particular issues. [Citations]

Here, the certification order merely reiterates Rule 23(b)(3)'s predominance requirement and is otherwise silent as to any reason why common issues predominate over individual issues certified under Rule 23(c)(4)(A). There has been no showing by Plaintiffs of how the class trial could be conducted. See e.g., Castano, 84 F.3d at 741–44. The district court abused its discretion by not adequately considering the predominance requirement before certifying the class. See *Dalkon Shield*, 693 F.2d at 856; cf. *Agent Orange*, 818 F.2d at 163–67; *School Asbestos*, 789 F.2d at 1010–11.

Last, but certainly not least, the district court must find that a class action is superior to other methods of adjudication. Fed.R.Civ.P. 23(b). Where classwide litigation of common issues will reduce litigation costs and promote greater efficiency, a class action may be superior to other methods of litigation. *See Dalkon Shield*, 693 F.2d at 856. A class action is the superior method for managing litigation if no realistic alternative exists. See Fed.R.Civ.P. 23(b)(3); 7A Wright et al., *supra*, § 1779 at 552. But here, as in *Dalkon Shield*, there has been no showing why the class mechanism is superior to alternative methods of adjudication, particularly when coupled with the discovery coordination that is made possible by the JPML consolidation. *See Dalkon Shield*, 693 F.2d at 856. Again, the certification order merely reiterates Rule 23(b)(3)'s superiority requirement but contains no discussion of alternatives or why class adjudication is superior.

The deficiencies in this certification are quite like those that caused the Sixth Circuit to reject the certification in American Medical, 75 F.3d at 1080–86. We similarly conclude that the district court abused its discretion by certifying particular issues for class adjudication. The district court's order is VACATED and the case is REMANDED for further proceedings.

Notes

1. *Valentino* addresses the four requirements in rule 23(a) which all cases must satisfy to be certified as a class action. It is often said that a fifth, unstated requirement for a class action is that an adequate definition of the class exist. *See* Federal Judicial Center, Manual for Complex Litigation § 21.222 (4th ed.2004). Why might this be important?

The *Valentino* court also assesses the requirements of rule 23(b)(3), one of the four specific types of class actions (rule 23(b)(1) contains two), each of which has its own separate and additional requirements for certification. Consider the predominance requirement of rule 23(b)(3), which the court finds was inadequately addressed by the trial court. This requirement is understood to require that common issues have greater significance or weight in the case than issues that are individual to each class member, such as damages. But rule 23(c)(4)(A) permits a case to be "brought or maintained" as a class action on limited issues. How can the predominance requirement of 23(b)(3) be reconciled with the authority for limited issue class actions in 23(c)(4)(A)? *Compare* Castano v. American Tobacco Co., 84 F.3d 734, 745 n.21 (5th Cir.1996) *with* Valentino v. Carter–Wallace, Inc., 97 F.3d 1227 (9th Cir.1996); In re Tetracycline Cases, 107 F.R.D. 719 (W.D.Mo. 1985); *see* Hines, Challenging the Issue Class Action End–Run, 52 Emory L.J. 709 (2003) (contending, based on text and history, that rule 23(c)(4)(A) does not authorize certification of a class that would not otherwise satisfy the requirements of rule 23(b)(3)).

2. What obstacles to certification of a products liability case as a class action emerge from this case? How realistic is it to expect that a many-claimant personal injury case will satisfy the obstacles identified by the *Valentino* court? What characteristics of the litigation would be essential for it to be certifiable? Note, particularly in this connection, the court's statement that the superiority criteria of rule 23(b)(3) require that no realistic alternative to a class action exist.

3. At this point, you should appreciate that plaintiffs both have control over the claims that will be at issue and often have a variety of claims that they can plausibly assert in a products liability case. The conventional wisdom among plaintiffs' lawyers is to assert as many different claims as they plausibly can. All plaintiffs have to do is persuade the jury on one, after all. Do you see why, in light of the predominance requirement of rule 23(b)(3), the conventional wisdom may be flawed?

4. Why was this case brought as a class action? Appreciate that in almost every instance, this decision is made by the lawyer and not by the client who serves as class representative. In what way were Mr. Valentino's interests furthered by pursuing this case as a class action? As you proceed through the remaining cases in this section, keep these questions in mind.

5. Suppose that you were consulted by a client who had just received notice of the certification of a rule 23(b)(3) class action consisting of all persons who had taken Felbatol and suffered injury as a result. Your client is a member of the class, having contracted aplastic anemia from taking the drug. What advice would you give your client about whether to opt out of the class?

JENKINS v. RAYMARK INDUSTRIES, INC.
United States Court of Appeals, Fifth Circuit, 1986.
782 F.2d 468.

Before GEE, ALVIN B. RUBIN and REAVLEY, CIRCUIT JUDGES.

REAVLEY, CIRCUIT JUDGE.

In this interlocutory appeal, the thirteen defendants challenge the decision of District Judge Robert M. Parker to certify a class of plaintiffs with asbestos-related claims. We affirm.

* * *

About 5,000 asbestos-related cases are pending in this circuit. Much, though by no means all, of the litigation has centered in the Eastern District of Texas. Nearly nine hundred asbestos-related personal injury cases, involving over one thousand plaintiffs, were pending there in December of 1984. Despite innovative streamlined pretrial procedures and large-scale consolidated trials of multiple plaintiffs, the dockets of that district's courts remained alarmingly backlogged. Plaintiffs had waited years for trial, some since 1979—and new cases were (and still are) being filed every day. It is predicted that, because asbestos-related diseases will continue to manifest themselves for the next 15 years, filings will continue at a steady rate until the year 2000.

In early 1985, ten of these plaintiffs responded by moving to certify a class of all plaintiffs with asbestos-related personal injury actions pending in the Eastern District on December 31, 1984. These plaintiffs hoped to determine in the class action one overarching issue—the viability of the "state of the art" defense. Because the trial of that issue consistently consumed substantial resources in every asbestos trial, and the evidence in each case was either identical or virtually so, they argued, a class determination would accelerate their cases.

II. THE PLAN

Following copious briefing and several hearings, the district court granted the motion. In his order of October 16, 1985, Judge Parker carefully considered the request under Rule 23(a), (b)(1) and (b)(3) of the Federal Rules of Civil Procedure. Finding a "limited fund" theory too speculative, he refused to certify the class under Rule 23(b)(1); by contrast, he found all of the elements for a 23(b)(3) action present. Drawing on his past experience, the judge concluded that evidence concerning the "state of the art" defense would vary little as to individual plaintiffs while consuming a major part of the time required for their trials. Considerable savings, both for the litigants and for the court, could thus be gained by resolving this and other defense and defense-related questions, including product identification, product defectiveness, gross negligence and punitive damages, in one class trial.[1] The court further found that the named representatives had "typical" claims, and that they and their attorneys would adequately represent the other class members. Accordingly, it certified the class as to the common questions, ordering them resolved for the class by a class action jury. The class jury would also decide all the individual issues in the class representatives' underlying suits; individual issues of the unnamed members would be resolved later in "mini-trials" of seven to ten plaintiffs. Although the class action jury would evaluate the culpability of defendants' conduct for a possible punitive damage award, any such damages would be awarded only after class members had won or settled their individual cases. The court subsequently appointed a special master to survey the class and prepare a report, detailing the class members and their claims, to apprise the jury of the gravity and extent of the absent members' claims and the typicality of the representatives' claims.

Defendants moved for reconsideration or, in the alternative, certification of the decision for interlocutory appeal. The court granted defendants' alternate motion.

On appeal, defendants challenge the court's decision on three grounds: (1) the class fails to meet the requirements of Rule 23; (2) Texas law proscribes a bifurcated determination of punitive damages and

---

1. The court pointed to the following general issues:

(a) which products, if any, were asbestos-containing insulation products capable of producing dust that contained asbestos fibers sufficient to cause harm in its application, use, or removal;

(b) which of the Defendants' products, if any, were defective as marketed and unreasonably dangerous;

(c) what date each Defendant knew or should have known that insulators and their household members were at risk of contracting an asbestos-related injury or disease from the application, use, or removal of asbestos-containing insulation products; and

(d) what amount of punitive damages, if any, should be awarded to the class as punishment for the Defendants' conduct.

actual damages; and (3) the contemplated class format is unconstitutional.

* * *

IV. RULE 23

Defendants argue that this class meets none of the Rule 23 requirements, except "numerosity." There is no merit to this argument.

The threshold of "commonality" is not high. Aimed in part at "determining whether there is a need for combined treatment and a benefit to be derived therefrom," *In re Agent Orange Product Liability Litigation*, 506 F.Supp. 762, 787 (E.D.N.Y.1980), the rule requires only that resolution of the common questions affect all or a substantial number of the class members. Defendants do not claim that they intend to raise a "state of the art" defense in only a few cases; the related issues are common to all class members.

The "typicality" requirement focuses less on the relative strengths of the named and unnamed plaintiffs' cases than on the similarity of the legal and remedial theories behind their claims. * * * Defendants do not contend that the named plaintiffs' claims rest on theories different from those of the other class members.

The "adequacy" requirement looks at both the class representatives and their counsel. Defendants have not shown that the representatives are "inadequate" due to an insufficient stake in the outcome or interests antagonistic to the unnamed members. [Citations] Neither do they give us reason to question the district court's finding that class counsel is "adequate" in light of counsel's past experience in asbestos cases, including trials involving multiple plaintiffs.

We similarly find no abuse in the court's determination that the certified questions "predominate," under Rule 23(b)(3). In order to "predominate," common issues must constitute a significant part of the individual cases. [Citations] It is difficult to imagine that class jury findings on the class questions will not significantly advance the resolution of the underlying hundreds of cases.

Defendants also argue that a class action is not "superior"; they say that better mechanisms, such as the Wellington Facility and "reverse bifurcation," exist for resolving these claims. Again, however, they have failed to show that the district court abused its discretion by reaching the contrary conclusion. We cannot find that the Wellington Facility, whose merits we do not question, is so superior that it must be used to the exclusion of other forums. Similarly, even if we were prepared to weigh the merits of other procedural mechanisms, we see no basis to conclude that this class action plan is an abuse of discretion.

Courts have usually avoided class actions in the mass accident or tort setting. Because of differences between individual plaintiffs on issues of liability and defenses of liability, as well as damages, it has been feared that separate trials would overshadow the common disposition for the class. See Advisory Committee Notes to 1966 Amendment to Fed. R.Civ.P. 23(b)(3). The courts are now being forced to rethink the alternatives and priorities by the current volume of litigation and more frequent mass disasters. [Citations] If Congress leaves us to our own devices, we may be forced to abandon repetitive hearings and arguments for each claimant's attorney to the extent enjoyed by the profession in the past. Be that as time will tell, the decision at hand is driven in one direction by all the circumstances. Judge Parker's plan is clearly superior to the alternative of repeating, hundreds of times over, the litigation of the state of the art issues with, as that experienced judge says, "days of the same witnesses, exhibits and issues from trial to trial."

This assumes plaintiffs win on the critical issues of the class trial. To the extent defendants win, the elimination of issues and docket will mean a far greater saving of judicial resources. Furthermore, attorneys' fees for all parties will be greatly reduced under this plan, not only because of the elimination of so much trial time but also because the fees collected from all members of the plaintiff class will be controlled by the judge. From our view it seems that the defendants enjoy all of the advantages, and the plaintiffs incur the disadvantages, of the class action—with one exception: the cases are to be brought to trial. That counsel for plaintiffs would urge the class action under these circumstances is significant support for the district judge's decision.

Necessity moves us to change and invent. Both the *Agent Orange* and the *Asbestos School* courts found that specific issues could be decided in a class "mass tort" action—even on a nationwide basis. We approve of the district court's decision in finding that this "mass tort" class could be certified.

V. OTHER CONTENTIONS

Defendants' remaining arguments challenge the bifurcated trials under Texas law and the United States Constitution. Defendants contend that, under Texas law, punitive damages cannot be determined separately from actual damages because the culpability of their conduct must be evaluated relative to each plaintiff. We disagree.

The purpose of punitive damages is not to compensate the victim but to create a deterrence to the defendant * * *. The focus is on the defendant's conduct, rather than on the plaintiff's. While no plaintiff may receive an award of punitive damages without proving that he suffered actual damages, * * * the allocation need not be made concurrently with an evaluation of the defendant's conduct. The relative timing of these assessments is not critical.

The critical issue in Texas punitive damages law is excessiveness or "reasonable proportionality." Whether a given award is excessive is a question of fact. *See Tatum v. Preston Carter Co.*, 702 S.W.2d 186, 188 (1986) [citations]. "The reasonable proportion rule does not, standing alone, serve to fix a particular ratio," *Tatum*, 702 S.W.2d at 188; that ratio will vary according to the facts of the case, *id.* at 188. In determining whether an award is excessive the court must consider: (1) the nature of the wrong; (2) the character of the conduct involved; (3) the degree of culpability of the wrongdoer; (4) the situation and sensibilities of the parties concerned; and (5) the extent to which such conduct offends a public sense of justice and propriety. [Citations]

The format in this case allows for the district court's review of the reasonableness of each plaintiff's punitive damage award and for our review of the standards which the court has applied. Texas law does not require more.

Defendants' constitutional challenges to bifurcation are equally unavailing. Like their other claims, these arguments only recast in constitutional terms their concern that, because the representatives' cases are "better" than the unnamed plaintiffs', the jury's view of the class claims will be skewed.

Although it fails to raise an issue of constitutional magnitude, this concern is nevertheless legitimate. Care must, of course, be taken to ensure fairness. Whatever the jury is told about the claims of the unnamed plaintiffs, it must be made aware that none of those claims have been proved; even after the class trial, they will still be mere allegations. The jury must not assume that all class members have equivalent claims: whatever injuries the unnamed plaintiffs have suffered may differ from the class representatives' as well as from one another's. Should the jury be allowed to award in the aggregate any punitive damages it finds appropriate, it must be instructed to factor in the possibility that none of the unnamed plaintiffs may have suffered *any* damages. Alternatively, the jury could be allowed to award an amount of money that each class member should receive for each dollar of actual damages awarded. Either way, the jury should understand that it must differentiate between proven and still-unproved claims, and that all class members, who recover actual damages from a defendant held liable for punitive damages, will share in the punitive award.

Furthermore, fairness as well as necessity dictates that both the parties and the court ensure that *all* of the necessary findings can be and are made in the class action trial. Sufficient evidence must be adduced for every one of each defendant's products to which a class member claims exposure so that the class jury can make the requisite findings as to *each* product and *each* defendant for such questions as periods of manufacture; areas and dates of distribution; "state of the art" knowledge for each relevant kind of product, use and user; when, if ever, conduct was grossly negligent; and dates and types of warnings if marketing defect is alleged.

The task will not be easy. Nevertheless, particularly in light of the magnitude of the problem and the need for innovative approaches, we find no abuse of discretion in this court's decision to try these cases by means of a Rule 23(b)(3) class suit.

AFFIRMED.

IN RE RHONE–POULENC RORER INC.
United States Court of Appeals, Seventh Circuit, 1995.
51 F.3d 1293.

POSNER, CHIEF JUDGE.

Drug companies that manufacture blood solids are the defendants in a nationwide class action brought on behalf of hemophiliacs infected by the AIDS virus as a consequence of using the defendants' products. The defendants have filed with us a petition for mandamus, asking us to direct the district judge to rescind his order certifying the case as a class action. We have no *appellate* jurisdiction over that order. An order certifying a class is not a final decision within the meaning of 28 U.S.C. § 1291; it does not wind up the litigation in the district court. And, in part because it is reviewable (at least in principle—the importance of this qualification will appear shortly) on appeal from the final decision in the case, it has been held not to fit any of the exceptions to the rule that confines federal appellate jurisdiction to final decisions. * * * Still, even nonappealable orders can be challenged by asking the court of appeals to mandamus the district court. Indeed, as a practical matter *only* such orders can be challenged by filing a petition for mandamus; an appealable order can be challenged only by appealing from it; the possibility of appealing would be a compelling reason for denying mandamus. For obvious reasons, however, mandamus is issued only in extraordinary cases. Otherwise, interlocutory orders would be appealable routinely, but with "appeal" renamed "mandamus." [Citations]

How to cabin this too-powerful writ which if uncabined threatens to unravel the final-decision rule? By taking seriously the two conditions for the grant of a writ of mandamus. The first is that the challenged order not be *effectively* reviewable at the end of the case—in other words, that it inflict *irreparable* harm. * * * Second, the order must so far exceed the proper bounds of judicial discretion as to be legitimately considered usurpative in character, or in violation of a clear and indisputable legal right, or, at the very least, patently erroneous. * * *

* * *

The suit to which the petition for mandamus relates, *Wadleigh v. Rhone–Poulenc Rorer Inc.*, 157 F.R.D. 410 arises out of the infection of a substantial fraction of the hemophiliac population of this country by the AIDS virus because the blood supply was contaminated by the virus before the nature of the disease was well understood or adequate methods of screening the blood supply existed. The AIDS virus (HIV–human immunodeficiency virus) is transmitted by the exchange of bodily fluids, primarily semen and blood. Hemophiliacs depend on blood solids that contain the clotting factors whose absence defines their disease. These blood solids are concentrated from blood obtained from many donors. If just one of the donors is infected with the AIDS virus the probability that the blood solids manufactured in part from his blood will be infected is very high unless the blood is treated with heat to kill the virus. * * *

First identified in 1981, AIDS was diagnosed in hemophiliacs beginning in 1982, and by 1984 the medical community agreed that the virus was transmitted by blood as well as by semen. That year it was demonstrated that treatment with heat could kill the virus in the blood supply and in the following year a reliable test for the presence of the virus in blood was developed. By this time, however, a large number of hemophiliacs had become infected. Since 1984 physicians have been advised to place hemophiliacs on heat-treated blood solids, and since 1985 all blood donated for the manufacture of blood solids has been screened and supplies discovered to be HIV-positive have been discarded. Supplies that test negative still are heat-treated, because the test is not infallible and in particular may fail to detect the virus in persons who became infected within six months before taking the test.

The plaintiffs have presented evidence that 2,000 hemophiliacs have died of AIDS and that half or more of the remaining U.S. hemophiliac population of 20,000 may be HIV-positive. Unless there are dramatic breakthroughs in the treatment of HIV or AIDS, all infected persons will die from the disease. * * *

Some 300 lawsuits, involving some 400 plaintiffs, have been filed, 60 percent of them in state courts, 40 percent in federal district courts under the diversity jurisdiction, seeking to impose tort liability on the defendants for the transmission of HIV to hemophiliacs in blood solids manufactured by the defendants. Obviously these 400 plaintiffs represent only a small fraction of the hemophiliacs (or their next of kin, in cases in which the hemophiliac has died) who are infected by HIV or have died of AIDS. One of the 300 cases is *Wadleigh*, filed in September 1993, the case that the district judge certified as a class action. Thirteen other cases have been tried already in various courts around the country, and the defendants have won twelve of them. All the cases brought in federal court (like *Wadleigh*)—cases brought under the diversity jurisdiction—have been consolidated for pretrial discovery in the Northern District of Illinois by the panel on multidistrict litigation.

The plaintiffs advance two principal theories of liability. The first is that before anyone had heard of AIDS or HIV, it was known that Hepatitis B, a lethal disease though less so than HIV–AIDS, could be transmitted either through blood transfusions or through injection of blood solids. The plaintiffs argue that due care with respect to the risk of infection with Hepatitis B required the defendants to take measures to purge that virus from their blood solids, whether by treating the blood they bought or by screening the donors—perhaps by refusing to deal with *paid* donors, known to be a class at high risk of being infected with Hepatitis B. The defendants' failure to take effective measures was, the plaintiffs claim, negligent. Had the defendants not been negligent, the plaintiffs further argue, hemophiliacs would have been protected not only against Hepatitis B but also, albeit fortuitously or as the plaintiffs put it "serendipitously," against HIV.

The plaintiffs' second theory of liability is more conventional. It is that the defendants, again negligently, dragged their heels in screening donors and taking other measures to prevent contamination of blood solids by HIV when they learned about the disease in the early 1980s. The plaintiffs have other theories of liability as well, including strict products liability, but it is not necessary for us to get into them.

The district judge did not think it feasible to certify *Wadleigh* as a class action for the adjudication of the entire controversy between the plaintiffs and the defendants. Fed.R.Civ.P. 23(b)(3). The differences in the date of infection alone of the thousands of potential class members would make such a procedure infeasible. Hemophiliacs infected before anyone knew about the contamination of blood solids by HIV could not rely on the second theory of liability, while hemophiliacs infected after the blood supply became safe (not perfectly safe, but nearly so) probably were not infected by any of the defendants' products. Instead the judge certified the suit "as a class action with respect to particular issues" only. Fed.R.Civ.P. 23(c)(4)(A). He explained this decision in an opinion which implied that he did not envisage the entry of a final judgment but rather the rendition by a jury of a special verdict that would answer a number of questions bearing, perhaps decisively, on whether the defendants are negligent under either of the theories sketched above. If the special verdict found no negligence under either theory, that presumably would be the end of all the cases unless other theories of liability proved viable. If the special verdict found negligence, individual members of the class would then file individual tort suits in state and federal district courts around the nation and would use the special verdict, in conjunction with the doctrine of collateral estoppel, to block relitigation of the issue of negligence.

[The court next addressed the plaintiffs' argument that there was no need for the court to intervene at this early stage of the litigation, because the class certification could be reviewed after final judgment.]

* * *

[Review of the final judgment] will come too late to provide effective relief to the defendants; and this is an important consideration in relation to the first condition for mandamus, that the challenged ruling of the district court have inflicted irreparable harm, which is to say harm that cannot be rectified by an appeal from the final judgment in the lawsuit. The reason that an appeal will come too late to provide effective relief for these defendants is the sheer *magnitude* of the risk to which the class action, in contrast to the individual actions pending or likely, exposes them. Consider the situation that would obtain if the class had not been certified. The defendants would be facing 300 suits. More might be filed, but probably only a few more, because the statutes of limitations in the various states are rapidly expiring for potential plaintiffs. The blood supply has been safe since 1985. That is ten years ago. The risk to hemophiliacs of having become infected with HIV has been widely publicized; it is unlikely that many hemophiliacs are unaware of it. Under the usual discovery statute of limitations, they would have to have taken steps years ago to determine their infection status, and having found out file suit within the limitations period running from the date of discovery, in order to preserve their rights.

Three hundred is not a trivial number of lawsuits. The potential damages in each one are great. But the defendants have won twelve of the first thirteen, and, if this is a representative sample, they are likely to win most of the remaining ones as well. Perhaps in the end, if class-action treatment is denied (it has been denied in all the other hemophiliac HIV suits in which class certification has been sought), they will be compelled to pay damages in only 25 cases, involving a potential liability of perhaps no more than $125 million altogether. These are guesses, of course, but they are at once conservative and usable for the limited purpose of comparing the situation that will face the defendants if the class certification stands. All of a sudden they will face thousands of plaintiffs. * * *

Suppose that 5,000 of the potential class members are not yet barred by the statute of limitations. And suppose the named plaintiffs in *Wadleigh* win the class portion of this case to the extent of establishing the defendants' liability under either of the two negligence theories. It is true that this would only be prima facie liability, that the defendants would have various defenses. But they could not be confident that the defenses would prevail. They might, therefore, easily be facing $25 billion in potential liability (conceivably more), and with it bankruptcy. They may not wish to roll these dice. That is putting it mildly. They will be under intense pressure to settle. [Citations] If they settle, the class certification—the ruling that will have forced them to settle—will never be reviewed. [Citations] Judge Friendly, who was not given to hyperbole, called settlements induced by a small probability of an immense judgment in a class action "blackmail settlements." Henry J. Friendly, *Federal Jurisdiction: A General View* 120 (1973). Judicial concern about them is legitimate, not "sociological," as it was derisively termed in *In re Sugar Antitrust Litigation*, 559 F.2d 481, 483 n.1 (9th Cir.1977).

* * *

We do not want to be misunderstood as saying that class actions are bad because they place pressure on defendants to settle. That pressure is a reality, but it must be balanced against the undoubted benefits of the class action that have made it an authorized procedure for employment by federal courts. We have yet to consider the balance. All that our discussion to this point has shown is that the first condition for the grant of mandamus—that the challenged ruling not be effectively reviewable at the end of the case—is fulfilled. The ruling will inflict irreparable harm; the next question is whether the ruling can fairly be described as usurpative. We have formulated this second condition as narrowly, as stringently, as can be, but even so formulated we think it is fulfilled. We do not mean to suggest that the district judge is engaged in a deliberate power-grab. We have no reason to suppose that he *wants* to preside over an unwieldy class action. We believe that he was responding imaginatively and in the best of faith to the challenge that mass torts, graphically illustrated by the avalanche of asbestos litigation, pose for the federal courts. But the plan that he has devised for the HIV-hemophilia litigation exceeds the bounds of allowable judicial discretion. Three concerns, none of them necessarily sufficient in itself but cumulatively compelling, persuade us to this conclusion.

The first is a concern with forcing these defendants to stake their companies on the outcome of a single jury trial, or be forced by fear of the risk of bankruptcy to settle even if they have no legal liability, when it is entirely feasible to allow a final, authoritative determination of their liability for the colossal misfortune that has befallen the hemophiliac population to emerge from a decentralized process of multiple trials, involving different juries, and different standards of liability, in different jurisdictions; and when, in addition, the preliminary indications are that the defendants are not liable for the grievous harm that has befallen the members of the class. These qualifications are important. In most class actions—and those the ones in which the rationale for the procedure is most compelling—individual suits are infeasible because the claim of each class member is tiny relative to the expense of litigation. That plainly is not the situation here. A notable feature of this case, and one that has not been remarked upon or encountered, so far as we are aware, in previous cases, is the demonstrated great likelihood that the plaintiffs' claims, despite their human appeal, lack legal merit. This is the inference from the defendants' having won 92.3 percent (12/13) of the cases to have gone to judgment. Granted, thirteen is a small sample and further trials, if they are held, may alter the pattern that the sample reveals. But whether they do or not, the result will be robust if these further trials are permitted to go forward, because the pattern that results will reflect a consensus, or at least a pooling of judgment, of many different tribunals.

For this consensus or maturing of judgment the district judge proposes to substitute a single trial before a single jury instructed in accordance with no actual law of any jurisdiction—a jury that will receive a kind of Esperanto instruction, merging the negligence standards of the 50 states and the District of Columbia. One jury, consisting of six persons (the standard federal civil jury nowadays consists of six regular jurors and two alternates), will hold the fate of an industry in the palm of its hand. This jury, jury number fourteen, may disagree with twelve of the previous thirteen juries—and hurl the industry into bankruptcy. That kind of thing can happen in our system of civil justice (it is not likely to happen, because the industry is likely to settle—whether or not it really is liable) without violating anyone's legal rights. But it need not be tolerated when the alternative exists of submitting an issue to multiple juries constituting in the aggregate a much larger and more diverse sample of decision-makers. That would not be a feasible option if the stakes to each class member were too slight to repay the cost of suit, even though the aggregate stakes were very large and would repay the costs of a consolidated proceeding. But this is not the case with regard to the HIV-hemophilia litigation. Each plaintiff if successful is apt to receive a judgment in the millions. With the aggregate stakes in the tens or hundreds of millions of dollars, or even in the billions, it is not a waste of judicial resources to conduct more than one trial, before more than six jurors, to determine whether a major segment of the international pharmaceutical industry is to follow the asbestos manufacturers into Chapter 11.

We have hinted at the second reason for concern that the district judge exceeded the bounds of permissible judicial discretion. He proposes to have a jury determine the negligence of the defendants under a legal standard that does not actually exist anywhere in the world. One is put in mind of the concept of "general" common law that prevailed in the era of *Swift v. Tyson*. The assumption is that the common law of the 50 states and the District of Columbia, at least so far as bears on a claim of negligence against drug companies, is basically uniform and can be abstracted in a single instruction. It is no doubt true that at some level of generality the law of negligence is one, not only nationwide but worldwide. Negligence is a failure to take due care, and due care a function of the probability and magnitude of an accident and the costs of avoiding it. A jury can be asked whether the defendants took due care. And in many cases such differences as there are among the tort rules of the different states would not affect the outcome. The Second Circuit was willing to assume *dubitante* that this was true of the issues certified for class determination in the Agent Orange litigation. *In re Diamond Shamrock Chemicals Co.*, 725 F.2d 858, 861 (2d Cir.1984).

We doubt that it is true in general, and we greatly doubt that it is true in a case such as this in which one of the theories pressed by the plaintiffs, the "serendipity" theory, is novel. * * * The law of negligence, including subsidiary concepts such as duty of care, foreseeability, and proximate cause, may as the plaintiffs have argued forcefully to us differ among the states only in nuance, though we think not, for a reason discussed later. But nuance can be important, and its significance is suggested by a comparison of differing state pattern instructions on negligence and differing judicial formulations of the meaning of negligence and the subordinate concepts. * * *

* * *

The plaintiffs' second theory focuses on the questions when the defendants should have learned about the danger of HIV in the blood supply and when, having learned about it, they should have taken steps to eliminate the danger or at least warn hemophiliacs or their physicians of it. These questions also may be sensitive to the precise way in which a state formulates its standard of negligence. If not, one begins to wonder why this country bothers with different state legal systems.

Both theories, incidentally, may be affected by differing state views on the role of industry practice or custom in determining the existence of negligence. In some states, the standard of care for a physician, hospital, or other provider of medical services, including blood banks, is a professional standard, that is, the standard fixed by the relevant profession. In others, it is the standard of ordinary care, which may, depending on judge or jury, exceed the professional standard. * * *

* * *

The third respect in which we believe that the district judge has exceeded his authority concerns the point at which his plan of action proposes to divide the trial of the issues that he has certified for class-action treatment from the other issues involved in the thousands of actual and potential claims of the representatives and members of the class. Bifurcation and even finer divisions of lawsuits into separate trials are authorized in federal district courts. Fed.R.Civ.P. 42(b); *Sellers v. Baisier*, 792 F.2d 690, 694 (7th Cir.1986). * * * However, as we have been at pains to stress recently, the district judge must carve at the joint. *Hydrite Chemicals Co. v. Calumet Lubricants Co.*, 47 F.3d 887, 890–91 (7th Cir.1995); cf. *McLaughlin v. State Farm Mutual Automobile Ins. Co.*, 30 F.3d 861, 870–71 (7th Cir.1994). Of particular relevance here, the judge must not divide issues between separate trials in such a way that the same issue is reexamined by different juries. The problem is not inherent in bifurcation. It does not arise when the same jury is to try the successive phases of the litigation. But most of the separate "cases" that compose this class action will be tried, after the initial trial in the Northern District of Illinois, in different courts, scattered throughout the country. The right to a jury trial in federal civil cases, conferred by the Seventh Amendment, is a right to have juriable issues determined by the first jury impaneled to hear them (provided there are no errors warranting a new trial), and not reexamined by another finder of fact. * * * *Gasoline Products Co. v. Champlin Refining Co.*, 283 U.S. 494, 500, 51 S.Ct. 513, 515, 75 L.Ed. 1188 (1931); *McDaniel v. Anheuser-Busch, Inc.*, 987 F.2d 298, 305 (5th Cir.1993); *Alabama v. Blue Bird Body Co.*, 573 F.2d 309, 318 (5th Cir.1978). * * *

The plan of the district judge in this case is inconsistent with the principle that the findings of one jury are not to be reexamined by a second, or third, or *n*th jury. The first jury will not determine liability. It will determine merely whether one or more of the defendants was negligent under one of the two theories. The first jury may go on to decide the additional issues with regard to the named plaintiffs. But it will not decide them with regard to the other class members. Unless the defendants settle, a second (and third, and fourth, and hundredth, and conceivably thousandth) jury will have to decide, in individual follow-on litigation by class members not named as plaintiffs in the *Wadleigh* case, such issues as comparative negligence—did any class members knowingly continue to use unsafe blood solids after they learned or should have learned of the risk of contamination with HIV?—and proximate causation. Both issues overlap the issue of the defendants' negligence. Comparative negligence entails, as the name implies, a comparison of the degree of negligence of plaintiff and defendant. [Citations] Proximate causation is found by determining whether the harm to the plaintiff followed in some sense naturally, uninterruptedly, and with reasonable probability from the negligent act of the defendant. It overlaps the issue of the defendants' negligence even when the state's law does not (as many states do) make the foreseeability of the risk to which the defendant subjected the plaintiff an explicit ingredient of negligence. [Citations] A second or subsequent jury might find that the defendants' failure to take precautions against infection with Hepatitis B could not be thought the *proximate* cause of the plaintiffs' infection with HIV, a different and unknown bloodborne virus. How the resulting inconsistency between juries could be prevented escapes us.

* * *

The defendants have pointed out other serious problems with the district judge's plan, but it is unnecessary to discuss them. The petition for a writ of mandamus is granted, and the district judge is directed to decertify the plaintiff class.

Notes

1. In 1998, rule 23 was amended to include a provision that permits, at the discretion of the court of appeals, an immediate appeal of a district court's decision granting or denying class certification. This new subsection, rule 23(f), was in response to concerns of the sort expressed by the court in *Rhone–Poulenc* and the increased use of mandamus to enable appellate courts to review class certifications of mass tort cases.

2. Did the court violate the *Eisen* prescription of not accounting for the merits? *See* In re Copley Pharmaceutical, Inc., 161 F.R.D. 456 (D.Wyo.1995). Recall that the discussion of the outcome of the previously-resolved cases was in connection with whether delayed review of the class certification would cause irreparable injury, thereby satisfying one of the elements for a writ of mandamus. Suppose plaintiffs had won, instead of lost, 12 of 13 prior cases? But if plaintiffs had that success rate, what would be the impact on their (more accurately, their lawyers') desire to proceed in a class action? Recall the *Fibreboard* class action.

3. Do the three concerns expressed by the *Rhone–Poulenc* court: 1) varying state laws applicable to the class; 2) running afoul of the reexamination clause of the Seventh Amendment by a different jury in the individual issues phase reconsidering matters already resolved in the common issues phase; and 3) imposing enormous pressure on defendants to settle because of the bet-your-company stakes in a personal injury class action) sound the death knell for all products liability class actions? Are there cases in which one or more of these objections would not exist? Are there ways in which class actions might be structured to overcome one or more of them? Would the *Fibreboard* class certification have satisfied the *Rhone–Poulenc* court?

For a critique of the third concern, excessive pressure to settle, see Silver, "We're Scared to Death": Class Certification and Blackmail, 78 N.Y.U. L.Rev. 1357 (2003).

4. Could subclasses be employed to deal with varying state laws? At this point in your study of products liability law, can you estimate how many different subclasses would be required to deal with variations in state law on the elements of a products liability claim? How many different interrogatories would have to be submitted to the jury for those subclasses to be able to fashion a verdict for a nationwide class? Can subclassing be reconciled with the manageability requirement of rule 23(b)(3)? *See* In re Telectronics Pacing Systems, Inc., 172 F.R.D. 271, 291–92 (S.D.Ohio1997) (identifying three possibilities: 1) state law is sufficiently similar that no subclassing is required; 2) state law is so varied that subclassing would not be feasible; 3) state laws, while having variations, can be reasonably grouped in a manageable number so as to permit subclassing of a nationwide class).

Could plaintiffs' agreement to prove liability under the most onerous state law solve the problem of establishing predominance in the face of different state laws? Are all differences among states merely a matter of linear increments in what must be established for liability? Could such an agreement be reconciled with the adequate representation requirement of rule 23(a)?

See generally Phair, Resolving the Choice of Law Problem in Rule 23(b)(3) Nationwide Class Actions, 67 U.Chi.L.Rev. 835 (2000) (discussing possibility of a number of subclasses); Kramer, Choice of Law in Complex Litigation, 71 N.Y.U.L.Rev. 547 (1996) (advocating a limited number of subclasses to deal with differing state laws).

AMCHEM PRODUCTS, INC. v. WINDSOR
Supreme Court of the United States, 1997.
521 U.S. 591, 117 S.Ct. 2231, 138 L.Ed.2d 689.

JUSTICE GINSBURG delivered the opinion of the Court.

This case concerns the legitimacy under Rule 23 of the Federal Rules of Civil Procedure of a class-action certification sought to achieve global settlement of current and future asbestos-related claims. The class proposed for certification potentially encompasses hundreds of thousands, perhaps millions, of individuals tied together by this commonality: each was, or some day may be, adversely affected by past exposure to asbestos products manufactured by one or more of 20 companies. Those companies, defendants in the lower courts, are petitioners here.

The United States District Court for the Eastern District of Pennsylvania certified the class for settlement only, finding that the proposed settlement was fair and that representation and notice had been adequate. That court enjoined class members from separately pursuing asbestos-related personal-injury suits in any court, federal or state, pending the issuance of a final order. The Court of Appeals for the Third Circuit vacated the District Court's orders, holding that the class certification failed to satisfy Rule 23's requirements in several critical respects. We affirm the Court of Appeals' judgment.

I

A

The settlement-class certification we confront evolved in response to an asbestos-litigation crisis. See *Georgine v. Amchem Products, Inc.*, 83 F.3d 610, 618, and n. 2 (C.A.3 1996) (citing commentary). A United States Judicial Conference Ad Hoc Committee on Asbestos Litigation, appointed by THE CHIEF JUSTICE in September 1990, described facets of the problem in a 1991 report:

> "[This] is a tale of danger known in the 1930s, exposure inflicted upon millions of Americans in the 1940s and 1950s, injuries that began to take their toll in the 1960s, and a flood of lawsuits beginning in the 1970s. On the basis of past and current filing data, and because of a latency period that may last as long as 40 years for some asbestos related diseases, a continuing stream of claims can be expected. The final toll of asbestos related injuries is unknown. Predictions have been made of 200,000 asbestos disease deaths before the year 2000 and as many as 265,000 by the year 2015.
>
> "The most objectionable aspects of asbestos litigation can be briefly summarized: dockets in both federal and state courts continue to grow; long delays are routine; trials are too long; the same issues are litigated over and over; transaction costs exceed the victims' recovery by nearly two to one; exhaustion of assets threatens and distorts the process; and future claimants may lose altogether."

Report of The Judicial Conference Ad Hoc Committee on Asbestos Litigation 2–3 (Mar.1991). Real reform, the report concluded, required federal legislation creating a national asbestos dispute-resolution scheme. * * * To this date, no congressional response has emerged.

In the face of legislative inaction, the federal courts—lacking authority to replace state tort systems with a national toxic tort compensation regime—endeavored to work with the procedural tools available to improve management of federal asbestos litigation. Eight federal judges, experienced in the superintendence of asbestos cases, urged the Judicial Panel on Multidistrict Litigation (MDL Panel), to consolidate in a single district all asbestos complaints then pending in federal courts. Accepting the recommendation, the MDL Panel transferred all asbestos cases then filed, but not yet on trial in federal courts to a single district, the United States District Court for the Eastern District of Pennsylvania; pursuant to the transfer order, the collected cases were consolidated for pretrial proceedings before Judge Weiner. See *In re Asbestos Products Liability Litigation (No. VI)*, 771 F.Supp. 415, 422–424 (Jud.Pan.Mult.Lit.1991).[1]

---

1. In a series of orders, the MDL Panel had previously denied other asbestos-case transfer requests. See *In re Asbestos and Asbestos Insulation Material Products Liability Litigation*, 431 F.Supp. 906, 910 (JPML 1977); *In re Asbestos Products Liability Litigation* (No. II), MDL–416 (JPML Mar. 13, 1980) (unpublished order); *In re*

The order aggregated pending cases only; no authority resides in the MDL Panel to license for consolidated proceedings claims not yet filed.

B

After the consolidation, attorneys for plaintiffs and defendants formed separate steering committees and began settlement negotiations. Ronald L. Motley and Gene Locks—later appointed, along with Motley's law partner Joseph F. Rice, to represent the plaintiff class in this action—co-chaired the Plaintiffs' Steering Committee. Counsel for the Center for Claims Resolution (CCR), the consortium of 20 former asbestos manufacturers now before us as petitioners, participated in the Defendants' Steering Committee. Although the MDL order collected, transferred, and consolidated only cases already commenced in federal courts, settlement negotiations included efforts to find a "means of resolving ... future cases." Record, Doc. 3, p. 2 (Memorandum in Support of Joint Motion for Conditional Class Certification); *see also Georgine v. Amchem Products, Inc.*, 157 F.R.D. 246, 266 (E.D.Pa.1994) ("primary purpose of the settlement talks in the consolidated MDL litigation was to craft a national settlement that would provide an alternative resolution mechanism for asbestos claims," including claims that might be filed in the future).

In November 1991, the Defendants' Steering Committee made an offer designed to settle all pending and future asbestos cases by providing a fund for distribution by plaintiffs' counsel among asbestos-exposed individuals. The Plaintiffs' Steering Committee rejected this offer, and negotiations fell apart. CCR, however, continued to pursue "a workable administrative system for the handling of future claims." [*Id.* at 270.]

To that end, CCR counsel approached the lawyers who had headed the Plaintiffs' Steering Committee in the unsuccessful negotiations, and a new round of negotiations began; that round yielded the mass settlement agreement now in controversy. At the time, the former heads of the Plaintiffs' Steering Committee represented thousands of plaintiffs with then-pending asbestos-related claims—claimants the parties to this suit call "inventory" plaintiffs. CCR indicated in these discussions that it would resist settlement of inventory cases absent "some kind of protection for the future." *Id.*, at 294; *see also id.*, at 295 (CCR communicated to the inventory plaintiffs' attorneys that once the CCR defendants saw a rational way to deal with claims expected to be filed in the future, those defendants would be prepared to address the settlement of pending cases).

Settlement talks thus concentrated on devising an administrative scheme for disposition of asbestos claims not yet in litigation. In these negotiations, counsel for masses of inventory plaintiffs endeavored to represent the interests of the anticipated future claimants, although

Asbestos School Products Liability Litigation, 606 F.Supp. 713, 714 (JPML 1985); *In re Ship Asbestos Products Liability Litigation*, MDL–676 (JPML Feb. 4, 1986) (unpublished order); *In re Leon Blair Asbestos Products Liability Litigation*, MDL–702 (JPML Feb. 6, 1987) (unpublished order).

those lawyers then had no attorney-client relationship with such claimants.

Once negotiations seemed likely to produce an agreement purporting to bind potential plaintiffs, CCR agreed to settle, through separate agreements, the claims of plaintiffs who had already filed asbestos-related lawsuits. In one such agreement, CCR defendants promised to pay more than $200 million to gain release of the claims of numerous inventory plaintiffs. After settling the inventory claims, CCR, together with the plaintiffs' lawyers CCR had approached, launched this case, exclusively involving persons outside the MDL Panel's province—plaintiffs without already pending lawsuits.[2]

C

The class action thus instituted was not intended to be litigated. Rather, within the space of a single day, January 15, 1993, the settling parties—CCR defendants and the representatives of the plaintiff class described below—presented to the District Court a complaint, an answer, a proposed settlement agreement, and a joint motion for conditional class certification.

The complaint identified nine lead plaintiffs, designating them and members of their families as representatives of a class comprising all persons who had not filed an asbestos-related lawsuit against a CCR defendant as of the date the class action commenced, but who (1) had been exposed—occupationally or through the occupational exposure of a spouse or household member—to asbestos or products containing asbestos attributable to a CCR defendant, or (2) whose spouse or family member had been so exposed. Untold numbers of individuals may fall within this description. All named plaintiffs alleged that they or a member of their family had been exposed to asbestos-containing products of CCR defendants. More than half of the named plaintiffs alleged that they or their family members had already suffered various physical injuries as a result of the exposure. The others alleged that they had not yet manifested any asbestos-related condition. The complaint delineated no subclasses; all named plaintiffs were designated as representatives of the class as a whole.

The complaint invoked the District Court's diversity jurisdiction and asserted various state-law claims for relief * * *.

A stipulation of settlement accompanied the pleadings; it proposed to settle, and to preclude nearly all class members from litigating against CCR companies, all claims not filed before January 15, 1993, involving compensation for present and future asbestos-related personal injury or death. An exhaustive document exceeding 100 pages, the stipulation presents in detail an administrative mechanism and a schedule of payments to compensate class members who meet defined asbestos-

---

2. It is basic to comprehension of this proceeding to notice that no transferred case is included in the settlement at issue, and no case covered by the settlement existed as a civil action at the time of the MDL Panel transfer.

exposure and medical requirements. The stipulation describes four categories of compensable disease: mesothelioma; lung cancer; certain "other cancers" (colon-rectal, laryngeal, esophageal, and stomach cancer); and "non-malignant conditions" (asbestosis and bilateral pleural thickening). Persons with "exceptional" medical claims—claims that do not fall within the four described diagnostic categories—may in some instances qualify for compensation, but the settlement caps the number of "exceptional" claims CCR must cover.

For each qualifying disease category, the stipulation specifies the range of damages CCR will pay to qualifying claimants. Payments under the settlement are not adjustable for inflation. Mesothelioma claimants—the most highly compensated category—are scheduled to receive between $20,000 and $200,000. The stipulation provides that CCR is to propose the level of compensation within the prescribed ranges; it also establishes procedures to resolve disputes over medical diagnoses and levels of compensation.

Compensation above the fixed ranges may be obtained for "extraordinary" claims. But the settlement places both numerical caps and dollar limits on such claims. The settlement also imposes "case flow maximums," which cap the number of claims payable for each disease in a given year.

Class members are to receive no compensation for certain kinds of claims, even if otherwise applicable state law recognizes such claims. Claims that garner no compensation under the settlement include claims by family members of asbestos-exposed individuals for loss of consortium, and claims by so-called "exposure-only" plaintiffs for increased risk of cancer, fear of future asbestos-related injury, and medical monitoring. "Pleural" claims, which might be asserted by persons with asbestos-related plaques on their lungs but no accompanying physical impairment, are also excluded. Although not entitled to present compensation, exposure-only claimants and pleural claimants may qualify for benefits when and if they develop a compensable disease and meet the relevant exposure and medical criteria. Defendants forgo defenses to liability, including statute of limitations pleas.

Class members, in the main, are bound by the settlement in perpetuity, while CCR defendants may choose to withdraw from the settlement after ten years. A small number of class members—only a few per year—may reject the settlement and pursue their claims in court. Those permitted to exercise this option, however, may not assert any punitive damages claim or any claim for increased risk of cancer. Aspects of the administration of the settlement are to be monitored by the AFL–CIO and class counsel. Class counsel are to receive attorneys' fees in an amount to be approved by the District Court.

D

On January 29, 1993, as requested by the settling parties, the District Court conditionally certified, under Federal Rule of Civil Procedure 23(b)(3), an encompassing opt-out class. The certified class included persons occupationally exposed to defendants' asbestos products, and members of their families, who had not filed suit as of January 15. Judge Weiner appointed Locks, Motley, and Rice as class counsel, noting that "[t]he Court may in the future appoint additional counsel if it is deemed necessary and advisable." Record, Doc. 11, p. 3 (Class Certification Order). At no stage of the proceedings, however, were additional counsel in fact appointed. Nor was the class ever divided into subclasses. In a separate order, Judge Weiner assigned to Judge Reed, also of the Eastern District of Pennsylvania, "the task of conducting fairness proceedings and of determining whether the proposed settlement is fair to the class." See 157 F.R.D., at 258. Various class members raised objections to the settlement stipulation, and Judge Weiner granted the objectors full rights to participate in the subsequent proceedings. *Ibid.*

In preliminary rulings, Judge Reed held that the District Court had subject-matter jurisdiction, see *Carlough v. Amchem Products, Inc.*, 834 F.Supp. 1437, 1467–1468 (E.D.Pa.1993), and he approved the settling parties' elaborate plan for giving notice to the class, see *Carlough v. Amchem Products, Inc.*, 158 F.R.D. 314, 336 (E.D.Pa.1993). The court-approved notice informed recipients that they could exclude themselves from the class, if they so chose, within a three-month opt-out period.

Objectors raised numerous challenges to the settlement. They urged that the settlement unfairly disadvantaged those without currently compensable conditions in that it failed to adjust for inflation or to account for changes, over time, in medical understanding. They maintained that compensation levels were intolerably low in comparison to awards available in tort litigation or payments received by the inventory plaintiffs. And they objected to the absence of any compensation for certain claims, for example, medical monitoring, compensable under the tort law of several States. Rejecting these and all other objections, Judge Reed concluded that the settlement terms were fair and had been negotiated without collusion. See 157 F.R.D., at 325, 331–332. He also found that adequate notice had been given to class members, see *id.*, at 332–334, and that final class certification under Rule 23(b)(3) was appropriate, see *id.*, at 315.

As to the specific prerequisites to certification, the District Court observed that the class satisfied Rule 23(a)(1)'s numerosity requirement, a matter no one debates. The Rule 23(a)(2) and (b)(3) requirements of commonality and preponderance were also satisfied, the District Court held, in that

> "[t]he members of the class have all been exposed to asbestos products supplied by the defendants and all share an interest in receiving prompt and fair compensation for their claims, while minimizing the risks and transaction costs inherent in the asbestos litigation process as it occurs presently in the tort system. Whether the proposed settlement satisfies this interest and is otherwise a

fair, reasonable and adequate compromise of the claims of the class is a predominant issue for purposes of Rule 23(b)(3)." *Id.*, at 316.

The District Court held next that the claims of the class representatives were "typical" of the class as a whole, a requirement of Rule 23(a)(3), and that, as Rule 23(b)(3) demands, the class settlement was "superior" to other methods of adjudication.

Strenuous objections had been asserted regarding the adequacy of representation, a Rule 23(a)(4) requirement. Objectors maintained that class counsel and class representatives had disqualifying conflicts of interests. In particular, objectors urged, claimants whose injuries had become manifest and claimants without manifest injuries should not have common counsel and should not be aggregated in a single class. Furthermore, objectors argued, lawyers representing inventory plaintiffs should not represent the newly-formed class.

Satisfied that class counsel had ably negotiated the settlement in the best interests of all concerned, and that the named parties served as adequate representatives, the District Court rejected these objections. [Citation] Subclasses were unnecessary, the District Court held, bearing in mind the added cost and confusion they would entail and the ability of class members to exclude themselves from the class during the three-month opt-out period. [Citation] Reasoning that the representative plaintiffs "have a strong interest that recovery for all of the medical categories be maximized because they may have claims in *any*, or several categories," the District Court found "no antagonism of interest between class members with various medical conditions, or between persons with and without currently manifest asbestos impairment." Declaring class certification appropriate and the settlement fair, the District Court preliminarily enjoined all class members from commencing any asbestos-related suit against the CCR defendants in any state or federal court. See *Georgine v. Amchem Products, Inc.*, 878 F.Supp. 716, 726–727 (E.D.Pa. 1994).

The objectors appealed. The United States Court of Appeals for the Third Circuit vacated the certification, holding that the requirements of Rule 23 had not been satisfied. See Georgine v. Amchem Products, Inc., 83 F.3d 610 (1996).

E

The Court of Appeals, in a long, heavily detailed opinion by Judge Becker, first noted several challenges by objectors to justiciability, subject-matter jurisdiction, and adequacy of notice. These challenges, the court said, raised "serious concerns." *Id.*, at 623. However, the court observed, "the jurisdictional issues in this case would not exist but for the [class action] certification." *Ibid*. Turning to the class-certification issues and finding them dispositive, the Third Circuit declined to decide other questions.

On class-action prerequisites, the Court of Appeals referred to an earlier Third Circuit decision, *In re General Motors Corp. Pick–Up Truck*

Fuel Tank Products Liability Litigation, 55 F.3d 768 (C.A.3), cert. denied, 516 U.S. 824, 116 S.Ct. 88, 133 L.Ed.2d 45 (1995) (hereinafter *GM Trucks*), which held that although a class action may be certified for settlement purposes only, Rule 23(a)'s requirements must be satisfied as if the case were going to be litigated. 55 F.3d, at 799–800. The same rule should apply, the Third Circuit said, to class certification under Rule 23(b)(3). See 83 F.3d, at 625. But cf. *In re Asbestos Litigation*, 90 F.3d 963, 975–976, and n. 8 (C.A.5 1996), cert. pending, Nos. 96–1379, 96–1394. While stating that the requirements of Rule 23(a) and (b)(3) must be met "without taking into account the settlement," 83 F.3d, at 626, the Court of Appeals in fact closely considered the terms of the settlement as it examined aspects of the case under Rule 23 criteria. See *id.*, at 630–634.

The Third Circuit recognized that Rule 23(a)(2)'s "commonality" requirement is subsumed under, or superseded by, the more stringent Rule 23(b)(3) requirement that questions common to the class "predominate over" other questions. The court therefore trained its attention on the "predominance" inquiry. [Citation] The harmfulness of asbestos exposure was indeed a prime factor common to the class, the Third Circuit observed. [Citation] But uncommon questions abounded.

In contrast to mass torts involving a single accident, class members in this case were exposed to different asbestos-containing products, in different ways, over different periods, and for different amounts of time; some suffered no physical injury, others suffered disabling or deadly diseases. See *id.*, at 626, 628. "These factual differences," the Third Circuit explained, "translate [d] into significant legal differences." *Id.*, at 627. State law governed and varied widely on such critical issues as "viability of [exposure-only] claims [and] availability of causes of action for medical monitoring, increased risk of cancer, and fear of future injury."[3] *Ibid.* "[T]he number of uncommon issues in this humongous class action," the Third Circuit concluded, *ibid.*, barred a determination, under existing tort law, that common questions predominated. [Citation]

The Court of Appeals next found that "serious intra-class conflicts preclude[d] th[e] class from meeting the adequacy of representation requirement" of Rule 23(a)(4). *Ibid.* Adverting to, but not resolving charges of attorney conflict of interests, the Third Circuit addressed the question whether the named plaintiffs could adequately advance the interests of all class members. The Court of Appeals acknowledged that the District Court was certainly correct to this extent: " '[T]he members of the class are united in seeking the maximum possible recovery for their asbestos-related claims.' " "But the settlement does more than simply provide a general recovery fund," the Court of Appeals immediately added; "[r]ather, it makes important judgments on how recovery is

---

3. Recoveries under the laws of different States spanned a wide range. Objectors assert, for example, that 15% of current mesothelioma claims arise in California, where the statewide average recovery is $419,-674—or more than 209% above the $200,000 maximum specified in the settlement for mesothelioma claims not typed "extraordinary."

to be *allocated* among different kinds of plaintiffs, decisions that necessarily favor some claimants over others." [Citation]

In the Third Circuit's view, the "most salient" divergence of interests separated plaintiffs already afflicted with an asbestos-related disease from plaintiffs without manifest injury (exposure-only plaintiffs). The latter would rationally want protection against inflation for distant recoveries. See *ibid*. They would also seek sturdy back-end opt-out rights and "causation provisions that can keep pace with changing science and medicine, rather than freezing in place the science of 1993." [Citation] Already injured parties, in contrast, would care little about such provisions and would rationally trade them for higher current payouts. [Citation] These and other adverse interests, the Court of Appeals carefully explained, strongly suggested that an undivided set of representatives could not adequately protect the discrete interests of both currently afflicted and exposure-only claimants.

* * *

The Court of Appeals similarly rejected the District Court's assessment of the superiority of the class action. The Third Circuit initially noted that a class action so large and complex "could not be tried." *Ibid*. The court elaborated most particularly, however, on the unfairness of binding exposure-only plaintiffs who might be unaware of the class action or lack sufficient information about their exposure to make a reasoned decision whether to stay in or opt out. [Citation] "A series of statewide or more narrowly defined adjudications, either through consolidation under Rule 42(a) or as class actions under Rule 23, would seem preferable," the Court of Appeals said. [Citation] The Third Circuit, after intensive review, ultimately ordered decertification of the class and vacation of the District Court's anti-suit injunction. * * *

We granted certiorari, and now affirm.

II

Objectors assert in this Court, as they did in the District Court and Court of Appeals, an array of jurisdictional barriers, [including lack of standing by exposure-only class members, lack of subject-matter jurisdiction for the same class members because the amount in controversy requirement was unsatisfied, and the absence of a justiciable case or controversy because the case had no disputed issue when it was filed. The Supreme Court declined to reach these issues because the "logically antecedent" class action certification issues were dispositive.]

* * *

III

* * *

In the 1966 class-action amendments, Rule 23(b)(3), the category at issue here, was "the most adventuresome" innovation. See Kaplan, A

Prefatory Note, 10 B.C. Ind. & Com. L.Rev. 497, 497 (1969) (hereinafter Kaplan, Prefatory Note). * * *

* * *

While the text of Rule 23(b)(3) does not exclude from certification cases in which individual damages run high, the Advisory Committee had dominantly in mind vindication of "the rights of groups of people who individually would be without effective strength to bring their opponents into court at all." Kaplan, Prefatory Note 497. As concisely recalled in a recent Seventh Circuit opinion:

> "The policy at the very core of the class action mechanism is to overcome the problem that small recoveries do not provide the incentive for any individual to bring a solo action prosecuting his or her rights. A class action solves this problem by aggregating the relatively paltry potential recoveries into something worth someone's (usually an attorney's) labor." *Mace v. Van Ru Credit Corp.*, 109 F.3d 338, 344 (1997).

* * *

In the decades since the 1966 revision of Rule 23, class action practice has become ever more "adventuresome" as a means of coping with claims too numerous to secure their "just, speedy, and inexpensive determination" one by one. See Fed. Rule Civ. Proc. 1. The development reflects concerns about the efficient use of court resources and the conservation of funds to compensate claimants who do not line up early in a litigation queue. See generally J. Weinstein, Individual Justice in Mass Tort Litigation: The Effect of Class Actions, Consolidations, and Other Multiparty Devices (1995); Schwarzer, Settlement of Mass Tort Class Actions: Order out of Chaos, 80 Cornell L.Rev. 837 (1995).

Among current applications of Rule 23(b)(3), the "settlement only" class has become a stock device. See, *e.g.*, T. Willging, L. Hooper & R. Niemic, Empirical Study of Class Actions in Four Federal District Courts: Final Report to the Advisory Committee on Civil Rules 61–62 (1996) (noting large number of such cases in districts studied). Although all Federal Circuits recognize the utility of Rule 23(b)(3) settlement classes, courts have divided on the extent to which a proffered settlement affects court surveillance under Rule 23's certification criteria.

In *GM Trucks*, 55 F.3d, at 799–800, and in the instant case, 83 F.3d, at 624–626, the Third Circuit held that a class cannot be certified for settlement when certification for trial would be unwarranted. Other courts have held that settlement obviates or reduces the need to measure a proposed class against the enumerated Rule 23 requirements. See, *e.g.*, *In re Asbestos Litigation*, 90 F.3d, at 975(C.A.5) ("in settlement class context, common issues arise from the settlement itself") (citing H. Newberg & A. Conte, 2 Newberg on Class Actions § 11.28, at 11–58 (3d ed.1992)); *White v. National Football League*, 41 F.3d 402, 408 (C.A.8 1994) ("adequacy of class representation . . . is ultimately determined by the settlement itself"), cert. denied, 515 U.S. 1137, 115 S.Ct. 2569, 132

L.Ed.2d 821 (1995); *In re A.H. Robins Co.*, 880 F.2d 709, 740(C.A.4) ("[i]f not a ground for certification per se, certainly settlement should be a factor, and an important factor, to be considered when determining certification"), cert. denied *sub nom. Anderson v. Aetna Casualty & Surety Co.*, 493 U.S. 959, 110 S.Ct. 377, 107 L.Ed.2d 362 (1989); *Malchman v. Davis*, 761 F.2d 893, 900 (C.A.2 1985) (certification appropriate, in part, because "the interests of the members of the broadened class in the settlement agreement were commonly held"), cert. denied, 475 U.S. 1143, 106 S.Ct. 1798, 90 L.Ed.2d 343 (1986).

* * *

IV

We granted review to decide the role settlement may play, under existing Rule 23, in determining the propriety of class certification. The Third Circuit's opinion stated that each of the requirements of Rule 23(a) and (b)(3) "must be satisfied without taking into account the settlement." 83 F.3d, at 626 (quoting *GM Trucks*, 55 F.3d, at 799). That statement, petitioners urge, is incorrect.

We agree with petitioners to this limited extent: settlement is relevant to a class certification. The Third Circuit's opinion bears modification in that respect. But, as we earlier observed, see *supra*, at 609, the Court of Appeals in fact did not ignore the settlement; instead, that court homed in on settlement terms in explaining why it found the absentees' interests inadequately represented. See 83 F.3d, at 630–631. The Third Circuit's close inspection of the settlement in that regard was altogether proper.

Confronted with a request for settlement-only class certification, a district court need not inquire whether the case, if tried, would present intractable management problems, see Fed. Rule Civ. Proc. 23(b)(3)(D), for the proposal is that there be no trial. But other specifications of the rule—those designed to protect absentees by blocking unwarranted or overbroad class definitions—demand undiluted, even heightened, attention in the settlement context. Such attention is of vital importance, for a court asked to certify a settlement class will lack the opportunity, present when a case is litigated, to adjust the class, informed by the proceedings as they unfold. See Fed. Rule Civ. Proc. 23(c), (d).[4]

And, of overriding importance, courts must be mindful that the rule as now composed sets the requirements they are bound to enforce. * * *

Rule 23(e), on settlement of class actions, reads in its entirety: "A class action shall not be dismissed or compromised without the approval

---

4. Portions of the opinion dissenting in part appear to assume that settlement counts only one way—in favor of certification. To the extent that is the dissent's meaning, we disagree. Settlement, though a relevant factor, does not inevitably signal that class action certification should be granted more readily than it would be were the case to be litigated. For reasons the Third Circuit aired, see 83 F.3d 610, 626–635 (1996), proposed settlement classes sometimes warrant more, not less caution on the question of certification.

of the court, and notice of the proposed dismissal or compromise shall be given to all members of the class in such manner as the court directs." This prescription was designed to function as an additional requirement, not a superseding direction, for the "class action" to which Rule 23(e) refers is one qualified for certification under Rule 23(a) and (b). Cf. *Eisen*, 417 U.S., at 176–177, 94 S.Ct., at 2151–2152 (adequate representation does not eliminate additional requirement to provide notice). Subdivisions (a) and (b) focus court attention on whether a proposed class has sufficient unity so that absent members can fairly be bound by decisions of class representatives. That dominant concern persists when settlement, rather than trial, is proposed.

The safeguards provided by the Rule 23(a) and (b) class-qualifying criteria, we emphasize, are not impractical impediments—checks shorn of utility—in the settlement class context. First, the standards set for the protection of absent class members serve to inhibit appraisals of the chancellor's foot kind—class certifications dependent upon the court's gestalt judgment or overarching impression of the settlement's fairness.

Second, if a fairness inquiry under Rule 23(e) controlled certification, eclipsing Rule 23(a) and (b), and permitting class designation despite the impossibility of litigation, both class counsel and court would be disarmed. Class counsel confined to settlement negotiations could not use the threat of litigation to press for a better offer, see Coffee, Class Wars: The Dilemma of the Mass Tort Class Action, 95 Colum. L.Rev. 1343, 1379–1380 (1995), and the court would face a bargain proffered for its approval without benefit of adversarial investigation, see, *e.g., Kamilewicz v. Bank of Boston Corp.*, 100 F.3d 1348, 1352 (C.A.7 1996) (Easterbrook, J., dissenting from denial of rehearing en banc) (parties "may even put one over on the court, in a staged performance"), cert. denied, 520 U.S. 1204, 117 S.Ct. 1569, 137 L.Ed.2d 714 (1997).

Federal courts, in any case, lack authority to substitute for Rule 23's certification criteria a standard never adopted—that if a settlement is "fair," then certification is proper. Applying to this case criteria the rulemakers set, we conclude that the Third Circuit's appraisal is essentially correct. Although that court should have acknowledged that settlement is a factor in the calculus, a remand is not warranted on that account. The Court of Appeals' opinion amply demonstrates why—with or without a settlement on the table—the sprawling class the District Court certified does not satisfy Rule 23's requirements.

A

We address first the requirement of Rule 23(b)(3) that "[common] questions of law or fact ... predominate over any questions affecting only individual members." The District Court concluded that predominance was satisfied based on two factors: class members' shared experience of asbestos exposure and their common "interest in receiving prompt and fair compensation for their claims, while minimizing the risks and transaction costs inherent in the asbestos litigation process as it occurs presently in the tort system." 157 F.R.D., at 316. The settling parties also contend that the settlement's fairness is a common question, predominating over disparate legal issues that might be pivotal in litigation but become irrelevant under the settlement.

The predominance requirement stated in Rule 23(b)(3), we hold, is not met by the factors on which the District Court relied. The benefits asbestos-exposed persons might gain from the establishment of a grand-scale compensation scheme is a matter fit for legislative consideration, see *supra*, at 2237–2238, but it is not pertinent to the predominance inquiry. That inquiry trains on the legal or factual questions that qualify each class member's case as a genuine controversy, questions that preexist any settlement.

The Rule 23(b)(3) predominance inquiry tests whether proposed classes are sufficiently cohesive to warrant adjudication by representation. See 7A Wright, Miller, & Kane 518–519. The inquiry appropriate under Rule 23(e), on the other hand, protects unnamed class members "from unjust or unfair settlements affecting their rights when the representatives become fainthearted before the action is adjudicated or are able to secure satisfaction of their individual claims by a compromise." See 7B Wright, Miller, & Kane § 1797, at 340–341. But it is not the mission of Rule 23(e) to assure the class cohesion that legitimizes representative action in the first place. If a common interest in a fair compromise could satisfy the predominance requirement of Rule 23(b)(3), that vital prescription would be stripped of any meaning in the settlement context.

The District Court also relied upon this commonality: "The members of the class have all been exposed to asbestos products supplied by the defendants...." 157 F.R.D., at 316. Even if Rule 23(a)'s commonality requirement may be satisfied by that shared experience, the predominance criterion is far more demanding. See 83 F.3d, at 626–627. Given the greater number of questions peculiar to the several categories of class members, and to individuals within each category, and the significance of those uncommon questions, any overarching dispute about the health consequences of asbestos exposure cannot satisfy the Rule 23(b)(3) predominance standard.

The Third Circuit highlighted the disparate questions undermining class cohesion in this case:

"Class members were exposed to different asbestos-containing products, for different amounts of time, in different ways, and over different periods. Some class members suffer no physical injury or have only asymptomatic pleural changes, while others suffer from lung cancer, disabling asbestosis, or from mesothelioma.... Each has a different history of cigarette smoking, a factor that complicates the causation inquiry.

"The [exposure-only] plaintiffs especially share little in common, either with each other or with the presently injured class members. It is unclear whether they will contract asbestos-related disease and, if so, what disease each will suffer. They will also incur different medical expenses because their monitoring and treatment will depend on singular circumstances and individual medical histories." *Id.*, at 626.

Differences in state law, the Court of Appeals observed, compound these disparities. See *id.*, at 627 (citing *Phillips Petroleum Co. v. Shutts*, 472 U.S. 797, 823, 105 S.Ct. 2965, 2980, 86 L.Ed.2d 628 (1985)).

No settlement class called to our attention is as sprawling as this one. Cf. *In re Asbestos Litigation*, 90 F.3d, at 976, n. 8 ("We would likely agree with the Third Circuit that a class action requesting individual damages for members of a global class of asbestos claimants would not satisfy [Rule 23] requirements due to the huge number of individuals and their varying medical expenses, smoking histories, and family situations."). Predominance is a test readily met in certain cases alleging consumer or securities fraud or violations of the antitrust laws. See Adv. Comm. Notes, 28 U.S.C.App., p. 697; see also *supra*, at 2246. Even mass tort cases arising from a common cause or disaster may, depending upon the circumstances, satisfy the predominance requirement. The Advisory Committee for the 1966 revision of Rule 23, it is true, noted that "mass accident" cases are likely to present "significant questions, not only of damages but of liability and defenses of liability, ... affecting the individuals in different ways." *Ibid.* And the Committee advised that such cases are "ordinarily not appropriate" for class treatment. Ibid. But the text of the rule does not categorically exclude mass tort cases from class certification, and district courts, since the late 1970s, have been certifying such cases in increasing number. See Resnik, From "Cases" to "Litigation," 54 Law & Contemp.Prob. 5, 17–19 (Summer 1991) (describing trend). The Committee's warning, however, continues to call for caution when individual stakes are high and disparities among class members great. As the Third Circuit's opinion makes plain, the certification in this case does not follow the counsel of caution. That certification cannot be upheld, for it rests on a conception of Rule 23(b)(3)'s predominance requirement irreconcilable with the rule's design.

B

Nor can the class approved by the District Court satisfy Rule 23(a)(4)'s requirement that the named parties "will fairly and adequately protect the interests of the class." The adequacy inquiry under Rule 23(a)(4) serves to uncover conflicts of interest between named parties and the class they seek to represent. See *General Telephone Co. of Southwest v. Falcon*, 457 U.S. 147, 157–158, n. 13, 102 S.Ct. 2364, 2370–2371, n.13, 72 L.Ed.2d 740 (1982). "[A] class representative must be part of the class and 'possess the same interest and suffer the same injury' as the class members." *East Tex. Motor Freight System, Inc. v. Rodriguez*, 431 U.S. 395, 403, 97 S.Ct. 1891, 1896, 52 L.Ed.2d 453 (1977) (quoting *Schlesinger v. Reservists Comm. to Stop the War*, 418 U.S. 208, 216, 94 S.Ct. 2925, 2930, 41 L.Ed.2d 706 (1974)).[5]

---

5. The adequacy-of-representation requirement "tend[s] to merge" with the commonality and typicality criteria of Rule 23(a), which "serve as guideposts for deter-

As the Third Circuit pointed out, named parties with diverse medical conditions sought to act on behalf of a single giant class rather than on behalf of discrete subclasses. In significant respects, the interests of those within the single class are not aligned. Most saliently, for the currently injured, the critical goal is generous immediate payments. That goal tugs against the interest of exposure-only plaintiffs in ensuring an ample, inflation-protected fund for the future. Cf. *General Telephone Co. of Northwest v. EEOC*, 446 U.S. 318, 331, 100 S.Ct. 1698, 1707, 64 L.Ed.2d 319 (1980) ("In employment discrimination litigation, conflicts might arise, for example, between employees and applicants who were denied employment and who will, if granted relief, compete with employees for fringe benefits or seniority. Under Rule 23, the same plaintiff could not represent these classes.").

The disparity between the currently injured and exposure-only categories of plaintiffs, and the diversity within each category are not made insignificant by the District Court's finding that petitioners' assets suffice to pay claims under the settlement. See 157 F.R.D., at 291. Although this is not a "limited fund" case certified under Rule 23(b)(1)(B), the terms of the settlement reflect essential allocation decisions designed to confine compensation and to limit defendants' liability. For example, as earlier described, see *supra*, at 2240–2241, the settlement includes no adjustment for inflation; only a few claimants per year can opt out at the back end; and loss-of-consortium claims are extinguished with no compensation.

The settling parties, in sum, achieved a global compromise with no structural assurance of fair and adequate representation for the diverse groups and individuals affected. Although the named parties alleged a range of complaints, each served generally as representative for the whole, not for a separate constituency. In another asbestos class action, the Second Circuit spoke precisely to this point:

> "[W]here differences among members of a class are such that subclasses must be established, we know of no authority that permits a court to approve a settlement without creating subclasses on the basis of consents by members of a unitary class, some of whom happen to be members of the distinct subgroups. The class representatives may well have thought that the Settlement serves the aggregate interests of the entire class. But the adversity among subgroups requires that the members of each subgroup cannot be bound to a settlement except by consents given by those who

mining whether ... maintenance of a class action is economical and whether the named plaintiff's claim and the class claims are so interrelated that the interests of the class members will be fairly and adequately protected in their absence." *General Telephone Co. of Southwest v. Falcon*, 457 U.S. 147, 157, n. 13, 102 S.Ct. 2364, 2370, n.13, 72 L.Ed.2d 740 (1982). The adequacy heading also factors in competency and conflicts of class counsel. Like the Third Circuit, we decline to address adequacy-of-counsel issues discretely in light of our conclusions that common questions of law or fact do not predominate and that the named plaintiffs cannot adequately represent the interests of this enormous class.

understand that their role is to represent solely the members of their respective subgroups."

In re Joint Eastern and Southern Dist. Asbestos Litigation, 982 F.2d 721, 742–743 (C.A.2 1992), modified on reh'g sub nom. *In re Findley*, 993 F.2d 7 (C.A.2 1993). The Third Circuit found no assurance here—either in the terms of the settlement or in the structure of the negotiations—that the named plaintiffs operated under a proper understanding of their representational responsibilities. See 83 F.3d, at 630–631. That assessment, we conclude, is on the mark.

C

Impediments to the provision of adequate notice, the Third Circuit emphasized, rendered highly problematic any endeavor to tie to a settlement class persons with no perceptible asbestos-related disease at the time of the settlement. *Id.*, at 633; cf. *In re Asbestos Litigation*, 90 F.3d, at 999–1000 (Smith, J., dissenting). Many persons in the exposure-only category, the Court of Appeals stressed, may not even know of their exposure, or realize the extent of the harm they may incur. Even if they fully appreciate the significance of class notice, those without current afflictions may not have the information or foresight needed to decide, intelligently, whether to stay in or opt out.

Family members of asbestos-exposed individuals may themselves fall prey to disease or may ultimately have ripe claims for loss of consortium. Yet large numbers of people in this category—future spouses and children of asbestos victims—could not be alerted to their class membership. And current spouses and children of the occupationally exposed may know nothing of that exposure.

Because we have concluded that the class in this case cannot satisfy the requirements of common issue predominance and adequacy of representation, we need not rule, definitively, on the notice given here. In accord with the Third Circuit, however, see 83 F.3d, at 633–634, we recognize the gravity of the question whether class action notice sufficient under the Constitution and Rule 23 could ever be given to legions so unselfconscious and amorphous.

V

The argument is sensibly made that a nationwide administrative claims processing regime would provide the most secure, fair, and efficient means of compensating victims of asbestos exposure. Congress, however, has not adopted such a solution. And Rule 23, which must be interpreted with fidelity to the Rules Enabling Act and applied with the interests of absent class members in close view, cannot carry the large load CCR, class counsel, and the District Court heaped upon it. As this case exemplifies, the rulemakers' prescriptions for class actions may be endangered by "those who embrace [Rule 23] too enthusiastically just as [they are by] those who approach [the rule] with distaste." C. Wright, Law of Federal Courts 508 (5th ed.1994); cf. 83 F.3d, at 634 (suggesting resort to less bold aggregation techniques, including more narrowly defined class certifications).

For the reasons stated, the judgment of the Court of Appeals for the Third Circuit is

Affirmed.

JUSTICE O'CONNOR took no part in the consideration or decision of this case.

JUSTICE BREYER, with whom JUSTICE STEVENS joins, concurring in part and dissenting in part.

Although I agree with the Court's basic holding that "settlement is relevant to a class certification," [citation] I find several problems in its approach that lead me to a different conclusion. First, I believe that the need for settlement in this mass tort case, with hundreds of thousands of lawsuits, is greater than the Court's opinion suggests. Second, I would give more weight than would the majority to settlement-related issues for purposes of determining whether common issues predominate. Third, I am uncertain about the Court's determination of adequacy of representation, and do not believe it appropriate for this Court to second-guess the District Court on the matter without first having the Court of Appeals consider it. Fourth, I am uncertain about the tenor of an opinion that seems to suggest the settlement is unfair. And fifth, in the absence of further review by the Court of Appeals, I cannot accept the majority's suggestions that "notice" is inadequate.

* * *

I

First, I believe the majority understates the importance of settlement in this case. Between 13 and 21 million workers have been exposed to asbestos in the workplace—over the past 40 or 50 years—but the most severe instances of such exposure probably occurred three or four decades ago. [Justice Breyer continued to detail the arterial-clogging nature of asbestos litigation for the nation's courts and the extraordinary transaction costs that it entailed—with only 39 cents of every dollar reaching asbestos victims, and many plaintiffs, with little or no symptoms, filing suit and recovering substantial amounts of money.]

I mention this matter because it suggests that the settlement before us is unusual in terms of its importance, both to many potential plaintiffs and to defendants, and with respect to the time, effort, and expenditure that it reflects. All of which leads me to be reluctant to set aside the District Court's findings without more assurance than I have that they are wrong. I cannot obtain that assurance through comprehensive review of the record because that is properly the job of the Court of Appeals and that court, understandably, but as we now hold, mistakenly, believed that settlement was not a relevant (and, as I would say, important) consideration.

* * *

Fourth, I am more agnostic than is the majority about the basic fairness of the settlement. *Ante*, at 2250–2252. The District Court's conclusions rested upon complicated factual findings that are not easily cast aside. It is helpful to consider some of them, such as its determination that the settlement provided "fair compensation ... while reducing the delays and transaction costs endemic to the asbestos litigation process" and that "the proposed class action settlement is superior to other available methods for the fair and efficient resolution of the asbestos-related personal injury claims of class members." 157 F.R.D., at 316 (citation omitted); see also *id.*, at 335 ("The inadequate tort system has demonstrated that the lawyers are well paid for their services but the victims are not receiving speedy and reasonably inexpensive resolution of their claims. Rather, the victims' recoveries are delayed, excessively reduced by transaction costs and relegated to the impersonal group trials and mass consolidations. The sickest of victims often go uncompensated for years while valuable funds go to others who remain unimpaired by their mild asbestos disease. Indeed, [these] unimpaired victims have, in many states, been forced to assert their claims prematurely or risk giving up all rights to future compensation for any future lung cancer or mesothelioma. The plan which this Court approves today will correct that unfair result for the class members and the ... defendants"); *id.*, at 279, 280 (settlement "will result in less delay for asbestos claimants than that experienced in the present tort system" and will "result in the CCR defendants paying more claims, at a faster rate, than they have ever paid before"); *id.*, at 292; Edley & Weiler, 30 Harv. J. Legis., at 405, 407 (finding that "[t]here are several reasons to believe that this settlement secures important gains for both sides" and that they "firmly endorse the fairness and adequacy of this settlement"). Indeed, the settlement has been endorsed as fair and reasonable by the AFL–CIO (and its Building and Construction Trades Department), which represents a " 'substantial percentage' " of class members, 157 F.R.D., at 325, and which has a role in monitoring implementation of the settlement, *id.*, at 285. I do not intend to pass judgment upon the settlement's fairness, but I do believe that these matters would have to be explored in far greater depth before I could reach a conclusion about fairness. And that task, as I have said, is one for the Court of Appeals.

Finally, I believe it is up to the District Court, rather than this Court, to review the legal sufficiency of notice to members of the class. The District Court found that the plan to provide notice was implemented at a cost of millions of dollars and included hundreds of thousands of individual notices, a wide-ranging television and print campaign, and significant additional efforts by 35 international and national unions to notify their members. *Id.*, at 312–313, 336. Every notice emphasized that an individual did not currently have to be sick to be a class member. And in the end, the District Court was "confident" that Rule 23 and due process requirements were satisfied because, as a result of this "extensive and expensive notice procedure," "over six million" individuals "received actual notice materials," and "millions more" were reached by the media campaign. *Id.*, at 312, 333, 336. Although the majority, in principle, is reviewing a Court of Appeals' conclusion, it seems to me that its opinion might call into question the fact-related determinations of the District Court. *Ante*, at 2252. To the extent that it does so, I disagree, for such findings cannot be so quickly disregarded. And I do not think that our precedents permit this Court to do so. See *Reiter*, 442 U.S., at 345, 99 S.Ct., at 2334; *Yamasaki*, 442 U.S., at 703, 99 S.Ct., at 2558–2559.

II

The issues in this case are complicated and difficult. The District Court might have been correct. Or not. Subclasses might be appropriate. Or not. I cannot tell. And I do not believe that this Court should be in the business of trying to make these fact-based determinations. That is a job suited to the district courts in the first instance, and the courts of appeal on review. But there is no reason in this case to believe that the Court of Appeals conducted its prior review with an understanding that the settlement could have constituted a reasonably strong factor in favor of class certification. For this reason, I would provide the courts below with an opportunity to analyze the factual questions involved in certification by vacating the judgment, and remanding the case for further proceedings.

Notes

1. Would it be wise in considering class actions to separate out the asbestos class actions from other mass products cases and treat the former as sui generis because of the unique demands asbestos litigation has imposed on the American court system? *See* Silicano, Mass Torts and the Rhetoric of Crisis, 80 Cornell L.Rev. 990 (1995) (generally debunking the notion that there is a crisis created by mass torts and arguing that asbestos claims could have been contained by proper handling); Davis, Toward the Proper Role for Mass Tort Class Actions, 77 Or.L.Rev. 157, 229 (1998) (arguing in favor of class action treatment for mass torts, but asserting that asbestos claims are unsuited for such treatment).

2. The *Amchem* settlement was driven by the defendants' desire to get out from continued asbestos litigation and to settle, once and for all, all (or virtually all) claims against them. Thus, *Amchem* consisted of a class of future-only asbestos claimants. In the aftermath of *Amchem* and the inadequacies identified by the Court, is there any realistic possibility of obtaining the "global peace" sought by defendants? In the years following the Supreme Court's decision in *Amchem*, numerous major asbestos manufacturers filed bankruptcy petitions. *See generally* Cabraser, Life After *Amchem:* The Class Struggle Continues, 31 Loy.L.A.L.Rev. 373 (1998).

3. Would subclassing solve problems identified by the Court with the proposed settlement? How many subclasses would be necessary? Recall *Rhone-Poulenc* and its concern with different tort law among the states. At what point would the number of subclasses, each with separate representation, become so unwieldy as to be impractical? Would the "back-end opt-out rights" be something defendants would find acceptable? How can effective notice be provided to those who do not currently have any asbestotic disease? Indeed, some may not even be aware that they were exposed to asbestos fibers.

4. In an article that preceded *Amchem*, Professor John Coffee assessed the new world of class actions in mass torts that many were arguing were essential to permit resolution of the enormous number of individual claims presented by asbestos and other mass products liability cases:

> In the race to a new system of group litigation in which lawyers represent "interests," rather than individuals, few in particular have looked for the perverse incentives that almost inevitably arise at such junctures when client control over attorneys is weakened. No opening generalization about the modern class action is sounder than the assertion that it has long been a context in which opportunistic behavior has been common and high agency costs have prevailed. If not actually collusive, non-adversarial settlements have all too frequently advanced only the interests of plaintiffs' attorneys, not those of the class members. * * *

* * *

> [O]ne must remember that the mass tort plaintiffs' attorney typically has an inventory of cases that the attorney represents on an individual basis. Often, the inventory may exceed several thousand cases. Normally, the individual cases in this inventory will move slowly through the litigation pipeline and settle only once a trial date has been set. Thus, the plaintiffs' attorney's tactical goal is to expedite cases, pushing them through the pipeline to the eve of trial (and predictable settlement). Conversely, defendants in the mass tort setting are concerned less about existing cases than future claimants, who may dwarf the number of present claimants because of the long latency period associated with mass torts.

> Given these different concerns, the possibilities for a deal between the two sides should become evident at this point: both sides have an incentive to trade a settlement of the plaintiffs' attorney's entire inventory (on terms favorable to the attorney) for a global settlement in a class action of all future claims (on terms favorable to the defendants). The advantages to the plaintiffs' attorney of such a trade are several: First, because plaintiffs' attorneys are almost invariably compensated on a contingency basis by their individual clients, the plaintiffs' attorney can expect to receive a substantial fraction (usually around thirty percent but sometimes more) out of the aggregate amount received by the clients from such an inventory settlement. Second, the inventory settlement telescopes into one year payments that might be delayed for many years. Thus, it gains the attorney the time value of money over

this period. Third, some cases that go to trial might lose, and other cases might be too weak on the merits to justify a settlement offer or to dare to take to trial (and thereby risk the attorney's credibility with the court). However, such cases can be included within the inventory settlement (which will typically encompass even unfiled cases so long as some medical evidence supporting the condition exists).

In return for the inventory settlement, the plaintiffs' attorney will be expected to serve as class counsel in a class action brought as a "settlement class" against the same defendants. By definition, a settlement class "action" cannot go to trial, and thus defendants need not fear litigation in the event that the two sides have a subsequent falling out. The critical step in this trade requires a special definition of the class: it must consist only of future claimants. Otherwise, if the proposed class covered present claimants, it would look suspicious that the attorneys representing the class had just settled similarly situated cases on a superior basis. This incongruity is avoided by defining the class as consisting of those persons having claims against the defendants with respect to the particular product, process, accident or incident at issue who have not filed suit prior to the date the class action is filed. Under this approach, the inventory settlements can be effected shortly before the class action is filed.

* * *

If one accepts the premise that an inventory settlement can be used as an inducement to the plaintiffs' attorney to enter into a non-adversarial settlement of a class action that disadvantages the class members, it follows logically that the person most susceptible to such an inducement will be the plaintiffs' attorney with the largest inventory of present claimants. Indeed, the more the plaintiffs' attorney maintains a high volume, low quality inventory of cases, the more the attorney may welcome a non-adversarial resolution of cases. In actual practice, defendants do seem to have targeted plaintiffs' attorneys who fit this profile of high volume "wholesalers."

* * *

5. Restricting Opt Outs: Mandatory Classes and the Limited Fund Theory.—Probably the most aggressive tactic that has been attempted recently in connection with a "friendly" mass tort settlement is the certification of a "mandatory" class action from which class members may not opt out. Normally, a class action seeking money damages must be certified pursuant to Federal Rule of Civil Procedure 23(b)(3), and in such a case, class members have an express right to opt out.

Because "small claimants" have little incentive to opt out and because future claimants have little ability to do so, a "mandatory" class action principally impacts "high stakes" present claimants who would otherwise pursue individual actions. In reality, certification of a Rule 23(b)(1)(B) mandatory class is a protection for defendants against the "danger" that high stakes individual claimants, dissatisfied with the terms of the settlement class, will opt out. If this were to happen, defendants would lose the benefit of the settlement because they might have to pay twice: once to the claims resolution facility established by the settlement, and again to individual claimants who opt out. Yet, the existence of substantial opt outs may be the best evidence that the original settlement was inadequate (and possibly collusive).

Attempts to obtain certification of a mandatory class action under Rule 23(b)(1)(B) usually seek to rely on the justification that, absent pooling and proration among all claimants, the defendant's limited assets soon will be exhausted to the prejudice of future claimants, who will not receive compensation. There are at least two short answers to this justification: First, bankruptcy handles this pooling function much better, and with superior safeguards and procedures, than does the class action. In particular, claimants in bankruptcy are protected by the "absolute priority" rule, which precludes the debtor's shareholders from participating in the reorganized company until all creditors have been paid in full. Second, the prediction that one's assets are insufficient to handle future claims is easily made, particularly by self-interested defendants. When the court accepts this claim, the defendant may be able to escape with a settlement that scales back its tort liability, whereas in bankruptcy, it would be forced to transfer virtually all its equity to its creditors. Until recently, possibly for these reasons in part, attempts to certify a "limited fund" class action have generally been reversed on appeal.

Coffee, Class Wars: The Dilemma of the Mass Tort Action, 95 Colum.L.Rev. 1343, 1347–48, 1373–75, 1382–83 (1995)

5. In an earlier portion of the article, Professor Coffee explained the perverse impact of the "reverse auction," a concern adverted to in the *Amchem* opinion:

One "old" form of collusion is not limited to the "small claimant" class action. It involves what this Article will call a "reverse auction," namely a jurisdictional competition among different teams of plaintiffs' attorneys in different actions that involve the same underlying allegations. The first team to settle with the defendants in effect precludes the others (who may have originated the action and litigated it with sufficient skill and zeal that the defendants were eager to settle with someone else).

* * *

The practical impact of this approach is that it allows the defendants to pick and choose the plaintiff team with which they will deal. Indeed, it signals to the unscrupulous plaintiffs' attorney that by filing a parallel, shadow action in state court, it can underbid the original plaintiffs' attorney team that researched, prepared and filed the action. The net result is that defendants can seek the lowest bidder from among these rival groups and negotiate with each simultaneously.

Coffee, *supra*, at 1370–72.

6. Coverage of class actions in this Section has necessarily been less than exhaustive of all of the issues that arise. For more comprehensive treatment of class actions, see Robert H. Klonoff & Edward K.M. Bilich,

Class Actions and Other Multi–Party Litigation (2000); Alba Conte & Herbert Newberg, Newberg on Class Actions (4th ed.2002); Charles Alan Wright, Arthur R. Miller & Mary Kay Kane, Federal Practice and Procedure §§ 1700–1821 (3d ed.2001).

Note on the Class Action Fairness Act of 2005

The increasing aversion by federal courts to certifying class actions in mass torts reflected in cases like *Rhone Poulenc* and *Amchem*, shifted some of the action into state courts. In one respect, state class actions afforded an advantage over nationwide classes in federal court: a class limited to state residents whose case would be governed by that state's laws avoided the choice of law problems presented when multiple states laws are implicated. Yet beyond avoiding the choice of law problem, there was a perception that state courts were more sympathetic to certifying mass tort class actions. For a plaintiff's lawyers explanation of the advantages of state court class actions, see Walker, Keep Your Case in State Court, Trial (Sept. 2004) at 22.

In response to this trend and perception, Congress enacted the Class Action Fairness Act of 2005 ("CAFA"), Pub.L.No. 109–2, § 5, 119 Stat. 4 (codified at 28 U.S.C.A. §§ 1332(d), 1453, 1711–15). The key feature of CAFA is an expansion of federal subject matter jurisdiction over state-law class actions containing at least 100 class members with an amount in controversy in excess of $5,000,000 (for the claims of all class members) and minimal diversity. Minimal diversity means that at least one plaintiff is a citizen of a different state from at least one defendant, a major change from the complete diversity required under the general federal diversity statute, 28 U.S.C. § 1332. Several exceptions to this broad opening of federal courthouse doors to class actions exist, but none of them is likely to exclude products liability class actions from the expanded federal jurisdiction provided in CAFA. Other provisions provide discretion to federal courts to decline to exercise the jurisdiction provided in CAFA; these are predominantly designed to keep class actions with a significant nexus to one state in state courts.

Other provisions in CAFA are designed to reduce perceived abuses that occur in consumer class actions in which cases are settled on a basis that provides class members with coupons whose value to class members is a fraction of their face value while separately providing cash with which to pay class counsel's attorney's fees. For examples of some of these coupon settlements, see Reig et al., The Class Action Fairness Act of 2005: Overview, Historical Perspective, and Settlement Requirements, 40 Tort Trial & Ins. Prac.L.J. 1087 (2005).

Note on Mandatory Class Actions

All of the class actions in this Chapter involved 23(b)(3) classes, in which class members are provided notice and, more importantly, the right to opt out of the class and pursue their claims on an individual basis. By contrast, 23(b)(1) class actions, to which Professor Coffee referred, are mandatory class actions in that they do not permit class members to opt out of the class. The idea behind 23(b)(1)(B) classes is that when multiple claimants are all seeking the same property or a fund that is limited and the claims conflict in the sense that the property or fund is inadequate to satisfy all claims, the claimants should be brought together into a single suit in which those claims can be adjudicated and resolved, thereby avoiding unseemly races to the courthouse and the unfairness of later-appearing claimants being shut out from recovery. The concern is much the same as that behind the procedural devices of interpleader and necessary parties and similar to bankruptcy, as we shall see.

These class actions are especially attractive to defendants in mass tort cases when negotiating settlements because they assure defendants "global peace," and they need not be concerned with opt outs. In the Bendectin litigation, the defendant, Merrell Dow, agreed to a settlement of $120 million in 1984, but on the condition that a 23(b)(1)(B) class be the mechanism by which the settlement was effectuated so that Merrell Dow could be assured that litigation over the drug would end. To effectuate the settlement, the trial court certified the class as a 23(b)(1)(B) class, even though the court had previously denied certification as a (b)(3) class. How might the trial court have found that a limited fund existed? Could the other subsection of 23(b)(1)—requiring that individual actions would create a risk of inconsistent adjudications that would create "incompatible standards of conduct" for Merrell Dow—justify certification?

The Sixth Circuit overturned the class action certification. Schreier v. Merrell Dow Pharmaceutical, Inc., 745 F.2d 58 (6th Cir.1984). Afterwards, Merrell Dow refused to settle by employing a 23(b)(3) class, and the Bendectin litigation continued for over a decade before petering out in the late 1990s.

The use of 23(b)(1)(B) classes to effectuate global settlements reached the Supreme Court in another asbestos case after *Amchem*, Ortiz v. Fibreboard Corp., 527 U.S. 815, 119 S.Ct. 2295, 144 L.Ed.2d 715 (1999), in which many of the concerns raised by Professor Coffee were present. Structured much like *Amchem*, *Ortiz* was a settlement of future asbestos claimants who would have claims against Fibreboard, a company that was struggling to pay current asbestos claims. As with *Amchem*, the *Ortiz* settlement arrangement involved settlements of existing asbestos claimants represented by class counsel outside the class action structure and a class consisting of future asbestos claimants. Complicating *Ortiz* was that Fibreboard was involved in a dispute with two insurers over whether their policies, which had no aggregate coverage limits, covered asbestos claims against Fibreboard. Fibreboard had obtained a determination that both policies provided coverage from a California state court, and the insurance companies appealed.

As the date for appellate resolution of the coverage dispute loomed, the insurance companies, asbestos plaintiffs' lawyers, and Fibreboard, with the assistance of two judges, reached an agreement that not only produced a 23(b)(1)(B) settlement class action, but also resolved several other major issues. The agreement included a contribution of $1.525 billion by the two insurance companies, $9.5 million from other insurance policies available to Fibreboard, and $500,000 from Fibreboard itself, for a total of $1.535 billion, settlement of existing claims of plaintiffs represented by the lawyers, and, finally, a 23(b)(1)(B) class action that would include all those who had or might have asbestos claims against Fibreboard but who had not yet filed suit. The agreement contemplated that the class action would result in an arrangement that would establish a claims facility for class members that, most significantly, would afford them more constrained options than simply filing their claims in court and obtaining recovery of any damages awarded. Most significantly, claims were capped at $500,000, punitive damages were barred, claims would be paid over a period of years, and no assurance was provided that the fund would not be depleted and the latest claimants would find any assets remaining.

After reviewing the history of the equitable procedure employed for limited fund cases and the history of Fed. R. Civ. P. 23(b)(1)(B), the Supreme Court derived three critical characteristics for any limited fund (i.e., 23(b)(1)(B)) class action: 1) a truly limited fund, inadequate to resolve all claims; 2) the totality of the fund used to pay the claims; and 3) equitable treatment among all claimants. The Supreme Court found flaws with the *Ortiz* settlement agreement in each of these three respects:

1. *Valuation of the limited fund.* To determine whether a limited fund truly existed required determining the assets available to satisfy the claims and the value of all claims. That assessment would require determining the value of the insurance policies with the two insurers, which, while they had no coverage limits, were practically limited by the net worth of each insurance company. Valuation of the insurance assets would also require discounting the net worth amount by the probability that the coverage decision would be reversed on appeal. In addition, the net worth of Fibreboard would be available to asbestos claimants and should be included in determining the amount of the fund. Using Fibreboard's "net worth" assumes that all of its other unsecured creditors will be paid fully. If future asbestos claimants are to recover less in a 23(b)(1) class action, why should other creditors of Fibreboard receive 100 cents on each dollar of their claims?

Once the value of the fund is determined, the amount of the claims by class members requires valuation. Experience with prior claims might permit determination of the value of claims, assuming that past and future claims were similar. More problematic, however, is determining the number of future claimants who will pursue claims. After hearing testimony from experts in hearings about the 23(b)(1) settlement class action in the Bendectin litigation and the wide range in their predictions of the number of future claimants, the trial judge observed, "The only conceivable suggestion I could make at this point is maybe we should have conferred with Jimmy the Greek." *See also* Weinstein, Ethical Dilemmas in Mass Tort Litigation, 88 Nw.U.L.Rev. 469, 509–10 (1994) (expressing lack of confidence in ability to determine number of future claimants).

The difficulty the Supreme Court found with the valuation process was that no adversarial process existed. The fund's value was determined by the parties in their settlement negotiations. Yet that is ordinarily the way that disputed issues are resolved. Why shouldn't the court accept that value? And, except in prominent case congregations like asbestos in which there are other plaintiffs' attorneys who are left out of the settlement and are therefore potential objectors, how is the court to conduct an adversarial hearing when, after the settlement, there are no adversaries?

Recognizing the first objection, the Court pointed to the conflict that existed for class counsel in representing their current claimants in settlement negotiations that were tied to settlement of the future-claimant class action: "In this case, certainly, any assumption that plaintiff's counsel could be of a mind to do their simple best in bargaining for the benefit of the settlement class is patently at odds with the fact that at least some of the same lawyers representing plaintiffs and the class had also negotiated the separate settlement of 45,000 pending claims, the full payment of which was contingent on a successful [settlement agreement]." *Ortiz,* 527 U.S. at 852.

Could the valuation problem have been solved by having separate counsel represent the present and future claimants? How could lawyers without existing asbestos clients adequately represent a class of future asbestos claimants?

2. *Equitable treatment of all class members.* The court identified two problems with the structure of the settlement, inconsistent with the requirement of equity among claimants. First was the exclusion from the class of some 45,000 asbestos plaintiffs who had filed suit and whose claims were settled on terms substantially more favorable than the terms provided to members of the 23(b)(1)(B) class. Second was the same conflict that arose in *Amchem* between class members whose claims were mature at the time of the settlement (even though they had not filed suit) and those whose claims would not mature until many years later. These two groups had different interests over how to allocate the fund among them in light of the uncertainty as to how many claims would be presented and how quickly the fund would be depleted. What about other conflicts among members of the class who would be treated better by the claims process established by the settlement than they would have been treated if they went to court and those who would be treated worse by the claims process than going to court? Would it be an adequate answer to respond that savings by employing a claims process rather than incurring the transaction costs of litigation would result in even the latter group being better off? In its opinion, the Court identified this issue, and wrote that it was "at least a legitimate question, which we leave for another day." 527 U.S. at 859–60.

In many prior class actions, courts have certified the class despite a variety of conflicting interests among class members, brushing them aside as merely "speculation" or "theoretical." *See* Waters v. Barry, 711 F.Supp. 1125, 1127 (D.D.C.1989); Hawk Indus. v. Bausch & Lomb, Inc., 59 F.R.D. 619, 623 (S.D.N.Y.1973). Are those cases distinguishable from asbestos classes like *Amchem* or *Ortiz* because the latter involve class members whose claims are large enough to be viable as individual actions while the former are too small to be individually viable?

3. *Fibreboard's retention of shareholder equity.* Finally, the Court addressed the feature of the settlement that involved a contribution of only $500,000 by Fibreboard, despite estimates that it was worth at least $235 million. Declining to rely on this ground because the prior two flaws were dispositive, the Court nevertheless observed that class members were to receive discounted recoveries, while Fibreboard would retain nearly all of its

net worth. Given that creditors have priority over stockholders when a company is insolvent and goes into bankruptcy, do you appreciate the attractiveness of a 23(b)(1)(B) settlement, such as *Ortiz*, to a company like Fibreboard?

The Supreme Court confronted, but declined to resolve, an important argument made by the class settlement proponents. Proponents of the class claimed that Fibreboard's retention of its net worth was justified because class members would be better off with the settlement class. The settlement class with its administrative claims facility would save a substantial amount of the transaction costs that would otherwise be consumed by individual litigation of asbestos claims against Fibreboard. With the transaction-cost saving exceeding Fibreboard's net worth, the argument went, class members would obtain more money in the class resolution, even without Fibreboard's contribution. After relating this argument, the Court declined to address and resolve it.

How should courts treat such an argument? Should it matter how the transaction-cost saving is distributed between the class and Fibreboard? What about individual class members with strong claims who, because of the administrative claims facility with categorical rather than individualized determinations, are worse off than pursuing an individual claim?

In any case, this unresolved question is also applicable to another alternative option for the true limited fund situation: bankruptcy. As you consider bankruptcy, keep in mind the question of whether claimants being better off (in terms of total recovery) in a 23(b)(1)(B) class rather than in bankruptcy court should be significant in determining which mechanism is better for resolution of limited fund cases.

Note on Bankruptcy Option for Mass Torts

Consideration of bankruptcy for resolution of mass torts is unavoidable when potential claims are sufficient to create a limited fund, in the sense that the assets available to a defendant are insufficient to pay all of the claims in full. Thus, bankruptcy provides an alternative mechanism for resolution of mass tort claims when the assets available to the defendant are insufficient to satisfy all of the claims against it. Detailed coverage of bankruptcy law would extend this text by hundreds of pages, but a brief description and some broad themes follow.

Jurisdiction over bankruptcy proceedings is exclusively in the federal courts. A Chapter 11 bankruptcy proceeding, which is the type most likely to be invoked with mass tort claimants, involves "reorganization" of the bankrupt company's debts. As with limited fund class actions, the idea is to have all claimants (creditors) present their claims in a single proceeding in which all of the claims can be addressed equitably while attempting to retain the value of the bankrupt as a going concern. Thus, suits by all creditors, including tort claimants, against the bankrupt are automatically stayed upon the filing of a bankruptcy petition and an injunction prevents the initiation of any other suits outside the bankruptcy proceedings. All creditors must submit their claims to the bankruptcy court. Future claims by those who had already been exposed to the bankrupt's toxic product but have not yet suffered disease have been included as claims in these reorganization plans.* Yet those claims present similar problems to the ones adverted to in the discussion of *Ortiz* when the bankruptcy court makes an estimation of the value of claims against the bankrupt, as the law requires.

Thus, the capacity of a bankruptcy court to aggregate all existing and future claims before it is unmatched. Could the *Windsor* and *Ortiz* class actions have included *all* current and future claimants? Yet the ability to aggregate is not equivalent to being able to resolve all of the claims—Congress has provided that personal injury claimants retain a right to jury trial for their claims. Unless an administrative scheme is established in the reorganization plan and is sufficiently attractive to claimants to divert them from litigation, bankruptcy provides little opportunity for more efficient resolution of mass claims. Yet the universal aggregation of claimants, the provisions for equitable treatment of all classes of creditors, and the substantial negotiation of interests in the bankruptcy proceeding frequently produce an administrative compensation scheme for tort claimants. Often the compensation system provides a back-end right to dissatisfied claimants to file suit in court, although this option is typically saddled with provisions making it unattractive for most.

The goal of a Chapter 11 bankruptcy is a reorganization plan that resolves the claims of all creditors and permits the bankrupt to continue operating with a discharge of all prior debts. Any reorganization plan is governed by detailed substantive and procedural protections for creditors. Creditors are separated into different classes with the idea that each class will have substantially similar types of claims and therefore interests. A majority (and two-thirds of the dollar value) of each class of creditors who will receive less than 100 cents on their dollar of claim must approve the plan, and the court must approve the plan as fair and in compliance with all requirements of the Bankruptcy code, after holding a hearing. How do you suppose current tort claimants decide whether to vote in favor of a plan? Should that cause concern?

A process exists to approve a reorganization plan in the absence of approval by a class of creditors, when the court finds, in essence, that the class is either receiving full payment of its claims or no class with junior rights is receiving any payment on its claims, i.e., all remaining funds of the bankrupt are devoted to the highest priority class of creditors.

Although many creditors will have liquidated claims, tort claimants are unliquidated. Before a reorganization plan can be developed and approved,

---

* In 1994, Congress amended the Bankruptcy code to provide coverage for future asbestos claimants in bankruptcy proceedings, provided certain protections were implemented in the bankruptcy proceedings. 11 U.S.C. § 524(g) & (h). *See* In re Joint E. & S. Dists. Asbestos Litig., 878 F.Supp. 473, 570–72 (E. & S.D.N.Y. 1995). *Compare* Epstein v. Official Committee of Unsecured Creditors, of the Estate of Piper Aircraft Corp., 58 F.3d 1573 (11th Cir.1995) (holding that future air crash victims who assert claims against the bankrupt, a manufacturer of general aviation airplanes, are not claimants within the meaning of the Bankruptcy code). *See* National Bankruptcy Review Commission, Treatment of Mass Future Claims in Bankruptcy (1997) (proposing modification of Bankruptcy code to include future tort victims as claimants in bankruptcy proceedings).

estimation of the value of the unliquidated tort claims is required. Recall the difficulties with determining future claims in *Ortiz* and the Bendectin litigations. An alternative to estimation is to try all of the claims to determine their value, but when there are large numbers of tort claimants, trials for each as a predicate to approval of a reorganization plan is infeasible and undesirable. For an explanation of the estimation process employed in the A.H. Robin bankruptcy for Dalkon Shield claimants, see McGovern, Resolving Mature Mass Torts, 69 B.U. L. Rev. 659 (1989).

In sum, bankruptcy seems to provide better structural protections for insuring similar (more equitable) treatment across the class of tort claimants and to make sure that tort claimants are treated fairly in relation to other creditors, a matter that mandatory class actions, such as *Ortiz,* do not. Yet the protections for classes of creditors and the cumbersome process of developing and obtaining approval of a reorganization plan imposes substantial administrative costs. While not the final word on this choice, consider the differing views from three federal judges, two of them writing in the decision that first affirmed the district court's certification of the *Ortiz* settlement class.

IN RE JOINT EASTERN & SOUTHERN DISTRICT ASBESTOS LITIGATION

United States Court of Appeals, Second Circuit, 1993.
14 F.3d 726.

WINTER, CIRCUIT JUDGE:

This is an appeal from Judge Weinstein's order issuing a preliminary injunction and certifying a mandatory limited-fund class action pursuant to Fed.R.Civ.P. 23(b)(1)(B). The underlying action's claim for relief is unique. It seeks a settlement with a mandatory class of all persons with present or future asbestos claims against Keene Corporation. Keene, however, does not claim that it has a right to such a settlement. * * *

Instead, it is clear that the complaint is an attempt to compel an adjustment of Keene's creditors' rights outside the Bankruptcy Code and is defended almost entirely by the argument that a mandatory class settlement of present or future asbestos claims would be better for all parties than a bankruptcy proceeding. Indeed, the process contemplated by Keene mirrors a bankruptcy proceeding. The finding of a limited fund corresponds to a finding of insolvency. The preliminary injunction serves much the same function as the automatic stay under Section 362(a) of the Bankruptcy Code. 11 U.S.C. § 362(a) (1988). The class representatives correspond to creditors' committees in Chapter 11 proceedings. *See* 11 U.S.C. § 1102 (1988). The proposed mandatory class settlement mirrors a reorganization plan and "cram-down,"[citations].

Keene's argument is self-defeating, however, because it is a self-evident evasion of the exclusive legal system established by Congress for debtors to seek relief. *See In re Johns Manville*, 982 F.2d at 735. The adoption of Keene's position would surely lead to further evasion of the

Bankruptcy Code as other debtors sought relief in mandatory class actions. Keene argues that such a precedent would be limited to situations, like Keene's, of mass torts in which some plaintiffs are not known at the time of the accident. We are dubious that a limit to unknown plaintiffs is feasible. Under the limited fund theory espoused here, a class representative for a large number of trade creditors might be appointed to seek a settlement on their behalf where a company was deemed to be a limited fund because of insolvency. The argument that the company and its creditors would all be better off in such an action than in bankruptcy would be as plausible in a case involving a large number of contract creditors as it is here. Breach of warranty cases involving numerous purchasers might also fall within the theory.

Moreover, even if limited to so-called mass torts with yet unknown plaintiffs, Keene's theory would cover a large number of cases. The use of aggregative techniques and inventive legal theories are causing mass torts to become rather routine. Certainly the theory pressed here would apply to many products liability cases, *see, e.g., In re Silicone Gel Breast Implants Prods. Liab. Litig.*, 793 F.Supp. 1098 (J.P.M.L.1992), environmental torts, *see, e.g., In re Love Canal Actions*, 92 A.D.2d 416, 460 N.Y.S.2d 850 (App.Div.1983), and even physical disasters. *See, e.g., Phillips v. Hallmark Cards, Inc.*, 722 S.W.2d 86 (Mo.1986) (en banc) (suit by firemen against owner of hotel in which skywalks collapsed for injuries, including emotional distress, sustained while rescuing trapped victims).

Evasion of bankruptcy is also not without costs or other perils. The injunction in the instant matter has already prevented execution of final judgments on supersedeas bonds and funds in escrow that are not Keene's assets. Moreover, class members in cases such as this would have no say in the conduct of the court-appointed class representatives and, unlike creditors in bankruptcy, are not able to vote on a settlement. *See* 11 U.S.C. § 1126. For them, it would be "cram-down" from start to finish. Finally, unlike a lawyer for a creditors' committee, the class representatives in matters like the present one may not be compensated unless a settlement is reached, a situation fraught with danger to the rights of plaintiffs. *See In re "Agent Orange" Prod. Liab. Litig.*, 818 F.2d 216, 222 (2d Cir.), cert. denied, 484 U.S. 926, 108 S.Ct. 289, 98 L.Ed.2d 249 (1987) (Fee arrangement creating incentives to settle without regard to merits is void.).

Keene argues passionately that bankruptcy will be a more costly route for the defendant class than this mandatory class action. It may be that the amount distributed to the class in a Keene bankruptcy will be less than in a settlement in the instant class action. Indeed, Keene has suggested that a trial be held on that issue. However, the function of federal courts is not to conduct trials over whether a statutory scheme should be ignored because a more efficient mechanism can be fashioned by judges.

[The court held that the complaint would have to be dismissed for lack of subject matter jurisdiction because the complaint asserted no claim at all, merely a request to certify a class that would require settlement negotiations between Keene and its asbestos claimants.]

IN RE ASBESTOS LITIGATION
United States Court of Appeals, Fifth Circuit, 1996.
90 F.3d 963, vacated and remanded, 521 U.S.
1114, 117 S.Ct. 2503, 138 L.Ed.2d 1008.

[This is the Fifth Circuit's opinion from its first consideration of the 23(b)(1)(B) class certified in Ortiz v. Fibreboard, *supra*. Challengers (intervenors) to the class certification objected, inter alia, that the mandatory class was an improper end run around the Bankruptcy Code.

After citing other cases that had certified 23(b)(1)(B) classes based on a limited fund to demonstrate that the Bankruptcy Code was not the exclusive forum for resolving claims against insolvent or potentially insolvent entitites, the court distinguished In re Joint Eastern and Southern District Asbestos Litigation, *supra*, after pointing out that its discussion of the propriety of a 23(b)(1)(B) class action was dicta.]

[*Ortiz's*] Global Settlement Agreement was undisputedly driven by insurance coverage litigation between Fibreboard and its insurers which created a serious risk for all parties to the agreement. The Global Health Claimant Class and Fibreboard faced the real possibility that Fibreboard would be insolvent simply on the basis of claims already settled. The Insurers, on the other hand, faced the possibility of virtually unlimited liability for damage caused by Fibreboard asbestos. This pressure, felt by all parties to the global settlement, is what finally brought them together on the eve of the coverage case appeal. The unique risks posed by the coverage cases distinguish [*Ortiz*] from a blatant attempt to circumvent the Bankruptcy Code such as occurred in *Keene*.

The facts of *Keene* further distinguish it from our case. First, an already weak Keene attempted to avoid impending bankruptcy by asking the court to coerce its tort victims to settle claims in a court where no claims were filed against Keene. Second, Keene attempted to utilize the 23(b)(1)(B) injunction to halt pending actions in other courts. Third, and most importantly, Keene's complaint was dismissed on the ground that it failed to present the court with any case or controversy because it requested only that the court compel all plaintiffs in suits against Keene to appear and negotiate.

[*Ortiz*] by comparison, presents us with claims against a healthy company for personal injuries and a proposed settlement of those claims. [*Ortiz*] presents no danger that Fibreboard may simply be abusing this proceeding to delay other actions or to improve its negotiating position with present claimants because it only enjoins future proceedings, not those already pending. We agree with the Keene court that under the facts presented to it, a 23(b)(1)(B) action was not appropriate. We also agree that, in the vast majority of cases, the Bankruptcy Code should govern the distribution of an insolvent entity's assets. However, where concerns such as the risk of an adverse judgment in the coverage litigation support an early resolution of the claims against an entity and all parties can benefit from a settlement under Rule 23(b)(1)(B), we see no legal or policy reason to deny the parties this benefit. The essential basis of any settlement is to avoid the uncertainty, risks, and expense of ongoing litigation. In our case, the risks facing Fibreboard, the Insurers, and the health claimants as a result of the California coverage litigation were real and enormous. Holding that the bankruptcy laws require the parties to wait until catastrophe befalls one or more of them as a result of the California litigation would be a denial of justice to the parties before us and unwarranted by the law.

* * *

[*Ortiz*] presented the district court with a superior alternative to the Bankruptcy Code and did so long before any bankruptcy court would have had jurisdiction over Fibreboard's assets. Indeed, one of the most important facts of this case is that, in spite of the threat posed by future personal injury litigation, Fibreboard is currently solvent and healthy. In the short term, no trade or tort creditor has the ability or the incentive to force Fibreboard into a Chapter 11 reorganization. It is also clear that shareholders and management, who stand to lose equity and/or employment if Fibreboard enters bankruptcy proceedings, will refuse to file a voluntary petition at least until the coverage dispute is resolved against it. That, of course, would be too late for the Global Health Claimant Class.

Even in the unlikely event that Fibreboard could be persuaded to file a voluntary bankruptcy petition, the Global Health Claimant Class would be worse off than it is under the Global Settlement Agreement. Under the Bankruptcy Code, representation for the class may not be available at all and courts that have allowed representation of future tort claimants have left them in an uncertain position that falls short of full "creditor" status. Additionally, full-blown bankruptcy proceedings would bring in all of Fibreboard's other creditors and impose large transactions costs on Fibreboard that, ultimately, would come out of any distribution. See Edward I. Altman, *A Further Empirical Investigation of the Bankruptcy Cost Question*, 39 J.Fin. 1067, 1077 (1984). In stark contrast to the uncertain and weak position afforded future tort claimants under the Bankruptcy Code, the plaintiff class and its representatives in [*Ortiz*] had center stage and ran no risk of encountering a cram-down reorganization approved only by trade creditors and rammed through over the objections of class representatives.

To the extent intervenors are arguing that certification is improper because Fibreboard fares better under the class action settlement than under a bankruptcy proceeding, we find their focus misplaced. The inquiry instead should be whether the class is better served by avoiding impairment of their interests. Fibreboard is clearly acting in its own interest in consummating the Global Settlement Agreement and thereby avoiding future insolvency. But the Global Settlement Agreement also serves the interests of the Global Health Claimant Class. Early settlement allows the class to recover far more as a group than it could if it was forced to wait until Fibreboard enters bankruptcy on its own and encounters the high transaction costs of insolvency. *See* Mark J. Roe, *Bankruptcy and Mass Tort*, 84 Colum.L.Rev. 846, 851–64, 905–17 (1984) (advocating early reorganizations because they avoid the waste of insolvency and distribute more to victims, but noting that no one with the ability to push the mass tortfeasor into an early reorganization has the incentive to do so). Precisely because it avoids the enormous transactions costs of litigation and insolvency, the Global Settlement Agreement can offer a deal from which all parties gain. Members of the Global Health Claimant Class receive more money in payment for their injuries and Fibreboard's shareholders keep their stake in a viable entity. The only loser under the Global Settlement Agreement is the asbestos litigation industry.

For all of these reasons, we find that the district court's decision to certify *Ortiz* as a 23(b)(1)(B) class action is an appropriate interpretation of Rule 23 that does not conflict with the Bankruptcy Code and upholds the principles of equity and fairness.

SMITH, CIRCUIT JUDGE, dissenting:

I. INTRODUCTION.

The district court and the majority undoubtedly are driven by a commendable desire to resolve voluminous personal injury claims against an otherwise strong American company and to ensure an orderly transfer of funds from the company's insurers to its victims. In order to accomplish this result, however, they have extinguished claims over which they have no jurisdiction and deprived thousands of asbestos victims of basic constitutional rights. The result is the first no-opt-out, mass-tort, settlement-only, futures-only class action ever attempted or approved.

Ironically, the willingness to jettison centuries-old legal precepts hurts the very victims they intend to help: The settlement forces asbestos victims to surrender their claims in exchange for a meager $10 million of Fibreboard's $225–250 million net worth. They also benefit from Fibreboard's settlement with its insurers, but Fibreboard and the insurers had powerful incentives to settle that dispute by themselves; in fact, they did so for $2 billion.

There was no need even to involve the class in those negotiations, much less to sacrifice its interests. "Thus, the class members appear to have traded Fibreboard's liability for nothing to which they did not already have a right."

On the other hand, the district court and the majority have bailed Fibreboard's shareholders out of a mammoth liability and awarded $43.7 million to class counsel. This suit was supposedly brought on behalf of Fibreboard's victims, but of the four entities directly affected by the settlement—Fibreboard, class attorneys, courts, and asbestos victims—the victims were the only entity absent from the bargaining table. Perhaps for that reason, they also were the only losers.

How could well-intentioned judges sanction—indeed, compel—such an untoward result? Apparently this is simply a case of judges—both trial and appellate—trying too hard to solve the vexing problems posed by unending asbestos litigation. Having certified at least two other high-profile asbestos class actions, then-Chief District Judge Parker was acutely aware of the problems posed by asbestos litigation. In the end, he appears to have become too close to both the overall problem and the instant settlement to continue to act in a judicial capacity in this case.

When Fibreboard and class counsel announced at a court hearing that they had reached a settlement, Chief Judge Parker referred to "extensive negotiations between counsel that the Court has participated in." Also at that time, and long before the fairness hearing, he said, "We will trust in the scholarship, the good judgment and common sense of the ... courts of appeal in the event this comes to their attention." In short, Chief Judge Parker tried his best to solve a perplexing problem, and it is our task to figure out whether that solution is legally sustainable.

There are two primary problems: (1) Fibreboard, class counsel, and Fibreboard's other creditors have combined to profit at the expense of absent class members; and (2) this case is an affront to the integrity of the judicial system. As we observed when reversing Chief Judge Parker's certification of another class action against Fibreboard: "The Judicial Branch can offer the trial of lawsuits. It has no power or competence to do more." Fibreboard, 893 F.2d at 712.

* * *

D. Constructive Bankruptcy.

* * * In bankruptcy, the claims of *all* of Fibreboard's creditors, not just its "future" personal injury victims, would be crammed-down. Permitting Fibreboard to effect a reorganization bankruptcy proceeding in the guise of a futures-only class action circumvents the detailed protections of the Bankruptcy Code for the express purpose of imposing the entire cost of the bailout on Fibreboard's most vulnerable creditors, to the betterment of its shareholders.

* * * The amicus brief of the Trial Lawyers for Public Justice puts the point more forcefully: "[I]nstead of protecting class members from the risk that their ability to obtain relief from Fibreboard will be 'substantially impaired,' certification of the proposed settlement class here ensures that the class members' ability to obtain relief from Fibreboard will be totally eliminated." [Citation]

* * *

In sum, the settlement fails either a customary legal analysis or a common-sense smell test. I respectfully but vehemently dissent from all but part III of the majority opinion.

Notes

1. Accepting the position of Judge Davis, representing the majority of the Fifth Circuit in In re Asbestos Litigation, how frequently will a 23(b)(1)(B) class action be justified when the limited fund consists of, inter alia, the assets of the product manufacturer? How frequently should it be?

2. For thumbnail sketches of three major bankruptcy proceedings occasioned by massive product liability claims, see Richard L. Marcus & Edward F. Sherman, Complex Litigation 203–08 (1998) (summarizing the Johns Manville, A.H. Robins, and Dow Corning bankruptcy proceedings); Paul Rheingold, Mass Tort Litigation § 18 (1996) (providing, in addition, information about over a dozen additional asbestos company bankruptcies). For detailed consideration of the Robins bankruptcy, in which the shareholders of Robins emerged with over $900 million, see Richard Sobol, Bending the Law (1991). For a detailed account of the trust fund established for Dalkon Shield claimants and its (apparently successful) administration, see Vairo, The Dalkon Shield Claimants Trust: Paradigm Lost (or Found?), 61 Fordham L.Rev. 617 (1992).

3. Professor Cohen, after reviewing *Ortiz* and considering the alternative of bankruptcy, concludes that in a 23(b)(1)(B) class action all of the defendant's assets cannot be devoted to the class, otherwise trade and other nontort creditors would be worse off than in a bankruptcy proceeding. *See* Cohen, The "Fair" Is the Enemy of the Good: Ortiz v. Fibreboard Corporation and Class Action Settlements, 8 Sup.Ct.Econ.Rev. 23, 88–94 (2000). Could a class action be certified with subclasses to account for each of the different creditor classes? Does this structure, even if permissible under the Federal Rules, so resemble bankruptcy that courts should be wary of invoking it?

4. Scholarly treatment of the debate between class actions and bankruptcy includes Brubaker, Bankruptcy Injunctions and Complex Litigation: A Critical Reappraisal of Non-debtor Releases in Chapter 11 Reorganizations, 1997 U.Ill.L.Rev. 959 (describing and criticizing bankruptcy courts providing a discharge to individuals and entities related to the debtor, such as officers and insurers, as part of the reorganization plan); Cohen, The "Fair" Is the Enemy of the Good: Ortiz v. Fibreboard Corporation and Class Action Settlements, 8 Sup.Ct.Econ.Rev. 23, 88–94 (2000)("bankruptcy may be the best alternative means for resolving mass tort litigation in this situation [yet] bankruptcy can be a very costly option for creditors as well as for the debtor"); Lyle, Mass Tort Claims and the Corporate Tortfeasor: Bankruptcy Reorganization and Legislative Compensation Versus the Common Law Tort System, 61 Tex.L.Rev. 1297 (1983); Smith, A Capital Markets Approach to Mass Tort Bankruptcy, 104 Yale L.J. 367 (1994) (arguing that strong structural and psychological forces result in future claimants not being fairly treated in bankruptcy proceedings).

5. Professor Elizabeth Gibson, in a study sponsored by the Federal Judicial Center, compared several limited fund class actions with bankruptcies. She concluded:

> I conclude that bankruptcy comes out ahead of limited fund class action settlements with respect to the fairness of the resolution process and the effectiveness of judicial review. The confirmation requirement of voting by individual creditors (including tort claimants), the substantive bankruptcy protections for individuals and classes that vote against the plan, and the practice of appointing a future claims representative provide greater protection and opportunity for input for absent tort claimants than is available to them when a district court approves a limited fund class action settlement. Moreover, tort claimants are treated more equitably in a bankruptcy reorganization with respect to the defendant's other creditors, because all are forced to share the defendant's shortfall; in a limited fund class action settlement, only the tort claimants are forced to compromise their claims.
>
> Judges presiding over bankruptcy reorganizations also have the advantage of having specific statutory standards for the confirmation of the reorganization plan. The standards for determining whether a limited fund class should be certified and whether a settlement should be approved, by contrast, remain ill defined. While neither method appears to have an advantage when it comes to estimating the defendant's total mass tort liability, a difficult task regardless of the resolution method used, bankruptcy judges are likely to have more expertise than district judges in determining the value of a defendant company. District judges, on the other hand, may be in a better position to assess the fairness of the treatment of the tort claimants in light of the merits of the claims.
>
> Where limited fund class action settlements come out ahead, in my view, is with regard to the efficiency of the resolution process and the likelihood that a defendant will invoke that resolution method. A limited fund class settlement can usually be achieved and approved by the court in much less time than it takes to achieve confirmation of a mass tort defendant's bankruptcy reorganization plan. Moreover, fewer parties, lawyers, and experts are generally involved in a limited fund class proceeding than in a Chapter 11 bankruptcy. Thus, a limited fund class action settlement should be achievable at much less cost than is required by a mass tort bankruptcy reorganization. A limited fund class action settlement in the past has most likely been seen by defendants as a more attractive option than bankruptcy, because it involves less stigma and presents no risk of loss of ownership of the company. However, the Supreme Court's recent Ortiz decision, by raising doubts about the validity of limited fund class action settlements of mass tort claims, may make a defendant more reluctant in the future to attempt such a settlement to resolve its mass tort liability.

Gibson, Cases Studies of Mass Tort Limited Fund Settlements and Bankruptcy Reorganizations 5–6 (2000).

6. **The Pre–Packaged Bankruptcy.** To streamline the bankruptcy process, companies have attempted "pre-packaged bankruptcy" filings. In

these bankruptcies, negotiations among the debtor and its creditors in advance of filing produces a Chapter 11 reorganization play with sufficient support among creditors for its immediate approval by the bankruptcy court. As with other efforts to provide global resolution of asbestos liabilities, the devil is often in the details.

In In re Combustion Engineering, Inc., 391 F.3d 190 (3d Cir.2005), the pre-packaged bankruptcy plan of the debtor was challenged. Overwhelmed by asbestos claims, Combustion Engineering negotiated a plan in which it would contribute half of its assets, along with available liability insurance to asbestos claimants. Under the plan, existing asbestos claimants would receive a percentage of the settled value of their claims, ranging from 37.5 to 95%. A separate fund was established for future claimants. Existing claimants would share in the futures fund to the extent of the shortfall (from 5 to 62.5%) in the payment that they received for the settled value of their claims; these claims on the future fund were denominated "stub claims."

In order to fund the settlement, two affiliated companies (subsidiaries of the same parent) would be sold and some of the proceeds of the sales contributed to pay asbestos claimants. In order for them to be sold, they would have to be freed of their asbestos liabilities. Hence, they were protected under the pre-packaged plan from suits by asbestos claimants in the same fashion as the debtor, Combustion Engineering.

The Third Circuit found several problems with the plan. Expert testimony in the lower court estimated that while current claimants would receive, on average, 59% of the settled value of their claims, future claimants would only receive 18% of the settled value of their claims. Exacerbating this disparity in the treatment of asbestos creditors was the manner in which approval of the plan from the future claimant class was obtained. All members of the existing claimant group were included in the future group for voting purposes because of the "stub claims" that existing claimants retained. Of the votes cast in favor the plan by the future asbestos claimant class, 90% were provided by the stub claimants. Finally, the Third Circuit found that the district court did not have jurisdiction, under the Bankruptcy Act, to adjudicate and resolve asbestos claims against companies affiliated with the debtor who had not filed for bankruptcy themselves, even though that resolution was crucial to the bankruptcy plan.

While the court made no categorical ruling about the validity of the pre-packaged plans, *Combustion Engineering* underscores the tension between existing and future asbestos claimants in any form of global resolution and the complexities of obtaining protection from future suits for those affiliated with a debtor seeking Chapter 11 reorganization.

*

Index

References are to Pages

ASSUMPTION OF RISK
See Comparative Fault

BREACH OF CONTRACT
Combined with warranty
    Express, 34
    Implied merchantability, 35
    Implied fitness, 35
Damages, 36
    Consequential economic loss, 36
    Economic loss, 36
Notice requirement, 51
    Purpose of, 51
    Remote sellers, 51
Privity, 34
    Horizontal, 34
    Relaxation of requirement, 34
    Vertical, 34
Proximate causation, 36
Relationships, 35
    Business family, 35
    Military family, 35
    Nephews, 35
    Nieces, 36
    Students, 36
    Tenants, 36
Remedies, 37
    Limitations, 47
        Conspicuousness, 49
        Contract interpretation, 45
        Gross unfairness, 49
        Failure of essential purpose, 47
        Impossibility of repair, 50
        Incidental damages, 50
        Independent limitations, 50
        Lack of bargaining power, 49
        Personal injury, 48
        Unconscionability, 47
    Replacement of defective parts, 47
Statutes of limitations, 51
    Discovery rule, 52
    Timing, 51
Statutes of repose, 52

BREACH OF WARRANTY
Generally, 13
Express Warranty, 15
    Affected parties, 17
    Contract interpretation, 16
    Fault, 18

BREACH OF WARRANTY—Cont'd
    Reliance, 20
    Remedial promise, 22
History of, 13
Implied warranty of fitness,
    Buyer's examination of goods, 32
    Buyer's intended use, 31
    Buyer's reliance, 31
    Combined with implied warranty of merchantability, 31
    Potential defendants, 31
    Seller's expertise, 31
Implied warranty of merchantability, 25
    Conformance with product label, 28
    Obvious defects, 28
    Opportunity to inspect, 28
    Potential defendants, 29
        Definition of merchant, 30
        Casual or inexperienced sellers, 30
    Standard of merchantability, 26
        Course of dealing, 28
        Industry Practice, 26
        Reasonable quality vs. perfection, 26
        Relationship to defect, 26
        Usage of trade, 28
    Unavoidable defect, 27
Types of warranty, 14

BYSTANDERS
See Defectiveness

CAUSATION
Causation in fact, 339
    But for test, 339
    Substantial factor test, 339
Proof of causation,
    See Proof of Causation
Proximate cause,
    See Proximate Cause

COMPARATIVE FAULT
Apportionment amount multiple defendants, 638
    Chain of distribution, 600
        Equitable indemnity doctrine, 646
        Governmental immunity, 649
        Imputed or constructive liability, 643
        Indemnity, 641
        Primary culpability, 643

COMPARATIVE FAULT—Cont'd
    Procedure, 608
    Secondary culpability, 643
    Spousal immunity, 649
    Timing of control, 630
  Comparative fault, 640
  Contribution, 649
    Apportionment of liability, 649
      Cause-in-fact apportionment, 650
      Comparative responsibility, 649
    Avoidable consequences, 652
    Comparison of causation, 651
    Contributory negligence, 652
    Different causes of action, 652
    Insolvent defendants, 641
    Mitigation of damages, 652
    Nomenclature of fault, 652
    Percentage bars, 653
    Post-accident plaintiff conduct, 652
  Employers, 657
    Exclusion of employers, 663
    Immunity, 657
    Worker's compensation, 657
  Joint and several liability, 639
    Distinct injuries, 639
    Indivisible causation, 639
    Indivisible injuries, 639
  Limitations on damages, 607
  Non-party defendants, 663
  Partial settlements, 653
    Comparative causation, 656
    Dollar credit, 654
    Mary Carter agreements, 657
    Percent credit, 654
    Pro-rata credit, 654
Consumer conduct defenses, 599
  Assumption of risk, 599, 606
    Express assumption of risk, 606
      Contractual assumption, 606
      Unconscionability, 607
    Implied assumption of risk, 607
      Proximate causation, 608
  Comparative responsibility, 613
    Assigning vs. comparing, 623
    Comparative causation, 623
    Defectiveness vs. conduct, 625
    Fault v. proximate causation, 626
    Quantifying fault, 625
    Strict tort liability, 627
  Contributory negligence, 600
    Breach of warranty, 601
    Misrepresentation, 602
    Negligence, 605
    Strict tort liability, 606
  Failure to discover or guard against risk, 605
  Misuse, 627
    Foreseeable risks, 629
    Legal vs. proximate causation, 631
    Negation of claim vs. defense, 636

COMPLEX LITIGATION
  Generally, 777
Bankruptcy option, 818
  Conflict with bankruptcy proceeding, 844
Class actions, 798
  Adequate definition of the class, 809
  Aggregative procedural devices, 788
  Class certification, 798
    Appealability, 800
    Cause of action, 801
    Mandamus, 806
    Merits, 801
  Choice of law, 823
  Mass accidents, 812
  Mass tort problems,
    Limited fund theory, 843
    Loss of client control, 842
    Mandatory classes, 843
    Reverse action, 844
    Special class treatment, 843
    Subclasses, 842
  Issue preclusion/collateral estoppel, 773
  Offensive collateral estoppel (Green), 788
  Seventh amendment, 821
  Strategic considerations, 788
Multi-district litigation, 791
  Consolidation, 791
  Forum non-conveniens statute, 796

CONTRIBUTION AND INDEMNITY
See Comparative Fault

CONTRIBUTORY NEGLIGENCE
See Comparative Fault

DAMAGES
  Generally, 548
American rule, 550
Apportionment, 548
Attorney's fees, 550
Compensatory damages, 548
  Mental distress, 561
    Bystanders, 562
    Exposure, 568
    Impact rule, 562
    Increased risk, 573
    Medical monitoring expenses, 572
    Physical harm requirement, 565
    Sub-clinical injury, 568
    Zone of danger, 565
  Pecuniary loss and harm to property, 550
    Component parts, 560
    Damage to product, 556
    De minimis rule, 561
    Necessity vs. luxury, 560
    Sudden and calamitous exception, 560

DAMAGES—Cont'd
General damages, 549
Medical monitoring, 573
Mental distress damages, 565
Pre-existing injuries, 509
Punitive damages, 575
    Constitutionality, 584
    Cost-benefit analysis, 581
    Evidence, 584
        Defendant's net worth, 535
        Profitability, 585
    Problems with punitive damages (Owen), 585
    Relevant factors, 589
    Standard of liability, 583
Special damages, 548
    Earning capacity, 548
    Lost property, 548
    Medical expenses, 548
Sub-clinical injuries, 567
Subsequent injuries, 548
Tort reform, 547
    Caps on damages, 550
    Collateral source rule, 550
Toxic tort cases, 548

DEFECTIVENESS
    See also, Design Defect; Manufacturing Defect; Warning Defect
    Generally, 81
Design defects, 98
    Abnormally dangerous activity, 173
    Allergies, 326
        Number of potential victims, 331
        Sensitizer vs. primary irritant, 330
    Alternative design, 151
        Alternative design vs. different product, 162
        Expert testimony, 162
        Liability without alternative design, 169
    Characterization of risk, 109
    Choosing the consumer, 96
        Average consumers, 108
        Expert testimony, 162
    Component part manufacturer, 189
    Consumer expectation test, 98, 171, 177
    Custom-made products, 187
    Foresight/hindsight, 158
    Idiosyncratic reactions, 326
    Ignorance of risk, 104
    Misuse, 144
        Foreseeable criminal misuse, 176
    Modification, 151
    Multi-functional machines, 187
    Non-delegable duty, 185
    Open and obvious risks, 99, 101, 109, 113
    Optional safety device, 183
    Ordinary users, 99
    Potential plaintiffs, 109
        Bystanders, 109
    Reasonably vs. completely safe, 151
    Technology, 152

DEFECTIVENESS—Cont'd
Timing of warning, 332
    Changes in technology, 334
    Component part manufacturer, 37
    Hindsight standard, 334
    Risks not discoverable at time of sale, 334
    Unavoidably unsafe products, 200, 211
        Pharmaceuticals, 211
    Worker's compensation, 184, 193
Tests,
    Consumer expectation test, 90, 95, 103
        Critique, 111
        Current viability, 113
        Justification, 113
        Used with risk-utility test, 112, 120, 129, 140
    Deviation from the norm test, 97, 136
    Foreign-natural test, 94
    Risk-utility test, 90, 114, 120, 126
        Burden of proof, 137
        Categorical risk-utility balancing, 176, 216
        Consumer vs. society, 131
        Cost-benefits analysis, 249
        Intervening causes, 249
        Limitation, 130
        Timing, 131
        Used with consumer expectation test, 112, 120, 129, 140
Warning defects, 234
    Adequacy of warning, 249
    Autonomy vs. safety, 244
    Causes of action,
        Breach of warranty, 241
        Negligence, 241
        Strict liability, 241
    Duty to warn, 234
        Of another manufacturer's product, 198
        Post-sale duty to warn, 332
    Effect of mass advertising, 311
    Failure to read warning, 264
    Instructions vs. warnings, 241, 262
    Learned intermediary doctrine, 303, 311
    Obvious or known dangers, 279
    Overlap with design defects, 241
    Pharmacist liability, 324
    Potential plaintiffs,
        Bystanders, 295
        Consumers, 295
        Users, 295
    Psychology of warnings, 274
    Risks,
        Foreseeable risks, 243
        Foresight/hindsight, 243
        Undiscoverable risks, 243
    Sophisticated user doctrine, 306

INDEX

References are to Pages

DEFENDANTS
See also Breach of Warranty; Comparative Fault; Parties Covered by Strict Liability
Farmers, 29
Pharmacists, 316

DESIGN DEFECT
See Defectiveness

EXPRESS WARRANTY
See Warranty

FAILURE TO WARN
See Defectiveness

FEDERAL RULES OF CIVIL PROCEDURE
Rule 23, p. 797

FEDERAL RULES OF EVIDENCE
Rule 104A, p. 413
Rule 401, p. 411
Rule 402, p. 411
Rule 403, p. 404, 415
Rule 702, pp. 403, 411, 432, 435, 437, 453, 462
Rule 703, pp. 413, 438, 462
Rule 706, p. 415, 434

FEDERAL STATUTES
Class Action Fairness Act of 2005, 845
Federal Insecticide, Fungicide and Rodenticide Act (FIFRA), 532
Multiparty, Multiform Trial Jurisdiction Act of 2002, 796

GOVERNMENT
See Parties Covered by Strict Liability

IMPLIED WARRANTY
See Warranty

MISREPRESENTATION
Duty to disclose, 10
Fraud, 9
    Elements of, 9
    Compared to breach of contract, 9
Innocent misrepresentation, 8
Intentional misrepresentation, 9
Justifiable reliance, 11
Negligent misrepresentation, 9
Potential plaintiffs, 11
Statements
    Materiality, 10
    Opinions, 10
    Promises, 10

NEGLIGENCE
Comparative negligence, 4
Contributory negligence, 4
Inherently dangerous, 3
Obvious dangers, 4
Privity of contract, 4
Reasonableness, 4

OBVIOUS OR KNOWN DANGERS
See Defectiveness

PARTIES COVERED BY STRICT LIABILITY
Generally, 691
Distributors, 691
Government contractors, 695
    Civilian products, 703
    Military contractor defense, 696
    Rubber stamp exception, 702
    Uniquely federal interests, 696
Retailers, 691
    Innocent retailers, 693
    Occasional sellers, 694
Successor corporations, 705
    Exceptions to the rule of non-liability, 706
        Continuity of enterprise exception, 706
        Mere continuation exception, 706
        Product line exception, 706
    Successor as liability conduit, 711
Wholesalers, 691

PREEMPTION
See Regulations

PRODUCT TYPES
Aircraft, 608, 622, 653, 676
    Airplane, 390
    Airplane repair, 763
    Helicopter, 696
Animals,
    Baby chickens, 27
Aphid-eating ladybugs, 163
Asbestos, 104, 309, 369, 508, 547, 567, 671, 678, 777, 796, 811, 823
    Special class action treatment, 813
Automobile, 32, 35, 48, 106, 340, 452, 528, 580, 674, 691
    Accelerator control system, 332
    Battery, 262
    Motorcycle, 576, 645
    Motorcycle shock absorbers, 151
    Pickup truck, 163
    Rental cars, 695
    SUV Rollover, 586, 596
    Tires, 48, 90, 231, 435, 692, 720, 767
    Tire rims, 288
    Transmission, 161
    Truck rental, 715
    Van, 393
    Wheels, 5
Blood, 215, 802
Boat, 32, 547
Boiled linseed oil, 347
Breast implants, 417, 792
Bullet-proof vest, 186
Bull tie, 247
Burglar alarm, 122
Chain/sprocket mechanism, 198
Chair, 402
Chitterling cleaning machine, 198
Cigarettes, 110, 130, 538
Construction crane, 98

PRODUCT TYPES—Cont'd
Contact lenses, 772
Conveyer, 395
Crane, 736
Deodorant, 326
Drink carton, 726
Dust collection bag, 198
Electric burner, 236
Fertilizer spreader, 169
Fishing boat, 153
Food, 34
    Cherry pie, 93
    Coffee, 398
    Mushrooms, 731
    Peanuts, 532
    Soda, 91, 218, 300
Forklift, 109, 143, 494
Freezer, 407
Furniture polish, 250
Gas furnace, 106
Gasoline can, 106
Golf,
    Driving range, 18
    Golfing Gizmo, 18
Grinder, 628
Gum turps, 347
Guns, 173
    Rifles, 7705
    Saturday Night Special, 177
Hair spray, 28
Hand drill, 270
Hannay Reel, 124
Harvesting combine, 445
Heat block, 262
Heating system, 745, 771
High lift loader, 134
Hoist, 601
Homes, 745
Hook, 247
Horse, 32
Hospital gown, 762
Hydraulic brakes, 129
Immunization clinic, 313
Insecticide, 260
Insulation, 778
Knives, 215
Ladder, 158
Latex gloves, 104
Lawn mower, 493
Lead arsenate, 257
Lounging robes, 31
Meat grinder, 102, 494
Medical devices, 142, 197, 215
Mercenaries, 735
Motor home, 262
Motorcycle helmet 464
Natural gas, 215, 270
Pesticides, 532
Pharmaceuticals, 199
    Bendectin, 409
    Birth control, 324
    Contact lenses, 772
    DES, 357
    Epilepsy drug, 802

PRODUCT TYPES—Cont'd
    Halcion, 199
    MER/29, 777
    Norplant system, 311
    Prescription drugs, 199, 269, 300, 311
Phosdrin, 162
Playpen, 403
Polychlorinate Biphenyls, 432
Power boat, 551
Power tools, 53
    Floor sander, 199
    Grinding wheel, 612
    Metal shearing machine, 279
    Metal straightening machine, 341
    Plastic molding machine, 487
    Punch press, 188
    Rip saw, 29
    Sanding machine, 114
    Table saw, 187
Prescription drugs, 138
Press brake, 623
Propane gas hose, 119
Publications, 731
    Books, 731
    Classified advertisements, 735
    Navigational charts, 736
    Product certifiers, 736
Railroad car, 723
Raw materials, 192
Refrigerator, 641
Reusable containers, 725
Rollover protective structure, 185
Rubber gaskets, 452
Securities, 801
Services, 761
    Airplane repair, 763
    Tire installation, 767
    Building design, 771
    Utility service, 770
Shirt, 234
Silica sand, 234
Skylight, 145
Stallion chain, 247
Stepladder, 399
Sulfuric acid, 215
Swimming pool liner, 170
Toxic chemicals, 144
Tractor, 155, 169, 185, 568
Used products, 714, 719, 736
Vaccines, 215

PROOF OF CAUSATION
    Generally, 341
Burden shifting, 350, 354, 370, 389
Deterioration of product, 436
Enhanced injuries, 352
    Crashworthiness, 352
Expert witnesses, 395
    Alternative design evidence, 449
    Daubert test, 409, 432
        Reliability prong, 413
        Relevance prong, 413
    Differential diagnosis, 454

PROOF OF CAUSATION—Cont'd
    Epidemiological evidence, 431, 456, 461
    Etiology, 454
    Exposure without injury, 431
    Falsifiability, 414, 432
    Frye test, 410
    General acceptance, 410
    General causation, 421
    Judge as amateur scientist, 432
    Junk science, 433
    Mass tort litigation, 417
    Specific causation, 421
    Technical and specialized knowledge, 435, 438, 462, 472
Multiple defendants, 339
    Circumstantial evidence, 366
    Market-share liability, 364
    Relevant market size, 403
Post-accident remedial measures, 403
Scientific evidence, 345
    See also, Expert Witnesses
Self-serving testimony of plaintiff, 351
Types of scientific evidence, 386
Warnings,
    Presumption, 342
    Rational disregard, 351
    Unread warnings, 351

PROOF OF DEFECT
    Generally, 390
Consumer expectations, 401
Expert opinions, 401
Industry standard and customs, 390
    Preemption, 385
    Safety standards, 359, 395
Non-specific defect, 222
State of the art, 333

PROXIMATE CAUSE
    Generally, 480
Foreseeability, 480
Foresight/Hindsight, 483
Manner of harm, 482
Overlapping policy limitations, 486
Relationship to apportionment of liability, 497
Type of harm, 480
Unforeseeable class of persons, 484
    Bystanders, 484
    Children, 485
    Consumers, 485
    Rescuers, 485
    Users, 485
Unforeseeable use of product, 491

PUNITIVE DAMAGES
See Damages

RECOVERY, THEORIES OF
Breach of warranty, 2, 13
Misrepresentation, 8,
Negligence, 3

RECOVERY, THEORIES OF—Cont'd
Strict tort liability, 48

REGULATIONS
    Generally, 464
Federal statutes, 515
Fraud in compliance, 537
Preemption, 533
    Express vs. implied preemption, 544
    Federal motor vehicle safety standards, 546
    Fraud on a federal agency, 545
    Medical devices, 546
Supremacy clause, 532
Voluntary industry standards, 521

RESTATEMENT (SECOND) OF TORTS
§ 299A, p. 217
§ 310, p. 10
§ 311, p. 10
§ 402A, pp. 57, 89, 99, 115, 182, 187, 193, 200, 212, 358, 392, 397, 490, 494, 562, 576, 603, 629, 694, 721, 734, 779
    comment a, p. 732
    comment f, p. 692
    comment g, pp. 91, 99, 105, 107, 110, 392, 483, 606
    comment h, pp. 238, 627
    comment i, pp. 100, 107, 110, 112, 116, 134
    comment j, pp. 241, 327, 348
    comment k, pp. 198, 213, 216
    comment m, p. 692
    comment n, pp. 603, 609
    comment p, pp. 193, 492, 630
    comment q, p. 187
§ 402B, pp. 8, 11, 602, 627
    comment j, p. 11
§ 433B, pp. 356, 376, 496
    comment f, p. 362
    comment g, p. 376
§ 436, pp. 565, 570
§ 520, p. 173
    comment l, p. 174
§ 549, p. 10
§ 552A, p. 602
§ 552B, p. 10
§ 552C, p. 11
§ 918, p. 652

RESTATEMENT (THIRD) OF TORTS
    Generally, 1, 397, 708, 807
§ 1, p. 714
    comment a, p. 1
    comment e, p. 693
§ 2, pp. 88, 143, 243, 301, 482, 694
    comment b, p. 168
    comment d, p. 397
    comment e, p. 176
    comment f, pp. 124, 129
    comment i, pp. 351, 613
    comment j, pp. 286, 345
    comment k, p. 330
    comment l, p. 257
    comment n, p. 1

INDEX 867
References are to Pages

RESTATEMENT (THIRD) OF TORTS
—Cont'd
  comment p, pp. 151, 493
§ 3, pp. 223, 229
§ 4, p. 511, 515
§ 5, p. 195
§ 6, pp. 215, 314
  comment a, p. 322
§ 7, p. 95
  comment b, p. 95
§ 8, pp. 622, 743
§ 9, p. 8
  comment b, p. 8
§ 10, pp. 336, 632
§ 11, p. 336
§ 12, p. 632
§ 13, p. 397, 712
§ 14, pp. 514, 729
§ 15, p. 493
§ 16, pp. 354, 511, 656
  comment d, p. 354
  comment g, p. 656
§ 17, pp. 626, 640
§ 18, p. 607
§ 19, pp. 217, 771
  comment c, p. 217
§ 20, p. 719
§ 21, p. 557
§ 22, p. 645
§ 23, p. 641
§ 24, p. 657
§ 26, p. 357, 651
  comment e, p. 383
§ 27, p. 340
§ 28, p. 389
§ 34, p. 505
§ 42, p. 713

SETTLEMENT
See Comparative Fault

STATUTES OF LIMITATIONS
  See also, Breach of Contract
    Generally, 665
Accrual of cause of action, 666
Discovery rule, 667
Extended latency periods, 671
Knowledge of the plaintiff, 671
Res judicata, 681
Shillady rule, 665
Single action rule, 678
Statutes of repose, 636
  Breach of warranty, 677
  Constitutionality, 672
  Tort reform, 676
Vexatious and oppressive litigation, 680
Wrongful death claims, 672

STRICT TORT LIABILITY
  Generally, 55
Basic elements, 58
Benefits of, 59
Judicially created, 57
History, 58

STRICT TORT LIABILITY—Cont'd
Underlying policies, 59
  Compared to negligence (Shavell), 73
  Consumer expectations, 60
  Cost internalization, 61
  Deterrence, 59
  Economic analysis (Posner), 72
  Economic justification of true strict liability, 91
  Enterprise liability theory (Klemme), 61
  Inconsistencies and inadequacies (Powers), 79
  Proof problems, 60

SUBSTANTIAL CHANGE
Product alteration, 487
  Burden of proof, 494
  Foreseeability, 489
  Removal/destruction of safety guard, 489
  Timing of alteration, 492
  Utility of alteration, 493
  Worker's compensation, 491

TORT REFORM
Through federal preemption 547

TRANSACTIONS COVERED BY STRICT LIABILITY
Bailments, 714
  Product demonstrations, 720
  Stream of commerce, 717
Franchises, 726
Leases, 714
Publications, 731
Real estate transactions, 745
  Implied warranty of habitability, 748
  Mass builders, 748
  Leased real estate, 750
Services, 761
  Essence of the transaction test, 769
  Hybrid transactions, 769, 772
  Professionals, 762, 768, 772
  Pure services, 761
  Warranty, 762
Trademark licenses, 726
Used products, 736
  Disclaimers, 737
  Refurbished or reconditioned, 742

UNIFORM COMMERCIAL CODE
Current sections,
  § 1–205, p. 29, 45
  § 2–102, pp. 14, 15, 714, 747, 767
  § 2–103, p. 15
  § 2–104, p. 29
  § 2–105, pp. 14, 747
  § 2–106, p. 15
  § 2–107, p. 15
  § 2–201, pp. 22, 28, 29
  § 2–202, pp. 22, 43, 45
  § 2–208, p. 45
  § 2–209, p. 45
  § 2–302, p. 48
  § 2–313, pp. 15, 20, 36, 49, 714, 720, 725

References are to Pages

UNIFORM COMMERCIAL CODE—Cont'd
§ 2–314, pp. 15, 25, 29, 121, 601, 638, 714, 720, 725
  comment 3, p. 745
  comment 6, p. 25
  comment 7, p. 26
  comment 8, p. 26
  comment 13, p. 608
§ 2–315, pp. 15, 27, 29, 714, 720, 725
  comment 2, p. 30
  comment 5, p. 32
§ 2–316, pp. 3, 29, 43, 45, 601
  comment 8, p. 603
  comment 9, p. 32
§ 2–318, pp. 34, 749
§ 2–401, p. 15
§ 2–607, p. 51
§ 2–715, pp. 24, 26, 37, 51, 601

UNIFORM COMMERCIAL CODE—Cont'd
§ 2–719, pp. 23, 43, 47, 607
§ 2–725, pp. 51, 677
Proposed changes,
  § 2–313, p. 22
  § 2–313A, p. 23
  § 2–313B, p. 24
  § 2–316, p. 4e
  § 2–318, p. 34

UNIFORM SALES ACT
§ 12, p. 21

WARRANTY
See Breach of Warranty

WORKER'S COMPENSATION
See Comparative Fault; Defect; Defendants; Proximate Cause

†